DESIGN OF ANALOG
INTEGRATED CIRCUITS
AND SYSTEMS

Electronics and VLSI Circuits

Senior Consulting Editor

Stephen W. Director, Carnegie Mellon University

Consulting Editor

Richard C. Jaeger, Auburn University

Also Available from McGraw-Hill

Schaum's Outline Series in Electronics & Electrical Engineering

Most outlines include basic theory, definitions and hundreds of example problems solved in step-by-step detail, and supplementary problems with answers.

Related Titles on the Current List Include:

Analog & Digital Communications
Basic Circuit Analysis
Basic Electrical Engineering
Basic Electricity
Basic Mathematics for Electricity & Electronics
Digital Principles
Electric Circuits
Electric Machines & Electromechanics
Electric Power Systems
Electromagnetics
Electronic Circuits
Electronic Communication
Electronic Devices & Circuits
Electronics Technology
Engineering Economics
Feedback & Control Systems
Introduction to Digital Systems
Microprocessor Fundamentals

Schaum's Solved Problems Books

Each title in this series is a complete and expert source of solved problems with solutions worked out in step-by-step detail.

Related Titles on the Current List Include:

3000 Solved Problems in Calculus
2500 Solved Problems in Differential Equations
3000 Solved Problems in Electric Circuits
2000 Solved Problems in Electromagnetics
2000 Solved Problems in Electronics
3000 Solved Problems in Linear Algebra
2000 Solved Problems in Numerical Analysis
3000 Solved Problems in Physics

Available at most college bookstores, or for a complete list of
titles and prices, write to:
Schaum Division
McGraw-Hill, Inc.
Princeton Road, S-1
Hightstown, NJ 08520

DESIGN OF ANALOG INTEGRATED CIRCUITS AND SYSTEMS

Kenneth R. Laker

University of Pennsylvania

Willy M. C. Sansen

Katholieke Universiteit Leuven
Belgium

McGraw-Hill, Inc.

New York   St. Louis   San Francisco   Auckland   Bogotá   Caracas
Lisbon   London   Madrid   Mexico City   Milan   Montreal
New Delhi   San Juan   Singapore   Sydney   Tokyo   Toronto

This book was set in Times Roman by Electronic Technical Publishing Services.
The editors were George T. Hoffman and John M. Morriss;
the production supervisor was Richard A. Ausburn.
The cover was designed by Carla Bauer.
Project supervision was done by Electronic Technical Publishing Services.
Arcata Graphics/Martinsburg was printer and binder.

DESIGN OF ANALOG INTEGRATED CIRCUITS AND SYSTEMS

 This book is printed on recycled, acid-free paper containing a minimum of 50% total recycled fiber with 10% postconsumer de-inked fiber.

2 3 4 5 6 7 8 9 0 AGM AGM 9 0 9 8 7 6 5 4

ISBN 0-07-036060-X

Library of Congress Cataloging-in-Publication Data

Laker, Kenneth R., (date).
   Design of analog integrated circuits and systems / Kenneth R.
Laker, Willy M. C. Sansen.
     p.   cm. — (McGraw-Hill series in electrical and computer
engineering. Electronics and VLSI circuits)
   Includes bibliographical references (p.) and index.
   ISBN 0-07-036060-X
   1. Linear integrated circuits—Design and construction.
I. Sansen, Willy M. C.   II. Title.   III. Series.
IN PROCESS
621.3815—dc20   93-49574

To our families
Mary Ellen, John, Chris, and Brian
Hadewych, Katrien, Sara, and Marjan

CONTENTS

3 Feedback and Sensitivity in Analog Integrated Circuits

PREFACE

In the short span of twenty five years, the field of analog integrated circuits and systems has developed and matured. During this same period, much has been made of the competition between analog and digital system design strategies. Advances in digital VLSI has enabled microprocessors and digital-signal processors to assume roles largely filled in the past by analog systems. However, there are three facts that render analog integrated circuits and systems increasingly important. First, the natural world is analog. Thus, analog systems are needed in information acquisition systems in order to prepare analog information for conversion to digital format. Second, there remain many important applications that are best addressed by mixed analog/digital VLSI systems. That is, analog and digital VLSI circuits coexist on the same die. Third, demanding digital systems can exhibit analog circuit qualities. Thus, a good grasp of analog IC design techniques is a valuable asset in the design and debugging of digital systems. The advances in both analog and digital VLSI has profoundly changed the way systems are partitioned to optimize integration and cost.

Much of the analog design during the 1960s and 1970s was done in bipolar and hybrid technologies. During this time, the operational amplifier emerged as an important subsystem. During subsequent years, the operational amplifier has been optimized and scaled to the degree that it is now considered a common component, like a resistor or capacitor. The 1980s was an era of rapid evolution of MOS analog integrated circuits, in particular CMOS. During the 1990s, we have seen the BICMOS technology (incorporating both bipolar and CMOS devices on the same die) emerge as a serious contender to the original technologies. Although somewhat more expensive to fabricate (e.g., more mask levels) than CMOS, BICMOS allows the designer to use both bipolar and MOS devices to their best advantage. At the same time, we have seen a proliferation of mixed analog/digital VLSI integrated circuits realized in state-of-the-art digital CMOS technologies to optimize cost and power dissipation in consumer products, many of which are pocket size and battery powered. For very high performance applications, BICMOS offers the opportunity to mix analog circuits on the same die with high-speed ECL digital circuits and dense CMOS logic.

It has become increasingly important for analog circuit designers to have a thorough appreciation of the similarities and differences between MOS and bipolar devices, and to be able to design with either, where appropriate. The same argument can be made for sampled-data and continuous-time design techniques. Thus, in this book, we combine the consideration of CMOS and bipolar circuits into a unified treatment. We also include combined CMOS-bipolar circuit realizations made possible by BICMOS technology. The text progresses smoothly from MOS and bipolar device modeling, to simple one- and two-transistor building block circuits (e.g., amplifiers, active loads, and sources). We then follow with a thorough treatment of the design of operational and transconductance amplifiers. The final two chapters present a unified coverage of sample-data and continuous-time signal processing systems. Earlier in the text, we thoroughly cover the concepts of feedback and sensitivity. These important topics, along with noise, nonlinear distortion, and power supply rejection are integrated, as needed, throughout the text.

The design of analog circuits relies heavily on insight gained from hand calculations based on first-order models. However, many important details of circuit behavior, such as precise gain, DC offsets, distortion, and noise, depend on second-order device characteristics that cannot be included in hand calculations. We use computer analysis the way it is most commonly employed in the engineering design process: as a tool to verify detailed circuit behavior beyond the scope of hand analysis. The circuit simulator called SPICE is the standard CAD tool for verifying integrated circuit performance. SPICE is available in a variety of forms on UNIX-based workstations and all popular PC platforms. With these thoughts in mind, we focus much of the text on the development of design intuition through hand calculations. Extensive use of SPICE is included thoughout the text, particularly as part of examples in the problem sets. The problem sets also include several open-ended design problems that expose the reader to practical situations.

Both authors have had extensive industrial experience in integrated-circuit (IC) design, as well as in the teaching of academic courses on this subject. The choice of the material covered in the body of the text and the problem sets is a reflection of our collective experience. We believe it to be a valuable resource for both IC designers and users. An understanding of the IC structure is extremely useful in evaluating the relative desirability of different designs. In addition, the IC user is in a much better position to interpret a manufacturer's data if he or she has a working knowledge of the internal operation of the integrated circuit in question.

This text was written to be used both as a text for students and as a reference book for practicing engineers. For class use, there are numerous worked problems in each chapter; the problem sets at the end of each chapter illustrate the practical applications of the material in the text. The contents of this book originated largely for the purpose of serving two courses on analog integrated circuit design offered at the University of Pennsylvania and the Katholieke Universiteit Leuven. The first of these is a senior level elective and the second is a first year graduate course. The book is structured so that it can be used as the basic text for such a two-course sequence. An outline of each chapter will follow shortly, together with suggestions for material to be covered in each course. We assume that each course consists of three hours of lecture per week over a 15-week semester. The users of this text are assumed to have a working knowledge of Laplace transforms and frequency-domain circuit analysis. We also assume that the readers have had an introductory course in electronics, such as that based on the text *Microelectronic Circuits* by A. Sedra and K. C. Smith. Thus, we expect readers to be familiar with the principles of transistor operation and with the functioning of simple analog circuits. We also expect that readers have an introductory knowledge of probability and statistics. We take advantage of the fact that an increasing number of students are exposed to sampled-data systems and the z-transform in their undergraduate curriculum. For those readers who have not been exposed to this material, and for those who wish to revitalize this knowledge, an introduction to sampled-data signals and systems is included in Appendix 7-1 at the end of Chapter 7.

The outline of the text is as follows:

Chapters 1 and 2 contain summaries of MOS and bipolar transistor models, respectively. This material is quite important in IC design because there is significant interaction between circuit and device design, as will be seen in later chapters. The components that are most crucial in achieving an accurate SPICE simulation are the device models. Thus, a thorough understanding of the influence of device fabrication on device characteristics and their models is essential. Both chapters in their entirety are required reading for both the undergraduate and graduate courses. We suggest spending one to two weeks on selected topics from these chapters, with the choice of topics depending on the background of the students.

Chapter 3 introduces the reader to the important concepts of feedback and sensitivity. Also included are the effects of feedback on transient response of second- and third-order systems. Some of this material will be review for some students, particularly at the graduate level. Particularly novel in this chapter is the inclusion of two powerful tools for designing feedback circuits, namely, Blackman's impedance relation and the asymptotic gain relation. In the undergraduate course, this chapter should be covered in full. It will require no more than two weeks to cover. For the graduate course, selected topics can be treated in class and the balance of the chapter as home reading. One week is allowed for this chapter in the graduate course.

Chapter 4 involves the use of transistors to construct elementary amplifier stages, buffers, impedance converter, active loads, and current sources. AC, DC, and transient performances are considered. Capacitances (both intentional and parasitic) give rise to poles and zeros that modify the input, output, and transfer relationships versus frequency. In all sections, the parallel between MOS and bipolar transistor stages is maintained; and the differences are highlighted. The configurations in this chapter represent the basic building blocks of modern analog IC design. Thus, in both courses this material should be covered in full with the exception of the appendices. A thorough treatment of this chapter will require three weeks. We recommend coverage of the full chapter for the undergraduate course and selected topics for the graduate course. For the graduate course, coverage is reduced to two weeks.

Chapter 5 is concerned with the modeling of operational and transconductance amplifier-based circuits from a behavioral point of view. A strong behavioral understanding is a prerequisite to undertaking the transistor level design of these amplifiers and/or the synthesis of higher level circuits that use them as components. The designer can greatly simplify the analysis and design of complex analog systems by using models for the amplifiers derived from behavioral descriptions rather than circuit schematics. Behavioral models developed in this chapter are used extensively in the analysis and design of analog signal processing systems in Chapters 7 and 8. Moreover, they are used in Chapter 6 to map detailed specifications to the attributes of transistor level circuit schematics. We recommend full coverage of this chapter in both courses, requiring two weeks.

Chapter 6 considers the transistor level analysis and design of several operational (op amp) and transconductance (OTA) amplifier schemes. They are developed by first considering the differential amplifier with active load, the simplest complete OTA. Succeeding schemes for CMOS, bipolar, and BICMOS, are developed with this basic OTA as a kernel. Fully differential or balanced schemes are also considered. Design plans are applied to all schemes, paying considerable attention to symmetry and matching, and also to other second-order effects (e.g., transient response, noise, nonlinearities, power supply rejection, offsets, common mode rejection, temperature effects), leading to a full set of specifications. Several design examples are worked in detail and important design tradeoffs are discussed. A thorough treatment of this chapter will require three weeks. We recommend coverage of the full chapter for both the undergraduate and graduate courses.

Chapter 7 is devoted to reviewing the fundamentals of linear active filtering in the continuous-time and sampled-data domains. For those readers who need to refresh their understanding of sampled-data systems, and z-transform, a brief review of these subjects is provided in Appendix 7-1. The fundamental schemes for integrated analog filters are introduced. Various performance requirements and methods for synthesizing efficient numerical transfer functions are considered. Models developed in Chapter 3 are used to estimate sensitivity and yield. A hybrid of discrete-time and analog circuit concepts are developed to facilitate the symbolic analysis and design of switched-capacitor circuits. A thorough treatment of this chapter requires three weeks. If Appendix 7-1 is reviewed in class, it can be adequately covered in two lectures. For the undergraduate course we recommend emphasizing continuous-time filters, providing an introduction to switched-capacitor filters. This involves all of Sections 7-1, 7-2, and 7-4, and parts of Sections 7-3, 7-5, and 7-6. This entire chapter is to be covered in the graduate course.

Chapter 8 builds on the materials in Chapters 5–7 to design and implement practical continuous-time and sampled-data integrated active filters. We consider concepts, circuit designs, circuit schematics, and design lore that have been found to result in robust integrated filters. Continuous-time and sampled-data realizations are considered with equivalent emphasis. Design and implementation is based on modular structures, where op amps, OTAs, and the passive structures are the building blocks. All schemes are analyzed, paying considerable attention to parasitics and matching, and also to other second-order effects (e.g., transient response, noise, nonlinearities, power supply rejection, and DC offsets). A thorough treatment of this chapter requires three weeks. There remains one week in the undergraduate course to cover selected sections. We recommend the coverage of Sections 8-1–8-3. The entire chapter is to be covered in the graduate course.

This book was conceived during W. Sansen's sabbatical leave with K. Laker at the University of Pennsylvania. The book was further developed during K. Laker's subsequent sabbatical leave at the Katholieke Universiteit Leuven. The funding for both sabbatical leaves were provided by the Penn-Leuven Faculty Exchange program. We are indeed grateful for this support. We wish to thank our students, colleagues, and the following reviewers for their careful evaluation of this book and their thoughtful comments: Stanley G. Burns, Iowa State University; L. Richard Carley, Carnegie Mellon University; Sherif Embabi, Texas A & M University; Sergio Franco, San Francisco State University; Edwin Greeneich, Arizona State University; Frank H. Hielscher, Lehigh University; Andrew L. Robinson, University of Michigan; Mani Soma, University of Washington; Bang-Sup Song, University of Illinois at Urbana–Champaign; and Gary Tuttle, Iowa State University. In particular, we wish to acknowledge the helpful suggestions from Professor Jan Van der Spiegel, University of Pennsylvania; Dr. T. R. Viswanathan, AT&T Microelectronics, Professor Michel Steyaert, Katholieke Universiteit Leuven, and Mr. A. Ganesan, Crystal Semiconductor.

Kenneth R. Laker
Willy M. C. Sansen

DESIGN OF ANALOG INTEGRATED CIRCUITS AND SYSTEMS

1

MOS TRANSISTOR
MODELS

INTRODUCTION

The design of analog circuits relies on an understanding of the transistor models used. For hand calculations, only first-order models can be used to evaluate circuit performance. However, many small details of circuit behavior, such as precise gain, distortion, and noise, depend on second-order transistor characteristics. Therefore, second-order characteristics must be included in the circuit verification. A full model will always be used to verify the circuit performance by means of a circuit simulator, such as SPICE. This book begins by discussing transistor modeling, and presents simplified models and full models.

We cannot learn circuit behavior just by running SPICE. Insight is obtained primarily by performing simple hand calculations. Thus, simple models must be used for qualitative results. SPICE can then be used to verify the assumptions made and to verify the circuit performance, if more complicated models are used. This book is intended to provide insight into analog circuit performance. Therefore, hand calculations and first-order models are emphasized.

Models of transistors are derived from semiconductor physics. It is difficult to determine where to start the discussion of model derivation. Although an understanding of basic physics is not necessary in order to use devices in analog circuits, too little knowledge of physics may not allow for an understanding of some second-order phenomena.

In this book we do not discuss device physics. If readers are not familiar with device physics they are encouraged to review this topic before continuing. (See Bibliography.)

For each device described, two models are given: the first-order model for hand calculations and the full model to be used in SPICE. Models are first given for the most important transistor, the MOS Transistor. JFET models are added next. The bipolar transistor is covered in Chap. 2, along with resistors and capacitances. Integrated or monolithic devices are discussed, as well as some compatible thin film devices. Thick film and discrete devices are omitted altogether.

1-1   MOSFET AND JUNCTION FET

For *Field Effect Transistors* (FETs), conductivity is controlled by a capacitance. The voltage across the capacitance controls the conductivity of the channel. If the controlling capacitance consists of a depletion layer capacitance, it gives rise to a *Junction FET* (JFET). If the controlling capacitance consists of an oxide layer, it gives rise to a *MOSFET* (MOST). These are depicted in Fig. 1-1a and 1-1b (Grove 1967; Tsividis 1988).

1-1-1   JFET

In Fig. 1-1a, a JFET cross section is portrayed. The degree of arcing (darkening) corresponds to each layer's degree of conductivity. A conductive channel connects two regions of high conductivity, source (S) and drain (D). Current can flow through the conducting channel between S and D, provided a voltage v_{DS} is applied across them.

In Fig. 1-1a, the JFET is of the n type. Thus, conduction is carried out by electrons. Both D and S must be biased positively relative to the substrate. The region that is most positively biased is the drain; the other is the source. For an n-channel JFET, the current flows from the drain through the channel to the source.

The channel is sandwiched between two depletion layers that isolate the channel from a top conductive layer (top gate) and a bottom conductive layer (substrate). These two depletion layers form junction capacitances between the channel to the top gate C_{GC} and to the bottom layer C_{BC}. The voltage across each capacitance controls the width of the depletion layer and hence, the width of the residual channel between both depletion layers. The voltages across C_{GC} and C_{BC} control the conductivity of the channel as well as its charge, and, as a result, the current through the channel. Either voltage across C_{GC} (at the gate) or across C_{BC} (at the substrate) can independently control the current through the channel.

1-1-2   MOST

In Fig. 1-1b the cross section of an n-channel MOST (nMOST) is shown. It contains two highly conductive regions connected by a conducting channel. Current can flow through this channel, provided a positive voltage is applied to one end (which becomes the drain); and the other end becomes the source. Then the current again flows from drain to source.

In this structure, however, the channel is sandwiched between an oxide layer and a depletion layer. They isolate the channel from a top conductive layer (gate) and a bottom conductive layer (substrate). These isolation layers again form capacitances between the channel to the top gate C_{GC} and between the channel to the bottom layer C_{BC}.

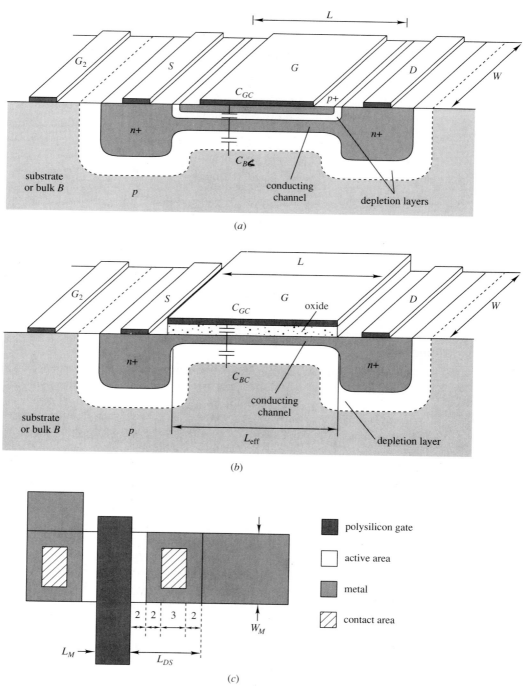

FIGURE 1-1   (a) n-channel JFET, (b) nMOST, and (c) layout nMOST.

In this case, however, C_{GC} is an oxide capacitance and C_{BC} is a depletion layer capacitance. Oxide capacitances are less efficient because the dielectric constant of silicon oxide ($\varepsilon_{\text{ox}} = 0.34$ pF/cm) is three times smaller than that of silicon ($\varepsilon_{\text{si}} = 1.06$ pF/cm). On the other hand, an oxide capacitance is independent of the voltage that is applied across it; this is not true for a depletion layer capacitance, which depends heavily on the voltage that is applied across it.

The voltages across the capacitances C_{GC} and C_{BC} control the charge in the residual channel. As a result, these voltages control the current through the channel. Independently, either voltage across C_{GC} (at the gate) or across C_{BC} (at the substrate) can control the current through the channel.

If the substrate (or bulk) voltage v_{BS} is kept constant with respect to the source, the current in the channel is only controlled by the gate voltage v_{GS}. The current in the channel between drain and source can only flow if the gate voltage v_{GS} is larger than a so-called threshold voltage V_T. Similarly, a substrate (or bulk) threshold voltage V_{TB} is found for a constant gate-source voltage v_{GS}, below which current cannot flow between drain and source. Since both the gate and substrate voltages v_{GS} and v_{BS} act on the same conducting channel, both values of V_T and V_{TB} depend upon each other. This is evidently the case for both structures in Fig. 1-1. The threshold voltages for these structures will be calculated in Sec. 1-2 and are calculated first for the nMOST of Fig. 1-1b.

1-1-3 nMOST and pMOST

Holes can be used for conduction instead of electrons. If we exchange all n regions in Fig. 1-1 by p regions, and vice versa, a pJFET and a pMOST are obtained. For instance, in complementary MOS (CMOS) technology, both pMOST and nMOST devices are used (see Fig. 1-2). Since the pMOST and nMOST devices require substrate material of opposite type of doping, at least two different CMOS technologies occur. In Fig. 1-2a the cross section of a p-well CMOS technology is shown. The nMOST is located in a deep, lowly doped p-well that serves as its bulk. The pMOST, on the contrary, is located directly on the n substrate material. The opposite is true for n-well CMOS technology. In a twin-well process both transistors are located in separate wells.

Differences between p-well and n-well CMOS technologies will be discussed later. However, an important difference can be made clear now. Typical doping levels for the substrate material are approximately 2×10^{14} to 10^{15} cm^{-3}. Since the wells are realized by means of diffusion, they are always doped at a higher level than the substrate itself. Typical doping levels of the wells are about 10^{16} cm^{-3}. As a result, the bulk doping level of an nMOST in a p-well CMOS technology is much higher than in an n-well CMOS technology. Typically, this ratio is a factor of 10 to 50. These two values of bulk doping levels will give different values of transistor parameters.

The reader must not be confused by the terms substrate, bulk, and well. The substrate is always the material just underneath the gate. For an n-well CMOS technology, the p-substrate is the substrate for the nMOST; on the other hand, the n-well is also the substrate for the pMOST (see Fig. 1-2b). The term bulk (B) is used instead of substrate to avoid confusion with the use of S to denote source.

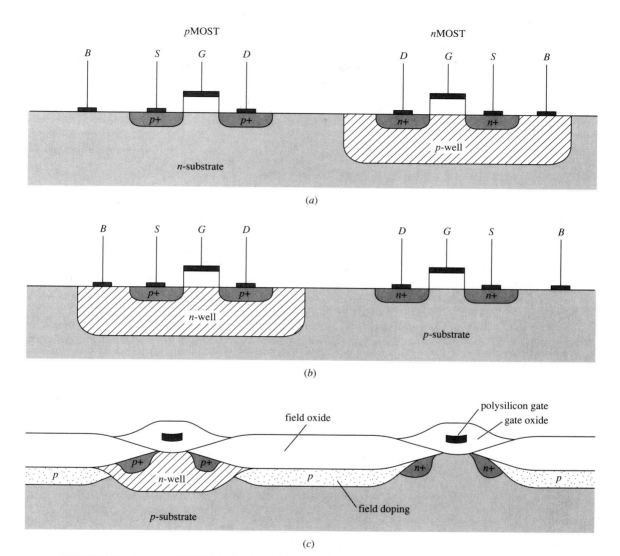

FIGURE 1-2   (*a*) *p*-well CMOS technology, (*b*) *n*-well CMOS technology, and (*c*) *n*-well CMOS technology.

1-2 CAPACITANCES AND MOST THRESHOLD VOLTAGES

1-2-1 MOS Capacitance

In order to calculate threshold voltages, the values of the controlling capacitances must first be calculated (Grove 1967; Sze 1981; Muller and Kamins 1986). For the *n*MOST of Fig. 1-1*b*, the actual layout is shown in Fig. 1-1*c*. The width of the gate is denoted by W and its length by L. The total gate channel capacitance is thus given by

$$C_{GC} = WLC_{\text{ox}} \qquad (1\text{-}1a)$$

in which

$$C_{\text{ox}} = \frac{\varepsilon_{\text{ox}}}{t_{\text{ox}}} \qquad (1\text{-}1b)$$

is the oxide capacitance per unit area. For example, for a gate oxide thickness of 50 nm (n = nano = 10^{-9}), the value of $C_{\text{ox}} = 6.8 \times 10^{-8}$ F/cm². For gate dimensions of $W \times L = 50 \times 5$ μm (μ = micro = 10^{-6}), $C_{GC} = 0.17$ pF or 170 fF (p = pico = 10^{-12} and f = femto = 10^{-15}).

1-2-2 Junction Capacitance

In a similar way, the total bulk channel capacitance is given by

$$C_{BC} = WLC_j \qquad (1\text{-}2a)$$

with

$$C_j = \frac{\varepsilon_{\text{si}}}{t_{\text{si}}} \qquad (1\text{-}2b)$$

in which t_{si} is the thickness of the depletion layer between channel and bulk (substrate). This thickness depends on the voltage across the depletion layer v_{BC} and on the doping level N_{SUB} of the substrate.

For a one-sided abrupt junction, an approximate expression can be used for t_{si}, as given by

$$t_{\text{si}} = \sqrt{\frac{2\varepsilon_{\text{si}}(\phi_j - v_{BC})}{q\,N_{\text{SUB}}}} \qquad (1\text{-}3a)$$

in which v_{BC} is the bulk to channel potential. We normally take its value at the source side, such that $v_{BC} = v_{BS}$. ϕ_j is the bulk-channel junction built-in voltage. For an abrupt junction it is given by

$$\phi_j = \frac{kT}{q} \ln \frac{N_C N_{\text{SUB}}}{n_i^2} \qquad (1\text{-}3b)$$

in which $n_i = 1.5 \times 10^{10}$ cm^{-3} at room temperature (27°C).

For example, for $N_{\text{SUB}} = 3 \times 10^{14}$ cm^{-3} and an estimated channel doping of 2×10^{17} cm^{-3}, $\phi_j = 0.68$ V. For zero applied voltage ($v_{BS} = 0$ V), $t_{\text{si}} = 1.73$ μm. As a result, $C_j = 0.67 \times 10^{-8}$ F/cm² and the total junction capacitance $C_{BC} = 15$ fF only.

It is worth noting that the value of C_{BC} is proportional to the square root of the substrate doping level (for an abrupt junction). For low capacitance, a low doping level is thus preferred. On the other hand, even for a high doping level, the value of C_{BC} is still much less than the value of C_{GC}. This is caused mainly by the thinner oxide thickness (50 nm), compared to the depletion layer thickness (1730 nm).

1-2-3 MOST and JFET

In the JFET structure of Fig. 1-1*a*, both controlling capacitances C_{GC} and C_{BC} are depletion layer capacitances. By definition, a FET device with channel conductivity controlled by the width of a junction depletion layer or by a junction depletion layer capacitance is called a *Junction Field Effect Transistor* (JFET). The structure of Fig. 1-1*a* is a double JFET.

By definition, a FET device with channel conductivity controlled by an oxide capacitance, is called a *Metal Oxide Semiconductor Transistor* (MOST). The structure of Fig. 1-1*b* is a parallel connection of a MOST and a JFET. The drain-source current can be controlled by the top (MOST) gate, by the bulk (JFET) gate or by both in parallel.

However, if several MOST transistor structures are realized on the same substrate, they share the same bottom (JFET) gate. Therefore, this bottom gate is not useful as an input gate to control the current of the device. On the other hand, the top (MOST) gate is well isolated from device to device resulting in only the top MOST gate being used. The device in Fig. 1-1*b* is a MOS Transistor. Its top MOST gate is the only gate used; its bottom JFET gate is handled as a parasitic effect.

The effect of the parasitic JFET in a MOST is represented in the threshold value V_T of the MOST by means of factor γ (gamma). This factor is the *body factor* or *bulk polarization* factor. It is given by

$$\gamma = \frac{\sqrt{2\varepsilon_{\text{si}} q\, N_{\text{SUB}}}}{C_{\text{ox}}} \tag{1-4a}$$

which has as a dimension $V^{1/2}$. By use of the expressions of C_{BC} and C_{GC}, this factor is also given by

$$\gamma = \frac{C_{BC}}{C_{GC}} 2\sqrt{\phi_j - v_{BS}} \tag{1-4b}$$

Body factor γ is directly proportional to the ratio of both controlling capacitances C_{BC} and C_{GC} (see Fig. 1-1). The proportionality factor is the voltage dependence of the bulk junction capacitance C_{BC}.

We will review the ratio of both controlling capacitances later in this book. For now, however, the ratio is represented by a specific parameter *n*, which is defined by

$$n - 1 = \frac{C_{BC}}{C_{GC}} = \frac{\gamma}{2\sqrt{\phi_j - v_{BS}}} \tag{1-5a}$$

Note that *n* depends on the applied voltage v_{BS}, whereas γ does not. Parameters γ and *n* are the first two parameters of the MOST model.

In circuit simulators, the best known of which is SPICE, MOS transistor parameters must be used (Antognetti and Massobrio 1988). They are obtained from measurements and are normally provided by the silicon foundry that produced the circuit simulators. Representative values for a standard 3 μm *p*-well CMOS process are listed in Table 1-1. For each parameter the expression in which this parameter has occurred first is added.

TABLE 1-1   NOMINAL SPICE PARAMETERS FOR A MOST (p-WELL CMOS)

Type	nMOS	pMOS	Dimension	Name	Equation or Table number
			Level 1		
VT0	0.6	−0.77	V	Zero bias threshold voltage	Eq. 1-6a
KP	4.0E-5	1.5E-5	A/V^2	Transconductance parameter	Eq. 1-9d
GAMMA	0.92	0.54	V$^{1/2}$	Bulk threshold parameter	Eq. 1-4a
LAMBDA	0.022	0.047	V^{-1}	Channel length modulation parameter	Eq. 1-24a
CGS0	5.2E-10	4.0E-10	F/m	GS overlap capacitance per meter channel width	Table 1-6
CGD0	5.2E-10	4.0E-10	F/m	GD overlap capacitance per meter channel width	
CGB0			F/m	GB overlap capacitance per meter channel width	
CJ	4.5E-4	3.6E-4	F/m^2	Zero bias junction capacitance	
MJ	0.5	0.5	—	Grading coefficient	
CJSW	6E-10	6E-10	F/m	Zero bias junction sidewall capacitance	
MJSW	0.33	0.33	—	Grading coefficient	
PB	0.6	0.6	V	Bulk junction potential	Eq. 1-3b
FC	0.5	0.5	—	Coefficient forward bias depletion capacitance	Table 2-4
JS	1E-3	1E-3	A/m^2	Bulk junction saturation current	Eq. 1-35
TPG	1.0	−1.0	—	Type of gate	Eq. 1-6b
LD	3.2E-7	3.2E-7	m	Lateral diffusion	Eq. 1-21a
RSH	20	50	Ω/□	Sheet resistance diffusion of D and S	Eq. 1-36
RS	15	20	Ω	Ohmic source resistance	Eq. 1-36
RD	15	20	Ω	Ohmic drain resistance	Eq. 1-36
			Process parameters		
TOX	5.2E-8	5.2E-8	m	Oxide thickness	Eq. 1-1b
PHI	0.60	0.60	V	Surface potential ($2\phi_F$)	Eq. 1-6d
NSUB	4.6E15	2.5E14	cm^{-3}	Substrate doping	Eq. 1-3b
NSS	5E10	5E10	cm^{-2}	Effect of surface charge (Q_{ox})	Eq. 1-6a
			Added for Level 2		
NFS	5E10	9E10	cm^{-2}	Effect of fast surface states	Eq. 1-5b
U0	500	200	cm^2/V	Surface mobility	Eq. 1-38a
UCRIT	1E6	5.2E4	V/cm	Critical field for mobility degradation	Eq. 1-38a
UEXP	0.01	0.17	—	Critical field exponent	Eq. 1-38a
UTRA	0.5	0.5	—	Transverse field coefficient	Eq. 1-38a
VMAX	1.0E5	1.0E5	cm/s	Maximum drift velocity	Eq. 1-38a

TABLE 1-1 (cont'd)

Type	nMOS	pMOS	Dimension	Name	Equation or Table number
NEFF	0.01	0.01	—	Total channel charge coefficient	Eq. 1-38a
XJ	4.0E-7	4.0E-7	m	Metallurgical junction depth	Eq. 1-21a
DELTA	1.6	1.9	—	Channel width factor (W)	Eq. 1-44
			Added for Level 3		
ETA	0.04	0.06	—	Static feedback effective parameter (L)	Eq. 1-45
THETA	0.05	0.12	V^{-1}	Empirical mobility modulation factor	Eq. 1-41
KAPPA	1	5	—	Field correlation factor	Eq. 1-38a
DL	0	0	μm	Change in L due to photolithography	Eq. 1-21a
DW	−0.4	−0.4	μm	Change in W due to photolithography	Eq. 1-21b
KF	2E-15	5E-17	A	Flicker noise coefficient	Eq. 1-68a
AF	1	1		Flicker noise exponent	Eq. 1-68a

The first MOST parameter introduced here is GAMMA (γ). The other parameter is n. In SPICE, parameter n also includes the effect of fast surface-states, denoted by NFS (in $cm^{-2}V^{-1}$). Its full expression is then given by

$$n = 1 + \frac{C_{BC}}{C_{ox}} + \frac{q\text{NFS}}{C_{ox}} \qquad (1\text{-}5b)$$

There are few surface states in state-of-the-art processing. Therefore the NFS in Eq. (1-5b) is usually negligible.

For the example, with $C_{ox} = 6.8 \times 10^{-8}$ F/cm^2 and $n_{SUB} = 3 \times 10^{14}$ cm^{-3}, the value of γ is readily calculated to be 0.15 V$^{1/2}$. For zero volts v_{BS}, the value of n is 1.09. However, for $n_{SUB} = 10^{16}$ cm^{-3}, $\gamma = 0.86$ V$^{1/2}$ and $n = 1.49$.

1-2-4 MOST Threshold Voltage

The expression of the threshold voltage of a MOST V_{T0} is obtained from semiconductor physics. For **zero bulk-source polarization** v_{BS}, V_{T0} is given by

$$V_{T0} = \phi_{GB} - \frac{Q_{ox}}{C_{ox}} + 2\phi_F \pm \frac{Q_D}{C_{ox}} \qquad (1\text{-}6a)$$

with + for an nMOST and − for a pMOST.

It is independent of the voltages applied. In SPICE it is denoted by V_{T0} (see Table 1-1). The four terms in V_{T0} are discussed below.

Parameter ϕ_{GB} is the difference in work-function potential between the gate material and the bulk material. It depends on the type of gate doping. In present-day processing, an $n+$ polysilicon gate is used with doping level N_G. The resulting expressions of ϕ_{GB} are then

for an nMOST (with p-bulk doping N_B):

$$\phi_{GB} = -\frac{kT}{q} \ln \frac{N_G N_B}{n_i^2} \quad \text{(TPG = 1 in SPICE)} \tag{1-6b}$$

for a pMOST (with n-bulk doping N_B):

$$\phi_{GB} = -\frac{kT}{q} \ln \frac{N_G}{N_B} \quad \text{(TPG = -1 in SPICE)} \tag{1-6c}$$

Charge Q_{ox} represents the positive charges (in Ccm^{-2}) at the silicon-oxide interface. Proper processing techniques try to reduce these charges as much as possible because they cause drift in V_{T0}. In the circuit simulator SPICE, Q_{ox} is represented by NSS (in cm^{-2}). Its value is then given by qNSS (in Ccm^{-2}).

Together, the first two terms in Eq. (1-6a) of V_{T0} form the flat-band voltage V_{FB}. It is the gate-source potential that causes no band bending in the silicon and is thus given by $V_{FB} = \phi_{GB} - Q_{ox}/C_{ox}$.

The surface potential at the source side of the channel under strong-inversion conditions is $2\phi_F$ (PHI in SPICE). Its value is obtained from the distance between the Fermi level (in the bulk) and the middle of the energy bandgap of the semiconductor material. It also represents the band bending in strong inversion. It is given by

$$\phi_F = \pm\frac{kT}{q} \ln \frac{N_{SUB}}{n_i} \tag{1-6d}$$

which is $+$ for an nMOST and $-$ for a pMOST.

Thus, parameter ϕ_F is a measure for the doping level, as well as for the conductivity in the semiconductor material.

The depletion charge Q_D is contained in the last term of V_{T0} in Eq. (1-6a). This charge depends on the depletion layer thickness t_{si} as given by $Q_D = qN_B t_{si}$. Therefore, the term $\pm Q_D/C_{ox}$ can also be written as

$$\pm\frac{Q_D}{C_{ox}} = \pm\gamma\sqrt{2|\phi_F|} \tag{1-6e}$$

as derived from Eqs. (1-3a) and (1-4a). Note that the built-in junction potential ϕ_j now equals $2|\phi_F|$.

Bulk polarization $\mathbf{v}_{BS}$ causes an increase in the depletion layer width as given by Eq. (1-3a). As a result, charge Q_D increases as well, as given by

$$\pm\frac{Q_D}{C_{ox}} = \pm\gamma\sqrt{2|\phi_F| - v_{BS}} \tag{1-7a}$$

Note that v_{BS} is negative such that $2|\phi_F|$ and v_{BS} add up in absolute value. The threshold voltage V_T can now be written as

$$V_T = V_{T0} \pm \gamma(\sqrt{2|\phi_F| - v_{BS}} - \sqrt{2|\phi_F|}) \tag{1-7b}$$

with $+$ for an nMOST and $-$ for a pMOST.

Q_D is the charge in the JFETs depletion layer. The term Q_D/C_{ox} or the term in γ in V_T thus represents the body effect or the effect of the parasitic JFET.

Example 1-1

Plot V_{T0} for values of $Q_{ox} = 5 \times 10^{10}$ qcm^{-2} and $N_G = 2 \times 10^{19}$ cm^{-3} at 27°C; N_{SUB} varies between 10^{14} and 10^{16} cm^{-3}. Note that 50 nm gate oxide thickness is used: $C_{ox} = 6.810^{-8}$ F/cm^2.

Solution. The values of V_{T0} are plotted versus N_{SUB} in Fig. 1-3a. Note that all terms of V_{T0} are also given in Table 1-2. They are negative for the pMOST. For the nMOST two terms are positive, i.e., $2|\phi_F|$ and $\gamma\sqrt{2|\phi_F|}$.

Increasing the bulk doping level also makes the value of the nMOST threshold voltage more positive, but makes the pMOST more negative. This is mainly a result of the body factor γ. It is clearly seen that for a low-bulk doping level, the threshold voltages of both transistors are negative. For increasing values of the bulk doping level, the value of the nMOST threshold voltage goes through zero to become positive.

A similar variation in threshold voltage can be obtained by variation of the bulk-source polarization v_{BS}. Indeed, Eq. (1-7b) shows how V_T changes. The curves are shown in Fig. 1-3b. The variation of V_T with v_{BS} is much weaker than with bulk doping N_B. As a result, both techniques, i.e., the variation of the bulk doping level N_B and the variation of the back gate-biasing v_{BS}, can be used to set the value of the threshold voltage to a desired value. Obviously, once the MOST devices have been realized in a specific technology, only the second technique is available to the designer: only v_{BS} can be used to modify V_T.

TABLE 1-2   COMPONENTS OF V_{T0}^*

	N_B(cm^{-3})	ϕ_{GB}	$-Q_{ox}/C_{ox}$	$2\phi_F$	$\pm Q_D/C_{ox}$	V_{T0}
nMOST	3×10^{14}	-0.799	-0.118	0.512	0.107	-0.298
	10^{16}	-0.890	-0.118	0.694	0.717	0.403
pMOST	3×10^{14}	-0.287	-0.118	-0.512	-0.107	-1.024
	10^{16}	-0.196	-0.118	-0.694	-0.717	-1.725

$^*t_{ox} = 50$ nm, $Q_{ox} = 5 \times 10^{10}$ q cm^{-2}, $n+$ gate $N_G = 2 \times 10^{19}$ cm^{-3}

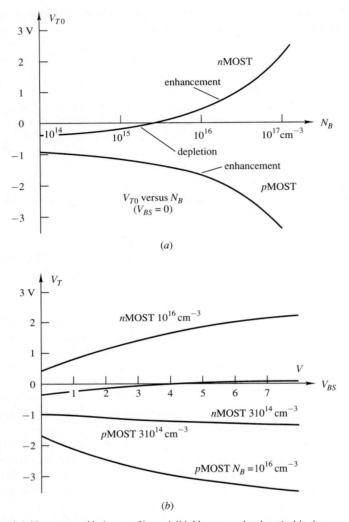

FIGURE 1-3   (a) V_{T0} versus N_3 ($v_{BS} = 0$), and (b) V_T versus back gate biasing.

1-2-5   Enhancement and Depletion MOST

An important question arises from an inspection of Fig. 1-3. What is the meaning of a positive or negative threshold voltage for an nMOST and pMOST?

In an nMOST, a drain-source current i_{DS} can flow provided the drain is made positive with respect to the source. The substrate is connected to the source. The drain then must be made positive. Otherwise the $n+$ drain would be forward biased with respect to the substrate, and would not be isolated from the substrate.

The drain-source voltage in an nMOST is always positive. Assume now that a positive gate-source voltage v_{GS} is required before drain-source current i_{DS} can flow. This gate-source voltage v_{GS} is the threshold voltage and is positive. The nMOST is an enhancement type. Its i_{DS} versus v_{GS} characteristic is shown in Fig. 1-4a.

Similarly for a pMOST the drain is now made negative with respect to the source. If the threshold voltage is negative, a pMOST of the enhancement type results (see Fig. 1-4b). The value of v_{GS} must be made larger (in absolute value, or more negative in real value) than V_T in order to allow current i_{DS} to flow.

However, if the threshold voltage of an nMOST is now negative, current i_{DS} already flows for zero v_{GS} as shown in Fig. 1-4c. This transistor is a depletion type. Despite its positive v_{DS}, its V_T is negative. Since the values of v_{DS} are always positive, the transistor can never be switched off.

FIGURE 1-4   (a) Transfer characteristic enhancement nMOST, (b) transfer characteristic enhancement pMOST, (c) transfer characteristic depletion nMOST, and (d) transfer characteristic depletion pMOST.

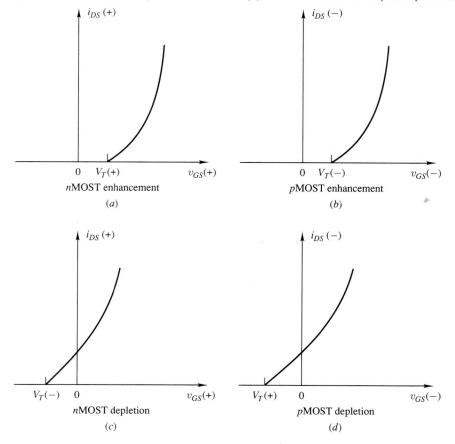

Similarly, a positive value of V_T gives rise to a pMOST of the depletion type. However, it is noted in Fig. 1-3 that positive values of V_T never occur for pMOSTs. Contrarily, nMOSTs can be of both the enhancement and depletion type, depending on their fabrication and substrate biasing. This is a result of the negative values of the threshold voltages at low substrate doping levels, caused by the presence of the parasitic JFET represented by parameter γ.

1-3   MOST LINEAR REGION AND SATURATION REGION

In order to fully understand what happens to all the charges in the MOST when voltages such as v_{GS}, v_{DS} and v_{BS} are applied, it is important to understand value of the charge, electric field, and potential distributions in a MOS transistor structure. These values can be obtained by first-order calculations,

1-3-1   Large v_{GS}, Small v_{DS}, and Zero v_{BS}

Under these conditions a large value of v_{GS} is applied, which is higher than V_{T0}. The other voltage v_{BS} is kept at zero and v_{DS} at nearly zero. An inversion channel is created underneath the gate oxide. The channel consists of mobile electrons with charge Q_m.

This charge Q_m is a result of the definition of the threshold voltage. It is given by

$$Q_m = C_{\text{ox}}(v_{GS} - V_T) \tag{1-8}$$

The mobile charge Q_m actually connects drain and source. It acts as a resistance connecting drain and source and is given by the sheet resistance under the gate. This sheet resistance is expressed in Ohms/$\square$. Its value is inversely proportional to this charge, as given by

$$R_{DS\square} = \frac{1}{\mu Q_m} \tag{1-9a}$$

For the actual value of the resistance, its dimensions W and L (see Fig. 1-1c) must be considered. This yields

$$R_{DS} = R_{DS\square}\frac{L}{W} = \frac{1}{\beta(v_{GS} - V_T)} \tag{1-9b}$$

with
$$\beta = \frac{W}{L}\text{KP} \tag{1-9c}$$

and
$$\text{KP} = \mu C_{\text{ox}} \tag{1-9d}$$

in which μ is the mobility in the channel.

Example 1-2

For $C_{ox} = 6.8 \times 10^{-8}$ F/cm^2, $\mu = 500$ cm^2/Vs and $W/L = 10$, calculate R_{DS} for $V_{GS} = 3.5$ and 5.5 V if $V_T = 0.9$ V.

Solution. From Eq. (1-9a) KP $= 34$ μA/V^2. If $W/L = 10$ then 10 $\square$'s are present; hence $\beta = 0.34$ mA/V^2. For $V_{GS} = 3.5$ V the value of $R_{DS\square} = 11.36$ k$\Omega/\square$ and R_{DS} is 10 times smaller or $R_{DS} = 1.136$ kΩ.

A small voltage V_{DS} across that resistance, e.g., of 0.1 V allows a current to flow of $I_{DS} = V_{DS}/R_{DS} = 88$ μA. For $V_{GS} = 5.5$ V the value of R_{DS} is 0.64 kΩ and $I_{DS} = 156$ μA.

For larger values of v_{DS}, this resistance R_{DS} becomes a function of v_{DS} as well. The current is then a nonlinear function of v_{DS}. A different calculation of the current is then necessary. As long as resistance R_{DS} does not depend on v_{DS}, the MOST is said to be in its linear region. The MOST can rightly be represented by a simple resistance R_{DS}, as given by Eq. (1-9).

Note that an important transistor parameter has been defined in Eq. (1-9d), i.e., transconductance parameter KP, which equals μC_{ox}. It is thus present in the list of SPICE parameters of Table 1-1. Some confusion may arise from the presence of μ (as U0) in the same list of parameters. It is sufficient to specify KP; parameter U0 is used to model mobility degradation effects (see higher-order models in Sec. 1-9).

1-3-2 Large v_{GS}, Large v_{DS}, and Zero v_{BS}

For larger values of v_{DS}, the value of Q_m is now given by

$$Q_m = C_{ox}[v_{GS} - V_T(v_{DS}) - v_{DS}] \qquad (1\text{-}10)$$

Note that the value of V_T now changes from source to drain because the depletion layer charge Q_D increases from source to drain. At the source side it is still given by Eq. (1-6e), but at the drain side it is given by Eq. (1-7a) with v_{DS} instead of v_{BS}.

Example 1-3

Take the nMOST with $C_{ox} = 6.8 \times 10^{-8}$C/cm^2, $N_B = 10^{16}$ cm^{-3} such that $V_{T0} = 0.4$ V (see Table 1-2) and $\gamma = 0.86$ V$^{1/2}$. Its $W/L = 10$ and $\mu = 500$ cm^2/Vs. Its $V_{GS} = 5$ V. Calculate the change of threshold voltage along the channel and the charges Q_D and Q_m for $V_{DS} = 1$ V.

Solution. The value of Q_D increases from 4.85×10^{-8} C/cm^2 at the source to 7.58×10^{-8} C/cm^2 at the drain. As a result, V_T increases from 0.4 V at the source to 0.45 V at the drain. On the other hand, the value of Q_m decreases from $Q_m = -1.76 \times 10^{-7}$ C/cm^2 at the source to -8.07×10^{-8} C/cm^2 at the drain.

The most important effect of raising the drain voltage is the reduction of the mobile charge Q_m at the drain side. The value of Q_m thus decreases from the source toward the drain. The resistance connecting drain and source is nonlinear. It can no longer be calculated by the simple Eq. (1-10). The technique consists of taking the integral of the resistance along the channel. This is discussed in Sec. 1-4.

Eventually the voltage v_{DS} can be increased to the extent that the mobile charge Q_m disappears altogether (see Fig. 1-5 at the drain side). At this point, the MOST is said to be in *saturation*. The value of v_{DS} at which saturation occurs is called v_{DSsat}. It can be extracted from Eq. (1-10) by putting Q_m to zero. Note, however, that V_T also depends on V_{DS} and hence changes along the channel. This calculation will be discussed later. An approximate or first-order value is obtained if the dependence of V_T on V_{DS} is neglected. This means that the value of V_T is then taken at the source side. The value of v_{DSsat} is simply given by

$$v_{DSsat} = v_{GS} - V_T \tag{1-11}$$

At this point, the potential in the channel has become independent of v_{DS}. Raising the value of v_{DS} even further does not change the potential. The end point of the channel is separated from the drain by a depletion layer, across which a voltage of $v_{DS} - v_{DSsat}$ is present (see Fig. 1-5). The width of this depletion layer x_{DCsat} is easily calculated in first-order by means of Eq. (1-3a), because the substrate doping and the voltage across the layer are known. This result cannot be expected to be accurate however, because of two-dimensional effects.

Finally, since the potential at the end of the channel is fixed, the voltage along the channel resistance is fixed as well, given by $v_{GS} - V_T$ (see Fig. 1-5). As a result, the current flowing between drain and source is constant. It has become independent of v_{DS}. The current is saturated. Therefore this region of values of v_{DS} where v_{DS} is greater than v_{DSsat}, is called the "saturation region."

FIGURE 1-5   (a) nMOST in saturation, and (b) longitudinal potential distribution.

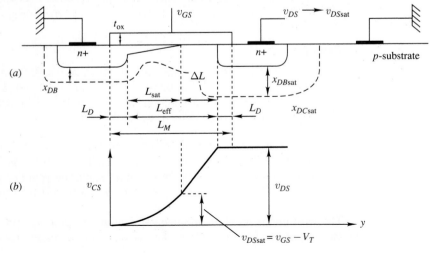

1-3-3 Large v_{GS}, Small v_{DS} and Large v_{BS}

Raising the bulk to source voltage by v_{BS} increases the voltage drop across the bulk to channel depletion region by the same amount. However, the potential in the channel itself is fixed by the fixed zero potentials of drain and source. Therefore it does not change.

The value of Q_m can also be derived from Eq. (1-8), as given by

$$Q_m = C_{ox}(v_{GS} - V_T(v_{BS})) \tag{1-12}$$

Let us stress that the value of V_T in Eq. (1-12) also depends on v_{BS}. Indeed, V_T depends on v_{BS} as given by Eq. (1-7b) because the depletion layer charge has increased.

For example, for $V_{BS} = -2$ V, the value of V_T is now increased from 0.4 V to 0.45 V. The value of Q_m is decreased from $Q_m = -1.76 \times 10^{-7}$ C/cm^2 to -1.28×10^{-7} C/cm^2.

Actually, the voltage v_{BS} could be increased so much that the mobile charge Q_m disappears completely when the MOST is said to be pinched off. The value of V_{BS} at which saturation occurs is the pinchoff voltage of the bulk JFET. This value could be extracted from Eq. (1-12) by putting Q_m to zero. Note, however, that V_T also depends on V_{BS}. Therefore, the exact calculation is not easily carried out. It would be found that large values of V_{BS} are required to pinch off the channel. Also, this value obviously depends on the value of V_{GS} used. Because this calculation concerns device physics, we will not consider it.

1-4 MOST CURRENT-VOLTAGE CHARACTERISTICS

In this section, the relation between the drain-source current i_{DS} and any combination of voltages v_{GS}, v_{DS}, and v_{BS} that can be applied is examined. For each case, the value of the mobile charge Q_m must be calculated as a function of these voltages. Integration of this charge between drain and source allows us to calculate the current. This value is first calculated for the linear region of the MOST, where the value of v_{DS} is small. An nMOST is taken for the derivation.

1-4-1 Linear Region

The value of the mobile charge for strong inversion has already been calculated in the previous section. For an nMOST, it is given by

$$Q_m(y) = C_{ox}[v_{GS} - V_T(v_{CS}(y)) - v_{CS}(y)] \tag{1-13}$$

in which $v_{CS}(y)$ is the channel potential with respect to the source and is a function of v_{DS} and v_{BS}. The y direction is the longitudinal direction along the channel from source to drain.

The current i_{DS} through the channel is directly proportional to the incremental voltage drop $dv_{CS}(y)$ across the incremental channel resistance dR_{DS}. Obviously, this resistance depends on the mobile channel charge Q_m as seen in Eq. (1-9) and as given by

$$dR_{DS} = R_{DS\square}\frac{dy}{W} = \frac{1}{\mu Q_m(y)}\frac{dy}{W} \qquad (1\text{-}14)$$

The current is simply given by $i_{DS} = dv_{CS}(y)/dR_{DS}$. After substitution of $Q_m(y)$ from Eq. (1-13), and after separation of the variables, we obtain the expression

$$i_{DS}dy = W\mu C_{\text{ox}}\{v_{GS} - V_T[v_{CS}(y)] - v_{CS}(y)\}dv_{CS}(y) \qquad (1\text{-}15)$$

The channel mobility μ also depends on the channel potential. Indeed, the mobility decreases slightly from source to drain. In first approximation, the mobility is given an average or effective value μ_{eff}, which is then independent of the position along the channel. Typical values are 500 cm^2/Vs for an nMOST and 200 cm^2/Vs for a pMOST.

In this expression, the dependence of the threshold voltage $V_T(v_{CS}(y))$ must be made explicit before integration can be carried out. It is obtained from Eq. (1-7b), in which v_{BS} is to be replaced by $v_{BS} - v_{CS}(y)$. This substitution and the integration of the left side of Eq. (1-15) from 0 to L and the right side from 0 to v_{DS}, yields an expression that can be simplified to

$$i_{DS} = \beta \left[\left(v_{GS} - V_{T0} - \frac{v_{DS}}{2}\right) v_{DS} \pm \gamma F(2/3) \right] \qquad (1\text{-}16a)$$

in which factor $F(2/3)$ always reduces the current in absolute value. It is given by

$$F\left(\frac{2}{3}\right) = (2|\phi_F|)^{1/2}v_{DS} + \frac{2}{3}[(v_{DS} + 2|\phi_F| - v_{BS})^{3/2} - (2|\phi_F| - v_{BS})^{3/2}] \quad (1\text{-}16b)$$

The MOST model of Eq. (1-16) has been implemented in several circuit simulators, such as SPICE. While the model is too complicated for hand calculations, it can be simplified as follows.

1-4-2   Linear Region: First-Order Model

In order to simplify the full model, it is assumed that the depletion layer charge is kept constant along the channel. The charge keeps the same value as at the source side. Hence, it does not depend on the variation of the channel potential. As a result, the depletion layer charge Q_D and threshold voltage V_T do not depend on the channel potential either. Their values are the same as they would be at the source side. The threshold voltage is simply V_{T0}. The expression of the current is again obtained by integration of both sides of Eq. (1-15), but after the replacement of $V_T(v_{CS}(y))$ by V_{T0}. It is also given by the first term of Eq. (1-16)

$$i_{DS} = \beta \left(v_{GS} - V_{T0} - \frac{v_{DS}}{2}\right) v_{DS} \qquad (1\text{-}17)$$

This is the most commonly used expression for hand calculations. Let us now investigate the circumstances under which both expressions Eq. (1-16) and Eq. (1-17) can provide nearly equal values for the current. This occurs in three cases:

1 When the *depletion layer charge* (and the threshold voltage) is kept constant and keeps the same value along the channel as at the source. In this case, Eq. (1-17) has been found.

2 When factor γ is small. This can only be the case when the substrate doping level is low (see Eq. (1-5a)), or when C_{ox} is high, i.e., when the oxide is quite thin.

3 When the drain-source voltage v_{DS} is very small with respect to $2|\phi_F|$, the second and the third term of the $F(2/3)$ factor can be developed in a series (for $v_{BS} = 0$). Truncation after the second term of the series again yields Eq. (1-17).

This means that for values of $V_{DS} \approx 10$ mV, Eq. (1-17) provides an exact value of the current. Therefore, this condition can be used to extract the value of V_{T0} and β from measurements.

If v_{BS} is not zero, then this requirement is less severe. Indeed, $|v_{DS}|$ must be smaller than only $2|\phi_F| - v_{BS}$.

Finally, for small values of v_{DS}, the term $v_{DS}/2$ is negligible with respect to $v_{GS} - V_{T0}$ in Eq. (1-17). As a result, the same expression is obtained as that in Eq. (1-9b), which had been derived for nearly zero v_{DS}. The value of the drain source resistance, as calculated by Eq. (1-9b) is accurate, provided $|v_{DS}|$ is much smaller than $2|\phi_F| - v_{BS}$.

1-4-3 MOST in Saturation: First-Order Model

For large values of v_{DS}, the saturation condition is reached. This means that v_{DS} has reached the value where the mobile charge Q_m has been reduced to zero at the drain side. This value of v_{DS} is called v_{DSsat} and is obtained by putting Q_m equal to zero in Eq. (1-10), then solving with respect to v_{DS}. If the threshold voltage is kept constant and equal to V_{T0}, Eq. (1-11) results. If, on the other hand, the expression of V_T is taken from Eq. (1-7b), with v_{BS} substituted by $v_{DSsat} - v_{BS}$, then a quadratic equation results in v_{DS}. This equation is solved exactly in SPICE. For hand calculations, however, it is never used; normally, the first-order Eq. (1-11) is used with V_{T0}.

The value of the current i_{DS} that is reached at $v_{DS} = v_{DSsat}$ is i_{DSsat}. It is obtained by substituting the actual value of v_{DSsat} by the actual current in Eq. (1-16).

For hand calculations it is easier, however, to substitute the first-order expression of v_{DSsat}, given by Eq. (1-11), into the first-order expression of i_{DS} in Eq. (1-17). This yields, after simplification

$$i_{DSsat} = \frac{\beta}{2}(v_{GS} - V_T)^2 \tag{1-18a}$$

in which V_T still depends on v_{BS} as given by Eq. (1-7b). This simple expression will be used for all hand calculations on MOST's in saturation. Thus it is important to know how accurate it is. This is demonstrated in the following example.

Example 1-4

Take the nMOST with $V_{T0} \approx 0.4$ V and $\gamma = 0.86$ V$^{1/2}$ from Example 1-3, where $W/L = 10$ and $\mu = 500$ cm^2/Vs. Calculate its current exactly and in first-order (also in saturation) for $V_{GS} = 3$ V, $V_{BS} = 0$ V and $V_{DS} = 1$ V.

Solution. This nMOST $\beta = 0.34$ mA/V^2. Its DC current is given by Eq. (1-16) and equals 0.64 mA. Its first-order value is given by Eq. (1-17) and equals 0.713 mA, which is larger than the actual value (0.64 mA). The actual value is about 10 percent smaller than the first-order value. For that reason factor β in Eq. (1-17) could be reduced to take this difference into account. This reduction will be included in a new parameter K', introduced later.

The first-order value $V_{DSsat} = 2.6$ V. The exact value, however, can be calculated as just explained (or from SPICE) and equals 1.92 V. This exact value is considerably smaller than the first-order value. The exact value of $I_{DSsat} = 0.82$ mA. The first-order Eq. (1-11) yields $I_{DSsat} = 1.146$ mA. The actual value is thus smaller than the first-order value by as much as 23 percent. Again, factor β in Eq. (1-17) could be reduced to take this difference into account and carried out by introducing a new parameter K', or by using factor n.

1-4-4 Parameters K' and n

In order to calculate the actual current by means of the simple Eq. (1-18a), a correction factor must be added to the $\beta/2$ factor in Eq. (1-18a). This factor is replaced by a factor K', out of which the ratio W/L is separated. The current is then given by

$$i_{DSsat} = K'\frac{W}{L}(v_{GS} - V_T)^2 \tag{1-18b}$$

Note that the factor $K'W/L$ is always smaller than factor $\beta/2$. For small values of γ, however, their values are very close.

In general, the value of K' is obtained from measurements in the saturation region. It provides a parabolic characteristic as shown in Fig. 1-6a. It can be extracted from the slope of the linear curve of $(I_{DSsat})^{1/2}$ versus v_{GS} as shown later in Fig. 1-9b. The intercept gives the value of V_T itself. For different v_{BS}, the curve shifts to the right (see Fig. 1-6a), corresponding to larger values of V_T as given by Eq. (1-7b).

This value of V_T (extracted from Fig. 1-9b) may be different from the value obtained for the MOST in the linear region for very small v_{DS}. This is the same as the difference between $K'W/L$ and β. The value of KP used in the circuit simulator SPICE (see Table 1-1) equals μC_{ox} such that $\beta =$ KP$W/L$. It is thus different from K'. A list of different K''s appears in Table 1-3.

An alternate way to reduce the current i_{DS} is to add n as a correction factor, as given by

$$i_{DSsat} = \frac{\beta}{2n}(v_{GS} - V_T)^2 = \frac{\text{KP}}{2n}\frac{W}{L}(v_{GS} - V_T)^2 \tag{1-18c}$$

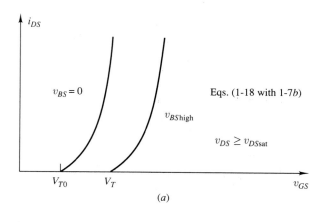

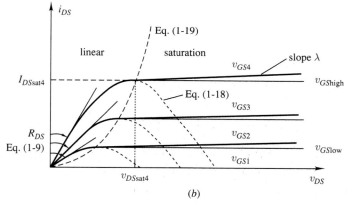

FIGURE 1-6 (a) i_{DS}/v_{GS} and (b) i_{DS}/v_{DS} (for $v_{BS} = 0$) characteristics of nMOST.

TABLE 1-3 K VALUES OF A MOST

Parameter	Expression	Expression for current i_{DS}	Equation number	Comment
β	$\mu C_{ox} \dfrac{W}{L}$	$\beta \left[(v_{GS} - V_T)v_{DS} - \dfrac{v_{DS}^2}{2} \right]$	Eq. (1-17)	linear region
β		$\dfrac{\beta}{2n}(v_{GS} - V_T)^2$	Eq. (1-18c)	saturation
KP	μC_{ox}	$\dfrac{KP}{2n}\dfrac{W}{L}(v_{GS} - V_T)^2$	Eq. (1-18c)	saturation SPICE parameter
KP_n	$\mu_n C_{ox}$	—	—	KP for nMOST
KP_p	$\mu_p C_{ox}$	—	—	KP for pMOST
K'	$< \dfrac{\mu C_{ox}}{2}$	$K'\dfrac{W}{L}(v_{GS} - V_T)^2$	Eq. (1-18b)	saturation parameter
K'_n		—	—	K' for nMOST
K'_p		—	—	K' for pMOST

in which n is always larger than unity as given by Eq. (1-5b). This expression may be used for hand calculations as well. SPICE users prefer this expression because KP can be used in the transistor model.

In this case, the first-order expressions of the current in the linear region Eq. (1-17) and v_{DSsat} Eq. (1-11) must be corrected as well, as given by

$$i_{DS} = \beta \left(v_{GS} - V_T - \frac{n}{2} v_{DS} \right) v_{DS} \qquad (1\text{-}18d)$$

and

$$v_{DSsat} = \frac{v_{GS} - V_T}{n} \qquad (1\text{-}18e)$$

1-4-5 Plots of i_{DS} versus v_{GS} and v_{BS}

Now that the current-voltage characteristics are known, they can be plotted as seen in Fig. 1-6. The first is the i_{DS} versus v_{GS} characteristic, with v_{BS} as a variable, also called the *transfer characteristic*. It is given by Eq. (1-18c), along with Eq. (1-7b), for the dependence on v_{BS}. It always forms a parabola, starting at $v_{GS} = V_T$. For larger values of v_{BS}, the curve shifts to the right, giving smaller values of i_{DS} for the same v_{GS}.

In the second curve (Fig. 1-6b), the i_{DS} versus v_{DS} characteristics are shown with v_{GS} as a variable. They are also called the *output characteristics*. For low values of v_{DS}, the characteristics are linear and well-approximated by Eq. (1-9). For larger values of v_{DS}, the full expressions must be used, given in first-order by Eq. (1-17). This is an inverted parabola, with its top on the onset of the saturation region. The portion of the parabola within the saturation region (represented by dotted lines) is thus not valid.

The saturation region is reached at v_{DSsat} in first-order, given by Eq. (1-11). Both regions are separated by the curve obtained from Eq. (1-18c) and Eq. (1-11) and described by

$$i_{DSsat} = \frac{KP}{2n} \frac{W}{L} (v_{GS} - V_T)^2 = \frac{KP}{2n} \frac{W}{L} (v_{DSsat})^2 \qquad (1\text{-}19)$$

which is another parabola, but with its top in the origin of the axes (represented by a dashed line in Fig. 1-6b).

Once the saturation region is reached, v_{DS} has no more influence on the current. Thus the current stays constant for increasing values of v_{DS}. Actually, the current increases slightly as a result of the extension of the depletion layer charge at the drain into the channel toward the source (see Fig. 1-5) over a distance ΔL. The voltage drop over ΔL is about $(v_{DS} - v_{DSsat})$. Thus the channel length is reduced over a distance ΔL from L to L_{sat}. This reduction in L in Eq. (1-18c) causes a slight increase in current. Therefore, the current in the saturation region is better represented by

$$i_{DSsat} = \frac{KP}{2n} \frac{W}{L} (v_{GS} - V_T)^2 (1 + \lambda v_{DS}) \qquad (1\text{-}20)$$

in which λ is a fit parameter. This parameter determines the slope of the output characteristic. For short channel lengths this parameter is larger than for long channel lengths, because the channel shortening is relatively more important. Parameter λ thus depends on L. It is an important parameter for all small-signal gain calculations and it will be discussed in more detail in Sec. 1-5.

1-4-6 Effective Channel Length and Width

Since the current is very sensitive to changes in channel length L, exact knowledge of L is important.

The effective channel length L_{eff} is given by

$$L_{\text{eff}} = L_M - 2\text{LD} - DL \qquad (1\text{-}21a)$$

where L_M is the channel length drawn in the layout (on the mask),

  LD is the underdiffusion and

  DL is a reduction because of photolithography and etching.

This latter reduction is not considered by SPICE and must be subtracted by hand. See Table 1-1 (Antognetti and Massobrio 1988).

The underdiffusion LD is a result of underdiffusion of the source and drain islands underneath the gate as seen in Fig. 1-5. It occurs on both the source and drain side of the channel. Typically it is about 80 percent of the source/drain junction depth XJ. Usually the value of LD is given directly in the parameter list (see Table 1-1). Note, however, that only parameter LD must be specified in the model. Parameter XJ is used only for the calculation of second-order effects, such as channel shortening (parameter DELTA) as seen in Sec. 1-9.

Similarly, the gate width W is reduced by DW as given by

$$W_{\text{eff}} = W_M + \text{DW} \qquad (1\text{-}21b)$$

This reduction is also listed in Table 1-1.

For very low and very high currents, the quadratic model Eq. (1-20) breaks down. At low currents, weak inversion occurs and a different model is required. On the other hand, velocity saturation does occur at very high currents, which also requires a different model. These models are discussed later in this chapter.

1-5 SMALL-SIGNAL MODEL IN SATURATION

In order to evaluate the response of gain stages to actual small signals, small-signal models must be used. Small signals are considered to be small variations on DC or biasing signals. For example, the total gate-source voltage v_{GS} can vary with time. Its DC component is then represented by V_{GS} and its variation by Δv_{GS}. The variations can have any nature. In this text, we use signals of sinusoidal or quasi-sinusoidal nature. So that v_{GS} can be expressed as a Fourier series of sinusoidal signals (see Chap. 7).

The variations always have a small amplitude; thus they are called *small signals*. Small signals are represented by v_{gs} and their amplitude by Δv_{GS} or, preferably, V_{gs}. Depending on what actual amplitude is meant, the peak value is represented by V_{gsp}, its RMS value by V_{gsRMS}, etc. Remember that $V_{gsRMS} = V_{gsp}/\sqrt{2}$. The full notation of symbols used is given in App. 1-1.

Let us now take an nMOST in the saturation region, that is biased by voltage source V_{GSQ} (see Fig. 1-7). Its i_{DS} versus v_{GS} characteristic (which represents Eq. (1-18c)) shows what the current is. It is given by the quiescent operating point Q. This current is the biasing current I_{DSQ}.

A small variation on the biasing voltage versus time causes a small variation in current as well. The peak amplitudes of these small signals are V_{gsp} and I_{dsp}, respectively. The time dependent amplitudes of these small signals are, respectively, V_{gs} and I_{ds}. Their values can be obtained from Eq. (1-18c). However, it is easier to have a direct relationship between the small-signal amplitudes. This is given by the small-signal model. Let us now derive this model for the MOST in the saturation region.

FIGURE 1-7 Transfer characteristics showing DC voltage amplification.

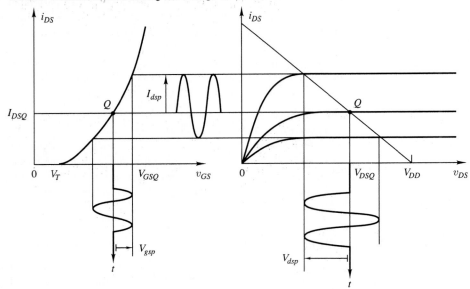

1-5-1   Transconductance g_m

The relationship between i_{ds} and v_{gs} is given by the slope of the i_{DS} versus v_{GS} characteristic at point Q. It is called the transconductance g_m. Indeed, it has the dimension of a conductance and it gives the ratio between the signal output current to the signal input voltage, i.e., the signal transfer.

This slope is actually the derivative of i_{DS} to v_{GS} in that point (Eq. (1-18c)), which yields

$$g_m = 2\frac{\text{KP}}{2n}\frac{W}{L}(V_{GSQ} - V_T) \tag{1-22a}$$

Alternative expressions are obtained by substitution, such as

$$g_m = 2\sqrt{\frac{\text{KP}}{2n}\frac{W}{L}I_{DSQ}} \tag{1-22b}$$

or

$$g_m = \frac{2I_{DSQ}}{V_{GSQ} - V_T} \tag{1-22c}$$

Remember that $\text{KP}/2n$ can always be replaced by K'. All these expressions will be used later during the design procedures, so the reader must be familiar with them all. Two out of the three variables I_{DSQ}, $V_{GSQ} - V_T$, and W/L are sufficient to determine g_m. This will later be exploited in the design procedures for amplifiers.

The transconductance is thus proportional to the square root of the current in Eq. (1-22b). Quadrupling the current only doubles the transconductance.

It is worth noting that comparison of Eq. (1-22a) and Eq. (1-9b) shows that the on resistance R_{DS}, in the linear region, is approximately the inverse of the transconductance g_m in the saturation region. It is difficult to find an intuitive reason for this, and yet it is worth considering. Insight into FET operation may be gained from this observation.

The small-signal model of the MOST in saturation is depicted in Fig. 1-8a. The input node at the gate is isolated. Its small-signal or AC voltage v_{gs} controls the current from drain to source i_{ds} by means of a voltage-controlled current source with value $g_m v_{gs}$.

FIGURE 1-8   Small-signal or AC equivalent circuitry.

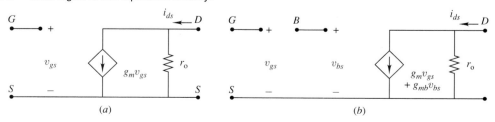

(a)   (b)

1-5-2   Bulk Transconductance g_{mb}

In the simple small-signal model, the bulk is connected to the source. If this is not so, a bulk node must be added. This is done in Fig. 1-8b, in which g_{mb} represents the transconductance from the bulk input-node voltage v_{bs} to the output current i_{ds}. This is called the bulk transconductance, but actually is the transconductance of the parasitic JFET. Its value can be obtained from differentiation of i_{DS} to v_{BS} as given by Eq. (1-18c) and Eq. (1-7b). It is given by

$$g_{mb} = \frac{\gamma}{2\sqrt{|2\phi_F - v_{BSQ}|}} g_m = \frac{C_{BSQ}}{C_{ox}} g_m = (n-1) g_m \qquad (1\text{-}23)$$

in which parameter γ has been implemented by means of Eq. (1-5a). Any of the above expressions can be used to calculate g_{mb}. The last expression is evidently the simplest, as the ratio of g_{mb} to g_m is simply $n - 1$.

1-5-3   Output Resistance r_o

One more parameter must be added to the small-signal model consisting of g_m and g_{mb}. It is the output resistance r_o or output conductance $g_{DS} = g_o = 1/r_o$. It is a result of the channel-shortening effect by v_{DS}. This causes the current to increase slowly for increasing values of v_{DS}, as shown in Fig. 1-6b and given by Eq. (1-20). The value of parameter r_o can be derived from Eq. (1-20). Its value is the inverse of the derivative of i_{DSsat} to v_{DS}. It is given by

$$r_o = \frac{1}{\lambda I_{DSsat}} \qquad (1\text{-}24a)$$

A first-order value of λ can be obtained by calculating the extension of the depletion layer (x_{DCsat} in Fig. 1-5) in the channel. This value can be erroneous, however, because of several two-dimensional effects. Therefore, an empirical expression is preferred.

Obviously, parameter λ depends on the channel length L, yet is assumed to be constant in SPICE. The model used in SPICE for Eq. (1-20) is only a very crude one. Therefore, another parameter is chosen, taking into account the dependence on channel length L. Equation (1-24a) is rewritten, as given by

$$r_o = \frac{1}{g_{DS}} = \frac{V_E L}{I_{DSsat}} \qquad (1\text{-}24b)$$

Comparison of Eq. (1-24a) and Eq. (1-24b) shows that the voltage V_E can be derived from λ, as given by

$$V_E = \frac{1}{\lambda L} \qquad (1\text{-}24c)$$

Parameter V_E is the *Early voltage* per unit-channel length in analogy with the Early voltage of a bipolar transistor (see Sec. 2-3). It is different for the nMOST and the pMOST because of the difference in substrate doping level. The extension of the depletion layer into the channel is inversely proportional to the substrate doping level (see Eq. (1-3a)). The larger the substrate doping, the larger the Early voltage.

Representative values for an n-well CMOS process are $V_{En} = 4$ V/μmL and $V_{Ep} = 7$ V/μmL. For the same channel length the output resistance of the nMOST is thus smaller than of the pMOST, in an n-well CMOS process. It is the opposite for a p-well CMOS process: $V_{Ep} = 4$ V/μmL and $V_{En} = 7$ V/μmL.

In SPICE, parameter λ is listed as LAMBDA (see Table 1-1). Thus we must convert Eq. (1-24) by hand. For each different channel length used, a different model card must be used.

In order to gain some familiarity with the small-signal model, a few simple examples are presented later in this chapter. But first we must verify the validity of this model at the low and high current ends.

1-6   WEAK INVERSION AND VELOCITY SATURATION

1-6-1   MOST In Weak Inversion

The characteristics previously given are all related to strong inversion (si) operation: the values of i_{DS} and of v_{GS} are large and the surface potential is larger than $2\phi_F$. However, for small values of the current i_{DS}, v_{GS} is barely larger than V_T (see Fig. 1-9a). For very small values of the current, v_{GS} can even be slightly smaller than V_T. This is the weak inversion region (Tsividis 1988).

Indeed, let us look at the i_{DS} versus v_{GS} characteristic in a plot of $\log(i_{DS})$ versus v_{GS} (see Fig. 1-9c). Below the threshold voltage, the current decreases exponentially towards zero. This is called the subthreshold region.

In this region of operation v_{GS} is less than V_T, so the mobile charge Q_m is already zero and the depletion charge Q_D is now larger. Previously considered to be the onset of strong inversion, the surface potential drop now is smaller than $2\phi_F$. This region is now properly called the weak-inversion (wi) region.

Actually the current still flows at the surface underneath the gate of the MOST, but it now flows in the depletion layer. Again, the current depends on both controlling capacitances C_{ox} and C_{BC}.

In the saturation region, v_{DS} must be larger than $v_{DS\text{sat}}$. This value is now about zero, however, because $v_{DS\text{sat}} \approx v_{GS} - V_T$ is about zero. Therefore it is sufficient that v_{DS} be larger than a few times kT/q or about 200 mV. The current is then given by

$$i_{DS\text{wi}} = \frac{W}{L} I_{D0} \exp\left(\frac{v_{GS}}{nkT/q}\right) \tag{1-25a}$$

in which coefficient n is given by Eq. (1-5b). This is the third occurrence of parameter n.

This expression clearly illustrates the exponential behavior of the subthreshold or weak inversion characteristic. The inverse slope (see Fig. 1-9c) is now larger than kT/q, (corresponding with 60 mV/decade); it is nkT/q. Therefore, factor n is also called the *subthreshold slope factor*. As a result, the easiest way to extract values of n is from the slope of the weak inversion characteristic.

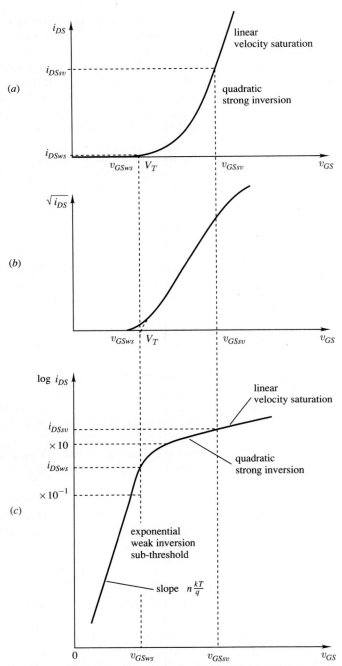

FIGURE 1-9 i_{DS}/v_{GS} characteristic with a (*a*) linear, (*b*) square root, and (*c*) logarithmic current scale.

In order to provide the full expression in the saturation region, Eq. (1-25a) must be multiplied by the same factor $(1 + \lambda v_{DS})$ as in Eq. (1-20). The same parameter λ can be used in strong and weak inversion.

For the weak inversion region, the *transconductance* g_m is again obtained by taking the derivative of i_{DS} versus v_{GS} in Eq. (1-25a), which yields

$$g_{mwi} = \frac{W}{L} \frac{I_{D0}}{nkT/q} \exp\left(\frac{v_{GSQ}}{nkT/q}\right) = \frac{i_{DSQ\text{wi}}}{nkT/q} \qquad (1\text{-}25b)$$

The transconductance is now directly proportional to the current. The transconductance is sketched on a bilogarithmic scale versus the current in Fig. 1-10a. The change in slope from 1 to 1/2, going from weak to strong inversion, is clearly seen.

1-6-2 Transconductance-Current Ratio

The transconductance is the most important parameter of the MOST because it reflects the transfer efficiency from input to output. A better criterion, however, is its transconductance to current ratio g_m/i_{DS}. This ratio shows how efficiently the current is used to generate transconductance.

FIGURE 1-10 (a) g_m and, (b) g_m/I_{DS} of MOST in saturation.

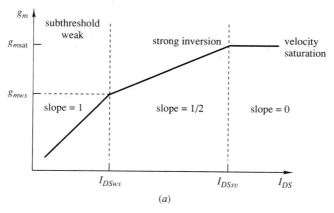

(a)

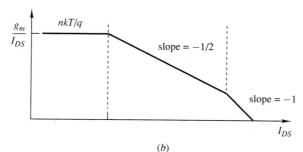

(b)

In strong inversion this ratio is obtained from Eq. (1-18) and Eq. (1-22), and is given by

$$\frac{g_m}{I_{DS}} = \frac{2}{V_{GS} - V_T} = 2\sqrt{\frac{KP}{2n} \frac{W}{L} \frac{1}{I_{DS}}} \tag{1-26a}$$

It is inversely proportional to the square root of the current, as shown in Fig. 1-10b. The smaller the current, the more efficiently it is used to generate transconductance. In weak inversion this ratio is obtained from Eq. (1-25) and is given by

$$\frac{g_{mwi}}{I_{DSwi}} = \frac{1}{nkT/q} \tag{1-26b}$$

which is independent of the current (see Fig. 1-10b). Moreover this is the highest ratio that can be achieved. For high gain this region is preferred.

1-6-3 Transition Weak-Strong Inversion

The transition from weak (w) to strong (s) inversion occurs when the currents meet at a current I_{DSws} in Figs. 1-9 and 1-10, or when the transconductances meet at g_{mws} in Fig. 1-10a. In order to find these values, the expressions of the current I_{DS}, the transconductance g_m and the ratio g_m/I_{DS}, are collected in Table 1-4. The ratio g_m/I_{DS} is given twice, once expressed as a function of $v_{GS} - V_T$ and once as a function of the current I_{DS} itself.

TABLE 1-4 EXPRESSIONS OF I_{DS}, g_m AND g_m/I_{DS} FOR MOST

	I_{DS}	g_m	$\dfrac{g_m}{I_{DS}} = f(v_{GS} - V_T)$	$\dfrac{g_m}{I_{DS}} = f(I_{DS})$
wi	$I_{D0} \dfrac{W}{L} \exp\left(\dfrac{v_{GS}}{nkT/q}\right)$ (1-25a)	$\dfrac{I_{D0}}{nkT/q} \dfrac{W}{L} \exp\left(\dfrac{v_{GS}}{nkT/q}\right)$ (1-25b)	$\dfrac{1}{nkT/q}$ (1-26b)	$\dfrac{1}{nkT/q}$ (1-26b)
ws			$(v_{GS} - V_T)_{ws} = 2n\dfrac{kT}{q}$	$I_{DSws} = \dfrac{KP}{2n} \dfrac{W}{L} \left(2n\dfrac{kT}{q}\right)^2$
si	$\dfrac{KP}{2n} \dfrac{W}{L}(v_{GS} - V_T)^2$ (1-18c)	$2\dfrac{KP}{2n} \dfrac{W}{L}(v_{GS} - V_T)$ (1-22a)	$\dfrac{2}{v_{GS} - V_T}$ (1-26a)	$2\sqrt{\dfrac{KP}{2n} \dfrac{W}{L} \dfrac{1}{I_{DS}}}$ (1-26a)
sv			$(v_{GS} - V_T)_{sv} = \dfrac{4nLC_{ox}v_{sat}}{KP}$	$I_{DSsv} = \dfrac{4WLC_{ox}^2 v_{sat}^2}{KP/2n}$
vs	$WC_{ox}v_{sat}(v_{GS} - V_T)$ (1-38b)	$WC_{ox}v_{sat}$ (1-39)	$\dfrac{1}{v_{GS} - V_T}$	$\dfrac{WC_{ox}v_{sat}}{I_{DS}}$

The transition current I_{DSws} is now easily found by equating g_m/I_{DS} in weak inversion to g_m/I_{DS} in strong inversion, both as functions of I_{DS} (see Table 1-4). This yields

$$I_{DSws} = \frac{\text{KP}}{2n}\frac{W}{L}\left(2n\frac{kT}{q}\right)^2 \tag{1-27a}$$

This expression can also be obtained by the equation of the expression of g_m/I_{DS} as a function of $v_{GS} - V_T$, which yields

$$(V_{GS} - V_T)_{ws} = 2n\frac{kT}{q} \tag{1-27b}$$

Substitution of this $(V_{GS} - V_T)_{ws}$ in Eq. (1-18c) yields Eq. (1-27a).

The transition is very smooth, provided KP, n, and I_{D0} have been given the appropriate values. Parameter KP is extracted from measured data in the linear region. Parameter n is extracted from the slope in weak inversion. Coefficient I_{D0} is the least known and depends exponentially on V_T and v_{BS}. It is normally obtained from measured data in weak inversion and adjusted to ensure continuity in the transition region. Often used values are $I_{D0} = 15$ to 20 nA.

There is no guarantee that the values of g_m undergo a continuous transition from the weak to the strong inversion region at the transition current I_{DSsw} given by Eq. (1-27a). This is not the case in SPICE, which results in a major deficiency and may create convergence problems. For hand calculations, however, we are not bothered by this discontinuity in g_m since, as designers, we know beforehand in what region we want the transistor to operate. In some other circuit simulators, more complicated models are used to ensure a continuous transition, but such models cannot be used for hand calculations.

In order to ensure that the transistor is working in the weak-inversion (or subthreshold) region, it must operate at a factor of at least eight to ten below the transition current. The same applies to the strong inversion (or quadratic) region. Thus first-order models can be used only at a distance from this weak-strong inversion transition current I_{DSws}.

The weak-inversion region is preferred for high gain. However, the current has become quite small in this region. The resulting high-frequency performance is poor. Therefore, a better biasing point is the strong inversion region close to the weak-inversion region. For example, at $V_{GS} - V_T \approx 0.2$ V, $g_m/I_{DS} \approx 10$, which is about a factor of seven above the transition current I_{DSws}. We suggest this choice for the input transistors of an operational amplifier for which a high value of g_m/I_{DS} is required (see Chap. 6).

Note that in SPICE, subthreshold conduction is considered to be a second-order effect. It cannot be described in the first-order (level 1) model. It is only included in the level 2 model provided NFS (see Eq. (1-5b)) is specified, whatever low value it may have.

Example 1-5

For the example of the nMOST with $V_{T0} = 0.4$ V, $\gamma = 0.86$ V$^{1/2}$ and $n = 1.49$ at zero v_{BS} (see Table 1-2), the $W/L = 10$ and KP $= 0.34$ mA/V^2. Calculate the transconductance at $I_{DS} = 0.1$ μA after you have determined if the transistor is in weak inversion.

Solution. Current I_{DSws} from Eq. (1-27a) is about 7 μA. which is about 70 times higher than the current given. Thus, the transistor is clearly in weak inversion. Its g_m/I_{DS}, obtained from Eq. (1-26), is 26, which is quite high. Thus its g_m is 2.6 μS.

1-6-4 MOST in Velocity Saturation

At high currents, the i_{DS} versus v_{GS} characteristic becomes linear rather than quadratic, as shown in Fig. 1-9a. This is a result of mobility degradation (see Sec. 1-9). The electrons are now moving at the highest possible velocity, i.e., the saturation velocity v_{sat}. Its value is about $v_{sat} \approx 10^7$ cm (Muller and Kamins 1986).

As a result, the transconductance has reached a constant value g_{msat} as shown in Fig. 1-10a. Also, the ratio g_m versus I_{DS} now decreases linearly with I_{DS} as shown in Fig. 1-10b.

The model for this region will be developed only in Sec. 1-9. It is already clear, however, that another transition current I_{DSsv} is present, going from strong inversion (s) to velocity saturation (v) (see Table 1-4).

There is no reason to use currents with values as high as I_{DSsv}. Indeed, the transconductance does not increase with more current. If high currents are to be used to push high-frequency performance to its limits, we suggest that the transconductance stays in the strong-inversion region, at a factor of eight to ten below I_{DSsv}.

1-7 EXAMPLES OF SMALL-SIGNAL ANALYSIS

In order to gain familiarity with the use of small-signal models, we present some examples here.

1-7-1 Example of Transconductance Amplifier

Let us first take an nMOST in a simple amplifier configuration (Fig. 1-11a). At the input a voltage source is applied with DC value V_{IN} and a small-signal component v_{in}. Its amplitude is V_{in}. The output is the small-signal transistor current itself i_{out}. The ratio i_{out}/v_{in} is a transconductance. Therefore, the amplifier is called a *transconductance amplifier*. The substrate is connected to ground.

Example 1-6

The transistor parameters are $V_{T0} \approx 0.7$ V, $\gamma = 0.86$ V$^{1/2}$, $n = 1.49$ ($V_{BS} = 0$) and its $K' = 30$ μA/V^2. What is the current output for 10 mV$_{RMS}$ signal input-voltage superimposed on $V_{IN} = 1.4$ V if $W/L = 50/5$ μm $= 10$?

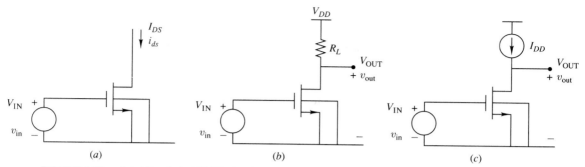

FIGURE 1-11   (a) AC gain in MOST with (b) resistive and (c) active load.

Solution. For $V_{\text{IN}} = 1.4$ V the current is given by Eq. (1-18c) to be $I_{\text{OUT}} = 0.147$ mA. The values of the transconductances are obtained from Eq. (1-22a) and are $g_m = 0.42$ mS (S = Siemens or mhos) and $g_{mb} = 0.206$ mS.

If at the gate a small-signal input voltage of $V_{\text{in}} = 10$ mV$_{\text{RMS}}$, is applied, the small-signal output current is $I_{\text{out}} = 4.2$ μA$_{\text{RMS}}$. Its peak value is then $4.2 . \sqrt{2} = 5.94$ μA$_p$. The maximum variation of the current is approximately 6/147 or 4 percent.

For an n-well CMOS process, the value $V_{En} = 4$ V$/\mu$mL, and thus $V_{En}L = 20$ V. Hence, the output resistance $r_o = 136$ kΩ.

Note the *design procedure*. Except for technological parameters, the input voltage V_{GS} and W/L are given. It is then a trivial task to calculate the current I_{DS} and the transconductance g_m from Eqs. (1-18b) and (1-22a). We could have given as input parameters W/L and I_{DS}, or even g_m and I_{DS}. For each case it is possible to find the other two parameters by means of Eqs. (1-18) and (1-22).

There are four variables to be determined for each MOST: V_{GS}, W/L, I_{DS}, and g_m. There are two equations, (1-18) and (1-22), so two parameters must be determined by the designer. This is the real design decision to be taken for each MOST in the circuit. The procedure to be followed is either a design procedure or a design plan (Gielen and Sansen 1991).

In the analog circuits Chaps. 4 and 6, the design procedure consists of deciding what two MOST parameters we will determine beforehand. We can choose them freely, but prefer to add constraints (such as speed, noise, etc.), until all parameters are determined automatically. A design procedure in which the number of variables equals the number of constraints can be solved in a numerical or analytic way. Such examples are given in Chap. 4.

1-7-2 Example of Voltage Amplifier with Active Load

Let us now take the same nMOST example used for voltage gain. The output current can be converted to an output voltage by means of a resistance or an active load (such as a current source). Both circuits are shown in Fig. 1-11b and c, respectively.

Example 1-7

We take the same transistor: $V_{T0} \approx 0.7$ V, $\gamma = 0.86$ V$^{1/2}$, $n = 1.49$ ($V_{BS} = 0$) and its $K' = 30$ μA/V^2. A resistive load is taken (see Fig. 1-11b). It is connected to a positive power supply with value of $V_{DD} = 8$ V. Choose a resistor such that the output voltage is half the supply voltage. This provides a maximum output voltage swing.

Solution. An output voltage of $V_{OUT} = 4$ V is obtained if the resistor has a value of $R_L = V_{OUT}/I_{DS} = 4/0.15 \times 10^{-3} = 27.2$ kΩ. The total resistance R'_L at the output is thus R_L in parallel with r_o, or $R_L /\!/ r_o$. Its value is $27.2 /\!/ 136 = 27.2 \times 136/(27.2 + 136) = 22.7$ kΩ or about 23 kΩ. The voltage gain is then given by

$$A_v = -g_m R'_L \tag{1-28a}$$

In this example $A_v = -9.5$. This value is quite low. Much higher values of gain can be obtained if the resistor is omitted and only r_o is left as a load. A current source is then required to allow the drain current to flow (see Fig. 1-11c). The value of the small-signal voltage gain is again given by Eq. (1-28) with r_o instead of R'_L, as given by

$$A_v = -g_m r_o \tag{1-28b}$$

The value of the gain has now increased to -57.

Substitution of g_m and r_o from Eq. (1-22c) and Eq. (1-24) in Eq. (1-28c) yields

$$A_v = -\frac{2I_{DS}}{V_{GS} - V_T}\frac{V_{En}L}{I_{DS}} = \frac{2V_{En}L}{V_{GS} - V_T} \tag{1-29}$$

which is a useful expression to calculate the gain as explained in the following design procedure.

The voltage gain is set by V_{GS} and L only (in strong inversion). We choose the smallest $V_{GS} - V_T$ possible, i.e., $V_{GS} - V_T \approx 0.2$ V. On the other hand, L must be taken as large as possible, e.g., $L = 10$ μm. $V_{En} = 4$ V/μmL, thus the voltage gain is now 400 or 52 dB.

However, we still must determine the W of the MOST. The larger the W, the larger the current I_{DS} and the transconductance g_m, but the smaller the output resistor r_o. We have no reason to drain more current than necessary. This could change later; e.g., high frequency performance does require larger currents. Now we limit W to a small value close to the minimum one: $W = 5$ μm and hence $I_{DS} = 6$ μA, $g_m = 60$ μS and $r_o = 6.7$ MΩ.

It is difficult, however, to set the current source I_{DD} at the correct value. The current in the transistor is determined only by the gate-source voltage V_{GS}. The values of V_{GS} and I_{DD} must be precisely tuned. This can be illustrated on Fig. 1-6b. A current source corresponds with a horizontal line. It must intersect the transistor characteristic in the saturation region, i.e., such that V_{DS} is greater than V_{DSsat}. Special biasing techniques that ensure such operation in saturation are developed in Chap. 4.

1-7-3 Example of a MOST Diode

The same transistor can also be used as a diode and its drain is then connected to its gate (Fig. 1-12a). This transistor is now always in saturation because $V_{GS} = V_{DS}$ (see Eq. (1-11)). Its current-voltage characteristic is quadratic, as given by Eq. (1-18) for positive values of V_{DS}. There is no conduction for negative values. Therefore, the transistor is said to be used as a diode.

First, let us assume that both the source and bulk are grounded. The DC voltage drop across the diode is easily derived from Eq. (1-18b), and given by

$$V_{GS} = V_T + \sqrt{\frac{I_{DSsat}}{K'W/L}} \qquad (1\text{-}30)$$

Thus its value can be set by both the current I_{DSsat} and W/L. Often, this configuration will be used in DC level shifter stages to provide biasing to consecutive MOST stages.

If an input AC current i_{in} is superimposed on the DC current, an AC voltage is generated across the diode. By analysis of the small-signal equivalent circuit of Fig. 1-12b, this voltage is easily found to be i_{in}/g_m.

FIGURE 1-12   (a), (c), and (d) MOST diode examples; (b) small signal equivalent circuit.

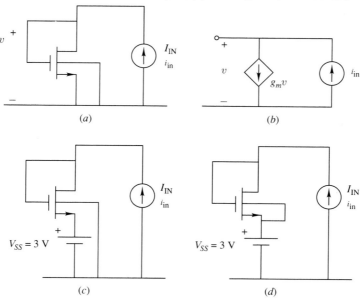

(a)

(b)

(c)

(d)

It is important to keep in mind that the small-signal or AC resistance of the diode equals $1/g_m$, which is normally of the order of magnitude of $k\Omega$'s. Actually, this resistance is shunted by the output resistance r_o, which is much larger. This reduces only slightly the resistance $1/g_m$.

If the diode now operates at a different voltage level somewhere in the middle of a circuit, for instance by addition of a constant voltage source in series (see Fig. 1-12c), the bulk is still connected to the ground. As a result, a value of V_{BS} must be included in the calculation of V_T in Eq. (1-18b) and Eq. (1-22), as indicated by Eq. (1-7b). Inclusion of V_{BS} increases the value of V_T hence increasing the value of the diode voltage drop V_{GS}. The value of g_m, however, is still the same because the current is the same due to the current drive.

Example 1-8

For the same transistor: $V_{T0} \approx 0.7$ V, $\gamma = 0.86$ V$^{1/2}$, $n = 1.49$ ($V_{BS} = 0$) and its $K' = 30$ μA/V^2, calculate the DC and AC voltages for a current drive of $I_{IN} = I_{DSsat} = 0.2$ mA. The AC current swing is 10 percent. Repeat the calculation for $V_S = 3$ V.

Solution. The voltage drop is $V_{DS} = V_{GS} = 0.7 + \sqrt{0.667} = 1.52$ V. At this current, $g_m = 0.49$ mS. Hence, $1/g_m = 2.04$ kΩ. With a peak amplitude of 10 percent in current, the AC voltage is 40.8 mV$_p$ or 29 mV$_{RMS}$. Resistance r_o, which is 100 kΩ, only slightly reduces the resistance to a value of about 2 kΩ.

For $V_S = 3$ V, the value of V_T increases from 0.7 V to 1.66 V (for $2\phi_F = 0.6$ V). As a result, the total DC voltage drop becomes 2.48 V.

In a p-well CMOS process, the bulk of the nMOST is the p-well. It is isolated from the substrate and thus can be connected to the source as in Fig. 1-12d. The body effect then does not apply. As a result, the value of the diode voltage drop is then the same, i.e., 1.52 V.

1-7-4 Example of Source Follower

A source follower is a unity-gain stage with high input resistance. It is as an ideal source follower if it is biased by a current source I_{SS}, as seen in Fig. 1-13. The current through the transistor cannot change because it has only a DC component (with value I_{SS}). Thus its V_{GS} cannot change either.

Let us assume that the nMOST is realized in a p-well CMOS process and that its *bulk is connected to the source* as in Fig. 1-13a. The body effect does not apply. The output voltage v_{OUT} is simply given by

$$v_{IN} - v_{OUT} = v_{GS} \tag{1-31a}$$

in which v_{GS} is given by Eq. (1-30). This is valid for both DC and AC. The small-signal voltage gain thus is unity. The output resistance equals $1/g_m = 2.04$ kΩ, the same as for a MOST diode, because the gate is at AC ground.

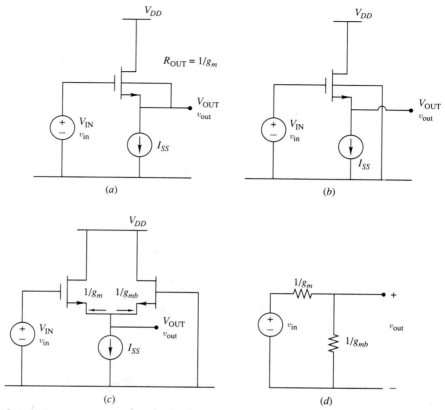

FIGURE 1-13   Gain and output resistance of source follower.

If, however, the *bulk is connected to ground* as seen in Fig. 1-13b, the values of V_T and of v_{GS} in Eq. (1-30) depend on the output voltage v_{BS}, which equals v_{OUT}. A quadratic equation results, given by

$$v_{OUT} = v_{IN} - V_{T0} - \gamma(\sqrt{2|\phi_F| + v_{OUT}} - \sqrt{2|\phi_F|}) - \sqrt{\frac{I_{SS}}{K'W/L}} \qquad (1\text{-}31b)$$

Again this expression is valid for both DC and AC. It can be solved exactly for v_{OUT} by calculation of the roots or by iteration.

However, the small-signal voltage gain is no longer at unity. It can, in principle, be extracted from Eq. (1-31b). Some additional insight is gained, however, when the parasitic JFET is drawn explicitly (see Fig. 1-13c). Its drain and source are common with the MOST, but its gate goes to ground. It presents a small-signal resistance of $1/g_{mb}$ to the output. Since the MOST itself exhibits an output resistance of $1/g_m$, a voltage division occurs at the output. This is illustrated by the small-signal equivalent circuit of Fig. 1-13d. The small-signal voltage gain is given by

$$A_v = \frac{\dfrac{1}{g_{mb}}}{\dfrac{1}{g_{mb}} + \dfrac{1}{g_m}} = \frac{1}{1 + \dfrac{g_{mb}}{g_m}} = \frac{1}{n} \tag{1-32}$$

in which n is given by Eq. (1-5b). The n is now used as the attenuation of an emitter follower, the bulk of which is connected to ground.

The output resistance R_{out} is now given by

$$R_{\text{out}} = \frac{1}{g_m + g_{mb} + g_o} \tag{1-33}$$

which is actually the parallel combination of all three resistances $1/g_m$, $1/g_{mb}$, and r_o. In most cases, the effect of the ouput resistance r_o is negligible.

Connecting the bulk to ground not only increases the value of V_{GS} but also decreases the small-signal gain. Both are a result of the body effect or the parasitic JFET between the channel and the bulk.

Example 1-9

For this example, $N_{\text{SUB}} = 10^{16}$ cm^{-3}, $C_{\text{ox}} = 6.8 \times 10^{-8}$ F/cm^2, $V_{T0} \approx 0.7$ V, $\gamma = 0.86$ V$^{1/2}$ and $n = 1.49$; find the DC output voltage and voltage gain for $V_{\text{IN}} = 3$ V and $I_{SS} = 0.2$ mA, if the source is connected to the source and to the ground, respectively.

Solution. For a bulk-to-source connection, $V_{\text{OUT}} = 2.3$ V but for a bulk-to-ground connection $V_{\text{OUT}} = 1.046$ V and $V_T = 1.137$ V. The value of g_m is the same as before because it is only determined by the current I_{SS}. Its value is thus $g_m = 0.49$ mS. Also, $g_{mb} = 0.24$ mS. The gain is now only 0.67. The resultant output resistance is 1.37 kΩ.

1-7-5   Example of MOST as a Switch with Resistive Load

A MOST can be used as a switch as well. This is a particularly important use of MOS transistors. For example, switched capacitor networks, discussed in Chap. 7, use such switches.

A configuration with an nMOST and a resistive load is shown in Fig. 1-14. The gate voltage is so high that the transistor behaves as a resistor. A resistive divider is then formed by the MOST and the resistive load R_L. If an AC component is added to the input signal source, attenuation occurs. Note that two configurations can occur. In Fig. 1-14a the substrate is connected to ground, whereas in Fig. 1-14b, the substrate is connected to the source. The second configuration is obviously only possible in a p-well CMOS technology. Also note that the drain is located on the left side because

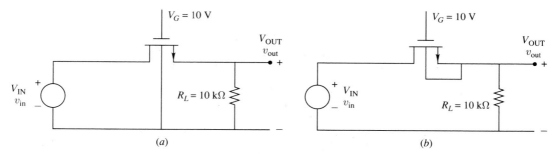

FIGURE 1-14   MOST as a switch with (*a*) *B* to ground or (*b*) *B* to source.

it is the more positive end. The source is located on the right side, i.e., at the output resistor.

The transistor is now intended to operate in the linear region. To ensure this, voltage V_G is usually made quite high. Since the MOST functions as a small resistance, the voltage drop across the transistor is very small. The output voltage v_{OUT} will then be only slightly smaller than the input voltage v_{IN}.

The resistance represented by the transistor is then given by Eq. (1-9), in which V_T still depends on V_{BS}, as given by Eq. (1-7b). However, this, latter voltage equals the output voltage itself (in the case of grounded bulk). A nonlinear equation thus results that is valid for both DC and AC. It is obtained by the combination of Eq. (1-9) and Eq. (1-7b), as given by

$$\frac{v_{OUT}}{v_{IN}} = \frac{R_L}{R_L + R_{DS}} \tag{1-34}$$

with

$$R_{DS} = \frac{1}{\beta \left[V_G - v_{OUT} - V_{T0} - \gamma \left(\sqrt{2|\phi_F| + v_{OUT}} - \sqrt{2|\phi_F|} \right) \right]}$$

It is clear that for small values of v_{IN}, v_{OUT} will be small as well. Since V_G is very large, the denominator of the expression of R_{DS} is also large and R_{DS} is small. The output voltage is then very close to the input voltage. As a first approximation, v_{OUT} can be replaced by v_{IN} in the expression of R_{DS} above and a new value of v_{OUT} can be calculated from the expression of Eq. (1-34). Such an iteration leads rapidly to a solution for v_{OUT}. Actually, for convergence, it is safer to rewrite Eq. (1-34) for $v_{IN} - v_{OUT}$ as a variable rather than v_{OUT} itself.

The resultant values of R_{DS} and v_{OUT} are plotted versus v_{IN} in Fig. 1-15a. The curves have been generated for an *n*MOST with $V_{T0} = 0.7$ V, $\gamma = 0.86$ V$^{1/2}$, KP = 34 μA/V^2, and $2\phi_F = 0.6$ V. The gate voltage $V_G = 10$ V and $R_L = 10$ kΩ. The curves are given for four different values of W/L.

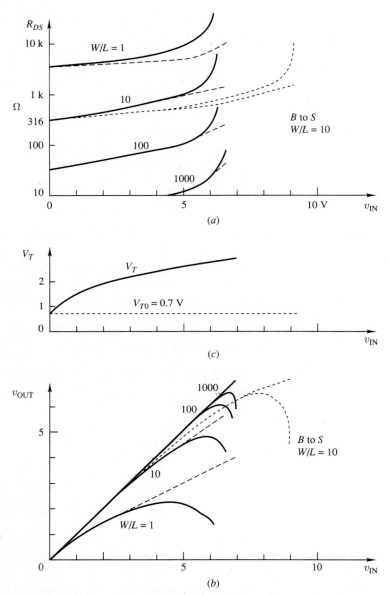

FIGURE 1-15   (a) MOST resistance; (b) output voltage when used as a switch; and (c) the threshold voltage.

The larger the transistor, the smaller the resistance and the more closely v_{OUT} follows v_{IN}. Also, the lower the input voltage, the smaller the resistance. For zero V_{IN} (and for $W/L = 10$), its value is easily found to be 316 Ω. For larger values of v_{IN} however, the value of V_{GS} becomes too low: the resistance increases drastically and the output voltage reaches a maximum. This occurs first for $W/L = 1$ (see Fig. 1-15b).

It is barely noticeable for $W/L = 1000$. Finally note that the value of V_T increases with v_{IN} as shown in Fig. 1-15c.

For larger values of v_{IN} however, the full Eq. (1-17) or maybe even Eq. (1-16) must be used rather than Eq. (1-9). Although an iterative solution is still possible, it is easier to use SPICE to obtain the output voltage. The obtained values of R_{DS} and v_{OUT} obtained, are added as Fig. 1-15 as dashed lines. For large values of W/L, they cannot be distinguished from the first-order results. For $W/L = 1$, however, the exact value of R_{DS} is always smaller (and v_{OUT} follows v_{IN} less closely (see Fig. 1-15b)). For example, at $V_{IN} = 5$ V, and for $W/L = 1$, they are 12.4 kΩ and 0.62 kΩ; for $W/L = 10$ they are 1.24 kΩ and 1 kΩ; for $W/L = 100$, they are 124 Ω and 120 Ω; finally for $W/L = 1000$, they are about the same, i.e., 12.4 Ω.

All calculations can now be repeated for the case where the substrate is connected to the source. In this case, the term in γ in Eq. (1-34) can be neglected, which considerably simplifies the calculations. The results are added as dotted lines in Fig. 1-15 for $W/L = 10$.

It is worth noting that resistance R_{DS} is smaller in this case, especially for larger values of v_{IN}. Moreover, the input voltage range, over which the switch can be used, is greatly extended. This configuration is preferred wherever possible.

The *small-signal model* for the switch arrangement of Fig. 1-14 is the same as for DC, at least as long as the transistor can be represented by a resistance. Indeed, the same resistive division factor $R_L/(R_{DS} + R_L)$ applies as much to the AC input voltage source as it does to the DC input voltage source. The AC attenuation is thus given by this factor itself.

If the MOST resistance becomes nonlinear, complicated calculations result. SPICE is thus used to find the exact value of the small-signal attenuation. The calculations are simpler in the case of Fig. 1-15b.

1-7-6 Example with a MOST as a Switch with Capacitive Load

An even more important switch arrangement in CMOS circuits is the one with a capacitive load of Fig. 1-16. This is the arrangement that is always used in CMOS logic and switched-capacitor circuits. It is a good application of the calculations above.

FIGURE 1-16   MOST as a switch with capacitance load; (a) B to ground, and (b) B to source.

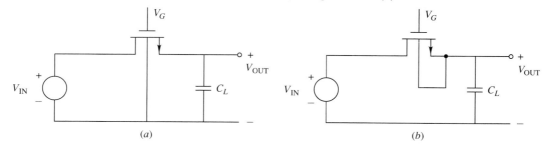

(a)   (b)

As soon as the gate voltage drive is switched on (see Fig. 1-17a), current starts flowing, charging up capacitance C_L. In the beginning the output voltage is still low. The value of v_{GS} is thus high, as is the current flow. The output voltage v_{OUT} thus rises rapidly (see Fig. 1-17b) and at this point, the value of R_{DS} is quite small (see Fig. 1-17c).

When v_{OUT} has become large and close to v_{IN}, v_{GS} and the current have decreased considerably. The output voltage only increases very slowly and R_{DS} has become large. Ultimately, the output voltage equals the input voltage. The current has become zero and R_{DS} has become large.

The value of R_{DS} increases continuously along the charging cycle, as shown in Fig. 1-17c. The output waveform cannot be characterized by a single time constant. An attempt could be made by taking the initial value of R_{DS} where v_{OUT} is still zero, but this underestimates the delay time. A better approach consists of taking R_{DS} at the point where v_{OUT} has reached half of its ultimate value (as shown in Fig. 1-17). This

FIGURE 1-17   Switching output voltage for: ————, B to ground; - - - - - - - , B to S; – – – – – ; R_{DS} = constant.

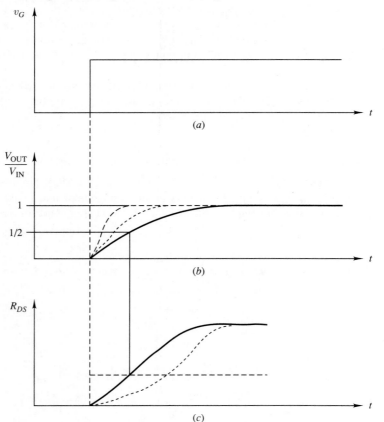

value of R_{DS} is then kept constant during the full charging cycle. The time constant is then approximately $R_{DS}C_L$. This still underestimates the delay time and the effect of the very long tail. If, however, five or seven time constants are taken, the effect of this long tail is more or less accounted for.

If the bulk is connected to the source, the value of R_{DS} is smaller and v_{OUT} increases faster, denoted by dotted lines in Fig. 1-17b and c. Remember, however, that this is only possible in a p-well CMOS process.

1-8 CAPACITANCES

At higher frequencies, capacitances become important as well, and they must be added in the small-signal model. They will be used to calculate the Bode diagrams in Chap. 4. Some of them have been mentioned in the beginning of this section and now all of them will be described in detail.

The capacitances can be subdivided in two categories: those belonging to the MOST device and those belonging to the interconnect circuitry between two devices. The capacitances of the MOST are discussed first. They are shown in the three dimensional drawing of Fig. 1-18 and listed in Table 1-5. For each capacitance, the contribution to the terminal capacitances C_{GS}, C_{GD}, C_{DB}, and C_{SB} must to be determined, as shown in Fig. 1-19. The terminal capacitances are listed in Table 1-6. Moreover, this is repeated for a MOST in the regions of operation, i.e., the linear region and the saturation region.

FIGURE 1-18   Capacitances in a MOST.

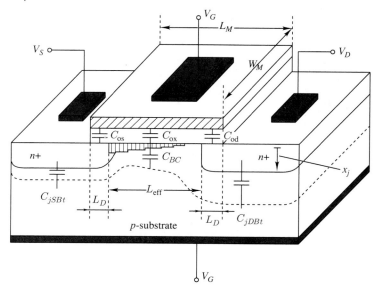

TABLE 1-5   MOST CAPACITANCES

$$C_{oxt} = C_{ox} WL_{eff} \qquad C_{ox} = \frac{\varepsilon_{ox}}{t_{ox}}$$

$$C_{BCt} = C_{jBC} WL_{eff} \qquad C_{jBC} = \frac{C_j}{\left(1 - \dfrac{V_{BC}}{\phi_j}\right)^{mj}}$$

$$C_{jSBt} = A_S C_{jSB} + P_S C_{jswSB} \qquad C_{jSB} = \frac{C_j}{\left(1 - \dfrac{V_{BS}}{\phi_j}\right)^{mj}} \qquad C_{jswSB} = \frac{C_{jsw}}{\left(1 - \dfrac{V_{BS}}{\phi_j}\right)^{mjsw}}$$

$$C_{jDBt} = A_D C_{jDB} + P_D C_{jswDB} \qquad C_{jDB} = \frac{C_j}{\left(1 - \dfrac{V_{BD}}{\phi_j}\right)^{mj}} \qquad C_{jswDB} = \frac{C_{jsw}}{\left(1 - \dfrac{V_{BD}}{\phi_j}\right)^{mjsw}}$$

$$C_{j(sw)} = \frac{\varepsilon_{si}}{t_{si}} = \left(\frac{\varepsilon_{si} q N_B}{2\phi_{j(sw)}}\right)^{1/2} \qquad m_j = 1/3, \ldots, 1/2$$

$$C_{jwellt} \approx (A_D + A_S + A_G) C_{jwell}$$

ϕ_j is the built-in junction
  potential (PB)
A_S is the source area
A_D is the drain area
P_D is the drain perimeter

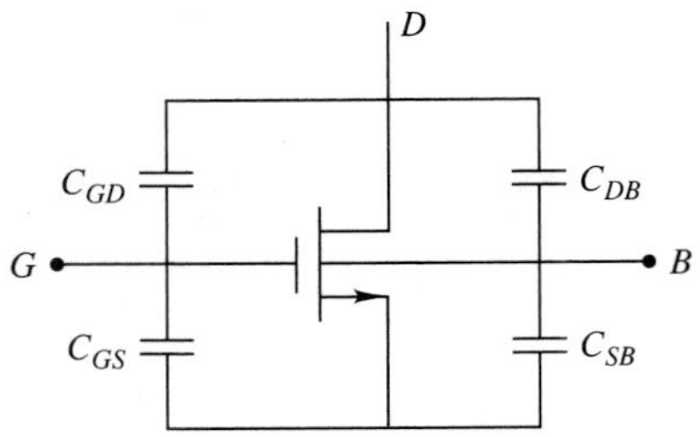

FIGURE 1-19   Terminal capacitances in a MOST.

TABLE 1-6   TERMINAL CAPACITANCES

In saturation	
$C_{GS} = C_{GS0} + 2/3 C_{oxt}$	$C_{SB} = C_{jSBt} + 2/3 C_{BCt}$
$C_{GD} = C_{GD0}$	$C_{DB} = C_{jDBt}$
In linear region	
$C_{GS} = C_{GS0} + 1/2 C_{oxt}$	$C_{SB} = C_{jSBt} + 1/2 C_{BCt}$
$C_{GD} = C_{GD0} + 1/2 C_{oxt}$	$C_{DB} = C_{jDBt} + 1/2 C_{BCt}$

1-8-1 MOST: Oxide Capacitance C_{ox}

This capacitance is the controlling capacitance of the MOST device. It gives rise to three capacitances:

- an overlap capacitance between gate and source C_{GS0}
- a gate to channel capacitance C_{GC}
- an overlap capacitance between gate and drain C_{GD0}

The *overlap* capacitances are a result of the gate overlapping source and drain by an amount LD (see Fig. 1-5). The corresponding capacitances C_{GS0} and C_{GS0} could easily calculated by WL_DC_{ox}. However, the overlap L_D is never known precisely and therefore, in the list of MOST SPICE parameters (Table 1-1), the capacitances C_{GS0} and C_{GD0} are given in Farad per meter channel width W.

It is obvious that C_{GS0} is directly added to terminal capacitance C_{GS} and that G_{GD0} is added to C_{GD} (see Table 1-6).

The contribution of the *gate-to-channel* capacitance C_{GC} to the terminal capacitances depends on the operation region of the device. Its total value C_{oxt} equals $C_{ox}WL_{eff}$ (as listed in Table 1-5).

In the linear region, this capacitance occurs between the gate and the channel, which connects source and drain and its value is evenly split between the terminal capacitances C_{GS} and C_{GD} (see Table 1-6). In the saturation region, however, the channel is discontinued at the drain end, as sketched in Fig. 1-5. Most of the capacitance (factor 2/3) is therefore added to the source terminal capacitance C_{GS} and nothing is added to C_{GD} (see Table 1-6). This factor of 2/3 is a result of field calculations.

The contribution of C_{oxt} to the terminal capacitances is also shown for the regions of operation in Fig. 1-20. In Fig. 1-20a, voltage V_{GS} is taken as a variable, whereas V_{DS} is as a constant. The linear and saturation regions are clearly distinguished. A similar plot is added in Fig. 1-20b with voltage V_{DS} as a variable and V_{GS} as a constant. The same results are obtained.

1-8-2 MOST Junction Capacitances

The source-channel-drain structure is isolated from the substrate by junction space charge depletion layers (see Fig. 1-18). Therefore, three *junction* capacitances must be added. They are:

- the channel bulk (or substrate) junction capacitance C_{BCt}
- the source-bulk junction capacitance C_{jSBt}
- the drain-bulk junction capacitance C_{jDBt}

If the MOST is in a well, a well-to-bulk junction capacitance C_{jwellt} is added.

The *channel-bulk junction capacitance* C_{BC} is the controlling capacitance of the parasitic JFET. Its total value C_{BCt} equals $C_{BC}WL_{eff}$, where C_{BC} was calculated in Eq. (1-2). It is also listed in Table 1-5. Its value is calculated with V_{BS} as bulk-channel voltage in order to obtain a worst case value.

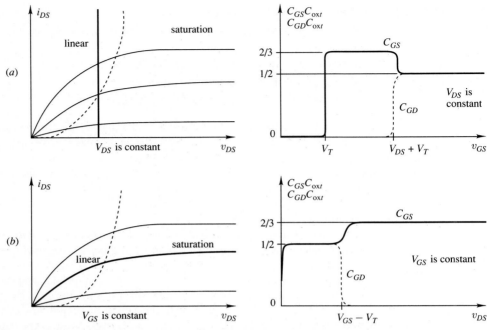

FIGURE 1-20   Capacitances C_{GS} and C_{GD} caused by oxide capacitance.

This capacitance C_{BCt} is divided over the terminal capacitances C_{SB} and C_{DB} in very much the same way as C_{oxt} is divided over C_{GS} and C_{GD}.

The *source-bulk* and *drain-bulk* junction capacitances consist of a bottom plate capacitance and a side wall capacitance. Their expressions are repeated in Table 1-5.

The *well-bulk* junction capacitance, C_{jwell}, depends on the voltage applied. It is loosely calculated, depending on how it is specified by the silicon foundry. It is also given in Table 1-5.

All values depend on the respective junction voltages. Note that in SPICE, the exponent m_j can be different for the bottom plate capacitance (i.e., MJ) than it is for the side-wall capacitance (MJSW). Normally, 0.5 is taken for an abrupt junction (such as the bottom plate capacitance) and 0.333 for a linear junction (such as for the side-wall capacitance). These values are indicated in the list of MOST parameters in Table 1-1.

Finally, a factor FC is present to limit the value of a junction capacitance in forward bias. It acts on both the bottom and the side-wall capacitances. Its effect is shown later in Fig. 2-10 and is given in Table 2-4.

These junction capacitances are added to the respective terminal capacitances, as indicated in Table 1-6.

1-8-3 MOST Junction Leakage Currents and Capacitances

Note that in SPICE (see Table 1-1), the values of the several capacitances are all calculated provided the values are given of the drain area AD (in m^2), the source area AS (in m^2), the drain perimeter PD (in m), and the source perimeter PS (in m) on each transistor card. The same parameters AD and AS are used to calculate the junction leakage currents. The total drain and source leakage currents are then, respectively, given by

$$I_{SD} = AD \cdot JS \qquad (1-35)$$

and

$$I_{SS} = AS \cdot JS$$

in which JS is the reverse current of the drain or source junctions per m^2 area. It is given in the SPICE parameter list (Table 1-1). The total junction leakage current can be specified as well. It is then specified by IS for any junction and it overrides the calculation of Eq. (1-35).

1-8-4 Interconnect Capacitances

Devices are always embedded in circuit and thus they must be connected to form a circuit. Moreover, they must be connected to input and output pads. Interconnections are discussed first.

Both metal lines and highly doped polysilicon lines can be used to realize interconnect lines. However, these lines create capacitances to the substrate and to each other at their crossing points. For large circuits, these interconnection lines can be quite long, and they give large capacitances that are often larger than MOST capacitances.

A metal interconnect line of width W_i and length L_i causes a capacitance to the substrate, shown in Fig. 1-21a. The dielectric is the field oxide with thickness t_{oxF}. This is made quite thick to avoid MOST operation under these lines. Indeed, the corresponding field oxide capacitance $C_{oxF} = \varepsilon_{ox}/t_{oxF}$ in Eq. (1-6a) is then quite small, which results in a large value of field threshold voltage V_{TF}. This value must be much larger than the supply voltage to avoid the creation of an inversion layer (leading to MOST operation) under the interconnect lines.

Example 1-10

Take a metal line of 5 μm width connecting two transistors 1 mm apart on the same chip. The field oxide thickness is 1 μm. What is the interconnect capacitance?

Solution. Since $\varepsilon_{ox} = 0.34$ pF/cm, $C_{oxF} = 3400$ pF/cm^2; the area of the line equals 5×10^{-5} cm^2, which yields a total capacitance of $C_{oxFt} = 0.17$ pF. Compared to normal MOST capacitances, which only have fF's, C_{oxFt} is quite large indeed.

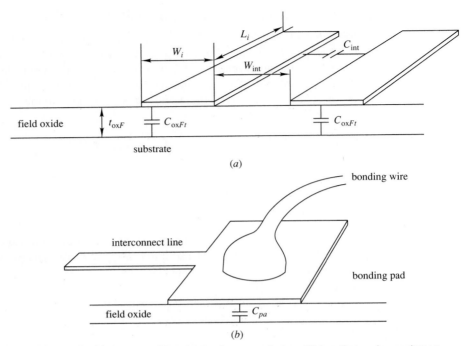

FIGURE 1-21   (*a*) Field oxide capacitance and interconnection capacitance; (*b*) bonding-pad capacitance.

Polysilicon lines are used for interconnect as well. They are commonly used as gate material and can therefore easily be extended for use as an interconnect material, despite their higher sheet resistance (typically 50 $\Omega/\square$). They create capacitance to the substrate in exactly the same way as a metal line. Depending on the process, the field oxide underneath the polyline may be somewhat less thick than under the metal. Therefore, the metal-to-substrate and the poly-to-substrate capacitances per unit area are usually specified by the silicon foundry and added to the SPICE parameters. An example of such data for the same process in Table 1-1 is given in Table 1-7.

If more polysilicon layers or metal layers are used, different isolation layers with different thicknesses must be used between them. Therefore, the capacitances between all layers must be specified separately. An example can be found in Table 1-7 for a double-poly double-metal process.

In SPICE, a transistor parameter can be added to take into account the capacitance caused by the extension of the polyline beyond the gate itself. It is the gate-bulk overlap capacitance per meter channel length $CGB0$ (see Table 1-1). It is also a field oxide capacitance and is therefore quite small. For this reason, it is either omitted altogether or included as part of the interconnect capacitance.

Two parallel interconnect lines in metal or in polysilicon have an interconnection capacitance to each other as well (see Fig. 1-21*a*) This capacitance C_{int} is smaller than

TABLE 1-7   VALUES OF PARASITIC CAPACITANCES

Double-poly n-well CMOS process of Table 1-1:

C_{oxm}	$C_{metal\ to\ substrate}$	$=$	5.2 nF/cm^2
C_{oxp}	$C_{poly\ to\ substrate}$	$=$	6.5 nF/cm^2
C_{mp}	$C_{metal\ to\ poly}$	$=$	12 nF/cm^2

Double-metal double-poly n-well CMOS process:

C_{mm}	$C_{metal\ to\ metal}$	$=$	2.5 nF/cm^2
C_{oxm}	$C_{metal\ to\ substrate}$	$=$	5.2 nF/cm^2
C_{oxp}	$C_{poly\ to\ substrate}$	$=$	6.5 nF/cm^2
C_{mp}	$C_{metal\ to\ poly}$	$=$	12 nF/cm^2

the capacitance to the bulk but it plays an important role in that it calculates cross-talk between clock lines, power supply lines, etc. This is why, in the layout of a mixed analog-digital chip, the digital signal lines are kept apart from the analog signal lines, from the ground lines, etc.

For example, the value of C_{int} between two metal lines of 1 mm long at a distance of $W_{int} = 5\ \mu$m is 34 fF if the metal is 1 μm thick ($C_{oxF} = 3400$ pF/cm^2), which is about one-fifth of the capacitance of each line to ground.

1-8-5 Bonding Pad Capacitance

In order for signals to go out of the chip, a bonding pad is required on which a bonding wire can be bonded (see Fig. 1-21b). This bonding pad is usually of the same metal as the interconnect line toward that pad and it rests on the same field oxide. It thus creates a capacitance towards the substrate, as calculated above.

A typical size of a bonding pad is 100 μm × 100 μm, resulting in a bonding pad capacitance of $C_{pa} = 0.34$ pF. Again, this is a large capacitance, which must be taken into account as a load in the design of off-chip driver circuits.

1-8-6 Package Pin Capacitance

The chip is normally packaged in a dual-in-line (DIL) or a chip-carrier package. For a DIL package, each pin has a capacitance of about 0.3 pF to adjacent pins and of about 0.7 pF to any other pin. This capacitance must be added to the pad capacitance once a signal is taken off-chip in a package. It is also clear that low pin capacitance is an important criterion in the design of new chip-carrier packages. Microwave packages easily achieve less than 0.1 pF pin capacitance.

These capacitors must also be taken into account in the design of off-chip drivers. If testing devices are added to perform production tests, their capacitances must be taken into account as well.

1-8-7   Protection Network Capacitance

A static discharge on the input gate of a MOST can destroy that gate. The gate oxide can only withstand about 800 V/μm, which is about 40 V for a gate oxide thickness of 50 nm. Static discharge voltages in dry environments can reach values of up to 6000 V, and thus a gate, which is connected to an input pad, must be protected during handling.

A simple protection network is shown in Fig. 1-22. It consists of a series resistance R_S and a parallel diode. It is reverse biased and breaks down at, say, 20 V. The diode has a series resistance as well, R_P. When the input voltage exceeds the breakdown voltage of the diode, the input gate is clamped at a voltage that is determined by the resistive divider R_S, R_P. If R_S is sufficiently large and/or R_P is sufficiently small, the voltage at the gate can be limited to 30 V, which is well below 40 V. However, requirements lead to large capacitance to the substrate. The more efficient the protection network, the more parallel capacitance it causes at the input. Again, these capacitors must be taken into account in the design of the off-chip drivers.

1-8-8   Total Capacitance Configurations

In order to show how all these capacitances add up in simple circuit configurations, a few examples are provided in Fig. 1-23. Figure 1-23a shows the terminal capacitances as given by Fig. 1-19 and Table 1-6. Parasitic capacitance C_{p1} has been added to the input and C_{p2} to the output to take into account interconnect, etc.

If the MOST is used as a simple amplifier, the capacitances around the transistor are easily found. They are added in Fig. 1-23b. Since the substrate is grounded, C_{SB} is shorted out.

A source follower is shown in Fig. 1-23c. Because the bulk is grounded, capacitance C_{DB} is also shorted out.

Note that these circuits contain two nodes and, as a consequence, three capacitances always connect these two nodes. This is always the case for a two-node circuit. The values of the capacitances, however, depend on the actual configuration of the transistor in that circuit.

FIGURE 1-22   MOST input gate protection network.

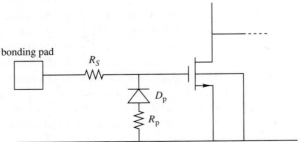

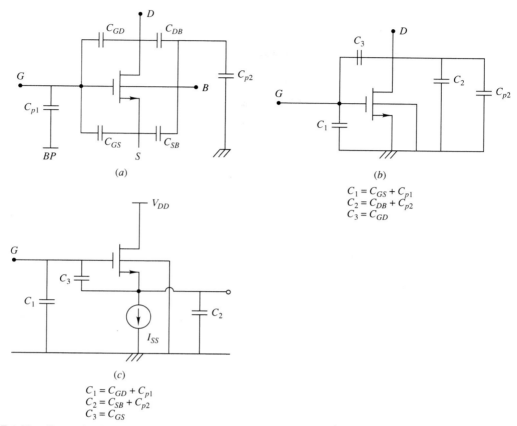

$$C_1 = C_{GS} + C_{p1}$$
$$C_2 = C_{DB} + C_{p2}$$
$$C_3 = C_{GD}$$

$$C_1 = C_{GD} + C_{p1}$$
$$C_2 = C_{SB} + C_{p2}$$
$$C_3 = C_{GS}$$

FIGURE 1-23   Determination of the (*a*) terminal capacitances for (*b*) an amplifier and (*c*) a source follower.

1-9   HIGHER-ORDER MODELS

Most of the important MOST parameters have already been discussed in previous sections. They describe the *I* versus *V* characteristics and capacitances of the MOS transistors with moderate and long channel lengths. For short channel lengths, however, deviations occur and additional model parameters must be introduced. These parameters cannot be used for hand calculations but they can be included in models used by circuit simulators, such as SPICE. Hand calculations are then used to predict first-order performance, whereas SPICE is used to verify actual performance and to weigh the importance of second-order effects (Antognetti and Massobrio 1988).

In this text, a limited number of parameters are added to cover higher-order effects. They closely correspond with the parameters added in the level 2 model of SPICE. For each, the physical reasoning is given along with the way they appear in the calculations. These additional parameters are also added in the list of MOST parameters of

Table 1-1. In this section, suggestions are given on how to use the MOST parameters in SPICE.

1-9-1 VT0-KP-GAMMA-LAMBDA or TOX-PHI-NSUB-NSS?

In SPICE, both electrical parameters and processing parameters can be specified. The first-order (level 1) electrical parameters are VT, KP, GAMMA, and LAMBDA (see Table 1-1). They can all be derived from the processing parameters TOX, PHI, etc. However, it is much safer from the point of predictability to specify these electrical parameters directly. The processing parameters are then not used by SPICE for these calculations and can be omitted. The only exception is TOX, which is required to calculate C_{ox} for the values of C_{GS} and C_{GD}.

1-9-2 Parasitic Resistances

The drain and source regions are realized by means of diffusion and therefore represent resistances, which can play an important role. They are calculated first and their effect on the operation of a MOST used in the saturation region or as a switch is examined next.

These effects can be described in both the level 1 and level 2 models of SPICE. They were not discussed earlier because they are of less importance for most circuits.

For a given sheet resistance RSH ($\Omega/\square$) of the drain and source diffusions, the series drain and source resistances are respectively given by

$$R_D = \text{RSH} \times \text{NRD} \tag{1-36}$$

$$R_S = \text{RSH} \times \text{NRS}$$

in which NRD and NRS are the number of squares of the drain and the source. An example is given in Sec. 1-10. The values of R_D and R_S can also be specified directly (as RD and RS), overriding the values calculated above (see Table 1-1).

The values of R_D and R_S are not always important. Let us investigate under what operating conditions they are to be included.

When the MOST is used as a *switch*, the values of R_D and R_S simply appear in series with the ON resistance (R_{DS}) of that transistor. Their values are added to the value of R_{DS}, given by Eq. (1-9). They are thus equally important and can never be left out if the value of R_{DS} is very small.

When the transistor is used as an *amplifier* in the saturation region, it is modeled as a current source. Resistance R_D is then too small relative to the large output resistance r_o of that current source and is thus negligible.

The source resistance, however, plays a significant role. If included in a simple amplifying stage, as shown in Fig. 1-24, it reduces the transconductance g_m of the MOST to a value g'_m, as given by

$$g'_m = \frac{g_m}{1 + g_m R_S} \tag{1-37}$$

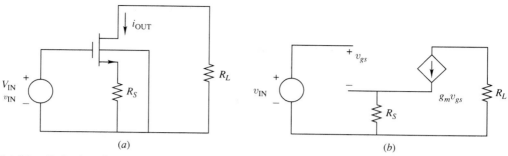

FIGURE 1-24   Reduction of g_m by source resistance R_S.

For large transistors with large values of g_m, this reduction can be considerable. Therefore, the source resistance must be made as small as possible. For example, a source metal contact must be applied to the full length of the source region (see design example).

1-9-3   Mobility Degradation due to Longitudinal Electric Field

Channel lengths have now been decreased to reach submicron values. However, the supply voltages used do not decrease that much. The transition from 5 V supply voltage to 3.3 V is carried out very slowly. Many systems operate at 5 V despite the small channel lengths used. As a result, the *longitudinal* electrical field has increased, which reduces mobility. Models are required in which the mobility is not a constant but is reduced with the voltage applied (Muller and Kamins 1986).

Mobility is a measure of the velocity acquired by the carriers as a result of the electric field applied, i.e., the velocity per unit electric field. For low values of electric field, the velocity increases proportionally. The slope is the mobility μ_0 (see Fig. 1-25). When the electric field becomes large, the velocity does not increase proportionally; it reaches a maximum or saturation velocity value v_{sat} (not to be confused with the saturation region for which we have used $v_{DS\text{sat}}$). Carriers at these velocities are called hot carriers. This occurs at a value of electric field called the *critical* electric field, represented by $\mathscr{E}_{\text{crit}}$. From Fig. 1-25, it is seen that the value of $\mathscr{E}_{\text{crit}}$ is approximately v_{sat}/μ_0. The value of the saturation velocity v_{sat} is about 10^5 m/s.

Several new parameters are introduced in SPICE to describe the reduction in mobility. They are U0 (μ_0), UCRIT ($\mathscr{E}_{\text{crit}}$), UEXP, UTRA, and VMAX (v_{sat}). They are listed in Table 1-1. Their values are obtained from fitting measured data. Do not try to change only one of them as they all belong together!

For small channel lengths, the model with constant mobility is no longer valid. In saturation, the current can then be derived from Eq. (1-18) after substitution of the electric field $\mathscr{E}$ by v_{sat}/μ_0. It is given by the simple expression

$$i_{DS\text{sat}} = W Q_m v_{\text{sat}} \tag{1-38a}$$

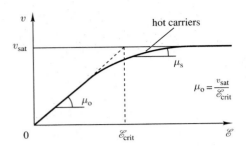

FIGURE 1-25   Mobility, velocity, and electric field for hot
carriers, described by factor θ.

in which Q_m is given by Eq. (1-10) and W is the gate width. It can be approximated
by omitting the term in v_{DS}. The current is thus also given by

$$i_{DSsat} = W C_{ox} v_{sat}(v_{GS} - V_T) \tag{1-38b}$$

This expression means that saturation is no longer defined at the point where the
mobile charge Q_m becomes zero, but at the point where the mobile carriers reach
their saturation velocity. It is the maximum current that can ever flow for the voltages
applied.

The maximum value of transconductance g_{msat} is now found by differentiation of
i_{DSsat} to v_{GS} and is given by

$$g_{msat} = W C_{ox} v_{sat} \tag{1-39}$$

This is the highest transconductance that can be achieved with a MOST. However,
g_m alone is not a good figure of merit. Another figure of merit that we have used
before is g_{msat} versus i_{DSsat}. At high frequencies, another figure of merit is better
used, i.e., g_{msat} versus C_{GS}, which has the dimension of a frequency. It is actually the
cutoff frequency or maximum frequency f_{max} of the operation of the device. Since
$C_{GS} \approx W L_{eff} C_{ox}$, this frequency is obtained from Eq. (1-18a) and Eq. (1-9b), yielding

$$f_{max} = \frac{1}{2\pi} \frac{g_{msat}}{C_{GS}} = \frac{1}{2\pi} \frac{\mu}{L_{eff}^2}(v_{GS} - V_T) \tag{1-40a}$$

which increases for shorter channel lengths. For very short channel lengths, this frequency is now limited by velocity saturation, given by

$$f_{max} = \frac{1}{2\pi} \frac{g_{msat}}{C_{GS}} = \frac{1}{2\pi} \frac{v_{sat}}{L_{eff}} \tag{1-40b}$$

This maximum frequency only depends on v_{sat} and the effective channel length.
It does not depend on the gate width W of the transistor nor on the capacitances
involved. It is thus truly an upper limit that can be achieved in silicon.

Example 1-11

What is the maximum value of current, transconductance, frequency, and figures of merit of an nMOST with $v_{GS} - V_T = 5$ V?

Solution. The value of C_{ox} (for 50 nm) is 6.8×10^{-8} F/cm^2. The value of Q_m is 3.4×10^{-7}C/cm^2 and the value of the maximum current is 34 mA per cm width (or 3.4 μA per μm width). The maximum transconductance is then 6.8 mS per cm width. The ratio g_{msat}/i_{DSsat} is simply the inverse of $(v_{GS} - V_T)$, which is 0.2 V^{-1} in this case. This ratio is quite low in comparison with what can be obtained in weak inversion ($\approx$ 20 V^{-1}). However, the absolute value of the transconductance obtained is the largest that can be obtained in silicon.

The maximum frequency is about 16 GHz for an effective channel length of 1 μm.

At small channel lengths, the value of λ and of the output resistance r_o must be modified as well. Parameter NEFF is used in model level 2 and KAPPA in model level 3 (see Table 1-1). It is easier, however, to use the empirical value of V_E instead, as given in Eq. (1-24).

It is important to know the current level at which the model in strong inversion (s) should be substituted for a model in velocity saturation (v). This transition current is I_{DSsv}. The relevant expressions are added in Table 1-4 on the bottom line. Equating the g_m/I_{DS} ratio in strong inversion to the one in velocity saturation (last column in Table 1-4) yields I_{DSvs}. Substitution of this value in Eq. (1-18c) then provides a value of $(v_{GS} - V_T)_{sv}$.

1-9-4   Mobility Degradation due to Transverse Electric Field

A *transverse* electrical field reduces the mobility in the channel as well. A transverse electrical field is caused by the gate voltage across the oxide-depletion layer structure. In order to model this, a parameter θ (Greek letter THETA) is introduced in model level 3. The mobility is then described by

$$\mu = \frac{\mu_0}{1 + \theta \, (v_{GS} - V_T)} \tag{1-41}$$

The value of θ depends on the oxide thickness and can be approximated by $2.3/t_{ox}$(nm).

It is to be noted that the reduction of the mobility has the same effect on the transconductance as a series resistance R_S in the source. Indeed, this resistance reduces the transconductance g_m by a factor $(1+g_m R_S)$ as given in Eq. (1-37). Factor θ reduces the g_m by a factor $(1 + \theta(v_{GS} - V_T))$ or $(1 + \theta g_m/(2K' \times W/L))$. As a result, the effect of factor θ is exactly the same as series resistance $R_{S\theta}$ with a value given by

$$R_{S\theta} = \frac{\theta}{2K'W/L} \tag{1-42}$$

For example, for $\theta = 0.05$, $K' = 34 \ \mu\text{A/V}^2$, and $W/L = 10$, the value of the resistance is $R_{S\theta} = 73 \ \Omega$.

Parameter θ can also be used to some extent to model the onset of the velocity-saturation region. Indeed, a large value of θ causes the current to level off. Substitution of μ of Eq. (1-41) in Eq. (1-18c) with $\text{KP} = \mu C_{\text{ox}}$, yields

$$i_{DS} = \frac{\mu_0 C_{\text{ox}}}{2n} \frac{W}{L} \frac{(v_{GS} - V_T)^2}{1 + \theta(v_{GS} - V_T)} \qquad (1\text{-}43a)$$

which becomes, for large values of θ

$$i_{DS\theta} = \frac{\mu_0 C_{\text{ox}}}{2n} \frac{W}{L} \frac{1}{\theta}(v_{GS} - V_T) \qquad (1\text{-}43b)$$

which is linear in $(v_{GS} - V_T)$ exactly as in Eq. (1-38b). Care must be exercised, however, to use Eq. (1-43b) since the mobility also depends on v_{DS}. This effect is not included in parameter θ. A more general expression of the mobility is

$$\mu = \frac{\mu_0}{1 + \theta(V_{\text{GS}} - V_{\text{T}}) + \theta_B V_{\text{BS}} + \theta_D V_{\text{DS}}} \qquad (1\text{-}43c)$$

in which θ_B is another constant and $\theta_D = \mu_0/L \, V_{\text{sat}}$.

Even more complex models, not discussed here, are used to achieve precise values of current transconductance.

1-9-5   Channel Width Factor DELTA

The depletion layer charge Q_D, which contributes to the threshold voltage V_T through factor γ as given by Eqs. (1-6a) and (1-7b), is not limited to the gate area itself. On both ends, additional charges Q_{DW} are required to terminate the depletion charge at the surface (see Fig. 1-26a). These additional charges are relatively unimportant for large values of gate width W and therefore they have been omitted in the calculation of V_T.

For small values of W, however, they cannot be neglected. The effective value of V_T will be larger than the value given by Eq. (1-6a) if the charges Q_{DW} are included. The threshold voltage is increased by a factor ΔV_T that equals twice the value of Q_{DW}/C_{oxt}. The value of Q_{DW} can be derived from Q_D by comparison of their respective geometries (see Fig. 1-26a). Charge Q_D is easily calculated for an abrupt junction.

In the level 2 model of SPICE, the value of ΔV_T calculated in this way, is multiplied by $\delta/4$ (δ is parameter DELTA) in order to take into account higher-order deviations

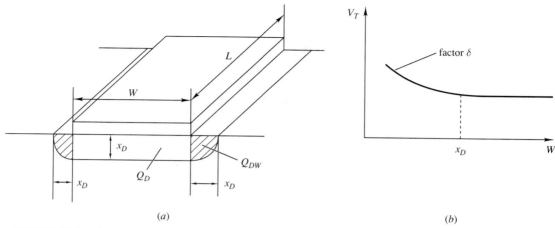

FIGURE 1-26 (a) Edge depletion charges; (b) threshold voltage V_T versus width W.

and to fit measured data. The value of ΔV_T in SPICE is given by

$$\Delta V_T = \frac{\delta}{4}\frac{\pi\varepsilon_{si}(2|\phi_F| - v_{BS})}{WC_{ox}} \qquad (1\text{-}44)$$

It is clear that the threshold voltage increases for small values of W, as sketched in Fig. 1-26b. Note that this increase is only important when W becomes comparable in size to the depletion layer width x_D.

1-9-6 Static Feedback Effect Parameter ETA

The depletion layer charge underneath the gate Q_D includes all the charge from source to drain. However, at both the drain and the source side, part of Q_D is not controlled by the gate voltage but by the drain and source voltages, respectively. These charges are denoted by Q_{DL} in Fig. 1-27a. These charges cannot be included in the calculation of V_T. They must be subtracted from Q_D to calculate V_T. The value of V_T must be decreased by ΔV_T, the value of which can be calculated in a very similar way as above. The value of ΔV_T is described in SPICE (model level 3) by a different expression given by

$$\Delta V_T = -8.15 \times 10^{-20}\eta\frac{v_{DS}}{L^3 C_{ox}} \qquad (1\text{-}45)$$

Parameter η (ETA) is introduced for fitting purposes. The expression clearly shows that the threshold voltage decreases for smaller values of channel length, as sketched in Fig. 1-27b.

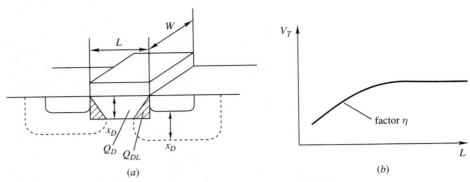

FIGURE 1-27   (a) Charge sharing charge; (b) threshold voltage V_T versus length L.

1-9-7   Onset of Short-Channel Effects

Rather than knowing how to calculate the short-channel effects described by δ and η, it is important to know whether they occur at all. It is also important to know whether they can be avoided by layout or use of supply voltages. For this purpose, Brews et al. (1980) use an expression in which all depletion layer effects are combined. It gives a minimum value of channel length L_{min}, above which the threshold voltage can still be considered to be independent of L. It is given by

$$L_{min} = 4\sqrt[3]{x_J t_{ox}\sqrt{x_D + x_S}} \qquad (1\text{-}46)$$

in which x_D and x_S are the thicknesses of the depletion layers at the drain and the source side, respectively, calculated as for abrupt junctions (see Eq. (1-3a)); t_{ox} is the oxide thickness; x_J is the junction depth. All dimensions are micrometers.

Example 1-12

Calculate the value of L_{min} for the nMOST of Sec. 1-2 with 5 V at the drain and zero bulk biasing (source at ground); $t_{ox} = 50$ nm, $N_B = 10^{16}$cm^{-3}, $x_J = 1$ μm, and $2\phi_F = 0.694$ V.

Solution. The values of x_D and x_S are, respectively, 0.87 μm and 0.30 μm and $L_{min} = 1.3$ μm. For all effective channel lengths larger than 1 μm, no short channel effects are taken into account.

1-9-8   Punchthrough and Substrate Currents

Short channel effects are not the only limitations that prevent the realization of MOST devices with short channel lengths. A more severe limitation is *punchthrough* from drain to source, illustrated in first-order in Fig. 1-28 (Sze 1981).

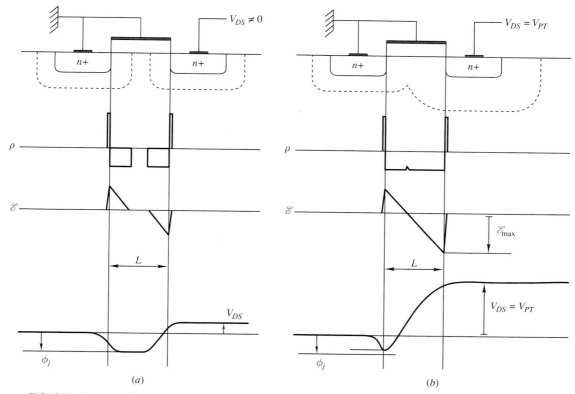

FIGURE 1-28   (a) Channel length L is larger than the sum of depletion widths; (b) punchthrough in nMOST.

In Fig. 1-28a, the cross section is given of an nMOST on an n substrate. A small voltage V_{DS} is applied to the drain. All other terminals are at ground potential. The distribution of the fixed ion charges of the depletion layers is sketched underneath. It corresponds with the electric field and potential distributions as shown.

The width of the depletion layer at the drain is wider than the one at the source because of the larger voltage across it. Its value is given by Eq. (1-3a). The built-in junction potential of the drain-bulk and source-bulk junctions is denoted by ϕ_j.

For this small value of V_{DS}, the channel length L is still larger than the sum of the depletion layer widths (see Fig. 1-28a). However, if the drain voltage V_{DS} increases, the corresponding depletion layer width increases as well. For a certain value of V_{DS}, the depletion layers touch each other as shown in Fig. 1-28b. At this point, a large current starts to flow from the source to the bulk and on to the drain. This is punchthrough.

This current is simply a result of lateral bipolar transistor operation. Indeed, this device is as much a lateral bipolar npn transistor as a pMOST, although it is never biased as a bipolar transistor as both junctions are always reverse biased. Nevertheless, if both depletion regions touch as in Fig. 1-28b, the drain voltage pulls down the potential across the source-bulk junction, forward biasing that junction. As a result, this source-bulk junction acts as an emitter and injects current into both the bulk, which now acts as a base, and into the drain, which now acts as a collector.

The value of this punchthrough current is difficult to calculate because the Poisson equations must be solved in two dimensions. The value of the voltage at which punchthrough occurs, however, is easy to calculate. Indeed, it is sufficient to equate the channel length L to the sum of the two depletion layer widths. The value of V_{DS} at which this occurs is the punchthrough voltage V_{PT}. For this calculation, the depletion layer at the source side is usually negligible. By use of Eq. (1-3a) the punchthrough voltage can be approximated by

$$V_{PT} \approx \frac{q N_D L^2}{2\varepsilon_{\text{si}}} - \phi_j \qquad (1\text{-}47)$$

Example 1-13

What is the punchthrough voltage for

1 an nMOST with $L = 3\ \mu$m on a substrate of $N_D = 10^{16}\ \text{cm}^{-3}$
2 an nMOST with $L = 1.25\ \mu$m on the same substrate?

Solution. For this junction, ϕ_j is about 0.7 V. For the first transistor, $V_{PT} = 68.6$ V; for the second transistor, $V_{PT} = 12.5$ V.

It is important to note that the punchthrough voltage strongly depends on the value of the channel length. For small channel lengths, the value of the punchthrough voltage is very small. Hence, it establishes the real lower limit of the values of channel length that can be used.

The above calculation is carried out only for abrupt junctions. For linear junctions, the value of V_{PT} is somewhat higher. On the other hand, the supply voltage can never be larger than about half of the value calculated in Eq. (1-47) to ensure that substrate currents cannot flow.

Note that the value of the punchthrough voltage is nearly independent of temperature. Indeed, if ϕ_j is negligible in Eq. (1-47), no temperature dependent factor is found. This property allows us to distinguish punchthrough from breakdown. The breakdown voltage always strongly depends on temperature. The temperature effects in a MOST are described in App. 2-1 after models for the bipolar transistor have been discussed.

1-10 DESIGN EXAMPLE

In order to gain insight into MOST parameters, a design example is now worked out. In Fig. 1-29, the cross section and the layout of an nMOST are shown in a p-well CMOS process. The parameters are given in Table 1-1. The field oxide thickness $t_{\text{ox}F}$ is 1 μm.

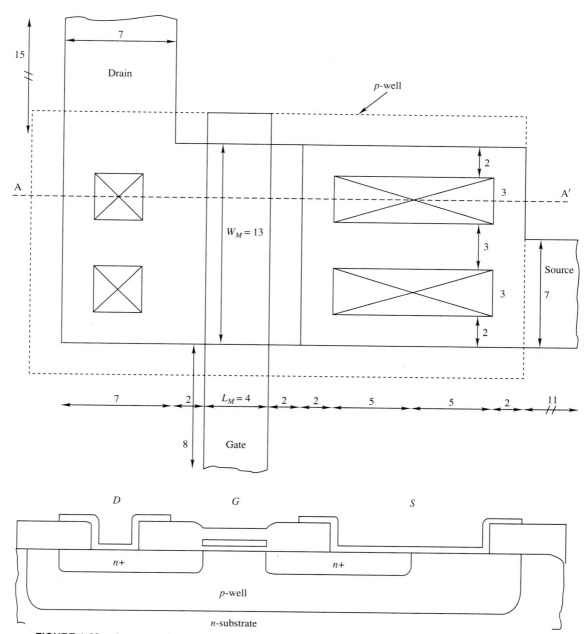

FIGURE 1-29   Layout and cross section of *n*MOST in *p*-well process (*B* connected to *S*), including some interconnect lines. All dimensions are in μm.

The transistor is biased at $V_{GS} = 3$ V, $V_{DS} = 5$ V and $V_{BS} = 0$. The following parameters must be calculated:

- the current I_{DS}
- the transconductances g_m and g_{mb}
- the output resistance r_o
- all capacitances C_{GS}, C_{DS}, and C_{GD}.
- the series resistances at the source

The resulting values are given in Table 1-8, which indicates the data taken from Fig. 1-29 and which expressions are used in what succession.

1-11 JUNCTION FETS

Junction field effect transistors are the oldest semiconductor devices. Their operation is based on the modulation of a conductive channel by means of depletion layers. While models have been developed specifically for JFETs, MOS field effect transistors have become much more important. Therefore, a JFET model is now derived from a MOST model. In this section, several models are compared but only the JFET derived from a MOST model will be used later in the book (Sze 1981; Das and Sansen 1980).

A p-channel JFET is shown in Fig. 1-30. The channel is isolated from the top gate G by a depletion layer with width h. The channel is also isolated from the substrate or bulk B by another depletion layer. Both depletion layers modulate the channel conductivity or pinch off the channel entirely. This can be done by reverse biasing the voltages across these depletion layers.

In CMOS only the top gate is used to control the transistor current. The bulk is either biased at a constant negative voltage or connected to the source. The depletion layer at the top gate G can then fully pinch off the channel, provided its thickness h_C is made equal to the thickness of the channel a_C. This can be done by reverse biasing the top gate G with respect to the source. The voltage v_{GS} required to fully pinch off the channel (for zero v_{DS}) is called the *pinchoff* voltage V_P.

The reverse bias of the bulk with respect to the source determines the value of the channel width a_C. The value of the pinchoff voltage thus depends on the bulk reverse bias. This is the bulk polarization effect. It plays exactly the same role in a MOST. It will be neglected here because the bulk is assumed to be connected to the source.

1-11-1 JFET Pinchoff Voltage

The pinchoff voltage V_P can be calculated in very much the same way as the punchthrough voltage of a MOST (see Eq. (1-47)). The thickness h_C of the depletion

TABLE 1-8 VALUES OF nMOST PARAMETERS (SEC. 1-11)

Input data	Parameter	Expression	Table or Equation number	Result
$L_M = 4\ \mu m$	L_{eff}	$L_{eff} = L_M - 2LD - DL$	(1-21a)	$3.36\ \mu m$
$W_M = 13\ \mu m$	W_{eff}	$W_{eff} = W_M - DW$		$13.4\ \mu m$
	W_{eff}/L_{eff}			4
	n	$n = 1 + \gamma/(2\sqrt{PB})$	(1-5a)	1.6
	i_{DSsat}	$KP/2n\ W/L\ (v_{GS} - V_T)^2$	(1-18c)	0.287 mA
	g_m	$KP/n\ W/L\ (v_{GS} - V_T)$	(1-22a)	0.239 mS
	g_{mb}	$(n-1)g_m$	(1-23)	0.143 mS
	r_o	$1/(\lambda i_{DSsat})$	(1-24)	158 kΩ
$GS0 = 13\ \mu m$	C_{GSO}	$C_{GSO} = CGS0 \times GS0$	Table 1-5	6.8 fF
$GD0 = 13\ \mu m$	C_{GDO}	$C_{GDO} = CGD0 \times GD0$		6.8 fF
	C_{ox}	$\varepsilon_{ox}/t_{ox} = 2 \times 10^{-7} F/cm^2$	(1-1b)	
$A_G = 13 \times 3.4\ \mu m^2$	C_{oxt}	$2/3\ C_{ox}\ W_{eff}L_{eff}$		60 fF
	C_{BCt}	$2/3\ C_j\ W_{eff}L_{eff}$		13.2 fF
$A_S = 13 \times 9\ \mu m^2$				
$P_S = 44\ \mu m$	C_{jSBt}	$A_S C_{j0} + P_S C_{jsw0}$	Table 1-1	79.0 fF
$A_D = 13 \times 9\ \mu m^2$				
$P_D = 44\ \mu m$	$C_{jDBt}(5V)$	$A_S C_j + P_S C_{jsw}$		25.9 fF
	C_{jw}	$\varepsilon_{si}/t_{si} = 6 \times 10^{-9} F/cm^2$	(1-2b)	
$A_{well} = 17 \times 31\ \mu m^2$	$C_{well,SUB}$	$C_{jw} \times A_{well}$		31.3 fF
$A_{pD} = 7 \times 15\ \mu m^2$	C_{pD}	$A_{pD} \times 5.2\ nF/cm^2$	Table 1-7	5.5 fF
$A_{pG} = 10 \times 4\ \mu m^2$	C_{pG}	$A_{pD} \times 6.5\ nF/cm^2$		$2.6\ \mu m$
$A_{pS} = 7 \times 11\ \mu m^2$	C_{pS}	$A_{pD} \times 5.2\ nF/cm^2$		4 fF
(Fig. 1-23b)	C_{p1}	$C_{p1} = C_{pG}$	Table 1-6	2.6 fF
	C_{p2}	$C_{p2} = C_{pD}$		5.5 fF
	C_{GS}	$C_{GS} = C_{GSO} + 2/3\ C_{oxt}$		66.8 fF
	C_{GD}			6.8 fF
	C_{DB}	$C_{DB} = C_{jDB}$		25.9 fF
	C_{SB}	$C_{SB} = C_{jSBt} + 2/3C_{BCt}$		87.8 fF
	C_1	$C_1 = C_{GS} + C_{p1}$		69.4 fF
	C_2	$C_2 = C_{DB} + C_{p2}$		31.4 fF
	C_3	$C_3 = C_{GD}$		6.8 fF
$R_{Ss} = 4/13\ \mu m$	R_S	$R_S = 15\ \Omega/\square \times R_{Ss}$		4.6 Ω

FIGURE 1-30 p-channel JFET.

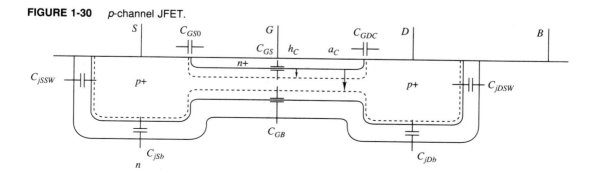

layer is obtained from Eq. (1-3a), for a channel with homogeneous doping level N_A, if the junction is assumed to be abrupt. At a reverse bias of V_P, the channel is pinched off. At this point, the thickness of the depletion layer equals the full channel thickness a_C. Substitution of V_{BC} by V_P and of t_{si} by a_C in Eq. (1-3a) yields:

$$V_P = \frac{q N_A a^2}{2\varepsilon_{si}} - \phi_j \tag{1-48}$$

in which ϕ_j is the gate-channel diode built-in voltage, given by Eq. (1-3b). This pinchoff voltage V_P consists of two terms that normally subtract from each other.

Example 1-14

If the top gate doping level equals 10^{19} cm^{-3} and $N_A = 10^{17}$ cm^{-3}, calculate the pinchoff voltage for $a_C = 0.2$ μm. What value of a_C is required to make $V_P = 3$ V and $V_P = 1$ V?

Solution. For the doping levels given, $\phi_j = 0.932$ V (see Eq. (1-3b)); the first term in Eq. (1-48) equals 3.019 V and hence $V_P = 2.087$ V. A reverse bias or positive voltage V_{GS} of about 2 V is thus required to pinch off the channel. In a similar way, for a channel thickness $a_C = 0.228$ μm, $V_P = 3$ V and $a_C = 0.16$ μm for $V_P = 1$ V.

The p-channel JFET of Fig. 1-30 is normally of the depletion type. The conducting channel already exists for zero applied V_{GS}. Its V_P must be positive, analogous with the V_T of a depletion pMOST. For this reason, the sign of V_{BC} was changed from Eq. (1-3a) to Eq. (1-47). In SPICE, the pinchoff voltage is denoted by VT0 (see Table 1-9). For a depletion pJFET the pinchoff voltage is positive.

By means of ion-implantation technology, even thinner channels than 0.2 μm can be realized. A value of V_P of about one volt is reached for a thickness a_C of about 0.16 μm and zero V_P for 0.11 μm. Transfer characteristics of JFETs with different pinchoff voltages are shown in Fig. 1-31. The pinchoff voltage can take values down to 0 V. However, the gate can only be forward biased over a few hundred mvolts, at which point a gate-source diode current starts to flow. This is gate leakage current and is to be avoided. This is actually the main disadvantage of the JFET. Additional circuitry is required to make sure the gate is never forward biased.

The characteristics of Fig. 1-31 are shown as a dashed line to indicate forward biasing. As a consequence, for small a_C or for small V_P, the input voltage range has become quite small (see curve 3 in Fig. 1-31). The most common value of V_P is about 1 V for JFETs with an implanted channel and 2 to 5 V for JFETs with channels realized by means of epitaxial layers.

For positive gate voltages larger than the pinchoff voltage, punchthrough may occur. A large current then starts flowing from gate to bulk. Obviously, this region of operation must be avoided as well and, again, the surrounding circuitry must ensure that punchthrough never occurs.

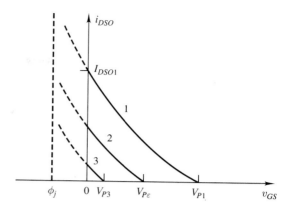

FIGURE 1-31 i_{DS} versus v_{GS} curves of JFET's with different V_P or I_{DSO}.

TABLE 1-9   NOMINAL SPICE PARAMETERS FOR A JFET

Type	n-JFET	p-JFET	Dimension	Name	Equation
VT0	−1	1	V	Zero bias threshold voltage	1-48
BETA	4E-4	2E-4	A/V²	Transconductance parameter	1-49b
LAMBDA	0.001	0.001	V⁻¹	Channel length modulation parameter	1-24a
CGS	5E-12	5E-12	F	Zero bias G-S junction capacitance	1-49c
CGD	1E-12	1E-12	F	Zero bias G-D junction capacitance	
PB	0.6	0.6	V	Bulk junction potential	1-3b
FC	0.5	0.5	—	Coefficient forward bias junction capacitance	T.2-4
IS	1E-13	1E-13	A	Bulk junction saturation current	
RS	20	50	Ω/□	Sheet resistance diffusion of S	1-36
RD	20	50	Ω/□	Sheet resistance diffusion of D	1-36
KF	2E-15	5E-17	A	Flicker noise coefficient	1-68a
AF	1	1		Flicker noise exponent	1-68a

1-11-2 JFET DC Model

A JFET behaves in very much the same way as a MOST. The current-voltage characteristics of a pJFET are sketched in Fig. 1-32. The i_{DS} versus v_{GS} characteristic (in Fig. 1-32a) is quadratic, as for a depletion MOST. It crosses the current axis at I_{DSO} and cannot be used for negative values of v_{GS}, as explained above.

The i_{DS} versus v_{DS} characteristic (in Fig. 1-32b) looks like the characteristic of a depletion MOS transistor. For small values of v_{DS} (e.g., when it is used as a switch) the JFET is in the linear region. For large values of v_{DS}, the JFET is in the saturation region. The current is then nearly independent of the drain voltage. The model of the JFET in the linear region is given first.

All expressions of the current that have been derived for a MOST can be directly applied to a JFET, provided the top oxide capacitance C_{ox} is replaced by the top

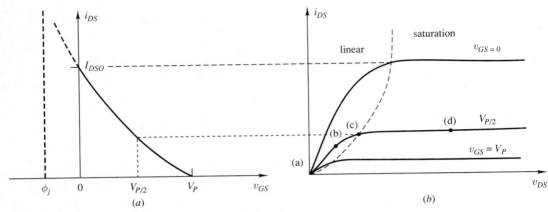

FIGURE 1-32   Characteristics i_{DS} versus v_{GS} (a) and i_{DS} versus v_{DS} (b).

junction capacitance C_{GC}. This is intuitively acceptable. The narrower the channel, the more the channel charge resembles the very narrow inversion layer charge spike of a MOST. Thus, the same model can be used for both devices.

This is certainly true for JFETs realized by means of ion-implantation. The channel and gate depth are only a few tenths of a micron and their pinchoff voltage is usually 1 V or less (type 3 in Fig. 1-31). This is not the case, however, for diffused JFETs. Their gate and channel depths can extend over several microns. As a result, their pinchoff voltages can be as high as 5 V (type 1 in Fig. 1-31). They can have two different models. If they are biased around $v_{GS} = V_{P1}$, their channel is very thin as well and they can be modeled by means of MOST models in the same way as ion-implanted devices. If they are biased around 0 V, their channel is wide open and a different model applies.

For this reason we introduce two models: the narrow-channel model and the wide-channel model. The narrow-channel model is copied from the MOST model. It applies to ion-implanted JFETs and diffused JFETs biased at their pinchoff voltage. The wide-channel model is not derived from the MOST model and applies to diffused JFETs, biased at I_{DS0} or at $v_{GS} \approx 0$ V. The narrow-channel model applies to most modern devices and is therefore taken first.

For narrow-channel devices biased around 0 V, either model can be used. The MOST model, however, is preferred because it is well known.

1-11-3   JFET: DC Model in Linear Region

For a narrow-channel JFET, the channel charge Q_m is almost fully taken up by the depletion layer charge of the top gate diode. The width of this depletion layer is a_C and hence the corresponding junction capacitance of the top gate diode is C_{GS}. In analogy with a MOST (see Eq. (1-9b)), the resistance R_{DS} of the JFET is given by

$$R_{DS} = \frac{1}{\beta(v_{GS} - V_P)} \tag{1-49a}$$

with

$$\beta = \frac{W}{L}\mu C_{GS} \tag{1-49b}$$

and

$$C_{GS} = \frac{\varepsilon_{si}}{a_C} \tag{1-49c}$$

Example 1-15

Calculate R_{DS} for $V_P = 1$ V ($a_C = 0.15$ μm) and $v_{GS} = 0$ V; note that $W/L = 10$; $\mu = 200$ cm^2/Vs; $N_A = 10^{17}$ cm^{-3} and $\phi_j = 0.932$ V (for 10^{19} cm^{-3} gate doping).

Solution. Capacitance $C_{GS} = 6.6 \times 10^{-8}$ pF/cm^2 and the model of Eq. (1-49) gives $\beta = 0.13$ mA/V^2 and $R_{DS} = 7547$ Ω. For a homogeneous resistor, the resistivity $\rho = (q\mu N_A)^{-1} = 0.31$ Ωcm. The length is L and the cross section is $a_C W$; the resultant $R_{DS} = 1953$ Ω, which is much larger than expected.

In SPICE (see Table 1-9) the value of β (BETA) is listed directly. For each W/L ratio, a different model is taken. Also, the value of C_{GS} is listed at zero-volt bias.

1-11-4 JFET DC Model: Onset of Saturation

For very small values of v_{DS}, the width of the depletion layer of the top gate diode is the same on both the drain and source side. This is the case in Fig. 1-30, which has been repeated in Fig. 1-33a. For larger values of v_{DS}, the width of the depletion layer increases on the drain side, as shown in Fig. 1-33b. The voltage drop across this depletion region increases from v_{GS} on the source side to $v_{GD} = v_{GS} - v_{DS}$ on the drain side. The value of v_{GD} is larger than v_{GS} because v_{GS} is positive and v_{DS} negative for a pJFET.

Even for larger values of v_{DS}, the depletion layer pinches off the channel (see Fig. 1-33c) and saturation occurs. At this point, the voltage drop v_{GD} evidently equals V_P. The value of v_{DS} at the onset of saturation is denoted by v_{DSsat} and it is approximately given by

$$v_{DSsat} = v_{GS} - V_P \tag{1-50}$$

in analogy to a MOST (see Eq. (1-11)).

Consider a pJFET with $V_P = 3$ V: $V_{GS} = 1$ V and $V_{DSsat} = -2$ V. Note that for $V_P = 1$ V, and $V_{GS} = 1$ V, $V_{DSsat} = 0$ V but the current i_{DS} is also zero. This is illustrated in Fig. 1-32b, in which the points of operation of Fig. 1-33 are indicated. For very small v_{DS}, the operating point is (a). The onset of saturation is indicated by point (c). This point shifts towards the zero of the axis if $v_{GS} = V_P$.

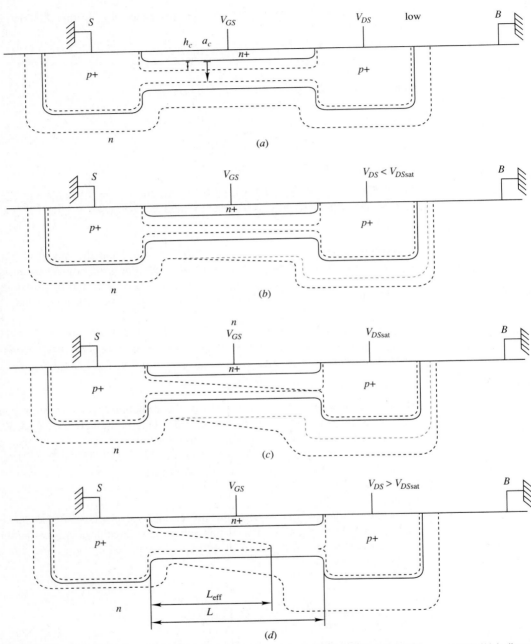

FIGURE 1-33   Channel depletion layers for constant V_{GS} and increasing V_{DS} (a) JFET as a switch (b) in linear region (c) at onset of saturation (d) in deep saturation.

For values of v_{DS} larger than v_{DSsat}, the channel is pinched off before it reaches the drain side (see Fig. 1-33d). The pinchoff point occurs where the voltage drop across the depletion layer equals V_P. Hence, the lateral voltage drop between the drain and the end point of the channel is given by $v_{DS} - v_{DSsat}$. This voltage drop causes a reduction in channel length from L to L_{eff}. This reduction $L - L_{\text{eff}}$ can be approximated by means of Eq. (1-3a) for one-sided abrupt junctions, in which N_D is substituted by channel doping level N_A.

The current i_{DS} in saturation is then approximately constant because it is determined by the lateral voltage drop between the end point of the channel and the source. This voltage drop is fixed at a value v_{DSsat}, independent of v_{DS} itself. The current increases slightly, however, because of the reduction in channel length (see point (d) in Fig. 1-32b).

The saturation mechanism described above is very similar to the same mechanism found in a MOST and will thus be derived from the MOST model.

1-11-5   JFET DC Model in Saturation

This model is quadratic and the current equals I_{DS0} at $v_{GS} = 0$ V. It is described by

$$i_{DSsat} = I_{DS0} \left(1 - \frac{v_{GS}}{V_P} \right)^2 \tag{1-51}$$

This model has the disadvantage that the parameters I_{DS0} and V_P depend on each other. Therefore, we prefer to convert this model of Eq. (1-51) into Eq. (1-52), given by

$$i_{DSsat} = \frac{\beta}{2}(v_{GS} - V_P)^2 \tag{1-52a}$$

in which β is given by (1-49b). This model closely resembles the MOS model in saturation (see Eq. (1-18a)). Comparison with Eq. (1-51) shows that i_{DSsat} can also be described by (Das and Sansen 1980)

$$i_{DSsat} = \frac{\beta}{2} V_P^2 \left(1 - \frac{v_{GS}}{V_P} \right)^2 \tag{1-52b}$$

Indeed, I_{DS0} and V_P are correlated, as clearly seen in Fig. 1-31. We can then use β and V_P rather than I_{DS0} and V_P.

The characteristic of Eq. (1-52) is also shown in Fig. 1-32a.

1-11-6   Model for Wide-Channel JFETs

If a JFET is built up by means of epitaxial layers, it has a wide channel (large a_C). In this case, the JFET in its linear region behaves as a resistor with length L and cross section $W a_C$. It is more interesting, however, to see the difference in the model if the JFET is used as an amplifier in the saturation region.

For the calculation of the current in saturation, the depletion layer width is always assumed to be given by Eq. (1-3a) as for a one-sided abrupt junction. The current i_{DS} is obtained by integrating the channel charge Q_m between source and drain. If this is carried out at the onset of saturation (see Fig. 1-33c), where $v_{DS} = v_{GS} - V_P$, the resultant current i_{DS} is i_{DSsat} (1981 Sze).

$$i_{DSsat} = I_{DSS}(1 - 3\phi_{GS} + 2\phi_{GS}^{3/2}) \tag{1-53}$$

with

$$I_{DSS} = \frac{W}{L}\mu\frac{q^2 N_A^2 a^3}{6\varepsilon_{si}}$$

and

$$\phi_{GS} = \frac{\phi_j + v_{GS}}{\phi_j + V_P}$$

The integration of an expression with a square root gives rise to a 3/2 power and is easily recognizable. The same 3/2 power has already occurred in the derivation of i_{DS} for a MOST. It is the coefficient of γ in Eq. (1-16).

It is clear from Eq. (1-53) that I_{DSS} is different from I_{DS0} and the current at zero v_{GS} from Eq. (1-53) is different from I_{DS0} or $(\beta/2)V_P^2$. We must keep in mind, though, that I_{DSS} is derived from first-order considerations. Therefore, we change the value of I_{DSS} such that I_{DS0} is the same in both Eq. (1-53) and Eq. (1-52b).

Even if the currents at zero v_{GS} are the same for both models, there is still a difference in curvature. Eq. (1-52b) has a quadratic relationship, whereas Eq. (1-53) contains a linear term and a 3/2 power term. Both are shown in Fig. (1-34) for the same current at zero v_{GS}. It is clear that the curve of Eq. (1-52b) is slighty more curved.

FIGURE 1-34 i_{DS} versus v_{GS} characteristics in saturation.

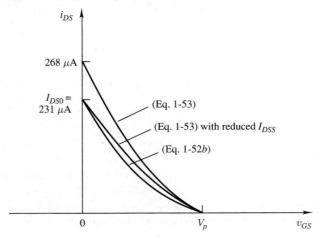

Example 1-16

Calculate the currents for both models for $a_C = 0.2$ μm, $V_P = 2.087$ V ($\phi_j = 0.932$ V), $W/L = 10$ and $\mu = 200$ cm^2/Vs. What value of I_{DSS} is required to ensure that both models provide the same I_{DS0}?

Solution. From Eq. (1-49c), $C_{GS} = 5.3 \times 10^{-8}$ pF/cm^2 and from (Eq. (1-49b), $\beta = 0.106$ mA/V^2. Hence, from Eq. (1-52b), $I_{DS0} = (\beta/2)V_P^2 = 0.231$ mA. From Eq. (1-53) $I_{DSS} = 0.644$ mA and the current at zero-volt v_{GS} is $i_{DSsat} = 0.268$ mA. We multiply I_{DSS} by a factor $0.231/0.268 = 0.862$ to obtain the same I_{DS0}. This situation is diagrammed in Fig. 1-34.

Because of its similarity with a MOST, the model of Eq. (1-52b) will be used from now on. If fabrication data is available, such as channel thickness a_C and channel doping level N_A, parameters V_P, C_{GS}, and β are easily calculated. On the other hand, if only measured data is available, V_P and I_{DS0} are easily extracted, and β is derived from Eq. (1-52c).

Note that there is still an important difference between the models of a MOST and a JFET because of the difference in nature between C_{ox} and C_{GS}. The first one is constant whereas the second one is a depletion layer capacitance, and thus depends on v_{GS}.

1-11-7 JFET DC Model in Saturation: Subthreshold Region

For very low current values, a subthreshold region occurs in very much the same way as it does for a MOST. The i_{DS0} versus v_{GS} characteristic is exponential. The slope of the semilogarithmic curve is again given by nkT/q in which n ($= 1 + C_{GS}/C_{BS}$) indicates the relative value of the controlling capacitance.

If both the top gate and the bottom gate (or bulk) are shorted together, then $n = 1$ and the same slope is achieved as for a bipolar transistor, i.e., 60 mV/decade. In general, the JFET does not have an isolated bulk and hence n has a typical value of 1.5 to 1.7.

In SPICE, the model of Eq. (1-52a) is used. Parameter β occurs in both Eq. (1-49) and Eq. (1-52a) and is listed as BETA in Table 1-9.

1-11-8 JFET Small-Signal Models

In saturation, the small-signal model is derived from the DC model of Eq. (1-52a) in exactly the same way as it was derived for a MOST. It consists of transconductance g_m which, in the quadratic region, is found by taking the derivative of Eq. (1-52a). The transconductance per unit current at zero v_{GS} is then given by

$$\frac{g_m}{i_{DSsat}}\bigg|_{v_{GS}=0} = \left|\frac{2}{V_P}\right| \tag{1-54}$$

This is a well-known result for JFETs: the smaller the pinchoff voltage, the larger the transconductance per unit current at zero v_{GS} (at I_{DS0}). In general, however, the JFET can be biased at any current between zero and I_{DS0} and hence g_m/i_{DSsat} can be made much larger than given by Eq. (1-54). As for a MOST, the smaller the current the larger the g_m/i_{DSsat} ratio (see Fig. 1-10b). In the subthreshold region, however, the ratio of g_m/i_{DSsat} reaches its maximum value and equals q/nkT.

The second small-signal model parameter is the output resistance r_o or r_{DS}. It depends on the current in exactly the same way as a MOST. In SPICE, it is also characterized by LAMBDA (λ). Hence, the relation between r_o and λ is again given by Eq. (1-24).

In addition to the transconductance and the output resistance, the capacitances must be added in the small-signal model. Again, the picture is very similar to a MOST except that C_{ox} is replaced by C_{GS} (see Fig. 1-30). Also, the gate overlap capacitances are replaced by the gate source and gate drain capacitances C_{GS0} and C_{GD0} respectively. These capacitances are much larger than the overlap capacitances in a MOST because their corresponding depletion regions are very thin as a result of the high doping levels on both sides.

For example, if the top gate is 0.2 μm deep and the doping level of both the gate and the drain (source) is 10^{19} cm^{-3}, then the depletion layer width is only about 0.024 μm ($\phi_j = 1.05$ V) and the overlap capacitance $C_{ov} = C_{GS0} = C_{GD0} = 8.8$ pF per cm width W, which is enormous.

In SPICE, the overlap capacitance C_{GS0} is included in CGS itself. The other capitance C_{GD0} is denoted by CGD at zero bias. Note that both capacitances in SPICE are total capacitances, not capacitances per unit area.

Example 1-17

Calculate the maximum frequency of operation $f_{max} = g_m/2\pi C_{GSt}$ in which C_{GSt} is the total gate capacitance. The pJFET has $L = 5$ μm, $\mu_p = 200$ cm^2/Vs at $V_{GS} - V_P = 1$ V. Repeat the calculation first with only an oxide capacitance of $C_{GSO} = 5.3 \times 10^{-8}$ F/cm^2 and then, after the addition of gate-source overlap capacitance, with value $C_{ov} = 8.8$ pF/cm.

Solution. The gate capacitance is $C_{GSt} = WLC_{GS}$ and the overlap capacitance is $C_{GStov} = 2WC_{ov}$. The frequency f_{max} is given by

$$f_{max} = \frac{1}{2\pi} \frac{g_m}{C_{GSt} + C_{GStov}} = \frac{1}{2\pi} \frac{\mu}{L^2} \frac{v_{GS} - V_P}{1 + \frac{2C_{ov}}{LC_{GS}}} \tag{1-55}$$

This provides $f_{max} = 127$ MHz without overlap capacitance but only 48 MHz with overlap capacitance

Note that this f_{max} is maximized for an nJFET with small channel length and biased at $v_{GS} = 0$. However, the reduction of the channel length is limited by punchthrough.

1-11-9   JFET Example: MESFET

A good example of a JFET with a small channel length L is a MESFET (see Fig. 1-35). It consists of a thin epitaxial channel that can be pinched off by the depletion layer of a top gate Schottky diode. Source and drain diffusions are not required and as a result, the lateral dimensions can be made quite small. A typical gate length is $L = 0.5$ μm. Usually GaAs is used instead of silicon, as it provides electron mobilities up to 1500 cm^2/Vs. As a result, the value of the maximum frequency (for $Vp = 1$ V and zero v_{GS}) is 95 GHz, which is a very high value indeed. This value can only be reached if the overlap capacitances are neglected.

A few more sophisticated realizations of silicon JFETs are shown in Fig. 1-36. The meander structure (Fig. 1-36a) uses only a small area for a resistance with a large value, whereas the round structure (Fig. 1-36b) provides minimum drain gate capacitance.

FIGURE 1-35   (a) nMESFET and (b) Pinch resistance as pJFET.

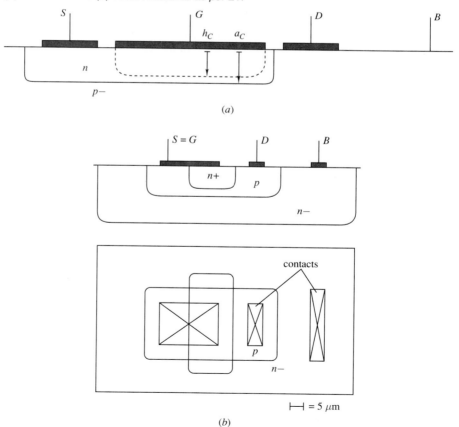

(a)

(b)

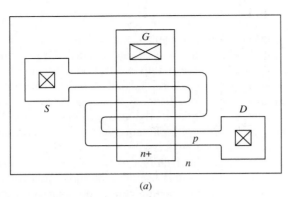
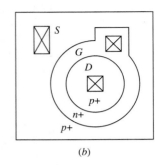

(a)   (b)

FIGURE 1-36   (a) Meander and (b) round JFET.

1-11-10   JFET Design Example

A *p*JFET has been realized with a double ion-implantation, resulting in gate and channel profiles as sketched in Fig. 1-37*a*. The depths are indicated, as are the average doping levels. The mobility in the channel is 275 cm^2/Vs. In Fig. 1-37*b*, the layout is given. All SPICE parameters (see also Fig. 1-7) are calculated at $V_{GS} = 0$.

At the biasing point $V_{GS} = 0$, the following specifications are obtained: I_{DS} ($V_{DS} = 10$ V), g_m, $g_m/I_{DS\text{sat}}$, and $f_{\max}$.

The results are collected in Table 1-10.

1-12   NOISE SOURCES IN FET

A JFET is used mainly to replace a MOST for low-noise applications. Therefore, the noise performance is investigated for both of them. However, since this is the first time that noise is discussed, elementary considerations of noise are provided (Ott 1988).

Noise is a signal with random amplitude versus time (see Fig. 1-38*a*). It is generated by all passive and active devices. Its average value over a certain period of time is zero and therefore its power is measured by the noise voltage v_N squared to v_N^2 and averaged over that time period (Fig. 1-38*b*).

The frequency spectrum of noise extends from nearly zero to frequencies up to 10^{14} Hz. In some cases, more noise is generated at low frequencies (see Fig. 1-39). At these low frequencies, the power decreases linearly with the frequency and is called $1/f$ (or pink) noise. At higher frequencies, all frequencies are equally present and it is called white noise. In order to be able to take into account frequency spectra with variable amplitude, an elementary small frequency band df is taken. The noise power in this band is then denoted by $\overline{dv_N^2}$ (see Fig. 1-39). The total noise in a given bandwidth from frequency f_1 to f_2 is given by

$$\overline{v_{12}} = \sqrt{\int_{f_1}^{f_2} \overline{dv_N^2} \ \mathrm{df}} \qquad (1\text{-}56a)$$

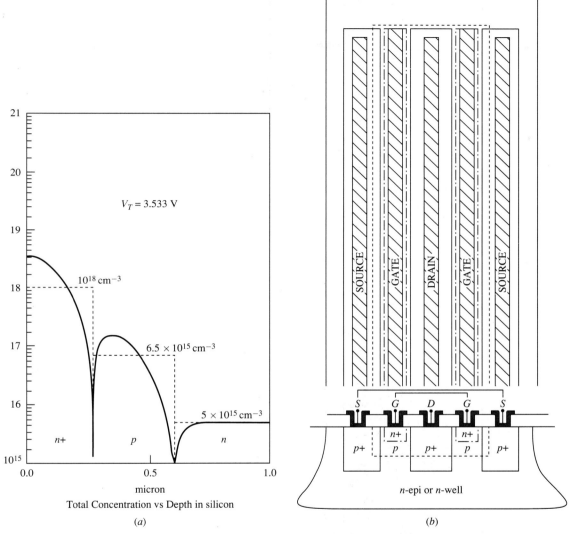

FIGURE 1-37   (a) Profile of doping level, for p-JFET; (b) Layout JFET: Note that the source stripes are connected together, and also the gate stripes.

This integration is easily carried out for white noise (see Fig. 1-39), given by

$$\overline{v_{12}} = \sqrt{(f_2 - f_1)\overline{dv_N^2}} \qquad (1\text{-}56b)$$

Note that for large frequency bands, the lower frequency f_1 is negligible with respect to f_2. Taking a value of zero for f_1 makes the calculation easier in Eqs. (1-56).

TABLE 1-10   VALUES OF JFET PARAMETERS (SEC. 1-11)

Input data	Parameter	Expression	Equation Number	Result
Fig. 1-37a	ϕ_j	$\dfrac{kT}{q}\ln(N_A N_D/n_i^2)$	(1-3b)	0.861 V
$a_C = 0.2\ \mu\text{m}$ Fig. 1-37b	V_P	$(qN_B a^2)/2\varepsilon_{si} - \phi_j$	(1-48)	1.1 V
$L_M = 18\ \mu\text{m}$ $W_M = 300\ \mu\text{m}$	L_{eff} W_{eff} $W_{\text{eff}}/L_{\text{eff}}$	$L_{\text{eff}} = L_M - 2LD$ $W_{\text{eff}} = 2xW_M$	(1-21a)	$14\ \mu\text{m}$ $600\ \mu\text{m}$ 43
	C_{GS}	$\dfrac{\varepsilon_{si}}{a_C} = 5.3 \times 10^{-8}\ \text{F/cm}^2$	(1-49c)	
$\mu = 275\ \text{cm}^2/\text{Vs}$	C_{GSt} β I_{DS0} g_m/I_{DS0} g_m λ	$W_{\text{eff}}L_{\text{eff}}C_{GS}$ $(W/L)_{\text{eff}}\mu C_{GS}$ $\beta/2V_P^2$ $2/V_P$ βV_P	(1-49b) (1-52c) (1-54) (1-24a)	4.45 pF $627\ \mu\text{A/V}^2$ $380\ \mu\text{A}$ 1.82 $691\ \mu\text{S}$ 0.001
Fig. 1-37b	C_{GS} C_{GS0}	$2/3\,C_{GSt}$ $C_{GS0} = C_{GS} \times 0.26\ \mu\text{m}$	(1-49c)	2.97 pF 1.38 pF/cm
Fig. 1-37a	C_{GD0} C_{GDtov}	$C_{GD0} = C_{GS0}$ $C_{GDtov} = W_{\text{eff}}C_{GD0}$		0.08 pF*
Fig. 1-37b	C_{DB}	$\dfrac{\varepsilon_{si}}{t_{si}} = 2.23 \times 10^{-8}\,\text{F/cm}^2$	(1-49c)	
$A_{DB} = 30 \times 300\ \mu\text{m}^2$	C_{DBt}	$C_{DBt} = A_{DB}\,C_{DB}$		2 pF
	f_{max}	$\approx g_m/(2\pi\,G_{GSt})$	(1-55)	36 MHz

* becomes 0.686 pF if the $n+$ and $p+$ regions touch; the capacitance C_{GD0} is then 11.44 pF/cm indeed.

FIGURE 1-38   Noise versus time.

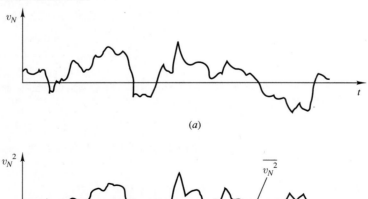

(a)

(b)

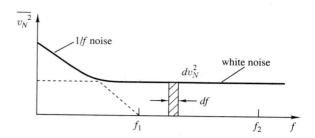

FIGURE 1-39 Noise signal versus frequency.

Calculations for noise signals other than white noise will be carried out later. Several noise sources are examined first.

1-12-1 Thermal or Johnson Noise

This kind of noise depends on temperature but not on current flow. It is white. A resistance R generates thermal noise, given by (Fig. 1-40a)

$$\overline{dv_R^2} = 4kTR \ df \tag{1-57}$$

in which k is Boltzmann's constant and T the absolute temperature. Factor kT is easily calculated by $kT = kT/q \times q = 25.86 \ \text{mV} \times 1.6 \times 10^{-19} \ \text{C} = 41.4 \times 10^{-22} \ \text{VC}$ or $\text{V}^2/\Omega \ \text{Hz}$.

Example 1-18

Calculate the noise voltage generated by a resistance of 1 kΩ and its total noise voltage between 100 Hz and 10 kHz.

Solution. $\overline{dv_R^2} = 16 \times 10^{-18} \ \text{V}^2/\text{Hz}$ or $4 \ \text{nV}_{\text{RMS}}/\sqrt{\text{Hz}}$. This is an easy result to obtain and is worth remembering.

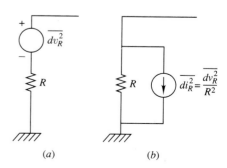

FIGURE 1-40 Thermal noise.

(a) (b)

The total noise between 100 Hz and 10 kHz is then $\overline{v_{12}} = 398$ nV$_{\text{RMS}}$. The approximate result (for $f_1 = 0$) is then 400 nV$_{\text{RMS}}$, which is sufficiently close to the exact result.

In Fig. 1-40a, thermal noise is represented by a voltage source in series. Its exact polarity is not important because its value will be squared anyway. The polarity is only indicated to apply the laws of Ohm and Kirchhoff, which are applicable only to voltages and currents, not to powers.

In some circuit configurations, it is advantageous to represent the thermal noise by a parallel current source, with value $\overline{di_R^2}$. It is obviously related to $\overline{dv_R^2}$ as indicated in Fig. 1-40b. Again, the polarity is indicated to carry out circuit calculations and it can be freely chosen.

Note that the higher the temperature of the resistor, the more thermal noise it generates, so cooling down the resistor reduces its noise contribution. This is not the case for shot noise, discussed next.

1-12-2 Shot Noise

Shot noise does not depend on temperature but on the current flow. It is also white noise. A junction diode always generates shot noise. Its value is given by (see Fig. 1-41a):

$$\overline{di_D^2} = 2q I_D \ df \tag{1-58}$$

and again, its polarity can be chosen.

Note that Eq. (1-58) is valid for forward bias current as well as for reverse bias current. In Fig. 1-41b, the diode is reverse biased and a small leakage current I_D flows, to which Eq. (1-58) is fully applicable.

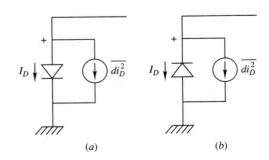

(a) $\qquad\qquad$ (b)

FIGURE 1-41 Shot noise.

Example 1-19

Calculate the noise generated by a diode that is

1 forward biased at a current of $I_D = 50$ μA; how is the noise related to the small-signal resistance $1/g_m$ of that diode?

2 reverse biased with a leakage current (for example, under influence of light or radiation) of $I_D = 0.5$ pA.

Solution. In forward bias, $\overline{di_D^2} = 16 \times 10^{-24}$ A^2/Hz or 4 pA$_{RMS}$/$\sqrt{Hz}$. This too is a useful result to remember.

At 50 μA, the small-signal resistance $1/g_m$ is $qI_D/kT = 517$ Ω. Comparison of Eq. (1-57), in which $\overline{di_D^2} = \overline{dv_R^2}/R^2$ with $R = 1/g_m$, shows that the diode generates only half of the noise power calculated from Eq. (1-57) with $1/g_m$ as resistance. Nevertheless, remember that g_m is a small-signal parameter that does not generate noise anyway.

In reverse bias, $\overline{dvi_R^2} = 16 \times 10^{-32}$ A^2/Hz or 0.4 fA$_{RMS}$/$\sqrt{Hz}$.

Note that this kind of noise can be reduced only by reducing the current, not by cooling down the device.

1-12-3 1/f Noise or Flicker Noise

To any of the noise sources described above, a $1/f$ noise source must be added. This kind of noise describes the quality of the conductive medium. The more homogeneous the material, the lower the $1/f$ noise. Also, the larger the conductive volume, the lower the $1/f$ noise. For planar devices, the $1/f$ noise is always inversely proportional to the size of the device.

The $1/f$ noise does not depend on temperature but rather is proportional to the current. It is not white but pink noise. Thus, the noise source $\overline{dv_R^2}$ of a resistor in Fig. 1-42 consists of a white noise component $\overline{dv_{RW}^2}$ and a $1/f$ noise component $\overline{dv_{RF}^2}$, given by

$$\overline{dv_{RF}^2} = KF_R \frac{R_\square^2}{A_R} V_R^2 \frac{df}{f} \tag{1-59}$$

in which A_R is the size or area of the resistor; V_R is the DC voltage across the resistor and KF_R is a technological $1/f$ noise constant. The resistor has been realized with sheet resistance $R_\square$. For a diffused or ion-implanted resistor, $KF_R \approx 5 \times 10^{-24}$ S^2 cm^2 (Das and Sansen 1980). For thick-film resistors, KF_R is about 10 times larger.

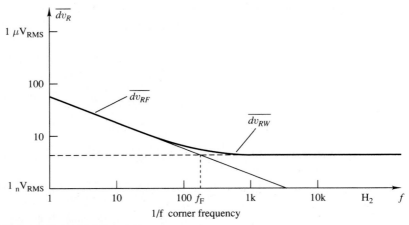

FIGURE 1-42 Noise voltage of 1 kΩ resistor.

Example 1-20

Draw the noise voltage of a resistor of 1 kΩ realized in drain resistance (50 Ω/□) that is 5 μm wide and in the frequency range 1 Hz to 100 kHz. The applied voltage is 1 V. At what frequency does the transition occur from $1/f$ to white noise?

Solution. With 50 Ω/□, twenty squares are needed to realize 1 kΩ. The length of the resistor is thus 20×5 μm $= 100$ μm and its area is $A_R = 100 \times 5$ μm $= 500$ μm² or 5×10^{-6} cm².

At 1 Hz, $\overline{dv_R^2} = 25 \times 10^{-16}$ V²/Hz or 50 nV$_{RMS}$/$\sqrt{Hz}$. At 100 Hz $\overline{dv_R^2} = 25 \times 10^{-18}$ V²/Hz or 5 nV$_{RMS}$/$\sqrt{Hz}$. The white noise level for 1 kΩ is at 4 nV$_{RMS}$/$\sqrt{Hz}$. Both characteristics intersect at about 160 Hz. This frequency is called the $1/f$ noise corner frequency f_F (see Fig. 1-42).

A $1/f$ noise source is also added to shot noise, i.e., to $\overline{di_D^2}$ in Fig. 1-41. Its value is given by

$$\overline{di_{DF}^2} = \frac{KF_I I_D}{A_D} \frac{df}{f} \tag{1-60}$$

in which A_D is the size of the diode, I_D the current through it, and KF_I, another technological noise constant. In general, $KF_I \approx 10^{-21}$ Acm². Experimental data has indicated that the exponent of I_D can differ from unity, but is normally at unity.

Example 1-21

Draw the noise current in the frequency range 1 Hz to 100 kHz of a diode biased at 50 μA. The size of the diode is 30×30 μm. What is the corner frequency?

Add curves for biasing currents of 0.5 mA and 5 mA. What happens to the corner frequency?

Solution. At 1 Hz, $\overline{di_{DF}^2} = 56 \times 10^{-22}$ A²/Hz or 75 pA$_{\text{RMS}}/\sqrt{\text{Hz}}$. At 100 Hz, $\overline{di_{DF}^2} = 56 \times 10^{-20}$ A²/Hz or 7.5 pA$_{\text{RMS}}/\sqrt{\text{Hz}}$. The white noise level is only 4 pA$_{\text{RMS}}/\sqrt{\text{Hz}}$. These characteristics intersect at a corner frequency of about 350 Hz. For a biasing current of 0.5 mA, which is 10 times higher than 50 μA, the white noise current decreases $\sqrt{10}\times$ but the $1/f$ noise current does not. The corner frequency thus increases by a factor of $\sqrt{10}$. The higher the DC current through the diode, the higher the corner frequency.

1-12-4 Other Noise Sources

A few more noise sources exist, which we mention here only in passing. The first is popcorn noise. It has a distinct behavior in the sense that on an oscilloscope it looks like regular noise except for a number of sudden pops at a low repetition rate. Its power has a $1/f^2$ spectrum. It is an indication of distinct recombination processes in the material, and a sign of bad quality processing. It should be avoided altogether.

The other noise source that occurs is associated with breakdown. Breakdown itself is a random phenomenom. Just before breakdown, excessive noise is generated and breakdown can be avoided by staying away from the breakdown voltage.

1-12-5 Total Noise

Assume that the bandwidth of the output noise of a resistor is limited by means of a capacitance (see Fig. 1-43a). The total output noise can then be calculated as given by Eq. (1-56a), provided its transfer function $H(f)$ is included. For a simple RC circuit, $H(f)$ is given by

$$H(f) = \frac{1}{1 + j\dfrac{f}{f_c}} \tag{1-61}$$

in which $f_c = 1/2\pi RC$ is the bandwidth. The total noise is obtained from Eq. (1-56a) and is given by

$$\overline{v_{\text{out}}} = \sqrt{\int_0^\infty \overline{dv_R^2} |H(f)|^2 df} \tag{1-62a}$$

Substitution of $\overline{dv_R^2}$ and of $H(f)$ allows integration. Noting that

$$\int \frac{x}{1+x^2}\,dx = \arctan x \quad \text{and that} \quad \int_0^\infty \frac{x}{1+x^2}\,dx = \frac{\pi}{2}$$

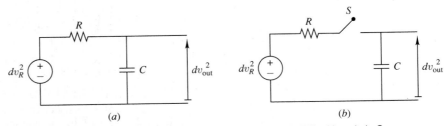

FIGURE 1-43   Output noise of resistor n with capacitance c, (a) without and (b) with switch S.

Eq. (1-62a) yields

$$\overline{v_{\text{out}}} = \sqrt{\frac{kT}{C}} \tag{1-62b}$$

This result could have been obtained from Eq. (1-56b) as well by working out the integral on $H(f)$ only. This yields

$$\overline{v_{\text{out}}} = \sqrt{f_c \frac{\pi}{2} \overline{dv_N^2}} \tag{1-63}$$

in which $f_c \pi/2$ is called the *noise bandwidth*. It is the bandwidth necessary to calculate the total white noise with the simplified Eq. (1-56b). Note that it is 57 percent larger than the bandwidth f_c itself, in order to include the effects of the finite slope of 20 dB/decade of a first-order filter. For higher-order filters (of order > 5), the noise bandwidth evidently equals f_c itself.

The result of Eq. (1-62b) is remarkable. It shows that the noise generated by a resistor depends only on its shunt capacitance. This is also true for very large R.

For charge amplifiers, where the input source is a capacitance, the noise is expressed as a noise charge or as a number of electrons. The noise charge is Cv_C, with v_C given by Eq. (1-62b). It is also given by qN_e, in which N_e is the number of electrons. Equating both yields

$$N_e = \frac{\sqrt{kT}}{q} \sqrt{C} \tag{1-64}$$

which equals $400\sqrt{C}$ if C is in pF. A charge amplifier with 2 pF input capacitance will thus exhibit about 456 electrons input noise.

Equation (1-62b) is valid if a switch is added in series with the resistor, as shown in Fig. 1-43b. The switch opens and closes periodically as in switched-capacitor circuits (see Chap. 7). It thus functions as a periodical sample-and-hold. Each time the switch opens, the output voltage is held. Because of the noise, the voltages held are slightly different. The random variation or the variance again equals $\sqrt{kT/C}$. For a 1 pF hold capacitance, the expected variation is thus as high as 64 μV_{RMS}. The only way to decrease this variance is to increase hold capacitance C.

1-12-6 FET Noise Models

Noise signals are small and can thus be added in the FETs small-signal model. This is shown in Fig. 1-44a for a FET in saturation. Two noise sources are included: thermal noise in the channel and gate leakage noise.

Channel resistance R_{ch} generates *thermal noise* $\overline{di^2_{DS}}$, shown in Fig. 1-40b. It is given by

$$\overline{di^2_{DS}} = \frac{4kT}{R_{ch}}\,\mathrm{df} \tag{1-65a}$$

Resistor R_{ch} is actually the drain-source resistance in the linear region, given by R_{DS} in Eq. (1-9). However, the drain-source resistance R_{DS} in the linear region approximately equals the inverse transconductance $1/g_m$ in the saturation region. Because of field effects in the channel, the noise is reduced by a factor of 0.6 to 0.7, or about 2/3. The resistive channel noise $\overline{di^2_{DS}}$ can thus be described by

$$\overline{di^2_{DS}} = \frac{8kT}{3}g_m\,df \tag{1-65b}$$

This is a truly important expression and definitely worth memorizing.

In order to be able to compare the noise generated by the FET to the input signal applied, the noise is referred to the input. It is then called the *equivalent input* noise voltage and is represented by $\overline{dv^2_{ieq}}$. Its value is obtained by division of $\overline{di^2_{DS}}$ of Eq. (1-65b) by g^2_m and is given by

$$\overline{dv^2_{ieq}} = \frac{8kT}{3}\frac{1}{g_m}\,df \tag{1-66}$$

FIGURE 1-44   Noise sources in a FET.

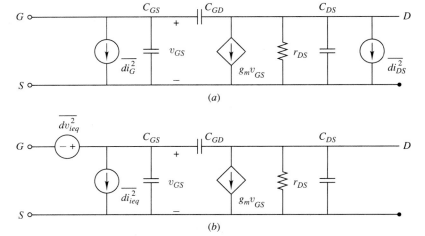

It occurs in series with the gate (see Fig. 1-44b). To this thermal noise source, a $1/f$ noise source is added. Referred to the input, it is given by an expression derived from Eq. (1-60). The current dependence disappears after division by g_m^2. and given by

$$\overline{dv_{ieqf}^2} = \frac{KF_F}{WLC_{\text{ox}}^2}\frac{df}{f} \tag{1-67}$$

in which W and L are in cm, and C_{ox} is in F/cm^2. Constant KF_F depends on the FET used. Empirical values are (Chang and Sansen 1991):

$$pJFET \qquad KF_F \approx 10^{-33}\text{C}^2/\text{cm}^2 \text{ (and } C_{GS} = C_{\text{ox}})$$

$$pMOST \qquad KF_F \approx 10^{-32}\ \text{C}^2/\text{cm}^2$$

$$nMOST \qquad KF_F \approx 4 \times 10^{-31}\ \text{C}^2/\text{cm}^2$$

These are obviously approximate values. Depending on the actual technology they can easily differ by more than a factor of two. Nevertheless these averages will be used in the remainder of this text.

Note that a JFET is about ten times higher in noise power (a factor of $\sqrt{10}$ in equivalent input voltage) than a pMOST of the same size. Also note that an nMOST is considerably worse than a pMOST.

Example 1-22

Derive the characteristic of $\overline{dv_{ieq}^2}$ versus frequency (as in Fig. 1-42 for a resistor) for a pMOST and a pJFET with $g_m = (1\ \text{k}\Omega)^{-1}$ and a gate area of $200 \times 5\ \mu\text{m}$. The controlling capacitance $C_{\text{ox}} = C_{GS} = 6.8 \times 10^{-8}\ \text{F/cm}^2$.

Solution. The white noise level is somewhat lower than for a resistor of 1 kΩ because of the 2/3 factor in Eq. (1-66). It is $\overline{dv_{ieq}} = 3.26\ \text{nV}/\sqrt{\text{Hz}}$ instead of 4 nV$_{\text{RMS}}/\sqrt{\text{Hz}}$. The $1/f$ noise is easily calculated to be 0.15 μV$_{\text{RMS}}/\sqrt{\text{Hz}}$ for a pJFET and 0.5 μV$_{\text{RMS}}/\sqrt{\text{Hz}}$ for a pMOST at 1 Hz. Both characteristics are sketched in Fig. 1-45. It is evident that a pMOST generates more noise at low frequencies. It has a corner frequency that is a factor of 10 larger than a JFET of the same gate size.

In Fig. 1-45, a noise curve is added for the same MOST biased at 10 times lower current. Note that its corner frequency is even lower than before, by a factor of $\sqrt{10}$.

1-12-7 $1/f$ Noise in SPICE

In SPICE, two parameters are added to characterize the $1/f$ noise. They are KF and AF (see Tables 1-1 and 1-9). The expression used is given by (Antognetti and

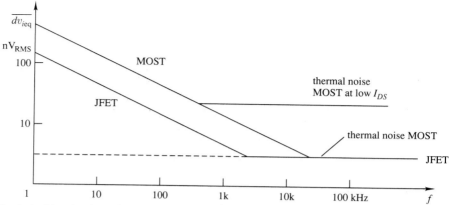

FIGURE 1-45   Equivalent input noise voltages of FETS with same g_m.

Massobrio 1988):

$$\overline{dv_{ieqf}^2} = \text{KF}\frac{I^{\text{AF}}}{g_m^2}\frac{df}{f} \qquad (1\text{-}68a)$$

in which $\text{AF} \approx 1$ and KF plays the same role as KF_F in Eq. (1-67) but has a different value. It includes, however, the influence of the gate area.

Equating Eqs. (1-67) and (1-68) shows that the relation between the technological constants KF_F and KF is

$$\text{KF} = \frac{4\text{KP}}{nL^2 C_{\text{ox}}^2} KF_F \qquad (1\text{-}68b)$$

in strong inversion and for $\text{AF} = 1$. For a pMOST with $C_{\text{ox}} = 6.8 \times 10^{-8}$ F/cm^2, $\text{KP}/n = 15 \times 10^{-6}$ A/V^2, and $L = 5 \times 10^{-4}$ cm, the coefficient of KF_F in Eq. (1-68b) is 5.2×10^{16} and $\text{KF} = 5.2 \times 10^{-16}$ A. Note that for each channel length L another value of KF must be taken.

1-12-8   Equivalent Input Noise Current

The capacitances in the small-signal circuit cause an equivalent input noise current to flow, as indicated in Fig. 1-44b. It is caused by the thermal channel noise and so it can be derived from Eq. (1-66) and is given by

$$\overline{di_{ieq}^2} = \frac{8kT}{3}\frac{1}{g_m}(\omega C_{GS})^2 df \qquad (1\text{-}69)$$

It is heavily frequency dependent, and thus it only becomes important at high frequencies, in applications of receivers or detectors, etc.

1-12-9   Gate Leakage Noise

The second noise source in the small-signal circuit of Fig. 1-44a is $\overline{di_G^2}$. It is shot noise caused by the gate leakage current. It is given by Eq. (1-58) where I_D is substituted by the leakage current i_G. For MOSTs, this current is quite small and its corresponding noise is negligible. If a protection network is added, however, the protection diode leakage current causes noise. This is also the case for a JFET in which the input gate diode leakage current causes noise. For MOSTs, however, it will be neglected in the remainder of this text.

Noise models will be developed further in the next chapter, after the introduction of the bipolar transistor.

SUMMARY

In this chapter, detailed attention has been paid to the model of a MOS Transistor, from which a JFET model has been derived. Emphasis was placed on first-order expressions for the i_{DS} versus v_{GS} characteristics, the transconductance, the capacitances, and the noise. Also, a full account was given of the MOST parameters as used in SPICE, necessary to verify circuit performance. Finally, the concept of a design plan or procedure was introduced for single-transistor amplifiers without capacitances. Such design plans with capacitances will be given in Chap. 4.

Temperature effects have not yet been discussed. They are collected in App. 2-1.

The next chapter is very similar in goal, where models of bipolar transistors will be discussed.

EXERCISES

1-1 Design an nMOST with equal controlling capacitances C_{GC} and $C_{BC}(n = 2)$. What is its γ in this case ($\phi_j = 0.6$ V)? Plot the required substrate doping N_{SUB} versus the oxide thickness t_{ox} if $v_{BS} = 0$. What value of N_{SUB} is reached at $t_{\text{ox}} = 50$ nm?

1-2 We want to realize a pMOST in an n-well of 10^{16} cm^{-3} with an oxide thickness $t_{\text{ox}} = 50$ nm. Calculate γ and the required V_{FB} to reach $V_{T0} = -1$ V. What is the required substrate bias v_{BS} to compensate for an overly small n-well doping? Plot v_{BS} versus N_{SUB} and give its value for a reduction in N_{SUB} of a factor of two.

1-3 Plot the i_{DS} versus v_{GS} and i_{DS} versus v_{DS} characteristics of an nMOST with $V_{Tn} = 0.8$ V, $\beta_n = 200$ μA/V^2, and $\lambda = 0.03$, for $V_{GS} = 1, 2, 3$, and 4 V and for V_{DS} from 0 to 5 V.

1-4 Plot the i_{DS} versus v_{GS} characteristic of an nMOST in both strong and weak inversion with $V_{Tn} = 1$ V, KP$_n = 50$ μA/V^2, $W/L = 10$ and $n = 1.5$. Choose I_{D0} for a best fit. Also take the derivative (or g_m).

1-5 A fit formula for g_m that ensures a continuous transition from weak to strong inversion is $G(i) = 1/\left(\sqrt{1 + 0.5\sqrt{i} + i}\right)$, in which $i = I_{DS}/2n\beta(kT/q)^2$ and $G(i) = g_m nkT/q I_{DS}$. Plot this expression and indicate the asymptotic lines for weak and strong inversion.

1-6 Plot g_m and g_o versus current for an nMOST with $V_{Tn} = 1$ V, $KP_n = 50$ μA/V^2, $W/L = 10$, and $\lambda = 0.02$, for currents from 1 nA to 1 mA. Also $n = 1.5$. Add ratios, such as g_m/I_{DS} and g_m/g_o.

1-7 Take an nMOST with $V_{Tn} = 1$ V, $KP_n = 50$ μA/V^2 ($n = 1.5$), $L = 1$ μm, and $C_{ox} = 10^{-7}$F/cm^2. Plot the W/L versus I_{DS}
   a for constant $V_{GS} - V_T$
   b for constant g_m
   going from weak to strong inversion and velocity saturation.

1-8 Develop a design procedure for a single-transistor amplifier with a resistive load R if V_{OUTDC} does not have to be half the supply voltage (5 V). The variables are thus A_v, R, g_m, I_{DS}, $V_{GS} - V_T$, W/L and V_{OUTDC}. We want a gain of 5, a $V_{OUTDC} = 3$ V and minimized I_{DS}. ($KP_n = 50$ μA/V^2 and $n = 1.5$)

1-9 Take a source follower consisting of a pMOST in an n-well process. Its $I_{SS} = 0.1$ mA, and its $V_{IN} = -4$ V. The pMOST parameters are $V_{Tp} = -0.8$ V, $KP_p = 20$ μA/V^2 ($n = 1.5$), $W/L = 5$, $\gamma = 0.9$ V$^{1/2}$, and $2\phi_F = -0.6$ V. What is the output voltage, the output resistance and the gain if
   a the bulk is connected to the source, and
   b the bulk is connected to the positive power supply (5 V).

1-10 Take an nMOST as a switch with a load resistor of 10 kΩ and $V_G = 5$ V (Fig. 1-14a). Plot R_{DS} and v_{DS} as a function of the output voltage; $V_{Tn} = 0.8$ V, $KP_n = 50$ μA/V^2, $W/L = 100$, $\gamma = 0.4$ V$^{1/2}$, and $2\phi_F = 0.6$ V. Repeat for i_{DS} versus v_{DS} (0 to 1 V).

1-11 A transmission gate consists of two transistors in parallel, i.e., an nMOST and a pMOST (see Fig. EX1-11). Plot the drain-source resistance for both transistors and for the total transmission gate, as a function of the applied input voltage V_{IN} if
   a bulk polarization can be neglected
   b an n-well process is used and only the pMOST bulk is connected to its source. Take $\beta_p = \beta_n = 400$ μA/V^2, $V_{Tn} = |V_{Tp}| = 1$ V, $\gamma_n = 0.4$ V$^{1/2}$ and $2|\phi_F| = 0.6$ V.

1-12 Sketch v_{OUT}/v_{IN} obtained by SPICE for Fig. 1-17. Use the nMOST of Exercise 1-10 and $V_{IN} = 1$ V, $V_G = 5$ V, and $C_L = 10$ pF.

FIGURE EX1-11   Transmission Gate

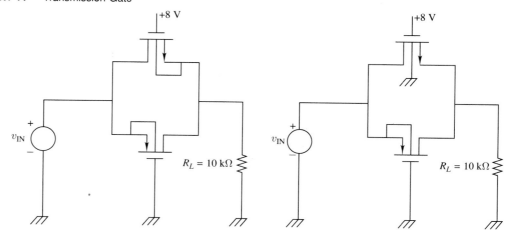

1-13 Plot f_{max} versus L_{eff} for L_{eff} between 0.1 μm and 100 μm, taking into account velocity saturation. Use a bilogarithmic scale and take $KP_n = 50$ μA/V^2, $C_{ox} = 10^{-7}$F/cm^2 and $V_{GS} - V_T = 1$ V.

1-14 For the values of δ and η given in Table 1-1, determine the W of an nMOST transistor with $L = 0.25$ μm to compensate for its ΔV_T's at $V_{DS} = 3$ V and $V_{BS} = 0$ V.

1-15 Indicate on a map, with scales in N_{SUB} and t_{ox}, where short-channel effects can be expected for an nMOST with $L = 5, 2.4, 1.2,$ and 0.8 μm. Take $V_{DS} = 3$ V and $V_{BS} = 0$ V. Also $\phi_j = 0.6$ V and $x_J = 0.6$ L.

1-16 Plot the punchthrough voltage V_{PT} of an nMOST versus its effective channel length L for $N_D = 10^{16}$ cm^{-3}; $N_G = 10^{19}$ cm^{-3}. What values of L are required to limit V_{PT} to 10 V ?

1-17 Repeat the design example of Sec. 1-10 for an nMOST with larger W such that three contacts can be accommodated.

1-18 Calculate g_m, g_{mb}, r_o, and the three terminal capacitances for the source follower of Fig. 1-23c. The current $I_{SS} = 100$ μA. The same nMOST is taken as in Sec. 1-10. What is the total output resistance and capacitance if the gate is AC shorted to ground?

1-19 Calculate the small-signal resistance $1/g_{mdi}$ and the parallel capacitance C_{di} of an nMOST connected as a diode as shown in Fig. 1-13a. Calculate its maximum frequency $f_{max} = g_{mdi}/2\pi C_{di}$. Take the nMOST with two drain contacts as given in Sec. 1-10.

Repeat for three drain contacts and derive the coefficients of the linear approximation of the capacitance as a function of width W, given by $C_{di} = C_{di0} + k_{di}W$, in which k_{di} is in fF/μm. Plot g_m, C_{di}, and f_{max} versus W.

1-20 Repeat Exercise 1-19 for the larger capacitances only: neglect all capacitances smaller than 10 percent of the total capacitance C_{di}. Find analytic expressions for g_m, C_{di}, and f_{max} versus W.

1-21 Compare the $g_m/2\pi C_{GS}$ frequency of a finger nMOST with that of a waffle nMOST, with the same W/L, as shown in Fig. EX1-21a and b. Take the data from Table 1-1 and Table 1-7 and use $V_{GS} - V_T = 0.25$ V for both. ($DW = DL = 0$).

1-22 Plot the i_{DS} versus v_{GS} and i_{DS} versus v_{DS} characteristics of a pJFET with $V_P = 3$ V and $I_{DS0} = 0.25$ mA for $V_{GS} = 0, 1, 2,$ and 3, V and for V_{DS} from 0 to 5 V.

1-23 Plot the i_{DS} versus v_{DS} characteristics of a pinch resistor (JFET) with channel doping 10^{17} cm^{-3} and 0.2 μm thickness (all $V = 0$). Its $W/L = 100$; $\mu = 200$ cm^2/Vs and $\phi_j = 0.9$ V.

1-24 Plot the i_{DS} versus v_{GS} and g_m versus v_{GS} characteristics for both models of a pJFET with $V_P = 1$ V and $I_{DS0} = 1$ mA ($\phi_j = 0.6$ V). What are the differences? Plot the difference versus v_{GS}.

1-25 An ion-implanted resistor of 100 kΩ is realized in 2.5 kΩ/$\square$. Its width is 10 μm and hence its length is 0.4 mm. Calculate its total integrated noise between 10 Hz and 50 kHz; 1 V is applied to it.

1-26 A JFET has a $1/f$ corner frequency of 350 Hz for a current of 0.25 mA and a $g_m = 1$ mS. In order to reduce the $1/f$ noise, four such JFETs are connected in parallel, which now draws 1 mA. What value of corner frequency do you expect now?

1-27 A radiation detector is shown in Fig. EX1-27. The diode has a capacitance of 10 pF. The light generates $i_D = 10$ μA at 10 MHz in the diode. Calculate the gain v_{OUT}/i_D, the total output noise and the S/N ratio at the output. The transistor has $g_m = 12$ mS and $C_{GS} = 2$ pF input capacitance.

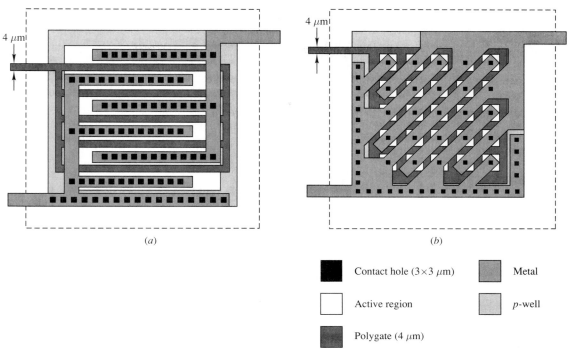

FIGURE EX1-21   Finger (a) and waffle (b) structures.

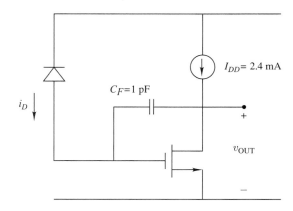

FIGURE EX1-27   Radiation detector.

1-28 In order to realize optimum noise matching for the radiation detector of Exercise 1-27, we want to
a modify its C_{GS} for minimum output noise (V^2/Hz) and
b modify its W, also modifying its C_{GS} and its g_m for minimum output noise.

1-29 Calculate the equivalent input noise voltage of the nMOST of the design example of Sec. 1-10 (Table 1-8). What is the total equivalent input noise voltage between 20 Hz and 20 kHz?

1-30 Calculate the equivalent input noise voltage of the JFET of Sec. 1-11 (Table 1-10). Also calculate the total input noise for frequencies from 20 Hz to 20 kHz. Change the current or the width W of the JFET such that its g_m is the same as for the nMOST of Exercise 1-29 and compare them.

1-31 A TL072 op amp has an input FET with a transconductance of $g_m = 34\ \mu S$ (obtained from its GBW). Its total equivalent input noise from 10 Hz to 20 kHz is 4 μV_{RMS}. What is the thermal noise, its $1/f$ noise, and its corner frequency?

Appendix 1-1

The currents, voltages, etc., in the electronic components can have DC values, AC values, total values, average values, quiescent values, RMS values, etc. Subscripts are used to indicate which ones are meant. The following notations are used.

As an example of a symbol, the output current i_{OUT} is taken. Note that the quiescent value coincides with the DC or average value if no distortion is present.

Notation of Symbols

	I_{OUT}	i_{OUT}	I_{out}	i_{out}
total instantaneous value		i_{OUT}		
- continuous time	—	$i_{OUT}(t)$	—	—
- discrete time	—	$i_{OUT}(kT)^*$	—	—
DC or average value	I_{OUT}	—	—	—
quiescent value	I_{OUTQ}	—	—	—
instantaneous value of AC component	i_{out}	—		
- continuous time	—	—	—	$i_{out}(t)$
- discrete time	—	—	—	$i_{out}(kT)$
amplitude of AC component	I_{out}	—		
- peak value	—	—	I_{outp}	—
- RMS value	—	—	I_{outRMS}	—
- Fourier $(j\omega)$ transform	—	—	$I_{out}(j\omega)$	—
- Laplace (s) transform	—	—	$I_{out}(s)$	—
z-transform	—	—	$I_{out}(z)$	—

*In discrete time and sampled systems, all signals are represented by a sequence of numbers $\{x(kT)\}$, equally or periodically spaced in time. The index kT refers to their periodic time instants, when k is a running integer (i.e., $k = 0, 1, 2, \ldots, N$) and T refers to the period. Sampling is discussed in Chap. 5.

Also note that only continuous time values are represented in the figure, whereas discrete time values are not. (See Fig. A1-1.)

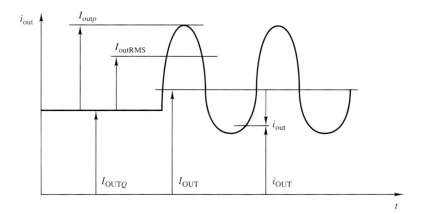

FIGURE A1-1   Symbols for distorted sinusoidal waveform.

REFERENCES

Antognetti, P., and G. Massobrio. 1988. *Semiconductor Device Modeling with SPICE*. New York: McGraw-Hill.

Brews, J., W. Fichtner, E. Nicollian, and S. Sze. 1980. "Generalized Guide for MOSFET Miniaturization." *IEEE Electron Devices Letters*, vol. EDL–1, no.1, pp. 2–4.

Chang, Z. Y., and W. Sansen. 1991. *Low-Noise Wide-Band Amplifiers in Bipolar and CMOS Technologies*. Norwell, MA: Kluwer Academic.

Das, C., and W. Sansen. 1980. "Design of ion-implanted resistors with low 1/f noise." *Microelectronics Journal*, vol. 11, no. 3, pp. 24–27.

Gielen, G., and W. Sansen. 1991. *Symbolic Analysis for Automated Design of Analog Circuits*. Norwell, MA: Kluwer Academic.

Grove, A. 1967. *Physics and Technology of Semiconductor Devices*. New York: Wiley and Sons.

Muller, R., and T. Kamins. 1986. *Device Electronics for Integrated Circuits*. New York: Wiley and Sons.

Ott, H. W. 1988. *Noise Reduction Techniques in Electronic Systems*. New York: Wiley and Sons.

Sansen, W., and C. Das. 1982. "A simple model of ion-implanted JFETs valid in both the quadratic and the subthreshold region." *IEEE Journal of Solid-State Circuits*, vol. SC-17, no. 4, pp. 658–666.

Sze, S. 1981. *Physics of Semiconductor Devices*. New York: Wiley and Sons.

Tsividis, Y. 1988. *The MOS Transistor*. New York: McGraw-Hill.

2

BIPOLAR
TRANSISTOR
MODELS

2-1 BIPOLAR TRANSISTOR OPERATION

While bipolar transistors are no longer the main component of microelectronic circuits, they are still as important for present-day circuitry as MOSTs. MOSTs can provide higher density (i.e., the number of transistors per cm^2) and allow low-power logic, but bipolar transistors offer better output current capability at high speed and provide less noise than MOSTs at low frequencies.

In this chapter, models of bipolar transistors are derived (Getreu 1976; Sze 1981; Muller-Kamins 1986). Their current versus voltage characteristics are derived first, followed by their small-signal characteristics and noise sources. Most of the model development presented in this chapter is focused on vertical devices. At the end of this chapter, the differences between lateral and vertical devices are discussed.

Also, MOSTs and bipolar transistors are compared from the designers point of view. Finally, passive components (e.g., resistors and capacitors) are discussed.

2-1-1 Structure

A bipolar transistor consists of two diodes connected back to back, such that the region in the middle is narrow. In this way, an *npn* transistor is formed by the connection of two short *np* diodes, as in Fig. 2-1a. The short middle region is called the base. The base width W_B is small, typically 0.5 to 0.8 μm, and its doping level N_B is medium (e.g., 2×10^{17} cm^{-3}). Normally, the left diode is forward biased. Its $n+$ region is called the emitter. It is heavily doped (e.g., $N_E = 10^{19}$ cm^{-3}) and has a width W_E of several μm. The right diode is normally reverse biased. Its n region, the *collector*,

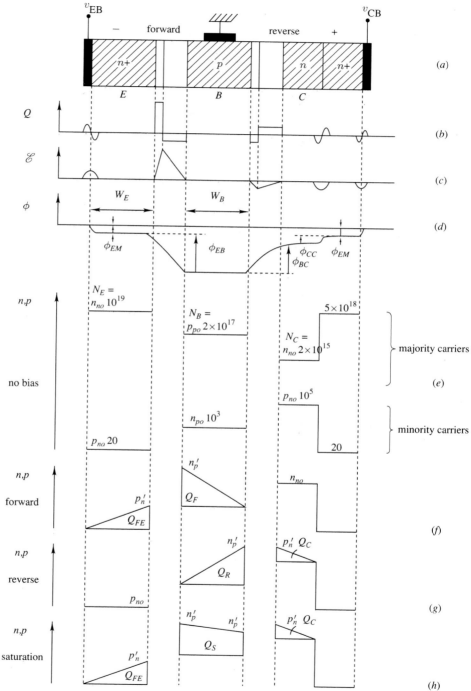

FIGURE 2-1   Bipolar transistor operation ($N_s = 10^{14}\,\text{cm}^{-3}$).

is only lightly doped (e.g., $N_C = 10^{15}$ cm^{-3}). In order to ensure an ohmic contact between the contact metal and the collector, an intermediate $n+$ layer is added that is doped almost as high as the emitter.

A realistic cross section of a bipolar transistor is shown in Fig. 2-2. The structure illustrated in Fig. 2-1 is easily recognized underneath the emitter. This illustration represents the intrinsic part of the bipolar transistor. The other parts are needed to allow all the currents to flow out from the transistor at the same surface. In this way the collector consists of an $n+$ buried layer, an n epitaxial layer that has a constant doping level, and an $n+$ contact at the surface. Finally, the substrate is doped $p-$ or π and serves as an isolator of the several transistors that are on the same chip. Therefore, the substrate-collector junction must always be reverse biased and the substrate potential is always the most negative voltage of the whole circuit, which is ground if there is no negative power supply.

The sketch of Fig. 2-2a is repeated in Fig. 2-2b. All doping levels and dimensions are collected in Table 2-1. The same transistor will be used in the design example at the end of this chapter.

In order to develop a first-order model, only the intrinsic part of the bipolar transistor is examined. The other parts will be added in Sec. 2-4, which discusses ohmic resistances.

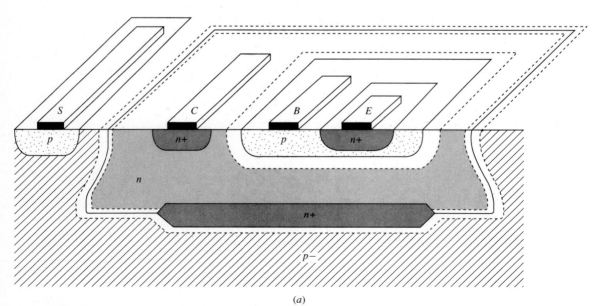

(*a*)

FIGURE 2-2*a*   Vertical *npn* bipolar transistor.

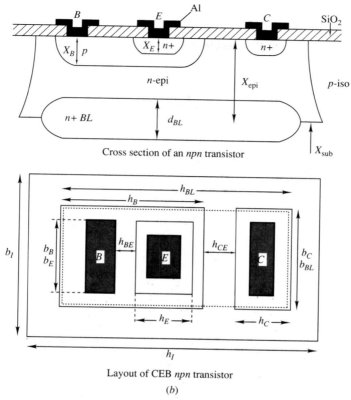

Cross section of an *npn* transistor

Layout of CEB *npn* transistor

(*b*)

FIGURE 2-2*b*   Cross section and layout of an *npn* transistor.

TABLE 2-1   BIPOLAR TRANSISTOR DATA OF FIG. 2-2*b*.

	Doping (cm^{-3})	Mobility (cm^2/Vs)			Dimensions (micrometers)	
		n	p			
Emitter	10^{19}	140	73	$x_E = 1$	$h_E = 15$	$b_E = 30$
Base	2×10^{17}	500	225	$x_B = 1.8$	$h_B = 50$	$b_B = 30$
					$h_{BE} = 10$	
Collector	2×10^{15}	1210	470	$x_{epi} = 12$	$h_C = 20$	$b_C = 50$
					$h_{CE} = 20$	
Buried Layer	5×10^{18}	175	115	$d_{BL} = 6$	$h_{BL} = 80$	$b_{BL} = 50$
Isolated Layer	10^{16}	—	—	$x_{iso} = 14$	$h_I = 120$	$b_I = 90$
Substrate	10^{16}	—	400	$x_{sub} = 250$		

2-1-2   Depletion Layers

In Fig. 2-2a, several regions are hatched according to their conductivity. The conductive regions of the bipolar transistors are separated by depletion layers. The fixed ion charges are sketched in Fig. 2-1b, the corresponding electric fields in Fig. 2-1c, and the potential diagram in Fig. 2-1d. Their values can all be calculated as for a conventional one-sided abrupt diode.

The junction potentials are thus easily derived from

$$\phi_{EB} = \frac{kT}{q} \ln \frac{N_E N_B}{n_i^2} \tag{2-1a}$$

and

$$\phi_{CC} = \frac{kT}{q} \ln \frac{N_{C1}}{N_{C2}} \tag{2-1b}$$

Note that ϕ_{CB} is found from Eq. (2-1a) after the substitution of E by C. Also note that the sum of the potential drops equals $\phi_{EB} = \phi_{CB} + \phi_{CC}$.

Example 2-1

Calculate all potential drops for the doping levels indicated in Fig. 2-1e. Note that $n_i^2 = 2.25 \times 10^{20}$ cm^{-6} and $kT/q = 25.86$ mV at room temperature (27°C).

Solution. From the above equations, $\phi_{EB} = 0.950$ V, $\phi_{CB} = 0.729$ V, $\phi_{CC} = 0.202$ V and $\phi_{EM} = 0.009$ V.

2-1-3   Base Doping

The conductive base region is bounded by the fixed changes of the *EB* and *CB* depletion layers. Its width is W_B. Its number of holes p_{po} (majority carriers) in equilibrium (without biasing) is N_B. Hence, its number of electrons n_{po} (minority carriers) is given by

$$n_{po} = \frac{n_i^2}{p_{po}} = \frac{n_i^2}{N_B} \tag{2-2}$$

This is illustrated in Fig. 2-1e for $N_B = 2 \times 10^{17}$ cm^{-3} and $n_i^2 = 2.25 \times 10^{20}$ cm^{-6}, the number of electrons is only $n_{po} = 1125$ cm^{-3} or about 10^3 cm^{-3}.

The same reasoning can be applied to the other regions. The doping levels are given in Fig. 2-1e.

2-1-4   Forward Biasing

The doping levels are sketched in Fig. 2-1e with no biasing applied. If the emitter and collector were then biased, the minority carrier distributions would visibly change.

They are redrawn for forward operation in Fig. 2-1f, for reverse operation in Fig. 2-1g, and for saturation in Fig. 2-1h.

In forward operation the EB junction is forward biased, i.e., the $(n+)$ emitter is biased negatively with respect to the (p) base.

The EB diode is forward biased and hence, injection occurs. Electrons from the emitter are injected in the base and holes from the base are injected in the emitter. This gives rise to an excess charge of electrons in the base Q_F (F of Forward) and an excess charge of holes in the emitter Q_{FE}. The excess electron concentration in the base on the side of the emitter is denoted by n'_p. It is related to the equilibrium concentration n_{po} by Boltzmann's factor $\exp(qV_{EB}/kT)$ as given by

$$n'_p = n_{po}\left(\exp\frac{v_{EB}}{kT/q} - 1\right) \tag{2-3a}$$

This equally applies to the excess hole concentration p'_n in the emitter on the side of the base. It is thus given by

$$p'_n = p_{no}\left(\exp\frac{v_{EB}}{kT/q} - 1\right) \tag{2-3b}$$

In Eqs. (2-3a and b), the second term of minus unity can be omitted because it is so small. For example, for $V_{EB} = 0.7$ V, the term $\exp(qV_{EB}/kT)$ is approximately 10^{12}, which is much larger than unity indeed. Also, $n'_p = 2 \times 10^{13}$ cm^{-3} which is much larger than $n_{po} = 2 \times 10^3$ cm^{-3}. Moreover, $p'_n = 2 \times 10^{11}$ cm^{-3}.

As for a diode, the excess carrier distribution decreases exponentially. However, since the base and emitter widths are so small, a first-order approximation is taken of this exponential. This is a straight line. Hence, the excess carrier concentration decays linearly away from the EB junction. As a result, triangular charge distributions are found in both the base and emitter (see Fig. 2-1f). In the base, the excess (electron) charge is Q_F and in the emitter it is Q_{FE}. Obviously, Q_F is much larger than Q_{FE} because n_{po} is much larger than p_{no}. In other words, Q_F is much larger than Q_{FE} because the emitter is doped much more heavily than the base.

The injection of electrons from the emitter to the base causes an excess charge of electrons in the base. However, the collector is biased positive, and the electrons arriving at the CB junction see a positive collector. Thus, they are subject to a negative electric field (see Fig. 2-1c) in the CB depletion layer. As a result, they are swept from B to C through the CB depletion layer. Once in the collector, they flow to the collector contact. In the base, a dynamic excess electron charge Q_F is established. This charge is continuously refilled from the emitter and emptied to the collector, causing an electron current to flow from the emitter to the collector through the base. Since by convention the current flow of holes is positive, a (positive) current flows from the collector through the base to the emitter. This is the collector current i_C.

Due to the above process, the electron concentration in the base is quite high on the left (n'_p) but is zero on the right, and a large gradient occurs. The electrons flow or diffuse from left to right as a result of this gradient and the resulting current i_n is thus a diffusion current, given by

$$i_n = q A_{EB} D_n \frac{dn'_p}{dx} \tag{2-4a}$$

in which A_{EB} is the EB junction area and D_n is the diffusion constant for electrons. It is related to mobility by Einstein's relation, given by $D_n = \mu_n kT/q$.

However, the slope of n'_p in the base is simply n'_p/W_B. After substitution of the differential in Eq. (2-4a), and by use of Eqs. (2-3a) and (2-2), the electron current is given by

$$i_n = \frac{q A_{EB} D_n n_i^2}{N_B W_B} \exp\left(\frac{v_{EB}}{kT/q}\right) \tag{2-4b}$$

in which A_{EB} is the emitter area. Note that this current is proportional to $1/N_B$, i.e., the lower the base doping the higher the current.

In fact, the hole injection from the base to the emitter creates a dynamic emitter charge Q_{FE}, as well. It also contributes to the emitter-base current. This hole current i_p is derived in the same manner as before, and is given by

$$i_p = \frac{q A_{EB} D_p n_i^2}{N_E W_E} \exp\left(\frac{v_{EB}}{kT/q}\right) \tag{2-4c}$$

It is, however, proportional to $1/N_E$ and therefore i_p is negligible with respect to i_n. The total collector current i_C is actually the sum of i_n and i_p, and is thus virtually equal to i_n. The collection current is thus given by

$$i_C = I_S \exp\left(\frac{v_{EB}}{kT/q}\right) \tag{2-5a}$$

with
$$I_S = \frac{q A_{EB} D_n n_i^2}{Q_B} \tag{2-5b}$$

in which $Q_B = N_B W_B$ is the integrated charge (per cm^2 emitter area) in the base.

This result has been derived for a constant doping level N_B in the base. However, it can be shown that Eq. (2-5b) is valid for any arbitrary base doping distribution with a total integrated base charge Q_B. As a consequence, this charge Q_B is by far the most important parameter of the bipolar transistor as nearly all other parameters depend on it. It is called the *Gummel number*. Typical values are 10^{11} to 10^{13} cm^{-2}.

In SPICE, parameter I_S is denoted by IS. It is listed in Table 2-2, along with all other transistor parameters (Getreu 1976; Antognetti and Massobrio 1988). Also, a fit factor NF is added in front of kT/q in Eq. (2-5a).

TABLE 2-2   NOMINAL SPICE PARAMETERS FOR A BIPOLAR TRANSISTOR

Name	Value	Dimension	Name	Eq. No.
IS	1.3E-16	A	Saturation current	2-5*b*
BF	200	—	Maximum current gain (forward current)	2-7
NF	1.0	—	Emission coefficient (forward current)	2-5
VAF	50	V	Early voltage (forward current)	2-18
IKF	1E-1	A	Corner current (forward current.)	2-38*a*
ISE	1E-13	A	B-E leakage saturation current	—
NE	2	—	B-E emission coefficient	2-13
BR	1	—	Maximum current gain (reverse current)	—
NR	1.0	—	Emission coefficient (reverse current)	—
VAR	50	V	Early voltage (reverse current)	—
IKR	1E-1	A	Corner current (reverse current)	—
ISC	1E-13	A	B-C leakage saturation current	—
NC	2	—	B-C emission coefficient	—
RB	340	Ω	Base resistance at low current	2-32
IRB	0.01	A	Current of half base resistance	2-32
RBM	50	Ω	Minimum base resistance at high current	2-32
RE	1	Ω	Emitter resistance	—
RC	500	Ω	Collector resistance	2-33
TF	2.5E-10	s	Transit time (forward current)	2-6*b*
XTF	0	—	Bias dependence of TF	—
VTF		V	Voltage dependence of TF	—
ITF		A	High current pararameter on TF	—
PTF	0.35	rad.	Excess phase at f_T	—
TR	1E-8	s	Transit time (reverse current)	—
CJE	2E-12	F	Zero bias B-E junction capacitance	T. 2-4
VJE	0.9	V	B-E junction potential	—
MJE	0.33	—	B-E junction grading coefficient	—
CJC	5E-13	F	Zero bias B-C junction capacitance	—
VJC	0.6	V	B-C junction potential	—
MJC	0.5	—	B-C junction grading coefficient	—
XCJC	1	—	Fraction of CJC to internal base	—
CJS	3.6E-12	F	Zero bias C-S junction capacitance	—
VJS	0.6	V	C-S junction potential	—
MJS	0.5	—	C-S junction grading coefficient	—
FC	0.5	—	Coefficient forward bias depletion capacitance	—
XTB	7E-3	/K	BETA's temperature coefficient	—
EG	1.11	V	Bandgap energy	A2-1*b*
XTI	3	—	Saturation current temperature exponent	A2-1*b*
KF	1E-16	A	Flicker noise coefficient	2-49*b*
AF	1		Flicker noise exponent	2-49*b*

2-1-5 Base Transit Time

Note that the current can also be written as

$$i_C = \frac{Q_F}{\tau_F} \tag{2-6a}$$

in which

$$\tau_F = \frac{W_B^2}{2D_n} \tag{2-6b}$$

This leads to the physical interpretation that τ_F is the average time in which the electrons diffuse through the base from the emitter side to the collector side, i.e., the base transit time. It is thus a measure of the maximum frequency $f_{T\,max}(= 1/2\pi\tau_F)$ of the transistor, given by

$$f_{T\,max} = \frac{1}{2\pi\tau_F} \tag{2-6c}$$

In SPICE, τ_F is denoted by TF (see Table 2-2).

Indeed, the base transit time t_{av} is given by the average electron velocity v_{av} in the base, which is given by W_B/v_{av}. Here, $v_{av} = i_C/qA_{EB}n'_{pav}$ and $n'_{pav} = n'_p/2$ for a triangular distribution, which yields $t_{av} = \tau_{av}$ and hence, $v_{av} = W_B/\tau_F$.

Note that the dynamic charge Q_F is not the same as the total integrated charge in the base Q_B. Indeed, Q_F depends on the forward bias v_{BE}, whereas Q_B is the charge that is physically present in the base. They are related by Eqs. (2-5) and (2-6a).

Note that Q_B and Q_F do not have the same dimensions: Q_B is the number of carriers per cm^2 whereas Q_F is the total charge in Coulombs.

Example 2-2

For the doping levels given in Fig. 2-1 or Fig. 2-2b and a base width of 0.8 μm (see Table 2-2), calculate the current in the transistor for $A_{EB} = 15 \times 30$ μm $= 4.5 \times 10^{-6}$ cm^2 and $V_{BE} = 0.72$ V (at room temperature). Also calculate the base transit time and the average velocity through the base. The mobility in the base is about $\mu_B = 500$ cm^2/Vs.

Solution. From the mobility we find $D_n = \mu_B kT/q = 500 \times 0.026 = 12.93$ cm^2/s. The base charge $Q_B = 1.6 \times 10^{13}$ cm^{-2}. From Eq. (2-5) $I_S = 1.31 \times 10^{-16}$ A. The injected charge is then $Q_F = 4 \times 10^{-14}$ Coulombs and the total collector current is $I_C = 0.162$ mA.

The base transit time is obtained from Eq. (2-6b) and becomes $\tau_F = 0.247$ ns. The maximum value of f_T is thus 643 MHz. Finally, the average velocity is 3.2 km/s or 11520 km/h, which is about ten times faster than the velocity of sound. However, it is only about 3.2 percent of the saturation velocity, which is 10^5 m/s.

All numerical values of this example are collected in Table 2-3, both per unit emitter area and in total.

TABLE 2-3   CHARGES AND CURRENTS FOR THE BIPOLAR TRANSISTOR
OF FIG. 2-2b WITH $V_{BE} = 0.72$ V

Parameter	Eq. No.	Per unit area	Total
Q_B	(2-5b)	$1.6 \times 10^{13}/\text{cm}^2$	7.2×10^7
qQ_B		2.56×10^{-6} C/cm^2	1.15×10^{-11} C
I_S	(2-5b)	2.91×10^{-8} A/cm^2	1.31×10^{-16} A
i_C	(2-5a)	35.9 A/cm^2	0.162 mA
Q_F	(2-6a)	8.9×10^{-9} C/cm^2	4×10^{-14} C
Q_F/q		5.56×10^{10} cm^{-2}	2.5×10^5

The injection of dynamic charges Q_F and Q_{FE} in the base and emitter, respectively, is a nonequilibrium process. These charges violate the charge equilibrium condition. More electrons are present in the base than what is given by Eq. (2-2). In order to compensate for this extra charge of electrons Q_F, an equal amount of holes must be added to the holes p_{po} or N_B, already present in the base. This extra quantity of holes (2.5×10^5; see Table 2-3) is nevertheless negligible with respect to Q_B (1.6×10^{13}). Therefore, they are not visible in Fig. 2-1. If the emitter base forward bias V_{BE} becomes very large, then n'_p becomes very large as well. If it becomes as large as the equilibrium doping level N_B, high injection conditions are met. This will be discussed later in Sec. 2-5.

2-2 THE TRANSISTOR BETA (β)

In contrast to a MOST, where the gate current is zero, the base current is not zero in a bipolar transistor. Therefore, in its symbol, the base lead is connected to the collector-emitter pathline, whereas the opposite is true in a MOS transistor. This base current is proportional to the collector current. The ratio of the collector current to the base current, i_C/i_B, is virtually constant. It is the beta of the transistor (Getreu 1976).

For an *npn* transistor, the collector current flows from the positive collector bias voltage through the transistor to the emitter. The base current then flows into the transistor base to the emitter. The emitter current is thus slightly larger than the collector current by the amount of the base current. As a result, the emitter current i_E is given by

$$i_E = i_C + i_B = i_C + \frac{i_C}{\beta_F} = \frac{\beta_F + 1}{\beta_F}(i_C) = \alpha_F i_C \qquad (2-7)$$

which defines the alpha (α_F) of the transistor. The indices F have been added to indicate the forward operation (see Fig. 2-2f). The value of β is determined by three phenomena, now briefly discussed (Grove 1967).

2-2-1   Beta Caused by Injection in the Emitter β_{IE}

As shown by Eq. (2-4c), the collector current is accompanied by the injection of holes from the base to the emitter, giving rise to current i_p. These holes are provided by the base terminal and thus constitute base current. The resulting beta β_{IE} is given by i_C/i_p or, after substitution, by

$$\beta_{IE} = \frac{N_E W_E}{N_B W_B}\left(\frac{D_n}{D_p}\right) \tag{2-8}$$

Since Q_E is much larger than Q_B, the value of β_{IE} is large. For the values of the example of Fig. 2-2b above, $\beta_{IE} = 342$. Note that the beta is very sensitive to the integrated base charge $Q_B = N_B W_B$. The slightest change in emitter diffusion changes the Q_B drastically and hence the beta.

2-2-2   Beta Caused by Recombination in the Base β_{RB}

As the excess electrons Q_F are passing from the emitter to the collector through the base, they recombine to some extent with the large number of holes p_{po} in the base. The recombination time constant is τ_{BF}. Holes are thus attracted from the base terminal, giving rise to another base current i_{BRB}, given by Q_F/τ_{BF}. The resultant beta is then given by i_C/i_{BRB} or, after substitution, by

$$\beta_{RB} = \frac{\tau_{BF}}{\tau_F} \tag{2-9}$$

The recombination in the base is quite limited, as the base is so thin. The electrons only spend a short time (τ_F) in the base. A typical value of τ_{BF} is about 1 μs. Hence, for the values of Example 2-2 ($\tau_F \approx 0.25$ ns) the $\beta_{RB} \approx 4000$.

It is obvious that β_{IE} is smaller than β_{RB} and is hence the dominant beta. This is usually the case in vertical npn transistors. In SPICE, the dominant beta is denoted by BF, the beta in forward direction (see Table 2-2).

Note that both kinds of base currents are proportional to the collector current. They thus depend exponentially on v_{BE}, i.e., they both contain the Boltzmann factor $\exp(qv_{BE}/kT)$, just as the collector current does. This is not the case for the third and last kind of base current now described.

2-2-3   Beta Caused by Recombination in the *EB* Space Charge Layer

As the electrons are passing from the emitter to the collector through the base, they pass through the *EB* depletion layer. In this narrow region, they recombine and generate base currents. The electrons recombine with holes, attracted from the base terminal, and this base current i_{BREB} again flows into the base.

This time, however, the recombination occurs in a region with high electric field. This region is nonresistive, in contrast to the base. The recombination mechanism is therefore different, governed by recombination centers that are most effective in the middle of the bandgap. Thus, a non-Boltzmann coefficient appears in its current. It has the form $\exp(q v_{BE}/2kT)$ rather than $\exp(q v_{BE}/kT)$. As a result, the beta depends on $\exp(q v_{BE}/2kT)$ and hence on the current itself. This dependence of the beta is a consequence of recombination in the EB space charge layer.

Also, the base current is different at the surface than in the bulk. It is given by

$$i_{BREB} = W_{EB} \left(\frac{A_{EB}}{\tau_{BRE}} + P_{EB} s_B \right) \frac{q n_i}{2} \exp \left(\frac{v_{EB}}{2kT/q} \right) \qquad (2\text{-}10)$$

where W_{EB} is the average width of the emitter base space charge layer,

A_{EB} is the emitter area,

P_{EB} is the emitter perimeter,

τ_{BRE} (in s) is the recombination time constant in the bulk EB space

charge layer

s_B (in cm/s) is the surface recombination velocity.

The total base current i_B is now obtained by the summation of all three terms. It is plotted versus v_{BE}, together with the collector current i_C, in Fig. 2-3a. For moderate and high values of v_{BE}, both i_C and i_B are Boltzmannian. The slope is kT/q, or about 60 mV/decade in current at room temperature. Their ratio is β and is thus constant, as shown in Fig. 2-3b.

However, for low values of v_{BE}, the base current due to recombination in the EB space charge layer dominates. The transition point is at V_{BET}. For values of v_{BE} smaller than V_{BET}, the beta decreases (see Fig. 2-3b).

2-2-4   AC Beta β_{AC}

An important consequence of the beta rolling off at low values of v_{BE} (or i_C), is that an AC beta β_{AC} must be distinguished that differs from β itself.

The definition of β_{AC} is taken from Fig. 2-4. It shows the i_C versus v_{CE} characteristics of a bipolar transistor for several values of base current i_B. The collector emitter voltage V_{CE} is kept constant. The beta at collector current i_{C5} is given by i_{C5}/i_{B5}.

Now we define an AC beta, denoted by β_{AC}, which is the ratio of the variations (rather than the absolute values) in current at a particular current. Hence, at current i_{C5},

$$\beta_{AC} = \frac{\Delta i_{C5}}{\Delta i_{B5}} \approx \frac{i_{C5} - i_{C4}}{i_{B5} - i_{B4}} \qquad (2\text{-}11)$$

These two beta's, while different, are still related. Their relationship is obtained by the differentiation of $i_C = \beta i_B$ to i_B. Substitution of di_C/di_B by β_{AC}

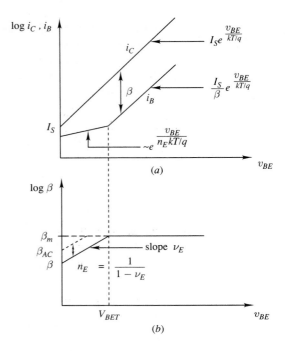

FIGURE 2-3   Asymptotic values of (a) i_C, i_B and (b) resulting beta's.

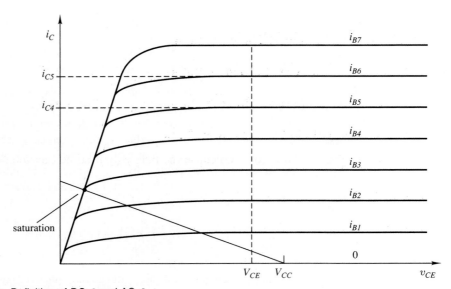

FIGURE 2-4   Definition of DC β and AC β_{AC}.

yields (Grove 1967):

$$\beta_{AC} = \frac{\beta}{\left(1 - \dfrac{d\beta}{di_C}\right)\dfrac{i_C}{\beta}} \tag{2-12}$$

This shows that if β depends on i_C, the differential in the denominator is not zero. The denominator is smaller than unity and $\beta_{AC} \geq \beta$. The asymptotic values of β_{AC} are plotted in Fig. 2-3 as a dashed line.

In modern devices, the region with $\exp(v_{BE}/2kT)$ only occurs at low values of current and is thus not easily distinguished. Therefore, two fit parameters are introduced. The first one is n_E or $v_E = 1 - 1/n_E$ (v is the Greek letter nu), which allows $\exp(qv_{BE}/2kT)$ to be replaced by $\exp(qv_{BE}/n_E kT)$. The other one is C_1.

The expression for β in SPICE is then given by

$$\beta = \frac{\beta_m}{1 + C_1 i_C^{-v_E}} \tag{2-13}$$

in which β_m (BF in Table 2-2) is the maximum value of β (see Fig. 2-3).

For large values of i_C, the second term in the denominator becomes negligible and $\beta = \beta_m$ as expected. For low values of i_C, the second term in the denominator is dominant. The slope of β versus i_C equals parameter v_E (or $1 - 1/n_E$). The transition current $I_{CT} = C_1^{1/v_E}$.

From Eq. (2-13), the value of β_{AC} is now easily calculated by the application of Eq. (2-12). It is given by

$$\beta_{AC} = \frac{\beta_m}{1 + (1 - v_E)C_1 i_C^{-v_E}} \tag{2-14}$$

It can be clearly seen that β_{AC} is larger than β for low values of i_C, but always smaller than β_m. The ratio β_{AC}/β is then $1/(1 - v_E)$ or n_E. In SPICE, n_E is represented by NE (Table 2-2).

Example 2-3

For $\beta_m = 100$, and $v = 0.35$, the current corresponding to V_{BET} is $I_{CT} = 1$ nA if $C_1 = 7.0 \times 10^{-4}$. Calculate the ratio β_{AC}/β at the transition current I_{CT} and at the currents 10 times lower and higher.

Solution. At 1 nA the value of β is 50 and of β_{AC}, 60.6. As a result, the ratio β_{AC}/β is 1.21. For 0.1 nA, the beta values are, respectively, 31 and 41 and their ratio is 1.32. For 10 nA, the beta values are, respectively, 69 and 77.5 and their ratio is 1.12.

The above equations model the bipolar transistor in the normal or forward mode of operation. This means that the emitter-base junction is *forward* biased and the collector-base junction is *reverse* biased. The electron current then flows from emitter to collector—the positive current flows from collector to emitter—in the case of an *npn* transistor. Since there are two junctions, there are three additional modes of operation, depending on which junction is forward or reverse biased.

In *reverse* (R) bias, the collector is forward biased and acts as an emitter. The emitter is then reverse biased. The same parameters can then be found as in the forward (F) mode (see Table 2-2). In the *off* mode, none of the junctions are forward biased and, in *saturation*, both junctions are forward biased. There is a third junction, the collector-substrate junction, which is always reverse biased in order to isolate the collector from the substrate.

A modified version of the Ebers-Moll model describes all four modes of operation. It allows the calculation of DC currents, regardless of the voltage applied. In analog design, only the forward mode is used, and thus this model is not presented. The reader is referred to Getreu (1976) and Sze (1981).

2-3   THE HYBRID-π SMALL-SIGNAL MODEL

Small-signal variations in v_{BE} cause small-signal variations in collector current i_C. Their relationship is given by a small-signal or AC model. Moreover, AC base current flows, which can also be represented in the AC model. Several other parasitic resistances, as well as capacitances, must also be included in the AC model. For the bipolar transistor, the most frequently used AC model has traditionally been called the *hybrid-π model*. Its parameters are now derived.

2-3-1   Transconductance g_m

Transconductance is the ratio of the variations of the collector current to the variations of the base-emitter voltage. It is obtained by taking the derivative of i_C to v_{BE}. Using Eq. (2-5), the transconductance g_m is given by

$$g_m = \frac{di_C}{dv_{BE}} = \frac{i_C}{kT/q} \tag{2-15}$$

It is directly proportional to the current itself, i.e., doubling the current doubles the transconductance. It is represented in the hybrid-π model by the voltage-controlled current generator g_m in Fig. 2-5.

The ratio g_m/i_C is always equal to q/kT or 1/26 mV at room temperature. This ratio is larger than its MOST counterpart. It is the maximum value that can be achieved with any kind of transistor.

2-3-2   Input Resistance r_π

Since AC collector current flows, AC base current flows as well, if a variation in v_{BE} is applied. The ratio of the AC v_{BE} and the AC i_B is the AC input resistance. It is

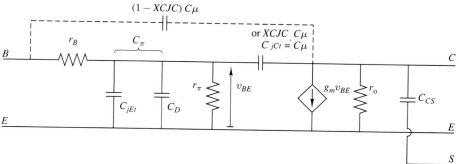

FIGURE 2-5   Hybrid-π model of bipolar transistor.

called r_π and is calculated as

$$r_\pi = \frac{dv_{BE}}{di_B} = \frac{dv_{BE}}{di_C}\frac{di_C}{di_B} = \frac{\beta_{AC}}{g_m} \qquad (2\text{-}16)$$

Its value decreases if the collector current increases. It is also represented in the hybrid-π model of Fig. 2-5. Its relationship with β and g_m is depicted in the diagram of Fig. 2-6. This diagram will be expanded upon later in the text.

2-3-3 Output Resistance r_o

In the hybrid-π model of Fig. 2-5, an output resistance r_o is present as well. It is the ratio of the AC variation of v_{CE} to the variation of i_C. It thus corresponds with the slope of the output characteristics shown in Fig. 2-4. The resistance r_o is given by

$$r_o = \frac{dv_{CE}}{di_C} \qquad (2\text{-}17a)$$

It is found that this resistance is inversely proportional to the collector current. Therefore, all curves of the output characteristics of Fig. 2-4 coincide at one point on the

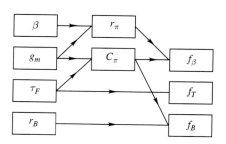

FIGURE 2-6   Relationships between hybrid-π parameters.

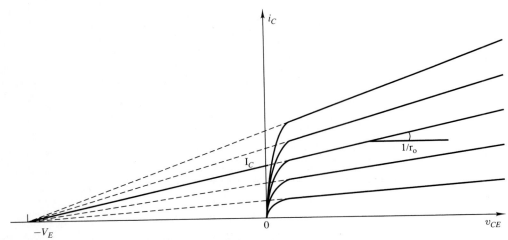

FIGURE 2-7   Output characteristics with finite output resistance.

v_{CE} axis, as shown in Fig. 2-7. This point is the Early voltage V_E. For a specific value of collector current I_C, the output resistance r_o is also given by

$$r_o = \frac{V_E}{I_C} \tag{2-17b}$$

It can be calculated as follows. The variations in v_{CE} can be decomposed, as given by $\Delta v_{CE} = \Delta v_{CB} + \Delta v_{BE} \approx -\Delta v_{BC}$, since the base-emitter voltage is about constant. Equation (2-17a) can then be rewritten as

$$r_o = -\frac{dv_{BC}}{di_C} = -\frac{dv_{BC}}{dQ_B}\left(\frac{dQ_B}{di_C}\right) \tag{2-17c}$$

Increasing the base-collector voltage by an amount Δv_{BC} increases the width of the depletion layer, as shown in Fig. 2-8. The depletion layer charge increases by an amount ΔQ_B. As a result, less base charge Q_B (present in Fig. 2-5b) is left. The base charge is decreased by the same amount, ΔQ_B. Also, the variation of the depletion layer charge ΔQ_B is linked to the depletion capacitance C_{jC} (in F/cm^2), as given by $q\Delta Q_B/\Delta v_{BC} = -C_{jC}$.

The second factor of Eq. (2-17c) is easily derived from Eq. (2-5). It is given by $\Delta Q_B/\Delta i_C = Q_B/i_C$. Substitution in Eq. (2-17c) and equating to r_o of Eq. (2-17b) yields

$$V_E = \frac{qQ_B}{C_{jC}} = \frac{qA_{BC}Q_B}{C_{jCt}} \tag{2-18}$$

in which A_{BC} is the total base-collector area and C_{jCt} the total base-collector junction capacitance underneath the emitter.

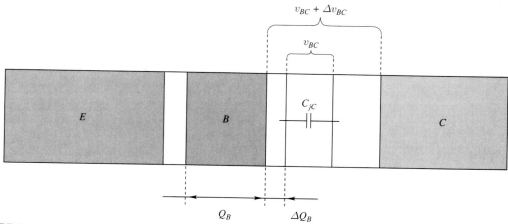

FIGURE 2-8   Relation between ΔQ_B and Δv_{BC} through C_{jC}.

Note that the Early voltage depends on the integrated base charge Q_B. Increasing the base charge increases the Early voltage. Remember that the beta is then decreased (see Eq. (2-8)). For two different values of beta, different values of Early voltage can be expected. This is illustrated in Fig. 2-9. In the first case the base charge is quite small. The beta is high but the Early voltage is quite small, leading to small values of r_o as well. In the other case (Fig. 2-9b), the base charge is much larger and thus the beta is much smaller. The Early voltage is much larger and so is the output resistance r_o. Large-beta transistors always have small V_E values.

In SPICE, the Early voltage is denoted by VAF in the forward direction and VAR in the reverse direction (see Table 2-2).

FIGURE 2-9   Dependence of Early voltage on Q_B.

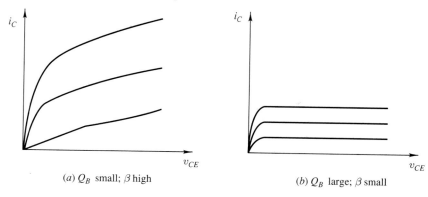

(a) Q_B small; β high   (b) Q_B large; β small

Example 2-4

Calculate the values of g_m, r_π, and r_o for a transistor with $\beta = 100$ and $V_E = 50$ V, which is biased at 0.01 mA, 0.1 mA and 1 mA.

Solution. The g_m values are, respectively, 0.38 mmhos, 3.8 mmhos, and 38.4 mmhos. The values of r_π are 260 kΩ, 26 kΩ and 2.6 kΩ, and the values of r_o are 5 MΩ, 500 kΩ and 50 kΩ.

2-3-4   Voltage Gain of Small-Signal Gain Stage

Now that we know the small-signal parameters, we can use them to calculate the gain of a gain stage. Such a stage has been studied with a MOST (see Fig. 1-11c). Now, a bipolar transistor is used, and the gain is given by

$$A_v = g_m r_o \tag{2-19a}$$

which becomes, after substitution of g_m and r_o,

$$A_v = \frac{V_E}{kT/q} \tag{2-19b}$$

This gain is quite large. For $V_E = 50$ V, it is about 2000, or 66 dB. Also, it is independent of the current, in contrast to a MOST.

2-3-5   Junction Capacitances

All regions of the bipolar transistor are separated by depletion layers, as shown in Fig. 2-2a. With each depletion layer there is a corresponding depletion-layer junction capacitance. They are added in the hybrid-π model of Fig. 2-5.

The junction capacitances are specified in Table 2-4. Note that only bottom junction capacitances are used and that the side-wall capacitances are neglected (compare with Table 1-5). In SPICE, the parameters are listed in Table 2-2. The base-emitter junction capacitance is denoted by C_{jEt}. It is normally forward biased. Therefore, $m_{jE} = 1/3$ is usually taken for its voltage dependence. The base-collector junction capacitance, C_{jCt}, is usually called C_μ in the hybrid-π model. It is normally reverse biased. A square root ($m_{jC} = 1/2$) is therefore taken for its voltage dependence.

The third junction capacitance is the collector-substrate junction capacitance C_{CS}. It is generally the largest junction capacitance because it covers the largest area and includes a side-wall capacitance. It is always reverse biased. A square root dependence ($m_{jS} = 1/2$) is taken for its voltage dependence.

In SPICE, there is one additional parameter, i.e., XCJC. This parameter indicates the fraction of C_μ that is connected to the internal base node (see Fig. 2-5). The rest is then connected to the external base node (shown by the dashed line in Fig. 2-5).

Finally, note that the value of C_j goes to infinity when the applied voltage V approaches ϕ_j (see Table 2-4), as shown in Fig. 2-10. However, at forward voltages

TABLE 2-4   JUNCTION CAPACITANCES

Parameter	Dimension	Name	Eq. No.
C_j	F/cm^2	Junction capacitance	(1-2)
$C_{jt} = A_j C_j$	F	CJ: Total junction capitance	
$C_{jt0} = A_j C_{j0}$	F	CJ0: Total junction capacitance at 0 V	
ϕ_j	V	VJ: Built-in junction potential	
m_j		M: Exponent	
for $V \leq$ FC VJ	$CJ = \dfrac{CJ0}{\left(1 - \dfrac{V}{VJ}\right)^M}$		
for $V \geq$ FC VJ	$CJ = \dfrac{CJ0}{(1 - FC)^M}\left(1 - FC(M+1) + M\dfrac{V}{VJ}\right)$		
$C_{jBEt0} = A_{BE} C_{jBE0}$	F	CJE0: Total base-emitter junction capacitance at zero V	
$C_{jBCt0} = A_{BC} C_{jBC0}$	F	CJC0: Total base-collector junction capacitance at zero V	
$C_{jCSt0} = A_{CS} C_{jCS0}$	F	CJS0: Total collector-substrate junction capacitance at zero V	

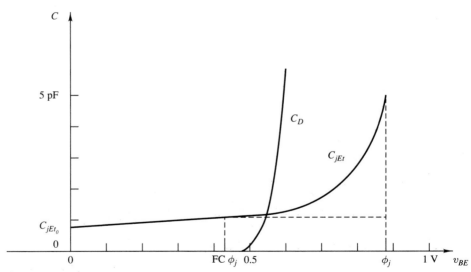

FIGURE 2-10   Capacitances C_{jEt} and C_D versus v_{BE}.

close to ϕ_j, the value of C_j cannot actually reach infinity but rather is limited to about two to three times C_{j0}. Another fit expression is then used. This allows the capacitance to increase only in a linear way in forward bias, as shown by the dashed line in Fig. 2-10. For this purpose, a new parameter is introduced, FC (see Table 2-4), and a new equation. A typical value of FC is 0.5.

2-3-6 Diffusion Capacitance C_D

A variation in base-emitter voltage Δv_{BE} causes a variation in injected charge ΔQ_F. This is the charge of minority carriers. It is always in equilibrium with a charge of majority carriers of the same size. The variation in v_{BE} thus causes a variation in majority carrier charge. The ratio of the variation in charge ΔQ_F to the variation Δv_{BE} has the dimensions of a capacitance, and is called the *diffusion* capacitance.

This kind of capacitance C_D can be derived as given by

$$C_D = \frac{dQ_F}{dv_{BE}} = \frac{dQ_F}{di_C}\frac{di_C}{dv_{BE}} = \tau_F g_m \qquad (2\text{-}20)$$

in which the first factor is obtained from Eq. (2-6a), which yields $1/\tau_F$. The diffusion capacitance is thus proportional to the current through g_m. It increases exponentially with v_{BE}, whereas C_{jEt} increases only with the square root of v_{BE} (see Fig. 2-10). Therefore, capacitance C_D is much larger than the junction capacitance C_{jEt} for values of v_{BE}, which are generally larger than 0.5 V. Thus, for all normal biasing currents, the diffusion capacitance is much larger than the base-emitter junction capacitance.

The diffusion capacitance C_D is put in parallel with C_{jEt} in the hybrid-π model (see Fig. 2-5) to form capacitance C_π. The relationship of Eq. (2-20) is depicted in Fig. 2-6.

The active region of the bipolar transistor is located directly underneath the emitter. This region is contacted by means of ohmic regions that add series resistance as well as additional capacitance.

For example, a series base resistance r_B is present between the base contact metal and the active base. It is the most important parasitic series resistance and is therefore included in the hybrid-π model (see Fig. 2-5). Also, emitter and collector resistance can be added (although they are usually omitted). The actual values of these resistances will be calculated in Sec. 2-4.

2-3-7 Common-Emitter Configuration with Current Drive

Several important parameters and characteristics can be derived by use of the hybrid-π model. They are all related to the operation of the bipolar transistor in common-emitter configuration, for which the hybrid-π model has actually been derived.

In the first example, we want to realize a current-gain amplifier. For this purpose we take a bipolar transistor amplifier, which has a large input source resistor R_S. The voltage source (in Fig. 2-11a), in series with R_S, has both a DC component V_{IN} and an AC component v_{in}. The AC input voltage is amplified and then short-circuited by means of a large capacitance C_∞ to ground, through which we can measure the output current i_{out}. Since the output is short-circuited, resistance r_o can be left out, as can capacitance C_{CS}. A current $i_C = i_{out}$ flows in the output short circuit.

The source resistance R_S is (much) larger than the input resistance $(r_B + r_\pi)$ of the transistor (see Fig. 2-11a). As a result, the transistor is current driven. Its input current is approximately $i_{in} = v_{in}/R_S$. Thus, in the hybrid-π model (see Fig. 2-11b), the input source v_{in} is replaced by current source i_{in} and $R_S = \infty$.

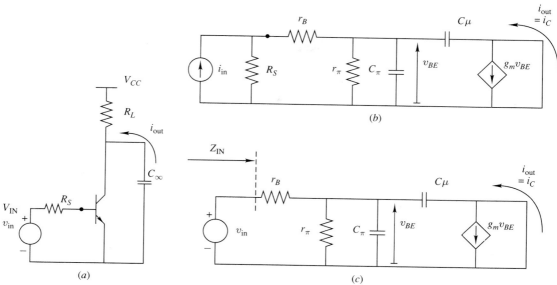

FIGURE 2-11   Bipolar transistor in CE configuration: (*a*) circuit schematic, (*b*) small-signal equivalent circuit (large R_S), and (*c*), idem as (*b*) but for small R_S.

At low frequencies, all capacitances can be omitted. The current gain A_I is then obviously given by $i_{out}/i_{in} = \beta_{AC}$. At high frequencies, however, the capacitances must be kept in the model.

The application of Kirchhoff's laws allows the calculation of the current gain at any arbitrary frequency. It is approximately given by

$$A_I = \frac{i_{out}}{i_{in}} = \frac{\beta_{AC}}{1 + jf/f_\beta} \tag{2-21a}$$

with

$$f_\beta = \frac{f_T}{\beta_{AC}} \tag{2-21b}$$

and

$$f_T = \frac{g_m}{2\pi(C_\pi + C_\mu)} \tag{2-21c}$$

The corresponding Bode diagrams are shown in Fig. 2-12. The top diagram shows the magnitude of the current gain, the bottom diagram its phase behavior. The frequency and magnitude scales are logarithmic and the phase scale is linear.

At low frequencies, the current gain equals β_{AC} and the phase difference is zero. At frequencies above f_β, however, the slope becomes minus unity, or -20 dB per decade in frequency (dB = 20 log). The phase is then shifted over $-90°$. At frequency f_β the magnitude is decreased by -3 dB (originating from $|1/(1+j)| = 1/\sqrt{2}$). The phase shift is halfway, i.e., $45°$.

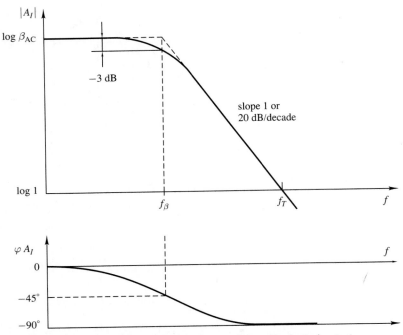

FIGURE 2-12   Bode diagrams of current driven CE bipolar transistor with shorted output.

At high frequencies, the line intercepts the axis of $|A_I| = 1$ at frequency f_T, the unity-gain frequency. It is an important transistor parameter, at least for a current driven transistor. It is a maximum frequency of usefulness and is therefore always used as a measure of high-frequency capability.

Note the similarity of this expression with the expression of a MOST in Eq. (1-40a). Indeed, capacitances $C_\pi + C_\mu$ form the input capacitance.

Frequency f_T depends on the biasing current I_C, as shown in Fig. 2-13a. Indeed, both g_m and the diffusion capacitance in C_π depend on I_C. After substitution of C_π, an expression is found that can be written as

$$f_T = \frac{1}{2\pi \tau_F} \frac{I_C}{I_C + I_{CfT}} \tag{2-21d}$$

with
$$I_{CfT} = (C_{jEt} + C_\mu)\frac{kT/q}{\tau_F}$$

The maximum value of f_T is reached at medium and high currents. It is uniquely determined by the base transit time τ_F, as already given by Eq. (2-6c). At low currents, f_T starts decreasing. This is mainly caused by the presence of the two junction capacitances. The transition current at which this occurs is denoted by I_{CfT}.

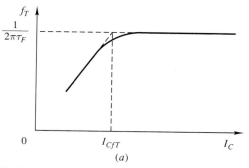
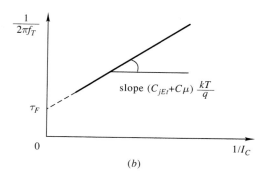

FIGURE 2-13   Unity-gain frequency f_T versus current I_C.

In order to separate τ_F from the junction capacitances, f_T is written as

$$\frac{1}{2\pi f_T} = \tau_F + (C_{jEt} + C_\mu)\frac{kT/q}{I_C} \qquad (2\text{-}21e)$$

This expression provides a linear relationship versus $1/I_C$, as shown in Fig. 2-13b. The extrapolated value for zero $1/I_C$ provides the value of τ_F. The slope itself contains both junction capacitances (remember that $C_\mu = C_{jCt}$). Note that the value of the emitter-base junction capacitance C_{jEt} in Eqs. (2-21d) and (2-21e) is its value in forward bias. Therefore, the plot of Fig. 2-13b is by far the easiest method to extract the value of C_{jEt} in forward bias.

Finally, f_T is specified for a bipolar transistor with a short-circuited (for AC signals) collector. If an ohmic series resistance r_C is present, the output can be shorted but there is still some collector resistance that remains. In this case, the expression of f_T must be slightly modified. A constant term $r_C C_\mu$ is added to τ_F in Eq. (2-21e), given by

$$\frac{1}{2\pi f_T} = \tau_F + (C_{jEt} + C_\mu)\frac{kT/q}{I_C} + r_C C_\mu \qquad (2\text{-}21f)$$

Example 2-5

Calculate the values of f_β and of f_T for a transistor with $\beta = 100$, $\tau_F = 0.25$ ns, $C_{jEt} = 5$ pF and $C_\mu = 1$ pF, at the currents of 0.01 mA, 0.1 mA, and 1 mA. What influence does a collector resistance of 30 Ω have on $f_{T\,\text{max}}$? Also, calculate the value of the transition current I_{CfT}.

Solution. The values are calculated to be 10 MHz, 88 MHz, and 393 MHz. The maximum frequency $f_{T\,\text{max}}$ equals 636 MHz. The addition of $r_C = 30$ Ω reduces this to 568 MHz. The current $I_{CfT} = 0.62$ mA. For all currents larger than this value, the maximum frequency $f_{T\,\text{max}}$ is obtained.

Parameter f_T is doubtlessly an important parameter. However, it has been specified for a bipolar transistor with an input current drive. Current drive conditions provide a low frequency gain of β_{AC}. This transistor parameter is highly unreproducible because it is so sensitive to processing conditions. Therefore, as well as for other reasons (see Chap. 4), voltage drive conditions are preferred.

2-3-8   Common-Emitter Configuration with Voltage Drive

This configuration is the same as in Fig. 2-11a, but now the source resistance R_S is much smaller than the input resistance r_π. The corresponding small-signal equivalent circuit (for zero R_S) is given in Fig. 2-11c.

At low frequencies, all capacitances can be neglected. The transconductance i_{out}/v_{in} (for zero R_S) is then given by g_m, provided $r_B < r_\pi$, which is generally the case.

At high frequencies, the transconductance A_G rolls off with a slope of unity again, as given by

$$A_G = \frac{i_{out}}{v_{in}} = \frac{g_m}{1 + jf/f_B} \tag{2-22a}$$

with
$$f_B = \frac{1}{2\pi r_B(C_\pi + C_\mu)} = \frac{1}{2\pi \tau_B} \frac{I_{CfT}}{I_C + I_{CfT}} \tag{2-22b}$$

and
$$\tau_B = r_B(C_{jEt} + C_\mu) + r_C C_\mu \tag{2-22c}$$

where, again, $r_B < r_\pi$.

The comparison of Eq. (2-22b) with Eq. (2-20b) shows that the cutoff frequency f_B is much larger than f_β. The ratio is approximately a factor of r_π/r_B, which is obviously much larger than unity. Note that the time constant $r_C C_\mu$ has been added again.

Frequency f_B can even be larger than f_T, provided r_B is smaller than $1/g_m$. This can be the case when the collector biasing current I_C is small. Frequencies f_B and f_T are equal at the current where $g_m r_B = 1$, or at the current

$$I_{CTB} = \frac{kT/q}{r_B} \tag{2-23}$$

The maximum value of f_B is now reached for currents smaller than I_{CfT}. This maximum depends only on the base resistance and both junction capacitances and is independent of the base transit time τ_F.

In general, it can be concluded that only the presence of r_B limits high frequency performance. For zero r_B, infinite bandwidth can be achieved. This clearly illustrates the importance of r_B in the bipolar transistor model. Considerable attention will be paid to its calculation in Sec. 2-4.

Example 2-6

Calculate the frequencies f_T and f_B for a bipolar transistor with $\beta = 100$, $\tau_F = 0.25$ ns, $C_{jEt} + C_{jCt} = 6$ pF and $r_B = 100$ Ω at the currents of 0.01 mA, 0.1 mA, and 1 mA. Also, calculate the value of the current I_{CTB}.

Solution. The f_T values have been given in Example 2-5 as 10, 88, and 393 MHz. The f_B values are, respectively, 261, 228, and 102 MHz. Current $I_{CTB} = 0.26$ mA.

Note that parameters f_β, f_T, and f_B are the most important parameters of a bipolar transistor. They all depend on the same fundamental parameters, shown in the diagram of Fig. 2-6. This diagram has been simplified with the omission of all junction capacitances. It is worth memorizing this schema to gain insight.

The fundamental parameters are β, g_m, τ_F, and r_B. Two of them are determined by the technology used, i.e., β and τ_F. The other two, g_m and r_B, are design variables. Parameter g_m can be varied continuously by varying the current i_C. Resistor r_B can be varied only by taking different (and especially larger) layouts, as explained in Sec. 2-4. The only true design parameter left is g_m. This result is in sharp contrast with a MOST, for which W/L is a true design parameter together with g_m.

2-3-9   Common-Collector and Common-Base Configurations

As a final example of the usefulness of the hybrid-π model, alternative configurations are discussed. The first one is the common-collector configuration or *emitter follower*. Its schematic is shown in Fig. 2-14a and closely resembles the schematic of Fig. 1-13a for a MOST source follower.

Two biasing sources are required. The first is a voltage source V_{IN} at the base. The second is a current source I_E at the emitter. This latter source determines the collector current within a small margin of error (equal to $1/\beta$). The first voltage source determines the output DC level V_{OUT}. Its value is approximately $V_{BE} \approx 0.7$ V lower than V_{IN}. An exact value for V_{BE} can be obtained from Eq. (2-5a) because the collector current is known. In this way, all DC voltages and currents are easily determined.

If an AC input voltage v_{in} is added, the current cannot change because it is determined by current source I_E. The AC current is thus zero and so is the AC base-emitter voltage v_{BE}. As a result, the AC input voltage v_{in} appears unattenuated at the output: $v_{out} = v_{in}$. Thus, the AC gain of this source follower is unity. Also, the AC input current is zero because it is $1/\beta$ of the collector current. As a result, the input resistance is quasi-infinity. In Chap. 4, we will show that the input resistance is not infinity at all. For now, we will simply assume this in order to examine the effect of the capacitances.

The main purpose of this configuration is to convert the impedance level from high to low values. The input impedance is high, as shown above, and the output impedance is low. In order to calculate the output impedance, the AC equivalent circuit is drawn. It is shown in Fig. 2-14b.

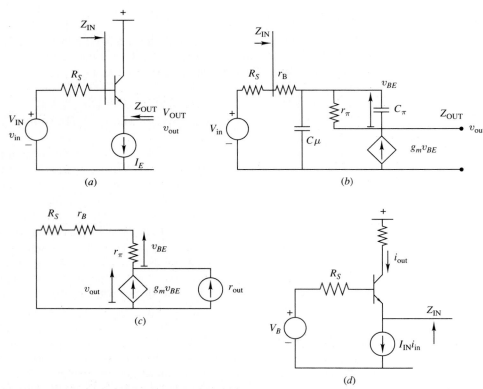

FIGURE 2-14 (a) Emitter follower. (b) Small signal equivalent circuit. (c) Equivalent circuit to calculate Z_{out} at low frequencies. (d) Common base configuration.

At low frequencies the capacitances can be omitted. The output resistance is then found by application of an output current source i_{out} and calculation of the output voltage v_{out} (see Fig. 2-14c). The resultant output resistance at low frequencies (LF) is given by

$$R_{OUTLF} = \frac{R_S + r_B + r_\pi}{1 + \beta_{AC}} \qquad (2\text{-}24a)$$

in which R_S is the source resistor. Usually, $\beta_{AC} \gg 1$, and Eq. (2-14a) can then be simplified to

$$R_{OUTLF} = \frac{1}{g_m} + \frac{R_S + r_B}{\beta_{AC}} \qquad (2\text{-}24b)$$

The second term is quite small if R_S is small and is therefore usually negligible. However, if R_S is large, this second term is dominant.

The first term, $1/g_m$, is also present in the output resistance of a MOST source follower (see Eq. (1-33)). However, for a source follower, there is no term for the source resistor R_S as there is for an emitter follower. A source follower thus always gives $1/g_m$ as an output resistance, regardless of the value of source resistor R_S. Thus, the impedance reduction from gate to source is nearly infinity. An emitter follower, on the other hand, is only capable of an impedance reduction from the base to the emitter of a factor β_{AC}.

At high frequencies the capacitances start playing a role as well. The full expression of the output impedance is then given by

$$Z_{OUT} = R_{OUTLF}\frac{1 + jf/f_B}{1 + jf/f_T} \qquad (2\text{-}25)$$

provided $g_m(r_B + R_S)C_\mu \ll C_\pi$.

All parameters R_{OUTLF}, f_B, and f_T are already known from Eq. (2-24a), (2-22b), and (2-21a), respectively. Since they all depend on the current, the values of Z_{OUT} are plotted versus current in Fig. 2-15.

In Fig. 2-15a, the asymptotic values of f_B and f_T are plotted versus current. These frequencies are the zero and pole frequencies of Eq. (2-15). This plot gives the positions of the zero and pole with current i_C as a variable and is therefore called the *pole-zero position plot*. The Bode diagrams for several values of the current are easily derived from the pole-zero position plot and are given in Fig. 2-15b. Only the amplitudes are shown; the phases are omitted.

At current I_{CTB}, $g_m r_B = 1$, as given by Eq. (2-23). The values of f_B and f_T are equal. A pure output resistance results. Its value is r_B itself. At lower currents, f_T is lower and the output impedance then rolls off versus frequency.

At higher currents, f_B occurs first. A region appears in which the output impedance increases with frequency. This region is called an *inductive region*. The larger the current the wider the inductive region. This inductance can cause instability if combined with parasitic capacitance at the output terminal, so it is safer to avoid it altogether by decreasing the source resistance or by decreasing the biasing current. This will be studied in more detail in Chap. 4.

The previous analysis has been conducted under the assumption that an AC or small-signal input has been applied to the base terminal in Fig. 2-14a. It was an AC voltage source superimposed on v_{IN}. The AC input can also be applied to the emitter by superimposing an AC emitter current on i_{IN} (see Fig. 2-14d). The base is then at a fixed voltage V_B. This is called the *common-base configuration* and the output is taken from the collector.

Obviously, all AC current that goes into the emitter also comes out at the collector (within a margin of error of $1/\beta_{AC}$). The current gain is thus unity.

The input impedance seen by the input current source is exactly the same as the output impedance of the emitter follower, shown in Fig. 2-14a, provided the source resistances are the same. As a result, the same diagrams can be used in Fig. 2-15. All conclusions drawn about the emitter follower output impedance are equally valid for the common-base stage input impedance.

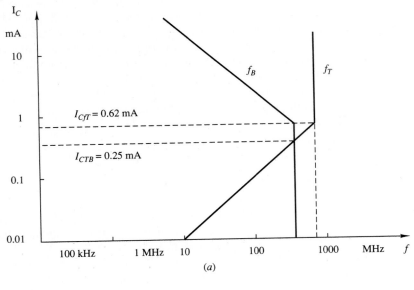

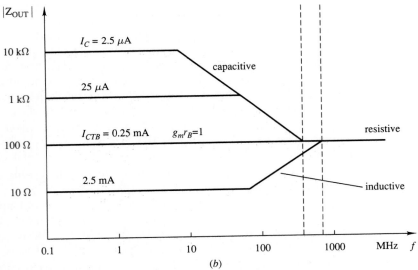

FIGURE 2-15   (a) Position of pole and zero, (b) Bode diagram of Z_{out} of emitter follower for $\beta = 100$, $r_B = 100 \ \Omega$, $\tau_F = 0.25$ ns, $C_{jEt} + C_\mu = 6$ pF.

It can be concluded that the high frequency performance of a bipolar transistor stage is governed by the parameters f_B and f_T, and especially by r_B. Remember, however, that the collector has always been short-circuited for AC signals. Voltage gain has never been realized. As a consequence, the multiplication effect of the feedback capacitance C_μ (called the "Miller effect") never had to be taken into account. This effect will be included in the evaluation of elementary circuits in Chap. 4.

Now, special attention is paid to the calculation and design aspects of the base resistance. In addition, the other ohmic resistances will be discussed.

2-4 THE OHMIC RESISTANCES

By far the most important ohmic resistance is the base resistance and therefore it is discussed first (Grove 1967).

2-4-1 The Base Resistance

There are two base resistances to be considered (see Fig. 2-16a). The first is the intrinsic base resistance r_{Bi}. It is located in the base region underneath the emitter. The other one is the extrinsic base resistance r_{Be}. It is the resistance from the edge of the emitter to the base contact. The latter one is the easiest one to calculate and is therefore treated first.

2-4-2 Extrinsic Base Resistance

For a region with sheet resistivity R_{Be} (in $\Omega/\square$) and the dimensions given in Fig. 2-16a, this resistance is given by

$$r_{Be} = R_{Be}\frac{h_B}{b_B} \tag{2-26}$$

For wide base contacts (large b_B), closely spaced to the emitter region (small h_B), the extrinsic base resistance will be small.

2-4-3 Intrinsic Base Resistance

The sheet resistivity R_{Bi} underneath the base is much higher than in the extrinsic base region. Indeed, the base is largely compensated by the emitter such that only a base depth W_B is left. Its sheet resistivity R_{Bi} (in $\Omega/\square$) is given by

$$R_{Bi} = \frac{1}{q\mu_n Q_B} \tag{2-27}$$

in which Q_B is the integrated base doping (in cm^{-2}) and μ_n the electron mobility in the base. Typical values of this sheet resistance are $R_{Bi} \approx 3$ to 5 $k\Omega/\square$.

This large resistivity creates a large lateral resistance underneath the emitter. This is the intrinsic base resistance, which will be calculated as follows.

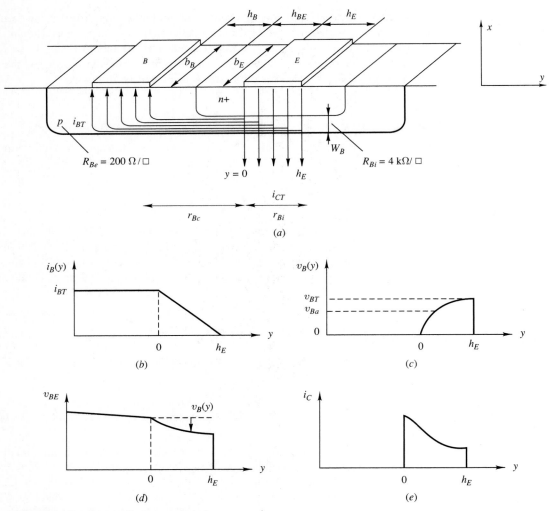

FIGURE 2-16   Base resistance calculation.

In Fig. 2-16a, the current lines of the collector are drawn. It is assumed that these lines are evenly spaced over the whole emitter contact. Each collector current line generates base current. As a consequence, the lateral base current is zero to the right of the emitter contact but reaches its total value i_{BT} to the left of the emitter contact. Because the collector current is evenly spread over the emitter contact, the base current i_B is a linear function (see Fig. 2-16b), as given by

$$i_B(y) = i_{BT}\left(1 - \frac{y}{h_E}\right) \qquad (2\text{-}28a)$$

The lateral voltage drop along the intrinsic base region is given by

$$v_B(y) = \int_0^{h_E} i_B dr_{Bi} = \frac{R_{Bi}}{b_E} \int_0^{h_E} i_B dy \qquad (2\text{-}28b)$$

in which dr_{Bi} is a small fraction of the lateral intrinsic base resistance.

The lateral base resistance r_{Bi} is defined as the ratio of the average lateral voltage drop v_{Ba} to the total base current i_{BT}. We have thus to take the average of v_B of Eq. (2-28b).

Substituting i_B from Eq. (2-28a) into Eq. (2-28b) and performing the integral yields

$$v_B(y) = \frac{R_{Bi}}{b_E} i_{BT} \left(y - \frac{y^2}{2h_E} \right) \qquad (2\text{-}29a)$$

This curve is given in Fig. 2-16c. Its maximum value v_{BT} is easily found by substitution of y by h_E in Eq. (2-29a). However, we must have its average value v_{Ba}. The average value of $v_B(y)$ is found from the following integral:

$$v_{Ba} = \frac{1}{h_E} \int_0^{h_E} v_B(y) dy \qquad (2\text{-}29b)$$

or

$$v_{Ba} = \frac{R_{Bi} h_E}{3b_E} i_{BT} \qquad (2\text{-}29c)$$

Then, the average lateral intrinsic base resistance is given by

$$r_{Bi} = \frac{v_{Ba}}{i_{BT}} = \frac{R_{Bi} h_E}{3b_E} \qquad (2\text{-}30)$$

This resistance is one third of the total lateral resistance of the intrinsic base region. The reduction factor is a result of the nonlinear voltage drop along that region. If two base contacts are present, one on each side of the emitter, the reduction factor is one-twelfth instead of one-third.

The voltage drop v_B must be subtracted from the applied base-emitter voltage v_{BE} (see Fig. 2-16d). As a result, the effective base-emitter voltage on the left of the emitter is larger than the base-emitter voltage on the right. Since the collector current depends exponentially on the base-emitter voltage, the collector current on the left is much larger than on the right (see Fig. 2-16e). This is called *emitter crowding*. Emitter crowding causes all the collector current to flow at the edge of the emitter on the side(s) of the base contact(s). This effect becomes important as soon as the lateral voltage drop is large with respect to kT/q. Thus, the onset of emitter crowding occurs at the current I_{Cec}, given by

$$I_{Cec} = \beta \frac{kT/q}{r_{Bi}} \qquad (2\text{-}31a)$$

or, after substitution of r_{Bi}, by

$$I_{Cec} = \beta \frac{3kT/q}{R_{Bi}} \frac{b_E}{h_E} \qquad (2\text{-}31b)$$

Note that this current does not depend on the base charge Q_B. It does, however, depend on the dimensions of the emitter. In order to avoid emitter crowding, current I_{Cec} must be made as large as possible. Therefore, long and narrow emitter contact stripes must be used, along with two base contacts, one on each side of the emitter.

Even lower intrinsic base resistances can be obtained by using more emitter stripes, always paralleled by base contact stripes. In this way, values down to Ω's can be reached. However, the emitter-base junction area can become very large, leading to a large emitter-base junction capacitance. This limits performance of such a device at high frequencies and necessitates a compromise.

The total base resistance consists of the sum of the extrinsic and intrinsic base resistances. However, this is the case only for low currents. At higher currents, all the current is injected on the left side of the emitter and only the extrinsic base resistance remains. This is depicted in Fig. 2-17, which clearly shows the current dependence of the base resistance.

In SPICE (see Table 2-2), an expression is used that provides the value of the total base resistance as a continuous function of the current (Antognetti and Massobrio 1988). It is given by

$$r_B = \text{RBM} + (\text{RB} - \text{RBM}) \left(\frac{1}{1 + \dfrac{I_C}{\text{IKF}}} \right) \qquad (2\text{-}32)$$

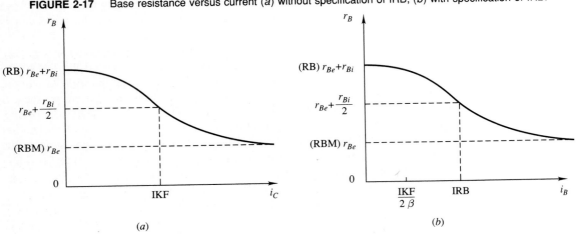

FIGURE 2-17   Base resistance versus current (a) without specification of IRB; (b) with specification of IRB.

in which RB $= r_{Be} + r_{Bi}$ is the limiting value at low currents (see Fig. 2-17a) and RBM= r_{Be} is the limiting value at high currents. Parameter IKF is a high-injection parameter. At this value of the collector current, the beta starts rolling off (see Sec. 2-5). Typical values of IKF for a small transistor are 20 to 50 mA. In Fig. 2-17a, IKF is that value of the collector current where the base resistance falls halfway to its minimum value.

If we prefer to separate the base-resistance roll-off from the high-injection effects (beta roll-off), we must specify a value for parameter IRB. As before, this causes a complicated expression to generate about the same curve (see Fig. 2-17b), an expression that is approximated by Eq. (2-32), but with I_B/IRB instead of I_C/IKF. Now, IRB is the base current where the base resistance falls halfway to its minimum value. Both curves (of Fig. 2-17a and b) coincide if IRB = IKF/2β. For IKF = 50 mA and $\beta = 200$, this value of IRB is 0.125 mA. Normally, IRB is much larger, as sketched in Fig. 2-17b (i.e., 20 to 50 mA). As a result, IRB is located in the region of the collector currents where high-injection effects already play an important role. The effects of the base resistance can no longer be distinguished.

Example 2-7

Calculate r_{Be} for $h_B = 10$ μm and $b_B = 30$ μm if $R_{Be} = 150$ $\Omega/\square$. Also, calculate the intrinsic base resistance and the current I_{Cec} for a transistor with a 1.6×10^{13} cm^{-2} base charge, $\beta = 100$, and hole mobility = 225 cm^2/Vs. The emitter dimensions are $b_E = 30$ μm and $h_E = 10$ μm. What is the total base resistance for one and two base contacts?

Solution. from Eq. (2-26), $r_{Be} = 50$ Ω. The value of $R_{Bi} = 1.736$ k$\Omega/\square$. From Eq. (2-30), $r_{Bi} = 289$ Ω. The value of I_{Cec} is then 8.95 mA. The total base resistance is 339 Ω for one base contact and 122 Ω for two base contacts.

2-4-4 The Collector Resistances

The collector current is injected by the emitter, crosses the base, and arrives in the collector region underneath the emitter. It must flow through three resistive regions before it arrives at the collector contact. Two of the resistive regions are located in the epitaxial region. This region is homogeneously doped and is thus characterized by a bulk resistivity ρ_{epi} in Ωcm or a doping level N_{epi} such that $\rho_{epi} = 1/q\mu_{epi}N_{epi}$. A typical value is $\rho_{epi} = 1$ Ωcm (see also Table 2-1).

The third region is the buried layer. It is included to reduce the resistivity of the collector region as much as possible. It is a result of a diffusion process step and is therefore characterized by a sheet resistivity R_{BL} in $\Omega/\square$. or a doping level N_{BL} (such that $N_{BL} = 1/d_{BL}q\mu_{BL}N_{BL}$). A typical value is 10 $\Omega/\square$. (see also Table 2-1).

The resultant resistances depend on the geometries of the collector region. They are given in Fig. 2-2b. The total resistance is then $r_C = r_{C1} + r_{C2} + r_{C3}$. It is found by inspection and given by

$$r_C = \rho_{\text{epi}} \left(\frac{x_{\text{epi}} - x_B - d_{BL}/2}{h_E b_E} \right) + R_{BL} \left(\frac{h_{CE}}{b_C} \right) + \rho_{\text{epi}} \left(\frac{x_{\text{epi}} - x_E - d_{BL}/2}{h_C b_C} \right) \quad (2\text{-}33)$$

These are obviously first-order calculations. The current is assumed not to spread out nor to be subject to crowding. Also, the underdiffusions are neglected so a large relative error can be expected. On the other hand, an exact value of collector resistance is usually not required.

In SPICE, the total collector resistance is denoted by RC (see Table 2-2).

Example 2-8

Find the collector resistances of the transistor of Fig. 2-2b with $R_{BL} = 12 \ \Omega/\square$ and $\rho_{\text{epi}} = 2.6 \ \Omega\text{cm}$.

Solution. $h_E = 15 \ \mu\text{m}$, $b_E = 30 \ \mu\text{m}$ and $x_{\text{epi}} - x_B - d_{BL/2} = 7.2 \ \mu\text{m}$, hence $r_{C1} = 413 \ \Omega$. Also, $h_{CE} = 20 \ \mu\text{m}$ and $b_C = 50 \ \mu\text{m}$; thus $r_{C2} = 4.7 \ \Omega$. Finally, $h_C = 20 \ \mu\text{m}$ and $x_{\text{epi}} - x_E - d_{BL/2} = 8 \ \mu\text{m}$, hence $r_{C3} = 206 \ \Omega$. The sum is $r_C = 624 \ \Omega$.

We clearly notice that the resistance due to the buried layer is negligible. The value of r_C obtained is an upper limit. It will usually be smaller because of the second-order effects mentioned above.

2-4-5   The Emitter Resistance

The emitter series resistance is the smallest resistance because the emitter is highly doped. A typical values is $R_E = 10 \ \Omega/\square$. On the other hand, the emitter resistance directly degrades the transconductance, as shown in Eq. (1-37), and therefore must be included as well.

If a similar calculation is tried for the emitter resistance as was tried for the collector resistances, the emitter resistance r_E is about 0.2 Ω. Usually, much larger values are measured—about 2 to 5 Ω. This difference is caused by the presence of metal contact resistance. Yet this resistance plays a role only if the product $g_m r_E$ becomes comparable to unity, i.e., at large collector currents. For this range of currents, high-injection effects and other second-order effects have become much more important.

In SPICE, the emitter resistance r_E is denoted by RE (see Table 2-2).

2-5   HIGH-INJECTION AND OTHER SECOND-ORDER EFFECTS

At high collector currents, some important phenomena occur, especially as a result of emitter crowding, which in turn is due to the large current density. All of this leads to drastic reduction in β and in f_T.

It is not easy to distinguish the several phenomena from one another, as they all occur at about the same current levels. Nevertheless, models can be devised for them.

They can be separated in high-injection effects in the base and high-injection effects in the collector (Muller and Kamins 1986).

2-5-1 High-Injection Effects in the Base

The onset of high injection occurs by definition at that value of v_{BE} where the injected minority carrier concentration in the base n'_p (see Fig. 2-1f) becomes equal to the majority carrier concentration in equilibrium p_{po} (see Fig. 2-18a). This value is denoted by V_{BEhi}. At that point, the actual majority carrier concentration p'_p is doubled (see Fig. 2-18b) because of the charge neutrality condition in the base.

The value of V_{BEhi} is obtained by equating p_{po} to n'_p (given by Eq. (2-3a). After the substitution of p_{po} by N_B and of n_{po} by n_i^2/N_B, the value of V_{BEhi} is approximately given by

$$V_{BEhi} = 2\frac{kT}{q}\ln\frac{N_B}{n_i} \tag{2-34}$$

For example, for a base doping of 2×10^{17} cm^{-3}, V_{BEhi} is approximately 0.84 V, which is quite a high value indeed.

As a consequence, the majority carrier (holes for an *npn* transistor) concentration is not homogeneous throughout the base. The concentration is higher on the emitter side than on the collector side (see Fig. 2-18b). As a result, the holes diffuse in the base from the emitter to the collector side.

FIGURE 2-18   (a) Low injection and (b) high injection conditions in the base.

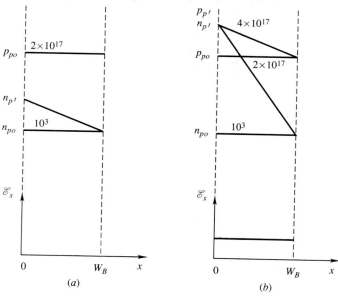

The holes cannot flow to the collector because the collector is positive, repelling holes. The hole current through the base must therefore be zero. An electric field $\mathscr{E}_x$ is created in the base to prohibit the diffusion of holes toward the collector side (see Fig. 2-18b).

The value of this electric field is calculated from the equation of the hole current p'_p to zero. Indeed this hole current density j_p $(= i_p/A_{EB})$ would result from drift current and diffusion current as given by

$$j_p = q\mu_p p_p \mathscr{E}_x - D_p\left(\frac{dp_p}{dx}\right) = 0 \tag{2-35}$$

From this expression, the value of the electric field $\mathscr{E}_x$ is extracted. An approximate expression is then obtained by use of Einstein's relationship $(D/\mu = kT/q)$ and, after substitution of the derivative, dp_p/dx by p_p/W_B. The electric field $\mathscr{E}_x$ is then approximately given by

$$\mathscr{E}_x = \frac{kT/q}{W_B} \tag{2-36}$$

For a linear hole distribution in the base (see Fig. 2-18), the electric field is constant.

Under low-level injection conditions (Fig. 2-18a), the electron current that is injected by the emitter and flows toward the collector is a result only of the diffusion in the base. For high-injection conditions (Fig. 2-18b), however, that electric field is present as well, causing additional drift. The current increases and an additional voltage drop appears across the base-emitter junction.

The collector current is given by

$$i_C = 2I_{\text{Shi}}\exp\left(\frac{v_{EB}}{2kT/q}\right) \tag{2-37a}$$

with

$$I_{\text{Shi}} = \frac{qA_{EB}D_n n_i}{W_B} = \left(\frac{N_B}{n_i}\right)I_S \tag{2-37b}$$

in which I_S is given by Eq. (2-5b).

This is an important result. It shows that the characteristic of collector current versus base-emitter voltage no longer contains the Boltzmann factor under high-injection conditions. Indeed, the coefficient in the denominator of the exponential is now $2kT/q$ instead of kT/q, as shown in Fig. 2-19a.

At low currents, represented in Fig. 2-19a, the graph is identical to Fig. 2-3. At high currents, the slope of the i_C characteristic is changed but not the slope of the i_B characteristic. As a result, the beta starts falling off at these high currents. The current where the slope changes is called the knee current I_{CK}. Its value is found by equating i_C from Eq. (2-5) to the one in Eq. (2-37). It is given by

$$I_{CK} = I_S\left(\frac{2N_B}{n_i}\right)^2 \tag{2-38a}$$

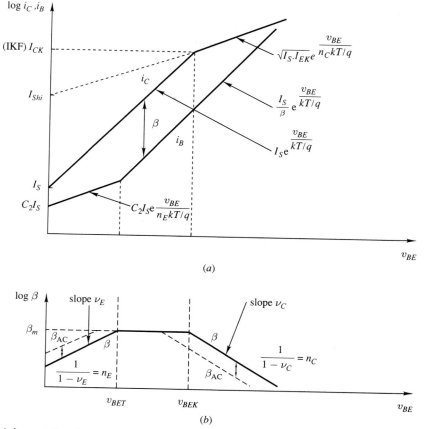

FIGURE 2-19   (a) Asymptotic values of i_C and i_B with (b) resulting beta's.

and the corresponding value of V_{BEK} is given by

$$V_{BEK} = 2\frac{kT}{q}\ln\frac{2N_B}{n_i} \qquad (2\text{-}38b)$$

This value is obviously very close to the one of Eq. (2-34).

Note that Eq. (2-37a) can now be rewritten as

$$i_C = \sqrt{I_S I_{CK}}\exp\left(\frac{v_{EB}}{2kT/q}\right) \qquad (2\text{-}37c)$$

In SPICE, parameter I_{CK} is called IKF (see Table 2-2). It is the knee or corner current in forward direction. In reverse direction it is called IKR.

2-5-2 High-Injection Model of Beta

Since the beta depends on the current, an AC beta can be distinguished that is now smaller than the DC beta. (see Fig. 2-19b). Indeed, another fit formula is used that again includes two fit parameters. At high currents, the region with $\exp(q v_{BE}/2kT)$ is better described by $\exp(q v_{BE}/n_C kT)$. The second fit parameter is C_2. The complete expression for β in SPICE is given by

$$\beta = \frac{\beta_m}{1 + C_1 i_C^{-v_E} + C_2 i_C^{v_C}} \tag{2-39}$$

in which $v_C = 1 - 1/n_C$. In comparison with Eq. (2-13), an extra term has been added to account for the drop in beta at high currents. The knee current I_{CK} is given by

$$I_{CK} = C_2^{-1/v_C} \tag{2-38c}$$

As before, the AC beta is easily derived from Eq. (2-39) by application of Eq. (2-12). It is plotted in Fig. 1-62b as well. It is clear that the AC beta starts falling off at a $(1 + v_C)$ lower collector current than the DC beta. Power transistors suffer considerably from this effect. Exponent v_C can be as high as 3 to 4. As a result, the AC beta drops to unexpectedly low values.

Exponent v_C can be so high because several effects are combined. Some of them are briefly discussed next. They include the effects of base resistance, the spreading of the collector current, high-injection effects in the collector, etc.

Example 2-9

For the transistor of Table 2-3, calculate the high-current i_C versus v_{BE} characteristics (calculate the knee current). Also calculate the AC beta at two times that knee current if we assume that $v_C = 2$.

Solution. That transistor has parameter $I_S = 1.3 \times 10^{-16}$ A. Factor N_B/n_i equals 1.3×10^7 and hence, from Eq. (2-37b), the value $I_{Shi} = 1.75 \times 10^{-9}$ A. The knee current is given by Eq. (2-38a) and is about $I_{CK} = 93$ mA. The corresponding value of V_{BE} is $V_{BEK} = 0.884$ V. The approximate value of the electric field is given by Eq. (2-36) and is only 323 V/cm.

From Eq. (2-38c), the constant C_2 is found to be $I_{CK}^{-v_C}$ or about 115. As a result the AC beta at 0.4 A can be obtained by application of Eq. (2-12) to Eq. (2-39), which yields

$$\beta_{AC} = \frac{\beta_m}{1 + (1 + v_C) C_2 i_C^{v_C}} \tag{2-40}$$

In this expression, $C_2 i_C^{v_C}$ equals 1 at 93 mA and equals 4 at twice that current (remember that $v_C = 2$). The AC beta is thus reduced to about 1/13 of the maximum value of β_m.

We also learn from this equation that the AC beta is always smaller than β_m and that its difference with the DC beta is larger if the slope v_C is larger (see Fig. (2-19b).

2-5-3 Base Resistance Effects

At high collector currents, the base current is high as well. It causes a lateral voltage drop ΔV_{BE} in the base region as a result of the presence of base resistance r_B. This resistance has been discussed in detail in Sec. 2-4.

This voltage drop must obviously be subtracted from the applied base-emitter voltage (see Fig. 2-20). As a result, the i_C versus v_{BE} characteristic flattens out and the beta is reduced. The expression of the collector current is then given by

$$i_C = I_S \exp\left(\frac{v_{BE} - r_B i_C/\beta}{kT/q}\right) \tag{2-41}$$

with I_S given by Eq. (2-5b).

2-5-4 Graded Base

In the discussions above, it has been assumed that the base is homogeneously doped, with doping level N_B. This is actually not the case, because the base is the result of two diffusions. For most of the base region, the doping level decreases toward the collector side. As a result, there is an aiding electric field that slightly increases the current and shortens the base transit time τ_F.

2-5-5 Collector Current Spreading

When the collector current becomes large, severe emitter crowding occurs. All collector current is then concentrated on the side of the base contact. The current path on the extreme side, denoted by W_B', is now much longer than underneath the emitter (see Fig. 2-21), where it is W_B. For that portion of the collector current, the recombination

FIGURE 2-20   Beta reduction by base resistance.

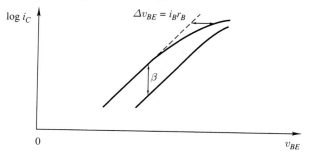

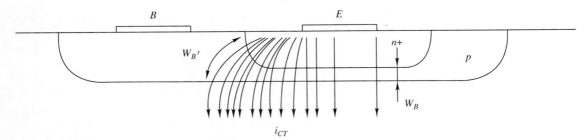

FIGURE 2-21   Collector current spreading.

in the base has increased considerably. For that portion, the beta is determined by recombination in the base and no longer by injection in the emitter. As a result, the beta drops considerably, the base transit time τ_F increases, and parameter f_T thus drops as well.

2-5-6   High-Injection Effects in the Collector

The collector of a bipolar transistor is separated from the base by a wide depletion layer. Its width is easily calculated if an abrupt junction can be assumed. For this purpose, Eq. (1.3a) can be used.

Moreover, it has been assumed that the depletion layer approximation holds, i.e., that the depletion layer only contains fixed ion charges (see Fig. 2-1b) and no mobile carriers (see Fig. 2-1f). For high currents, this no longer holds true. A large number of electrons flow continuously through the base-collector depletion layer, and this flow represents a negative charge in that collector-base depletion layer. The doping levels in the depletion layers on both sides of that junction must therefore be modified by a quantity N_I, given by

$$N_I = \frac{i_C}{q A_{EB} v_{\text{sat}}} \tag{2-42}$$

in which v_{sat} is the maximum carrier velocity ($\approx 10^5$ m/s), which has been introduced for FETs as well (see Eq. (1-38a)).

For a transistor of 30×15 μm and a current of 13 mA, N_I is about 1.8×10^{15} cm^{-3}. This doping level is comparable indeed to the doping level of the collector itself (2×10^{15} cm^{-3}). Thus, high-injection effects occur in the collector. The result is that for high currents, the effective base width W_B increases, leading to considerable reductions in beta (due to recombination) and frequency f_T (Sze 1981).

2-5-7   Bipolar Transistors for VLSI

The bipolar transistor diagrammed in Fig. 2-2 with f_T values of about 500 to 700 Mhz, is the most conventional one. The base diffusion is 2 to 3 μm deep ($W_B = 0.5$ to

0.8 μm) and the epitaxial layer is 6 to 10 μm, depending on the required breakdown voltage. Its main disadvantage is the enormous area lost for the isolation diffusion.

Recent devices are fully realized by means of ion-implantation. All vertical dimensions decrease by a factor of ten. Base widths of less than 0.1 μm are obtained, resulting in f_T's of over 30 GHz. Both the base and the collector are contacted by highly doped plugs (see Fig. 2-22a) in order to reduce the parasitic resistances r_B and r_C as much as possible.

An even further decrease in lateral dimensions is obtained by use of local oxidation. Oxides are used to isolate the devices instead of the depletion layers of isolation diffusions (see Fig. 2-22b). Moreover, the emitter is contacted through a polysilicon layer that boosts the beta and makes it temperature insensitive. The base is contacted through a polysilicon layer as well. This allows more spacing between the emitter and base contacts, resulting in smaller devices.

For these high-frequency transistors, several second-order effects play a role. They can be modeled by additional parameters in SPICE (see Table 2-2), which act on

FIGURE 2-22 Recent bipolar transistor structures.

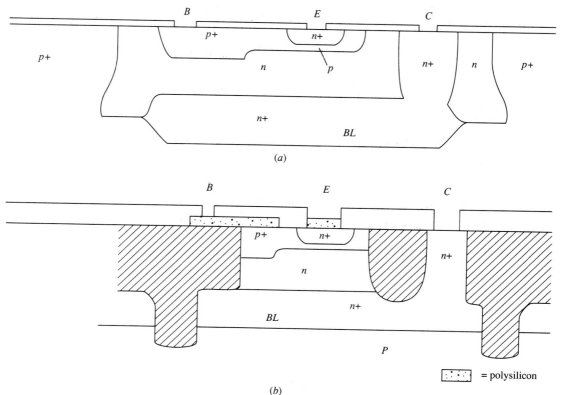

the base transit time τ_F. For example, τ_F can be made biasing dependent, voltage dependent, etc.

One parameter in particular is worth mentioning here—the excess phase parameter PTF. This parameter indicates how many degrees phase shift must be added to current source g_m (in the hybrid-π model) at frequency $f_T (= 1/2\pi\tau_F)$. This extra phase shift can be used to fit measured phase shifts at frequency f_T.

2-6 LATERAL *pnp* TRANSISTORS

Bipolar devices of opposite polarity can be realized together with the vertical *npn* transistors of Fig. 2-2 (Muller and Kamins 1986). Two kinds of *pnp* transistors can be distinguished, namely, vertical and lateral *pnp* devices. We will first discuss vertical devices.

Vertical pnp transistors are hampered by the fact that the collector is always the substrate and are thus also called substrate *pnp*. This is caused by the fact that the epitaxial *n*-region, which is the collector for a normal vertical *npn* transistor, is now used as the base (see Fig. 2-23*a*). It is contacted through a *n*+ diffusion, which corresponds to the emitter of the vertical *npn*.

The underlying *p*-substrate then acts as the collector. It is a common collector for all the vertical *pnp* devices on the same chip. As a consequence, the vertical *pnp* transistor can only be used in the common-collector configuration, i.e., it can only be used as an emitter follower in an output stage or a buffer stage.

The *lateral pnp transistor* is shown in Fig. 2-23*b*. Again, the epitaxial region is the base. Both the emitter and collector are realized in the same *p*-region of the base of the vertical *npn* transistor. Note that a buried layer is now present as well and that the lateral device is circular. The reasons for these changes will be made clear later on.

In some present-day technologies, an extra diffusion or ion-implantation is often carried out, such that vertical *pnp*'s can be realized. The advantage of such technology is that the vertical *pnp*'s characteristics are considerably improved upon. Their f_T's, especially, are close to the f_T's of vertical *npn*'s. In this text, such devices are not discussed as they are not commonly available.

For both kinds of *pnp* devices, the most important characteristics are now derived. These characteristics include the parameters I_S, beta, and f_T. The hybrid-π model, however, is exactly the same for a *pnp* transistor as for an *npn* transistor and is therefore not repeated. Applications and second-order effects will be considered. The simplest device, substrate *pnp*, is discussed first.

2-6-1 Substrate *pnp* Transistors

The substrate or vertical *pnp* behaves as a conventional bipolar transistor. Only its base is quite wide (d_v in Fig. 2-23*a*) and the base doping is quite low. Its doping level is determined by the collector vertical *npn*, for which a typical value is $N_B = 10^{15}$ cm^{-3} (see Table 2-1). As a result, the integrated base charge Q_B (per cm^2) is of the same order of magnitude as for a vertical *npn* transistor.

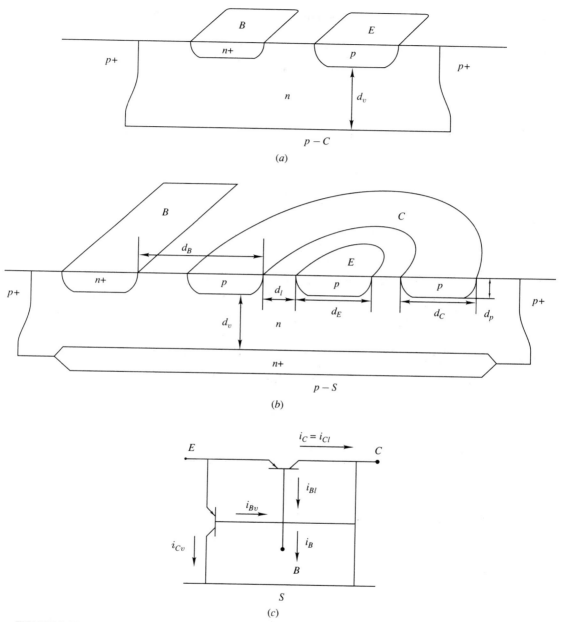

FIGURE 2-23 *pnp* devices in the bipolar process: (*a*) vertical; (*b*) lateral; and (*c*) with symbols.

Parameter I_S, which determines the i_C versus v_{BE} relation (see Eq. (2-5b)), is also given by Eq. (2-5b), with the exception of D_n now substituted by D_p. It is also of the same order of magnitude.

The picture is different for the beta value. Because the base width is so much larger compared to a vertical npn, base recombination in the base dominates, rather than injection into the emitter. Its expression is given by Eq. (2-9). It depends on the base transit time τ_F, given by Eq. (2-6b), after again substituting D_n by D_p. The recombination time constant is again approximately $\tau_{BF} \approx 1$ μs. The beta value is usually somewhat lower for a vertical pnp transistor than for a vertical npn transistor.

At both low and high currents, the beta falls off in very much the same way as before (see Eq. (2-39), such that the AC betas are different from the DC betas.

The maximum value of f_T is again determined by the base transit time τ_F, given by Eq. (2-21e). The junction capacitances determine the f_T values at low current.

Here, we consider the effect of adding a buried layer in the vertical pnp transistor. Indeed, the buried layer, not present in Fig. 2-23a, is added in Fig. 2-23b. This buried layer is highly doped (10^{18} to 10^{19} cm^{-3}, see Table 2-1) and extends over a few micrometers. It thus represents a charge of about 10^{15} cm^{-2}.

This charge must be added to the base charge Q_B, which then becomes at least two orders of magnitude larger than before. As a result, the value of I_S decreases by more than two orders of magnitude. On the other hand, the injected charge Q_F now has a rectangular rather than a triangular distribution (see Fig. 2-1f). The injected charge is thus doubled and the net effect is that, for the same value of v_{BE}, the collector current is two orders of magnitude smaller. Moreover, the base recombination increases, reducing the beta value of that transistor. For these reasons, a buried layer is not used in a substrate pnp transistor.

Example 2-10

A vertical pnp transistor has a circular emitter with a 30 μm diameter. Its dimensions are $d_v = 6$ μm and $A_{EB} = 706$ μm^2. The doping level of the emitter is 2×10^{17} cm^{-3} and of the base (epitaxial layer) 2×10^{15} cm^{-3}. Mobilities of holes and electrons are, respectively, 470 and 500 cm^2/Vs. What is the current at 0.66 V emitter-base voltage? Calculate the base transit time, the betas, ($\tau_{BF} = 1$ μs), and the maximum value of f_T.

Solution. The base charge is $Q_B = 1.2 \times 10^{12}$ cm^{-2}. The value of D_n is derived from the mobility; its value is $D_p = 12.1$ cm^2/s. The value of I_S is then 2.6×10^{-15} A. For a base-emitter voltage of 0.66 V, the current is 320 μA. The base transit time is $\tau_F = 14.8$ ns, resulting in a maximum f_T of 10.7 MHz. The beta, as a result of the recombination, is $\beta_R = 67$. The beta as a result of injection in the emitter is only about $\beta_I = 47$, comparable in size to β_R. The net resulting beta can be obtained from

$$\frac{1}{\beta} = \frac{1}{\beta_R} + \frac{1}{\beta_I} \tag{2-43}$$

which is about 28. While this is a low value, it is nevertheless higher than what we can obtain from lateral devices, as explained next.

2-6-2 Lateral *pnp* Transistors

A lateral *pnp* transistor is shown in Fig. 2-23b. The emitter is circular and completely surrounded by the collector. This is necessary to collect as much of the emitted current as possible and to keep the injection around the emitter as evenly distributed as possible. The base width is denoted by d_l. This parameter is not imposed by technology, as it is for a vertical *npn*, it is in fact a design parameter.

Three *pnp* transistors can be distinguished in the same structure. A vertical *pnp* is present from each *p* region to the substrate and also between the two *p* regions. All three transistors are shown in Fig. 2-23c. The vertical *pnp* from the collector is always off and can thus be left out, but the other vertical *pnp*, from the emitter, is always on. As a result the lateral *pnp* transistor always operates in parallel with a vertical *pnp* transistor, which injects current i_{Cv} in the substrate. This parasitic effect can be minimized by the addition of a buried layer, but it can never be avoided altogether. As previously explained, the buried layer merely decreases the vertical current i_{Cv} by a few orders of magnitude.

Currents will now be calculated.

The i_C versus v_{BE} characteristic is determined by parameter I_S and is given by Eq. (2-5a) after the substitution of D_n by D_p. Note that the injection area A_{EB} is now the perimeter of the emitter. For the circular emitter shown, the emitter is given by $\pi d_E d_p$. The resultant value of I_S is usually of the same order of magnitude as the resultant value for a vertical *npn* transistor.

The beta of the lateral *pnp* is also dominated by base recombination with time constant τ_{BF}. Indeed, its base width d_l is quite large. Moreover, two base current components are present (see Fig. 2-23c) as both the lateral *pnp* transistor and the parasitic vertical *pnp* transistor draw base current. The total base current is given by

$$i_B = i_{Bl} + i_{Bv} = i_{Bl}(1 + K_{vl}) \qquad (2\text{-}44a)$$

with
$$K_{vl} = \frac{i_{Bv}}{i_{Bl}} = \frac{2A_{EBv}d_v}{A_{EBl}d_l} = \frac{d_E d_v}{2d_p d_l} \qquad (2\text{-}44b)$$

and
$$i_{Bl} = \frac{Q_F}{\tau_{BF}} \qquad (2\text{-}44c)$$

A reduction factor K_{vl} has been introduced to account for the parasitic *pnp*. A factor of two is added to take into account that the injected charge Q_F in the vertical transistor is rectangular rather than triangular.

The resultant beta is taken from Eq. (2-9), and is given by

$$\beta = \frac{\tau_{BFp}}{\tau_F} \frac{1}{1 + K_{vl}} \qquad (2\text{-}45)$$

with
$$\tau_F = \frac{d_l^2}{2D_p}$$

and τ_{BFp} is the recombination time constant in the epitaxial region (about 1 μs). The base transit time τ_F is obtained from Eq. (2-6b). It is striking to see that the beta of the lateral transistor is seriously degraded by the presence of the parasitic vertical transistor by means of factor K_{vl}.

The actual base transit time of the lateral *pnp* is not τ_F but rather $\tau_F(1 + K_{vl})$. Indeed, since charge is injected in both the lateral and vertical bases, the total majority carrier charge to be displaced by v_{BE} is the sum of the Q_F charges of both transistors. The diffusion capacitance includes the effect of both charges as does the base transit time. Thus, the f_T also suffers seriously from the presence of the parasitic vertical *pnp*.

Example 2-11

Consider a lateral *pnp* with a round emitter, as pictured in Fig. 1-23b. The dimensions are $d_v = 6$ μm, $d_l = 8$ μm, $d_E = d_C = 30$ μm and $d_p = 3$ μm. The doping level of the emitter is 2×10^{17} cm^{-3} and for the base (epitaxial layer), it is 2×10^{15} cm^{-3}. Mobilities of holes and electrons are, respectively, 470 and 500 cm^2/Vs. What is the current at 0.66 V emitter-base voltage? Calculate the base transit time, the betas ($\tau_{BF} = 1$ μs), and the maximum value of f_T.

Solution. For the lateral *pnp*, $A_{EB} = 283$ μm^2 and for the vertical *pnp*, $A_{EB} = 707$ μm^2. Factor K_{vl} thus equals 3.75.

The lateral base charge $Q_B = 1.6 \times 10^{12}$ cm^{-2} and the vertical base charge is 1.2×10^{12} cm^{-2}. The value of D_p is again $D_p = 12.1$ cm^2/s. The value of I_S is then 7.7×10^{-16} A. For a base-emitter voltage of 0.66 V, the current is 95.5 μA. The values of the injected charge Q_F are, for the lateral *pnp*, 5.5×10^{12} cm^{-2} and, for the vertical *pnp*, 8.3×10^{12} cm^{-2}. The lateral base transit time without parasitic *pnp* would be 26.3 ns, but its actual value is as large as 125 ns. The resulting value of maximum f_T is therefore only 1.3 MHz.

The beta as a result of the recombination is 38 and the presence of the vertical *pnp* reduces this value to a mere 8. The beta as a result of injection in the emitter is approximately 35. This latter beta value is indeed higher and can thus be neglected.

We conclude that the performance of a lateral *pnp* transistor is quite poor. Both beta and f_T values are two orders of magnitude lower compared to the vertical *npn* transistor. Note, however, that reduction of the base width can improve performance. Actually, all parameters in factor K_{vl} can be worked on to improve performance. From the technological point of view, deep p diffusions (d_p) should be used, along with a shallow epitaxial layer (d_v). From the designers point of view, the emitter (d_E) and the base width (d_l) should both be small.

2-6-3   Base Width, Early Voltage, and Punchthrough

From the above analysis, it is clear that the base width d_l should be made as small as possible. However, two phenomena limit this: Early voltage and punchthrough.

The lateral *pnp* is a lateral device, very similar to a MOST. Most considerations concerning Early voltage and punchthrough made for a MOST apply here as well. For instance, the reduction in base width for a MOST is also limited by punchthrough (see Eq. (1-47)). Both the beta (from Eq. (2-45)), and the punchthrough voltage (from Eq. (1-47)), are sketched versus the base width in Fig. 2-24. The smaller the base width, the smaller the punchthrough voltage and the Early voltage, and the smaller the output resistance r_o. For a lateral *pnp* $V_E \approx 6$ V/μm base width d_l is a representative value.

A compromise must be made. Lateral *pnp* devices with large output resistances r_o and large breakdown voltage will thus have low betas.

2-6-4   Base Resistance and Emitter Crowding

For the substrate *pnp* transistor of Fig. 2-23a, previous discussion on the vertical *npn* is equally valid. For the lateral transistor, however, the base contact is located on the collector side (see Fig. 2-23b). As a result, the base resistance is quite high and emitter crowding already occurs at low values of the collector current. A rule of thumb: the maximum collector current that can be allowed before beta and f_T start to fall off is about 2 μA per μm emitter perimeter. For the transistor with an emitter diameter of 30 μm in Example 2-10, the maximum current allowed is about 200 μA. Lateral *pnp* transistors that must deliver mA's will thus take up an exceedingly large area.

2-6-5   Applications with *pnp*'s

The applications of *pnp* transistors are very limited (Gray and Meyer 1984). The substrate transistor is the best *pnp*, but it can only be used as an emitter follower. It is found quite often as such at the end of an output stage.

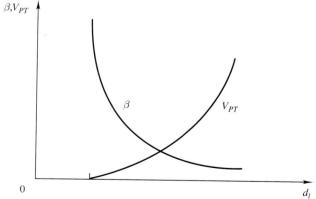

FIGURE 2-24   Beta and punchthrough voltage versus base width for a lateral *pnp*.

On the other hand, the lateral *pnp* has very low values of beta and f_T and yet it cannot be missed in analog IC design because it may be the only complementary device available. Its most important application is a current mirror, shown in Fig. 2-25.

The layout is shown in Fig. 2-25*a*. The collector is subdivided into four regions. Since the current is evenly emitted from the perimeter of the emitter, each collector collects a current that is proportional to its relative fraction of the total circle. Currents i_{C1} and i_{C2} are about equal, whereas i_{C3} is proportionally larger and i_{C4} smaller.

Two symbolic representations of such current mirrors are given in Fig. 2-25*b* and *c* respectively. These representations are equivalent. The transistor structure is connected as a current mirror in Fig. 2-25*d* and *e*. For this purpose, one of the transistors (the first one in the figure) is connected as a diode. Since the base-emitter voltages are all the same, the relative collector currents are determined only by the relative length of their collector regions. In other words, their relative I_S values are scaled to their relative lengths.

Since the current in the diode is now set by the current source I_{CS}, all other currents are defined. The output resistance at each collector is the resistance r_o, determined by the Early effect. Its value is high and thus each transistor acts as a controlled current source. Moreover, the output capacitance is quite low. Indeed, the most important capacitance is normally the collector-substrate capacitance. This does not exist in a lateral *pnp* transistor because the collector is screened from the substrate by the base (epitaxial) region. Thus, the high value of output impedance can be maintained until it reaches high frequencies. Such a current mirror will be used to bias other stages (see Chap. 6).

The main shortcoming of the current mirror of Fig. 2-25*d* is that all the base current $\Sigma i_C / \beta$ flows together with the collector current of the first (diode connected) transistor. This generates an error of the order of magnitude $1/\beta$. Since the β is very low, the error is large. It is better to divide this base current by another *pnp* transistor, as shown in Fig. 2-25*e*. This latter transistor is obviously chosen to be a substrate *pnp* because of its high beta. The error current i_ε then equals the sum of the collector currents, divided by the lateral *pnp* beta and the vertical *pnp* beta. Errors of less than one percent can be obtained in this way. More details on current mirrors will be given in Chap. 4.

Of course, lateral *pnp* transistors of square or rectangular shape can be laid out as well. However, the injection of the current in the corners is not as reproducible. The error in the distribution of the current over the several collectors is larger and the matching between the respective current sources is worse.

Lateral *pnp* transistors are normally available in a bipolar process because the same diffusions are used that were employed for vertical *npn* transistors. However, they are also available in a conventional CMOS process. The well acts as a base and the emitter is the normal source and drain region. For the vertical transistor, the substrate acts as a collector. For the lateral device, both collector and emitter are realized in the source and drain diffusion.

Usually, the vertical device has high beta values but only moderate f_T's, because of its wide base. Again, the lateral device has too low a beta to be useful here. This

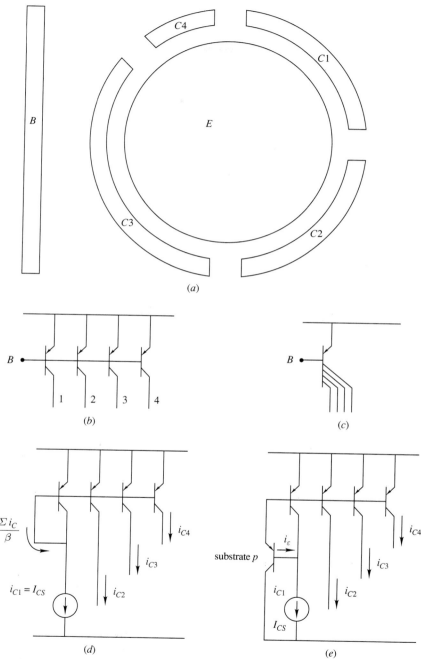

FIGURE 2-25   Use of lateral *pnp* as a controlled current source.

is the result of the parasitic vertical device, no longer inactivated by a buried layer. In addition, the source and drain regions are too shallow to yield useful betas.

2-7 NOISE

The noise sources of a bipolar transistor can be added in its small-signal or hybrid-π model, shown in Fig. 2-26a. One thermal noise source and two shot noise sources are present (Ott 1988; Chang and Sansen 1991).

2-7-1 Input Noise Sources

The thermal noise source is associated with the only ohmic resistance in the model, base resistance r_B. The associated thermal noise source is derived from Eq. (1-57) and given by

$$\overline{dv_B^2} = 4kTr_B df \tag{2-46}$$

Since a bipolar transistor consists of two junctions, it contains two sources of shot noise. There are several ways to represent them and the most appropriate way is shown in Fig. 2-26a. The first shot noise source is associated with the DC base current I_B. It is derived from Eq. (1-58) and given by

$$\overline{di_B^2} = 2qI_B df \tag{2-47}$$

FIGURE 2-26   (a) Noise sources in a bipolar transistor and (b) equivalent noise sources in bipolar transistor.

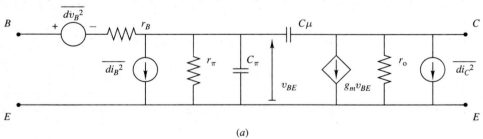

(a)

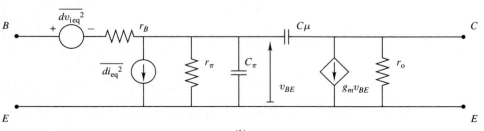

(b)

In the same way, a shot noise source is associated with the collector current I_C. This is given by

$$\overline{di_C^2} = 2qI_C df \tag{2-48}$$

The $1/f$ noise is normally added to the base shot noise, as given by

$$\overline{di_{Bf}^2} = \frac{KF_B I_B}{A_{EB}} \frac{df}{f} \tag{2-49a}$$

in which A_{EB} is the injecting emitter area. Constant KF_B depends on the technology. For a conventional vertical *npn* transistor, an approximate value is $KF_B \approx 10^{-3}$ Acm^2.

In SPICE, a somewhat simpler expression is used (see Table 2-2), given by

$$\overline{di_{Bf}^2} = KF I_B^{AF} \left(\frac{df}{f} \right) \tag{2-49b}$$

Parameter KF plays the same role as KF_B in Eq. (2-49a), except that it does not include the size of the emitter. For each transistor size, a different value of KF is required. Parameter AF is approximately equal to unity and is taken to be unity for practical purposes.

2-7-2 Equivalent Input Noise Sources

In order to compare the magnitude of the noise to that of the incoming input signal, equivalent noise sources are defined. All three noise sources of Fig. 2-26a can be replaced by an equivalent input noise voltage source $\overline{dv_{ieq}^2}$ and an equivalent input noise current source $\overline{di_{ieq}^2}$, shown in Fig. 2-26b.

In order to calculate the *equivalent input noise voltage* $\overline{dv_{ieq}^2}$, the input must be shorted. In practice, a large capacitance can be connected between the input terminal and ground. In this case, the equivalent input noise current is shorted to ground and can thus be left out of the circuit. The output is shorted as well and the output noise current is calculated through that short. This current must be equal to the current in the shorted output of the total circuit of Fig. 2-26a, with shorted input. The resultant equivalent input noise voltage is given by

$$\overline{dv_{ieq}^2} = 4kT \left(r_B + \frac{1/2}{g_m} \right) df \tag{2-50a}$$

where the beta is assumed to be much larger than unity and the base resistance r_B is assumed to be much smaller than r_π.

The base resistance clearly appears in this expression. It is followed by a term that originates from the collector shot noise and it dominates for low collector currents. It is very similar to the term in g_m in the equivalent input noise voltage of a MOST (see Eq. (1-66)). The difference between two-thirds and one-half is quasi-negligible. It can be concluded for low currents that the equivalent input noise voltage of a MOST and a bipolar transistor are nearly the same and inversely proportional to g_m.

At currents larger than $kT/2qr_B$, the base resistance limits the noise performance. It is the lowest value of equivalent input noise voltage that can be achieved with a bipolar transistor.

The *equivalent input noise current* can be calculated by leaving the base open. The equivalent input noise voltage source can then be left out. Equation of the currents through the shorted outputs of both configurations of Fig. 2-26b yields

$$\overline{di_{ieq}^2} = 2q \left(I_B + \frac{K F_B I_B}{A_{EB} f} + \frac{I_C}{|\beta(j\omega)|^2} \right) df \qquad (2\text{-}50b)$$

The term $I_C/|\beta(j\omega)|^2$ contains the frequency dependent beta of that transistor. The beta starts decreasing at frequency f_β or f_T/β. At high frequencies, this term becomes the most important term but at low frequencies the base current I_B is the dominant noise source.

With two noise sources, namely, the equivalent input noise voltage source $\overline{dv_{ieq}^2}$ and the equivalent input noise current source $\overline{di_{ieq}^2}$ the question of which source is dominant depends on the value of the source resistance R_S used. For small source resistance, the input is nearly shorted and the equivalent input noise voltage source is dominant. If the transistor is current driven, then the equivalent input noise current source is dominant.

However, several reasons have already been mentioned to prefer a voltage drive for a bipolar transistor. As a result, the equivalent input noise voltage source $\overline{dv_{ieq}^2}$ is usually the most important. The influence of R_S is better expressed by means of the noise figure.

2-7-3 Noise Figure

For an arbitrary source resistance R_S, the noise figure NF compares the combined noise of the amplifier and the source resistance to the noise of the source resistance alone. It is defined as the ratio of the signal-to-noise ratio before the amplifier to the same ratio after the amplifier. This indicates how far the signal-to-noise ratio of the source S has been degraded by the addition of the amplifier A.

The noise figure is given by

$$NF = \frac{(S/N)_S + (S/N)_A}{(S/N)_S} = \frac{N_S + N_A}{N_S} = 1 + \frac{N_A}{N_S} \qquad (2\text{-}51a)$$

Note that all symbols represent powers. They must all be taken either at the input terminal or at the output terminal.

The noise power of the amplifier N_A is expressed in terms of the equivalent input signal noise sources. The resultant expression of the noise figure NF is given by

$$NF = 1 + \frac{\overline{dv_{ieq}^2} + R_S^2\overline{di_{ieq}^2}}{4kTR_Sdf} \tag{2-51b}$$

The noise figure is usually expressed in dB. Since it only contains powers, it is obtained by taking $10 \cdot \log(NF)$.

2-7-4   Optimum R_S

The noise figure is obviously a function of the source resistance. For a voltage drive, $\overline{dv_{ieq}^2}$ dominates and the noise figure is inversely proportional to that source resistance. For a current drive, $\overline{di_{ieq}^2}$ dominates and NF increase with R_S. This is shown in Fig. 2-27.

A minimum occurs where both terms of the numerator in Eq. (2-51b) are equal (i.e., the derivative of NF to R_S is zero). The optimum value of the source resistance is given by

$$R_{Sopt} = \sqrt{\frac{\overline{dv_{ieq}^2}}{\overline{di_{ieq}^2}}} \tag{2-52}$$

FIGURE 2-27   Noise figure of bipolar transistor with $r_B = 100\ \Omega$ and $\beta = 100$, and FET at 10 μA.

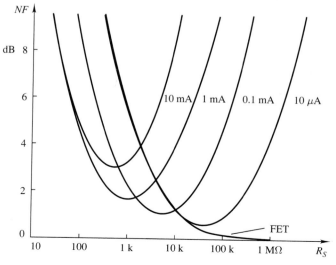

At low currents (lower than $kT/2qr_B$), substitution of the equivalent input noise sources by Eq. (2-50) yields $R_{Soptlo} = \sqrt{\beta}/g_m$. For large currents, source resistance is given by $R_{Sopthi} = \sqrt{2r_\pi r_B}$. It equals R_{Soptlo} multiplied by $\sqrt{2g_m r_B}$.

Note that the optimum value of source resistance depends on the current. The larger the current, the lower the optimum source resistance, and the higher the noise figure. This is illustrated clearly in Fig. 2-27.

In the same figure, the noise figure is sketched for a MOST, with the same transconductance g_m as a bipolar transistor at 10 μA. Since a MOST does not exhibit any equivalent input current noise, no minimum occurs. The noise figure is inversely proportional to the source resistance. Thus, for large source resistances, a FET is always a better choice than a bipolar transistor.

This in fact is one of the pecularities of the noise figure. Since the noise of the amplifier is compared to the noise of the source resistance, the noise figure improves as the source resistance becomes larger. It appears as if the amplifier is better the larger the source resistance. This is why the noise figure is used only in systems with a standardized source resistance. Examples are a cable TV with $R_S = 50\ \Omega$ and a telephony with $R_S = 600\ \Omega$. In all other applications, equivalent input noise sources are better used to describe the noise behavior of a circuit.

2-7-5   Optimum *NF*

Optimum *NF* is the smallest noise figure that can be reached with a bipolar transistor at large currents (see Fig. 2-27). It is found by substitution of R_{Sopthi} in Eq. (2-51*b*). This yields

$$NF_{\text{opthi}} = 1 + \frac{r_B}{R_S} = 1 + \sqrt{\frac{2g_m r_B}{\beta}} = 1 + \sqrt{\frac{2r_B}{r_\pi}} \tag{2-53}$$

This value is clearly limited by the base resistance, repeated several times in the above equation. Transistors with very low base resistance are required to achieve ultimate noise performance.

2-7-6   Optimum *I_C*

For a given value of source resistance, the optimum collector current can be calculated as well. It is obtained by solving I_C out of Eq. (2-52) with Eq. (2-50*a*). This yields a quadratic equation out of which I_{Copt} can be calculated. It is given by

$$I_{Copt} = I_{Co}\left(1 + \sqrt{1 + \frac{kT/q}{r_B I_{Co}}}\right) \tag{2-54}$$

with

$$I_{Co} = \frac{\beta r_B kT/q}{R_S^2}$$

Example 2-12

Take a bipolar transistor with $\beta = 100$ and $r_B = 200 \; \Omega$. The transition current $kT/2qr_B$ is 64.6 μA. Calculate the values of the equivalent input noise sources at a current of 0.5 mA, followed by the optimum source resistance and the noise figure. Finally, calculate the noise figure for a source resistance R_S of 600 Ω and the optimum collector current.

Solution. At that current, $g_m = 19.3$ mS and $r_\pi = 5.17$ kΩ . The equivalent input noise voltage $\overline{dv_{ieq}^2}$ is obtained from Eq. (2-50a) and equals $\overline{dv_{ieq}^2} = 3.7 \times 10^{-18}$ V^2/Hz or $\overline{dv_{ieq}} = 1.93$ nV$_{\text{RMS}}/\sqrt{\text{Hz}}$. The equivalent input noise current (without $1/f$ noise) is obtained from Eq. (2-50b) and equals $\overline{di_{ieq}^2} = 1.610^{-24}$ A^2/Hz or $\overline{di_{ieq}} = 1.26$ pA$_{\text{RMS}}/\sqrt{\text{Hz}}$. The optimum source resistance is then given by Eq. (2-152) and is 1.53 kΩ. The noise figure is then 1.278 kΩ or 5.65 dB. For a source resistance of $R_S = 600 \; \Omega$, however, the noise figure is larger. It is 1.43 kΩ or 8.3 dB. The optimum collector current would be 2.9 mA.

2-8 DESIGN EXAMPLE

Lay out a vertical *npn* with two base contacts using the dimensions of the emitter and base contacts of Fig. 2-2b, vertical *npn* transistors, and a lateral and a substrate *pnp* transistor.

All SPICE parameters must be calculated at $V_{BE} = 0$ V (for $V_{CE} = 5$ V) and in the biasing point of 0.16 mA (for $V_{BE} = 0.72$ V). Also, the hybrid-π model must be derived and f_β, f_T, and f_B calculated.

The results are collected in Table 2-5. The reader should repeat this design example for other processing conditions in order to gain familiarity with such calculations.

2-9 OTHER COMPONENTS

In addition to MOSTs, JFETs, and bipolar transistors, integrated circuits use other components as well. The most common ones are resistors and capacitors. Inductors have also been used but they fail to realize high quality factors and will therefore be discussed only briefly.

In bipolar technology, resistors of various types are commonly available but it is difficult to find a good capacitor. The opposite is true for CMOS technology in that capacitors of high precision are available but the only resistors available have low resistivity. A CMOS process to which resistors with high resistivity have been added is often called an analog CMOS process. These components are now described in detail.

2-9-1 Base Diffusion Resistors

Resistors are characterized by their sheet resistivity (in $\Omega/\square$). For example, the sheet resistivity of a base diffusion in a conventional bipolar process is about $\rho_B = 150 \; \Omega/\square$.

TABLE 2-5   VALUES OF BIPOLAR TRANSISTOR PARAMETERS WITH ONE ($B1$) AND TWO ($B2$) BASE CONTACTS IN FORWARD OPERATION (SEC. 2-8)

Input data	Parameter	Eq. or Table No.	$B1$	$B2$	Dimension
$A_{EB} = 30 \times 15 \ \mu m^2$	IS	(2-5b)	0.13	0.13	fA
	BF	(2-7)	342	342	
	IKF	(2-38a)	92	92	mA
See Example 2-7	RB	(2-32)	339	146	Ω
	RBM		50	25	Ω
	RE		0.2	0.2	Ω
See Example 2-8	RC(1/3)	(2-33)	208	208	Ω
	TF	(2-6b)	0.247	0.247	ns
See Fig. 2-1	$VJE = \phi_{jEB}$	(2-1a)	0.95	0.95	V
	$C_{JE}(0)$	T. 2-4	134	134	nF/cm²
$A_{EB} = 30 \times 15 \ \mu m^2$	$CJE = C_{JEt}(0)$		0.60	0.60	pF
	$C_{JEt}(0.72)$		1.22	1.22	pF
	$VJC = \phi_{jCB}$	(2-1a)	0.73	0.73	V
	$C_{JC}(0)$	T. 2-4	49	49	nF/cm²
$A_{BC} = 50 \times 50 \ \mu m^2$	$CJC = C_{JCt}(0)$		1.235		pF
	$C_{JCt}(-5)$		0.44		pF
$A_{BC} = 70 \times 50 \ \mu m^2$	$CJC = C_{JCt}(0)$			1.715	pF
	$C_{JCt}(-5)$			0.61	pF
Only BL	$VJS = \phi_{jCB}$	(2-1a)	0.85	0.85	V
	$C_{JSt}(0)$	T. 2-4	31.5	31.5	nF/cm²
$A_{BLS} = 80 \times 50 \ \mu m^2$	$CJS = C_{JSt}(0)$		1.26		pF
	$C_{JSt}(-5)$		0.48		pF
$A_{BLS} = 100 \times 50 \ \mu m^2$	$CJS = C_{JSt}(0)$			1.57	pF
	$C_{JSt}(-5)$			0.6	pF
	V_E	(2-18)	146	146	V
	KF	(2-49b)	0.22	0.22	fA
At $V_{BE} = 0.72$ V	I_C	(2-5a)	162	162	μA
	g_m	(2-15)	6.26	6.26	mS
	r_π	(2-16)	54.6	54.6	kΩ
	r_o	(2-17b)	901	901	kΩ
	C_D	(2-20)	1.55	1.55	pF
	$r_C C_\mu$		91	127	ps
	f_T	(2-21c)	258	234	MHz
	f_β	(2-21b)	0.75	0.68	MHz
	f_B	(2-22b)	125	220	MHz
	I_{CfT}	(2-22d)	174	196	μA

A resistor that uses this layer is shown in Fig. 2-28. Its resistance is approximately given by

$$R_B = \rho_B \frac{L}{W} \tag{2-55}$$

In Fig. 2-28, the resistor counts about five squares. Its value is thus $5 \times 150 = 750 \ \Omega$.

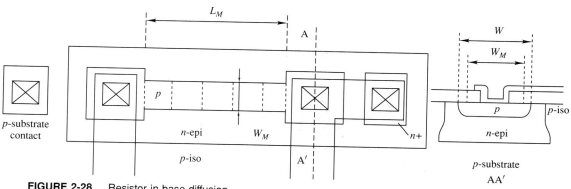

FIGURE 2-28 Resistor in base diffusion.

Note that several sources of inaccuracy are present. First, base diffusion resistivity is known only within, at best, 10 percent accuracy. A resistor with absolute accuracy is hard to realize.

Second, only the mask dimensions are known. The actual width W is larger than W_M because of underdiffusion (which is about 0.8 times the junction depth). The larger the width of the mask, the less relative the error.

The exact length L is not known either, because of the contact areas. About half a square resistance must be added to take the contact areas into account (Glaser and Subak-Sharpe 1977).

Finally, note that the resistor is embedded in an n-epi well for isolation. The well must be connected to the positive power supply or to the most positive side of the resistor, as shown in Fig. 2-28. In this way, reverse biasing is always achieved.

2-9-2 Other Resistors

Resistance can be realized in all resistive layers of a bipolar process. Various resistors are listed in Table 2-6. Small resistors can be more easily realized in the emitter diffusion layer. Large resistors can be realized with the *pinch-resistor* structure in Fig. 2-29. It uses the base diffusion underneath the emitter, which results in much larger resistivity values.

Actually, such a structure is a JFET: the p channel corresponds with the base and the top gate corresponds with the emitter. The cross section and layout are similar to their counterparts in a bipolar transistor. The difference is that the gate (emitter) laterally overlaps the p-region (base). Also, the gate and source are normally connected together and the drain voltage is low, and thus the JFET operates in the linear region. Sheet resistances of 3 to 5 kΩ/$\square$ are normally obtained.

The absolute accuracy of a pinch-resistor is much less, as is its breakdown voltage (which is actually the emitter-base breakdown voltage, about 7 V). The resistor of Fig. 2-29 corresponds with about 9 kΩ. This would require 60 squares in a base diffusion layer. This can be done in a serpentine layout, shown in Fig. 2-30. Additional

TABLE 2-6   RESISTORS

Process	Type	$\rho\square$ $\Omega/\square$	absolute accuracy percent	temperature coefficient percent/°C	voltage coefficient percent/V	breakdown voltage V
Bipolar	base diffusion	150	10	0.12	2	50
	emitter diffusion	10	20	0.02	0.5	7
	pinch resistance	5 k	40	0.33	5	7
	epi layer	1 k	10	0.3	1	60
	aluminum	50 m	20	0.01	0.02	90
	ion-implantation	2 k	1	0.02	0.2	20
	ion-implantation	200	0.3	0.02	0.05	20
CMOS	S/D diffusion	20-50	20	0.2	0.5	20
	well	2.5 k	10	0.3	1	20
	poly gate	50	20	0.2	0.05	40
	poly resistance	1.5 k	1	0.05	0.02	20
	aluminum	50 m	20	0.01	0.02	90
Thin film	NiCr(Ta)	200	1	0.005	0.005	90
	aluminum	50 m	20	0.01	0.02	90

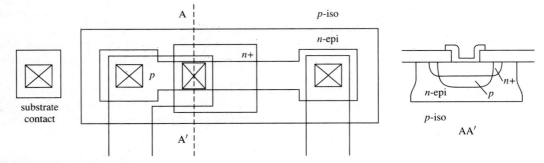

FIGURE 2-29   Pinch-resistor.

errors then occur in the corners, which add about 0.6 squares. Note that in this layout, the substrate of the resistor (the epi-layer) is connected to the positive power supply.

The epitaxial layer itself can be used as well, as can the aluminum metallization for very small resistors.

In some bipolar processes, additional ion-implants are available as resistances. This provides very attractive resistors because of their high resistivity and high absolute accuracy.

2-9-3   Temperature Coefficient

Most resistors of Table 2-6 are realized in semiconducting material. Thus, the resistance depends on temperature as does the mobility (see App. 2-1). The higher the

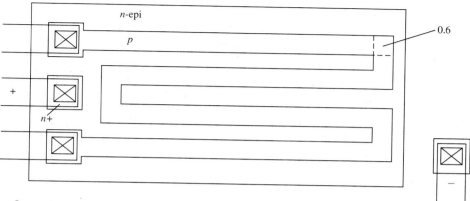

FIGURE 2-30   Serpentine resistor.

resistivity, the higher the temperature coefficient (see Table 2-6). The ion-implanted resistor is an exception because of its special annealing step. In this case, the temperature coefficient very much depends on the actual annealing performed. The values of Table 2-6 are thus only approximate. The exact values must be obtained from the manufacturer. Moreover, the metal resistor has a very low temperature coefficient.

2-9-4 Voltage Coefficient

Resistors that are isolated from their substrate by means of a depletion layer have a large voltage coefficient. In this sense they behave as JFETs with a large pinchoff voltage (and hence with small transconductance or voltage sensitivity). Typical values are given in Table 2-6.

2-9-5 Frequency Dependence

For each resistor, a parallel capacitance is associated with its substrate. As a result, a resistor forms a lowpass filter. The cutoff frequency can be obtained from distributed line considerations (Glaser and Subak-Sharpe 1977) and is approximately given by

$$f_{RC} = \frac{2.43}{2\pi R_R C_R (L/W)^2} \tag{2-56}$$

in which R_R is the sheet resistance ($\Omega/\square$), C_R is the capacitance (per $\square$) and L/W is the number of squares. In order to reach a high cutoff frequency, the number of squares must be small.

Example 2-13

What is the cutoff frequency for a 1 kΩ resistor, realized in p-base diffusion with $R_R = 130\ \Omega/\square$ and $C_R = 0.2$ pF/$\square$. Calculate the frequency at which the parasitic capacitance causes a phase shift of 10° with respect to low frequencies.

Solution. For 1 kΩ, 8 squares are needed. As a result, $f_{RC} = 15$ GHz/$(L/W)^2$ or 15 GHz/64 = 230 MHz. A phase shift of 10° is reached at the frequency f_{10} where $tg(10°) = f_{10}/f_{RC}$ or at about 40 MHz.

2-9-6 Absolute and Relative Accuracy

To realize a resistor with absolute accuracy is difficult, but layout tricks can be applied to reduce the uncertainties. For example, the contact and corner areas can be covered with $p+$ islands. Nevertheless, good design must never be based on absolute values. Relative values such as resistor ratios must be used. The relative errors obtained are about one-tenth of the absolute accuracies given in Table 2-6. Obviously, the larger the dimensions, the better the relative accuracy that can be achieved.

This is illustrated in Fig. 2-31 for both diffused (base diffusion: 150 $\Omega/\square$) resistors. The relative accuracy improves more or less proportionally to the resistor width. Moreover, the relative error is approximately a factor of three smaller for ion-implanted devices than for diffused ones. In order to reach a relative error of 0.1 percent, ion-implanted resistances must be taken with about 40 μm width.

Many other layout tricks (see Sec. 6-7) can be applied to improve matching.

FIGURE 2-31   Matching of resistors with width W.

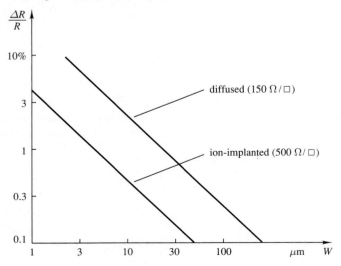

2-9-7 Resistors in a CMOS Process

In a conventional n-well CMOS process, several resistances are available. They are the source/drain resistance, the polysilicon gate and the n-well region. However, none of these are intended to be used as a resistor. The control on the accuracy of the resistivity is very poor (see Table 2-6). An analog CMOS process quite often includes an additional polysilicon resistor with excellent properties. Its temperature and voltage coefficient are then low as well.

2-9-8 Thin Film Resistors

On top of a chip, a thin-film resistor can be easily deposited. Actually, the aluminium metallization layer is such a resistor, albeit with very low resistivity. A higher resistivity is obtained with NiCr or Ta, which yield values from 100 to 4 k $\Omega/\square$. The control on its resistivity is excellent and so are its temperature and voltage coefficient. This is why they are used for very high precision circuits and for circuits at very high frequencies.

2-9-9 Capacitors

In a bipolar process, junction capacitance is available at each junction. The most useful is the collector-base junction capacitance (see Table 2-7), shown in Fig. 2-32. It is not very accurate, however, and it is very voltage dependent (see Table 1-5). This applies to all other junction capacitances as well.

Note that the capacitance on the bottom side is always connected by a parasitic capacitance C_p to the substrate. This capacitance is always a fixed fraction of the useful capacitance and cannot be avoided.

Much more accuracy can be obtained with a MOS capacitance in a CMOS process (see Fig. 2-33). Not only is its value larger, but its accuracy is much higher, especially for the poly-to-poly capacitance. Also, the temperature and voltage coefficients are quasi-nihil. Its parasitic capacitance from the bottom plate to ground is decreased to

TABLE 2-7   CAPACITORS

Process	Type	C nF/cm^2	absolute accuracy percent	temperature coefficient percent/$^\circ$C	voltage coefficient percent V	breakdown voltage V
Bipolar	C_{CB}	16	10	0.02	2	50
	C_{EB}	50	10	0.02	1	7
	C_{CS}	8	20	0.01	0.5	60
CMOS	$C_{ox}(50\ \text{nm})$	70	5	0.002	0.005	40
	$C_{m,poly}$	12	10	0.002	0.005	40
	$C_{poly,poly}$	56	2	0.002	0.005	40
	$C_{poly,substrate}$	6.5	10	0.01	0.05	20
	$C_{m,substrate}$	5.2	10	0.01	0.05	20
	$C_{poly,substrate}$	6.5	10	0.01	0.05	20

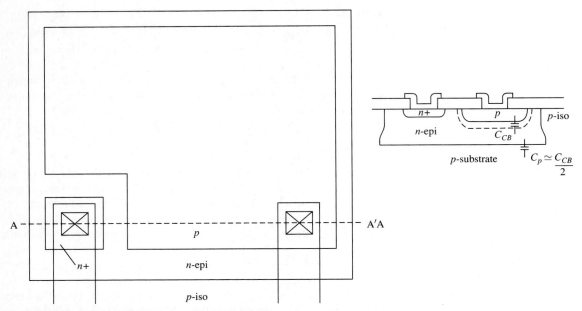

FIGURE 2-32   Collector-base junction capacitance.

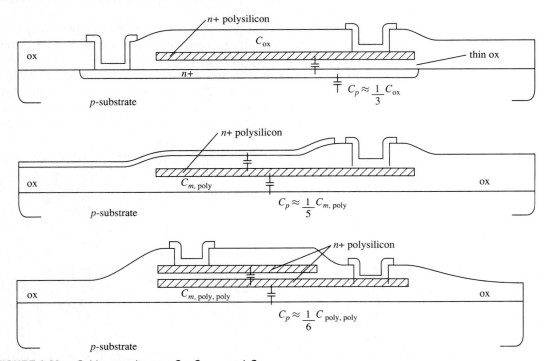

FIGURE 2-33   Oxide capacitances C_{ox}, $C_{m,poly}$ and $C_{poly,poly}$.

one-sixth. Its relative error or matching is about 0.2 percent, with capacitor sizes of only 30 × 30 μm. It improves with the square root of the capacitor side ratio (see Fig. 2-34).

Care must be taken to avoid the creation of a parasitic MOST operation under the capacitance areas. This is the reason why an $n+$ layer is present under the oxide capacitance C_{ox} (see Fig. 2-33). Additional biasing tricks may be necessary in some cases.

For optimum matching, all capacitors must have equal size and an equal area to perimeter ratio (see Sec. 6-7). This is illustrated in Fig. 2-35 for a capacitance ratio of $7/2 = 3.5$. Note that tabs are used to either connect or disconnect the unit capacitances. They are always present, however, to make sure that each unit capacitance is exactly the same and constantly presents the same parasitic capacitance.

2-9-10 Inductors

All structures discussed until now have been planar, i.e., two-dimensional. In order to realize coils, which are inherently three-dimensional, a thick metal layer is required. Also, the coil wires or layers must be closely paced (small d_L in Fig. 2-36a). In this way, inductors can be realized of the order of magnitude of a few tens of nH's (Glaser and Subak-Sharpe 1977).

The main problem is the quality factor Q. The equivalent circuit of such a coil is shown in Fig. 2-36b. A parasitic parallel capacitance C_p causes self-resonance. Moreover, the parasitic impedances to the substrate consist of a series capacitance C_S in series with a resistance due to the substrate R_s. This resistance prevents reaching Q factors much higher than 10 (since $Q = L\omega/R$). Thus, only low-Q filters can be realized.

FIGURE 2-34   Matching of capacitors with side S.

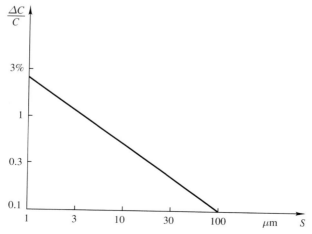

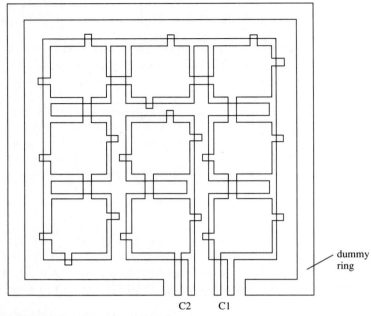

FIGURE 2-35   Example of matched C ratio of 3.5.

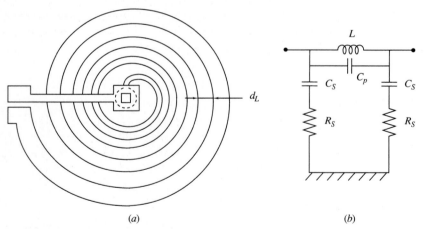

(a)   (b)

FIGURE 2-36   (a) Spiral inductor; (b) model.

2-10 COMPARISON BETWEEN MOSTS AND BIPOLAR TRANSISTORS

The technology of the future is probably BICMOS, which combines both bipolar and CMOS technologies on the same chip. Most companies offer such processes. A good example of such BICMOS technology is shown in Fig. 2-37. It is the LinBICMOS

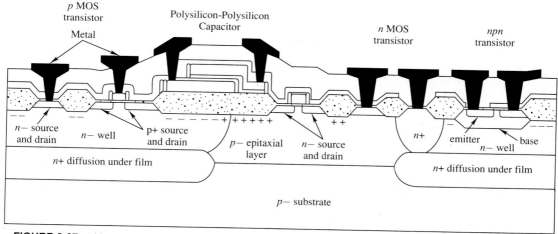

FIGURE 2-37   Linear BICMOS process.

process of Texas Instruments. Besides conventional *n*MOS, *p*MOS, and vertical *npn* transistors, it also offers poly-poly capacitors for linear applications. Other companies use twin-tub isolation or trench isolation for their BICMOS processes. The exact process is of no importance here. It is important only to realize that both CMOS and bipolar technologies are available on the same chip, and hence it is important for a designer to understand which transistor to use in which position. For this purpose, a comparison is now given between a MOST and a bipolar transistor from the designers point of view. We will look at DC and AC characteristics, noise, and at design difficulties. The results are summarized in Table 2-8. DC aspects will be discussed first.

2-10-1 Input Current

Both devices carry current under control of a gate (base) voltage. However, the gate does not draw current whereas the base does. The input base current is the collector current divided by beta. This is true for both DC and AC currents. As a result, the input resistance of a bipolar transistor is small compared to that of a MOST.

2-10-2 DC Saturation Voltage

In saturation, each device behaves as a voltage-controlled current source. The minimum output voltage has been denoted by $V_{DS\text{sat}}$ ($V_{CE\text{sat}}$). This voltage is only a few times kT/q for a bipolar transistor. For a MOST, it depends on the size W/L and current I_{DS} and in first-order it is given by

$$V_{DS\text{sat}} = V_{GS} - V_T = \sqrt{\frac{I_{DS}}{K'(W/L)}} \qquad (2\text{-}57)$$

TABLE 2-8 COMPARISON OF MOSTS AND BIPOLAR TRANSISTORS

	Specification		MOST	Bipolar transistor
1.	I_{IN}		0	I_C/β
	R_{IN}		∞	$r_\pi + r_B$
2.	V_{DSsat}		$V_{GS} - V_T = \sqrt{\dfrac{I_{DS}}{K'W/L}}$	few kT/q
3.	$\dfrac{g_m}{I}$	wi	$\dfrac{1}{nkT/q}$	$\dfrac{1}{kT/q}$
		si	$\dfrac{2}{V_{GS} - V_T}$	$\dfrac{1}{kT/q}$
		vs	$\dfrac{1}{V_{GS} - V_T}$	$\dfrac{1}{kT/q}$
4.	Design planning		$\dfrac{W}{L}, V_{GS} - V_T$	kT/q
5.	I-range		2 decades	5 decades
6.	Max f_T	low I	C_{GS}, C_{GD}	C_{jEt}, C_μ
		high I	v_{sat}/L_{eff}	v_{sat}/W_B
7.	Noise	Therm.	$4kT\left(\dfrac{2/3}{g_m} + R_G\right)$	$4kT\left(\dfrac{1/2}{g_m} + R_B\right)$
		1/f	10×	
	Offset		10×	

This voltage can be made quite small provided the size W/L is quite large (see Fig. 2-38). In this instance, a bipolar transistor is certainly smaller in area than a MOST.

Given such a large W/L, the MOST is already operating close to the weak inversion region. This point is reached when the value of W is larger than W_{wi}, given by

$$W_{wi} \approx \frac{LI_{DS}}{K'(kT/q)^2} \qquad (2\text{-}58)$$

At this value of W, the value of V_{Dsat} simply becomes kT/q.

As an example, for $I_{DS} = 0.1$ mA, $K' = 30$ μA/V^2 and $L = 3$ μm, $W_{wi} = 15$ cm, at which value $V_{DSsat} = 26$ mV. For $V_{DSsat} = 260$ mV, the value of W can be one hundred times smaller, or about 150 μm ($W/L = 50$).

It can thus be concluded that the range of values of V_{DS} in which a MOST is in saturation can be increased by increasing W. This region is always at its maximum range for a bipolar transistor.

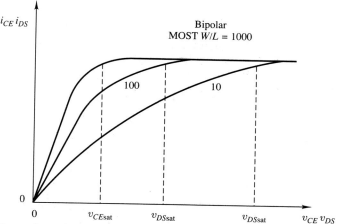

FIGURE 2-38   Comparison of saturation voltages.

2-10-3   Transconductance-Current Ratio

This ratio g_m/I_{DS} has been discussed in detail for a MOST and the ratios for both transistors are repeated in Fig. 2-39. The maximum value is always reached for a bipolar transistor where it is $(kT/q)^{-1}$. For a MOST, it is only $(nkT/q)^{-1}$, but this value is only reached at very small currents, i.e., in weak inversion. At higher currents, this ratio decreases with the square root of the current.

Thus, at intermediate currents, the bipolar transistor offers a better current drive capability. Less input voltage is required to drive a larger output current.

FIGURE 2-39 g_m/I for bipolar transistor and MOST.

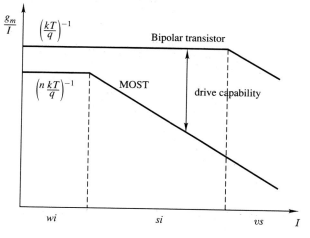

2-10-4   Design Planning

A bipolar transistor is much easier to include in a design plan because it has less parameters to consider. In Fig. 2-40, these parameters are displayed. For a bipolar transistor, the g_m and current I_{CE} are linked through kT/q, which is a constant. For a MOST, the g_m and current I_{CE} are linked through two parameters, W/L and $V_{GS} - V_T$, which can both be changed by the designer. The design planning for a MOST is thus much more complicated as it requires a judicious planning stage as part of the design task.

2-10-5   Current Range

A bipolar transistor exhibits an exponential i_{CE} versus v_{BE} characteristic, that can be maintained over many decades. For example, this is the case from 0.1 nA to 1 mA, which is 7 decades. If we want to stay away from these limiting currents by a factor of ten, we still have 5 decades left.

In a MOST, it is important to stay in strong inversion for reasons of current predictability. The limiting currents of the weak-inversion and the velocity-saturation region are only about four decades apart. Indeed, both currents I_{DSws} and I_{DSvs} are given in Table 1-4. Their ratio is approximately

$$\frac{I_{DSvs}}{I_{DSws}} = \left(\frac{2Lv_{\text{sat}}}{\mu kT/q}\right)^2 \tag{2-59}$$

which is only about four decades. If we want to stay away from these limiting currents by a factor of ten, we have only about 2 decades left, which is much less than with a bipolar transistor. Also note that the smaller L becomes, the less operating region is left.

2-10-6   Maximum Frequency of Operation

The maximum frequency of operation is f_T, but it could also be the unity-gain frequency of an amplifier. Let us now assume f_T, as amplifiers will be discussed later.

FIGURE 2-40   Relationship between design variables.

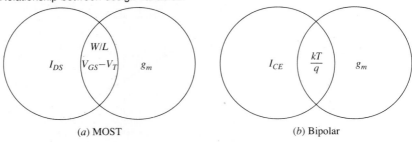

(a) MOST   (b) Bipolar

At low currents, this frequency is determined by gate oxide for a MOST and by junction capacitances for a bipolar transistor. The MOST can be made smaller in area and therefore has less capacitance and its f_T would then be larger at low currents.

At high currents, the channel (base) transit time τ_F is given by

$$\tau_F = \frac{L_{\text{efft}}}{v_{\text{sat}}} \text{ or } \frac{W_B}{v_{\text{sat}}} \tag{2-60}$$

which is likely to be smaller for a bipolar transistor than for a MOST because the vertical W_B is easier to make smaller than the lateral L_{eff}. For 0.1 μm, this time constant is about 1 ps and the corresponding maximum frequency is about 160 GHz.

This maximum frequency f_T can be plotted versus current as shown in Fig. 2-41. At some current I_{MB}, the bipolar transistor takes over in f_T. This current is normally about 10 to 100 μA.

2-10-7   Noise

For thermal noise, both devices have about the same expression (see Table 2-8). This is especially the case at low currents. At higher currents, the bipolar transistor has a base resistor but the MOST has a gate resistor and thus they are equivalent.

The $1/f$ noise, on the other hand, is about ten times worse for a MOST, depending, of course, on the area. The MOST can be made larger to compensate for this but the capacitances would then increase and the maximum frequency would go down. For equal areas, the bipolar transistor performs better.

Note that a JFET performs as well in this respect as a bipolar transistor. It is not in Table 2-8 because it is an addition to a conventional process.

FIGURE 2-41   Maximum frequency versus current.

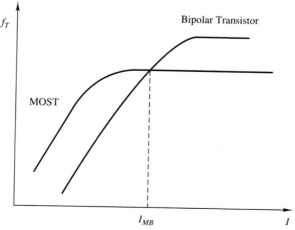

Finally, note that offset is added in the table as well and is also ten times worse for a MOST as for a bipolar transistor. Offset is actually the difference between the gate (base) voltage between two "equal" devices. The devices are actually not quite equal, the difference being expressed by their offset. This is explained in greater detail in Chap. 6.

This concludes our comparison of MOST and bipolar transistor devices. It is clear that neither device on its own can fully satisfy the range of each priority specification, and thus other devices may have to be selected. This is a challenge that is currently met only by BICMOS and is thus certainly a challenge for designers in the future.

SUMMARY

In this chapter, the model of a bipolar transistor has been derived. Most of the emphasis was on the i_{CE} versus v_{BE} characteristics, the transconductance, the capacitances, and the noise. First-order expressions were given priority in order for hand calculations to be used. On the other hand, a full list of the parameters to be used in SPICE is provided. The temperature effects are given in the appendix.

Also, other passive components were discussed, such as resistors, capacitors, and, briefly inductors. These components are necessary to build circuits of larger complexity and better linearity.

This chapter concluded with a short comparison of the capabilities of a MOST versus a bipolar transistor. In view of the upcoming BICMOS processes, a designer must have a clear insight into the advantages of both.

Before we engage in the analysis and design of elementary circuits, a chapter is devoted to the analysis techniques of circuits, both in time and in frequency.

EXERCISES

2-1 Plot both betas β_{IE} and β_{RB} versus base width W_B for values of the base width from 0.1 μm to 10 μm. Use the missing data from Table 2-1 ($\tau_{BF} = 1$ μs). Which beta is dominant in each region?

2-2 Plot the DC and AC beta versus current for a bipolar transistor with $\beta_m = 400$ and $v_E = 0.35$. C_1 is such that the beta drops to 1/2 at $I_C = 1$ nA; Take a log-log plot for the current from 0.1 nA to 1 A. Repeat for $v_C = 4$ and C_2 such that the beta drops to 1/2 at $I_C = 0.1$ A.

2-3 A plot of i_C and i_B versus v_{BE} is given in Fig. EX2-3. Extract the values of β_m, C_1, and v_E.

2-4 Plot the small-signal parameters g_m, r_π, r_o, and C_D versus collector current from 1 μA to 0.1 A. Use bilogarithmic scales.

2-5 Plot the small-signal parameters f_β, f_B, and f_T versus collector current from 1 μA to 10 mA. Other parameters are $\beta = 100$, $\tau_F = 0.25$ ns, $C_{jEt} = 5$ pF, $C_\mu = 1$ pF, $r_B = 100$ Ω, and $r_C = 0$. Use bilogarithmic scales.

2-6 Repeat Exercise 2-5 with $\beta = 50$, $\tau_F = 0.10$ ns, $C_{jEt} = 0.08$ pF, and $C_\mu = 0.04$ pF.

2-7 Develop a design procedure for a single-transistor amplifier with a resistive load R if $V_{OUTDC} = 2$ V. The possible variables are A_v, R, g_m, and I_{CE}. We want to minimized I_{CE}.

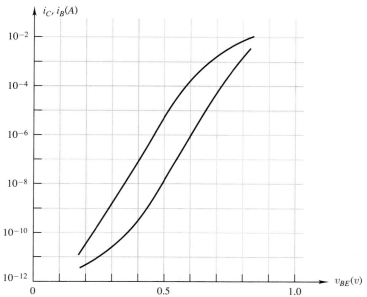

FIGURE EX2-3   Plot of currents i_C and i_B versus v_{BE} (see Exercise 2-3).

2-8 Give the pole-zero position and Bode diagrams of the output impedance of an emitter follower with $\beta = 100$, $r_B = 100\ \Omega$, $R_S = 10\ k\Omega$, $\tau_F = 0.25$ ns, $C_{jEt} + C_\mu = 6$ pF with I_{CE} as a variable.

2-9 Take an emitter follower with $\beta = 100$, $r_B = 100\ \Omega$, $\tau_F = 0.25$ ns, $C_{jEt} + C_\mu = 6$ pF at $I_C = 0.2$ mA. Give the pole-zero position plot and the corresponding Bode diagram for the source resistor R_S as a variable.

2-10 Plot r_B and C_{jEt} and the product $r_B C_{jEt}$ versus n, which is the number of emitter stripes for $n = 1, \ldots, 10$. For $n = 1$, there is one emitter stripe and 2 base contact stripes; for $n = 2$, there are 2 emitter stripes and 3 base contact stripes, etc. The stripes are all 100 μm long, i.e., $b_B = b_E = 100$ μm (Fig. 2-16). Use also $h_B = h_{BE} = h_E = 10$ μm and take the necessary capacitance data from Table 2-5.

2-11 Repeat the calculations of Table 2-5 for the bipolar transistor of Fig. 2-2 but with a base depth of $x_B = 1.5$ μm (see Table 2-1). What are the base transit time τ_F and $f_{T\,max}$ now?

2-12 Derive a vertical *pnp* transistor from the *npn* transistor of Fig. 2-2b, by simple omission of the emitter area and buried layer. Assume an additional collector contact all around the transistor. Calculate the SPICE parameters as in Table 2-5.

2-13 For the lateral *pnp* transistor of Example 2-11, plot its beta β, $f_{T\,max}$, and punch-through voltage V_{PT} versus base width d_1 (see Fig. 2-23b) for d_1 going from 1 to 30 μm.

2-14 Plot the equivalent voltage noise of a bipolar transistor versus current. Plot the equivalent current noise versus current I_C with frequency as a parameter. Take the data from Table 2-5.

2-15 Plot the noise figure versus current I_C for a constant $R_S = 1$ kΩ. Calculate all characteristic values. Take the necessary data from Table 2-5. Omit $1/f$ noise.

2-16 At what current do we have to bias a bipolar transistor amplifier with $R_S = 50$ Ω for minimum noise figure? Use $\beta = 50$, $r_B = 20$ Ω, $\tau_F = 50$ ps, and $C_{jEt} + C_\mu = 1.2$ pF. What are the equivalent input noise sources and what is the resultant noise figure? Omit $1/f$ noise.

2-17 Calculate the transition current I_{MB} in Fig. 2-41 for a MOST of $W/L = 20$ with $L = 1.2$ μm and $t_{ox} = 25$ nm. The bipolar transistor has a $f_{T\,max}$ of 12 GHz and $C_{jEt} + C_\mu \approx 2$ pF.

2-18 Compare a MOST with a bipolar transistor of exactly the same area. Make first-order estimates of the capacitances and use the data from Tables 1-8 and 2-5.

APPENDIX 2-1

Temperature effects are important in power applications, in space, in biomedical applications, etc. For this reason, they have been collected in this appendix for all three devices.

The *reverse current of a junction* is dominated by a generation-recombination current that depends on temperature through n_i. Its full expression is given by

$$n_i = 3.88 \times 10^{16} T^{3/2} \exp\left(-\frac{E_{g0}}{2kT}\right) \tag{A2-1a}$$

where E_{g0} is the extrapolated width of the bandgap of silicon, given by

$$E_g = E_{g0} - \beta T \tag{A2-1b}$$

with $E_{g0} = 1.206$ eV and $\beta = 2.8 \times 10^{-4}$/K is a constant. At 300 K, $E_g = 1.122$ eV, $2kT = 2(0.02586\text{ eV}) = 0.05172$ eV, and $n_i = 1.50 \times 10^{10}$ cm^{-3}.

The temperature coefficient of n_i is then given by

$$\frac{1}{n_i}\frac{dn_i}{dT} = \frac{1}{T}\left(\frac{3}{2} + \frac{E_{g0}}{2kT}\right) \tag{A2-2}$$

which is $(1.5+23.32)/300 = 0.0827$/K at 300 K. It is largely dominated by the exponential in Eq. (A2-1) or by the term with E_{g0} in Eq. (A2-2). This shows that n_i doubles every 8.4 K around 300 K. Also, n_i increases (decreases) by a factor of 10 at 30°C above (25°C below) the room temperature of 300 K. As a result, the reverse leakage current I_{Dg} is a very sensitive function of temperature.

In SPICE, the value of Eg (not E_{g0}) must be put in as EG. Also, the factor $T^{3/2}$ is replaced by $T^{XTI/2}$ such that the temperature coefficient can be made to fit experimental data.

The *junction built-in potential* depends on temperature as well. From Eq. (1-3b) it is found to be

$$\frac{d\phi_j}{dT} = \frac{\phi_j}{T} - 2\frac{kT}{q}\left(\frac{1}{n_i}\frac{dn_i}{dT}\right) = \frac{1}{T}\left(\phi_j - 3\frac{kT}{q} - \frac{E_{g0}}{q}\right) \tag{A2-3}$$

after substitution of the temperature coefficient of n_i from Eq. (A2-2). The built-in potential usually decreases with increasing temperature because the influence of n_i is dominant.

Example A2-1

Calculate the variation in temperature of ϕ_j for a diode with doping levels of 10^{18} and 10^{16} cm^{-3} around room temperature (300 K). Repeat this for 30 K higher and lower.

Solution. At room temperature Eq. (1-3b) gives $\phi_j = 0.813$ V. The first term of Eq. (A2-3) gives 2.71 mV/K, the second, 4.28 mV/K (with the temperature coefficient of n_i taken from Eq. (A2-2) to be 0.0827), which yields as a total −1.57 mV/K. At 30 K higher these values are $\phi_j = 0.765$ V and −1.595 mV/K; at 30 K lower they are $\phi_j = 0.859$ V and −1.543 mV/K. It can be concluded that the built-in potential does indeed decrease with temperature but its change with temperature is approximately constant and equals −1.5 to −2 mV.

MOST Threshold Voltage Temperature Coefficient

In the expression V_T as given in Eq. (1-6a), parameter ϕ_F occurs several times and therefore its temperature dependence plays a dominant role. The expression of ϕ_F is given by Eq. (1-6d). Its temperature dependence is derived as for ϕ_j in Eq. (A2-3) above. In this expression, the temperature dependence of n_i is more important than the term with T itself. After substitution, the temperature dependence of ϕ_F is given by

$$\frac{d\phi_F}{dT} = \frac{1}{T}\left[\phi_F \pm \left(\frac{3}{2}\frac{kT}{q} + \frac{E_{g0}}{2q}\right)\right] \tag{A2-4}$$

in which − is used for an nMOST and + for a pMOST. Parameter ϕ_F always decreases in absolute value when the temperature increases. The term with E_{g0} is dominant. As a result, for an nMOST, ϕ_F is positive and its $d\phi_F/dT$ is negative. Since the nMOST is usually of the enhancement type, its threshold voltage decreases in absolute value. On the other hand, for a pMOST, ϕ_F is negative and $d\phi_F/dT$ is positive. The threshold voltage thus decreases in absolute value as well.

Now the temperature dependence of V_T itself can be calculated. It is derived from Eq. (1-6a) and is given by

$$\frac{dV_{T0}}{dT} = \frac{d\phi_{GB}}{dT} + \left(2 \pm \frac{\gamma}{\sqrt{2|\phi_F|}}\right)\frac{d\phi_F}{dT} \tag{A2-5}$$

with + for an nMOST and − for a pMOST.

It is assumed that the oxide charge is temperature independent.

Many authors assume that the work function difference ϕ_{GB} is independent of temperature as well. However, the term $d\phi_{GB}/dT$ can easily be derived from Eq. (1-6c). Since it contains kT/q, a dependence on temperature seems to be present.

On the other hand, for $n+$ doped silicon gate transistors, the doping level is actually so high that other second-order effects occur. The temperature dependence is then not easily determined. Therefore, $d\phi_{GB}/dT$ is assumed to be zero and the temperature dependence of V_T only depends on the temperature dependence of ϕ_F.

Example A2-2

Calculate the temperature dependence of the threshold voltage of the nMOST on 10^{16} cm^{-3} substrate doping and of the pMOST on 3×10^{14} cm^{-3}.

Solution. From Eqs. (A2-4) and (A2-2), the value of $d\phi_F/dT = 1.16 - 2.14 = -0.98$ mV/K. From Eq. (A2-5), then $dV_T/dT = -2.97$ mV/K. In a similar way, for the pMOST, $d\phi_F/dT = -0.85 + 2.14 = 1.29$ mV/K and $dV_T/dT = 2.31$ mV/K.

Note that the values obtained are close to 2 mV/K.

Temperature Coefficient of KP

The transconductance parameter KP depends on temperature because of the mobility, as shown by Eq. (1-9d). The mobility can be a strong function of temperature, depending on the doping level (see Fig. A2-1) given by $\mu = C_\mu T^{-n_\mu}$, in which C_μ is a constant and n_μ is the slope of the curve of Fig. 1-8. The temperature coefficient itself is then given by

$$\frac{1}{\mu}\left(\frac{d\mu}{dT}\right) = -\frac{n_\mu}{T} \tag{A2-6}$$

For low doping levels, the value of n_μ is about 1.5. For high doping levels such as in drains and sources, the value of n_μ is about zero. The channel has an average doping level that is at least the doping level of the bulk (i.e., strong inversion condition). Therefore, the bulk doping level is used to obtain the value of n_μ in Fig. A2-1. This procedure usually leads to a value of close to 1.5 as well.

Current Temperature Dependence

For a MOST in saturation, the expression of the current in its simplest form is given by Eq. (1-18c). The temperature coefficient of the current is then easily derived by taking the derivative with respect to temperature, which yields

$$\frac{1}{i_{DSsat}}\left(\frac{di_{DSsat}}{dT}\right) = -\frac{n_\mu}{\mu} - \frac{2}{V_{GS} - V_T}\left(\frac{dV_T}{dT}\right) \tag{A2-7}$$

Since the V_T of an nMOST has a negative temperature coefficient, the second term is positive, whereas the first term is negative. Thus, a biasing point exists where both terms have equal amplitude and hence yield a zero temperature coefficient. This point is obtained by equating Eq. (A2-7) to zero. The resultant value of V_{GST} is given by

$$V_{GST} = V_T - \frac{2T}{n_\mu}\left(\frac{dV_T}{dT}\right) \tag{A2-8}$$

Example A2-3

What is the temperature coefficient of KP for an nMOST with mobility 500 cm^2/Vs? At what $V_{GST} - V_T$ is the point reached with zero temperature coefficient?

Solution. The answer is $-1.5/300 = -0.5$/K. For an nMOST the second term is negative. The value of V_{GST} is thus slightly larger than V_T. For the nMOST with

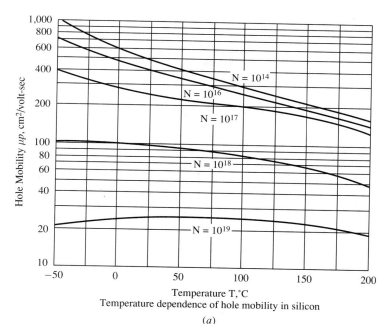

Temperature dependence of hole mobility in silicon

(a)

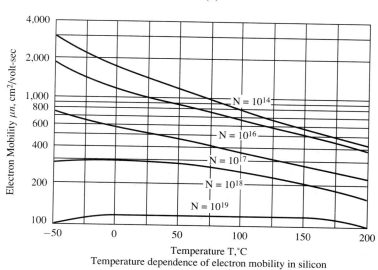

Temperature dependence of electron mobility in silicon

(b)

FIGURE A2-1   (a) Temperature dependence of hole mobility in silicon and temperature dependence of electron mobility in silicon (b) Temperature dependence of electron mobility in silicon

$dV_T/dT = -2.97$ mV/K, the second term equals $V_{GST} - V_T = 1.188$ V. If the nMOST is biased at higher values of V_{GS}, the negative temperature coefficient of the mobility dominates. The current then decreases with temperature, stabilizing the biasing point.

For a JFET the only temperature dependent parameter in V_P is ϕ_j (see Eq. (1-48)). For large values of V_P the relative temperature dependence is negligible. However, for small values of V_P, ϕ_j constitutes a large fraction of V_P. The relative temperature dependence is higher, the smaller the value of V_P. On the other hand, the absolute temperature coefficient $\Delta V_P/\Delta T$ is the same as for ϕ_j, i.e., $\Delta\phi_j/\Delta T$. It has been calculated above and is given by Eq. (A2-3)

Since ϕ_j decreases for increasing temperature, V_P increases with temperature.

This is not the case for I_{DSO}, however. From Eq. (1-52b), it is seen that I_{DSO} will decrease with increasing temperature as a result of the presence of the mobility. The i_{DS} versus v_{GS} characteristic rotates to become flatter. The value of g_m decreases twice for increasing temperature: once because of the increasing V_P and once for the decreasing μ in β.

An even more important effect, however, is the influence of the temperature on the gate input current. This is the current of a reverse biased diode and it increases drastically with temperature. For this reason, JFETs are not desirable at high temperatures and MOST devices are preferred.

Since a bipolar transistor consists of two diodes, all temperature effects discussed concerning diodes apply to a bipolar transistor as well. This is especially true for all junction leakage currents and the saturation current I_S (given by Eq. (2-5b)). The temperature coefficient of I_S is denoted by XTI in SPICE (see Table 2-2).

The forward current is given by Eq. (2-5a). If the current is maintained at a fixed value, the temperature sensitivity of the base-emitter voltage equals about -2 mV/K. Only $1°$C difference in temperature between two equal transistors causes a difference in voltage of 2 mV and a difference in current of 8 percent. A difference in current of a factor of two is caused by a difference in input voltage of 18 mV, or barely $9°$C.

Beta

The beta has a positive temperature coefficient as a result of two opposite effects. The first one is bandgap narrowing. The emitter is doped very highly and therefore the bandgap in the emitter has become smaller than the bandgap in the base by an amount ΔE_g. In the expression of the beta, as a result of injection in the emitter (see Eq. (2-8)), a term must be added such that

$$\beta \sim \exp\left(-\frac{\Delta E_g}{kT}\right) \tag{A2-9}$$

The beta thus increases for increasing temperatures.

The reason why beta decreases with temperature is that the ratio of the diffusion constants occurs (see Eq. 2-8). This is the same as the ratio of the mobilities. The emitter is very highly doped and therefore the mobility of the holes in the emitter hardly changes with temperature (see Fig. A2-1). This is not true for the base, where the mobility of the electrons changes with temperature with an exponent of about -1.4 (for 2×10^{17} cm^{-3} in Fig. A2-1b). The beta would thus decrease with temperature.

The net effect is that the beta increases with temperature with a temperature coefficient of about 0.7 %/°C around room temperature. This temperature coefficient is denoted by XTB in the SPICE model (see Table 2-2). The bandgap itself is denoted by EG. Its value at room temperature is approximately $E_g = 1.11$ V.

Base Transit Time

The base transit time is given by Eq. (2-6b). Only the diffusion constant D_n depends on temperature. As shown above, it is proportional to $T^{-1.4}$, but since $D_n = \mu_n kT/q$, D_n is proportional to $T^{-0.4}$. The base transit time increases by the same ratio and the maximum f_T decreases accordingly. This is only a weak temperature dependence.

Actually, the base transit time also appears in the beta if the recombination in the base is dominant (see Eq. (2-9)). The recombination time constant always decreases with temperature. As a result, the beta decreases with temperature in this case. Obviously, this is only the case for lateral transistors or transistors with wide bases and hence low values of f_T.

REFERENCES

Antognetti, P., and G. Massobrio. 1988. *Semiconductor Device Modeling with SPICE*. New York: McGraw-Hill.

Chang, Z. Y., and W. Sansen. 1991. *Low-Noise Wide-Band Amplifiers in Bipolar and CMOS Technologies*. Norwell, MA: Kluwer Academic.

Getreu, I. 1976. *Modeling the Bipolar Transistor*. Tektronix, Inc., Beaverton, OR.

Glaser, A., and G. Subak-Sharpe. 1977. *Integrated Circuit Engineering*. Englewood Cliffs, NJ: Addison-Wesley.

Gray, P., and R. Meyer. 1984. *Analysis and Design of Analog Integrated Circuits*. New York: Wiley and Sons.

Grove, A., 1967. *Physics and Technology of Semiconductor Devices*. New York: Wiley and Sons.

Muller, R., and T. Kamins. 1986. *Device Electronics for Integrated Circuits*, New York: Wiley and Sons.

Ott, H. W., 1988. *Noise Reduction Techniques in Electronic Systems*. New York: Wiley and Sons.

Sze, S., 1981. *Physics of Semiconductor Devices*. New York: Wiley and Sons.

3

FEEDBACK AND SENSITIVITY IN ANALOG INTEGRATED CIRCUITS

INTRODUCTION

Feedback is a fundamental concept and a means of control in electronic circuits and systems. Moreover, feedback appears in most physical systems, inherently or by design. In fact, feedback is a crucial mechanism in many social processes, such as corporate management, politics and government, and economics. Simply described, feedback is a process that links the current operation of a system (or process) to information about its past performance. In other words, feedback introduces a dependency between current behavior and past behavior. Feedback is often used to help a system (or process) converge to some particular objective. (See Black 1934; Blackman 1943; Bode 1945, 1960; Desoer and Kuh 1969; Geiger, Allen, and Strader 1985; Ghausi 1985; Rosenstark 1986; Sariant 1964; Schaumann, Ghausi, and Laker 1990; Sedra and Smith 1991; Waldhauer 1982.)

Let us assume that we have a process "A", such that "A" responds to events $\{x\}$ with outcomes $\{y\}$. That is, $\{y\}$ depends on $\{x\}$ and "A", but $\{x\}$ and "A" are unaffected by $\{y\}$. When we interject a means for outcomes $\{y\}$ to affect events $\{x\}$ or process "A", we have introduced feedback between $\{y\}$ and $\{x\}$ or "A". Clearly, in a causal situation, the current $\{x\}$ or "A" can only depend on past $\{y\}$.

For example, a restaurant manager may wish to improve the quality of service delivered by the restaurant staff. Let $\{x\}$ be the service, "A" be the restaurant staff, and $\{y\}$ be the reactions that customers have to the service $\{x\}$. There is a clear cause-and-effect relationship that forces $\{y\}$ to depend on $\{x\}$, but not vice versa. A simple way for the manager to introduce feedback so that $\{x\}$ is affected by $\{y\}$ is to ask all customers to comment on the service they have received and then to share these comments with the staff. This feedback can also be used in decisions regarding the firing and promotion of staff members, thus making "A" depend on $\{y\}$. If well managed, such feedback will be constructive. Thus, service quality will improve and staff satisfaction will be high. When not well managed, feedback can be destructive, causing service quality and customer satisfaction to decline. In electronic systems, feedback provides a similar double-edged sword; a fact of nature that will become increasingly evident as the reader progresses through this chapter.

One of the potentially destructive outcomes of feedback is instability. *Stability* in electronic circuits and systems is a condition in which all bounded excitations $\{x\}$ yield bounded responses $\{y\}$. Passive RLC circuits are stable by their very nature, i.e., the fundamental conservation of energy principles (Schaumann, Ghausi, and Laker 1990). Since these circuits do not contain internal energy sources they cannot have divergent responses. Active networks, on the other hand, do contain internal energy sources that can combine with the input excitation to cause the output to increase indefinitely or sustain oscillations. Circuits and systems that yield an unbounded response to any bounded input excitation are unstable. Since 0 or ground is a bounded excitation, unstable feedback systems can yield unbounded responses, even in the absence of an input. Even if a feedback system is stable, how it responds to transients is very important in many applications. Thus, controlling the degree of stability is often an important design criterion, particularly in amplifier design.

The practical realization of precision VLSI analog circuits and systems is complicated by the fact that physical circuit components (e.g., resistors, capacitors, operational amplifiers, etc.) deviate from nominal values, or design intent, due to a variety of statistical and deterministic effects. The consequence of these unavoidable deviations is that the circuit performance changes in a proportional manner. Some changes may in fact cause circuits to no longer meet design requirements. *Sensitivity* is the cause-and-effect relation (or transfer function) between a component change and the resulting change in performance (Geiger, Allen, and Strader 1990; Schaumann, Ghausi, and Laker 1990). The consequence of varying components and sensitivity is that less than 100 percent of the fabricated circuits will perform in accordance to the specifications (specs) or design objectives. The percentage of circuits fabricated that meet specs, when tested in their final packages, is called the *yield*. (Becker and Jensen 1977; Calahan 1968; Geiger, Allen, and Strader, 1990; Mukherjee and Carley 1991; Murphy 1964.) Percent yield is the bottom line measure of success in integrated circuit design and fabrication. As we will soon discover, sensitivity can be greatly affected by feedback.

In this chapter, our purpose is to review the principles of feedback; the mathematical theory and practical ramifications of its use in circuits. Two important consequences that we consider in detail are the impacts on stability and sensitivity. A model will be developed that relates yield to sensitivities and thus to controllable feedback parameters. In the chapters that follow, we will make sophisticated use of feedback to produce a variety of useful functions and effects. To become a proficient analog IC designer and to receive maximum benefit from this text, it is important that the reader master both the rigor and application of feedback.

3-1   FEEDBACK THEORY

The theory that permits the rigorous study of feedback and the design of feedback systems was developed by electronic engineers, who were largely interested in the design of electronic amplifiers and repeaters for telephony (Black 1934, Blackman 1943, Bode 1960). In particular, Harold S. Black, who was an electronics engineer at Bell Laboratories, is heralded as inventing the feedback amplifier in 1927 (Black 1934). It is reported that he first sketched this revolutionary concept on a copy of the *New York Times* while commuting to work on the Lackawanna Ferry (Waldhauer 1982). Since then, feedback has become so widely used that it is an important consideration in nearly all analog and digital electronic systems.

In the subsequent chapters of this text, we will deliberately apply feedback to amplifier circuits in order to produce a variety of interesting functions and effects. For example, in Chap. 4 we show how feedback is used to stabilize the DC operation point of a transistor amplifier. Feedback is also applied to tailor the amplifier's AC performance and two-port characteristics. In many cases, feedback is present due to parasitic components, whether it is wanted or not. Such feedback is difficult, if not impractical, to control, and it limits performance to some degree. In Chaps. 1 and 2, we have already encountered several examples of inherent or parasitic feedback. In one example, the source resistance R_S (not to be confused with the signal-source resistance R_s) associated with the MOST transistor, introduces feedback in the common-source amplifier of Fig. 1-24. As shown in Eq. (1-37) of Chap. 1, this feedback reduces and limits the effective transconductance of the MOST. In another example, the base-collector junction capacitance C_μ, associated with the bipolar transistor, provides feedback in the common-emitter amplifier of Fig. 2-11. In this case, C_μ significantly reduces the bandwidth of the amplifier, as described in Sec. 4-1-5. The impact of C_μ is magnified by the feedback; an outcome that is referred to as the *Miller effect*. The resulting effective capacitance is called the *Miller capacitance*. We will say more about these parasitic feedback situations later. The Miller effect will reappear on several occasions in this and subsequent chapters.

As we will see, feedback can take the form of either *negative feedback* or *positive feedback*. In the design of linear electronic circuits, negative feedback is used to accomplish a variety of important effects. On the other hand, positive feedback often enhances tendencies toward unstable behavior. Hence, when positive feedback is used, it is applied with some degree of caution.

To further motivate the discussion, let us consider the practical example of a MOST single-transistor common-source amplifier in Fig. 3-1a. In this circuit, we introduce feedback via resistor R_F. To connect this example with the general discussion in the previous paragraphs, let $\{x\} = V_i$, $\{y\} = V_o$, and "A" = the amplifier with no feedback (i.e., with $R_F = \infty$). We see that feedback via R_F forces $\{x\}$ to depend on $\{y\}$, thus affecting change in the response observed at the output of "A". For this example, let the small-signal high-frequency operation of the MOST be modeled by the equivalent circuit in Fig. 3-1b. In this model, C'_{DG} is the Miller capacitance (analogous to the

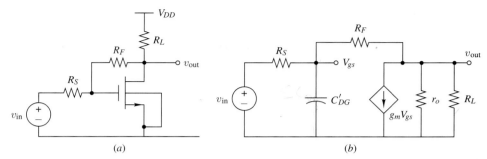

FIGURE 3-1   (*a*) A single MOST common-source feedback amplifier, and (*b*) its small-signal equivalent circuit.

previously mentioned capacitance associated with C_μ). Analysis of Fig. 3-1*b* for the voltage gain $A_v = V_{out}/V_{in}$ yields the following expression:

$$A_v = \frac{V_{out}}{V_{in}} = \frac{-\left(g_m - \dfrac{1}{R_F}\right)R'_L}{1 + \dfrac{R'_L}{R_F} + (1 + g_m R'_L)\dfrac{R_S}{R_F} + sC'_{DG}R_S\left(1 + \dfrac{R'_L}{R_F}\right)} \tag{3-1}$$

where $R'_L = R_L /\!/ r_o$. If we assume that $g_m R'_L \gg 1$, $R'_L \ll R_F$, and $1/g_m \ll R_F$, then A_v can be rewritten in the following convenient form:

$$A_v \approx \frac{\dfrac{-g_m R'_L}{1 + g_m R'_L \dfrac{R_S}{R_F}}}{1 + s\dfrac{C'_{DG}R_S}{1 + g_m R'_L \dfrac{R_S}{R_F}}} = \frac{A_{v0}}{1 + \dfrac{s}{p}} \tag{3-2}$$

where,

$$A_{v0} = \frac{-g_m R'_L}{1 + g_m R'_L \dfrac{R_S}{R_F}} = \frac{(A_{v0})_{OL}}{1 - (A_{v0})_{OL}\dfrac{R_S}{R_F}} \tag{3-3a}$$

$$\omega_{3dB} = p = \frac{1 + g_m R'_L \dfrac{R_S}{R_F}}{C'_{DG}R_S} = \frac{1 - (A_{v0})_{OL}\dfrac{R_S}{R_F}}{C'_{DG}R_S} \tag{3-3b}$$

and

$$\omega_t = 2\pi\, GBW = |A_{v0}|\omega_{3dB} = \frac{g_m R'_L}{C'_{DG}R_S} \tag{3-3c}$$

The quantity ω_t or GBW, i.e., gain-bandwidth product, is an often used measure of quality for amplifier circuits. It is defined as the product of DC (or midband) gain and 3 dB bandwith. In this text, GBW will always refer to the gain-bandwidth expressed in Hz and $\omega_t = 2\pi GBW$ to the gain-bandwidth expressed in rps.

For our example, observe that when $R_F = \infty$, then $g_m R'_L (R_S/R_F) = 0$ and there is no feedback. Thus,

$$A_{v0} = (A_{v0})_{OL} = -g_m R'_L \tag{3-4a}$$

and

$$\omega_{3\text{dB}} = (\omega_{3\text{dB}})_{OL} = \frac{1}{C'_{DG} R_S} \tag{3-4b}$$

$$\omega_t = (\omega_t)_{OL} = \frac{g_m R'_L}{C'_{DG} R_S} \tag{3-4c}$$

When the feedback is reduced to zero, e.g., $R_F = \infty$, the circuit is said to be an *open-loop* (i.e., the feedback loop is open-circuited). The subscript OL refers to open-loop.

In contrast to the open-loop condition, let us consider the closed-loop condition $g_m R'_L (R_S/R_F) \gg 1$, i.e., the feedback is large. Thus,

$$A_{v0} = (A_{v0})_{CL} = -\frac{R_F}{R_S} \tag{3-5a}$$

and

$$\omega_{3\text{dB}} = (\omega_{3\text{dB}})_{CL} = \frac{g_m R'_L \dfrac{R_S}{R_F}}{C'_{DG} R_S} \tag{3-5b}$$

$$\omega_t = (\omega_t)_{CL} = \frac{g_m R'_L}{C'_{DG} R_S} \tag{3-5c}$$

The subscript CL refers to **closed-loop**. Since there is a 180° phase difference between input and output, this amplifier is referred to as an inverting amplifier. We also note that since $g_m R'_L$ and R_S/R_F are nonnegative, the quantity $1 + g_m R'_L (R_S/R_F) \geq 1$.

Using Eqs. (3-1) through (3-5), let us highlight some of the more prominent benefits of negative feedback:

The Control and Desensitization of Gain   The gain of an active device can be modified and controlled with negative feedback, as illustrated in Fig. 3-1. Concurrently, feedback serves to render the gain less dependent on (or less sensitive to) device parameters that may vary significantly with manufacturing tolerances, temperature, and aging. To appreciate this effect, let us compare Eqs. (3-4a) and (3-5a). In the absence of feedback, i.e., $R_F = \infty$, we find that A_{v0} is directly proportional to the MOST g_m. However, when the feedback is increased such that the quantity

$g_m R_L (R_S / R_F) \gg 1$, A_{v0} becomes very nearly independent of g_m. This is perhaps one of the most attractive benefits of negative feedback, and one that will be used repeatedly throughout this text.

The Extension of the Bandwidth   When using negative feedback, gain can be traded for bandwidth and, at the same time, enhance the parametric control of the circuit's frequency response. This trade is demonstrated in Eqs. (3-3a) and (3-3b). We observe that as $g_m R_L$ (R_S / R_F) increases, A_{v0} decreases and ω_{3dB} increases, and vice versa. Note, however, that in Eqs. (3-3) thru (3-5) the gain-bandwidth product remains constant, independent of the applied feedback, i.e.,

$$(GBW)_{OL} = (GBW)_{CL} = GBW = \frac{1}{2\pi} A_{v0} \omega_{3dB}$$

This basic conservation principle is used extensively in the design of active-RC and switched-capacitor filters.

The Control Over Input and Output Impedance   With feedback, the input and output impedances of a circuit can either be increased or decreased as desired. Impedance control is particularly important in achieving isolation and peak power performance from amplifiers. It is also the basis for the Miller effect, discussed in more detail and applied in Chap. 4.

A general illustration of the Miller effect is given in Fig. 3-2. In Fig 3-2a, impedance Z_a is connected between port-1 and port-2 of an arbitrary linear circuit $\mathcal{N}$. The currents and voltages at these terminals are defined as I_1, V_1, I_2, V_2, and $V_2/V_1 \equiv -A_v$. In Fig. 3-2b, we show an alternative representation where Z_a is reflected across both port-1 and port-2, i.e.,

$$Z_1 = \frac{Z_a}{1 + A_v} \quad \text{and} \quad Z_2 = \frac{Z_a}{1 + \dfrac{1}{A_v}} \qquad (3\text{-}6a)$$

FIGURE 3-2   The Miller effect: (a) general linear circuit with impedance Z_a connected between ports -1 and -2; and (b) the equivalent with Z_a reflected across ports -1 and -2.

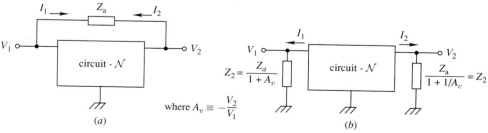

That is, the effect of Z_a as seen at port-1 is reduced by a factor of $1 + A_v$. At port-2, Z_a's impact is reduced by $1 + 1/A_v$. Note that when $A_v \gg 1$,

$$Z_1 \approx \frac{Z_a}{A_v} \quad \text{and} \quad Z_2 \approx Z_a \tag{3-6b}$$

When Z_a is a capacitor, i.e., $Z_a = 1/sC_a$, the effective capacitances at ports-1 and -2 are

$$C_1 = C_a(1 + A_v) \quad \text{and} \quad C_1 = C_a\left(1 + \frac{1}{A_v}\right) \tag{3-6c}$$

Thus, in an amplifier, the Miller effect magnifies the influence of particular transistor parasitic capacitances (e.g., C_{DG} or C_μ for common-sourceand common-emitter amplifiers, respectively). These capacitances, in particular C_1, are referred to as the Miller capacitors. We leave it to the reader to show that Figs. 3-2a and 3-2b are completely equivalent.

The Reduction in Nonlinear Distortion   The concept of linear active circuits is an idealization that can be achieved to a close approximation, particularly at small-signal levels. Nonlinear distortion degrades the quality of the output signal and reduces the *dynamic range* of the active circuit. Note that by dynamic range we mean the range of input signal levels for which the active circuit will perform according to specifications. Noise usually limits the low end of the signal range, and nonlinear distortion limits the high end of the signal range. The high-end degradation can be directly reduced with the application of feedback. At the low end, feedback systems can be designed that lessen the impact of noise under very specific conditions. These specific conditions will be explored momentarily.

In each of the above cases, the price paid for one or more of these desired effects is reduced gain. This is often a small price to pay, particularly in an operational amplifier (or op amp) circuits where the op amp open-loop voltage gain is usually very large (> 60 dB in the frequency range of interest). We have shown that feedback reduces gain and increases bandwidth by the common factor $1 + g_m R_L' (R_S/R_F) \geq 1$. This factor, an important quantity in feedback systems, is referred to as the *return difference* (or the *amount of feedback*). As we will show, it is also the factor by which nonlinear distortion is decreased and gain sensitivity is decreased, etc.

Gain reduction is a fundamental characteristic of negative feedback; negative feedback works to reduce gain, i.e., closed-loop gain is always less than the open-loop gain. On the other hand, *positive feedback* works to increase gain. As we will see, sufficiently large amounts of positive feedback can lead to a gain that grows uncontrollably, with output signal amplitude limited only by the supply voltages. This instability is useful in the design of oscillators and switching circuits but it is catastrophic when it occurs in amplifiers, filters and other linear signal conditioning circuits. Nonetheless, small amounts of positive feedback can be useful in linear applications. For example, positive feedback is employed in the design of many active filters to reduce component spreads, i.e., R_{max}/R_{min} and/or C_{max}/C_{min}, which in turn reduces the chip area required for IC implementation. However, positive feedback must always be used with due caution to the threat of instability and increased sensitivity. The stability issue will be covered in detail in the next section.

3-1-1 Basic Feedback Concepts and Definitions

In the previous section, we used a restaurant management task and a single MOST transistor amplifier as examples to introduce the concept of feedback. Let us now cast the subject of feedback into a more general and rigorous framework. Figure 3-3 shows the block diagram or *signal-flow graph* for a basic feedback circuit. The terminal variables can either be voltages, as shown, or currents. The Laplace transformed functions $\mathcal{A} = \mathcal{A}(s)$ and $\mathcal{H} = \mathcal{H}(s)$ are the *open-loop gain* and *feedback factor*, respectively. Also, the voltage functions $V_{in}(s)$, $V_{out}(s)$, $V_f(s)$, and $V_\varepsilon(s)$ are the Laplace transforms of the source, output, feedback, and "error" voltage signals (all defined with respect to ground). We note that signal-flow diagrams provide convenient schematic representations for circuits, systems, and algorithms that are independent of both technology and implementation. In fact, some performance qualities in circuits are largely signal-flow graph dependent, and thus are common to all circuit implementations of the graph.

Implicit in the signal-flow graph description in Fig. 3-3 is that the source, the output, the feedback circuitry $\mathcal{H}$ and the open-loop circuit $\mathcal{A}$ do not interact (depend on, or load) with each other. With feedback, these seemingly ideal conditions can often be arranged in practice (feedback circuits involving op amps are the most celebrated examples). Referring to Fig. 3-3, we can write the following basic relations:

$$V_{out} = \mathcal{A}V_\varepsilon \quad V_f = \mathcal{H}V_{out} \quad \text{and} \quad V_\varepsilon = V_{in} - V_f \tag{3-7}$$

Noting the subtraction in the relation for the signal V_ε, we observe that the negative feedback tends to reduce the "error" at the input to the open-loop circuit and when $V_{in} = V_f$, the "error" V_ε is zero. Solving Eq. (3-7) for V_{out} in terms of V_{in} yields:

$$V_{out} = \left(\frac{\mathcal{A}}{1 + \mathcal{A}\mathcal{H}} \right) V_{in}$$

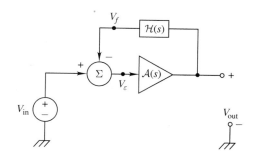

FIGURE 3-3   Block diagram for a basic feedback circuit.

or

$$A_{CL}(s) = \frac{V_{\text{out}}}{V_{\text{in}}} = \frac{\mathcal{A}}{1 + \mathcal{A}\mathcal{H}} = \frac{\mathcal{A}}{1 + \mathcal{T}} \tag{3-8}$$

where A_{CL} is the closed-loop voltage gain, and the quantity $(\mathcal{T} = \mathcal{A}\mathcal{H})$ is called the *loop-gain*, a name derived from the flow diagram in Fig. 3-3. Referring to our earlier amplifier example, we see that at $\omega = 0$, the loop-gain is $\mathcal{T}(j0) = -g_m R'_L (R_S/R_F)$ and $a(j0) = (A_{v0})_{OL}$.

Observe that for negative feedback, the loop-gain must be positive $(\mathcal{T} > 0)$ such that $|1 + \mathcal{T}| > 1$. Hence, the closed-loop gain is smaller than the open-loop gain, i.e., $A_{CL} < \mathcal{A}$. In fact, A_{CL} will be smaller than $(\mathcal{A})$ by the factor $(1 + \mathcal{T})$, which is called the *return difference* or the *amount-of-feedback*. Recall that mention of these terms with reference to the amplifier example was made in the previous section. If $|1 + \mathcal{T}| < 1$, the feedback is positive. It is noted that the quantity $|1 + \mathcal{T}|$ is generally frequency dependent; hence, a feedback system can exhibit both negative and positive feedback for different frequencies. This occurs frequently in active filter circuits. One technique for determining the loop-gain is shown in Fig. 3-4. With the loop cut open at the point of feedback and the system source set to zero, the loop-gain is the voltage transfer function V_{out}/V_1. The reader can verify this result by inspection. An important equation in the characterization of feedback systems is obtained by equating the return difference to zero, i.e.,

$$1 + \mathcal{A}(s)\mathcal{H}(s) = 1 + \mathcal{T}(s) = 0 \tag{3-9}$$

The roots of Eq. (3-9), called the *characteristic equation*, are the natural frequencies of the closed-loop system. Hence, for a stable closed-loop system, the roots must all lie in the left-half s-plane.

In many cases, in particular op amp circuits, the loop gain is large, i.e., $\mathcal{T} \gg 1$. Under this condition we can write the following approximate expression for the closed-

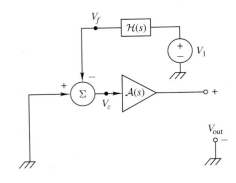

FIGURE 3-4   Breaking the loop to measure loop gain.

loop gain A_{CL}:

$$A_{CL}(s) \approx \frac{1}{\mathcal{H}} \tag{3-10}$$

Equation (3-10) implies that the closed-loop gain is virtually independent of open-loop gain $\mathcal{A}$ and almost entirely determined by the feedback factor $\mathcal{H}$. This is precisely the result we obtained in Eq. (3-5) of the previous section. Comparing Eqs. (3-5) and (3-10), we determine that $1/\mathcal{H} = (A_{v0})_{CL}|_{T \to \infty} = -R_F/R_S$. By rearranging the terms in Eq. (3-8), we can express $A_{CL}(s)$ in the following alternative form

$$A_{CL}(s) = \frac{\mathcal{A}}{1 + \mathcal{A}\mathcal{H}} = \frac{1}{\mathcal{H}} \left(\frac{1}{1 + \dfrac{1}{\mathcal{A}\mathcal{H}}} \right) \tag{3-11}$$

Let us define the function $\varepsilon_{rr}(s) = 1/\mathcal{A}\mathcal{H} = 1/\mathcal{T}$. If $A_{CL}(s) = 1/\mathcal{H}$ is the desired gain, then $\varepsilon_{rr}(s)$ represents the error that occurs due to finite loop-gain $\mathcal{A}\mathcal{H}$, i.e., $\varepsilon_{rr} \to 0$ as $\mathcal{A} \to \infty$. Since open-loop gain $\mathcal{A}$ is usually a function of transistor parameters (e.g., g_m's) and feedback factor $\mathcal{H}$ is not, the designer can often define $\mathcal{H}$ with somewhat greater precision than $\mathcal{A}$. Thus, using large negative feedback is an elegant, yet simple, means of obtaining precision gain functions. We will return to Eq. (3-11) in Chap. 5, when we consider a variety of different feedback circuits using op amps.

Another useful equation is obtained from Eqs. (3-7) by relating the feedback voltage V_f to the system source V_{in}, i.e.,

$$V_f = \frac{\mathcal{T}}{1 + \mathcal{T}} V_{in} \quad \text{and} \quad V_\varepsilon = \frac{1}{1 + \mathcal{T}} V_{in} \tag{3-12a}$$

For the condition $\mathcal{T} \gg 1$, we observe that $V_f \approx V_{in}$; the negative feedback attenuates the "error" signal $V_\varepsilon \approx (1/\mathcal{T})V_{in}$. Equation (3-12a), with $\mathcal{T} \gg 1$, leads to an intuitively appealing result; namely,

$$\frac{V_\varepsilon}{V_{in}} \approx \frac{1}{\mathcal{T}} = \varepsilon_{rr}(s) \tag{3-12b}$$

i.e., when $\mathcal{T} \gg 1$, $\varepsilon_{rr}(s)$ is the error transfer function. Let us now consider four examples that illustrate several of the concepts and properties of negative feedback that we have discussed.

Example 3-1

Consider a feedback amplifier where the open-loop gain $\mathcal{A} = 100$. (a) Determine the value of $\mathcal{H}$ that will produce a closed-loop gain of $A_{CL} = 5$, exactly. (b) Derive the relation between the fractional change in A_{CL} (i.e., dA_{CL}/A_{CL}) and the fractional change in $\mathcal{A}$ (i.e., $d\mathcal{A}/\mathcal{A}$). (c) If $\mathcal{A}$ decreases by 20 percent, calculate the corresponding percentage change in A_{CL}.

Solution. (a) Let us use the expression for A_{CL} given in Eq. (3-11), i.e.,

$$A_{CL} = \frac{1}{\mathcal{H}} \left(\frac{1}{1 + \dfrac{1}{A\mathcal{H}}} \right) \tag{3-13a}$$

The value for $\mathcal{H}$ required to reduce the closed-loop gain to $A_{CL} = 5$ is computed by solving Eq. (3-13a) for $\mathcal{H}$, i.e.,

$$\mathcal{H} = \frac{1}{A_{CL}} - \frac{1}{A} = 0.20 - 0.01 = 0.19 \tag{3-13b}$$

In Eq. (3-13b) we calculated the precise $\mathcal{H}$ needed to compensate for the finite open-loop gain, namely $A = 100$. Note that when $A \rightarrow \infty$, then $\mathcal{H} \rightarrow 1/A_{CL} = 0.20$. In practice, A will be frequency dependent and highly variable from circuit to circuit and with temperature. Consequently, to be truly effective, compensation would necessitate customizing $\mathcal{H}$ for each circuit, and perhaps with frequency and temperature. In other words, we would like $\mathcal{H}$ to track the changes that occur in A. This may seem to be an impossible task. However, with automatic tuning techniques and matched components, one can come close to realizing this ideal tracking condition. We will say more about these techniques in Chap. 8. (b) To determine the fractional change in A_{CL}, let us start by differentiating the right-hand side of Eq. (3-13a) with respect to A, i.e.,

$$\frac{d A_{CL}}{d A} = \left[\frac{1}{A\mathcal{H}} \left(\frac{1}{1 + \dfrac{1}{A\mathcal{H}}} \right) \right]^{2} \tag{3-14}$$

Dividing Eq. (3-14) by the right-hand side of Eq. (3-8) yields the desired relation

$$\frac{d A_{CL}}{A_{CL}} = \frac{1}{A\mathcal{H}} \left(\frac{1}{1 + \dfrac{1}{A\mathcal{H}}} \right) \frac{d A}{A} = \frac{1}{1 + T} \cdot \frac{d A}{A} \tag{3-15}$$

where

$$\frac{1}{A\mathcal{H}} = \frac{1}{19} = 0.0526$$

Equation (3-15) shows us that the $d A_{CL}/A_{CL}$ is smaller than $d A/A$ by a factor equal to the amount of feedback $(1+T)$. Note that Eq. (3-15) is based on differential or small $d A_{CL}/A_{CL}$ and $d A/A$. For larger variations, which occur frequently in integrated circuits, the analysis requires the use of finite differences rather than differentials. That is, if $\Delta A_{CL} = A'_{CL} - A_{CL}$ and $\Delta A = A' - A$, where A'_{CL} and

A' represent the changed values and A_{CL} and A represent the nominal or original values, we can use Eq. (3-8) to write

$$\Delta A_{CL} = A'_{CL} - A_{CL} = \frac{1}{\mathcal{H}}\left(\frac{1}{1 + \dfrac{1}{A'\mathcal{H}}}\right) - \frac{1}{\mathcal{H}}\left(\frac{1}{1 + \dfrac{1}{A\mathcal{H}}}\right)$$

Dividing both sides by A_{CL} and rearranging yields

$$\frac{\Delta A_{CL}}{A_{CL}} = \frac{1}{A'\mathcal{H}}\frac{1}{\left(1 + \dfrac{1}{A'\mathcal{H}}\right)}\frac{\Delta A}{A} \tag{3-16}$$

Note that Eqs. (3-15) and (3-16) approach equality as $\Delta A \to 0$.

(c) Calculating dA_{CL}/A_{CL} using Eq. (3-15), with $dA/A = 20$ percent (or 0.2), yields $dA_{CL}/A_{CL} = 0.99$ percent (or 0.0099). To use the more exact Eq. (3-16), we must first determine

$$A' = 80 \text{ and } \frac{1}{A'\mathcal{H}} = \frac{1}{15.2} = 0.0658$$

Substituting these values into Eq. (2-16) yields $\Delta A_{CL}/A_{CL} = 1.23$ percent (or 0.0123). It should be pointed out that $\Delta A/A = 20$ percent used in this example is not an exaggerated figure. We cannot overstate the fact that amplifier open-loop gains can vary widely with manufacturing tolerances and temperature. Fortunately, the negative feedback is seen to desensitize A_{CL} to changes in the open-loop gain A.

Example 3-2

Consider an open-loop amplifier whose frequency response is characterized by the one-pole transfer function

$$A(s) = \frac{A_0}{1 + \dfrac{s}{\omega_p}} = \frac{A_0}{1 + \dfrac{s}{2\pi f_p}} \tag{3-17}$$

In the above equation, A_0 is the DC open-loop gain and ω_p is the open-loop 3 dB cutoff radian frequency. (a) Assuming a feedback system with a signal-flow graph, as in Fig. 3-3, determine the 3 dB cutoff frequency for the closed-loop system in terms of A_0 and f_p. (b) With $A_0 = 10^4$, $\mathcal{H} = 0.0999$, and $\omega_p = 2\pi(100)$ rps, compute the closed-loop 3 dB cutoff frequency f'_p.

Solution. (a) Form $A_{CL}(s)$ by substituting Eq. (3-17) into Eq. (3-8), obtaining

$$A_{CL}(s) = \frac{A_0/(1 + A_0\mathcal{H})}{1 + \dfrac{s}{\omega_p'}} = \frac{A_{0CL}}{1 + \dfrac{s}{2\pi f_p'}} \qquad (3\text{-}18a)$$

where $A_{0CL} = A_{CL}(j0)$ and ω_p' is the closed-loop 3 dB cutoff frequency expressed by

$$\omega_p' = \omega_p(1 + A_0\mathcal{H}) \quad \text{in rps, or} \quad f_p' = f_p(1 + A_0\mathcal{H}) \quad \text{in Hz} \qquad (3\text{-}18b)$$

Also note that

$$A_{0CL} \to \frac{1}{\mathcal{H}} \text{ as } A_0 \to \infty \quad \text{and} \quad \varepsilon_{rr}(s) = \frac{1}{A_0\mathcal{H}}\left(1 + \frac{s}{\omega_p}\right) \qquad (3\text{-}19)$$

Again we see that the negative feedback has served to reduce the DC gain and increased the 3 dB cutoff or bandwidth by $1 + \mathcal{T}$, i.e., *GBW* is once again invariant. (b) To compute the closed-loop 3 dB frequency, we simply substitute $A_0 = 10^4$, $\mathcal{H} = 0.0999$, and $f_p = 100$ Hz into Eq. (3-18b), i.e.,

$$f_p' = 10^5 \text{ Hz}$$

Note that f_p' can be adjusted over a wide range of values by simply adjusting the feedback $\mathcal{H}$. It is instructive to examine the effect positive feedback has on the closed-loop cutoff f_p'. With positive feedback, where $A_0\mathcal{H} < 0$, f_p' is seen to decrease with decreasing (becoming more negative) loop gain ($A_0\mathcal{H}$) and becomes zero when $A_0\mathcal{H} = -1$. At this point, the system pole has moved to the origin of the s-plane and the output oscillates (at 0 Hz). Any further decrease in loop gain will result in instability.

Example 3-3

Consider the feedback amplifier in Fig. 3-5 in which a disturbance is introduced via the distortion generator v_D. We note that the input v_{IN}, the output v_{OUT}, and the disturbance v_D are assumed to be total signals, including AC and DC components. Also, since v_D is usually dependent on some other voltage (or current) in the circuit, we show v_D in Fig. 3-5 to be a dependent voltage source. This somewhat simple model is often used to account for nonlinear distortion in linear amplifiers produced by internal nonlinearities. This distortion will appear on the output waveform and degrade amplifier performance. For this analysis, let us assume that the distortion is sufficiently small for the system to remain approximately linear in operation, such that amplifier (A') can be modeled as a distortionless amplifier (A_0) and an additive distortion generator. Derive the relation that characterizes the amount that the distortion has been reduced by the feedback and discuss the result.

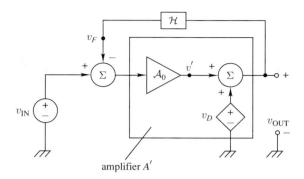

FIGURE 3-5   Feedback configuration with nonlinear distortion source for Example 3-3.

amplifier A'

Solution. In the absence of feedback, we can write

$$v_{\text{OUT}} = A_0 v_{\text{IN}} + v_D \qquad (3\text{-}20)$$

Now, analyzing the circuit with feedback, we obtain the relations

$$v' = A_0(v_{\text{IN}} - \mathcal{H}v_{\text{OUT}}) \quad \text{and} \quad v_{\text{OUT}} = v' + v_D \qquad (3\text{-}21)$$

Solving Eqs. (2-21) for v_{OUT} in terms of v_{IN} and v_D yields

$$v_{\text{OUT}} = \left(\frac{A_0}{1 + A_0 \mathcal{H}}\right) v_{\text{IN}} + \left(\frac{1}{1 + A_0 \mathcal{H}}\right) v_D \qquad (3\text{-}22)$$

In practice, to obtain a quantitative analysis, we note that one must either be given or derive a nonlinear model for the distortion signal v_D, i.e., $v_D = A_2 v^2 + A_3 v^3 + ... + A_N v^N$. Comparing Eqs. (3-20) and (3-22), we see that the nonlinear distortion has been reduced by a factor equal to the amount of feedback (or the loop gain, since $A_0 \mathcal{H} \gg 1$). Since the distortionless output has also been reduced by the same amount, the *signal-to-distortion ratio (S/D)* has not improved. The feedback has, however, improved the linearity of the amplifier system by reducing the gain. The positive impact of this operation is that the closed-loop system can process a wider range of input signal amplitudes than can the open-loop system, before a given distortion level is reached. Without the feedback effect in Eq. (3-22), op amps (where $A_0 > 10^3$) would be of little value in linear circuit applications (see the open-loop op amp transfer characteristic in Fig. 5-5).

Example 3-4

The signal-to-disturbance ratio can be reduced under certain conditions. Consider the case in Fig. 3-6a where an amplifier (A_0) has as inputs the signal v_{IN} and disturbance v_D. This is the typical model when the disturbance is noise, i.e., noise

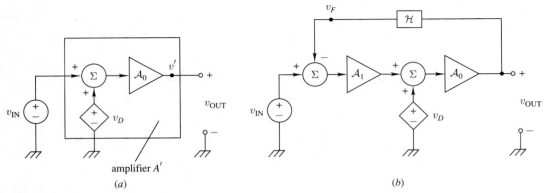

FIGURE 3-6 (a) Amplifier with distortion source at the input, and (b) feedback configuration with "noise free" preamplifier for Example 3-4.

generated by the input differential pair of an op amp, or noise generated by the power supply hum in an audio power amplifier, etc. The signal-to-disturbance ratio for this configuration is

$$S/D = \left| \frac{v_{\text{IN}}}{v_D} \right|$$

How can we increase S/D?

Solution. Let us consider the insertion of a *disturbance free,* or *noise free,* preamplifier (A_1) within the feedback loop and in front of the disturbance, as shown in Fig. 3-6b. This configuration has been widely used in audio amplifier design, where a power amplifier (with low voltage gain) is preceded by a high voltage gain, low noise preamplifier (with low power gain) to reduce the annoying power supply hum of the power amplifier. The expression for the output v_{OUT}, in terms of v_{IN} and v_D, is readily found (using analysis methods that should be becoming rather familiar by now), i.e.,

$$v_O = \left(\frac{A_1 A_0}{1 + A_1 A_0 \mathcal{H}} \right) v_{\text{IN}} + \left(\frac{A_0}{1 + A_1 A_0 \mathcal{H}} \right) v_D \qquad (3\text{-}23a)$$

The closed loop gain (A_{CL}) and the signal-to-disturbance ratio (S/D) are then

$$A_{CL} = \frac{A_1 A_0}{1 + A_1 A_0 \mathcal{H}} \quad \text{and} \quad S/D = A_1 \left| \frac{v_{\text{IN}}}{v_D} \right| \qquad (3\text{-}23b)$$

Referring to Eq. (3-23b), it is clear that significant improvement in S/D requires a large preamplifier gain A_1. One can use amplifier gain (A_1) and feedback $\mathcal{H}$ as design parameters to adjust the signal-to-disturbance ratio while maintaining a constant overall closed-loop system gain. Observe that if $A_1 = 1$ in Eq. (3-23b), which corresponds to eliminating the noiseless preamplification, then S/D is unaffected by the feedback. Note that the negative feedback tends to reduce nonlinear distortion produced by either or both amplifiers.

3-1-2 Feedback Configurations and Classifications

In the feedback configuration shown in Fig. 3-3, the open-loop amplifier $\mathcal{A}(s)$ and the feedback $\mathcal{H}(s)$ blocks are idealized in the sense that both blocks are modeled as noninteracting, ideal voltage-controlled voltage sources. In practice, the feedback block is usually a passive circuit (for our purposes an RC circuit) that may load or interact with the open-loop amplifier. Furthermore, amplifiers are not ideal voltage-controlled voltage sources. The ideal behavior depicted in Fig. 3-3 can be achieved approximately when the following *basic transmission assumptions* are satisfied:

1 The forward transmission through the feedback circuit is negligible in comparison with the forward transmission through the open-loop amplifier.

2 The reverse transmission through the open-loop amplifier is negligible in comparison with the reverse transmission through the feedback circuit.

Both assumptions are typically met in practice when the feedback is through a passive RC circuit and the *open-loop amplifier* is an active circuit with gain. Most practical feedback circuits will fall into this category. Circuits involving op amps will prove to be particularly cooperative subjects in this respect. As we have seen, further simplification occurs when the loading of the open-loop amplifier by the feedback circuit can be assumed to be negligible. Again, this condition is frequently valid when the open-loop amplifier is an op amp.

Let us now consider the common feedback connections used in practice; namely, the *series-shunt, shunt-series, series-series,* and *shunt-shunt* feedback configurations shown in Fig. 3-7. In each case, the feedback system is represented as a two-port network comprised of four interconnected two-ports representing the open-loop amplifier circuit, the feedback circuit, the source, and the load. To keep this discussion somewhat general, we model the amplifier circuit as a controlled source with gain A, input impedance $Z_{\text{in}a}$, and output impedance $Z_{\text{out}a}$. In a similar fashion, the feedback circuit is modeled as a controlled source with gain F, input impedance $Z_{\text{in}f}$, and output impedance $Z_{\text{out}f}$. The unilateral nature of the models for the open-loop amplifier and feedback circuits in Fig. 3-7 is based on the transmission assumptions above.

Since the feedback connections in Fig. 3-7 are covered in many undergraduate electronic circuit texts, we assume that the reader has been previously exposed to the detailed analysis of these schemes. However, it is useful to take a moment to briefly review their salient features. In all cases, increasing the amount of feedback can be shown to desensitize the closed-loop gain to the characteristics of the open-loop amplifier (thus increasing precision and control over the closed-loop gain) and to increase bandwidth in direct proportion to the reduction in the closed-loop gain.

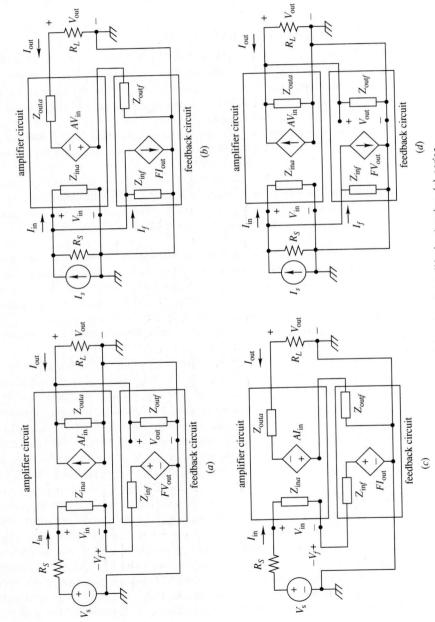

FIGURE 3-7 The four basic feedback connections: (a) series-shunt, (b) shunt-series, (c) series-series, and (d) shunt-shunt.

Series-Shunt Connection   In the series-shunt configuration shown in Fig. 3-7*a*, the output voltage is sensed by the feedback network, fed back as a voltage V_f and added in series with the input voltage. With this scheme, (as we will see in Table 3-1 for all four schemes) the closed-loop input impedance (Z_{inCL}) is magnified and the output impedance (Z_{outCL}) is reduced by the amount of the applied feedback, i.e., $(1 + T)$. Consequently, applying large amounts of feedback in this scheme tends to produce a high quality voltage-controlled voltage source.

Series-shunt feedback is used in applications where electrical isolation and voltage amplification are important, such as buffer amplifiers, the output drive for op amps, and many kinds of signal processing circuits. The series-shunt scheme, as we will find in Chaps. 5, 7, and 8, is widely used in continuous-time active filters and noninverting op amp based feedback circuits.

Shunt-Series Connection   In the shunt-series configuration shown in Fig. 3-7*b*, the output current is sensed by the feedback network, fed back as a current I_f, and added in parallel with the input current. With this scheme, the closed-loop input impedance is reduced and the output impedance is magnified by the factor $(1 + T)$. Consequently, applying large amounts of feedback in this scheme tends to produce a high quality current-controlled current source.

Series-Series Configuration   In the series-series configuration shown in Fig. 3-7*c*, the output current is sensed by the feedback network, fed back as a voltage V_f, and added in series with the input voltage. In this case, the closed-loop input and output impedances are both magnified by $(1 + T)$. Consequently, applying large amounts of feedback in this scheme tends to produce a high quality transconductance amplifier or a voltage-controlled current source. Transconductance amplifiers are very important linear circuit building blocks, and they will receive considerably more attention in Sec. 5-5 and in various sections of Chap. 6.

However, in an amplifier, unintended series-series feedback can degrade performance. In Eq. (1-37) and Fig. 1-24 of Chap. 1, we observed the work of parasitic series-series feedback in a common-source MOST amplifier via the source resistance R_S (not to be confused with the signal-source resistance R_s). In Eq. (1-37), it was shown that the effect of R_S was to reduce, and thus limit, the effective MOST g_m, i.e.,

$$g'_m = \frac{g_m}{1 + g_m R_S} = \frac{g_m}{1 + T}$$

Shunt-Shunt Configuration   In the shunt-shunt configuration shown in Fig. 3-7*d*, the output voltage is sampled by the feedback network, fed back as a current I_f, and added in parallel with the input current. The closed-loop input and output impedances for this scheme are both reduced by $(1 + T)$. Consequently, applying large amounts of feedback in this scheme tends to produce a high quality transresistance amplifier or current-controlled voltage source. The amplifier in Fig. 3-1 is an example of the shunt-shunt connection. Note that in this case, the circuit is voltage driven and the source resistance $Z_1 = R_S$ is in series. One can shift between the current drive with parallel R_S and the voltage drive with series R_S, by using Norton and Thévenin transformations.

Shunt-shunt feedback is widely used in active filters and inverting op amp-based feedback circuits, as we will find in Chap. 5, 7, and 8. Perhaps the most celebrated example of this scheme is the Miller effect, illustrated in Fig. 3-2. In Chap. 4, we will see that in amplifiers the Miller effect magnifies certain parasitic capacitances, thus limiting the available bandwidth. Later in the text, this effect will be turned into an advantage in designing op amps that are stable within a wide range of feedback schemes. This process is known as *frequency compensation.*

It should be evident to the reader that the open-loop amplifiers modeled in Fig. 3-7 represent arbitrary configurations, e.g., single-stage amplifiers or multistage amplifiers or op amps. Although many practical feedback networks can be identified as one of the four configurations in Fig. 3-7, there are exceptions that cannot be classified in this manner. For example, we have only considered single-loop feedback systems. In practice most analog circuits involve multiple feedbacks, some by design and some parasitic. In most cases, the feedback loops are nested such that they can be dealt with independently, e.g., the open-loop amplifiers in Fig. 3-7 may also use feedback to achieve certain properties. The simple common-source feedback amplifier in Fig. 3-1 has two feedbacks, namely, a designed shunt-shunt feedback via R_F and a parasitic shunt-shunt feedback via C_{DG} (i.e., the Miller effect). Such multiple-loop feedback schemes can be addressed with ordered repetitions of the principles in Fig. 3-7 and Fig. 3-8.

3-2   ANALYSIS OF FEEDBACK AMPLIFIER CIRCUITS

Two obvious methods for analyzing feedback circuits are to perform a brute-force circuit analysis with pencil-and-paper or to use SPICE. (Vladimirescu, Newton, and Pederson 1980) Since feedback circuits with seemingly little complexity can lead to equations that call for tedious algebraic manipulations, brute-force pencil-and-paper analysis is all too likely to be a frustrating and error-fraught process. A natural remedy to this dilemma is to let SPICE and the computer do the work. SPICE is a wonderful, proven tool for detailed design verification, but SPICE analysis rarely provides the insights that designers get from well-formed equations. An alternative set of software tools are emerging that are based on symbolic simulation, such as Mathematica (Wolfram 1991). Tools such as ISAAC (Gielen and Sansen 1991) and Nodal (Nodal 1992) provide symbolic expressions rather than tabular or plotted output. At this early stage in the development of symbolic circuit simulators, the management of the complexity (e.g., truncation and approximation) of the resulting expressions is largely left to the user.

Hence, the approach of this section is to seek systematic analytical methods that lead to the desired insight with reduced labor and opportunity for error. Let us first consider an analysis strategy for cases where the feedback circuit can be identified as one of the schemes in Fig. 3-7. We will then use Blackman's impedance relation

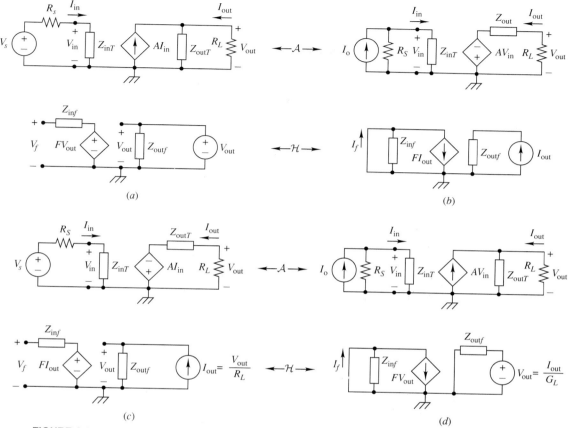

FIGURE 3-8 Circuits for separately determining $\mathcal{A}$ and $\mathcal{H}$ associated with the four feedback schemes in Fig. 3-7: (a) series-shunt, (b) shunt-series, (c) series-series and (d) shunt-shunt.

(Blackman 1943) and Rosenstark's asymptotic gain relation (Rosenstark 1974) to expand this restricted strategy to more general feedback structures.

3-2-1 Analysis When the Feedback Network is One of the Basic Configurations in Fig. 3-7

Simple and systematic analysis strategies can be formulated for feedback circuits identified as one of the schemes in Fig. 3-7. The detailed examination of these basic schemes is usually accomplished with the theory of two-port networks. As we noted earlier, these developments can be found in several popular undergraduate texts on electronic circuits, e.g., Murphy (1964, Chap. 12), and Ghausi (1985, Chap. 10). Leaving the details of the development to these texts, we conveniently summarize the important relations and characteristics for the four feedback schemes in Table 3-1.

TABLE 3-1 SUMMARY OF RELATIONS FOR THE BASIC FEEDBACK CONFIGURATIONS (WHERE ADMITTANCES $X_{IT} = X_{IA} + X_{IF}$, $X_{OT} = X_{OA} + X_{OF}$ WITH $X = Z$ OR Y).

	series-shunt	shunt-shunt	shunt-series	series-series
$A_{i,v} =$	$\dfrac{-A}{(R_s + Z_{iT})(G_L + Y_{oT})}$	$\dfrac{AG_L}{(G_s + Y_{iT})(G_L + Y_{oT})}$	$\dfrac{-A}{(G_s + Y_{iT})(R_L + Z_{oT})}$	$\dfrac{AR_L}{(R_s + Z_{iT})(R_L + Z_{oT})}$
$\mathcal{H}_{i,v} =$	F	$-\dfrac{F}{G_L}$	F	$-\dfrac{F}{R_L}$
$(A_{i,v})_{CL} =$	$\dfrac{A_v}{(1 + T)}$	$\dfrac{A_i}{(1 + T)}$	$\dfrac{A_i}{(1 + T)}$	$\dfrac{A_v}{(1 + T)}$
$Z_{inCL} =$	$(R_s + Z_{iT})(1 + T)$	$\dfrac{1/(G_s + Y_{iT})}{1 + T}$	$\dfrac{1/(G_s + Y_{iT})}{1 + T}$	$(R_s + Z_{iT})(1 + T)$
$Z_{outCL} =$	$\dfrac{1/(G_L + Y_{oT})}{1 + T}$	$\dfrac{1/(G_L + Y_{oT})}{1 + T}$	$(R_L + Z_{oT})(1 + T)$	$(R_L + Z_{oT})(1 + T)$

The entries in Table 3-1 are based on the two-port models in Figs. 3-7 and 3-8. In addition, we define the parameters $A_{i,v}$, $\mathcal{H}_{i,v}$, and $(A_{i,v})_{CL}$ as follows:

for series-shunt and series-series

$$A_v = \frac{V_{\text{out}}}{V_s}\Big|_{F=0} \qquad \mathcal{H}_v = \frac{V_f}{V_{\text{out}}}\Big|_{I_{\text{in}}=0} \qquad (A_v)_{CL} = \frac{V_{\text{out}}}{V_s}$$

$$Z_{inCL} = \frac{V_s}{I_{\text{in}}} \qquad \text{and} \qquad Z_{outCL} = \frac{V_{\text{out}}}{I_{\text{out}}} \tag{3-24a}$$

for shunt-series and shunt-shunt

$$A_i = \frac{I_{\text{out}}}{I_s}\Big|_{F=0} \qquad \mathcal{H}_i = \frac{I_f}{I_{\text{out}}}\Big|_{V_{in}=0} \qquad (A_i)_{CL} = \frac{I_{\text{out}}}{I_s}$$

$$Z_{inCL} = \frac{V_i}{I_s} \qquad \text{and} \qquad Z_{outCL} = \frac{V_{\text{out}}}{I_{\text{out}}} \tag{3-24b}$$

where subscripts i, v designate A, $\mathcal{H}$, and A_{CL} as either current or voltage transfer relations. We can easily shift between current- and voltage-based relations using $I_{\text{out}} = -V_{\text{out}}/R_L$ and $I_s = V_s/R_S$ as follows:

$$A_v = -\frac{R_L}{R_S}A_i \text{ and } (A_v)_{CL} = -\frac{R_L}{R_S}(A_i)_{CL} \tag{3-25a}$$

Hence, $1 + \mathcal{A}_v \mathcal{H}_v = 1 + \mathcal{A}_i \mathcal{H}_i = 1 + \mathcal{A}\mathcal{H}$, i.e., the loop-gain is independent of whether the circuit is voltage or current driven, and we can write:

$$\mathcal{H}_v = -\frac{R_S}{R_L}\mathcal{H}_i \tag{3-25b}$$

The definitions for $\mathcal{A}_{i,v}$ and $\mathcal{H}_{i,v}$ in Eqs. (3-24) and (3-25) form the basis for the analysis procedure described in (Geiger, Allen, and Strader 1990; Ghausi 1985). This process determines $\mathcal{A}_{i,v}$ and $\mathcal{H}_{i,v}$ from a decomposition of the feedback circuit into subcircuits that represent the open-loop amplifier and feedback factor, separately. Note that setting the feedback to zero, i.e., $F = 0$ in Table 3-1, does not relieve $\mathcal{A}_{i,v}$ of the loading due to the input and output impedances of the feedback circuit, i.e.,

$$Z_{inT} = Z_{ina} + Z_{inf} \qquad \text{and} \qquad Z_{outT} = Z_{outa} + Z_{outf} \tag{3-25c}$$

The procedures for determining $\mathcal{A}_{i,v}$ and $\mathcal{H}_{i,v}$ are illustrated in Fig. 3-8 for all four schemes. The closed-loop A_{CL}, Z_{inCL} and Z_{outCL} are then determined by making the appropriate substitutions for $\mathcal{A}_{i,v}$, $\mathcal{H}_{i,v}$, Z_{inT}, Z_{outT}, (or Y_{inT}, Y_{outT}) into the relations in Table 3-1.

Example 3-5

Consider the feedback circuit in Fig. 3-9a. The open-loop amplifier, with voltage gain $-A_0$, is assumed to have infinite input impedance and zero output impedance.

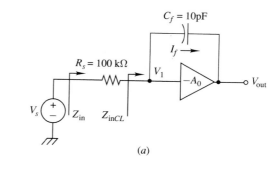

(a)

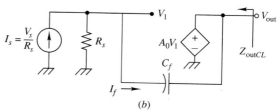

FIGURE 3-9   (a) Shunt-shunt feedback circuit for Example 3-5, and (b) equivalent circuit with open-loop amplifier modeled as an ideal VCVS.

(b)

Let $A_0 = 100$, $R_s = 100$ kΩ and $C_f = 10$ pF. (a) Determine $\mathcal{A}_v$, $\mathcal{H}_v$, and $(A_v)_{CL}$, (b) use the Miller equivalence to determine the Miller capacitance C_{in} and to verify the results in (a). (c) Determine input impedance R_{in} for the closed-loop circuit.

Solution. Modeling the open-loop amplifier as a VCVS and replacing the source with its Norton equivalent, we can redraw Fig. 3-9a as Fig. 3-9b.

(a) Let us then decompose Fig. 3-9b to determine $\mathcal{A}$ and $\mathcal{H}$, as indicated in Fig. 3-10a and Fig. 3-10b, respectively. Analyzing these equivalent circuits yields:

$$\mathcal{A}_v = \frac{V_{out}}{V_s} = \frac{-A_0}{1 + sR_sC_f} = \frac{-100}{1 + s10^{-6}} \tag{3-26a}$$

$$\mathcal{H}_v = \frac{R_sI_f}{V_{out}} = -sR_sC_f = -s10^{-6} \tag{3-26b}$$

$$(A_v)_{CL} = \frac{\mathcal{A}_v}{1 + \mathcal{A}_v\mathcal{H}_v} = \frac{-1}{sR_sC_f + \dfrac{1}{A_0}(1 + sR_sC_f)} \tag{3-26c}$$

$$= \frac{-100}{1 + s(1.01)(10^{-4})}$$

Dividing numerator and denominator by $\mathcal{A}_v\mathcal{H}_v$, and rearranging terms, we express $(A_v)_{CL}$ in the following insightful manner, i.e.,

$$(A_v)_{CL} = -\frac{1}{sR_sC_f}\left(\frac{1}{1 + \dfrac{1}{\mathcal{A}_v\mathcal{H}_v}}\right) = -\frac{1}{sR_sC_f}\left(\frac{1}{1 + \varepsilon_{rr}}\right) \tag{3-27a}$$

where

$$\varepsilon_{rr} = \frac{1}{A_0}\left(1 + \frac{1}{sR_sC_f}\right) \tag{3-27b}$$

Note that as $A_0 \to \infty$, $(A_v)_{CL} \to -1/sR_sC_f$, that is, an inverting integrator.

(b) Using the Miller equivalence in Fig. 3-2, we find that the Miller capacitance is $C_{in} = C_f(1 + A_0) = 1010$ pF and Fig. 3-9b can be redrawn as Fig. 3-10c. We leave it to the reader to verify that deriving V_{out}/V_s, yields the result in Eq. (3-26c).

(c) The shunt-shunt input impedance Z_{inCL}, shown in Fig. 3-9a, is then derived according to Table 3-1, i.e.,

$$Z_{inCL} = \frac{R_s // \dfrac{1}{j\omega C_f}}{1 + \mathcal{A}_v\mathcal{H}_v} = \frac{R_s}{1 + j\omega(1 + A_0)C_fR_s} \approx \frac{10^5}{1 + j\omega10^{-4}} \tag{3-28a}$$

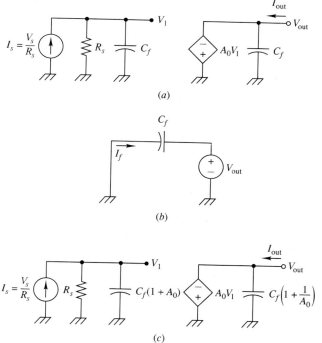

(a)

(b)

(c)

FIGURE 3-10   The feedback circuit in Example 3-5: (a) the circuit to determine $\mathcal{A}_V$, (b) the circuit to determine $\mathcal{H}_V$, and (c) equivalent circuit based on Miller's theorem.

Note that if $\mathcal{A}_v \mathcal{H}_v \gg 1$ (or $\omega[1 + A_0]C_f R_s \gg 1$), then Eq. (3-28a) reduces to the Miller capacitance, i.e.,

$$Z_{inCL} \approx \frac{1}{j\omega(1 + A_0)C_f} \tag{3-28b}$$

Referring to Figs. 3-9a and 3-9b, we see that Z_{inCL} is the impedance looking into the input of the open-loop amp (i.e., V_1). The input impedance looking from the voltage source V_s is then

$$Z_{in} = R_s + Z_{inCL} = 2R_s \frac{1 + j\omega\left(\dfrac{1 + A_0}{2}\right)C_f R_s}{1 + j\omega(1 + A_0)C_f R_s} \tag{3-29a}$$

and for $\mathcal{A}_v \mathcal{H}_v \gg 1$, Eq. (3-29a) reduces to

$$Z_{in} \approx R_s = 100 \text{ k}\Omega \tag{3-29b}$$

3-2-2 Blackman's Impedance Relation

It should be clear by this point that by using negative feedback, one can control the impedances at various points within the closed loop circuit. More than thirty years ago, R. B. Blackman offered his method for determining the impedances in feedback amplifiers (Blackman 1943). Although his method is simple and general, it has unfortunately been ignored in most texts on feedback amplifier design. Many texts restrict their consideration to the four basic schemes in Fig. 3-7 and their specialized impedance relations. However, there are times when a feedback circuit does not conform to one of the basic configurations, and hence a more general technique is needed to derive impedance relations.

Let us consider a feedback circuit that includes a general controlled source, as shown in Fig. 3-11. In this circuit, X_j is the controlled source quantity (either voltage or current), X_i is the controlling quantity (either voltage or current), and X_i, X_j are related by the parameter k, i.e., $X_j = kX_i$. The impedance at any two terminals a and b of a feedback circuit can be determined by *Blackman's impedance relation*, i.e.,

$$Z_{ab} = \frac{V_{ab}}{I_{ab}} = Z_{ab}^0 \frac{1 + \mathcal{T}_{sc}}{1 + \mathcal{T}_{oc}} \tag{3-30}$$

where Z_{ab} is the feedback circuit impedance determined between terminals a
    and b,
V_{ab} is the Laplace transform of the voltage at terminals a and b,
I_{ab} is the Laplace transform of the current at terminals a and b,
Z_{ab}^0 is impedance Z_{ab} in the reference condition with controlled source
    $X_j = kX_i$ set to zero (i.e., this is equivalent to setting the open loop
    gain to zero),
$\mathcal{T}_{sc}$ is the loop gain with terminals a and b short-circuited,
$\mathcal{T}_{oc}$ is the loop gain with terminals a and b open-circuited.

Recall that Fig. 3-4 illustrates a means for breaking the loop to measure loop gain. In an analogous fashion, loop gains $\mathcal{T}_{sc}$ and $\mathcal{T}_{oc}$ can be determined by replacing a controlled source $X_j = kX_i$ by an independent source of value k, setting all other independent sources to zero, and deriving the relation for the voltage (or current)

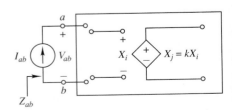

FIGURE 3-11   Circuit for deriving Blackman's impedance
relation.

variable X_i in the resulting circuit. Note that the dimension of k depends on the dimensions of X_i and X_j. For example, when both X_i and X_j are voltages (or currents), k is dimensionless. The loop gains $\mathcal{T}_{sc}$ and $\mathcal{T}_{oc}$ are then expressed by

$$\mathcal{T}_{sc} = -X_i|_{V_{ab}=0} \quad \text{and} \quad \mathcal{T}_{oc} = -X_i|_{I_{ab}=0} \qquad (3\text{-}31)$$

where terminals a and b are short-circuited and open-circuited, respectively. Note that $\mathcal{T}_{sc}$ and $\mathcal{T}_{oc}$ are dimensionless, and so is X_i, when $X_j = k$. This is equivalent to setting independent voltage source V_1 in Fig. 3-4 to $\mathcal{A}(s)$ and determining the voltage V_ε. With this assignment, referring to Fig. 3-4, we observe that

$$V_\varepsilon = -\mathcal{A}(s)\mathcal{H}(s) = -\mathcal{T}(s) \qquad (3\text{-}32)$$

In the case of multistage feedback networks that have several controlled sources, one must be selected as the reference for replacement by an independent source of value k. The same result will be achieved regardless of the one selected, and hence the choice should be made on the basis of convenience.

Since we expect that Blackman's impedance relation is unfamiliar to many readers, let us take a moment to derive Eq. (3-30). Referring to Fig. 3-11, let us write a pair of two-port relations using I_{ab} and X_j as sources, and V_{ab} and X_i as outputs, i.e.,

$$V_{ab} = AI_{ab} + BX_j \qquad (3\text{-}33a)$$

$$X_i = CI_{ab} + DX_j \qquad (3\text{-}33b)$$

Solving for the ratio V_{ab}/I_{ab}, we obtain the following relation for Z_{ab}

$$Z_{ab} = A\frac{1 - \dfrac{k(AD - BC)}{A}}{1 - kD} \qquad (3\text{-}34)$$

To complete the derivation, we now need to interpret each of the terms in Eq. (3-34).

First, from Eq. (3-33a), we have $A = V_{ab}/I_{ab}|_{X_j=0}$, which corresponds to the definition of Z_{ab}^0. Next, if $V_{ab} = 0$, which implies that terminals a and b are short circuited, and $X_j = k$, then Eqs. (3-33a) and (3-33b) can be manipulated to eliminate I_{ab} such that

$$X_i|_{V_{ab}=0} = \frac{k(AD - BC)}{A} = -\mathcal{T}_{sc} \qquad (3\text{-}35)$$

Finally, if $I_{ab} = 0$ and $X_j = k$, then from Eq. (3-33b),

$$X_i|_{I_{ab}=0} = kD = -\mathcal{T}_{oc} \qquad (3\text{-}36)$$

The derivation is complete.

Let us verify Blackman's relation and Eqs. (3-31) by using these new tools to evaluate the series-shunt circuit in Fig. 3-7a.

Example 3-6

Determine $\mathcal{T}_{sc}$, $\mathcal{T}_{oc}$, Z_{ab}^0, and Z_{ab}, where a and b are at the voltage source input, for the series-shunt feedback circuit in Fig. 3-7a. Use Blackman's formula and the method advocated in Eq. (3-31).

Solution. For this choice of entry, $Z_{ab} = Z_{inCL}$. Let us choose the reference dependent source to be $X_j = kX_i \rightarrow V_f = FV_{out}$, such that $\mathcal{T}_{sc}$, $\mathcal{T}_{oc}$ are determined using the circuit in Fig. 3-12 and

$$Z_{ab}^0 = Z_{inCL}|_{F=0} = R_S + Z_{inT} \tag{3-37}$$

From Fig. 3-12, we readily determine that

$$\mathcal{T}_{oc} = -V_{out}|_{I_{in}=0} = 0 \text{ and } \mathcal{T}_{sc} = -V_{out}|_{V_{ab}=0} = \frac{AF}{(R_S + Z_{inT})(G_L + Y_{outT})} \tag{3-38}$$

Hence, $\mathcal{T}_{sc} = \mathcal{A}\mathcal{H} = \mathcal{T}$ and the impedance Z_{ab} equals the series-shunt Z_{inCL} in Table 3-1, i.e.,

$$Z_{ab} = Z_{ab}^0(1 + \mathcal{A}\mathcal{H}) = Z_{inCL} \tag{3-39}$$

It is comforting to find that all roads, which are said to lead to Rome, do indeed go to Rome!

Note that one can always determine the impedance at any terminal-pair by employing brute-force mesh or nodal analysis to determine the current I_{ab} and voltage V_{ab}. However, we submit that Blackman's relation is a more intuitive approach, clearly showing the effect of feedback on impedance. Moreover, it will often be more efficient

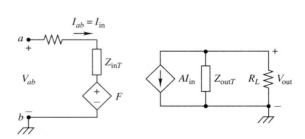

FIGURE 3-12   Series-shunt circuit in Fig. 3-7a rearranged for determining $\mathcal{T}_{ox}$ and $\mathcal{T}_{sc}$ in Example 3-6.

and reliable to calculate Z_{ab} using Eq. (3-30). In fact, in many cases either T_{sc} or T_{oc} is zero, and the nonzero loop gain corresponds to the system loop gain. Hence, the only new quantity required in this method is Z_{ab}^0. As we observed in the previous example, this is indeed the case for the input and output impedances associated with the basic schemes in Fig. 3-7.

Let us consider an example involving a transistor amplifier and resistive series-series feedback.

Example 3-7

Derive the input impedance for the voltage follower circuit in Fig. 3-13a. The equivalent circuit for this configuration is shown in Fig. 3-13b.

Solution. Setting controlled source $g_m V_{be}$ to zero, one can readily determine Z_{ab}^0 to be

$$Z_{ab}^0 = r_\pi + R_e + R_S \tag{3-40}$$

Replacing controlled current source $g_m V_{be}$ with an independent source of value g_m and setting independent voltage source $V_{in} = 0$, we may consider the derivation of the loop gains T_{sc} and T_{oc}, i.e.,

$$T_{sc} = -V_{be}|_{V_{ab}=0} \qquad \text{and} \qquad T_{oc} = -V_{be}|_{I_{ab}=0} \tag{3-41}$$

Clearly, when terminals a and b are open-circuited such that $I_{ab} = 0$, then $V_{be}r_\pi = I_{ab} = 0$ and $T_{oc} = 0$. To determine T_{sc}, we first convert current source $g_m V_{be}$ to a voltage source $g_m r_o V_{be}$. We then find V_{be} in Fig. 3-14, with dependent source $g_m r_o V_{be}$ set to $g_m r_o$, and terminals a and b shorted such that $V_{ab} = 0$. This

FIGURE 3-13   (a) The emitter follower for Example 3-7, and (b) its hybrid-π equivalent circuit.

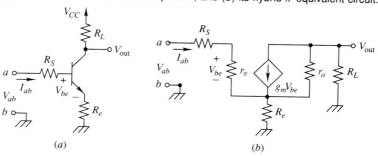

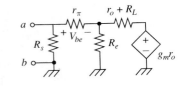

FIGURE 3-14 The rearranged emitter follower equivalent circuit to determine $\mathcal{T}_{sc}$ in Example 3-7, where the current source g_m is transformed into an equivalent voltage source $g_m r_o$.

process yields:

$$\mathcal{T}_{sc} = \frac{g_m r_\pi r_o R_e}{(R_S + r_\pi) R_e + (R_L + r_o) R_e + (R_L + r_o)(R_S + r_\pi)} \tag{3-42}$$

$$= \frac{g_m r_\pi r_o R_e}{(R_S + r_\pi + R_e)(R_L + r_o + R_e) - (R_e)^2}$$

Please note that if $\mathcal{A}\mathcal{H} = \mathcal{T}_{sc}$ were computed using Fig. 3-8a and Table 3-1, one would find that

$$\mathcal{A}\mathcal{H} = \frac{g_m r_\pi r_o R_e}{(R_S + r_\pi + R_e)(R_L + r_o + R_e)} \tag{3-43}$$

The difference between Eqs. (3-42) and (3-43) is due to the reverse transmission through R_e that is ignored in Eq. (3-43). Finally, substituting these results for Z_{ab}^0, $\mathcal{T}_{oc}$, and $\mathcal{T}_{sc}$ into Blackman's relation in Eq. (3-30) yields

$$Z_{ab} = \frac{V_{ab}}{I_{ab}} = Z_{ab}^0 \frac{1 + \mathcal{T}_{sc}}{1 + \mathcal{T}_{oc}} = (R_S + r_\pi + R_e)\{1 + \mathcal{T}_{sc}\} \tag{3-44}$$

3-2-3 The Asymptotic Gain Relation

The asymptotic gain relation is a simple relation used to compute the closed-loop gain for arbitrary feedback circuits (Rosenstark 1974). Like Blackman's relation, it is particularly useful when the feedback circuit under consideration does not readily stand out as one of the basic schemes in Fig. 3-7. The asymptotic gain relation is stated as follows

$$A_{CL} = K \frac{\mathcal{T}}{1 + \mathcal{T}} + \frac{G_0}{1 + \mathcal{T}} \tag{3-45}$$

where A_{CL} is the closed-loop gain

G_O is the direct transmission term, i.e $G_0 = A_{CL}|_{\mathcal{T}=0}$

K is the asymptotic gain, i.e., $K = A_{CL}|_{\mathcal{T}=\infty}$

$\mathcal{T}$ is loop-gain

To discuss the determination of these quantities, let us use Fig. 3-15, where again the feedback network is assumed to consist of at least one controlled source $X_j = kX_i$. One can derive the asymptotic gain relation in Eq. (3-45) using arguments similar to those used in the derivation of Blackman's impedance relation. In this case, let us consider V_1 and X_j as sources and V_2 and X_i as outputs. Accordingly, we may characterize the network with the following relations

$$V_2 = AV_1 + BX_j \qquad (3\text{-}46a)$$

$$X_i = CV_1 + DX_j \qquad (3\text{-}46b)$$

where $X_j = kX_i$.

Solving for the voltage gain ratio V_2/V_1, we obtain the following relation:

$$A_{CL} = \frac{V_2}{V_1} = \left(1 - \frac{BC}{D}\right)\frac{-kD}{1 - kD} + \frac{A}{1 - kD} \qquad (3\text{-}47)$$

Interpreting the terms in Eq. (3-47), we see that if $V_1 = 0$ and $X_j = k$, we find from Eq. (3-46b) that $X_i = kD$. Consequently, the loop gain is $T = -X_i = -kD$. Loop gain is derived in a manner analogous to the method used to determine T_{sc} and T_{oc} for Blackman's impedance relation.

The asymptotic gain K is determined by substituting $X_j = kX_i$ in Eqs. (3-46a) and (3-46b), algebraically eliminating X_i, solving for the ratio V_2/V_1, and taking the limit as k approaches infinity, i.e.,

$$K = \frac{V_2}{V_2}|_{k\to\infty} = \lim_{k\to\infty}\left(\frac{A - k(AD + BC)}{1 - kD}\right) = A + \frac{BC}{D} \qquad (3\text{-}48a)$$

$$= A_{CL}|_{k\to\infty} = A_{CL}|_{T\to\infty}$$

From the relation $T = -kD$, it should be clear that the condition $k \to \infty$ is equivalent to the condition $T \to \infty$. Let us now consider what happens to X_i when $k \to \infty$. This can be readily determined by setting $X_j = kX_i$ in Eq. (3-46b) and solving the result for X_i in terms of V_1, i.e., $X_i = [C/(1 - kD)]V_1$. Hence, for a finite V_1, $X_i|_{k\to\infty} = 0$. Note that for large loop gain (i.e., $T \gg 1$), which is usually the case, A_{CL} will approximately equal the asymptotic gain K. Referring back to Eq. (3-10), it should be clear that the asymptotic gain is $K = 1/\mathcal{H}$.

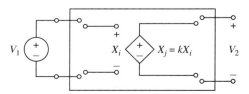

FIGURE 3-15 Circuit for deriving the asymptotic gain relation.

Correspondingly, the direct transmission term G_0 is determined by taking the limit as $k \to 0$, i.e.,

$$G_0 = \frac{V_2}{V_2}|_{k \to 0} = \lim_{k \to 0} \left[\frac{A - k(AD + BC)}{1 - kD} \right] = A \qquad (3\text{-}48b)$$

$$= A_{CL}|_{k \to 0} = A_{CL}|_{T \to 0} \qquad (3\text{-}49)$$

This term is equivalent to the forward transmission though the feedback circuit, which is usually a passive network. Remember that in the previous section we assumed the forward transmission through the feedback network to be negligible. Typically, $G_0 \ll KT$ and

$$A_{CL} \approx K \frac{T}{1 + T} = \left(1 - \frac{BC}{D} \right) \frac{-kD}{1 - kD} \qquad (3\text{-}50)$$

Comparing Eqs. (3-45) and (3-50), one can interpret the first term in the asymptotic gain relation in Eq. (3-46) as being the dominant term, particularly for large loop-gain ($T \gg 1$). The second term can be interpreted as a corrective term, which modifies the relation when the loop-gain (the amount of feedback) is not very large compared to unity. Under this condition, the basic transmission assumptions expressed in Sec. 3-1-2, and the approximations they suggest, are no longer valid. We now see that the asymptotic gain relation is a rather general, powerful, and insightful relation for computing closed-loop-gain. Its use is not tied to specific feedback configurations, and it is applicable when the loop-gain is large or small.

Remember that in the case of multistage feedback circuits with several controlled sources, one controlled source must be selected as a reference source. This controlled source is replaced by an independent source of value k in the determination of loop-gain T. This source is also set to infinity when determining asymptotic gain K, and set to zero for evaluating the direct transmission term G_0. The same result will be achieved no matter which one is selected and hence the choice should be made solely on the basis of convenience.

3-3 STABILITY CONSIDERATIONS IN LINEAR FEEDBACK SYSTEMS

Stability in electronic circuits and systems occurs when all bounded excitations produce bounded responses. In practical terms, the output of a stable circuit cannot diverge (i.e., to a limit set by the power supply rail(s)) for any input that has limited amplitude (Bode 1945; Daryanani 1976; Desoer and Kuh 1969; Geiger, Allen, and Strader 1990; Rosenstark 1986; Savant 1964; Schaumann, Ghausi, and Laker 1990; Sedra and Smith 1991; Waldhauer 1982). Also, a stable circuit cannot sustain oscillations in the absence of an applied source. Passive RLC circuits are stable by their very nature, since they do not contain energy sources that might inject additional energy into the circuit. Active networks, on the other hand, do contain energy sources that can combine constructively to produce unstable behavior. Circuits and systems that produce unbounded responses to bounded excitations are said to be *unstable*.

Oscillators are very useful analog functions, but the occurrence of unwanted oscillations is a serious performance degradation and represents borderline instability in linear feedback systems. An important objective in the design of feedback circuits used in linear signal processing applications is to avoid even potential instability. In other words, the goal is to design a circuit that is stable under all input signal conditions and for all ranges of component values. A system that is stable under any and all conditions is referred to as *unconditionally stable*, or *absolutely stable*. Absolute stability occurs only in the simplest of feedback systems and is generally not a realistic design objective. Since circuit components can and will change from their nominal values due to statistical manufacturing errors, temperature, and aging, it is important to employ safety margins when designing for stability. In this context, we will introduce the concepts of *gain margin* and *phase margin*. These margins are either readily determined analytically, calculated from computer simulations, or measured experimentally. They lend significant insight into the current stability condition of a circuit and they can also be helpful in determining the amount of feedback $\mathcal{H}$, needed to produce particular stability objectives. At a minimum, designs must guarantee stability over the full range of allowed circuit components and ambient operating conditions.

In a feedback system, such as the general structure of Fig. 3-3, the open-loop-gain $\mathcal{A}(s) = N_a(s)/D_a(s)$ is generally a function of frequency and is more accurately referred to as the *open-loop transfer function*. Although in many of our discussions we have assumed that the feedback factor $\mathcal{H}$ is frequency independent, derived from an all-resistor feedback network, we know this is also generally not the case. In fact, we have discussed some very practical yet simple applications of frequency dependent feedback, the most notable being the integrator type circuit in Fig. 3-10. In general, we will refer to $\mathcal{H}(s) = N_f(s)/D_f(s)$ as the *feedback transfer function*. It then follows that the closed-loop transfer function $A_{CL}(s)$ is expressed as

$$A_{CL}(s) = \frac{N(s)}{D(s)} = \frac{\mathcal{A}(s)}{1 + \mathcal{A}(s)\mathcal{H}(s)} = \frac{N_a(s)D_f(s)}{D_a(s)D_f(s) + N_a(s)N_f(s)} \qquad (3\text{-}51)$$

It should be well known to the reader that the stability of the circuit/system is assured if all the poles of $A_{CL}(s)$, i.e., the roots of the characteristic equation $D(s)$, are in the left-half of the s-plane (i.e., $\sigma < 0$). Otherwise, the circuit/system either oscillates or is unstable. This suggests a straightforward way for checking stability; evaluate the closed-loop transfer function $A_{CL}(s)$ and factor the denominator $D(s)$ to determine the locations of its roots. This procedure, although conceptually simple and at times useful, usually requires the factoring of a high-order polynomial—a task that can readily be accomplished on a computer used for specific numerical cases. The results of this exercise, however, offer little indication as to the margins by which stability is achieved and they do not add additional design insight. For design purposes, we want symbolic and graphical methods of determining stability that also provide insight into the relationship between $\mathcal{A}\mathcal{H}$ and the degree of stability.

It should be evident that stability must be guaranteed at all frequencies from DC to infinity, not just within the passband or some limited frequency range of operation.

In other words, the effect of all nondominant poles and excess phase shifts, deemed ignorable in an approximate frequency response calculation, must be taken into account if stability is to be guaranteed. This implies that accurate models or experimental data must be used in stability calculations. In this section, we explore alternative and more insightful techniques for examining stability.

Let us assume that the open-loop circuit $A(s)$ is lowpass, i.e., it passes DC and all frequencies $\omega < \omega_C$ with constant gain A_0. The gain $|A(s)|$ then declines with frequency as determined by poles and zeros occurring at frequencies $\omega \geq \omega_C$. To simplify matters, let us assume that at low frequencies the feedback $\mathcal{H}(s)$ reduces to a constant value $(\mathcal{H}_0)$. Hence, at low frequencies $(\omega < \omega_C)$, the loop-gain $T(s) = A(s)\mathcal{H}(s) = A_0\mathcal{H}_0$ is also constant, and positive if the feedback is negative. What then happens at higher frequencies (i.e., $\omega > \omega_C$)?

For physical or sinusoidal steady state frequencies, i.e., $s = j\omega$, Eq. (3-51) becomes

$$A_{CL}(j\omega) = \frac{A(j\omega)}{1 + T(j\omega)} \tag{3-52}$$

Thus the loop-gain $A(j\omega)\mathcal{H}(j\omega)$ is a complex number that can also be represented in terms of magnitude and phase, i.e.,

$$T(j\omega) \equiv A(j\omega)\mathcal{H}(j\omega) = |A(j\omega)\mathcal{H}(j\omega)|e^{j\varphi(\omega)} \tag{3-53}$$

The stability or instability can then be ascertained by observing the manner in which the loop-gain varies with frequency. For example, consider the frequency (ω_φ) at which the phase angle $\varphi(\omega)$ becomes equal to π radians or $180°$. At this frequency, the loop-gain is a negative, real number and the feedback is positive. If $|T(j\omega_\varphi)| < 1$, then $1 + T(j\omega_\varphi) < 1$ and $A_{CL}(j\omega_\varphi) > A(j\omega_\varphi)$. Nevertheless, the feedback system is still stable. If, on the other hand, $|T(j\omega_\varphi)| = 1$, then $1 + T(j\omega_\varphi) = 0$ and $A_{CL}(j\omega_\varphi) = \infty$. In this case, the closed-loop system has a nonzero output for a zero input, and the system oscillates at the frequency ω_φ.

What then happens when $|T(j\omega_\varphi)| > 1$? The answer, though not obvious from Eq. (3-52), is that the system will oscillate and the oscillation will grow in magnitude until some nonlinearity (by design or inherence) reduces the loop-gain to unity, at which time oscillation is sustained. An example of an inherent nonlinearity is the saturation that occurs when the output reaches limits set by the power supply rails. We point out that this type of limiting has proven to be very effective in the realization of sinusoidal oscillators that have very robust start-up properties (Sedra and Smith 1991). We will assume for now that oscillations represent intolerable system performance, and that they are to be prevented at all cost.

3-3-1   Effect of Feedback on the System Natural Frequencies

It is insightful to explore how the poles of the open-loop transfer function shift with the application of feedback. Let us assume for simplicity that the open-loop transfer function is comprised of only stable, real poles and no finite zeros (that is, all the zeros are at $s = \infty$ and N_a is a constant). Let us also assume for now that the feedback is resistive, i.e., $\mathcal{H}$ is real and independent of frequency. These assumptions will simplify the symbolic analysis, and permit us to focus on the fundamental concepts.

One-Pole System   Let us consider the case where $\mathcal{A}(s)$ is a single-pole function, i.e.,

$$\mathcal{A}(s) = \frac{A_0}{1 + s/\omega_p} \tag{3-54}$$

Please note that ω_p is a real valued quantity. This type of system was discussed earlier in Example 3-2. The corresponding loop-gain and closed-loop transfer functions are given, respectively, as

$$\mathcal{T}(s) = \mathcal{A}(s)\mathcal{H} = \frac{A_0\mathcal{H}}{1 + s/\omega_p} \tag{3-55a}$$

$$A_{CL}(s) = \frac{A_0/(1 + A_0\mathcal{H})}{1 + s/\omega_p(1 + A_0\mathcal{H})} \tag{3-55b}$$

Dividing numerator and denominator of the term $A_0/(1 + A_0\mathcal{H})$ by $A_0\mathcal{H}$, yields the following useful reformulation of Eq. (3-55b):

$$A_{CL}(s) = \frac{\dfrac{1}{\mathcal{H}}\left(\dfrac{1}{1 + A_0\mathcal{H}}\right)}{1 + s/\omega_p(1 + A_0\mathcal{H})} = \frac{A_{CL0}}{1 + s/\omega_{CLp}} \tag{3-56a}$$

In many instances, the loop-gain $A_0\mathcal{H} \gg 1$, which leads to the often used approximation

$$\frac{\dfrac{1}{\mathcal{H}}\left(\dfrac{1}{1 + A_0\mathcal{H}}\right)}{1 + s/\omega_p(1 + A_0\mathcal{H})} \approx \frac{\dfrac{1}{\mathcal{H}}\left(1 - \dfrac{1}{A_0\mathcal{H}}\right)}{1 + s/\omega_p A_0\mathcal{H}} = \frac{\dfrac{1}{\mathcal{H}}\left(1 - \dfrac{1}{A_0\mathcal{H}}\right)}{1 + s/\omega_{CLp}} \tag{3-56b}$$

We see that increasing the low frequency or DC loop-gain $A_0\mathcal{H}$ from zero shifts the pole along the negative real axis, as illustrated in Fig. 3-16a. The closed-loop pole location is then given by $\omega_{CLp} = \omega_p(1 + A_0\mathcal{H})$. The closed-loop gain decreases correspondingly, approaching the value $1/\mathcal{H}$, as $A_0\mathcal{H}$ becomes very large. The Bode magnitude plot in Fig. 3-16b (although not shown, a corresponding Bode plot for the phase can be drawn) indicates that at low frequencies (i.e., $\omega < \omega_p$), the difference between the open-loop and closed-loop functions is $-20\log(1 + A_0\mathcal{H}) \approx -20\log(A_0\mathcal{H})$ for $A_0\mathcal{H} \gg 1$. However, at higher frequencies (i.e., $\omega > \omega_{CLp}$) the two characteristics coincide, following the same -6 dB/octave (or -20 dB/decade) asymptote. One can verify that this is indeed the case by determining the limits of $\mathcal{A}(s)$ and $A_{CL}(s)$ in Eqs. (3-54) and (3-56b), respectively, as $\omega \to \infty$, i.e.,

$$\mathcal{A}(s) \approx A_{CL}(s) \approx \frac{A_0\omega_p}{s} = \frac{\omega_t}{s} \tag{3-57}$$

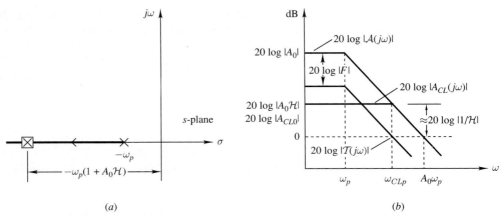

(a)   (b)

FIGURE 3-16   Effect of feedback on (a) pole location and (b) closed loop gain for a feedback circuit with a single-pole open-loop transfer function.

Physically, Eq. (3-57) is the consequence of the feedback $(1 + \mathcal{A}(s)\mathcal{H})$ being reduced, due to the roll off of $|\mathcal{A}(j\omega)|$ with frequency, to the point of being ineffective.

Note that since the pole never leaves the left-half plane for any value of $\mathcal{H}$, we conclude that a single-pole feedback system is absolutely or unconditionally stable. This result is physically appealing, since the phase lag associated with a single-pole response can be no larger than 90°. Consequently, the system never reaches the 180° degree phase shift needed for the feedback to become positive.

Two-Pole System   Let us now consider the application of resistive feedback to a two-pole open-loop system, given by

$$\mathcal{A}(s) = \frac{A_0}{(1 + s/\omega_{p1})(1 + s/\omega_{p2})} \tag{3-58}$$

where ω_{p1} and ω_{p2} are real, and $\omega_{p1} \ll \omega_{p2}$. We note that for op amps, the pole frequencies ω_{p1} and ω_{p2} are usually spaced widely apart such that $\omega_{p2} > A_0\omega_{p1}$. In such cases, ω_{p1} is said to be the *dominant pole* (ω_d) and ω_{p2} the *nondominant pole* (ω_{nd}); see Apps. 3-1 and 3-2.

The corresponding loop-gain transfer function is $T(s) = \mathcal{A}(s)\mathcal{H}$, such that

$$T(s) = \frac{A_0\mathcal{H}}{(1 + s/\omega_{p1})(1 + s/\omega_{p2})} \tag{3-59a}$$

$$\approx \frac{(A_0\mathcal{H})\omega_{p1}}{s(1 + s/\omega_{p2})} \qquad \text{for } s \gg \omega_{p1} \tag{3-59b}$$

If, in addition, $\omega_{p2} > (A_0\mathcal{H})\omega_{p1}$ in Eq. (3-59b), then ω_{p1} is a dominant pole and the loop gain-bandwidth product is $\omega_{CLp1} = (A_0\mathcal{H})\omega_{p1}$. For second-order and higher-order systems, the ω_{CLp1} and the unity-gain-frequency do not necessarily coincide. The exact calculation for ω_u as function of $\omega_{p2}/\omega_{CLp1}$ is discussed in App. 3-2 (where in App 3-2, let $\omega_{CLp1} \rightarrow \omega_t$ or loop gain-bandwidth product).

Using Eqs. (3-59), the closed-loop transfer function can be written as

where

$$A_{CL}(s) = \frac{A_0\omega_{p1}\omega_{p2}}{1 + \mathcal{A}(s)\mathcal{H}} \tag{3-60a}$$

$$1 + \mathcal{A}(s)\mathcal{H} = s^2 + s(\omega_{p1} + \omega_{p2}) + (1 + A_0\mathcal{H})\omega_{p1}\omega_{p2} \tag{3-60b}$$

Note that for $s \gg \omega_{p1}, \omega_{p2} > (A_0\mathcal{H})\omega_{p1}$, and $A_0\mathcal{H} \gg 1$, Eq. (3-60b) reduces to

$$1 + \mathcal{A}(s)\mathcal{H} \approx s^2 + s\omega_{p2} + (A_0\mathcal{H})\omega_{p1}\omega_{p2}$$

$$= s^2 + s\omega_{p2} + \omega_{CLp1}\omega_{p2} \tag{3-60c}$$

The closed-loop pole locations are then determined by setting $1 + \mathcal{A}(s\mathcal{H}) = 0$ in Eq. (3-60b) and solving for the roots s_1 and s_2, i.e.,

$$s_1, s_2 = -\frac{1}{2}(\omega_{p1} + \omega_{p2}) \pm \frac{1}{2}\sqrt{(\omega_{p1} + \omega_{p2})^2 - 4(1 + A_0\mathcal{H})\omega_{p1}\omega_{p2}} \tag{3-61a}$$

$$\approx -\frac{1}{2}\omega_{p2} \pm \frac{1}{2}\sqrt{\omega_{p2}^2 - 4\omega_{CLp1}\omega_{p2}} \tag{3-61b}$$

where in Eq. (3-61b) we assume the dominant pole condition represented by Eq. (3-60c). The error associated with the dominant pole approximation is analyzed in App. 3-1.

The locations of the poles (s_1, s_2), as the DC loop-gain $A_0\mathcal{H}$ is increased from zero, are illustrated in the pole location plot in Fig. 3-17. This plot is referred to as a *root locus diagram*. Following the shift of the poles, as $A_0\mathcal{H}$ increases, reveals that the poles initially move toward each other. They become coincident at $\sigma = -(\omega_{p1} + \omega_{p2})/2$, when $(\omega_{p1} + \omega_{p2})^2 - 4(1 + A_0\mathcal{H})\omega_{p1}\omega_{p2} = 0$ or for the value of $A_0\mathcal{H} = (A_0\mathcal{H})_1$ given by

$$(A_0\mathcal{H})_1 = \left[\frac{(\omega_{p1} + \omega_{p2})^2}{4\omega_{p1}\omega_{p2}}\right] - 1 \approx \frac{(\omega_{p1} + \omega_{p2})^2}{4\omega_{p1}\omega_{p2}}$$

$$\approx \frac{\omega_{p2}}{4\omega_{p1}} \qquad \text{for } \omega_{p2} \gg \omega_{p1}$$

For $A_0\mathcal{H} > (A_0\mathcal{H})_1$, the poles are complex conjugate, i.e., $s_2 = s_1^*$, and move along the vertical line shown in Fig. 3-17. The root locus shows that the poles remain in the left-half s-plane for all values of $(A_0\mathcal{H})$; this second-order feedback system is absolutely stable. This result is consistent with the physical observation that the phase lag for a two-pole system asymptotically approaches $180°$ as $\omega \rightarrow \infty$. Consequently, there is no finite frequency for which $|1 + \mathcal{A}(s)\mathcal{H}| = 0$. Even though stability is assured, the design of a second-order system that satisfies specific transient response

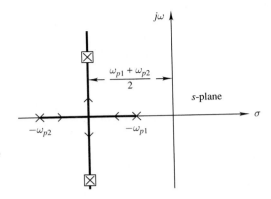

FIGURE 3-17   Effect of feedback on the pole location for a feedback circuit with a second order open-loop transfer function comprised of two real poles.

requirements requires more careful consideration of the location of the system poles. In amplifier design, we generally want to avoid situations where $|1 + \mathcal{A}(s)\mathcal{H}| \approx 0$, to ensure that the transient response is well behaved. On the other hand, in filter design (see Chaps. 7 and 8), feedback is often used to locate poles so that $|1 + \mathcal{A}(s)\mathcal{H}| \approx 0$, in order to realize highly selective filters. These issues are discussed next.

Second-order feedback systems are very important in amplifier and active filter applications. Let us take a moment to examine the fine structure of their frequency domain and transient behavior. Second-order characteristic equations are often expressed in the following standard forms:

$$D(s) = s^2 + s\left(\frac{\omega_0}{Q_p}\right) + \omega_0^2 = s^2 + s(2\zeta\omega_0) + \omega_0^2 = 0 \qquad (3\text{-}62)$$

$$= (s + s_1)(s + s_1^*)$$

Where ω_0 is the *resonant frequency*, Q_p is the *pole quality factor*, and ζ $(\zeta = 1/2Q_p)$ is the *damping ratio*. The relationships for these parameters are best illustrated geometrically, using the simple diagram in Fig. 3-18a. From this diagram we discern that

$$Re(s_1) = \omega_0\zeta, \; Im(s_1) = \omega_0\sqrt{1 - \zeta^2} = \omega_p, \qquad \text{and} \qquad |s_1| = \omega_0.$$

where ω_p is the peak or pole frequency. Note that when $\zeta \ll 1$ or $Q_p \gg 1$, $\omega_p \approx \omega_0$.

Using these relations, we can write the expression for the polar angle θ in Fig. 3-18a of the complex poles as follows:

$$\theta = \arctan\left(\frac{Im(s)}{Re(s)}\right) = \arctan\sqrt{\frac{1}{\zeta^2} - 1} = \arctan\sqrt{4Q_p^2 - 1}$$

We see that quality factor Q_p is inversely proportional to the distance the pole lies from the $j\omega$-axis. That is, as the complex pole pair approaches the $j\omega$-axis, the $Q_p \to$ large and $\theta \to 90°$. We note that the poles are found to be complex for $Q_p > 0.5$

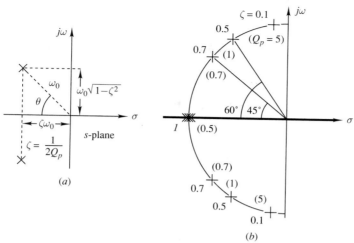

FIGURE 3-18   (a) Relationships between pole location and quality factor Q_p, damping ratio ζ, and resonant frequency ω_0; (b) pole locations for various values of damping ratio ζ (and quality factor Q_p).

or $\zeta < 1$ and lie exactly on the $j\omega$-axis when $Q_p = \infty$ or $\zeta = 0$. Pole positions for several values of ζ are shown in Fig. 3-18b.

For the second-order feedback system under study, the parameters ω_0, Q_p, and ζ are expressed as

$$\omega_0 = \sqrt{(1 + A_0 \mathcal{H}) \omega_{p1} \omega_{p2}} \approx \sqrt{(A_0 \mathcal{H}) \omega_{p1} \omega_{p2}} = \sqrt{\omega_{CLp1} \omega_{p2}} \qquad (3\text{-}63a)$$

$$Q_p = \frac{\sqrt{(1 + A_0 \mathcal{H}) \omega_{p1} \omega_{p2}}}{\omega_{p1} + \omega_{p2}} \approx \frac{\sqrt{(A_0 \mathcal{H}) \omega_{p1} \omega_{p2}}}{\omega_{p2}} = \sqrt{\frac{\omega_{CLp1}}{\omega_{p2}}} \qquad (3\text{-}63b)$$

and

$$\zeta = \frac{1}{2} \frac{\omega_{p1} + \omega_{p2}}{\sqrt{(1 + A_0 \mathcal{H}) \omega_{p1} \omega_{p2}}} \approx \frac{1}{2} \frac{\omega_{p2}}{\sqrt{(A_0 \mathcal{H}) \omega_{p1} \omega_{p2}}} = \frac{1}{2} \sqrt{\frac{\omega_{p2}}{\omega_{CLp1}}} \qquad (3\text{-}63c)$$

The gain $G(\Omega)$ and phase $\varphi(\Omega)$ responses for a second-order closed loop system are shown as a function of normalized frequency ($\Omega = \omega / \omega_p$) in Fig. 3-19. Peaking in the response, as shown in Fig. 3-19a, occurs at $\omega = \omega_p$ when $\zeta < 0.707 (Q_p > 0.707)$. The amount of peaking increases with decreasing ζ (or increasing Q_p), i.e.,

$$A_p = 20 \log \frac{1}{2 \zeta \sqrt{1 - \zeta^2}} = 20 \log \frac{Q_p}{\sqrt{1 - \frac{1}{4 Q_p^2}}} \text{ dB} \qquad (3\text{-}63d)$$

When $\zeta = 0.1$ or $Q_p = 5$, we observe that the amount of peaking is about $A_p = 14$ dB. For $\zeta = 0.5$ or $Q_p = 1$, the poles are at $\theta = \pm 45°$ and A_p is only 1.25 dB.

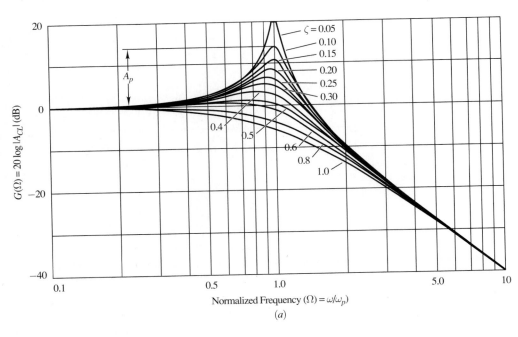

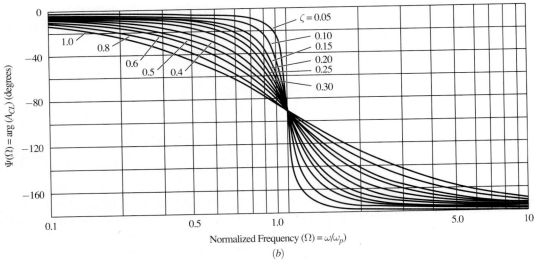

FIGURE 3-19   Second-order circuit frequency responses for values of damping ratio ζ (and quality factor Q_p); (a) gain versus ω and (b) phase versus ω.

For $\zeta = Q_p = 0.707$ (or $1/\sqrt{2}$), the pole angles are less than $\pm 30°$ and $A_p/A = 1$, i.e., the frequency response is *maximally flat*. When $\zeta = 1$ or $Q_p = 0.5$, the poles become real and coincide. For $\zeta > 1$, the poles are real and split apart; the damping is actually no longer defined. We also observe that the slope of the phase $(d\varphi/d\Omega)$, at and near $\Omega = 1$, increases as the damping ζ decreases (i.e., Q_p increases). As we will discuss in Chap. 5, $d\varphi/d\Omega$ is proportional to the group delay $(\tau(\Omega) = -d\varphi(\Omega)/d\Omega)$. In Chaps. 7 and 8 we will often use feedback circuits, with pole Q_p's of 5 or more $(\zeta \leq 0.1)$, to realize filters with high out-of-band discrimination.

In the design of op amps (Chap. 6), particularly those used in switched-capacitor filters (Chap. 8), the transient response of second-order feedback systems is an important design objective. The typical vehicle for evaluating this behavior is the step response; i.e., the response due to a unit step excitation $u(t)$, where $u(t) = 1$ for $t \geq 0$ and $u(t) = 0$ for $t < 0$. The system transfer function is given by

$$A(s) = \frac{\omega_0^2}{s^2 + s(2\zeta\omega_0) + \omega_0^2} \tag{3-64a}$$

The step response, solved by taking the inverse Laplace transform of $R_U(s) = (1/s)A(s)$, can be written as

$$r_u(t) = \left[1 + \frac{1}{\sqrt{1 - \zeta^2}}e^{-\zeta\omega_0 t}\sin\left(\omega_0\sqrt{1 - \zeta^2}t + \varphi\right)\right]u(t) \tag{3-64b}$$

where

$$\varphi = \arctan\frac{\sqrt{1 - \zeta^2}}{\zeta}.$$

Examining the plots of $r_u(t)$ in Fig. 3-20a and Eq. (3-64b), we find that for the values of $\zeta > 0$, the step responses ultimately converge to a *steady-state* of $r_{ss} = r_u(\infty) = 1$, i.e., they *settle* to a value of unity, or the envelope of the unit step, after some period of time. This period of time is called the *settling time* (t_s), as shown in Fig. 3-20a. In practice, t_s is defined in terms of the time required to settle to some specified percent of the final or steady-state value (e.g., 99 percent or $\varepsilon = 0.01$ or 99.9 percent or $\varepsilon = 0.001$). We use the notation $t_s(\varepsilon)$ to indicate the specific definition used. When $\zeta = 0$, $r_u(t)$ freely oscillates at frequency ω_0 about a pedestal of unity.

For $0 < \zeta < 1$, $r_u(t)$ is seen to overshoot and settle to the steady-state value of unity in an oscillatory manner. The maximum or peak overshoot r_p always occurs at the first overshoot. To determine the time of the peak overshoot, we set the derivative $dr_u(t)/t = 0$ and solve for $t = t_p$ of the first peak, i.e.,

$$t_p = \frac{\pi}{\omega_0\sqrt{1 - \zeta^2}} \tag{3-64c}$$

Substituting Eq. (3-64c) back into Eq. (3-64b) for t, we obtain the value for the peak overshoot r_p, i.e.,

$$r_p = r_u(t_p) = 1 + e^{-\pi\zeta/\sqrt{1 - \zeta^2}} \tag{3-64d}$$

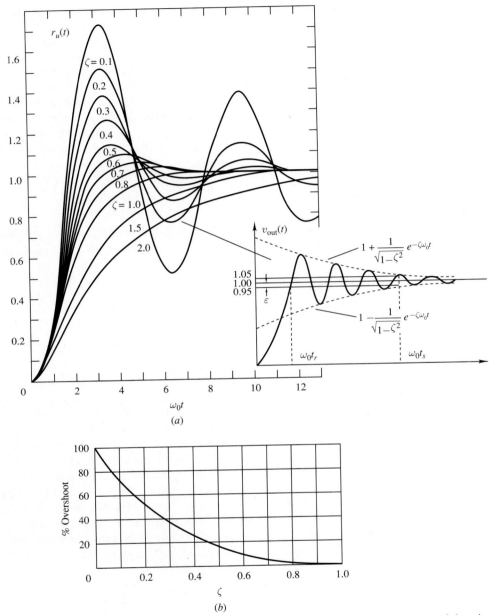

FIGURE 3-20   Second-order circuit step response: (a) plots of $r_u(t)$ in Eq. (3-64b) for various values of damping ratio ζ and (b) percent overshoot as function of ζ. Shown as an insert in (a) are the definitions for rise-time t_r and settling-time t_s. Note that the time scale is normalized to $\omega_0 t$.

Percent overshoot is then defined as

$$\% \text{ overshoot} = \frac{r_p - r_{ss}}{r_{ss}} \times 100\% \qquad (3\text{-}65)$$

In Fig. 3-20b, we plot percent overshoot as a function of ζ.

It is evident that both overshoot and settling time increase as ζ decreases. Comparing Fig. 3-19a and Fig. 3-20a, we see that peaking in the frequency response corresponds to overshoot in the step response. When $\zeta \geq 1$, the roots are real and the overshoot (and peaking) are nonexistent. When $\zeta > 1$, the system is said to be *overdamped*, and t_s increases with increasing ζ. In contrast, the system is *underdamped* when $\zeta < 1$, and we have already noted that for such cases t_s increases as ζ decreases. When $\zeta = 1$, the system is said to be *critically damped*.

Three-Pole System Let us increase the complexity of the open-loop transfer function by one more pole and consider the three-pole situation illustrated in the root locus diagram in Fig. 3-21. As indicated, increasing the loop-gain moves the highest frequency pole ω_{p3} outward along the negative real-axis and moves the two lower frequency poles ω_{p1}, ω_{p2} toward each other in a manner similar to the two-pole case. Increasing the loop-gain further causes poles ω_{p1}, ω_{p2} to become coincident and then to become complex and conjugate. With sufficiently large $(A_0 \mathcal{H})$, the complex conjugate poles cross the $j\omega$-axis into the right-half plane. The system is then unstable.

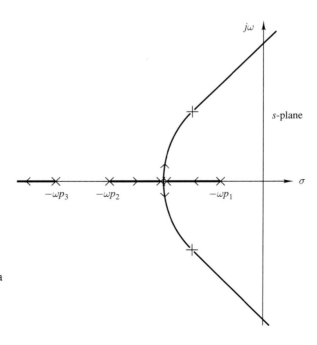

FIGURE 3-21   Root-locus of pole locations for a feedback circuit comprised of an all-pole third-order open-loop $A(s)$ and a resistive feedback factor $\mathcal{H}$.

Recognizing that the three pole loop transfer function has a phase lag of $270°$ as ω approaches ∞, one should expect a $180°$ phase shift to occur at a finite frequency (ω_φ). From the root locus we observe that a stable system can be maintained by ensuring that $(A_0 \mathcal{H})$ is never sufficiently large (either by design or by error due to manufacturing tolerances, temperature, aging, etc.) to shift the poles out of the left-half plane. In other words, there is a maximum value for loop-gain $(A_0 \mathcal{H})$ above which results in instability. Correspondingly, there is a minimum value for low frequency closed-loop gain A_{CL0} that can be realized before instability occurs. To realize lower closed-loop gains, one must alter the loop transfer characteristic $A\mathcal{H}$. This process, *compensation*, is an important aspect of feedback amplifier design. In Sec. 5-3 and again in Chap. 6, we will develop the concept of compensation in more detail when we discuss the design of op amps.

Note that the construction of a root locus diagram for systems higher than third-order and/or that have finite transmission zeros is a time consuming process. Fortunately, a systematic procedure does exist for constructing root locus diagrams and computer programs (e.g., in MATLAB (1988; 1990)) exist that automate this process. This procedure will not be covered here, so the interested reader is referred to any one of several electronic circuits texts (Ghausi 1985; Sedra and Smith 1991) or feedback control texts (e.g., Savant 1964) to review root locus construction.

The three-pole case demonstrates the importance of including nondominant open-loop poles (and zeros) when analyzing stability. The added phase lag of a third nondominant real pole, in an otherwise approximate second-order system, is suffi-cient to cause instability for large enough loop-gain. In other words, a nondominant open-loop pole can become a dominant closed-loop pole when sufficient feedback is applied. Adding more poles to the open-loop response further aggrevates the problem. Consequently, one must be particularly careful about making approximations in the open-loop transfer function when analyzing and designing feedback systems, particu-larly when evaluating stability. In the next section, we will consider the use of Bode plots in the determination of stability and stability margins. One very attractive feature of this approach is that experimental measurements can be used directly, eliminating concern over the accuracy of the open-loop model.

3-3-2 The Use of Bode Plots in Stability Analysis

From previous discussions, we know that we can determine stability by examining the loop-gain $T(j\omega)$ as a function of frequency. Bode plots, for sketching asymptotic approximations for the magnitude and phase of $T(j\omega)$ as defined in Eq. (3-53), are very convenient and effective tools for conducting this examination. Magnitude and phase characteristics, or Bode plots, can be drawn directly from experimental data or SPICE simulation. We assume in this section that the reader has a basic familiarity with the Bode plot technique. We refer readers who feel a need to review this method to any one of several texts that cover this material, (e.g., Daryanani 1976; Ghausi 1985; Sedra and Smith 1991).

The technique to be employed is illustrated in Fig. 3-22. In this illustration, four parameters are displayed, namely, ω_φ, ω_u, PM, and GM. The frequencies ω_φ and ω_u

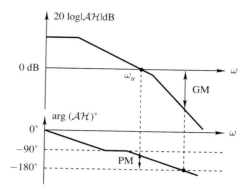

FIGURE 3-22   Determination of gain and phase margins from Bode plots.

are the frequencies where the phase is $-180°$ and the magnitude is unity (or 0 dB), respectively. In the context of stability analysis, these frequencies are sometimes referred to, respectively, as the *phase-crossover* and *gain-crossover frequencies*. Note that the gain-crossover frequency is the unity-gain frequency discussed in the previous subsection. The parameter PM, an abbreviation for *phase margin*, is defined as the difference between the phase $\varphi(j\omega_u) = \arg[T(j\omega_u)]$ and $-180°$ when $|T| = 1$. Referring to Fig. 3-22, we can express PM as follows:

$$\text{PM} = \varphi(j\omega_u) - (-180°) \tag{3-66}$$

Phase margin is an important measure of stability, as it represents the number of degrees of additional phase lag permitted before the feedback system becomes unstable.

The parameter GM, an abbreviation for *gain margin*, is defined as the difference between the gain $20 \log |T(j\omega_\varphi)|$ and 0 dB (or unity gain) $\varphi = 180°$. Referring again to Fig. 3-22, we can express GM as follows:

$$\text{GM} = 0 \text{ dB} - 20\log |T(j\omega_\varphi)| = -20\log |T(j\omega_\varphi)| \text{ dB} \tag{3-67}$$

Gain margin is an alternative measure of stability, since it represents the additional loop-gain (in dB) permitted before the feedback system becomes unstable.

Based on our previous discussions regarding stability, the reader should find Eqs. (3-66) and (3-67) intuitively appealing. We note that for stable systems, both PM and GM are positive quantities. Consequently, zero phase (or gain) margin implies the system can oscillate and negative phase (or gain) margin implies instability. Since absolute stability is an unrealistic expectation, stable feedback systems are designed to have sufficient gain and phase margins to allow for the inevitable changes in loop-gain due to manufacturing tolerances, temperature, aging, etc. Moreover, with amplifiers we must also be concerned about peaking and overshoot.

In the previous subsection we demonstrated that one-pole and two-pole feedback systems are absolutely stable. It should be expected that the phase margin for a one-pole feedback system is positive and PM $\geq 90°$, depending on the location of the closed-loop pole. Correspondingly, the phase margin for the two-pole feedback system is positive and PM $\geq 0°$, depending on the location of the closed-loop pole-pair. For complex pole-pairs, it is intuitive that PM decreases as the damping ratio ζ decreases. Thus, as PM decreases, both the peaking in the frequency response and the overshoot in the step response increase as illustrated in Fig. 3-19 and Fig. 3-20. For $\zeta < 1$ (or PM $< 76°$) we can write the following useful formulas that relate PM to ζ and Q_p, i.e.,

$$\zeta = \frac{1}{2Q_p} = \frac{1}{2}\sqrt{\frac{\omega_{p2}}{\omega_{CLp1}}} = \frac{\sin(\text{PM})}{2\sqrt{\cos(\text{PM})}} \tag{3-68a}$$

or

$$\text{PM} = \arccos[\sqrt{1 + 4\zeta^4} - 2\zeta^2] \tag{3-68b}$$

These relationships are shown graphically in Fig. 3-23. The interested reader can find the development of these expressions in App. 3-2 (recall that $\omega_{p2} = \omega_{nd}$). Also, when $\zeta \ll 1$ (or PM $\ll 76°$), the following approximate expression can be written for settling-time $t_s(\varepsilon)$ in terms of PM and ω_{CLp1}:

$$t_s(\varepsilon) = \frac{2\pi}{\omega_{CLp1}}\left\{\frac{2\cos(\text{PM})}{\sin^2(\text{PM})}\left[\ln(\varepsilon) + \frac{1}{2}\ln\left(1 - \frac{\sin^2(\text{PM})}{4\cos(\text{PM})}\right)\right]\right\} \tag{3-69}$$

From previous discussions, it is evident that PM has a profound effect on the shape of the closed-loop magnitude response (and correspondingly to the transient or step response). To further examine this relationship, let us consider a feedback amplifier with a large low frequency loop-gain, i.e., $A_0\mathcal{H} \gg 1$. It follows that the closed-loop

FIGURE 3-23   Plots of (a) damping ζ versus phase margin PM and (b) phase margin PM versus $\omega_{p2}/\omega_{CLp1}$ for a second-order system.

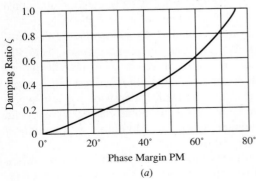

(a)

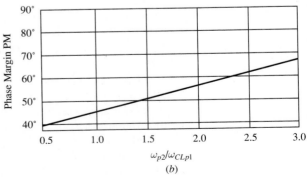

(b)

gain is $A_{CL}(j\omega) \approx 1/\mathcal{H}$. Let us now express the loop-gain, at the unity gain frequency (ω_u), as follows:

$$T(j\omega_u) = A(j\omega_u)\mathcal{H} = 1 \times e^{j\varphi(j\omega_u)} \tag{3-70}$$

where $\varphi(j\omega_u) = PM - 180°$. Using Eq. (3-69), we can write closed-loop gain as

$$A_{CL}(j\omega_u) = \frac{A(j\omega_u)}{[1 + A(j\omega_u)\mathcal{H}]} = \left(\frac{1}{\mathcal{H}}\right)\frac{e^{j\varphi(j\omega_u)}}{[1 + e^{j\varphi(j\omega_u)}]} \tag{3-71}$$

It is noted that feedback amplifiers are usually designed for low overshoot, say PM > 45° (or $\zeta > 0.42$) and in many cases it is desired that PM $\approx$ 60°. Let us then compute $A_{CL}(j\omega_u)$ for a phase margin of 45°, or $\varphi(j\omega_u) = -135°$. We compute the resulting closed-loop gain to be

$$|A_{CL}(j\omega_u)| = \left(\frac{1}{\mathcal{H}}\right)\frac{1}{|1 + e^{j\varphi(j\omega_u)}|} = 1.3\frac{1}{\mathcal{H}} \tag{3-72}$$

Equation (3-72) tells us that designing the system with a phase margin of 45° yields a closed-loop gain that peaks by a factor of 1.3 (or 2.6 dB) above the low frequency value of $(1/\mathcal{H})$. This is consistent with the value of A_p, calculated using Eq. (3-63d). It should be evident that the peaking can be reduced by increasing PM. Also, reducing PM $\rightarrow$ 0 causes $|1 + e^{j\varphi(j\omega_u)}| \rightarrow 0$ and $|A_{CL}(j\omega_u)| \rightarrow \infty$, and thus the system becomes unstable.

Example 3-8

Let us now consider the feedback amplifier in Fig. 3-24. For this example, the open-loop amplifier is an ideal voltage-controlled voltage source with gain $A(s)$, and the feedback is of the series-shunt type via the voltage divider formed by resistors R_A, R_B. Let $A(s)$ be represented by a three-pole transfer function of the form

$$A(s) = \frac{A_0}{(1 + s/\omega_{p1})(1 + s/\omega_{p2})(1 + s/\omega_{p3})} \tag{3-73a}$$

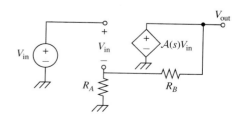

FIGURE 3-24   Series-Shunt feedback system for Example 3-8.

where $A_0 = 10^5$ (or 100 dB), $\omega_{p1} = 2\pi\,10^3$ rps, $\omega_{p2} = 2\pi\,10^5$ rps, and $\omega_{p3} = 2\pi\,10^7$ rps. Determine the phase margin and the stability for this feedback circuit. As we will see in Chaps. 5 and 6, Eq. (3-73a) is a typical voltage transfer function for an open-loop operational amplifier. This closed-loop scheme realizes a noninverting amplifier with $A_{CL} \approx 1/\mathcal{H}$.

Solution. The expression for the feedback factor $\mathcal{H}$ is

$$\mathcal{H} = \frac{R_A}{(R_A + R_B)} \tag{3-73b}$$

To investigate the stability of this amplifier, the Bode magnitude and phase plots for the loop-gain are drawn in Fig. 3-25 for the unity gain case where $\mathcal{H} = 1$ (i.e., $R_B = 0$ and/or $R_A = \infty$). In this case, the loop-gain is equal to the open-loop-gain, i.e., $\mathcal{A}(s)\mathcal{H} = \mathcal{A}(s)$. In this figure, the slanted dashed lines indicate the asymptotes for each of the poles and the heavy solid line plots are the overall gain and phase of the loop-gain. Noting that the frequency scale is logarithmic, unity gain frequency can be determined either graphically from the Bode plot or by solving the relation $|\mathcal{A}(j\omega_u)\mathcal{H}| = 1$ for ω_u, yielding:

$$\omega_u = 2\pi \times 7.5(10^6) \text{ rps}$$

FIGURE 3-25   Magnitude and phase Bode plots for the loop gain of a three-pole high gain amplifier.

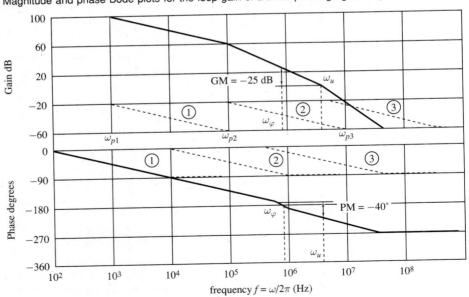

The corresponding phase margin is determined either directly from the Bode plot or by calculating $\varphi(j\omega_u) = \arg(\mathcal{A}(j\omega_u)\mathcal{H}) = -220°$ and substituting the result into Eq. (3-66), which yields

$$\text{PM} = -220° - (-180°) = -40°$$

Consequently, the amplifier is definitely unstable. In addition, we note that $\omega_\varphi = 2\pi \times 7.5(10^5)$ rps and GM $= -25$ dB.

Can the feedback circuit in Example 3-8 be made stable? The answer is yes, but something will have to be altered. One way to make this circuit stable is to reduce the loop-gain by making $\mathcal{H} \ll 1$. This is accomplished by adjusting R_A and R_B to appropriate finite values, where $R_B \gg R_A$. Since in this case $\mathcal{H}$ is real and independent of frequency, reducing $\mathcal{H}$ will decrease the magnitude of the loop-gain while leaving its phase unchanged. The Bode diagrams in Fig. 3-25 can be used to adjust $\mathcal{H}$ to achieve the desired phase margin. This is accomplished by first adding the desired PM to $-180°$ in order to determine the proper phase at the unity-gain frequency. The new unity-gain frequency ω_u' is then read directly from the Bode phase plot where $\varphi(j\omega_u') = -180° + \text{PM}$. To complete the process, a new value for $\mathcal{H}$, namely $\mathcal{H}'$, is calculated to shift the loop-gain to 0 dB at ω_u', i.e.,

$$20\log|\mathcal{A}(j\omega_u')\mathcal{H}'| = 0 \text{ dB} \quad \text{or} \quad 20\log(\mathcal{H}') = -20\log|\mathcal{A}(j\omega_u')| \qquad (3\text{-}74)$$

For example, in Fig. 3-26, $\mathcal{H}$ has been reduced to the value $\mathcal{H}'$ in order to achieve a phase margin of 45°. The required decrease in loop-gain is

$$20\log(\mathcal{H}') \approx -57 \text{ dB} \qquad \text{which implies} \qquad \mathcal{H}' \approx 1.41 \times 10^{-3}$$

To arrive at the required values for R_A and R_B, we choose R_A to be some convenient value, say $R_A = 1$ kΩ, then R_B can be computed by solving Eq. (3-73b) for R_B in terms of R_A and $\mathcal{H}'$, i.e.,

$$R_B = R_A \frac{(1 - \mathcal{H}')}{\mathcal{H}'} \approx 708.2 \text{ k}\Omega$$

The resulting crossover frequencies and stability margins, as indicated in Fig. 3-26, are $\omega_u' \approx 2\pi \times 10^5$ rps (also $\omega_\varphi' = 2\pi \times 7.5 \times 10^5$ rps), and PM $= 45°$ (also GM ≈ 32 dB), which represent adequate stability margins.

Before we conclude our study of stability, let us consider a variation of the loop-gain Bode plot approach just discussed. An alternative, that can be somewhat simpler, is to construct a Bode plot of the open-loop gain $\mathcal{A}$, rather than the loop-gain ($\mathcal{T} = \mathcal{A}\mathcal{H}$).

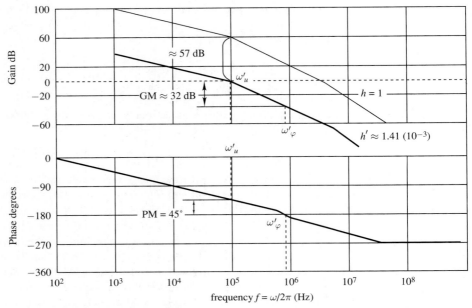

FIGURE 3-26   Magnitude and phase Bode plots for the loop gain in Fig. 3-25 compensated for stability by reducing the feedback factor $\mathcal{H}$.

Assuming for the present that $\mathcal{H}$ is independent of frequency, we can plot $20\log(1/\mathcal{H})$ as a straight horizontal line. The difference between these two curves is the loop-gain expressed in dBs, i.e.,

$$20\log|\mathcal{A}(j\omega)| - 20\log\left(\frac{1}{\mathcal{H}}\right) = 20\log|\mathcal{A}(j\omega)\mathcal{H}| \qquad (3\text{-}75)$$

Note that at the frequency where these curves coincide, there exists the relation

$$20\log|\mathcal{A}(j\omega)| = 20\log\left(\frac{1}{\mathcal{H}}\right) \quad \text{or} \quad 20\log|a(j\omega)\mathcal{H}| = 0 \qquad (3\text{-}76)$$

That is, the frequency at which coincidence occurs is $\omega = \omega_u$. Moving down to the Bode phase plot, PM is determined in the usual manner. This procedure is demonstrated in Fig. 3-27. If one desires to question the stability for different value of $\mathcal{H}$, (e.g., $\mathcal{H}_1$, $\mathcal{H}_2$, and $\mathcal{H}_3$ in Fig. 3-27), then one needs only to draw the horizontal lines for $20\log(1/\mathcal{H}_1)$, $20\log(1/\mathcal{H}_2)$, and $20\log(1/\mathcal{H}_3)$, find the gain crossover frequencies ω_{g1}, ω_{g2}, and ω_{g3}, and read the phase margins PM_1, PM_2, and PM_3 on the Bode phase plot.

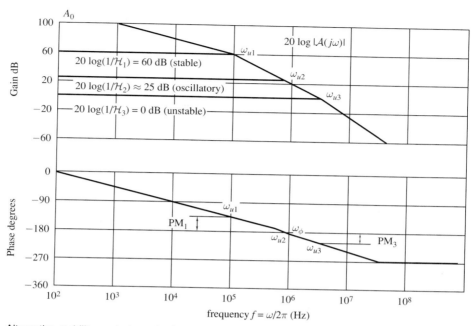

FIGURE 3-27   Alternative stability analysis method using Bode magnitude and phase plots for open-loop gain $\mathcal{A}$.

3-4 SENSITIVITY, COMPONENT MATCHING, AND YIELD

The practical realization of precision VLSI analog circuits (e.g., amplifiers, integrators, active-filters, etc.) is complicated by the fact that physical circuit components (e.g., resistors, capacitors, op amps, etc.) deviate from nominal values or design intent due to a variety of statistical and deterministic effects. The consequence of these unavoidable deviations is that the circuit performance will change in a proportional manner. What concerns the designer is that the changed circuit(s) may or may not satisfy the design requirements or specifications (of course we assume that the initial or nominal circuit design was verified to satisfy these specs, usually with some degree of margin). The consequence of varying components and sensitivity, is that less than 100 percent of the fabricated circuits will perform in accordance to the specifications (specs) or design objectives. The percentage of circuits fabricated that meet specs, when tested in their final packages, is called the *yield*. We will say more about yield later in this section.

The effects that cause components to vary from their nominal or average values include fabrication tolerances, environmental changes (such as in temperature and humidity), aging, varying chemical reactions in components, and inaccuracies in modeling due to second order effects. Some of these causes have been addressed in Chaps. 1 and 2 for transistor characteristics and IC components. In this chapter, we have discussed the use of feedback to reduce the dependence of the closed-loop gain on the detailed characteristics of the open-loop $\mathcal{A}(s)$ such that $A_{CL} \approx 1/\mathcal{H}$. If circuit parameter or component $x(j\omega)$ (where $x(j\omega) = A_0(j\omega)$, or $= g_m$, or $= R$, or $= C$, etc.) deviates from its nominal, intended, or ideal value by $\Delta x(j\omega)$ due to any one or combination of these effects, the actual value $x'(j\omega)$ can be modeled as follows:

$$x'(j\omega) = x(j\omega)\left(1 + \frac{\Delta x(j\omega)}{x(j\omega)}\right) = x(j\omega)\{1 + \varepsilon_\Delta(\omega)e^{j\theta\Delta(\omega)}\} \qquad (3\text{-}77a)$$

$$\approx x(j\omega)\{1 + \varepsilon_\Delta(\omega) + j\theta_\Delta(\omega)\} \qquad (3\text{-}77b)$$

where ε_Δ and θ_Δ represent the magnitude and phase of the relative or normalized component deviation $\Delta x/x$. The approximation in Eq. (3-77b) can be written when the deviations are incremental, i.e., $|\Delta x/x| \ll 1$ for all ω of interest. This simplifying approximation is often used and justified in practice. We note that $\Delta x/x$ can be frequency dependent and complex, even though x is real and frequency independent. This occurs when ε_Δ and θ_Δ account for second-order errors in a passive component, e.g., the finite distributed capacitance associated with an integrated resistor. We can also model an IC capacitor's parasitic and second-order effects, such as the finite dissipation factor and lead inductance, as deviations from an ideal lumped capacitor of value C by introducing the appropriate frequency dependent $\varepsilon_\Delta, \theta_\Delta$ into Eqs. (3-77). As we will see in Chap. 5, nonideal op amps are conveniently modeled in this manner.

In general, $\Delta x/x$, ε_Δ, and θ_Δ are statistical or random variables. For example, if x is a capacitor with actual value C' and nominal or average value C, we can model the error due to fabrication tolerances as $C' = C(1 + \varepsilon_{\Delta c})$, where $\varepsilon_{\Delta c} = \Delta C/C$ varies in a random fashion. Fabrication tolerances are *statistical* quantities, and hence in such cases each $\Delta x/x$ (or the ε_Δ and/or θ_Δ) is usually characterized as a *gaussian* random variable (Papoulis 1965), symmetrically distributed about a zero average or nominal value with standard deviation σ_x (or σ_ε and/or σ_θ) as shown in Fig. 3-28. The standard deviation σ_x is defined such that the probability of $\Delta x/x$ being in the range $-3\sigma_x < \Delta x/x < 3\sigma_x$ is[1]

$$P\left(-3\sigma_x < \frac{\Delta x}{x} < 3\sigma_x\right) = 0.9974 \quad \text{or} \quad 99.74\% \qquad (3\text{-}78a)$$

with

$$P\left(-\beta\sigma_x < \frac{\Delta x}{x} < \alpha\sigma_x\right) = \int_{-\beta\sigma_x}^{\alpha\sigma_x} \frac{1}{\sqrt{2\pi}\sigma_x} e^{-(\eta^2/2\sigma_x^2)} d\eta$$

$$= \text{erf}(\alpha) + \text{erf}(\beta) \qquad (3\text{-}78b)$$

where $\eta = \Delta x/x$, $\text{erf}(\cdot)$ is the error function (Papoulis 1965), and, usually, $\alpha = \beta = n$ (an integer). Since our circuit performance functions, such as closed-loop voltage gain and input/output impedance, are multilinear functions of the component x, the

---

[1]In addition, $P(-n\sigma_x < \Delta x/x < n\sigma_x) = 0.9545$ for $n = 2$ and 0.6827 for $n = 1$.

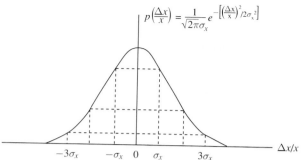

FIGURE 3-28 Plot of gaussian distribution $p(\Delta x/x)$ versus $\Delta x/x$.

statistics of the normalized variation in performance (e.g., $\Delta A_{CL}/A_{CL}$ in Eqs. (3-15) and (3-16)) can also be characterized at each frequency as gaussian.

3-4-1 Component Matching

Fortunately, ratios x_i/x_j of IC components of a similar type and fabricated using the same process steps (e.g., resistors, capacitors, or MOST g_m's) can be realized with significantly higher accuracy than the individual components x_i, x_j. That is, the variations in two or more components (let us say two capacitors), fabricated using the same process steps and located in close proximity on the chip, will track closely and nearly cancel in the ratio. Such components are said to be *matched*. It cannot be overemphasized that variations in fabrication, which cause components to vary from site to site, chip to chip, and wafer to wafer, are unavoidable in IC realization. Hence, matching between two like components is one of the most important design features in analog circuit design.

The cancellation of such errors when matched components appear in ratios may at first seem like magic, but it can be readily verified. For example, let us assume that because of natural fabrication variations, capacitors C_1 and C_2 are fabricated with errors $\Delta C_1/C_1$ and $\Delta C_2/C_2$, respectively. With the actual capacitor values expressed as $C_1' = C_1(1 + \Delta C_1/C_1)$ and $C_2' = C_2(1 + \Delta C_2/C_2)$, let us form the ratio C_2'/C_1', i.e.,

$$\frac{C_2'}{C_1'} = \frac{C_2}{C_1}\frac{1 + \dfrac{\Delta C_2}{C_2}}{1 + \dfrac{\Delta C_1}{C_1}} = \frac{C_2}{C_1}\frac{\left(1 + \dfrac{\Delta C_2}{C_2}\right)\left(1 - \dfrac{\Delta C_1}{C_1}\right)}{1 - \left(\dfrac{\Delta C_1}{C_1}\right)^2} \approx \frac{C_2}{C_1}\left(1 + \frac{\Delta C_2}{C_2} - \frac{\Delta C_1}{C_1}\right)$$

$$(3\text{-}79a)$$

$$\approx \frac{C_2}{C_1} \quad \text{if} \quad \frac{\Delta C_2}{C_2} = \frac{\Delta C_1}{C_1} \quad \text{and} \quad \left(\frac{\Delta C_1}{C_1}\right)^2, \left(\frac{\Delta C_2}{C_2}\right)^2 \ll 1 \qquad (3\text{-}79b)$$

Let us allow $\Delta C_i/C_i$, for $i = 1, 2$, to take into account finite dissipation and parasitic lead inductance such that C_i' is complex and frequency dependent:

$$C_i'(j\omega) = C_i\{1 + \varepsilon_{\Delta_i}(\omega) + j\theta_{\Delta_i}(\omega)\} \quad \text{for } i = 1, 2 \tag{3-80}$$

In this case, if $\varepsilon_{\Delta_1} = \varepsilon_{\Delta_2}$ and $\theta_{\Delta_1} = \theta_{\Delta_2}$, and $|\Delta C_i(j\omega)/C_i|^2 << 1$ for all ω, then the cancellation of errors expressed in Eqs. (3-79) will also occur when the deviations are complex and frequency dependent.

The condition $\Delta x_2/x_2 = \Delta x_1/_1$, called "perfect" matching or tracking, rarely occurs in practice because of unavoidable variations in photolithography, etching, oxide gradients, and the like. Moreover, to achieve the tracking of complex errors due to parasitics and second-order effects requires careful layout. Hence, tracking is imperfect and the exact cancellation of errors expressed in Eqs. (3-79) do not usually occur. However, with proper layout and well controlled fabrication, the designer can expect that

$$\left| \frac{\Delta(x_2/x_1)}{x_2/x_1} \right| \ll \left| \frac{\Delta x_2}{x_2} \right| \quad \text{or} \quad \left| \frac{\Delta x_1}{x_1} \right| \tag{3-81}$$

Typically, the larger the components in value and in chip area, the tighter the matching will be. Hence, high precision and small chip area are often conflicting objectives and tradeoffs must usually be considered.

In multivariable gaussian random processes, the statistical equivalent of tracking or matching is called *correlation*.[2] Two zero average value gaussian random variables, say η_1 and η_2, are said to be correlated if their joint *expected value* is nonzero, i.e.,

$$E[\eta_1, \eta_2] = \rho_{12}\sigma_1\sigma_2 \neq 0 \tag{3-82}$$

The quantity $-1 \le \rho_{12} \ge 1$ is called the *correlation coefficient* for η_1 and η_2. If η_1, η_2 are uncorrelated or statistically independent, then $\rho_{12} = 0$, if they are correlated and track in direct proportion to one another, then $\rho_{12} = 1$, and if they track in inverse proportion to one another, then $\rho_{12} = -1$. Also, partial tracking occurs if $0 < \rho_{12} < 1$.

Consequently, synthesis based on ratios of matched parameters is indeed a fundamental concept in all IC design lore, independent of technology. Much more will be said about this as the reader progresses through the text.

3-4-2 Sensitivity Problem in Precision Analog Circuits

The cause-and-effect relationship between circuit component deviations and the resulting changes in the response is called *sensitivity* (Becker and Jensen 1977; Daryanani

---

[2]It is beyond the scope of this text to provide a review of probability and statistics. For detailed definitions and explanations of the various statistical terms used in this section, e.g., expected value, correlation, standard deviation, variance, we refer the reader to such texts as Gielen and Sansen (1991), and Nodal Circuit Design Software (1990).

1976; Schaumann, Ghausi, and Laker 1990).[3] Let $P' \equiv P(j\omega, x + \Delta x) = P(j\omega, x')$ be the actual circuit response or performance function due to component change $\Delta x/x$ and $P' \equiv P(j\omega, x)$ be the nominal response function with $\Delta x/x = 0$. To determine the fractional or relative variation in response[4] $\Delta P/P = (P' - P)/P$ due to component deviation $\Delta x/x$, we expand $P(j\omega, x')$ in a Taylor series about $x' = x$ (or $\Delta x/x = 0$). Performing this expansion along with some algebraic manipulation, we write

$$\frac{\Delta P}{P} = \frac{P(j\omega, x') - P(j\omega, x)}{P(j\omega x)} = \left(\frac{x}{P}\right) \frac{\partial P(j\omega, x)}{\partial x} \left(\frac{\Delta x}{x}\right)$$
$$+ \left(\frac{x^2}{2P}\right) \frac{\partial^2 P(j\omega, x)}{\partial x^2} \left(\frac{\Delta x}{x}\right)^2 + \cdots \tag{3-83}$$

If we restrict our consideration to $|\Delta x/x| \ll 1$ such that the curvature of $\Delta P/P$ is not "large" in the vicinity of x, then we approximate Eq. (3-83) as follows

$$\frac{\Delta P}{P} \approx \frac{x}{P} \frac{\partial P}{\partial x} \frac{\Delta x}{x} = S_x^P \frac{\Delta x}{x} \tag{3-84a}$$

To be more realistic, $\Delta P/P$ is usually due to simultaneous variations of several circuit parameters. Hence, we generalize Eq. (3-84a) as follows

$$\frac{\Delta P}{P} \approx \sum_{i=1}^{k} S_{x_i}^P \frac{\Delta x_i}{x_i} \tag{3-84b}$$

where $k =$ total number of components or parameters that define the circuit, and S_x^P is the *Bode* or *relative sensitivity*[5] of P to component x, where

$$S_x^P = \frac{x}{P} \frac{\partial P}{\partial x} = \frac{\partial (\ln P)}{\partial (\ln x)} \tag{3-84c}$$

In Eq. (3-84b) the $\Delta x_i/x_i$ are determined by the IC technology and layout, while the $S_{x_i}^P$ are determined by the details of the circuit design, i.e., the response function,

---

[3]It is beyond the scope of this text to provide an exhaustive treatment of the subject of sensitivity. Our objective is to provide a sufficient set of analytical tools for the designer to expeditiously derive insight that can be incorporated into the design. Detailed sensitivity analyses and statistical simulations can be obtained from CAD tools such as SPICE (Calahan 1968 and SPICE 26-6 user manual).

[4]We note that relative changes $\Delta P/P$ and $\Delta x/x$ are often referred to as the *variability* of P and x, respectively.

[5]There are several useful identities that can be used to simplify sensitivity calculations, i.e.,

(1) $S_x^P = -S_x^{1/P}$, (2) $S_x^P = -S_{1/x}^P$, (3) $S_x^{P_1 P_2} = S_x^{P_1} + S_x^{P_2}$, (4) $S_x^{P_1/P_2} = S_x^{P_1} - S_x^{P_2}$, (5) $S_x^{P^n} = -n S_x^P$

It is left for the reader to verify these formulas and others in the exercises.

the circuit schematic and the nominal component values. The $\Delta x_i / x_i$ data is usually supplied by the fabricator and the $S_{x_i}^P$ are determined by the designer (or a CAD package). Often, the $\Delta x_i / x_i$ data compiled will be intended for a combination of components and component ratios; representing a compromise between what is deemed most useful by circuit designers and what is economically measured. Component ratio variations should be used for $\Delta x_i / x_i$ in Eq. (3-84b) when possible, since their smaller magnitudes will tend to increase the accuracy of the linear approximation. Hence, the IC designer can exercise some control of $\Delta P / P$ by designing the circuit for low sensitivity and by adhering to layout practices that maximize the component matching (see Sec. 2-9) referred to in Eq. (3-81).

Depending on the specific form of P, sensitivities $S_{x_i}^P$ can be complex and/or frequency dependent (Daryanani 1976; Schaumann, Ghausi, and Laker 1990). We have already established, based on the model in Eq. (3-77), that $\Delta x_i / x_i$ can be complex, frequency dependent, and random. However, the $S_{x_i}^P$ depend on the nominal or average values for x_i and are always deterministic quantities. Let us now consider a useful formulation of Eqs. (3-84) in which P and $\Delta P / P$ are complex, e.g., when P is a circuit voltage gain function. We then express P in terms of its magnitude and phase, i.e.,

$$P(j\omega) = M(\omega)e^{j\varphi(\omega)} \qquad \text{or} \qquad \ln P(j\omega) = \ln M(\omega) + j\varphi(\omega) \qquad (3\text{-}85)$$

Also, we may express $G(\omega) = 20\log M(\omega) = 8.686[\ln M(\omega)]$ dBs. Hence, applying Eq. (3-85) to Eq. (3-84c) we obtain[6]

$$S_{x_i}^P = \frac{\partial(\ln P)}{\partial(\ln x_i)} = \frac{\partial(\ln M)}{\partial(\ln x_i)} + j\frac{\partial\varphi}{\partial(\ln x_i)} = S_{x_i}^M + jQ_{x_i}^\varphi \qquad (3\text{-}86a)$$

$$= \frac{1}{8.686}Q_{x_i}^G + jQ_{x_i}^\varphi \qquad (3\text{-}86b)$$

where

$S_{x_i}^M = Re(S_{x_i}^P)$ is the relative sensitivity of M to x_i

$Q_{x_i}^\varphi = Im(S_{x_i}^P)$ is the semi-relative sensitivity[7] of φ to x_i

$Q_{x_i}^G = 8.686Re(S_{x_i}^P)$ is the semi-relative sensitivity of G[8] to x_i

Combining Eqs. (3-86) and (3-77) with Eqs. (3-84), we can express $\Delta P / P$ in the following forms:

$$\frac{\Delta P}{P} \approx \sum_{i=1}^{k}\left[S_{x_i}^M \varepsilon_{\Delta_i} - Q_{x_i}^\varphi \theta_{\Delta_i}\right] + j\sum_{i=1}^{k}\left[Q_{x_i}^\varphi \varepsilon_{\Delta_i} + S_{x_i}^M \theta_{\Delta_i}\right] \qquad (3\text{-}87a)$$

---

[6]We note that $\ln P = 1$ or $P = e$ is equivalent to $20\log e = 8.686$ dB.

[7]Semi-relative sensitivity, a special case of the Bode sensitivity, is $Q_{x_i}^P = x\partial P/\partial x = \partial(P)/\partial(\ln x)$. The identities in footnote 5 also apply to relative sensitivities, with S replaced by Q.

[8]We note that $Q_{x_i}^G = \dfrac{\partial G}{\partial(\ln x_i)} = \dfrac{\partial(20\log M)}{\partial(\ln x_i)} = 8.686\,S_{x_i}^M$ expressed in dBs.

or

$$\frac{\Delta P}{P} \approx \sum_{i=1}^{k} \left[\frac{1}{8.686} Q_{x_i}^G \varepsilon_{\Delta_i} - Q_{x_i}^\varphi \theta_{\Delta_i} \right] + j \sum_{i=1}^{k} \left[Q_{x_i}^\varphi \varepsilon_{\Delta_i} + \frac{1}{8.686} Q_{x_i}^G \theta_{\Delta_i} \right] \quad (3\text{-}87b)$$

The components of $\Delta P/P$ in Eqs. (3-87) can then be interpreted as follows

$$\frac{\Delta M}{M} \approx \sum_{i=1}^{k} \left[S_{x_i}^M \varepsilon_{\Delta_i} - Q_{x_i}^\varphi \theta_{\Delta_i} \right] \quad (3\text{-}88a)$$

$$\Delta G \approx \sum_{i=1}^{k} \left[Q_{x_i}^G \varepsilon_{\Delta_i} - 8.686 Q_{x_i}^\varphi \theta_{\Delta_i} \right] \quad (3\text{-}88b)$$

$$\Delta \varphi \approx \sum_{i=1}^{k} \left[Q_{x_i}^\varphi \varepsilon_{\Delta_i} + S_{x_i}^M \theta_{\Delta_i} \right] = \sum_{i=1}^{k} \left[Q_{x_i}^\varphi \varepsilon_{\Delta_i} + \frac{1}{8.686} Q_{x_i}^G \theta_{\Delta_i} \right] \quad (3\text{-}88c)$$

We note that $\Delta M/M$ is dimensionless, ΔG is in dBs, and $\Delta \varphi$ is in degrees.

Finally, consider the case where the $\theta_{\Delta_i} = 0$ for all i, and the ε_{Δ_i}'s are zero average value gaussian random variables with statistics $\sigma_i = \sqrt{E(\varepsilon_{\Delta i})^2}$ and $\rho_{ij} \sigma_i \sigma_j = E(\varepsilon_{\Delta_i} \varepsilon_{\Delta_j})$. Note that when similar IC components, fabricated using the same process steps, are correlated, their ratios are similarly correlated. Since $\Delta M/M$, ΔG, and $\Delta \varphi$ are assumed to be linear functions of $\varepsilon_{\Delta i}$, they will also be gaussian as long as this assumption holds. Moreover, since the average values for ε_{Δ_i} are zero, the average values for $\Delta M/M$, ΔG, and $\Delta \varphi$ will also be zero (approximately), i.e., $E[\Delta M/M] \approx 0$, $E[\Delta G] \approx 0$ and $E[\Delta \varphi] \approx 0$. Hence, we may express the standard deviations $\sigma(\Delta M/M)$, $\sigma(\Delta G)$, and $\sigma(\Delta \varphi)$ as follows[9]

$$\sigma\left(\frac{\Delta M}{M}\right) \approx \sqrt{E\left[\left(\frac{\Delta M}{M}\right)^2\right]} \approx \left[\sum_{i=1}^{k} (S_{x_i}^M)^2 \sigma_i^2 + \sum_{i=1}^{k} \sum_{j\neq i}^{k} S_{x_i}^M S_{x_j}^M \rho_{ij} \sigma_i \sigma_j \right]^{1/2} \quad (3\text{-}89a)$$

$$\sigma(\Delta G) \approx \sqrt{E[(\Delta G)^2]} \approx \left[\sum_{i=1}^{k} \left(Q_{x_i}^G\right)^2 \sigma_i^2 + \sum_{i=1}^{k} \sum_{j\neq i}^{k} Q_{x_i}^G Q_{x_j}^G \rho_{ij} \sigma_i \sigma_j \right]^{1/2} \quad (3\text{-}89b)$$

$$\sigma(\Delta \varphi) \approx \sqrt{E[(\Delta \varphi)^2]} \approx \left[\sum_{i=1}^{k} \left(Q_{x_i}^\varphi\right)^2 \sigma_i^2 + \sum_{i=1}^{k} \sum_{j\neq i}^{k} Q_{x_i}^\varphi Q_{x_j}^\varphi \rho_{ij} \sigma_i \sigma_j \right]^{1/2} \quad (3\text{-}89c)$$

[9]Note that for random variable η we find $\sigma(\eta) \equiv \sqrt{E[(\eta - m)^2]} = \sqrt{E[\eta^2]}$ when $m = E[\eta] = 0$.

Note that $\sigma(\Delta M/M)$, $\sigma(\Delta G)$, and $\sigma(\Delta\varphi)$ are frequency dependent, and hence Eqs. (3-89) estimate the standard deviations at each frequency. The designer may then estimate the $\pm n\sigma$ range for the variation in the particular response function of choice at each frequency of interest. For circuit optimization, it is convenient to have a single measure of circuit variability (Vladimirescu, Newton, and Pederson 1980). For this purpose, the $\sigma'(\cdot)s$ in Eqs. (3-89) can be integrated over a frequency range, say $\omega_1 \le \omega \le \omega_h$, to obtain the "average value" for $\sigma(\cdot)$ over ω.

3-4-3 Yield Considerations in Analog Integrated Circuits

As mentioned earlier, the consequence of varying components and sensitivity is that less than 100 percent of the fabricated circuits will be usable or sellable circuits. Those circuits that do not meet specs are either discarded or used in other applications where relaxed specs can be used. Failures due to varying components, second-order effects, and sensitivity are called *soft failures*, as opposed to *hard failures*, which render circuits inoperable, i.e., resulting in either short or open circuits. Hard failures are usually due to catastrophic errors in the fabrication process and/or defects in materials. Hard failures are usually unrelated to the robustness of the design. On the other hand, soft failures are typically the result of component variations, and can often be reduced with improved design.

In order to effectively model yield, it is important to understand the steps associated with the production of an integrated circuit. The IC production process is illustrated in Fig. 3-29. First, the wafer substrates are processed to fabricate the bipolar or CMOS circuits as a matrix of chips, which will later be separated and individually packaged. Prior to separation, each chip on the wafer is probed and tested to verify proper operation. At this stage, hard and soft failures are identified. The percentage of circuits fabricated that meet specs, i.e., pass all wafer probe tests, is called the *wafer probe yield Y_{tw}*,

$$Y_{tw} = Y_{hw}Y_{sw} \tag{3-90a}$$

FIGURE 3-29 The integrated circuit production cycle from fabrication through final test.

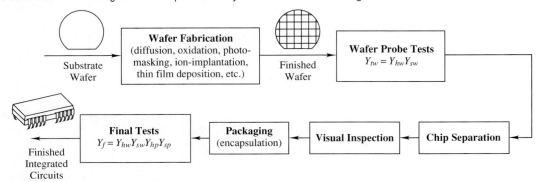

where Y_{sw} is due to soft failures, predicted using Eqs. (3-89), and Y_{hw} is due to the hard failures. We will soon discuss Y_{sw} and Y_{hw} in greater detail. After the wafer probe, the wafer is separated into individual chips and only the chips that passed the wafer probe tests are inspected and packaged. After packaging, the same tests performed at the wafer probe are repeated to identify chips lost due to errors in the packaging process (e.g., incomplete wire bonds, scratches, etc.). The final yield Y_f represents the percentage of circuits passing both the wafer probe and the final tests, i.e.,

$$Y_f = Y_{tw} Y_{tp} = Y_{hw} Y_{sw} Y_{hp} Y_{sp} \qquad (3\text{-}90b)$$

Typically, for larger chips that involve precision analog circuits, $Y_{tw} \ll Y_{tp}$ and $Y_f \approx Y_{tw}$. Since Y_{tp} is largely due to human error, it is not readily modeled in analytic form, and is maximized by careful handling and strict quality control.

Y_{sw} can be estimated using Eqs. (3-89) and the definition of the gaussian distribution in Eq. (3-78b). This estimate is linked directly to the margin allocated in the specifications for $\Delta M/M$, or ΔG, or $\Delta\varphi$. For example, if the spec for gain G is a nominal gain G_n and a margin defined, with α, β constants, i.e.,

$$G_n - \beta\sigma(\Delta G) < G < G_n + \alpha\sigma(\Delta G) \qquad (3\text{-}91a)$$

then

$$Y_{sw} = P(-\beta\sigma(\Delta G) < \Delta G < \alpha\sigma(\Delta G)) = \operatorname{erf}(\alpha) + \operatorname{erf}(\beta) \qquad (3\text{-}91b)$$

Note that although $\sigma(\Delta G)$ is a function of frequency, Y_{sw} is independent of frequency as long as α, β are independent of frequency. If α, β are frequency dependent, $Y_{swi}(\omega_i)$ must be evaluated at each frequency and the overall $Y_{sw} = \min(Y_{swi})$ is the yield at the most challenging frequency.

$Y_{hw} < 100$ percent is due to a combination of factors associated with the fabrication and packaging of the IC chips (Geiger, Allen, and Strader 1990). The first, and most significant, source of yield loss is due to pin-like defects of various kinds that occur during the photoresist and diffusion steps of fabrication. The impact of such defects on yield is related to process quality control as measured by the average defect density D (typically 1 to 2 defects/cm^2 for industrial bipolar and CMOS processes) and the chip or die area A in cm^2 consumed by the circuit. One of the factors in defining D is the number of mask steps in the process. With all other factors being equal, the process requiring the most mask steps will likely have the larger D. If one of these defects occurs in the active area of an IC die, particularly on a transistor, it is likely the IC will be non-functional. It is arguable that the damage will be reduced if the defect occurs on a resistor or a capacitor, and reduced further if it occurs on the interconnect wiring. Clearly, if the defect fortuitously occurs on an open space, it has no impact at all. Hence, densely packed chips will tend to be more sensitive to defects, but loosely packed chips will involve a larger die area and more defects. For a given circuit, a dense layout or a loose layout will likely result in similar yields. However, the loosely packed layout will produce fewer good circuits per wafer, which increases the cost per circuit.

A simple model for the statistics of defects in ICs is based on the Poisson distribution (Papoulis 1965) and the assumption that defects are randomly distribute over the entire wafer. If we further assume, perhaps somewhat pessimistically, that one or more defects anywhere on the chip will cause a hard failure, the Poisson model for Y_{hw} due to defects in fabrication is

$$(Y_{hw})_P = e^{-AD} \tag{3-92a}$$

Clearly, when $A \to 0$ or $D \to 0$, then $Y_{hw} \to 100$ percent. Also, Y_{hw} decreases rapidly as A or D become large. Since defects have greater impact in the active area of the chip where the transistors, resistors and/or capacitors reside, a more realistic model is obtained if we separate the die area into active and inactive regions, such that $A = A_A + A_I$ such that

$$Y_{hw} = e^{-(A_A D_A + A_I D_I)} \tag{3-92b}$$

where $D_A > D_I$ allows for the relative importance of defects in the two regions to be taken into account. This partitioning is particularly important in analog circuits, which typically have a larger percentage of inactive area than digital circuits of similar complexity.

The Poisson model tends to be overly pessimistic in predicting Y_{hw} for larger chip sizes. An alternative model, suggested by Murphy (Sedra and Smith 1991), has been found to predict Y_{hw} more accurately when $A \gg 1/D$. This model is expressed as follows:

$$(Y_{hw})_M = \left(\frac{1 - e^{-AD}}{AD} \right)^2 \tag{3-92c}$$

The Y_{hw} for $D = 1/\text{cm}^2$ and $2/\text{cm}^2$ have been calculated and plotted in Fig. 3-30 using the Poisson and Murphy models. Readers wishing to calculate the curve for a particular process will need to obtain from the fabricator a value for D (or D_A and D_I), and assistance in choosing the proper yield model.

Let us illustrate the concepts in this section with the following example.

Example 3-9

Let us calculate the estimated yield for a CMOS inverting amplifier, as shown in Fig. 3-31a. This circuit uses one CMOS op amp and two p-well resistors. A model for studying the performance of this circuit is given in Fig. 3-31b. We will say much more about Fig. 3-31 in Chap. 5. For this circuit, assume that it was designed for $A_{CL\infty} = 10$ with $A_0 = 10^3$. The D and component statistics, provided by the fabricator, are $D = 2/\text{cm}^2$ and $\sigma_{R_1} = \sigma_R = 0.2$, $\sigma_{A_0} = 0.5$, $\rho_{RA_0} = \rho_{R_{1A0}} = 0$. Based on the layout, the area was determined to be $A = 0.1 \text{ cm}^2$.

(a) For $M_{CL} = |A_{CL}|$, derive the sensitivities $S_{R_1}^{M_{CL}}$, $S_R^{M_{CL}}$ and $S_{A_0}^{M_{CL}}$. (b) Determine $\sigma(\Delta G_{CL})$, where $G_{CL} = 20 \log |A_{CL}|$, for the two cases $\rho_{R_1 R} = 0.95$ and

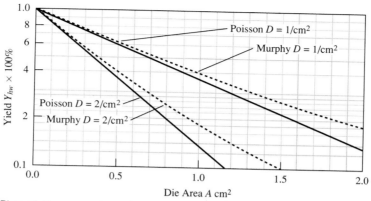

FIGURE 3-30 Plots of Y_{hw} versus area A, according to the Poisson $(Y_{hw})_P$ and Murphy $(Y_{hw})_M$ models. We show Y_{hw} for defect densities $D = 1/cm^2$ and $2/cm^2$.

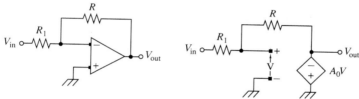

FIGURE 3-31 CMOS inverting amplifier for Example 3-9: (a) op amp circuit, (b) VCVS based model.

$\rho_{R1R} = 0$. (c) Determine the estimated yield Y_{tw} at wafer probe if the specification is for $G_{CL} = G_{CL_\infty} \pm 0.75$ dB.

Solution. (a) The expression for A_{CL}, determined from analysis of the model in Fig. 3-31b, is as follows:

$$A_{CL} = -\frac{R}{R_1} \left[\frac{1}{1 + \frac{1}{A_O(s)}\left(1 + \frac{R}{R_1}\right)} \right] \tag{3-93}$$

Taking the derivatives and forming the sensitivities, we obtain

$$S_R^{M_{CL}} = 1 + \frac{A_{CL}}{A_O} \approx 1 \tag{3-94a}$$

$$S_{R_1}^{M_{CL}} = -S_R^{M_{CL}} \approx -1 \tag{3-94b}$$

and

$$S_{A_0}^{M_{CL}} \approx \frac{1}{A_0} \left(1 + \frac{R}{R_1}\right) = \frac{1}{A_0}\left(1 - A_{CL\infty}\right) \tag{3-94c}$$

Note that in Eqs. (3-94) we have used $1/A_0 \ll 1$ in the approximations.

(b) We may compute $\sigma(\Delta G_{CL})$ using the relation $\sigma(\Delta G_{CL}) = 8.686\sigma(\Delta M_{CL}/M_{CL})$, i.e.,

$$\sigma(\Delta G_{CL})$$
$$= 8.686\sqrt{(S_R^{M_{CL}})^2\sigma_R^2 + (S_{R_1}^{M_{CL}})^2\sigma_{R_1}^2 + \left(S_{A_0}^{M_{CL}}\right)^2\sigma_{A_0}^2 + \left(2S_R^{M_{CL}}S_{R_1}^{M_{CL}}\right)\rho_{R_1 R}\sigma_{R_1}\sigma_R}$$

Substituting Eqs. (3-94) and the data into $\sigma(\Delta G_{CL})$ yields:

(i) for $\rho_{R_1 R} = 0.95$

$$\sigma(\Delta G_{CL})$$
$$\approx 8.686\sqrt{(1)^2(0.2)^2 + (-1)^2(0.2)^2 + \left(\frac{11}{10^3}\right)^2(0.5)^2 + (2)(1)(-1)(0.95)(0.2)(0.2)}$$

Hence, $\sigma(\Delta G_{CL}) \approx .56$ dB.

(ii) for $\rho_{R_1 R} = 0$

$$\sigma(\Delta G_{CL}) \approx 8.686\sqrt{(1)^2(0.2)^2 + (-1)^2(0.2)^2 + \left(\frac{11}{10^3}\right)^2(0.5)^2} = 2.46 \text{ dB}$$

(c) To estimate wafer probe yield we must first determine Y_{sw} from $\sigma(\Delta G_{CL})$ and the specs. For $\rho_{R_1 R} = 0.95$, $\Delta G_{CL} = \pm 0.75$ dB, which corresponds to $\pm 3\sigma(\Delta G_{CL})$. Hence, Y_{sw} is estimated to be

$$Y_{sw} = P(-3\sigma(\Delta G) < \Delta G < 3\sigma(\Delta G)) = 2 \text{ erf}(3) = 0.9974 \quad \text{or} \quad 99.74\%$$

For $\rho_{R_1 R} = 0$, $\Delta G_{CL} = \pm 0.75$ dB corresponds to $\pm 0.6\sigma(\Delta G_{CL})$. Hence, Y_{sw} is estimated to be

$$Y_{sw} = P(-0.6\sigma(\Delta G) < \Delta G < 0.6\sigma(\Delta G)) = 2 \text{ erf}(0.6) = 0.4515 \quad \text{or} \quad 45.15\%$$

The impact of the resistor matching is quite evident.

The Y_{hw} is determined from the chip area $A = 0.1$ cm^2, $D = 2/$cm^2, and either Eq. (3-92a) or Fig. 3-30. Note that $A \ll 1/D$, and hence both Y_{hw} models give nearly the same results. Using the Poisson model in Eq. (3-92a), we obtain

$$Y_{hw} = e^{-(0.1)(2)} = 0.82 \quad \text{or} \quad 82\%$$

The total wafer probe yield is then estimated to be

$$Y_{tw} = Y_{sw}Y_{hw} = (0.9974)(0.82) = 0.82 \quad \text{or} \quad 82\% \quad \text{for} \quad \rho_{R_1 R} = 0.95$$

and

$$Y_{tw} = Y_{sw}Y_{hw} = (0.4515)(0.82) = 0.37 \quad \text{or} \quad 37\% \quad \text{for} \quad \rho_{R_1 R} = 0$$

Note that the impact of σ_{A_0} in this example was small in comparison to the variations in σ_R and σ_{R_1}. This was due to the fact that $A_{CL_\infty} \ll A_0$. If, for the same A_0, the sensitivity $S_{A_0}^{M_{CL}}$ increases in direct proportion to A_{CL_∞}, then, for sufficiently large A_{CL_∞}, the effect of σ_{A_0} will dominate Y_{sw}. It should be emphasized that the yields estimated in this example are based on the approximation that ΔG is linearly dependent on the component variations. If the designer needs a more accurate estimate, CAD simulators using *Monte Carlo methods* (Calahan 1968) should be used.

SUMMARY

In this chapter we reviewed the fundamentals of feedback and introduced the reader to several of its roles in analog integrated circuits. We observed that feedback appears in most physical systems, either inherently or by design. Two examples from Chaps. 1 and 2 where used to show how model parameters associated with transistors provide built-in feedback in transistor amplifiers. We saw that the source resistance R_S of the MOST transistor introduces a series-series feedback in common-source amplifiers and the base-collector junction capacitance C_μ of the bipolar transitor provides a shunt-shunt feedback in common-emitter amplifiers. Both feedbacks play profound roles in the performance of these amplifier circuits.

We introduced feedback in a controlled fashion, or by design, to regulate bandwidth, gain, input impedance, output impedance, sensitivity, and signal-to-noise. In Sec. 3-2 we offered several methods for evaluating and designing feedback circuits. The magnitude or gain response, within a specified frequency range, is most sensitive to poles (and zeros) within or near this band. Such poles are called dominant poles, because they dominate in determining the character of this response. Poles (or zeros) far removed for the band of interest, play a much lesser or even negligible role and are said to be nondominant. Hence, in approximate models for the analysis and design of electonic circuits, nondominant poles and zeros are often discarded. The error incurred in making such approximation is calculated in App. 3-1.

One peril associated with introducing feedback is potential instability and the opportunity for unwanted oscillation. Stability and stability margin are seen in Sec. 3-3 to be determined by a confluence of gain and phase. Thus, we showed that both dominant and nondominant poles contribute equally to the determination of a feedback circuit's stability condition. Even if stable, how a circuit responds to transients is very important in applications that include data communications, control, video, and sampled-data systems. In Sec. 3-2 we related important transient response qualities to stability margin. Regulating the degree of stability is an important objective in the design of analog integrated circuits.

The practical realization of precision VLSI analog circuits and systems is complicated by the fact that physical circuit components (e.g., resistors, capacitors, operational amplifiers, etc.) deviate from nominal values, or design intent, due to a variety of statistical and deterministic factors. The consequence of these unavoidable deviations, as related in Sec. 3-4, is that the circuit performance changes in a proportional manner. Some changes may in fact cause circuits to no longer meet design requirements. Percent yield, i.e., the percentage of circuits fabricated that satisfy all design objectives, was related to component variations and sensitivities. Sensitivities, relating component change to circuit performance, were shown to be affected and regulatable by feedback. The principles introduced in this chapter will be further developed, applied, and demonstrated in subsequent chapters.

EXERCISES

3-1 Formulate the restaurant management example, described in the introduction of this chapter, as a block diagram or model that makes the feedback most visible.
  a Consider the case when customer comments are shared with employees, and
  b when customer reaction is used to judge restaurant employees.

3-2 Using the transistor amplifier circuit in Fig. EX3-2:
  a derive Eqs. (3-1) thru (3-5);
  b for $g_m = 1$ mS, $C'_{DG} = 100$ pF, $R_S = 10$ KΩ, and $R'_L = 50$ KΩ, determine A_{v0} and ω_{3dB} when $1/R_F = 0$.
  c Using the same parameters as in **b**, calculate $g_m R'_L (R_S/R_F)$, A_{v0}, ω_{3dB}, $(A_{v0})_{CL}$, and $(\omega_{3dB})_{CL}$ for $R_F = 100$ KΩ and 10 KΩ;
  d Compare and discuss the results obtained in **c**.

3-3 Consider the variation to A_{v0} in Eq. (3-3a) that occurs when the nMOST g_m for the amplifier in Fig. EX3-2 changes (due to a variety of causes such as temperature, back bias, etc.). The normalized variation in A_{v0} due to change in g_m (Δg_m) is expressed

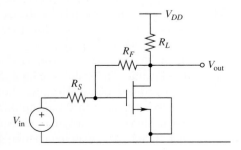

FIGURE EX3-2

as follows:

$$\frac{\Delta A_{v0}}{A_{v0}} = \frac{A'_{v0}(g_m + \Delta g_m) - A_{v0}(g_m)}{A_{v0}(g_m)} \tag{EX3-1}$$

Using the parameters in Exercise 3-2, determine $\Delta A_{v0}/A_{v0}$ when $\Delta g_m/g_m = 0.1$ (or 10%) of the two feedback cases $R_F = 100$ KΩ and 10 KΩ. Compare and discuss the results for the two feedback cases.

3-4 The Miller effect is illustrated in Fig. 3-2. Show that Figs. 3-2a and 3-2b are completely equivalent, i.e., derive Eq. (3-6a).

3-5 Let us consider the hybrid-π model for the bipolar transistor given in Fig. 2-5, i.e., Use the Miller equivalence in Fig. 3-2 to simplify the hybrid-π transistor model in Fig. EX3-5.

3-6 Assume the transistor parameters $L = 3$ μm, $v_{GS} - V_T = 1$ V, $K' = 30$ μA/V^2, $C_{ox} = 6.810^{-8}$ F/cm^2, and $C_{DG0} = C_{GS0} = 0.1$ pF. In addition, let us assume that $C_{SB} = C_{DB} = 0, \gamma = 0$.

   a With $R_S = 10$ KΩ, design the amplifier in Fig. EX3-2 for an open-loop DC gain of $|A_{v0}| = 20$ dB and a closed-loop bandwidth of $f_{3dB} = 1$ MHz (i.e., find W and R_F).

   b Calculate the resulting closed-loop DC gain.

3-7 In Fig. EX3-7 let $A = \dfrac{A_{v0}}{s + 2\pi \times 100}$. Determine the A_{v0} and $\mathcal{H}$ that will result in $|A_{CL}| = 2$ with error $|\varepsilon_{rr}| \le 0.1$ percent over the frequency range $f \le 10$ kHz.

3-8 In Fig. EX3-7 let $A(s) = (s^2 + 3)/(s^2 + 0.4s + 4)$ and let $\mathcal{H} = 0.1$ be frequency independent. Determine and sketch the return difference $F = |1 + T|$ as a function of frequency.

   a For what frequencies is the feedback negative? For what frequencies is the feedback positive?

   b Derive $A_{CL}(s)$ and describe the effect of the feedback on the closed-loop behavior.

3-9 Consider the feedback schemes in Fig. EX3-9 involving two stage amplifiers.

   a Let $\mathcal{A}_1 = \mathcal{A}_2 = 10^2$, and determine $\mathcal{H}_1$ and $\mathcal{H}_2$ for $A_{CL1} = A_{CL2} = 10$.

   b For $d\mathcal{A}_1/\mathcal{A}_1 = d\mathcal{A}_2/\mathcal{A}_2 = 0.05$, determine dA_{CL1}/A_{CL1} and dA_{CL2}/A_{CL2}.

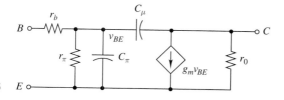

FIGURE EX3-5

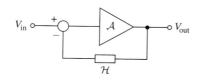

FIGURE EX3-7

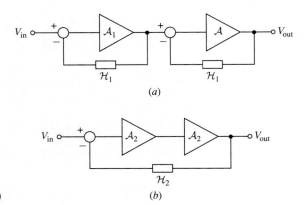

(a)

(b)

FIGURE EX3-9

3-10 For the feedback schemes in Fig. EX3-9, with $\mathcal{A}_1 = \mathcal{A}_2 = \mathcal{A}$ and $A_{CL1} = A_{CL2}$, it can be shown that

$$\frac{dA_{CL2}}{A_{CL2}} = f(\mathcal{A}, \mathcal{H}_1)\frac{dA_{CL1}}{A_{CL1}} \tag{EX3-2}$$

Determine $f(\mathcal{A}, \mathcal{H}_1)$.

3-11 Derive the expressions in Table 3-1 for the series-shunt feedback configuration.

3-12 Derive the expressions in Table 3-1 for the shunt-shunt feedback configuration.

3-13 Derive the expressions in Table 3-1 for the shunt-series feedback configuration.

3-14 Derive the expressions in Table 3-1 for the series-series feedback configuration.

3-15 Verify Eqs. (3-26) in Example 3-5.

3-16 Consider the four stage bipolar amplifier in Fig. EX3-16. Let the load resistors and transistors be matched such that $R_{C1} = R_{C2} = R_{C3} = R_L = R$, and $Q1 = Q2 = Q3 = Q4$. Using the hybrid-π model, with $r_B = 0$, determine the expressions for the low frequency $\mathcal{A}_i$, $\mathcal{H}_i$, $(A_i)_{CL}$, Z_{inCL}, and Z_{outCL}.

FIGURE EX3-16

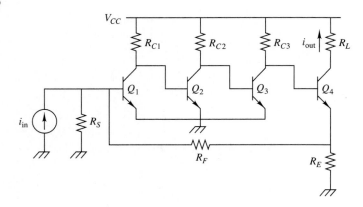

3-17 Let the parameters for all the transistors in the amplifier of Fig. EX3-16 be $r_B = 0$, $\beta = 100$, $V_E = 50$ V, $I_C = 0.1$ mA. For the resistor values $R_{C1} = R_{C2} = R_{C3} = R_L = 10$ KΩ, $R_S = 1$ MΩ, $R_F = 2$ KΩ, and $R_E = 100$ Ω:

a Calculate the low frequency $\mathcal{A}_i$, $\mathcal{H}_i$, $(A_i)_{CL}$, Z_{inCL}, and Z_{outCL}.

b If the collector current I_C increases by 20 percent to 0.12 mA, calculate the effect on $(A_i)_{CL}$, Z_{inCL}, and Z_{outCL}.

3-18 Use Blackman's impedance relation to verify the Z_{outCL} derived in Exercise 3-16.

3-19 Consider the feedback structure in Fig. EX3-19, where the feedback is introduced via an arbitrary three-terminal passive RC circuit. Let us define $T_{12} = V_1/V_2|_{V_3=0} = N_{12}/D_{12}$ and $T_{13} = V_1/V_3|_{V_2=0} = N_{13}/D_{13}$. Using the asymptotic gain relation, determine $A_{CL} = V_{out}/V_{in}$:

a in terms of T_{12}, T_{13}, A_0; and

b N_{1j}, D_{1j} as $A_0 \rightarrow \infty$ (note that D_{12} and D_{13} are related, i.e., the natural frequencies of the RC circuit).

3-20 Consider the feedback structure in Fig. EX3-20, where feedback is introduced via an arbitrary three-terminal passive RC circuit and the resistor divider r_1, r_2. Let us employ the definitions for T_{12} and T_{13} imposed in Exercise 3-19. Using the asymptotic gain relation, determine $A_{CL} = V_{out}/V_{in}$:

a in terms of T_{12}, T_{13}, A_0, k; and

b N_{1j}, D_{1j}, k as $A_0 \rightarrow \infty$ (note that D_{12} and D_{13} are related, i.e., the natural frequencies of the RC circuit).

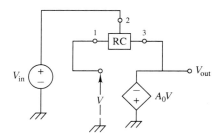

FIGURE EX3-19

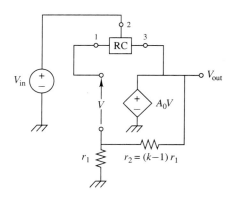

FIGURE EX3-20

3-21 An amplifier has a transfer function characterized by a low frequency gain of 500 and three negative real poles at $f = 100$ kHz, 200 kHz, and 500 kHz. Constant feedback is applied such that $\mathcal{H} = 0.03$.
  a Is the closed-loop amplifier stable?
  b Calculate the phase and gain margins.

3-22 Using the same open-loop amplifier as in Exercise 3-21,
  a sketch the gain (dB) and phase (degrees) versus frequency (log scale) for the open-loop gain.
  b determine the maximum value of $\mathcal{H}$ that will yield a stable closed-loop amplifier.
  c determine the value of $\mathcal{H}$ required to achieve a phase margin of PM $= 60°$.

3-23 An amplifier has a transfer function with low frequency gain of 80 dB and three negative real poles at $f = 1$ kHz, 200 kHz, and 5 MHz.
  a If resistive feedback is applied to this amplifier to realize a low frequency closed-loop gain of $|A_{CL}| = 500$, determine the resulting phase margin.
  b Repeat a for $|A_{CL}| = 50$.

3-24 A feedback amplifier is characterized as follows:

$$A(s) = \frac{10}{(1 + s/2\pi \times 10^6)^2(1 + s/4\pi \times 10^6)^2} \quad \text{and} \quad \mathcal{H} = 0.1 \qquad \text{(EX3-3)}$$

  a Sketch the gain (dB) and phase (degrees) versus frequency (log scale) for the open-loop gain $A(s)$.
  b Sketch the root-locus for the closed-loop $A_{CL}(s)$ as a function of $\mathcal{H}$;
  c Determine the phase margin for the specified $\mathcal{H}$.

3-25 Feedback is to be applied to an open-loop amplifier, characterized as

$$A(s) = \frac{10^5 \left[1 + s/2\pi(150 \times 10^3) \right]}{(1 + s/2\pi(80))(1 + s/2\pi(100 \times 10^3))} \qquad \text{(EX3-4)}$$

  a Sketch the root-locus for $A_{CL}(s)$ as $\mathcal{H}$ varies $0 \le \mathcal{H} \le 1$;
  b Determine the values for $\mathcal{H}$ required to realize $A_{CL}(0) = 10$, and $A_{CL}(0) = 1$
  c Determine the closed-loop pole/zero locations and phase margins for the values of $\mathcal{H}$ determined in **b**.

3-26 A feedback amplifier is specified to realize the unit-step response sketched in Fig. EX3-26.
  a Determine the closed-loop $A_{CL}(s)$ that realizes Fig. EX3-26;
  b With the open-loop amplifier given as

$$A(s) = \frac{A_0}{(s/p + 1)(s/0.2p + 1)} \qquad \text{(EX3-5)}$$

determine A_0, p, and feedback $\mathcal{H}$ that realizes $A_{CL}(s)$ in **a**.

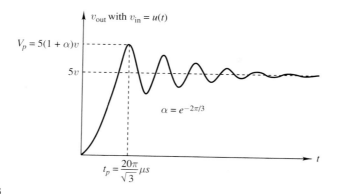

FIGURE EX3-26

3-27 The following data represents the measured gain and phase responses for an open-loop feedback amplifier:

Frequency (kHz)	$\|A(j\omega)\|$ (dB)	arg $A(j\omega)$ (°)
0.01	60	−5
0.1	58	−20
1	46	−80
5	39	−120
10	32	−200
50	0	−260

a If resistive feedback is applied to $A(s)$, determine the value of $\mathcal{H}$ required to achieve a phase margin of 60°;

b Determine the range of $\mathcal{H}$ and the resulting values of A_{CL} at 10 Hz, for which the feedback scheme is stable.

3-28 The gain of an amplifier is determined by the ratio of two integrated circuit resistors, i.e., $A_{CL} = -R_1/R_2$. The data for these resistors are as follows: $R_1 = 25$ kΩ, $R_2 = 15$ kΩ, with absolute tolerance $= \pm 15$ percent, temperature coefficient $= +0.12 \pm 0.02$ percent/°C (from room temperature at 27°C). If the amplifier is tested at 75°C, determine the worst case percentage deviation in A_{CL}.

3-29 Derive Eqs. (3-89).

3-30 Prove the following useful relationships using the definition of relative sensitivity in Eq. (3-84c):

a $S_x^{P_1 P_2} = S_x^{P_1} + S_x^{P_2}$

b $S_x^{P_1/P_2} = S_x^{P_1} - S_x^{P_2}$

c $S_x^{P_1+P_2} = \dfrac{P_1 S_x^{P_1} + P_1 S_x^{P_2}}{P_1 + P_2}$

d If $P = f(y)$ and $y = g(x)$, $S_x^P = S_y^P S_x^y$

3-31 Use the relationships in Exercise 3-30 to verify the following relations:

    a $S_x^{P^n} = n S_x^P$

    b $S_x^{P+c} = \frac{P}{P+c} S_x^P$

    c $S_{\sqrt{x}}^P = 2 S_x^P$

3-32 For the feedback schemes in Fig. EX3-9, with $\mathcal{A}_1 = \mathcal{A}_2 = \mathcal{A}$ and $A_{CL1} = A_{CL2}$, show that the sensitivities are related as

$$S_a^{A_{CL2}} = \frac{1}{1 + \mathcal{A}\mathcal{H}_1} S_a^{A_{CL1}}$$

3-33 For the circuit in Fig. EX3-2:

    a determine $|S_{gm}^{(A_{v0})_{CL}}|$

    b with $R_S = 10$ KΩ, $R_L' = 50$ KΩ, calculate $|S_{gm}^{(A_{v0})_{CL}}|$ for $R_F = 100$ KΩ and 10 K Ω;

    c discuss the results from a feedback theory perspective.

3-34 For the circuit in Fig. EX3-16:

    a determine $|S_{gm}^{(A_i)_{CL}}|$;

    b determine $|S_{I_C}^{(A_i)_{CL}}|$.

3-35 Consider the amplifier circuit in Exercise 3-2 with $R_F = 100$ KΩ and $r_{DS} \gg R_L$. Let the component statistics be $\sigma_{R_S} = \sigma_{R_S} = \sigma_{R_F} = 0.2$, $\sigma_{gm} = 0.5$, $\rho_{R_i gm} = 0$, and $\rho_{R_i R_j} = 0.95$.

    a Determine $\sigma(\Delta A_{v0})$, where A_{v0} is given in Eq. (3-3a).

    b Calculate the estimated yield Y_{sw} if the specification is $A_{v0} \pm 2\sigma(\Delta A_{v0})$.

APPENDIX 3-1: Approximate Calculations for a Two-Pole System when the Poles are Real and Widely Separated

In design, it insightful to factor the roots of symbolic circuit polynomials to preserve the relationships between the root locations and the component values. This can be done in many practical cases with little labor if approximations are made. The purpose of this appendix is to provide tools for deriving such relations. The special case of real-valued roots that are widely separated occurs with sufficient frequency to justify added attention.

Let us start with the quadratic equation in s, given by

$$1 + \beta s + \alpha s^2 = 0 \tag{A3-1}$$

the roots can be calculated by the well known expression:

$$s\pm = \frac{-\beta \pm \sqrt{\beta^2 - 4\alpha}}{2\alpha} \tag{A3-2}$$

However, this calculation can be greatly simplified provided the two roots are real and have values that are widely separated. This is the case when $\beta^2 \gg 4\alpha$.

Let us call the smaller value of $s\pm$ the dominant pole $s_d \approx s_+$ and the larger value the nondominant pole $s_{nd} \approx s_-$. They correspond to time constants τ_d and τ_{nd}, respectively. Thus, the quadratic form in Eq. (A3-1) can be rewritten as

$$(1 + \tau_d s)(1 + \tau_{nd} s) = 0 \qquad \text{(A3-3)}$$

or, when multiplied out, as

$$1 + (\tau_d + \tau_{nd})s + \tau_d \tau_{nd} s^2 = 0 \qquad \text{(A3-4)}$$

Since we assume that $s_d \ll s_{nd}$ or $\tau_d \gg \tau_{nd}$, Eq. (A3-4) can be approximated by

$$1 + \tau_d s + \tau_d \tau_{nd} s^2 = 0 \qquad \text{(A3-5)}$$

Comparing Eq. (A3-5) with Eq. (A3-1), we see that

$$\tau_d = \beta \qquad \text{and} \qquad \tau_{nd} = \frac{\alpha}{\beta} \qquad \text{(A3-6)}$$

Also note that $\tau_d \tau_{nd} = \alpha$.

In a sinusoidal steady state, where $s = j\omega$, the approximate values of the resulting frequencies are given by

$$\omega_d = -\frac{1}{\tau_d} \approx -\frac{1}{\beta} \quad \text{or} \quad f_d = -\frac{1}{2\pi \tau_d} \approx -\frac{1}{2\pi \beta} \qquad \text{(A3-7a)}$$

and

$$\omega_{nd} = -\frac{1}{\tau_{nd}} \approx -\frac{\beta}{\alpha} \quad \text{or} \quad f_{nd} = -\frac{1}{2\pi \tau_{nd}} \approx -\frac{\beta}{2\pi \alpha} \qquad \text{(A3-7b)}$$

If the roots are not widely spread apart, using Eqs. (A3-7) will lead to error in evaluating the roots. In order to make an estimate of this error, let us introduce a relative error measure, given by the ratio of the actual value of the root to the approximative value. Measures for the dominant and nondominant roots are given by

$$E_d = -\beta s_+ \qquad \text{(A3-8a)}$$

and

$$E_{nd} = \frac{-\alpha}{\beta} s_- \qquad \text{(A3-8b)}$$

Also note that

$$E_d E_{nd} = \alpha s_+ s_- = 1 \tag{A3-9}$$

The relative error on the dominant root (or pole) can be further developed using Eq. (A3-2), which yields

$$E_d = \frac{2}{1 + \sqrt{1 - \dfrac{4\alpha}{\beta^2}}} = \frac{2}{1 + \sqrt{1 - \dfrac{4\omega_d}{\omega_{nd}}}} \quad \text{and} \quad E_{nd} = \frac{1}{E_d} \tag{A3-10}$$

where $4\omega_d/\omega_{nd} = 4 f_d/f_{nd}$.

Note that the error ratios depend only on the ratio $4\alpha/\beta^2$. They are plotted in Fig. A3-1. However, since $\omega_d/\omega_{nd} \approx \alpha/\beta^2$, they have been added to the horizontal axis of Fig. A3-1. As a rule of thumb, the value of the error equals the value of the ratio itself. At $\omega_d/\omega_{nd} = 0.1$, E_d is larger than unity. The actual value of the dominant pole frequency ω_d is then about 10 percent, (more precisely 12.7 percent), larger than the approximate value given by Eq. (A3-7a). Also, the actual value of ω_{nd} is 12.7 percent smaller than the value given in Eq. (A3-7b).

FIGURE A3-1

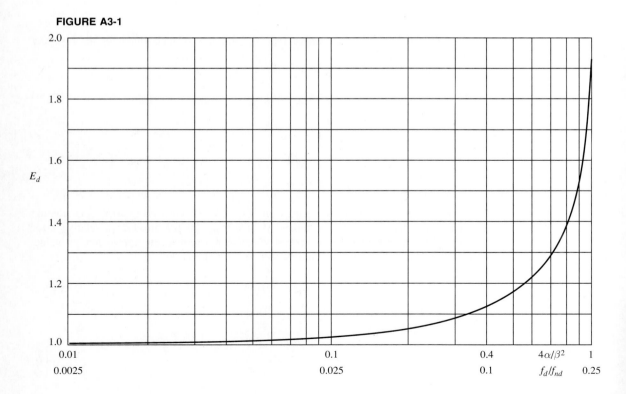

APPENDIX 3-2: Exact Calculation of the Bode Diagram for Two-Pole Systems

In Fig. A3-2, we show the magnitude and phase characteristics for the two-pole gain $A(s)$, where

$$A(j\omega) = \frac{A_0}{\left(1 + j\dfrac{\omega}{\omega_d}\right)\left(1 + j\dfrac{\omega}{\omega_{nd}}\right)} \tag{A3-11}$$

Pole frequencies $\omega_d = 2\pi f_d$ and $\omega_{nd} = 2\pi f_{nd}$ are the dominant and nondominant poles, respectively. In a Bode plot, the magnitude characteristic $|A|$ is approximated by two straight-line asymptotes, with corners at ω_d and ω_{nd}. In addition, there are two more frequencies where the gain and/or phase of $A(j\omega)$ are important. They are ω_t, where $\omega_t \equiv A_0\omega_d$ (or $GBW \equiv A_0 f_d$); and ω_u, where $|A(j\omega_u)| \equiv 1$. At ω_u we determine phase margin PM, as defined in Eq. (3-66).

Exact or very accurate calculations are often required in the following four cases illustrated in Fig. A3-2:

- $A(j\omega_d)$; where we can define the gain reduction factor as the ratio $r_d = |A(j\omega_d)|/A_0$.
- $A(j\omega_{nd})$; where we can define the gain reduction factor as the ratio $r_{nd} = |A(j\omega_{nd})|/A_0$.
- The value of the frequency ω_u.
- The value of the phase margin PM

FIGURE A3-2

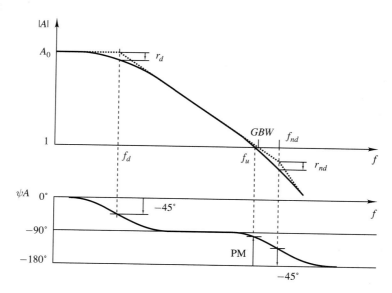

If $A_0 \gg 1$ and $\omega_{nd} > A_0\omega_d$, then at the dominant pole-frequency ω_d, the factor $1 + j(\omega_d/\omega_{nd}) \approx 1$. Thus, at $\omega = \omega_d$, Eq. (A3-11) reduces to

$$A(j\omega_d) \approx \frac{A_0}{1+j} \quad \text{and} \quad r_d = \frac{1}{\sqrt{2}} = 0.707(\text{ or } -3 \text{ dB}) \qquad \text{(A3-12)}$$

Since $\omega_{nd} \gg \omega_d$, Eq. (A3-11) can be simplified at $\omega = \omega_{nd}$ to

$$A(j\omega_{nd}) \approx \frac{A_0\omega_d}{j\omega_{nd}(1+j)} \quad \text{and} \quad r_{nd} = \frac{1}{\sqrt{2}}\frac{\omega_d}{\omega_{nd}} \qquad \text{(A3-13)}$$

To calculate frequency ω_u, let us assume that ω_u is in the vicinity of ω_{nd}. Thus, we set $|A(j\omega_u)| = 1$ in Eq. (A3-11), which yields

$$1 \approx \left| \frac{A_0}{\left(j\dfrac{\omega_u}{\omega_d} \right)\left(1 + j\dfrac{\omega_u}{\omega_{nd}} \right)} \right| \qquad \text{(A3-14}a\text{)}$$

or

$$1 \approx \frac{A_0}{\left(\dfrac{\omega_u}{\omega_d} \right)\sqrt{1 + \left(\dfrac{\omega_u}{\omega_{nd}} \right)^2}} \qquad \text{(A3-14}b\text{)}$$

Equation (A3-14b) can be expressed by the form

$$y^4 = \eta^2(y^2 + 1) \qquad \text{(A3-15}a\text{)}$$

where $\omega_{nd}/\omega_t = f_{nd}/GBW = \eta$ and $\omega_{nd}/\omega_u = f_{nd}/f_u = y$. Solving Eq. (A3-15a) for y yields

$$y = \frac{\omega_{nd}}{\omega_u} = \sqrt{\frac{\eta\sqrt{\eta^2 + 4} + \eta^2}{2}} \qquad \text{(A3-15}b\text{)}$$

For the special case where $\omega_t = \omega_{nd}$ (or $GBW = f_{nd}$); i.e., $\eta = 1$, Eq. (A3-15b) gives

$$y = \frac{\omega_{nd}}{\omega_u} = \sqrt{\frac{\sqrt{5} + 1}{2}} = 1.272 \qquad \text{(A3-15}c\text{)}$$

We note that at $\omega_{nd} = \omega_t$, the phase equals $-135°$, but the phase is only $-128°$ at frequency ω_u. If $\omega_t \neq \omega_{nd}$, the solution of Eq. (A3-15a) is better written in terms of the phase margin, as discussed next.

Using Eq. (3-66), let us determine the phase margin for $A(j\omega)$ in Eq. (A3-11) for the case when frequency ω_u is close to ω_{nd}, i.e.,

$$PM = 90° - \arctan\left(\frac{\omega_u}{\omega_{nd}}\right) \tag{A3-16}$$

We leave it to the reader to show that Eq. (A3-16) can be rewritten in either of the following two forms

$$PM = \arctan\left(\frac{\omega_{nd}}{\omega_u}\right) = \arctan(y) \tag{A3-17a}$$

or

$$PM = \arcsin\left(\frac{\eta}{y}\right) \tag{A3-17b}$$

Solving Eq. (A3-17b) for η, we obtain $\eta = y\sin(PM)$. Substituting $\eta = y\sin(PM)$, Eq. (A3-15a) can be solved to determine the following expression for PM:

$$PM = \arccos\left\{\sqrt{\left[\left(\frac{\eta}{2}\right)^2 + 1\right]} - \frac{\eta}{2}\right\} \tag{A3-18}$$

$$= \arccos\left\{\sqrt{\left[\left(\frac{\omega_{nd}}{2\omega_t}\right)^2 + 1\right]} - \frac{\omega_{nd}}{2\omega_t}\right\}$$

Also, frequency ω_u can be expressed in terms of PM, i.e.,

$$\omega_u = \omega_t \sin(PM) \quad \text{or} \quad \omega_u = \frac{\omega_{nd}}{\tan(PM)} \tag{A3-19}$$

If, on the contrary, the values of ω_t and PM are given, then ω_u is given by Eq. (A3-19); and ω_{nd} is obtained from Eq. (A3-17b), i.e.,

$$\omega_{nd} = \omega_u \tan(PM) = \omega_t \frac{\sin^2(PM)}{\cos(PM)} \tag{A3-20}$$

REFERENCES

Becker, P. W., and F. Jensen. 1977. *Design of Systems and Circuits for Maximum Reliability and Production Yield.* New York: McGraw-Hill.

Black, H. S. 1934. "Stabilized Feedback Amplifiers." *Bell Syst. Tech. J.*, vol. 13, pp. 1–18.

Blackman, R. B. 1943. "Effect of Feedback on Impedance," *Bell Syst. Tech. J.*, vol. 22, pp. 269–277.

Bode, H. W. 1945. *Network Analysis and Feedback Amplifier Design.* New York: Van Nostrand.

Bode, H. W. 1960. "Feedback–The History of an Idea." *Proceedings of the Symp. on Active Networks and Feedback Sys.*, Polytechnic Institute of Brooklyn. (Also published 1964. *Selected Papers on Mathematical Trends in Control Theory.* New York: Dover.

Calahan, D. A. 1968. *Computer Aided Network Design.* New York: McGraw-Hill.

Daryanani, G. 1976. *Principles of Active Network Synthesis and Design.* New York: Wiley and Sons.

Desoer, C. A., and E. S. Kuh. 1969. *Basic Circuit Theory.* New York: McGraw-Hill.

Geiger, R. L., P. E. Allen, and N. R. Strader. 1990. *VLSI Design Techniques for Analog and Digital Circuits.* New York: McGraw-Hill.

Ghausi, M. S. 1985. *Electronic Devices and Circuits: Discrete and Integrated,* New York: Holt, Rinehart and Winston.

Gielen, G., and W. Sansen. 1991. *Symbolic Analysis for Automated Design of Analog Circuits.* Norwell, MA: Kluwer Academic.

MATLAB: *Signal Processing Tool Box User's Guide.* 1988. South Natic, MA: The Math-Works, Inc.

MATLAB: *Control Systems Toolbox User's Guide.* 1990. South Natic, MA: The Math-Works, Inc.

Mukherjee, T., and L. R. Carley. 1991. "Rapid Yield Estimation as a Computer Aid for Analog Circuit Design," *IEEE J. Solid-State Circuits,* vol. 26, no. 3, pp. 291–299.

Murphy, B. T. 1964. "Cost-Size Optima of Monolithic Integrated Circuits," *Proc. IEEE*, vol. 52, pp. 1537–1545.

Nodal™ Circuit Design Software. 1990. Macallan Consulting.

Papoulis, A. 1965. *Probability, Random Variables, and Stochastic Processes.* New York: McGraw-Hill.

Rosenstark, S. 1974. "A Simplified Method Feedback Amplifier Analysis," *IEEE Transactions on Education*, vol. E-17, no. 4, pp. 192–198.

Rosenstark, S. 1986. *Feedback Amplifier Principles.* New York: Macmillan.

Savant, C. J. 1964. *Control System Design.* New York: McGraw-Hill.

Schaumann, R., M. S. Ghausi, and K. R. Laker. 1990. *Design of Analog Filters.* Englewood Cliffs, N.J.: Prentice-Hall.

Sedra, A. S., and K. C. Smith. 1991. *Microelectronic Circuits.* New York: Holt, Rinehart and Winston.

Vladimirescu, A., A. R. Newton, and D. O. Pederson. 1980. "SPICE Version 26.1 User's Guide." Berkeley: University of California, Dept. of Electrical Engineering and Computer Science.

Waldhauer, F. D. *Feedback.* 1992. New York: Wiley and Sons.

Wolfram, S. 1991. *Mathematica: A System for Doing Mathematics by Computer*, Sec. Ed. Reading, MA: Addison-Wesley.

4

ELEMENTARY
TRANSISTOR STAGES

INTRODUCTION

Models of several transistors were discussed in preceding chapters. Many parameters were discussed because there are so many different specifications in analog circuits. Because performance depends on many second-order effects, second-order transistor parameters must be included. In Chap. 3, specifications are given for amplifiers as black boxes. It is shown how amplifiers can be analyzed and how their performance can be represented.

In this chapter, transistors are used to construct amplifiers. Elementary amplifier functions have already been discussed in the first chapters that discussed the small-signal models, as have source followers. All of them have used only a single transistor and no capacitances were added. In this chapter, however, capacitances are added on all nodes, giving rise to poles and zeros that modify the output-input relationship versus frequency. Such calculations are the main subject of this chapter.

In every circuit there is, in principle, always a capacitance present from each node to ground. They are stray capacitances, device output capacitances, load capacitances, etc. Each such capacitance to ground represents a pole in the transfer characteristic, and hence causes attenuation at high frequencies. In this chapter, only elementary circuits are considered. Their complexity is limited to two or sometimes three nodes, thus only two or three poles can be present. This leads to transfer characteristics of second order, or occasionally third order. Only second-order systems are discussed in detail, since it is shown that most amplifiers can be well represented by second-order systems. This also applies to full operational amplifiers, as will be discussed in Chap. 5 and Chap. 6.

In order to study the high-frequency performance of these elementary stages, Bode diagrams are used throughout. However, designers are always interested to learn how one single parameter in the circuit may influence the performance (reflected in the Bode diagram). Therefore, they must repeat this Bode diagram for several values of that parameter. A pole-zero position diagram is added (see Fig. 2-15a) to give the evolution of poles and zeros of a particular transfer function with one single parameter (such as transconductance) as a variable. It provides insight into the role of that parameter with respect to the high frequency performance. Moreover, it allows derivation of the Bode diagram in a straightforward way. Pole-zero position diagrams will therefore be used throughout this chapter to illustrate the regions of instability, pole-zero cancellation points, etc.

There are several classification methods for elementary transistor stages. They can be classified by the number of transistors used or we can classify by single-transistor stages followed by two-transistor stages, etc. Another method, however, is to classify stages by the number of nodes. Power supplies and ground do not carry AC signals, and thus are not considered. A single-node circuit is, for example, a diode connected to ground, which presents some impedance to a source. Two nodes are much more common. All amplifiers that have only one input and one output node can be handled as two-node stages. The amplifier may have an extra internal node, raising the node count to three, etc.

In Chap. 6, amplifier design is organized according to the number of nodes. In this chapter however, we begin with a single-transistor amplifier. This stage may seem too elementary to dwell on; nevertheless, it already contains two nodes, i.e., the input node and the output node. As such, it is representative of all two-node amplifiers, and thus is analyzed in detail. Important characteristics such as gain, input and output impedance, and noise are discussed. Other important phenomena such as pole-splitting are also introduced, even in this simple configuration.

The simple transistor amplifiers are followed by impedance converter stages such as source and emitter followers. The buffering capabilities from high to low versus frequency are investigated. Impedance conversion from low to high can be realized by means of cascode transistor stages. They are the last single-transistor stages to be discussed in this section.

Note that often different names are used for the three conventional single-transistor configurations. The amplifier stage consists of a transistor in common source (emitter) configuration. The source (emitter) follower contains a transistor in common drain (collector) configuration and the cascode stage contains a transistor in common gate (base) configuration. All three configurations are shown in Fig. 4-1.

The first two-transistor stage is the well-known CMOS inverter. It consists of an nMOST and a pMOST. It is followed by cascode amplifiers and by differential stages, both of which consist of two nMOST transistors or two pMOSTs. Finally, current mirrors are discussed. They are of vital importance in construction of biasing blocks and active loads for amplifying stages. In their simplest form, they also consist of only two transistors.

Throughout this chapter, the parallel between MOST and bipolar transistor stages is maintained. Differences are highlighted and discussed. As such, the analyses are directly applicable to BICMOS technologies, an important aspect of this chapter.

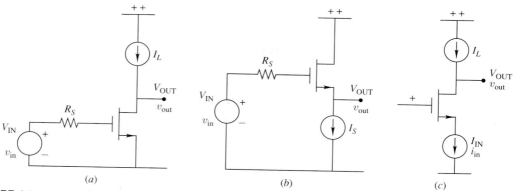

FIGURE 4-1   (a) Amplifier; (b) source follower; (c) cascode.

Each analog designer must decide if a bipolar transistor or a MOST is to be used for a particular function. Familiarity with the tradeoffs of both technologies in all elementary configurations is of paramount importance.

In this chapter, analysis is still dominant over synthesis. It is essential that the reader becomes familiar with sound analysis techniques before risking the slippery path of design procedures and, especially, of automated design synthesis. Nevertheless, on a few occasions a design plan is outlined in order to prepare the reader for full design tasks, as described in Chap. 6.

4-1 MOST SINGLE-TRANSISTOR AMPLIFYING STAGES

4-1-1 Biasing

A single-transistor amplifier is shown in Fig. 4-1a. It is biased by a voltage source V_{IN}, which is connected to the gate through source resistor R_S. The load could be a resistor, as well. For high gain, however, we prefer an active load, consisting of a current source with current I_L. How such a current source can be realized will be discussed in Sec. 4-8, on current mirrors. For the time being, an ideal independent current source can be assumed.

An input voltage source always includes some internal impedance, called the source impedance. In principle, this source impedance can be either resistive, capacitive, or inductive. For example, an antenna can be capacitive or inductive. A microphone usually can be represented by a capacitance. The input source can be a current source as well, with a resistance, capacitance, or inductance in parallel. A radiation detector can be represented by current source in parallel with a capacitance. In this first section an input voltage source is taken with a simple source resistance R_S in series (see Fig. 4-1a) (Sedra and Smith 1987).

The input voltage source also contains an AC component v_{in}. It is amplified to generate v_{out} at the drain. The ratio of the amplitudes V_{out}/V_{in} is the voltage gain A_v. If both voltages are small, the gain can be calculated after substitution of the transistor by its small-signal equivalent circuit. The gain is the most important characteristic and the reason why the circuit is made. Nevertheless, the AC currents are superimposed on the DC currents. Thus, they must be determined first.

Biasing in the configuration of Fig. 4-1a is provided by the DC component V_{IN} of the input voltage source v_{IN}. Its value equals the gate-source voltage V_{GS} of the MOST, such that a drain current I_L can flow. It is thus given by

$$V_{\text{IN}} = V_{GS} = V_T + \sqrt{\dfrac{I_L}{K'W/L}} \tag{4-1}$$

in which V_T is the threshold voltage of that MOST, W/L its ratio and K' its transconductance factor ($K' = KP/2n$).

Most often the input source does not provide this specific value of V_{IN}. Also, we may prefer (for example, for safety reasons in a biomedical amplifier) to couple the input source with a coupling capacitor C_C. Then resistive biasing can better be used as shown in Fig. 4-2. The DC gate voltage V_{GS} is now completely decoupled from DC component V_{DC} of the input source. Its value is derived from the supply voltage V_{DD} by the potentiometric divider, consisting of R_1 and R_2. It is thus given by

$$V_{GS} = \dfrac{R_2}{R_1 + R_2} V_{DD} \tag{4-2}$$

The task of the designer is to select R_1 and R_2 such that V_{GS} of Eq. (4-1) equals that of Eq. (4-2).

A resistor R_L is used as a load. It determines the DC output voltage V_{OUT} as given by

$$V_{\text{OUT}} = V_{DD} - R_L I_L \tag{4-3}$$

We may want to set the output voltage at half the supply voltage, or we may want to use this DC voltage V_{OUT} to bias the next stage of a following circuit. Although

FIGURE 4-2   Single transistor amplifier with resistive load and biasing resistors.

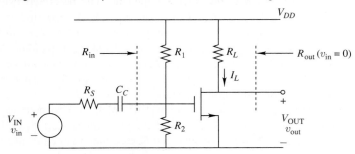

there will be other criteria to consider later, now we must be certain that the MOST is maintained in its saturation region for all output signal voltages, i.e., $V_{DS} > V_{GS} - V_T$. A good rule of thumb is to set the DC output voltage at half the supply voltage, if no other constraints are present.

Example 4-1

Bias the amplifier of Fig. 4-2 consisting of a nMOST with $V_T = 1$ V, $K'_n = 25$ μA/V^2 and $W/L = 50$ at $I_L = 0.2$ mA. Set its output voltage at $V_{\text{OUT}} = 4$ V for $V_{DD} = 12$ V. Calculate values for the biasing resistors. Also calculate the maximum output swing around $V_{\text{OUT}} = 4$ V.

Solution. From Eq. (4-3) we find that R_L must be 40 kΩ and from Eq. (4-1) we find that the square root equals 0.4 V. Hence $V_{GS} = 1.4$ V. The resistor ratio is of Eq. (4-2) is thus 1.4/12 or 0.1167. Let us allow a current through the biasing resistors of not more than 10 percent of the MOST current. This current is then 0.02 mA. The values of the biasing resistors are then $R_2 = 1.4/0.02$ k$\Omega = 70$ kΩ and $R_1 = 10.6/0.02$ k$\Omega = 530$ kΩ.

In order to calculate the maximum output swing around $V_{\text{OUT}} = 4$ V, we must find the minimum output voltage to keep the MOST from entering the linear region. This minimum is $V_{GS} - V_T = 0.4$ V. The largest excursion from 4 V to 0.4 V is thus 3.6 V. The largest swing will thus be 7.2 V_{ptp} (volts peak to peak).

Only about 7.2/12 or 60 percent of the total range is thus used. A larger swing can be obtained if the MOST is biased such that the V_{OUT} is 6 V. In this case the total swing would be $2(6 - 0.4) = 11.2$ V_{ptp}, which corresponds to 93 percent of the total supply voltage.

Resistive biasing is by no means the only way to bias a MOST amplifier. Switched capacitors can also be used, as we will explain in Chap. 7. If more transistors are allowed, several biasing techniques become available. The most elegant way to bias a MOST amplifier is to include it in a differential stage, discussed in Sec. 4-7. Feedback can be used as well, leading to even more complex circuitry.

Let us now investigate how much AC or small-signal gain we have achieved with the simple single-transistor configurations of Fig. 4-1a and 4-2.

4-1-2   Low Frequency Gain

The AC component of v_{IN}, denoted by v_{in}, generates an AC drain current and hence an AC output voltage v_{out}. The voltage gain A_v can be calculated by using the small-signal equivalent circuit, provided the AC voltages are small. This is shown in Fig. 4-3.

The transistor is represented by its g_m-generator. Its output resistance is r_{DS} and it is found in parallel with the load resistor. Thus it can be represented by a single resistor R'_L which is R_L // to r_{DS}. The sign // means that both resistors are put in parallel; hence $R'_L = R_L r_{DS}/(R_L + r_{DS})$. The biasing resistors are combined in resistor R_{12}, which can be represented by R_1//R_2.

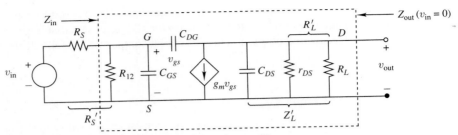

FIGURE 4-3   Small-signal equivalent circuit of single-transistor amplifier.

At low frequencies, all capacitances in Fig. 4-3 can be omitted. The voltage gain is denoted by A_{v0} and is then

$$A_{v0} = \frac{v_{\text{out}}}{v_{\text{in}}} = -\frac{R_{12}}{(R_S + R_{12})} g_m R'_L \qquad (4\text{-}4)$$

This expression contains two factors and a minus sign. The minus sign indicates a phase inversion from input to output, which is characteristic of all single-transistor amplifying stages. The first factor represents the attenuation caused by the biasing resistors. The other factor $g_m R'_L$ is the actual gain, and depends mainly on only one transistor parameter, i.e., transconductance g_m.

The value of g_m is derived in detail in Sec. 1-1. It is obtained from Eq. (1-22), and is given by

$$g_m = 2\sqrt{K'_n \frac{W}{L} I_{DS}} = \frac{2I_{DS}}{V_{GS} - V_T} \qquad (4\text{-}5)$$

The transconductance g_m and the gain A_{v0} increase with the square root of the current I_{DS} and the aspect ratio W/L. Also for a given biasing current, the MOST is best used with a small value of $V_{GS} - V_T$ (or large W/L). All parameters are related, however, and therefore exercises are mandatory.

Example 4-2

Take the amplifier of Fig. 4-2 with the values of Example 4-1. Source resistor $R_S = 10$ kΩ. Calculate its low-frequency gain. Repeat with an Early voltage of 20 V.

Redesign this amplifier for a gain of -10 with the same transistor and load resistor, but with minimum current.

Solution. Since $I_{DS} = 0.2$ mA and $V_{GS} - V_T = 0.4$ V, g_m is given by the second expression in Eq. (4-5), which is 1 mS (S stands for Siemens or mho and is

A/V). Factor $g_m R'_L$ is thus 40. The attenuation, because of the biasing resistors, is calculated: resistance $R_{12} = R_1//R_2 = 70//530$ k$\Omega = 61.83$ kΩ. The attenuation is thus 0.86. The total low-frequency gain A_{v0} is -34.4.

If the Early resistance r_{DS} is taken into account, then $r_{DS} = V_E/I_{DS} = 20/0.2$ k$\Omega = 100$ kΩ. The total output resistance $R'_L = R_L//r_{DS} = 40//100$ k$\Omega = 28.6$ kΩ. The gain now decreases by the same ratio, $28.6/40$ to $A_{v0} = -24.6$.

The redesign for a gain of -10 can be cumbersome if all effects are included (see Exercise 4-1). Therefore, a few engineering approximations are made. The reductions of both the biasing resistors and the presence of the Early resistance r_{DS} are both estimated to be about -15 percent. We will use SPICE to verify this estimate later. Factor $g_m R_L$ must be about 30 percent larger than 10 to accommodate these two reductions, i.e., $g_m R_L \approx 13$. Since $R_L = 40$ kΩ, $g_m \approx 0.325$ mS. From the first expression in Eq. (4-5) we obtain the value of I_{DS}, which is about 53 μA. The required value of V_{GS} is then about 1.277 V. The biasing resistors must be modified to $R_1 = 536$ kΩ and $R_2 = 64$ kΩ. A SPICE run with these values gives about $A_{v0} = -8.9$. This is about 10 percent too low. Thus the current must be increased by about 20 percent.

It is obvious from these calculations that high accuracy can never be expected. Even for exact calculations, a large deviation in K' must be expected, causing a large spread in resulting gain values.

The largest values that can be expected are obtained when the output is biased at half of the supply voltage. At that point, the current is $I_{DS} \approx V_{DD}/2R_L$. Substitution of this value in the second expression of g_m in Eq. (4-5), yields for the gain A_{v0} about $V_{DD}/(V_{GS} - V_T)$. Even for low values of $V_{GS} - V_T$, such as 0.2 V (without going in weak inversion), the gain is only $12/0.2 = 60$ for 12 V supply voltage. Higher values of gain are difficult to achieve with a MOST with a resistor as load.

For higher gains, *active loads* are required. Assume that we replace the load resistor R_L of 40 kΩ in Fig. 4-2 by a current source of $I_L = 0.2$ mA, as shown in Fig. 4-1a. As a result R'_L (which was 28.6 kΩ) is substituted in the expression of the gain by r_{DS} only, which is 100 kΩ. Thus the resulting gain is larger by a factor of three. Moreover, its dependence on the current changes drastically, since both g_m and r_{DS} depend on the current. The gain decreases with increasing current, as explained in Sec. 1-1. This capability will be explored further after we have found a solution to the biasing problem of such an active load, i.e., when we discuss active loads in differential stages in Sec. 4-7.

After the gain, the most important characteristics of the amplifying stage are its *input impedance* and *output impedance*. Indeed they will tell us how much interaction we can expect with the different stages (see Chap. 3).

If no capacitances are present, the input impedance becomes resistive only and is thus an input resistance. It is indicated in Fig. 4-2. This input resistance can be obtained by application of a small-signal voltage source v_{in} and calculation of the resulting small-signal input current i_{in}. Actually, we obtain the same result by application of a current source i_{in} and measurement of the resulting v_{in}. Application to the small-signal equivalent circuit of Fig. 4-3 (without capacitances) yields

$$R_{in} = \frac{v_{in}}{i_{in}} = R_{12} \qquad (4\text{-}6)$$

If we managed to bias the transistor without the bias resistors, then the input resistance would be infinity. This is probably one of the most attractive results of a MOST in comparison to a bipolar transistor. The input resistance may not be infinity because of some leakage currents, but it is certainly very, very high.

The *output resistance* can be obtained similarly. It is obtained by application of a small-signal voltage source v_{out} at the output and calculation of the resulting small-signal input current i_{out}. Again, we obtain the same result by application of a current source i_{out} and measurement of the resulting v_{out}. Remember that the input voltage source must be shorted out, but the source resistance R_S is still present. Also note that we have included the load resistance in the amplifier itself, as clearly shown in Figs. 4-2 and 4-3. We find that

$$R_{out} = \frac{v_{out}}{i_{out}} = R_L' \qquad (4\text{-}7)$$

or r_{DS} (in the case of an active load). Thus the output resistance is fairly high, but this cannot be avoided because the output resistance must be high for high gain. If we want a low output resistance, we must apply feedback, or add other stages with low output resistance, as discussed in Sec. 4-3.

Instead of an nMOST, a pMOST transistor can be used as well. Its small-signal model is exactly the same, however, and also given by Fig. 4-3. However, a pMOST stage provides a gain that is a factor of two to three times lower than an nMOST stage, because holes have lower mobility (in K') than electrons. Therefore, nMOSTs are preferred as amplifying devices.

4-1-3   Bandwidth

Inclusion of the capacitances in the small-signal equivalent circuit of Fig. 4-3 will cause the gain to change versus frequency. Because of the capacitances from both input and output nodes to ground, the gain will roll off with frequency. The bandwidth is defined to be that frequency where the gain is decreased by 3 dB with respect to the gain at low frequencies.

However, in order to calculate the bandwidth, all capacitances must be included. Since the transistor contains two nodes, all transistor and parasitic capacitances can be lumped into three terminal capacitances:

1 one from the input node to ground, which is called C_{GS}
2 one from the output node to ground, called C_{DS}
3 one from output to input, called C_{DG} (or C_{GD}).

The gain transfer function A_v can then be calculated as a function of complex frequency by means of Laplace transforms. Each capacitance can be represented by its impedance $1/sC$ in which $s = j\Omega$. This also applies to the input and output impedances versus complex frequency.

The denominator of the transfer function is only of the second order, because the three terminal capacitances in Fig. 4-3 form a loop. This transfer function will be analyzed in detail, because most amplifier configurations that occur and that will be discussed in this book can be simplified to the configuration in Fig. 4-3. It is important to understand this circuit in order to understand the remainder of this book.

This expression of the gain, and input and output impedance, are found by application of the current and voltage laws of Kirchhoff. They yield complex equations that are not easily interpreted. Therefore we will begin by examining the effect of each capacitance separately.

Effect of C_{GS} Only   If only the input capacitance C_{GS} is present, the small-signal equivalent circuit of Fig. 4-3 can be simplified, as in Fig. 4-4a. The *voltage gain* A_v is examined first. If the input capacitance C_{GS} is present and both other capacitances are left out, the expression of the gain A_v is readily found to be

$$A_v = \frac{A_{v0}}{1 + jf/f_{c1}} \tag{4-8}$$

in which

$$f_{c1} = \frac{1}{2\pi R'_S C_{GS}} \tag{4-9}$$

and in which $R'_S = R_S//R_{12}$ is the resistance seen by C_{GS}. (Sedra and Smith 1987)

Frequency f_{c1} is the crossover frequency. Since it occurs in the denominator, it provides a single pole in the Bode diagram of the gain characteristic, as seen in Fig. 4-4b. Thus it is the bandwidth.

This Bode diagram is very simple because it includes only one single pole. Thus it corresponds to a lowpass filter characteristic. At low frequencies, the term f/f_{c1} in the denominator is smaller than unity and thus negligible. Hence $A_v = A_{v0}$ as expected. At high frequencies the term jf/f_{c1} is larger, and hence dominant with respect to unity. The gain then rolls off with a slope of unity or -20 dB/decade, as shown in Fig. 4-4b. Remember that these lines are asymptotes. At the corner frequency, the corner is actually rounded, i.e., the amplitude is decreased by 3 dB. Also note that the vertical scale is a log scale when the actual values are displayed. The corresponding linear scale in dB ($= 20\log$) is shown, as well.

The corresponding phase diagram is also given in Fig. 4-4b. It is described by arctan (f/f_{c1}). When the amplitude characteristic is constant, the phase is ideally zero. In the region of -20 dB/decade, the phase is ideally $-90°$. At the corner frequency, it is $-45°$. The actual phase characteristic is a fluent curve connecting these points. Note that the slope of this curve at the crossover frequency hits the $0°$ and $-90°$ lines at a factor of about 5 from that frequency.

Note that if the source resistance R_S were zero, this pole frequency would occur at infinity. Unfortunately, this is never the case. Every realistic input source includes some resistance (or capacitance or inductance), however small it may be.

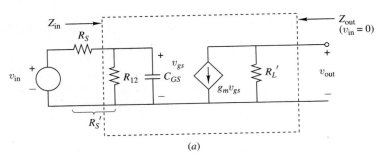

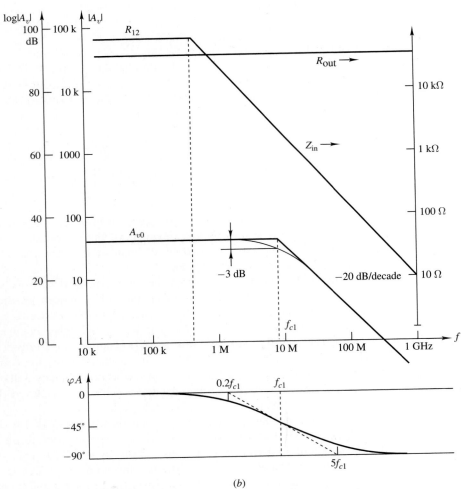

FIGURE 4-4 (a) Small-signal equivalent circuit with C_{GS} only; (b) gain A_v input impedance Z_{in} and output resistance R_{out} of nMOST amplifier with $C_{GS} = 4$ pF only

As an example, take the nMOST operating at 0.2 mA, which provides $g_m = 1$ mS (see example 4-2). With $R'_L = 40$ kΩ, the value of $A_{v0} = -40$. With $R'_S = 5$ kΩ and $C_{GS} = 4$ pF, the pole frequency $f_{c1} = 8$ MHz. This is shown in Fig. 4-4b.

The input impedance Z_{in} now consists of the input resistance R_{12} in parallel with the input capacitance C_{GS}. It is thus given by

$$Z_{in} = \frac{v_{in}}{i_{in}} = \frac{R_{12}}{1 + R_{12}C_{GS}s} \tag{4-10}$$

This characteristic is also illustrated in Fig. 4-4b. Note that at high frequencies $Z_{in} = 1/j\Omega C_{GS}$. Thus it is purely capacitive. Its amplitude decreases with a slope of 20 dB/decade as also seen in Fig. 4-4b. At 10 MHz, its absolute value is about $|Z_{in}| \approx 4$ kΩ.

The amplifier thus presents a capacitance at its input. This capacitance heavily interacts with the source resistance because it causes the pole given in Eq. (4-9).

The *output impedance* is determined as shown in Fig. 4-4a. However, since no capacitance is demonstrated, it is the output resistance which is already given by Eq. (4-7). It is also illustrated in Fig. 4-4b.

It can be concluded that capacitance C_{GS} causes a single pole in the gain characteristic. Also, the resulting input impedance becomes capacitive at high frequencies. The pole of Eq. (4-9) is listed in Table 4-1. All other poles and zeros are included on the list for easy comparison.

Effect of C_{DS}   Each amplifier has a load connected to it by a piece of wire. That piece of wire adds capacitance to this output capacitance. Therefore, we must understand quite clearly what this capacitance does to the frequency response.

If this C_{DS} is the only capacitance present, the small-signal equivalent circuit of Fig. 4-3 can be simplified again. The analysis is similar to that given previously. The expression of the gain A_v contains again a single pole, which is now given by

$$f_{c2} = \frac{1}{2\pi R'_L C_{DS}} \tag{4-11}$$

The Bode diagram is not given, since it has the same shape as that in Fig. 4-4b. Frequency f_{c2} is also listed in Table 4-1.

The *input impedance* is easily calculated. In the absence of any input-node capacitance, the value of the input impedance is resistive and given by R_{12}.

The *output impedance* is easily calculated as well. Because an output node capacitance C_{DS} is present, the output impedance simply consists of a parallel RC circuit, as given by

$$Z_{out} = \frac{v_{out}}{i_{out}} = \frac{R'_L}{1 + jf/f_{c2}} \tag{4-12}$$

Note that this characteristic has a pole at the same frequency f_{c2} as the gain.

TABLE 4-1   LIST OF TIME CONSTANTS IDENTIFIED IN THE MOST SINGLE-TRANSISTOR AMPLIFIER WITH SMALL-SIGNAL MODEL GIVEN IN FIG. 4-3.

Time constant τ	Value (ns)	f_{-3dB} ($=1/2\pi\tau$)	Value** (159 MHz/τ(ns))	Equation No.
$R_S{}'C_{GS}$	20	f_{c1}	8.0	(4-9)
$R_L{}'C_{DS}$	100	f_{c2}	1.6	(4-11)
$MR_S C_{DG}$	245	f_{c3}	0.64	(4-13b)
C_{DG}/g_m	1	f_{c4}	160	(4-13d)
$R_L{}'C_{DG}$	40	f_{c5}	4.0	(4-17b)
$(C_{GS}+C_{DS})/g_m$	6.5	f_{c6}	24.5	(4-24)
$R_S(C_{GS}+MC_{DG})$ $+R_L{}'C_{DS}$	365	f_{c7}	0.44	
$R_L{}'R_S C^2/\tau_7$	0.9	f_{c8}	176	
$R_S C_{GS}+R_L{}'C_{DS}$	120	f_{c9}	1.3	(4-25c)
$R_S R_L{}'C_{GS}C_{DS}/\tau_9$	16.7	f_{c10}	9.54	(4-26b)
$R_S(C_{GS}+MC_{DG})$	265	f_{c11}	0.6	(4-29b)
$R_S R_L{}'C_{GS}C_{DG}/\tau_{11}$	3.0	f_{c12}	52.6	Ex. 4-7
$R_S(C_{GS}+C_{DG})$	25	f_{c13}	6.4	(4-21b)
C_{GS}/g_m	4	$f_{c14}=f_T$	40	(4-32b)
$R_S R_L{}'C^2/\tau_9$	27.5	f_{c15}	5.8	(4-29b)
$R_L{}'(C_{DS}+C_{DG})$	140	f_{c16}	1.135	(4-20b)
$R_L{}'C^2/(C_{GS}+C_{DG})$	132	f_{c17}	1.2	
$R_S{}'C'^2/(C_{GS}+C'_{DS})$	20	f_{c18}	7.9	(4-56b)

Values: $R_S = 5$ kΩ, $R_L' = 40$ kΩ, $1/g_m = 1$ kΩ, $A_{v0} = -40$, $M = 49$, $C_{GS} = 4$ pF, $C_{DS} = 2.5$ pF, $C_{DG} = 1$ pF, $R_L' R_S C^2 = 3300$(ns)^2, $C_L = 10$ pF
$C^2 = 16.5$ (pF)^2, $C'^2(C'_{DS}$ instead of $C_{DS}) = 66.5$ (pF)^2

** only two significant figures, unless it is a 4, 5, or 6.

It can be concluded that addition of a capacitance at the output has very much the same effect as connecting a capacitance at the input. A single pole appears in the gain characteristic. The output impedance becomes capacitive, but the input impedance remains resistive.

Let us now investigate what happens if a capacitance is connected *between* both nodes.

Effect of C_{DG} Only   The importance of capacitance C_{DG} is that it couples the output node to the input node and thus is seen from both the output and input terminals. It behaves as a feedback capacitance from output to input. Actually, any feedback capacitance will have the same effect as C_{DG}. Therefore, its effect must be studied thoroughly as it will be used to stabilize feedback amplifiers as well as in filter design.

The small-signal equivalent circuit of Fig. 4-3 can be simplified as shown in Fig. 4-5a. The biasing resistors have been left out to simplify this illustration.

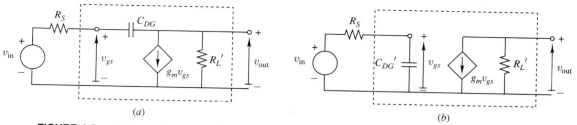

FIGURE 4-5   (a) Small-signal equivalent circuit with C_{DG} only; and (b) Miller capacitance $C'_{DG} = MC_{DG}$.

The expression of the *gain* A_v is obtained by straight application of Kirchhoff's laws. Without any approximations, it is given by

$$A = A_{v0} \frac{1 - jf/f_{c4}}{1 + jf/f_{c3}}$$

(4-13a)

in which

$$f_{c3} = \frac{1}{2\pi M R_S C_{DG}}$$

(4-13b)

and

$$M = 1 + \frac{R'_L}{R_S} - A_{v0}$$

(4-13c)

and

$$f_{c4} = \frac{g_m}{2\pi C_{DG}}$$

(4-13d)

This characteristic now contains a pole at frequency f_{c3} and a zero at frequency f_{c4}. It is illustrated asymptotically in Fig. 4-6a. Both f_{c3} and f_{c4} are also listed in Table 4-1.

At low frequencies, obviously $|A_v| = A_{v0}$. At high frequencies the pole is usually dominant over the zero, i.e., it comes in at a lower frequency. The reason is that M appears in f_{c3}, which contains A_{v0} and thus is large. This factor M stands for Miller effect, which will be explained next.

Miller Effect   It is striking that now the -3 dB frequency f_{c3} is not generated by a simple RC product. A multiplier M is added to the RC product. The largest contribution to factor M is the low frequency gain A_{v0} itself. This is the so-called Miller effect (Sedra and Smith 1981). The dominant pole is caused by the product of the coupling capacitance C_{DG} and the source resistance R_S, multiplied by the low

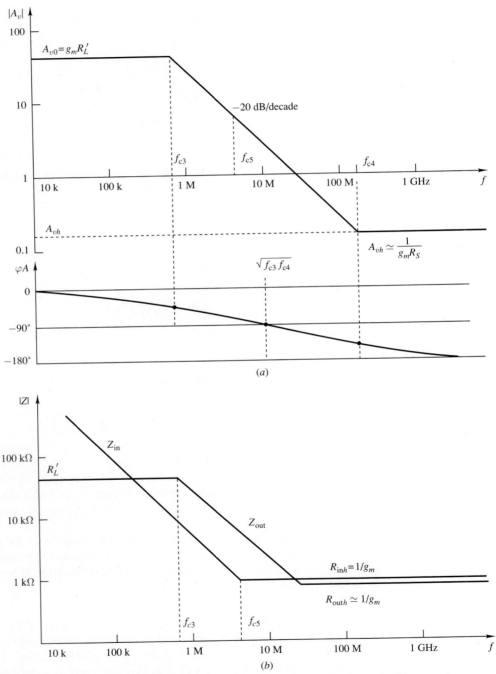

FIGURE 4-6   (a) A_v if only $C_{DG} = 1$ pF is present; and (b) Z_{in} and Z_{out} if only $C_{DG} = 1$ pF is present.

frequency gain A_{v0} of that amplifying stage. Remember that A_{v0} is negative such that all terms add up in absolute value in Eq. (4-13c).

Since the source resistance appears in the expression of the pole, it generates the same value of pole frequency when a capacitance C'_{DG} is put from the input node to ground (see Fig. 4-5b). Comparison of Eqs. (4-13b) and (4-9) shows that

$$C'_{DG} = M C_{DG} \approx |A_{v0}| C_{DG} \qquad (4\text{-}14)$$

As a result, C'_{DG} is an equivalent input capacitance, called the Miller capacitance, which causes the same pole in the gain characteristic as does coupling capacitance C_{DG} (see Chap. 3).

At still higher frequencies, the zero of Eq. (4-13a) comes in. This occurs at a frequency f_{c4}. Above that frequency, the frequency response of the gain (see Fig. 4-6a) is flat and reaches a value A_{vh}, which is resistive. It can easily be obtained by dropping both terms 1 in Eq. (4-13a). This yields

$$A_{vh} \approx \frac{R'_L}{M R_S} = \frac{1}{g_m R_S} \qquad (4\text{-}15)$$

In Fig. 4-6a it is easy to see that the ratio f_{c4}/f_{c3} equals the ratio A_{v0}/A_{vh} in absolute values. Indeed, the slope between frequencies f_{c3} and f_{c4} equals unity, or -20 dB/decade.

Positive Zero   Note that the pole in Eq. (4-13a) is negative, whereas the zero is positive. This does not change the amplitude characteristic of the gain A_v, but it does change its phase characteristic. In Fig. 4-7, the characteristics are given for both the amplitude (with asymptotes) and the phase for two different gain expressions. The first has a negative zero, whereas the other has a positive zero. As clearly seen, the amplitude characteristic is exactly the same. The phase at high frequencies, however, differs over $180°$ as a result of the minus sign. Note that all phases are relative with respect to the phase (of zero degrees) at low frequencies.

Remember that A_{v0} contains a minus sign as well, which corresponds with another phase difference of $180°$. Thus, at low frequencies there is a phase difference of $180°$ between input and output. At high frequencies there actually is no phase difference, or $360°$. This agrees with the intuitive picture that can be formed by inspection of the circuit (Fig. 4-5a). At high frequencies the capacitance behaves as a short circuit and the output follows the input, albeit in attenuated form, but without phase shift.

The input impedance with only one single capacitance C_{DG} can be calculated by use of Fig. 4-5a or 4-5b. The biasing resistors have been removed. Input impedance Z_{in} is then given by

$$Z_{in} = \left(\frac{1}{1 - A_{v0}} \right) \frac{1 + R'_L C_{DG} s}{s C_{DG}} \approx \frac{1}{s C'_{DG}} \qquad (4\text{-}16)$$

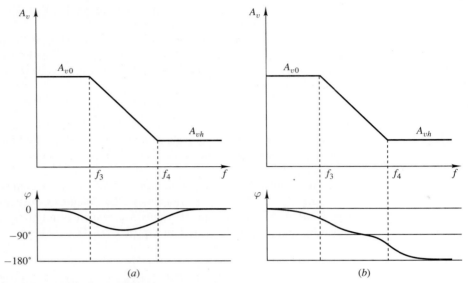

FIGURE 4-7   Difference in phase for (a) a negative and (b) a positive zero.

with

$$f_{c5} = \frac{1}{2\pi R'_L C_{DG}} \tag{4-17}$$

It shows that for low frequencies, the capacitance seen at the input is the Miller capacitance (see Fig. 4-5b).

At frequencies higher than f_{c5}, the zero becomes important in Eq. (4-16). At these high frequencies, the input impedance is resistive and equals $R_{inh} \approx 1/g_m$, as indicated in Fig. 4-6b.

It is no surprise to see $1/g_m$ as input resistance at high frequencies. Replacement of C_{DG} by a short circuit in Fig. 4-5a gives exactly the same result. If this connection (between drain and gate) is also realized in DC, as seen in Fig. 4-8, then we immediately recognize the resulting diode configuration. We know that the small-signal resistance of a diode (shown in Fig. 4-8b) is given by $1/g_m$ (see Chap. 1). This obviously applies to the output resistance as well.

The calculation of the output impedance is also carried out by use of the equivalent circuit of Fig. 4-5. This gives

$$Z_{out} = R'_L \frac{1 + jf/Mf_{c3}}{1 + jf/f_{c3}} \tag{4-18}$$

At low frequencies the value of Z_{out} is given by R'_L (see Fig. 4-6b). Also, the pole at f_{c3} is the same as for the gain, and thus contains the Miller capacitance as well. The zero always occurs at higher frequencies.

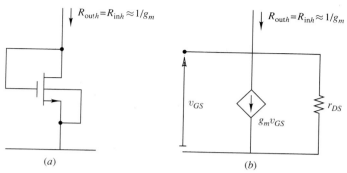

(a) (b)

FIGURE 4-8   Input and output resistance of a diode-connected MOST.

At very high frequencies, the value of Z_{out} becomes resistive as well, and is denoted by R_{outh}. Its value is found by omission of all the numeral ones in Eq. (4-18) and is given again by $R_{\text{outh}} = R'_L/M \approx 1/g_m$, as also shown in Fig. 4-6b.

Example 4-3

Take a single transistor amplifier with $g_m = 1$ mS, $R_S = 5$ kΩ ($R_{12} = \infty$) and $R'_L = 40$ kΩ. Capacitance $C_{DG} = 1$ pF. Calculate the gain, and the input and output impedances versus frequency.

Solution. From Eq. (4-4), $A_{v0} = -40$ and from Eq. (4-13c), the value of factor $M = 49$. For $C_{DG} = 1$ pF, $f_{c3} = 640$ kHz and $f_{c4} = 160$ MHz are obtained from Eq. (4-13b and d). The Bode diagrams are shown in Fig. 4-6a. The attenuation at high frequencies is about $1/g_m R_S \approx 0.16$. The input impedance diagram is governed by f_{c5}, which is obtained from Eq. (4-17) and is 4 MHz. Its Bode diagrams are shown in Fig. 4-6b. The output impedance diagrams can now easily be drawn as given by Eq. (4-18) and shown in Fig. 4-6b.

In conclusion, we see that capacitance from the input node to ground or from the output node to ground, generates a pole in the gain characteristic. A capacitance between the input and nodes, however, also generates a positive zero, causing a large phase shift that will cause problems in feedback amplifiers later. Let us now analyze the single-transistor amplying stage with all capacitances present.

4-1-4   Full Circuit Performance at High Frequencies

If none of the three terminal capacitances are omitted, complex expressions emerge for all three characteristics of the gain, input, and output impedance. They all can be obtained from straightforward but tedious hand calculations, or from a symbolic simulator, such as ISAAC, using the circuit of Fig. 4-2b (Gielen and Sansen 1991).

The expression of the gain A_v is given by

$$A_v = A_{v0} \left(\frac{1 - s(C_{DG}/g_m)}{1 + [R_S(C_{GS} + MC_{DG}) + R'_L C_{DS}]s + R_S R'_L C^2 s^2} \right) \qquad (4\text{-}19a)$$

with

$$C^2 = C_{DG}C_{GS} + C_{DG}C_{DS} + C_{GS}C_{DS} \qquad (4\text{-}19b)$$

The input impedance Z_{in} is given by

$$Z_{\text{in}} = \left\{ \frac{1}{[C_{GS} + (1 - A_{v0})C_{DG}]s} \right\} \left\{ \frac{1 + R'_L(C_{DS} + C_{DG})s}{1 + \left[\dfrac{R'_L C^2 s}{[C_{GS} + (1 - A_{v0})C_{DG}]s} \right]} \right\} \qquad (4\text{-}20a)$$

with

$$f_{c16} = \frac{1}{2\pi R'_L(C_{DS} + C_{DG})} \qquad (4\text{-}20b)$$

and the output impedance Z_{out} by

$$Z_{\text{out}} = R'_L \left\{ \frac{1 + R_S(C_{GS} + C_{DG})s}{1 + [R_S(C_{GS} + MC_{DG}) + R'_L C_{DS}]s + R_S R'_L C^2 s^2} \right\} \qquad (4\text{-}21a)$$

with

$$f_{c13} = \frac{1}{2\pi R_S(C_{GS} + C_{DG})} \qquad (4\text{-}21b)$$

We will now study all three characteristics in detail. The values used in the following examples are $g_m = 1$ mS, $R_S = 5$ kΩ, $R'_L = 40$ kΩ, $C_{GS} = 4$ pF, $C_{DS} = 2.5$ pF, and $C_{DG} = 1$ pF, which gives $A_{v0} = -40$ and $M = 49$.

In order to provide better insight into the role of each transistor parameter and capacitance, the characteristics of A_v, Z_{in}, and Z_{out} are examined. All three capacitances are always present. However, only one of them or some other transistor parameter is now used each time as a variable. This means that we have six parameters to use, i.e., g_m, R'_S, R'_L, and the tree capacitances ($R_{12} = \infty$) (see Fig. 4-3). Thus, we can redraw the same Bode diagram of the gain A_v six times, each time with a different parameter as a variable. Actually, we can repeat this with Z_{in} and Z_{out}, leading to 18 Bode diagrams. We will limit ourselves to only a few.

First, capacitance C_{DG} is taken as a variable. Since the effect of C_{DG} is multiplied by the Miller factor M, capacitance C_{DG} is the best choice to set the bandwidth of the amplifier at a given value. An external capacitance can then be added to capacitance

C_{DG} in order to obtain a specific cut-off frequency. Thus, it is important to study the characteristics of this amplifier for low and high values of C_{DG} as well.

The Gain A_v with C_{DG} as a Parameter   Let us first take a very low value of C_{DG}, i.e., zero. For zero C_{DG}, Eq. (4-19a) is reduced to

$$A_v = A_{v0} \frac{1}{(1 + jf/f_{c1})(1 + jf/f_{c2})} \tag{4-22}$$

which shows two poles. They occur at frequencies f_{c1} and f_{c2}, which have been derived in Eqs. (4-9) and (4-11), respectively, and which are already listed in Table 4-1. They are a direct result of the presence of the capacitances C_{GS} and C_{DS} at the input and output nodes, respectively. For this example, f_{c2} is the dominant pole and is denoted by f_d, since it occurs at the lower frequency, i.e., 1.6 MHz. This could be expected because R_S is usually small (kΩ's), whereas R'_L is usually large in order to obtain large gain.

Now we will allow capacitance C_{DG} to increase. In order to keep track of what happens to the poles, a pole-zero position diagram is used. In this diagram the poles and zeros are plotted versus C_{DG}, as seen in Fig. 4-9a. It has been derived by assuming that two separate poles are present at widely different frequencies (see App. 3-2). The two poles are clearly seen for small values of C_{DG}, i.e., if C_{DG} is smaller than approximately 0.5 pF.

Since the pole-zero position diagram is not yet commonly used, it will be worked out here in detail. It will be used in several exercises, so that the reader can become familiar with it.

The second important case is where C_{DG} has been made large in order to reduce the bandwidth. In this case, Eq. (4-19a) is reduced to

$$A_v = A_{v0} \frac{1 - s\,(C_{DG}/g_m)}{1 + MR_S C_{DG} s + R_S R'_L C_{DG}(C_{GS} + C_{DS})s^2} \tag{4-23}$$

The dominant pole is now caused by the Miller capacitance MC_{DG} and is located at frequency f_{c3}. The dominant pole is thus decreased, as can be expected.

The value of the other or nondominant pole can be easily approximated by omission of the first term in the denominator and division by s (see App. 3-2). It is then given by

$$f_{c6} = \frac{M}{2\pi R'_L(C_{GS} + C_{DS})} \approx \frac{g_m}{2\pi(C_{GS} + C_{DS})} \tag{4-24}$$

in which M has been approximated by $A_{v0} = g_m R'_L$.

In this example, $f_{c6} = 24.5$ MHz. This nondominant pole thus occurs at frequencies that are much higher than either f_{c1} or f_{c2}. As a result, the increase of C_{DG} has split the poles apart. This situation is illustrated in Fig. 4-9a. *Pole splitting* is clearly seen from the values of C_{DG} of $C_{DGt} = 0.5$ pF on.

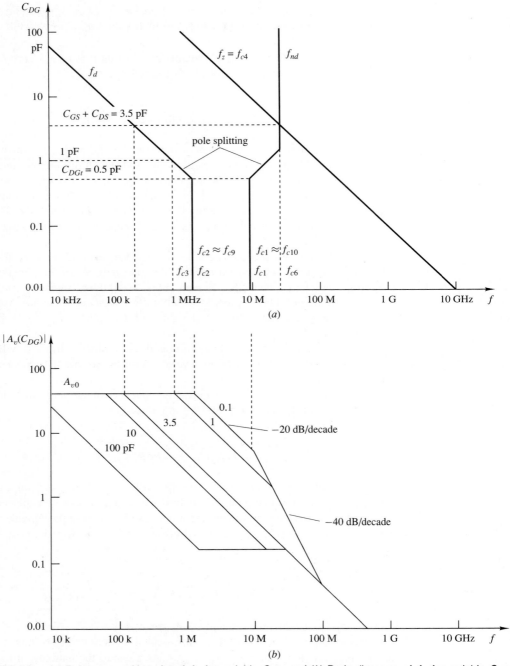

FIGURE 4-9   (a) Pole zero position plot of A_v for variable C_{DG}; and (b) Bode diagrams of A_v for variable C_{DG} (phase omitted).

This threshold value C_{DGt} obviously depends on other capacitances. It can be extracted from the expression of the dominant pole f_d, which is drawn in Fig. 4-9a. It can be obtained from Eq. (4-19a) since this curve for f_d can be constructed from the terms in s of the denominator. Since we deal with the dominant pole only, we can leave out the term in s^2. The curve for f_d is then approximated by

$$f_d = \frac{f_{c9}}{1 + C_{DG}/C_{DGt}}$$

(4-25a)

with

$$C_{DGt} = \frac{1}{2\pi M R_S f_{c9}}$$

(4-25b)

and

$$f_{c9} = \frac{1}{2\pi (R_S C_{GS} + R'_L C_{DS})}$$

(4-25c)

For low values of C_{DG}, frequency f_{c9} establishes the dominant pole. Its value is close to f_{c2} (see Table 4-1). Substitution of f_{c9} by f_{c2} in Eq. (4-25b) gives

$$C_{DGt} \approx \frac{C_{DS}}{g_m R_S}$$

(4-25d)

Example 4-4

Take an amplifier with $g_m = 1$ mS, $R_S = 5$ kΩ, $R'_L = 40$ kΩ, $C_{GS} = 4$ pF, $C_{DS} = 2.5$ pF, and $C_{DG} = 1$ pF, which gives $A_{v0} = -40$ and $M = 49$. Calculate the pole-zero position diagram with all breakpoints.

Solution. The break frequencies are $f_{c2} = 1.6$ MHz, $f_{c1} = 8$ MHz, $f_{c3} = 0.64$ MHz, and $f_{c6} = 24.5$ MHz. The diagram is given in Fig. 4-9a.

In this example, $C_{DS} = 2.5$ pF and $g_m R_S = 5$. As a result, the value of C_{DGt} is 0.5 pF.

In a similar way (see App. 4-1), the expression of the nondominant pole f_{nd} can be obtained. It is derived from Eq. (4-19a) by omission of the one in the denominator and division by s. It can then be approximated by

$$f_{nd} = f_{c10} \frac{1 + \left(\dfrac{C_{DG}}{C_{DGt}} \right)}{1 + \left(\dfrac{C_{DG}}{C_{DGu}} \right)}$$

(4-26a)

with
$$f_{c10} = \frac{f_{c1} f_{c2}}{f_{c9}} \tag{4-26b}$$

and
$$C_{DGu} = \frac{C_{GS} C_{DS}}{C_{GS} + C_{DS}} \tag{4-26c}$$

For low values of C_{DG}, the nondominant pole f_{nd} is at frequency f_{c10}, which is very close to f_{c1} (see Table 4-1), given by Eq. (4-9).

As clearly seen, pole splitting occurs simultaneously at C_{DGt} for both poles. Also note that the nondominant pole moves away from the dominant pole over a ratio f_{c6}/f_{c2}, given by Eqs. (4-24) and (4-11):

$$\frac{f_{c6}}{f_{c2}} = A_{v0} \left(\frac{C_{DS}}{C_{GS} + C_{DS}} \right) \tag{4-27}$$

Hence, the more low-frequency gain A_{v0} is available, the more the nondominant pole moves out as a result of increasing C_{DG}. Pole splitting is proportional to the gain. In this example, this ratio is only a factor of 16. For values of C_{DG}, which are larger than 16 times C_{DGt}, or 8 pF, the nondominant pole is constant at frequency f_{c6} (see Fig. 4-9a).

The zero f_z of Eq. (4-19a) is also plotted in Fig. 4-9a. The larger C_{DG}, the more it shifts to lower frequencies. For high values of C_{DG}, the zero is found between both poles. In order to understand this, we first must look at the corresponding Bode diagrams.

The Bode diagrams of the gain A_v have been constructed in Fig. 4-9b for several values of C_{DG}. Because the phase diagrams are omitted (since they can easily be derived from the amplitudes), only the amplitudes are shown.

The dominant pole decreases for larger C_{DG}. For very large C_{DG} the effect of the zero is clearly seen. A flat part appears with value R_L' versus $M R_S$ (≈ 0.16).

For a specific value of C_{DG}, the zero coincides with the nondominant pole and a single-pole characteristic emerges. This value of C_{DG} is found by equating the frequency of the zero f_{c4}, to frequency f_{c6} (see Fig. 4-9a). This value of C_{DG} is $C_{GS} + C_{DS}$. Its value is 3.5 pF in Example 4-4.

For this value of C_{DG}, a perfect first-order characteristic results. The slope of -20 dB/decade is maintained over all frequencies. For lower values of C_{DG} a steep, second-order part appears in the characteristic, whereas for higher values of C_{DG} a flat part appears. Neither of these characteristics are desirable if a single-order characteristic is required. This will be the case, as well, in all operational amplifier characteristics discussed in Chap. 6.

It must be clear by now how easy it is to construct the Bode diagrams (Fig. 4-9b) from the pole-zero position diagram of Fig. 4-9a. Therefore, we will continue to use this dual set of diagrams to study the influence of parameters.

The expression of the input impedance is given by Eq. (4-20). We can analyze it the same way we analyzed the gain. The diagrams are not given because they are studied in the exercises.

The expression of the output impedance is given by Eq. (4-21). It has the same denominator for the gain as Eq. (4-19). Therefore the positions of the poles for variable C_{DG} are the same as for the gain, clearly showing pole splitting. Diagrams for pole splitting are studied in the exercises, as well.

Remember, however, that both the input impedance and the output impedance exhibit a resistive part at higher frequencies (see Fig. 4-6b). Again, the transistors' drain and gate can be considered to be short-circuited together, resulting in a diode configuration with resistance value of about $1/g_m$.

Three characteristics with C_{DG} as a variable have been analyzed, leading to three Bode diagrams. We could have used a parameter other than C_{DG}, such as one of the capacitances or a transistor parameter such as g_m. By inspecting the equivalent circuit of Fig. 4-2b, we find the three capacitances, the source and load resistance, and the transconductance as parameters, totaling six parameters. Remember that we can derive eighteen pole-zero position and Bode diagram combinations.

We only discuss a few of the pole-zero positions in the text and exercises. It is imperative that the reader learns to draw the Bode diagram as derived from the pole-zero position plot, and thus the reader is given many opportunities to derive these diagrams.

The Bode diagram, studied next, is one with g_m as a parameter. This is of particular importance because g_m sets the gain A_{v0} itself, and depends on the current. Therefore it is the most useful parameter to use in the design process.

The Gain A_v with g_m as a Parameter The poles and zero of the gain A_v with g_m as a variable are again given by Eq. (4-19). They are plotted in Fig. 4-10a.

The expression of the dominant pole f_d, which is valid for all values of g_m, is extracted as before from the terms in s in the denominator of Eq. (4-19). It is given by

$$f_d = f_{c9}\left(\frac{1}{1 + g_m/g_{mt}}\right) \tag{4-28a}$$

with

$$g_{mt} = \frac{\tau_9}{R_S R'_L C_{DG}} \tag{4-28b}$$

and

$$f_{c9} = \frac{1}{2\pi \tau_9} = \frac{1}{2\pi (R_S C_{GS} + R'_L C_{DS})} \tag{4-28c}$$

as already given by Eq. (4-25c) (see Table 4-1). In Example 4-4, g_{mt} is 0.6 mS. From that value on, the dominant pole becomes even more dominant (see Fig. 4-10a). Note that τ_9 simply contains the input and output time constants.

The expression of the nondominant pole f_{nd} is given by

$$f_{nd} = f_{c15}(1 + g_m/g_{mt}) \tag{4-29a}$$

with

$$f_{c15} = \frac{g_{mt}C_{DG}}{2\pi C^2} = \frac{\tau_9}{2\pi R_S R'_L C^2} \tag{4-29b}$$

which is 5.8 MHz in this example.

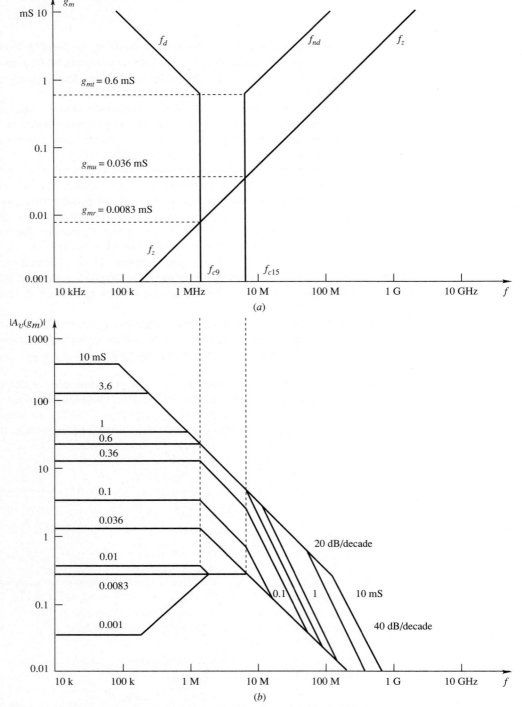

FIGURE 4-10 (a) Pole zero position plot of A_v for variable g_m of MOST; and (b) Bode diagram of A_v for variable g_m (phase omitted).

For low values of g_m (see Fig. 4-10a), the two poles are given by f_{c9} and f_{c15}. For values of g_m larger than g_{mt}, pole splitting occurs again, and keeps increasing for even higher values of g_m. A large value of g_m (or gain) thus is a requirement for effective pole splitting.

The zero f_z is added in Fig. 4-10a as well. It increases with increasing g_m. This is exactly the opposite, compared to Fig. 4-9a, where the zero moves in with increasing C_{DG}. There are thus two techniques to cause pole splitting, i.e., by increasing C_{DG} and by increasing g_m (or the gain). The latter is preferred by far, because the positive zero then moves out to higher frequencies. In the op amp design in Chap. 6, we will see that we need a transistor with high g_m under capacitance C_{DG}. Therefore, we usually prefer a bipolar transistor in that position (in a BICMOS process, where we have a choice).

The Bode diagrams of the gain A_v are easily derived from Fig. 4-10a. They are shown in Fig. 4-10b. At low frequencies, $|A_{v0}|$ is linearly proportional to g_m, since it equals $g_m R_L$. The gain can thus be set by either g_m or by R_L, or both. At higher frequencies two different possibilities are clearly shown.

For large values of g_m, a region of first-order (-20 dB/decade), is always followed by a region of second-order, (-40 dB/decade). Where g_m equals g_{mt} (0.6 mS), the region with a slope of -40 dB/decade is the largest.

In general, we do not want regions of -40 dB/decade. When the amplifier is used in a feedback configuration, this amplifier may cause peaking and ringing, as explained in Chap. 3.

For very low values of g_m, the zero f_z is dominant. A peaked characteristic results in a broad peak between f_{c9} and f_{c15} (at 2.7 MHz). This zero is a direct result of feedthrough of the input signal to the output through C_{DG}.

For intermediate values of g_m, however, a perfect first-order characteristic can be obtained twice: (1) where the zero crosses the nondominant pole (at $g_m = g_{mu}$) and (2) where the zero crosses the dominant pole (at $g_m = g_{mr}$). The value of g_{mu} is found by equating the zero f_z to f_{c15} (see Table 4-1). It is given by C_{DG}/τ_{15}, which is 0.036 mS. The value of g_{mr} is found by equating f_{c9} to the zero f_z, which gives C_{DG}/τ_9 (8.3 μS). Both operating points can be of interest because they lead to wide-band amplifiers.

Since the zero involved is a positive zero, the phase diagrams of a few gain characteristics are given in Fig. 4-11. The curves of $|A_v|$ for $g_m = 1$ mS and 1 μS, are taken from Fig. 4-10b and repeated in Fig. 4-11. Note that all phase values reach $-270°$ at high frequencies, and invariably change by $-90°$ at each (negative) pole or (positive) zero.

4-1-5 Unity-Gain Frequency and Gain-Bandwidth Product

Now that we know how to draw the Bode diagrams, we have to define a number of characteristic frequencies. We will use these frequencies during the designs, during the optimizations and during comparison of the frequency performance of different amplifiers. Some of the characteristic frequencies are already known to us, such as the dominant pole, nondominant pole, and the zero.

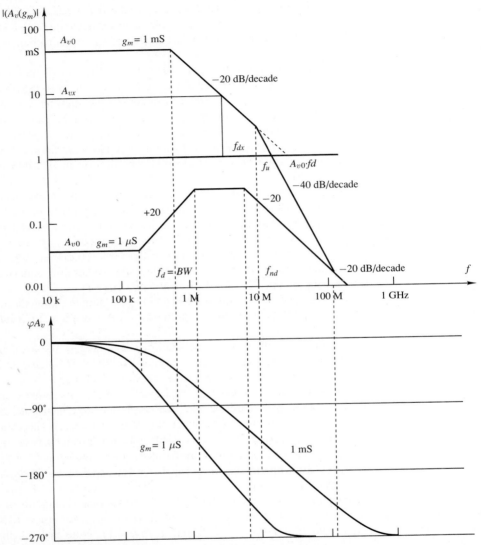

FIGURE 4-11   Bode diagrams for A_v for $g_m = 1$ mS and 1 μS

The frequency where the -20 dB/decade slope starts is the frequency of the dominant pole f_d (see Fig. 4-11). At this point, the actual gain is at -3 dB (or $1/\sqrt{2}$ with respect to the flat level). It is also called the "-3 dB frequency," or more commonly the "bandwidth (BW)".

The frequency where the gain reaches a value of unity is called the "unity-gain frequency f_u." The product of the low-frequency gain A_{v0} with the dominant pole

f_d is denoted by $A_{v0}f_d$. All these frequencies are all indicated in Fig. 4-11. Do not confuse frequency $A_{v0}f_d$ with the gain-bandwidth product. This term is reserved for a different frequency, as explained next.

Remember that the slope of -20 dB/decade is actually a slope of unity. As a result, if the gain is modified for some reason (such as feedback) from A_{v0} to A_{vx}, the bandwidth is modified from f_d to f_{dx}, as shown in Fig. 4-11. The resulting product is the same, i.e., $A_{vx}f_{dx} = A_{v0}f_d$. A reduction in gain yields the same increase in bandwidth. Gain and bandwidth can be freely exchanged. The product is always constant.

However, this product is not constant for points on the slope of -40 dB/decade. This is the case for the points on the curve close to unity (see Fig. 4-11). We must avoid the region of -40 dB/decade for all values of the gain A_v between A_{v0} and unity. This can be done by moving out the nondominant pole to higher frequencies as sketched in Fig. 4-12.

In Fig. 4-12, the Bode diagrams are sketched for an amplifier with two poles. The zero is left out to keep it simple. In Fig. 4-12a both poles are relatively close together, whereas in Fig. 4.12c the dominant pole is really dominant, i.e., it occurs at very low frequencies. The nondominant pole occurs at very high frequencies, beyond the point where the gain A_v is unity.

The characteristic frequencies f_d, f_{nd}, f_u, and $A_{v0}f_d$ are always indicated. In Fig. 4-12a, the frequency $A_{v0}f_d$ is much larger than f_u, in Fig. 4-12b they coincide, and in Fig. 4-12c curve $A_{v0}f_d$ is much smaller. The slope of -20 dB/decade clearly extends to gains below unity only in Fig. 4-12c. Therefore, the frequency $A_{v0}f_d$ is called the "gain-bandwidth product (GBW)." In the first and second part of Fig. 4-12, the GBW is not defined because the slope of -20 dB/decade does not extend over all values of the gain A_v from A_{v0} to unity.

The most sensitive parameter to measure the position of the nondominant pole with respect to GBW is the phase at the GBW frequency. Rather than the phase itself, the difference is taken from $-180°$, counting upwards. This phase difference is called the "phase margin" and is denoted by ϕ_m or PM. For Fig. 4-12b, f_u nearly coincides with the GBW and f_{nd}; hence PM = 45°. The phase margin is smaller for Fig. 4-12a and larger for Fig. 4-12c. Note that even in Fig. 4-12c, the unity-gain frequency f_u is not quite the same as the GBW, but the difference is very small. Indeed, the f_u is the frequency where $|A_v| = 1$ and the GBW is the first-order extrapolated frequency at $|A_v| = 1$.

To avoid ringing and peaking in later designs, we will aim at phase margins of around 70°, which require a nondominant pole at about three times GBW (see Chap. 3). We will use this important rule of thumb for the remainder of this list. The nondominant pole should be at about $3 \cdot GBW$. The question remains as to how we can make sure that the nondominant pole is high enough in frequency. The answer is pole splitting.

We have seen that pole splitting is caused by an increase of g_m or of capacitance C_{DG}. In Fig. 4-10b, we have seen that increasing g_m shifts the nondominant pole to higher frequencies. A value of g_m between 5 to 10 mS seems sufficient. Application to the curves of the gain (Fig. 4-11) gives for $g_m = 1$ mS a value of about $f_{nd} = 20$

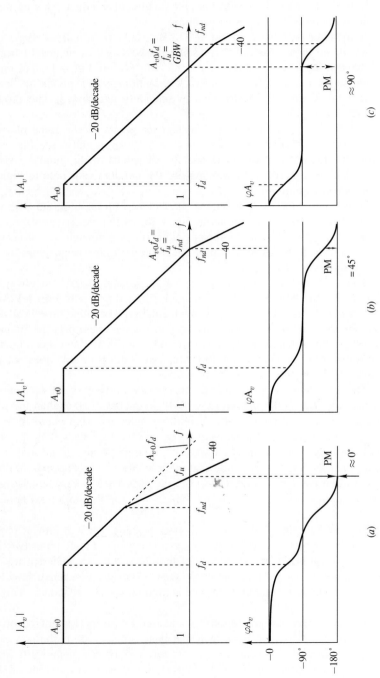

FIGURE 4-12 Bode diagrams with definition of *GBW* for several positions of poles f_d and f_{nd}.

MHz, where $|A_v| = 1$. The value of GBW that can be obtained with 70° phase margin will thus be one-third, or about 6.7 MHz.

Increasing either g_m or C_{DG} to realize a PM of about 70° by means of pole splitting is also called *compensation*. We compensate parasitic capacitive effects, increasing the nondominant pole. Remember that the result is always a decrease of dominant pole, hence a decrease in GBW.

From the designer's point of view, we always want to achieve a maximum value of GBW for current consumption. If we increase the current, and hence g_m, we can see in Fig. 4-10a that the GBW (for $|A_v| = 1$) does not increase beyond about 40 MHz. The maximum achievable GBW seems to be $GBW_{max} = 40$ MHz. What is the origin of this number?

Maximum GBW with Dominant Miller Effect   The value of GBW_{max} is easily extracted from Eq. (4-19) as being the product of A_{v0} and the dominant pole f_d, for large values of g_m. Under these conditions, the gain is large; thus we can safely assume that the Miller capacitance is dominant such that

$$GBW_{max} = A_{v0}\frac{1}{2\pi R_S M C_{DG}} \approx \frac{1}{2\pi R_S C_{DG}} \tag{4-30}$$

which is 32 MHz in this example. If the full expression is taken, but only dominant pole considered, $GBW_{max} = 29$ MHz, which is close to the previous value.

Still, some correction factors may be necessary because the zero is present as well as other minor effects. We should not be overly concerned, however, because the transistor parameters are never known accurately.

Maximum GBW with Dominant Input Capacitance   The value of GBW_{max} is caused by the Miller capacitance MC_{DG}. Circuit techniques are available, however, to reduce the Miller effect such that it is no longer dominant. For example, we can use cascode transistors, as will be explained in Sec. 4-6, or we can use feedback.

In this case, only the time constants $R_S C_{GS}$ and $R'_L C_{DS}$ remain to be considered. The dominant pole frequency is now considerably extended toward f_{c9}, given by Eq. (4-25c) and repeated in Eq. (4-28). The value of GBW_{max} is then given by

$$GBW_{max} = \frac{g_m R'_L}{2\pi(R_S C_{GS} + R'_L C_{DS})} \approx A_{v0} f_{c9} \tag{4-31}$$

The denominator is the sum of the input time constant $R_S C_{GS}$, and the output time constant $R'_L C_{DS}$. Depending on the application and specific values of R'_L and R_S, either time constant can be dominant.

For a low value of R'_L (and low amplification factor A_{v0}), the input time constant is dominant. In this case the maximum value GBW_{max} is given by

$$GBW_{max} = \left(\frac{1}{2\pi}\right)\left(\frac{R'_L}{R_S}\right)\left(\frac{g_m}{C_{GS}}\right) \tag{4-32a}$$

As a result, this time constant C_{GS}/g_m is often considered to be the ultimate limiting time constant of a MOST. This time constant C_{GS}/g_m is characterized by frequency f_{c14}, given by

$$f_{c14} = f_T = \left(\frac{1}{2\pi}\right)\left(\frac{g_m}{C_{GS}}\right) \tag{4-32b}$$

which is called f_T in analogy with a bipolar transistor.

However, this value of GBW_{max} depends on g_m. For $C_{GS} = 4$ pF and $g_m = 1$ mS, $GBW_{max} = 107$ MHz, which can still be increased by increasing g_m. However, both C_{GS} and g_m are set by the transistor width. Substitution of C_{GS} by WLC_{ox} and of g_m by Eq. (1-22a) yields

$$GBW_{max} = \left(\frac{R'_L}{R_S}\right) f_{max} \tag{4-32c}$$

with

$$f_{max} = \frac{1}{2\pi}\frac{2K'}{C_{ox}}\frac{1}{L^2}(V_{GS} - V_T) \approx \frac{1}{2\pi}\frac{\mu}{L^2}(V_{GS} - V_T) \tag{4-32d}$$

which is independent of W [see Eq. (1-40)]. Many authors denote f_{max} by f_T in analogy with a bipolar transistor (Sze 1981).

Design Procedure   Now that we know the GBW_{max} is an important parameter, we want to optimize GBW_{max} and f_{max} by using a design plan. For maximum f_{max}, L is to be made as small as possible for a given technology, as shown by Eq. (4-32c). For example, $L = 3$ μm. Factor $V_{GS} - V_T$ must be made large, which will inevitably lead to low gain (see Sec. 4-1-2). Let us choose $V_{GS} - V_T = 1$ V, This yields for $K' = 30$ μA/V^2 and for $C_{ox} = 6.8 \times 10^{-8}$ F/cm^2, a value of $f_{max} = 1.6$ GHz. The choice of W then fixes the values of I_{DS}, g_m, and C_{GS}. As a result, all three parameters I_{DS}, g_m, and C_{GS} are linearly proportional to the width W.

In general, the choice of $V_{GS} - V_T$ and W sets all the characteristics of the transistor (if L is fixed at its minimum value).

On the other hand, the transistor may already have been designed and realized. Then, only its $V_{GS} - V_T$ can be chosen, not its W nor L. The choice of $V_{GS} - V_T$ then sets the values of f_{max} and of g_m and I_{DS}. For larger $V_{GS} - V_T$, f_{max} increases linearly; g_m also increases linearly but I_{DS} increases with the square, such that g_m/I_{DS} decreases linearly.

Example 4-5

An nMOST with an effective gate length of 1.2 μm is to be used to construct an amplifier with $GBW > 20$ MHz (PM $\approx 70°$) for a source resistance of 600 Ω. An active load is used for optimum gain. What minimum current and transistor size are required? Would the addition of a cascode transistor help?

The transistor parameters are $K' = 30 \ \mu A/V^2$, $V_E = 20$ V, $C_{GS} = 1$ pF, and $C_{DG} = 0.4$ pF. The output capacitance C_{DS} includes some interconnect (and other) load capacitance and is $C_{DS} = 1$ pF. The maximum value of $V_{GS} - V_T = 1$ V.

Solution. On first sight this seems to be an easy task. Indeed, it is obvious that the Miller effect is going to be the dominant factor. The load resistance and gain are both intended to be high. From Eq. (4-30) we obtain $GBW_{max} = 662$ MHz, which is above the required 20 MHz. But what about the current and the nondominant pole?

For a 70° phase margin, the nondominant pole must be at about $3 \cdot GBW$ or 60 MHz. We may need pole splitting to achieve this, and for this purpose we could increase g_m. Figure 4-10a shows that pole splitting starts at the value of g_{mt} given by Eq. (4-28b). The output time constant $R'_L C_{DS}$ is certainly larger than the input time constant $R_S C_{GS} (= 0.6$ ns). As a result, g_{mt} is simplified to $g_{mt} \approx C_{DS}/R_S C_{DS} = 4.17$ mS. At that point, the current (for $V_{GS} - V_T = 1$ V) is given by Eq. (1-24c) and is $I_{DS} = 2.1$ mA. The output resistance is then $r_{DS} = V_E/I_{DS} = 20/2.1 = 9.6$ kΩ. The output time constant $r_{DS} C_{DS} = 9.6$ ns, which corresponds with $1/2\pi(9.6 \times 10^{-9}) = 16.6$ MHz. Thus we need a pole splitting factor of 3. The required current is then $3^2 = 10 \times 2.1$ mA, or about 21 mA. This is a large value for which we need a $W/L = I_{DS}/K'(V_{GS} - V_T)2 = 700$ and $W = 0.84$ mm. The low frequency gain A_{v0} is $g_m r_{DS} = 4.17 \times 9.7 \approx 40$ and the bandwidth is $20/40 = 0.5$ MHz. The SPICE input file that corresponds with this example is given in Table 4-2.

If a cascode is allowed, the Miller effect disappears. The input time constant is $R_S C_{GS} = 0.6$ ns, which corresponds with 265 MHz. The output time constant is still the same at that current of 2.1 mA, i.e., 9.6 ns, giving 16.6 MHz. Unless

TABLE 4-2   INPUT FILE FOR SPICE FOR THE SINGLE-TRANSISTOR *n*MOST AMPLIFIER OF EXAMPLE 5 IN SEC. 4-1-5.

```
* Ex. 4-5 (TEMPERATURE = 27.000 DEG C)
* CIRCUIT DESCRIPTION
M1 2 1 0 0 NMOS W=840U L=1.2U
IB 4 2 21M
VDD 3 0 DC 1.9 AC 1
CGS 1 0 1P
CDG 2 1 0.4P
CL 2 0 10P
RL 2 0 100K
RS 3 1 600
.MODEL NMOS NMOS LEVEL=2 VTO=0.9 KP=50E-6 GAMMA=0.01
+ LAMBDA=0.05
.PRINT AC VDB(2) VP(2)
.PLOT AC VDB(2) VP(2)
.WIDTH OUT = 75
.END
```

we find a trick to get rid of that output time constant, a cascode will not help. We will see later that a buffer stage can be inserted between the output and the output capacitance, reducing the transistor capacitance C_{DS} to approximately 0.1 pF. The output time constant yields 166 MHz in this case, allowing a GBW of up to about 1/3 or 55 MHz.

From this example the reader will realize that the design has become systematic. From the technological parameters and the specifications, one particular set of design results has been obtained. In this example, only the GBW and the PM (or the position of the nondominant pole) had to be designed. We still had some choices to make. In other words, we still had some degrees of freedom left, such as the $V_{GS} - V_T$. Everything else was determined automatically and no compromises had to be taken.

Design becomes different if we specify such characteristics as the output swing, noise, or gain. Then compromises are necessary. Then we must decide which specifications have priority. Most real-life design problems have more specifications than degrees of freedom. Thus, an interactive database will be required to indicate the possible compromises between the specifications and the free-design variables.

This problem can be relieved by adding more transistors, which usually adds more free-design variables. Efficient design means that only those transistors are added that add more degrees of freedom. In this way, the number of specifications can be matched by the number of free-design variables.

Noise is an important specification. In Chap. 6 we will discuss many more specifications.

4-1-6 Noise Performance

The noise behavior of the single-transistor amplifier is analyzed by use of the noise sources developed in Chap. 1. These are included in the small-signal equivalent circuit at low frequencies of Fig. 4-3, shown in Fig. 4-13a.

The transistor itself is represented by its equivalent input noise voltage $\overline{dv_{ie}^2}$. The noise voltage of the source resistor R_S is given by $\overline{dv_S^2}$. The noise current of the load resistor R_L is denoted by $\overline{di_L^2}$, and the noise current biasing resistors R_{12} is denoted by $\overline{di_{12}^2}$. All noise sources, except that of R_S, now can be lumped into one, total

FIGURE 4-13   Small-signal equivalent circuit of single-transistor amplifier at low frequencies with noise sources.

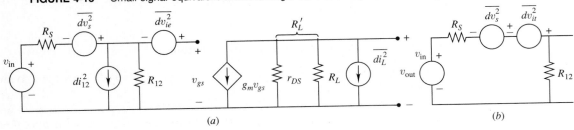

(a) *(b)*

equivalent, input noise voltage source $\overline{dv_{it}^2}$ at the input, in series with $\overline{dv_S^2}$, (as shown in Fig. 4-13b). Its value can be found by equation of the total output noise of the circuit in Fig. 4-13a, with all the noise sources to the total output noise of the circuit in Fig. 4-13b, with the total equivalent input noise source $\overline{dv_{it}^2}$. This yields (assuming that $R_S \ll R_{12}$):

$$\overline{dv_{it}^2} = \overline{dv_{ie}^2} + R_S^2 \overline{di_{12}^2} + \frac{\overline{di_L^2}}{g_m^2} \tag{4-33}$$

We commonly introduce an excess noise factor y, which gives the ratio of the equivalent input noise $\overline{dv_{it}^2}$ to that of the input transistor $\overline{dv_{ie}^2}$ only. It is obtained by substitution of $\overline{dv_{ie}^2}$ by $4kT/1.5g_m$ (see Chap. 1) and of $\overline{di_{12}^2}$ by $4kT/R$, which yields:

$$y = \frac{\overline{dv_{it}^2}}{\overline{dv_{ie}^2}} \approx 1 + 1.5 g_m R_S \left(\frac{R_S}{R_{12}} \right) + \frac{1.5}{g_m R_L} \tag{4-34}$$

It can be concluded that the equivalent input noise of the amplifier depends mainly on the noise of the transistor itself. Only large input source resistances could add some noise. For low noise applications, the transistor transconductance must be made large. We have already done that in order to increase the gain and/or the pole splitting.

4-2 BIPOLAR SINGLE-TRANSISTOR AMPLIFYING STAGES

In the previous section, the high-frequency performance of a MOST has been thoroughly studied. Now we will investigate a bipolar transistor. It is different than a MOST because of its base resistance and base current. Therefore, the resulting pole-zero position plots and the Bode diagrams are slightly more complicated. The biasing circuitry is discussed first.

An amplifying stage can be formed with a bipolar transistor, as shown in Fig. 4-14a. Again, an npn as a pnp transistor (see Fig. 4-14b) can be used as well. Appropriate biasing circuitry is required to set the collector at a specific value. A biasing current source I_{IN} can be taken as well, rather than a biasing voltage source V_{IN} (see Fig. 4-14). For a biasing current, a source resistance R_S is taken in parallel, whereas for a biasing voltage the source resistance R_S is in series with the voltage source. In the case of a current source, the transistor is current driven. For a voltage source, the transistor is voltage driven. Both drive types have their uses. The exact point of transition between these two modes of operation is examined.

4-2-1 Biasing

The difference between the bipolar transistor and the MOST is that biasing current flows into the base of the npn transistor, whereas biasing current is zero (of the order of pA) for a MOST. This biasing current or base current I_{IN} is a $1/\beta$ fraction of the collector current I_T. Its value will be assumed to be larger than 50 throughout this

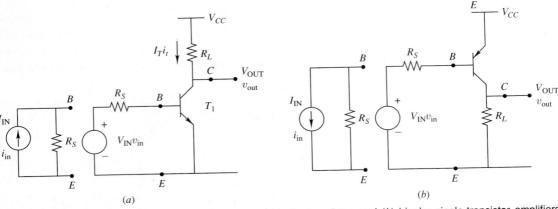

FIGURE 4-14   (a) Amplifying stage formed with a bipolar transistor; and (b) bipolar single-transistor amplifiers with resistive load.

text. Typical values are even larger, ranging from 100 to 500. For *pnp* transistors, however, we must keep in mind that their beta can be as low as 5 in older, standard bipolar processes. They will require more elaborate biasing schemas. Nowadays, betas of *pnp* transistors can also reach values higher than 100.

The collector current or transistor current I_T is determined mainly by the base-emitter voltage V_{BE} by the exponential I_C versus V_{BE} relationship described in Chap. 2. The output voltage is only determined by current I_T and output resistance R_L, as given by Eq. (4-1), with V_{CC} instead of V_{DD} being the supply voltage.

The biasing circuits for bipolar amplifiers can be divided into two classes: the circuits for discrete amplifiers and the circuits for integrated amplifiers. Biasing of discrete amplifiers relies on the availability of resistors and capacitors. Some config-urations are shown in Fig. 4-15. In the first, (Fig. 4-15a), the base current is provided by base resistor R_B. Its value is approximately given by

$$R_B = \frac{V_{CC} - V_{BEON}}{I_C/\beta} \tag{4-35}$$

in which $V_{BEON} \approx 0.7$ V. The resulting collector current depends heavily on tem-perature, because β is strongly temperature dependent ($\approx 0.7\%/°C$). Therefore, lo-cal feedback is better used as in Fig. 4-15b and 4-15c. This also affects the gain (and bandwidth) unless the feedback resistor can be shunted out. This is the case in Fig. 4-15c, in which capacitance C_E shunts out R_E for all frequencies of interest. Even better is using a voltage divider, as in Fig. 4-15d. The input source is always capacitively coupled through C_S.

However, in this text we concentrate on integrated amplifiers. By far the easiest way to bias the bipolar transistor is to take two equal (matched) transistors and to connect them either in a differential pair (see Sec. 4-7) or in a current mirror (see Sec. 4-8). An example of such a current mirror biasing schema is shown in Fig. 4-15e.

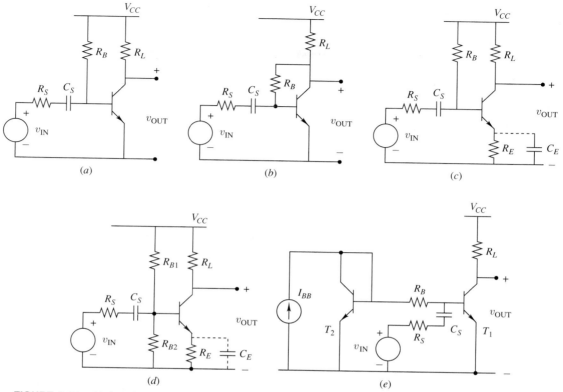

FIGURE 4-15 Various biasing configurations for a bipolar transistor amplifier and (e) biasing by use of current mirror.

For not-too-large values of R_B, both transistors have about the same V_{BE}, hence the same collector current, which equals I_{BB}. The exact value of I_{C1} is obtained from the difference in V_{BE}, as given by

$$V_{BE2} - V_{BE1} = \frac{R_B I_{C1}}{\beta} \qquad (4\text{-}36a)$$

Since $I_C = kT/q \ln(I_C/I_S)$, this is easily converted into

$$I_{C1} = I_{C2} \exp\left(-\frac{R_B I_{C1}}{\beta V_t}\right) \qquad (4\text{-}36b)$$

with $V_t = kT/q$ (25.86 mV at 300 K or 27° C). For small values of R_B, the exponent is about unity. We cannot make the exponent zero, though, which would decrease the input resistance to $1/g_m$ of transistor T2.

In the subsequent analyses the biasing resistances are included in the source resistance R_S.

4-2-2   Gain for Voltage and Current Drive

A variation of v_{IN} or i_{IN} generates a variation in i_T and hence in v_{OUT}. The relation between these small-signal components v_{in}, i_{in}, i_t, and v_{out} can be calculated by means of the small-signal model, shown in Fig. 4-16. At low frequencies, all capacitances can be omitted. The voltage gain is then given by

$$A_{v0} = -\left(\frac{r_\pi}{R_S' + r_\pi} \right) g_m R_L' \tag{4-37}$$

with $R_S' = R_S + r_B$ and $R_L' = R_L // r_o$. Again, the minus sign indicates an inversion in phase. The value of g_m has been calculated before. It is given by I_T / V_t.

For a *voltage-driven* transistor, the value of the source resistance R_S must be smaller than the input resistance $r_\pi + r_B$. Since the value of r_B is usually small, this results in the condition that $R_S' \ll r_\pi$. Eq. (4-37) is then reduced to:

$$A_{v0V} = \frac{v_{out}}{v_{in}} = -g_m R_L' \tag{4-38a}$$

For a *current-driven* transistor, $R_S' \gg r_\pi$, which allows us to convert Eq. (4-37) to:

$$A_{v0I} = \frac{v_{out}}{v_{in}} = -\beta \left(\frac{R_L'}{R_S'} \right) \tag{4-38b}$$

When the input current source configuration is preferred ($R_S' \gg r_\pi$), resistive gain is provided with value

$$A_{r0} = \frac{v_{out}}{i_{in}} = \beta R_L' \tag{4-38c}$$

Both Eq. (4-38b) and Eq. (4-38c) provide the same result because the voltage and current small-signal sources are related by $v_{in} = R_S' \cdot i_{in}$.

Equations (4-38b) and Eq. (4-38c) demonstrate why a bipolar transistor should never be current driven. Parameter β is not well-defined. Its reproducibility is low. Variations on β can be as high as 50 percent from batch to batch; therefore, it is

FIGURE 4-16   Small-signal equivalent circuit.

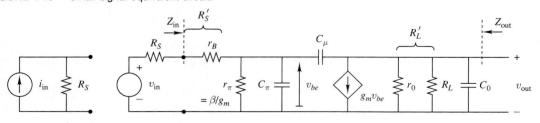

not an acceptable design parameter. The situation is different if discrete transistors are used, because their values of β can be measured separately and considered in the design procedure. For integrated circuit design, however, this is not possible, resulting in bipolar transistors that are always voltage driven. The gain is given by Eq. (4-38a), which is exactly the same expression as that of a MOST (see Eq. (4-4)), but with different g_m.

When a *pnp* transistor is used instead of an *npn* transistor (see Fig. 4-14b), its DC output voltage is given by $R_L I_T$. Its small-signal model, however, is exactly the same as for a *npn* transistor, and is also represented in Fig. 4-16. Its gain is given by Eq. (4-37), as well. Moreover, since g_m only depends on the current and not on the mobility of carriers, it is the same for both *npn* and *pnp* transistors operating at the same DC current.

Bipolar transistors provide a ratio g_m/I_C of $1/V_t$, which is about 38.5 V^{-1}. The gain that can be realized is thus 38.5 per Volt DC voltage drop over R'_L. For a supply voltage of 10 V, half of which can be used, values of gain up to 190 can be reached. This is a factor of nearly four times more than for a MOST. With two transistor configurations, even higher gain can be realized. It is important to remember this factor of four.

4-2-3 Frequency Performance

In order to study the frequency performance, all capacitances must be added. The capacitances in and around a bipolar transistor can be modeled by three capacitances, as shown in Fig. 4-16. They are called C_π, C_μ, and C_o. We must keep in mind, though, that any external capacitance added at the output node can be lumped into C_o. This is not entirely true for external capacitance between collector and base. This capacitance occurs before r_B, whereas C_μ occurs after r_B. SPICE allows redistributing part of C_μ over r_B (see parameter XCJC in Table 2-2). Since r_B is a small resistance, this distinction is neglected in most cases. In a few cases, e.g., for the calculation of Z_{in}, this distinction must be made.

Moreover, addition of external capacitance between base and collector increases the order of the frequency characteristic. Addition of capacitance to C_μ does not increase the order. The three capacitances in Fig. 4-16 form a loop that results in a characteristic of only second-order. It can still be handled by straightforward analysis.

Now we will derive the frequency characteristics of the gain, the input and output impedance. They will be used to generate some Bode diagrams later.

Gain A_v By use of Kirchhoff's current and voltage laws, the gain characteristic is given by

$$A_v = A_{v0} \left\{ \frac{1 - j\left(\dfrac{f}{f_{c4}}\right)}{1 + \dfrac{R'_S}{r_\pi} + \left[R'_S(C_\pi + MC_\mu) + R'_L\left(1 + \dfrac{R'_S}{r_\pi}\right)C_o \right]s + R'_S R'_L C^2 s^2} \right\}$$

$$(4\text{-}39a)$$

with

$$M = 1 + \frac{R'_L}{R'_S} + g_m R'_L = 1 + \frac{R'_L}{R'_S} - A_{v0} \tag{4-39b}$$

and

$$C^2 = C_\pi C_\mu + C_\pi C_o + C_\mu C_o \tag{4-39c}$$

and

$$f_{c4} = \frac{g_m}{2\pi C_\mu} \tag{4-39d}$$

All characteristic frequencies for the bipolar transistor amplifier are listed in Table 4-3. The first frequency is f_{c4}.

For a *voltage* drive ($R_S + r_B \ll r_\pi$), this is reduced to

$$A_{vV} = A_{v0V} \left\{ \frac{1 - j\left(\dfrac{f}{f_{c4}}\right)}{1 + [R'_S(C_\pi + M C_\mu) + R'_L C_o]s + R'_S R'_L C^2 s^2} \right\} \tag{4-40}$$

which is exactly the same as Eq. (4-19) for a MOST. A voltage-driven bipolar transistor behaves like a MOST. We will see this conclusion repeated frequently.

TABLE 4-3   LIST OF TIME CONSTANTS IDENTIFIED IN THE BIPOLAR SINGLE-TRANSISTOR AMPLIFIER WITH SMALL-SIGNAL MODEL GIVEN IN FIG. 4-16

Time constant τ	Value τ (ns)	f_{-3dB} ($= 1/2\pi\tau$)	Value (MHz)	Equation no.
$M r_\pi C_\mu = \beta R_L C_\mu$	6000	f_{c1}	0.026	(4-50)
$R'_L C_o$	100	f_{c2}	1.6	
$M R'_S C_\mu$	781	f_{c3}	0.2	
C_μ / g_m	0.15	f_{c4}	1060	(4-39d)
$(C_\pi + C_\mu)/g_m$	0.95	$f_{c5} = f_T$	170	
$R'_S(C_\pi + C_\mu)$	11.4	f_{c6}	14	
$R'_S C_{jE} + R'_L C_o$	107	f_{c9}	1.5	(4-45b)
$\tau_F + R'_L C_\mu$	60.2	f_{c10}	2.64	(4-45d)
$R'_S C^2/C_o$	13.3	f_{c15}	12	(4-46b)
$r_\pi(C_\pi + C_\mu)$	95	f_{c16}	1.7	

$R_s = 1\ k\Omega$	$R'_L = 40\ k\Omega$	$1/g_m = 100\ \Omega$	$\beta = 100$	$r_\pi = 10\ k\Omega$
$r_B = 200\ \Omega$	$C_{jE} = 6\ pF$	$C_\mu = 1.5\ pF$	$C_o = 2.5\ pF$	
$R'_S = 1.2\ k\Omega$	$\tau_F = 0.2\ ns$	$\tau_F g_m = 2\ pF$	$C_\pi = 8\ pF$	
$A_{v0} = -400$	$M = 434$	$C^2 = 27.75\ (pF)^2$		

For a *current* drive ($r_\pi \ll R_S + r_B$), Eq. (4-39) can be converted to

$$A_{vI} = A_{v0I} \left\{ \frac{1 - j\left(\dfrac{f}{f_{c4}}\right)}{1 + [r_\pi(C_\pi + MC_\mu) + R'_L C_o]s + r_\pi R'_L C^2 s^2} \right\} \tag{4-41}$$

In both Eq. (4-40) and Eq. (4-41), the dominant pole is caused by the Miller capacitance MC_μ. For a voltage drive, however, this capacitance sees a resistance R'_S (in Eq. (4-40), which is much smaller than the current drive resistance r_π (in Eq. (4-41)). The frequency of the dominant pole thus is much higher for a voltage drive than for a current drive. This is another reason why a bipolar transistor should always be voltage driven.

Input Impedance Z_{in}   In a similar way the expression of Z_{in} is easily derived and is given by

$$Z_{in} = (r_\pi + r_B) \left\{ \frac{1 + [r_B(C_\pi + MC_\mu) + R'_L C_o]s + r_B R'_L C^2 s^2}{1 + [r_\pi(C_\pi + g_m R'_L C_\mu) + R'_L C_o]s + r_\pi R'_L C^2 s^2} \right\} \tag{4-42}$$

Output Impedance Z_{out}   The output impedance Z_{out} depends on the source resistance. For a voltage drive, it is given by

$$Z_{outV} = R'_L \left\{ \frac{1 + (R_S + r_B)C_\mu s}{1 + [(R_S + r_B)(C_\pi + MC_\mu) + R'_L C_o]s + (R_S + r_B)R'_L C^2 s^2} \right\} \tag{4-43}$$

For a current drive, it is given by

$$Z_{outI} = R'_L \left\{ \frac{1 + r_\pi C_\mu s}{1 + [r_\pi(C_\pi + MC_\mu) + R'_L C_o]s + r_\pi R'_L C^2 s^2} \right\} \tag{4-44}$$

Equation (4-44) is the last expression we will consider for a current drive. Henceforth in this text, only a voltage-driven bipolar transistor is used. If circuits in which bipolar transistors are examined are current driven, alternative circuitry should be devised in order to avoid the disadvantages of a current drive.

Now that gain expressions have been derived, the input and output impedances can be used to generate the relevant Bode diagrams.

4-2-4 Gain-Bandwidth Product

For the bipolar transistor, Bode diagrams can be drawn for the gain A_v, the input impedance Z_{in}, and the output impedance Z_{out}, using all parameters which occur in the expressions as variables. Only the most important parameters are given here, but others are used in the exercises.

Doubtless, the most important frequency characteristic is the gain A_v, with g_m as a variable, and therefore this characteristic is given first.

The expression of the gain A_v versus frequency is given in Eq. (4-40). The position of the poles and the zero versus g_m is given in Fig. 4-17a, whereas the actual Bode diagram (of the amplitude only) is given in Fig. 4-17b. Note the similar characteristics of a MOST, given in Fig. 4-10a and 4-10b.

The *dominant pole* of the gain can be written as a function of g_m, as given by

$$f_d = f_{c9} \left(\frac{1}{1 + \dfrac{g_m}{g_{mt}}} \right) \tag{4-45a}$$

with

$$f_{c9} = \frac{1}{2\pi (R'_S C_{jE} + R'_L C_o)} \tag{4-45b}$$

and

$$g_{mt} = \left(\frac{1}{R'_S} \right) \left(\frac{f_{c10}}{f_{c9}} \right) \tag{4-45c}$$

and

$$f_{c10} = \frac{1}{2\pi (\tau_F + R'_L C_\mu)} \tag{4-45d}$$

The value of the nondominant pole can be approximated by

$$f_{nd} = f_{c15} \left(1 + \frac{g_m}{g_{mt}} \right) \tag{4-46a}$$

with

$$f_{c15} = \frac{C_o}{2\pi R'_S C^2} \tag{4-46b}$$

Example 4-6

The transistor parameters are $r_B = 200\ \Omega$; $\beta = 100$; $\tau_F = 0.2$ ns, $C_{jE} = 6$ pF, $C_\mu = 1.5$ pF, $C_o = 2.5$ pF. It is biased at a current such that $g_m = 10$ mS. The resistances are $R'_L = 40$ kΩ and $R_S = 1$ kΩ ($R'_S = 1.2$ kΩ), yielding $A_{v0} = -400$; $M = 434$, and $C^2 = 27.75$ (pF)^2. Calculate f_{c9}, f_{c10}, g_{mt}, and f_{c15}.

Solution. First, $R'_S C_{jE} = 7.2$ ns, $R'_L C_o = 100$ ns, and $f_{c9} = 1.5$ MHz; $R'_L C_\mu = 60$ ns and $f_{c10} = 2.64$ MHz; finally, $g_{mt} = 1.47$ mS. Also, $f_{c15} = 12$ MHz.

We will use these equations to interpret two cases. In the first, the gain is large because R'_L is large; due, for example, to an active load. Then the output time constant $R'_L C_o$ and the Miller effect are dominant. In this case, the large gain will be used in a feedback loop in order to increase the bandwidth. Therefore, we must ensure that the circuit is stable, i.e., that a phase margin of at least 70° is realized. This means that the nondominant pole is about a factor of three times the *GBW*. This is obviously the case of a bipolar transistor used in an operational amplifier.

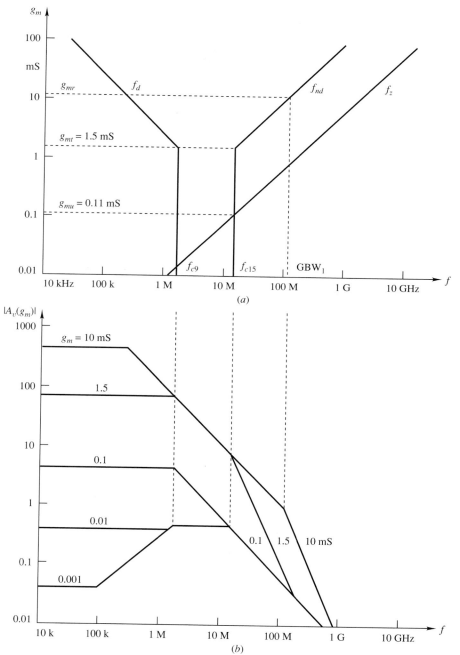

FIGURE 4-17   (*a*) Pole zero position plot of $A_v(g_m)$ for bipolar transistor; (*b*) Bode diagram of $A_v(g_m)$.

In the other case, such as in wide-band amplifiers, we do not use feedback. The gain is not large; resistor R'_L is much smaller. Here the input time constant $R'_S C_\pi$ is likely to be dominant. The bandwidth is optimized, whereas the *GBW* is not defined. We will analyze this case in the exercises.

Let us now consider the case where R'_L is large. For low values of g_m, $f_d = f_{c9}$, and the dominant time constant is $R'_L C_o$ at the output node (100 ns or 1.6 MHz). It is independent of g_m up to g_{mt}, at which point pole splitting starts (see Fig. 4-17a). The nondominant pole f_{nd} is also constant at f_{c15}. The zero depends on g_m, as well. The zero cancels the nondominant pole at a value of g_m, which is denoted by g_{mu} (see Fig. 4-17a). Its value is not calculated here, but it is approximately 0.11 mS.

In this case, we will most probably operate in the region where pole splitting occurs, i.e., for larger g_m than g_{mt}. In this region the equations (Eqs. (4-45)) of the poles can be approximated by

$$f_d \approx \frac{1}{2\pi R'_S g_m R'_L C_\mu} \tag{4-47a}$$

and

$$f_{nd} \approx \frac{g_m C_\mu}{2\pi C^2} \tag{4-47b}$$

Also,

$$g_{mt} \approx \frac{1}{R'_S} \frac{C_o}{C_\mu} \tag{4-47c}$$

The value of the gain-bandwidth product *GBW* is easily obtained from Eq. (4-47a) and is given by

$$GBW = \frac{1}{2\pi R'_S C_\mu} \tag{4-48}$$

In order to ensure a slope of −20 dB/decade down to a gain A_{v0} of unity, g_m must have a minimum value g_{mr}, such that the value of the nondominant pole equals three times the value (for 70° phase margin) of the gain-bandwidth product *GBW*. From Eq. (4-48) and Eq. (4-47b) this value of g_m is given by

$$g_{mr} \approx \frac{3C^2}{R'_S C_\mu^2} \tag{4-49}$$

For the example, *GBW* = 88.3 MHz and g_{mr} = 30.9 mS. The corresponding value of the gain is A_{v0r} = 1203.

The maximum value GBW_{max} is obtained for minimum R'_S, hence for $R_S = 0$. Thus it is determined by the $r_B C_\mu$ time constant, establishing the ultimate limit of what can be achieved with a bipolar transistor. In this example, the time constant is 0.3 ns; thus GBW_{max} is 530 MHz.

Example 4-7

A bipolar transistor is used once again to construct an amplifier with $GBW > 20$ MHz (PM $\approx 70°$) for a source resistance of 600 Ω (see Example 4-5). For optimum gain, an active load is used. What minimum current is required?

The transistor parameters are the same as those used for the examples above. They are summarized in Table 4-3.

Solution. Assume again that the Miller effect is the dominant factor. We also know that the GBW_{max} is well above the required 20 MHz. What about the current and, especially, the nondominant pole?

For 70° phase margin, the nondominant pole must be at about 3· GBW, or 60 MHz. We will need pole splitting to achieve this. This will determine the minimum current.

Fig. 4-17a shows that pole splitting starts at the value of g_{mt} given by Eq. (4-47c), which is about 2.1 mS. For stability the minimum value of g_m is g_{mr}, given by Eq. (4-49), which is 46.2 mS. At that point, the gain $g_m R'_L = 1848$, $f_d = 72$ kHz, and $f_{nd} = 396$ MHz. The GBW is 132 MHz, much more than needed. The current is $I_{CE} \approx 1.2$ mA.

Note that the required current is much smaller than that of a MOST, which was 21 mA.

A SPICE input file is again given in Table 4-4.

It can thus be concluded that higher values of GBW can be realized with bipolar transistors than with MOSTs. This is a result of larger values of g_m for a particular current. This conclusion is only valid if the Miller capacitance dominates.

TABLE 4-4   INPUT FILE FOR SPICE FOR THE SINGLE-TRANSISTOR WIDE-BAND *n*MOST AMPLIFIER OF EXAMPLE 7 IN SEC. 4-2-3.

```
* Ex.4-7 (TEMPERATURE = 27.000 DEG C)
* CIRCUIT DESCRIPTION
Q1 2 1 0 NPNT
IB 4 2 1.2M
VDD 4 0 DC 5
VIN 3 0 DC 0.785 AC 1
CL 2 0 10P
RL 2 0 100K
RS 3 1 600
.MODEL NPNT NPN BF=100 RB=200 TF=0.2N CJE=2P CJC=2P VAF=50
* CONTROL CARDS
.AC DEC 10 10K 100 MEG
.PRINT AC VDB(2) VP(2)
.PLOT AC VDB(2) VP(2)
.WIDTH OUT = 75
.END
```

4-2-5   Input Impedance

The input impedance is of particular importance because we know that input current can flow in a bipolar transistor. As a result, the input impedance can be expected to be much smaller than in a MOST. It is analyzed by use of Eq. (4-42). The pole-zero position plot of Z_{in} in function of g_m is easily derived as shown in Fig. 4-18a. The dominant pole is given by

$$f_{c1} \approx \frac{1}{2\pi \beta R'_L C_\mu} \tag{4-50}$$

It is dominated by Miller capacitance $g_m R'_L C_\mu$, which forms with resistance r_π, a time constant $\beta R'_L C_\mu$ (see Table 4-3). It is independent of g_m.

The dominant zero is approximated by

$$f_{z1} \approx \frac{1}{2\pi g_m r_B R'_L C_\mu} \tag{4-51}$$

which depends on g_m; $f_{z1} = 1.32$ MHz for $g_m = 10$ mS. Note that the zero coincides with the pole at a value of g_m, where $r_B = r_\pi$ (given by β / g_m).

The nondominant pole and nondominant zero cancel each other such that both the numerator and denominator are always of first order in complex frequency s.

The corresponding Bode diagram is given in Fig. 4-18b. At low frequencies, the input resistance equals $r_\pi + r_B$, the value of which depends on g_m. At high frequencies, however, all curves coincide at the ratio f_{c1}/f_{z1} with a value r_B.

For sake of completeness, the phase characteristic is given as well (Fig. 4-18c). A single-pole, single-zero system always has a minimum in phase at the frequency $f_m = \sqrt{f_{c1} \cdot f_z}$ as indicated in Fig. 4-18c for $g_m = 100$ mS. The values of f_{c1}, f_z, and f_m are 26 kHz, 132 kHz, and 59 kHz, respectively.

A better known way to display the input impedance Z_{in} is the *polar diagram*. The imaginary part of Z_{in} is then plotted versus its real part. It is possible to show that this plot always yields a half circle (see exercises). Such circles are given in Fig. 4-18d for several values of g_m and in Fig. 4-18e for $g_m = 100$ mS. Therefore, the polar diagram is also called the *circle diagram*.

At very low frequencies, the imaginary point at which the input resistance is $r_\pi + r_B$ is zero. At very high frequencies, the real axis is reached again, but now at a value r_B. The diameter of the circle thus equals r_π. The larger the current, the larger the g_m and the smaller the circle.

The bottom point of the circle is f_{c1}. A straight line between the bottom point and the origin provides all points of equal phase, and thus crosses the circle at f_z (see Fig. 4-18e). The point of maximum phase (or tangent to the circle) is f_m.

The circle diagram is well-known because it allows easy extraction of the most important bipolar transistor parameters. Knowledge of the current yields g_m. From the diameter, r_π and β_{AC} is extracted. Frequency f_β is the same as f_{c1}, i.e., the bottom point of the circle. Frequency f_T is the product $\beta_{AC} f_\beta$. From this, the value of $(C_\pi + C_\mu)$ is easily extracted. Care must be taken, however, not to use the data

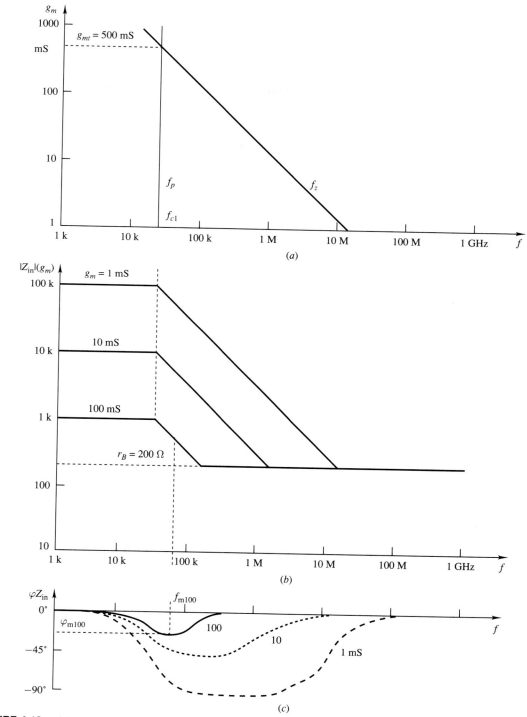

FIGURE 4-18 (*a*) Pole zero position plot of Z_{in} with g_m as variable. (*b*) Bode diagrams of Z_{in} with g_m as variable and magnitude $|Z_{in}|$. (*c*) Phase.

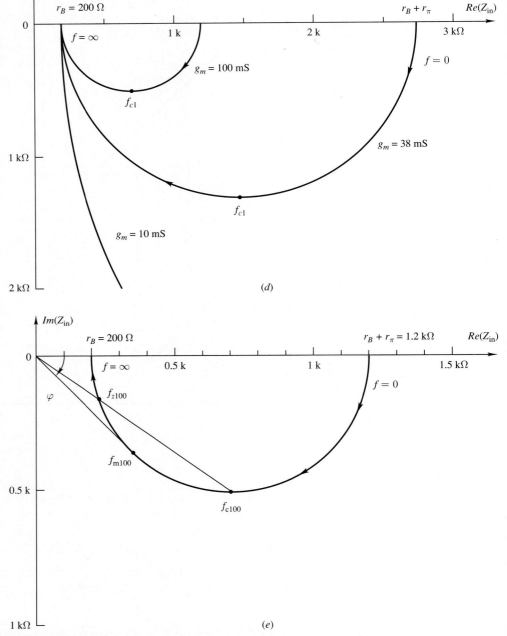

FIGURE 4-18 (cont'd) (*d*) Circle diagram of Z_{in}; and (*e*) circle diagram of Z_{in} for $g_m = 100$ mS.

points beyond frequency f_m (see Fig. 4-18e). From that frequency on, the experimental data points tend to go toward the origin, rather than to r_B on the real axis. This is a result of the distributed character of r_B over both junction capacitances. Frequency f_m can thus be used as an upper limit of validity of the simple hybrid-π model presented (Getreu 1976).

Similarly, all three diagrams for the gain A_v, the input impedance Z_{in}, and the output impedance Z_{out} can be evaluated for all circuit parameters (R_S, R_L, r_π, C_π, C_μ, C_o, and g_m) as variables. This gives rise to 21 diagrams for a bipolar transistor, single-transistor amplifier stage.

In this amplifier stage, the emitter is taken as a reference (or small-signal ground). Therefore, this transistor is connected in a so-called common-emitter configuration. However, the same transistor can also be used with its collector connected to the reference (common-collector configuration), or with its base connected to the reference (common-base configuration). This gives rise to an additional 42 diagrams. Not all the diagrams are independent and not all are equally important. We will discuss only a few of them in detail, but will use others in the exercises.

In the common-collector configuration, the transistor is used as an emitter follower. This latter term is more common among designers. On the other hand, a more common name for a bipolar transistor in the common-gate configuration is a cascode transistor. We will discuss this nomenclature in Secs. 4-3 and 4-4.

As with a bipolar transistor, a MOS transistor (or JFET) can be connected with its drain to the reference (common-drain or source follower), or with its gate to the reference (common-gate or cascode configuration). They give rise to another 36 diagrams (r_π is not present). Many of the diagrams are similar to those of a bipolar transistor. We will study some in more detail because they will help us understand the role of each different configuration and each transistor parameter.

4-3 SOURCE AND EMITTER FOLLOWERS

In the previous section, a MOST has been applied in a common-source configuration, in order to generate gain and bandwidth. However, gain is not the only function to be realized. Quite often an impedance must be transformed or converted. Both types of impedance conversion occur: from high to low and vice-versa. In this section the impedance down converter stage is analyzed. Its goal is to provide buffering between input and output node. The ideal model of such a converter simply consists of an isolated input node (see Fig. 4-19a), followed by a voltage generator with unity gain. It is ideal because the gain is unity, the input impedance is infinity, and the output impedance zero.

In order to illustrate the converter's buffering capability, it is included in the first-order circuit of Fig. 4-19b. The cutoff frequency of this circuit is determined by time constant $R_{IN}C_L$. After the ideal buffer is inserted (see Fig. 4-19c), the time constant has become zero, which extends the frequency performance of that circuit to infinity.

We will now examine how a source (emitter) follower can be an ideal buffer. For the discussion the same models and analysis techniques are used as in the previous section. We start with the source follower.

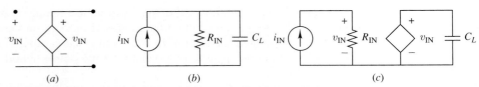

FIGURE 4-19   Model of ideal buffer (a) first-order circuit (b) without buffer; (c) with buffer.

4-3-1   Source Followers

The configuration of the source follower is shown in Fig. 4-20a and 4-20b. Both are common-drain configurations because the drain is connected to the positive power supply, which is ground for small signals. The input is at the gate and the output at the source. The transistor is biased at current I_T by a current source with high, but finite, output resistance R_T. The load is represented by capacitance C_L.

The substrate can be connected to the source (Fig. 4-20a) or to DC ground (Fig. 4-20b). The first configuration is only possible for an nMOST in a p-well CMOS process and for a pMOST in an n-well CMOS process. The first configuration is easier to analyze and therefore is discussed first.

Normally, the DC input voltage V_{IN} is provided by the previous circuit. It is also possible to bias the gate by means of resistors (see Fig. 4-20a), although this is more common for discrete circuits. Note that the output voltage is always at a lower DC voltage than its input. This circuit can also be used for DC level shifting. Therefore, we will examine this function before we explore gain, input, and output impedance.

DC Level Shift   The DC level shift from input to output is easy to calculate from first-order transistor characteristics. It is the V_{GS} of transistor T1, operating at current

FIGURE 4-20   (a) Source follower with zero V_{BS} and (b) source follower.

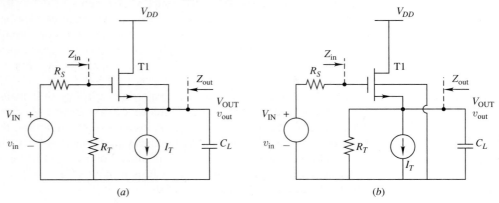

I_T. It is given by (Fig. 4-20a):

$$V_{IN} - V_{OUT} = V_{T0} + \sqrt{\frac{I_T}{K'W/L}} \tag{4-52}$$

This value can be set at any specific value larger than V_{T0}, by setting the aspect ratio W/L and K', after the current I_T has been selected.

When the bulk is connected to ground (Fig. 4-20b), the transistor has a bulk-source polarization V_{BS}, which equals V_{OUT}. It increases the value of V_{T0} (see Chap. 1). The DC level shift is derived in Eq. (1-31b), then is given by

$$V_{IN} - V_{OUT} = V_{T0} + \gamma \left(\sqrt{2\phi_F + V_{OUT}} - \sqrt{2\phi_F} \right) + \sqrt{\frac{I_T}{K'W/L}} \tag{4-53a}$$

where γ is the bulk polarization factor, and $2\phi_F \approx 0.6$ V. is In this case, the DC level shift is larger, and also depends on the actual value of the output voltage. The DC output voltage is now a nonlinear function of the DC input voltage.

In both cases, the DC output voltage as plotted versus W/L in Fig. 4-21 for $I_T = 250$ μA, $V_{T0} = 1$ V, $K' = 30$ μA/V^2, $2\phi_F = 0.6$ V and $\gamma = 0.86$ V$^{1/2}$ where $V_{IN} = 8$ V. For small values of W/L, the DC level shift becomes too large to be accommodated by the input voltage. The current source does not have sufficient output voltage to be operational. In this area the curve is denoted by a dashed line in Fig. 4-21.

FIGURE 4-21 Output voltage of source follower for $V_{in} = 8$ V and variable W/L.

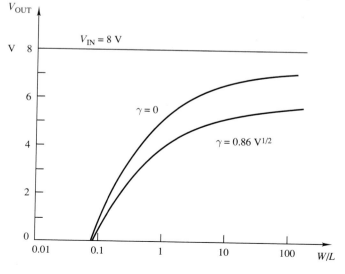

As we can see, the source follower is an attractive level shifter. All DC voltages can be reached with easy control by means of W/L. It plays an important role in BICMOS for exactly this reason.

Low-Frequency Impedance Conversion   For small-signal analysis, the transistor must be replaced by its small-signal equivalent, as shown in Fig. 4-22a, which can be further simplified to the circuit of Fig. 4-22b.

At low frequencies, all capacitances can be omitted, which leads to near ideal buffering performance: the input resistance is infinitely high. Including a large source resistance, does not make any difference.

The small-signal gain is always smaller than unity, however, but very close to unity as explained in Sec. 1-1. The output at the source "follows" the input. This is the origin of the name source follower. When the bulk is connected to ground, however, the parasitic JFET becomes active. The gain is considerably lower than unity, as given by Eq. (1-32) in Sec. 1-1.

At the output, the output resistance of the transistor r'_{DS} is put in parallel with the output resistance of the current source and the g_m and g_{mb} current generators (see Fig. 4-22a). As a result,

$$R_{\text{out}} = \frac{1}{g_m + g_{mb} + 1/r_{DS} + 1/R_T} \tag{4-53b}$$

FIGURE 4-22   (a) Small-signal equivalent circuit of source follower. (b) Simplified circuit.

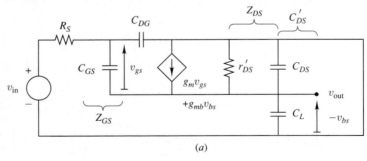

(a)

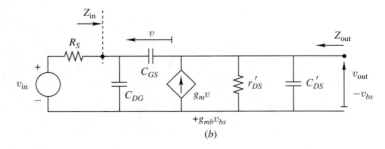

(b)

For example, for $r_{DS} = 50$ kΩ, $R_T = 1$ MΩ, $g_m = 1$ mS, and $g_{mb} = 0.5$ mS is $R_{\text{out}} = 0.58$ kΩ. Although this is not zero, it is quite low. Thus, a resistive down conversion is realized from infinity down to 0.58 kΩ. If the bulk is connected to the source, g_{mb} drops out of Eq. (4-54), and R_{out} slightly increases to about 1 kΩ.

The importance of this impedance conversion can now be illustrated by adding a load capacitance of $C_L = 10$ pF. This value could represent a clock line over a certain distance on chip. For a source resistance of $R_S = 50$ kΩ, this capacitance would cut off all frequencies above $(2\pi C_L R_S)^{-1}$ or 0.3 MHz. With the impedance converter with $R_{\text{out}} = 0.58$ kΩ, the cutoff frequency is increased to $(2\pi C_L R_{\text{out}})^{-1}$, or 16 MHz.

High Frequency Gain Inclusion of the capacitances allows prediction of the values of gain, and input and output impedances at high frequencies. The small-signal equivalent circuit of Fig. 4-22a is used. This model is valid for both configurations in Figs. 4-20a and b. Only the values of C_{DS} are slightly larger when the substrate is connected to ground. Indeed, the parasitic JFET value of C_{GS} is then added to it. Load capacitance C_L can be added to C_{DS} also, since both are connected between output and small-signal ground.

The transfer characteristic of this circuit (see Fig. 4-22b) is of second order (three capacitances in a loop). The gain characteristic is analyzed first.

Straightforward analysis gives an expression for the gain, which is given by

$$A_v = \left\{ \frac{1 + \left(\dfrac{C_{GS}}{g_m}\right) s}{1 + \left[\left(1 + \dfrac{R_S}{r_{DS}}\right)\dfrac{C_{GS}}{g_m} + \dfrac{C'_{DS}}{g_m} + R_S C_{DG}\right] s + \left(\dfrac{R_S}{g_m}\right) C'^2 s^2} \right\} \tag{4-54}$$

in which C'^2 is given by Eq. (4-19b), using C'_{DS} instead of C_{DS}. To simplify the analysis the gain is assumed to be unity at low frequencies.

The pole-zero position plot of this expression versus g_m is given in Fig. 4-23a. The actual Bode diagram of $|A_v|$ is shown in Fig. 4-23b.

The expression of the dominant pole is given by

$$f_d = f_{c6} \left(\frac{1}{1 + \dfrac{g_m}{g_{mr}}} \right) \tag{4-55a}$$

with

$$g_{mr} = \left(\frac{1}{R_S}\right)\left(\frac{C_{GS} + C'_{DS}}{C_{DG}}\right) \tag{4-55b}$$

in which f_{c6} is already given in Table 4-1. For $g_m = 1$ mS, the value of $g_{mr} = 3.3$ mS.

The expression of the nondominant pole is given by

$$f_{nd} = f_{c18}\left(1 + \frac{g_m}{g_{mr}}\right) \tag{4-56a}$$

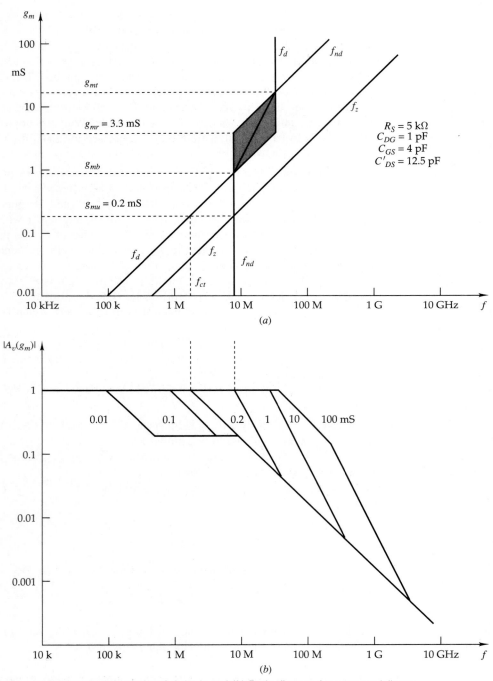

FIGURE 4-23   (a) Pole zero position plot of $A_v(g_m)$; and (b) Bode diagram for a source follower.

with
$$f_{c18} = \frac{C_{GS} + C'_{DS}}{2\pi R_S C'^2} \qquad (4\text{-}56b)$$

For values of g_m smaller than g_{mr}, f_{nd} equals f_{c18}, which is 7.9 MHz ($C'^2 = 66.5$ pF^2).

It is interesting to note, however, that the lines of the poles cross each other. The enclosed area is denoted by hatch marks in Fig. 4-23a. Since the nondominant pole cannot occur at frequency values lower than the dominant pole, something is wrong with the approximations. The reason is that for values of g_m, (which correspond with the hatched area), two complex poles occur at the frequencies represented by the thick line connecting the extremes of the hatched area.

Complex poles lead to peaking, and thus must be avoided. Peaking is maximum in the middle at $g_m = g_{mr}$ (3.3 mS), but starts at the bottom of the hatched area at g_{mb} and continues up to its top at g_{mt}, (calculated as in the example of App. 4-1). The ratio of g_{mt} (13.3 mS) to g_{mb} (0.8 mS) is easily calculated to be

$$\frac{g_{mt}}{g_{mb}} = 1 + \frac{C_{DGt}}{C_{DG}} \qquad (4\text{-}57a)$$

with
$$C_{DGt} = \frac{C_{GS} C'_{DS}}{C_{GS} + C'_{DS}} \qquad (4\text{-}57b)$$

Ratio g_{mt}/g_{mb} equals 16 in the example. Obviously, this ratio depends on the load capacitance C'_{DS} and C_{GS}, as well as on compensating capacitance C_{DG}. This ratio can never be made smaller than or equal to unity.

The hatched area is minimum as soon as C_{DG} is larger than C_{DGt}, or 3 pF in this example. Note, however, that C_{DG} is actually all the capacitance from the gate to ground, forming a lowpass filter at the input with time constant $R_S C_{DG}$. This lowpass filter is required to avoid peaking.

Note that there is one zero proportional to g_m. It is not positive, however, it is negative. A single-pole characteristic can be obtained at the value of g_m, where this zero cancels the nondominant pole. The approximate value of g_m is given by

$$g_{mu} = \frac{1}{R_S} \qquad (4\text{-}58a)$$

(see Fig. 4-23a).

Its value is 0.2 mS. At this value of g_m and for $C_{DG} = C_{DGt}$, the cutoff frequency is given by

$$f_{ct} = \frac{1}{2\pi R_S (2C'_{DS})} \qquad (4\text{-}58b)$$

Its value equals 9.6 MHz (for $C_{DG} = 1$ pF) and 8.1 MHz (for $C_{DG} = 3$ pF).

This value of g_{mu} can be realized easily at low currents. For large values of R_S, however, this rule is impractical. The transconductance cannot be lowered to that level, because the current becomes very small, as well. Take, for example, $R_S = 50$ MΩ. Then, $g_m < 20$ nS, which is obtained for currents around 1 nA. With a low value of drain current, current is insufficient to charge and discharge capacitance C'_{DS} (including C_L), resulting in slew rate distortion. Thus larger currents are taken. In order to avoid peaking under these conditions, capacitance C_{DG} must be increased. It then functions as a compensation capacitance, or as an input filter, as already explained.

The time constant in Eq. (4-58b) is obviously $R_S C'_{DS}$. It is the dominant time constant because C'_{DS} includes the large load capacitance. This dominant pole value is the same as if the output capacitance C'_{DS} were connected directly to the source resistance R_S, without an intervening transistor. In other words, the transistor, which should buffer output from input, merely causes peaking if we try to increase the bandwidth. The main culprit is, of course, the presence of C_{GS}, which directly connects output to input. We use capacitance C_{DG}, however, to stabilize (or compensate) this stage, even for values of g_m larger than g_{mu}.

For very large values of g_m, two single poles occur (see Fig. 4-23a), the second of which always is closely followed by the zero. All values of g_m can now be used for peaking without danger.

It can be concluded that the addition of input capacitance to C_{DG} stabilizes the source follower. It decreases the value of the dominant pole such that only one critical value of g_m is left. The minimum value of C_{DG} is given by Eq. (4-57b). The critical value of g_m, which is better avoided, is given by Eq. (4-55b).

Example 4-8

Let us design a source follower for a load capacitance of $C_L = 100$ pF. What is its minimum W/L, and/or drain current I_{DS}? What bandwidth is then achieved?

We use as parameters the values of Table 4-1. However, in order to take into account the dependence of C_{GS} and C_{DG} with W/L, we take $C_{GS} = 0.01 \times W/L$ pF and $C_{DG} = C_{GS}/4$.

Solution. We will need a large current to drive 100 pF. Thus, the transistor will have a large value of W/L. The critical value of g_m is taken from Eq. (4-55b) and can be expressed as $g_{mr} \approx [2/(W/L)]S$ if $C_{GS} < 100$ pF. On the other hand, the minimum value of C_{DG} is given by Eq. (4-57b) and can be expressed as $C_{DGt} \approx C_{GS} = 0.01 \, W/L$ pF again, if $C_{GS} < 100$ pF. An optimization could be carried out, but a good compromise for a designer is $W/L \approx 200$. This yields $g_{mr} \approx 10$ mS. Let us take twice g_{mr} or $g_m = 20$ mS. The compensation capacitance is $C_{DGt} = 2$ pF. Thus it will cost us a large area to allow this large current, either in transistor size or in capacitor size! The bandwidth is determined by f_{c6}, which is a result of the 100 pF load, seeing $1/g_m$ (or 50 Ω) at the output node. Thus it is about 32 MHz.

Decreasing W/L will decrease the current, but will increase the compensation capacitance and will decrease the bandwidth.

Input Impedance   The expression of input impedance of the source follower (Fig. 4-22a) is given by (if $g_m r'_{DS} \gg 1$):

$$Z_{in} = \left(\frac{1}{\left(C_{DG} + \dfrac{C_{GS}}{g_m r'_{DS}} \right) s} \right) \left(\frac{1 + j \left(\dfrac{f}{f_{c6}} \right)}{1 + \dfrac{r'_{DS} C^2 s}{C_{GS} + g_m r'_{DS} C_{DG}}} \right) \qquad (4\text{-}59)$$

in which f_{c6} is given in Table 4-1.

Obviously, the input impedance is capacitive. At low frequencies, the input capacitance is about C_{DG}. Capacitance C_{GS} is bootstrapped out because of the large value of $g_m r'_{DS}$ (50 in the example). If a really high input impedance or low input capacitance is required, then C_{DG} must be reduced to below $C_{GS}/g_m r'_{DS}$ (a mere 0.06 pF).

At higher frequencies one pole and one zero are included; these nearly cancel each other.

Output Impedance   The expression of the output impedance is derived from Fig. 4-20b with $C_L = 0$, and is given by

$$Z_{out} = \frac{1}{g_m} \left\{ \frac{1 + j \left(\dfrac{f}{f_{c13}} \right)}{1 + \left[\left(1 + \dfrac{R_S}{r_{DS}} \right) \left(\dfrac{C_{GS}}{g_m} \right) + \dfrac{C'_{DS}}{g_m} + R_S C_{DG} \right] s + \left(\dfrac{R_S}{g_m} \right) C'^2 s^2} \right\}$$
$$(4\text{-}60)$$

If $g_m r'_{DS} \gg 1$. Frequency f_{c13} is given in Table 4-1. The low-frequency value (see Eq. (4-53)) has been reduced to g_m for simplicity.

Note that the poles are the same as the gain, given by Eq. (4-54). The pole-zero position plot versus g_m, and the Bode diagram of $|Z_{out}|$ are studied in the exercises. The only important result is that values of g_m around g_{mr} (given by Eq. (4-55b)) should once again be avoided.

There are several other characteristics that should be studied. For example, capacitance C_{DG} is the input node capacitance of the source follower. In order to investigate how well the source follower can screen the effect of this input node capacitance, the output impedance could be examined with C_{DG} as a variable. Also, in order to investigate to what extent the source follower is able to convert high input resistances into the low output resistance of $1/g_m$, $|Z_{out}|$ could be plotted for different values of R_S. These plots are considered in the exercises.

The conclusion always holds that the main advantage of the MOST source follower is the reduction of the impedance from ∞ to $1/g_m$ up to f_{c6}, a high frequency indeed. To avoid peaking, a relation exists between R_S, g_m, and the capacitances. As a result, a minimum value is required for g_m, which is g_{mr}. A minimum value, especially, is required for input capacitance C_{DG}.

After source followers, the emitter followers are discussed in order to see how closely they can realize ideal buffering, compared to their MOST equivalents.

4-3-2 Emitter Followers

The emitter follower configurations, with an *npn* transistor and a *pnp* transistor, are shown in Figs. 4-24a and 4-24b. They are biased by a current source with output resistance I_T. The load is represented by capacitance C_L.

The DC level shifting possible with a bipolar transistor is much less useful than that of a MOST. In fact, the voltage drop between input and output is simply given by its V_{BE}, which is always about 0.7 V. Hence, several emitter followers must be used in series if a larger DC shift is to be realized.

Low-Frequency Impedance Conversion   In order to calculate the gain, and the input and output resistance at low frequencies, the small-signal equivalent circuit as represented in Fig. 4-25a is used. It can be further simplified to that shown in Fig. 4-25b. At low frequencies all capacitances can be omitted.

The main difference between the bipolar transistor and the MOST source follower is that the *input resistance* is not infinity, but has a much lower value. This is evident because of the presence of r_π at the input node (in Fig. 4-25b). At low frequencies, it is given by

$$R_{in} = r_B + r_\pi + (\beta + 1)r'_o \qquad (4\text{-}61a)$$

in which $r'_o = r_o \ // \ R_T$. By far the largest contribution is given by $\beta r'_o$. For example, if $\beta = 100$ and $r'_o = 40$ kΩ, then $R_{in} = 4$ MΩ, which is still high, but not infinity.

The *output resistance* is given by (also see Eq. (2-24b))

$$R_{out} = \left(\frac{1}{g_m} + \frac{R_S + r_B}{\beta + 1} \right) \ // \ r_o \qquad (4\text{-}61b)$$

FIGURE 4-24   (a) Emitter follower with *npn* transistor. (b) Emitter follower with *pnp* transistor.

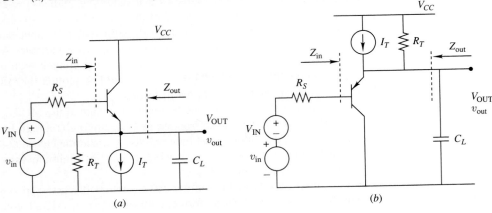

(a)   (b)

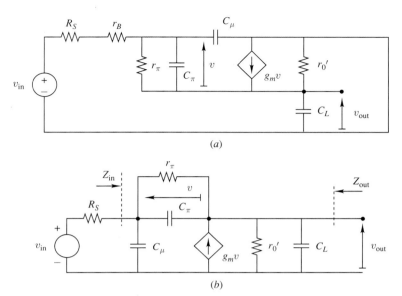

FIGURE 4-25   (a) Small-signal equivalent circuit of emitter follower. (b) Simplified circuit.

in which the effect of r_o is usually negligible. In the Example with $R_S = 1$ kΩ and $r_B = 200$ Ω, $R_{out} = 112$ Ω.

The *output resistance* is linearly proportional to the source resistance. The input resistance can thus be "seen" from the output terminal. The buffering capability of the emitter follower is rather limited. The MOST source follower is much better in this respect because the output resistance is only $1/g_m$ whatever the value of the source resistance.

The *gain* of the emitter follower is readily calculated from the diagram of Fig. 2-25a, and is given by

$$A_{v0} = \frac{1}{1 + \dfrac{R_{out}}{r'_o}} \tag{4-61c}$$

which is only slightly less than unity (for $g_m = 10$ mS, $A_{v0} = 0.9975$). Note that the gain depends on the source resistance through R_{out}.

High Frequency Performance   In order to evaluate the high-frequency performance of the emitter follower, all capacitances must be included in the small-signal equivalent circuits (see Fig. 4-25a and Fig. 4-25b). Note that the collector-substrate capacitance is short-circuited, but load capacitance C_L is present. Also, resistance r_B is omitted, because it plays only a minor role in an emitter follower. Additional input capacitance can be added, by grouping it together with C_μ.

The expression of the gain can then be calculated as

$$A_v = \frac{1 + \left(\dfrac{C_\pi}{g_m}\right) s}{1 + \left[\left(1 + \dfrac{R'_S}{r'_o}\right)\dfrac{C_\pi}{g_m} + \left(1 + \dfrac{R'_S}{r_\pi}\right)\dfrac{C_L}{g_m} + R'_S C_\mu\right] s + \left(\dfrac{R'_S}{g_m}\right) C^2 s^2} \qquad (4\text{-}62)$$

with $R'_S = R_S + r_B$ and $C^2 = C_\pi C_\mu + C_\pi C_L + C_\mu C_L$.

Three approximations have been made to derive Eq. (4-62):

1 The low frequency gain equals unity: $A_{v0} = 1$
2 $g_m r'_o \gg 1$ ($g_m r'_o = 400$ in the example)
3 $R'_S \ll \beta r'_o$ ($R'_S = 1.2$ kΩ and $\beta r'_o = 4$ MΩ)

The last approximation is a result of the requirement that an emitter follower can never be current driven, but always voltage driven. As a result, $R'_S \ll R_{\text{in}}$.

The gain A_v will now be examined, using g_m as a variable. The poles and zero can be derived from Eq. (4-62). Note that the value of C^2 depends on g_m, as well. Also, the value of R'_S is assumed to be smaller than r'_o, and even smaller than r_π. The pole-zero position plot has been derived as a prototype calculation in App. 4-1. We discuss the most important results here. The curves are similar to those of a MOST source follower given in Fig. 4-23a and 4-23b, so are not repeated. (See App. 4-1.)

Again, two complex poles occur around the value of $g_m = g_{mr}$. This value is taken from App. 4-1, and is given by

$$g_{mr} = \left(\frac{1}{R_S}\right)\left(\frac{C_{jE} + C_L}{C_\mu + \tau_F/R_S}\right) \qquad (4\text{-}63a)$$

In the example its value is $g_{mr} = 8$ mS. For this value severe peaking occurs, so we will not use it.

Note that Eq. (4-63) corresponds with Eq. (4-55b) for a MOST. The same conclusion thus can be drawn here as was drawn for a MOST. A minimum value of C_μ is necessary to avoid peaking. This value is given by

$$C_{\mu r} = \frac{C_{jE} C_L}{C_{jE} + C_L} \qquad (4\text{-}63b)$$

Again, the effect of C_μ is such that a lowpass filter is present at the input. For instance, input capacitance can be added in order to increase C_μ. In this example, C_μ must be increased to 3.75 pF.

The resulting bandwidth is given by

$$f_d = \frac{1}{2\pi(\tau_F + R_S C_\mu)} \qquad (4\text{-}63c)$$

in which the input time constant is dominant, as if no emitter follower were present.

Example 4-9

Let us design an emitter follower with the same load as that of the MOST in Example 4-8. The source resistor $R_S = 20$ kΩ. The load capacitance $C_L = 100$ pF. What is its minimum drain current I_{CE}? What bandwidth can now be achieved?

We use as parameters the values of Table 4-3, which correspond to a minimum-size bipolar transistor.

Solution. The critical value of g_m is given by Eq. (4-63a) and is now 3.5 mS. Thus only a current larger than 91 μA current is required. However, the minimum value of C_μ is given by Eq. (4-63b) and equals about C_{jE} or 6 pF. This is a large value of compensation capacitance, indeed. The bandwidth is given in Eq. (4-63c) and equals about 5 MHz. This is much lower than what could be obtained with the MOST (32 MHz). It is a result of the large input capacitance of 6 pF. Decreasing this capacitance will increase the ringing, however. Thus there is no other choice.

Input Impedance   The expression of the input impedance is calculated for the equivalent circuit of Fig. 4-25b. It is given by

$$Z_{\text{in}} = R_{\text{in}} \left\{ \frac{1 + \left(\dfrac{C_\pi + C_L}{g_m} \right) s}{1 + \left[r_\pi \left(C_\pi + g_m r_o' C_\mu \right) + r_o' C_L \right] s + r_\pi r_o' C^2 s^2} \right\} \qquad (4\text{-}64)$$

in which R_{in} is given by Eq. (4-61a). For this derivation it is assumed that $g_m r_o' \gg 1$. Note that this expression has the same denominator as Eq. (4-42), in the section on amplifier stages. However, the load R_L' is replaced by the current source resistance r_o' ($r_o /\!/ R_T$).

The most important variable for Z_{in} is parameter C_L. We already know that an emitter follower allows a resistance to be seen through. This lack of buffering capability can be found easily at higher frequencies, as well. The characteristics are similar to those of a MOST, so we will use them in the exercises.

Output Impedance   From the equivalent circuit of Fig. 4-25b, the expression of the output impedance is readily calculated. It is given by

$$Z_{\text{out}} = R_{\text{out}} \left\{ \frac{1 + (R_S' /\!/ r_\pi)(C_\pi + C_\mu)s}{1 + \left[\left(1 + \dfrac{R_S'}{r_o'} \right) \dfrac{C_\pi}{g_m} + \left(1 + \dfrac{R_S'}{r_\pi} \right) \dfrac{C_L}{g_m} + R_S' C_\mu \right] s + \dfrac{R_S'}{g_m} C^2 s^2} \right\}$$
$$(4\text{-}65)$$

in which R_{out} is given by Eq. (4-61) and the denotations and approximations used are the same as those used for A_v, given in Eq. (4-62).

As expected from previous analyses, the expressions of Z_{out} and A_v have the same denominators, hence the same poles. The zero is different, however. In order to learn about the buffering capabilities of an emitter follower, it is useful to study the influence of g_m, R_S, and C_L on Z_{out}. Only the first two are discussed here.

For the analysis of Z_{out} with g_m as a variable, R'_S is assumed to be smaller than r'_o and r_π. In this example, $R'_S = 1.2$ kΩ. Thus the assumption is quite acceptable. The positions of the poles and zero, with g_m as a variable, are shown in Fig. 4-26a and 4-26b.

The poles are on the same locations as those for A_v in Fig. A4-1 (in App. 4-1). Thus, peaking occurs at $g_m = g_{mr}$, as given by Eq. (4-63). The zero, however, is at a much lower frequency. As a result, for high values of g_m, the output impedance is inductive. The limiting value of g_m, above which this inductance appears, is the value of g_m where the zero cancels the dominant pole. This value is given by

$$g_{mu} = \left(\frac{1}{R'_S}\right)\left(\frac{C_{jE} + C_L}{C_{jE} + C_\mu}\right) \tag{4-66}$$

which is 1.8 mS, in this example.

If the value of C_μ is increased to reduce the size of the hatched region in Fig. 4-26a as much as possible, this condition comes closer to $g_{mu} \approx 1/R'_S$.

Together, the source resistance and base resistance determine at what value of g_m (or current) the output impedance is inductive or capacitive.

The output impedance is purely resistive for $g_m = g_{mu}$. Even for $R'_S = 0$, some base resistance is left such that only low values of currents result. For example, if $R'_S = 0$ and $r_B = 200$ Ω, the required current is 25 mV/200 $\Omega = 0.13$ mA.

The value of Z_{out} is also examined, with the source resistance R'_S as a variable. Indeed we would like to know how efficient the emitter follower can be to buffer a high source resistance R'_S at high frequencies. Now R'_S can be larger than r_π. The value of R'_S is always assumed to be smaller than r'_o, however. The positions of the poles and zero are shown in Fig. 4-27a. The magnitude of Z_{out} or $|Z_{out}|$ is shown in Fig. 4-27b.

For very small and very large values of R_S, the output impedance is always capacitive. However, for values of R'_S somewhat smaller than $\beta R'_{St}$, the output impedance becomes inductive again. The value of R'_{St} is given by

$$R'_{St} = \frac{1}{g_m}\left(\frac{C_\pi + C_L}{C_\mu + C_L/\beta}\right) \tag{4-67}$$

which is 600 Ω in the example. Hence, $\beta R'_{St} = 60$ kΩ. For values of R'_S around 600 Ω, complex poles appear.

As before, this region of complex poles can be reduced by increasing C_μ or the input capacitance of the emitter follower; this is done at the cost of bandwidth, however.

Thus it can be concluded that an emitter follower has much less buffering capability than its MOST counterpart. This is a clear message for BICMOS designers. For certain combinations of source resistance R_S and g_m, peaking and ringing can occur. In order to avoid this, a minimum value of g_m, i.e., g_{mr} of Eq. (4-55b), should be used. Moreover, a lowpass filter must precede the follower.

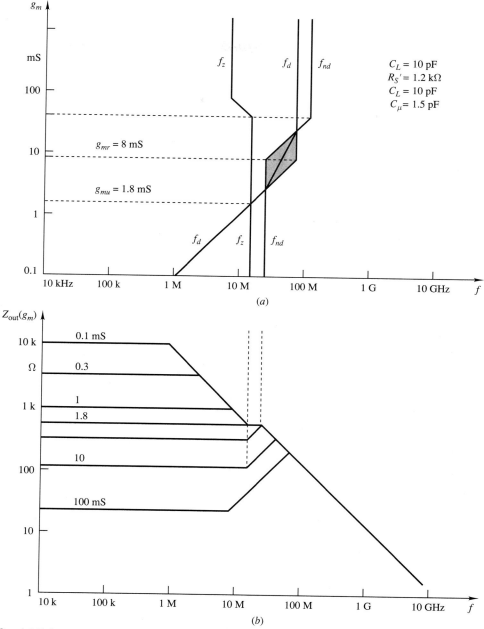

FIGURE 4-26   (*a*) Pole zero position plot of Z_{out} (g_m); and (*b*) Bode diagram for an emitter follower.

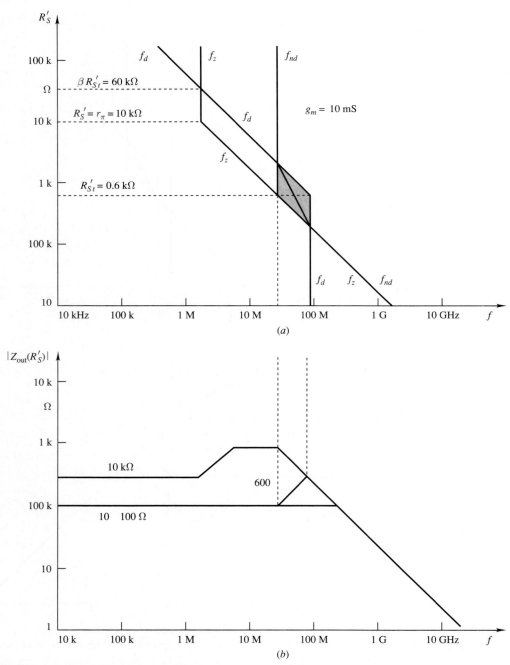

FIGURE 4-27   (a) Pole zero position plot of Z_{out} (R); and (b) Bode diagram of an emitter follower.

We will conclude this section on source and emitter followers by investigating their noise performance.

4-3-3 Noise Performance

Only the noise behavior of the emitter follower given in Fig. 4-28a is analyzed. It is very similar to that of a source follower but not repeated here.

The noise voltage of the source resistor R_S is given by $\overline{dv_S^2}$. The two equivalent input noise sources of the transistor are denoted by $\overline{dv_{ie}^2}$ and $\overline{di_{ie}^2}$. The output noise current of current source I_T is given by $\overline{di_T^2}$. Moreover, an amplifying stage is added with gain A. Its equivalent input noise sources are denoted by $\overline{dv_A^2}$ and $\overline{di_A^2}$.

All noise sources, except that of R_S, can now be joined into a total equivalent input noise voltage source $\overline{dv_i^2}$, as shown in Fig. 4-28b. Its value can be found by equation of the total output noise of the circuit in Fig. 4-28a to the total output noise of the circuit of Fig. 2-28b. This yields

$$\overline{dv_i^2} = \overline{dv_{ie}^2} + \overline{dv_A^2} + \left(R_S - \frac{1}{g_m} \right)^2 \overline{di_{ie}^2} + \frac{(\overline{di_T^2}) + \overline{di_A^2}}{g_m^2} \tag{4-68}$$

assuming that $R_S < \beta R_T$.

For low values of R_S and high values of g_m, only the first two terms of the right-hand side are important.

FIGURE 4-28   (a) Emitter follower with noise sources and noisy post amplifier, and (b) Equivalent input noise source of emitter follower.

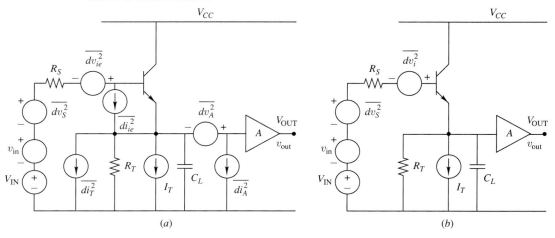

(a)   (b)

The excess noise factor, which gives the ratio of the equivalent input noise $\overline{dv_i^2}$ to that of the first input transistor $\overline{dv_{ie}^2}$, is then given by

$$y = \frac{\overline{dv_i^2}}{\overline{dv_{ie}^2}} \approx 1 + \frac{\overline{dv_A^2}}{\overline{dv_{ie}^2}} \tag{4-69}$$

It can be concluded that the equivalent input noise of the emitter follower of the fact that the emitter follower only provides a gain of unity and hence does not reject the noise of the next stage. For low noise applications, both the emitter follower itself and the next amplifier must be designed for low noise.

Followers are impedance-down converters. Let us now discuss impedance-up converters, or cascodes.

4-4 CASCODE TRANSISTORS

In this section the impedance-up converter stage is analyzed. This stage provides buffering between an input and an output node. The ideal model of such a converter consists of a short-circuited input node (see Fig. 4-29) followed by a current generator with unity gain. It is ideal because the gain is unity, the input impedance is zero, and the output impedance infinity.

We will now examine how a cascode configuration can be an ideal buffer. For this analysis, we will use the same models and analysis techniques as before. We start with the MOST cascode.

4-4-1 MOST Cascode

Cascode configurations are shown in Fig. 4-30. Both are common-gate configurations because the gate is connected to a positive reference voltage V_{GG}, which is ground for small signals. Normally it is derived from the positive power supply voltage by means of resistors, which are represented by an equivalent series resistor R_G.

The input is at the source and the output at the drain. The transistor is biased at current I_{IN} by a current source with high, but finite, output resistance R_T. The load is represented by capacitance C_L.

The substrate can be connected to the source (Fig. 4-30a) or to DC ground (Fig. 4-30b), in exactly the same way as in a source follower configuration.

DC Conditions   First let us look at the DC conditions of the MOST cascode. The current through the transistor is determined by current source I_{IN}, which also flows

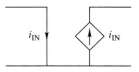

FIGURE 4-29   Model of ideal buffer

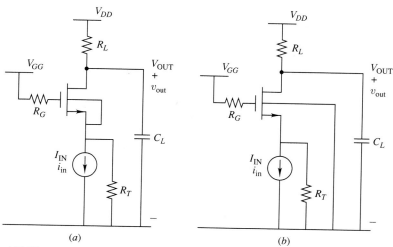

FIGURE 4-30   *n*MOST cascode with bulk (*a*) to source (*b*) to ground.

through the output resistor R_L. As a result, the output voltage is determined by the voltage drop across R_L, as given by Eq. (4-3). The DC voltage at the source follows the biasing voltage V_{GG} as for a source follower. Thus, the DC voltage drop between gate and source is also given by Eq. (4-52). In this way, the DC currents and voltages are all known.

Low Frequency Analysis   To study the low-frequency performance of the cascode, let us consider its small-signal equivalent circuit illustrated in Fig. 4-31. At low frequencies all capacitances can be omitted. We now must verify whether the current gain is unity, the input resistance is small, and the output resistance large. Let us start with the current gain.

FIGURE 4-31   Small-signal equivalent circuit of cascode.

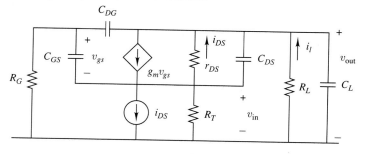

On first sight the *current gain* is unity, because all current pulled from the source must come out of the load resistor. However, close inspection of the small-signal circuit in Fig. 4-31 shows that two resistances are present that shunt the current generators $g_m v_{gs}$ and i_{in}. They are r_{DS} and R_T. A detailed analysis is required (Abidi 1990).

Application of Kirchhoff's laws allows us to write the output current i_{out} as a function of the input current i_{in}. This ratio is the current gain A_i. The output voltage v_{out}, as a function of the input current i_{in}, is then the transresistance $A_r = A_i \cdot R_L$. The current gain A_i is given by

$$A_i = \frac{i_l}{i_{in}} = \frac{R_T(g_m r_{DS} + 1)}{R_L + R_T(g_m r_{DS} + 1) + r_{DS}} \tag{4-70}$$

in which $R_T(g_m r_{DS} + 1) + r_{DS}$ in the denominator is a very large resistance (denoted by R_{Lc}). This expression is plotted in Fig. 4-32a and shows that for all values of R_L smaller than R_{Lc}, the current gain A_i is unity. The transresistance A_r is plotted in Fig. 4-32b. It increases proportionally to R_L until R_{Lc} is reached, at which point A_r reaches a constant maximum value of R_{Lc}.

Thus, for large gain, a cascode must have a large R_L. Once values are used higher than R_{Lc}, no extra gain is achieved.

In order to gain some more insight into the operation of the cascode, let us also calculate the current i_{ds} flowing through the transistor output resistance r_{DS}. This is obtained from straightforward analysis and given by

$$\frac{i_{ds}}{i_{in}} = \frac{R_T(g_m R_L - 1)}{R_L + R_T(g_m r_{DS} + 1) + r_{DS}} \tag{4-71}$$

also plotted in Fig. 4-32a. This clearly shows that for large values of R_L, a large current flows through r_{DS}, which is provided by the $g_m v_{gs}$ generator. It is much larger than i_{in} itself. This current will have an enormous effect on the input resistance R_{in}, calculated next.

The input resistance R_{in} is given by

$$R_{in} = \frac{v_{in}}{i_{in}} = \frac{R_T(R_L + r_{DS})}{R_L + R_T(g_m r_{DS} + 1) + r_{DS}} \tag{4-72a}$$

which is also plotted in Fig. 4-32b. It shows that for small load resistors, the input resistance is $1/g_m$, as expected. However, for large load resistors, the input resistance increases and reaches a value as high as R_T, when $R_L = R_{Lc}$. At this point, the transistor itself exhibits an input resistance infinity such that the resistance at the source is determined by the input current source's output resistance. This means that no buffering effect is obtained; the large load resistance is clearly visible at the source, through r_{DS}. Moreover, the input resistance is low (i.e., $1/g_m$) only when R_L is low. This is the case only in some types of wide-band amplifiers. In operational amplifier type circuits, active loads are used, and hence R_L can be very large.

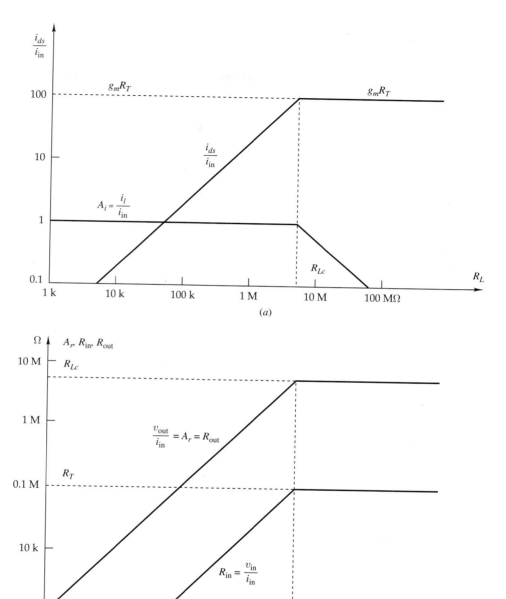

FIGURE 4-32   (*a*) Current ratios in a cascode; (*b*) resistance levels in a cascode.

The only characteristic left for discussion is the output resistance R_{out}. This resistance is the parallel combination of the load resistor R_L with the resistance at the drain looking into the transistor. This latter resistance is readily calculated to be R_{Lc}. The output resistance is thus A_r, as already seen in Fig. 4-32b. An example will make this clear.

Example 4-10

Plot the curves of Fig. 4-32 for the nMOST of Table 4-1 with the additional information that $r_{DS} = 60$ kΩ and $R_T = 100$ kΩ. What are the values of the gain A_r, R_{in}, and R_{out} if $R_L = 100$ kΩ?

Solution. The critical value of R_L is R_{Lc}. Its value is obtained from Eq. (4-70) and is $R_{Lc} = 6.16$ MΩ. This is much higher than 100 kΩ. Hence, $A_r = 100$ kΩ as well. The curves are the ones shown in Fig. 4-32. For values of R_L smaller than R_{Lc}, an approximate expression can be used for R_{in}. It is derived from Eq. (4-72a) by neglecting R_L in the denominator and is given by

$$R_{in} \approx \frac{1}{g_m} \left(1 + \frac{R_L}{r_{DS}} \right) \qquad (4\text{-}72b)$$

Since the second term is 2.66, R_{in} is 2.66 kΩ. Note that this expression shows the presence of $1/g_m$ more explicitly. It is a useful expression to remember when designing cascodes. Finally, the value of R_{out} is simply 100 kΩ as well.

High Frequency Performance Now all capacitances must be included in Fig. 4-31. This gives us a system of third order. Thus it is not easy to evaluate. Therefore, we will simplify the circuit before we attempt to analyze it.

Resistance R_G can be made small by addition of a large (external) capacitance to ground at the gate of the cascode. If $R_G = 0$, capacitance C_{DG} can be added to C_L, which becomes C_L', and C_{GS} becomes the input capacitance from source to ground. This is now a second-order system that can be analyzed with pole-zero position diagrams, as before. However, we will calculate the poles assuming that only one capacitance is present. We will later decide if we want to draw a full pole-zero position plot.

For capacitance C_L', the pole is easy to calculate because the time constant is simply $R_{out}C_L'$. The pole position plot with R_L' as variable is derived from Fig. 4-32b and is shown in Fig. 4-33. The larger the R_L', the smaller the pole frequency. Finally, note that the curves of Fig. 4-33 have been calculated for the numerical values of Example 4-10, with $C_L' = 10$ pF, $C_{GS} = 4$ pF, and $C_{DS} = 2.5$ pF.

Another pole easy to calculate is that associated with C_{GS}. This capacitance is connected from source to ground. Thus it generates a pole with R_{in}. Its position is again derived from Fig. 4-32b and is also shown in Fig. 4-33. It occurs at much higher frequencies than that of C_L', except for very low values of C_L'. Both poles coincide

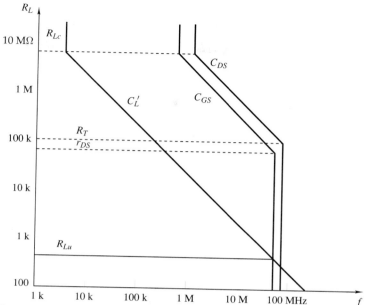

FIGURE 4-33   Dominant pole positions for C_L, C_{GS}, and C_{DS} separately.

at the value of R'_L, which is denoted by R_{Lu} and given by

$$R_{Lu} = \frac{1}{g_m} \left(\frac{C_{GS}}{C'_L} \right)$$

(4-72c)

At this value a complex pole pair occurs. It is a result of resonance between C_{GS} and C'_L. Therefore, this range is to be avoided.

The pole due to C_{DS} is more difficult to calculate. The easiest way to calculate the resistance is seen by C_{DS} in Fig. 4-31 at low frequencies. This is r_{DS} in parallel with a resistance, which is easily calculated to be $1/g_m\ (1 + R_L/R_T)$. The resulting pole positions are given in Fig. 4-33. The pole due to C_{DS} is of the same order of magnitude as that of C_{GS}. Together they form the nondominant pole for most values of R_L, except around R_{Lu}, where both C_{DS} and C_{GS} contribute to the complex pole pair.

It is clear from the pole-zero position plot of Fig. 4-33 that a dominant pole can be recognized for most values of R_L. This is not the case around R_{Lu}, where two complex poles occur. Therefore the full analysis with pole-zero position diagrams is not carried out.

4-4-2 Bipolar Transistor Cascodes

Substitution of the nMOST by an npn bipolar transistor in the cascode configuration of Fig. 4-30a gives us a bipolar transistor cascode. Rather than going through a full analysis again, we will limit the discussion to the differences between both.

The main difference with a MOST is that a bipolar transistor draws base current. The collector current thus is always $1/\beta$ smaller than the emitter (input) current. The *current gain* of this cascode is never unity. This is an important disadvantage of the bipolar transistor cascode.

Because of the base current, the base resistance is never negligible. It establishes a minimum value for resistance R_G in Fig. 4-30a. Also, this resistance can be seen at the emitter through r_π. The input resistance thus will be even higher than with the MOST cascode. In very much the same way as the load resistor R_L is visible through r_{DS} at the input, the base resistor R_G is now visible through r_π. The input resistance R_{in} can thus be derived from Eq. (2-24b) and Eq. (4-72b), as given by

$$R_{in} \approx \frac{1}{g_m} \left(1 + \frac{R_G}{r_\pi} + \frac{R_L}{r_{DS}} \right) \tag{4-73}$$

Thus the input resistance can be even larger than with a MOST, depending on the actual value of base resistor R_G.

At high frequencies the situation is much more complicated. The same small-signal equivalent circuit can be used (see Fig. 4-31). Remember, a resistance r_π must be added in parallel with C_{GS}, now called C_π. Also, R_G includes the base resistance r_B. Since R_G can never be omitted, we must always deal with a third-order system. Thus the analysis is cumbersome. Let us look for some simplifications.

Two capacitances are likely to dominate the high-frequency performance. They are the capacitances C_{GS}, now C_π, and the load capacitance C_L. The time constant associated with C_L is easy to calculate. It is the product with R_{out} or A_r, which is $A_i R_L$ where A_i is given by Eq. (4-70). If R_L is made large (for large gain), then this time constant $A_i R_L C_L$ is most probably going to provide the dominant pole.

The time constant associated with C_π is not this easy to obtain. None of its terminals are connected to ground, making the analysis cumbersome. When we replace the input current source by a transistor, we will find other capacitances more important than C_π. This is discussed in Sec. 4-6, on the full cascode configurations, so we will not calculate the pole associated with C_π now.

It can be concluded that for large values of R_L, the high frequency performance of the bipolar transistor cascode will be dominated by the output time constant in exactly the same way as for a MOST cascode.

4-4-3 Noise Performance

A cascode transistor is shown again in Eq. (4-34a), in which its equivalent input noise voltage is denoted by $\overline{dv_{ie}^2}$. The noise voltage of R_G is denoted by $\overline{dv_G^2}$. The question becomes what fraction of these noise sources reaches the output. The answer is zero, at least if load resistor R_L is small.

Indeed, the circuit functions as a source follower for the noise sources. The gate voltage, consisting of the noise voltages, appears unattenuated at the source. The current through the transistor, however, is not affected by the gate voltage. The current is only determined by the cascode biasing and input current I_{IN}. As a result, the output noise current $\overline{di_{out}^2}$ caused by the noise voltage sources $\overline{dv_{ie}^2}$ and $\overline{dv_G^2}$, is zero.

The zero output noise current is one of the most important advantages of the cascode transistor because it does not contribute noise to the output. It is unusual to be able to add a transistor to a circuit without deteriorating its noise performance. This is an exception.

Unfortunately, this is only true if load resistance R_L is small. If we take into account the finite output resistance R_T of the current source (see Fig. 4-34a), and the drain-source resistor r_{DS}, we find as gain

$$A_{vn} = \sqrt{\frac{\overline{dv_{out}^2}}{\overline{dv_{ie}^2}}} \approx \frac{R_L}{R_T} \left(\frac{1}{1 + \dfrac{R_L + R_T + r_{DS}}{R_{Lc}}} \right) \qquad (4\text{-}74)$$

This relation is sketched in Figure 4-34b. It shows that the above approximations are only valid for small R_L. Indeed, for most values of load resistance $R_L (< R_{Lc})$, the input noise contributions $\overline{dv_{ie}}$ and $\overline{dv_G}$ are amplified by R_L/R_T, thus increasing with increasing R_L.

With these considerations, we have finished the study of the single-transistor configurations. For more gain or more bandwidth, we need more transistors. We will see that all two- and more-transistor circuits are simple combinations of the single-transistor configurations studied up to now. Therefore, the reader must understand the preceding section before proceeding.

Next, we will discuss two-transistor amplifier configurations.

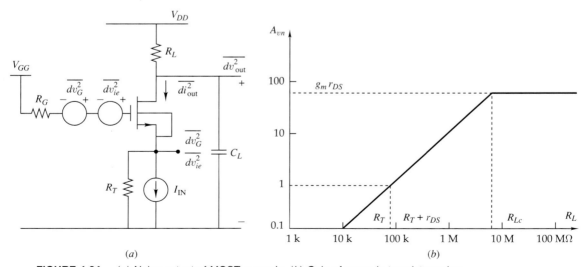

(a)   (b)

FIGURE 4-34   (a) Noise output of MOST cascode. (b) Gain of cascode transistor noise.

4-5   CMOS INVERTER STAGES

In order to generate more gain, the product $g_m R_L$ must increased. This can be done only by substituting R_L with a transistor. This is an active load. The simplest configuration of an nMOST amplifier with active load is shown in Fig. 4-35a. The pMOST acts as an active load. It is biased at some DC voltage V^+ between supply voltage V_{DD} and ground. The bulk is shorted to the source for each transistor. As a result, we will not have problems with the body effect (factor γ). The output is inverted with respect to the input. Therefore, this stage is called an inverter stage. It is an important building block in digital electronics. In this text, however, we will examine its properties as an analog amplifier.

The most common way to provide V^+ is to connect the gate of the pMOST to the input voltage source itself, as shown in Fig. 4-35b. The output is inverted again. Thus this stage is called a CMOS inverter, as well.

First we will examine the DC operating conditions for the latter configuration. Similar stages with bipolar transistors rather than MOST are discussed later in Sec. 4-5-7.

4-5-1   DC Analysis of CMOS Inverters

CMOST Inverter with Parallel Input   This configuration is shown in Fig. 4-35b. The I_{DS} versus V_{DS} characteristics for each transistor are shown in Figs. 4-36a and b. For both transistors, the current is a positive flow from supply line to ground. Also, both voltages are taken positive in the same direction, i.e., directed toward the positive supply V_{DD} (see Fig. 4-35a). For the nMOST this is conventional, but for the

FIGURE 4-35   (a) CMOS inverter with active load; (b) CMOS inverter with parallel input.

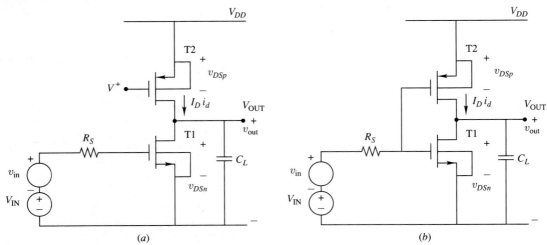

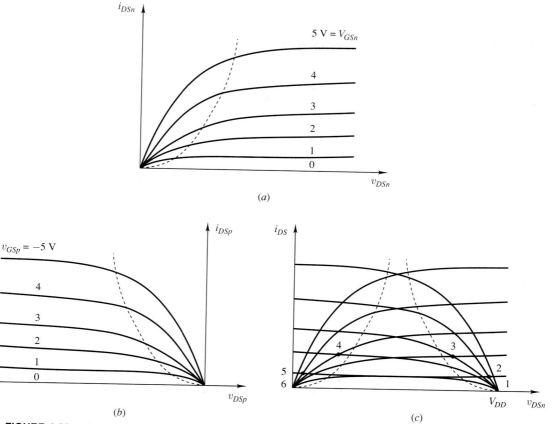

FIGURE 4-36 i_{DS} versus v_{DS} curves for (a) the nMOST; the (b) pMOST; and (c) the inverter.

pMOST, the current plotted is I_{SDp}; V_{DSp} points the other way. For both diagrams, the curves are indicated for values of V_{GS} ranging from 0, 1, 2, ..., 5 V with a supply voltage $V_{DD} = 5$ V.

To find the current in the inverter, the appropriate i_{DS} versus v_{DS} characteristics must be compared. Since the current is always the same for both transistors, we must take the curves with the V_{GS} values indicated by V_{IN}, in the points where

$$V_{GSn} = V_{\text{IN}}$$

$$V_{GSp} = V_{DD} - V_{\text{IN}}$$

$$V_{DSn} + V_{SDp} = V_{DD}$$

$$I_D = I_{DSn} = I_{SDp} \tag{4-75}$$

In order to realize these equations in a graphic way, the I_{DS} versus V_{DS} curves are shown one on top of the other for the same value of V_{IN}. This is repeated for the values of $V_{IN} = 0, 1, 2, \ldots, 5$ V in Figs. 4-37. They are repeated in their final position in Fig. 4-36c.

By inspection of Fig. 4-37b, for $V_{IN} = 1$ V, it is clear that the crosspoint of the curves for $V_{GSn} \doteq 1$ V and $V_{GSp} = -4$ V determines the current I_{D2}. This crosspoint

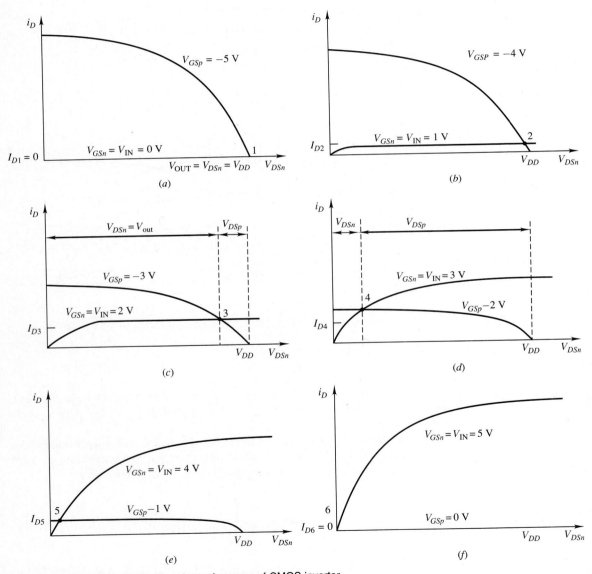

FIGURE 4-37   Derivation of transfer curve of CMOS inverter.

also determines the values of V_{DSn} and V_{SDp}. It is labeled point 2 in both Fig. 4-37b and 4-36c. This graphic way to find I_D and the values of V_{DSn} and V_{SDp} must be repeated for all values of V_{IN}.

Also, for any particular value of V_{IN}, the output voltage is given by $V_{\text{OUT}} = V_{DSn}$. It is plotted in Fig. 4-38a. The corresponding currents I_D are plotted in Fig. 4-38b.

$V_{\text{IN}} = 0$:

$V_{GSn} = 0$ and the nMOST is off, prohibiting any current to flow: $I_D = 0$. However, $V_{SGp} = 5$ V($= V_{DD}$). The only possible crosspoint is at $V_{DSn} = 0$ V (see Fig. 4-37a) and $V_{SDp} = 5$ V. Also, $V_{\text{OUT}} = 5$ V. This is point 1 in Fig. 4-37a, Fig. 4-36c, and Fig. 4-38.

$V_{\text{IN}} > V_{Tn}$:

$V_{GSn} (= V_{\text{IN}})$ is larger than V_{Tn} and current can start to flow. V_{DSn} increases whereas V_{SDp} and V_{OUT} decrease. This is point 2 in Fig. 4-37b, Fig. 4-36c, and Fig. 4-38.

V_{IN} large:

the I_{DS} versus V_{DS} curve of the nMOST keeps increasing, whereas the curve of the pMOST continues to decrease. When V_{IN} reaches 5 V, no V_{SGp} is left and the pMOST does not allow any current to flow. Again, the current $I_D = 0$. $V_{DSn} = 0$ V and $V_{SDp} = 5$ V. Thus, $V_{\text{OUT}} = 0$. This is point 6.

Somewhere between points 3 and 4, a maximum in current I_{Dm} is reached (see Fig. 4-38b). It is the point where the I_{DS} versus V_{DS} curves cross each other when their slopes are lowest (see, e.g., Figs. 4-37c and d). As a result, the values of V_{DS} change rapidly in this region. Also, the curve of v_{OUT} versus v_{IN} (Fig. 4-38a) is quite steep in that region.

The small-signal gain A_v is defined as $dv_{\text{OUT}}/dv_{\text{IN}}$, which is the slope (or the derivative) of the $v_{\text{OUT}}/v_{\text{IN}}$ curve. This slope is given in Fig. 4-38c. Clearly, its maximum is in the same region where the current also reaches its maximum. This point is calculated in the next section.

Finally, note that the $v_{\text{OUT}}/v_{\text{IN}}$ characteristic (Fig. 4-38a), called the *DC transfer characteristic*, displays a true inverter behavior indeed. If v_{IN} is low, v_{OUT} is high, and vice versa. For linear applications, however, only the steep middle region is used, where the gain is high.

Let us now calculate the value of the maximum current. In the region of points 3 and 4, the i_{DS} versus v_{DS} characteristics show that both transistors are in saturation (see Fig. 4-36c). For both transistors, the quadratic characteristic can be used. This yields for the nMOST and pMOST, respectively,

$$i_D = K'_n \left(\frac{W}{L}\right)_n (v_{\text{IN}} - V_{Tn})^2 (1 + \lambda_n v_{\text{OUT}}) \tag{4-76a}$$

$$i_D = K'_p \left(\frac{W}{L}\right)_p (V_{DD} - v_{\text{IN}} - V_{Tp})^2 [1 + \lambda_p (V_{DD} - v_{\text{OUT}})] \tag{4-76b}$$

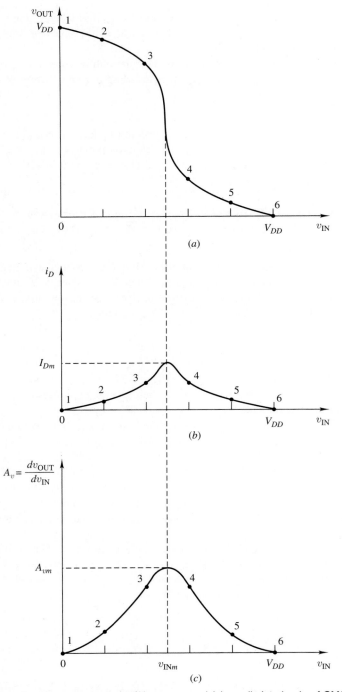

FIGURE 4-38   (*a*) Transfer characteristic; (*b*) current; and (*c*) small-signal gain of CMOS inverter.

Elimination of i_D yields a relation between v_{OUT} and v_{IN} that can be written as

$$v_{OUT} = \frac{K_i(1 + \lambda_p V_{DD}) - 1}{\lambda_n + K_i \lambda_p} \tag{4-77a}$$

with
$$K_i = \frac{K_p'(W/L)_p}{K_n'(W/L)_n} \left(\frac{V_{DD} - V_{Tp} - v_{IN}}{v_{IN} - V_{Tn}} \right)^2 \tag{4-77b}$$

Both these relations are sketched in Fig. 4-39a. They are only valid if both transistors are in saturation (if $V_{DS} \geq V_{GS} - V_T$) as shown in Fig. 4-39b. The region in the middle is the only region where both transistors operate in saturation, and thus is where a linear characteristic is obtained. The values of v_{OUT} are centered around V_{OUTm}, which corresponds with V_{INm}. The range over which v_{OUT} can vary is limited by the threshold voltages V_{Tn} and V_{Tp}.

We will carry out calculations only in this region, where both transistors are in saturation. For regions denoted by hatch marks in Fig. 4-39b, only one transistor is in the saturation region. The other is in its linear region. Because the analytic evaluation is quite cumbersome, we have omitted it.

If we want a symmetrical output swing, V_{OUTm} must be halfway V_{DD}, i.e., $V_{OUTm} = V_{DD}/2$. Input voltage V_{INm} is calculated from Eq. (4-77) to be

$$V_{INm} = \frac{V_{DD} - V_{Tp} + V_{Tn} KC}{1 + KC} \tag{4-78a}$$

with
$$KC = \sqrt{K_i' \left(\frac{K_n'(W/L)_n}{K_p'(W/L)_p} \right)} \tag{4-78b}$$

and
$$K_i' = \frac{1 + \lambda_n V_{DD}/2}{1 + \lambda_p V_{DD}/2} \tag{4-78c}$$

The value of K_i' is always close to unity. If $V_{Tn} = |V_{Tp}| = V_T$ and $\lambda_n = \lambda_p = \lambda$, then $K_i' \approx 1$. Also, if we design $K_n'(W/L)_n = K_p'(W/L)_p$, then $KC = 1$, and finally,

$$V_{INm} = \frac{V_{DD} - V_{Tp} + V_{Tn}}{2} \tag{4-78d}$$

which is about $V_{DD}/2 \; (= 2.5 \text{ V})$.

In this case, the maximum current I_{Dm} and the maximum voltage gain A_{vm} are easily calculated. Indeed, the relationship Eq. (4-76a) can be rewritten as

$$I_{Dm} = K_n' \left(\frac{W}{L} \right)_n \left(\frac{V_{DD}}{2} - V_T \right)^2 \left(1 + \lambda \frac{V_{DD}}{2} \right) \tag{4-79}$$

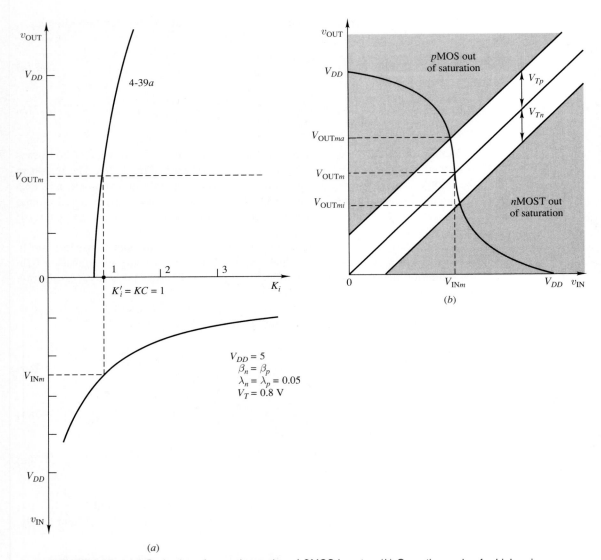

(a)

FIGURE 4-39   (a) Derivation of operating region of CMOS inverter; (b) Operating region for high gain.

Note that the requirement of the designer to make $K'_n(W/L)_n = K'_p(W/L)_p$ leads to larger W/L ratios for the pMOST than for the nMOST, since

$$\frac{(W/L)_p}{(W/L)_n} = \frac{\mu_n}{\mu_p} \qquad (4\text{-}80)$$

which is normally a little more than a factor of two, but less than three.

Before we carry out more calculations on gain, bandwidth, etc., let us have a look at the CMOS inverter with active load. We will see that its DC biasing is different, but that most of the conclusions on gain and bandwidth apply to both inverters.

CMOS Inverter with Active Load   The current in the inverter with parallel input (see Fig. 4-35b) is set by the supply voltage, as shown by Eq. (4-79). This is a disadvantage. It is not practical to modify the supply voltage when the current must be modified. Also, it is difficult to obtain low values of current in a reproducible way. The supply voltage, then, must be equal to $V_{Tn} + V_{Tp}$. This value is subject to large variations because of processing variations. For these reasons the current can be set better by an independent biasing voltage V^+ as shown in Fig. 4-35a. The pMOST transistor on top then behaves as an active load.

In this inverter, additional circuitry must be added to determine the value of V^+. The advantage is, however, that V^+ accurately determines V_{GSp} hence current I_D. An additional requirement is that the value of V_{IN} must be such that the nMOST takes the same current I_D, and V_{OUT} is in about the middle of the supply voltage V_{DD}.

In order to illustrate this point, the DC transfer characteristics are shown for several values of V^+ in Fig. 4-40. It is clear that for a specific value of biasing voltage V^+, a corresponding value of V_{IN} is required if the transistor is to be biased in the region with maximum slope or gain. Moreover, only specific combinations of V^+ and V_{IN} can be used that guarantee both transistors are kept in saturation.

How V^+ and its corresponding V_{IN} can be derived to obtain a specific current I_D, is the subject of Chap. 6. Now it is important to examine what values of gain and bandwidth can be realized for the several values of current I_D.

FIGURE 4-40   Transfer curves of CMOS inverter with active load, for different V^+.

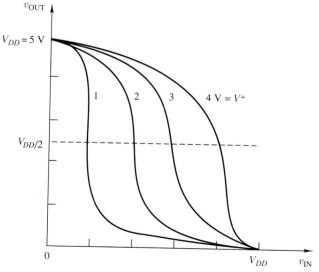

4-5-2 Low Frequency Gain

In order to calculate the small-signal gain, the small-signal equivalent circuit is used at the maximum current I_{Dm} (see Fig. 4-41). At this point, the maximum voltage gain A_{vm0} is obtained. At low frequencies, all capacitances can be omitted. The maximum gain A_{vm0} is then given by

$$A_{vm0} = -\frac{g_{mn} + g_{mp}}{g_{DSn} + g_{DSp}} \tag{4-81a}$$

For small signals both transistors operate in parallel to provide small-signal gain. Since g_m can be rewritten by use of Eq. (1-22b) and $g_{DS} = 1/r_o$ by use of Eq. (1-24b), this maximum gain is also given by

$$A_{vm0} = -V_E \sqrt{\frac{K'_n(W/L)_n}{I_{Dm}}} \tag{4-81b}$$

if $V_E = V_{En} L_n = V_{Ep} L_p$, and $K'_n(W/L)_n = K'_p(W/L)_p$.
Substitution of I_{Dm} from Eq. (4-79) finally yields:

$$A_{vm0} \approx -\frac{2V_E}{V_{DD}/2 - V_T} \tag{4-81c}$$

for small values of λ or large values of V_E.

Even if we cannot assume that $V_{En} L_n = V_{Ep} L_p$, the error is not large. In Eq. (4-81a), the dominant value of g_{DS} must be taken, i.e., the smaller value of V_E must be taken in Eq. (4-81c), or more accurately $V_E = V_{En} \cdot V_{Ep}/(V_{En} + V_{Ep})$.

For example, for $V_E = 30$ V, $V_T = 0.8$ V, $A_{v0} = 60/1.7 = 35.3$. Also, $I_{Dm} = 0.68$ mA for $W/L = 10$ and $K'_n = 30$ μA/V^2. Equation (4-81c) shows that the gain is inversely proportional to the supply voltage. For larger values of V_{DD}, the current I_{Dm} increases. Then the transconductance g_m increases only with the square root of the current, whereas g_{DS} increases linearly with the current. This results in a decrease of the gain with the square root of the current, as given by Eq. (4-81b). The curves of g_m, r_{DS}, and the gain A_{vm0} are illustrated in Fig. 4-42.

FIGURE 4-41   Small-signal equivalent circuit of CMOS inverter ($g_{DS} = 1/r_{DS}$).

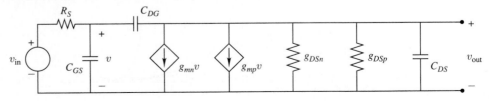

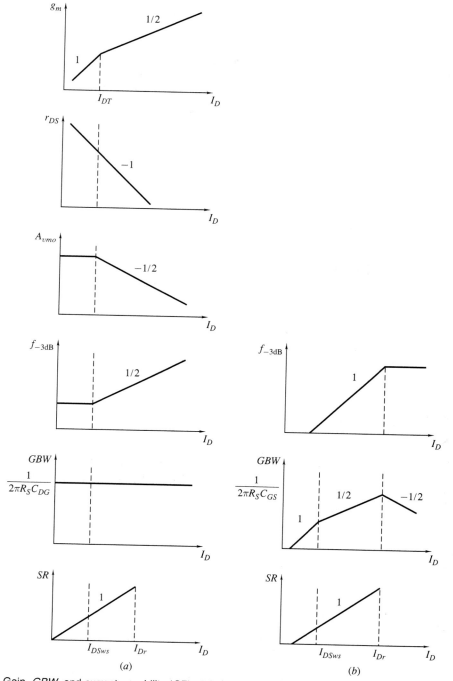

FIGURE 4-42   Gain, *GBW*, and current capability (*SR*) of CMOS inverter for (*a*) Miller Capacitance and (*b*) negligible C_L limitations in f_{-3dB}.

For high gain, the current must be low. For zero current, Eq. (4-81*b*) gives infinitely high gain. Obviously, some previously made assumption must be wrong. Indeed, for ever decreasing current, the weak inversion region is reached. The value of v_{GS} is lower than V_T. The i_{DS} versus v_{GS} characteristic becomes exponential rather than quadratic (see Sec. 1-2). The transition current I_{DSws} is given by Eq. (1-27). Its value is close to $\beta_n(kT/q)^2$.

In weak inversion, the value of the maximum gain A_{vm0} is still given by Eq. (4-81*a*). Now, however, $g_m = I_D/(nkT/q)$, which leads to

$$A_{vm0} = -\frac{V_E}{nkT/q} \tag{4-82}$$

if again $V_E = V_{En}L_n = V_{Ep}L_p$.

The gain is now quite high and independent of current (see Fig. 4-42). For example, if $V_E = 30$ V for both transistors, and $n = 1.5$, $A_{vm0} = 773$. Now the current has become quite low. For an nMOST with $(W/L)_n = 10$, $\beta = 0.4$ mA/V^2 and $I_{DSws} = 0.27$ μA.

Example 4-11

Design a CMOS inverter with parallel input for a voltage gain of 10 and a symmetrical output swing. The supply voltage is $V_{DD} = 10$ V. The transistor parameters are $V_T = 1$ V, $K'_n = 40$ μA/V^2 and $K'_p = 15$ μA/V^2; $V_{En} = 5$ V/μm and $V_{Ep} = 8$ V/μm. Calculate the current and the W's and L's required.

Solution. From Eq. (4-81*c*) we learn that an effective value of $V_E = 20$ V is required. Hence, $V_{En} = V_{Ep} = 40$ V. As a result, $L_n = 8$ μm and $L_p = 5$ μm. The maximum current is obtained from Eq. (4-79): per unit $(W/L)_n$ the current is about 0.64 mA. Minimum W's thus can be taken: both $W_n = W_p = 4$ μm, which yields $I_{Dm} = 0.32$ mA. Note that Eq. (4-80) is satisfied as well by following this procedure. This current is fairly high because the supply voltage value is high. The SPICE input file is given in Table 4-5. From the output we find 0.22 mA current and 24 dB gain.).

4-5-3 Bandwidth

To calculate the inverter bandwidths in Fig. 4-35, and their gain-bandwidth product, the capacitances must be present in the small-signal equivalent circuit of Fig. 4-43. For the inverter with active load (Fig. 4-35*a*):

$$
\begin{aligned}
g_m &= g_{mn} \\
r_{DS} &= r_{DSn}//r_{DSp} \\
C_{GS} &= C_{GSn} \\
C_{DG} &= C_{DGn} \\
C_{DS} &= C_{DSn} + C_{DSp} + C_L + C_{DGp}
\end{aligned} \tag{4-83a}
$$

TABLE 4-5 INPUT FILE FOR SPICE FOR THE CMOS INVERTER AMPLIFIER OF
EXAMPLE 11 IN SEC. 4-5-2

```
*Ex.4-11 (TEMPERATURE =27.000 DEG C)
* CIRCUIT DESCRIPTION
M1 2 1 0 0 NMOS W=4U L=8U
M2 2 1 4 4 PMOS W=4U L=57
VDD 4 0 DC 10
VIN 3 0 DC 4.5 AC 1
CL 2 0 10P
RL 2 0 1MDG
RS 3 1 1K
.MODEL NMOS NMOS LEVEL=2 VTO=1 KP=60E-6 GAMMA=0.01 LAMBDA=0.025
.MODEL PMOS PMOS LEVEL=2 VTO=-1 KP=24E-6 GAMMA=0.01 LAMBDA=0.025
* CONTROL CARDS
.DC VIN 4 6 0.025
.PRINT DC V(2) I(VDD)
.PLOT DC V(2)
.AC DEC 10 1K 10K
.PRINT AC VDB(2)
.WIDTH OUT=75
.END
```

and for the inverter with parallel input (Fig. 4-35b):

$$g_m = g_{mn} + g_{mp}$$
$$r_{DS} = r_{DSn} // r_{DSp}$$
$$C_{GS} = C_{GSn} + C_{GSp}$$
$$C_{DG} = C_{DGn} + C_{DGp}$$
$$C_{DS} = C_{DSn} + C_{DSp} + C_L$$

(4-83b)

The small-signal circuit has been thoroughly analyzed. For high gain and not too large C_L, the Miller capacitance determines the bandwidth, which is then given by

$$f_{-3dBM} \approx \frac{1}{2\pi R_S M C_{DG}}$$

(4-84a)

with
$$M \approx |A_{vm0}| \approx g_m r_{DS}$$

The gain-bandwidth product GBW is given by

$$GBW_M = A_{vm0} f_{-3dBM} = \frac{1}{2\pi R_S C_{DG}}$$

(4-84b)

Their values are shown as a function of current in Fig. 4-42. For $C_{DG} = 1$ pF and $R_S = 10$ kΩ, $GBW_M = 16$ MHz.

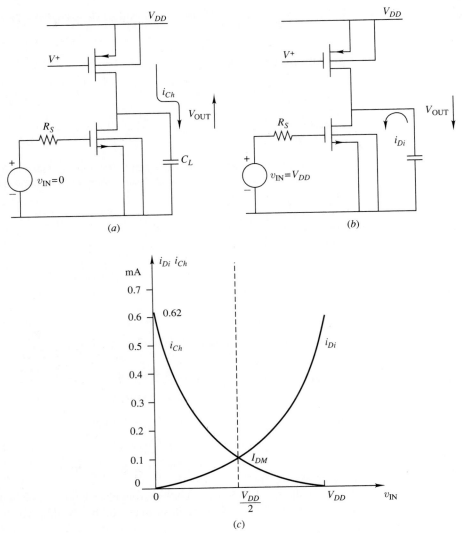

FIGURE 4-43   Definition of (a) charging and (b) discharging current. (c) Values of charging (i_{Ch}) and discharging currents (i_{Di}) versus input drive.

However, when R_L is small, the gain is small. The Miller effect is then negligible. In this case, Eq. (4-84a) and Eq. (4-84b) become

$$f_{-3\text{dB}} = \frac{1}{2\pi(R_S C_{GS} + r_{DS} C_{DS})} \qquad (4\text{-}85a)$$

and

$$GBW = \frac{g_m}{2\pi \left(\dfrac{C_{GS} R_S}{r_{DS}} + C_{DS} \right)} \tag{4-85b}$$

Both are shown in Fig. 4-42. For very large currents, r_{DS} is quite small. The term in C_{GS}, in the denominator of Eq. (4-85b), equals C_{DS} at current I_{Dr}, given by

$$I_{Dr} = \frac{C_{DS}}{C_{GS}} \frac{V_E}{R_S} \tag{4-86}$$

For $C_{DS} = 10$ pF, $C_{GS} = 5$ pF, $V_E = 30$ V and $R_S = 10$ kΩ, $I_{Dr} = 6$ mA. The curves are added for both regions in Fig. 4-42. A maximum appears in the curve of GBW at I_{Dr}. This maximum is mainly determined by the output conductances and the source resistance of the inverter.

The expression of GBW_{max} is obtained from Eq. (4-85b) and is given by

$$GBW_{max} = \frac{1}{2} \frac{g_{mr}}{2\pi C_{DS}} \tag{4-87}$$

in which g_{mr} is to be calculated at I_{Dr}. At this high current the transistor is still in strong inversion, but may even be at the onset of velocity saturation. Hence, for $K'_n = 30$ μA/V^2 and $W/L = 10$, $g_{mr} = 2.7$ mS at 6 mA. Since $C_{DS} = 10$ pF, $GBW_{max} = 21.6$ MHz. Also, $A_{vm0} = 13.4$ since $r_{DS} = 5$ kΩ only and $f_{-3dB} = 1.6$ MHz.

This maximum is worth pursuing, especially for large values of R_S, the value of GBW being already low. For instance, for $R_S = 5$ MΩ, $I_{Dr} = 6$ μA only, which is about one decade above the weak inversion limit.

4-5-4 Current Capability and Slew Rate

The gain and the bandwidth, calculated earlier, all refer to small signals. At low frequencies, the output voltage is never allowed to enter the hatched region (as seen in Fig. 4-39b). Otherwise, the signals are no longer small, and distortion results. The value of this maximum output voltage is simply given by

$$V_{OUT\,max} = V_{Tn} + V_{Tp} \tag{4-88}$$

for the inverter with parallel input (Fig. 4-35b). For the inverter with independent biasing, a similar maximum output voltage can be found.

At high frequencies, however, the output capacitances (mainly C_L) must be charged and discharged over the same value of $V_{OUT\,max}$, as at low frequencies. This requires additional current from the pMOST in order to increase v_{OUT} (current I_{Ch} in Fig. 4-43a), or additional current to the nMOST (I_{Di} in Fig. 4-43b) in order to decrease v_{OUT}. For increasing v_{OUT}, the pMOST acts as a source of additional current, charging C_L. On the other hand, for decreasing v_{OUT}, the nMOST acts as a sink for additional current, discharging C_L.

These currents flow in addition to the DC current that already flows through both transistors. These currents take time to flow, because it takes time to charge and discharge a capacitance. Therefore, the bandwidth is lowered for large output voltage at higher frequencies.

A second important consequence of these additional charging and discharging currents is that they cause additional power dissipation. Both phenomena will be studied into more detail.

Slew Rate of Inverter with Active Load   In this inverter (Fig. 4-35a), the value v_{SGp} is constant, hence i_{SDp} is about constant since the pMOST is in saturation. Thus the current available to charge C_L is I_{SDp}. During this charging time, v_{OUT} increases at a rate given by:

$$SR = \frac{dv_{OUT}}{dt} = \frac{I_{SDp}}{C_L} \qquad (4\text{-}89)$$

Note that C_L actually includes other capacitances, as well (see Eq. (4-83)). Since I_{SDp} is constant, v_{OUT} linearly increases in time. The rate given in Eq. (4-89) is the slew rate (SR) as defined in Chap. 3. It is the positive SR because v_{OUT} increases.

For example, for $I_{SDp} = 0.10$ mA and $C_L = 10$ pF, the $SR = 10$ V/μs. For a maximum output voltage of ($V_{Tp} + V_{Tn} =)1.6$ V, it takes 0.16 μs. For a sine wave, which can be approximated by a triangular wave, a full period is covered by this time multiplied by 4, or 0.64 μs. The corresponding maximum frequency thus would be 1.8 MHz.

Note that both SR and GBW are related to each other through current I_{SD}. This will be discussed later.

The negative SR discharging current can be made much larger than the charging current. By allowing v_{IN} to increase up to V_{DD}, a large value of $v_{GS}(= V_{DD} - V_{Tn})$ is available to draw a large value of $I_{DSn} = I_{Di}$.

It is given by:

$$I_{Di} = I_{DSn} = K'_n \left(\frac{W}{L}\right)_n (V_{DD} - V_{Tn})^2 \qquad (4\text{-}90)$$

Hence, the negative SR is much higher. The time it takes to discharge is therefore negligible. For example, if $I_{DSn} = 0.68$ mA with $V_{GSn} - V_{Tn} = 1.7$ V, then I_{DSn} is 6.2 times larger or 4.25 mA for $V_{GSn} - V_{Tn} = 4.2$ V ($V_{Tn} = 0.8$ V). To discharge $C_L = 10$ pF over 1.6 V, a $SR = 425$ V/μs is available, which causes a 1.6 V voltage drop in 3.7 ns.

Since the discharging current is 17.6 times larger, it takes a factor of 17.6 less time than charging the same capacitance (10 pF) over the same voltage (1.6 V). As a result, the discharge time is negligible and the maximum frequency of 1.8 MHz, which is calculated above, is valid as a limiting value.

At low frequencies the power dissipation is given by

$$P_{DS} = V_{DD}I_D = V_{DD}I_{SDp} \qquad (4\text{-}91)$$

where I_{SDp} is determined by its $V_{SGp} = V_{DD} - V^+$. The power dissipation is constant as long as the pMOST is still in saturation. Its value is quite large, which is typical for a class A operation.

At high frequencies, nothing changes because I_{SDp} is a constant. Hence the power dissipation is the same.

Slew Rate of Inverter with Parallel Input   In this configuration (see Fig. 4-35b), both transistors are directly driven by the input voltage source. The calculation for the discharging current through the nMOST can now be repeated for the charging current through the pMOST. Thus, both the discharging and charging currents are considerably larger than the maximum quiescent current I_{Dm} at low frequencies, given by Eq. (4-79). The voltage drive at I_{Dm} for the nMOST is only $0.5 \times V_{DD} - V_{Tn}$. The voltage drive during the discharging of C_L is $V_{DD} - V_{Tn}$, yielding a current that is about 6.2 times larger than I_{Dm}. As a result, if $K'_n(W/L)_n = K'_p(W/L)_p$, then both currents are 6.2 times larger than I_{Dm}. The available current is shown versus v_{IN} in Fig. 4-43c. Clearly it shows that this CMOS inverter acts as a class AB amplifier. For large output swing, more current is available to charge and discharge the load than in quiescent state (for small-signals). This ratio is 6.2 in the example.

This additional current also causes additional power dissipation. Per charging cycle, an amount of charge is drawn from V_{DD}, given by

$$Q_D = \frac{C_L(V_{Tn} + V_{Tp})^2}{2} \qquad (4\text{-}92)$$

since $V_{Tn} + V_{Tp}$ is the maximum signal amplitude. The dynamic power dissipation is then given by

$$P_{DD} = fQ_D \qquad (4\text{-}93)$$

in which f is the clock frequency. This power consumption must be added to the static power dissipation previously calculated. Notice that P_{DD} is proportional to frequency. For example, for $C_L = 10$ pF and $V_{Tn} + V_{Tp} = 1.6$ V, at $I_{DT} = 0.68$ mA, $P_{DS} = 3.4$ mW. Also, $Q_D = 10$ pC. At $f = 20$ MHz, $P_{DD} = 0.2$ mW.

The dynamic power is still negligible with respect to the static power dissipation. This contrasts with the dissipation of a digital CMOS inverter. It consumes no power in its two quiescent points (points 1 and 6 in Fig. 4-38b). All power dissipation is then of a dynamic nature, as given by Eq. (4-92) and Eq. (4-93), but with full output swing V_{DD}.

This above calculation is only approximate, however. More exact expressions show that the current only increases linearly with V_{DD} rather than with V_{DD}^2.

Now that we know how to calculate the gain of a CMOS inverter, its gain-bandwidth, and its slew rate, let us explain a systematic design procedure.

4-5-5 Design Procedure

Let us assume that a CMOS inverter is to be designed with parallel input. The specifications of the GBW are given for a given load capacitance C_L and source resistance R_S. The supply voltage V_{DD} is fixed.

It is obvious that we maintain the requirements for symmetry, i.e., $K'_n(W/L)_n = K'_p(W/L)_p$ from Eq. (4-80), and $V_{En} = V_{Ep} = V_E$ from Eq. (4-81), which fixes the gain A_{vm0} (Eq. (4-81)). The GBW, however, requires some more discussion.

We are considering a typical two-node circuit, as we have studied in the beginning of this chapter. Both nodes and ground are connected by three capacitances. The input node is dominant if the Miller capacitance is dominant, or if source resistance R_S is large.

For a large load capacitance C_L, however, the dominant pole is created at the output node. Let us assume that C_L is large. The GBW is then obtained from Eq. (4-85b), in which $R_S \approx 0$ and in which C_{DS} includes capacitance C_L, as given by

$$GBW = \frac{g_{mn}}{2\pi(C_{DS} + C_L)} \tag{4-94a}$$

or by

$$GBW = \frac{2\sqrt{K'_n(W/L)_n I_D}}{2\pi(C_{DS} + C_L)} \tag{4-94b}$$

Since C_L is large, C_{DS} is negligible with respect to C_L. For a given value of GBW, the required value of g_{mn} is obtained from Eq. (4-95a).

The second part of the design task is to ensure that the second pole is at least $3 \cdot GBW$ (see Fig. 4-12c). The second pole is now given by Eq. (4-84a). This condition can be written as $f_{-3dB} \geq 3 \ GBW$, or more explicitly

$$\frac{C_{DS} + C_L}{C_{DG}} \geq 3 g_m r_{DS} g_m R_S \tag{4-95a}$$

which means, on first sight, a minimum value of C_L is required. However, r_{DS} depends on the current as well. Rewriting Eq. (4-95a) versus current yields (in strong inversion):

$$\frac{C_{DS} + C_L}{C_{DG}} \geq 12 K'_n W_n V_{En} R_S \tag{4-95b}$$

in which V_{En} is the early voltage per μm channel length.

It is concluded that Eq. (4-95b) sets the width W_n of the nMOST. If we use the length L_n at its minimum value (i.e., 3μm), then the size of the transistors are determined. The current is then obtained from Eq. (2-94b).

Example 4-12

Design an inverter with parallel input with $GBW = 1$ MHz for $C_L = 10$ pF and $R_S = 1$ kΩ ($K'_n = 30$ μA/V^2 and $V_{En} = 5$ V/μm). Approximate values of the capacitances are $C_{DS} = 2$ pF, $C_{DG} = 1$ pF and $C_{GS} = 5$ pF.

Solution. From Eq. (4-95b) we find, as minimum value, $W_n = 6.6$ μm, if $L_n = 3$ μm is chosen. From Eq. (4-94b), $I_D = 21.6$ μA.

In order to automate the design even more, we must first generalize the formulation. All design equations are collected in Table 4-6 with the design parameters in the last column of the table. There are seven design parameters: W_n, L_n, W_p, W_p, A_{vm0}, GBW, and I_D. The other parameters C_{DS} and C_{DG} cannot be modified; they are a result of the dimensions (W_n, L_n, ...) and the technology used. Parameters R_S, C_L, and V_{DD} have been set beforehand. The remaining parameters, such as K'_n, V_{En}, etc. also have been determined by the technology used.

In Table 4-6 we have five equations to determine seven parameters. This means that two parameters can be freely chosen. Normally, these are GBW and the gain A_{vm0}. These two parameters become the two "specification" parameters, from which all other parameters can be derived by means of straightforward analysis.

In this case, the design procedure has become very simple. Only parameter W_n occurs in the last equation of Table 4-6, i.e., Eq. (4-95b). Thus, its value is obtained from

$$W_n \leq \left(\frac{C_{DS} + C_L}{C_{DG}}\right)\left(\frac{1}{12K'_n V_{En} R_S}\right) \tag{4-96}$$

On the other hand, parameter L_n occurs only in the third equation of Table 4-6, i.e., Eq. (4-81). Its value is

$$L_n = A_{vm0}\frac{V_{DD}/2 - V_T}{2V_{En}} \tag{4-97}$$

Parameter L_p is determined from the second equation of Table 4-6, and W_p from the first.

Finally, the current is determined from Eq. (4-94b), as given by

$$I_D \approx 3(2\pi GBW)^2(C_{DS} + C_L)C_{DG}V_{En}L_n R_S \tag{4-98}$$

This concludes the design procedure.

TABLE 4-6   DESIGN EQUATIONS FOR THE CMOST INVERTER

Number	Equation	Equation no.	Design parameters
1	$\dfrac{(W/L)_p}{(W/L)_n} = \dfrac{\mu_n}{\mu_p}$	(4-80)	$(W/L)_n, (W/L)_p$
2	$V_E = V_{En}L_n = V_{Ep}L_p$	(4-81b)	L_n, L_p
3	$A_{vm0} \approx -\dfrac{2V_E}{V_{DD}/2 - V_T}$	(4-81c)	A_{vm0}, L_n
4	$GBW = \dfrac{2\sqrt{K_n'(W/L)_n I_D}}{2\pi(C_{DS}+C_L)}$	(4-94b)	$GBW, I_D, (W/L)_n$
5	$\dfrac{C_{DS}+C_L}{C_{DG}} \geq 12K_n'W_n V_{En}R_S$	(4-95b)	W_n

Example 4-13

Repeat the design of Example 4-12 for $GBW = 1$ MHz and $A_{vm0} = 10$. Also, $C_L = 10$ pF and $R_S = 1$ kΩ. The transistor parameters are $K_n' = 30$ μA/V^2 and $V_{En} = 5$ V/μm; $K_p' = 15$ μA/V^2 and $V_{Ep} = 8$ V/μm. All $|V_T|$ are 1 V. Approximate values of the capacitances are $C_{DS} = 2$ pF, $C_{DG} = 1$ pF, and $C_{GS} = 5$ pF. The supply voltage $V_{DD} = 5$ V.

Solution. Following the design procedure just discussed yields $W_n = 6.7$ μm; also, $L_n = 1.5$ μm and $(W/L)_n = 4.5$. For equal output resistances (second equation in Table 4-6), $L_p = 1$ μm; from the first equation $(W/L)_p = 9$ and $W_p = 9$ μm. Finally, from Eq. (4-94b) $I_D \approx 1$ mA. The transconductance is then $g_m = 0.73$ mS and the $V_{GS} - V_T = 2.74$ V. The transistor already operates close to velocity saturation.

As a designer we could plot L_n and L_p versus C_L to see whether these specifications can be met with a 2.4 μm CMOS technology. We could also plot the current versus GBW, or even the required W_n versus L_n, etc. A designer can find many alternatives to explore.

Finally, in order to verify the performance of this inverter, refer to its SPICE input file in Table 4-5. The results match the specifications very closely.

The value of W_n thus has an upper limit, and I_D is found to be proportional to $(GBW)^2$. This could be expected since the transistor operates in strong inversion.

In this design procedure, GBW and the gain thus have been taken as specifications or independent variables. Alternative procedures are quite possible for other specifications, such as GBW and I_D, or A_{vm0} and I_D, etc. These are considered in the exercises.

4-5-6   Other MOST Inverters

The CMOS inverters with parallel input and independent biasing are the important inverters, but not the only inverters. Many others have been realized, but very few have comparable performance. Some of these inverters are discussed here, as well as in the exercises.

Invertor with Resistive nMOST Load in Saturation   Instead of a pMOST active load, an nMOST can be used, such that two nMOSTs are now present. This nMOST is connected in diode configuration, however, (see Fig. 4-44a) and thus transistor T2 is always in saturation. Its bulk is connected to its source, such that the body effect is avoided. This is only possible in a p-well CMOS process, however. Otherwise, the bulk is connected to ground as in Fig. 4-44b.

The DC output voltage is now fixed by subtraction of V_{GS2} from V_{DD}. We must ensure that transistor T1 is always in saturation. Hence, $(V_{DD} - V_{GS2})$ must be larger than V_{DSsat1}, or $(V_{GS1} - V_T)$ or $(V_{IN} - V_T)$. Because of this voltage drop, the output voltage is only a fraction of the supply voltage. This is illustrated by the output characteristics of both transistors in Fig. 4-44c. The corresponding transfer characteristics are given in Fig. 4-44d. The quiescent point Q must be in the middle of the linear region. This linear region exists as long as both transistors are in saturation. Their second-order i_{DS} versus v_{GS} characteristics compensate each other, such that a linear region results. This is easily verified for small-signal operation.

The small-signal gain now is much smaller than it was because a diode connected MOST offers only $1/g_{m2}$ as a small-signal load resistance. Therefore, this inverter is called *inverter with resistive MOST load in saturation*. For the inverter of Fig. 4-46a (see Sec. 4-5-7), the gain is given simply by

$$A_{v0} = -\frac{g_{m1}}{g_{m2}} = -\sqrt{\frac{(W/L)_1}{(W/L)_2}} \tag{4-99a}$$

Its value is fixed only by the relative sizes of the transistors and thus is independent of the K' factors or mobilities. In this way precision amplification can be achieved, albeit with low value. This precision is not available for the inverter of Fig. 4-44b because g_{mb2} intervenes, depending on v_{OUT} in a nonlinear way. Its gain is now

$$A_{v0} = -\frac{g_{m1}}{g_{m2} + g_{mb2}} \tag{4-99b}$$

The dominant pole is most probably found at the input node because the output node has a low impedance $1/g_{m2}$ to ground. On the other hand, the Miller effect is small as well. A large bandwidth thus can be achieved. The exact calculations and design procedures are covered in the exercises.

Inverter with Resistive nMOST Load in Linear Region   If a full output swing is required, it is better to bias the gate at a voltage V_{GG}, which is higher than V_{DD} (see Fig. 4-45a). In this case, however, transistor T2 operates in the linear region. Its g_{m2} is larger than that in Fig. 4-44b and its gain $A_{v0} = g_{m1}/g_{m2}$ thus is smaller. The gain is no longer independent of K'_n or from V_{GG}. Thus, this inverter is much less

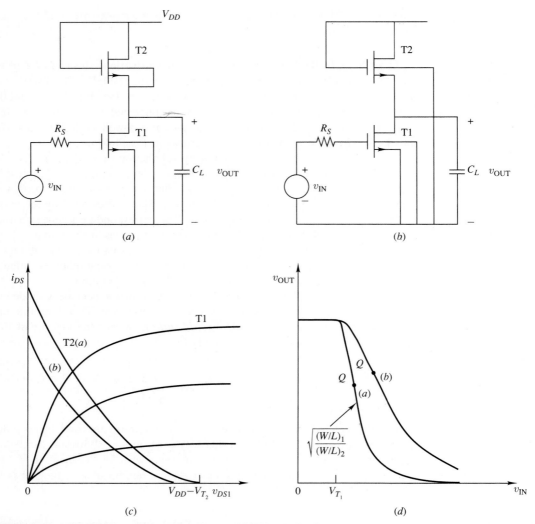

FIGURE 4-44 (a) MOST inverters with resistive MOST load (b) with bulk to ground; (c) output characteristics; (d) transfer characteristics.

attractive. It is mainly used in digital applications where a larger g_{m2} is required to reduce the output time constant g_{m2}/C_L.

Folded nMOST Inverter with Resistive nMOST Load in Saturation Instead of connecting the nMOST resistive load to the positive power supply, we can also connect such load to ground as shown in Fig. 4-45b. Transistor T3 performs the same function as transistor T2 in Fig. 4-44a; it always operates in saturation. An easy way

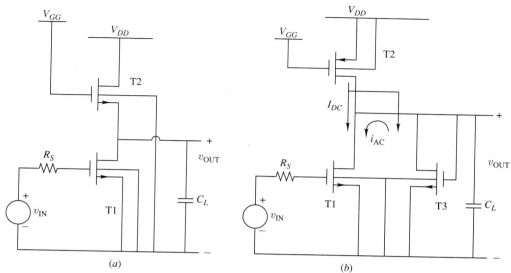

FIGURE 4-45   CMOST inverters (a) with separate gate bias; (b) with nMOST resistive load.

to realize this biasing condition is to enforce the input and output DC voltages to be the same. Then both transistors have the same V_{GS}. Their currents are proportional to their widths (if their lengths are the same). The DC output current I_{DC} from transistor T2 is then shared by both transistors T1 and T3.

The AC current i_{AC} in T3, however, is equal in magnitude but opposite in sign, compared to the AC current in the input transistor T1. The AC current is thus folded from T1 to T3. The gain and gain-bandwidth are the same as for the nMOST inverter with resistive nMOST load in saturation of Fig. 4-44a. The gain is thus again given by Eq. (4-99a) and is independent of K' values.

4-5-7   Bipolar Transistor Inverter Stages

An inverter with bipolar transistors instead of MOSTs is readily copied from Fig. 4-35a and shown in Fig. 4-46a. The pnp transistor is on top and is biased as an active load for the bottom npn transistor, which carries out the amplification function. Most of the calculations and comments made on the MOST inverter apply equally to the bipolar transistor inverter.

However, an important difference between a MOST and a bipolar transistor, is their output characteristic.

Output Characteristic   In Sec. 2-10, we discussed a comparison between the output characteristics of a MOST and a bipolar transistor. In Fig. 2-38, the i_D versus

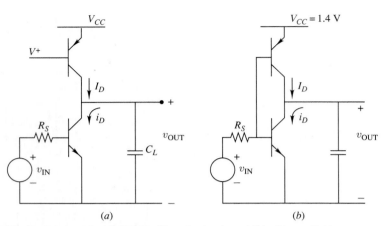

FIGURE 4-46   Bipolar transistor inverters (*a*) with active load; and (*b*) with parallel input.

v_{DS} characteristics are plotted for a MOST with several values of the width, together with the i_{CE} versus v_{CE} characteristic of a typical bipolar transistor. The current is the same and the values of V_{DS} and V_{CE} are large, for all values.

For a bipolar transistor, the V_{CEsat} is quite small, i.e., of the order of magnitude of 100 to 300 mV. For a MOST, the value of V_{DSsat} depends on the size W/L and the current of the transistor, as given by

$$V_{DSsat} = V_{GS} - V_T = \sqrt{\frac{I_{DS}}{K'W/L}} \tag{4-100}$$

(see Eq. (1-11)).

For increasing values of W, the value of V_{DSsat} decreases. For small V_{DSsat}, the values of W required become quite large. Then, the MOST already operates close to the weak inversion region.

Transfer Characteristic   As a result, if the transfer characteristics of a bipolar transistor inverter (see Fig. 4-47) is compared with that of a MOST inverter (Fig. 4-38*a*), then we notice that the middle region with the steepest slope is much larger. The region 3–4 nearly extends over the full range of v_{OUT}. In this area, both bipolar transistors are in their linear region, i.e., when $v_{IN} = V_{BEon} \approx 0.7$ V. Their current I_{Cm} is set by the biasing voltage V^+ at the base of the active load transitor. The slope is maximum, hence the small-signal gain is maximum as well.

Note that the transfer characteristic does not reach either the value of V_{CC} or zero at the extreme points 1 and 6 (see Fig. 4-38*a*). In point 1, the *npn* transistor is off and the *pnp* transistor is in saturation. Its value of V_{CEsat} is then a few tens of mV, but not zero. It is derived from the Ebers-Moll model (Getreu 1976).

Similarly, in point 6, the *pnp* transistor provides its maximum current I_{Cm}, as dictated by V^+, but the V_{BE}, and thus I_B, of the *npn* transistor are much larger than

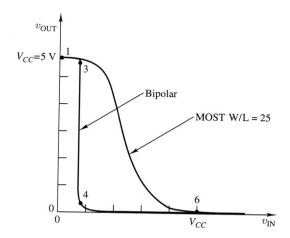

FIGURE 4-47   Transfer characteristic of bipolar inverter.

required to accommodate this current. Thus, the *npn* is in saturation. The voltage across it is small, but never zero.

It is possible to construct a bipolar transistor inverter with parallel input (see Fig. 4-46*b*) in the same way as the MOST inverter of Fig. 4-35*b*. The two bases must then be connected to form the input terminal. However, since the i_{CE} versus v_{BE} characteristic of a bipolar transistor is exponential, rather then quadratic as in a MOST, it is difficult to set the supply voltage V_{CC} to an accurate value, such that the maximum current I_{Cm} is well controlled. Remember, only 60 mV is required to change the collector current by a decade. It is only 18 mV for a ratio of a factor of two, 10.5 mV for a deviation of 50 percent, and 2.5 mV for a deviation of 10 percent.

Special biasing techniques can be used, however, to limit the current to a nonexcessive value. The simplest technique is to set V_{CC} at about $2V_{BEon} \approx 1.4$ V. Since current only flows during switching from one state to the other, only current spikes occur. For digital applications, this is acceptable. For analog applications, however, more sophisticated biasing schemes must be used.

Small-Signal Performance   The small-signal performance of the bipolar transistor inverter of Fig. 4-46*a* is actually that of a single-transistor amplifier with an active load (see Sec. 4-2). The total output capacitance is given by

$$C'_L = C_L + C_{CSN} + C_{CSP} + C_{\mu P} \tag{4-101}$$

in which all indices *N* refer to the *npn* transistor and *P* to the *pnp* transistor.

Curves of g_m, r_o, A_v, f_{-3dB}, *GBW*, and *SR* can be derived as for a MOST inverter. They are given in Fig. 4-48. Some of these curves are calculated next.

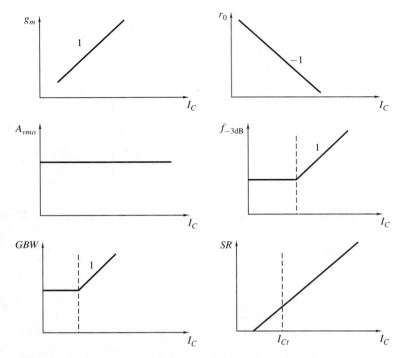

FIGURE 4-48   Gain, *GBW*, and current capability (*SR*) for bipolar transistor inverters of Fig. 2-45*d*.

The gain is independent of the current. It is given by

$$A_{vm0} = \frac{V_{EN}//V_{EP}}{kT/q} \tag{4-102}$$

and thus is quite high. For instance, for $V_{EN} = 50$ and $V_{EP} = 60$ V, $A_{vm0} = 1050$. Note that V_{EP} can be made larger by increasing the distance between collector and emitter (see Chap. 2).

The value of the bandwidth $f_{-3\text{dB}}$ depends on the relative values of $C_{\pi N}$, C'_L and $C_{\mu N}$. Since no cascode transistors are used, the Miller effect is dominant. The curves in Fig. 4-48 are given within this assumption.

For small currents i_C, $r_{\pi N}$ is large and $(R_S + r_{BN})$ determines the resistance level at the input, hence $f_{-3\text{dB}}$. For large currents, $r_{\pi N}$ is smaller than $(R_S + r_{BN})$ and determines the value of $f_{-3\text{dB}}$. The transition current is determined by $r_{\pi N} = R_S + r_{BN}$ and occurs at the current I_{Ct} given by

$$I_{Ct} = \beta \frac{kT/q}{R_S + r_{BN}} \tag{4-103}$$

which is 2.17 mA for $\beta = 100$ and $R_S + r_{BN} = 1.2$ kΩ .

For small currents, the value of $f_{-3\text{dB}}$ is given by

$$f_{-3\text{dB}} = \frac{1}{2\pi(R_S + r_{BN})A_{vm0}C_{\mu N}} \tag{4-104}$$

and *GBW* is given by

$$GBW = \frac{1}{2\pi(R_S + r_{BN})C_{\mu N}} \tag{4-105}$$

For example, for $C_{\mu N} = 1$ pF, the values of $f_{-3\text{dB}} = 126$ kHz and $GBW = 132.5$ MHz.

For currents larger than I_{Ct}, both $f_{-3\text{dB}}$ and *GBW* increase linearly with current.

Actually, the curves of Fig. 4-48 are similar to those of a MOST inverter in Fig. 4-42, Only the current A_{vm0} is now constant. Also, I_{Ct} is three orders of magnitude larger than I_{DSws}. *GBW* is also different. Its value increases with a larger I_C. This latter difference is an advantage when using bipolar transistors, as illustrated in Fig. 2-41.

For large input voltages, there are slew rate limitations because the output load capacitance C'_L is present. The output swings between the positive voltage supply and ground. The slew rate can be different, however, for an increasing output voltage than for a decreasing one.

For the inverter of Fig. 4-45a, the slew rate for a decreasing output voltage is caused by charging up C'_L by means of the maximum current I_{Cm}, controlled by the *pnp* transistor. The slew rate *SR* thus is given by I_{Cm} versus C'_L.

For positive output voltages, the discharge current through the *npn* transistor can be much larger because the input voltage of the *npn* can be overdriven. Thus, the slew rate is not constant and the switching time is shorter.

For the inverter with parallel input (Fig. 4-45b), the input is overdriven in both directions and the switching times are quite short in both directions. The actual calculation of these switching times depends on the transistor parameters and the drive voltage specifications. This subject would be more appropriate in a text on switching phenomena in bipolar transistors.

4-5-8 Noise Performance

In order to evaluate the noise behavior of an inverter, the CMOS inverters in Fig. 4-35 are analyzed. The CMOS inverter with parallel input (Fig. 4-35b) is considered first. The equivalent input noise voltages of the transistors (see Fig. 4-49a) can be lumped into one equivalent noise voltage source $\overline{dv_{iT}^2}$, as shown in Fig. 4-49b. Its value is found by equation of the output noise voltages of both circuits. It is given by

$$\overline{dv_{iT}^2} = \overline{dv_{\text{in}}^2}\left(\frac{g_{mn}}{g_{mn} + g_{mp}}\right)^2 + \overline{dv_{ip}^2}\left(\frac{g_{mp}}{g_{mn} + g_{mp}}\right)^2 \tag{4-106a}$$

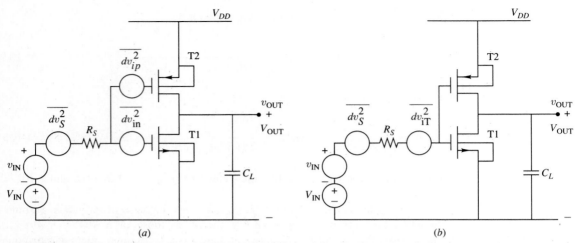

FIGURE 4-49   (a) Noise sources in CMOS inverter with parallel input, and (b) same inverter with equivalent input noise source.

The excess noise factor y for white noise is given by

$$y = \frac{\overline{dv_{iT}^2}}{\overline{dv_{in}^2}} = \frac{1}{2} \tag{4-106b}$$

since, usually, $g_{mn} = g_{mp}$ or $K_n'(W/L)_n = K_p'(W/L)_p$.

This is an excellent result. The equivalent input noise voltage is $\sqrt{2}$ lower than that of a single-transistor amplifier. In fact, by paralleling the two input devices, the gain increases by a factor of two but the noise increases only by $\sqrt{2}$. The equivalent input noise voltage thus is reduced by $\sqrt{2}$.

For a CMOS inverter with active load (see Fig. 4-50a), a similar calculation can be carried out. Note, however, that the output noise of the biasing voltage $\overline{dv_B^2}$ must be included. The value of the total equivalent input noise voltage $\overline{dv_{iT}^2}$ in Fig. 4-50b is given by:

$$\overline{dv_{iT}^2} = \overline{dv_{in}^2} + \left(\overline{dv_{ip}^2} + \overline{dv_B^2}\right)\left(\frac{g_{mp}}{g_{mn}}\right)^2 \tag{4-107a}$$

and the excess noise factor y is now given by:

$$y = \frac{\overline{dv_{iT}^2}}{\overline{dv_{in}^2}} = 2 + \frac{\overline{dv_B^2}}{\overline{dv_{in}^2}} \tag{4-107b}$$

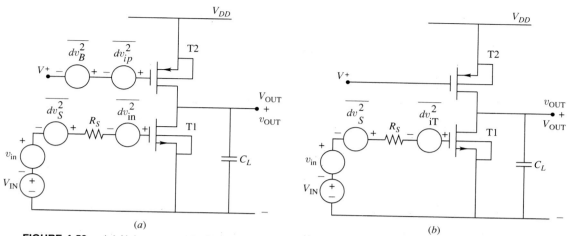

FIGURE 4-50   (a) Noise sources in CMOS inverter with active load, and (b) same inverter with equivalent input noise source.

It is important to note that the equivalent input noise is now larger than that of the inverter with parallel input. This is true especially if the noise of the biasing source $\overline{dv_B^2}$ cannot be eliminated by means of a large capacitance at that point.

All the inverters studied in the preceding sections consist of two transistors of the amplifier type (see Fig. 4-1). Now we will discuss the two-transistor configurations in which one transistor is of the amplifier type and the other of the cascode type. These are the cascode stages.

4-6 CASCODE STAGES

In the calculations of the bandwidth, it has always been assumed that the effect of the Miller capacitance can be avoided by specific circuitry. In this way much larger values of bandwidth have been achieved. The cascode circuit is one example of such a circuit. It is used frequently in high-performance circuitry, such as deflection circuitry for TV, etc. In such circuits, high-supply voltages are combined with high-frequency performance.

A cascode stage always consists of a transistor that provides amplification and a cascode transistor. Several configurations are possible.

4-6-1 Cascode Configurations

In their simplest form, cascode configurations consist of two transistors in series, as shown in Fig. 4-51a. The bottom transistor T1 acts as an amplifying device (in common-source configuration). Its output current is determined by the input voltage source. This current is fed to another transistor T2, which is biased by V^+ in cascode

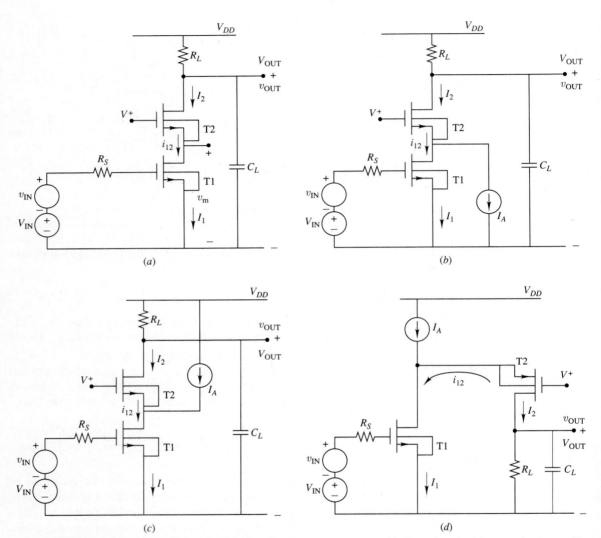

FIGURE 4-51   (*a*) Cascode stage with $I_1 = I_2$; (*b*) cascode stage with $I_2 = I_1 + I_A$; (*c*) cascode stage with $I_1 = I_2 + I_A$; and (*d*) cascode stage with $I_A = I_1 + I_2$.

or common-gate configuration. The output is taken at the collector of the cascode transistor.

In this configuration, the total current through both transistors is the same. This is not necessarily always the case. In Fig. 4-51*b*, *c*, and *d*, several alternatives are shown. They are used to meet particular design criteria, discussed later.

In Fig. 4-51*b* and *c*, the DC currents in the transistors are clearly different because of how they use a DC current source. The AC current is the same in both transistors, however. In Fig. 4-51d, the DC current I_1 in transistor T1 is set by the DC input voltage V_{IN}. The current difference $I_A - I_1$ is then forced through transistor T2. Again, the AC current i_{12} is the same in both transistors.

All the configurations in Fig. 4-51a, b, and c have in common AC currents that flow from the positive power supply V_{DD} to ground through both transistors. In the configuration of Fig. 4-51d, however, the AC current circles through both transistors and ground, without going through the positive power supply. The AC current flow through transistor T2 is equal in magnitude, but opposite in direction compared to transistor T1. The AC current thus is folded back. Therefore, the cascode of Fig. 4-51d is called the folded cascode.

The small-signal gain of all four configurations is $-g_m R_L$. The bandwidth depends on the configuration, as well as on the sizes of the transistors used. Thus it can be made the same for all four configurations, as will be explained in Sec. 4-6-2.

However, an important difference between the several configurations is the over-drive and recovery characteristics. If the input transistor of the folded cascode (Fig. 4-51d) is overdriven (high V_{in}), all current I_A is sunk to T1, which enters the linear region. The source of T2 is pulled down to ground. Transistor T2 thus is switched off. To recover, the source of T2 must rise until it reaches $V^+ + V_{GS}$. During that time all capacitances at this point must charge up through the high impedance of the drain of T1. Thus, a large recovery time results.

On the other hand, if T1 is switched off, transistor T2 remains active because it carries current I_A. Thus, the drain of T1 remains at a low impedance level ($1/g_{m2}$) at voltage $V^+ + V_{GS}$. Transistor T1 thus can switch in quite rapidly.

The same phenomenon occurs in the cascode of Fig. 4-51c, but in the opposite order. If T1 is switched off, the source of T2 increases up to V_{DD}. It takes a long time to bring this point down to $V^+ - V_{GS2}$. If T1 is overdriven, T2 simply enters the linear region and fast recovery is evident.

None of these phenomena occur in the cascodes of Fig. 4-51a and b. If T1 is overdriven, T2 simply enters the linear region. If T1 is switched off, T2 is off in Fig. 4-51a. As soon as T1 is on again, T2 follows T1. In Fig. 4-51b, T2 always remains on and thus follows T1 even faster.

4-6-2 Bandwidth of Cascode with Low R_L

For wide-band amplifiers the gain is small, but the bandwidth is pushed to high values. For this purpose, the load R_L is small. The gain is $-g_m R_L$. We will analyze this bandwidth next. High values of R_L are studied in the next section.

The output impedance of T1 (looking into the drain of T1) is high, whereas the input impedance of T2 (looking into the source of T2) is low, provided R_L is low. Thus, both stages are well isolated from each other. The small-signal calculations thus can be performed separately for each transistor. As load for T1, the input impedance of T2 is taken. As source for T2, the output impedance of T1 is taken.

As seen before, the input impedance of T2 equals $1/g_{m2}$ over a large range of frequencies. The most important pole of T1 thus is formed at the input node. Indeed, the cutoff frequency is given by

$$f_{p1} = \frac{1}{2\pi R_S(C_{GS} + M_c C_{DG})} \qquad (4\text{-}108a)$$

with

$$M_c = 1 + \frac{g_{m1}}{g_{m2}} + \frac{1}{g_{m2} R_S} \qquad (4\text{-}108b)$$

The gain (from G to D) of this stage is the Miller effect M_c. It equals only about g_{m1}/g_{m2}. Typically, its value is 1 to 3. Therefore, the Miller multiplication M_c of C_{DG} is small. Hence, the Miller effect is practically negligible. This is the main advantage of a cascode stage. Feedback capacitance C_{DG} is not multiplied by the total gain but only by 1 to 3, depending on the actual g_m values.

The most important pole of the output transistor T2 is realized at its drain, where the impedance is high. Its time constant is simply $R_L C_L$. We have seen this earlier, for a single amplifying stage and for a common-gate stage.

Which pole is dominant for the whole cascode stage, depends on the relative values of R_L and R_S. If an active load is used for R_L, the dominant pole is most certainly realized at the drain of T2. This stage then delivers high gain. The second pole then occurs at the input node. Moreover, a distant third pole is present at the middle node, which complicates matters considerably. Gain, bandwidth, and stability must be examined further.

4-6-3 Cascode with Active Load

For an active load (see Fig. 4-52a), the load resistor R_L is large because it consists of output resistances r_o. The gain is then given by

$$A_{v0} = g_{m1}(r_{\text{out1}} /\!/ r_{\text{out2}}) \qquad (4\text{-}109)$$

where

$$r_{\text{out1}} = r_{o3}$$

and

$$r_{\text{out2}} = r_{o1} + r_{o2}(1 + g_{m2}r_{o1}) \approx r_{o2}(1 + g_{m2}r_{o1})$$

The value of r_{out2} is much larger than r_{out1} because of the local feedback (with $T = g_{m2}r_{o1}$). In order to fully exploit the presence of this high resistance for high gain, a second cascode transistor must be added, as shown in Fig. 4-52b. The value of r_{out1} is then given by

$$r_{\text{out1}} = r_{o3} + r_{o4}(1 + g_{m4}r_{o3}) \approx r_{o4}(1 + g_{m4}r_{o3}) \qquad (4\text{-}110)$$

The gain A_{v0} then can be simplified (if $g_m r_o \gg 1$) to

$$A_{v0} = \frac{1}{2} g_{m1} r_{o1} g_{m2} r_{o2} \qquad (4\text{-}111)$$

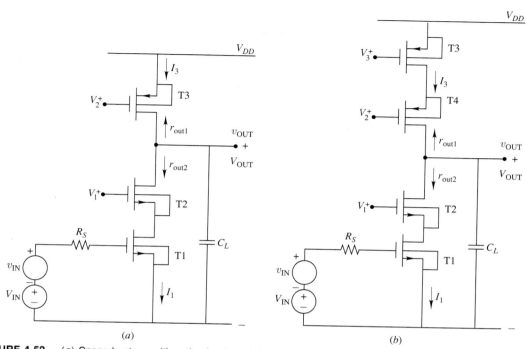

FIGURE 4-52   (a) Cascode stage with active load; and (b) cascode stage with cascode active load.

if r_{out1} is made larger than r_{out2} and $I_1 = I_3$. This value of A_{v0} can be made quite large. It is nearly twice (in dB) as large as the gain of a single transistor stage with active load. It depends on the current in the same way, however. In weak inversion $g_m r_o$ equals $V_E/(nkT/q)$, which is of the order of 50 dB. Thus, this cascode easily realizes 100 dB of gain. In strong inversion, however, this gain decreases linearly in proportion to the current.

The evolution of the gain versus R_L is given in Fig. 4-53. Both the gains from the input to the intermediate node v_m/v_{in} and from the input to the output v_{out}/v_{in} are given. The gain v_m/v_{in} is easily calculated by use of Eq. (4-72b). Note that both r_{o1} and r_{o2} are now included. For $R_L < r_{o2}$, the gain is indeed given by $-g_{m1}R_L$. Also, the gain of the first transistor is only $-g_{m1}/g_{m2}$, such that no Miller multiplication is present. For $R_L > r_{o1}(g_{m2}r_{o2})$, however, the Miller multiplication factor is much larger, i.e., $g_{m1}r_{o1}$. Capacitance C_{DG1} thus will also be multiplied by this factor and the maximum total gain is reached, as given by Eq. (4-111).

The approximate bandwidth is given by

$$f_d \approx \frac{1}{2\pi (r_{out1}//r_{out2})C_L} \qquad (4\text{-}112a)$$

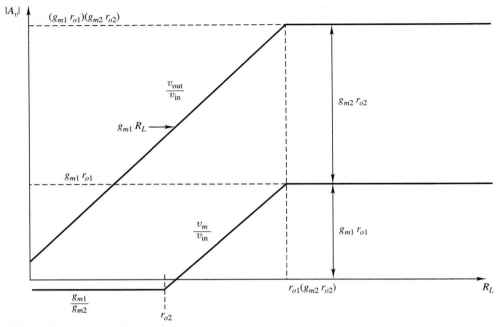

FIGURE 4-53   Gains versus R_L of cascode stage (Fig. 2-51a).

provided the value of R_L and of C_L are large, such that the dominant pole occurs at the output. In this case, the value of the gain-bandwidth product GBW is again given by

$$GBW = \frac{g_{m1}}{2\pi C_L} \qquad (4\text{-}112b)$$

The value of GBW thus is exactly the same as a single-transistor amplifier with active load. As a consequence, the cascode transistors realize more gain at low frequencies, but not more GBW (see Fig. 4-54a). Only the dominant pole occurs at lower frequencies and thus has become more dominant.

The Miller capacitance of the cascode transistor is not present in the GBW. This is the main advantage in using a cascode configuration.

One can wonder if the Miller effect is really absent because, after all, the impedance at the middle node increases for increasing load resistance. The gain over T1 is $g_{m1}r_{o1}$ for large values of R_L (see Fig. 4-53a). Therefore, the analysis is repeated with only two capacitances, i.e., C_L and C_{DG1}.

The voltage gain is calculated to be given by

$$A_v = -\frac{g_{m1}g_{m2}(1 - C_{DG1}/g_{m1}s)}{(g_{o1}g_{o2} + g_{m2}G_L) + (g_{m2}C_L + g_{DG1}C_{DG1})s + F_S C_L C_{DG1}s^2} \qquad (4\text{-}113)$$

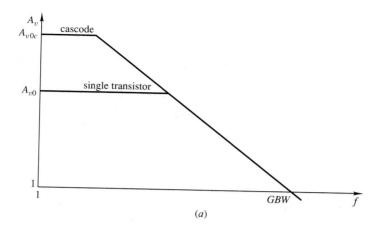

(a)

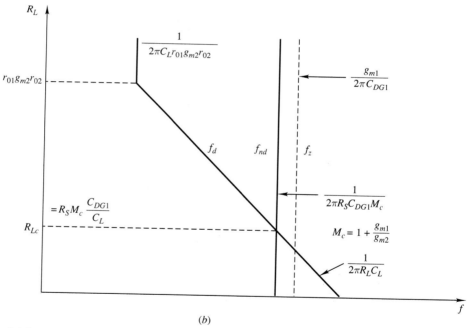

(b)

FIGURE 4-54   (a) A cascode has larger A_v, but the same GBW has a single transistor amplifier. (b) Pole-zero position diagram for cascode (Fig. 4-51a) for $C_L \gg C_{DG1}$.

with $g_{DG1} = F_S G_L + (1 + g_{m1} R_S) g_{o2}$

and $F_S = 1 + M_c g_{m2} R_S$

and $M_c = 1 + \dfrac{g_{m1}}{g_{m2}}$

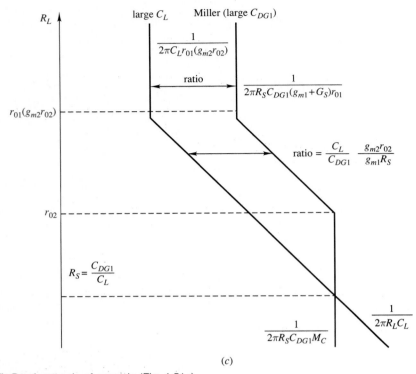

(c)

FIGURE 4-54 (cont'd) Dominant pole of cascode (Fig. 4-51a).

The pole-zero position plot for large $C_L > C_{DG1}$ is given versus R_L in Fig. 4-54b. The characteristic frequencies are added in the figure. It is clear that the Miller effect due to C_{DG1} would only be a consideration if R_L is very small (less than R_{Lc}, which is $\approx R_S M_c C_{DG1}/C_L$). This is never the case, however, because the gain would be too small as well. Thus, the conclusions with respect to the bandwidth and GBW above are valid.

If, on the other hand, the output capacitance is small, then a different picture emerges. The pole position diagram for $C_{DG1} > C_L$ is given in Fig. 4-54c. The dominant pole for $C_L > C_{DG1}$ is taken from Fig. 4-54b and is added for sake of comparison. It is seen from the ratio indicated in the figure, that whether C_L or C_{DG1} will provide the dominant pole depends on which numerical values are used. Normally, C_L is larger and the picture of Fig. 4-54b is valid.

From this plot (Fig. 4-54b), a design procedure can be derived. In order to ensure stability, we must ensure that the nondominant pole occurs at frequencies well beyond GBW. Since we have three nodes, we have a third-order system. The effects of two more capacitances must be added to the pole position plot of Fig. 4-54b. They are the input capacitance to ground C_{GS1}, and the capacitance from the middle node to ground $C_m = C_{DS1} + C_{GS2}$. Only the two extreme cases are examined, i.e., for R_L very small ($< r_{o2}$) and for R_L very large ($> r_{o1}(g_{m2}r_{o2})$). We will always assume that capacitance C_L is dominant.

For very small R_L, two poles and one zero are present (see Fig. 4-54b). Capacitance C_{GS1} can simply be added to C_{DG1}. It is clear that the two poles coincide around $R_{Lc} \approx R_S M_c C_{DG1}/C_L$. Thus, this point should be avoided.

For very large R_L, there is a dominant pole and a nondominant pole. We must be sure that the separation between both is sufficient. The nondominant pole must be at three times the GBW (given by Eq. (4-113)). This condition becomes

$$\frac{C_L}{C_{DG1}} \geq 3g_{m1}R_S M_c \tag{4-114}$$

It can be concluded that most cascodes behave as a two-pole system. The value of R_L and C_L can be used to set the values of the gain and the gain-bandwidth product.

Example 4-14

Design a cascode for a GBW of 10 MHz for a load of 10 pF. The source resistance is 1 kΩ. The low-frequency gain must be larger than 60 dB. Take $K'_n = 40 \ \mu A/V^2$, $K'_p = 15 \ \mu A/V^2$, $V_{En} = 5 \ V/\mu m$, and $V_{Ep} = 8 \ V/\mu m$.

Solution. From Eq. (4-112b) we obtain a minimum value of $g_m = 0.63$ mS. From Eq. (4-114) we learn (for $M_c \approx 2$) that C_{DG1} must be smaller than about 2.5 pF, which should not be a problem.

In order to obtain that gain we will need a double cascode, as in Fig. 4-52b. From Eq. (4-111) we learn that we need $g_{m1}r_{o1}g_{m2}r_{o2} = 2000$, in which $g_{m1} = 0.63$ mS. Substitution of g_m and r_o in these two equations allows us to determine the current I_1 and the transistor sizes.

We can carry out this design procedure in a more systematic way. Equations (4-112b), (4-114), and (4-111) give us three equations to use with five design parameters, i.e., current I_1 and transistor sizes W_1, L_1, W_2, and L_2. Two of the parameters thus can freely chosen. The design result will be dependent upon parameters we have chosen.

We have chosen the size of the input transistor. It is an amplifying device. Therefore, we take its length at its minimum value, i.e., $L_1 = 2 \ \mu m$ and its $(W/L)_1 = 10$; hence $W_1 = 20 \ \mu m$. All other values are now determined: from the value of g_{m1} we obtain $I_1 = 0.25$ mA. Also, $L_2 = 10 \ \mu m$ and $W_2 = 40 \ \mu m$. It is straightforward to determine the transistor sizes of T3 and T4 because the current is known, and $g_{m3}r_{o3}g_{m4}r_{o4} = 2000$ as well.

Again, the designer can now start manipulating data in order to gain some more insight. He can plot L_2 and I_1 versus I_1, etc. Software is easily written to generate all plots required for close inspection.

The SPICE file for this Example is given in Table 4-7.

TABLE 4-7   INPUT FILE FOR SPICE FOR THE *n*MOST CASCODE AMPLIFIER OF EXAMPLE 4-14 IN SEC. 4-6-3.

```
*Ex.4-14 (TEMPERATURE = 27.000 DEG C)
* CIRCUIT DESCRIPTION
M1 2 1 0 0 NMOS W=20U L=2U
M2 5 9 2 2 NMOSC W=40U L=10U
M3 6 7 4 4 PMOS W=50U L=2U
M4 5 8 6 6 PMOSC W=40U L=10U
VDD 4 0 DC 10
VIN 3 0 DC 1.255 AC 1
VC1 7 0 DC 8.741
VC2 8 0 DC 6.5
VC3 9 0 DC 3.5
CL 5 0 10P
RL 5 0 10MEG
RS 3 1 1K
.MODEL NMOS NMOS LEVEL=2 VTO=1 KP=60E-6 GAMMA=0.01 LAMBDA=0.1
.MODEL NMOSC NMOS LEVEL=2 VTO=1 KP=60E-6 GAMMA=0.01 LAMBDA=0.02
.MODEL PMOS PMOS LEVEL=2 VTO=-1 KP=24E-6 GAMMA=0.01 LAMBDA=0.066
.MODEL PMOSC PMOS LEVEL=2 VTO=-1 KP=24E-6 GAMMA=0.01 LAMBDA=0.0125
* CONTROL CARDS
.DC VIN 1.24 1.27 0.001
.PRINT DC V(5) V(VDD)
.AC DEC 10 100 1MEG
.PRINT AC VDB(5) VP(5)
.PLOT AC VDB(5) VP(5)
.WIDTH OUT = 75
.END
```

4-6-4 Noise Performance

The equivalent input noise of the cascode stage is the same as that of a single transistor stage. This is the second major advantage of using a cascode configuration.

The equivalent input noise $\overline{dv_2^2}$ of transistor T2 (in Fig. 4-55*a*) does not contribute to its drain current, if R_L is small. The situation is depicted in Fig. 4-55*b*. In an ideal source follower, the input voltage appears unattenuated at the source. Hence, its AC voltage v_{GS2} is zero; thus the AC current in the cascode transistor T2 is zero as well.

If an active load is used, such as that in Fig. 4-52*b*, the value of R_L can be quite high. As a result, the resistance at the middle node is coupled to R_L through r_{o2} (see Eq. (4-72*b*) and Fig. 4-53). The gain from the second transistor noise voltage $\overline{dv_2^2}$ to the output thus will also increase with increasing R_L. This gain is obtained by low-frequency analysis of the circuit in Fig. 4-55*b*, in which both r_{o1} and r_{o2} must be present. It is given by

$$\frac{\overline{dv_{\text{out}}}}{\overline{dv_2}} = \frac{R_L}{r_{o1}} \frac{1}{1 + \dfrac{R_L}{r_{o1} g_{m2} r_{o2}}} \tag{4-115}$$

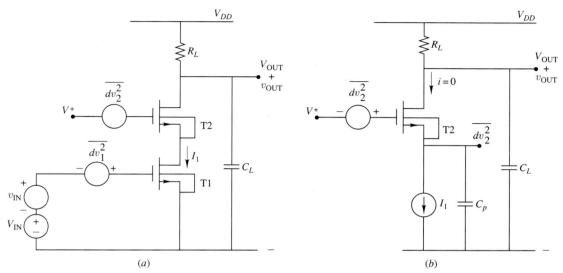

FIGURE 4-55   (a) Cascode stage with two equivalent input noise sources; and (b) the noise output of the cascode transistor is zero.

For small values of R_L, the gain increases proportionally. For very large values of R_L, the gain equals $g_{m2}r_{o2}$. This is a high value. It is actually the gain over the cascode transistor itself, as shown in Fig. 4-53. In this case, the noise of transistor T2 is as important as the noise of the input transistor T2.

The transistors T1 and T3 in Fig. 4-54b contribute equally to the output noise (see Sec. 4-5-8). As a result, all four transistors in Fig. 4-54b will provide comparable contributions to the output noise. Therefore, it is difficult to design a high-gain cascode stage with low noise.

4-6-5   High Voltage Cascode

It has become clear that the transistors in a normal cascode (Fig. 4-51a) serve a different function. Transistor T1 must generate transconductance and hence, gain. Transistor T2 screens the load R_L from transistor T1. This property can be exploited in a high-voltage cascode, where the positive supply voltage can increase up to high values (> 1000 V). Transistor T1 is optimized for high g_m. Its length L_1 is made as small as possible in order to realize a large ($W/L)_1$ value. As a result, its breakdown voltage is small, too, due to punchthrough. Bias voltage V^+ is small as well.

Transistor T2 is optimized for large breakdown voltage. Its length L_2 is made very large. This combination of high voltage with high gain is a third major advantage of using cascodes.

Note that for all cascode transistors, a decision must be made whether or not the bulk is connected to the source. Evidently this applies only to the nMOST in a p-well process and vice versa. If the bulks are connected to the substrate, the values of V_T

increase and the values of g_m decrease. In general, these effects are not important, provided they are considered in the choice of the biasing voltage V^+.

4-6-6   Cascode Stages with Bipolar Transistors

Cascode stages can be built with bipolar transistors in very much the same way they are with MOST. Again, four types can be distinguished (see Fig. 4-51). Two of them are given in Fig. 4-56: the normal cascode stage (Fig. 4-56a) and the folded cascode stage (Fig. 4-56b).

The advantages of the cascode stage amplifier are still valid, i.e., the Miller effect can be avoided such that larger values of GBW can be obtained.

If the pole at the output node is dominant, again the GBW is given by Eq. (4-112b). If the input capacitance or input resistance is large, the expression of the GBW in Eq. (4-32a) results. In this expression, C_{GS} must be replaced by $C_\pi + C_\mu$. For large currents, C_π is much larger than C_μ (see Chap. 1) and equals $g_m \tau_F$. Hence, the maximum value of GBW is given by

$$GBW_{\max} = \left(\frac{1}{2\pi}\right)\left(\frac{R'_L}{R_S}\right)\left(\frac{1}{\tau_F}\right) = \left(\frac{1}{2\pi}\right)\left(\frac{R'_L}{R_S}\right) f_{T\,\max} \qquad (4\text{-}116)$$

The second advantage of a cascode is that the noise of the cascode transistor does not occur because the output current is determined solely by driver transistor T1, not by cascode transistor T2. This is also valid for a bipolar cascode stage, if R_L is small.

FIGURE 4-56   (a) Cascode stage with $I_1 = I_2$; and (b) folded cascode stage $I_A = I_1 + I_2$.

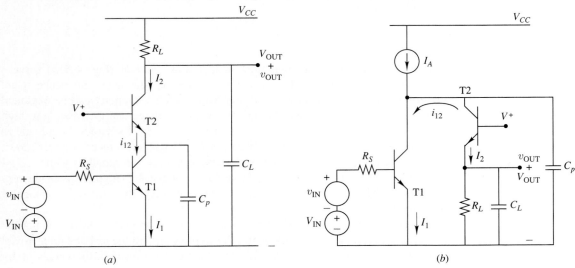

(a)   (b)

There is only one important difference between the bipolar transistor cascode and the MOST cascode. The impedance at the source of MOST T2 is always resistive and equals about $1/g_{m2} \cdot (1 + R_L/r_{o2})$. However, the impedance at the emitter of bipolar transistor T2 can be inductive because its base resistance interacts C_π. This inductance can form a resonant circuit with parasitic capacitance C_P (see Fig. 4-56) and generate peaking that can also appear at the output. Although this capacitance C_P is generally quite small with MOSTs, it is not small with bipolar transistors. With bipolar transistors, separate collector islands must be used. On the other hand, this capacitance is never large because no connections are made to this point. This has been studied in Sec. 4-3-2.

In a BICMOS process, a MOST or a bipolar transistor can be used in each position. Since we already have four configurations (see Fig. 4-51), we can now distinguish 16 different cascode stages. If different types of transistors are used for the input device and cascode, different currents can be used. Here, the configurations of Fig. 4-51b, c, and d, can be used. The current can be optimized in a different way for each separate device.

4-6-7 Feedforward in Cascode Amplifiers

Very high values of *GBW* can be obtained if feedforward is applied to the cascode transistor in the folded cascode of Fig. 4-57a (Sansen and Chang 1990). This is necessary, especially if the *pnp* transistor is of the lateral type; its f_T is fairly low (5 to 10 MHz). Therefore, it is advantageous to bypass a lateral transistor at high frequencies by means of a feedforward capacitance C_{FF}.

FIGURE 4-57 (a) Feedforward in cascode stage; and (b) small-signal equivalent circuit.

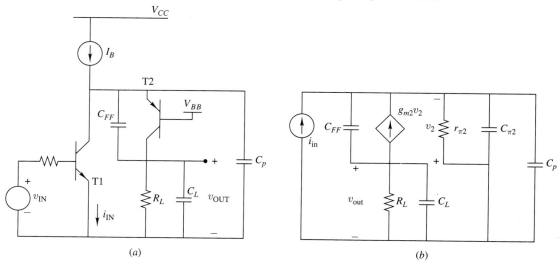

For analysis, transistor T1 is represented in Fig. 4-57b by a pure current source with value $i_{IN} = g_{m1} v_{IN}$. The output capacitance of T1 and the large input capacitance of T2 are lumped together in C_P. Transistor T2 is represented by $r_{\pi 2}$, $C_{\pi 2}$, and g_{m2}. Remember that $C_{\pi 2}$ can be large because the value of f_T is low.

The gain is obtained by straightforward analysis, as given by

$$\frac{v_{OUT}}{i_{IN}} \approx R_L \frac{1 + \dfrac{C_{FF}}{g_{m2}} s}{1 + \left(R_L C_L + \dfrac{C_{FF}}{g_{m2}} \right) s + \dfrac{R_L C^2}{g_{m2}} s^2} \tag{4-117}$$

with

$$C^2 = C_L(C_\pi + C_P) + C_{FF}(C_\pi + C_P + C_L)$$

in which $g_m R_L \gg 1$ is assumed and $C_\pi = C_{\pi 2}$.

Its pole-zero position plot is given in Fig. 4-58. For nearly zero value of C_{FF}, a dominant pole, a nondominant pole, and a zero occur. The characteristic frequencies are indicated in the diagram. The dominant pole is caused by the $R_L C_L$ time constant, as expected. The nondominant pole is caused by the parasitic capacitances C_π and C_P.

FIGURE 4-58   Pole-zero position diagram of cascode with feedforward capacitance C_{FF}.

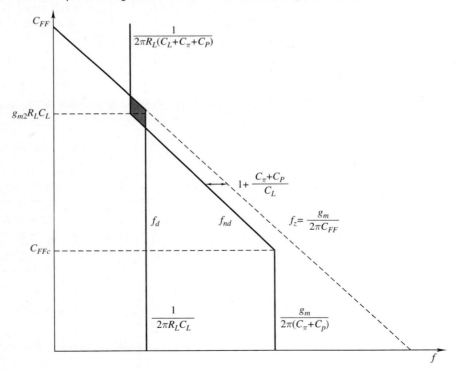

It occurs at frequencies that are not high enough to ensure stability. For this reason, C_{FF} is applied.

For increasing values of C_{FF} a zero occurs. It nearly coincides with the nondominant pole at values of C_{FF}, which are larger than C_{FFc}, given by

$$C_{FFc} = \frac{C_L(C_\pi + C_P)}{C_L + C_\pi + C_P} \tag{4-118}$$

At this point, the zero nearly compensates for the effect of the nondominant pole. But the compensation is never complete, because the nondominant pole and zero never actually cancel each other. There are several improvements possible on this schema in order to achieve exact cancellation (Sansen and Chang 1990). One such example is the addition of a resistance in series with the emitter of T2. Such actions lead to third-order systems, however, and are not discussed further in this text.

We have analyzed inverters and cascode stages. The most important two-transistor amplifiers, however, are the differential stages. They are the cornerstones of all analog integrated circuits. Therefore, they are analyzed in considerable detail in the next section.

4-7 DIFFERENTIAL STAGES

The most important analog building block is, without doubt, a differential pair. It is the input stage of an operational amplifier (op amp) and most integrated filters. Therefore, we must study it closely.

The differential pair is mainly composed of two equal (or matched) transistors. An example of such a differential pair with MOSTs is shown in Fig. 4-59. It consists of two equal transistors and a current source with value I_B, which biases both transistors T1 and T2 at the same current $I_B/2$. As a result, two input and two output terminals are available. For easy analysis, two other input voltages and output voltages are defined, each derived from the terminal voltages.

4-7-1 Definitions

The differential-mode input voltage v_{Id} and the average, or common-mode input voltage v_{Ic}, are derived from the applied input voltages v_{I1} and v_{I2}, as defined by

$$v_{Id} = v_{I1} - v_{I2} \tag{4-119a}$$

$$v_{Ic} = \frac{v_{I1} + v_{I2}}{2} \tag{4-119b}$$

In a similar way, at the output

$$v_{Od} = v_{O1} - v_{O2} \tag{4-120a}$$

$$v_{Oc} = \frac{v_{O1} + v_{O2}}{2} \tag{4-120b}$$

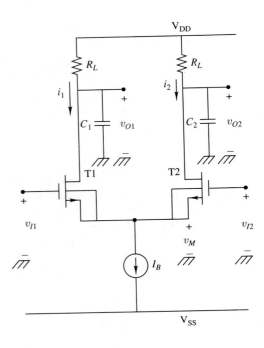

FIGURE 4-59   MOST differential stage.

Some designers take half the difference of v_{Id} and v_{Od}. This does not impair the following analysis. Note that all symbols v contain a DC and AC component as well.

The first goal of the differential stage is to amplify the differential component v_{Id} and only v_{Id}. The common-mode component v_{Ic} must be rejected. For example, if disturbances (such as power-supply hum and radio frequencies) are induced on both inputs, they generate a signal v_{Ic}. This signal must not be amplified by the differential stage; it must be rejected. To formally describe this rejection of common mode signals v_{Ic}, all gains must first be defined.

The four voltages defined by Eq. (4-119) and Eq. (4-120) allow us to define four gains, as given by

$$v_{Od} = A_{dd}v_{Id} + A_{dc}v_{Ic} \qquad (4\text{-}121a)$$

$$v_{Oc} = A_{cd}v_{Id} + A_{cc}v_{Ic} \qquad (4\text{-}121b)$$

Only the differential output voltage v_{Od} is of interest. Thus, only the gains A_{dd} and A_{dc} are to be investigated in more detail.

Obviously, gain A_{dd} is the real differential gain, which is the main purpose of this stage. According to Eq. (4-121a), however, v_{Od} can also be generated by a common-mode input signal v_{Ic}. The circuit schematic shows that v_{Od} can only be generated by v_{Ic} if asymmetry is present in the input transistors or load resistors. The threshold voltages V_T or values of K' can be slightly different, leading to a nonzero value of A_{dc}.

The measure of A_{dc}, with respect to A_{dd}, is the *Common Mode Rejection Ratio* (*CMRR*). It is defined as

$$CMRR = \frac{A_{dd}}{A_{dc}} \tag{4-122}$$

It also reflects the amount of common-mode input voltage v_{Ic} that is amplified or, in other words, the asymmetry in the input devices and load resistors. Typical values of *CMRR* are 80 dB for bipolar transistor differential stages and 60 dB for CMOST stages. The origin of this difference will be explained in Sec. 6-6.

In this chapter it is assumed that the input devices and loads are perfectly matched. Their parameter values are identical, hence $A_{dc} = 0$ and $CMRR = \infty$. For all further considerations on matching and finite *CMRR*, the reader is referred to Sec. 6-6.

First the transfer characteristic of the differential stage is analyzed. Then its small-signal performance is derived at low, as well as high frequencies. Finally, active loads are added with and without cascode stages. MOST devices are considered first.

4-7-2 MOST Differential Stages

DC Transfer Characteristic In Fig. 4-59, the value of v_{Od} is given by

$$v_{Od} = -R_L i_{Od} \tag{4-123a}$$

in which

$$i_{Od} = i_1 - i_2 \tag{4-123b}$$

Also,

$$I_B = i_1 + i_2 \tag{4-123c}$$

The currents i_1 and i_2 can be extracted from the two expressions above. They are given by:

$$2i_1 = I_B + i_{Od} \tag{4-124a}$$

$$2i_2 = I_B - i_{Od} \tag{4-124b}$$

On the other hand, the input voltages are related by:

$$v_{id} = v_{GS1} - v_{GS2} \tag{4-125}$$

$$v_{GS1} = V_T + \sqrt{\frac{i_1}{K'_n(W/L)}} \tag{4-126a}$$

$$v_{GS2} = V_T + \sqrt{\frac{i_2}{K'_n(W/L)}} \tag{4-126b}$$

in which $(W/L)_1 = (W/L)_2 = (W/L)$. The last two expressions are obtained by use of the simple quadratic i_{DS} versus v_{GS} relationship of a MOST and by neglecting output conductances. Also note that v_{BS} is zero for both transistors.

Substitution of v_{GS1} and v_{GS2} from Eq. (4-126) in Eq. (4-125) then yields

$$v_{Id} = \frac{1}{\sqrt{K_n'(W/L)}} \left(\sqrt{i_1} - \sqrt{i_2} \right) \tag{4-127}$$

Finally, substitution of i_1 and i_2 from Eq. (4-124) in Eq. (4-127) yields

$$\sqrt{1 + \frac{i_{Od}}{I_B}} - \sqrt{1 - \frac{i_{Od}}{I_B}} = \sqrt{\frac{2K_n'(W/L)}{I_B}} v_{Id} \tag{4-128}$$

This equation has the form

$$\sqrt{1 + y} - \sqrt{1 - y} = x \tag{4-129a}$$

in which $$y = \frac{i_{Od}}{I_B}$$

and $$x = \sqrt{\frac{2K_n'(W/L)}{I_B}} v_{Id} \quad \text{or} \quad = \frac{v_{Id}}{V_{GS} - V_T}.$$

The solution is given by

$$y = x\sqrt{1 - \frac{x^2}{4}} \tag{4-129b}$$

These relations are shown in Fig. 4-60. They are only valid if $|y| \leq 1$ or if $|x| \leq \sqrt{2}$. For larger values of x (or v_{Id}), y simply remains (+ or −) unity . This means that for $x = \pm\sqrt{2}$, $v_{Id} = \pm\sqrt{I_B/K_n'(W/L)}$, or $\pm\sqrt{2}(V_{GS} - V_T)$, all current flows in one transistor only. The other transistor is off. For larger values of v_{Id}, the transistor that is on acts as a source follower. The common source point (at voltage v_M) follows the input voltage (see Fig. 4-60c) with a difference of V_{GS} corresponding to I_B. For negative v_{I1}, the value of v_M is maintained at the same V_{GS} below zero volt (v_{I2}).

Small-Signal Behavior   For small values of v_{Id} or x, $y \approx x$, or by using Eqs. (4-127), (4-129a), and (4-129b):

$$v_{Od} = -R_L \sqrt{2K_n'(W/L)I_A} v_{Id} \tag{4-130a}$$

which can be written as

$$v_{Od} = -g_m R_L v_{Id} \tag{4-130b}$$

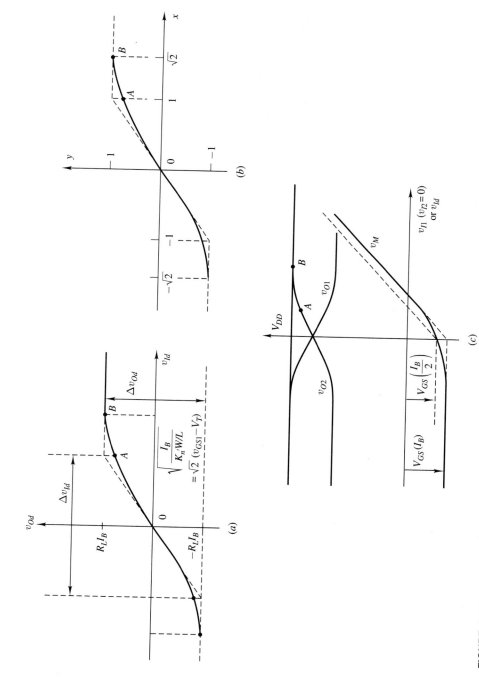

FIGURE 4-60 (a) Transfer curve of CMOS differential stage; and (b) expression (4-129b) of $y = x\sqrt{1 - (x^2/4)}$ for $|x| \leq \sqrt{2}$; and (c) node voltages for large v_{Id}

Note that $g_m = g_{m1} = g_{m2}$ is the transconductance of one transistor at current $I_B/2$. The small-signal gain thus is the same as that of a single transistor operating at the same current $I_B/2$, as each of the transistors of the differential stage.

The small-signal current in each transistor must be the same in magnitude, but opposite in sign. Any current that flows in transistor T1 must flow entirely through transistor T2 in the opposite direction. This is true because the DC current source does not take any AC current. The AC current $g_m v_{Id}$ thus circles around through both transistors and resistors R_L. Thus, the small-signal values of v_{GS} are also the same in magnitude but with opposite polarity. As a result, the small-signal value of v_M equals $(v_{I1} + v_{I2})/2$. In other words, it is zero for a symmetrical input drive, i.e., if $v_{I2} = -v_{I1}(v_{Id} = 2v_{I1}$ and $v_{Ic} = 0)$ (see Fig. (4-61a). It equals v_{I1} if $v_{I2} = v_{I1}(v_{Id} = 0$ and $v_{Ic} = v_{I1})$. In the latter case, no small-signal current can flow in either transistor because I_B is generated by an ideal DC current source that does not allow AC current to flow (see Fig. 4-61b).

There is a third possibility, i.e., when an input voltage v_{I1} is applied to one input only, and at the other one $v_{I2} = 0$ (see Fig. 4-61c). In this case $v_{Id} = v_{I1}/2$ and $v_M = v_{I1}/2$, as well. The AC current is now only half of what was obtained in the first case.

Where $v_{Id} = v_{I1}$ and $v_{Ic} = 0$, there is a purely symmetrical or differential drive and $v_M = 0$ for all small signals. Thus, the small-signal equivalent circuit of the differential stage falls into two separate, equal single-transistor equivalent circuits with grounded source. The analysis for a single transistor amplifying stage also applies to the gain, as it does for the bandwidth and the gain-bandwidth product. Finally, at all points the impedances are easily found. The impedance at the common source point corresponds with the output impedance of two ideal source followers in parallel. At low frequencies it equals $1/2g_m$.

Active Loads   In order to increase the gain, active loads can be used (see Fig. 4-62a) to lead to exactly the same small-signal analysis as for a single transistor amplifier with active load.

FIGURE 4-61   Differential- and common-mode voltages for a differential stage under different drive conditions.

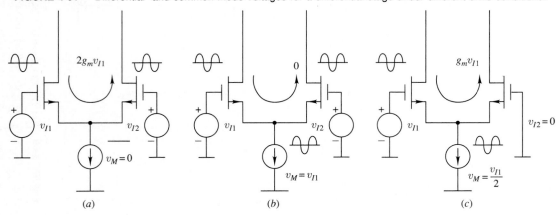

(a)   (b)   (c)

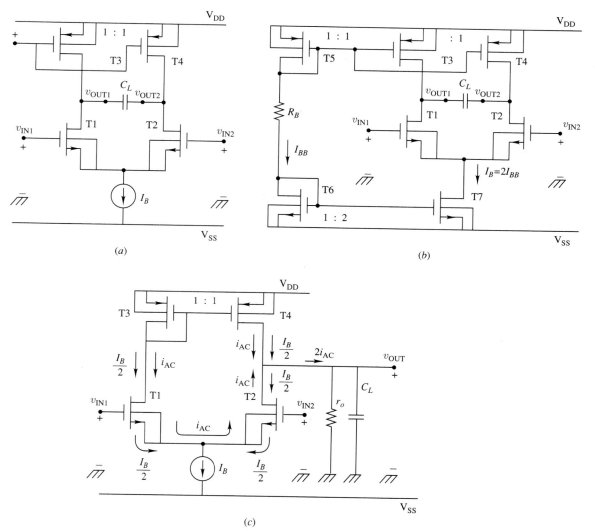

FIGURE 4-62   (a) Differential stage with active loads; (b) differential stage with active load and biasing network; and (c) self biasing differential stage with active load.

However, a biasing problem occurs. An active load acts as a current source. Thus it must be biased with V^+ such that their currents add up exactly to I_B. In practice this is quite difficult. Thus, a feedback circuit is required to ensure this equality. An example of such a (common-mode) feedback circuit is shown in Fig. 4-62b.

Transistors T5 and T6 are connected as a diode. Together with R_B, they define current I_{BB} as given by $(V_{DD} - V_{SS} - V_{SD5} - V_{DS6})/R_B$.

On the other hand, transistors T3, T4, and T5 all have the same W/L ratio. They also have the same voltage v_{GS}, hence the same drain current I_{BB}. Also, transistors

T6 and T7 have the same V_{GS}, but their aspect ratio's W/L differ by a factor of two. The current in T7 thus is $2I_{BB}$ or I_B. It is exactly the sum of the currents through T1 and T2.

The combination T6 and T7 is a *current mirror*. T3, T4, and T5 also form a current mirror. One transistor is always connected as a diode and drives the other transistors. Their value of V_{GS} is the same. Thus their currents depend only on their respective W/L ratios. They will be studied in more detail in Sec. 4-8.

Mismatching between the transistors and differences in V_{DS} can cause errors in the output current matching. The schematic of Fig. 4-62*b* performs well in first order, but fails to function properly because of second-order effects. Therefore we do not consider it further.

Direct use of a current mirror as a load for a differential stage, leads to the self-biasing circuit of Fig. 4-62*c*. If transistors T3 and T4 are well-matched, then the DC currents are the same in all transistors, i.e., $I_B/2$.

For small signals, the picture is very different. The output load is made up by the output resistances and is denoted by r_o. Current mirror T3, T4 mirrors the small-signal currents, as well. The currents in T3 and T4 thus have the same small-signal component i_{AC}. This current i_{AC} flows through T1, but is reversed in T2, since no AC current can be taken up by the current source I_B. The small-signal current that flows out of the differential stage to ground, through C_L and the output resistance r_o, is $2i_{AC}$. This is different from the previous circuit (Fig. 4-62*a*), where the AC current flows through the two top transistors, then in parallel through C_L and the output resistance r_o. This is a much more symmetrical arrangement than that seen in Fig. 4-62*c*. On the other hand, the self-biasing circuit of Fig. 4-62*c* provides a double-to-single conversion. The output can be taken from one single output node, yet is functionally a differential output.

Symmetry is broken in Fig. 4-62*c*. Transistor T3 offers only a low DC voltage drop (V_{GS3}) and a low AC impedance ($1/g_{m3}$ at low frequencies) to T1. Transistor T3 offers a much larger DC voltage drop (V_{DS4}) and much higher AC output impedance (r_{o4} at low frequencies) to T2. This usually results in offset and other effects that will be discussed in Chap. 6.

The gain is the same as before. Indeed, current i_{AC} equals $g_m v_{id}$. Thus, the gain is simply given by

$$A_{v0} = g_m r_o \tag{4-131}$$

with $r_o = r_{o2}//r_{o4}$ and $g_m = g_{m1} = g_{m2}$. Note that factor 2 has dropped out.

Only transistor T3 does not directly figure in the calculations, since it is the same as transistor T4.

Detailed Analysis of the Low Frequency Gain   The actual AC current flow is more complicated than the simple Eq. (4-131) suggests. The exact situations for the different cases are depicted in Fig. 4-63. In these figures the resistances r_o are shown explicitly to show how the currents actually flow through them.

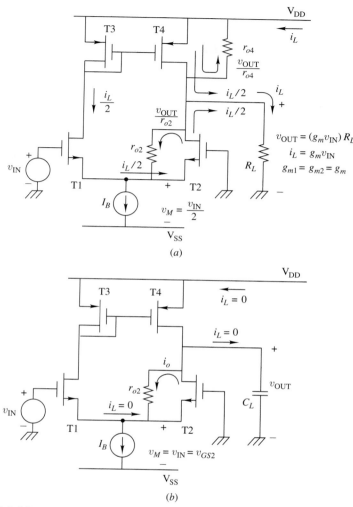

FIGURE 4-63   (a) AC currents in differential pair with $R_L \ll r_{o2}$, r_{o4}; (b) AC currents in differential pair with $R_L \gg r_{o2}$, $r_{o4} = \infty$ at low frequencies.

The resistances r_{o1} and r_{o3} are never shown. The AC voltage at the drain of T1 is always small because T3 only represents a resistance of $1/g_{m3}$. Thus this AC voltage is always small. The currents through r_{o1} and r_{o3} are quite low and negligible. Therefore, r_{o1} and r_{o3} are omitted in the following analyses. That this is the case can be easily verified by SPICE.

In the first example, the load resistance R_L is assumed to be much smaller than either r_{o2} or r_{o4}. An AC current thus is drawn from the output of this stage through R_L to ground. This AC current is denoted by i_L. This current is always drawn from

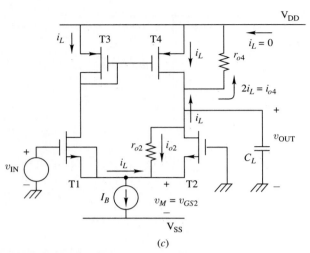

FIGURE 4-63 (cont'd) AC currents in differential pair at low frequencies.

the positive power supply V_{DD}. As expected, it is given by $i_L = g_m v_{IN}$, where the g_m's of the input transistors are taken as the same. The voltage gain is simply $g_m R_L$. Note, however, that additional AC current flows through the resistances r_{o2} and r_{o4} (as indicated in Fig. 4-63a). On the other hand, at the common-source point the AC voltage is exactly $v_M = v_{IN}/2$, as expected.

If the load resistor is omitted, the currents are different. In Fig. 4-63b the resistance R_L is replaced by a capacitance C_L. At low frequencies, this represents an infinite impedance. Hence, current i_L is zero at low frequencies. At higher frequencies this capacitance represents a finite impedance and again we have the situation as shown in Fig. 4-63a.

In the case of Fig. 4-63b the situation is simplified because r_{o4} is taken infinite and only r_{o2} is left. This can be realized quite easily if L_4 is given a large value. In this case straightforward analysis shows that AC current only flows in transistor T2 and r_{o2}. Its value is $g_m v_{IN}$. It determines the gain A_{dd}, which is $g_m r_{o2}$ as expected. As a result the full input voltage v_{IN} appears across T2, i.e., $v_{GS2} = v_{IN}$ and $v_M = v_{IN}$ as well.

Finally, the most general situation is shown in Fig. 4-63c. The analysis is now much more complicated. All transistors again carry an AC current, denoted by i_L. The current i_{o4} through r_{o4} equals v_{OUT}/r_{o4}. This current must be equal to $2i_L$, because no AC current is drawn from the power supply V_{DD}; no AC current is flowing through C_L, either. As a result, a current i_L is required from T2. This current i_L is obviously flowing through T1 also. The only remaining question is how much current is flowing through r_{o2} and what are the values of v_{GS1} and v_{GS2} (which equals $-v_M$)?

The governing circuit equations are given by

$$v_{IN} = v_{GS1} - v_{GS2}$$

$$i_L = g_{m1}v_{GS1}$$

$$i_L + i_{o2} = -g_{m2}v_{GS2}$$

$$v_{OUT} - v_M = i_{o2}r_{o2}$$

$$v_{OUT} = 2i_L r_{o4}$$

$$v_M = -v_{GS2}.$$

(4-132a)

From these equations we easily find that the gain A_{dd} is given by Eq. (1-131), provided $g_m r_{o4} \gg 1$. Also,

$$v_{GS1} = \frac{v_{IN}}{2(1 + r_{o4}/r_{o2})}$$

(4-132b)

$$v_M = -v_{GS2} = -\frac{1 + 2r_{o4}/r_{o2}}{2(1 + r_{o4}/r_{o2})}v_{IN}$$

(4-132c)

We notice that v_{GS2} is larger than v_{GS1} in magnitude. This is a result of the asymmetry of the active load configuration T3, T4.

We also notice that with a capacitive load, no AC current is drawn from C_L nor from the power supply V_{DD} at low frequencies. The higher the frequency, however, the more current is taken up by C_L, and hence returned by power supply V_{DD}. In this case we again observe the situation illustrated in Fig. 4-63a.

Gain-Bandwidth Product   The bandwidth is evidently given by

$$f_{-3dB} = \frac{1}{2\pi r_o C_L}$$

(4-133a)

and the gain-bandwidth GBW by

$$GBW = \frac{g_m}{2\pi C_L}$$

(4-133b)

as expected.

Remember, however, that the node capacitance at the drain of T1 also forms a nondominant pole. Since v_M at the common-source point is not always zero (as in Fig. 4-63c), a second nondominant pole can be present. A detailed design procedure is given in Chap. 6.

An interesting problem arises when we consider the simplest differential amplifier of Fig. 4-59, where load capacitances C_L is connected from both drains of T1 and T2 to ground. Does this configuration have two poles (because there are two capacitances) or only one?

Two capacitances on two different nodes would normally give rise to a two-pole system. On the other hand, comparison with Fig. 4-62a leads us to believe that the same effect can be realized with only one capacitance, albeit with value $C_L/2$. The circuit of Fig. 4-62a certainly is a first-order system. There is only one capacitance. A detailed analysis (see exercises) shows that both circuits behave as a single-pole system. It is located at the same frequency, provided the load capacitance of Fig. 4-62a is $C_L/2$.

This is also true if the load resistances are slightly different. Then two poles occur. The effect of the second pole is compensated, however, by a zero between both poles (see exercises), resulting again in a first-order characteristic.

Slew Rate In a differential stage with active load, an input voltage of $\sqrt{I_B/K'_n(W/L)}$ or $\sqrt{2}(V_{GS} - V_T)$ is sufficient to draw all the current I_B through one input transistor only (see Fig. 4-60). When we apply an input voltage that is much larger, slew rate limiting occurs.

The current mirror follows this current drive instantaneously, such that a constant current with value I_B is forced through the load capacitances. Then the slope of the output voltage is limited and given by the slew rate, which is obviously I_B versus C_L.

The ratio SR/GBW thus is given by

$$\frac{SR}{2\pi GBW} = \frac{I_B}{g_m} \qquad (4\text{-}134a)$$

For MOST in strong inversion, this is also given by

$$\frac{SR}{2\pi GBW} = \sqrt{\frac{I_B}{2K'_n(W/L)}} = V_{GS} - V_T \qquad (4\text{-}134b)$$

This value is small for large currents. Relatively large SR's thus can only be obtained deep in the strong inversion region (where $V_{GS} - V_T$ is large). For this reason, MOSTs are used quite often for the differential input stages in high performance operational amplifiers.

Parasitic capacitances on the other nodes cause the actual charging current to be slightly different from I_B. Both situations for positive and negative switching input voltage are depicted in Fig. 4-64. Hence, the positive SR slightly differs from the negative SR. For example, during the charging cycle (Fig. 4-64a), capacitance C_{p1} must be charged up, as well. It draws additional current from the positive power supply, increasing SR_+. This effect is slightly compensated by the very small discharge of C_{p2} (V_{GS3} hardly changes). When C_L is discharging, capacitance C_{p1} discharges as well, decreasing the current I_B available for the SR_-. Thus, the positive SR_+ is smaller than the negative SR_- in this configuration.

Noise Performance The noise performance of the self-biasing differential stage of Fig. 4-62c will be analyzed first. For this purpose, the noise-source powers of all transistors must be added together. In Fig. 4-65, the drain-source thermal noise

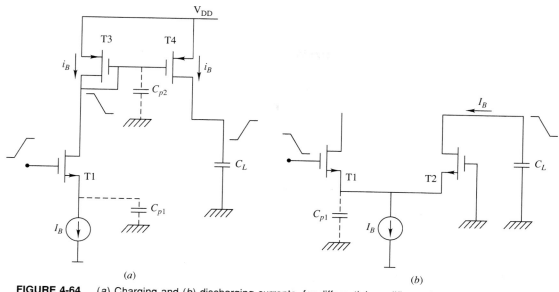

(a)   (b)

FIGURE 4-64   (a) Charging and (b) discharging currents, for differential amplifier under overdrive (or slew rate) conditions.

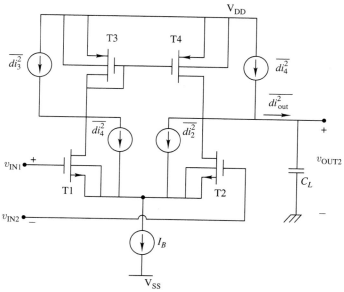

FIGURE 4-65   Differential stage of Fig. 4-62c with the noise current sources added.

current generator is shown for all four transistors. Their contribution to the output load is easily observed in the figure. The total output noise current power is given by

$$\overline{di_{\text{out}}^2} = \frac{8kT}{3}(g_{m1} + g_{m2} + g_{m3} + g_{m4})df \qquad (4\text{-}135)$$

Note that $8kT/3 = 1.1 \times 10^{-20}$ VC or W at 27°C. The equivalent input noise voltage power is then given by

$$\overline{dv_{ieq}^2} = \frac{\overline{di_{\text{out}}^2}}{g_{m1}^2} = \frac{8kT}{3}\frac{y}{g_{m1}}df \qquad (4\text{-}136a)$$

in which

$$y = 2\left(1 + \frac{g_{m3}}{g_{m1}}\right) \qquad (4\text{-}136b)$$

is the excess noise factor; note that for reasons of symmetry $g_{m1} = g_{m2}$ and $g_{m3} = g_{m4}$. This factor y indicates how many times a particular circuit provides more noise power than a single transistor amplifier.

For optimum noise performance, g_{m3} must be made smaller than g_{m1}. Then $y \approx 2$, and the equivalent input noise voltage power is twice that of a single transistor amplifier, the equivalent input noise voltage is $\sqrt{2}$ times worse than the equivalent input noise voltage of a single transistor amplifier, running at the same current as each transistor of the differential pair.

How can a designer make the ratio g_{m3}/g_{m1} smaller? This ratio is given by

$$\frac{g_{m3}}{g_{m1}} = \sqrt{\frac{\mu_3(W/L)_3}{\mu_1(W/L)_1}} \qquad (4\text{-}137)$$

For the configuration of Fig. 4-65, in which the pMOST transistors are on top, the ratio μ_3/μ_1 is about 1/2. Therefore, $(W/L)_3$ must also be made smaller than $(W/L)_1$, which is easy to do.

For symmetrical gain we have also tried to make $r_{o3} = r_{o1}$, which leads to

$$\frac{L_3}{L_1} = \frac{V_{En}}{V_{Ep}} \qquad (4\text{-}138)$$

In an n-well CMOS process $V_{Ep} > V_{En}$, thus $L_3 < L_1$, which makes it easy to realize $(W/L)_3 > (W/L)_1$, as well.

Similar conclusions can be drawn for the differential amplifier of Fig. 4-62b. Expressions similar to those above are valid here, as well. Moreover, the noise generated by all common-mode components such as T5, T6, T7, and R_B is cancelled by taking a differential output. Obviously this is also the case for the noise associated with current source I_B and the power supply voltages V_{DD} and V_{SS} in Fig. 4-65. None of these contribute to the output voltage.

For the differential amplifier with resistive loads (see Fig. 4-59), the noise contribution of resistor R_L is usually negligible with respect to the noise contribution of the transistor itself. Actually, this is the case as soon as $g_m R_L > 3/2$.

As a result, the current excess factor y can always be reduced to a factor of two. This is the same result as that of a differential stage with active loads.

This equivalent input noise voltage power of Eq. (4-136a) can be added in series with either terminal of the differential amplifier (see Fig. 4-66), because the noise generators represent powers, which do not have a polarity.

Example 4-15

Let us design a MOS differential amplifier for a voltage gain of 50 dB and a symmetrical input range of 1 V. The transistor parameters are $V_T = 1$ V, $K'_n = 40$ μA/V^2 and $K'_p = 15$ μA/V^2; $V_{En} = 5$ V/μm and $V_{Ep} = 8$ V/μm. Calculate the current and the W's and L's required if noise is to be minimized, as well.

Solution. From Eq. (4-129) with the input range we find that the minimum value of $V_{GS} - V_T = 0.5/\sqrt{2} = 0.35$ V. From Eq. (4-131) of the gain (which is 50 dB or 330), we obtain an expression from which the current has disappeared (since $g_m/I_{DS} = 2/(V_{GS}-V_T)$). For $r_{o2} = r_{o4}$, this equation is $V_{En}L_1 = 330(V_{GS}-V_T) = 115$ V. This yields $L_1 = 23$ μm. Also, since $L_3/L_1 = 5/8$, we find $L_3 \approx 14$ μm. Note that $g_{m1} = 0.16$ mS.

The values of the width W will now determine the current: the larger the W, the larger the current. We choose $(W/L)_1 \approx 4$ such that $W_1 \approx 100$ μm. The current is then 20 μA and $I_B = 40$ μA. For low noise we must take $(W/L)_3 \ll (W/L)_1$. Therefore, we take $W_3 = 4$ μm such that $(W/L)_3 = 0.3$. The excess noise factor is about 2.2, which is very close to the optimum of 2. The equivalent input noise itself is 12 nV$_{RMS}/\sqrt{Hz}$.

In Table 4-8, a SPICE input file is given for this differential stage. The results show that the gain is slightly less (47 dB) and that the noise is somewhat larger (16 nV$_{RMS}/\sqrt{Hz}$).

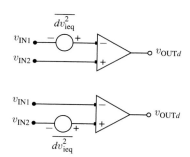

FIGURE 4-66   Inclusion of the equivalent input noise voltage in a MOST differential amplifier.

TABLE 4-8   INPUT FILE FOR THE SPICE FOR THE MOST DIFFERENTIAL AMPLIFIER OF EXAMPLE 4-15 IN SEC. 4-7-2.

```
* Ex.4-15 (TEMPERATURE = 27.000 DEG C)
* CIRCUIT DESCRIPTION
M1 4 1 5 5 NMOS W=100U L=23U
M2 2 0 5 5 NMOS W=100U L=23U
M3 4 4 6 6 PMOS W=4U L=14U
M4 2 4 6 6 PMOS W=47 L=14U
VDD 6 0 DC 5
VSS 7 0 DC -5
VIN 3 0 DC 0.006 AC 1
CL 2 0 10P
RL 2 0 10MEG
RS 3 1 1K
IB 5 7 40U
.MODEL NMOS NMOS LEVEL=2 VTO=1 KP=60E-6 GAMMA=0.01 LAMBDA=0.009
.MODEL PMOS PMOS LEVEL=2 VTO=-1 KP=24E-6 GAMMA=0.01 LAMBDA=0.009
* CONTROL CARDS
.DC VIN 0 0.01 0.001
.PRINT DC V(2)
.AC DEC 10 1K 1 MEG
.PRINT AC VDB(2) VP(2)
.PLOT AC VDB(2) VP(2)
.NOISE V(2) VIN 10
.WIDTH OUT = 75
.END
```

4-7-3 Bipolar Transistor Differential Stages

The differential stage with bipolar transistors behaves in very much the same way as it does with MOSTs. It is shown in Fig. 4-67. The differential-mode and common-mode input and output voltages are defined as before. Also, all definitions and remarks made on the various gains and the *CMRR* are valid, as well. A bipolar transistor's transfer characteristic is analyzed first.

Transfer Characteristic   In a bipolar transistor, the collector current i_C and the base-emitter voltage v_{BE} are related by the well-known exponential relationship (see Chap. 2) given by

$$i_C = I_{CS} \exp\left(\frac{v_{BE}}{V_t}\right) \tag{4-139}$$

in which I_{CS} is the saturation current and $V_t = kT/q$ (26 mV at 29°C or 302 K).

The differential output voltage is given, in general, by Eq. (4-120a) and now equals $v_{0d} = -R_L i_{0d}$, in which

$$i_{0d} = i_1 - i_2 = I_{CS}\left[\exp\left(\frac{v_{BE1}}{V_t}\right) - \exp\left(\frac{v_{BE2}}{V_t}\right)\right] \tag{4-140}$$

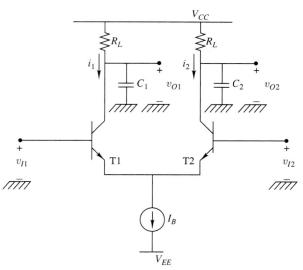

FIGURE 4-67   Bipolar transistor differential stage.

The sum of the collector currents is kept constant and equals current I_B of the ideal current source. As a consequence,

$$i_B = i_1 + i_2 = I_{CS} \left[\exp\left(\frac{v_{BE1}}{V_t} \right) - \exp\left(\frac{v_{BE2}}{V_t} \right) \right] \qquad (4\text{-}141)$$

On the other hand, the differential input voltage is again given by Eq. (4-119a), in which

$$v_{Id} = v_{BE1} - v_{BE2} \qquad (4\text{-}142)$$

Substitution of v_{BE1} from Eq. (4-142) in Eq. (4-140) and Eq. (4-141) allows elimination of v_{BE1}. Division of Eq. (4-140) by Eq. (4-141) also allows elimination of v_{BE2}, which then yields

$$\frac{i_{Od}}{I_B} = \frac{\exp\left(\dfrac{v_{Id}}{V_t} \right) - 1}{\exp\left(\dfrac{v_{Id}}{V_t} \right) + 1} \qquad (4\text{-}143a)$$

or

$$\frac{i_{Od}}{I_B} = \tanh\left(\frac{v_{Id}}{2V_t} \right) \qquad (4\text{-}143b)$$

The latter expression is depicted in Fig. 4-68. It contains a region around the origin where the slope is constant. This slope is the small-signal gain. It is easily derived

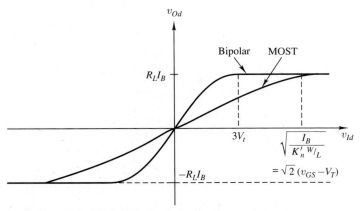

FIGURE 4-68   Transfer characteristic of bipolar transistor differential stage.

from Eq. (4-143b) for small values of v_{Id}. For $x < 1$, $\tanh(x) \approx x$ and

$$v_{Od} = -R_L I_B \frac{v_{Id}}{2V_t} \tag{4-144a}$$

or for small signals

$$v_{Od} = -g_{m1} R_L v_{Id} \tag{4-144b}$$

as could be expected. For large values of v_{Id} (actually a few times V_t or $3V_t$ in Fig. 4-68), all current flows in transistor T1, whereas transistor T2 is off.

Then the output voltage simply equals $R_L I_B$ and the small signal gain is zero. An exponential tail connects the region of constant (small-signal) gain to the region of zero gain.

In Fig. 4-68, the transfer characteristic of a MOST (see also Fig. 4-60a) is added for comparison. It is clear that the MOST has a much flatter characteristic. This region can be considered in the design, however. It has an additional design parameter that is sufficient to work close to the weak inversion region where $v_{GS} - V_T$ is small to realize a similar characteristic as for a bipolar transistor. For a bipolar transistor, it is not part of the design procedure. It is always approximately $3kT/q$. As a consequence, the design procedure is simpler for a bipolar transistor (see Sec. 2-10).

Active Loads   In order to increase the gain of a bipolar transistor differential stage, active loads can be used in much the same way as they are for MOST differential stages. Again, biasing networks are required in order to ensure exact ratios of the currents flowing. A self-biasing differential stage is shown in Fig. 4-69. It operates in the same way as its MOST equivalent in Fig. 4-62c. It is not the best solution for symmetry, but it does allow easy biasing.

The expressions of the gain, *GBW*, and slew rate have already been discussed for the MOST differential stage. They are exactly the same as given by Eq. (4-131) through Eq. (4-134).

Noise Performance   Another important difference between a MOST and a bipolar transistor is that base current flows in a bipolar transistor. Hence, shot noise is associated with this current (see Chap. 2), which gives rise to an equivalent input noise current generator $\overline{di_i^2}$ at the input, which is not present in a MOST. As a result, each transistor in Fig. 4-67 and Fig. 4-69 has two equivalent input noise generators, i.e., $\overline{dv_i^2}$ and $\overline{di_i^2}$. The noise of the current source I_B is in negligible first-order, because a differential output is taken (see Chap. 6).

All eight noise sources are shown in Fig. 4-70. They can be represented by one equivalent input noise voltage source, $\overline{dv_{ieq}^2}$, and one equivalent input current source, $\overline{di_{ieq}^2}$. Since they do not have a polarity, they can be connected to either input terminal of the differential amplifier. Thus, four different ways exist to connect them, two of which are shown in Fig. 4-71.

In order to calculate the value of $\overline{di_{ieq}^2}$, the input terminals must be grounded such that the effect of $\overline{di_{ieq}^2}$ is made nihil. Calculation of the output current shows that

$$\overline{dv_{ieq}^2} = 2(\overline{dv_1^2} + \overline{dv_3^2})\qquad(4\text{-}145a)$$

FIGURE 4-69   Self-biasing differential stage with active lead.

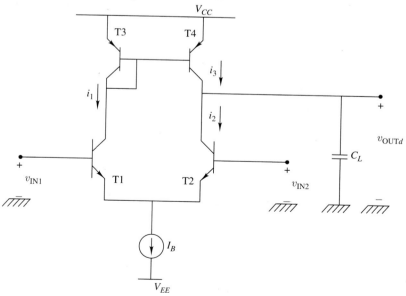

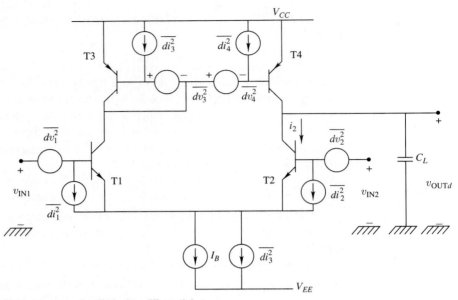

FIGURE 4-70   Noise sources of self-biasing differential stage.

which is exactly the same result as for a MOST differential stage with active loads. This can also be written as

$$\overline{dv_{ieq}^2} = y\overline{dv_1^2} \qquad (4\text{-}145b)$$

in which y is the excess noise factor. It is thus given by

$$y = 2\left(1 + \frac{\overline{dv_3^2}}{\overline{dv_1^2}}\right) = 2\left(1 + \frac{g_{m1}}{g_{m3}}\right) = 2(1+1) = 4 \qquad (4\text{-}145c)$$

FIGURE 4-71   Inclusion of equivalent input noise sources in a bipolar transistor differential amplifier.

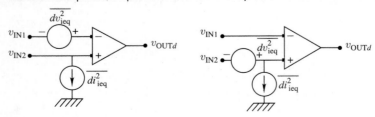

This is a surprising result. It shows that all four transistors contribute equally to the output noise. Also, this is a factor of two worse than what can be achieved with MOST transistors!

In order to calculate the value of $\overline{di_{ieq}^2}$, the input terminals must be left open so that the sources $\overline{dv_i^2}$ do not play a role. Calculation of the output currents then shows that

$$\overline{di_{ieq}^2} = 2\overline{di_1^2} \qquad (4\text{-}146)$$

This result is of little importance, however, because a bipolar transistor differential pair is never current driven; it is always voltage driven. For this purpose the source resistance must be made low, i.e., less than r_π. The effect of the $\overline{dv_{ieq}^2}$ source is then dominant.

Example 4-16

Let us use a bipolar transistor differential amplifier at $I_B = 40\ \mu\text{A}$. What are the values of the voltage gain, the input range, and the noise, in comparison to those of the MOST differential stage of Example 4-15? The transistor parameters are given in Table 4-3 with $V_E = 40$ V.

Solution. The output resistance r_o is V_E versus I_{CE}, which is 2 MΩ. The total output resistance is thus half of the resistance, which is 1 MΩ. Also, $g_m = 0.77$ mS. From Eq. (4-131) of the gain, we obtain an expression from which the current has disappeared again (since $g_m/I_{CE} = q/kT$). The gain is thus half of qV_E/kT, which is 770 (or 58 dB). It is a little larger than that of the MOST amplifier.

The input range, however, is only about 6 kT/q or about 150 mV, which is a factor of 6 lower than that with MOSTs. Is this an advantage or a disadvantage? For conventional amplifiers this is an advantage, since less drive is needed. As soon as distortion specifications are considered, however, this is a disadvantage. The MOST differential amplifier can take about six times more input drive before distortion appears.

The excess noise factor is 4, nearly two times as much as that of MOSTs. However, if we calculate the values of the equivalent input noise voltage $\overline{dv_{ieq}}$, then we have approximately 7.6 nV$_{\text{RMS}}/\sqrt{\text{Hz}}$ for the bipolar stage, which is smaller than the 12 nV$_{\text{RMS}}/\sqrt{\text{Hz}}$ of the MOST differential stage.

BICMOS Differential Stages   In BICMOS technology we can realize many different differential amplifiers (as in Fig. 4-62c): two types of full CMOS differential amplifiers (nMOST input devices or pMOST input devices), two types of bipolar amplifiers, and four types of BICMOS amplifiers (nMOST or pMOST, or npn or pnp input devices), totaling eight choices. The differences between MOST and bipolar devices have been highlighted in Sec. 2-10. Therefore, it will depend on the actual specifications to which the designer gives priority. For example, for high slew rate or for zero input biasing current, MOST input devices are preferred. For lower input noise, bipolar devices seem to do better. This compromise will be amply illustrated by means of the operational amplifiers examples in App. 6-2.

In this chapter, gain, high frequency performance, and noise of single and two-transistor amplifiers and buffer stages have been analyzed. With these stages, operational amplifiers and other analog integrated circuits will be designed in Chap. 6.

Before we attempt to do this, however, current mirrors must be described. These have been used as active loads, but they can be used as amplifiers as well. They are essential building blocks in biasing networks, too. As a consequence, they are the most important analog building blocks, other than the differential stages.

4-8 CURRENT MIRRORS

4-8-1 Definitions

A current mirror has already been used as an active load in the self-biasing MOST stage of Fig. 4-62c. It is a circuit that must mirror the current. After the differential stage, it is the most important circuit block. Therefore, it will be discussed in detail (Gray and Meyer 1984).

The current mirror is represented in ideal form in Fig. 4-72a. Its most simple realization is shown in Fig. 4-72b. It consists of two transistors with identical v_{GS}. One is connected as a diode and is driven by i_{IN}. The other one provides output current i_{OUT} at a high impedance level. Since their v_{GS}'s are the same, the ratio of their currents is given by

$$\frac{i_{OUT}}{i_{IN}} = B = \frac{(W/L)_2}{(W/L)_1} \tag{4-147}$$

By choosing this ratio, the output current can be set at any arbitrary value with high precision. Usually the channel length L is kept the same for both transistors to

FIGURE 4-72 (a) Principle of current mirror and (b) a simple MOST current mirror.

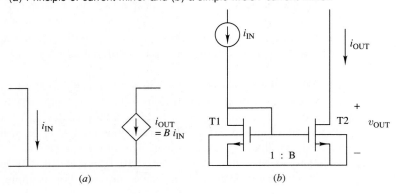

achieve good matching (see Chap. 6). Then the ratio B is set by the transistor widths W. Several errors occur, however, that cause deviations from ideal behavior.

The requirements of an ideal current source are the following:

- the current ratio B is precisely set by the (W/L) ratio, independent of temperature.

- the output impedance is very high, i.e., high R_{OUT} and low C_{OUT}. As a result, the output current is independent of the output voltage, DC and AC.

- the input resistance R_{IN} is very low.

- the compliance (voltage) is low, i.e., the minimum output voltage V_{OUTc}, for which the output acts as a current source, is low.

These requirements are now considered for the simple CMOS current mirror.

4-8-2 Simple MOST Current Mirror

The most important characteristic of a current mirror is its current ratio. Therefore it is investigated first.

Current Ratio   The current ratio is given by Eq. (4-147). An error occurs because the finite output resistance of both transistors is present. Transistor T1 operates at low $v_{DS1} = v_{GS1}$, whereas T2 operates at another $v_{OUT} = v_{DS2}$, which is probably much higher. Its value is determined by the load, which could be a resistor, a differential stage, etc. Thus, an error in current Δi_{OUT} occurs, as shown in Fig. 4-73. It is given by

$$\frac{\Delta i_{OUT}}{i_{OUT}} = \lambda(v_{DS2} - v_{DS1}) = \frac{v_{DS2} - v_{DS1}}{V_{En}L_2} \tag{4-148}$$

The error can be reduced by using large values of transistor length L_2, but especially by enforcing equal v_{DS} values on both transistors. This can be realized by addition of more transistors, as explained in Sec. 4-8-3.

At high frequencies the current ratio is impaired as well. The small-signal equivalent circuit of the current mirror seen in Fig. 4-72b is given in Fig. 4-74. All transistor capacitances are included. It is clear that the current mirror behaves as any other two-node amplifier, as has already been studied. Thus it has two poles and one zero.

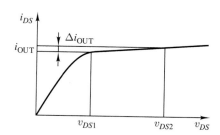

FIGURE 4-73   Current error because of different v_{DS}

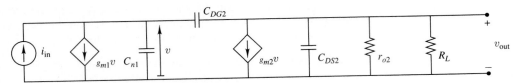

FIGURE 4-74   Small-signal equivalent circuit of current mirror.

The input node is at an impedance level that is quite low, i.e., $1/g_{m1}$. Therefore the effect of C_{DG2} is usually negligible.

The dominant pole of the current ratio transfer characteristic is then given by

$$f_p = \frac{g_{m1}}{2\pi C_{n1}} \tag{4-149}$$

in which $C_{n1} = C_{GS1} + C_{GS2} + C_{DS1}$.

This pole is normally situated at quite high frequencies because of the low value of g_{m1}. Thus, the current mirror operates well up to high frequencies.

The dominant pole can also occur at the output node, as we will discuss.

Output Impedance   The output impedance is simply the output resistance r_{o2} of the output transistor (see Fig. 4-72b) in parallel with an output capacitance. It is independent of the impedance of the current source with which the input transistor is driven. The value r_{o2} can be made high by increasing the transisor length L. Very high values are difficult to realize, however. Therefore, other configurations are required, such as those used with cascodes, as given in the next section and as shown in Fig. 4-76.

The output capacitance is simply $C_{DS2} + C_{DG2}$ (see Fig. 4-74) in which C_{DS2} is normally dominant. This is the junction capacitance of the drain (see Chap. 1). Thus values smaller than that are difficult to achieve; this can be a severe limitation at high frequencies.

Input Resistance   The input resistance is quite low because it is given by $1/g_{m1}$. Thus, it is easy to design a current source with value i_{IN}, which has an output resistance much higher than the resistance $1/g_{m1}$.

Compliance V_{OUTc}   The compliance voltage V_{OUTc} is the minimum output voltage at which the current mirror still provides a high output resistance. It is given by the value $V_{DS\text{sat}2}$ of the output transistor. For lower values of V_{DS}, the output transistor enters the linear region and the output resistance drops drastically.

This also equals $V_{GS1} - V_T$ and is determined by how far the transistors operate in strong inversion. For a given current, the value of $V_{GS1} - V_T$ can be decreased by taking large values of (W/L). In strong inversion it is given by

$$V_{\text{OUT}c} = V_{GS1} - V_T = V_{DS\text{sat}2} = \sqrt{\frac{I_{\text{OUT}}}{K_n'(W/L)_2}} \qquad (4\text{-}150)$$

It is shown as a function of $(W/L)_2$ in Fig. 4-75 for $I_{\text{OUT}} = 0.1$ mA and $K_n' = 30 \ \mu\text{A/V}^2$.

The current mirror of Fig. 4-72b is the simplest and thus it is used more often than any other. Nevertheless, for precision circuits there is a need for a current mirror with higher output resistance r_{o2} and with less error in current Δi_{OUT}. We will introduce other configurations that have less error.

4-8-3   Other MOST Current Mirrors

More MOS transistors are required to correct the Δi_{OUT} and to increase the output resistance. Several configurations are given in Fig. 4-76. Let us compare them.

In Fig. 4-76a, two current mirrors have been cascoded. The two transistors T1 and T2, which determine the current ratio, are designed to have the same value of v_{DS}. The error Δi_{OUT} thus is greatly reduced. Now it is only a result of mismatches between T1 and T2. These effects will be discussed in Chap. 6.

The output resistance of the current mirror (of Fig. 4-76a) is increased, as well. Indeed, T4 acts as a cascode transistor. Its output resistance r_{o4} thus is multiplied by $g_{m4}r_{o2}$ as we have already seen (see Sec. 4-6). The output capacitance is reduced as well, because C_{DS4} sees a high resistance provided by T2, such that its effect is reduced by the same factor $g_{m4}r_{o2}$.

An alternative configuration is given in Fig. 4-76b. Now T2 is connected as a diode rather than transistor T1. Again, the v_{DS} of both transistors T1 and T2 is made equal easily, reducing Δi_{OUT} to a minimum. Also, the output resistance is increased due to the effect of the negative feedback. Its loop gain is $g_{m1}r_{o1}$. As a result, the output resistance r_{o4} is increased and the output capacitance is decreased by the same amount $g_{m1}r_{o1}$.

Normally the current mirrors are driven by current sources with value i_{IN}. They can be driven by voltage sources as well. The expression of the output current then contains g_m rather than a ratio of transistor sizes as in Eq. (4-147). It is best to avoid

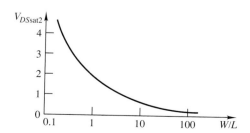

FIGURE 4-75   Saturation voltage versus W/L (0.1 mA; 30 μA/V^2)

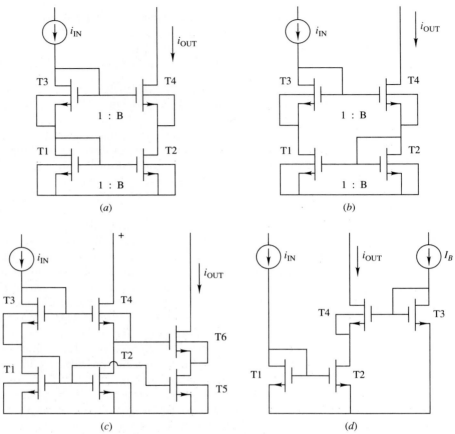

FIGURE 4-76   (a) Cascode current mirror; (b) feedback current mirror; (c) low output voltage current mirror; and (d) low output voltage current mirror with extra current source I_B.

this. However, the last current mirror must always be driven by a current source, the output resistance of which is much higher than r_{o1}. If it is driven by a voltage source or by a current source with large output capacitance, the loop gain is decreased, decreasing the output resistance of the current mirror. This decrease is a disadvantage, especially when compared to the current mirror in Fig. 4-76a.

The main disadvantage of both circuits of Fig. 4-76a and b is their high output compliance voltage V_{OUTc}. Both transistor T2 and T4 must be kept in saturation. The minimum output voltage is thus $v_{GS2} + v_{DSsat4}$, which is always larger than V_T. For this reason the following configurations are preferred.

The current mirror of Fig. 4-76c has properties similar to that in Fig. 4-76a. The error in current ratio Δi_{OUT} is negligible, except for mismatching effects. The output resistance is high because of cascode transistor T6. Moreover, the output compliance

V_{OUTc} is only $v_{DSsat5} + v_{DSsat6}$, which can be made quite small if the transistors operate close to weak inversion or if large transistors are used.

It is not obvious how the transistor sizes are to be determined, however, because all transistors T2, T5, and T6 must be kept in saturation (see Exercise 4-51). In practice, it is difficult to make $v_{DS5} = v_{DS1}$, which results in some error Δi_{OUT}. Also, the output transistor T6 is usually given a high W/L ratio. These are the prices to pay, however, for a lower output compliance voltage.

A simpler configuration with a lower output compliance voltage V_{OUTc} is shown in Fig. 4-76d. It is easier to design than the previous one. This will be discussed in Exercise 4-52.

4-8-4 Bipolar Transistor Current Mirrors

Bipolar transistors can also be used to construct current mirrors. They give rise to configurations similar to MOSTs. However, bipolar transistors exhibit base current. This is another important cause of errors. Several configurations are shown in Fig. 4-77. The simplest configuration is analyzed first.

FIGURE 4-77   Bipolar current mirrors. (c) Widlar; (d) Wilson.

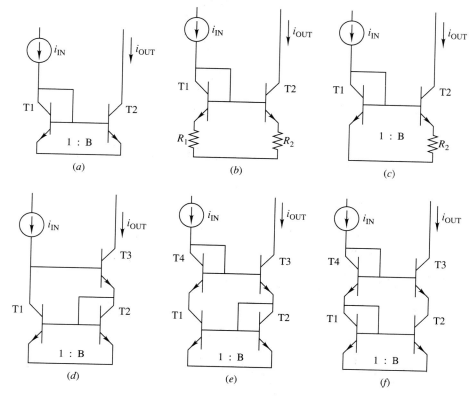

The simple bipolar transistor current mirror behaves in a way similar to its MOST counterpart. Its current ratio is determined by the ratio of the emitter areas. In practice, the emitter area is not scaled, a number of equal-sized transistors are put in parallel, which provides better matching. For example, if T1 consists of two transistors in parallel and T2 of seven, then $B = 3.5$.

Again, the output resistance is only r_{o2}. The output compliance, on the other hand, is excellent because of the very low $v_{CE\text{sat}}$ of only a few times kT/q of a bipolar transistor (see Fig. 2-38).

The output resistance can be increased by means of local feedback, as shown in Fig. 4-77b. The ouput resistance is increased by the loop gain, i.e., a factor of $(1 + g_{m2}R_2)$. The resistances can also be used to set the current ratio. In fact, the current ratio $i_{\text{OUT}}/i_{\text{IN}}$ is given by

$$\frac{i_{\text{OUT}}}{i_{\text{IN}}} = \frac{R_1}{R_2} \left(\frac{1 + \dfrac{1}{g_{m1}R_1}}{1 + \dfrac{1}{g_{m2}R_2}} \right) \tag{4-151}$$

which is about equal to R_1/R_2. The error is inversely proportional to the loop gain and thus is about $1/g_{m2}R_2$. In this case, mismatch between T1 and T2 is not as important. Now it is the matching between R_1 and R_2 that dominates and can be better than using transistors.

The third current mirror is named after Widlar. It has as a goal to generate very large current ratios, such that very small output currents can be derived from average input currents. The current ratio can be derived from the solution of

$$v_{BE1} = v_{BE2} + R_2 i_{\text{OUT}} \tag{4-152a}$$

or
$$\frac{i_{\text{IN}}}{i_{\text{OUT}}} = \frac{1}{B} \exp\left(\frac{R_2 i_{\text{OUT}}}{kT/q} \right) \tag{4-152b}$$

in which B is the number of transistors in the output branch. For example, for a voltage drop of 60 mV across R_2 (and $B = 1$), the current i_{OUT} is ten times smaller than the current i_{IN}. Since i_{OUT} is small, this leads to large values of R_2, which may be difficult to integrate. Temperature behavior is another problem.

In contrast with all other current mirrors discussed, the current ratio is temperature dependent because of kT/q in Eq. (4-152b). All previous current ratios only had transistor sizes in their expressions. These do not depend on temperature. This is the first current ratio that is different.

The first three current sources all suffer from an error in current ratio because of the base current. The base currents of both transistors are subtracted from the input current source (see Fig. 4-77a), causing an error that depends on the beta values. The exact relation between the input and output currents for the configuration of Fig. 2-77a is given by

$$i_{IN} = i_{OUT} \left(\frac{1}{B} + \frac{1}{\beta} + \frac{1}{\beta B} \right) \tag{4-153}$$

For $B = 1$, the error is $2/\beta$. For lateral *pnp* transistors with low β, this error can be quite large.

The Wilson current mirror of Fig. 4-77d remedies this. A feedback loop with loop gain β reduces the error to about $2/\beta^2$ (see Exercise 4-55). Moreover, its output resistance increases by β as well, provided the output resistance of the i_{IN} current source is larger than r_{o1}. This circuit configuration is actually the same as for the current mirror of Fig. 4-76b. This becomes clearer if transistor T4 is added, as in Fig. 4-77e. Transistor T4 establishes equal values of v_{CE} across transistors T1 and T2, which determine the current ratio. The error in current ratio thus can be expected to be quite small.

A similar circuit of the current mirror in Fig. 4-76a is shown in Fig. 4-77f. It provides a current ratio with low error and with high output resistance, because of the cascode transistor T3.

The last three current mirrors (Fig. 4-77d, e, f) all suffer from large output compliance voltage V_{OUTc}. Indeed, all three circuits stack two transistors, thus requiring an output voltage of at least $v_{BEon} + v_{CEsat}$.

An alternative configuration that reduces the error due to β without stacking transistors, is shown in Fig. 4-78a. It is derived from the configuration of Fig. 4-77a. The base current is divided, however, by the beta of T3, before it is subtracted from the input current source i_{IN}. The resulting error thus is proportional to $2/\beta^2$ (see exercises). Since these base currents are fairly small, the current through transistor T3 may be quite small. As a result, its β may be considerably reduced. Therefore, a resistor R_1 is added in order to increase the collector current of T3. In this way, transistor T3 operates at higher currents where its β is larger.

Caution must be exerted to ensure stability. The capacitances are shown explicitly in Fig. 4-78b. Capacitance C_3 is mainly the diffusion capacitance of T3. If each transistor is modeled by its g_m and r_π, the current ratio is calculated to be

$$\frac{i_{OUT}}{i_{IN}} = \frac{1 + \dfrac{C_3 s}{g_{m3}}}{1 + \left[\dfrac{C_1}{g_{m1}\beta_3} + \dfrac{C_2}{g_{m1}} \left(1 + \dfrac{2}{g_{m3}r_{\pi 3}} \right) + \dfrac{C_3}{g_{m3}} \right] s + \dfrac{C^2 s^2}{g_{m1} g_{m3}}} \tag{4-154a}$$

$$\approx \frac{1 + \dfrac{C_3 s}{g_{m3}}}{1 + \left(\dfrac{C_2}{g_{m1} + \frac{C_3}{g_{m3}}} \right) s + \dfrac{C^2 s^2}{g_{m1} g_{m3}}} \tag{4-154b}$$

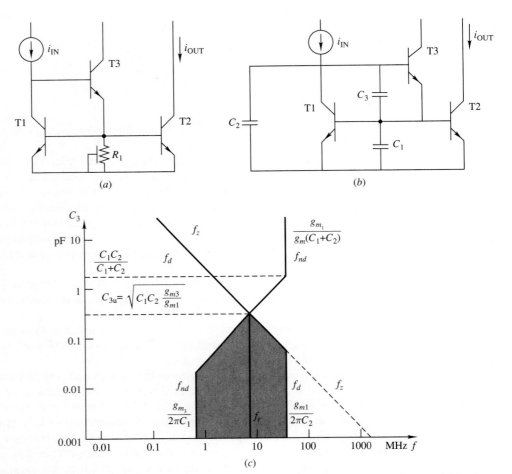

FIGURE 4-78   (a) Current mirror with reduction of β error; (b) capacitances of current mirror; and (c) pole-zero position plot of current mirror.

in which $C^2 = C_1C_2 + C_1C_3 + C_2C_3$. The corresponding pole-zero position plot is given in Fig. 4-78c. The output current can have a peaked response because two complex poles can occur if $C_3 \leq C_{3u}$, with

$$C_{3u} = \sqrt{C_1C_2 \frac{g_{m3}}{g_{m1}}} \qquad (4\text{-}155)$$

For smaller values of C_3, the resonant frequency is given by

$$f_r = \frac{1}{2\pi}\sqrt{\frac{g_{m1}g_{m3}}{C_1C_2}} \qquad (4\text{-}156a)$$

For larger values of C_3, the first pole f_d and the zero f_z cancel. As a result, the bandwidth is determined by the other pole f_{nd} and is given by

$$BW = \frac{1}{2\pi} \frac{g_{m1}}{C_1 + C_2} \qquad (4\text{-}156b)$$

Its value is higher than that of the resonant frequency. The bandwidth thus can be increased by increasing C_3 to a value higher than $C_1 C_2/(C_1 + C_2)$, as shown in Fig. 4-78c.

Another way to reduce the region of complex poles is to reduce the ratio f_d/f_{nd} for small C_3 (see Fig. 4-78c). This ratio is given by

$$\frac{f_d}{f_{nd}}\bigg|_{C3=0} = \frac{g_{m1}}{g_{m3}} \frac{C_1}{C_2} \qquad (4\text{-}156c)$$

for which it is clear that this ratio can be decreased if g_{m3} is made larger. This means that the current in transistor T3 must be increased, e.g., by addition of a current source instead of R_1 (see Fig. 4-78a).

From these conclusions, a comparison is readily made between the BICMOS current mirror of Fig. 4-79 and the full bipolar current mirror. The current error Δi_{OUT} is about zero because the MOST does not draw gate current. On the other hand, its capacitance C_3 is smaller, such that stability problems are likely to occur. For correct operation, the condition in Eq. (4-155) must be verified to determine if C_{GS} must be increased.

4-8-5   Noise Output of Current Mirrors

Current mirrors also generate noise. The noise sources in the simple MOST current mirror are shown in Fig. 4-80. The transistors' noise is represented by noise current sources $\overline{di_1^2}$ and $\overline{di_2^2}$. We have taken the output noise current sources rather than the

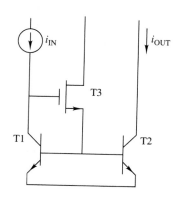

FIGURE 4-79   BICMOS current mirror

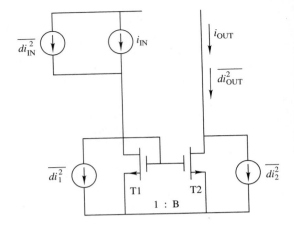

FIGURE 4-80   Noise in single MOST current mirror.

equivalent input noise sources (see Chap. 2), because we want to calculate the total output noise, not the equivalent input noise. The noise generated by the input current source i_{IN} is denoted by $\overline{di_{IN}^2}$. Its value can be quite large if many transistors are used.

The total output noise $\overline{di_{OUT}^2}$ is then given by

$$\overline{di_{OUT}^2} = (\overline{di_{IN}^2} + \overline{di_1^2})B^2 + \overline{di_2^2} \tag{4-157a}$$

After substitution of the noise current generators by the expression $\overline{di^2} = (8kT/3)\times (g_m df)$ (see Chap. 2), this expression becomes

$$\overline{di_{OUT}^2} = B^2\overline{di_{IN}^2} + \frac{8kT}{3}(B+1)g_{m2}\, df$$

or

$$= B^2\overline{di_{IN}^2} + \frac{16kT}{3}(B+1)\sqrt{K_n'\left(\frac{W}{L}\right)_2 i_{OUT}}\, df \tag{4-157b}$$

As a result, for a given output current, the noise output current becomes smaller if B and/or $(W/L)_2$ are assigned small values. In the best case, $B = 1$. However, if we make $(W/L)_2$ small, then its $V_{GS2} - V_T$ is large, which causes a large output compliance voltage V_{OUTc}. Large $V_{GS2} - V_T$ is also better for matching (see Chap. 6). A compromise must be made here.

At low frequencies, the noise output can be reduced by connecting a large capacitance at the common-gate point. Only $\overline{di_2^2}$ is left as output noise. Application of large capacitances is only practical in discrete circuits, however.

Series Resistance   The best technique to reduce the output noise is reducing the $(W/L)_2$ to very small values. An alternative consists of inserting series resistances as shown in the MOST current mirror of Fig. 4-81.

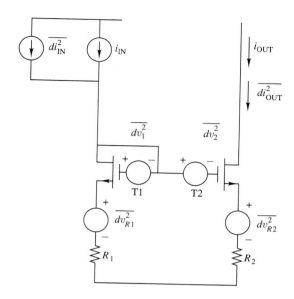

FIGURE 4-81   Reduction of noise by series R.

All noise sources are shown explicitly in Fig. 4-81. The total output noise is then given by

$$\overline{di_{\text{OUT}}^2} = \left(\frac{R_1}{R_2}\right)^2 \overline{di_{\text{IN}}^2} + \frac{\overline{dv_1^2} + \overline{dv_2^2}}{R_2^2} + \frac{\overline{dv_{R1}^2} + \overline{dv_{R2}^2}}{R_2^2} \qquad (4\text{-}158a)$$

provided $R_1 > 1/g_{mi}$ for both transistors $i = 1, 2$. Substitution of the several noise sources by their expressions, and noting that $B = R_1/R_2$, yields

$$\overline{di_{\text{OUT}}^2} = B^2 \overline{di_{\text{IN}}^2} + \frac{4kT}{R_2}\left[B + 1 + \frac{4\left(\sqrt{B}+1\right)}{g_{m2}R_2}\right] df \qquad (4\text{-}158b)$$

The first terms between the square brackets are a result of the resistors. Thus their contribution decreases with increasing R_2. The last term is due to the transistors. Their contribution thus decreases with increasing R_2^2. The noise contributions of the resistors are larger than those of the transistors. They all can be made quite small, provided R_2 is made quite large. The resistors have no effect, however, on the noise contribution of the input current source. Thus attention must be paid to that noise source.

The expressions of Eq. (1-158) are only valid if the resistors R_1 and R_2 are larger than $1/g_{m1}$ and $1/g_{m2}$, respectively. For smaller resistors, the noise contributions of the resistors are simply added to those of the transistors. For $B = 1$, the relative contributions to the total output noise are illustrated in Fig. 4-82. For small resistors, the transistors are the main contributors to the output noise, whereas for large resistors the resistors provide most of the output noise, as given by Eq. (4-158b).

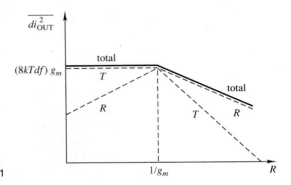

FIGURE 4-82   Noise contributions of transistors and resistors for current mirror of Fig. 4-81

Example 4-17

Design a low-noise two-transistor current mirror with ratio $B = 4$ with $I_{OUT} = 100$ μA. Take small sizes for T1 and T2, in order to reduce the output capacitance as much as possible (in a 2 μm CMOS process). What is the output current S/N ratio? What value of R_2 would be required to reduce the output noise current by half?

Solution. In order to obtain a large output resistance, we increase the length L_1 and L_2 to 10 μm. For minimum size let us take $W_1 = 4$ μm and $W_2 = 16$ μm, which yields $B = 4$. The output noise is then given by Eq. (4-157b) which yields $\overline{di^2_{OUT}} = 7.7 \times 10^{-24} A^2/Hz$ or 2.8 pA$_{RMS}/\sqrt{Hz}$. The output current S/N is 3.6×10^7, or 151 dB. A SPICE file for this example is given in Table 4-9.

In order to further decrease the output noise, we can insert a resistor R_2 in the source of T2. Then $R_1 = 4R_2$, but both transistors are equal: $W_1 = W_2 = 2$ μm. In this case, $g_{m2} = 49$ μS and $1/g_{m2} \approx 20$ kΩ. In order to reduce the output noise current by a factor of two, we must reduce the output noise power by a factor of four (see Fig. 4-82). Hence, $R_2 = 44$ kΩ. The output noise is now given by Eq. (4-158), which yields $\overline{di^2_{OUT}} = 2.1 \times 10^{-24} A^2/Hz$ or 1.5 pA$_{RMS}/\sqrt{Hz}$.

We may be surprised by the large value of R_2, which is difficult to realize. Moreover, the DC voltage drop across such a resistor can be prohibitive. In Example 4-17, the voltage drop across R_2 is 4.4 V, which is not practical for low power supplies. Therefore, series resistors are used mainly with bipolar transistor current mirrors, in which g_{m2} is larger.

Concluding Remarks on Current Mirrors   From the several current mirrors, current references can easily be derived. In a current mirror a precise relationship exists between the output and input currents. This precision is obtained by use of scaled transistor sizes, by ratios of numbers of equal transistors, by use of resistances and capacitances, etc. Current references, on the other hand, yield output currents that are not related to any input voltage or current. The output current is derived from

TABLE 4-9   INPUT FILE FOR SPICE FOR LOW-NOISE CURRENT MIRROR OF EXAMPLE
4-17 IN SEC. 4-8-5.

```
* Ex.4-17 (TEMPERATURE = 27.000 DEG C)
* CIRCUIT DESCRIPTION
M1 2 2 1 1 NMOS W=4U L=10U
M2 4 2 3 3 NMOS W=16U L=10U
VDD 5 0 DC 5
VD2 6 0 DC 5
IIN 5 2 DC 25U AC 1
CL 4 0 10P
RL 6 4 10K
R1 1 0 1
R2 3 0 1
.MODEL NMOS NMOS LEVEL=2 VTO=1 KP=60E-6 GAMMA=0.01 LAMBDA=0.0125
* CONTROL CARDS
.AC DEC 10 10K 10MEG
.PRINT AC 1(VD2)
NOISE V(4) IIN 10
.WIDTH OUT = 75
.END
```

a combination of voltages with transistor parameters and resistors. If the output current is linearly proportional to an input voltage, the circuit is called a V/I converter.

Such a current reference, or such a V/I converter, is necessary to drive a current mirror. The input signal of a current mirror is always provided by a current source. An elementary current source is a large resistor connected to the power supply line. Also, a string of diode-connected transistors can be used as input current source. By far the best solution, however, is to use a real current reference or a V/I converter.

It has been shown that current mirrors can be designed with highly accurate current ratios. It is sufficient to bias the transistors, which carry out the actual current mirroring, at exactly the same output voltages v_{DS} (or v_{CE}) and v_{BS}. Errors will always appear, however, because of mismatches between these transistors. Mismatches and design techniques to reduce these effects are discussed in Sec. 6-5.

SUMMARY

In this chapter the most important two-transistor amplifiers have been discussed. There are many more, however. For example, the *Darlington amplifier* is well-known. It consists of two transistors configured as shown in Fig. 4-83. Its goal is to reduce the input biasing current. It is a three-node amplifier, though, which may be difficult to analyze at high frequencies. Some aspects are handled in the exercises.

Another well-known configuration is the so-called super *pnp*, which is often used in power applications. It is aimed at the realization of a *pnp* with superior characteristics, i.e., with superior g_m and/or β. It is shown in Fig. 4-84a. A super *pMOST* can be realized in the same way as shown in Fig. 4-84b. Its model is shown in Fig. 4-84c.

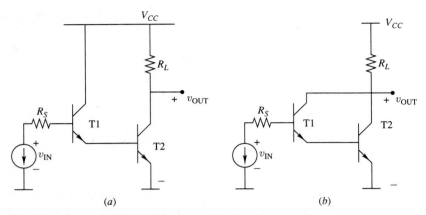

FIGURE 4-83   Darlington configurations (*a*) without and (*b*) with common collector.

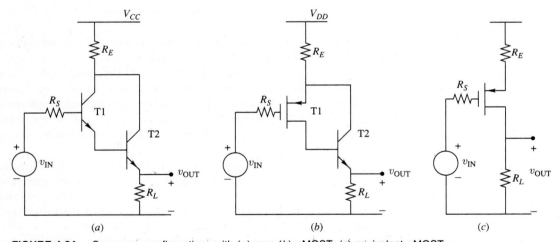

FIGURE 4-84   Super *pnp* configurations with (*a*) *pnp*; (*b*) *p*MOST; (*c*) equivalent *p*MOST.

In the configurations of Fig. 4-84, local feedback is applied by means of resistor R_E. A four-node amplifier results. Thus, resistor R_E considerably increases the complexity of the analysis at high frequencies. Again, this is discussed in the exercises.

It is always possible to connect several amplifying stages in series. This is called *cascading*. Such a cascade amplifier is shown in Fig. 4-85. It is a three-node amplifier. This, too, is discussed in the exercises.

In this chapter, techniques have been detailed to analyze and design elementary transistor circuits. We have analyzed the single-transistor in its three configurations, i.e., the amplifier, the source follower, and the cascode configuration. Then we ana-

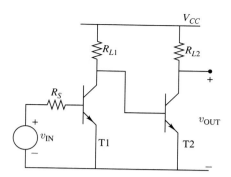

FIGURE 4-85   Cascade amplifier.

lyzed two-transistor circuits such as a CMOS inverter, a differential pair, a cascode amplifier, and a current mirror.

Complexity has always been limited to two nodes, which results in systems of only second order. This may seem to be a limitation. However, the vast majority of the circuits discussed in later chapters can be simplified to two-node equivalents. Therefore, it is important that the reader be thoroughly familiar with the analyses in this chapter.

All too often, analysis is confused with running a SPICE program. Too many designers hope to gain insight by running SPICE. They are warned, however, that SPICE is only a tool for verification. It allows insight only drop-by-drop. This is typical for numerical circuit simulators. Symbolic simulators are much more useful in understanding this subject because they indicate the governing parameters in analytic form.

This chapter has been aimed at the generation of analytic tools that help us understand the operation of the circuits. We have relied on extreme simplification and on hand calculations. New diagrams have been given, too, such as the pole-zero position plot, to better visualize and better understand the results.

The elementary cells described in this chapter have been limited to differential pairs, cascade amplifiers, and current mirrors. Joined together, they yield full amplifier configurations. This has already been illustrated in Fig. 4-62c for the self-biasing differential pair with active load. This circuit already possesses most of the characteristics of an operational amplifier. The design of these amplifiers is discussed in detail in Chap. 6. Before the design is touched upon, however, the basics of an operational amplifier as a "black box" must be explained. This is done in Chap. 5.

EXERCISES

4-1 Design a single-transistor amplifier with resistive load and biasing resistors (Fig. 4-2) with $V_{DD} = 5$ V and $R_S = 5$ kΩ. Its $V_{T0} = 0.8$ V, $K'_n = 35$ μA/V^2. We want a voltage gain of 20 and a symmetrical output swing. Plot the W/L and R_L versus output current and select a current of about 0.1 mA on this plot.

4-2 Derive the expression for the input impedance of the amplifier of Fig. 4-5a with $g_m = 1$ mS, $R_L = 40$ kΩ, and $C_{DG} = 1$ pF. If we want to represent this input impedance by a series RC to ground, what are the resistor and capacitor values?

4-3 Give the pole-zero position and Bode diagrams of the input impedance Z_{in} of an nMOST amplifier with C_{DG} as a variable. What is the maximum value of C_{DG} for which Z_{in} can be represented by a single capacitance? Use the transistor parameters of Table 4-1.

4-4 Give the pole-zero position and Bode diagrams of the output impedance Z_{out} of an nMOST amplifier with C_{DG} as a variable. What is the value of C_{DGt} at which pole splitting starts? Use the transistor parameters of Table 4-1.

4-5 What is the maximum GBW we can obtain for a single-transistor amplifier with active load, if the source resistor is 600 Ω and the transistor parameters in Table 4-1 can be used? What is the minimum value of g_m, and of the current if we limit W/L to 200? Repeat if we limit the current to 10 mA.

4-6 Give the pole-zero position and Bode diagrams of the output impedance Z_{out} of an nMOST amplifier with g_m as a variable. What is the maximum value of g_m at which pole splitting starts? Use the transistor parameters of Table 4-1.

4-7 Derive the pole-zero position and Bode diagrams of the gain A_v of an nMOST amplifier, with C_{DS} as a variable. Use the transistor parameters of Table 4-1.

4-8 Derive the pole-zero position and Bode diagrams of the output impedance Z_{out} of an nMOST amplifier, with C_{DS} as a variable. Use the transistor parameters of Table 4-1.

4-9 Design an nMOST amplifier with resistive load and biasing resistors (Fig. 4-2) with $V_{DD} = 5$ V. We want a voltage gain of at least 20 and a symmetrical output swing. The equivalent input noise must be less than 2 $nV_{RMS}/\sqrt{Hz}$.

4-10 Repeat Exercise 4-1 for the bipolar transistor amplifier of Fig. 4-15d with $R_E = 0$ and $\beta = 100$. Select again 0.1 mA as current.

4-11 Repeat Exercise 4-5 for a bipolar transistor with $f_{T\,max} = 2.5$ GHz, in which $C_\mu = 0.5$ pF and $C_{jE} = 1.5$ pF. Also, $C_L = 1$ pF.

4-12 A circle diagram for a bipolar transistor is given at 5 mA (see Fig. EX4-12). Its $C_\mu = 0.05$ pF. Find its f_T, β, and r_B. What maximum GBW can be obtained with this transistor if the Miller effect dominates?

4-13 Repeat Exercise 4-9 for a bipolar transistor, with $r_B = 100$ Ω.

4-14 Derive the pole-zero position and Bode diagrams of the gain A_v of a bipolar transistor amplifier with a feedback resistor R_F between collector and base; take this

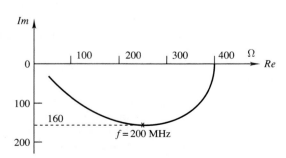

FIGURE EX4-12   Circle diagram bipolar transistor at $I_{CE} = 5$ mA.

resistor R_F as variable. Use the transistor parameters of Table 4-3, but neglect output capacitance C_o.

4-15 Take a high-frequency bipolar transistor at 5 mA, with $\tau_F = 15$ ps, $C_{jE} = 100$ fF, $C_\mu = 50$ fF and $r_B = 100 \ \Omega$. Derive the pole-zero position and Bode diagrams of f_T of that transistor after inclusion of an emitter resistor R_E; take this resistor R_E as variable.

4-16 Take a bipolar transistor amplifier as shown in Fig. EX4-16 with a load resistor $R_L = 50 \ k\Omega$ and an emitter resistor $R_E = 10 \ k\Omega$. The current is 100 μA. Only one transistor capacitance is present: $C_\pi = 6$ pF. We have connected a capacitance C_E across R_E to compensate for the pole caused by C_π. Use the pole-zero position diagram to find the compensation value of C_E.

4-17 Realize a level shifter of 2.5 V with the MOST of Exercise 4-1, with $\gamma = 1\sqrt{V}$ in a p-well CMOS process, and then in an n-well CMOS process. Take $I_{DS} \approx 50 \ \mu$A.

4-18 Repeat the diagrams of the source follower of Fig. 4-23 with larger C_{DG} ($= 3$ pF). What can you conclude about the region of complex poles?

4-19 Derive the pole-zero position and Bode diagrams of the gain A_v of an nMOST source follower with load capacitance C_{DS} as a variable. Use the transistor parameters of Table 4-1.

4-20 Derive the pole-zero position and Bode diagrams of the output impedance Z_{out} of an nMOST source follower with g_m as a variable. Use the transistor parameters of Table 4-1 with C_{DG} increased to 3 pF.

4-21 Derive the pole-zero position and Bode diagrams of the output impedance Z_{out} of an nMOST source follower, with capacitance C_{DG} as a variable. What is the minimum value of C_{DG} to avoid complex poles? Use the transistor parameters of Table 4-1.

4-22 Derive the pole-zero position and Bode diagrams of the input impedance Z_{in} of an nMOST source follower, with load capacitance C_{DS} as a variable. Use the transistor parameters of Table 4-1.

4-23 Derive the pole-zero position and Bode diagrams of the gain A_v of an emitter follower, with g_m as a variable. Load capacitance C_L is 10 pF. Use the transistor parameters of Table 4-3.

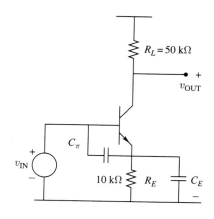

FIGURE EX4-16   Amplifier with emitter impedance.

4-24 Derive the pole-zero position and Bode diagrams of the input impedance Z_{in} of an emitter follower, with load capacitance C_L as a variable. Use the transistor parameters of Table 4-3.

4-25 A microphone preamplifier is shown in Fig. EX4-25. Calculate the gain and the output signal-to-noise ratio for a 10 mV$_{RMS}$ input signal with 20 kHz -3dB bandwidth. Does this ratio improve if we omit the source follower? For the MOST, $K' = 30$ μA/V^2 and $W/L = 1000$; for the bipolar transistor $\beta = 500$, $V_E = 52$ V, and $r_B = 100$ Ω. Repeat for a source resistor of 1 MΩ.

4-26 For the wide-band cascode amplifier in Fig EX4-26, calculate the gain and sketch the Bode diagrams. The transistor parameters are $\beta = 50$ and $r_B = 50$ Ω.

4-27 Two amplifier configurations are compared for gain and signal-to-noise ratio. They are shown in Fig EX4-27. The MOSTs all have $V_T = 1$ V, $K' = 25$ μA/V^2, and $W/L = 80$. Use $V_{GS} = 1.5$ V.

4-28 Plot the gain A_v and the current I_{Dm} versus V_{DD} for a CMOS inverter, with $|V_{Tp}| = V_{Tn} = 1$ V; $K'_n = 30$ μA/V^2; $K'_p = 15$ μA/V^2; $(W/L)_n = 5$; $(W/L)_p = 10$; $V_{En} = 5$ V/μm; and $V_{Ep} = 8$ V/μm. Find all dimensions if $V_E = 20$ V.

4-29 Design an inverter with parallel input for a $GBW = 30$ MHz for $C_L = 5$ pF, with $R_S = 100$ Ω. Use as parameters $|V_{Tp}| = V_{Tn} = 1$V; $K'_n = 30$ μA/V^2;

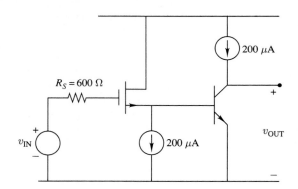

FIGURE EX4-25   Microphone preamplifier.

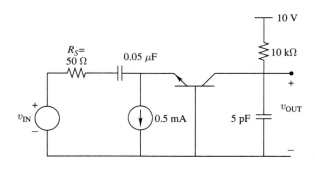

FIGURE EX4-26   Cascode amplifier

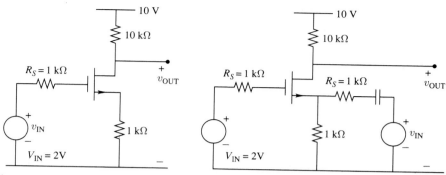

FIGURE EX4-27   Low-noise amplifiers.

$K'_p = 15\ \mu\text{A/V}^2$; $V_{En} = 5\ \text{V}/\mu\text{m}$; $V_{Ep} = 8\ \text{V}/\mu\text{m}$; $C_{DS} = 1\ \text{pF}$; $C_{DG} = 0.1\ \text{pF}$; $C_{GS} = 0.4\ \text{pF}$; and $L_{\min} = 1.25\ \mu\text{m}$. What are the current and W_n if $V_{DD} = 5\ \text{V}$?

4-30 Develop a design procedure as in Sec. 4-5-5 if both MOSTs are fully operating in velocity saturation. Take $C_{\text{ox}} = 10^{-7}\ \text{C/cm}^2$ and $v_{\text{sat}} = 10^7\ \text{cm/s}$.

4-31 Derive expressions for the transfer characteristic of the inverter of Fig. 4-44a, as sketched in Fig. 4-44d. Also calculate the required DC input voltage to keep the output voltage at half the supply voltage. Calculate all values for the transistor parameters of Exercise 4-29 with $V_{DD} = 10\ \text{V}$ and a gain of 5.

4-32 Design an inverter as shown in Fig. 4-44a for a gain of 3.2, such that $(W/L)_1 = 20$. Make sure that $V_{\text{OUT}} = 2.5\ \text{V}$ for $V_{DD} = 5\ \text{V}$. Calculate the GBW for $C_L = 5\ \text{pF}$.

4-33 Derive an expression for the signal-to-noise ratio of a single-transistor amplifier, with capacitive source $R_S = 0$ and $R_L = R_1 = R_2 = \infty$ (see Fig. 4-2). Only include C_{GS} and C_{DG}, whereas $C_{DS} = 0$. Plot the signal-to-noise ratio versus C_C and versus C_{DG}.

4-34 The input noise voltage of the inverter with parallel input is $\sqrt{2}$ better than that with one transistor. Is the equivalent noise of the inverter then the same as for one single nMOST with W/L two times as large?

4-35 Design an nMOST cascode with $I_2 = I_1 + I_A$ (Fig. 4-51b), with active load such that $A_v > 1000$. For the cascode transistor $g_{m2}R_{S2} = 1$, in which $R_{S2} = 200\ \Omega$ is the gate resistor of T2. Take the minimum current for T1, but $(W/L)_{\min} = 20$. Also $K'_n = 30\ \mu\text{A/V}^2$ and $V_{En} = 5\ \text{V}/\mu\text{m}$; $L_{1\min} = 1.2\ \mu\text{m}$.

4-36 Design an nMOST cascode with $I_2 = I_1$ (Fig. 4-51a), with active load and $C_L = 5\ \text{pF}$. Realize $GBW > 50\ \text{MHz}$ for $R_S = 200\ \Omega$ and $C_{DG} = 0.4\ \text{pF}$. Take $(W/L)_{\min} = 20$ and $L_{\min} = 1.2\ \mu\text{m}$. Also, $K'_n = 30\ \mu\text{A/V}^2$ and $V_{En} = 5\ \text{V}/\mu\text{m}$.

4-37 Realize a bipolar transistor folded cascode with $I_2 = I_1 = I_A/2 = 0.2\ \text{mA}$ (Fig. 4-51d), with active load such that GBW is maximum ($C_L = 5\ \text{pF}$). Transistor parameters are $f_{T\max 1} = 600\ \text{MHz}$, $f_{T\max 2} = 10\ \text{MHz}$, all $C_\mu = 0.5\ \text{pF}$, $V_E = 50\ \text{V}$, $C_{jE} = 1\ \text{pF}$, $C_{CSn} = 1.5\ \text{pF}$.

4-38 Compare the BICMOS cascodes shown for gain, GBW, and nondominant pole in Fig. EX4-38. The load currents I_2 and capacitances C_L are the same.

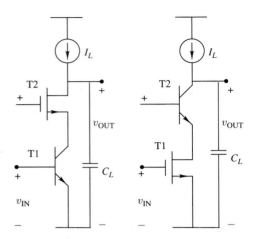

FIGURE EX4-38   BICMOS cascode amplifiers.

4-39 Design a wide-band cascode with nMOSTs and $R_S = 50\ \Omega$, $R_L = 500\ \Omega$, and $C_L = 5$ pF. Use the parameters of Table 4-1. Ensure first-order roll-off down to unity gain.

4-40 Take an nMOST differential amplifier with $V_{Tn} = 1$ V; $K'_n = 25\ \mu\text{A/V}^2$; $(W/L)_n = 8$; $R_L = 20$ kΩ and 21 kΩ (5% difference) and $V_{DD,SS} = \pm 5$ V. The current source is replaced by a resistor of $R_E = 7.5$ kΩ. The input voltages are $v_{I1} = 110$ mV and $v_{I2} = 104$ mV. Calculate the V_{OUT}, A_{dd}, A_{dc} and $CMRR$.

4-41 Calculate the transfer characteristic for a bipolar transistor differential pair with $I_B = 0.2$ mA, with emitter resistors of 1 kΩ. Realize the same characteristic with nMOSTs with $K'_n = 30\ \mu\text{A/V}^2$, i.e., what W/L is necessary to realize the same small-signal gain?

4-42 Design a MOST differential pair with active load (Fig. 4-62c) for maximum gain and maximum output swing: $V_{DD} = 5$ V; $K'_n = 30\ \mu\text{A/V}^2$; $K'_p = 15\ \mu\text{A/V}^2$; $V_{En} = 5$ V/μm; and $V_{Ep} = 8$ V/μm. What current and W/L are required?

4-43 Design a MOST differential pair with active load (Fig. 4-62c) for maximum gain and minimum equivalent input noise: $V_{DD} = 5$ V; $K'_n = 30\ \mu\text{A/V}^2$; $K'_p = 15\ \mu\text{A/V}^2$; $V_{En} = 5$ V/μm; and $V_{Ep} = 8$ V/μm. What current is required ($I_{B\ \text{max}} = 100\ \mu$A)? Compare with a bipolar stage at the same current ($V_E = 52$ V).

4-44 For the differential amplifier of Fig. 4-59, draw the Bode diagrams if the R_L's are different by a small amount ΔR_L. Is this a first- or second-order characteristic?

4-45 Feedback is applied in an nMOST differential amplifier by inserting R_E between both sources (see Fig. EX4-45). What value of C_E is required to compensate the effect of the C_{GS} capacitances in the transistors? Use a pole-zero position diagram.

4-46 Optimize the ratio $R_{\text{out}}/R_{\text{in}}$ for the simple two-transistor current mirror of Fig. 4-72b, if $B = 1$. Use $V_{En} = 5$ V/μm and $L_{2\text{max}} = 10\ \mu$m.

4-47 Design the current mirror shown in Fig. EX4-47 (in a p-well process). Transistor parameters are $K'_n = 25\ \mu\text{A/V}^2$, $V_T = 0.8$ V and $n = 1.5$.

4-48 Design a current mirror as in Fig. 4-76a and b for a large $R_{\text{out}}/R_{\text{in}}$ ratio ($B = 1$), and low V_{outc}. Plot for both the output current versus V_{out} and indicate V_{outc}.

4-49 Compare the frequency performance of the current mirrors of Fig. 4-76a and b, if all capacitances C_{GS} are introduced ($B = 1$).

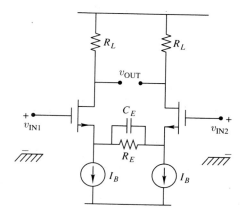

FIGURE EX4-45   Differential amplifier with feedback.

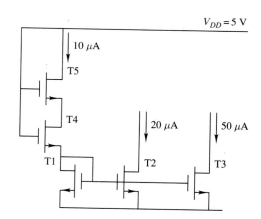

FIGURE EX4-47   Current mirror.

4-50 Compare the noise performance of the current mirrors of Fig. 4-76a and b ($B = 1$).

4-51 Design the current mirror of Fig. 4-76c for $i_{\text{IN}} = i_{\text{OUT}} = 0.1$ mA and minimum V_{outc}. Calculate all W/L for $V_T = 1$ V; $K'_n = 30$ μA/V^2.

4-52 Design the current mirror of Fig. 4-76d for $i_{\text{IN}} = i_{\text{OUT}} = 0.1$ mA and minimum V_{outc}. Calculate all W/L for $V_T = 1$ V; $K'_n = 30$ μA/V^2; take T1 = T2 = T4.

4-53 Take the current mirror amplifier shown (Fig. EX4-53) with $I_L = 100$ μA and $R_S = 5$ kΩ. Determine the W/L values and B for maximum GBW, and low equivalent input noise ($C_L = 5$ pF). Repeat after including series resistors, in both sources of $R_E = 5$ kΩ and $B = 1$.

4-54 Design a Widlar current mirror (Fig. 4-77c) for $I_{\text{IN}} = 100$ μA and $I_{\text{OUT}} = 2$ μA, Plot R_2 for $B = 2, 3$, and 4 to 10.

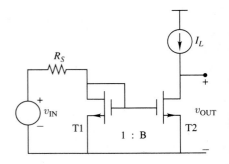

FIGURE EX4-53 Current mirror amplifier.

4-55 Calculate the exact expressions of the error in output current Δi_{OUT}, and the output resistance R_{out} for the current mirrors of Fig. 4-77d and 4-78a ($B = 1$).

4-56 Compare the frequency performance of the current mirrors of Fig. 4-77e and f, if all capacitances C_π are introduced ($B = 1$).

4-57 Design a current mirror of the type in Fig. 4-78a, for $I_{\mathrm{IN}} = I_{\mathrm{OUT}} = 500\ \mu\mathrm{A}$. Transistor parameters are $f_{T\,\max} = 600$ MHz, all $C_\mu = 0.5$ pF, $C_{jE} = 1.5$ pF, and $C_{CS} = 2$ pF. Repeat for lateral pnps, for which $f_{T\,\max} = 5$ MHz, all $C_\mu = C_{jE} = 0.5$ pF. Also $\beta_N = 100$ and $\beta_P = 10$.

4-58 Compare the high frequency performance of the current mirrors of Fig. 4-78a and Fig. 4-77(e), if all capacitances C_π are included ($B = 1$).

4-59 Compare the BICMOS current mirrors shown in Fig. EX4-59 for the error in output current Δi_{OUT} and the output resistance R_{out}.

4-60 Compare the Darlington configuration of Fig. 4-83a with the single-transistor amplifier of Fig. 4-14a, for the gain and input resistance.

4-61 Calculate the *GBW* of the amplifier of Fig. 4-84 configurations if only capacitances C_π (or C_{GS}) and C_L are included.

4-62 Calculate the *GBW* of the amplifier of Fig. 4-84 configurations if only capacitances C_μ (or C_{DG}) and C_L are included.

FIGURE EX4-59 BICMOS current mirrors.

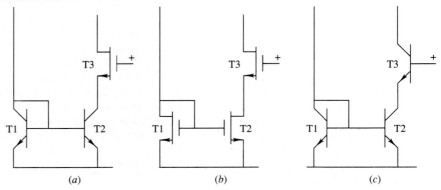

APPENDIX 4-1: The Pole-Zero Position Diagram: Evaluation of a Transfer Characteristic for Different Parameters

Let us assume that a transfer characteristic is given as a function of complex frequency. Commonly, this characteristic is evaluated by plotting its amplitude (magnitude) and phase versus frequency (Bode diagram). However, this characteristic usually depends on several circuit parameters, such as transconductance, resistances, and capacitances. In order to gain insight into the role of each circuit parameter, we must change its value and verify the corresponding changes in the Bode diagram. A better approach consists of drawing a separate plot of the poles and zeros of this characteristic, with this circuit parameter as a variable. This is the pole-zero position diagram (Sansen and Chang 1990). An example is completed to illustrate this technique. We have taken a complicated example in which the analysis has been carried out in great detail. In most text examples, the analyses are not taken to this extent.

As an example, the voltage gain A_v of an emitter follower is taken. The transfer characteristic appeared in Eq. (4-62) and is repeated here. It is given by

$$A_v = \frac{1 + \left(\dfrac{C_\pi}{g_m}\right) s}{1 + \left[\left(1 + \dfrac{R'_S}{r'_o}\right) \dfrac{C_\pi}{g_m} + \left(1 + \dfrac{R'_S}{r_\pi}\right) \dfrac{C_L}{g_m} + R'_S C_\mu\right] s + \left(\dfrac{R'_S}{g_m}\right) C^2 s^2}$$

and can be simplified to

$$A_v = \frac{1 + \left(\dfrac{C_\pi}{g_m}\right) s}{1 + \left(\dfrac{C_\pi + C_L}{g_m + R_S C_\mu}\right) s + \left(\dfrac{R_S}{g_m} C^2\right) s^2} \qquad (A4\text{-}1a)$$

with

$$C^2 = C_\pi C_\mu + C_\pi C_L + C_\mu C_L \qquad (A4\text{-}1b)$$

which can also be written as

$$C'^2 = C_{jE} C_\mu + C_{jE} C_L + C_\mu C_L \qquad (A4\text{-}1c)$$

since

$$C_\pi = C_{jE} + g_m \tau_F \qquad (A4\text{-}1d)$$

with

$$C^2 = C'^2 + g_m \tau_F (C_L + C_\mu) \qquad (A4\text{-}1e)$$

In this expression, there are six independent variables, i.e., g_m, R_S, C_μ, C_{jE}, C_L, and τ_F. Each can be used to generate different Bode diagrams. Some are instructive, e.g., those diagrams with variables R_S and C_L. In this example, however, we want to evaluate the positions of the zero and the two poles with g_m as a variable. Indeed, g_m depends on the current and is an often-used design parameter.

The numerical values are taken from Table 4-3. They are $R_S = 1.2$ kΩ, $C_\mu = 1.5$ pF, $C_{jE} = 6$ pF, $C_L = 10$ pF, and $\tau_F = 0.2$ ns. As a result, $C^2 = 107$ (pF)^2 and $C'^2 = 84$ (pF)^2.

Poles and Zeros   Each pole and zero must be written as a function of g_m and plotted versus frequency, as shown in Fig. A4-1a.

The expression of the zero is given by

$$f_z = \frac{g_m}{2\pi C_\mu} \tag{A4-2}$$

which is linearly proportional to g_m. For $g_m = 10$ mS, $f_z = 1.06$ GHz. The zero is plotted in Fig. A4-1a. It increases with increasing g_m.

FIGURE A4-1

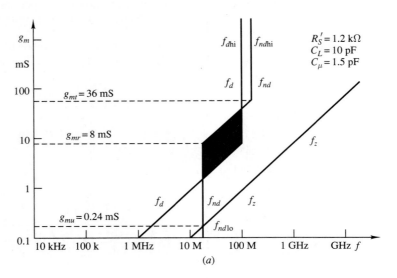

(a)

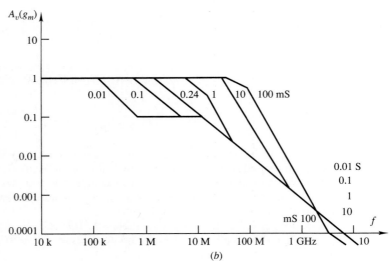

(b)

The expression of the dominant pole is found by assuming that the pole at lowest frequency is dominant. Its value is then extracted from the coefficient in s in the denominator of Eq. (A4-1a). (See App. 3-1.) It is given by

$$f_d = \frac{g_m}{2\pi \left[(C_\pi + C_L) + g_m R_S C_\mu \right]} \tag{A4-3a}$$

in which C_π is a function of g_m, as well, as given by Eq. (A4-1e). Taking g_m as a variable allows us to rewrite Eq. (A4-3a), as given by

$$f_d = \left[\frac{g_m}{2\pi (C_{jE} + C_L)} \right] \left(\frac{g_m}{1 + \frac{g_m}{g_{mr}}} \right) \tag{A4-3b}$$

with
$$g_{mr} = \frac{C_{jE} + C_L}{\tau_F + R_S C_\mu} \tag{A4-3c}$$

The curve of f_d in Fig. A4-1a has a breakpoint at $g_m = g_{mr}$ ($= 8$ mS in this example). At high values of g_m the dominant pole is constant. It occurs at frequency

$$f_{d\text{hi}} = \frac{g_{mr}}{2\pi (C_{jE} + C_L)} = \frac{1}{2\pi (\tau_F + R_S C_\mu)} \tag{A4-4}$$

which is 80 MHz, in this example.

The expression of the nondominant pole is given by the ratio of the coefficient in s to that in s^2 in the denominator (see App. 3-1). It is given by

$$f_{nd} = \frac{C_\pi + C_L + g_m R_S C_\mu}{2\pi R_S C^2} \tag{A4-5a}$$

in which both C_π and C^2 depend on g_m. Thus it can be rewritten as

$$f_{nd} = \left(\frac{C_{jE} + C_L}{2\pi R_S C^2} \right) \left(\frac{1 + \frac{g_m}{g_{mr}}}{1 + \frac{g_m}{g_{mt}}} \right) \tag{A4-5b}$$

in which g_{mr} is given above, and g_{mt} is given by

$$g_{mt} = \frac{C'^2}{\tau_F (C_\mu + C_L)} \tag{A4-5c}$$

or 36.5 mS, in this example.

Thus, the curve of f_{nd} in Fig. A4-1a has two breakpoints, one at g_{mr} and one at g_{mt}. For low values of $g_m (< g_{mr})$, the value of f_{nd} is constant and given by

$$f_{ndlo} = \frac{C_{jE} + C_L}{2\pi R_S C'^2} \tag{A4-6}$$

which is 25.2 MHz in this example. For high values of $g_m (> g_{mt})$, the value of f_{nd} is constant again and given by

$$f_{ndhi} = f_{ndlo} \left(\frac{g_{mt}}{g_{mr}} \right) = \frac{C_\mu + \tau_F/R_S}{2\pi \tau_F (C_\mu + C_L)} \tag{A4-7}$$

which is 138 MHz. Now, the full curve of f_{nd} is easily added in Fig. A4-1a.

Complex Poles   It is striking to note, however, that for values of g_m around 10 mS, the value of the nondominant pole is lower than the value of the dominant pole. Obviously, this is wrong. Thus, the approximations that have allowed us to calculate f_d and f_{nd} are wrong. For all values of g_m, where $f_{nd} < f_d$, the poles are complex. This region is denoted by hatch marks in Fig. A4-1a.

Both complex poles are then given by the coefficient of the term in s^2 (see App. 3-1), as given by

$$f_c = \frac{1}{2\pi} \sqrt{\frac{g_m}{R_S C^2}} \tag{A4-8a}$$

in which C^2 depends on g_m. This can be rewritten as

$$f_c = \frac{1}{2\pi} \sqrt{\frac{g_m}{R_S C'^2 \left(1 + \dfrac{g_m}{g_{mr}}\right)}} \tag{A4-8b}$$

This curve is represented by the solid line in the middle of the hatched region of Fig. A4-1a, connecting the two extreme points where f_d and f_{nd} coincide.

Where complex poles occur, peaking can occur as well. Therefore, this region must be made as small as possible, if not completely avoided. Therefore, the boundaries of this region are subject to closer investigation. In the frequency domain, the boundary frequencies are simply given by f_{dhi} and f_{ndlo}. Their ratio is given by

$$\frac{f_{dhi}}{f_{ndlo}} = \frac{C'^2}{(C_\mu + \tau_F/R_S)(C_{jE} + C_L)} \tag{A4-9}$$

or 3.2 in this example.

In the g_m domain, on the contrary, the boundary values still must be derived. On the high g_m side, the value of g_{mhi} is found at the crosspoint of f_{nd} and f_{dhi}. It is given by

$$g_{mhi} = \frac{R_S C'^2}{(\tau_F + R_S C_\mu)^2} \tag{A4-10}$$

On the other hand, the value of g_{mlo} is found at the crossing of f_d and f_{ndlo}. It is given by

$$g_{mlo} = \frac{(C_{jE} + C_L)^2}{R_S C'^2} \tag{A4-11}$$

The (harmonic) average value of g_m in the hatched region is obviously $g_{mr} = \sqrt{g_{mhi} g_{mlo}}$. The ratio of both g_{mhi}/g_{mlo} is easily found. By use of Eq. (A4-7), it can be written as

$$\frac{g_{mhi}}{g_{mlo}} = \left(\frac{f_{dhi}}{f_{dlo}}\right)^2 \tag{A4-12}$$

which is hardly a surprise, since all slopes in Fig. A4-1a are integers with value 2, 1, and 0 (horizontal line).

In order to make the hatched region as small as possible, the ratio f_{dhi}/f_{dlo} must be made small. This ratio can also be approximated by (if $R_S C_\mu > \tau_F$):

$$\frac{f_{dhi}}{f_{dlo}} = 1 + \frac{C_{\mu r}}{C_\mu} \tag{A4-13a}$$

with

$$C_{\mu r} = \frac{C_{jE} C_L}{C_{jE} + C_L} \tag{A4-13b}$$

which is 3.5 and 3.75 pF.

It is clear that this ratio can never be smaller than unity. Thus, complex poles are always present at $g_m = g_{mr}(= 8 \text{ mS})$. This ratio can be made small by increasing C_μ. It is not worth increasing C_μ more than its critical value $C_{\mu r}$. As a result, however, the -3 dB frequency will decrease.

If $C_\mu = C_{\mu r}$ and $\tau_F < R_S C_\mu$, the value of g_{mr} can be simplified to

$$g_{m\mu r} = \frac{1}{R_S}\left(\frac{(1+x)^2}{x}\right) \tag{A4-14}$$

with $x = C_{jE}/C_L$.

For given values of R_S and g_m, Eq. (A4-14) shows at what values of C_L the emitter follower is unstable, even for an optimal value of C_μ, given by Eq. (A4-13b).

For low values of g_m, a cancellation occurs between f_{ndlo} and f_z (see Fig. A2-5) at the value of $g_m = g_{mu}$. It is given by

$$g_{mu} = \frac{C_\mu(C_{jE} + C_L)}{R_S C'^2} \tag{A4-15}$$

At this value of g_m, a single pole results. Hence, a single-pole characteristic is obtained (see Fig. A4-1b). Its -3 dB frequency is derived from Eq. (A4-3b), and is given by

$$f_{du} = \frac{g_{mu}}{2\pi(C_{jE} + C_L)} \tag{A4-16}$$

This value obviously decreases with increasing C_L.

For values of g_m lower than g_{mu}, the zero occurs between both poles. This causes a resistive (flat) region in the transfer characteristic (Fig. A4-1b). This region is a result of a capacitive division. The value of the gain in that region is given by

$$A_{vm} = \frac{C_\mu}{2\pi(C_{jE} + C_L)} \tag{A4-17}$$

which is 0.094 (but is 0.22 if $C_\mu = C_{\mu r} = 3.5$ pF).

At high values of g_m (for $g_m > g_{mt}$), two distinct poles occur. Still, the dominant pole f_d is at lower frequencies than the nondominant pole f_{nd}. This is pure coincidence, however. The ratio of f_{ndhi} to f_{dhi} is easily calculated from Eqs. (A4-7) and (A4-4). It is given by

$$\frac{f_{ndhi}}{f_{dhi}} = \frac{(\tau_F + R_S C_\mu)2}{\tau_F R_S(C_\mu + C_L)} \tag{A4-18a}$$

which can be further simplified, if $\tau_F < R_S C_\mu$, to

$$\frac{f_{ndhi}}{f_{dhi}} = \frac{R_S C_\mu^2}{\tau_F(C_\mu + C_L)} \tag{A4-18b}$$

In order for the poles to avoid becoming complex, this ratio must be larger than unity, or, (if $C_\mu < C_L$),

$$C_\mu > \sqrt{\frac{\tau_F C_L}{R_S}} \tag{A4-19}$$

which is 1.3 pF in this example. For a given value of R_S, the minimum value of C_μ is an increasing function of load capacitance. On the other hand, for a given C_μ, source resistance R_S has a minimum value given by Eq. (A4-18b). Finally, for given values of C_μ and R_S, Eq. (A4-18b) gives the value of the maximum load capacitance C_L, and this value increases with increasing R_S.

Finally, at very high frequencies, not all curves coincide (see Fig. A4-1b). The gain can be approximated by

$$A_{vhif} = \frac{C_\mu}{R_S C'^2(1 + g_m/g_{mt})s} \tag{A4-20}$$

with g_{mt} given by Eq. (A4-5c). All curves coincide if $g_m < g_{mt}$ (36 mS). They give a value of $A_{vhif} = 2.4 \times 10^{-4}$ at 10 GHz. For higher values of g_m, the resulting curves are lower (see the curve of 100 mS in Fig. A4-1b). Of course, at those frequencies, the model is probably no longer valid.

In this way, the transfer characteristic given by Eq. (4-62) is fully analyzed with g_m as a parameter. This procedure can be repeated with any of the other five circuit parameters as a variable. It is strongly urged that the reader go through at least one such analysis to ensure familiarity with the procedure.

REFERENCES

Abidi, A. 1988. "On the operation of cascode gain stages," *IEEE Journal of Solid-State Circuits*, vol. 23, no. 6, pp. 1434–1437.

Antognetti, P., and G. Massobrio. 1988. *Semiconductor Device Modeling with SPICE*. New York: McGraw-Hill.

Chang, Z. Y., and W. Sansen. 1991. *Low-Noise Wide-Band Amplifiers in Bipolar and CMOS Technologies*. Norwell, MA: Kluwer Academic.

Getreu, I. 1976. "Modeling the bipolar transistor." Tektronix.

Gielen, G., and W. Sansen. 1991. *Symbolic Analysis for Automated Design of Analog Circuits*. Norwell, MA: Kluwer Academic.

Gray, P., and R. Meyer. 1984. *Analysis and Design of Analog Integrated Circuits*. New York: Wiley and Sons.

Ott, H. W. 1988. *Noise Reduction Techniques in Electronic Systems*. New York: Wiley and Sons.

Sansen, W., and Z. Y. Chang. 1990. "Feedforward Compensation Techniques for High-Frequency CMOS Amplifiers," *IEEE Journal of Solid-State Circuits*, vol. 25, no. 6, pp. 1590–1595.

Sedra, A., and K. Smith. 1987. *Microelectronic Circuits*. New York: Holt, Reinhart, and Winston.

Sze, S. 1981. *Physics of Semiconductor Devices*. New York: Wiley and Sons.

5

BEHAVIORAL MODELING OF OPERATIONAL AND TRANSCONDUCTANCE AMPLIFIERS

INTRODUCTION

We now turn to the study of operational and transconductance amplifiers, and their applications in analog systems, from a behavioral point of view. A strong understanding of behavioral issues is a prerequisite to the undertaking of the transistor level design of these amplifiers and/or the synthesis of higher level circuits that use them as components. Fortunately, we can greatly simplify the analysis and design of complex analog systems, involving many such amplifiers, using approximate models for the amplifiers based on behavioral descriptions rather than circuit schematics. The behavioral models developed in this chapter will be used extensively in the analysis and design of analog systems in Chaps. 7 and 8. Moreover, as we will learn in Chap. 6, such models are useful aids in mapping detailed specifications to the attributes of an amplifier's transistor level circuit schematic.

The *operational amplifier* or *op amp* is one of the most versatile and widely used building blocks in linear circuit applications. (Allen and Holberg 1987; Daryanani 1976; Ghausi 1985; Gray, Hodges, and Broderson 1980; Gray and Meyer 1984; Grebene 1984; Moschytz 1975; Schaumann, Ghausi, and Laker 1990; Sedra and Smith 1991; Soclof 1985). The availability of high-performance yet inexpensive op amps has had a dramatic influence on the electronics industry. Today, integrated circuit op amps can be obtained off-the-shelf, packaged as single and multiple unit devices. It is not unusual to find ten or more op amps incorporated into the implementation of a mixed analog/digital very large scale integrated (VLSI) chip. High quality integrated circuit op amps have reached component level prices, on the order of $0.1 per op amp (or less when incorporated into a VLSI device). Their cheap price, general availability, near ideal performance, and versatility justify their wide acceptance among circuit

408

designers and their emphasis in this text. Consequently, the balance of coverage in this chapter is heavily weighted toward the op amp.

Basically, op amps are direct coupled differential amplifiers with extremely high voltage gain, extremely high input impedance, and very low output impedance. They are usually used with external feedback to achieve precision gain and bandwidth control. In fact, for linear circuit applications, external feedback is a necessity. Due to the importance of feedback in the application of op amps, the concepts of feedback and stability were reviewed in Chap. 3. Today, op amps are realized as silicon integrated circuits using both bipolar CMOS and BICMOS technologies. BICMOS (Nayebi and Wooley 1988), as described in Chap. 2, is a high performance analog technology that incorporates the major features of both bipolar and CMOS transistors. In addition, GHz (10^9 Hz) op amps have been fabricated with GaAs technology for research purposes. Currently, GaAs op amps are relatively expensive and not generally available.

The design lure for MOS op amps initially developed around the NMOS technology (Gray, Hodges, and Broderson 1980). Limited by design constraints associated with the lack of complimentary devices, even the most creative NMOS op amp designs could not deliver the high quality performance readily achievable in a straightforward bipolar design. In the past ten years, there has been significant progress in the development of design techniques to realize high performance, very compact, and low power CMOS op amps for switched-capacitor (SC) filters, A/D converters, and a vast variety of analog systems (Allen and Holberg 1987; Gray, Hodges, and Broderson 1980; Gray and Meyer 1984; Grebene 1984). Attracted by low power dissipation and considerable design flexibility, CMOS is also becoming the principal technology for a growing number of digital VLSI designs. Consequently, with its capabilities for supporting high quality analog and digital circuitry, CMOS has evolved as the technology of choice for the realization of mixed analog/digital VLSI devices.

The recent attention given to the realization of precision, fully integrated active-RC filters at frequencies well above the audio band (i.e., $f > 1$ MHz), has stimulated renewed interest in the *transconductance amplifier*, also called the *operational transconductance amplifier* or *OTA* (Geiger and Sanchez-Sinencio 1985; Schaumann, Ghausi, and Laker 1990; Unbehauen and Cichocki 1989). An OTA is a voltage-controlled current source with a specified transconductance gain G_m. The OTA and the op amp are related in that the core of an OTA is essentially an op amp differential input stage. Hence, being somewhat simpler than conventional op amps, OTAs offer the potential for retaining near ideal behavior at higher frequencies. Moreover, the design and implementation of bipolar and CMOS OTAs have benefited directly from advances that have occurred in the op amp area.

As we will see in this chapter, op amp-based circuits derive significant advantages from their elegant use of large amounts of external feedback. In fact, the use of feedback is essential when op amps are used in linear applications. In contrast, feedback is not required in the use of OTAs in linear circuits. However, in the absence of feedback, the designer must complicate the basic OTA structure with added circuitry to acquire important performance characteristics (e.g., linearity over a wide range of signal amplitudes) that come painlessly with the use of external feedback in op amp circuits. Techniques to linearize OTAs for filter applications are reserved for Chap. 8. Nonetheless, it appears that OTAs will play an increasingly important role in VLSI analog circuits and systems, particularly where operation is required at frequencies beyond the comfort range for standard op amps, i.e., $f > 100$ kHz.

In this chapter, we study the behavioral or "black box" specification and modeling of both op amps and OTAs. That is, our concern is with specifying and modeling the behavior of these circuits as seen at their input/output interfaces or terminals. Switched-capacitor circuits, being sampled data systems, represent an important departure from the traditional use of op amps in continuous-time circuits. To assist in the behavioral modeling of switched-capacitor circuits, z-domain equivalent circuits will be developed in Chap. 7.

As you will discover in subsequent chapters, well designed op amps and OTAs achieve near ideal performance over a broad range of conditions. Hence, a vast majority of the analog circuits designed with either op amps or OTAs as their active components work very close to their predicted theoretical performance. This simplifies the design of such circuits considerably and simple behavioral models are often quite sufficient for the design of practical circuits. Several examples that demonstrate this fact and illustrate the application of the design principles to the realization of several fundamental analog functions will be given. The reader is not to be misled into the notion that he or she does not need to master the inner details of the op amp and OTA circuits. For demanding and cost sensitive applications, one may be required to design a custom op amp, modify an existing op amp design, or evaluate a given op amp circuit at the transistor level. In particular, OTAs are typically custom designed for each application. The transistor level analysis and design of op amps and OTAs, treated in Chap. 6, are facilitated by the behavioral understanding developed in this chapter.

5-1   THE OP AMP SCHEMATIC SYMBOL AND IDEAL MODEL

A conventional op amp has three signal-bearing terminals, illustrated in the op amp circuit symbol given in Fig. 5-1. The terminals labeled v^+, v^- are inputs and the terminal labeled v_{out} is the output. They are designated by the total instantaneous voltages v^+, v^-, and v_{out}, and defined as total instantaneous voltages[1] between the respective terminals and ground. The op amp triangle is the standardized graphic symbol used to designate the generic op amp in circuit schematics. Since the op amp is an active circuit, it requires appropriate DC power to operate properly. It has been conventional practice to operate analog devices over a $2V_B$ volt range, centered about a zero volt or ground potential reference. Consequently, many op amps are powered from two external DC supplies, one a positive voltage ($V_{DD} = +V_B$ volts) and the other a negative voltage ($V_{SS} = -V_B$ volts), as shown in Fig. 5-2. More recently, with power from a single positive $V_{DD} = +V_B$ volt supply becoming standard for digital

---

[1] To avoid confusion, please take note of the notation used in this book with regard to voltages and currents, and their respective transforms listed in App. 1-1.

FIGURE 5-1   Op amp circuit symbol showing only the signal bearing terminals.

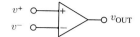

CMOS VLSI devices, compatible CMOS op amps have been designed to operate over a 0 to $+V_B$ volt range, with a reference level of $V_B/2$ volts.

Note that many practical integrated circuit op amps provide additional terminals to permit the use of external circuitry to customize specific support functions. Such functions include frequency compensation, DC offset nulling, and gain bandwidth adjustment, all of which will be explained in subsequent sections. When op amps are embedded in a VLSI device, the input/output signals are routed from/to internal circuits and all the required support functions except power are implemented on the chip. In these cases, the original op amp terminals are generally unavailable for external use.

The function of the op amp is rather simple and it is graphically characterized in the circuit symbol. That is, the op amp produces at the output terminal a signal v_{OUT}, derived as the product of the input voltage difference $(v^+ - v^-)$ and the gain A_0, i.e.,

$$v_{OUT} = A_0(v^+ - v^-) \qquad (5\text{-}1)$$

The ideal op amp operates like an ideal *voltage-controlled voltage source* (VCVS) as per Fig. 5-3. That is, the input impedance of the ideal op amp is infinite (i.e., $Z_{inc} = Z_{ind} = \infty$) and the output impedance is zero ($Z_{out} = 0$). Hence, the ideal op amp draws no current through its input terminals and its output voltage is always governed by the relation in Eq. (5-1), independent of the load connected across the output terminal and ground. Note that the output v_{out} is in phase with input v^+ and 180 degrees out of phase with input v^-. Consequently, the v^+ input terminal is referred to as the *noninverting terminal* and the v^- input terminal is referred to as the *inverting terminal*.

Reflecting on Eq. (5-1), the ideal op amp is observed to respond only to the *difference* or *differential* between the noninverting and inverting inputs, while any signal components that are common between the two inputs are exactly canceled.

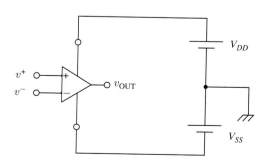

FIGURE 5-2   Op amp circuit symbol with DC power terminals also shown.

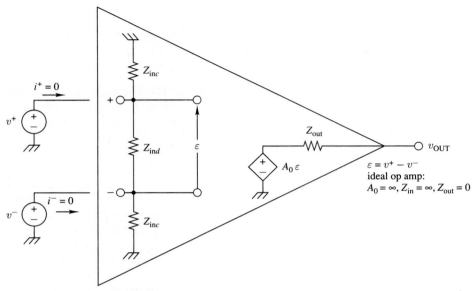

FIGURE 5-3   Behavioral model for ideal differential input, single-ended output op amp.

This latter property is referred to as *common-mode rejection*. It is seen to be infinite in the case of the ideal op amp. The finite common-mode rejection of practical op amps will be discussed later. Due to the differential input property, the ideal op amp is more precisely referred to as an ideal *differential input, single-ended output amplifier*. Later in the chapter we will consider an op amp that provides two output terminals for balanced, differential output signals v_{OUT}^+ and v_{OUT}^-, as shown in Fig. 5-4.

The gain A_0, appropriately referred to as the op amp *differential gain*, is very large—approaching infinity for the ideal op amp over the infinite frequency range $0 \leq \omega = 2\pi f \leq \infty$. This introduces another important characteristic of the op amp; it amplifies signals at frequencies as low as zero Hz (or DC). Because of this quality, op amps are also referred to as *direct coupled* or *DC amplifiers*. As we will discuss later, practical op amps do not have infinite gain and bandwidth. Their gain, particularly at low frequencies, is finite but very large (80 to 100 dB) and its frequency dependence is a lowpass characteristic. The input and output impedances

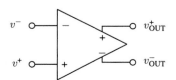

FIGURE 5-4   Differential input-differential output op amp.

are also finite. As shown in Fig. 5-3, input impedance has two components: (1) a differential input impedance Z_{ind} connected across the two input terminals; and (2) a common-mode input impedance Z_{inc} connected between each input terminal and ground. In the usual frequency ranges of interest, Z_{inc} and Z_{ind} are resistive and very large, i.e., $R_{ic} > 100$ MΩ and $R_{id} \approx 10$ MΩ. Thus, $|Z_{inc}| \gg |Z_{ind}|$ and hence Z_{inc} is usually ignored and the input impedance of the op amp is $Z_{in} = Z_{ind}$. The output impedance Z_{out} is typically resitive and small, such that 100 $\Omega \leq R_{out} \leq 10$ kΩ; depending upon the application and microcircuit technology involved. It is fortunate for many applications that the large low frequency gain, very high input impedance and very low output impedance, of practical op amps provides near ideal performance. Thus, the *ideal op amp* (infinite gain, infinite bandwidth, infinite input impedance, zero output impedance and infinite common-mode rejection) is often a good approximation to the actual device. Making use of this approximation greatly simplifies the analysis and synthesis of circuits that use op amps.

Before leaving the subject of the ideal op amp, more should be said about the very large, ideally infinite, differential gain A_0. The transfer characteristic for a typical op amp is shown in Fig. 5-5. Due to the large gain, the range of input (differential) voltage for linear operation is very small. This range is expressed as

$$\varepsilon = v^+ - v^- = \frac{v_{OUT}}{A_0} \approx 0 \qquad (5\text{-}2)$$

FIGURE 5-5   Typical op amp transfer characteristic.

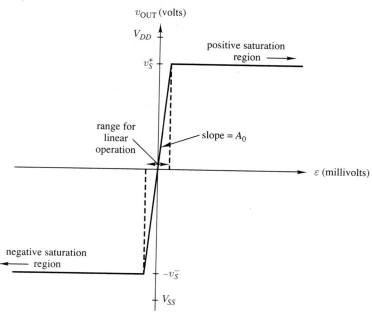

Equation (5-2) implies that ε must be very small. Note that the op amp saturates for large positive and negative voltages, i.e., $\max(v_{\text{OUT}}) = v_S^+ < V_{DD}$ and $\min(v_{\text{OUT}}) = -v_S^- > V_{SS}$. In general, these operating limits are not symmetrical, i.e., $v_S^+ \neq v_S^-$. However, in Chap. 6 the reader will learn that v_S^+, v_S^- are determined by the supply voltages V_{DD}, and V_{SS}, the device parameters for the IC technology in use, and the particular design of the op amp. In many applications the op amp design goals require the designer to make the saturation voltages as symmetrical and as close to the supply voltages as possible.

Based on the characteristic in Fig. 5-5, one justifiably questions the utility op amps in linear applications. The remedy to this dilemma is the use of feedback. In linear applications, the op amp is never used in an open-loop configuration; instead it is always embedded in some sort of feedback circuit or closed-loop configuration (e.g., Fig. 3-7) In this context the gain A_0 is often referred as the *op amp open-loop gain*.

When the input differential exceeds the linear range, the op amp operates as a nonlinear device. This property is used in many nonlinear applications (Allen and Holberg 1987; Ghausi 1985; Gray and Meyer 1984; Grebene 1984; Sedra and Smith 1991; Soclof 1985), such as in comparator, oscillator, and Schmitt trigger circuits.

5-2 ANALYSIS OF CIRCUITS INVOLVING OP AMPS

In this section, we use the behavioral or "black box" model of the ideal op amp to perform pencil-and-paper analyses of various op amp circuits. The techniques discussed are only valid for linear circuits. With the general availability of high powered personal computers (PCs), workstations, and/or main frame computers, reasonable questions to ask are: Why do we need idealized models? Why do we perform pencil-and-paper analyses? First, analyses with ideal op amp models are quick, very efficient and usually provide rather accurate results. Second, computer simulations yield numerical data for only the particular circuit conditions addressed; while pencil-and-paper analyses yield equations and parameters that address a range of conditions and provide insights that lead to a better understanding of the circuit. When the circuit becomes sufficiently complex, brute-force pencil-and-paper analysis of the circuit is not practical. In these cases, the op amp's near ideal VCVS conditions permit large circuits, involving several op amps, to be partitioned into a collection of smaller subcircuits. Each subcircuit is then individually analyzed with pencil and paper and the results mathematically combined to yield the overall result. Let us now analyze a few op amp circuits to get a feel for what is involved and to establish several useful op amp "building-block" circuits.

5-2-1 Inverting Configuration

Let us consider the circuit, referred to in the literature as the *inverting configuration*, shown in Fig. 5-6a. The name given to this circuit is very descriptive of its function, i.e., it inverts the input signal by introducing a $180°$ phase shift. This circuit consists of one op amp and two passive (complex and frequency dependent) impedances Z_1 and Z. These are driving-point or input impedances for passive resistor-capacitor (RC)

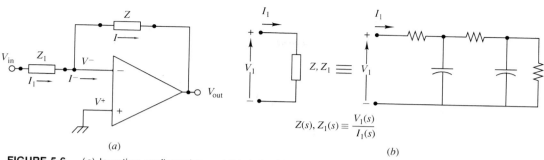

FIGURE 5-6   (a) Inverting configuration and (b) derivation of driving-point impedance functions Z and Z_1.

networks, shown in Fig. 5-6b. As we will soon see, Z_1 and Z represent networks that range from single elements (i.e., resistors and capacitors) to complex RC subcircuits. When this circuit is designed properly, its detailed function is determined largely by the properties of Z and Z_1.

In this circuit, impedance Z_1 is connected between the input[2] V_{in} and the op amp inverting input terminal V^-. Impedance Z introduces a negative feedback path between the output V_{out} and V^-. Finally, the noninverting op amp input terminal V^+ is connected to ground. If impedance Z were connected between the output and V^+, or if we could replace Z with a $-Z$, then the sense of the feedback would be inverted and the result would be positive feedback. Recalling the feedback configurations in Fig. 3-7, this feedback arrangement is recognized to be of the shunt-shunt type. In any event, connecting Z and Z_1 in this manner enables the designer to scale, shape, and regulate the closed-loop gain of the circuit rather precisely.

To simulate and design the inverting configuration, we construct the equivalent circuit in Fig. 5-7. In this circuit we use the op amp model in Fig. 5-3 with $Z_{in} = \infty$, $Z_{out} = 0$, and $V^+ = 0$. Note the inversion in the polarity of the VCVS in Fig. 5-7. This inversion is the result of connecting the signal input to the V^- or inverting terminal. It also follows from Fig. 5-3 and Eq. (5-1) when $V^+ = 0$. Since Z_1, Z, and A_0 are generally complex and frequency dependent (i.e., $Z_1 = Z_1(j\omega)$, $Z = Z(j\omega)$, and $A_0 = A_0(j\omega)$), we express the currents, voltages, and impedances in the frequency domain as either Fourier or Laplace transforms. The reader is reminded that the notations used in this text to represent the various definitions for current and voltage are given in App. 1-1, located at the end of Chap. 1.

With reference to Eq. (5-2), we note that with very large A_0 (i.e., $A_0 \to \infty$), $V^- \approx V^+$. With the noninverting terminal V^+ connected to ground, it follows that $V^- \to 0$ as $A_0 \to \infty$. Because the V^- terminal is connected to zero potential in this indirect manner, it is referred to as a *virtual ground*. As the reader becomes more experienced in working with op amps, he or she will develop a great appreciation for

---

[2]Please note that V_{in}, V^+, V^-, and V_{out} represent the Laplace transforms of these terminal voltages.

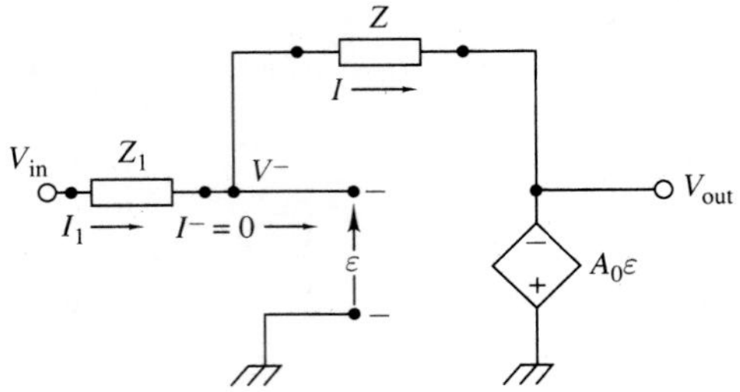

FIGURE 5-7   Equivalent circuit for the inverting configuration using the op amp model in Fig. 5-3 with $Z_{in} = \infty$ and $Z_{out} = 0$.

the value of the virtual ground. Although ideally large, in practice $|A_0(j\omega)|$ decreases rapidly as ω increases. Thus, it limits the near ideal behavior of the closed-loop $A_{CL}(s)$ to a somewhat narrow bandwidth. Moreover, $A_0(s)$, combined with the feedback introduced by $Z(s)$ and $Z_1(s)$, can result in instability or an undesirable transient response (as described in Chap. 3). Later in this chapter, and in Chap. 6, we show how to shape A_0 to counter these effects.

With an elementary circuit analysis of Fig. 5-7, we can straightforwardly determine the closed-loop gain $A_{CL}(s) = V_{out}/V_{in}$. We begin the analysis with an accounting of the currents branching from the virtual ground; namely,

$$I^- = I_1 - I = 0 \tag{5-3}$$

where

$$I_1 = \frac{(V_{in} - V^-)}{Z_1} \quad \text{and} \quad I = \frac{(V^- - V_{out})}{Z} \tag{5-4}$$

Combining Eqs. (5-3) and (5-4) yields

$$\frac{(V_{in} - V^-)}{Z_1} + \frac{(V_{out} - V^-)}{Z} = 0 \tag{5-5}$$

where

$$V^- = -\frac{V_{out}}{A_0(s)} \tag{5-6}$$

or

$$\frac{V_{in}}{Z_1} + \frac{V_{out}}{Z} = V^- \left(\frac{1}{Z_1} + \frac{1}{Z} \right) = -\frac{V_{out}}{A_0(s)} \left(\frac{1}{Z_1} + \frac{1}{Z} \right) \tag{5-7}$$

Rearranging terms to form the ratio V_{out}/V_{in} yields the desired relation for the closed-loop gain $A_{CL}(s)$, i.e.,

$$A_{CL}(s) = \frac{V_{out}}{V_{in}} = -\frac{Z}{Z_1} \left(\frac{1}{1 + \dfrac{1}{A_0(s)} \left(1 + \dfrac{Z}{Z_1} \right)} \right) = -\frac{Z}{Z_1} \left(\frac{1}{1 + \varepsilon_{rr}(s)} \right) \tag{5-8a}$$

For the ideal op amp where $A_0 = \infty$ (or $1/A_0 = 0$), $\varepsilon_{rr} = 0$ and $A_{CL}(s)$ reduces to the well known expression

$$A_{CL\infty}(s) = \frac{V_{\text{out}}}{V_{\text{in}}} = -\frac{Z}{Z_1} \tag{5-8b}$$

We use the ∞ subscript to designate the ideal op amp closed-loop gain.

The function $\varepsilon_{rr}(s)$ represents the error due to the nonideal op amp gain A_0, or $1/A_0 \neq 0$, i.e.,

$$\varepsilon_{rr}(s) = \frac{1}{A_0}\left(1 + \frac{Z}{Z_1}\right) = \frac{1}{A_0(s)}(1 - A_\infty) \tag{5-8c}$$

For $s = j\omega$ and for $|\varepsilon_{rr}(j\omega)| \ll 1$, we can conveniently express ε_{rr} in terms of magnitude and phase, i.e.,

$$\varepsilon_{rr}(j\omega) = m_{rr}(\omega)e^{j\varphi_{rr}(\omega)} \approx m_{rr}(\omega) + j\varphi_{rr}(\omega) \tag{5-8d}$$

Clearly, the ε_{rr} decreases in magnitude as A_0 increases, and in fact reduces to zero as $1/A_0 \to 0$. Also, we see that ε_{rr} depends on the ratio of the external impedances Z/Z_1. Since in general A_0, Z, and/or Z_1 are complex and frequency dependent, ε_{rr} will also be complex and frequency dependent. Moreover, $|\varepsilon_{rr}|$ will usually increase with frequency (i.e., as $A_0(s)$ decreases).

Example 5-1

Derive the expression for the Bode sensitivity $S_{A_0}^{A_{CL}(s)}$, defined in Eq. (3-84c) for the inverting configuration modeled in Fig. 5-7.

Solution. Referring to Eq. (3-84c), our task is to determine

$$S_{A_0}^{A_{CL}(s)} = \frac{A_0}{A_{CL}(s)}\frac{\partial A_{CL}(s)}{\partial A_0} \tag{5-9}$$

where the derivative $\partial A_{CL}(s)/\partial A_0$, with $A_{CL}(s)$ given in Eq. (5-8a), can be written as

$$\frac{\partial A_{CL}(s)}{\partial A_0} = \frac{\dfrac{Z}{Z_1}\dfrac{1}{A_0^2}\left(1 + \dfrac{Z}{Z_1}\right)}{\left[1 + \dfrac{1}{A_0}\left(1 + \dfrac{Z}{Z_1}\right)\right]^2} \tag{5-10a}$$

Thus, the sensitivity is determined to be

$$S_{A_0}^{A_{CL}(s)} = \frac{\dfrac{1}{A_0}\left(1 + \dfrac{Z}{Z_1}\right)}{1 + \dfrac{1}{A_0}\left(1 + \dfrac{Z}{Z_1}\right)} \approx \frac{1}{A_0}\left(1 + \frac{Z}{Z_1}\right) = \varepsilon_{rr} \tag{5-10b}$$

We see that ε_{rr} is a good measure of the sensitivity of closed-loop $A_{CL}(s)$ to the op amp's open-loop A_0. Ideally, we would like this sensitivity to be zero. In Sec. 5-3-1, we consider schemes to reduce this error; in particular to widen the frequency range over which $|\varepsilon_{rr}| \ll 1$.

When we assume that the op amp is ideal, the analysis leading to Eq. (5-8b) can be shortened significantly. The simplification is based on the ideal virtual ground at V^- achieved when $1/A_0 = 0$. Setting $V^- = 0$ in Eqs. (5-4) and (5-5), we see that $A_{CL\infty}$ can be obtained directly from Eq. (5-5). With practice, the reader should find it straightforward to write circuit equations like Eq. (5-5) directly from inspection of the schematic. Examining Eq. (5-8b), one observes that $A_{CL\infty}$ is dependent only on the external feedback circuit; namely, the ratio of impedances Z_1 and Z. This is an important result which, as we will see in Chap. 7, enables us to realize active-RC and switched capacitor filters with precise characteristics. Even when the op amp is not ideal, which is clearly what we have in practice, we can still design the op amp and/or limit the feedback circuit such that, at least, $1/A_0(1 + Z/Z_1) \ll 1$. With this assumption we can write a convenient approximate expression for Eq. (5-8a), namely,

$$A_{CL}(s) \approx -\frac{Z}{Z_1}\left[1 - \frac{1}{A_0(s)}\left(1 + \frac{Z}{Z_1}\right)\right] = -\frac{Z}{Z_1}[1 - \varepsilon_{rr}(s)] \tag{5-11}$$

This expression is intuitively appealing in that the ε_{rr} function appears as a variation in $A_{CL}(s)$, i.e., $\Delta A_{CL}(s)$. Also, as we will see later, this approximation simplifies the expression for $A_{CL}(s)$ to a form which is convenient for back-of-the-envelope calculations.

Two important characteristics in the specification and design of inverting configurations are the input impedance Z_{inCL} and output impedance Z_{outCL}. They are particularly important when interfacing a particular design with other circuits and/or measurement equipment. The output impedance for the inverting configuration is the output impedance of the op amp scaled by $1/(1 + \mathcal{A}\mathcal{H})$, which is typically very small as noted earlier. Hence, for much of our work, we assume that the circuit has been designed such that $Z_{outCL} \approx 0$ or significantly less than the input impedance of the circuit it feeds. If this is not the case we use a buffer device to reduce the effective Z_{outCL}. Buffers will be discussed in the next subsection. The input impedance is readily derived using Eq. (5-4), i.e.,

$$Z_{inCL} = \frac{V_{in}}{I_1} = \frac{Z_1}{1 + \dfrac{A_{CL}(s)}{A_0(s)}} \approx \frac{Z_1}{1 + \dfrac{A_{CL\infty}(s)}{A_0(s)}} \tag{5-12a}$$

or, for the ideal op amp

$$Z_{inCL\infty} = \frac{V_{in}}{I_1}\Big|_{A_0=\infty} = Z_1 \tag{5-12b}$$

That is, although the op amp input impedance is very large (and infinite in the ideal op amp), the input impedance for the inverting configuration is rather finite and approximately equal to Z_1. Moreover, specifying $A_{CL\infty}$ and $Z_{inCL\infty}$ uniquely determine the Z_1 and Z, i.e., $Z_1 = Z_{inCL\infty}$ and $Z = -A_{CL\infty}Z_1$.

Example 5-2

Consider the inverting configuration in Fig. 5-8a. (a) Derive the closed-loop gain $A_{CL}(s)$ for this circuit, with op amp specs $A_0(s) = A_0/(1 + s/\omega_p)$, $Z_{in} = \infty$, and $Z_{out} = 0$. (b) Determine $A_{CL}(s)$ when the op amp is ideal, and (c) determine the ε_{rr} function.

Solution. (a) First derive the impedance functions Z_1 and Z, i.e.,

$$Z_1 = R_1 + \frac{1}{sC_1} = \frac{sC_1R_1 + 1}{sC_1}$$

$$Z = R_2 // \frac{1}{sC_2} = \frac{R_2\left(\dfrac{1}{sC_2}\right)}{R_2 + \dfrac{1}{sC_2}} = \frac{R_2}{sC_2R_2 + 1}$$

Hence, using Eq. (5-8a) we obtain

$$A_{CL}(s) = \frac{V_{out}}{V_{in}}$$

$$= -\frac{sC_1R_2}{(sC_1R_1 + 1)(sC_2R_2 + 1)}\left\{\frac{1}{1 + \dfrac{1}{A_0(s)}\left(1 + \dfrac{sC_1R_2}{(sC_1R_1 + 1)(sC_2R_2 + 1)}\right)}\right\}$$

$$(5\text{-}13a)$$

(b) $A_{CL\infty}$ for an ideal op amp is readily determined by setting $1/A_0 = 0$ in Eq. (5-13a), i.e.,

$$A_{CL\infty}(s) = -\frac{sC_1R_2}{(sC_1R_1 + 1)(sC_2R_2 + 1)} = -\frac{sC_1R_2}{\left(\dfrac{s}{\omega_{p1}} + 1\right)\left(\dfrac{s}{\omega_{p2}} + 1\right)} \qquad (5\text{-}13b)$$

(c) The ε_{rr} function is evaluated using Eq. (5-8c), i.e.,

$$\varepsilon_{rr}(s) = \frac{1}{A_0(s)}(1 - A_{CL\infty}(s)) = \frac{\dfrac{s}{\omega_p} + 1}{A_0}\left[1 + \frac{sC_1R_2}{\left(\dfrac{s}{\omega_{p1}} + 1\right)\left(\dfrac{s}{\omega_{p2}} + 1\right)}\right] \qquad (5\text{-}13c)$$

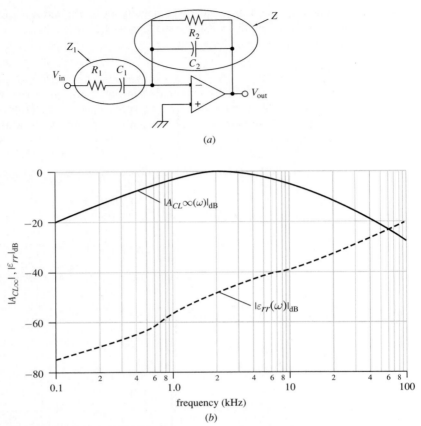

FIGURE 5-8   (a) Inverting configuration circuit and (b) plot of $|A_{CL\infty}(2\pi f)|$ and $|\varepsilon_{rr}(2\pi f)|$ for Example 5-2.

where $A_0(s) = A_0/(1+s/\omega_p)$ is a typical open-loop gain for a practical op amp. As we discuss in Sec. 5-3, DC gain $A_0 > 1000$ and pole $\omega_p < 2\pi \times 1000$ rps, such that $\omega_{p1}, \omega_{p2} \gg \omega_p$. Note that as $s \to \infty$, $1/A_0(s) \to s/A_0\omega_p$ and $1 - A_{CL\infty}(s) \to 1$, and hence at high frequencies ε_{rr} is dominated by $1/A_0(s)$. To make this example come to life, let us insert some numbers, i.e., let us use $1/(C_1 R_2) = 2\pi(10^3)$, $\omega_{p1} = 1/(C_1 R_1) = 2\pi(1.5 \times 10^3)$, $\omega_{p2} = 1/(C_2 R_2) = 2\pi(3.0 \times 10^3)$, $\omega_p = 2\pi(0.1 \times 10^3)$ and $A_0 = 10^4$. Using these numbers, we plot in Fig. 5-8b $|A_{CL\infty}|$ and $m_{rr}(2\pi f) = |\varepsilon_{rr}|$ in dBs, as per Eqs. (5-13). Over the frequency range shown, the error magnitude $m_{rr}(2\pi f) = |\varepsilon_{rr}(2\pi f)| < -20$ dB. Consequently, in this range, $|A_{CL}(2\pi f)|$ is nearly indistinguishable from $|A_{CL\infty}(2\pi f)|$.

Our example circuit in Fig. 5-8a is an active-RC filter that realizes the second-order voltage transfer function in Eq. (5-13b) and the frequency response shown in

Fig. 5-8b. As we will learn in Chaps. 7 and 8, second-order active filters serve as convenient building blocks for for the reader to recognize that the circuit in Fig. 5-8a is one realization, not *the* (only) realization of $A_{CL\infty}$ in Eq. (5-13b). There are numerous circuits offered in the active filter literature to realize transfer functions equivalent to Eq. (5-13b), but only a few are truly appropriate for realizing high-quality integrated active filters. In Chap. 7 we will probe this issue in greater detail and develop a small cadre of excellent circuit structures for realizing integrated second-order active filters.

To be more specific, let us now consider a few of the more widely used inverting configurations, namely, the inverting amplifier in Fig. 5-9, the inverting integrator in Fig. 5-10, and the inverting summing configurations in Figs. 5-11 and 5-12. Equations (5-8), (5-11), and (5-12) provide the information needed to characterize these circuits.

Inverting Amplifier   The simplest and perhaps most widely used inverting configuration is the inverting amplifier in Fig. 5-9, where $Z_1 = R_1$ and $Z = R$. The expressions for $A(s)$, A_∞, ε_{rr}, and Z_{inCL} for this circuit are readily obtained using Eqs. (5-8), (5-11), and (5-12), i.e.,

$$A_{CL}(s) = -\frac{R}{R_1}\left[\frac{1}{1 + \dfrac{1}{A_0(s)}\left(1 + \dfrac{R}{R_1}\right)}\right] \tag{5-14a}$$

$$A_{CL\infty} = -\frac{R}{R_1} \tag{5-14b}$$

$$\varepsilon_{rr} = \frac{1}{A_0(s)}\left(1 + \frac{R}{R_1}\right) \tag{5-14c}$$

and

$$Z_{inCL} \approx \frac{R_1}{1 - \dfrac{1}{A_0(s)}\left(\dfrac{R}{R_1}\right)} \tag{5-14d}$$

An important observation that can be derived from these expressions is that the effect of $1/A_0$ is magnified by closed-loop gain $A_{CL\infty}$. That is, as the amount of feedback is increased to reduce $A_{CL}(s)$, the effect of finite A_0 decreases. This is in fact a

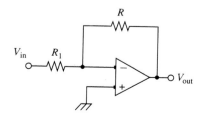

FIGURE 5-9   Inverting amplifier with $Z_1 = R_1$ and $Z = R$.

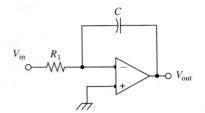

FIGURE 5-10   Inverting integrator circuit.

demonstration of one of the fundamental tradeoffs in feedback circuits. This tradeoff, along with other aspects of feedback circuits, were discussed in Sec. 3-3.

Inverting Integrator   Another important inverting configuration is the *inverting integrator*, shown in Fig. 5-10. In this case, Z_1 is a resistor and Z is a capacitor, i.e., $Z_1 = R_1$ and $Z = 1/sC$, which yields

$$A_{CL}(s) = \frac{V_{out}}{V_{in}} = -\frac{1}{sR_1C} \left[\frac{1}{1 + \frac{1}{A_0(s)}\left(1 + \frac{1}{sR_1C}\right)} \right] \tag{5-15a}$$

$$A_{CL\infty}(s) = \frac{-1}{sR_1C} \quad \text{or} \quad V_{out} = -\frac{1}{sR_1C}V_{in} \tag{5-15b}$$

$$\varepsilon_{rr}(s) = \frac{1}{A_0(s)}\left(1 + \frac{1}{sR_1C}\right) \tag{5-15c}$$

and

$$Z_{inCL} \approx \frac{R_1}{1 - \frac{1}{A_0(s)}\left(\frac{1}{sR_1C}\right)} \tag{5-15d}$$

We will say much more about the ramifications of Eqs. (5-15) in Sec. 5-3.

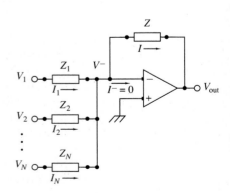

FIGURE 5-11   General multiple-input inverting summer configuration.

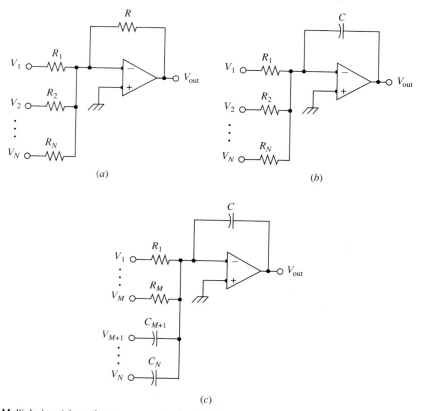

FIGURE 5-12   Multiple-input inverting summer circuits: (*a*) summing amplifier, (*b*) summing integrator, and (*c*) summing integrator-amplifier combination.

When the op amp is ideal, Eq. (5-15*b*) describes the frequency domain operation for an inverting integrator, scaled by the factor $1/R_1C$. That is, in the time-domain, $v_{\text{out}}(t)$ is the definite integral (where we assume that the initial condition on C is zero):

$$v_{\text{out}}(t) = -\frac{1}{R_1 C} \int_0^t v_{\text{in}}(\tau)d\tau \tag{5-16}$$

Inverting Summer Configurations   Let us consider a generalization of the basic inverting configuration; namely the *multiple-input inverting summer configuration* in Fig. 5-11. In this circuit, multiple inputs $V_1, V_2, \ldots, V_N$ feed into the op amp virtual ground through impedances $Z_1, Z_2, \ldots, Z_N$. The application of feedback through impedance Z forces the output to track the sum of the inputs, each scaled or weighted by a factor determined by the ratios of the feedback resistor and the feed-in resistors. The summation operation can be understood by carrying out an analysis similar to that for the single input case. First, we know that the input currents $I_1, I_2, \ldots, I_N$ are given according to Ohm's Law as:

$$I_1 = \frac{V_1 - V^-}{Z_1}, \; I_2 = \frac{V_2 - V^-}{Z_2}, \ldots, \; I_N = \frac{V_N - V^-}{Z_N} \quad \text{and} \quad I = \frac{V^- - V_{\text{out}}}{Z}$$

Reusing the analysis conducted in Eqs. (5-3) through (5-8), we obtain

$$\frac{V_1}{Z_1} + \frac{V_2}{Z_2} + \cdots + \frac{V_N}{Z_N} + \frac{V_{\text{out}}}{Z} = \left\{ \frac{1}{Z} + \sum_{i=1}^{N} \frac{1}{Z_i} \right\} V^-$$

Substituting $V^- = -V_{\text{out}}/A_0(s)$ and rearranging terms leads to the desired result

$$V_{\text{out}} = -\frac{\displaystyle\sum_{i=1}^{N} \frac{Z}{Z_i} V_i}{1 + \dfrac{1}{A_0(s)} \left[1 + \displaystyle\sum_{i=1}^{N} \frac{Z}{Z_i} \right]} \tag{5-17a}$$

$$= -\sum_{i=1}^{N} \frac{Z}{Z_i} V_i \quad \text{for} \quad A_0(s) = \infty \tag{5-17b}$$

Recognize that the simplicity of Eq. (5-17b), and the simple input/output relations for all the inverting configurations, is due to the handy work of the virtual ground.

To make the configuration in Fig. 5-11 a useful circuit, we must be more specific with regard to impedances Z_i and Z. Hence, in Fig. 5-12, we show three of the more widely used special cases of the general structure. The first is the inverting summer amplifier, where $Z_i = R_i$ and $Z = R$, shown in Fig. 5-12b. Mentally inserting $Z_i = R_i$ and $Z = R$ into Eqs. (5-15), we observe that each input V_i is scaled by a ratio R/R_i and each scaling can be independently adjusted by altering the value of R_i. We leave the the remaining analysis of this circuit as an exercise for the reader.

In another useful summer circuit, illustrated in Fig. 5-12b, summation and integration are combined within a single structure. This is accomplished by replacing $Z_i = R_i$ and $Z = 1/sC$. When $1/A_0(s) = 0$, the output of this circuit is the inverted, weighted sum of the integrals of the input signals, i.e.,

$$V_{\text{out}} = -\sum_{i=1}^{N} \frac{1}{sCR_i} V_i \tag{5-18}$$

The integration time constants are then individually controlled via the input feed-in resistors R_i.

In a third scheme, shown in Fig. 5-12c, the summing amplifier and summing integration functions are combined into a single structure. In this scheme, the first M voltage inputs feed the op amp via resistors (i.e., $Z_i = R_i$ for $1 \leq i \leq M$) and the remaining $N - M$ voltage inputs feed via capacitors (i.e., $Z_i = 1/sC_i$ for $M + 1 \leq i \leq N$). The output voltage for this circuit is then expressed, with $1/A_0(s) = 0$, by

$$V_{\text{out}} = -\sum_{i=1}^{M} \frac{1}{sCR_i} V_i - \sum_{i=M+1}^{N} \frac{C_i}{C} V_i \qquad (5\text{-}19)$$

The reader is warned that the choice of feedback and feed-in components (Z, Z_i) in Fig. 5-6 and Fig. 5-11 is constrained by the requirement to maintain a DC path to ground in order to prevent *DC instability* (i.e., the buildup of DC offset until the output is pinned to either V_{DD} or V_{SS}). This requirement prohibits the embedding of op amps in a network comprised entirely of capacitors. In Chaps. 7 and 8 we construct some very useful circuits using op amps, capacitors, and switched-capacitors (i.e., comprised of capacitors and MOSFET switches). In these circuits, switched-capacitors replace the function of conventional, "continuous" resistors, and provide the needed DC stability.

5-2-2 Noninverting Configuration

The noninverting configuration in Fig. 5-13a illustrates another important feedback arrangement. In this configuration the input signal V_{in} is fed into a noninverting V^+ op amp terminal and the inverting V^- terminal is connected to arbitrary impedances Z_A and Z_B. Also, Z_A is connected to ground and Z_B is connected to the output terminal V_{out}. Again, we caution the reader that the requirement to provide a proper DC path to ground also applies to the noninverting scheme. Hence, either Z_A or Z_B must have a resistive component (i.e., without series capacitance).

FIGURE 5-13   (a) Noninverting configuration and (b) equivalent circuit using the op amp model in Fig. 5-3 with $Z_{\text{in}} = \infty$ and $Z_{\text{out}} = 0$.

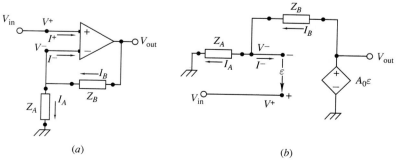

(a)   (b)

Let us analyze the equivalent circuit in Fig. 5-13b to derive the closed-loop gain $A_{CL}(s) = V_{out}/V_{in}$. The equations for this circuit are

$$\left[\frac{1}{Z_A} + \frac{1}{Z_B}\right] V^- - \frac{1}{Z_B} V_{out} = 0 \tag{5-20a}$$

$$V^+ = V_{in} \tag{5-20b}$$

$$\varepsilon = V^+ - V^- = \frac{V_{out}}{A_0(s)} \tag{5-20c}$$

Solving Eqs. (5-20) for V_{out}/V_{in} and rearranging terms, we obtain $A(s)$ in the following familiar form

$$A_{CL}(s) = \left(1 + \frac{Z_B}{Z_A}\right) \frac{1}{1 + \frac{1}{A_0(s)}\left(1 + \frac{Z_B}{Z_A}\right)} = A_{CL\infty}(s)\frac{1}{1 + \varepsilon_{rr}(s)} \tag{5-21a}$$

where

$$A_{CL\infty}(s) = 1 + \frac{Z_B}{Z_A} \tag{5-21b}$$

and

$$\varepsilon_{rr}(s) = \frac{1}{A_0(s)}\left(1 + \frac{Z_B}{Z_A}\right) \tag{5-21c}$$

The input and output impedances for the noninverting configuration are the input and output impedances (Z_{in}, Z_{out}) of the op amp scaled by the loop-gain, as described for series-shunt configuration in Table 3-1, i.e.,

$$Z_{inCL} = Z_{in}(1 + \mathcal{A}\mathcal{H}) > Z_{in} \quad \text{and} \quad Z_{outCL} = \frac{Z_{out}}{1 + \mathcal{A}\mathcal{H}} < Z_{out} \tag{5-21d}$$

Note that Z_{inCL} and Z_{outCL} are independent of the individual values of Z_A and Z_B. Hence, the designer can scale external impedances Z_A and Z_B with greater flexibility in this configuration than in the inverting configuration, where $Z_1 = Z_{inCL}$ must be large.

At the risk of being redundant, we point out that $A_{CL}(s) = A_{CL\infty}(s)$ when $1/A_0 = 0$ for an ideal op amp. Moreover, $A_{CL\infty}(s)$ is clearly noninverting and controlled by the impedance ratio Z_B/Z_A. The reader should note that $A_\infty(s)$, for an ideal op amp, can be derived simply and directly by setting $V^+ = V^-$ in Eq. (5-20). Once again, the $\varepsilon_{rr}(s)$ allows the designer to characterize the deviation in $A_{CL}(s)$ due to finite A_0. If the op amp is designed and/or the external Z_A, Z_B are limited such that $|(1/A_0)(1 + Z_B/Z_A)| \ll 1$, then $A_{CL}(s)$ can be written in the following convenient form

$$A_{CL}(s) = A_{CL\infty}(s)(1 - \varepsilon_{rr}(s)) \tag{5-22}$$

Let us be more specific by focusing attention on a few of the more widely used noninverting configurations. As the reader may expect, many important noninverting configurations are the noninverting duals of the inverting circuits in Figs. 5-9 through 5-12. These noninverting circuits are shown in Figs. 5-14, 5-15, and 5-17. Equations (5-20) through (5-21) provide the information needed to characterize these circuits.

Noninverting Amplifier   The noninverting amplifier in Fig. 5-14a is obtained by selecting $Z_A = R_A$ and $Z_B = R_B$. Likewise, $A_{CL\infty}$, and ε_{rr} for this circuit are readily obtained by inserting these substitutions into Eq. (5-21), i.e.,

$$A_{CL\infty} = 1 + \frac{R_B}{R_A} \tag{5-23a}$$

$$\varepsilon_{rr}(s) = \frac{1}{A_0(s)} \left(1 + \frac{R_B}{R_A} \right) \tag{5-23b}$$

Note that $A_{CL\infty}$ has a minimum value of unity when either $R_B = 0$ (a short circuit) and/or $R_A = \infty$ (an open circuit). In fact, for these particular connections, $A_{CL\infty} \equiv 1$, independent of all circuit components. In contrast, for the inverting amplifier, $A_{CL\infty} = -R/R_1 = -1$ is achieved only when $R_1 = R$. Hence, $A_{CL\infty}$ will vary from -1 as resistors R and R_1 drift from equal values. The *unity gain amplifier* or *voltage follower circuit* or *buffer amplifier*, obtained when $R_A = \infty$ and $R_B = 0$, is shown in Fig. 5-14b. The virtue of this circuit is that, in practice, it achieves unity gain and behaves as a near ideal VCVS over a wide range of frequencies. Moreover, $Z_{inCL} \to \infty$ and $Z_{outCL} \to 0$, as noted earlier for the more general configuration. The near ideal behavior at high frequencies can be derived from $\varepsilon_{rr}(s)$ in Eq. (5-23b) with $R_B = 0$, i.e.,

$$\varepsilon_{rr}(s) = \frac{1}{A_0(s)} \tag{5-24}$$

In contrast, the ε_{rr} for a unity gain inverting amplifier, obtained by setting $R_1 = R$ in Eq. (5-14c), is larger by a factor of two. With these ideal characteristics, voltage followers make excellent isolation and input/output buffer devices.

FIGURE 5-14   (a) Noninverting amplifier and (b) unity gain amplifier or voltage follower.

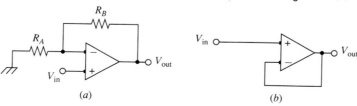

(a)   (b)

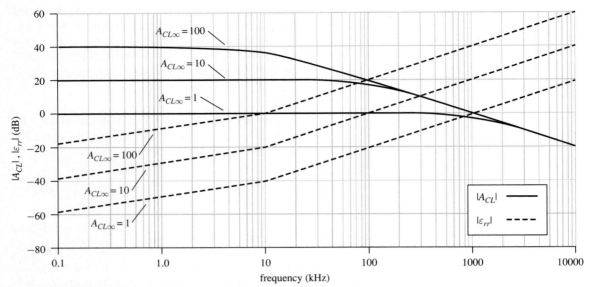

FIGURE 5-15   Plot of $|A_{CL}(2\pi f)|$ and $|\varepsilon_{rr}(2\pi f)|$ for the noninverting amplifier with $A_{CL\infty} = 100$, 10, and 1.

To demonstrate the relationship between $A_{CL\infty}$ and $\varepsilon_{rr}(s)$ (i.e., Eq. (5-21)) and the corresponding impact on $A_{CL}(s)$, we plot (in Fig. 5-15) $|A_{CL}(j2\pi f)|$ and $|\varepsilon_{rr}(j2\pi f)|$ versus frequency for three values of $A_{CL\infty}$, namely, $A_{CL\infty} = 100$ (or 40 dB), 10 (or 20 dB), 1 (or 0 dB). Recall that for $1/A_0 = 0$, $A_{CL}(s) = A_{CL\infty} = 1 + R_B/R_A$, a constant for all frequencies. It should be evident that $A_{CL\infty} = 100$, 10, and 1 are realized with resistor ratios $R_B/R_A = 99$, 9, and 0, respectively. For this demonstration, let us use the model $A_0(s) = A_0/(1 + s/\omega_p)$, with $A_0 = 10^4$ and $\omega_p = 2\pi \times 100$ rps for the open-loop op amp. We see in Fig. 5-15 that the $|\varepsilon_{rr}(j2\pi f)|$ curves increase with frequency and scale directly with $A_{CL\infty}$, i.e., the $|\varepsilon_{rr}(j2\pi f)|$ curves are separated by 20 dB intervals. The impact on $|A_{CL}(j2\pi f)|$ is clearly demonstrated. For the high gain case where $A_{CL\infty} = 40$ dB, we see that $|A_{CL}(j2\pi f)| \approx A_{CL\infty}$ with a 3 dB-bandwidth of about 10 kHz. One can verify that the 3 dB-bandwidths of $|A_{CL}(j2\pi f)|$ for $A_{CL\infty} = 20$ dB and 0 dB are 100 kHz and 1 MHz, respectively. That is, if we increase $A_{CL\infty}$ by 20 dB, the 3 dB-bandwidth for $|A_{CL}(j2\pi f)|$ will down scale by exactly a factor of 10 and vice versa. The trade of gain for bandwidth is one of the fundamental products of negative feedback, studied in Chap. 3.

Noninverting Integrators   A noninverting integrator can be realized using the single noninverting op amp circuit in Fig. 5-16. Let us determine the closed loop gain function $A_{CL\infty}(s) = V_{out}(s)/V_{in}(s)$. We leave the derivation of $A_{CL}(s)$ and $\varepsilon_{rr}(s)$ as exercises for the reader. To begin, let us develop the expressions for V^+ and V^-, i.e.,

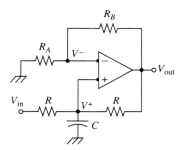

FIGURE 5-16   A single op amp noninverting integrator circuit.

with $1/A_0 = 0$:

$$\left(\frac{1}{R_A} + \frac{1}{R_B} \right) V^- - \frac{1}{R_B} V_{\text{out}} = 0 \qquad (5\text{-}25a)$$

$$\left(\frac{2}{R} + sC \right) V^+ - \frac{1}{R} V_o - \frac{1}{R} V_{\text{in}} = 0 \qquad (5\text{-}25b)$$

Solving for V^- and V^+ yields:

$$V^- = \left[\frac{1}{1 + \dfrac{R_B}{R_A}} \right] V_{\text{out}} \qquad (5\text{-}26a)$$

$$V^+ = \left[\frac{1}{2 + sCR} \right] V_{\text{out}} + \left[\frac{1}{2 + sCR} \right] V_{\text{in}} \qquad (5\text{-}26b)$$

Assuming the ideal op amp condition $V^+ - V^- = 0$, we form Eq. (5-26):

$$\left[\frac{1}{2 + sCR} - \frac{1}{1 + \dfrac{R_B}{R_A}} \right] V_{\text{out}} + \left[\frac{1}{2 + sCR} \right] V_{\text{in}} = 0$$

Rearranging terms and forming the ratio $V_{\text{out}}/V_{\text{in}}$ yields:

$$A_{CL\infty}(s) = \frac{V_{\text{out}}}{V_{\text{in}}} = \frac{\left(1 + \dfrac{R_B}{R_A} \right)}{2 + sCR - \left(1 + \dfrac{R_B}{R_A} \right)} \qquad (5\text{-}27)$$

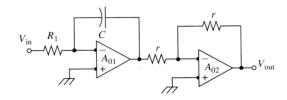

FIGURE 5-17   An alternative two op amp noninverting integrator circuit that is less dependent on the passive components.

Setting $R_A = R_B = r$, we obtain the transfer function for a noninverting integrator, i.e.,

$$A_{CL\infty}(s) = \frac{V_{out}}{V_{in}} = \frac{2}{sCR} \tag{5-28}$$

Recalling the inverting integrator in Fig. 5-10, we note that integration operation was achieved inherently by the circuit structure and did not require any pre-selection of component values. In contrast, the noninverting integrator requires that $R_A = R_B$ and that the two resistors—labeled R, and connected to the V^+ terminal—be made equal as shown. Unfortunately, we cannot expect the resistors to be fabricated with exactly equal values. Consequently, an IC realization of Eq. (5-28) cannot be achieved exactly, even with an ideal op amp. The actual transfer function will be determined by Eq. (5-27), using the actual component values (C', R', R'_A, and R'_B) for each implementation. This unfortunate, but unavoidable, situation is a manifestation of the *sensitivity* problem discussed in Sec. 3-4. The most unfortunate situation occurs when R_B, and R_A vary such that $1 + R_B/R_A > 2$. For such cases, the circuit is unstable and will oscillate at a finite frequency.

The circuit in Fig. 5-17 is a brute-force, two op amp realization of a noninverting integrator that avoids this particular sensitivity problem. In this circuit, an inverting integrator is connected in tandem, or *cascade*, with a unity gain inverting amplifier. Although in practice the resistors labeled r will not be exactly equal, we leave it to the reader to verify that the circuit still functions as an ideal integrator (assuming an ideal op amp) and only the time constant of the integrator is effected by errors in the components. Aside from the extra cost of the second op amp, the price paid for this arrangement is that the effect of $A_0(s)$, i.e., $\varepsilon_{rr}(s)$, increases. We leave it to the reader to verify, for matching op amps (i.e., $A_{01} = A_{02} = A_0$), that

$$\varepsilon_{rr}(s) \approx (\varepsilon_{rr}(s))_{II} + (\varepsilon_{rr}(s))_{IA} = \frac{1}{A_0(s)}\left(3 + \frac{1}{sR_1C}\right) \tag{5-29}$$

where subscripts II and IA refer to the inverting integrator and inverting amplifier used in the Fig. 5-17 realization.

Noninverting Summer Configurations   Unfortunately, there is no truly elegant and general noninverting summer configuration to complement the inverting configuration in Fig. 5-11. However, there are some interesting and useful special purpose circuits. We will demonstrate two of these circuits in Examples 5-3 and 5-4.

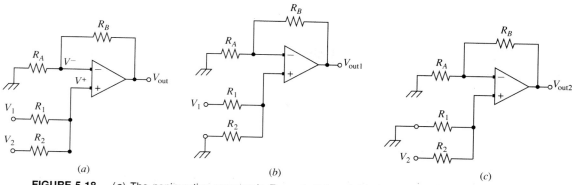

FIGURE 5-18   (a) The noninverting summer in Example 5-3 and the analysis using superposition, with (b) the circuit with $V_2 = 0$ and (c) the circuit with $V_1 = 0$.

Example 5-3

Figure 5-18a shows a noninverting summing amplifier, with inputs V_1, V_2 and output V_{out}. Assuming an ideal op amp: (a) Find the expression for the output V_{out} in terms of the inputs V_1 and V_2. (b) Determine the values for R_A, R_B, R_1, and R_2 to realize the input/output relation:

$$V_{\text{out}} = a_1 V_1 + a_2 V_2 = 2V_1 + 4V_2 \tag{5-30}$$

Solution. The analysis of the circuit in Fig. 5-18a can proceed in several ways. An efficient means for dealing with multiple input linear circuits is to use the principle of superposition, which the reader should be familiar with from prior course work. That is, decompose the analysis of the two input circuit into the analyses of two single input circuits by first reducing V_2 to zero in one circuit and V_1 to zero in the other circuit, as has been done in Figs. 5-18b and 5-18c, respectively. We then know that the output V_{out} is the superposition of the two output components, namely, $V_{\text{out}} = V_{\text{out}1} + V_{\text{out}2}$.

Let us proceed first with the circuit in Fig. 5-18b. Comparing this circuit with the noninverting circuit in Fig. 5-14a, one observes that they are identical with the exception of the voltage division at the input, i.e.,

$$V^+ = \left(\frac{R_2}{R_1 + R_2} \right) V_1 = V^-$$

Combining this expression with Eq. (5-23a), we obtain

$$V_{\text{out}1} = \left(\frac{R_2}{R_1 + R_2} \right) \left(1 + \frac{R_B}{R_A} \right) V_1 \tag{5-31a}$$

Performing the same analysis on the circuit in Fig. 5-18c yields

$$V_{\text{out2}} = \left(\frac{R_1}{R_1 + R_2}\right)\left(1 + \frac{R_B}{R_A}\right)V_2 \qquad (5\text{-}31b)$$

Hence, the total output V_{out} is

$$V_{\text{out}} = \left(\frac{R_2}{R_1 + R_2}\right)\left(1 + \frac{R_B}{R_A}\right)V_1 + \left(\frac{R_1}{R_1 + R_2}\right)\left(1 + \frac{R_B}{R_A}\right)V_2 \qquad (5\text{-}32)$$

To perform the design required in part (b) of this example, substitute the designated values for R_A and R_B into Eq. (5-32) and equate the resulting coefficients of V_1 and V_2 with those in Eq. (5-30), i.e.,

$$\left(1 + \frac{R_B}{R_A}\right)\left(\frac{R_2}{R_1 + R_2}\right) = a_1 = 2 \qquad (5\text{-}33a)$$

and

$$\left(1 + \frac{R_B}{R_A}\right)\left(\frac{R_1}{R_1 + R_2}\right) = a_2 = 4 \qquad (5\text{-}33b)$$

The ratio R_B/R_A can be found by adding these to relations in order to eliminate the dependence on R_1 and R_2. Adding these relations yields:

$$1 + \frac{R_B}{R_A} = 6 \quad \text{or} \quad \frac{R_B}{R_A} = 5 \qquad (5\text{-}34a)$$

Substituting this result into either Eq. (5-33a) or Eq. (5-33b), one can solve the resulting relation for the ratio R_1/R_2 (or R_2/R_1). Using Eq. (3-31a) yields:

$$1 + \frac{R_1}{R_2} = 3 \quad \text{or} \quad \frac{R_1}{R_2} = 2 \qquad (5\text{-}34b)$$

Note that in this case the design led to the specification of two resistor ratios, rather than specific values for individual resistors. This is a convenient result that fortunately occurs quite frequently in the design of active circuits. These relations give the designer the flexibility to adjust or *scale* the resistors R_1, R_2 and R_3, R_4 to values convenient for the particular fabrication technology being used. More importantly perhaps, the ratios of IC components of the same kind (e.g., resistors, capacitors, or MOSFET g_m's) can be realized with significantly higher accuracy than as individual components (see Sec. 3-1). It is important for the reader to remember that variations in fabrication, which cause components to vary from site to site, chip to chip, and wafer to wafer, are unavoidable in IC realization.

Let us complete the design task initiated in Example 5-3 by determining practical values for R_A, R_B, R_1, and R_2. Hence, we assign the values $R_A = 10$ kΩ and $R_1 = 10$ kΩ and calculate, using Eq. (5-33), the values $R_B = 50$ kΩ and $R_1 = 20$ kΩ. Observe that the minimum resistor value is $R_{\text{min}} = 10$ kΩ and the maximum value is $R_{\text{max}} = 50$ kΩ, giving a maximum-to-minimum spread ($R_{\text{max}}/R_{\text{min}}$) of 5.

The ratio R_{max}/R_{min} is typically a measure of chip real-estate or cost required in the realization. Also, the value of R_{min} usually limits the precision of the resistor value and its corresponding ratios (see Sec. 2-9 and Sec. 3-4). That is, large component values consume more chip area than small component values, but large component values can be fabricated more accurately. Hence, there are practical limits at both ends of the spectrum for any given technology. To ensure that these concerns are factored into the design, these parameters are often specified as part of the design objectives.

In the next example, we show another useful circuit that combines the functions of inverting and noninverting amplification with summation.

Example 5-4

Figure 5-19a shows a two input configuration, with input V_1 to the V^- terminal and V_2 to the V^+ terminal. Assuming an ideal op amp, determine the output V_{out} in terms of the two inputs V_1 and V_2.

Solution. Using superposition as applied in the previous example, we can draw the two circuits in Fig. 5-19b and 5-19c with inputs V_1 and V_2 alternately set to zero. Working first with the circuit in Fig. 5-19b, we note that with V_2 at ground and the op amp $I^+ = 0$, no current flows through resistors R_2 and R_A. Consequently, V^+ is at ground potential and the circuit reduces to a simple inverting amplifier where

$$V_{out1} = -\left(\frac{R_B}{R_1}\right) V_1 \tag{5-35}$$

Moving on to Fig. 5-19c, we obtain the following expressions for V^+ and V^- :

$$V^+ = \left[\frac{R_A}{R_2 + R_A}\right] V_2 \quad \text{and} \quad V^- = \left[\frac{R_1}{R_1 + R_B}\right] V_{out2}$$

FIGURE 5-19   (a) The noninverting circuit for Example 5-4 and the analysis using superposition, with (b) the circuit with $V_2 = 0$ and (c) the circuit with $V_1 = 0$.

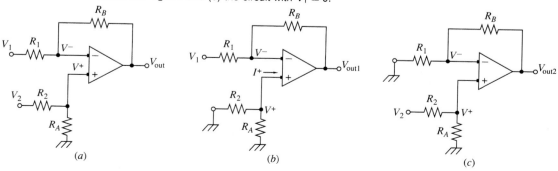

Forming the relation $V^+ - V^- = 0$ and solving for V_{out2} in terms of V_2 yields:

$$V_{\text{out2}} = \frac{(1 + R_B/R_1)}{(1 + R_2/R_A)} V_2 \qquad (5\text{-}36)$$

Combining Eqs. (5-35) and (5-36) yields the desired result, namely,

$$V_{\text{out}} = -\frac{R_B}{R_1} V_1 + \frac{(1 + R_B/R_1)}{(1 + R_2/R_A)} V_2 \qquad (5\text{-}37)$$

This circuit performs weighted subtraction. The generalization of this circuit to N inputs is straightforward and left for the reader to consider. Note that if $R_B/R_1 = R_A/R_2$ then

$$V_{\text{out}} = \left(\frac{R_B}{R_1} \right) (V_2 - V_1) \qquad (5\text{-}38)$$

The output in Eq. (5-38) describes the operation of a *differential amplifier*, producing an output V_{out} proportional to the difference between input signals V_2 and V_1. The differential amplifier has important applications in the areas of instrumentation and signal analysis.

5-3 PRACTICAL OP AMP CHARACTERISTICS AND MODEL

In previous sections we have assumed the luxury of working with an idealized op amp. The ideal op amp is, as previously mentioned, an approximation that usually provides a very good first-order fit to the real-life op amp. However, if a designer is going to design an op amp and/or design circuits using op amps, then he or she must be thoroughly familiar with the characteristics of practical op amps and how they effect typical op amp based circuits and systems. These nonideal properties will, at the very least, limit the performance and range of operation of circuits and systems realized using op amps. The particular choice of op amp design or selection of designs for a given application will often be determined by carefully scrutinizing many of the nonideal characteristics discussed in this section.

5-3-1 Gain-Bandwidth and Compensation

It was demonstrated in Sec. 3-3 that an unstable feedback circuit can be made stable by reducing the loop gain via the feedback factor $\mathcal{H}$. However, in practice, this is usually not a viable design option. For example, if our design objective is to realize a feedback amplifier with a specific closed-loop gain, then decreasing $\mathcal{H}$ to achieve a particular stability margin may conflict with this objective. There are many cases, such as with filters, where the design requirements are achieved by realizing specific values of $\mathcal{H}$. We must then explore alternative means for stabilizing op amps that do not require altering the external feedback circuitry. The only parameter left to work with in the loop-gain relation $\mathcal{T} = \mathcal{A}(s)\,\mathcal{H}$ is the open-loop transfer function $\mathcal{A}(s)$.

One such technique is to use RC circuits to introduce additional poles and/or zeros into $\mathcal{A}(s)$ so as to increase the gain and phase margins. This is the method of *frequency compensation* (Daryanani 1976; Gray and Meyer 1984; Grebene 1984; Sedra and Smith 1991; Schaumann, Ghausi, and Laker 1990) which we alluded to earlier in Sec. 5-1.

Let us consider an op amp modeled by the following three-pole open-loop transfer function:

$$\mathcal{A}(s) = \frac{A_0}{(1 + s/2\pi f_{p1})(1 + s/2\pi f_{p2})} \frac{1}{1 + s/2\pi f_{p3}} \tag{5-39a}$$

where A_0 is the op amp DC gain, and $f_{p1} < f_{p2} < f_{p3}$ are poles that limit the op amp's open-loop frequency response. Poles f_{p1} and f_{p2} are determined by the stray capacitances connected to the high impedance nodes of the op amp's gain stage. A small-signal model of a two-pole CMOS gain stage is illustrated in Fig. 5-20a. In this circuit, G_{m1} and G_{m2} are transconductances and g_a and g_b and C_a and C_b, represent the accumulated physical conductances and capacitances attached to nodes a and b, respectively. The two stages are shown to be decoupled, with f_{p1} and f_{p2} determined independently. An analysis of this circuit reveals that

$$A_0 = \frac{G_{m1}G_{m2}}{g_a g_b}, \qquad f_{p1} = \frac{1}{2\pi}\frac{g_a}{C_a}, \quad \text{and} \quad f_{p2} = \frac{1}{2\pi}\frac{g_b}{C_b} \tag{5-39b}$$

Let us attach some numbers to our discussion by letting $G_{m1} = 26.5\ \mu\text{S}$, $G_{m2} = 246\ \mu\text{S}$, $g_a = 0.0075\ \mu\text{S}$, $g_b = 8.7\ \mu\text{S}$, $C_a = 1.2$ pF, and $C_b = 13.8$ pF. With these components, we calculate $A_0 = 10^5$, $f_{p1} = 1$ kHz, and $f_{p2} = 100$ kHz. Note that $f_{p1} \ll f_{p2}$, thus f_{p1} is a dominant pole. We recall from Chap. 3 that the phase margin PM increases as the ratio f_{p1}/f_{p2} increases. Thus, the further f_{p1} and f_{p2} can be split apart, the higher the phase margin for $\mathcal{A}(s)$.

Missing from the model in Fig. 5-20a is an important capacitance C_c added in Fig. 5-20b. The details of the construct of this model, and its relationship to actual layouts of IC op amp circuits, are deferred to the next chapter. In CMOS (and bipolar) op amp circuits, C_c is either a transistor parasitic capacitance or a larger intentional capacitance (in parallel with an inherent and much smaller parasitic capacitance, usually < 0.1 pF). In either case, C_c provides a path for feedback and feedforward to occur within the gain stage. Recall our discussion the Miller effect in Sec. 3-1. The reader should recognize C_c as a Miller capacitance. The effect of adding C_c is reflected in the transfer function:

$$\mathcal{A}(s) = \frac{A_0(1 - s/2\pi f_{cz})}{(1 + s/2\pi f_{cp1})(1 + s/2\pi f_{cp2})} \frac{1}{1 + s/2\pi f_{p3}} \tag{5-40a}$$

As C_c is increased, the two poles split further apart; shifting the first pole lower in frequency (so that $f_{cp1} < f_{p1}$) and the second pole higher in frequency (so that $f_{cp2} > f_{p2}$). The third pole f_{p3} is created by circuitry (not shown) outside of the Miller feedback loop and remains unchanged. Finally, the feedforward leakage through the

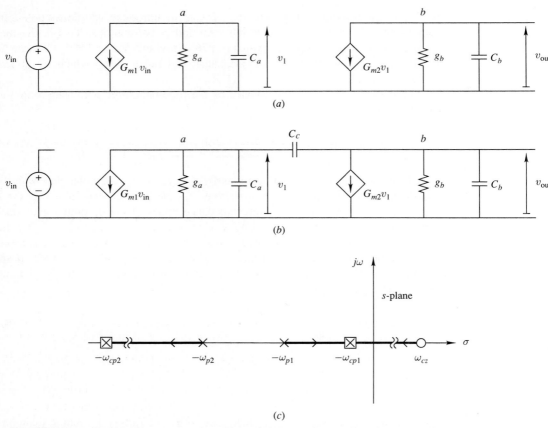

FIGURE 5-20   Single-pole compensation: (a) uncompensated two-pole gain stage; (b) compensated two-pole gain stage; (c) root locus plot illustrating the pole-splitting achieved by the compensation. In (c) the starting pole locations are those realized with (a). The poles and zero shift as functions of C_c in (b).

total Miller capacitance produces a real-valued zero at f_{cz} in the right-half plane. This zero moves in the direction of the origin as C_c is increased. These pole-zero shifts are depicted in Fig. 5-20c. Analyzing the circuit in Fig. 5-20b, with the assumption that $G_{m2} \gg g_a$ or g_b, results in the following expressions:

$$A_0 = \frac{G_{m1}G_{m2}}{g_a g_b} \qquad f_{cp1} \approx \frac{1}{2\pi}\frac{G_{m1}}{A_0 C_c} \qquad f_{cp2} \approx \frac{1}{2\pi}\frac{G_{m2}C_c}{C_a C_b + C_c(C_a + C_b)} \qquad \text{and}$$

$$f_{cz} \approx -\frac{1}{2\pi}\frac{G_{m2}}{C_c}$$

(5-40b)

Using the numbers that were associated with the evaluation of Eq. (5-39b), let us calculate the value for C_c needed to shift f_{p1} to $f_{cp1} = 10$ Hz. Thus, we obtain

$C_c \approx 4.2$ pF. The corresponding values for f_{cp2} and f_{cz} are 2.1 MHz and 9.3 MHz, respectively. We see that C_c has split the poles sufficiently far so that the compensated $\mathcal{A}(s)$ is essentially a one-pole system (we assume that $f_{p3} > 1$ MHz), i.e.,

$$\mathcal{A}(s) \approx \frac{A_0}{(1 + s/2\pi f_{cp1})} \tag{5-41a}$$

Note that in most applications, the frequencies of interest are $f_{cp1} \ll f \ll f_u$, where f_u is the unity-gain frequency described in Sec. 3-3-2. Within this frequency range, $\mathcal{A}(s)$ in Eq. (5-41a) approximates an ideal integrator, i.e.,

$$\mathcal{A}(s) \approx \frac{A_0 2\pi f_{cp1}}{s} = \frac{\omega_t}{s} \tag{5-41b}$$

The quantity $\omega_t = 2\pi A_0 f_{cp1}$ or $GBW = A_0 f_{cp1}$ is the *op amp gain-bandwidth product*. Note also that single-pole compensation force $\omega_u \rightarrow \omega_t$. This result is both simple and appealing from a stability point of view (recall Sec. 3-3). Consequently, Eq. (5-41b) is widely used to represent the "actual" open-loop frequency characteristic of an op amp. For audio-frequency (i.e., $f < 20$ kHz) applications, op amps are typically designed for $GBW \geq 1$ MHz.

The frequency compensation technique described in Eq. (5-40) and Fig. 5-20 is called *pole splitting* (Gray and Meyer 1984; Grebene 1984; Sedra and Smith 1991). Since $|\mathcal{A}(s)|$ in Eq. (5-41) largely follows a single-pole rolloff, this method is also called *single-pole compensation*. Capacitance C_c, when used for this purpose, is called a *compensation capacitance*. This capacitance can either be externally applied, to pins reserved for this purpose on the op amp package, or the capacitance can be fabricated as part of the op amp integrated circuit. The latter case is referred to as an *internally compensated* op amp. In the former case, the op amp is said to be *uncompensated* until the *external compensation circuit* is applied. External C_c provides the designer with the flexibility to easily customize the compensation and to use precise components. Internal compensation removes this flexibility, but the integrated system fully realizes the cost and size advantages of VLSI.

We have shown in Eqs. (5-39) and (5-40) that we can substantially alter the pole locations for $\mathcal{A}(s)$ with relatively small values of C_c. The net result is that high frequency characteristics of $\mathcal{A}(s)$ are changed in a direction that increases the gain and phase margins, as illustrated in Fig. 5-21. The numbers used in this figure for the uncompensated and compensated $\mathcal{A}(s)$ are those associated with Eqs. (5-39) and (4-40), with the addition of $f_{p3} = 5$ MHz. As shown in Fig. 5-21, the phase margin for the compensated $\mathcal{A}(s)$ is PM $\approx 70°$. The op amp is now sufficiently stable for general use in feedback configurations. In comparison, the uncompensated op amp with PM $\approx -35°$ is likely to be unstable when feedback is applied.

A limitation associated with the single-pole compensation method can be observed by comparing the compensated and uncompensated low frequency loop gains in Fig. 5-21. There is a significant reduction in open-loop gain due to the compensation, for example at 1 kHz, where the gain is reduced from 100 dB to 60 dB due

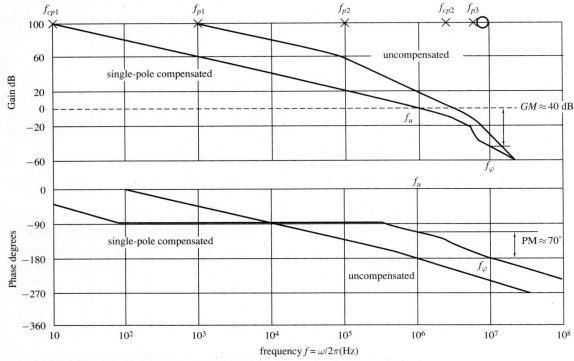

FIGURE 5-21   Illustration of the single-pole frequency compensation method.

to the roll off of the first pole at f_{cp1}. As we will see in Chap. 8, such reduction in loop gain can seriously alter the frequency response of an active-RC filter.

To attack this problem, alternative compensation techniques have been developed that achieve the desired stabilization while maintaining a large low frequency open-loop gain. One scheme that has been used successfully in the realization of precision audio frequency active-RC filters is the *double-pole compensation* scheme that introduces two poles and zero into $\mathcal{A}(s)$. The compensated op amp open-loop transfer function then takes the form

$$\mathcal{A}(s) = \frac{A_0(1 + s/\omega_z)}{(1 + s/\omega_{cp1})(1 + s/\omega_{cp2})} \qquad (5\text{-}42)$$

where $\omega_z > \omega_{cp1}, \omega_{cp2}$. This scheme can be shown to provide, approximately, an order of magnitude more open-loop gain in the audio frequency range than that obtained with single-pole compensation (Daryanani 1976; Moschytz 1975). These compensation schemes tend to be more complicated, involving more passive components than in the single-pole scheme. Consequently, in spite of its limitations, single-pole compensation is the most widely used method of frequency compensation. The circuit design details for implementing frequency compensation in integrated circuit op amps are given in Chap. 6.

Example 5-5

Consider (a) the inverting integrator and (b) the noninverting integrator circuits in Fig. 5-10 and Fig. 5-17, respectively. Use the approximate op amp open-loop gain model in Eq. (5-40) to evaluate the integration error that occurs due to the finite gain-bandwidth ω_t. Assume that the op amp input and output impedances are ideal.

Solution. The analysis of both circuits is carried out using the model in Fig. 5-22. (a) The circuit equations for the inverting integrator are readily written as

$$\left(\frac{1}{R_1} + sC\right) V' = \left(\frac{1}{R_1}\right) V_{in} + sC V_{out} \quad \text{and} \quad V_{out} = -\frac{\omega_t}{s} V'$$

Solving for the closed-loop transfer function V_{out}/V_{in}, we obtain

$$A(s) = \frac{V_{out}(s)}{V_{in}(s)} = \frac{-1}{s R_1 C} \left[\frac{1}{1 + \dfrac{s}{\omega_t} + \dfrac{1}{\omega_t R_1 C}} \right]$$

At low frequencies, where $\omega \ll \omega_t$, we make the following approximation

$$A(s) = \frac{-1}{s R_1 C}(1 - \varepsilon_{rr}(s)) \approx \frac{-1}{s R_1 C}\left(1 - \frac{s}{\omega_t} - \frac{1}{\omega_t R_1 C}\right)$$

where the complex and frequency dependent $\varepsilon_{rr}(s)$ represents the integrator error. Evaluating $\varepsilon_{rr}(s)$ at physical frequencies $s = j\omega$, we obtain (for $|\varepsilon_{rr}| \ll 1$, e.g., Eq. (5-8d)):

$$\varepsilon_{rr}(j\omega) \approx m_{rr}(\omega) + j\varphi_{rr}(\omega) = \frac{1}{\omega_t R_1 C} + \frac{j\omega}{\omega_t} \tag{5-43a}$$

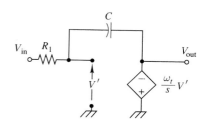

FIGURE 5-22   Equivalent circuit for the inverting integrator, with the approximate op amp open-loop characteristic $A_0(s) = \omega_t/s$.

where

$$m_{rr}(\omega) = \frac{1}{\omega_t R_1 C} \ll 1 \quad \text{and} \quad \varphi_{rr}(\omega) = \frac{\omega}{\omega_t} \ll 1 \tag{5-43b}$$

Note that $m_{rr}(\omega) = \varphi_{rr}(\omega) = 0$ for the ideal op amp where $\omega_t = \infty$. For finite ω_t, $m_{rr}(\omega)$ and $\phi_{rr}(\omega)$ are inversely proportional to ω_t. Hence, for the circuit to perform accurately as an integrator, $\omega \ll \omega_t$. As we will see in Chaps. 7 and 8, the error related to the finite ω_t of actual op amps limits the performance of active-RC filters.

(b) Following the same line of reasoning used in (a), the transfer function for a noninverting integrator can be expressed as

$$A(s) = \frac{-1}{s R_1 C} \left[\frac{1}{1 + \dfrac{s}{\omega_t} + \dfrac{1}{\omega_t R_1 C}} \right] \left(\frac{-r}{r} \right) \left[\frac{1}{1 + \dfrac{2s}{\omega_t}} \right]$$

$$= \frac{1}{s R_1 C} \left(\frac{1}{1 + \dfrac{s}{\omega_t} + \dfrac{1}{\omega_t R_1 C}} \right) \left(\frac{1}{1 + \dfrac{2s}{\omega_t}} \right)$$

With $\omega \ll \omega_t$, the reader can verify that the magnitude and phase errors are approximately expressed as

$$m_{rr}(\omega) \approx \frac{1}{\omega_t R_1 C} \quad \text{and} \quad \varphi_{rr}(\omega) \approx \frac{3\omega}{\omega_t} \tag{5-44}$$

We see in Eq. (5-44) that the use of the additional inverting unity gain amplifier has increased the phase error by a factor of 3 and left the magnitude error unchanged.

In Fig. 5-23, we summarize the error results for a variety of interesting inverting and noninverting integrator structures. The basic structures in Figs. 5-23a and 5-23c have been characterized in Eqs. (5-43) and (5-44), respectively. The phase-lag noninverting structure in Fig. 5-23d, where an inverting unity gain amplifier is placed in the feedback loop to create the effect of a negative capacitance $(-C)$, results in a phase error $\varphi_{rr}(\omega)$ that is nearly equal and opposite in sign to that of the inverting integrator in Fig. 5-23a. The reader should verify that simply inverting the sign of the v_{out} fed back through C will not provide the compensation required to realize the $\varphi_{rr}(\omega)$ expressed in Fig. 5-23d. In fact, the reader should further verify that matched op amp open-loop gains (i.e., $A_1 = A_2 = \omega_t/s$) is a necessary condition for the

Inverting Integrators

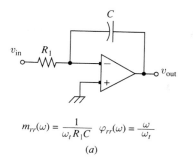

$$m_{rr}(\omega) = \frac{1}{\omega_t R_1 C} \quad \varphi_{rr}(\omega) = \frac{\omega}{\omega_t}$$

(a)

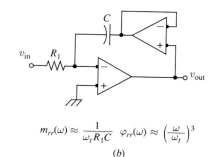

$$m_{rr}(\omega) \approx \frac{1}{\omega_t R_1 C} \quad \varphi_{rr}(\omega) \approx \left(\frac{\omega}{\omega_t}\right)^3$$

(b)

Noninverting Integrators

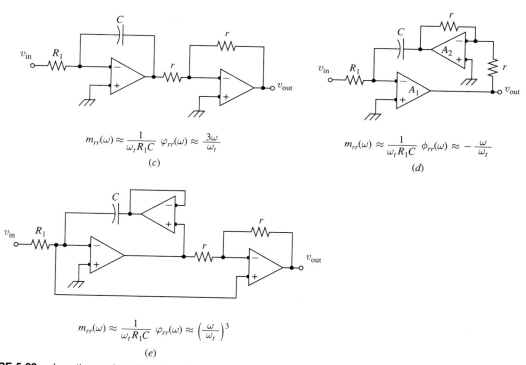

$$m_{rr}(\omega) \approx \frac{1}{\omega_t R_1 C} \quad \varphi_{rr}(\omega) \approx \frac{3\omega}{\omega_t}$$

(c)

$$m_{rr}(\omega) \approx \frac{1}{\omega_t R_1 C} \quad \phi_{rr}(\omega) \approx -\frac{\omega}{\omega_t}$$

(d)

$$m_{rr}(\omega) \approx \frac{1}{\omega_t R_1 C} \quad \varphi_{rr}(\omega) \approx \left(\frac{\omega}{\omega_t}\right)^3$$

(e)

FIGURE 5-23   Inverting and noninverting integrator structures: (a) conventional inverting integrator, (b) actively compensated inverting integrator, (c) conventional noninverting integrator, (d) phase lag noninverting integrator, and (e) actively compensated noninverting integrator.

desired compensation to occur. In Chap. 8, we describe several active-RC filters that use tandem connections of inverting and noninverting integrators. For these cases, the phase-lag inverting integrator would appear to be an appealing structure because the phase error for the tandem would nearly cancel to zero.

Due to the positive feedback introduced by inverting the signal fed back through C, one must always be concerned about stability when using this phase-lag structure. This is particularly the case in active filters where it is likely that integrators are embedded in another feedback loop or even in multiple feedback loops. The structures in Figs. 5-23b and 5-23e are called actively compensated (Schaumann, Ghausi, and Laker 1990) integrators because additional active circuitry is used to reduce $\varphi_{rr}(\omega)$. However, the magnitude errors $m_{rr}(\omega)$ in all cases are seen to be nearly identical. As in the phase-lag case, matched op amp dynamics are necessary conditions for these active compensation schemes to operate, as advertised in Fig. 5-23. The reader is encouraged to verify these results. It should be clear that this error analysis can be applied to a large variety of circuits, e.g., active filters. Some interesting circuits are considered in the exercises at the end of this chapter.

5-3-2   Step Response and Settling

The rise time t_r and settling time t_s, associated with an op amp's closed-loop step response, are important performance specifications for transient response sensitive applications. Such applications include instrumentation electronics, control systems, and sampled data systems, such as switched-capacitor filters. In these applications, op amp phase margins of PM $< 45°$ (or $\zeta < 0.707$) are not desirable because the excessive underdamping results in large overshoot and ringing in the step response (recall Fig. 3-19 and Fig. 3-20). We see in Fig. 5-24 that, for such cases, the rise time $(t_r)_u$ is quite fast, but the settling time $(t_s)_u$ is rather long. In Fig. 3-20, the ringing was shown to decay with envelope

$$1 \pm \frac{1}{\sqrt{1-\zeta^2}} e^{-\zeta \omega_o t}$$

At the other end of the spectrum, a severely overdamped design will cause the output to respond slowly $((t_r)_o \gg (t_r)_u)$ and undershoot the final value. In this case, the output settles slowly $((t_s)_o \approx (t_r)_o)$ as it rises toward the final value. For a given feedback configuration, the op amp step response and settling characteristics are related to the op amp open-loop transfer function and the closed-loop stability margins. An op amp's step response is typically measured with the op amp connected as a unity gain voltage follower (i.e., with maximum feedback) as shown in Fig. 5-14b.

Exactly how near the final value the op amp output settles is determined by the finite gain of the op amp. Consequently, even if the op amp of a unity gain follower (Fig. 5-14b) has infinite bandwidth, it will not reach the step input voltage as its steady-state response. In other words, if a unit step (of height 1 V) is applied to a unity gain follower comprised of an op amp with infinite bandwidth and finite DC gain (A_0), the output will settle to a value $(1 - \varepsilon)$ V. The difference or error ε is a function of $(1/A_0)$. Note that the single-pole model for the op amp yields a step response that rises exponentially towards the final value. This is demonstrated by considering the unity gain follower comprised of an op amp with finite gain and bandwidth represented

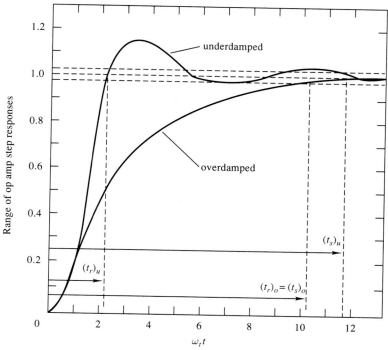

FIGURE 5-24   Range of closed-loop op amp step responses from underdamped to overdamped. Also shown are the relevant rise and fall times: $(t_r)_u$, $(t_s)_u$ for the underdamped response and $(t_r)_o$, $(t_s)_o$ for the overdamped response.

by the single-pole model, i.e.,

$$A(s) = \frac{A_0}{1 + \dfrac{s}{\omega_p}} \tag{5-45}$$

The transfer function for the unity gain follower is readily determined to be

$$A_{CL}(s) = \frac{1}{1 + 1/A(s)} = \frac{1}{(1 + 1/A_0) + s/A_0\omega_p} \approx \frac{(1 + 1/A_0)^{-1}}{1 + s/A_0\omega_p} \tag{5-46}$$

Noting the relation $V_{\text{out}}(s) = A_{CL}(s)V_{\text{in}}(s)$, the step response associated with unity gain follower is determined to be

$$v_{\text{out}}(t) = \left(\frac{1}{1 + 1/A_0}\right)\left(1 - e^{-\omega_t t}\right)u(t) \tag{5-47}$$

where $\omega_t = A_0\omega_p$. Note that the final value for $v_{\text{out}}(t)$, expressed as $v_{\text{out}}(t)|_{t=\infty} = (1 + 1/A_0)^{-1} \approx 1 - 1/A_0 = 1 - \varepsilon$, is indeed less than the unity final value for the unit step input. Also, the output is seen to rise toward final value with a slope nearly equal to ω_t. Consequently, the settling time is proportional to the op amp ω_t. This response is sketched for a single pole system in Fig. 5-25. The step response for a given op amp phase margin and frequency compensation can be obtained by conducting a similar analysis using the higher order op amp model, e.g., Eqs. (5-39) and (5-42). If the op amp load is capacitive, the size of the load capacitance will influence the step response by effectively reducing the phase margin associated with an unloaded system (see Exercise 5-16). We point out that Eq. (5-47) occurs only for small-signal amplitudes (i.e., a few mV's). For larger amplitudes, the op amp slew rate limits the rise time to less than ω_t. Slew rate is the topic of the next subsection.

In the design and realization of switched-capacitor filters, we are concerned with the settling characteristics of inverting integrator stages. In sampled data systems, the actual effect of an unsettled integrator will depend highly on how and when sampling is accomplished. Usually, many samples are taken within the time span of a signal period. Thus, the changes in amplitude at each sample are small and so settling is not limited by slew rate. These and other properties of sampled-data filters will be treated in detail in Chaps. 7 and 8.

5-3-3 Slew Rate and Full Power Bandwidth

In the previous sections, our analyses and observations were based on the assumption that the op amp was operating as a linear device. This assumption is due in part to the concept of small-signal operation, which implies that the output voltages are quite small. In fact, signal amplitudes are significantly smaller than the op amp's full scale output capability. For example, consider an op amp powered by a single +5 V supply. Such an op amp is usually rated to accommodate a peak-to-peak signal swing of up to 3.5 or 4.0 V. However, small signal operation implies an output swing of about 1 V. As the signal amplitude increases, the nonlinearities associated with the

FIGURE 5-25   Step response for a unity gain follower using a single-pole op amp model.

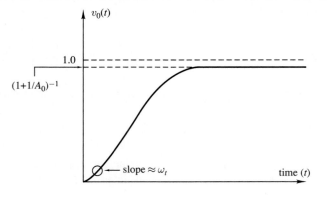

transistors within the op amp will cause the output to distort. If the output is made large enough, the output waveform will become clipped as the op amp saturates. Due to the dynamics of the op amp, the distortion will also depend strongly on how fast the output must change in order to follow the input signal (i.e., the frequency of the input). This dependence on input signal frequency is referred to as *slew rate (SR) limiting*. Slew rate limiting produces a softer form of distortion than that produced by clipping.

One way to observe slew rate limiting is to drive a unity gain voltage follower with a sine wave input that has an amplitude equal to the full scale peak-to-peak signal swing rating of the op amp. For example, let us consider the response of a unity gain follower stage (see Eq. (5-46)) to a 3.5 V peak-to-peak sine wave input (with the op amp full-scale output limited by a single +5 V supply). Let the frequency of this input be sufficiently high, say at ω_t (the closed-loop 3 dB frequency). With such an input, we find the output sine wave to be distorted in shape and its frequency somewhat lower than the input frequency. This phenomenon is illustrated in the sketch in Fig. 5-26a. Note that the rate of change of the output at the zero crossings is smaller than that of the sine wave input. The reader is encouraged to try this experiment using a square wave input, as shown in Fig. 5-26b, with the same period as the sine wave (i.e., $2\pi/\omega_t$). As might be expected, the distortion effect for the square wave input is visibly increased, compared to that of the sine wave input, due to the enhanced distortion of the square wave's higher frequency components.

Slew rate limiting is physically associated with the finite speed in which the capacitors in the op amp, which include the compensation capacitance and numerous parasitic capacitances, can be charged or discharged in response to the input. The rate

FIGURE 5-26   Slew rate limiting causing distortion in the op amp output: (*a*) for sinusoidal inputs and (*b*) for square wave inputs. In (*b*) the constant slope $= i_{MAX}/C$ is evident at the transitions of the square wave.

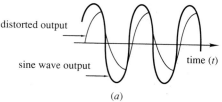

distorted output

sine wave output

time (t)

(*a*)

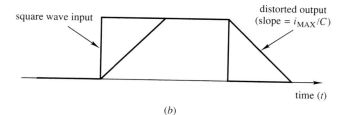

square wave input

distorted output
(slope $= i_{MAX}/C$)

time (t)

(*b*)

at which voltage charges across a capacitor is given by the relation

$$\frac{dv}{dt} = \frac{i}{C} \tag{5-48}$$

In a physical op amp, the available current is limited to some maximum value i_{MAX}. Hence, the maximum rate at which the voltage across the capacitor can be changed is

$$\left(\frac{dv}{dt}\right)_{max} = \frac{i_{MAX}}{C} = SR \tag{5-49}$$

If the output across the capacitor is required to change faster than the slew rate SR, the output distorts in the manner shown in Fig. 5-26. For the square wave input in Fig. 5-26b, we observe that output is forced to ramp up and down with a fixed slope, i.e., the slew rate. This is in fact the easiest means for measuring slew rate. Although the positive and negative slopes are shown as equal, they are not necessarily so. That is, depending on circuit configuration, the slew rates for positive and negative output swings may be different. The relationship between Eq. (5-49) and the actual op amp circuit parameters is reserved for Chap. 6.

An op amp's slew rate is usually specified on its data sheet in units of volts per micro second (V/μs). It is most readily measured by applying a square wave input to the op amp (under test), connected as a unity gain follower. The slew rate is then determined by measuring the slope of the ramp edges of the distorted output.

Slew rate is related to the op amp's *full power bandwidth* f_M. An op amp's f_M is defined as the frequency at which a sine wave output, whose amplitude is set at the maximum rated output voltage, begins to show distortion due to slewing. This maximum amplitude is usually 1 V, or smaller than the supply voltage(s) due to unavoidable voltage drops within the op amp. For example, let the input to the unity gain voltage follower be a sine wave with amplitude equal to the maximum rated output (peak-to-peak) V_{max}, i.e., $v_{OUT}(t) = (V_{max}/2)\sin(\omega t)$. Taking the derivative of $v_{OUT}(t)$ with respect to t yields the rate at which the output changes. i.e.,

$$\frac{dv_{OUT}(t)}{dt} = \frac{\omega V_{max}}{2}\cos(\omega t) \tag{5-50}$$

The maximum value for $dv_{OUT}(t)/dt$ occurs at the zero crossings, hence

$$\left[\frac{dv_{OUT}(t)}{dt}\right]_{max} = \omega\frac{V_{max}}{2} \tag{5-51}$$

Given the definition of full power bandwidth, we can write

$$SR = 2\pi f_M \frac{V_{max}}{2} \times 10^{-6} \qquad \text{or} \qquad f_M = \frac{SR}{\pi V_{max}} \times 10^{6} \tag{5-52}$$

Where SR is expressed in V/μs, which gives rise to the 10^{-6} and 10^{6} multipliers in the expressions for SR and f_M, respectively. In essence, Eq. (5-49) is a worst-case relation that defines the limits of the linear operating range for an op amp. In fact, if the output amplitude becomes larger than V_{max}, the op amp will saturate and clipping occurs. For output amplitudes that are constrained to be smaller than V_{max}, frequencies higher than f_M can be processed without incurring slew rate distortion.

Example 5-6

If the specified slew rate for an op amp is 2 V/μs, at its maximum rated output of ± 3.5 V, then (a) determine the full power frequency and (b) if the op amp is connected as an inverting amplifier with a closed-loop gain $A_{CL} = -2$ and the input is $v_{IN}(t) = V_a \cos \omega t$, with $V_a \leq 0.5$ V, determine the frequency f_{max} at which slew rate limiting occurs.

Solution. (a) Using Eq. (5-52) we obtain

$$f_M = \frac{2}{\pi \times 7.0} \times 10^6 = 90.945 \text{ kHz}$$

(b) The output of the inverting amplifier is $v_{OUT}(t) = -2V_a \cos \omega t$ and the output amplitude is constrained $|v_{OUT}| \leq 2V_a = 1.0$ V. Carrying out this analysis in the same manner as Eqs. (5-50) and (5-51) yields

$$SR = \left[\frac{dv_{OUT}(t)}{dt} \right]_{max} \times 10^{-6} = 2V_a f_{max} \times 10^{-6} = 4\pi f_{max} \times 10^{-6}$$

or

$$f_{max} = SR/4\pi \times 10^6 = 159.155 \text{ kHz}.$$

In Fig. 5-27, we plot V_{max} as a function of f_M, for $SR = 2$ V/μs. This graph illustrates the trade of increased f_M for reduced V_{max}, given a constant SR. Note that the curve limits at $V_{max} = 7$ V for $f_M < 90.945$ kHz. Similar curves are often included in op amp specification sheets.

Before moving to the next section, it is useful to discuss the concept of *dynamic range*, defined as the ratio of the maximum usable output voltage to the minimum usable output voltage. The maximum usable output voltage will be limited by slew rate and ultimately V_{max}, as previously discussed. The amount of distortion tolerated for a given application is specified in terms of *total harmonic distortion*. Total harmonic distortion can be experimentally determined by applying a sine wave input at some mid-range frequency, say 1 kHz. The output power is then measured after the fundamental component at the input frequency (in this case 1 kHz) is removed by a notch or bandreject filter (see Chap. 7). The ratio of the measured output power (representing the total distortion) to the power in the fundamental component, multiplied

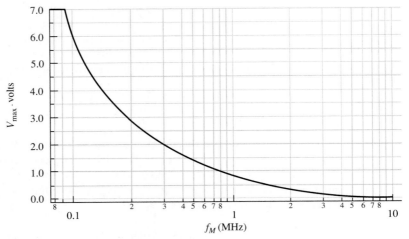

FIGURE 5-27   Plot of V_{max} versus f_M for $SR = 2$ V/μs.

by 100, gives the *percent total harmonic distortion*. For high quality audio systems, the percent total harmonic distortion is limited to be less than 1 percent. The minimum usable signal, on the other hand, is limited by the internally generated noise voltages. Clearly, if the signal level is less than the noise level, the noise obscures the useful signal. The amount by which the signal must exceed the noise to constitute a useful signal is specified in terms of the minimum *signal to noise ratio*. Typically, linear systems involving op amps have dynamic ranges between 75 and 125 dB.

5-3-4   DC Offsets and DC Bias Currents

In an ideal op amp, if the input signal is zero, the output will also be zero. In an actual op amp, imperfections in the circuit components cause a DC voltage V_{out} to exist at the output, even when the input voltage is zero, as established in Fig. 5-28a. The response at DC is not always critical, but excessive DC offset will alter the output waveform symmetry about zero volts; possibly causing the waveform to clip over a smaller range of signal amplitudes than would occur if the DC offset were absent. In other words, positive (or negative) DC offset may cause clipping to occur for positive (or negative) signal swings at a lower amplitude than for negative (or positive) swings. Consequently, the dynamic range for the op amp is reduced. This is particularly a problem in high gain situations, such as biomedical and sensor applications, that involve the processing of small input signals. In such applications, a few millivolts of DC offset is amplified, with the signal, into the 1 V range. Applications like analog-to-digital converters require the DC voltages that represent digital codes to be determined very accurately. In these applications, internal offsets must be reduced to insignificance by *offset nulling* or *auto-zero* circuitry (see Chap. 8).

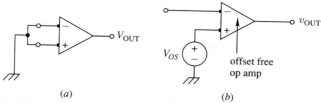

(a)   (b)

FIGURE 5-28   (a) Schematic representation and (b) model of DC offset in op amps.

A convenient way of schematically representing DC offset is with an equivalent voltage source at the noninverting input to the op amp, as shown in Fig. 5-28b. The voltage source in Fig. 5-28b is called the *input referred* offset voltage, $V_{OS} = V_{OUT}/A_0$ and is typically on the order of ± 5 millivolts (mV) for bipolar op amps and ± 20 mV for MOS op amps. Offset voltage can change or *drift* with time and temperature. The linear temperature coefficient for V_{OS} drift, typically expressed in mV/°C, is often specified in op amp data sheets. Offset drifts while often small, can be important when offset nulling is required.

Let us examine the effect of V_{OS} on the performance of closed-loop op amp systems. Consider the inverting amplifier configuration in Fig. 5-29, with the signal source set to ground and the input referred DC offset represented by voltage source V_{OS}. Note that examining a noninverting scheme in the same manner would result in the same schematic as Fig. 5-29. That is, from the point of view of DC offset, the inverting and noninverting configurations are identical. Analyzing this circuit yields the following relation for the output offset

$$V_{OUT} = \left(1 + \frac{R_2}{R_1}\right) V_{OS} \tag{5-53}$$

Hence, in actual operation, the output of the inverting amplifier will have a DC offset superimposed onto the output signal of value $(1 + R_2/R_1)V_{OS}$. If several stages similar to Fig. 5-29 are cascaded, each stage will accumulate and amplify the offsets from

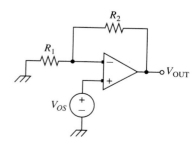

FIGURE 5-29   Representing DC offset in the inverting and noninverting configurations.

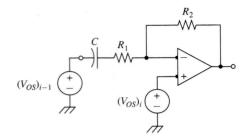

FIGURE 5-30 The use of AC coupling to reduce the output
due to DC offsets.

previous stages (in addition to its own input referred offset). Consequently, a large
DC offset can build up, even if the input offsets are quite small. In some applications,
especially those where the closed-loop system is not required to pass DC, it is possible
to keep the offsets under control by using capacitive, high pass, or *AC coupling* as
shown in Fig. 5-30. The advantage here is that DC offsets are neither accumulated nor
amplified, and the overall output offset is equal to the V_{OS} of the last stage (i.e., the
circuit in Fig. 5-30 appears to its input referred DC offset as a unity gain follower).
The disadvantage of this approach is the low frequency roll off accumulation due to
the high pass characteristic associated with each AC coupled stage. A consequence
of this problem is that the capacitors required may become too large for practical
integrated circuit realization.

One major source of DC offset for bipolar op amps is associated with input bias
currents, as shown in Fig. 5-31. Such bias currents are nearly nonexistent in MOSTs.
In an ideal op amp, the input impedance is infinite and no current flows through its
input leads. In actual op amps, small currents, needed to bias the input transistors, do
flow into these terminals. These currents are represented as I_{B1} and I_{B2} in Fig. 5-31.
In op amp data sheets, these currents are usually specified in terms of *input bias
current* I_{BS}, which is the average value of I_{B1} and I_{B2}, and the *input offset current*
I_{OS}, which is the difference between these currents. The expressions that relate I_{BS}

FIGURE 5-31 Representation of input bias currents by two current sources.

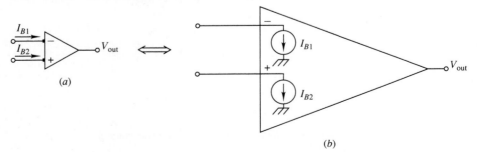

and I_{OS} to I_{B1} and I_{B2} are

$$I_{BS} = \frac{I_{B1} + I_{B2}}{2} \quad \text{and} \quad I_{OS} = I_{B1} - I_{B2} \tag{5-54}$$

The currents I_{B1} and I_{B2} tend to track, and I_{OS} is a measure of the degree of tracking that occurs. Typical values for these parameters are $I_{BS} = 100$ nA and $I_{OS} = 10$ nA for bipolar op amps and 10 pA for MOS op amps. The effect of these currents is to produce a small amount of DC offset, as illustrated in the following example.

Example 5-7

Again, consider the inverting amplifier with a closed-loop gain of $A_{CL} = -5$, realized with resistors $R_1 = 10$ kΩ and $R_2 = 50$ kΩ, as shown in Fig. 5-32. If the input bias current is 100 nA and the input offset current is in the range between ± 10 nA, what is the resulting maximum output offset voltage?

Solution. Analyzing the circuit in Fig. 5-32 yields

$$\left(\frac{1}{R_1} + \frac{1}{R_2}\right) V^- - \left(\frac{1}{R_2}\right) V_{\text{OUT}} = -I_{B1}$$

where $V^- = 0$, due to the virtual ground condition at the inverting terminal. Consequently, the output offset is given by

$$V_{\text{OUT}} = I_{B1} R_2 \tag{5-55}$$

To determine the maximum DC offset voltage, we must compute the maximum value for I_{B1}. This value is seen to be $(I_{B1})_{\max} = (2I_{BS} + (I_{OS})_{\max})/2 = 105$ nA. The resulting output offset is $V_{\text{out}} = 5.25$ mV. Clearly, Eq. (5-55) places an upper limit on the value of R_2, through which the biasing current is provided.

There is a very effective technique for reducing the value of the DC offset voltage created by the input bias currents. The technique involves the use of a resistance in the noninverting lead that is used to balance out the input offset currents. The application of the technique is shown in Fig. 5-33a for the inverting amplifier (Fig. 5-9) and

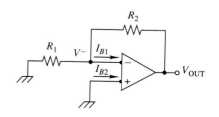

FIGURE 5-32   Analysis of inverting amplifier, accounting for input bias currents.

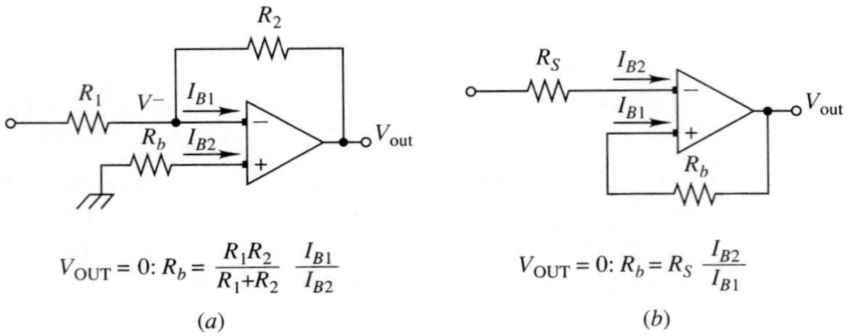

R_2
R_1
$V-$
I_{B1}
R_b
I_{B2}
V_{out}
$V_{OUT} = 0$: $R_b = \frac{R_1R_2}{R_1+R_2}\frac{I_{B1}}{I_{B2}}$
(a)
R_S
I_{B2}
I_{B1}
R_b
V_{out}
$V_{OUT} = 0$: $R_b = R_S\frac{I_{B2}}{I_{B1}}$
(b)

FIGURE 5-33 Use of balancing resistor to cancel bias currents in an (*a*) inverting amplifier and (*b*) a unity gain follower.

for the unity-gain follower (see Fig. 5-14*b*) in Fig. 5-33*b*. The determination of the values for R_b required to mathematically cancel the output offset is left as a homework exercise. Note that, in practice, exact cancellation will rarely occur due to unavoidable variations in resistor values and due to the input offset current.

5-3-5 Common-Mode Signals

As previously discussed, the output of an ideal op amp is proportional to the difference signal $\varepsilon = v^+ - v^-$, i.e., $v_{out} = \mathcal{A}(s)\varepsilon$. Hence, if an ideal op amp is connected in the common-mode, as shown in Fig. 5-34, then the output is identically zero. In an actual op amp, this is not the case, and the ratio of the resulting output voltage to the common-mode input voltage is called the *common-mode gain* $\mathcal{A}_{CM}$. The gain $\mathcal{A}_{DM} = \mathcal{A}$ is then referred to as the *differential-mode gain*, where $\mathcal{A}$ is also the op amp's open-loop gain. We note that, in general, $\mathcal{A}_{DM}$ and $\mathcal{A}_{CM}$ are frequency dependent.

A measure of the degree to which the common-mode signal is suppressed, relative to the difference-mode signal, is expressed by the *common-mode rejection ratio* or *CMRR*. *CMRR* is defined as

$$CMRR = \frac{|\mathcal{A}_{DM}|}{|\mathcal{A}_{CM}|} = \frac{|\mathcal{A}|}{|\mathcal{A}_{CM}|} \tag{5-56}$$

v_{OUT}
v_{IN}
$\alpha_{CM} = \frac{v_{OUT}}{v_{IN}}$

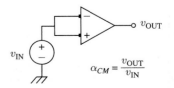

FIGURE 5-34 Configuration to measure finite *CMRR* of an op amp.

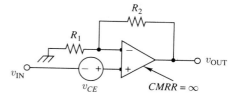

FIGURE 5-35   Analysis of noninverting amplifier, accounting for finite *CMRR*.

Typically, *CMRR* is specified in dB, i.e., $CMRR = 20 \log\{|\mathcal{A}|/|\mathcal{A}_{CM}|\}$ dB. *CMRR* is frequency dependent, decreasing in value as frequency increases. Typical values at low frequencies are 80 dB or larger.

The finite *CMRR* is unimportant in inverting configurations (Fig. 5-6), since the noninverting input is at virtual ground and the common-mode input is very near zero. In the noninverting configuration (Fig. 5-13) the input is a "virtual" common-mode input, due to the very large $\mathcal{A}$. Hence, when applying the noninverting configuration to applications with very demanding requirements, the finite *CMRR* will have to be taken into account as an error term.

A simple method for including finite *CMRR* in the closed-loop analyses is to define an input referred common-mode error voltage $v_{CE} = v_{\mathrm{IN}}/CMRR$. Note that when we multiply v_{CE} by the difference mode gain $|\mathcal{A}|$, we get the common-mode output $v_{\mathrm{OUT}} = |\mathcal{A}_{CM}|v_{CE}$ obtained using the configuration in Fig. 5-34. This error voltage can then be included as an additional input signal to an ideal op amp, as shown in Fig. 5-35. Taking into account *CMRR* (via v_{CE}) in the noninverting amplifier, we determine v_{OUT}

$$v_{\mathrm{OUT}} = \left(1 + \frac{R_2}{R_1}\right)\left(1 + \frac{1}{CMRR}\right)v_{\mathrm{IN}} = A_{CL}(1 + \Delta A_{CL})v_{\mathrm{IN}}$$

The finite *CMRR* is seen to result in a closed-loop percent gain error $\Delta A_{CL} = (1/CMRR) \times 100$ percent.

5-3-6 Noise

As discussed earlier, the minimum usable signal is limited by the small external and internally generated spurious signals. External spurious sources include a power supply ripple, 60 Hz pickup, and cross talk due to electromagnetic radiation. These sources are typically deterministic, and can be modeled as independent voltage or current sources, appropriately located in the circuit. The internally generated sources are the random noises associated with the circuit components (e.g., transistors and resistors in the op amp and feedback circuits). Any or all of the spurious signals can be represented as input referred voltage or current sources at the two op amp input terminals. The effect of these spurious sources can then be analyzed in a manner similar to the way DC offsets were considered in Sec. 5-3-4. The only difference here is that these spurious signals are frequency dependent and/or random and need to be characterized accordingly.

Let us step back for a moment to review a few facts and definitions associated with noise. As noise is a random (or at least quasi-random) function of time, it cannot be assigned a specific frequency or phase. Furthermore, its average or DC value is zero. However, noise can be characterized and measured in the mean-square or root-mean-square (rms) over a given frequency range or bandwidth. The mean-square value of a noise voltage or current is symbolized by $\overline{x_n^2}$ and its rms value $\overline{x_n} = \sqrt{\overline{x_n^2}}$, where $x = v$ or i. For microelectronic circuits, $\overline{v_n^2}$, $\overline{i_n^2}$ are usually expressed in the units $(nV)^2$, $(pA)^2$, and $\overline{v_n}$, and $\overline{i_n}$ in nV_{RMS}, pA_{RMS}, respectively. Noise, although usually very broad band, must be measured by instruments with limited bandwidth. Consequently, it is often convenient to express noise in terms of per-unit-bandwidth; i.e., $\overline{dx_n^2} = \overline{x_n^2}/\Delta f$ or $\overline{dx_n} = \overline{x_n}/\sqrt{\Delta f}$. The $\overline{dx_n^2}$ and $\overline{dx_n}$ are defined as the voltage (current) square and rms densities, respectively. Since power is proportional to the square of the current or voltage, $\overline{dx_n^2}$ is also called the power spectral density (PSD) and labeled $S_n(f)$. The frequency argument in $S_n(f)$ reminds us that PSDs (and $\overline{x_n^2}$, etc.) are generally frequency dependent (e.g., such is the case for noise created by transistors, as shown in Chaps. 1 and 2). The simple relation $\overline{x_n^2} = S_n(f)\Delta f$ strictly applies when $S_n(f)$ is constant with frequency. However, when $S_n(f)$ varies with frequency, the relation between the $\overline{x_n^2}$ and $S_n(f)$ is more complex, i.e.,

$$\overline{x_n^2} = \int_0^\infty S_{nI}(f)df \quad \text{one-sided PSD} \tag{5-57a}$$

or

$$\overline{x_n^2} = \int_{-\infty}^\infty S_{nII}(f)df \quad \text{two-sided PSD} \tag{5-57b}$$

The subscripts I and II differentiate between the one-sided and two-sided spectral densities, respectively. Since $S_n(f)$ are symmetrical about zero Hz, the conversion between one-sided and two-sided PSDs is accomplished as $S_{nII}(f) = 1/2S_{nI}(f)$. For microelectronic circuits, spectral densities are usually expressed in the units $(nV)^2/Hz$ or $nV_{RMS}/\sqrt{Hz}$ and $(pA)^2/Hz$ or $pA_{RMS}/\sqrt{Hz}$.

Let us now focus our attention on the random noise generated internally by the op amp. This topic is covered in greater depth in Chaps. 1 and 2. The primary sources of noise in an op amp are the thermal $(\overline{dv_R^2}$ in Eqs. (1-57) and (2-46)) and flicker $(\overline{dv_{RF}^2}$ in Eqs. (1-59) and (2-49)) noises associated with the op amp's input devices. Recall that thermal noise, also called *Nyquist noise*, is caused by the random thermal motion of mobile charge carriers in the resistive and semiconducting materials associated with IC resistors and conducting channels of transistors. It is directly proportional to both the magnitude of the resistance and its absolute ambient temperature. Also, flicker noise ($1/f$ noise) is due to the semiconductor surface imperfections that occur in the emission and diffusion processes. This noise is important at low frequencies and can

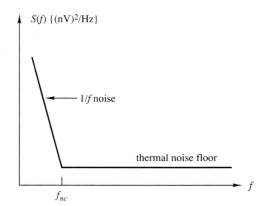

FIGURE 5-36   Sketch of noise power spectral density for an op amp MOS or bipolar input device.

be reduced considerably by careful, well-controlled processing. It is also inversely proportional to the area of the device.

The power spectral density $S(f)$ for a typical transistor (MOS or bipolar), due to the combination of thermal and $1/f$ noise, is sketched in Fig. 5-36. We note that the thermal and $1/f$ noise sources are uncorrelated and add in the rms. At low frequencies the $1/f$ component dominates, decreasing inversely proportional to frequency toward the thermal noise floor. The thermal noise floor is reached at the corner frequency f_{nc}, after which the noise remains constant over the remaining noise bandwidth of the op amp. In continuous systems, the $1/f$ noise tends to be more important than the thermal noise. In sampled-data systems, the converse tends to be true, with the thermal noise and noise bandwidth usually being of prime importance because of aliasing. Aliasing and noise in sampled-data filters are reserved for consideration in Chap. 7.

To calculate the noise output in closed-loop op amp systems, it is convenient to model the noisy op amp as a noiseless op amp, with equivalent input referred mean-square noise voltage and current sources connected to its input terminals, as shown in Fig. 5-37. The input noise voltage and current are usually specified in the op amp data sheet as a function of frequency. This data is sketched in Fig. 5-38 for $\overline{dv_{ni}}$ and $\overline{di_{ni}}$. The total noise output is then best determined by superposition and the addition of the mean-square output noise components due to the two noise sources.

FIGURE 5-37   Noisy op amp modeled as noiseless op amp excite by equivalent-input, mean-square, noise voltage and current sources.

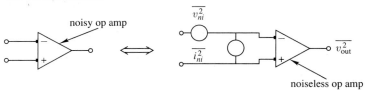

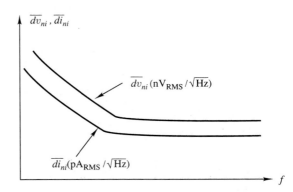

FIGURE 5-38   Sketch of typical op amp input rms noise voltage and current versus frequency.

5-4 DIFFERENTIAL AND BALANCED CONFIGURATIONS

In the integration of analog circuits, the designer must be concerned with a host of second-order disturbances that can build up and limit circuit performance. Unavoidable parasitics, associated with all silicon ICs, provide numerous paths for unwanted disturbances to couple into the signal path of an analog circuit via the substrate, the power supplies rails, the ground lines and/or even directly from nonideal components. The disturbances from all these sources can accumulate, potentially leading to serious loss in signal-to-noise and dynamic range. Throughout this chapter, we have used op amps that have a differential input and a single-ended output, as shown in Fig. 5-39a. Op amps can also be designed to be fully differential and/or balanced, thus maintaining positive and negative signal paths throughout. In fact, to reduce the impact of parasitic couplings, designers of analog ICs often realize their circuits as *differential* structures rather than the *single-ended* schemes that we have studied thus far in this chapter. Yet even further improvement is obtained if the analog circuit is not only differential but *balanced* as well (Gregorian and Temes 1986; Schaumann, Ghausi, and Laker 1990; Schaumann and Laker 1993). That is, it is realized with dual inverting and noninverting signal paths, in a completely symmetrical layout, such that all parasitic injections couple equally into both signal paths as common-mode signals. The differential nature of these circuits causes these common-mode disturbances to cancel (or at least nearly cancel) such that their impact is reduced significantly. Of course, fully balanced design does not come without cost; because, as we shall see, it requires duplication of much of the circuitry.

Throughout this chapter, we have used op amps that have a differential input and a single-ended output, as shown in Fig. 5-39a. Op amps can be designed to be fully differential and/or balanced, thus maintaining positive and negative signal paths throughout. It is important to clearly distinguish between the three kinds of op amps shown in Fig. 5-39. First, we have the conventional *single-ended* (differential input-single-ended output) op amp shown in Fig. 5-39a. The op amp in Fig. 5-39b is a *differential* (differential input-differential output) op amp. The output of the latter is defined as the difference between the two output terminal voltages. The values of the

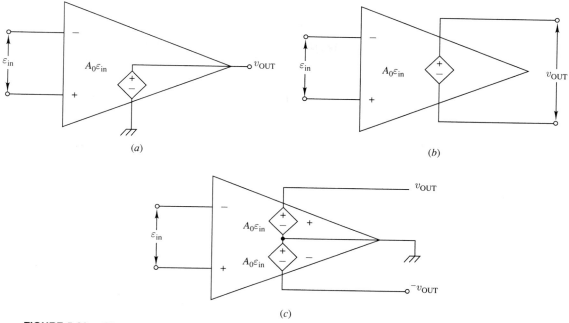

FIGURE 5-39   Three types of op amps (a) single-ended output, (b) differential output, and (c) balanced differential output.

terminal voltages, with respect to ground, are not in this case individually defined. In contrast, the *balanced differential* (differential input-balanced differential output) op amp is shown in Fig. 5-39c. In this case, the individual differential outputs are accurately balanced and defined with respect to ground. In fact, in balanced systems, with dual inverting and noninverting signal paths, the outputs are completely symmetrical with respect to ground, as illustrated in Fig. 5-40.

The device level design of balanced op amps is deferred to Chap. 6. However, it is instructive to examine a rather straightforward implementation based on the interconnection of two single-ended op amps, as shown in Fig. 5-41. Although this scheme does not lead to an optimum design, it has been used because it works and it is easy to implement (Gregorian and Temes 1986). Its primary disadvantage is that both signals see different hardware, namely, one single-ended op amp versus

FIGURE 5-40   Block diagram for a balanced differential system.

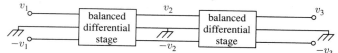

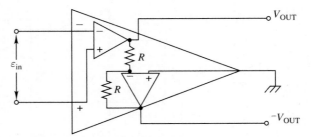

FIGURE 5-41   Implementation of balanced differential output op amp based on an interconnection of two single-ended op amps.

two single-ended op amps. Hence, at high frequencies, the phase difference (recall Fig. 5-23) caused by the second op amp can destroy the balance between the two outputs. For voice frequency ($f < 4$ kHz), this simple implementation has been found to give good results.

Let us consider the differential input-differential output scheme in Fig. 5-42 with inputs v_{IN1}, and v_{IN2} and outputs v_{OUT1} and v_{OUT2}, defined with respect to ground. Connected to this op amp are admittances G_1, G_2, G_3, and G_4, which represent arbitrary passive RC networks. Analyzing this system we write the following equations

$$G_2(v_{OUT1} - v_1) = G_1(v_1 - v_{IN1}) \tag{5-58a}$$

$$G_4(v_{OUT2} - v_2) = G_3(v_2 - v_{IN2}) \tag{5-58b}$$

where

$$v_{OUT1} = A_1(v_1 - v_2) \quad \text{and} \quad v_{OUT2} = -A_2(v_1 - v_2) \tag{5-58c}$$

FIGURE 5-42   A single differential input-differential output op amp configured with differential gains A_1, A_2 and external feedback in the dual signal paths determined by admittances G_1, G_2, G_3, and G_4. The inputs v_{IN1} and v_{IN2} and output v_{OUT1} and v_{OUT2} are defined with respect to ground.

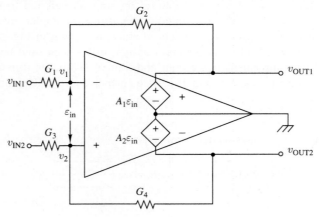

Solving Eqs. (5-58) for v_{OUT1} and v_{OUT2} in terms of v_{IN1} and v_{IN2} yields:

$$v_{OUT1} = -\sqrt{\frac{A_1}{A_2}} \frac{\dfrac{G_1}{G_1+G_2}v_{IN1} - \dfrac{G_2}{G_3+G_4}v_{IN2}}{\dfrac{G_2}{G_1+G_2}\sqrt{\dfrac{A_1}{A_2}} + \dfrac{G_4}{G_3+G_4}\sqrt{\dfrac{A_2}{A_1}} + \dfrac{1}{\sqrt{A_1 A_2}}} \qquad (5\text{-}59a)$$

$$\approx -\sqrt{\frac{A_1}{A_2}} \frac{\dfrac{G_1}{G_1+G_2}v_{IN1} - \dfrac{G_3}{G_3+G_4}v_{IN2}}{\dfrac{G_2}{G_1+G_2}\sqrt{\dfrac{A_1}{A_2}} + \dfrac{G_4}{G_3+G_4}\sqrt{\dfrac{A_2}{A_1}}}$$

$$v_{OUT2} = -\sqrt{\frac{A_2}{A_1}} \frac{\dfrac{G_3}{G_3+G_4}v_{IN2} - \dfrac{G_1}{G_1+G_2}v_{IN1}}{\dfrac{G_2}{G_1+G_2}\sqrt{\dfrac{A_1}{A_2}} + \dfrac{G_4}{G_3+G_4}\sqrt{\dfrac{A_2}{A_1}} + \dfrac{1}{\sqrt{A_1 A_2}}} \qquad (5\text{-}59b)$$

$$\approx -\sqrt{\frac{A_2}{A_1}} \frac{\dfrac{G_3}{G_3+G_4}v_{IN2} - \dfrac{G_1}{G_1+G_2}v_{IN1}}{\dfrac{G_2}{G_1+G_2}\sqrt{\dfrac{A_1}{A_2}} + \dfrac{G_4}{G_3+G_4}\sqrt{\dfrac{A_2}{A_1}}}$$

In these approximations it is assumed that $A_1, A_2 \gg 1$.

For balanced operation we require that $G_1 = G_3$, $G_1 = G_4$, $A_1 = A_2$, and $v_{IN1} = -v_{IN2} = v_{IN}$. Substituting these conditions into Eq. (5-59) yields

$$v_{OUT1} \approx -2\sqrt{\frac{A_1}{A_2}} \frac{\dfrac{G_1}{G_2}v_{IN}}{\sqrt{\dfrac{A_1}{A_2}} + \sqrt{\dfrac{A_2}{A_1}}} = -\frac{2}{1+\dfrac{A_2}{A_1}}\frac{G_1}{G_2}v_{IN} = -\frac{G_1}{G_2}v_{IN} \quad (5\text{-}60a)$$

$$v_{OUT2} \approx 2\sqrt{\frac{A_2}{A_1}} \frac{\dfrac{G_1}{G_2}v_I}{\sqrt{\dfrac{A_1}{A_2}} + \sqrt{\dfrac{A_2}{A_1}}} = -\frac{2}{1+\dfrac{A_1}{A_2}}\frac{G_1}{G_2}(-v_{IN}) = \frac{G_1}{G_2}v_{IN} \quad (5\text{-}60b)$$

Hence, for the balanced differential circuit, we have terminal voltages v_{IN}, v_{OUT} in signal path 1 and terminal voltages $-v_{IN}$, $-v_{OUT}$ in signal path 2.

To see the practical value of balanced design, let our balanced differential circuit be perturbed by some external disturbance v_D. In practice, this disturbance enters both signal paths via parasitic components, which we can assume are nearly equal. Moreover, the degree of match that occurs in the parasitics is highly related to the degree of match achieved in realizing the desired components. Hence, for simplicity let us assume that v_D adds directly to inputs $+v_{IN}$ and $-v_{IN}$ with unity gain (in practice, since the parasitic components, are somewhat smaller than the desired components, this gain will usually be $\ll 1$) as shown in Fig. 5-43. With this assignment the reader can easily verify that

$$v_{OUT1} \approx -\frac{G_1}{G_2}(v_{IN} + v_D) \qquad \text{and} \qquad v_{OUT2} \approx -\frac{G_1}{G_2}(-v_{IN} + v_D) \qquad (5\text{-}61)$$

If we then take the difference $v_{OUT1} - v_{OUT2}$, the desired signal components add and the disturbance components subtract such that

$$v_{OUT1} - v_{OUT2} = -\frac{G_1}{G_2}(v_{IN} + v_D) + \frac{G_1}{G_2}(-v_{IN} + v_D) = -2\frac{G_1}{G_2}v_{IN} \qquad (5\text{-}62)$$

In addition to the cancellation of the disturbance, we see in Eq. (5-62) that the desired signal swing is doubled. It is important at this point to distinguish between correlated or deterministic disturbances and random noise. The cancellation in Eq. (5-62) can only occur if v_D's in both signal paths are correlated, i.e., deterministic and identical. When v_D's are random (and uncorrelated) noise, than the noise powers in both paths will add in accordance with the discussion in Sec. 5-3-6. Even if v_D in both signal paths are from the same noise source, the mismatches in the two paths is sufficient to uncorrelate the two noises. Consequently, the noise voltages add in the rms, or as $\sqrt{2}$, which contrasts with the doubling of the desired signals indicated in Eq. (5-62). Hence, even for random noise, the use of balanced differential structures yields a $2/\sqrt{2}$ improvement in signal-to-noise.

It is important to remember that the equal valued components (i.e., $G_1 = G_4$, $G_2 = G_4$, and $A_1 = A_2$) needed to implement the balance in Eq. (5-60) and to achieve the cancellation in Eq. (5-62) are realized in practice with some error. In this

FIGURE 5-43   A balanced differential configuration with external disturbances v_D corrupting both signal paths.

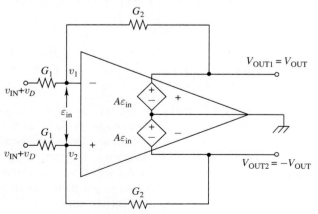

case, Eq. (5-59) can be used to evaluate mismatch in v_{OUT1} and v_{OUT2} due to these unavoidable component mismatches. We will make valuable use of balanced structures when we consider the realization of fully integrated active-RC and switched capacitor filters in Chaps. 7 and 8.

Note that we will usually find it convenient to develop our analog circuits and systems as single-ended structures at the start of the design. We take this approach because the derivation of single-ended structures and their operation are easier to understand than those of balanced differential structures. There are also important circumstances, such as battery powered circuits, where the need for minimal power dissipation dictates the use of single-ended configurations. Moreover, since balanced structures consume nearly twice the chip area of equivalent single-ended structures, the prudent approach for cost sensitive designs is to determine whether specifications can be met with a single-ended design before committing to the more complex structure. In any event, once a single-ended structure has been found, we will see that it is straightforward to translate it to a balanced differential structure, if required. In fact, we can view the single-ended schematic as a versatile notation that can serve as either the illustration for a single-ended design or as a short hand drawing for an equivalent fully balanced design.

The following procedure can be used to implement this translation: (a) draw the singled-ended circuit and its mirror image reflected about ground, duplicating all the elements, as illustrated in Fig. 5-44a; (b) merge each mirrored single-ended op amp pair into a single balanced differential input-differential output op amp, as shown in Fig. 5-44b. With signals of both polarities now available, sign inversions (i.e., as realized by a unity gain inverting amplifier) can be implemented by a simple cross coupling of the input or output leads, as illustrated in Fig. 5-45. This can result in

FIGURE 5-44   Realizing a balanced differential inverting integrator: (a) the mirrored signal paths using duplicate single-ended structures and (b) the balanced differential structure in which the two mirrored, single-ended op amps are replaced with a single differential input-differential output op amp.

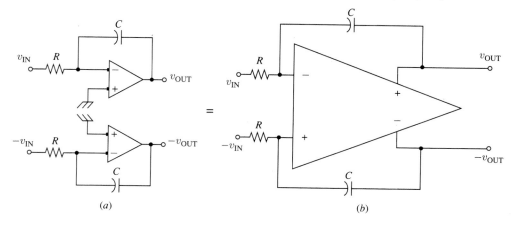

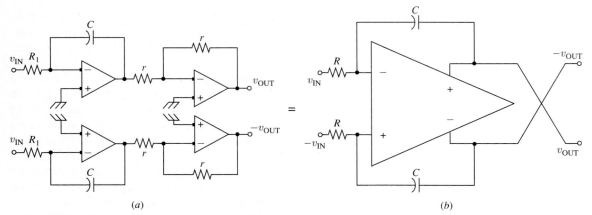

FIGURE 5-45   Realizing a balanced differential noninverting integrator: (*a*) the mirrored signal paths using duplicate single-ended structures and (*b*) the balanced differential structure in which the redundant inverting unity gain amplifiers are replaced by the cross coupling of the dual outputs.

the saving of several op amps that would otherwise be required in a single-ended structure. These savings reduce the cost difference between balanced differential and single-ended designs. Even more interesting is the fact that in some cases, balanced structures can be derived that have no exact single-ended counterpart. In Chap. 8, we examine interesting balanced filter structures that offer important performance advantages not available in equivalent single-ended schemes.

Caution should be raised before the reader eliminates all the so-called redundant op amps from his or her design. In many op amp circuits, additional op amps are used for active compensation or to realize a strategic phase change. The op amps used in the feedback loops of the integrator structures in Figs. 5-23*b*, 5-23*d*, and 5-23*e* are good cases in point. To remove these seemingly redundant op amps would also eliminate the corrective functions they provide. Consequently, these additional op amps are to be retained in the translation, as demonstrated in Fig. 5-46. We note that if the active devices being mirrored have precise single-ended gains (say K for example), then we divide all the translated gains by two and invert the sign of all the mirrored active elements (i.e., K splits into $K/2$ and the mirror $-K/2$).

Before ending this discussion, let us make one more interesting observation. The availability of outputs with both signs not only permits one to eliminate op amps, but perhaps even more interesting balanced system structures can be derived that have no exact single-ended counterpart. As we will see in Chap. 8, there are some interesting balanced switched-capacitor filter structures that offer important performance advantages which are not available in equivalent single-ended schemes.

5-5   THE OPERATIONAL TRANSCONDUCTANCE AMPLIFIER (OTA)

An *operational transconductance amplifier (OTA)* (Geiger and Sanchez-Sinencio 1985; Schaumann, Ghausi, and Laker 1990; Schaumann and Laker 1993; Unbehauen and

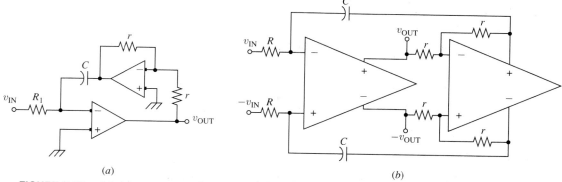

(a)   (b)

FIGURE 5-46   A balanced differential phase-lag compensated noninverting integrator: (a) the single-ended structure (Fig. 5-20d) and (b) the balanced differential structure. In this case, the inverting unity gain amplifier in the feedback loop is retained.

Cichocki 1989), also called a transconductance element or a transconductor, is a device that translates voltage inputs to current outputs such that $i_{OUT} = G_m v_{IN}$. The *transconductance gain* G_m can usually be varied over a wide range by adjusting an external DC bias current I_B. When G_m is a filter parameter, I_B can be used to control or to program the characteristics of the filter. Recently, OTAs have emerged as compelling alternatives to conventional op amps in the realization of fully integrated continuous-time active filters (i.e., *active-G_m/C* filters) (Schaumann, Ghausi, and Laker 1990; Schaumann and Laker 1993; Unbehauen and Cichocki 1989), particularly at frequencies above 100 kHz. Part of the interest in OTAs stems from their relative simplicity in comparison to a standard op amp. For example, CMOS OTAs are single stage circuits, essentially comprised of a simple differential stage described in Secs. 4-8 and 4-9. Hence, at high frequencies where large excess phase significantly degrades the performance of a conventional op amp, a properly designed OTA can still maintain near ideal behavior.

5-5-1   Ideal Model

The circuit symbol for the OTA is shown in Fig. 5-47a. The OTA is seen to be a three input, one output device. The three inputs are voltage signals v^+, v^-, and current I_B, and the output is a current signal i_{out}. Although in linear filter applications I_B is a DC source used to control G_m, some interesting nonlinear functions can be realized if I_B is a more general signal. To simplify notation in filter schematics, the bias current I_B is often dropped from the symbol. It is emphasized that dropping I_B from the symbol is not to imply that I_B has been eliminated or that it is unimportant. In fact, the control of G_m with I_B is crucial to the use of OTAs in precision filters (Schaumann, Ghausi, and Laker 1990; Schaumann and Laker 1993; Unbehauen and Cichocki 1989).

In Fig. 5-47b, the small-signal model for an ideal OTA is seen to be a differential input voltage-controlled current source (VCCS), with infinite input and infinite output

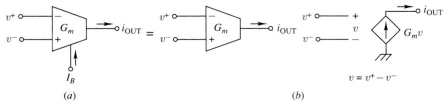

FIGURE 5-47   The differential OTA (*a*) symbol and (*b*) ideal model.

impedances, i.e.,

$$i_{OUT} = G_m(v^+ - v^-) \tag{5-63a}$$

For linear filter applications where I_B is used to control G_m, it is highly desirable that the G_m dependence on I_B be linear. Hence, the G_m for the ideal OTA is assumed to be

$$G_m = G_m(I_B) = \eta I_B \tag{5-63b}$$

where η is a constant determined by process parameters, temperature, and input device geometries (see Sec. 6-1). The linear dependence in Eq. (5-63*b*) occurs when the OTA (MOS or bipolar) operates in the weak inversion or low current region.

5-5-2 OTA Building Block Circuits

Several building block circuits (Geiger and Sanchez-Sinencio 1985; Schaumann, Ghausi, and Laker 1990; Schaumann and Laker 1993) that will be useful in applications considered in subsequent chapters are given in Fig. 5-48. Also given are the ideal transfer functions and the relevant input or output impedances. The transfer function and impedance formulas for each circuit can be readily verified by substituting the ideal model in Fig. 5-47*b* for each OTA and performing a straightforward circuit analysis on the resulting equivalent circuit. The reader is encouraged to verify the circuits in Fig. 5-48 as study exercises.

There are several observations worthy of discussion regarding the behavior of circuits in Fig. 5-48. Let us first compare the general operation of these OTA building blocks with their equivalent op amp-based counterparts. In the case of op amp building blocks, we recall in Sec. 5-2 that specific voltage gains (or transfer functions) are realized by surrounding the op amp with large amounts of external negative feedback in order to significantly desensitize the closed-loop performance to the characteristics of the open-loop op amp. In fact, for ideal operation, the closed-loop performance of these circuits is independent of the op amp's open-loop behavior; determined only by the external passive components in the feedback network (e.g., see Fig. 5-6 through Fig. 5-13). In other words, the open-loop gain of the op amp is a second-order effect in these circuits. Moreover, the feedback guarantees linear operation over a wide range

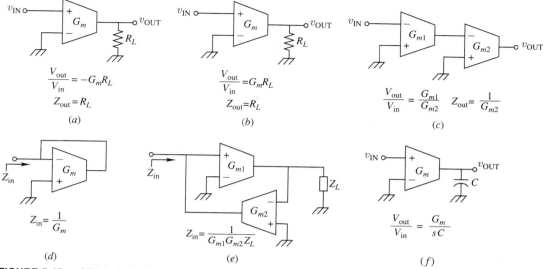

FIGURE 5-48   OTA building block circuits: (a) inverting voltage amplifier with load R_L, (b) noninverting voltage amplifier with load R_L, (c) inverting voltage amplifier with load $1/G_{m2}$, (d) controlled resistance, (e) impedance inverter, and (f) noninverting integrator.

of conditions, in spite of the op amp's very high open-loop gain. In contrast, OTA building blocks use no external feedback and their transfer and impedance functions depend directly on OTA G_m's (e.g., see Figs. 5-47a, b, c, and f). In other words, the G_m of the OTA is a first-order effect in OTA-based circuits. This requires a significant change in design strategy from that practiced for op amp-based circuits and systems. The strategy for OTA-based circuits and systems places far greater emphasis on custom design, optimization, and control of the OTA parameters.

Let us now make some specific observations regarding the OTA building block circuits in Fig. 5-48. Based on the inverting and noninverting voltage amplifiers, it should be obvious that an inverting integrator can be realized by reversing the polarity of the input terminals for the OTA in the noninverting integrator in Fig. 5-48f. Also note that if we set Z_L of the impedance inverter in Fig. 5-48e to a capacitor, i.e., $Z_L = 1/sC$, then $Z_{in} = sC/G_{m1}G_{m2}$ looks like an inductor of value $L = C/G_{m1}G_{m2}$. Finally, we point out that the large terminal impedances associated with OTA-based circuits can present potential loading problems when two or more are interconnected in a circuit. OTAs can be followed by unity gain buffers to reduce output impedance and loading. However, the frequency response of the buffer may degrade the inherent high frequency performance of the OTA.

5-5-3 Practical Considerations

There are three major areas of nonideal behavior that limit the use of OTAs in linear circuits, namely, the nonlinearity of G_m, the high variability of G_m with process and temperature, and parasitic elements that limit the frequency range. The important parasitic elements are shown in the nonideal model in Fig. 5-49. Since OTAs and op amps have similar input circuitry, the noise, DC offset, and power supply rejection for an OTA is similar to that of an op amp with similar sized input devices. Hence, the discussion in the previous section regarding these matters is relevant to OTA operation. Moreover, the use of balanced OTA structures, such as that depicted in Fig. 5-50, enable the designer to extend the dynamic range of OTA-based circuits. In Fig. 5-50b, the balanced OTA in Fig. 5-50a is conceptually realized as two identical single-ended OTAs, mirrored about ground and controlled with a common bias current I_B. Here, as in the case of finite amplifier gains, the single-ended G_m splits into a dual pair of mirrored VCCS's with transconductances $G_m/2$ and $-G_m/2$.

The most limiting nonideal behaviors are the nonlinearity and high variability of G_m. These limitations are further exaggerated by the role G_m plays in the first-order behavior of OTA-based circuits. The intrinsic nonlinearity of G_m is the first crucial limitation that must be dealt with by the designer. For example, to achieve a sufficiently linear G_m (> 80 dB dynamic range) the input signal swing may be required to be restricted to as little as 10 to 50 mV peak-to-peak. For this reason, linearization schemes (Unbehauen and Cichocki 1989) are usually required to achieve sufficiently linear operation over any practical input signal range, say ± 1 V or more for ± 3 V supplies. Furthermore, the value of G_m will vary significantly due to unavoidable variations in the fabrication process and ambient temperature. Consequently, several phase locking schemes have been offered for using I_B to adjust and control the value of G_m's for OTAs used in active filters. Linearization and control techniques for OTAs are developed further in Chap. 8.

FIGURE 5-49   Model for a nonideal OTA

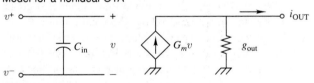

FIGURE 5-50   Balanced differential input-differential output OTA: (a) the symbol and (b) conceptual implementation based on the use of two identical single-ended OTAs.

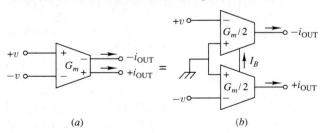

SUMMARY

In this chapter, we studied the op amp and closed-loop op amp systems, viewing the op amp as "black box." We also considered the balanced-differential systems and OTAs.

Initially we defined the ideal op amp with infinite gain, bandwidth, input impedance, and output conductance. We then developed the operation of actual, nonideal op amps by adding layers of detail on top of the ideal op amp model. The ideal op amp was seen to be a good approximation for closed-loop transfer function analyses as long as the loop gain $T \gg 1$. A good grasp of the detailed operation of the nonideal op amp will enhance the reader's abilities to use the op amp creatively and robustly. Chapters 7 and 8 will provide more complex signal processing applications, several of which will stress one or more of the nonideal op amp characteristics. Moreover, detailed familiarity is required if the reader intends to design op amps for custom applications. Note that op amp design is the focus of the next chapter.

Finally, we examined operational transconductance amplifiers or OTAs, and their role in the realization of linear circuits. The OTAs, in comparison to op amps, were shown to present the linear circuit designer with a different, and perhaps complimentary, array of alternatives and tradeoffs.

EXERCISES

5-1 a Derive the input impedance Z_{in} for the inverting configuration in Fig. EX5-1; and
   b determine $Re(Z_{in}(\omega))$ and $Im(Z_{in}(\omega))$ when $A_0(j\omega) = 10^4$, $R_1 = 10\text{ k}\Omega$, $R_2 = 50$ kΩ, $R_3 = 20$ kΩ, and $C_2 = 100$ pF.

5-2 Let the open-loop gain of the op amp be modeled as $A_0(s) = \omega_t/s$, and compare the 3 dB bandwidths of inverting and noninverting unity gain amplifiers in Fig. EX5-2. Assume that the op amp $R_{in} = \infty$ and $R_{out} = 0$.

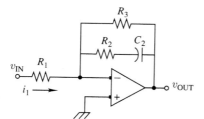

FIGURE EX5-1

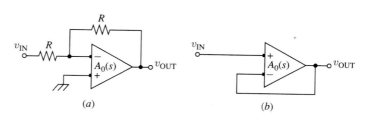

(a)   (b)

FIGURE EX5-2

5-3 Consider the inverting integrator circuit in Fig. EX5-3, with an op amp characterized by open-loop gain $A_0(s)$, input resistance R_{in}, and output resistance R_{out}. Using the op amp model in Fig. 5-3, derive the closed-loop voltage gain V_{out}/V_{in} for the integrator.

5-4 For the inverting integrator and op amp in Exercise 5.3,
   a determine the expression for error $\varepsilon_{rr}(s)$;
   b evaluate $|\varepsilon_{rr}(j2\pi f)|$ when $R_1 = 100$ kΩ, $C = 100$ pF, $R_{in} = 5$ MΩ, $R_{out} = 100$ Ω, and

$$A_0(s) = \frac{10^5}{[1 + s/2\pi(10)][1 + s/2\pi(2 \times 10^6)]}.$$

5-5 Assuming an ideal op amp,
   a determine the input impedance $Z_{in} = V_{in}/I_1$ for the circuit in Fig. EX5-5;
   b discuss the result derived in **a** in terms of the functionality and application of this circuit.

5-6 Assuming an ideal op amp,
   a determine the the input impedance $Z_{in} = V_{in}/I_1$ for the circuit in Fig. EX5-6;
   b discuss the result derived in **a** in terms of the functionality and application of this circuit.

5-7 Verify Eq. (5-29).

5-8 Consider the inverting integrator in Fig. EX5-3. With $R_1 = 1$ MΩ, $C = 100$ pF, and $A_0(s) = A_0$; Determine the minimum value for A_0 that will limit the error to $|\varepsilon_{rr}(2\pi f)| \leq 0.1$ dB over the frequency range 10 Hz $< f \leq 20$ kHz.

5-9 Consider the inverting integrator in Fig. EX5-3. With $R_1 = 1$ MΩ, $C = 100$ pF, and $A_0(s) = 2\pi f_t/s$: Determine the minimum value for f_t that will limit the error to $|\varepsilon_{rr}(2\pi f)| \leq 0.1$ dB over the frequency range $0 < f \leq 20$ kHz.

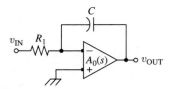

FIGURE EX5-3

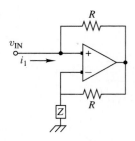

FIGURE EX5-5

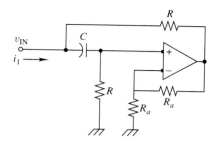

FIGURE EX5-6

5-10 Verify Eq. (5-44).

5-11 Consider the actively compensated integrator in Fig. EX5-11.
  a For $A_1 = A_2 = \omega_t/s$, show that $m_{rr}(\omega) \approx 1/\omega_t R_1 C$ and $\varphi_{rr}(\omega) \approx (\omega/\omega_t)^3$;
  b determine $m_{rr}(\omega)$ and $\varphi_{rr}(\omega)$ with A_2 ideal (i.e., $A_2 = \infty$);
  c compare **a** and **b**.

5-12 Let us consider the passively compensated inverting integrator in Fig. EX5-12. With $A(s) = \omega_t/s$,
  a derive $\varepsilon_{rr}(j\omega)$;
  b determine the value for R_c that will force $\varphi_{rr}(\omega) = 0$;
  c discuss the practical limitations of this approach.

5-13 Let us consider the passively compensated inverting integrator in Fig. EX5-13. With $A(s) = \omega_t/s$,
  a derive $\varepsilon_{rr}(j\omega)$;
  b determine the value for C_c that will force $\varphi_{rr}(\omega) = 0$;
  c discuss the practical limitations of this approach.

5-14 Consider the unity gain noninverting amplifier in Fig. EX5-2. With $A_0(s) = 10^5/(1 + s/2\pi(10))(1 + s/2\pi(2 \times 10^6))$,
  a Determine the closed-loop voltage gain $A_{CL}(s)$;
  b determine the phase-margin;
  c determine the transient response $v_{out}(t)$, if $v_{in}(t) = u(t)$; determine the peak overshoot r_p and settling time $t_s(\varepsilon = 0.01)$. Note that these terms are defined in Chap. 3.

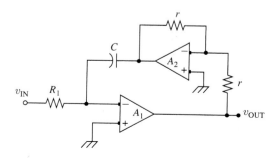

FIGURE EX5-11

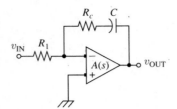

FIGURE EX5-12

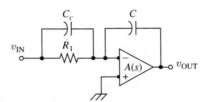

FIGURE EX5-13

5-15 Consider the unity gain noninverting amplifier in Fig. EX5-2. With the op amp specified as $A_0(s) = 10^5/(1 + s/\omega_a)(1 + s/\gamma\omega_a)$, where $\gamma \gg 1$,
   a determine the value of γ that will achieve a phase margin PM = 60°;
   b recalculate γ to achieve a percent overshoot = 5 percent.
5-16 Consider the noninverting integrator circuit in Fig. EX5-16, with the op amp open-loop gain $A_0(s) = \omega_t/s$.
   a Derive the voltage transfer function $V_{\text{out}}/V_{\text{in}}$;
   b explain the effect finite ω_t has on the integrator's response.
5-17 In Fig. EX5-17 we have a unity gain noninverting amplifier driving a capacitive load of C_L. With the op amp specified as $A_0(s) = 10^5/(1 + s/30)$, $R_{\text{in}} = \infty$, and $R_{\text{out}} = 1$ KΩ, show how the presence of C_L effects the step response.
5-18 Calculate the phase margin and % overshoot for the circuit in Exercise 5-17 when $C_L = 150$ pF.

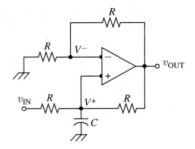

FIGURE EX5-16

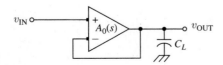

FIGURE EX5-17

5-19 An op amp having $A_0 = 10^4$, $f_t = 10$ MHz, $R_{ind} = 10$ MΩ , and $R_{inc} = 100$ MΩ is used in a noninverting amplifier configuration realizing a closed-loop gain of $A_{CL} = 11$. If the op amp open-loop gain is modeled as $A_0(s) = \omega_t/s$, determine the equivalent circuit for the closed-loop input impedance.

5-20 An op amp powered by ± 5 V supplies, has a slew rate of $SR = 0.5/\mu S$. The op amp is to be used in a feedback amplifier that will achieve a gain 7.0 at $f = 10$ kHz.

   a Determine the largest input amplitude that can be applied at $f = 10$ kHz such that the output is without distortion;

   b Repeat the calculation for $f = 100$ kHz.

5-21 The input stage of an op amp, compensated with a capacitance $C = 50$ pF, supplies a maximum current of 100 μA.

   a calculate the slew rate;

   b if the maximum rated output voltage is ± 3 V, determine the value for the op amp's full power bandwidth f_M.

5-22 Consider the noninverting amplifier in Fig. EX5-22. Let the closed-loop gain be $A_{CL} = 10$ and $R = 10$ MΩ; and the op amp's DC offset specs be $V_{OS} = 10$ mV, $I_{BS} = 200$ nA, and $I_{OS} = 20$ nA.

   a Calculate the output offset voltage;

   b if the op amp output saturation levels are at ± 3 V, determine the maximum amplitude of the sinusoidal signal that can be applied to the input without the output clipping;

   c repeat **a** and **b** if $A_{CL} = 1000$.

5-23 Consider the inverting integrator in Fig. EX5-23, where $R = 200$ KΩ and $C = 250$ pF. Let the DC offset specs for the op amp be $V_{OS} = 2$ mV, $I_{BS} = 200$ nA, and $I_{OS} = 20$ nA.

   a With $v_{IN}(t) = 0$, determine and sketch $v_{OUT}(t)$ versus time;

   b if the op amp output saturates at ± 3 V, calculate the time at which saturation occurs.

5-24 **a** Reconsider Exercise 5-23 after placing a resistor of value $R = 10$ MΩ in parallel with the integrating capacitor C;

   b compare offset and AC responses with those of the inverting integrator in Fig. EX5-23.

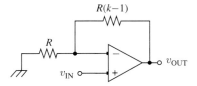

FIGURE EX5-22

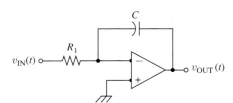

FIGURE EX5-23

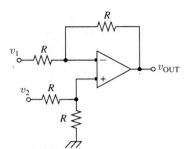

FIGURE EX5-25

5-25 Consider the difference amplifier in Fig. EX5-25, where $R = 10$ kΩ and the common-mode rejection of the op amp is $CMRR(f) = 80$ dB for $f \leq 25$ kHz and rolls off at -40 db/decade for $f > 25$ kHz. Determine the common-mode output when v_1 and v_2 are 1 V sinusoids at 10 kHz and 50 kHz, respectively.

5-26 Consider a noisy amplifier of gain $A(jf) = A_0/1 + j(f/f_a)$, and input referred noise that has a constant or "white" spectral density S_{in}. Referring to Eq. (5-57), the noise at the output of an amplifier can be expressed as

$$\overline{x_{on}^2} = \int_0^\infty S_{on}(f)df = \int_0^\infty |A(jf)|^2 S_{in}df = S_{in}\int_0^\infty |A(jf)|^2 df$$

Let us replace $|A(jf)|$ with an equivalent rectangular frequency response such that $|A(jf)|_{eq} = A_0$ for $0 \leq f \leq f_N$ and $|A(jf)|_{eq} = 0$ for $f > f_N$. The equivalent output noise is then

$$\overline{x_{oneq}^2} = \int_0^\infty |A(jf)|_{eq}^2 S_{in}df = S_{in}(A_0)^2 f_N$$

The noise bandwidth for an amplifier is defined as the frequency f_N for which the noise $\overline{x_{oneq}^2} = \overline{x_{on}^2}$. Show that $f_N = 1.57 f_a$.

5-27 Calculate the output rms noise voltage for a noninverting amplifier with $A_{CL} = 10$. The op amp is specified with open-loop gain $A_0(jf) = 10^4/1 + j(f/100)$ and $\overline{dv_{ni}} = 10$ nV/$\sqrt{\text{Hz}}$ for all f.

5-28 Verify Eqs. (5-60).

5-29 A differential output op amp can be constructed from two single-ended output op amps, as shown in Fig. EX5-29.
  a Show the operation of this circuit when both op amps are ideal;
  b if the op amps have matched open-loop gains $A(s) = \omega_t/s$, show the effect on the differential outputs.

5-30 Assuming ideal OTAs, verify that the circuit in Fig. 5-48c realizes the voltage transfer function $V_{out}/V_{in} = -G_{m1}/G_{m2}$ and output impedance $Z_{out} = 1/G_{m2}$.

5-31 Assuming ideal OTAs, verify that the circuit in Fig. 5-48e realizes the input impedance $Z_{in} = 1/G_{m1}G_{m2}Z_L$.

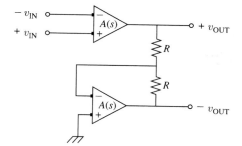

FIGURE EX5-29

5-32 Consider the OTA integrator circuit in Fig. EX5-32a. The nonideal OTA is modeled for finite input and output impedances as shown in Fig. EX5-32b. Let us assume that the input signal amplitude is sufficiently small that the OTA behaves as a linear circuit.

 a Show that the ideal voltage transfer function (i.e., with $C_{in} = 0$, $g_{out} = 0$) is
 $V_{out}/V_{in} = G_m/sC$;

 b when C_{in} and g_{out} are nonzero, express V_{out}/V_{in} in the following form $V_{out}/V_{in} = G_m/sC[1/1 + \varepsilon_{rr}(s)]$;

 c with $C = 100$ pF, $G_m = 5$ μS, $C_{in} = 0.5$ pF, and $g_{out} = 50$ nS, sketch V_{out}/V_{in}.

5-33 Fig. EX5-33 is comprised of three differential input-differential output OTAs. Using the OTA model in Fig. EX5-32b (with $C_{in} = 0$ and $i_{OUT}^+ = I_{OUT}^-$ for all OTAs). Determine the relation between the differential utput voltage $(v_{OUT}^+ - v_{OUT}^-)$, in terms of the differential input voltages (i.e., $v_1^+ - v_1^-$ and $v_2^+ - v_2^-$).

5-34 Determine the voltage transfer function (V_{out}/V_1) for the differential input-differential output circuit in Fig. EX5-34.

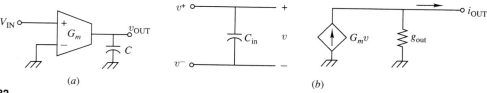

(a)   (b)

FIGURE EX5-32

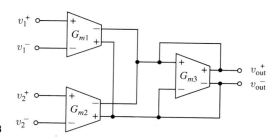

FIGURE EX5-33

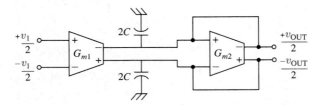

FIGURE EX5-34

REFERENCES

Allen, P. E., and D. R. Holberg. 1987. *CMOS Analog Circuit Design.* New York: Holt, Rinehart and Winston.

Daryanani, G. 1976. *Principles of Active Network Synthesis and Design.* New York: Wiley and Sons.

Geiger, R. L., and E. Sanchez-Sinencio. 1985. "Active Filters Using Operational Transconductance Amplifiers: A Tutorial," *IEEE Circuits and Devices Magazine,* vol. 1, pp. 20–32.

Ghausi, M. S. 1985. *Electronic Devices and Circuits: Discrete and Integrated.* New York: Holt, Rinehart and Winston.

Gray, P. R., D. A. Hodges, and R. W. Broderson, eds. 1980. "Analog MOS Integrated Circuits," *IEEE Press Selected Reprint.* New York: Wiley and Sons.

Gray, P. R., and R. G. Meyer. 1984. *Analysis and Design of Analog Integrated Circuits.* New York: Wiley and Sons.

Grebene, A. B. 1984. *Bipolar and MOS Analog Integrated Circuit Design.* New York: Wiley and Sons.

Gregorian, R., and G. C. Temes. 1986. *Analog MOS Circuits and Systems.* New York: Wiley and Sons.

Moschytz, G. S. 1975. *Linear Integrated Networks: Design.* New York: Van Nostrand-Reinhold.

Nayebi, M., and B. A. Wooley. 1988. "A 0.5 Ghz BiCMOS Op-Amp." *Symposium on VLSI Circuits Digest of Technical Papers.*

Schaumann, R., M. S. Ghausi, and K. R. Laker. 1990. *Design of Analog Filters.* Englewood Cliffs, NJ: Prentice-Hall.

Schaumann, R., and K. R. Laker. 1993. "Active Filter Design." Chap. 10, in *Reference Data for Engineers: Radio, Electronics, Computer, and Communications,* edited by E. C. Jordan, 8th ed. Indianapolis: Howard W. Sams.

Sedra, A. S., and K. C. Smith. 1991. *Microelectronic Circuits.* 3rd ed., Philadelphia: Sanders College Publishing.

Soclof, S. 1985. *Applications of Analog Integrated Circuits.* Englewood Cliffs, NJ: Prentice-Hall.

Unbehauen, R., and A. Cichocki. 1989. *MOS Switchec-Capacitor and Continuous-Time Integrated Circuits and Systems.* Berlin: Springer-Verlag.

6

OPERATIONAL
AMPLIFIER DESIGN

INTRODUCTION

Operational amplifiers are the prototypes of analog integrated circuits. All problems related to gain-bandwidth (GBW), gain, stability, and biasing are encountered in operational amplifier design (Gray and Meyer 1984; Allen and Holberg 1987; Gregorian and Temes 1986). Therefore, we will discuss this topic in detail.

In Chap. 5, the operational amplifier is used as a black box. It is represented by a behavioral model. In this chapter the model is derived from components that make up the operational amplifier. These are transistors, capacitors, and, occasionally, resistors. The gain stages studied in Chap. 4 could easily become the first stage of an operational amplifier. None, however, provide the required combination of high gain and high gain-bandwidth while maintaining a symmetrical input configuration. Therefore, we will discuss an alternative configuration. It will be analyzed and its specifications will be derived. This configuration will serve as a basis with which to compare other operational amplifier configurations.

In this chapter considerable attention is paid to symmetry and matching, as well as to other second-order effects, to determine a full set of operational amplifier specifications.

Throughout this chapter, a transconductance amplifier (OTA) is used as an operational amplifier (op amp). An OTA has a large open-loop output resistance at low frequencies. Its gain is characterized by a transconductance G_m that can be quite large. An op amp provides a large voltage gain. Its open-loop output resistance at low frequencies is very low. In general, an op amp can be built by adding an output buffer, such as a class AB stage or a source follower, to the output of the OTA. The difference between the two is explained in detail in Chap. 5.

There are several ways to classify circuits. For example, we can count the number of transistors. We began studying circuits in Chap. 4 by calling them single-transistor amplifiers, two-transistor amplifiers, etc. In this chapter we will classify the circuits according to the number of nodes. A node is counted only if it has a high impedance with respect to ground. For example, the single-transistor amplifier is a two-node circuit. It has an input node and an output node. The input node is connected to the input source v_{IN} over a source resistance R_S. The CMOS inverter is a two-node circuit, as well. The differential amplifier with active load (see Fig. 4-62c) is still a two-node circuit. The input terminals do not count as nodes because they are connected directly to an input voltage source, with zero impedance to ground. The cascode amplifiers of Fig. 4-56a and b, on the other hand, are all three-node circuits.

The advantage of classifying the circuits by the number of nodes is that we know beforehand what complexity we must consider when analyzing that circuit. Each node is at a finite impedance with respect to ground. From each node there is a resistance R_n to ground and a capacitance C_n. Hence, a pole is established at each node. The pole frequency is $1/(2\pi R_n C_n)$. As a result, a two-node circuit will have two poles. A three-node circuit will have three poles, etc.

In order to determine which poles are dominant, we must monitor the impedance levels. The capacitances C_n are all of the same order of magnitude (pF's), but the resistances R_n can vary considerably. When the resistance is high, a dominant pole is formed. In simple transistor circuits all resistance levels are either determined by output resistances r_o, or by transconductances g_m. In the first case the resistance level is high, whereas in the latter the resistance level is low.

For example, the CMOS inverter with low source resistance R_S is a two-node amplifier with one high-resistance (output) node and one low-resistance (input) node. In this case, the dominant pole and the *GBW* are determined by the output node. Then the nondominant pole is realized at the input node. This latter pole determines the phase margin.

The cascode amplifier of Fig. 4-51a is a three-node amplifier. It has one high-resistance node at the output and two low-resistance nodes at the input and the intermediate point. The dominant pole and the *GBW* are realized at the output. The two nondominant poles determine the phase margin.

The differential amplifier with active load (Fig. 4-62c) is a two-node circuit. Its output has two output resistors r_o in parallel and thus is at high level. The output node determines the dominant pole and the *GBW*. The other node only has a resistance level of $1/g_m$. It is low and determines the nondominant pole and the phase margin. This amplifier will be analyzed first. It is the simplest complete OTA structure. Therefore, it is called the simple CMOS OTA.

After we examine this simple OTA, we will add an inverter stage to form the Miller CMOS OTA. This gives rise to a three-node amplifier with two high-resistance nodes. A compensation capacitance is necessary to connect these two nodes in order to realize pole splitting. The third low-resistance node gives an additional nondominant pole. This amplifier is representative of many designs, and thus will be analyzed in detail. Matching, *PSRR*, and many more specifications are also examined.

After we discuss the Miller CMOS OTA, we will analyze more OTAs, such as the symmetrical OTA, a folded cascode, etc. A design procedure will be given for all.

6-1 DESIGN OF A SIMPLE CMOS OTA

In Fig. 6-1a, a simple CMOS OTA is shown. Its symbolic representation is shown in Fig. 6-1b. The simple CMOS OTA consists of a self-biasing MOST differential stage with active load. Transistors T1 and T2 form a matched transistor pair. They have equal W/L ratios $(W/L)_1$. Transistor T3 and T4 have equal W/L ratios $(W/L)_4$, as well. All current levels are determined by current source I_B, half of which flows through T1 and T3, with the other half flowing through T2 and T4. Note that all substrates are connected to the sources in order to exclude the body effect and to improve matching (see Sec. 6-5).

FIGURE 6-1   (a) Configuration of simple CMOS OTA. (b) Symbol of OTA

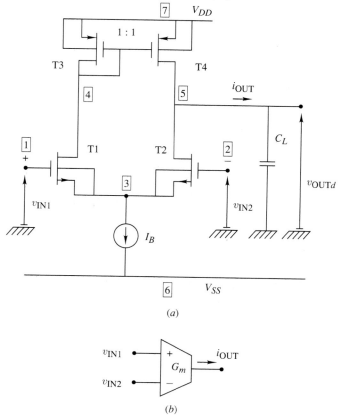

The design of this CMOS OTA consists of the derivation of all transistor sizes W/L from the given specifications such as GBW, phase margin, gain, etc. Although there are several approaches to the solution of this design problem, we will discuss a systematic design procedure that always provides the optimum result and that can be easily implemented in a software package.

6-1-1   Gain of the Simple CMOS OTA

At low frequencies, the transconductance of the OTA is given by $G_m = g_{m1} = g_{m2}$. It is also given by

$$G_m = \sqrt{2K'_n I_B \left(\frac{W}{L}\right)_1}$$ (6-1)

in which $(W/L)_1$ is the aspect ratio of the input transistors; K'_n is the transconductance parameter for an nMOST in saturation. Also note that the current I_B in Eq. (6-1) is the total current, which is twice the current through one transistor.

A voltage gain can be calculated as well, because the output resistance R_{OUT} at the output terminal consists of the two output resistances r_{o2} and r_{o4} in parallel. In order to realize a high value of R_{OUT}, both values of r_o must be equally large and equal to each other.

The output resistance of a MOST is determined by the Early voltage and its channel length. If $r_{o2} = r_{o4} = r_o$, the value of R_{OUT} can be written as

$$R_{OUT} = \frac{r_{o2}}{2} = \frac{V_{En} L_1}{I_B}$$ (6-2)

in which L_1 is the length of transistor T1. For an nMOST in an n-well CMOS process, V_{En} is smaller than that of a pMOST. Typical values of V_E are $V_{En} = 4.5$ V/μm and $V_{Ep} = 8.3$ V/μm. As a result, for equal r_o the gate length of the pMOST will be smaller than for the nMOST, using the same ratios as the values of V_{En} and V_{Ep}.

The voltage gain A_v is then given by

$$A_v = G_m R_{OUT} = V_{En} \sqrt{\frac{2K'_n W_1 L_1}{I_B}}$$ (6-3a)

which can also be written as (see Chap. 1)

$$A_v = \frac{V_{En} L_1}{V_{GS1} - V_T}$$ (6-3b)

Parameters $K'_n (\approx KP_n/2n)$ and V_{En} are given by the processing engineers and are thus technological constraints. Parameters W_1, L_1, and I_B are design parameters. They are variables and can be chosen for optimum performance. Let us calculate two more resistances with important values. The resistance at node 4 with respect to ground R_{n4}, is easily ascertained. It is output resistance r_{o1} in parallel with resistance $1/g_{m3}$ of the diode connected MOST T3. Since r_{o1} is much larger than $1/g_{m3}$, the resistance at node 4, i.e., R_{n4}, can be approximated by $1/g_{m3}$ or by

$$R_{n4} \approx \frac{1}{g_{m3}} = \frac{1}{\sqrt{2K'_p I_B \left(\frac{W}{L}\right)_4}} \qquad (6\text{-}4)$$

in which $(W/L)_4 = (W/L)_3$ is the aspect ratio of both transistors T4 and T3; K'_p is the transconductance parameter for a pMOST.

Finally, the resistance of node 3 with respect to ground, denoted by R_{n3}, is given (for both inputs shorted to ground) by

$$R_{n3} = \frac{1}{2g_{m1}} \qquad (6\text{-}5)$$

in which g_{m1} can be detailed, as well. However, node 3 is a common-mode point and will only play a role in common-mode and *CMRR* considerations. For differential gain, *GBW*, and *SR* considerations, it does not play a role. Therefore it is not calculated.

Example 6-1

Calculate the voltage gain and all node resistances for a simple CMOS OTA with $K'_n \approx 20 \ \mu A/V^2$ and $K'_p \approx 10 \ \mu A/V^2$. Its $L_1 = L_4 = W_4 = 5 \ \mu m$ and $W_1 = 50 \ \mu m$, and $I_B = 10 \ \mu A$.

Solution. The OTA transconductance is $G_m = 63.2 \ \mu S$. Its $(W/L)_1 = 10$ and for $I_B = 10 \ \mu A$, $R_{OUT} = 2.25 \ M\Omega$ and $A_v = 142$. Also, $V_{GS1} - V_T = 0.16$ V, and for $(W/L)_4 = 1$, $R_{n4} = 71 \ k\Omega$.

6-1-2 The *GBW* and Phase-Margin

Only two nodes are available that can cause poles. Thus we have a two-pole system. One of the poles is dominant; it occurs at frequency f_d. The other is the nondominant pole at frequency f_{nd}. The resistance levels at these two nodes are in Example 6-1, $R_{n4} = 71 \ k\Omega$ and $R_{n5} = 2.25 \ M\Omega$. These values are largely different. The node capacitances, however, have similar values of the order of magnitude of pF's. The dominant pole thus is likely to occur on the node with the highest resistance level. Capacitance on node 5, i.e., C_{n5} thus would create a dominant pole on node 5, about 30 times earlier in frequency than on node 4. Moreover, the load capacitance C_L must be added to C_{n5}, since it is also present on node 5. Thus, node 5 is even more dominant. Because the source resistance is assumed to be about zero, no Miller effect is present.

Thus, the -3 dB cut-off frequency or the dominant pole is created on node 5 and is given by

$$f_d = \frac{1}{2\pi R_{\text{OUT}}(C_{n5} + C_L)} \tag{6-6}$$

in which $C_{n5} = C_{GD4} + C_{DB4} + C_{GD2} + C_{DB2} + C_{DS2} + C_{DS4}$.

Capacitances C_{GD4} and C_{DB4} are the capacitances that are connected to the drain of transistor T4; C_{GD2} and C_{DB2} are the capacitances connected to the drain of transistor T2.

The value of the gain-bandwidth product (*GBW*) is then obtained by multiplication of Eq. (6-3) by Eq. (6-6). It is given by

$$GBW = A_v f_d = \frac{g_{m1}}{2\pi (C_{n5} + C_L)} \tag{6-7a}$$

This expression for *GBW* is very general. Later we will see that the *GBW* is always determined by the input transistors g_m and the dominant capacitance. In the case of an OTA with only one high-resistance node, the dominant capacitance is the load capacitance C_L. In the case of an OTA with two high-resistance nodes, the Miller (compensation) capacitance connects these two nodes (see Sec. 6-2).

The *GBW* for a given C_L is determined by g_{m1}. This transconductance can have three different expressions (see Eqs. (1-22)), depending on what parameters are given. We already know that we always have two free variables for each MOST. Therefore, we must set g_{m1} by choosing I_B and $(W/L)_1$ or by choosing I_B and $(V_{GS} - V_T)_1$, etc. The choice made depends on the design plan, discussed in the next section.

On the other hand, in order to avoid peaking for all feedback conditions down to unity-gain feedback, the phase margin must be at least $60°$. This can be realized by placing the nondominant pole at 2 to 3 times the *GBW* (see Chap. 5).

The nondominant pole is obviously created on node 4. It is given by

$$f_{nd} = \frac{1}{2\pi R_{n4} C_{n4}} \tag{6-8}$$

in which $R_{n4} \approx 1/g_{m3} = 1/g_{m4}$ and $C_{n4} = C_{GD1} + C_{DB1} + C_{DB3} + C_{GS3} + C_{GS4} + C_{GD4} + C_{GB3} + C_{GB4} + C_{DS1} + C_{DS4}$.

Note that there is no Miller effect considered for capacitance C_{GD4}, because the voltage gain has already become quite small at these high frequencies. This value of f_{nd} normally is larger than the value of *GBW*. From this value of f_{nd}, the phase margin PM is easily calculated.

However, this nondominant pole acts on only half the signal. It acts only on node 4, not on node 5. A thorough analysis (see App. 6-1) shows that, when a pole acts on only half the signal, the effect is the same as having a pole at that frequency and a zero at twice that frequency, both operating on the full signal.

The phase margin is given by

$$\text{PM} = 90° - \arctan\frac{GBW}{f_{nd}} + \arctan\frac{GBW}{2f_{nd}} \tag{6-9}$$

Example 6-2

Calculate the *GBW*, unity-gain frequency, nondominant pole and phase margin for the simple CMOS OTA of Example 6-1: with $L_1 = L_4 = W_4 = 5$ μm and $W_1 = 50$ μm, and $I_B = 10$ μA. Take $C_L = 5$ pF, $C_{n5} = 3$ pF, and $C_{n4} = 0.37$ pF.

Solution. For $(W/L)_1 = 10$ and for $I_B = 10$ μA, $g_{m1} = 63.2$ μS; $GBW = 0.9$ MHz and $f_d = 8.84$ kHz. For $C_{n4} = 0.37$ pF, $f_{nd} = 4.4$ MHz. The phase margin is about 84°. Remember that the actual unity-gain frequency f_u (where $|A_v| = 1$) is slightly smaller than the *GBW*: $f_u = GBW \sin(\text{PM}) \approx 0.89$ MHz (see Chap. 3).

Equation (6-9) clearly shows that the phase shift of the zero compensates the nondominant pole such that the phase margin is always larger than 70°. However, because of settling time (see Sec. 6-3), we do not want this pole-zero doublet to occur in the useful range of frequencies, i.e., the frequency range up to *GBW*. Therefore, as a rule, the minimum value of the f_{nd} is taken to be the *GBW* itself. The effect of pole-zero pairs on settling time, etc., is discussed in App. 6-1.

For subsequent analysis we will allow the values of f_{nd} and *GBW* to coincide. Equation of f_{nd} to *GBW* leads to the expression

$$\frac{g_{m3}}{C_{n4}} = \frac{g_{m1}}{C_{n5} + C_L} \tag{6-10a}$$

Substitution of g_m, and assumption of $K_n' \approx 2K_p'$, yields

$$(W/L)_4 \approx 2(W/L)_1 \left(\frac{C_{n4}}{C_L + C_{n5}}\right)^2 \tag{6-10b}$$

Condition Eq. (6-10b) clearly illustrates the importance of the node capacitances C_n. The larger C_{n4}, the more extra capacitance C_L is required. The values of C_n can be minimized by clever design. They are mainly functions of $(W/L)_1$ and $(W/L)_4$, as we will discuss later.

Equation (6-10b) provides the necessary condition to ensure sufficient phase margin and no pole-zero doublet. Thus it must be used in the design plan. Up to now, two equations that govern such a design plan have been obtained. The first contains the *GBW* (Eq. (6-7a)), the second contains the position of the nondominant pole (Eq. (6-10)).

6-1-3 Design Plan

Assume that we are asked to design a simple CMOS OTA with a certain GBW for a given load capacitance C_L. Equations (6-7a) and (6-10b) show that we must find three variables: I_B, $(W/L)_1$, and $(W/L)_4$. One equation is missing, however. Of course we could simply choose $(W/L)_4$ and use the two equations to solve for $(W/L)_1$ and I_B. However, there is a better way.

Since transistor T1 must provide amplification, its g_m/I ratio must be high. Thus we choose its $V_{GS1} - V_T$ to be small, i.e., 0.2 V. It then operates in strong inversion, but close to weak inversion, where its g_m/I is large. This serves as our third equation. Now we can derive all values of $(W/L)_1$, $(W/L)_4$, and I_B.

From GBW and C_L we determine g_{m1} by means of Eq. (6-7a), since C_{n5} is negligible with respect to C_L. Ratio $(W/L)_1 = g_{m1}/2K_n'(V_{GS1} - V_T)$. The required current is then $I_B = g_{m1}/(v_{GS1} - V_T)$. Finally, ratio $(W/L)_4$ is determined from Eq. (6-10b).

An alternative procedure consists of taking $V_{GS4} - V_T = 0.5$ V for matching (see Sec. 6-5), or choosing $(W/L)_4 = 1$ for minimum area. For each method a different design results. Several of these designs are studied in the exercises.

Example 6-3

Take the simple CMOS OTA of Example 6-1. Calculate the maximum GBW for $I_B = 10$ μA and $C_L = 10$ pF, if we fix $(W/L)_4 = 1$, which gives $C_{n4} = 0.37$ pF. What is the required $(W/L)_1$?

Solution. Since I_B and $(W/L)_4$ are known, we can calculate $g_{m4} = 14$ μS and $f_{nd} = 6$ MHz (from Eq. (6-8)). As a result, the maximum GBW is one third, or 2 MHz. The required g_{m1} is 126 μS (from Eq. 6-7a) and $(W/L)_1 \approx 40$.

We cannot require the GBW to be arbitrarily high, however. There is a limit on the value of the GBW that can be obtained.

6-1-4 Optimization for Maximum *GBW*

The expression of GBW, given by Eq. (6-7a), can also be rewritten as given by

$$GBW = \frac{g_{m1}}{2\pi(C_{n5} + C_L)} = \frac{\sqrt{2K_n'I_B}}{2\pi} \frac{\sqrt{(W/L)_1}}{C_{n5} + C_L} \tag{6-7b}$$

If C_L is given, then GBW is proportional to the square root of $(W/L)_1$. This is shown in Fig. 6-2 for $C_L = 5$ pF. For each value of $(W/L)_1$, a value of $(W/L)_4$ can be derived by means of Eq. (6-10b). For example, for $C_L = 5$ pF, at $(W/L)_1 = 10$, the value of GBW is given by Eq. (6-7a) to be 1.26 MHz. Also, from Eq. (6-10b), $(W/L)_4 = 4$.

In these calculations, we have assumed that the node capacitances C_{n4} and C_{n5} are independent of the sizes of the transistors connected to these nodes. This is not the case, however. The larger the aspect ratios are, the larger the node capacitances

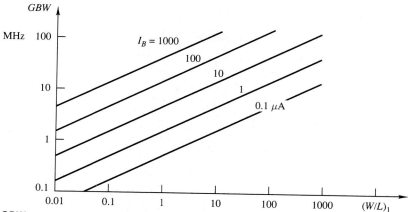

FIGURE 6-2 GBW versus $(W/L)_1$ for variable I_B (μA) and $C_L = 5$ pF ($C_{n4} = 4$ pF; $C_{n5} = 3$ pF)

become, as well. If this were not the case, unlimited values of GBW could be obtained (see Fig. 6-2).

A model is required to link the values of the node capacitances to the transistor sizes. This has been illustrated in Chap. 1. It is now shown that the resulting GBW reaches a maximum or optimum value.

After a certain size, the capacitances grow linearly with the sizes of the transistors. The node capacitance are modeled as given by

$$C_n = C_{n0} + k\frac{W}{L} \qquad (6\text{-}11a)$$

These values can be calculated from several layouts using different sizes of transistors. Values for a 3 μm CMOS processes are, for example, taken to be $C_{n0} = 0.5$ pF, $k = 0.1$ pF. These are relatively large values. For present-day dense layout, $C_{n0} \approx 0$ and $k \approx 2$ to 5 fF. From Eq. (6-11a), it is clear that node capacitance C_{n4} depends on the sizes of both transistors T1 and T3. A more accurate model is therefore

$$C_{n4} = C_{n04} + k_1\left(\frac{W}{L}\right)_1 + k_3\left(\frac{W}{L}\right)_3 \qquad (6\text{-}11b)$$

Not to complicate things, however. We will use the simplified equation Eq. (6-11a) in the subsequent analysis.

Substitution of C_{n5} and C_{n4} by C_n (from Eq. (6-11)), in both Eqs. (6-7b) and (6-10), provides two equations that are nonlinear in the variables $r_1 = (W/L)_1$ and $r_4 = (W/L)_4$, as given by

$$GBW = \frac{\sqrt{2K_n'I_B}}{2\pi}\frac{\sqrt{r_1}}{C_L' + k(r_1 + r_4)} \qquad (6\text{-}12a)$$

with

$$\sqrt{\frac{r_4/2}{r_1}} = \frac{C_{n0} + k(r_1 + r_4)}{C'_L + k(r_1 + r_4)} \tag{6-12b}$$

and with $C'_L = C_L + C_{n0}$. Numerical techniques are required to solve these equations. An easy way to find solutions is to evaluate these equations for the limiting cases, i.e., for low and high values of r_1.

For low values of r_1, the values of r_4 are small, as well. Equations (6-12) can then be approximated by

$$GBW = \frac{\sqrt{2K'_n I_B}}{2\pi} \frac{\sqrt{r_1}}{C'_L} \tag{6-13a}$$

and by

$$\sqrt{\frac{r_4/2}{r_1}} = \frac{C_{n0}}{C'_L} \text{ or } r_4 = 2r_1 \left(\frac{C_{n0}}{C'_L}\right)^2 \tag{6-13b}$$

As a result, the values of GBW increase proportionally to $\sqrt{(W/L)_1}$, as expected. They are plotted in Fig. 6-3. The value of r_4 is quite small, but increases proportionally to r_1. It is plotted in Fig. 6-3, as well. For the example in which $C_{n0} = 0.5$ pF and $C'_L = 5.5$ pF, for $r_1 = 1$, $GBW = 0.58$ MHz and $r_4 = 0.016$.

For high values of r_1, Eqs. (6-12) can now be approximated by

$$GBW = \frac{\sqrt{2K'_n I_B}}{2\pi} \frac{\sqrt{r_1}}{k(r_1 + r_4)} \tag{6-14a}$$

and

$$r_4 \approx 2r_1 \tag{6-14b}$$

FIGURE 6-3 GBW versus $(W/L)_1$ for variable I_B (μA) and $C_L = 5$ pF ($C_{n0} = 0.5$ pF; $k_1 = k_4 = 0.1$ pF)

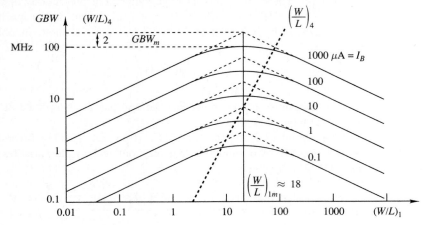

Elimination of r_4 in Eq. (6-14a) yields

$$GBW = \frac{\sqrt{2K_n'I_B}}{2\pi}\frac{1}{3k\sqrt{r_1}} \tag{6-15}$$

It is striking to note that the values of GBW now decrease with $\sqrt{(W/L)_1}$ (see Fig. 6-3). Also, the value of r_4 is much larger, for example, for $r_1 = 100$, $r_4 \approx 200$ and $GBW = 1.06$ MHz.

For intermediate values of $(W/L)_1$, an optimum GBW is obtained. It occurs at values of $(W/L)_1$, which are found by equating Eq. (6-13a) to Eq. (6-15). This yields a value, called $(W/L)_{1m}$, which is given by

$$\left(\frac{W}{L}\right)_{1m} = \frac{C_L'}{3k} \tag{6-16}$$

In this example: $C_L' = 5.5$ pF, $k = 0.1$, and $(W/L)_{1m} = 18.3$. This value is quite acceptable.

At this point, the value of GBW reaches a maximum value GBW_m. It is obtained by substitution of $(W/L)_1$ by $(W/L)_{1m}$ in Eq. (6-15) or in Eq. (6-18). This yields the asymptotic value. For the real value we must divide by two (see Fig. 6-3), which yields

$$GBW_m = \frac{1}{2}\frac{\sqrt{2K_n'I_B}}{2\pi}\frac{1}{\sqrt{3kC_L'}} \tag{6-17}$$

For the example with $I_B = 10$ μA, in which $C_L' = 5.5$ pF and $k_1 = 0.1$, $GBW = 1.24$ MHz. This maximum value increases with $\sqrt{I_B}$ and decreases with $\sqrt{C_L'}$. For larger output capacitance C_L', the input transistors must be larger, and GBW_m again decreases. Also, the smaller the k can be made, the larger GBW_m becomes.

Also note that another value of $(W/L)_4$ belongs to each value of $(W/L)_1$. It increases very rapidly from very small values (see Eq. (6-13b)) to $2(W/L)_1$ (see Eq. (6-14b)). The exact values of $(W/L)_4$ can be solved from Eq. (6-12). They are given versus $(W/L)_1$ in Fig. (6-3), as well. Reasonable values of $(W/L)_4$ are around unity, i.e., within 0.1 and 10. This means that $(W/L)_1$ can only have values between 3 and 20. Good choices are $(W/L)_1 = C_{n0}/k$, which yields 5, and $(W/L)_4 = 0.29$. For minimum area it would be better to take the minimum size for T4: hence $(W/L)_4 = 1$ and $(W/L)_1 = 9.2$, or about 10 (all at $I_B = 10$ μA). This provides a value of GBW that is close to GBW_m, i.e., 1.2 MHz. Remember this value as a rule of thumb: a 3 μm CMOS process provides about 1 MHz GBW at an input stage current of about 10 μA.

Finally, the maximum value of GBW_m can still be increased by increasing the current I_B. The maximum still occurs at $(W/L)_{1m}$, though. For increasing current, however, the values of $(W/L)_4$ may become impractically large. Also, the values of $V_{GS} - V_T$, which are required to accommodate the current, become too large, leading to mobility degradation due to velocity saturation. At that point, a different model must be used (see Chap. 1).

There is no need, however, to try to remember Eq. (6-17) for GBW_m. The GBW is still given by $g_{m1}/2\pi(C_L + C_{n5})$ (see Eq. (6-7a)). We now know that we reach an optimum for about $(W/L)_1 \approx 20$ for large currents. At that point we obtain GBW_m. Now we must select the largest current possible to avoid velocity saturation. For $(W/L)_1 \approx 20$ let us assume that this current occurs at about 2 mA. These two values completely determine the parameters of transistor T1: $g_{m1} = 1.8$ mS and $GBW_m = 52$ MHz.

Example 6-4

A matrix layout for a large nMOST yields $k \approx 5$ fF and $C_{n0}(W/L)_1 = C_{n0}/k = 1$ pF. What maximum GBW can be obtained with 0.1 mA? The load capacitance is 10 pF.

Solution. Ratio $(W/L)_1 = C_{n0}/k = 200$. With $V_{GS1} - V_T = 0.2$ V, $g_{m1} = 2I_B/(V_{GS1} - V_T) = 0.1$ mS. The resulting $GBW_m = 1.6$ MHz.

Until now we have concentrated on two characteristics only, i.e., the GBW and the position of the nondominant pole, leading to two design equations. In order to obtain an optimum design, we must choose as a third equation the operating point of the input transistors. We could have taken another specification as a third equation, as well, such as slew rate, the input impedance, the output impedance, the equivalent input noise, etc. Several of these specifications have already been analyzed in Sec. 4-7. The slew rate and the equivalent input noise are among the most important specifications, thus would be the best choice as a third equation.

It can be concluded that the simple CMOS OTA provides appreciable values of gain and GBW that are easy to design and to predict. However, the gain is never high. For this purpose, a second stage must be added.

6-2   THE MILLER CMOS OTA

6-2-1   Operating Principles and Biasing

A two-stage OTA in CMOS is shown in Fig. 6-4. It consists of two stages, the first of which is a differential stage with pMOST input devices T1 and T2 and the current mirror T3 and T4 acting as an active load. The second stage is a simple CMOS inverter with T6 as driver and T5 acting as an active load. Its output is connected to its input, i.e., to the output of the differential stage by means of compensation capacitance C_c. Since the compensation capacitance actually acts as a Miller capacitance in that stage, the op amp is called a *Miller OTA*. It is shown that for most of the frequency range, the output impedance is low. Hence, the Miller OTA behaves as a Miller op amp for most of the frequency range.

The OTA configuration could be inverted as well, i.e., nMOSTs could be used as input devices and a pMOST current mirror. There is no difference for the subsequent analysis. However, for better matching (discussed in Sec. 6-5), the sources of the input devices are better connected to their substrate, which is a common n-well. The

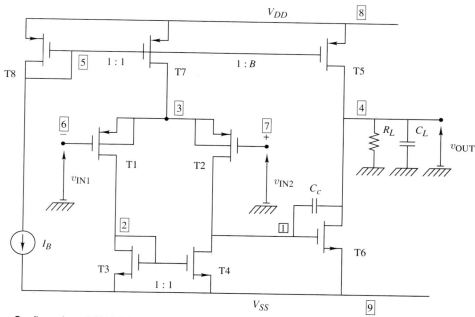

FIGURE 6-4   Configuration of CMOS Miller OTA: $V_{DD,SS} = \pm 2.5$ V; $I_B = 2.5$ μA; $B = 10$.

configuration of Fig. 6-4 thus is only possible in an n-well CMOS process and the inverted configuration in a p-well CMOS process. Note that for all other transistors the substrate is connected to the source. This is why the substrate contacts are only shown for the input transistors in Fig. 6-4. As a result, body-biasing effects do not occur and all values of V_T are equal in absolute value.

We have fully analyzed this op amp. The transistor parameters used are listed in Table 6-1. The transistor geometries are given in Table 6-2. The biasing current I_B is 2.5 μA, the value of compensation capacitance C_c is 1 pF, the load impedance $C_L = 10$ pF, and the power supply voltages are ± 2.5 V.

The Miller op amp is biased by an independent current source I_B. Transistors T7 and T8 have equal sizes. Thus, current I_B also flows in the differential input stage. Transistor T5 is much larger (about ten times as large). Thus, the current in the second stage is much larger, as well. All currents are known. They are listed in Table 6-2 for all transistors.

The DC voltages on all points can be calculated, as well, provided assumptions are made with respect to the input and output voltages. Let us assume that the op amp is connected in unity gain configuration with the inputs grounded. Hence, $V_{IN-} = V_{IN+} = V_{OUT} = 0$ V. As a result all values of V_{GS} and V_{DS} can easily be calculated. They are also given in Table 6-2, as they have been obtained from a SPICE run (the SPICE input file is given in Table 6-3). The value of V_{GS} is not given explicitly, but

TABLE 6-1   TECHNOLOGICAL PARAMETERS FOR A STANDARD 3 μm
CMOS N-WELL TECHNOLOGY

Parameter	nMOST	pMOST	Dimensions
V_{T0}	0.9	−0.9	V
V_{Early}	4.5	8.3	V/μm
K' (hand calculation)	19	6.5	μA/V^2
(KP; SPICE)	50	17	μA/V^2
n	1.4	1.4	—
LD	0.22	0.35	μm
GAMMA	0.3	0.5	$\sqrt{V}$
PHI	0.7	0.7	V
CGS0	0.18	0.28	fF/μm
CGD0	0.18	0.28	fF/μm
CJ	0.07	0.33	fF/μm^2
CJSW	0.39	0.44	fF/μm
MJ	0.5		—
MJSW	0.33		—
JS	10^{-3}		A/m^2
NFS	10^{11}		cm^{-2}
UCRIT	10^{4}		V/cm
RSH	25	45	Ω
DL	0	0	μm
DW	−0.4	−0.4	μm
KF (1/f noise)	10^{-8}	5×10^{-10}	V$^2\mu$m^2
Minimum W_M	5		μm
Minimum L_M	5		μm
t_{ox}	42.5		nm
C_{ox}	0.8		fF/μm^2
$C_{polyI-polyII}$	0.8		fF/μm^2
$C_{n well-substrate}$	0.06		fF/μm^2

rather $V_{GS} - V_T$, which only differs over a fixed amount of $|V_T| = 0.9$ V. Since for all transistors the substrate is connected to the source, body biasing effects do not occur and all values of V_T are equal in absolute value in Table 6-2.

It is important to note that all values of V_{DS} are considerably larger than $V_{GS} - V_T$. As a consequence, all transistors operate under saturation conditions. The actual values of V_{DSsat} are added, as well, as they have been obtained from SPICE. They are all slightly smaller than $V_{GS} - V_T$. Hence, all transistors are in the saturation region.

Moreover, the values of $V_{GS} - V_T$ are always larger than the weak inversion limit, which is normally a few hundred mV (see Chap. 1) and which corresponds with currents I_{DSwi}. Indeed, all currents I_{DS} are larger than I_{DSwi}. Thus all transistors

TABLE 6-2   PARAMETER VALUES OF THE TRANSISTORS OF THE MILLER OTA OF FIG. 6-4. ALL VALUES ARE TAKEN FROM SPICE (TABLE 6-3). NOTE THAT $V_{N1} = -1.39$ V, $V_{N2} = -1.36$ V, $V_{N3} = 1.24$ V, AND $V_{N5} = 1.07$ V.

MOST	N/P	W_M (μm)	L_M (μm)	$K'W/L$ (μA/V^2)	I_{DS} (μA)	I_{DSwi} (μA)	$V_{GS} - V_T$ (V)	V_{DSsat} (V)	V_{DS} (V)
T1	P	26	16	14	1.25	0.07	0.34	0.26	2.59
T2	P	26	16	14	1.25	0.07	0.34	0.26	2.63
T3	N	10	10	24	1.25	0.13	0.24	0.21	1.14
T4	N	10	10	24	1.25	0.13	0.24	0.21	1.11
T5	P	55	5	107	25.2	0.56	0.53	0.42	2.5
T6	N	115	5	626	25.2	3.3	0.21	0.18	2.5
T7	P	13	10	11	2.5	0.06	0.53	0.42	1.26
T8	P	13	10	11	2.5	0.06	0.53	0.42	1.43

MOST	g_m (μS)	g_{mb} (μS)	g_o (μS)	C_{GS} (fF)	C_{GD} (fF)	C_{SB} (fF)	C_{DB} (fF)
T1	7.5	2.1	0.006	216	7	97	50
T2	7.5	2.1	0.006	216	7	97	50
T3	10.3	1.7	0.024	49	2	17	12
T4	10.3	1.7	0.024	49	2	17	12
T5	95.5	2.53	0.61	141	15	195	101
T6	246	41.6	1.18	302	20	124	68
T7	9.5	2.5	0.013	65	3	52	34
T8	9.5	2.5	0.013	65	3	52	33

operate in strong inversion. The strong inversion model is used to calculate their g_m. The values are given in Table 6-2. The values of the output conductances g_o can be calculated, as well. They are also given in Table 6-2.

It is important to note that the values of gate length and width have mask dimensions. The effective dimensions are usually somewhat smaller (see Chap. 1).

All DC biasing conditions are now known, together with all the conductances. The small-signal gain and *GBW* can now be calculated.

Notice that this amplifier is a three-node amplifier. Two of them are at a high-resistance level. They are connected by compensation capacitance C_c. The third node (number 2 in Fig. 6-4) is at a low-resistance level. We will carry out the analysis of gain, *GBW*, and phase margin focusing on the two high-resistance nodes. Then we will verify how much node 2 affects the phase margin.

6-2-2   Gain of the Miller OTA

Now the gain of the Miller CMOS OTA is calculated at low frequencies. For this purpose we use the small-signal equivalent circuit of Fig. 6-5. Note that node 2 has been omitted. A two-node circuit results, in which compensation capacitance C_c acts as a feedback element.

TABLE 6-3   SPICE LIST FOR THE CALCULATION OF THE GAIN A_{dd} FOR THE MILLER CMOS OTA

```
* MILLER OTA (TEMPERATURE = 27.000 DEG C)
* CALCULATION OF THE DIFFERENTIAL GAIN ADD
* CIRCUIT DESCRIPTION
M1 2 6 3 3 PMOS W=25.2U L=15.3U AD=234P AS=234P PD=44U PS=44U
M2 1 7 3 3 PMOS W=25.7U L=15.3U AD=234P AS=234P PD=44U PS=44U
M3 2 2 9 9 NMOS W=9.2U L=9.56U AD=90P AS=90P PD=28U PS=28U
M4 1 2 9 9 NMOS W=9.38U L=9.56U AD=90P AS=90P PD=28U PS=28U
M5 4 5 8 8 POUT W=54.2U L=4.3U AD=495P AS=495P PD=73U PS=73U
M6 4 1 9 9 NOUT W=114.2U L=4.56U AD=1035P AS=1035P PD=133U PS=133U
M7 3 5 8 8 PMOS W=12.2U L=9.3U AD=117P AS=117P PD=31U PS=31U
M8 5 5 8 8 PMOS W=12.2U L=9.3U AD=117P AS=117P PD=31U PS=31U
IB 5 0 DC 2.5U
VDD 8 0 DC 2.5
VSS 9 0 DC -2.5
VIN 7 0 DC 0 AC 1
CL 4 0 10P
RL 4 0 100K
CC 4 1 1P
* DC-FEEDBACK
EFB 10 0 4 0 1
RFB 10 6 1G
CFB 6 0 1
* SPECIAL 3U N-WELL PARAMETERS
* W = WEFF = WM + 2*DW ; FOR NMOS AND PMOS: WEFF = WM - 0.8
* L = LEFF = LM + 2*DL - 2*LD : FOR NMOS: LEFF = LM - 0.44
*                               FOR PMOS: LEFF = LM - 0.7
*OUTPUT CONDUCTANCE: FOR NMOS : LAMBDA = 1/4.5*L**1.1
*                    FOR PMOS : LAMBDA = 1/8.3*L**1.14
.MODEL NMOS NMOS LEVEL=2 VTO=0.9 KP=50E-6 GAMMA=0.30 PHI=0.70
+ CGSO=1.76E-10 CGDO=1.76E-10 CJ=0.7E-4 MJ=0.5 CJSW=3.9E-10
+ MJSW=0.33 JS=1E-3 TOX=42.5N NFS=1E11 LD=0 UCRIT=1E4 RSH=25
+ LAMBDA=0.019
.MODEL NOUT NMOS LEVEL=2 VTO=0.9 KP=50E-6 GAMMA=0.30 PHI=0.70
+ CGSO=1.76E-10 CGDO=1.76E-10 CJ=0.7E-4 MJ=0.5 CJSW=3.9E-10
+ MJSW=0.33 JS=1E-3 TOX=42.5N NFS=1E11 LD=0 UCRIT=1E4 RSH=25
+ LAMBDA=0.042
.MODEL PMOS PMOS LEVEL=2 VTO=-0.9 KP=17E-6 GAMMA=0.50 PHI=0.69
+ CGSO=2.8E-10 CGDO=2.8E-10 CJ=3.3E-4 MJ=0.5 CJSW=4.4E-10
+ MJSW=0.33 JS=1E-3 TOX=42.5N NFS=1E11 LD=0 UCRIT=1E4 RSH=25
+ LAMBDA=0.005
.MODEL POUT PMOS LEVEL=2 VTO=-0.9 KP=17E-6 GAMMA=0.50 PHI=0.69
+ CGSO=2.8E-10 CGDO=2.8E-10 CJ=3.3E-4 MJ=0.5 CJSW=4.4E-10
+ MJSW=0.33 JS=1E-3 TOX=42.5N NFS=1E11 LD=0 UCRIT=1E4 RSH=25
+ LAMBDA=0.023
* CONTROL CARDS
.OPTIONS LIMPTS=1000
.AC DEC 10 1 100MEG
.NODESET V(1)=-1.4 V(2)=-1.4 V(3)=1.3 V(4)=0 V(5)=1.1
+ V(6)=0 V(7)=0 V(8)=2.5 V(9)=-2.5
.PRINT AC VDB(4) VP(4)
.PLOT AC VDB(4) VP(4)
.WIDTH OUT = 75
.END
```

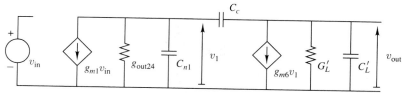

FIGURE 6-5   Equivalent circuit of the CMOS Miller OTA.

$$g_{m1} = 7.5 \ \mu\text{S}; \ g_{m6} = 246 \ \mu\text{S}; \ g_{o24} = g_{o2} + g_{o4} = 0.03 \ \mu\text{S}; \ C_c = 1 \ \text{pF}$$

$$G_L' = G_L + g_{o5} + g_{o6} = 11.8 \ \mu\text{S}; \ C_{n1} = 0.37 \ \text{pF}; \ C_L' = C_L + C_{n4} = 10.2 \ \text{pF}$$

The first stage is a simple CMOS OTA as has been discussed in Sec. 6-1. Its gain is given by

$$A_{v10} = \frac{g_{m1}}{g_{o24}} \tag{6-18}$$

where $g_{o24} = g_{o2} + g_{o4}$ is the load conductance of the first stage. The second stage is a simple inverter. Its gain has been calculated before in Sec. 4-5. It is given by

$$A_{v20} = \frac{g_{m6}}{G_L'} \tag{6-19}$$

where $G_L' = G_L + g_{o5} + g_{o6}$ is the total load conductance of the last stage. The overall gain at low frequencies thus is given by the product of both, or by

$$A_{v0} = A_{v10} A_{v20} = \left(\frac{g_{m1}}{g_{o24}} \right) \left(\frac{g_{m6}}{G_L'} \right) \tag{6-20}$$

Example 6-5

Calculate the values of the gains for the parameters of Table 6-2.

Solution. $A_{v10} = 250$ or 48 dB; $A_{v20} = 20.8$ or 26.3 dB. The overall gain thus is $A_{v0} = 5200$ or 74.3 dB.

6-2-3 Gain-Bandwidth Product and Phase-Margin

For high-frequency performance, the values of the capacitances must be added. Since all transistors operate in saturation, the capacitances can easily be calculated (see Table 1-3 to 1-5 in Chap. 1). Their values are also given in Table 6-2.

Poles and Zeros Without Compensation Capacitance   Now the poles and zeros of the Miller op amp can be calculated. First, the compensation capacitance C_c is omitted. Each node represents one pole. The input nodes can be omitted because the OTA is driven by low-resistance input sources. The common-mode node 3 can be omitted as well, because only differential mode gain is considered here. Common-mode gain is discussed in Sec. 6-5.

Three nodes are left, i.e., node 1, 2, and 4, and thus we have a three-pole system. The impedance at node 1 is the highest in the circuit, because only r_o's connect it to ground. It is most likely to be the node of the dominant pole. Its value is given by

$$f_{p1} = \frac{g_{o24}}{2\pi C_{n1}} \tag{6-21}$$

with $C_{n1} = C_{GD2} + C_{DB2} + C_{GD4} + C_{DB4} + C_{GS6}$ (see Table 6-8 on page 506), as explained in Chap. 1.

For the example, C_{GS6} is by far the largest one; $C_{n1} = 0.373$ pF and $g_{o24} = g_{o2} + g_{o4} = 0.030\ \mu S$, which yields $f_{p1} = 18.3$ kHz, a low value indeed. Still, it is higher than the dominant pole of an op amp that is typically 100 Hz. The reason is that there is not yet compensation capacitance C_c. As a result, the dominant pole is considerably higher.

The other poles are created on nodes 2 and 4. The second pole f_{p4} is created on the output node or node 4. It is given by

$$f_{p4} = \frac{G'_L}{2\pi (C_L + C_{n1})} \tag{6-22}$$

with $C_{n4} = C_{GD5} + C_{DB5} + C_{DB6}$.

For the example, $C_{n4} = 0.184$ pF, which is obviously negligible with respect to the large load capacitance of 10 pF. As a result, since $G'_L = G_L + g_{o5} + g_{o6} = 11.8\ \mu S$, $f_{p4} = 184$ kHz.

The pole on node 2 is given by

$$f_{p2} = \frac{g_{m3}}{2\pi C_{n2}} \tag{6-23}$$

with $C_{n2} = C_{GS3} + C_{DB3} + C_{GS4} + C_{GD4} + C_{GD1} + C_{DB1}$

Note that no Miller effect is taken into account on C_{GD4} because the gain at that frequency is quite low.

For the example, $C_{n2} = 0.170$ pF and $f_{p2} = 9.6$ MHz. It is clear that this pole can be omitted. Moreover, this pole acts on half the signal only. As a result, it causes a pole at that frequency and a zero at twice that frequency (see App. 6-1). At the frequency of the GBW, which is about 1 MHz, the error in phase, as a result of the omission of this pole-zero doublet, is only about arctan $(GBW / f_{p2}) - $ arctan $(GBW / 2 f_{p2}) \approx 2.8°$.

The small-signal equivalent circuit of the OTA is shown in Fig. 6-5. The resulting Bode diagram of the Miller OTA is shown in Fig. 6-6a. The two poles are spaced closely together, resulting in a negative phase margin PM_0. The op amp thus will show peaking in unity-gain configuration. Compensation capacitance must be added

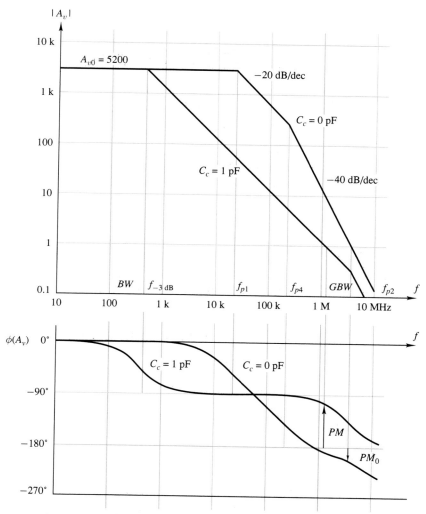

FIGURE 6-6a   Bode diagram of Miller OTA with $C_c = 0$ pF and $C_c = 1$ pF.

to increase the phase margin PM to a value of about 70°. Assume that $C_c = 1$ pF is added as indicated in Fig. 6-4 and in Fig. 6-5. In this way, we obtain a two-pole system with feedback capacitance, as has already been thoroughly analyzed in Chaps. 3 and 4.

Bode Diagrams With Compensation Capacitance   The pole on node 1 now has become even more dominant than before (see Fig. 6-6a). The −20 dB/dec line crosses the unity-gain axis just above 1 MHz. The *GBW* product thus is well-defined. The phase margin PM is now positive. Its value is larger than $45°$. The second pole is situated somewhere between 1 and 10 MHz. The exact values are now calculated.

The Miller OTA is represented by the two-pole system of Fig. 6-5. The dominant pole is a result of the Miller effect of capacitance C_c. The dominant pole or *bandwidth* BW is approximately given by

$$BW \approx f_d = f_{-3\text{dB}} \approx \frac{g_{o24}}{2\pi A_{v20} C_c} \qquad (6\text{-}24a)$$

Its value is $BW = 228$ Hz.

The gain-bandwidth product GBW is obtained by the product of this pole frequency and the open-loop gain, given by Eq. (6-20). Thus it is approximately given by

$$GBW \approx \frac{g_{m1}}{2\pi C_c} \qquad (6\text{-}25a)$$

An exact analysis on the circuit of Fig. 6-5 yields

$$GBW = \frac{g_{m1}}{2\pi C_c} \frac{1}{1 + \varepsilon_{GBW}} \qquad (6\text{-}25b)$$

with

$$\varepsilon_{GBW} = \frac{G_L'}{g_{m6}} \left(1 + \frac{C_{n1}}{C_c}\right) + \frac{g_{o24}}{g_{m6}} \left(1 + \frac{C_L'}{C_c}\right)$$

In this example, $A_{v0} = 5200$ and Eq. (6-25a) gives $GBW = 1.19$ MHz. The error ε_{GBW} is only 6.7 percent.

The bandwidth BW can now be written better as a function of the GBW, for use in later derivations. It is given by

$$BW = \frac{g_{o24}}{2\pi A_{v20} C_c} = \frac{g_{o24} G_L'}{2\pi g_{m6} C_c} = \frac{g_{m1}}{2\pi A_{v0} C_c} = \frac{GBW}{A_{v0}} \qquad (6\text{-}24b)$$

The nondominant pole still occurs on the output node 4. Its value is derived by straightforward analysis of the circuit of Fig. 6-5. It is given by

$$f_{nd} = \frac{g_{m6}}{2\pi C_L'} \frac{1 + \varepsilon_{GBW}}{1 + \dfrac{C_{n1}}{C_c} + \dfrac{C_{n1}}{C_L'}} \approx \frac{g_{m6}}{2\pi C_L'} \qquad (6\text{-}26)$$

in which the approximation is valid if $C_{n1} \ll C_c$, C_L' (see also Eq. (4-24) with $C_{GS} \ll C_{DS}$). At these high frequencies, the compensation capacitance acts as a short circuit. Transistor T6 thus is connected as a diode. Its impedance, which is the same as the output impedance, thus has become resistive with value $1/g_{m6}$. The value of f_{nd} is about 3.8 MHz, which is about a factor of three larger than the value of the GBW. This is no surprise because that is why the compensation capacitance C_c has been chosen.

The *phase-margin* PM is now given by

$$PM = 90° - \arctan \frac{GBW}{f_{nd}} \tag{6-27}$$

which yields 72.6°. Note that this factor of three between the nondominant pole and the *GBW* is an excellent rule of thumb to realize phase margins of about 70°.

In this two-pole system a positive zero occurs, as well. Its value is given by

$$f_z = \frac{g_{m6}}{2\pi C_c} \tag{6-28}$$

which yields 39 MHz. It can be ignored because its contribution can be derived by an expression similar to Eq. (6-26). Its contribution to the phase margin is only −1.7°.

Finally, remember that we still have a pole-zero doublet on node 2. Its contribution to the phase margin was calculated, after Eq. (6-23) and was only −2.8°. We can ignore this, as well.

These characteristic frequencies have been collected in Table 6-4. They will be used in later calculations, as well.

As a result of the compensation capacitance, a stable response is achieved without peaking, even under unity-gain feedback conditions. To clarify the actual effect of the compensation capacitance C_c, Fig. 6-6b gives the pole-zero position diagram, with C_c as a variable. Also, the Bode diagram is repeated in Fig. 6-6b for several values of C_c.

TABLE 6-4 CHARACTERISTIC EQUATIONS OF CMOS MILLER OTA

Parameter	Expression	Value	Reference	Temperature Coefficient
I_{DS1}	1	1.25 μA	Table 6-2	constant
K'_n	—	19 μA/V^2	Table 6-2	T^{-a}
g_{m1}	$2\,I_{DS1}/(V_{GS1} - V_T)$ $2(I_{DS1} K'_n W/L)^{0.5}$	7.5 μS	Eq. 6-1	T^{-a}
g_{m6}	$2\,I_{DS6}/(V_{GS6} - V_T)$	246 μS	Eq. 6-1	T^{-a}
$g_{o24} = 1/r_{o24}$	$(V_{Ep} \cdot L_2 + V_{En} \cdot L_4)/I_{DS1}$	0.03 μS	Eq. 6-2	constant
A_{v10}	g_{m1}/g_{o24}	250	Eq. 6-18	T^{-a}
A_{v20}	g_{m6}/G'_L	20.8	Eq. 6-19	T^{-a}
A_{v0}	$A_{v10} \cdot A_{v20}$	5200	Eq. 6-20	T^{-a}
GBW	$g_{m1}/2\pi C_c$	1.19 MHz	Eq. 6-25a	$T^{-a/2}$
$f_d, f_{p1}, f_{-3dB}, BW$	GBW/A_{v0}	228 Hz	Eq. 6-24a	$T^{a/2}$
f_{z1}	$G'_L/2\pi C'_L$	186 kHz		constant
f_{p2}, f_{nd}	$g_{m6}/2\pi C'_L (1 + C_{n1}/C_c)$	2.85 MHz	Eq. 6-26	$T^{-a/2}$
	$\approx g_{m6}/2\pi C'_L$	3.8 MHz	Eq. 6-26	$T^{-a/2}$
	$\approx 3\,GBW$	3.6 MHz		
f_z, f_{z2}	$g_{m6}/2\pi C_c$	39.2 MHz	Eq. 6-28	$T^{-a/2}$
f_{z3}	$g_{o24}/2\pi C_c$	5.3 kHz	Eq. 6-49	constant
f_{z4}	$g_{m6}/2\pi C_{n1}$	105 MHz	Eq. 6-60	$T^{-a/2}$
PM	$90° - \arctan(GBW/f_{nd})$	72°	Eq. 6-27	constant
	$90° - \arctan(GBW/f_z)$	67°		constant
f_u	$GBW \cdot \sin(PM)$	1.10 MHz	App. 6-1	$T^{-a/2}$

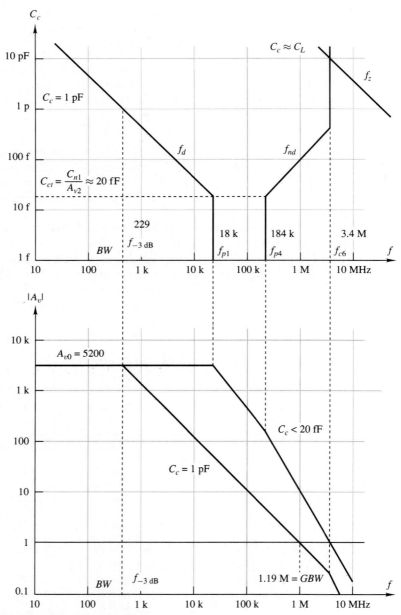

FIGURE 6-6*b* Bode diagram of A_v for variable C_c.

Without compensation capacitance, the poles at nodes 1 and 4 are dominant. Clearly, pole splitting starts for C_{ct}, as given by Eq. (4-25b) or $C_{ct} = C_{n1}/A_{v20} \approx 20$ fF (exact value is 17.9 fF). Only for $C_c = 1$ pF, however, is the phase margin sufficiently large. The nondominant pole is fixed at a frequency f_{c6}, obtained by Eq. (4-24), and given by Eq. (6-26). Its value is 3.8 MHz. The zero f_z occurs at even larger frequencies. It coincides with f_{nd} if $C_c \approx C_L$, as explained for Eq. (4-9a).

Now that we know all the relevant equations, how do we actually design a Miller CMOS OTA?

6-2-4 Design Plan

Previously, values of currents and transistor sizes were given. Depending on the application, values of *GBW* or other specifications are given. It is the task of the designer to derive all transistor dimensions. Also, the current consumption and input noise must always be made as small as possible.

Let us take the specifications given in Table 6-5. The design equations have already been given; they are the expressions for g_{m1}, *GBW*, and f_{nd} and are collected in Table 6-4. We know that, with respect to phase margin, avoiding peaking (phase margin PM > 70°) requires the nondominant pole to be about three times the *GBW* (see Table 6-4).

Determine Compensation Capacitance C_c   In contrast to the design procedures of the simple CMOS OTA, the size of the input transistor is not readily determined from the *GBW*. Now the expression of the *GBW* contains compensation capacitance C_c instead of the load capacitance C_L. Capacitance C_L is known, but C_c is not. Therefore, C_c is to be found first from the phase margin or other considerations.

The *GBW* and PM are determined by three variables, g_{m1}, g_{m6}, and C_c, by means of Eqs. (6-25) and (6-27). One of the variables can be freely chosen. Rather than choosing one we will introduce a third constraint (equation). In this way we obtain three equations in three variables. The solution of this set of equations provides us with an exact and optimum solution.

TABLE 6-5   DESIGN SPECIFICATIONS FOR THE MILLER CMOS OTA WITH $V_{DD,SS} = \pm 2.5$ V.

Parameter	Specifications	Calculation	SPICE	
GBW	1	1.19	1.12	MHz
SR	2	2.27	2.2	V/μs
A_{v0}	≥ 60	74	74	dB
PM	≥ 60	67	66	°
$V_{out,max}$	± 2	± 2.08		V
$V_{in,cm}$	± 0.5	± 0.84		V
I_{B1}	2.5	2.5	2.5	μA
$I_{tot,max}$	30	27.7	27.7	μA

As a third equation, the total area of the op amp is taken. It must be as small as possible. We could have chosen, as well, another constraint, such as minimum noise, maximum *SR*, maximum output swing, a large *PSRR*, etc. We have chosen minimum total area, however, because we want to avoid transistors that become exceedingly large because of the optimum-design procedure. The total area A_T of the amplifier depends mainly on the sizes of the output transistors T5 and T6, and on the size of the compensation capacitance. Hence, as a simplified expression we take $A_T \approx A_5 + A_6 + A_c$.

From this third expression, i.e., the total area of the amplifier, the current $I_5 = I_6$ will be derived. Of course, the value of that current could be taken directly as a third equation, e.g., $I_5 = 50 \ \mu A$. We prefer the equation with A_T, however, because it is a bit more complicated.

As a result, three variables g_{m1}, g_{m6}, and C_c must be obtained from three expressions of *GBW*, PM, and A_T. The compensation capacitance C_c is determined from the position of the nondominant pole. Since g_{m6} determines the nondominant pole, it is taken first. We do not take g_{m6} as a variable, but rather I_6. The procedure could then be as follows:

1 Choose $I_6 (= I_5)$ as an independent variable to begin
2 For T6:
   - Choose $V_{GS6} - V_T$ (≈ 0.2 V)
   - calculate g_{m6} and $(W/L)_6$; remember that $g_{m6} = 2I_6/(V_{GS6} - V_T)$ and $(W/L)_6 = g_{m6}/(2K'_n(V_{GS6} - V_T))$
   - choose minimum $L_6 = 5 \ \mu m$
   - calculate W_6
   - calculate size A_6 of T6; take as model $A_6 = A_G + 2A_S = W(18 + L) \ \mu m^2$
   (see Chap. 1):
3 Repeat step 2 for T5 (but for $V_{GS5} - V_T \approx 0.5$ V)
4 Calculate C_{n1} from the sizes of T5 and T6 (see Chap. 1)
5 Calculate C_c from the exact Eq. (6-26)
6 Calculate size A_c of C_c for 0.4 fF/μm2
7 Total size $A_T = A_5 + A_6 + A_c$

This procedure can be repeated for a wide range of currents I_6. Since transistor T6 provides gain, it is set for maximum g_m/I without going into weak inversion. Hence, $V_{GS6} - V_T = 0.2$ V. Transistor T5 is not that critical since it merely serves as a current source. For optimum matching, it is suggested to take its $V_{GS5} - V_T$ large. Hence, $V_{GS5} - V_T = 0.5$ to 1 V. It limits the positive output voltage swing, however. Therefore, $V_{GS5} - V_T = 0.5$ V, still allowing 2 V output excursion for $v_{DD}+ = 2.5$ V.

The total areas of the two transistors and of the compensation capacitance are given in Fig. 6-7. The total area is given, as well.

From this figure it can be concluded that $I_6 = 25 \ \mu A$ is a good choice. Thus, this is now our third equation. The use of lower currents is prohibited by the rapidly increasing value of the size of C_c. This can be seen from Eq. (6-26). Decreasing g_{m6} by decreasing the current, drastically increases C_c in order to keep the nondominant

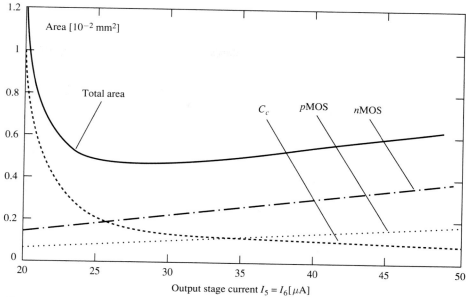

FIGURE 6-7   Output stage area versus current.

pole at $3 \cdot GBW$. Hence, if the current is lower than about 20 μA, no solution is possible, i.e., Eq. (6-26) would give a negative value of C_c.

For $GBW = 1$ MHz and $C_L = 5$ pF, the resultant values are: for $I_5 = I_6 = 25$ μA, $C_c = 1$ pF and $A_T = 0.005$ mm^2.

Determine $(W/L)_1$ and I_1   Now that C_c is known, the same design procedure can be followed as for the simple CMOS OTA. From Eq. (6-25) of the GBW, the g_{m1} can now be determined. Since transistor T1 provides gain as well, it is set again at $V_{GS1} - V_T = 0.2$ V. As a result $(W/L)_1 = g_{m1}/(2K'_n(V_{GS1} - V_T)) = 1.6$. The current $I_1 = g_{m1}(V_{GS1} - V_T)/2 = 1.25$ μA and thus the biasing current $I_B = 2I_1 = 2.5$ μA. For minimum $1/f$ noise, the input transistors are made larger in area. As a result we have chosen for $L_1 = 16$ μm, and thus $W_1 = 26$ μm.

Finally for maximum symmetry in the input stage (see Sec. 6-5), we must ensure that the voltages on nodes 1 and 2 are equal. Hence, $V_{GS3} - V_T = V_{GS4} - V_T = 0.2$ V. The dimensions of T3 and T4 are easily derived. Again they are given by $(W/L)_3 = (W/L)_4 = g_{m3}/(2K'_p(V_{GS3} - V_T))$. All dimensions are listed in Table 6-2.

This design procedure is by no means unique. The designer must decide which specifications carry the largest weight. A weighted combination of specifications could be used. It is common that when a circuit is optimized to fulfill only one or two specifications, the other characteristics may become nonsense. It is important in an optimization procedure to decide beforehand which specifications should be used in that procedure. On the other hand, since this OTA has only three independent variables, only three specifications can be used in the design procedure.

Ideally, all specifications should be included. This leads to an optimization problem, however. Usually only the most important specifications are included, such as *GBW*, *SR*, total current, noise, and total area. The other characteristics must be monitored very carefully during that optimization. They are, for example, the output swing and the common-mode input range. Design packages exist that provide a user interface, which allows monitoring of all the specifications. An example is the DONALD interface in ARIADNE (Swings and Sansen 1992).

In order to draw the attention of the designer to all other characteristics, they are all derived for the Miller CMOS OTA in Sec. 6-3.

6-2-5   BICMOS Miller OTAs

At this point let us compare BICMOS alternatives. Although we could consider bipolar alternatives as we saw in Chap. 2, BICMOS combines the advantages of both technologies. Now let us see in what sense the BICMOS Miller OTA may perform better than its CMOS equivalent.

The first alternative is shown in Fig. 6-8a. MOST T6 is replaced by a bipolar transistor in order to increase the pole splitting (see Sec. 4-1-4). Indeed, its transconductance is larger than that of a MOST. For the same currents, a smaller compensation capacitance C_c is required, increasing the *GBW*.

There is no point substituting the input devices, since a large input impedance and a large *SR/GBW* ratio is required.

On the other hand, the impedance at node 1 decreases drastically because of the low input resistance ($r_{\pi6}$) of transistor T6. As a result, the gain of the first stage decreases as well. Thus the total gain will be much less than before. Moreover, the DC voltages at nodes 1 and 2 are difficult to make the same. Thus the drain voltages of the input devices leading to offset are different (see Sec. 6-5). Therefore we prefer the configuration in Fig. 6-8b.

Instead of one bipolar transistor, a Darlington configuration is used (see Fig. 4-83). Its input impedance is much higher, such that the total gain is high. Also, a three-transistor current mirror (see Fig. 4-78) is taken, such that the voltages at the nodes 1 and 2 are the same. However, there are two drawbacks.

We introduced two more nodes into the circuit, leading to two more nondominant poles. Thus the phase margin decreases. Also, the bipolar transistor T4 has a large collector-to-substrate capacitance C_{CS}. This increases node capacitance at node 1, which necessitates a slightly larger compensation capacitance.

As a result, it is not clear whether the substitution of MOST T6 by a bipolar transistor has improved the performance. It seems that some characteristics have improved, whereas others have deteriorated.

6-3   FULL SET OF CHARACTERISTICS OF THE MILLER OTA

In the previous section, the design procedure has been spelled out to provide a certain amount of *GBW*. Several other characteristics have been overlooked, however. In this section we will calculate second-order characteristics. All numerical values are taken from the first-order analysis of the CMOS Miller OTA in the previous section.

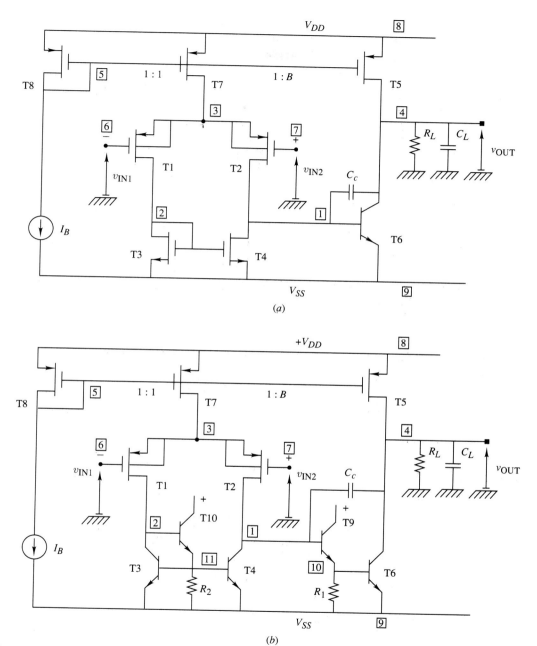

FIGURE 6-8   Miller BICMOS OTAs.

It is our aim to derive a full set of characteristics for the CMOS Miller OTA. A complete analysis is the best way to learn about all the intricacies of a circuit.

Doubtless the most important characteristics are those for which the circuit has been designed. They are usually the AC characteristics and especially those at high frequencies. However, all AC circuit operation depends on the DC operation. Therefore, a circuit must always be analyzed for its DC operation first.

The DC operating point for the CMOS Miller OTA is given in Table 6-2 for supply voltages $V_{DD} = 2.5$ V and $V_{SS} = -2.5$ V. All currents are set by the current source I_B, which has been chosen to be 2.5 μA. The DC voltage levels of the nodes are determined, however, by the supply voltage levels. The OTA has been designed such that all transistors are in the saturation region. This is guaranteed for zero input voltages. This may not be the case, however, if the common-mode (or average) input voltage is too high or too low, nor if the output voltage excursion is too large.

The input common-mode range, for which all transistors are in the saturation region, is examined first.

6-3-1   Full DC Analysis: Common-Mode Input Voltage Range Versus Supply Voltage

The common-mode input voltage is the average input voltage. It is thus given by

$$v_{ICM} = \frac{v_{IN1} + v_{IN2}}{2} \tag{6-29}$$

Its range is limited to the voltage levels where any transistor goes out of saturation (i.e., where $V_{DS} \leq V_{GS} - V_T$). If both input voltages increase, the common-source voltage (node 3 in Fig. 6-4) increases as well, reducing v_{DS} of the current source transistor T7. The limit is reached when T7 enters the linear region. The input voltage excursion limit thus is given by

$$V_{ICM\,max} = V_{DD} - V_{DS\,sat7} - V_{GS1} \tag{6-30a}$$

which is $2.5 - 1.66 = 0.84$ V, using the values of Table 6-2. This value tracks the positive power-supply line V_{DD}, as shown in Fig. 6-9.

If both input voltages decrease, the input transistors enter the linear region. At this point, the limit $V_{ICM\,min}$ is reached. It is given by

$$V_{ICM\,min} = V_{SS} + V_{GS3} + V_{DS\,sat1} - V_{GS1} \tag{6-30b}$$

which is $-2.5 + 0.16 = -2.34$ V, using the values of Table 6-2.

For variable power-supply lines $V_{DD} = |V_{SS}|$, the limits $V_{ICM\,max}$ and $V_{ICM\,min}$ are shown in Fig. 6-9. They both track the power-supply lines. The total range is only 3.18 V on 5 V at $V_{DD} = |V_{SS}| = 2.5$ V. It is not symmetrical with respect to zero volts. A large loss is encountered due to current source transistor T7.

It is possible to extend the common-mode input voltage range to include the negative power-supply line. This may be necessary if we use only a single-supply voltage

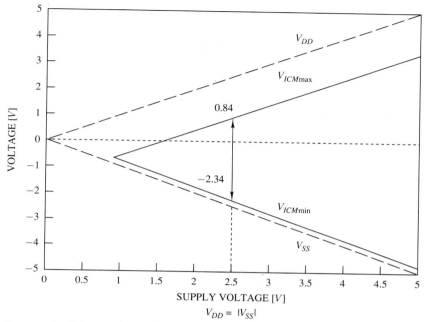

FIGURE 6-9   Common-mode input voltage range versus supply voltage for the Miller op amp.

and the OTA must operate between, for example, 0 and 5 V. We may want the OTA to be operational, even when the input voltages are at 0 volts. For this purpose it is sufficient to make V_{GS1} more than 0.16 V larger (see Eq. (6-30b)). However, this also decreases $V_{ICM\,max}$ by the same amount. As a result, the total range does not change, but merely shifts downward and now includes the negative power-supply line.

6-3-2 Full DC Analysis: Output Voltage Range Versus Supply Voltage

The output voltage range is limited by two phenomena:

- one output transistor is driven out of saturation, or
- too little current is available to drive the load.

The maximum current available from T5 to drive the load R_L of 100 kΩ is 25.2 μA. Thus the limits for the positive swing are given by

$$V_{OUT\,max} = \min[V_{DD} - V_{DS\,sat5}, R_L \cdot I_{DS5}] \qquad (6\text{-}31a)$$

which is min [2.08, 2.52] = 2.08 V. The limits for the negative swing are given by

$$V_{OUT\,min} = V_{SS} + V_{DS\,sat6} \qquad (6\text{-}31b)$$

which is -2.32 V. Transistor T6 can always be driven sufficiently high to sink much more current than 25 μA.

At $V_{DD} = |V_{SS}| = 2.5$ V, the available output voltage swing is symmetrical around zero volts. The output voltage range is shown for variable $V_{DD} = |V_{SS}|$ in Fig. 6-10. It closely tracks the full power-supply range. Symmetry can be maintained up to $V_{DD} = |V_{SS}| = 3$ V. At that point, the finite current from T5 in R_L limits the positive output voltage swing to about 2.5 V.

6-3-3   Full DC Analysis: Maximum Output Current (Source and Sink)

The maximum *source* output current is the maximum current that can be delivered to the load. Thus it is the current available from transistor T5 that is $I_{DS5} = 25.2$ μA (see Table 6-2).

The maximum *sink* output current is much larger. As shown in Fig. 6-10, the maximum negative excursion is -2.32 V, sinking (taking up) 23.2 μA from load resistance R_L (100 kΩ). Transistor T6 can sink much more current, however. This current could be taken up from a large capacitive load.

The maximum current is reached when input voltage v_{IN2} (on the + side) is pulled down heavily. Node voltage 1 increases, causing T6 to draw (or sink) a large current.

FIGURE 6-10   Output voltage range versus supply voltage for the Miller op amp.

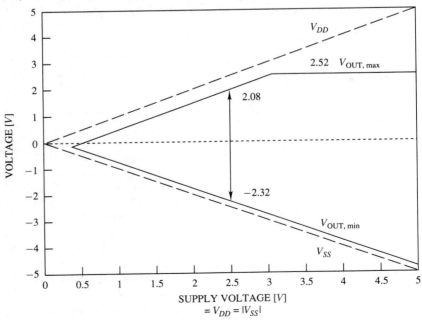

The limit is reached when transistor T2 enters the linear region. Hence

$$V_1 = V_{IN2} + V_{GS2} - V_{DSsat2} \tag{6-32a}$$

and thus
$$V_{GS6} = V_1 - V_{SS}$$

$$= V_{IN2} + V_{GS2} - V_{DSsat2} - V_{SS}$$

which is $V_{IN2} + 3.48$ V using the values of Table 6-2.

The resulting current, assuming that T6 is still in saturation, is given by

$$I_{sink} = I_{DS6} = K'_n \left(\frac{W}{L} \right)_6 (V_{GS6} - V_T)^2 - I_{DS5} \tag{6-32b}$$

For $V_{IN2} \approx -1$ V$(V_{IN1} = 0$ V$)$, this current is 3.8 mA.

This concludes the full DC analysis of the CMOS Miller OTA. We will discuss the AC analysis next.

6-3-4 AC Analysis: Low Frequencies

For a full analysis of the AC characteristics, the small-signal parameters of Table 6-2 are used. At each node the impedance is calculated with respect to ground. In this way the designer can determine which nodes will play a dominant role in the gain-frequency characteristic. Remember, however, that such node impedances depend on the load of the amplifier, which differs if the output is shorted to ground. Sometimes a shorted output is required (Sedra and Smith 1987).

The resistive part of the impedance at node i is denoted by R_{oi} and the capacitive part by C_{oi}. They are given by the approximate expressions listed in Table 6-6. Their numerical values are in Table 6-7, together with all other relevant numerical values.

For the calculation of a node impedance, Blackman's rule must be used (see Sec. 3-2). If no feedback is present, this impedance can also be found by inspection.

The expressions of the node resistances are straightforward (see Table 6-6). Those of the node capacitances, on the other hand, deserve more attention. All C_{ni} denote the node capacitances without taking into account Miller effect. As can be seen in Table 6-8, Miller effect (subscript M) occurs twice, i.e., on nodes 1 and 4. The Miller multiplication factor occurs on node 1 so that C_{n1M} is much larger than C_{n1}. On node 4, a capacitive division occurs, such that C_{n4M} is smaller than C_{n1}.

The numerical values are repeated in Table 6-7. The small-signal equivalent circuit of Fig. 6-5 is used again. The open-loop pole frequencies $f_o = 1/2\pi R_o C_o$ are added. It is obvious that the lowest (dominant) pole frequency is obtained on node 1. The second pole occurs on node 2. Node 3, on the other hand, does not come in because it is a common-mode point for a differential drive.

The values of the gains from the input to node i are added in Table 6-7, as well. The expressions have already been given in Table 6-4; the low-frequency gain on node 1 is $A_{v10} = 250$ and the total gain on node 4 is A_{v0}, which is 5200.

TABLE 6-6   EXPRESSIONS OF NODE RESISTANCES AND CAPACITANCES

Node	Node resistance R_o Expression	Value (kΩ)	Node capacitance C_o Expression	Value (pF)
1	$R_{o1} = 1/g_{o24}$	33300	$C_{o1} = C_{n1} + C_{n1M}$	22.7
			$C_{n1} = C_{GD2} + C_{DB2}$	
			$\quad + C_{GD4} + C_{DB4} + C_{GS6}$	0.373
			$C_{n1M} = C_c'(1 + |A_{v20}|)$	22.3
2	$R_{o2} = 1/g_{m3}$	97.1	$C_{o2} = C_{n2} = C_{GS3} + C_{DB3}$	
			$\quad + C_{GS4} + C_{GD4} + C_{GD1} + C_{DB1}$	0.17
3	$R_{o3} = 1/(g_{m1} + g_{m2})$	66.7	$C_{o3} = C_{n3} = C_{well1} + C_{DB7}$	
			$\quad + C_{GD7} + C_{GS1} + C_{DB1} + C_{GS2} + C_{DB2}$	0.68
4	$R_{o4} = 1/(g_{m6} + g_{o56})$ (no R_L, no C_L)	4	$C_{o4} = C_{n4} + C_{n4M}$	0.46
			$C_{n4} = C_{GD5} + C_{DB5} + C_{DB6}$	0.184
			$C_{n4M} = (C_c' \cdot C_{n1}/(C_c' + C_{n1})$	0.28
5	$R_{o5} = 1/g_{m8}$	105.3	$C_{o5} = C_{n5} = C_{GS8} + C_{DB8}$	
			$\quad + C_{GS7} + C_{GD7} + C_{GS5} + C_{GD5}$	0.32
			$C_c' = C_c + C_{GD6}$	

TABLE 6-7   NODE IMPEDANCES OF CMOS MILLER OTA; NOTE THAT THE DC VOLTAGES $V(6) = V(9)$ = 0 V; $V(8) = 2.5$ V AND $V(9) = -2.5$ V.

Node	V_{DC} (V)	R_o (kΩ)	C_n (pF)	C_o (pF)	f_o (Hz)	A_{v0}	A_{vc0}
1	−1.39	33300	0.373	22.7	2.1 k	−250	−0.048
2	−1.36	97.1	0.17	0.17	9.36 M	0.36	7.10^{-5}
3	1.24	66.7	0.68	0.68	3.5 M	0	1
4	0	4.0	0.18	0.46	86.4 M	5200	1
5	1.07	105.3	0.32	0.32	4.72 M	0	0

TABLE 6-8   CHARACTERISTICS OF CMOS MILLER OTA UNDER DIFFERENT PARAMETER CONDITIONS

Parameters	A_o (dB)	GBW (MHz)	PM (°)	I_{tot} (μA)
nominal	74.1	1.02	66	27.7
Slow $T = 27°$	67.3	0.67	70	22.5
$T = 80°$	62.6	0.58	71	22.5
Fast	81.1	1.35	62	32.5

In a unity-gain closed-loop configuration, the gains A_{vc} at low frequencies are denoted bt A_{vc0}. They are derived from the open-loop values by dividing by A_{v0}. The *GBW*, however, requires more explanation.

6-3-5 Gain-Bandwidth Versus Biasing Current

The AC characteristics at higher frequencies are completely dominated by the *GBW* and the phase margin (PM). We know that the PM must always be approximately 70°. The *GBW* is now investigated in great detail for the existing Miller CMOS OTA. We vary the biasing current I_B from the biasing current I_B^* of 2.5 μA for which it has been designed, and we look at the *GBW* that can be obtained. Note that all parameter values with an asterisk* refer to the values of the parameters at $I_B^* = 2.5$ μA as they are given in Table 6-2.

The exact expression of the CMOS Miller OTAs *GBW* has been derived before (see Eq. (6-25b)). The *GBW* depends on the biasing current I_B through the transconductance and the output conductance of the transistors. The actual dependence on the biasing current is related to the operation region of these transistors: weak inversion, strong inversion, or velocity saturation.

Remember (from Chap. 1) that the expressions of the transconductances are given by

- in weak inversion: $g_{mwi} = I_{DS}/nkT/q$
- in strong inversion: $g_{msi} = 2\sqrt{K'W/LI_{DS}}$
- in velocity saturation: $g_{mvs} = WC_{ox}v_{max}$

whereas the output conductance g_o is always directly proportional to the current: $g_o = I_{DS}/V_E L$.

All Transistors in Strong Inversion   If all transistors T1 to T6 operate in strong inversion and the conductances g_m and g_o can be normalized to the values g_m^* and g_o^*, they have at $I_B^* = 2.5$ μA. From the expressions above we see that g_m is proportional to the square root of the current, whereas the output conductance g_o is directly proportional to the current, as given by:

$$g_m = g_m^* \sqrt{\frac{I_B}{I_B^*}} \text{ and } g_o = g_o^* \frac{I_B}{I_B^*}$$

Equation (6-25b) of the *GBW* can then be rewritten, as given by

$$GBW = \frac{a\, I_B}{b + \left(c\sqrt{I_B}\right) + dI_B} \tag{6-33a}$$

in which

$$a = \frac{1}{2\pi C_c} \frac{g_{m1} * g_{m6}^*}{I_B^*} \qquad c = \frac{g_{m6}^*}{\sqrt{I_B^*}}$$

$$b = G_L' \left(1 + \frac{C_{n1}}{C_c}\right) \qquad d = \left(1 + \frac{C_L'}{C_c}\right) \frac{g_{o24}^*}{I_B^*}$$

As a result, for small biasing currents, GBW is proportional to I_B. For moderate biasing currents, the GBW is proportional to $\sqrt{I_B}$, and for high biasing currents, the GBW has become constant. This behavior is sketched asymptotically in Fig. 6-11.

The first breakpoint, at low currents, is obtained from $b = c\sqrt{I_B}$ and given by $I_{B1} = (b/c)^2$, which is 7.8 nA.

The second breakpoint, at high currents, is obtained from $c\sqrt{I_B} = dI_B$ and given by $I_{B2} = (c/d)^2$, which is 1.34 A.

However, the GBW behavior described above is not valid for small (weak inversion) and large (velocity saturation) biasing currents. For low currents, the input transistors go into weak inversion. Another expression is required.

FIGURE 6-11 GBW versus biasing current I_B for Miller CMOS OTA with the following specifications: $g_{m1}^* = 7.5\ \mu S$; $g_{m6}^* = 246\ \mu S$; $g_{024}^* = 0.03\ \mu S$; $G_L' = 11.8\ \mu S$; $C_c + C_{n1} = 1.373$ pF; $C_c + C_L + C_{n4} = C_c + C_L' = 11.18$ pF; $1 + C_{n1}/C_c = 1.37$; $1 + C_L' = 11.18$.

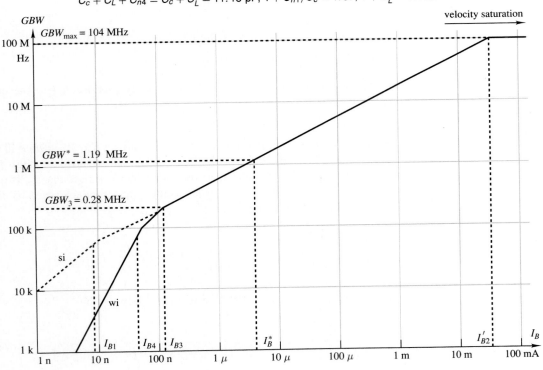

Input Transistors in Weak Inversion If the input transistors operate in weak inversion, then the expression Eq. (6-25b) of GBW can be shown to be

$$GBW = \frac{a' I_B^2}{b' + c' I_B + d' I_B^2} \tag{6-33b}$$

in which the coefficients are derived in Exercise 6-8.

This expression is also plotted in Fig. 6-11. At low currents, the values for weak inversion are plotted in solid lines, whereas those for strong inversion are plotted in dashed lines.

At low currents the GBW is proportional to I_B^2. The transition point at I_{B1} is now shifted to I_{B4}. The most important breakpoint occurs at I_{B3}, however, where the weak inversion region changes into the strong inversion region. This current I_{B3} is given by

$$I_{B3} = 2I_{DSwi1} \tag{6-34}$$

which is 0.14 μA (see Table 6-2).

Thus, this current is the lower limit of the strong inversion region where the GBW is proportional to $\sqrt{I_B}$ (see Fig. 6-11). At this point, the value of GBW is given by

$$GBW_3 = GBW * \sqrt{\frac{I_{B3}}{I_B^*}} \tag{6-35}$$

which is 0.28 MHz (see Fig. 6-11).

Now we will examine the upper limit of GBW, which occurs at very high currents.

High Current Limit: Velocity Saturation At currents higher than I_{B2} (1.34 A), the GBW becomes constant and thus reaches its maximum value GBW_{max}. Remember that the transistors are still in strong inversion. The value of GBW_{max} thus is still obtained from Eq. (6-25b) and is given by

$$GBW_{max} = \frac{a}{d} \approx \frac{g_{m1}}{2\pi C_c} \tag{6-36}$$

For g_{m1} taken at I_{B2}, $GBW_{max} = 104.5$ MHz (see Fig. 6-11).

However, at that high current, velocity saturation may already be reached. The maximum value of g_{m1} that can be reached is $W_1 C_{ox} v_{sat}$, which is 2.1 mS for transistor T1 (for $v_{sat} \approx 10^7$ cm/s). The corresponding value of GBW is 330 MHz, with $I_{DS1} = 190$ mA. This current is a lot smaller than I_{B2} (1.34 A). We want to stay in strong inversion away from velocity saturation. Therefore, we take a current which is smaller by a factor of about ten. As a result, $I_{DS1} = 19$ mA and $I'_{B2} = 2I_{DS1} = 38$ mA. The maximum of GBW_{max} is then $\sqrt{10}$ times smaller, or 104 MHz.

It is clear that velocity saturation will only come in if input transistors are used with very small dimensions, giving rise to a small value of I_{DSsv}. This is clearly not the case for our CMOS Miller OTA.

High Current Limit: Current Saturation   At high currents, the transistors need a larger V_{DS} in order to stay in saturation, and to avoid ending up in the linear region. In first order this minimum V_{DS} is $V_{DSsat} = V_{GS} - V_T$. Voltage V_{GS} increases with increasing current.

The resulting output voltage without distortion equals the supply voltage minus voltage V_{DS} (see previous section). The resulting output voltage decreases. Let us assume that we want to ensure a minimum output voltage V_{OUTM}. For sinusoidal operation this corresponds with a peak value of V_{OUTM} and an RMS value of $V_{OUTM}/\sqrt{2}$.

Let us now investigate the maximum value of the biasing current I_B before placing any transistors into the linear region (we always take $V_{OUTM} = 1$ V):

1 In order to keep T7 in saturation: $V_{DS7} < V_{DD} - V_{GS1} I_{B\max 7} \approx 4$ mA

2 In order to keep T1, T2, and T6 in saturation: $V_{DS1,2,6} < V_{SS} - V_{GS6} + V_{GS1}$; $I_{B\max 1,2,6} \approx 0.62$ mA

3 In order to keep T1, T2, and T3 in saturation: $V_{DS1,2,3} < V_{SS} - V_{GS3} + V_{GS1}$; $I_{B\max 1,2,3} \approx 0.5$ mA

4 In order to keep T5 in saturation: $V_{DS5} < V_{DD} - V_{OUTM} I_{B\max 5} \approx 0.017$ mA

5 In order to keep T6 in saturation: $V_{DS6} < V_{SS} - V_{OUTM} I_{B\max 6} \approx 0.115$ mA

This calculation shows that increasing I_B pushes T5 into the linear region first, causing distortion. The real limitation for very large GBW thus lies in the output transistors. Of course, we could realize a new design: we could increase the dimensions of the output transistors T5 and T6. This would increase the capacitance C_{n1}, however, requiring a larger compensation capacitance C_c. This in turn would decrease the GBW, etc. The design cycle starts all over again.

This illustrates that all characteristics of an op amp are related and that none can be increased without observing all the other characteristics.

Looking at Fig. 6-11, we can draw some final conclusions. The input devices of an op amp will most probably operate in strong inversion. At the weak inversion side, the GBW decreases too drastically. At the velocity saturation side, large values of GBW can be reached, provided the designer takes into account other important specifications, such as output voltage amplitude, etc. Let us discuss several of these specifications.

6-3-6 Slew Rate Versus Load Capacitance

Slewing is obtained when a large input signal is applied to the op amp. For a large positive input voltage step, transistor T2 is cut off almost instantaneously (see Fig. 6-4). The current from the current source T7 then flows through transistors T1 and T3, causing the same current to be drawn through T4. Since T2 is off, this current can only be drawn through capacitance C_c. A constant current I_B through a capacitance C_c generates a voltage ramp with slope $\Delta V/\Delta t = I_B/C_c$. However, the voltage at node 1 is fixed because it is V_{GS6}, and transistor T6 is always on. In fact, transistor T5 always provides sufficient current to T6. As a result, the voltage ramp appears at node 4.

For a large negative input voltage step, transistor T2 is heavily pulled on, and leaves T1 off. Thus transistors T3 and T4 are also off. The current from T2 is now pushed through C_c, causing a negative voltage ramp with the same slope I_B/C_c at the output.

The slew rate is given by

$$SR_{int} = \frac{I_B}{C_c} \qquad (6\text{-}37)$$

the value of which is 2.5 V/μs. It is called the *internal SR* because node 1 is the limiting node and an internal node.

Capacitance C_c is not the only capacitance that must be charged and discharged, however. Load capacitance C_L must be charged and discharged, as well. Discharging C_L is no problem because transistor T6 can pull (or sink) a lot of current when overdriven. Charging C_L, however, can only be realized in a finite time, because C_L is charged by means of the current from T5. This current is actually only $I_5 - I_B$, since C_c takes I_B away. As a consequence, for a positive input voltage step, the voltage at the internal node 1 decreases, also decreasing the current through T6. Current $I_5 - I_B$ then charges C_L, resulting in a positive voltage ramp with a slope given by

$$SR_{ext} = \frac{I_5 - I_B}{C_L} \qquad (6\text{-}38)$$

This is called the *external SR* because the external (output) node is the limiting node. For example, current $I_5 - I_B$ is 22.3 μA (see Table 6-2) and $SR_{ext} \approx 2.2$ V/μs. It is smaller than the previous SR_{int}. As a result, the overall slew rate SR is the smaller, about 2.2 V/μs.

The SR versus the load capacitance is shown in Fig. 6-12. The breakpoint value between the SR_{int} and the SR_{ext} is given by

$$C_{Lc} = C_c \frac{I_5 - I_B}{I_B} - C_{n4} \qquad (6\text{-}39)$$

which is 8.9 pF in Fig. 6-12. For larger values of C_L, the external SR_{ext} is dominant, due to the charging of the load capacitance C_L.

6-3-7 Output Voltage Range Versus Frequency

The output voltage is an important characteristic. It is useless to design a 100 MHz op amp that only can deliver 100 mV. There is clearly a compromise to be made, as we discussed in Sec. 6-3-5.

The output voltage range is limited by the supply voltage at lower frequencies (see Sec. 6-3-2) and by the slew rate at higher frequencies (see Chap. 3).

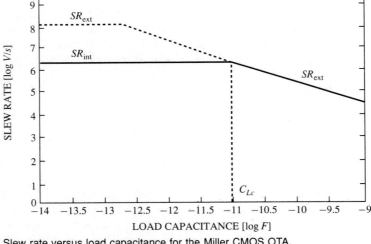

FIGURE 6-12   Slew rate versus load capacitance for the Miller CMOS OTA.

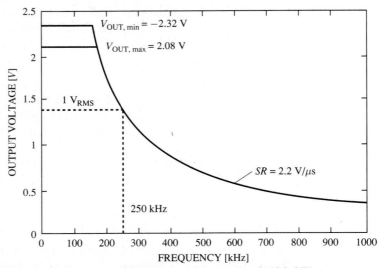

FIGURE 6-13   Output voltage range versus frequency for the Miller CMOS OTA.

At low frequencies the output voltage range is limited by $V_{OUT\,max} = 2.08$ V or $V_{OUT\,min} = -2.32$ V, as shown in Fig. 6-10 and repeated in Fig. 6-13.

At high frequencies, the maximum output voltage is given by

$$V_{OUT\,max\,SR} = \frac{SR}{2\pi f} \qquad (6\text{-}40)$$

which gives a hyperbola in Fig. 6-13. The breakpoints are at 171 and 153 kHz. This latter bandwidth is often called the *power bandwidth* of the amplifier.

For 1 V_{RMS} output voltage (1.42 V_{peak}), the maximum frequency is 250 kHz; for 1 V_{peak}, the maximum frequency is 355 kHz. At the frequency of the *GBW*, the output voltage is only 0.3 V_{peak}.

6-3-8 Settling Time

The OTA of Fig. 6-4 can be used in a feedback configuration to generate gain with a well-controlled and precise value A_v. Its value can be between 1 and its open-loop gain A_{v0}. Both feedback resistors and capacitors can be used to set the gain A_v (see Chap. 5).

Since the *GBW* of the OTA is fixed, the bandwidth *BW* in first-order is given by $BW = GBW/A_v$. A time constant τ_d corresponds with this frequency *BW*, given by $\tau_d = 1/2\pi BW$. If the phase margin is larger than approximately 70°, this circuit behaves as a first-order system with time constant τ_d.

For a step input (Fig. 6-14a), the output (Fig. 6-14b) initially slews, then slowly settles toward its final value, determined by the gain A_v. The slew rate is governed by the availability of biasing current to charge the capacitance at the dominant node. The settling time, however, is governed by small-signal time constants. In a first-order system it is governed by time constant τ_d.

In a first-order analysis, we can assume that the slewing time is short with respect to the settling time. In this case, the output voltage reaches its final value by means of an exponential characteristic (see Fig. 6-14c), with time constant $\tau_d = 1/2\pi f_d$.

For the CMOS Miller OTA, the phase margin PM is 67°. This is close enough to 90° to be regarded as a first-order system. The settling time $t_s(\varepsilon)$ is approximated by

$$t_s(\varepsilon) \approx \tau_d \ln\left(\frac{1}{\varepsilon}\right) \approx \frac{A_v}{2\pi GBW} \ln\left(\frac{1}{\varepsilon}\right) \tag{6-41}$$

in which ε is the error when settling occurs (see Sec. 5-3-2).

If the phase margin is much smaller than 76°, the expression is more complicated. It is given in App. 6-1.

For 0.1 percent, $\ln(1/\varepsilon) = 6.9$ and for *GBW* = 1.19 MHz, $\tau_d = 0.134$ μs, such that t_s (0.1 percent) = 0.92 μs, in unity-gain configuration ($A_v = 1$). For 0.01 percent, $\ln(1/\varepsilon) = 9.2$ and t_s (0.01 percent) = 1.23 μs. The 0.1 percent settling time thus is about 6 μs. For an input voltage step of 0.2 V, the output voltage must change over 2 V. With a slew rate of 2.2 V/μs (see previous example), this would only take 0.9 μs, which is comparable with respect to the 0.1 percent settling time of 0.92 μs. It should be added to the settling time in order to obtain a worst-case value (see Fig. 6-14d).

The results of a SPICE simulation for the CMOS Miller OTA are shown in Fig. 6-15. A small input step of only 10 mV is taken. The gain is unity, such that the output settles to 10 mV, as well. In this way, slew rate limitations are negligible. The rise time and settling time are all due to the time constant τ_d. Two different vertical scales are used to evidence the overshoot. The resulting settling times can be read on

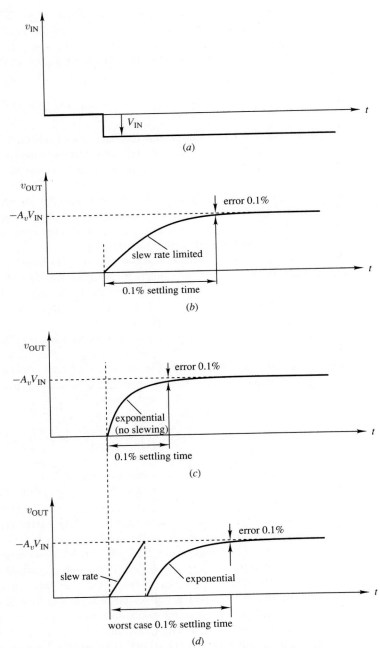

FIGURE 6-14   Settling time includes effects of (*b*) slew rate, (*c*) time constant exponential, or (*d*) both.

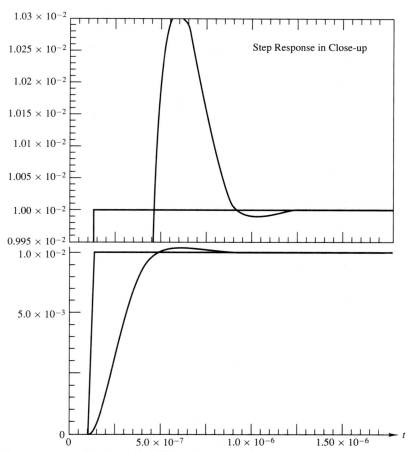

FIGURE 6-15   Step response of Miller CMOS OTA.

the top graph, about t_s (0.1 percent) $\approx 0.7\ \mu$s and t_s (0.01 percent) $\approx 1.0\ \mu$s. These values are shorter than those calculated because of the relatively small phase margin and the small overshoot allowed.

6-3-9   Input Impedance

As with any op amp, the Miller CMOS OTA has two input terminals. Hence, three different input impedances can be defined, as shown in Fig. 6-16a: C_+ and C_- from either terminal to ground, and C_d between both terminals. The input resistances are nearly infinitely high and therefore have been omitted.

Now several capacitances are calculated for the OTA in open-loop configuration. We will short one of the inputs to ground, in order to calculate the capacitance at the other input.

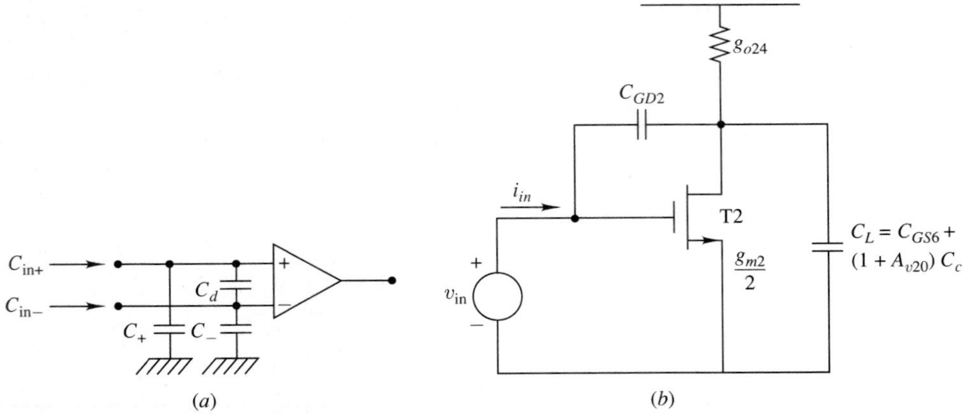

FIGURE 6-16   (a) Input impedance capacitances. (b) Equivalent circuit to calculate C_+

Noninverting Input is Grounded   In this case the input capacitance C_{in-} is given by $C_{in-} = C_d + C_-$ (see Fig. 6-16a). In the circuit of Fig. 6-4, we look into the gate of transistor T1. This transistor has, as source impedance, $1/g_{m2}$ in parallel with capacitances C_{GS2} and the output capacitance of current mirror transistor T7. Its load resistor is $1/g_{m3}$. Thus the gain of transistor T1 from gate to drain is low. The Miller effect of capacitance C_{GD1} can be ignored. As a result, the input capacitance of transistor T1 is approximately $C_{GS1}/2$. The factor 2 is to include the effect of $1/g_{m2}$ in its source.

The input capacitance C_{in-} thus is approximately given by

$$C_{in-} = C_d + C_- \approx \frac{C_{GS1}}{2} \tag{6-42}$$

Inverting Input is Grounded   In this case, the input capacitance C_{in+} is given by $C_{in+} = C_d + C_+$ (see Fig. 6-16a). We now look into the gate of transistor T2 in the circuit of Fig. 6-4. This transistor has as load conductance g_{o24}, in parallel with the input capacitance of transistor C_{GS6} and the compensation capacitance C_c, multiplied by the gain of the second stage A_{v20} (Miller effect). This is given by Eq. (6-19) and equal to 20.8, for this OTA. The input capacitance C_{in+} is approximately given by

$$C_{in+} = C_d + C_+ \approx \frac{C_{GS2}}{2} + (1 + A_{v10})C_{GD1} \tag{6-43}$$

Now we can identify the capacitances from Eqs. (6-42) and (6-43) to be (note that $C_{GS1} = C_{GS2}$):

$$C_d \approx \frac{C_{GS1}}{2}$$

$$C_- \approx 0 \tag{6-44a}$$

$$C_+ \approx (1 + A_{v10})C_{GD2}$$

The value of C_+ only holds for very low frequencies, however. For frequencies higher than the open-loop bandwidth (228 Hz for this OTA), capacitances C_{GS6}, and especially C_c, short-out conductance g_{o24}; thus the value of A_{v10} decreases. The value of C_+ versus frequency can easily be calculated by means of the simplified circuit of Fig. 6-16b. Transconductance g_{m2} has been divided by two in order to include the effect of $1/g_{m1}$ in the source of transistor T2. The input capacitance C_+ is given by

$$C_+ \approx A_{v10}C_{GD2}\frac{1 + \left(\dfrac{C_{GD2}}{g_{m2}}\right)s}{1 + A_{v10}\dfrac{(C_{GD2} + C_L)}{g_{m2}}s} \qquad (6\text{-}44b)$$

with $C_L = C_{GS6} + (1 + A_{v20})C_c$, provided $A_{v10} \gg 1$ (250 for this OTA),

For our Miller OTA, the value of C_{in-} is C_d, which is $C_{GS1}/2$ or 0.11 pF. The corresponding value of Z_{in-} is sketched in Fig. 6-17. At 1 kHz it is 1.45 GΩ.

The low frequency values $A_{v10} = 250$ and $A_{v20} = 20.8$ are taken from Table 6-4. The low frequency value of C_+ thus is 1.76 pF and the value of C_{in+} 1.87 pF. The pole of A_{v2} occurs at the open-loop BW of the OTA, which is 228 Hz (see Table 6-4). The characteristic of A_{v2} versus frequency is shown in Fig. 6-17a for the sake of comparison.

FIGURE 6-17a   Gain factors of Miller CMOS OTA.

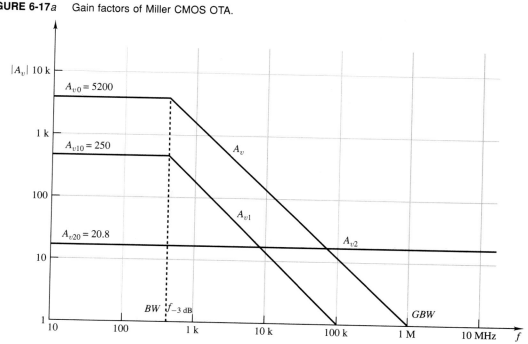

For frequencies up to 228 Hz, the absolute value of Z_{in+} thus corresponds to a capacitance of 1.87 pF. From 228 Hz on, Z_{in+} is constant until it hits the impedance line corresponding to C_d only, or 0.11 pF (see Fig. 6-17b). In that frequency region, the input impedance is thus resistive. Its value is easily extracted from Eq. (6-44b) and is given by

$$R_{in+} = \frac{1}{g_{m2}}\left(1 + \frac{C_L}{C_{GD2}}\right) \tag{6-45a}$$

which is about 420 MΩ ($C_L = 22.2$ pF). Resistance R_{in+} coincides with Z_{in-} at frequency f_{in+}, after which Z_{in+} and Z_{in-} coincide.

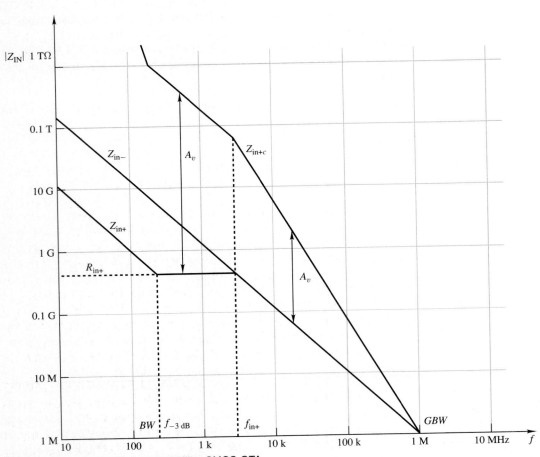

FIGURE 6-17b   Input impedances of Miller CMOS OTA.

This frequency is found by equation of $Z_{in-} = 2/2\pi C_{GS1}$ and R_{in+} and is given by

$$f_{in+} = \frac{2g_{m2}}{2\pi C_{GS1}} \frac{1}{\left(1 + \dfrac{C_L}{C_{GD2}}\right)} \tag{6-45b}$$

which is about $f_{in+} = 3.5$ kHz.

The zero in Eq. (6-44b) of C_+ can be neglected, because it only occurs on 186 MHz (see Table 6-4).

Closed-Loop Input Impedance Versus Frequency   For unity-gain feedback, the input capacitance must be divided by the loop gain (see Chap. 5). It is given by

$$C_{in+c} = \frac{C_{in+}}{1 + A_v} = \frac{C_d + C_+}{1 + A_v} \tag{6-46}$$

At low frequencies, (for A_{v0}, $A_{v10} \gg 1$) it is given by

$$C_{in+c0} \approx \frac{C_{GS1}}{2} \frac{1}{A_{v0}} + C_{GD2} \frac{A_{v10}}{A_{v0}} \tag{6-47}$$

Since $A_{v0} = 5200$ and $A_{v10} = 250$ (see Table 6-4), the first term is only 0.02 fF and the second 0.53 fF, totaling 0.55 fF, which is 2.8 GΩ at 100 Hz.

At low frequencies, below $BW = 228$ Hz, both capacitances are reduced by the loop gain A_{v0}. The effect of C_{GD2} is dominant because of its Miller effect. The value of C_{GD2} is only reduced by the gain of the second stage A_{v20} (which has a value of 20.8).

From frequencies above 228 Hz on, both A_v and A_{v1} decrease, but A_{v2} stays constant (see Fig. 6-17a). The effect of C_{GS1} starts increasing, whereas the effect of C_{GD2} stays constant. As a result, the effect of C_{GS2} becomes dominant at the frequency where both terms of Eq. (6-46) have become equal. This frequency is the same as in Eq. (6-45b), which is about 3.5 kHz for our OTA. From that frequency on, the capacitance C_{in+c} increases with frequency. Thus, the corresponding Z_{in+c} decreases with twice that slope (-40 dB/dec) until the GBW is reached. For even higher frequencies, it coincides with the open-loop values (see Fig. 6-17b).

These considerations are for unity-gain feedback. For other levels of feedback, similar derivations are easily carried out. We must remember, however, that the input capacitance will be larger for less loop gain. The unity-gain configuration always provides minimum input capacitance, and thus is an ideal stage for buffer applications.

6-3-10   Output Impedance

The output impedance is another important characteristic of an OTA. This is especially true for an OTA in contrast with an op amp, because an OTA has no output stage to lower the output impedance.

The output impedance in open-loop configuration can be modeled by an output resistance in parallel with an output capacitance. For the calculation of the output impedance of the OTA in Fig. 6-4, the output load consisting of R_L and C_L usually is omitted. This is not always the case, however. The output impedance value, with the output load included, is interesting, especially because C_L is part of the stabilization scheme. In this analysis, the output-load components R_L and C_L are omitted. They can be placed in parallel, if necessary.

The output impedance is found by application of a current source to the small-signal circuit of Fig. 6-5, as shown in Fig. 6-18a. The output impedance then equals the ratio of the resulting voltage v_{out} to that current i_{out}. Since the output load components R_L and C_L are omitted, load $G'_L (= G_L + g_{o5} + g_{o6})$ has been substituted by g_{o56} $(= g_{o5} + g_{o6})$. The output impedance is then easily calculated to be

$$Z_{\text{OUT}} = \frac{1}{g_{o56}} \left[\frac{1 + \left(\dfrac{C_c + C_{n1}}{g_{o24}} \right) s}{1 + \left(\dfrac{g_{m6}}{g_{o24} g_{o56}} \right) C_c s \left(1 + \dfrac{C_{n1}}{g_{m6}} s \right)} \right] \tag{6-48}$$

if $g_{m6} \gg g_{o24}$ and g_{o56}, which is clearly the case.

At low frequencies, Z_{OUT} equals $1/g_{o56}$, which is about 556 kΩ. The plot of Z_{OUT} versus frequency is shown in Fig. 6-18b. The first pole occurs at a frequency of about $f_{p1} = 35$ Hz. The second pole only occurs at 71 MHz and therefore is not shown in Fig. 6-18b.

Also, a zero occurs (at about 5.3 kHz). This zero is an important break frequency because it occurs in the middle of the frequency band of interest. It is given by

$$f_{z3} = \frac{g_{o24}}{2\pi C_c} \tag{6-49}$$

and is also listed in Table 6-4.

For intermediate frequencies larger than $f_{z3} = 5.3$ kHz, the output impedance is resistive and low. Its value is obtained from Eq. (6-45) and is given by

$$R_{\text{OUT}im} = \frac{1}{g_{m6}} \left(1 + \frac{C_{n1}}{C_c} \right) \approx \frac{1}{g_{m6}} \tag{6-50}$$

Since $1/g_{m6} = 4.1$ kΩ, this value is about 5.6 kΩ. Since the second pole occurs at around 70 MHz, this low resistance is maintained up to very high frequencies.

This result is not unexpected. An output impedance of $1/g_m$ has already been found for all previous OTA stages (see Chap. 4). Indeed, for all frequencies larger than f_{z3}, the compensation capacitance C_c acts as a short. In this way transistor T6 acts as a diode, giving rise to an input and output resistance of $1/g_{m6}$. To our surprise, an

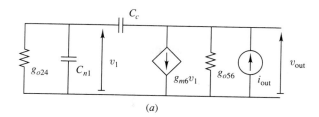

(a)

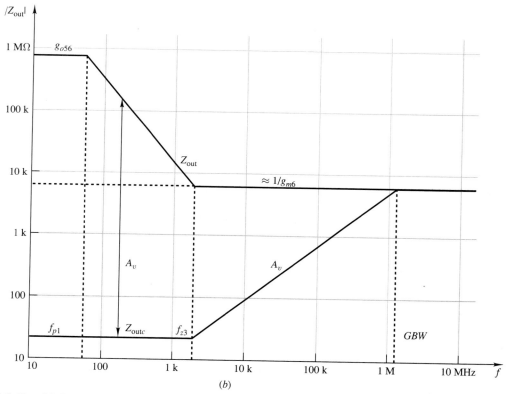

(b)

FIGURE 6-18   (a) Equivalent circuit of the Miller OTA for the calculation of Z_{out} (derived from Fig. 6-5), and (b) output impedances of Miller CMOS OTA.

$$g_{m6} = 246 \ \mu S;$$

$$g_{o24} = g_{o2} + g_{o4} = 0.03 \ \mu S;$$

$$g_{o56} = g_{o5} + g_{o6} = 1.8 \ \mu S;$$

$$C_{n1} = 0.37 \text{ pF}; \quad C_c = 1 \text{ pF}$$

OTA does not exhibit a high output resistance, as suggested by output resistance g_{o56}. It exhibits merely $1/g_{m6}$ for most of the useful frequency range. Only at very low frequencies is the output resistance g_{o56}. Therefore, this OTA can be used as an op amp in most applications.

For unity-gain feedback, the value of the output impedance must be divided by the total loop gain $(1 + A_v)$. The resulting closed-loop output impedance Z_{outc} is also given in Fig. 6-18b. The open-loop gain A_v is now much larger, however, because we have omitted R_L, raising A_{v0} from 5200 to 35000. Also, the dominant pole is decreased by the same ratio, i.e., from 228 to 35 Hz. Remember that the dominant pole of the gain is also the dominant pole of the open-loop output impedance. The GBW depends only on g_{m1} and C_c, and thus remains the same.

The closed-loop output impedance Z_{outc0}, at very low frequencies, is approximately given by

$$Z_{\text{OUT}c0} \approx \frac{Z_{\text{OUT}}}{A_{v0}} = \left(\frac{1}{g_{o56}}\right)\left(\frac{g_{o24}}{g_{m1}}\right)\left(\frac{g_{o56}}{g_{m6}}\right) = \frac{g_{o24}}{g_{m1}g_{m6}} = \frac{1}{A_{v10}g_{m6}} \qquad (6\text{-}51)$$

which is 16 Ω (see Fig. 6-18b). It does not change at the dominant-pole frequency f_{p1} of 35 Hz.

The zero f_{z3} that occurs at 5.3 kHz in the open-loop characteristic, also occurs in closed loop. From that frequency on, the output impedance increases with frequency, similar to an inductor. At the frequency of the GBW, no more loop gain is available. Thus, both open and closed loop characteristics coincide at value $1/g_{m6}$.

Now that gain and input and output-impedance have been studied, we must consider temperature behavior.

6-3-11 Temperature Effects

In order to study the influence of temperature variations, the following realistic assumptions are made:

- The biasing current I_B is independent of temperature
- The load components R_L and C_L are independent of temperature
- All capacitances are independent of temperature
- All transistors stay in saturation
- The Early voltage V_E is independent of temperature

The only parameter assumed to depend on temperature is mobility, which decreases with temperature. It is contained in the gain factor K'_n, which thus varies as $K'_n \cdot T^{-a}$. Coefficient a depends on the doping level and is about 1.5.

The other temperature dependencies can be easily calculated. They have been added in the last column of Table 6-4. The low-frequency gain, the GBW, the second pole, and the zero decrease with increasing temperature, while the first pole increases. As a result, the phase margin that depends only on the relative position of the second pole with respect to GBW is almost independent of temperature.

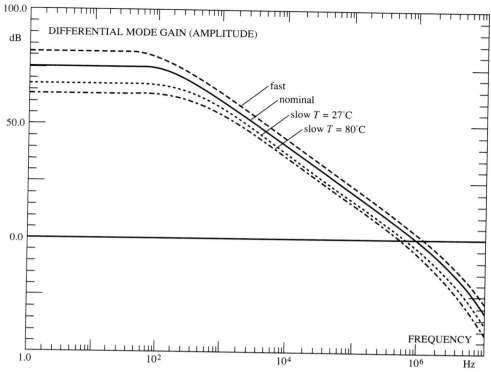

FIGURE 6-19*a*

Several SPICE plots have been made for verification. The temperature limits are 27° and 80°. Also, the K'_n factor has been changed to simulate "slow" and "fast" devices. The plots are shown in Fig. 6-19*a* (above) and Fig. 6-19*b* (shown on the following page) and the results are summarized in Table 6-8. It shows that the *GBW* varies considerably with K'_n, and thus with temperature.

6-4 NOISE ANALYSIS OF OTAs

After we have studied several characteristics of the Miller CMOS OTA, we will analyze its noise performance. The Miller OTA is a two-stage amplifier, however, so we must consider the noise contributions of both stages. Since this is the first time that we must analyze the noise of a two-stage amplifier, we will carry out the analysis in general. The specific case of the Miller OTA then is taken for the sake of illustration.

Each transistor contributes white noise and $1/f$ noise. The equivalent input noise voltage $\overline{dv_n^2}$ of a MOST thus is given by (see Chap. 1)

$$\overline{dv_n^2(f)} = \frac{8kT}{3}\frac{1}{g_m}df + \frac{K_F}{WL}\frac{df}{f} \qquad (6\text{-}52)$$

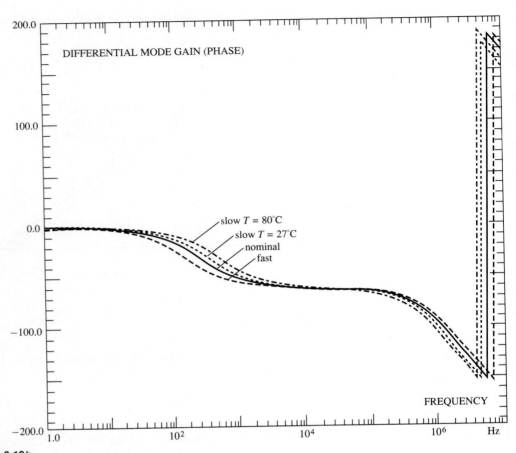

FIGURE 6-19*b*

The K_F values for a standard 3 μm n-well CMOS process (for $t_{ox} = 42.5$ nm) have been discussed in Chap. 1. They are $K_{Fn} = 9.8 \times 10^{-9}$ V$^2\mu$m^2 for an nMOST, and $K_{Fp} = 0.49 \times 10^{-9}$ V$^2\mu$m^2 for a pMOST.

The values of the equivalent input noise voltages $\overline{dv_{ni}^2}$ can now be calculated for each transistor Ti as given by Eq. (6-52). (see Table 6-9 and 6-10). The transistor dimensions and g_m values are taken from Table 6-2.

6-4-1 Noise Performance at Low Frequencies

In order to calculate the noise performance at low frequencies, all capacitances are omitted. The transistor noise voltage sources can be added to one equivalent input noise voltage $\overline{dv_{nie}^2}$ by use of the following expression:

$$\overline{dv_{nie}^2} = \sum_{i=1}^{n} \overline{dv_{ni}^2} \left(\frac{A_{vni}}{A_{v0}} \right)^2 \qquad (6\text{-}53)$$

TABLE 6-9 EQUIVALENT INPUT NOISE VOLTAGES OF TRANSISTORS OF CMOS MILLER OTA

MOST	N/P	W (μm)	L (μm)	g_m (μS)	$\overline{dv_{niw}}$ white ($nV_{RMS}/\sqrt{Hz}$)	$\overline{dv_{nif}}$ $1/f$ at 1 Hz ($\mu V_{RMS}/\sqrt{Hz}$)
T1, T2	P	26	16	7.5	38.3	1.13
T3, T4	N	10	10	10.3	32.7	10.56
T5	P	55	5	95.5	10.7	1.45
T6	Na	115	5	246	6.7	4.34
T7,T8	P	13	10	9.5	34.0	2.08

TABLE 6-10 CONTRIBUTIONS OF TRANSISTOR NOISE SOURCES TO THE TOTAL OUTPUT NOISE.
$A_{V10} = \frac{G_{M1}}{G_{O24}} = 250$; $A_{V20} = \frac{G_{M6}}{G_L'} = 20.8$; $A_{V0} = A_{V10}A_{V20} = 5200$

MOST	A_{vni0}	$\dfrac{A_{vni0}}{A_{v0}}$	$\overline{dv_{ni}^2}\left(\dfrac{A_{vni0}}{A_{v0}}\right)^2$	white $\left(10^{-18}\ V_{RMS}^2/Hz\right)$	$(1/f)_{1\ Hz}$ $\left(10^{-12}\ V_{RMS}^2/Hz\right)$
T1, T2	A_{v0}	1	$\overline{dv_{n1}^2}$	1467	1.277
T3, T4	$\dfrac{g_{m3}}{g_{m1}}A_{v0}$	1.37	$\overline{dv_{n3}^2}\left(\dfrac{g_{m3}}{g_{m1}}\right)^2$	2007	209
T5	$\dfrac{g_{m5}}{G_L'} = \dfrac{g_{m5}}{g_{m6}}A_{v20}$	1.56×10^{-3}	$\overline{dv_{n5}^2}\left(\dfrac{g_{m5}}{g_{m6}}\dfrac{1}{A_{v10}}\right)^2$	2.8×10^{-4}	5×10^{-6}
T6	A_{v20}	4×10^{-3}	$\overline{dv_{n6}^2}\dfrac{1}{A_{v10}^2}$	7.2×10^{-4}	3×10^{-4}
T7	$\dfrac{g_{m7}}{2\,g_{m3}}\dfrac{g_{o13}}{g_{m1}}A_{v0}$	1.9×10^{-3}	$\overline{dv_{n7}^2}\left(\dfrac{g_{m7}}{2\,g_{m3}}\dfrac{g_{o13}}{g_{m1}}\right)^2$	4.2×10^{-3}	1.6×10^{-5}
T8	$A_{vn70} - A_{vn50}$	3×10^{-4}	$\overline{dv_{n8}^2}\left(A_{vn70} - A_{vn50}\right)^2$	1×10^{-4}	4×10^{-7}
			total sum is	6948	420

in which $\overline{dv_{ni}^2}$ is the equivalent input noise voltage of transistor Ti and A_{vni} is the gain from that noise source to the output.

The gains are calculated first, then multiplied by the noise sources. All expressions and numerical values are collected in Table 6-10. However, a few of them require some additional attention.

The equivalent input noise voltage $\overline{dv_{n7}^2}$ of transistor T7 causes a noise drain-source current i_7, which splits into two equal currents (see Fig. 6-4) flowing through both input transistors. A simplified equivalent circuit is given in Fig. 6-20. One current $i_7/2$ is mirrored by T3–T4 and subtracted from the other current. The resulting output current flows into the load of the first stage. The resulting voltage is then amplified

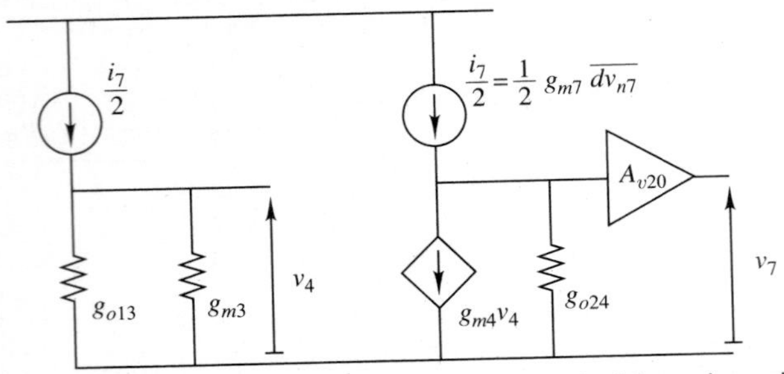

FIGURE 6-20   Equivalent circuit to calculate the gain ($= v_7/i_7$) of the noise voltage of transistor T7.

by the second stage, as indicated by the expression in Table 6-10. The resulting gain A_{vn70} is 9.6.

The noise current through transistor T8 has two paths to the output: one through T7 and the first stage (with the same gain $A_{vn70} = 9.6$ as for the noise from T7), and one through T5 with gain $A_{vn50} = 8.1$. The expression is also given in Table 6-10. It is clear from the numerical values that both noise currents nearly cancel each other. The current component's contribution through the first stage is only little larger.

Division of the gains in the first column of Table 6-10 by the total gain A_{v0} provides the values of the second column. Multiplication of these values by the equivalent input noise voltages squared (from Table 6-9), yields the output noise voltage powers.

The total white output noise is 6948×10^{-18} V²/Hz or 83 nV$_{RMS}/\sqrt{Hz}$; the total $1/f$ output noise at 1 Hz is 420×10^{-12} V²/Hz or 20.5 μV$_{RMS}/\sqrt{Hz}$. Note that only devices of the input stage play an important role, as could be expected. Also note that for white noise all four input stage transistors give an important contribution. The $1/f$ noise, on the other hand, is fully dominated by the load devices T3 and T4.

The sum of the terms in the middle column of Table 6-10 can be approximated by

$$\overline{dv_{nie}^2} \approx 2\left[\overline{dv_{n1}^2} + \overline{dv_{n3}^2}\left(\frac{g_{m3}}{g_{m1}}\right)^2\right] \tag{6-54}$$

Remember, however, that the equivalent input noise voltage consists of both white noise and $1/f$ noise components, as given by

$$\overline{dv_{nie}^2} = \overline{dv_{niew}^2} + \overline{dv_{nief}^2} \tag{6-55}$$

At all intermediate frequencies the white noise is dominant. Substitution of all terms $\overline{dv_{ni}^2}$ by their expression $8kT/3g_{mi}df$ yields, for the white noise excess factor

$$y_w = \frac{\overline{dv_{niew}^2}}{\overline{dv_{n1}^2}} = 2\left(1 + \frac{g_{m3}}{g_{m1}}\right) \tag{6-56}$$

which is 2×2.37 or 4.75 (with $\overline{dv_{n1}} = 38.3 \text{ nV}_{\text{RMS}}/\sqrt{\text{Hz}}$ from Table 6-9 and $\overline{dv_{niew}} = 83.4 \text{ nV}_{\text{RMS}}/\sqrt{\text{Hz}}$).

At low frequencies the $1/f$ noise is dominant. It can be written as

$$y_f = \frac{\overline{dv_{nief}^2}}{\overline{dv_{n1}^2}} = 2\left[1 + \frac{K_{Fn}}{K_{Fp}}\frac{(WL)_1}{(WL)_3}\left(\frac{g_{m3}}{g_{m1}}\right)^2\right] \tag{6-57}$$

which is 313 (with $\overline{dv_{nf1}} = 1.13 \ \mu\text{V}_{\text{RMS}}/\sqrt{\text{Hz}}$ at 1 Hz from Table 6-9 and $\overline{dv_{nief}} = 20 \ \mu\text{V}_{\text{RMS}}/\sqrt{\text{Hz}}$ at 1 Hz).

Since the $1/f$ noise source voltage decreases with frequency and the white noise voltage is constant, it will become equal at the so-called corner frequency f_c. Its value is given by the ratio $\overline{dv_{nief}^2}/\overline{dv_{niew}^2}$ or 57 kHz. This value seems to be high, but is very typical for small MOSTs.

Until now, only the noise has been calculated at low frequencies where capacitances are not a factor. Therefore, all white noise is expressed per $\sqrt{\text{Hz}}$ and the $1/f$ noise per $\sqrt{\text{Hz}}$ at 1 Hz. The total noise can be found by integration over frequency. This will be discussed for white noise later in Sec. 6-4-3. First let us explore what happens at high frequencies, when all capacitances come in.

6-4-2 Noise Performance at High Frequencies

At intermediate and high frequencies, the effects of all capacitances must be included. At these frequencies the $1/f$ noise can be ignored.

The CMOS Miller OTA consists of two stages, both having a different gain versus frequency characteristic. The equivalent input noise sources of the transistors thus are amplified toward the output, with different gain versus frequency characteristics.

The equivalent input noise of the first stage is denoted by $\overline{dv_1}$ (as shown in Fig. 6-21). It is caused mainly by the four input transistors T1 through T4. Its value is simply given by $\overline{dv_{niew}}$ in Eq. (6-84), or $83.4 \text{ nV}_{\text{RMS}}/\sqrt{\text{Hz}}$. Its gain versus frequency characteristic is the open-loop gain characteristic A_v of the OTA, as shown in Fig. 6-6

FIGURE 6-21   Noise model for the Miller CMOS OTA

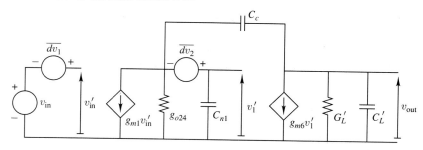

and in Fig. 6-22a. It has the form

$$A_v = A_{v0} \frac{\left(1 - j\dfrac{f}{f_z}\right)}{\left(1 + j\dfrac{f}{f_{p1}}\right)\left(1 + j\dfrac{f}{f_{p2}}\right)} \tag{6-58}$$

Its low-frequency value is $A_{v0} = 5200$ and the poles occur at $f_{p1} = 228$ Hz and at $f_{p2} \approx 3.8$ MHz (see Table 6-4). It also has a positive zero at $f_z \approx 39$ MHz (not shown in Fig. 6-22a).

FIGURE 6-22a   Open-loop gains A_v and A_{v2} of the Miller OTA.

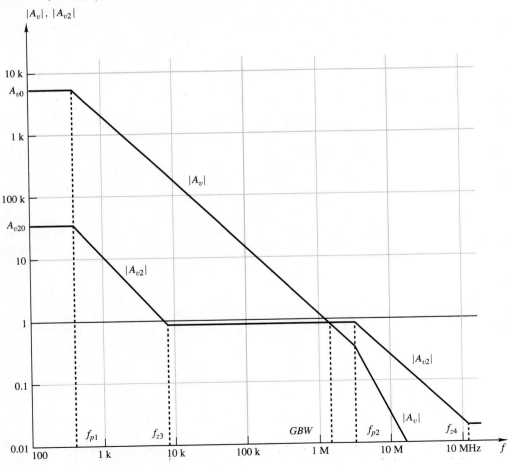

The equivalent input noise of the second stage is denoted by $\overline{dv_2}$ (as shown in Fig. 6-21). It is caused mainly by the two second-stage transistors T5 and T6. Its value is given by an expression similar to Eq. (6-54), as given by

$$\overline{dv_2^2} \approx \overline{dv_{n6}^2} + \overline{dv_{n5}^2}\left(\frac{g_{m5}}{g_{m6}}\right)^2 \tag{6-59}$$

which is 62×10^{-18} V^2/Hz or 7.88 nV$_{\text{RMS}}/\sqrt{\text{Hz}}$ (with the values of Table 6-4). Its gain to the output again is at low frequencies given by A_{v20}. The gain versus frequency characteristic of $\overline{dv_2^2}$ is very different, however, as a result of the unusual position of the voltage source $\overline{dv_2}$ in the circuit (see Fig. 6-21). Straightforward analysis of this gain A_{v2} yields

$$A_{v2} = A_{v20}\frac{\left(1 + j\dfrac{f}{f_{z3}}\right)\left(1 + j\dfrac{f}{f_{z4}}\right)}{\left(1 + j\dfrac{f}{f_{p1}}\right)\left(1 + j\dfrac{f}{f_{p2}}\right)} \tag{6-60}$$

in which f_{z3} has already been derived for the output impedance (see Fig. 6-18b) by Eq. 6-49, and

$$f_{z4} = \frac{g_{m6}}{2\pi C_{n1}}$$

All characteristic frequencies are listed in Table 6-4, as well. The characteristic of A_{v2} is also shown in Fig. 6-22a. Remember that $A_{v20} = 20.8$ and $f_{z3} = 5.3$ kHz.

It may be a surprise to see that a zero occurs in the middle of the useful frequency region., i.e., at 5.3 kHz. This zero is a result of the interaction of the output conductance g_{o24} of the first stage and the compensation capacitance C_c, which governs the frequency performance of the second stage. It does not appear in the total gain characteristic A_v, but it does appear in the gain of the second stage A_{v2}, as clearly shown in Fig. 6-22a.

The contributions of the noise sources $\overline{dv_1}$ and $\overline{dv_2}$ to the output in open loop are now shown in Fig. 6-22b. Source $\overline{dv_1}$ is simply amplified by the total gain $|A_v|$. The noise of the second stage $\overline{dv_2}$ is amplified by $|A_{v2}|$. The total open-loop output noise power $\overline{dv_{\text{out}}^2}$ (voltage squared) is the summation of both contributions given by

$$\overline{dv_{\text{out}}^2} = |A_v|^2\overline{dv_1^2} + |A_{v2}|^2\overline{dv_2^2} \tag{6-61}$$

At intermediate frequencies, almost the entire output noise arises from the first stage. At higher frequencies, however, when $|A_v|$ decreases below unity, the second-stage noise exceeds the contribution of the first stage.

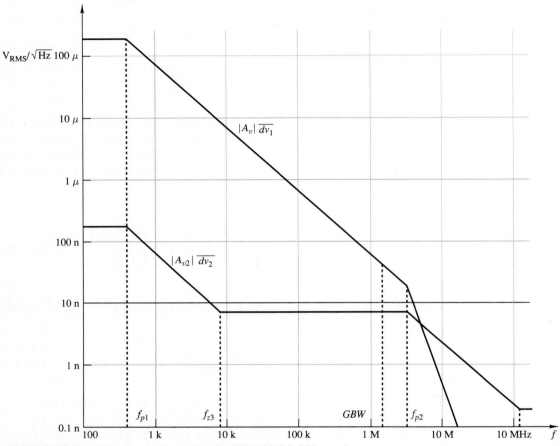

FIGURE 6-22b   Open-loop output noise of a Miller CMOS OTA.

This is clearly noticeable when we plot the equivalent input noise versus frequency, as shown in Fig. 6-22c. It is given by

$$\overline{dv_{in}^2} = \frac{\overline{dv_{out}^2}}{|A_v|^2} = \overline{dv_1^2} + \frac{|A_{v2}|^2}{|A_v|^2}\overline{dv_2^2} \tag{6-62a}$$

Substitution of A_v and A_{v2} from Eqs. (6-58) and (6-60), respectively, yields

$$\overline{dv_{in}^2} = \overline{dv_1^2} + \overline{dv_2^2}\left(1 + j\frac{f}{f_{z3}}\right)\left[\frac{\left(1 + j\dfrac{f}{f_{z4}}\right)}{\left(1 - j\dfrac{f}{f_z}\right)}\right] \tag{6-62b}$$

$$\approx \overline{dv_1^2} + \overline{dv_2^2}\left(1 + j\frac{f}{f_{z3}}\right)$$

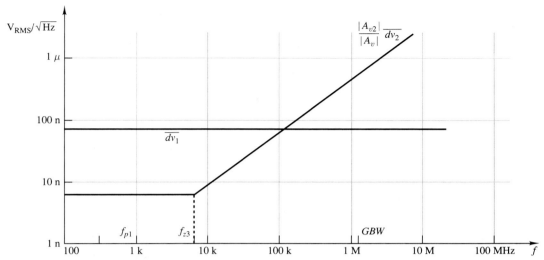

FIGURE 6-22c   Open-loop input noise of a Miller CMOS OTA.

since frequencies f_{z4} and f_z are higher than 40 MHz (see Table 6-4). Thus the zero f_{z3} causes the noise of the second stage to become dominant at higher frequencies.

When *feedback* is applied to the CMOS Miller OTA, the output noise power $\overline{dv_{out}^2}$ is reduced by $|1 - T(f)|^2$ where $T(f)$ is the loop-gain. For unity-gain feedback, the loop gain $T(f)$ equals the open-loop gain A_v, given by Eq. (6-58), such that

$$1 - T(f) = 1 + A_v(f) \approx A_{v0}\frac{\left(1 + j\dfrac{f}{GBW}\right)}{\left(1 + j\dfrac{f}{f_{p1}}\right)} \tag{6-63}$$

if we neglect all poles and zeros above 40 MHz.

The closed-loop output voltage $\overline{dv_{outc}^2}$ thus is given by

$$\overline{dv_{outc}^2} = \frac{\overline{dv_{out}^2}}{|1 + A_v(f)|^2}$$

$$\approx |A_{vc}|^2\overline{dv_1^2} + |A_{v2c}|^2\overline{dv_2^2} \tag{6-64}$$

with
$$A_{vc} = \frac{1}{\left(1 + j\dfrac{f}{GBW}\right)\left(1 + j\dfrac{f}{f_{p2}}\right)}$$

and
$$A_{v2c} = \frac{A_{v20}}{A_{v0}} \frac{\left(1 + j\dfrac{f}{f_{z3}}\right)}{\left(1 + j\dfrac{f}{GBW}\right)\left(1 + j\dfrac{f}{f_{p2}}\right)}$$

Both closed-loop gains A_{vc} and A_{v2c} are given in Fig. 6-23a. The output noise contributions $|A_{vc}|\overline{dv_1}$ and $|A_{v2c}|\overline{dv_2}$ are given in Fig. 6-23b. The total output noise voltage is given in Fig. 6-23c. It is the equivalent input noise voltage because the gain is unity. The $1/f$ noise has been added, as well.

At all intermediate frequencies the output noise is approximately equal to the first-stage input noise $\overline{dv_1}$. With increasing frequency, the loop gain decreases below unity. The influence of feedback vanishes, such that the influence of the second-stage noise increases.

It is clear from Fig. 6-23b that at high frequencies beyond the GBW, the output noise at frequencies around the gain-bandwidth can form an important contribution to the total integrated output noise. Remember that the axes are logarithmic and that noise adds up linearly. Already we can conclude that the Miller OTA can have poor high-frequency noise behavior, compared to a simple OTA, if it is not properly designed.

6-4-3   Total Integrated Output Noise

In order to obtain the total integrated noise, the integral of the noise voltage power must be carried out over all frequencies (see Chap. 3). Carrying out integrals over expressions such as that in Eq. 6-64 is important, and therefore we will take some approximations. We will take all noise contributions separately and assume that we must deal only with first-order expressions.

The total integrated output noise contains three contributions. (see Fig. 6-23c). They are

- the $1/f$ noise at low frequencies up to corner frequency f_c
- the white noise $\overline{dv_1}$ up to frequencies around GBW
- the white noise $\overline{dv_2}$ at frequencies higher than f_{p2}.

The first integrated noise component is given by

$$v_{of}^2 = \int_{f_1}^{f_c} \overline{dv_{nief}^2} \frac{df}{f} \tag{6-65a}$$

in which $\overline{dv_{nief}^2}$ is derived from Eq. (6-56), and in which the lower integration boundary is arbitrarily taken to be $f_1 = 1$ Hz. This can be worked out to

$$v_{of} = \sqrt{\overline{dv_{nief}^2} \ln(f_c)} \tag{6-65b}$$

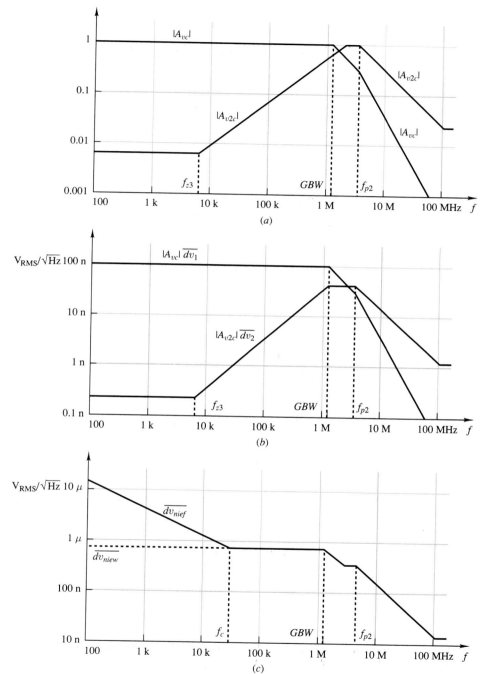

FIGURE 6-23   (a) Closed-loop gains of Miller CMOS OTA. (b) Closed-loop output noise contributions. (c) Equivalent input noise voltage of a Miller OTA.

For $\overline{dv_{nief}} = 20\ \mu V_{RMS}/\sqrt{Hz}$ and $f_c = 57$ kHz, this first noise component is $v_{of} = 68\ \mu V_{RMS}$. This is quite a large value.

The second noise source extends from zero to GBW, with a first-order roll off. Thus the noise bandwidth is $GBW\,(\pi/2)$. Its value is then given by

$$v_{ow2} = \sqrt{\overline{dv_{niew}^2}\,GBW\,\frac{\pi}{2}} \tag{6-65c}$$

in which $\overline{dv_{niew}^2}$ is obtained from Eq. (6-56). For $\overline{dv_{niew}} = 84\ nV_{RMS}/Hz$ and $GBW = 1.19$ MHz, this second noise component is $v_{ow2} = 114\ \mu V_{RMS}$. Thus it is larger than the $1/f$ noise component, but not by much.

The third noise source $\overline{dv_2^2}$ has been calculated in Eq. (6-59). As an approximation, it is taken from zero to f_{p2}, with a first-order roll off at f_{p2}. Its value is then given by

$$v_{ow3} = \sqrt{\overline{dv_2^2}\,f_{p2}\,\frac{\pi}{2}} \tag{6-65d}$$

For $f_{p2} = 3.8$ MHz, this third noise component is $v_{ow3} = 19.2\ \mu V_{RMS}$. This is low because $\overline{dv_2^2}$ is low. It is not negligible, however.

The white noise of the first stage is clearly dominant, closely followed by the $1/f$ noise of the first stage. The total integrated output noise is $\sqrt{114^2 + 68^2 + 19^2} = 134\ \mu V_{RMS}$, if the $1/f$ noise is taken from 1 Hz.

If a different design optimization is carried out to reduce the $1/f$ noise (large WL input devices), the white noise can be made more dominant. In this case, the expression of v_{ow2} can be rewritten by means of Eqs. (6-56), (6-25a), and (6-65c), which yields

$$v_{ow2} = \sqrt{y_w\,\frac{2}{3}\,\frac{kT}{C_c}} \tag{6-66}$$

which again is $114\ \mu V_{RMS}$.

As has already been explained in Chap. 1, the total integrated noise of a first-order system is independent of the gain or transconductance in exactly the same way as the integrated noise of a resistor is independent of its value. The total noise depends on the capacitance of the first-order time constant, which is the compensation capacitance C_c for the CMOS Miller OTA.

Example 6-6

After a a CMOS OTA and a bipolar OTA have been optimized for noise, let us compare their noise performance (the integrated white noise). Both have a $GBW = 1$ MHz; the CMOS OTA has $C_c = 1$ pF, whereas the bipolar one has $C_c = 2$ pF. Which OTA performs better?

Solution. Both have equal integrated white noise. In fact, y_w is a factor of two smaller in the MOST (after optimization), offset by the C_c, which is two times lower.

6-5 MATCHING CHARACTERISTICS

Matching components, such as two resistors, two capacitances, two transistors, etc., is one of the most important design features in analog circuit design. Until now the input transistors of a differential pair have been assumed to be exactly identical. In practice, however, this is never the case. Because of photolithography, etching, etc., the characteristics of two matched transistors are slightly different. The larger the devices, the less of a role these differences play.

These small differences do not influence the main specifications, such as the gain and *GBW*. Thus, other characteristics must be added to quantify these matching properties. They are, for example, offset and *CMRR*, defined in Chap. 5. These characteristics are calculated in this section for CMOS differential stages. Offset and *CMRR* are also calculated for the Miller CMOS OTA. Guidelines are given for design of low mismatching. Finally, these characteristics are calculated for bipolar differential stages, as well.

6-5-1 Transistor Mismatch Model

Definition   The most important parameters of an nMOST at DC and low frequencies are V_T, K, and γ. Therefore, differences (deltas) must be introduced for all three parameters. The case of a simple differential pair with resistive loads (see Fig. 6-24) is discussed first. The deltas are:

- ΔV_T: difference in threshold voltage between two matched transistors is a result of differences in oxide thickness, substrate doping, etc. Its value will be calculated later, but is typically 10 to 25 mV.

- ΔK: difference in gain factor $K = K_n' \cdot W/L$; is a result of differences in oxide thickness and mobility; its typical value can be as high as 0.1 or 10 percent.

- $\Delta \gamma$: difference in body factor is a result of differences in oxide thickness, the substrate doping, etc., and is typically as high as 0.05 or 5 percent.

Finally, the load resistances can be slightly different as well: ΔR_L is the difference in R_L. Typical values depend on the size (see Chap. 1). When we need a value for an example, we will use $\Delta R_L/R_L = 5$ percent.

These deltas can occur between two adjacent devices in the same circuit layout: between two devices with the same function in two adjacent chips on the same wafer, between two wafers, and between two batches. These deltas can be classified into two categories.

The latter are a result of *global* variations, which occur over a wafer or from batch to batch. The second category is a result of *local* variations, which refer to adjacent components on the same wafer and even in the same circuit. The first category

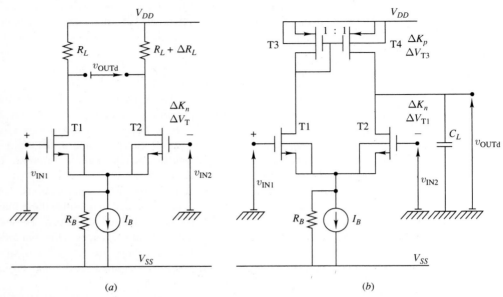

FIGURE 6-24   Differential pairs with mismatched components.

influences absolute values, whereas the other influences matching. We are interested mainly in the latter. Absolute values are difficult to realize. If they are required in precision analog design, we must to use laser trimming and other trimming techniques.

These deltas occur in a *statistical* way (see Chap. 3). They have the value of a variance, which is defined as follows. A variable x with randomly distributed values around its average or mean x_a, has a standard deviation σ_x, such that 90 percent of its values occur within $\pm 3\sigma_x$. The variance is then σ_x^2 and $\Delta x = \sigma_x$. They are now derived from experimental data for a MOST.

Threshold Voltage Mismatch V_T.   The technological parameters that contribute most to deviations in V_T are the oxide thickness and the bulk doping level. In modern VLSI MOS processing, the oxide thickness is reproducible. As a result, its contribution to ΔV_T can be ignored. Variations in bulk doping level are the main source of mismatch ΔV_T. However, bulk doping level refers both to the original bulk doping of the wafer and to subsequent modifications by means of ion-implants. The more ion-implants, the more deviation occurs.

Experiments (Lakshmikumar et al. 1989, Pelgrom et al. 1988) have shown that the variance σ_{VT} or mismatch ΔV_T is described by

$$\frac{\sigma_{V_T}}{V_T} = \frac{\sigma_{0V_T}}{V_T \sqrt{WL}} \tag{6-67}$$

in which $\overline{V_T}$ is the average or mean value of V_T and $\sigma_{0V_T} \approx 0.016$ V $\cdot \mu$m for an nMOST and about 50 percent more for a pMOST in a standard 3 μm CMOS n-well process. Note that the dimension of σ_{0V_T} is V$\cdot\mu$m, whereas the dimension for σ_{V_T} is V.

As expected for local variations, the larger the size, the smaller the variance or mismatch ΔV_T. The variance is larger for a pMOST because of its higher number of threshold voltage adjustments with ion-implantation.

Finally, note that ΔV_T is normally expressed in mV's; we do not use $\Delta V_T / V_T$ in percentages.

Gain Factor Mismatch K   Gain factor K includes both the K' parameter ($\approx \mu C_{ox}$) and the gate dimensions W and L. Its variance can be written as

$$\frac{\sigma_K}{\overline{K}} = \left[\frac{\sigma_{K0}^2}{WL} + \sigma_{KWL}^2 \left(\frac{1}{W^2} + \frac{1}{L^2} \right) \right]^{0.5} \tag{6-68}$$

in which $\overline{K}$ is the average value of K, and in which $\sigma_{K0} \approx 0.0056$ μm and $\sigma_{KWL} \approx 0.02$ μm for an nMOST; both are about 50 percent larger for a pMOST. Even for larger devices, the first term with σ_{K0} is usually negligible. Variations in K thus are due mainly to photolithographic variations of W and L and to much less extent variations in mobility (or K'_n) or in oxide thickness.

In principle the deviation in mobility (in K') depends on deviations in the bulk doping level and thus could be correlated to ΔV_T. This effect is small, however. Also, both $\Delta K'$ and ΔV_T could be correlated through variation in oxide thickness. As previously stated, the oxide thickness can be made homogeneous. As a result, ΔV_T and ΔK are assumed not to be correlated.

Body Factor Mismatch γ   This factor includes mainly the bulk doping level and oxide thickness. As stated before, the variation in bulk doping level is most important. It can be written as given by

$$\frac{\sigma_\gamma}{\overline{\gamma}} = \frac{\sigma_{\gamma 0}}{\sqrt{WL}} \tag{6-69}$$

in which $\overline{\gamma}$ is the average value of γ and in which $\sigma_{\gamma 0} \approx 0.016$ μm for an nMOST and 0.012 μm for a pMOST. Again, note that σ_γ has $\sqrt{\text{V}}$ as dimensions whereas $\sigma_{\gamma 0}$ has μm.

However, since the sources are connected to the respective substrates in all applications in this section, the body factor mismatch can be ignored. Thus, $\Delta \gamma$ will no longer be of concern.

6-5-2 Offset Voltage Definition

In general, when both input voltages of an open-loop amplifier are connected to ground, the output voltage is not zero. The offset voltage V_{os} is, per definition, the input voltage required to force the output to zero volts (see Chap. 5).

This offset voltage can be caused by random mismatches, such as ΔR_L, ΔV_T, and ΔK in Fig 6-24a. It is then called *random offset*. The offset voltage also can be caused by asymmetry in circuit configuration, as is the case in Fig. 6-24b. Then it is called *systematic offset*. Random offset is calculated first.

Random Offset   It is not difficult to calculate the relationship between the Δ's in Fig. 6-24 and the offset voltage V_{os}, because V_{os} is a small signal. Its effect thus can be calculated by use of the small-signal parameters in a small-signal model.

No Δ's   If no Δ's are present, application of the differential input voltage V_{os} gives a differential output voltage V_{odos}, which is given by (see Fig. 6-24)

$$V_{odos} = g_m R_L V_{os} \tag{6-70}$$

The effects of the Δ's now can be calculated as follows.

Effect ΔR_L: Both inputs are connected to ground. If only ΔR_L is present, the current I_B still is equally divided over both transistors. The output voltage with respect to V_{DD} at the drain of transistor T1 thus is $-R_L I_B/2$. On the drain of transistor T2, the output voltage is $-(R_L + \Delta R_L)I_B/2$. This difference causes an output voltage V_{odR}, which is given by

$$V_{odR} = \Delta R_L \frac{I_B}{2} \tag{6-71a}$$

Effect ΔV_T: Both inputs again are connected to ground. If only ΔV_T is present, the drain currents through both transistors will be slightly different. The difference is $\Delta I_{DS} = g_m \Delta V_T$. Since ΔV_T can be regarded as a small-signal input voltage, it will be amplified to the output by small-signal gain $g_m R_L$. The output voltage V_{odT} thus is given by

$$V_{odT} = g_m R_L \Delta V_T \tag{6-71b}$$

Effect ΔK: Both inputs are connected to ground. The drain currents through both transistors again are slightly different. The difference is now $\Delta I_{DS} = I_{DS}\Delta K/K$. Since each transistor carries about $I_B/2$, this difference in current is $I_B/2 \Delta K/K$. The output voltage V_{odK} is then given by

$$V_{odK} = \frac{R_L I_B}{2} \frac{\Delta K}{K} \tag{6-71c}$$

Total Random Offset: The total random offset V_{osr} can be found by equation of Eq. (6-70) to the sum of Eqs. (6-71a and b). It provides the random offset voltage V_{osr} that would be present if all three Δ's were taken into account simultaneously.

After division by the gain $g_m R_L$, this yields

$$V_{osr} = \frac{I_B}{2} \frac{1}{g_m} \left(\frac{\Delta R_L}{R_L} \right) + \Delta V_T + \frac{I_B}{2 g_m} \left(\frac{\Delta K}{K} \right) \tag{6-72}$$

In strong inversion, $g_m = 2 I_{DS}/(V_{GS} - V_T) = I_B/(V_{GS} - V_T)$. In this case Eq. (6-72) can be converted into

$$V_{osr} = \Delta V_T + \frac{V_{GS} - V_T}{2} \left(\frac{\Delta R_L}{R_L} + \frac{\Delta K}{K} \right) \tag{6-73}$$

Note that all deltas have arbitrary signs $+$ or $-$. Their effects thus are added statistically. This means that their absolute values are only added in rare cases.

Also, the influence of ΔR_L and ΔK becomes smaller by biasing the transistors at smaller values of $V_{GS} - V_T$. In this case, the transistors operate closer to weak inversion. ΔV_T is then the main factor influencing V_{osr}.

For a given current, however, small values of $V_{GS} - V_T$ lead to large values of W/L. As a conclusion, mismatch depends on deltas and on biasing points, as well. One design rule has already become apparent; low offset can be achieved by using low values of $V_{GS} - V_T$. For a given current, this means that the W/L ratios must be large (since $W/L = I_{DS}/K'(V_{GS} - V_T)^2$).

Example 6-7

Calculate the maximum value of V_{osr} for $\Delta V_T = 20$ mV; relative errors in R_L and K are 5 percent and 10 percent, respectively. The transistors are biased at $V_{GS} - V_T = 0.5$ V. Compare with the result if $V_{GS} - V_T = 0.2$ V.

Solution. The maximum value of $V_{osr} = 20 + 250(0.15) = 57.5$ mV for $V_{GS} - V_T = 0.5$ V and 35 mV for $V_{GS} - V_T = 0.2$ V.

6-5-3 Mismatch Effects on a Current Mirror

In the previous section, mismatch in a differential pair was shown to generate a random offset voltage, which can be reduced by biasing the transistors at low $V_{GS} - V_T$. For a fixed current this means that the W/L must be large. A current mirror uses two matched transistors, as well. The question arises whether or not the same design rules apply to a current source.

Mismatch is indicated again by ΔV_T and ΔK (see Fig. 6-25a). In this case, however, we are interested to know the relative variation in the output current $\Delta I_{OUT}/I_{OUT}$ as a result of the deltas.

The variation in current ΔI_{OUT} is easily calculated as in the previous section. It is given by

$$\Delta I_{OUT} = g_m \Delta V_T + \frac{\Delta K}{K} I_{OUT} \tag{6-74}$$

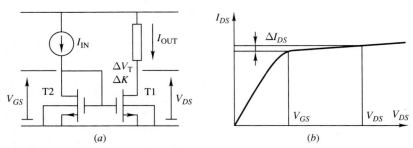

FIGURE 6-25   Current mismatch as a result of different values in V_{DS}.

Since in strong inversion $g_m = 2I_{\text{OUT}}/(V_{GS} - V_T)$, the ratio $\Delta I_{\text{OUT}}/I_{\text{OUT}}$ becomes

$$\frac{\Delta I_{\text{OUT}}}{I_{\text{OUT}}} = \frac{2}{V_{GS} - V_T}\Delta V_T + \frac{\Delta K}{K} \qquad (6\text{-}75)$$

This is the *random* current variation. It can be made small by biasing the transistors at large values of $V_{GS} - V_T$. Hence, they must operate deeply in strong inversion. This also means that for a given current, transistors must be used with small W/L ratios. The conclusions are thus exactly the opposite as for a differential pair.

There is also a *systematic* current variation, however. Both transistors in Fig. 6-25a may have different values of V_{DS}. As a results, the currents are slightly different (see Fig. 6-25b) because of the slope of the $I_{DS} - V_{DS}$ curve (Early effect). The relative difference in current is given by

$$\frac{\Delta I_{DSs}}{I_{DS}} = \frac{V_{DS} - V_{GS}}{L V_E} \qquad (6\text{-}76)$$

in which V_E is the Early voltage per unit gate length (see Chap. 1). The voltage difference $V_{DS} - V_{GS}$ depends on the DC output voltage, which is set by a feedback network or the subsequent circuit. Thus it is a fixed quantity that depends on design, not a random quantity. Therefore, $\Delta I_{DSs}/I_{DS}$ is called a systematic error. Actually, this source of systematic error is the most important one for DC performance in analog circuits, as will be illustrated later.

Note that this error is a systematic offset component caused by asymmetry in DC biasing. Thus it is only present in DC performance evaluation. In first-order it is not detectable in small-signal performance. Random errors, on the other hand, play a role in both DC and AC performance.

6-5-4   Differential Stage With Active Load

A differential stage with an active load is actually a combination of a single differential pair and a current mirror (see Fig. 6-24b). Both random and systematic errors thus will occur. The total *random offset voltage* can be written as

$$V_{osr} = V_{os12} + \frac{\Delta I_{34}}{g_{m1}} \tag{6-77}$$

in which V_{os12} is offset due to mismatch between transistors T1 and T2, and ΔI_{34} is offset due to mismatch between transistors T3 and T4. After filling in V_{os12} and ΔI_{34} from Eqs. (6-73) and (6-75), respectively, this expression becomes

$$V_{osr} = V_{os12} + \frac{I_{DS1}}{g_{m1}} \left[\left(\frac{\Delta K_{34}}{K_{34}} \right) + \frac{2 \Delta V_{T34}}{V_{GS3} - V_T} \right] \tag{6-78a}$$

or since $g_m = 2I_{DS}/(V_{GS} - V_T)$, in strong inversion,

$$V_{osr} = V_{os12} + \frac{V_{GS1} - V_T}{V_{GS3} - V_T} \Delta V_{T34} + \frac{V_{GS1} - V_T}{2} \left(\frac{\Delta K_{12}}{K_{12}} \right) + \frac{V_{GS3} - V_T}{2} \left(\frac{\Delta K_{34}}{K_{34}} \right) \tag{6-78b}$$

Also, a *DC systematic offset component* V_{oss} is caused by asymmetry in the DC biasing. Systematic offset occurs as soon as the output voltage differs from the DC drain voltage of T1 and T3 (see Fig. 6-24b), which we denote by V_{D13}. This difference in voltage is thus $V_{OUTd} - V_{D13}$. The currents through T3 and T4 are then different, as is the current through T1 and T2. The systematic offset V_{oss} is derived from Eq. (6-76) and can be written as

$$V_{oss} = \frac{V_{OUTd} - V_{D13}}{2} \left(\frac{V_{GS3} - V_{Tp}}{L_4 V_{Ep}} - \frac{V_{GS1} - V_{Tn}}{L_2 V_{En}} \right) \tag{6-79}$$

Note that for the first time, a difference in absolute value is taken into account between the V_T of an *n*MOST and the V_T of a *p*MOST.

The same conclusions thus can be drawn as that of a simple differential pair. The offset can be made small by:

* reducing the systematic error as much as possible (by making node voltages $V_{OUTd} = V_{D13}$
* biasing the input transistors at low values of $V_{GS} - V_T$, i.e., close to weak inversion, which means that all W/L ratios must be made large for a given current.
* biasing the load transistor at an intermediate value such that ΔK_{34} dominates for higher values of $V_{GS3} - V_T$, and ΔV_T dominates for lower values of $V_{GS3} - V_T$.

It can be concluded that in a proper design, ΔV_T between two matched transistors is the main source of concern. Therefore, techniques will be described to reduce ΔV_T by means of layout manipulation. In Chap. 8, techniques will be given to reduce the effects of offset by means of clever circuit design.

However, besides the random offset V_{osr} and the DC systematic offset V_{oss} caused by asymmetry in DC biasing, there is a third source of offset. It is the systematic offset V_{oscm} caused by the *common-mode input voltage drive*.

Let us denote the common-mode or average input voltage of the differential stage (see Fig. 6-24*b*) by v_{Icm}, which is given by $(v_{IN1} + v_{IN2})/2$. The purest common-mode drive is realized by connecting both gates to an input voltage source v_{Icm}. A current then flows through resistance R_B, which is given by $i_{cm} = v_{Icm}/R_B$ (provided $1/g_{m1} \ll R_B$). Half this current i_{cm} then flows through transistor T1 and T2.

The effect of this current can be calculated from the equivalent circuit of Fig. 6-24*b*, which is simplified to that given in Fig. 6-26. In this equivalent circuit, both transistors T1 and T2 are represented by the independent current sources with equal current $i_{cm}/2$. Load transistor T3 is represented by its small-signal resistance $1/g_{m3}$; transistor T4 acts as an ideal current-controlled current source with the same current i as through T3. The output current is taken as output signal. It flows through r_{o2} in parallel with r_{o4}, which is in parallel with the load capacitance C_L.

First we will carry out the calculations for intermediate frequencies, where the load capacitance acts as a short circuit to ground, shorting out the output resistances r_{o2} and r_{o4}. Thus, the output current flows through this short to ground.

The output current i_{out}, caused by current i_{cm}, is obtained by straightforward calculation to be

$$\frac{i_{\text{out}}}{i_{cm}/2} = \frac{1/g_{m3}}{r_{o1} + 1/g_{m3}} \approx \frac{1}{g_{m3}r_{o1}} \tag{6-80}$$

or, after substitution of i_{cm} by v_{Icm}, this becomes

$$\frac{i_{\text{out}}}{v_{Icm}} = \frac{1}{2R_B} \frac{1}{g_{m3}r_{o1}} \tag{6-81}$$

The differential input voltage, which is required to compensate for this output current i_{out}, is simply i_{out}/g_{m1}. This input voltage is the systematic offset v_{oscm} caused by a

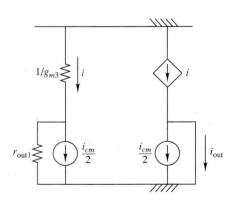

FIGURE 6-26   Equivalent circuit of differential pair for common-mode drive

common-mode input voltage drive v_{Icm}, given by

$$v_{oscm} = \frac{i_{out}}{g_{m1}} = \frac{v_{Icm}}{2g_{m1}R_B} \frac{1}{g_{m3}r_{o1}} \tag{6-82}$$

Since both $g_{m1}R_B$ and $g_{m3}r_{o1}$ usually have large values, v_{oscm} is quite small; it only plays a role if v_{Icm} is large.

At very low frequencies and DC, the output current flows through r_{o2} (r_{o4} is still taken to ∞), which causes a large output voltage. The differential voltage gain is then large, as well. It is easy to verify (see exercises) that the resulting equation is exactly the same as that given by Eq. (6-82). We must keep in mind, however, that a DC voltage v_{ICM} is always applied. In fact, it is the common reference point for the input voltages. Normally, this is ground and thus $v_{ICM} = V_{SS}$ or V_{DD}. There is always a DC systematic offset V_{oscm} caused by the input gate biasing.

If the differential stage has a purely differential drive, i.e., if the input voltages are the same in amplitude but with opposite phase, then the AC components of v_{Icm} and v_{oscm} are zero, but not the DC ones.

Example 6-8

For a simple CMOS OTA with $I_B = 20$ μA, $V_{DD,SS} = \pm 2.5$ V, $C_L = 10$ pF, $(W/L)_1 = 10$ and $(W/L)_4 = 1$ with $L_1 = L_3 = 5$ μm; also: $V_{Tn} = V_{Tp} = 1$ V, $K_n' = 30$ μA/V, $K_p' = 15$ μA, $V_{Ep} = 8$ V/μm, and $V_{En} = 5$ V/μm. We assume the DC input and output voltage at 0 V. The deltas are $\Delta V_T = 5$ mV, $\Delta K/K = \Delta R_L/R_L = 0.1$, and finally, $R_B = 2$ MΩ. Find all relevant offset voltages if we assume that they all add up (the extreme worst case).

Solution. Since I_{DS} and $(W/L)_1$ is known, we can calculate $V_{GS1} - V_T = \sqrt{I_{DS}/K_n'(W/L)}_1 = 0.18$ V and $g_{m1} = 2I_{DS}/(V_{GS1} - V_T) = 111$ μS; similarly, for the load transistor, $V_{GS3} - V_T = 0.82$ V and $g_{m3} = 24.5$ μS. For the input devices Eq. (6-73) yields $V_{os12} = 5 + 18 = 23$ mV. Eq. (6-79) then gives $V_{osr} = 23 + 1.1 + 9 + 40.8 = 77$ mV. The difference in DC output voltage is $2.5 - 1.82 = 0.68$ V. Therefore, Eq. (6-78b) gives $V_{oss} = 0.34(20.8 - 7.3) = 4.4$ mV. Finally the input voltage is at 0 V. The common-mode voltage V_{Icm} is thus 2.5 V and Eq. (6-82) gives $V_{oscm} = 2.5/2.7 \times 10^4 = 0.09$ mV.

The largest terms are the random offset of the input devices and especially of the active load.

6-5-5 Offset Drift

The offset voltage V_{os} can change versus time and temperature (also versus stress gradients, radiation, etc.). Both are called *drift*. The drift versus time is attributed to charge changes in the oxide due to chemical reactions occurring in time. Since they can be controlled by appropriate processing, we will disregard them in this text.

The change of offset versus temperature for a differential pair with active load depends on the changes of ΔV_T, and of ΔK versus temperature. The change of ΔV_T versus temperature is quite small, usually a few mV per °C.

The variation of ΔK versus temperature is considerably larger because it includes mobility. Hence, the ratio $\Delta K/K$ depends on temperature as well. As a result, the drift of the offset voltage versus temperature $\Delta V_{os}/\Delta T$ is not negligible at all. We will discuss this topic further after we have examined the bipolar transistor with respect to offset and drift.

6-5-6 CMRR

The common-mode rejection ratio of a differential pair has been defined in Chap. 3. It is the ratio of A_{dd}/A_{dc}, in which A_{dd} is the differential output voltage for a pure differential drive and A_{dc} is the differential output voltage for a pure common-mode drive. For the simple differential pair of Fig. 6-24a, the gain $A_{dd} = A_{v0} = g_{m1}r_{024}$.

The gain A_{dc} is easily calculated, provided both inputs are connected to the common-mode input voltage v_{ic}, as shown in Fig. 6-27. Both transistors are then operating as two source followers in parallel. For an ideal current source $I_B(R_B = \infty)$, no current can ever flow as a result of the input voltage v_{ic}. Hence, the resulting output voltage v_{od} is zero and $A_{dc} = 0$, and, as a result, $CMRR = \infty$.

However, a current source is never ideal. Its output resistance is never infinitely high. Its output resistance is represented by R_B in parallel with the current source (see Fig. 6-27). Also, a capacitance C_B is present. This capacitance is ignored. It will be included in Sec. 6-5-9.

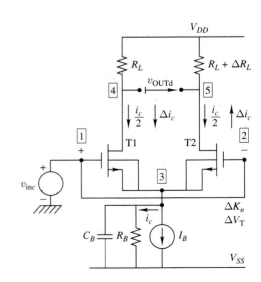

FIGURE 6-27 Circuit for calculation of A_{dc}

The input voltage source v_{ic} causes a current to flow in both transistors, about $i_c/2$ or $v_{ic}/2R_B$. Both currents flow through the loads R_L, as well. They cause an output voltage v_{od} as soon as mismatches occur.

Mismatch ΔR_L   For a difference in R_L only, the output is calculated as before. It is given by $v_{odR} = i_c \Delta R_L/2$, whence

$$v_{odR} = \Delta R_L \frac{i_c}{2} = \frac{\Delta R_L}{R_B} \frac{v_{ic}}{2} \tag{6-83a}$$

Mismatch ΔV_T   Only in V_T, the currents caused by v_{ic} that flow in T1 and T2 are slightly different. This difference Δi_c causes an output voltage of $v_{odT} = 2R_L \Delta i_c$.

This current Δi_c is a circular current flowing through only T1, T2, and both load resistances (Fig. 6-27). Thus it is given by $\Delta i_c = g_{m1} \Delta V_T/2$ with $g_{m1} = 2I_{DS1}/(V_{GS1} - V_T)$. As a result

$$v_{odT} = g_{m1} R_L \Delta V_T = \frac{R_L}{R_B} \frac{\Delta V_T}{V_{GS} - V_T} v_{ic} \tag{6-83b}$$

Mismatch ΔK_n   For ΔK_n only a circular current flows, again given by

$$\Delta i_c = \frac{\Delta K_n}{K_n} \frac{i_c}{2}$$

As a result

$$v_{odK} = \frac{R_L}{2} \frac{\Delta K_n}{K_n} \frac{v_{ic}}{R_B} \tag{6-83c}$$

The total gain A_{dc} is then given by

$$A_{dc} = \frac{\Sigma v_{od}}{v_{ic}} = \frac{1}{2} \frac{R_L}{R_B} \left(\frac{2\Delta V_T}{V_{Gs} - V_T} + \frac{\Delta R_L}{R_L} + \frac{\Delta K_n}{K_n} \right) \tag{6-84}$$

and the corresponding random $CMRR_r$ thus is given by

$$CMRR_r = \frac{A_{dd}}{A_{dc}} = \frac{2g_{m1} R_B}{\dfrac{2\Delta V_T}{V_{GS} - V_T} + \dfrac{\Delta R_L}{R_L} + \dfrac{\Delta K_n}{K_n}} \tag{6-85}$$

Note that the $CMRR_r$ can be improved by increasing the input transconductance g_{m1}, and by taking a current source with high output resistance R_B.

Example 6-9

What is the random offset V_{osr} and the $CMRR_r$ for the input devices of the previous Example 6-8 if all deltas add up?

Solution. In this Example, $g_{m1} = 111$ μS and its $V_{GS1} - V_T = 0.18$ V. The denominator of the Eq. (6-85) thus is 0.255. With $R_B = 2$ MΩ, The numerator is 444 such that $CMRR_r = 1741$, or 65 dB, if the effects of all deltas add up. This is a typical value for MOST differential stages and op amps. Remember, this $CMRR_r$ is a minimum or worst-case value. The offset itself is $0.255 \times (V_{GS1} - V_T)/2$ or 90 mV, which is 23 mV (see Eq. 6-73).

6-5-7   Relation Between Random V_{osr} and $CMRR_r$

Actually, both $CMRR_r$ (in Eq. (6-95)) and random V_{osr} (in Eq. (6-73)) contain the same deltas. Indeed, it is the asymmetry in the differential amplifier that causes a nonzero value of V_{os} and a finite value of $CMRR$.

We then have two different characteristics, described by the same sources of asymmetry. Let us combine them by taking the product of both.

This yields

$$V_{osr} \cdot CMRR_r = \frac{V_{GS1} - V_T}{2} (2g_{m1}R_B) \qquad (6\text{-}86a)$$

or, since $g_{m1} = I_B/(V_{GS1} - V_T)$, we have

$$V_{osr} \cdot CMRR_r = I_B R_B \qquad (6\text{-}86b)$$

However, for a single-transistor current source I_B, the output resistance is simply the Early resistance (see Chap. 1) given by $R_B = V_{En}L_B/I_B$. Hence,

$$V_{osr} \cdot CMRR_r = V_{En}L_B \qquad (6\text{-}87)$$

This result is remarkable. It shows that random offset and $CMRR_r$ are unambiguously connected. For example, for $V_{En} = 4.5$ V and a channel length of 5 μm, the early voltage of the current source transistor is then 22.5 V. When the random offset V_{osr} is 10 mV, then $CMRR_r = 2250$ or 67 dB.

Higher $CMRR_r$ can be reached only if V_{osr} can be made smaller, and vice versa. Also, techniques to reduce V_{osr} will automatically increase $CMRR_r$. For example, laser trimming R_L to an V_{osr} of 100 μV, directly generates 107 dB $CMRR_r$.

This remarkable relationship only holds for random offset. However, a differential pair with active load also generates a DC systematic offset if it is not symmetrically biased. The question arises whether or not there is a similar relationship for systematic offset.

6-5-8   Relation Between Systematic V_{oss} and $CMRR_s$

In the case of DC systematic offset, a DC difference in output voltage is present. This difference is divided by the small-signal gain to give rise to the systematic offset. However, the small-signal model is not affected by it. The values of the parameters of the small-signal model are not changed because of the presence of DC systematic offset. Hence, the calculation of the gains A_{dd} and A_{dc} are not affected by DC systematic offset. As a result, a systematic $CMRR_s$ cannot be derived in this way.

Obviously, there is a relationship between the systematic offset v_{oscm}, as a result of a common-mode drive, and the $CMRR_s$. The $CMRR_s$ can be rewritten as given by

$$CMRR_s = \frac{A_{dd}}{A_{dc}} = \frac{v_{OUT}/v_{oss}}{v_{OUT}/v_{ic}} = \frac{i_{OUT}/v_{oss}}{i_{OUT}/v_{ic}} = \frac{v_{ic}}{v_{oss}} \qquad (6\text{-}88)$$

in which i_{OUT} is the output current in the capacitive load in parallel with $r_{o2}//r_{o4}$. (see Fig. 6-24b). It is the output current obtained by the amplification of v_{oss} with factor A_{dd}. It is also the output current obtained by the amplification of the common-mode voltage v_{ic}, with factor A_{dc}. By definition, the currents are the same in both cases. In other words, v_{ic} is the common-mode input voltage required to compensate for the effect of offset voltage v_{oss}.

The relation between the $CMRR_s$ and the systematic offset v_{oss} is obtained by Eq. (6-82) and Eq. (6-88), as given by

$$CMRR_s = \frac{v_{Icm}}{v_{oscm}} = 2g_{m1}R_B g_{m3}r_{o1} \qquad (6\text{-}89)$$

As a result, we have two expressions for the $CMRR$, one that depends on random offset $CMRR_r$, given by Eq. (6-85), and one given by systematic offset caused by a common-mode input drive $CMRR_s$, given by Eq. (6-89). The resulting $CMRR$ is then given by

$$\frac{1}{CMRR} = \frac{1}{CMRR_r} + \frac{1}{CMRR_s} \qquad (6\text{-}90)$$

As a result, the smaller $CMRR$ is always dominant.

Example 6-10

What is the systematic $CMRR_s$ for the input devices of the previous Example 6-8? Compare the result with the random $CMRR_r$ of Example 6-9.

Solution. From Example 6-8 we take $CMRR_s = 2.7 \times 10^4$, or 88 dB. Since $CMRR_r = 1741$ or 65 dB, we obtain a total $CMRR$ of about 64 dB. The random $CMRR_r$ thus is dominant.

This leads to the interesting conclusion that the total of the $CMRR$ depends on the way it is calculated or measured. From a SPICE run, or a hand calculation (in which no deltas are introduced), only values for the systematic offset v_{oss} and $CMRR_s$ can be obtained. The DC systematic offset is obtained as the DC input voltage to be applied to create the output current or voltage zero. Both gains A_{dd} and A_{dc} can be obtained separately from SPICE. Their ratio is the $CMRR_s$. Remember that for a purely differential drive, no AC current flows in the current source such that $CMRR_s = \infty$. This is one method to separate the effects of random and systematic offset at intermediate frequencies.

The random offset and $CMRR_r$ can only be evaluated by introduction of ΔV_T, $\Delta R_L/R_L$, or $\Delta K/K$.

From measurements, total values of offset and $CMRR$ are obtained, which are combinations of the two other ones.

6-5-9 *CMRR* Versus Frequency

Random $CMRR$ and systematic $CMRR$ are only present if current is flowing in R_B (see Fig. 6-27). Thus, they are influenced by the capacitances at the circuit nodes. Two of the capacitances play an important role: they are the capacitance across R_B denoted by C_B and the capacitance across transistor T3. The latter causes the nondominant pole f_{nd} in the A_{dd} characteristic. The first, however, causes a zero in the A_{dc} characteristic.

The zero due to C_B is given by

$$f_B = \frac{1}{2\pi R_B C_B} \tag{6-91}$$

Both gains are shown in Fig. 6-28. The dominant pole f_d occurs in both characteristics. The resulting $CMRR$ is then easily obtained by division of A_{dd} by A_{dc}. It is also shown in Fig. 6-28. The -3 dB frequency for the $CMRR$ thus is also f_B. It is vitally important to realize current sources with very low output capacitance C_B, if high $CMRR$ is required at high frequencies.

6-5-10   Offset and *CMRR* of the Miller CMOS OTA

For the Miller CMOS OTA, the DC systematic offset caused by DC biasing is calculated first. It is easily obtained from Table 6-7, with the DC voltage levels at all nodes. The difference in voltage between nodes 1 and 2 of the first stage is only 30 mV. Since the gain A_{v10} of the first stage is about 250 (see Eq. (6-18)), the DC systematic offset is only about $30/250 \approx 0.1$ mV. It thus is negligible.

In order to find the *random offset*, asymmetry must be introduced. Assume, for example, that the difference between the transconductances of the input transistors is a mere 1 percent. This can be caused by a relative error of 1 percent in K or by a difference of a few mV's in V_T, or by a combination of both.

In the case of only a relative error of 1 percent in K, the random offset is easily obtained from Eq. 6-73 to be $V_{osr} = 1.7$ mV, since for the input transistors the values of $V_{GS} - V_T = 0.34$ V, as given in Table 6-2.

The corresponding $CMRR_r$ then can be obtained from Eq. (6-85), provided the output resistance R_B is known for the current source transistor T7. This value is again given by Table 6-2 to be $R_B = 77$ MΩ. Since $I_B = 2.5$ μA, the product $V_{osr} \cdot CMRR_r = 192$ V. Hence, $CMRR_r = 1.13 \times 10^5$ or 101 dB. This is the low-frequency value. It is quite large because we have assumed only 1 percent variation in K.

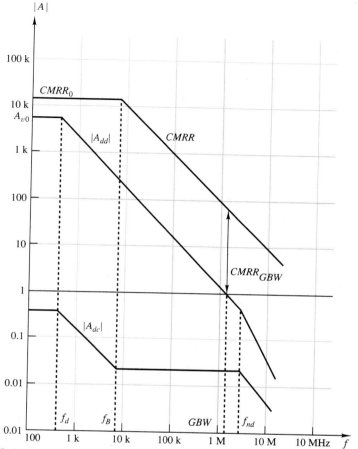

FIGURE 6-28 Gains and *CMRR* versus frequency.

The $CMRR_s$ as a result of common-mode input drive is given by Eq. (6-89). All values are easily obtained from Table 6-2. As a result, $CMRR_s = 1/2 \times 577 \times 1717 = 4.95 \times 10^5$, or 114 dB. The resultant *CMRR* at low frequencies is then obtained from Eq. (6-90) and given by 87100 or 98.8 dB.

At high frequencies, the capacitance from node 3 to ground (see Fig. 6-4) begins to play an important role. Let us call this capacitance C_3. It has a value given by

$$C_3 = C_{DB7} + C_{\text{well1}} \qquad (6-92)$$

in which C_{well1} is the well-to-substrate capacitance of the input transistors. Its value is 0.17 pF at 0 V (see parameter in Table 6-1), and 0.1 pF at 1.26 V biasing voltage in the circuit. Capacitance $C_{DB7} = 34$ fF (see Table 6-2). The resultant value of C_3 thus is 0.134 pF.

Capacitance C_{n2} on node 2 plays a role as well. Its value has been calculated before to be 0.17 pF (see Table 6-7). Both capacitances C_3 and C_{n2} control the CMRR behavior at high frequencies. Their ratio $C_{n2}/C_3 = 1.26$.

Taking into account Δg_{m1} and the systematic offset, the total CMRR versus frequency is obtained from straightforward analysis. It is given by

$$CMRR = \frac{g_{m1}}{A + Bs + Cs^2} \tag{6-93}$$

with

$$A = \left(g_{o1} + \frac{g_{o7}}{2}\right)\frac{\Delta g_{m1}}{g_{m1}} + \frac{g_{o7}}{2}\frac{g_{o13}}{g_{m3}}$$

and

$$B = \left(\frac{\Delta g_{m1}}{g_{m1}} + \frac{g_{o13}}{g_{m3}}\right)\frac{C_3}{2} + \frac{g_{o7}}{g_{m3}}\frac{C_{n2}}{2} \quad \text{and} \quad C = \frac{C_3}{2}\frac{C_{n2}}{g_{m3}}$$

This expression is now evaluated for either random offset or for systematic offset only.

Systematic Offset Only   If random offset is zero, i.e., if $\Delta g_{m1} = 0$, then Eq. (6-93) can be simplified to

$$CMRR_s = \frac{2g_{m1}r_{o13}g_{m3}r_{o7}}{(1 + r_{o7}C_3s)(1 + r_{o13}C_{n2}s)} \tag{6-94}$$

in which $r_{o13} = r_{o1}//r_{o3} = 33 \text{ M}\Omega$ (see Table 6-2). At low frequencies, the expression corresponds to Eq. (6-89). The two poles are clearly distinguished. They correspond to the two capacitances C_3 and C_{n2}. For capacitance C_3, one pole occurs at 15.4 kHz and the other at 28 kHz.

Random Offset Only   If Δg_{m1} is introduced such that

$$\frac{\Delta g_{m1}}{g_{m1}} \gg \frac{g_{o13}}{g_{m3}} \quad \text{and} \quad \gg \frac{C_{n2}}{C_3}\frac{g_{o13}}{g_{m3}}$$

which is 0.29 percent and 0.37 percent respectively, then Eq. (6-93) can be simplified to

$$CMRR_r = \frac{g_{m1}r_{o1}}{\dfrac{\Delta g_{m1}}{g_{m1}}\left(1 + \dfrac{r_{o1}C_3}{2s}\right)} \tag{6-95}$$

For relatively large random offset (if $\Delta g_{m1}/g_{m1} = 1$ percent), the low frequency value is 1.25×10^5 or 102 dB. As shown in Eq. (6-95), the pole then no longer depends on Δg_{m1}. It has become constant, with a time constant $r_{o1}C_3$, corresponding to 7 kHz.

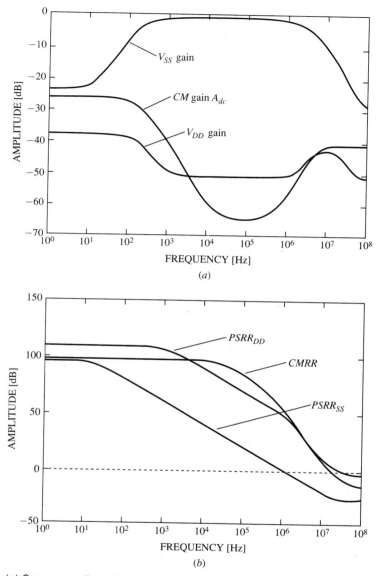

FIGURE 6-29 (a) Common-mode and power supply gains of Miller CMOS op amp, and (b) CMRR and PSRR of Miller CMOS op amp.

The characteristics of the common-mode gain and the resultant $CMRR_r$ for $\Delta g_{m1}/g_{m1} = 1$ percent, are shown in Fig. 6-29a and 6-29b. They have been calculated with SPICE. It is clear that around 10 kHz the $CMRR$ starts rolling off. It is not clear, however, which is the slope of the roll off, since both $CMRR_s$ and $CMRR_r$ play a role.

6-5-11 Design for Low Offset and Drift

The effects of random offset can be minimized by design and layout rules. It has been previously indicated that in a differential pair, transistors must be designed with a small value of $V_{GS} - V_T$ (see Eq. (6-73)). For transistors in a current mirror, however, a large value of $V_{GS} - V_T$ must be taken (see Eq. (6-75)). In this section, attention is paid to the reduction of the deltas themselves by means of layout rules.

Two kinds of errors can cause mismatch: global errors and local errors (Lakshmikumar, Hadaway, and Copeland 1989). Global errors are associated with changes of underetching over the wafer, of diffusion depths, etc. Local errors are associated with the definition of the line edges of the devices. The edges can be jagged, rounded off, distorted, etc. The importance of local errors always decreases with the size of the device dimensions, which is not necessarily the case with global errors. In a simple model, the effect of local errors decreases with the dimensions of the device, whereas the effect of the global errors is constant. For example, the deviation of V_T can be described by

$$\Delta V_T = \Delta V_{T0} \sqrt{P_{gl} + \frac{P_{loc}}{WL}} \qquad (6\text{-}96)$$

in which P_{gl} and P_{loc} are proportionality constants for the global errors and local errors, respectively. Their value must be extracted from experimental data.

For resistances, the curves with experimental data are given in Fig. 2-31. For capacitances, the curves are given in Fig. 2-34. Large sizes are thus used to reduce the effects of mismatch.

Several other layout design rules can be distinguished as well. They are a result of the experience of many analog designers and have been collected from various sources. They can be described in the following sequence:

1 Only try to match devices of equal nature. Do not match MOSTs with JFETs, nor diffused resistances with ion-implanted ones, nor MOS capacitances with diffused ones, etc.

2 The devices to be matched must operate on the same temperature. Power devices present on the chip are sources of heat and they generate thermal gradients (see Fig. 6-30). For this reason, it is important to know the isotherms (lines of equal temperature) on the chip and to realign the devices on the same isotherm, i.e., on a line of constant temperature.

3 Increasing the size of the devices for better matching is always a good option.

4 Lay out the devices at a minimum distance from each other. This may not be as important for resistances as it is for capacitances and hence it is also important for MOST's, because of the large contribution of global errors.

5 Lay out devices with the same orientation with respect to the silicon crystal, putting them in parallel (see Fig. 6-31) such that the currents take the same direction. MOSTs have slightly different mobilities in different orientations.

6 All devices to be matched must have the same area to perimeter ratio. In this way, they have the same ratio of global to local errors, which optimizes matching.

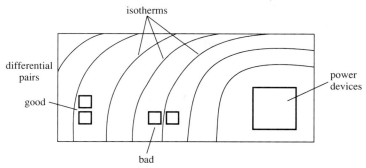

FIGURE 6-30   Chip layout with isotherms.

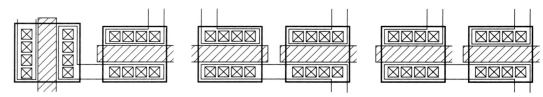

FIGURE 6-31   Matched transistor pairs in increasing order of matching.

For example, consider a current mirror with a ratio of two. It is better to take two times the same transistor than to take a single transistor with double width W (see Fig. 6-32).

7 It is easier to match round devices than square devices. This is especially true of corners, given the uncertainty involved and thus the potential for mismatch. For the same reason, the number of bends and corners in the connections between pairs must be the same. This rule is especially applicable for lateral *pnp* transistors.

8 Try a *centroid layout* for the devices to be matched. An example of a centroid layout for a differential pair is illustrated in Fig. 6-33. Both transistors of the dif-

FIGURE 6-32   Current mirror 4:4:2:1:2 with end dummies.

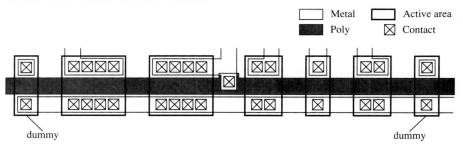

ferential pair are doubled and connected pairwise in parallel. In this manner, global errors are averaged out. However, care must be taken to avoid differences in source resistance. Only one resistance is added in the drain of T1a to realize a crossover.

In Fig. 6-34, a centroid layout is shown for a capacitor array. All squares represent unit capacitances. The central capacitance is marked with a cross. All capacitances that are equally hatched are put in parallel and they thus form capacitance

FIGURE 6-33   Cross-coupled differential pair.

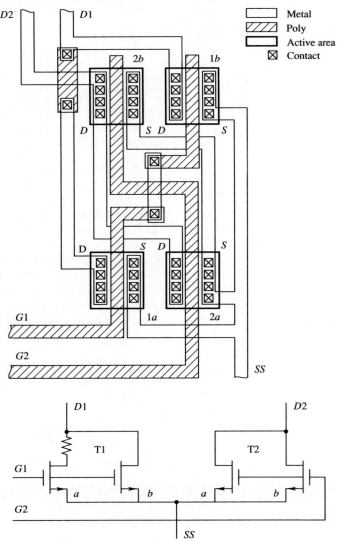

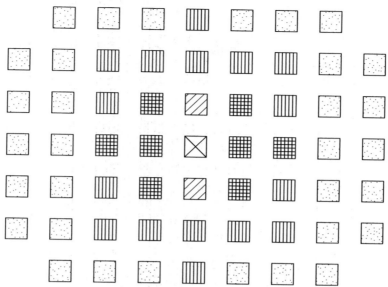

FIGURE 6-34   Capacitor array in centroid layout.

ratios with the binary ratios of 1-2-4-8-... etc. Note that the point of gravity is the same; always in the middle of the central capacitance (crossed in Fig. 6-34).

9 Add dummy devices at both ends of a series of equal devices. The first and the last devices in a series have different etch effects and are mismatched. (see Fig. 6-32). Also, add a dummy ring around a resistor or capacitor bank (see Fig. 2-35).

10 We show in the next section that a pair of bipolar transistors have a ΔV_{BE} that is always about a factor of ten smaller than for a pair of equal-sized MOSTs. Thus, the use of bipolar transistors is recommended whenever matching is required. Of course, this design rule may only be of importance in a BIMOS process.

11 If design rules are not sufficient to reduce mismatch, trimming must be applied. Three kinds of trimming are available (Grebene 1984):

- A laser can be used to trim one of the load resistances (see Fig. 6-34). In this way, a ΔR_L is introduced to compensate for a ΔV_T or ΔK. This only works at one specific point of biasing and temperature and thus the drift is unpredictable.

- Diodes can be applied in parallel to parts of the load resistance. "Zapping" some of these diodes allows the designer to short out parts of that resistance.

- Fuses can be applied in parallel to parts of the load resistance. A fuse is a thin aluminum strip. A large current through the fuse causes the aluminum to melt, which in turn opens the connection.

Trimming must be carried out on a per device basis and is thus costly. As a consequence, designs that avoid trimming are preferred.

6-5-12   Offset in JFET Differential Amplifiers

JFETs can easily replace MOSTs in a differential pair (see Fig. 6-24a). In fact, models for JFETS and MOSTS are very similar. The single significant alteration is that the threshold voltage V_T must be replaced by the pinchoff voltage V_P (see Eq. (1-52)). It is thus sufficient to investigate the random offset caused by the pinchoff voltage (given by Eq. (1-48)).

Taking the derivative of V_P to N_A and a gives

$$V_{osr} = \Delta V_P = V_P \left(\frac{\Delta N_A}{N_A} + 2 \frac{\Delta a}{a} \right) \tag{6-97}$$

Both N_A and a are accurately controlled by means of ion-implantation. As a result, the relative deviations are of the order of 1 to 2 percent. A V_P of about 1 V thus yields offsets that are less than 10 mV. This is a lot lower than what can be achieved with MOSTs, and of the same order of magnitude of what can be realized with bipolar transistors.

Note that diffused JFETs are much worse in this respect, because a diffusion step is less controllable than an ion-implant. the relative deviations are an order of magnitude worse, as are the offsets.

6-5-13   Offset and *CMRR* in Bipolar Differential Amplifiers

Until this point, the mismatch characteristics have been examined for a differential amplifier with only MOSTs and JFETs. With bipolar transistors, a similar account can be given. Again, both random and systematic offset occurs and, as before, systematic offset can be made negligible by appropriate design (and will thus not be repeated). Random offset on the other hand determines the $CMRR_r$. It can thus be concluded that the treatment for a bipolar differential pair is very similar for the MOST differential pair.

However, the bipolar transistor is modeled by different parameters and the collector current is modeled by saturation current I_{CS} (see Chap. 2). Moreover, the bipolar transistor needs a finite input bias current, i.e., the base current. This current is modeled by the beta of the transistor. For this reason, we need to investigate how these two parameters determine the random offset V_{osr} and eventually the $CMRR_r$.

Random Offset   A bipolar differential pair is depicted in Fig. 6-35. Mismatches, which cause random offset, have been introduced by means of ΔI_{CS}, $\Delta \beta$ and ΔR_L. Their contribution to the random offset V_{osr} can be calculated in exactly the same way as for MOST transistors.

For a voltage drive, the input bias currents, and hence the β's, do not play a role. As a result, $\Delta \beta$ can also be left out. The resultant expression of the offset voltage is given by

$$V_{osr} = \frac{kT}{q} \left(\frac{\Delta I_{CS}}{I_{CS}} + \frac{\Delta R_L}{R_L} \right) \tag{6-98}$$

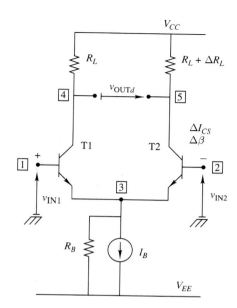

FIGURE 6-35   Bipolar differential pair with mismatches.

in which ΔI_{CS} is the mismatch in saturation current I_{CS}, mainly due to variations in base charge Q_B and in emitter area A_E. For a ΔI_{CS} of 5 percent and in R_L of 1 percent, its value is about 1.5 mV. This value is a lot smaller than for a MOST. The main reason is that the offset is now only proportional to kT/q (≈ 26 mV), whereas for a MOST the offset is proportional to $V_{GS} - V_T$, which is usually around 0.2 to 0.5 V. As a result, the offset of the bipolar transistor pair is an order of magnitude smaller than for a MOST pair.

If the source resistances or the base resistance r_B are large, then mismatch in beta also plays a role. In this case, a term must be added to Eq. (6-98), given by

$$V_{osr\beta} = r_B I_{BB} \frac{\Delta\beta}{\beta} \tag{6-99}$$

in which I_{BB} is the base current. This may especially show up for lateral *pnp*'s, where the betas are lower and the base resistances higher.

Relationship Between Offset and *CMRR*   The random offset V_{osr} of a bipolar transistor pair is related to the $CMRR_r$ by a simple expression similar to the expression found in Eq. (6-87) for a MOST differential pair. For a bipolar transistor pair, it is easy to show that the product of random offset and $CMRR$ is given by

$$V_{osr} \cdot CMRR_r = 2g_m R_B \frac{kT}{q} \tag{6-100a}$$

in which R_B is the output resistance of the current source (see Fig. 6-35). A single-transistor current source is used, such that $R_B = r_o = V_E/I_C$. Since $g_m = qI_C/kT$, however, Eq. (6-100a) can be further simplified to

$$V_{osr} \cdot CMRR_r = V_E \tag{6-100b}$$

For a typical 600 MHz bipolar process, $V_E \approx 35$ V. As a result, for $V_{osr} = 1.5$ mV, the $CMRR_r \approx 23{,}000$ (87 dB). This is a representative value for bipolar transistor differential amplifiers and operational amplifiers. It is typically 20 dB (ten times) larger than for MOST differential pairs, because the offset is typically ten times smaller.

Remember that the systematic offset has been made negligible by proper design (or symmetry).

Example 6-11

Consider a transistor with $V_E = 35$ V and $r_B = 300$ Ω. Its base current is 100 nA. Take 10 percent mismatch in beta and 5 percent for the other ones. What random offset and $CMRR$ are expected?

Solution. Equation (6-98) gives $V_{osr} = 3.9$ mV, if all mismatches add up (which is never the case). Equation (6-99) gives only $V_{osr\beta} = 3$ μV, which is negligible. The $CMRR_r$ is obtained from Eq. (6-100b) and is approximately 9000 or 79 dB.

Offset Drift   The drift of the offset versus temperature is easily obtained from Eq. (6-98) by taking the derivative with respect to temperature. It is given by

$$\frac{\Delta V_{osr}}{\Delta T} = \frac{V_{osr}}{T} \tag{6-101}$$

which is only about 5 μV/°C for the example with 1.5 mV offset. This is a small value compared to MOSTs.

More importantly, the offset drift $\Delta V_{osr}/\Delta T$ is proportional to the offset V_{osr} itself. Techniques to reduce random offset thus also reduce the drift. They can both be made small with the same effort. This is a considerable advantage over MOSTs, where offset and drift are not related and thus bipolar transistors are by far the best option if good performance in offset and drift are required.

6-5-14   Bias Current, Offset and Drift

In contrast with MOSTs, bipolar transistors require input biasing currents. These are the DC base currents that flow into the base if *npn* transistors are used (see Fig. 6-36). They flow out of the base if *pnp* transistors are used. They depend on the betas of the bipolar transistors and thus also on the temperature.

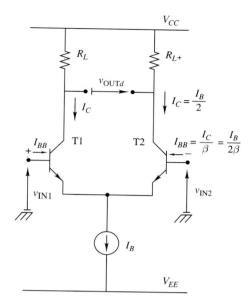

FIGURE 6-36   Bias currents in bipolar differential pair.

The *bias current* I_{bias} of a bipolar differential pair (or a bipolar operational amplifier) is then simply defined as base current I_{BB} or I_C/β. The *bias current offset* I_{bos} is the difference in bias current between the two inputs,

$$I_{bos} = \frac{I_C}{\beta} \left(\frac{\Delta R_L}{R_L} + \frac{\Delta \beta}{\beta} \right) \qquad (6\text{-}102)$$

A typical value of relative error on β is 10 percent. The offset I_{bos} is thus about 10 percent of the current I_{bias}.

For a pure voltage drive, the effect of parameter β is negligible, but this is not the case for precision applications. In Chap. 5, the effect of a bias current on precise gain is investigated. In this type of application, an op amp is preferred with MOSTs or JFETs in the input stage, as no bias current flows and the gain is very precise. Alternatives are discussed in the next paragraph.

Design for Low Input Bias Current   For high precision applications, it is not sufficient to select MOSTs or JFETs as input devices. The input bias currents are low but the errors due to offset are larger. This issue requires further investigation.

The input bias currents are compared for bipolar transistors, MOSTs, and JFETs in Fig 6-37. The bias current is highest for a conventional bipolar transistor. It decreases with temperature, however, because β increases with temperature (about 0.7 percent/°C). To decrease the bias current, superbeta bipolar transistors are introduced. They have values of about 2000 to 5000 but they have breakdown voltages of only a few volts (see Chap. 1). Superbeta bipolar transistors require a deeper emitter diffusion, which is a modification in standard processing and thus may not be available.

A JFET seems to be a good alternative. However, this is only true at room temperature. At high temperatures, the junction reverse current of the gate doubles about every 8°C (see Fig. 6-37) and thus becomes quite high at high temperatures. Only MOSTs perform better at all temperatures, provided they are not equipped with protection diodes, which have similar junction reverse currents as the input gates of the JFETs.

While MOSTs provide very low bias currents, they also provide the highest offset. For low offset, bipolar transistors must be used. In order to reduce the bias currents, superbeta transistors must be added to the process. Circuit tricks can also be used to reduce the bias currents, examples of which are given in Fig. 6-38.

In the first example (from op amp OP27), the current is measured in the collector ($I_B/2$) by transistor T4. Its base current ($I_B/2\beta$) is mirrored by the *pnp* current mirror T5-T6 and provided to the input terminal, where it equals the bias current required ($I_B/2\beta$). Mismatches limit the bias current of this current compensation scheme to about 5 to 10 percent. Moreover, the noise performance is bad because too many transistors are used on both sides.

A better alternative (also from op amp OP27) is shown in Fig. 6-38*b*. The current is now derived from a separate current source with value $I_B/2$. The base currents are derived from transistors T3-T4 and mirrored by T5-T6-T7 to the input terminals. With these techniques, the input biasing currents can be reduced by approximately a factor of ten. Mismatch prohibits further reductions.

FIGURE 6-37   Input bias currents for several transistors.

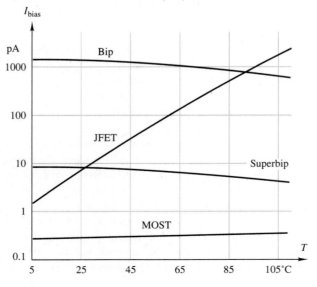

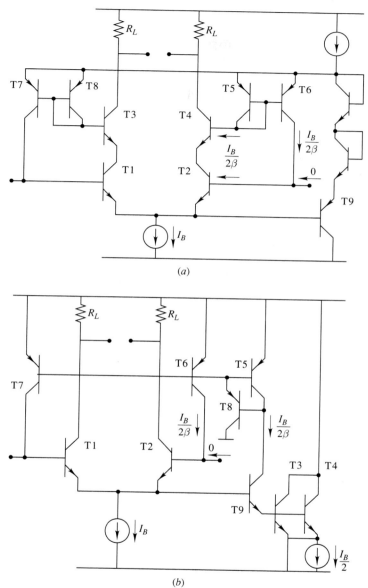

FIGURE 6-38   Bias current compensation according to (a) op amp OP07 and (b) op amp OP27.

Another important difference between these circuits is that the compensation circuit in Fig. 6-38a provides local (differential) feedback, whereas the one in Fig. 6-38b provides common-mode feedback, i.e., the stability conditions are different.

6-6 POWER SUPPLY REJECTION RATIO

In modern IC designs, analog and digital functions are joined together on the same chip, and as a result, interaction is possible between both parts. This interaction consists of spikes, which are generated by clocks (from digital parts or from switched capacitor circuits), by output drivers, etc. Spikes are generated on the supply lines, on ground, and on the substrate. These spikes are easily coupled to the analog circuits. One of the important characteristics of modern analog blocks is their insensitivity to spikes on the supply lines. This is expressed by their Power Supply Rejection Ratios (*PSRR*s).

If we reduce the power consumption of analog blocks, the impedance levels at their terminals increase, as does their sensitivity to spurious signals. Spikes on the supply lines are therefore detected much more easily. This is a second reason to worry about *PSRR*; The more this ratio becomes degraded, the less power becomes available.

One of the peculiar difficulties associated with *PSRR* is that high values of *PSRR* can be obtained at low frequencies but not at high frequencies. However, it is especially at high frequencies that a high *PSRR* is required. The spikes on the power supply lines are short time spikes and thus contain many high frequency components. As a consequence, a high *PSRR* at only intermediate and high frequencies is required.

Hand calculations of *PSRR* pose several problems. One such problem is that with the positive power supply line as an AC input, many connections are made to that input. Hence, we must deal with a multiple input amplifier, which we do not often analyze. The hand calculations yield expressions that easily become cumbersome. The use of SPICE is of no help here because the role of each transistor parameter is hidden by numbers. As a result, only symbolic analysis is useful to study *PSRR*. Such a simulator is ISAAC (Gielen and Sansen 1991). In fact, several expressions used in this section have been generated and verified by means of ISAAC.

In this section, we analyze the *PSRR* of several elementary amplifiers. The simple CMOS OTA is analyzed first, followed by the Miller CMOS OTA.

An amplifier has several terminals: one or two for the input, one for the output, one connected to the positive power supply line and one connected to the negative power supply line. For all of them, a common ground is used as a reference terminal. For each terminal, a gain can be defined to the output terminal. For the input terminal, this is the voltage gain A_v. For the positive power supply V_{DD}, the gain $A_{DD} = v_{OUT}/v_{DD}$. For the negative power supply V_{SS}, the gain is $A_{SS} = v_{OUT}/v_{SS}$.

We want the gains A_{DD} and A_{SS} to be low in comparison to A_v. In analogy to the definition of the *CMRR*, the $PSRR_{DD}$ and $PSRR_{SS}$ can be defined as

$$PSRR_{DD} = \frac{A_v}{A_{DD}} = \frac{v_{OUT}}{v_{IN}} \frac{v_{DD}}{v_{OUT}} = \frac{v_{DD}}{v_{IN}} \qquad (6\text{-}103a)$$

$$PSRR_{SS} = \frac{A_v}{A_{SS}} = \frac{v_{OUT}}{v_{IN}} \frac{v_{SS}}{v_{OUT}} = \frac{v_{SS}}{v_{IN}} \qquad (6\text{-}103b)$$

The different gains are now calculated in order to evaluate the *PSRR*'s (Steyaert and Sansen 1992).

6-6-1 *PSRR$_{DD}$* of a Simple CMOS OTA

A simple CMOS OTA consists of a differential input stage with an active load. The scheme of Fig. 6-39 has been copied from Fig. 6-1a. Only the capacitance C_L is present as a load. The ideal current source has been replaced by a real one, formed by a simple current mirror, which is driven by a current source I_B.

Several characteristics are already known for this OTA: the gain A_v, the bandwidth BW, and the gain-bandwidth GBW. These characteristics are taken from Sec. 6-1.

$PSRR_{DD}$ without Coupling Capacitances   With V_{DD} as an input terminal, the circuit can be simplified to the one shown in Fig. 6-40a. The input devices T1 and T2 are simply replaced by their output resistances r_{o1} and r_{o2}. Also, the current source is replaced by its output resistance r_{oB}.

From this circuit, a small-signal equivalent circuit can be derived, shown in Fig. 6-40b. Transistor T3 is replaced by $1/g_{m3}$ and transistor T4 is replaced by an ideal current dependent current generator i. Moreover, we have assumed that $R_B \gg r_{o2,4}$. Under the assumption that $g_{m3} \gg g_{oB}/2$, the gain A_{DD} is obtained from straightforward analysis:

$$A_{DD} = \frac{v_{\text{out}}}{v_{DD}} = \frac{1}{1 + j\dfrac{f}{BW}} \tag{6-104}$$

FIGURE 6-39   Simple CMOS OTA.

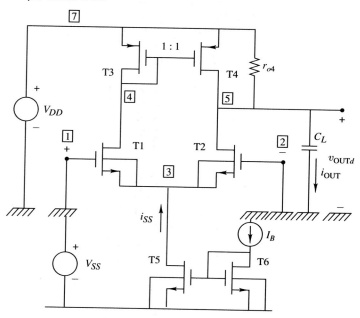

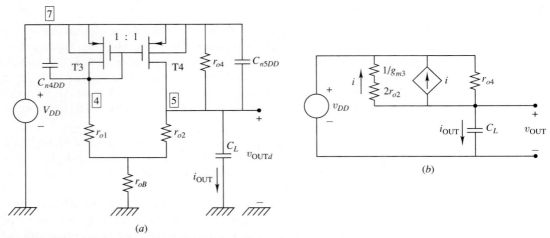

FIGURE 6-40   (a) Equivalent circuit of simple CMOS OTA for calculation of $PSRR_{DD}$. (b) Small-signal equivalent circuit of Fig. 6-40a.

in which
$$BW = \frac{g_{o24}}{2\pi C_L}$$

The gain A_{DD} is thus unity for all frequencies up to the bandwidth BW of that circuit.

The gain characteristics A_v and A_{DD} are sketched in Fig. 6-41 for $C_L = 5$ pF and for $I_B = 10$ μA, which yields $g_{m1} = 63.2$ μS and $g_{o24} = 0.444$ μS. The gain $A_{v0} = 142$. The BW and GBW are, respectively, 14 kHz and 2 MHz. The break frequency of the A_{DD} is thus also $BW = 14$ kHz.

The $PSRR_{DD}$ is given by the ratio of both gains, i.e.,

$$PSRR_{DD} = \frac{A_v}{A_{DD}} = A_{v0} \qquad (6\text{-}105)$$

It is constant because the break frequencies (i.e., the BW) in both A_v and A_{DD} are the same (see Fig. 6-49). The $PSRR_{DD}$ is thus large and constant up to frequencies beyond GBW. Of course, this is only possible because the parasitic capacitances have hitherto been omitted.

For the calculations in Eqs. 6-104 and 6-105, we have used voltage gain. In the subsequent calculations, however, we will use transconductance, as simpler calculations result. To illustrate this point, we will repeat the calculations above with transconductances and then proceed to more complex derivations.

The output current through load capacitance C_L is now taken as the output quantity rather than the output voltage (see Fig. 6-40). Of course, we can only do that provided the current through C_L is larger than the current through g_{o24}. This is the case for all frequencies larger than the BW. These analyses thus always assume that we are only interested in frequencies larger than the BW.

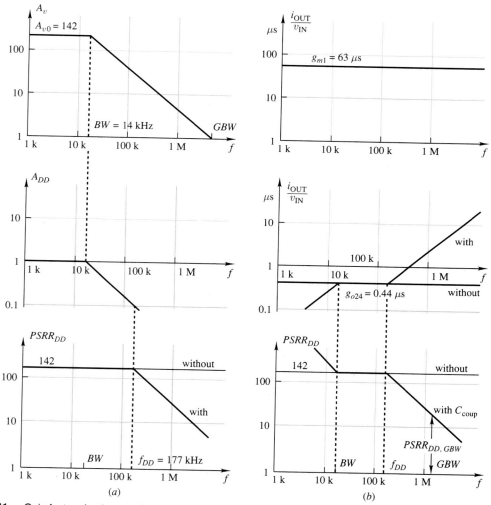

FIGURE 6-41 Gain factors for the calculation of $PSRR_{DD}$ (a) voltage gains, and (b) transconductances of a simple CMOS OTA.

The output current through load capacitance C_L, as a result of the input voltage, is simply g_{m1}. The output current through load capacitance C_L for the circuit of Fig. 6-40b is easily derived, as for Eq. (6-104). It is given by

$$\frac{i_{OUT}}{v_{DD}} = g_{o24} \frac{j \dfrac{f}{BW}}{1 + j \dfrac{f}{BW}} = g_{o24} \frac{C_L s}{g_{o24} + C_L s} \qquad (6\text{-}106)$$

For intermediate and high frequencies, i.e., for all frequencies higher than BW, the above expression is reduced to g_{o24}. Both transconductances are shown in Fig. 6-41b. The $PSRR_{DDif}$ is then given by

$$PSRR_{DDif} = \frac{\dfrac{i_{OUT}}{v_{IN}}}{\dfrac{i_{OUT}}{v_{DD}}} = \frac{g_{m1}}{g_{o24}} \tag{6-107}$$

The $PSRR_{DD}$ is also shown in Fig. 6-41b, and it is obviously the same as in Fig. 6-41a. It is large and constant up to frequencies beyond GBW. Do not forget, however, that this is because the coupling capacitances have been omitted.

The only difference between the $PSRR$ of Fig. 6-41a and 6-41b is that in Fig. 41b, we have omitted the break frequency BW such that the calculations have become simpler.

Let us now include all the small parasitic and coupling capacitances, and repeat the calculations.

$PSRR_{DD}$ With Coupling Capacitances

At intermediate and higher frequencies, all small capacitances of the transistors and of the interconnections come in. The most important ones are the coupling capacitances between the supply line V_{DD} and the output, because they are in parallel with g_{o24}. They are coupling capacitances C_{n4DD} and C_{n5DD} between nodes 4 and 5, respectively, and the supply line V_{DD} (see Fig. 6-40a). They can be calculated partially from transistor geometries. Note that interconnect and other small capacitances must also be added and therefore C_{n4DD} and C_{n5DD} are never precisely known, nor do they appear in the list of parameters in Table 6-2.

It is readily verified that the easiest way to include the effect of these capacitances is to substitute g_{o24} by $g_{o24} + (C_{n4DD} + C_{n5DD})s$ in the above expressions.

The $PSRR_{DDif}$ is now given by

$$PSRR_{DDif} = \frac{\dfrac{i_{OUT}}{v_{IN}}}{\dfrac{i_{OUT}}{v_{DD}}} = \frac{g_{m1}}{g_{o24}} \frac{1}{1 + \dfrac{(C_{n4DD} + C_{n5DD})s}{g_{o24}}} \tag{6-108}$$

which is valid for all frequencies higher than BW. It is also shown in Fig. 6-41b, in which the curve is labeled "with C_{coup}" where evidently $C_{\text{coup}} = C_{n4DD} + C_{n5DD}$.

The pole of the $PSRR_{DDif}$ occurs at the frequency f_{DD}, which is given by

$$f_{DD} = \frac{g_{o24}}{2\pi (C_{n4DD} + C_{n5DD})} \tag{6-109}$$

If we assume C_{n4DD} and $C_{n5DD} = 0.2$ pF, then break frequency f_{DD} is about 177 kHz, as shown in Fig. 6-41b.

At high frequencies, i.e., at frequencies higher than f_{DD}, the $PSRR$ is denoted by $PSRR_{DDhi}$ and is given by

$$PSRR_{DDhi} = \frac{g_{m1}}{(C_{n4DD} + C_{n5DD})s} \tag{6-110}$$

Of particular importance is the $PSRR_{DD}$ obtained at the frequency of the GBW itself, which is the maximum useful frequency of that circuit. Remember that the GBW is given by

$$GBW = \frac{g_{m1}}{C_L s} \tag{6-111}$$

such that the $PSRR$ at GBW is given by

$$PSRR_{DD,GBW} = \frac{C_L}{C_{n4DD} + C_{n5DD}} \tag{6-112}$$

Indeed, g_{m1} occurs in both $PSRR_{DDhi}$ and GBW. By taking g_{m1} out in this way, a normalized $PSRR_{DD}$ at high frequencies is obtained. Also, the frequency dependence is taken out and it is thus an excellent measure for $PSRR$ at high frequencies.

Using the above values, the value of $PSRR_{DD,GBW}$ is $5/0.4 = 12.5$ or 22 dB. While this is not a large value, remember that this is at 2 MHz. It is proportionally larger at lower frequencies (see Fig. 6-41b).

6-6-2 $PSRR_{SS}$ of a Simple CMOS OTA

In order to evaluate the $PSRR_{SS}$, we again refer to Fig. 6-39. The gain of the V_{SS} supply to the output is the product of two gain factors. They are

- the current i_{SS} at the output of the current mirror as a result of v_{SS}, and
- the output current i_{OUT} as a result of current i_{SS}.

To simplify the expressions, we again calculate the current through load capacitance C_L. This is valid for frequencies larger than $BW = 14$ kHz.

The driving current I_B of the current mirror is ideal. It is a pure DC current source. Hence, no AC current flows into T6. As a result, the only AC current that can flow through T5 is through its output resistance r_{o5}. The current i_{SS} caused by v_{SS} is simply given by

$$\frac{i_{SS}}{v_{SS}} = \frac{1}{r_{o5}} \tag{6-113}$$

If the differential stage is perfectly symmetrical, the output current i_{OUT} caused by i_{SS} is zero. In this case, the gain A_{SS} is zero and $PSRR_{SS}$ is infinity.

However, if we assume mismatches in the input transistors, i.e., if the input transistors have different transconductances, then the current ratio is given by

$$\frac{i_{OUT}}{i_{SS}} = \frac{\Delta g_{m1}}{2g_{m1}} \tag{6-114}$$

The resulting $PSRR_{SSif}$ is thus given by

$$PSRR_{SSif} = \frac{\dfrac{i_{OUT}}{v_{IN}}}{\dfrac{i_{OUT}}{v_{SS}}} = \frac{g_{m1}}{g_{o5}} \frac{2g_{m1}}{\Delta g_{m1}} \tag{6-115}$$

If we assume mismatches in the load transistors, i.e., if the load transistors have different transconductances, then the current ratio is instead given by

$$\frac{i_{OUT}}{i_{SS}} = \frac{\Delta g_{m3}}{2g_{m3}} \tag{6-116}$$

and the $PSRR_{SSif}$ changes accordingly.

Equation (6-115) shows that the $PSRR_{SS}$ is usually much larger than the $PSRR_{DD}$. Both contain a similar ratio g_m/g_o, which corresponds to the gain of the amplifier. The $PSRR_{SS}$, however, is increased by the inverse mismatch ratio, which is 100 for 1 percent mismatch.

At high frequencies, coupling capacitances must be introduced. The most important one is coupling capacitance C_{n3SS} i.e., the coupling capacitance between node 3 and supply line V_{SS}. It shunts g_{o5} at frequencies higher than f_{SS}, given by

$$f_{SS} = \frac{g_{o5}}{2\pi C_{n3SS}} \tag{6-117}$$

At this frequency, the $PSRR_{SS}$ starts rolling off.

Note that for both input transistors, the bulks are connected to the sources. If this is not the case, then the bulk transconductances are mismatched as well. The total expression of the $PSRR_{SSif}$ is then given by

$$PSRR_{SSif} = \frac{\dfrac{i_{OUT}}{v_{IN}}}{\dfrac{i_{OUT}}{v_{SS}}} = \frac{g_{m1}}{(g_{o5} + C_{n3SS})\,s} \frac{1}{\dfrac{\Delta g_{m1}}{2g_{m1}} + \dfrac{\Delta g_{mb1}}{2g_{mb1}}} \tag{6-118}$$

The worst mismatch determines the $PSRR_{SSif}$. Do not forget that the signs have been taken arbitrarily. The sign of the mismatches are impossible to predict.

At high frequencies, the $PSRR_{SS,GBW}$ is given by

$$PSRR_{SS,GBW} = \frac{C_L}{C_{n3SS}} \frac{2g_{m1}}{\Delta g_{m1}} \tag{6-119}$$

if both input transistors are in the same well. The $PSRR_{SS,GBW}$ depends on both the capacitive ratio and on matching and is thus hard to predict.

Example 6-12

Calculate the break frequency f_{SS} and the $PSRR_{SS,GBW}$ for $C_L = 5$ pF if 5 percent mismatch is present in input transconductance ($GBW = 2\text{MHz}$). The current source has an output resistance of 2 MΩ in parallel with 0.2 pF.

Solution. From Eq. (6-117), $f_{SS} = 0.4$ MHz. At the GBW, $PSRR_{SS,GBW} = 2000$, or 66 dB. This is an excellent result because of the small output capacitance of the current source.

Equation (6-119) provides the $PSRR$ at the GBW frequency as a result of a small coupling capacitance to the common source point of the differential pair (node 3 in Fig. 6-39). However, there is another capacitance at that point that is as important: the capacitance C_{well1} between the common well and the substrate. Indeed, it is always advantageous to put input transistors in a common well for better matching. As a result, the common source point is connected to that well, which has a large capacitance with respect to the substrate.

The well for nMOSTs (see Fig. 6-39) is of the p-type and the substrate is of the n-type. It must be connected to the positive power supply. We thus obtain another expression for the $PSRR_{DD}$, which is of the same nature as the $PSRR_{SS}$, given in Eq. (6-119). It is given by

$$PSRR_{DDw,GBW} = \frac{C_L}{C_{well1}} \frac{2g_{m1}}{\Delta g_{m1}} \tag{6-120}$$

Its value obviously depends on the minimum value of C_{well1} that can be achieved. In Eq. (6-92), we have used a value of $C_{well1} = 0.1$ pF. The values of Example 6-7 then yield $PSRR_{DDw,GBW} = 72$ dB, which is an excellent result. Unless C_{well1} is large, the $PSRR_{DDw,GBW}$ can be neglected with respect to the $PSRR_{DD,GBW}$ of Eq. (6-112), which was only 22 dB.

6-6-3 $PSRR_{DD}$ of the Miller CMOS OTA

The schematic of the Miller OTA is shown in Fig. 6-4. We must calculate the output voltage v_{OUT} as a result of variations in V_{DD}, denoted by v_{DD}. Two different inputs are connected to V_{DD}, and they allow currents through transistors T7 and T5. The contributions of two different currents are calculated to find v_{OUT} and the $PSRR_{DD}$.

Current Through Transistor T7   Transistor T7 serves as a current source. Because its v_{GS} has no AC component, the transistor can only carry AC current through its output conductance g_{o7}. If we assume that all mismatches are contained in the input pair, the analysis is the same as for the current source of the simple CMOS OTA in Sec. 6-6-2.

The current i_{OUT7} through transistor T7 due to v_{DD} is determined by r_{o7} and the coupling capacitance C_{n3DD} in parallel with it. A fraction $\Delta g_{m1}/2g_{m1}$ of this current reaches node 1, where it is amplified by a factor $1/C_c s$ to contribute to the output voltage. The output voltage v_{OUT7} is given by

$$\frac{v_{OUT7}}{v_{DD}} = \frac{(g_{o7} + C_{n3DD}s)}{C_c s}\frac{\Delta g_{m1}}{2g_{m1}} \tag{6-121}$$

For this calculation we have assumed that the gain of the OTA can be simplified to $A_v = g_{m1}/C_c s$. This is obviously only valid for frequencies larger than the open-loop bandwidth, which is about 230 Hz (see Table 6-4) for this Miller OTA.

Current Through Transistor T5   The current through this transistor provides an output voltage, which is easy to calculate only if we know the impedance Z_{6c} represented by the T6-C_c combination as seen from its drain. We therefore calculate it separately.

The equivalent circuit is shown in Fig. 6-42. Transistors T2 and T4 are replaced by their output conductance g_{o24}. The impedance $Z_{6c} = v_{6c}/i_{6c}$ is approximately given by

$$Z_{6c} \approx \frac{1}{g_{m6}}\frac{1 + j\dfrac{f}{f_{z3}}}{1 + j\dfrac{f}{f_{z4}}} \tag{6-122}$$

in which f_{z3} and f_{z4} have already been defined for calculation of the output impedance in Eq. (6-60). Both break frequencies are also listed in Table 6-4. For the Miller OTA of the example, $f_{z3} = 5.3$ kHz and $f_{z4} = 105$ MHz. Note that in Eq. (6-122), g_{o24} has been neglected with respect to g_{m6}. Indeed, g_{o24} is only 0.03 μS (see Table 6-2) and g_{m6} is 246 μS.

For intermediate frequencies larger than 5.3 kHz, the impedance Z_{6c} can be simplified to $1/g_{m6}$. The compensation capacitance C_c shorts drain and gate together. As a result, the impedance of this diode-connected MOST is $1/g_{m6}$.

The effect of the current through T5 is now easily calculated. This current is determined by r_{o5} and its parallel coupling capacitance C_{n4DD} between node 4 and the V_{DD} supply line. The resulting output voltage is thus given by

$$\frac{v_{OUT5}}{v_{DD}} = \frac{g_{o5} + C_{n4DD}s}{g_{m6}} \tag{6-123}$$

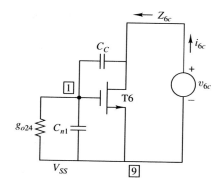

FIGURE 6-42 Equivalent circuit of Miller OTA for the calculation of impedance Z_{6c}

and the resulting $PSRR_{DD}$ is given by

$$PSRR_{DD} = \frac{\dfrac{v_{OUT_d}}{v_{IN}}}{\dfrac{v_{OUT7} + v_{OUT5}}{v_{DD}}} = \frac{g_{m1}}{(g_{o7} + C_{n3DD}s)\dfrac{\Delta g_{m1}}{2g_{m1}} + \dfrac{g_{o5} + C_{n4DD}s}{g_{m6}}C_c s} \qquad (6\text{-}124)$$

Its value at intermediate and high frequencies can be found by taking the coefficients in s only, as given by

$$PSRR_{DDif} = \frac{g_{m1}}{C_{n3DD}s\dfrac{\Delta g_{m1}}{2g_{m1}} + \dfrac{C_{n4DD}s}{g_{m6}}C_c s} \qquad (6\text{-}125a)$$

The high frequency $PSRR_{DD,GBW}$ is ultimately given by

$$PSRR_{DD,GBW} = \frac{1}{\dfrac{C_{n3DD}}{C_c}\dfrac{\Delta g_{m1}}{2g_{m1}} + \dfrac{g_{o5}}{g_{m6}}} \qquad (6\text{-}125b)$$

since $GBW = g_{m1}/2\pi C_c$. This is an excellent result, but it depends on matching. The maximum value is g_{m6}/g_{o5}, which is 403, or 52 dB. If $C_{n3DD} = 0.2$ pF, 1.2 percent matching would be required to achieve this maximum value.

At very low frequencies (mains, supply frequency, etc.) compensation capacitance C_c cannot be regarded as a short. The low frequency component of Eq. (6-124) must then be modified (see Exercise 6-19) as given by

$$PSRR_{DD0} = \frac{g_{m1}}{-\dfrac{g_{o7}}{2}\left(\dfrac{\Delta g_{m1}}{g_{m1}} + \dfrac{g_{o13}}{g_{m3}}\right) + \dfrac{g_{o5}}{g_{m6}}g_{o24}} \qquad (6\text{-}126)$$

Let us take as an example the values of Table 6-2. The term g_{o13}/g_{m3} is only 0.0029. The mismatch term $\Delta g_{m1}/g_{m1}$ is dominant in this expression. The value of $PSRR_{DD0}$ varies, depending on the sign of the mismatch. If $g_{m2} > g_{m1}$ by 1 percent, then $PSRR_{DD0} = (-)8 \times 10^5$, or 118 dB. In the opposite case, when $g_{m2} < g_{m1}$, $PSRR_{DD0} = 1.4 \times 10^4$, or 83 dB.

6-6-4 $PSRR_{SS}$ of the Miller OTA

We now calculate the output voltage v_{OUT} as a result of v_{SS}. Since there are three inputs, three different currents must be calculated to find v_{OUT}. Moreover, the input well capacitance is also connected to the V_{SS} supply line.

Current Through Transistor T3   This transistor is connected as a diode. The AC current through it is thus determined by r_{o1} and its parallel capacitance. This capacitance is C_{n23}, which is the parasitic coupling capacitance between nodes 2 and 3, which mainly consists of C_{DB1}.

This current through transistor T3 flows through transistor T2 to node 1, where it is amplified by $1/C_c s$ to reach the output. The output voltage is given by

$$\frac{v_{OUT3}}{v_{SS}} = \frac{g_{o1} + C_{n23}s}{C_c s} \tag{6-127}$$

Current Through Transistor T4   The current is now determined by the output conductance g_{o4} of transistor T4, in parallel with coupling capacitance C_{n1SS}. This current is also amplified by $1/C_c s$ to reach the output. The output voltage is now given by

$$\frac{v_{OUT4}}{v_{SS}} = \frac{g_{o4} + C_{n1SS}s}{C_c s} \tag{6-128}$$

Current Through T6   In order to gain insight into the effect of v_{SS} on the output voltage through T6 and capacitance C_c, the simplified circuit of Fig. 6-43a is used. The first stage is represented by g_{m1}. The second stage is represented by a gain stage, with gain $A_{v2} = g_{m6}R'_L$, across which the compensation capacitance C_c is applied. The output conductance g_{o24} of the first stage is omitted. The error caused by this omission will be verified later.

This circuit can then be further simplified, as shown in Fig. 6-43b. Straightforward analysis yields

$$\frac{v_{OUT6}}{v_{SS}} = \frac{1}{1 + \dfrac{C_c + C_{n1SS}}{A_{v2}C_c}} \tag{6-129}$$

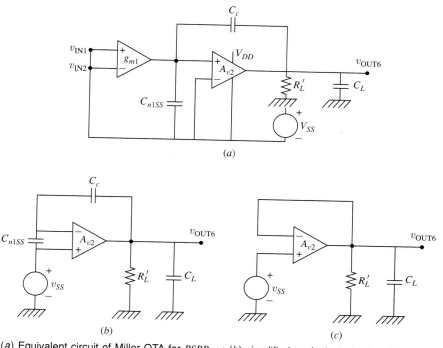

FIGURE 6-43   (a) Equivalent circuit of Miller OTA for $PSRR_{SS}$; (b) simplified equivalent circuits of Miller OTA for calculation of $PSRR_{SS}$, and; (c) the simplest model.

Even for small values of A_{v2}, this expression yields at approximately unity. The signals v_{SS} of the negative power supply thus reach the output unattenuated. This is caused by the compensation capacitance C_c, which shorts drain to gate for these frequencies, as shown in Fig. 6-43c. The resulting impedance of T6 is thus again $1/g_{m6}$. Our assumption that g_{o24} can be neglected is thus verified, and note that conductance g_{o24} is indeed much smaller than $1/g_{m6}$.

Current Due to the Input Well Capacitance   The input MOSTs of the Miller OTA (see Fig. 6-4) are put in an n-well. To provide better matching, the n-well is connected to the sources. A large well to substrate capacitance C_{well1} results between node 3 and the p-type substrate, which is connected to the V_{SS} supply line. Its contribution must thus add up to the other three contributions.

The current from v_{SS} is determined by the coupling capacitance C_{well1}. A fraction $\Delta g_{m1}/2g_{m1}$ of this current reaches node 1, where it is amplified by a factor $1/C_c s$ to contribute to the output voltage. The output voltage $v_{OUTwell1}$ is thus given by

$$\frac{v_{OUTwell1}}{v_{SS}} = \frac{C_{well1}}{C_c} \frac{\Delta g_{m1}}{2g_{m1}} \tag{6-130}$$

Thus, $PSRR_{SS}$ consists of four contributions, and it is given by

$$PSRR_{SS} = \frac{\dfrac{v_{OUT}}{v_{IN}}}{\dfrac{v_{OUT}}{v_{SS}}} = \frac{g_{m1}}{g_{o24} + (C_{n23} + C_{n1SS} + C_{well1} + C_c)s} \qquad (6\text{-}131)$$

since $g_{o1} = g_{o2}$.

At intermediate and high frequencies, the $PSRR_{SSif}$ is given by

$$PSRR_{SSif} = \frac{g_{m1}}{(C_{n23} + C_{n1SS} + C_{well1} + C_c)s} \qquad (6\text{-}132a)$$

Finally, at the $GBW\,(= g_{m1}/2\pi C_c)$, the $PSRR_{SS,GBW}$ is given by

$$PSRR_{SS,GBW} = 1 + \frac{C_{n23} + C_{n1SS}}{C_c} \qquad (6\text{-}132b)$$

To our surprise, this value is approximately unity. This result is nevertheless quite acceptable. At these frequencies, the compensation capacitance C_c acts as a short circuit. Hence, transistor T6 is connected as a diode. It thus represents only $1/g_{m6}$, which is small compared to the load impedance. Note that signals on V_{SS} reach the load unattenuated.

This is probably the most important disadvantage of the Miller OTA. Spurious signals on the negative power supply line reach the output without any rejection, and circuit modifications are required to remedy this problem. An example of this is provided in the next section.

At very low frequencies, compensation capacitance C_c can no longer be regarded as a short circuit. The low frequency component of Eq. (6-130) is then modified (see Exercise 6-20) to

$$PSRR_{SS0} = \frac{g_{m1}}{g_{o1}\dfrac{\Delta g_{m1}}{2g_{m1}} + \dfrac{g_{o6}}{g_{m6}}g_{o24}} \qquad (6\text{-}133)$$

We will again use the values of Table 6-2 for the following example. The second term, rather than the mismatch term, is dominant in this expression. In this case, the $PSRR_{SS0}$ is even larger than the open-loop gain. They would be the same if the load were r_{o6} and not R'_L.

Depending on the sign of the mismatch, the value of $PSRR_{SS0}$ can vary slightly. If $g_{m2} > g_{m1}$ by 1 percent then $PSRR_{SS0} = 9 \times 10^4$, or 99 dB. In the opposite case, $PSRR_{SS0} = 3.7 \times 10^4$ or 91 dB.

Results have been obtained with SPICE for both $PSRR_{DD}$ and $PSRR_{SS}$, and are given in Fig. 6-29. Mismatches of 1 percent are assumed between the transconductances of the input transistors whenever necessary. Of note is the bad $PSRR_{SS}$, which is approximately unity around GBW (1 MHz).

TABLE 6-11   CHARACTERISTICS OF THE MILLER CMOS OTA

Parameter	Specifications	Calculations	SPICE	
I_B	2.5	2.5	2.5	μA
$I_{tot,max}(\pm 2.5\ V)$	30	27.7	27.7	μA
Total active area		0.01		mm^2
GBW	1	1.19	1.12	MHz
SR	2	2.27	2.2	V/μs
A_{v0}	≥ 60	74	74	dB
PM	≥ 60	67	66	$^\circ$
$V_{out,max}$	± 2	± 2.08		V
$V_{in,cm}$	± 0.5	± 0.84		V
$C_{in}(-)$	0.11	0.1		pF
$R_{out,0}$		556		kΩ
Output noise v_o		134		μV$_{RMS}$
System offset		0.1	0.1	mV
Random offset ($\Delta g_m = 1\%$)		1.7	1.6	mV
$CMRR_0$		98.8	98.8	dB
$PSRR_{DD,0}$ ($g_{m1} = 1.01 \cdot g_{m2}$)		83	83	dB
$PSRR_{SS,0}$ ($g_{m1} = 1.01 \cdot g_{m2}$)		91	91	dB

All the characteristics of the Miller CMOS OTA are listed in Table 6-11. Some of them are repeated from Table 6-5. For the total active area, the layout of Fig. 6-44 (on the following page) has been used. In this layout, all transistors are easily recognizable by means of the dimensions given in Table 6-2.

Now that we have fully analyzed the Miller OTA, we move on to the analysis of other configurations. Of course, we are unable in this text to cover these other configurations in the same depth as the Miller OTA. We thus limit ourselves to the expressions of the *GBW* and few other important characteristics. Of course, the reader is encouraged to develop the full set of characteristics, if so inclined.

After the analysis of these configurations, we focus on some design options and discuss a number of existing op amp designs for the sake of illustration.

6-7   DESIGN OF OTHER OTAS

Until this point, we have discussed only the simple CMOS OTA and the Miller CMOS OTA derived from it. Their input stage consists of a differential pair loaded by a current mirror. This load is thus very asymmetrical. Therefore, we may prefer the symmetrical CMOS OTA, which provides the same load to both input devices.

6-7-1   Symmetrical CMOS OTA

The circuit schematic of the CMOS OTA with symmetrical input stage is given in Fig. 6-45. The differential pair is formed by input transistors T1 and T2. They drive their output currents in two transistors, T3 and T4, which are connected as diodes.

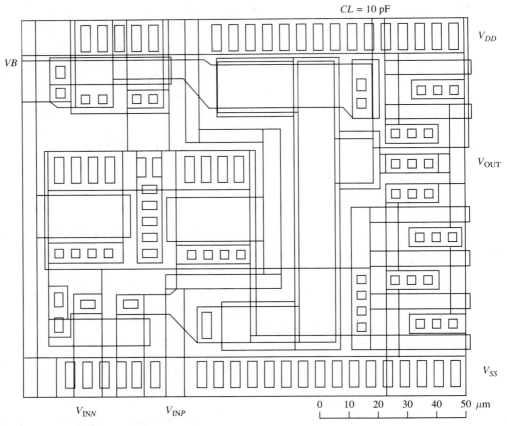

FIGURE 6-44   Layout of Miller CMOS OTA of Fig. 6-4.

They are the inputs of two current mirrors with current muliplication factor B. Typical values are $B = 1$ to 3. The output current of transistor T5 (see Fig. 6-45) is then mirrored once more in current mirror T7, T8, with $B = 1$, as indicated.

Gain of the Symmetrical CMOS OTA   At nodes 4, 5, and 6, a diode connected FET is driven by a current source. A diode connected FET represents only a small signal resistance of $1/g_m$, whereas the current sources have an output resistance r_o, which is much higher than $1/g_m$. As a result, at each of these nodes, the small-signal resistance with respect to ground is quite small, i.e., $1/g_m$.

The small-signal resistance is high only at the output node 7. It is formed by the two output resistances r_{o6} and r_{o8} in parallel. For equal values of $r_{o6} = r_{o8}$, output resistance R_{OUT} equals $r_{o6}/2$. On the other hand, the transconductance of the OTA is now a factor B higher than for the simple OTA, i.e., Bg_{m1}.

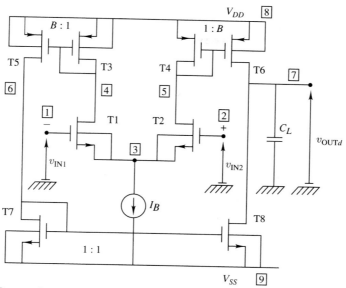

FIGURE 6-45 Symmetrical CMOS OTA (p-well).

The voltage gain A_v is then given by multiplication of the transconductance and R_{OUT}, or by

$$A_v = B g_{m1} \frac{r_{o6}}{2} = V_{Ep} L_6 \sqrt{\frac{2K_n'}{I_B} \left(\frac{W}{L} \right)_1} \qquad (6\text{-}134)$$

after substitution of the MOST parameters (see Chap. 1).

Note that factor B is not present in the expression of the gain A_v. The transconductance increases B times, whereas R_{OUT} decreases B times. Yet, in comparison with A_v in Eq. (6-3a), an additional design factor appears in Eq. (6-134), which is L_6. Its value can be taken as larger than L_1. The voltage gain A_v can thus be increased by increasing the value of r_{o6} or L_6. With this additional degree of freedom, the output resistance R_{OUT} and the voltage gain A_v can be increased without affecting the OTA transconductance.

Up until this point, the total gain A_v of the OTA has been considered. The gain of the first stage A_{v1} alone is important as well, as it determines the noise performance of the OTA. It is given by the ratio of $(v_5 - v_4)/v_{\text{IN}1}$, if $v_{\text{IN}2}$ is grounded. It is found by inspection (see Sec. 6-1) to be

$$A_{v1} = \frac{g_{m1}}{g_{m3}} = \sqrt{\frac{K_n'}{K_p'}} \sqrt{\frac{(W/L)_1}{(W/L)_3}} \qquad (6\text{-}135)$$

For low noise purposes, we must ensure that the noise of the input stage is dominant over the noise of the output transistors referred to the input. Therefore, the gain must be larger than unity, i.e., the gain must have a minimum value of three, the reasons for which will be explained shortly.

As a result, a new design constraint can be introduced. For a given value of $(W/L)_1$, the value of $(W/L)_3$ must be smaller than $0.22 (W/L)_1$, if $K_n'/K_p' \approx 2$.

GBW of the Symmetrical CMOS OTA   The values of the dominant and non-dominant poles can be determined, as well as the value of the *GBW*, in much the same way in which they were determined for a simple OTA. However, since more nodes are carrying signal voltages, more nondominant poles are present. They must be shifted to sufficiently high frequencies in order to ensure a phase margin of more than 60°.

The dominant pole f_d is evidently realized at node 7, which exhibits the highest resistance, i.e., R_{OUT}. Its value is given by

$$f_d = \frac{1}{2\pi R_{\text{OUT}}(C_{n7} + C_L)} \tag{6-136}$$

in which C_{n7} includes all capacitances connected to node 7, due to the OTA (see Fig. 6-45). The value of *GBW* is given by

$$GBW = A_v f_d = \frac{B g_{m1}}{2\pi (C_{n7} + C_L)} = B \frac{\sqrt{2K_n' I_B}}{2\pi} \frac{\sqrt{(W/L)_1}}{C_{n7} + C_L} \tag{6-137}$$

after substitution of the MOST parameters.

In comparison with the *GBW* of the simple OTA, given by Eqs. (6-7a) and (6-7b), the *GBW* of the symmetrical OTA is *B* times larger. Note, however, that the total current consumption is $(B + 1)$ times larger as well. The value of *GBW* is thus increased, but at the expense of more current consumption.

On the other hand, let us not forget that the increased symmetry of the input stage is an additional advantage, which has not yet been represented by numbers. This will be done later. In order to be able to effectively use this value of *GBW*, the nondominant poles are evaluated first. The calculation of the phase margin will show that the factor of *B* can never be made large.

Phase Margin PM of the Symmetrical CMOS OTA   Nondominant poles occur at all other nodes, i.e., at nodes 4, 5, and 6, due to the capacitances on these nodes. Nodes 4 and 5 carry small signals, which have the same amplitude but the opposite phase. Therefore, the poles at nodes 4 and 5 are the same. Together, they form one single nondominant pole f_{nd5} (see also App. 6-1).

It is found by inspection and is given by

$$f_{nd5} \approx \frac{g_{m4}}{2\pi C_{n5}} = \frac{\sqrt{2K'_p I_B}}{2\pi} \frac{\sqrt{(W/L)_4}}{C_{n5}} \qquad (6\text{-}138)$$

The other nondominant pole occurs at node 6, i.e., f_{nd6}, but acts on only half of the output signal. Indeed, only the current flowing in T3, T5, T7, and T8 is subject to this pole. A thorough analysis (see App. 6-1) shows that, when a pole acts on only half of the signal, a zero must be added at twice the frequency. A pole-zero doublet is thus created. This pole is again found by inspection and is given by

$$f_{nd6} \approx \frac{g_{m7}}{2\pi C_{n6}} = \frac{\sqrt{2K'_n I_B}}{2\pi} \frac{\sqrt{B(W/L)_7}}{C_{n6}} \qquad (6\text{-}139)$$

and
$$f_{z6} = 2 f_{nd6}$$

The value of the phase margin PM is given by

$$PM = 90° - \varphi_{n5} - \varphi_{n6} \qquad (6\text{-}140)$$

with
$$\varphi_{n5} = \arctan \frac{GBW}{f_{nd5}} = \arctan B A_{v1} \frac{C_{n5}}{C_L + C_{n7}}$$

and
$$\varphi_{n6} = \arctan \frac{GBW}{f_{nd6}} - \arctan \frac{GBW}{2 f_{nd6}}$$

$$= \arctan \sqrt{\frac{B(W/L)_1}{(W/L)_7} \frac{C_{n6}}{C_L + C_{n7}}} - \arctan \frac{1}{2} \sqrt{\frac{B(W/L)_1}{(W/L)_7} \frac{C_{n6}}{C_L + C_{n7}}}$$

after substitution of GBW, f_{nd5}, and f_{nd6}. Also $K'_n \approx 2K'_p$ and gain A_{v1} has been taken from Eq. (6-135).

It can be concluded that the phase margin PM can be increased by

- decreasing node capacitances C_{n5} and C_{n6}
- decreasing B
- increasing $(W/L)_7$

(provided we keep constant $A_{v1} = 3$ and constant C_L).

It is not acceptable to decrease B too much. Factor B is normally increased to increase the slew rate (as we will see later in this section). A good compromise is $B = 3$. For a given C_L, this leaves us thus only $(W/L)_7$ to play with to ensure sufficient phase margin.

However the phase margin is not very sensitive to $(W/L)_7$ because φ_6 is only a very weak function of $(W/L)_7$. As a result, other design plans may be more suitable, as explained later.

Example 6-13

Take a symmetrical OTA with $I_B = 10 \ \mu A$, $B = 3$, $V_{Ep} = 8.3 \ V/\mu m$, $L_6 = 10 \ \mu m$, $L_1 = 5 \ \mu m$ and $W_1 = 50 \ \mu m$ ($K_n' = 20 \ \mu A/V^2$, $K_p' = 10 \ \mu A/V^2$). Calculate the gains and the *GBW* for $C_L = 10$ pF.

Find the PM for $(W/L)_7 = 10$ and $A_{v1} = 3$ if $C_{n5} = C_{n6} = 1$ pF. Repeat for $B = 1$.

Solution. The resulting values are $R_{OUT} = 2.77 \ M\Omega$, the OTA transconductance $Bg_{m1} = 190 \ \mu S$ and $A_v = 524$. For $C_L = 10$ pF (C_{n7} is negligible), *GBW* $= 0.3$ MHz. The PM $= 90° - \varphi_{n5} - \varphi_{n6} = 90° - 42° - 4.9° = 43.1°$. For $B = 1$, the respective values are $R_{OUT} = 8.3 \ M\Omega$, $Bg_{m1} = 63.3 \ \mu S$, but $A_v = 524$ is the same. For $C_L = 10$ pF, *GBW* $= 0.1$ MHz. The PM $= 90° - 16.7° - 2.85° = 70.4°$.

Design Plan   The design plan is very similar to the plan for a simple OTA. Again, it is carried out in two steps. The *GBW* is determined at the dominant node, which is the output node, as given by Eq. (6-137). Second, the phase margin is determined by the two nondominant poles at the two other nodes.

Assume that C_L is given. For a given current I_B, a given $(V_{GS1} - V_T)$, and a given *GBW*, the size of the input transistor $(W/L)_1$ is obtained from Eq. (6-137). The sizes of the transistors $(W/L)_4$ and $(W/L)_7$ must be such that the phase margin, given in Eq. (6-140), is sufficiently large. Two extra variables are added, i.e., the gain of the first stage A_{v1} and the current multiplier B.

As a result, we have four variables I_B, $(W/L)_1$, $(W/L)_4$, and $(W/L)_7$ to satisfy four specifications: *GBW*, PM, A_{v1}, and B, provided C_L is given. An exact solution can thus be found.

We can also relax the specifications. After all, B is present because of the slew rate and A_{v1} is present because of the noise. Let us first calculate these characteristics exactly before we make a decision about the design plan.

Slew Rate   Again, for the symmetrical OTA, the slew rate is determined by the load capacitance. The current available to charge this capacitance is now BI_B. The slew rate is given by

$$SR = B \frac{I_B}{C_L + C_{n7}} \tag{6-141}$$

It is B times larger than the slew rate for the simple OTA, which yields a considerable advantage. Remember, however, that the current consumption was $(B + 1)$ times larger as well.

Noise Performance   The total output noise voltage power $\overline{dv_{out}^2}$ is the sum of the equivalent input noise voltage powers $\overline{dv_{in}^2}$ of each transistor, multiplied by their gain squared. The equivalent input noise voltage power $\overline{dv_{in}^2}$ is then obtained by division of the total gain squared. This yields

$$\overline{dv_{in}^2} = 2\overline{dv_1^2} + 2\left(\frac{g_{m4}}{g_{m1}}\right)^2 \overline{dv_4^2}$$

$$+ \frac{2}{B^2}\left[\left(\frac{g_{m6}}{g_{m1}}\right)^2 \overline{dv_6^2} + \left(\frac{g_{m7}}{g_{m1}}\right)^2 \overline{dv_7^2}\right] \tag{6-142}$$

Substitution of all $\overline{dv_{in}^2}$ by their expression $8kT\,df/3g_{mi}$ yields

$$y = \frac{\overline{dv_{in}^2}}{\overline{dv_1^2}} = 2 + 2\frac{g_{m4}}{g_{m1}} + \frac{2}{B^2}\left[\frac{g_{m6}}{g_{m1}} + \frac{g_{m7}}{g_{m1}}\right] \tag{6-143a}$$

Note that the total equivalent input noise has been normalized to the equivalent input noise of one input transistor only. This is the so-called excess noise y.

Remembering that $g_{m1}/g_{m4} = A_{v1}$ and that $g_{m6}/g_{m4} = B$, the previous expression becomes

$$y = 2\left\{1 + \frac{1}{A_{v1}}\left[1 + \frac{1}{B}\left(1 + \sqrt{\frac{K_n'(W/L)_7}{K_p'(W/L)_5}}\right)\right]\right\} \tag{6-143b}$$

The total equivalent input noise can thus be reduced to the equivalent input noise of only the two input transistors, provided the gain of the first stage A_{v1} is large. Since this impairs the stability, as shown by Eq. (6-140), a compromise is taken for A_{v1}, such as three to five. Increasing B helps, but it also reduces the phase margin. A good compromise for B is one to three.

Example 6-14

Calculate the excess noise and the total input noise voltage for the amplifier of Fig. 6-45, from Example 6-13 with $B = 1$ in unity gain configuration (i.e., output connected to a noninverting input terminal). Also, calculate the maximum signal-to-noise S/N ratio for a sinusoidal output with a ± 2.5 V supply voltage.

Solution. Since $(W/L)_1 = 10$ and $A_{v1} = 3$, Eq. (6-135) yields $(W/L)_3 = 2.2$; also, $(W/L)_5 = (W/L)_3 = 2.2$ because $B = 1$. Hence, the total equivalent input noise voltage power is $y = 5.3$ times that of only the input transistor. For this transistor T1, $g_{m1} = 63.3$ μS, which yields $\overline{dv_1^2} = 1.75 \times 10^{-16}$ V^2/Hz and $\overline{dv_{in}^2} = 9.3 \times 10^{-16}$ V^2/Hz. For a bandwidth of 0.1 MHz with a single-pole characteristic, the noise bandwidth is $\pi/2$ times as much (see Chap. 5), or 0.16 MHz. The equivalent input noise is thus 1.5×10^{-10} V^2 or 12 μV$_{RMS}$. The peak output amplitude for a sine waveform is 2.5 V and its RMS value is $2.5/\sqrt{2} = 1.77$ V$_{RMS}$. As a result, the maximum S/N ratio is 1.5×10^5, or 103 dB.

BICMOS Alternatives In a BICMOS process with an n-well, the symmetrical OTA can be realized, as shown in Fig. 6-46. To obtain better matching, the sources of the input devices are connected to their common well. The input devices are MOSTs, because of the high input impedance and the high SR/GBW ratio. The nMOST current mirrors have been replaced by npn transistor mirrors.

The advantages of using a BICMOS process are as follows. First, the minimum voltage across a bipolar transistor is only a few hundred mV's, allowing a larger output swing. Second, the transconductance of a bipolar transistor is smaller. This causes the impedances at nodes 4 and 5 to be smaller. At these nodes, however, the capacitance is higher because of the collector-to-substrate capacitances. As the main nondominant pole is determined at these nodes, it will depend on the actual values used, whether the phase margin is smaller or not.

However, the noise performance will always be worse. The gain A_{v1} will probably be less than unity, giving rise to a large contribution by all transistors (see Eq. (143b)). In the CMOS circuit, we can effectively limit the noise contributions to the noise of two input transistors only, which is the best that can be achieved with any differential circuit.

FIGURE 6-46   Symmetrical BICMOS OTA (n-well).

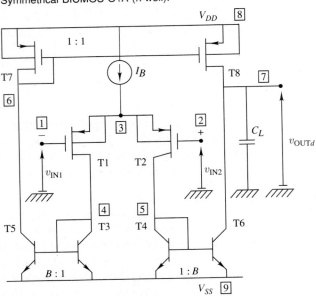

Note that current mirrors can be substituted by more complicated mirrors to increase the symmetry. Since this primarily involves the use of cascode transistors, we devote a separate section to this possibility.

6-7-2   Cascode Symmetrical CMOS OTA

In order to increase the open-loop gain and the symmetry, cascode transistors can be added. Of course, cascodes can be added in any OTA circuit. As an example, let us add cascodes in the symmetrical CMOS OTA discussed in the previous section. The circuit schematic is given in Fig. 6-47. Transistors M7 to M10 are cascode transistors. They are biased by a separate biasing network consisting of transistors M15 to M18, the current in which is set by current source I_B and transistor M14.

Gain   The only high impedance point in this circuit is the output node. All other such points are at a resistance level of $1/g_m$. The output resistance R_{OUT} consists of a resistance toward transistor M8, called $R_{OUT8}(= 1/g_{OUT8})$, and one toward M10, called $R_{OUT10}(= 1/g_{OUT10})$. It is given by

$$R_{OUT} = \frac{1}{g_{OUT8} + g_{OUT10}} \tag{6-144}$$

with

$$g_{OUT8} = \frac{g_{o8}g_{o6}}{g_{m8}}$$

FIGURE 6-47   Cascode symmetrical CMOS OTA (*n*-well).

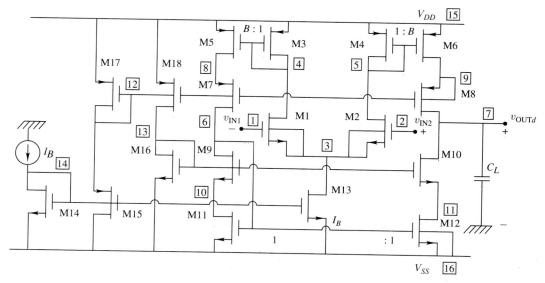

and
$$g_{OUT10} = \frac{g_{o10} g_{o12}}{g_{m10} + g_{mb10}}$$

The gain A_{v0} is thus given by

$$A_{v0} = g_{m1} R_{OUT} \tag{6-145}$$

Note that this circuit is realized in an n-well CMOS process. The n-well bulk of pMOST M8 is connected to its source. This is not possible for nMOST M10, however. As a result, g_{mb10} appears in the expression of g_{OUT10}. Also, note that both g_{OUT8} and g_{OUT10} can be made very small, yielding a very large output resistance R_{OUT}. This is a direct result of the use of the cascode transistors M8 and M10.

GBW and Phase Margin PM   Since there is only one high impedance node, the GBW is simply given by

$$GBW = \frac{B(g_{m1} + g_{mb1})}{2\pi (C_L + C_{n7})} \tag{6-146}$$

which is the same expression for the symmetrical OTA, except for the addition of g_{mb1}. In order to be able to effectively use this value of GBW, the nondominant poles and the phase margin PM must be evaluated.

Nondominant poles occur at all other nodes, i.e., at nodes 4, 5, 8, 9, 6, and 11. Nodes 4 and 5 carry signals with the same amplitude but opposite phase. Therefore, nodes 4 and 5 form one single nondominant pole f_{nd5} (see App. 6-1), given by

$$f_{nd5} \approx \frac{g_{m4}}{2\pi C_{n5}} \tag{6-147}$$

The same applies to nodes 8 and 9. They form a single pole, given by

$$f_{nd9} \approx \frac{g_{m8}}{2\pi C_{n9}} \tag{6-148}$$

The other nondominant poles occur at node 6, node 10, and node 11. They are given by

$$f_{nd6} \approx \frac{g_{m11}}{2\pi C_{n6}} \tag{6-149}$$

and
$$f_{nd10} \approx \frac{g_{m9} + g_{mb9}}{2\pi C_{n10}} (1 + G_{11}) \tag{6-150}$$

and
$$f_{nd11} \approx \frac{g_{m10} + g_{mb10}}{2\pi C_{n11}} \tag{6-151}$$

in which G_1 is the loopgain (at high frequencies) around transistor T11. As a result, the phase shift due to f_{nd10} is the smaller one and can be neglected.

All three poles act on only half of the output signal. All three generate a zero at double the frequency (see App. 6-1), and therefore their contribution to the phase margin can be made negligible.

We can conclude that the phase margin PM is determined mainly by poles f_{nd5} and f_{nd9}.

Design Plan   The design is very similar to the design for the symmetrical OTA, and is carried out in two steps. First, the *GBW* is determined at the output node. Second, the phase margin is determined mainly by the nondominant poles on nodes 5 and 9. The sizes of the transistors $(W/L)_4$ and $(W/L)_8$ must be such that the phase margin is sufficiently large.

As a result, we have six variables; namely I_B, $(W/L)_1$, $(W/L)_4$, $(W/L)_6$, $(W/L)_8$, and $(W/L)_{10}$ to satisfy the four specifications *GBW*, PM, A_{v1}, and *B*, provided C_L is given. Obviously, we have more variables than constraints. We can now choose other $(V_{GS} - V_T)$ values. We can also involve the slew rate, the noise, and a few other specifications.

We will not calculate the values for slew rate and noise, as they are exactly the same values obtained for the symmetrical OTA (see Sec. 6-7-1). The cascode transistors should not contribute to the noise, assuming they are properly designed (see Sec. 4-5-4).

Such a cascode symmetrical CMOS OTA has been realized. Its essential features are discussed in Sec. 6-9-1 and its dimensions are presented in App. 6-2.

6-7-3 Symmetrical Miller CMOS OTA With High *PSRR*

In order to increase the open-loop gain of a symmetrical OTA, a second stage can be added, as it was for the Miller OTA. The new schematic is given in Fig. 6-48 (Steyaert and Sansen 1990).

A *p*-well CMOS process is used, which explains why the input devices are *n*MOSTs. Cascode transistors M11 and M12 have been added to increase the input load symmetry and the gain. The second stage consists of transistors M13 and M14. Load transistor M14 is driven by transistor M3 of the first stage.

The compensation capacitance C_c normally connected between the output and the input of the second stage transistor M13, is guided through cascode transistor M11. The advantage of doing so is the increase of the $PSRR_{SS}$, as explained next.

The gain, *GBW*, PM, *SR*, and *y* have been discussed often and thus the calculations are left to the reader. There cannot be any doubt that the *GBW* is given by $g_{m1}/2\pi C_c$. We now focus on the $PSRR_{SS}$.

In order to suppress the feedforward path from V_{SS} over the compensation capacitance C_c to the output, a unidirectionally operating device, such as a MOST M11 is used. That part of the circuit is repeated in Fig. 6-49a. Transistor M11 is readily

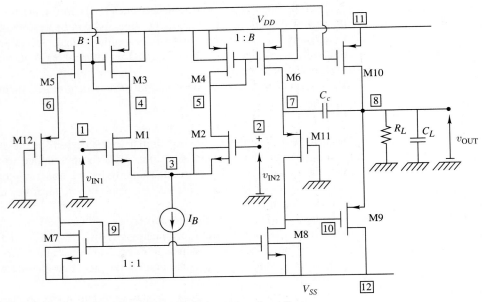

FIGURE 6-48   Miller symmetrical CMOS OTA with high $PSRR_{SS}$ (p-well).

recognized. Its biasing is left out, but it must ensure that the MOST always operates in saturation. The parasitic capacitance from the gate of M13 to V_{SS} is denoted by C_{n1SS}.

For analysis, the transistor is substituted by its small-signal equivalent circuit, shown in Fig. 6-49b. Note that the parasitic capacitance to ground C_p at the drain of the MOST cannot be neglected.

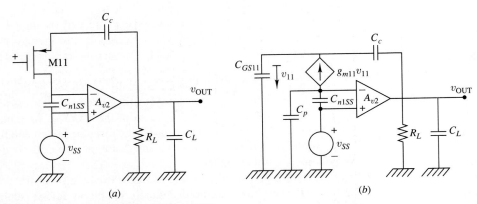

FIGURE 6-49   Principle schematic of OTA with high $PSRR_{SS}$.

Straightforward analysis of this circuit yields

$$\frac{v_{\text{out}}}{v_{SS}} = \frac{C_p}{C_c}\left(1 + j\frac{f}{f_{11}}\right)$$

(6-152)

with

$$f_{11} = \frac{g_{m11}}{2\pi(C_c + C_{GS11})}$$

if

$$A_{v2} > \frac{C_{n1SS} + C_p}{C_c}\left(1 + j\frac{f}{f_{11}}\right)$$

which is normally no problem.

For a large f_{11}, g_{m11} must also be large, but then C_p increases as well. Let us take for M11 a transistor that is equal in size to M1. In this case, $f_{11} \approx GBW$. If $C_{1nSS} = 0.2$ pF, and $C_p = 0.1$ pF, then the gain v_{OUT}/v_{SS} is 0.1, or -20 dB. This condition is easy to fulfill if $A_{v2} > 0.3$, which should not present a problem.

The high frequency $PSRR_{SS,GBW}$ is then given by

$$PSRR_{SS,GBW} = \frac{C_c}{C_p}$$

(6-153)

which is 10 if $C_c = 1$ pF and $C_p = 0.1$ pF. In comparison with unity for the Miller CMOS OTA, a factor of 10 has been gained by insertion of transistor M11. While it is always better to add the transistor, an extra node is added to the circuit, and this means that extra calculations will be necessary for the phase margin.

Such a symmetrical Miller CMOS OTA has been realized. Its features are discussed in Sec. 6-9-1 and its dimensions and characteristics are given in App. 6-2.

6-7-4 Folded-Cascode CMOS OTA

The main disadvantage of the cascode symmetrical CMOS OTA of Section 6-7-2 is its limited output swing. For this purpose, and for other reasons that will be made clear, a folded-cascode CMOS OTA is preferred. The circuit schematic is given in Fig. 6-50. Transistors M5 and M6 are cascode transistors. Transistors M7 to M9 form a cascoded current mirror. The cascode transistors are biased by a separate biasing network (not shown), which provides V_{B1} and V_{B2}. The currents are set by current source I_B and transistors M11 to M13. Normally, the current through transistor M3 is twice the current through transistor M1. As a result, the current through transistors M5–9 is the same as through the input transistors M1 and M2.

Gain If v_{in} is the differential AC input voltage, then $g_{m1}v_{\text{in}}/2$ is the AC current flowing in the input transistors. This current flows from transistor M1 through transistor M6 to the output. The current through transistor M2 flows through transistor M5 and is mirrored by transistors M8 and M9 through transistor M7 to the output.

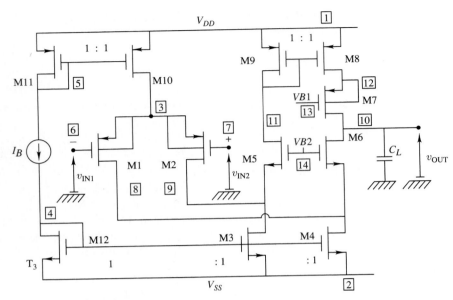

FIGURE 6-50   Folded Cascode CMOS OTA.

The only high impedance point in this circuit is the output node. All other nodes are at a resistance level of $1/g_m$. The output resistance R_{OUT} consists of a resistance toward M7, called $R_{OUT7}(= 1/g_{OUT7})$, and one toward M6, called $R_{OUT6}(= 1/g_{OUT6})$. It is given by

$$R_{OUT} = \frac{1}{g_{OUT7} + g_{OUT6}} \tag{6-154}$$

with

$$g_{OUT7} = \frac{g_{o7}g_{o9}}{g_{m7}}$$

and

$$g_{OUT6} = \frac{g_{o6}(g_{o4} + g_{o1})}{g_{m6} + g_{mb6}}$$

The gain A_{v0} is given by

$$A_{v0} = g_{m1}R_{OUT} \tag{6-155}$$

Note that this circuit is realized in a n-well CMOS process. The n-well bulk of pMOST M7 is connected to its source. This is also the case for both input devices, but it is impossible for the nMOST M6. As a result, g_{mb6} appears in the expression of g_{OUT6}. Also note that a very large output resistance R_{OUT} can be realized.

GBW and Phase Margin PM   Since there is only one high impedance node, the *GBW* is given by

$$GBW = \frac{g_{m1}}{2\pi(C_{n10} + C_L)} \tag{6-156}$$

which is the same expression given for the simple OTA. For the phase margin PM, the nondominant poles must be evaluated.

Nondominant poles occur at all other nodes, i.e., at nodes 8, 9, 11, and 12. Nodes 8 and 9 carry signals with the same amplitude but opposite phase. Therefore, nodes 8 and 9 form one single nondominant pole f_{nd8} (see App. 6-1), given by

$$f_{nd8} \approx \frac{g_{m6} + g_{mb6}}{2\pi C_{n8}} \tag{6-157}$$

The other nondominant poles occur at node 11 and 12. They are given by

$$f_{nd11} \approx \frac{g_{m8}}{2\pi C_{n11}} \tag{6-158}$$

and
$$f_{nd12} \approx \frac{g_{m7}}{2\pi C_{n12}} \tag{6-159}$$

However, both poles act only on half the output signal, and thus both generate a zero at double the frequency (see App. 6-1).

The value of the phase margin PM is then given by

$$PM = 90° - \varphi_{n8} - \varphi_{n11} - \varphi_{n12} \tag{6-160}$$

with
$$\varphi_{n8} = \arctan \frac{GBW}{f_{nd5}} = \arctan \frac{g_{m1}}{g_{m6} + g_{mb6}} \frac{C_{n8}}{C_L + C_{n10}}$$

and
$$\varphi_{n11} = \arctan \frac{GBW}{f_{nd11}} - \arctan \frac{GBW}{2f_{nd11}}$$

$$= \arctan \frac{g_{m1}}{g_{m8}} \frac{C_{n11}}{C_L + C_{n10}} - \arctan \frac{1}{2} \frac{g_{m1}}{g_{m8}} \frac{C_{n11}}{C_L + C_{n10}}$$

and φ_{n12} is given by a similar expression as that given for φ_{n11}.

We can conclude that the phase margin PM is mainly determined by pole f_{nd8}.

Design Plan   Again, the design is carried out in two steps. The *GBW* is determined at the output node and the phase margin is determined mainly by the nondominant pole on node 8.

The independent variables are I_B, $(V_{GS1} - V_T)$, $(V_{GS3} - V_T)$, $(V_{GS5} - V_T)$, $(V_{GS7} - V_T)$, $(V_{GS9} - V_T)$, and the biasing voltages V_{B1} and V_{B2}.

Assume that C_L is known. For a given current I_B and a given GBW, the size of the input transistor $(W/L)_1$ is obtained from a choice in $(V_{GS1} - V_T) \approx 0.2$ V (because they are amplifying devices). The sizes of the transistors $(W/L)_{5,6}$ must be such that the phase margin PM is sufficiently large.

Obviously, we have more variables than constraints. We can now make choices in the other $(V_{GS} - V_T)$ values and/or we can allow the slew rate, the noise, and other specifications to come into play. For example, for the current mirrors, $(V_{GS3} - V_T) = (V_{GS9} - V_T) \approx 0.5$ V for matching and all other $(V_{GS} - V_T) \approx 0.3$ V. Also, $V_{B1} = 0.1$ V and $V_{B2} = -0.1$ V, etc.

Let us now calculate the slew rate and the noise. The calculation of other characteristics are left to the reader.

Slew Rate   The slew rate is obviously determined by the load capacitance. The current available to charge this capacitance is now the DC current through transistor M10, denoted by I_{B10}. The slew rate is given by

$$SR = \frac{I_{B10}}{C_L + C_{n10}} \qquad (6\text{-}161)$$

Noise Performance   The total output noise voltage power $\overline{dv_{out}^2}$ is the sum of the equivalent input noise voltage powers $\overline{dv_{in}^2}$ of each transistor, multiplied by their gain squared.

This yields (approximately)

$$\overline{dv_{in}^2} = 2\overline{dv_1^2} + 2\left(\frac{g_{m3}}{g_{m1}}\right)^2 \overline{dv_3^2} + 2\left(\frac{g_{m8}}{g_{m1}}\right)^2 \overline{dv_8^2} \qquad (6\text{-}162)$$

Substitution of all $\overline{dv_{in}^2}$ by their expression $8kT\,df/3g_{mi}$ yields, as excess noise factor,

$$y = \frac{\overline{dv_{in}^2}}{\overline{dv_1^2}} = 2\left(1 + \frac{g_{m3}}{g_{m1}} + \frac{g_{m8}}{g_{m1}}\right) \qquad (6\text{-}163)$$

The total equivalent input noise can thus be reduced to the equivalent input noise of only the two input transistors, provided g_{m3} and g_{m8} are small. Remember that this depends on their sizes and/or their $(V_{GS} - V_T)$ values.

Such a folded-cascode CMOS OTA has been realized. Its prime features are discussed in Sec. 6-9-1 and its dimensions and characteristics are provided in App. 6-2.

BICMOS Folded-Cascode OTA   Several BICMOS folded-cascode OTAs can be derived from the CMOS OTA. A good example is shown in Fig. 6-51. The input devices are pMOSTs because there is an n-well CMOS process available. In this way, their sources can be connected to their bulk to avoid bulk biasing.

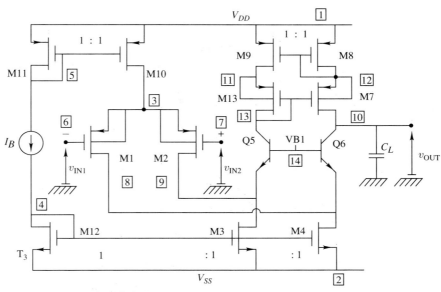

FIGURE 6-51   Folded Cascode BICMOS OTA.

We set up the cascode transistors as *npn* transistors in order to realize a low impedance at nodes 8 and 9, and in turn a high phase margin is easy to realize. All current mirror devices are MOSTs. As a load, a symmetrical current mirror is used (see Fig. 4-76*b*) with high output resistance. The major drawback of this mirror is its high voltage drop.

The design plan is very much the same as the CMOS version. Only this time we do not have to include the size or the $(V_{GS} - V_T)$ of transistors M5 and M6. We have one variable less and thus less choices to make.

6-7-5 Operational Current Amplifier (OCA)

Sometimes currents must be amplified rather than voltages, (e.g., for photodiodes), and it is then better to use a current-mode OTA (Sedra and Smith, 1987). A CMOS configuration is shown in Fig. 6-52. Since this circuit takes a current as an input, it is called an operational current amplifier (OCA). The simplest OCA is a current mirror. However, a current mirror is not differential. Differential configurations with current mirrors are thus OCA's. The configuration of Fig. 6-52 is a simple one because four simple current mirrors are used. Each of the current mirrors can be substituted by more sophisticated ones (see Sec. 4-8-3) to improve performance, but let us first perform a first-order analysis.

The operation is fairly straightforward. Transistors M1 and M3 are input transistors. They can sink or source the input current i_{IN}. Assume that the input current is positive such that the current is sourced by transistor M1. It is then amplified by current mirror

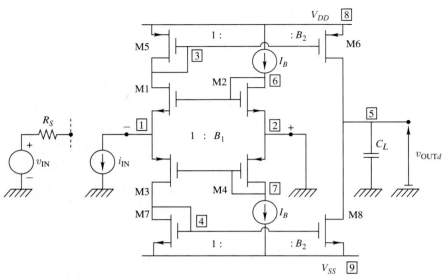

FIGURE 6-52   Operational current amplifier (OCA).

M5,6 by a factor B_2 to reach the output. The current gain is thus B_2, which is a transistor ratio, and can thus be set at very predictable and precise values. Typical values are 5 to 10.

The input transistors are biased by devices M2,4 that carry a DC current I_B, which is a factor B_1 smaller. Typical values are 0.1 to 1.

Note that this circuit is mirrored with respect to the horizontal axis. As a result, $g_{m2} = g_{m1}$, $g_{m7} = g_{m5}$, etc. Mismatches will thus play an important role. Let us first discuss the elementary characteristics, such as the gain.

Gain   This OTA is normally current-driven and its input impedance must thus be low. Indeed, it is only $1/2g_{m1}$ (since $g_{m3} = g_{m1}$). The only high impedance point in this circuit is the output node. All the other nodes are at a resistance level of the order of magnitude of $1/g_m$. The current gain is $A_{IN0} = B_2$. We can also take the output voltage as we have done for the OTA, and we obtain a transresistance A_R. At low frequencies it is given by

$$A_{R0} = \frac{v_{OUT}}{i_{IN}} = \frac{B_2}{g_{o68}} \tag{6-164a}$$

in which $g_{o68} = g_{o6} + g_{o8}$. Since the output conductance is proportional to the current, A_{R0} is given by

$$A_{R0} = \frac{v_{OUT}}{i_{IN}} = \frac{1}{g_{o13}} \tag{6-164b}$$

which depends only on the current and the channel length of the input transistors.

_BW_ and Phase Margin PM   Since there is only one high impedance node, the _BW_ is given by

$$BW = \frac{g_{o68}}{2\pi (C_L + C_{n5})} \tag{6-165}$$

Note that we cannot define the _GBW_. Indeed, the gain is a resistance A_R and there is no point where $|A_R| = 1$. When we apply a lot of feedback, i.e., when the external feedback resistor R_F is small, the closed-loop transresistance is simply R_F and a large closed-loop bandwidth BW_F is achieved. It is approximately given by

$$BW_F = \frac{1}{2\pi R_F (C_L + C_{n5})} \tag{6-166}$$

If this bandwidth is close to the nondominant poles, the phase margin may become too small. It is clear that the position of the nondominant poles limits the maximum achievable bandwidth BW_F for the OCA as well as for the OTA.

Nondominant poles occur at all other nodes, i.e., at nodes 1, 3, 4, 6, and 7. Input node 1 forms a nondominant pole f_{nd1}, as given by

$$f_{nd1} \approx \frac{2g_{m1}}{2\pi C_{n1}} \tag{6-167}$$

Nodes 3 and 4 carry signals with the same amplitude but opposite phase, and therefore nodes 3 and 4 form one single nondominant pole f_{nd3} (see also App. 6-1), given by

$$f_{nd3} \approx \frac{g_{m5}}{2\pi C_{n3}} \tag{6-168}$$

The other nondominant pole at node 6 does not come into play because it appears at the gate of cascode transistor M1 (see Sec. 4-6-2). The same applies to the pole at node 7.

A zero appears across transistor M6, given by

$$f_{z3} \approx \frac{g_{m6}}{2\pi C_{GD6}} \tag{6-169}$$

The value of the phase margin PM is thus given by

$$\text{PM} = 90° - \varphi_{n1} - \varphi_{n3} + \varphi_{z3} \tag{6-170}$$

with $\qquad \varphi_{n1} = \arctan \dfrac{BW_F}{f_{nd1}} \quad$ and $\quad \varphi_{n3} = \arctan \dfrac{BW_F}{f_{nd3}}$

and $\qquad \varphi_{z3} = \arctan \dfrac{BW_F}{f_{z3}}$

All of these values depend on the actual amount of feedback applied and thus on resistor R_F.

It is possible to define a *GBW* if we use a voltage source v_{IN} with source resistor R_S at the input as shown in Fig. 6-52. Of course, we must ensure that resistor R_S is always larger than $1/2g_{m1}$. If not, the input current i_{IN} is given by the input resistance:

$$\frac{i_{IN}}{v_{IN}} = \frac{1}{R_{IN}} = \frac{1}{R_S + 1/2g_{m1}} \tag{6-171}$$

and the voltage gain is given by

$$A_{v0} = \frac{v_{OUT}}{i_{IN}} = \frac{A_{R0}}{R_{IN}} = \frac{1}{g_{o13}(R_S + 1/2g_{m1})} \tag{6-172}$$

which indeed depends on R_S. The *GBW* is determined by the dominant pole, i.e., capacitance C_L, as given by

$$GBW = \frac{1}{2\pi R_S(C_L + C_{n5})} \tag{6-173}$$

which evidently depends on R_S as well. If we keep R_S constant and vary only the feedback resistor R_F, we obtain a *GBW* as we did for an OTA. However, if instead we vary R_S, then *GBW* varies as well, and we can no longer consider a *GBW*. In the latter case, the BW_F is constant, as given by Eq. (6-166).

Design Plan   The design is carried out, not surprisingly, in two steps. The *BW* is determined at the output node and the phase margin is determined by the nondominant poles and zero.

The independent variables are I_B, $(V_{GS1} - V_T)$, $(V_{GS5} - V_T)$, B_1, and B_2, and we assume that C_L is given and a certain *BW* is required. The output resistance $1/g_{o68}$ is thus determined. For a reasonable channel length $L_{6,8}$, the output current I_{DS68} and the width $W_{6,8}$ is determined. Parameter B_2 is determined on the basis of the current gain, the power consumption, and especially the nondominant poles. The sizes of the transistors $(W/L)_{1,3}$ are then determined as well. Parameter B_1 is not critical; it merely fixes the sizes of the transistors $(W/L)_{2,4}$.

It is obvious that we have more constraints than variables. Such a simple OCA is full of compromises and it is therefore better to substitute the simple current mirrors by more sophisticated ones. This substitution somewhat relaxes the compromises.

Let us now calculate the slew rate and the noise, as we have done for the other amplifiers.

Slew Rate   The slew rate is not determined by the load capacitance this time. The current that is available to charge this capacitance can be quite large because it is B_2 times the input current. There is thus no slew rate limitation as there is for a conventional OTA or op amp. This is probably the main advantage of OCAs and current amplifiers.

Noise Performance   The total output noise current power $\overline{di_{\text{out}}^2}$ is the sum of the noise currents $\overline{di_{\text{in}}^2}$ of each transistor multiplied by their gain squared. This gives approximately

$$\overline{di_{\text{out}}^2} = 2\left[\left(\overline{di_1^2} + \overline{di_5^2} + 2\frac{\overline{di_2^2}}{B_1^2}\right)B_2^2 + \overline{di_6^2}\right] \tag{6-174}$$

Substitution of all $\overline{di_{\text{in}}^2}$ by their expression $8kTg_{mi}df/3$ yields, for the equivalent input noise current,

$$\overline{di_{\text{in}}^2} = \frac{\overline{di_{\text{out}}^2}}{B_2^2} = \frac{16kT}{3}\left[g_{m1}\left(1 + \frac{1}{B_1}\right) + g_{m5}\left(1 + \frac{1}{B_2}\right)\right] \tag{6-175}$$

The total equivalent input noise can thus be limited to the noise of the two input transistors, provided g_{m5} is small and B_1 and B_2 are large. This is yet another extra compromise.

The design does not become easier by employing a BICMOS process rather than a CMOS process. It is an obvious choice to replace the four input transistors M1 to M4 by bipolar transistors in order to realize a low input resistance. However, in order to maintain symmetry, we need a *pnp* transistor with the characteristics of a *npn* transistor. This is the case only if we have a vertical *pnp*, which is not a standard component.

6-8 DESIGN OPTIONS

In previous sections, a simple CMOS OTA, a symmetrical CMOS OTA, and a Miller OTA have been analyzed in great detail. Moreover, all characteristics (except distortion) have been derived for the CMOS Miller OTA. The design aspects have been limited to a few characteristics, such as the *GBW* and stability. In this section, more attention is paid to the design aspects.

In the following three subsections, design alternatives are discussed. The first alternative is the relation between optimum *GBW* or *SR*. The second alternative handles the stability problem caused by the right hand zero. The third alternative discusses the merits and the pitfalls of the use of cascodes.

This chapter concludes with the discussion of a number of op amp configurations in different technologies and combinations of technologies. The advantages and disadvantages are indicated, yet with a minimum of detail. These configurations are only representative for each technology and new ones can always be added. The schematics and specifications for these op amp configurations are present in App. 6-2.

6-8-1 Design for Optimum *GBW* or *SR*

Design procedures have been given for the optimum *GBW* (see Sec. 6-3-5). Design procedures can also be given for the optimum *SR*. Both characteristics reflect high-frequency performance. Linear amplifiers are better characterized by their GBW. Switched-capacitor filters, on the other hand, reach higher frequencies if their OTAs have a higher slew rate. Which one do we choose? How far can the GBW be increased at the cost of the SR, or vice versa?

In order to illustrate this design compromise, let us refer to the example of the CMOS Miller OTA, which we now know quite well. Its $GBW = 1.19$ MHz and its $SR = 2.23$ V/μs (see Table 6-5). As a result, the maximum output voltage that can be obtained at the frequency of the GBW is obtained from Eq. (6-40) and is given by

$$V_{\text{out}M} = \frac{SR}{2\pi GBW} \qquad (6\text{-}176)$$

which is 0.3 V. This output voltage is SR-limited (see Fig. 6-13) and thus has a triangular waveform. Such a triangle has about 10 percent third harmonic distortion. If we aim to limit the distortion to 1 percent, then we must divide the output amplitude by $\sqrt{10}$, since third harmonic distortion is proportional to the square of the output voltage amplitude. As a consequence, the maximum output voltage that we obtain at 1.19 MHz (with less than 1 percent distortion) is only about $0.3/\sqrt{10} \approx 0.1$ V or 0.07 V$_{\text{RMS}}$. This result is quite disappointing.

The only remedy is to increase the $SR/2\pi GBW$ ratio by proper design. In order to derive the consequent design rules, we first have a look at the simplest configuration, i.e., the simple CMOS OTA of Fig. 6-1.

Both the GBW and the SR are then determined by the load capacitance C_L as given by Eqs. (6-7) and (6-18). The resultant ratio is given by

$$\frac{SR}{2\pi GBW} = \frac{I_B}{g_{m1}} \qquad (6\text{-}177)$$

Note that this ratio is expressed in volts. In order to increase this ratio, the transconductance g_{m1} of the input transistor must be made small with respect to its DC current $I_B/2$. Usually, we must design for a large input transconductance. This is an exception and probably the only one we encounter. This expression indicates that we must design for a small transconductance. Actually, this is not true—we do not have to design for a small transconductance but rather for a small transconductance to current ratio. Let us examine how this can be realized in several technologies.

With MOS transistors, the ratio in Eq. (6-177) can be further evaluated: it is equal to $(V_{GS} - V_T)$. The input transistors must thus operate with large $(V_{GS} - V_T)$ values and in strong inversion. This conclusion is the opposite of what has been reached for large GBW and for small mismatch. A compromise must then be taken.

For example, if at $I_B = 10$ μA and $(W/L)_1 = 10$, $GBW = 0.9$ MHz ($K'_n = 20$ μA/V^2) and $SR = 1.25$ V/μs for 8 pF load. The ratio in Eq. (6-177) is only 0.22 V. This value can be increased only (for constant I_B) by decreasing $(W/L)_1$. The input transistors then operate in stronger inversion. For $(W/L)_1 = 1$, the ratio in Eq. (6-177) and $(V_{GS1} - V_T)$ increase by a factor $\sqrt{10}$, or about 3, and so does the SR.

Note that the same conclusions that are valid for MOSTs are valid for JFETS.

For bipolar transistors, the ratio in Eq. (6-151) is not a design parameter: i.e., we cannot modify it. Indeed, this ratio is simply $2kT/q$, or about 52 mV at room temperature and is thus always small. The application of emitter resistors increases this ratio by a factor $(1 + g_m R_E)$. However, it also causes additional offset and noise, considerably degrading the noise performance of the OTA. This is why the input stage in BICMOS usually consists of MOSTs.

For the Miller CMOS OTA of Fig. 6-4, the ratio of Eq. (6-176) is easily calculated from Eqs. (6-25) and (6-37) or (6-38). If internal SR is the limiting factor, then Eq. (6-37) is the expression to be used. The compensation capacitance then drops out and the same conclusions are valid for the input stage of the simple CMOS OTA.

If, however, the external SR is the limiting factor, Eq. (6-54) is used. The ratio in Eq. (4-150) is then given by

$$\frac{SR}{2\pi GBW} = \frac{I_5}{g_{m1}} \frac{C_c}{C_L} \tag{6-178}$$

The best way to increase this ratio is to increase I_5. Indeed, g_{m1} and C_c determine the GBW, whereas C_L is given. However, I_5 can only be increased insofar as the external SR is still the limiting factor. If I_5 is increased even more, the internal SR dominates again. This minimum value of I_5, which ensures that the external SR is not the limiting factor, is obtained by comparison of Eqs. (6-37) and (6-38). It is given by

$$I_{5\text{min}} = I_B \left(1 + \frac{C_L}{C_c}\right) \tag{6-179}$$

For the Miller OTA, this is 11 times I_B, or 27.5 μA. Since $I_5 - I_B = 22.5$ μA, this condition is not fulfilled. The external SR is thus the limiting SR, although the difference is small.

If extremely large values of SR are required, or if we prefer that the input devices have small values of $(V_{GS} - V_T)$, then *transconductance reduction stages* can be used. An example is given in Fig. 6-53 (Schmoock 1975). Two pairs of transistors are used. The external transistors M1 and M4 are n times larger (in (W/L)) than the internal transistors M2 and M3. Two equal biasing sources are required with value I_B.

For small input signals, the internal transistors only operate at $I_B/(n + 1)$ biasing current. Their transconductance can thus be made small and the currents through the external transistors are then lost to ground.

For large input signals, e.g., for a large input voltage at the gates of T1 and T2, both T1 and T2 are shut off. All current I_B of their current source then flows through T3 to the output. The ratio in Eq. (6-177) is then multiplied by a factor $(n + 1)$.

Mismatches can somewhat limit the efficiency of this design trick, but all op amps with very large SRs use it, albeit in different implementations.

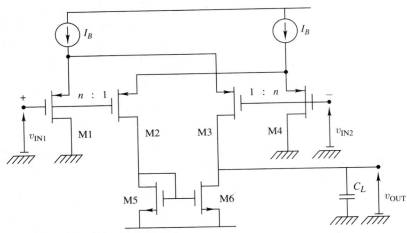

FIGURE 6-53 Transconductance reduction technique.

6-8-2 Compensation of the Positive Zero

The use of a Miller compensation capacitance C_c causes a positive zero, i.e., a zero that is located in the right-hand complex plane. This zero is particularly harmful for the stability of the OTA (see Fig. 6-7), especially if its value is close to the GBW. This zero must then be compensated.

Several design techniques exist. In Fig. 6-54a, a simplified schematic is given of a Miller OTA. Its small-signal equivalent circuit is given in Fig. 6-54b. The corresponding expressions of GBW, f_z, and f_{nd} are given in the first column of Table 6-12. Note that the zero depends on the transconductance g_{m2} of the second stage. If a bipolar transistor is used, or a MOST with large g_m, the zero frequency may be sufficiently high so that no compensation is required. This is why the second stage in a BIMOS process should consist of a bipolar transistor.

In all other cases, an additional stage (or component) must be inserted in series with the compensation capacitance C_c. Three possibilities are generally discussed. In the first, a unity-gain buffer stage is used (see Fig. 6-54c). In the second, (see Fig. 6-54f) a series resistance is inserted. In the last one (see Fig. 6-54h), a cascode transistor is used, as in Fig. 6-48. The buffer stage solution is examined first.

This buffer stage can easily be realized by means of a source follower (see Fig. 6-54d). Its gain can be less than unity and is therefore denoted by A_c. Its equivalent circuit is shown in Fig. 6-54e. After insertion in the equivalent circuit of Fig. 6-54b, the voltage gain can easily be calculated, and it is given by

$$A_v = \frac{A_{v0}}{1 + [R_1 C_1 + R_2 C_2 + R_1 C_c (1 + A_c g_{m2} R_2)]s + R_1 R_2 C_2 (C_1 + C_c)s^2} \quad (6\text{-}180)$$

with $A_{v0} = g_{m1} g_{m2} R_1 R_2$. From this expression, the GBW, zero, and nondominant pole are easily derived. They are listed in Table 6-12, together with the expressions when

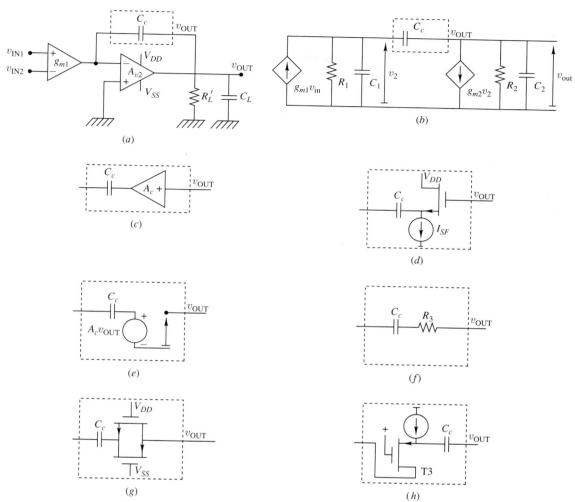

FIGURE 6-54   (a) Simplified schematic of Miller OTA, and (b) small-signal equivalent circuit.

no buffer is present. For all expressions in Table 6-12, it is assumed that $C_c > C_1$ and C_2.

The positive zero has clearly disappeared. This situation is independent of the gain of the buffer. The *GBW* does not change, provided the gain is unity and the nondominant pole is hardly affected.

We can conclude that the use of a source follower is an efficient way to eliminate the positive zero caused by the compensation capacitance. The intuitive reason for this is that this buffer stage acts as an unidirectional voltage follower, which does not allow the feedforward current to pass from the input of the A_{v2} ampli-

TABLE 6-12 CHARACTERISTIC FREQUENCIES FOR THE ZERO COMPENSATION ($C_C > C_1, C_2$) FOR A SOURCE FOLLOWER (GAIN A_C) OR A RESISTOR R_3.

	Without	A_c	$R_3 = \dfrac{1}{g_{m2}}$
GBW	$\dfrac{g_{m1}}{2\pi\, C_c}$	$\dfrac{g_{m1}}{2\pi\, A_c\, C_c}$	$\dfrac{g_{m1}}{2\pi\, C_c}$
f_z	$-\dfrac{g_{m2}}{2\pi\, C_c}$	∞	∞
f_{nd}	$\dfrac{g_{m2}}{2\pi\,(C_1 + C_2)}$	$\dfrac{A_c\, g_{m2}}{2\pi\, C_2}$	$\dfrac{g_{m2}}{2\pi\,(C_1 + C_2)}$
f_3	—	—	$\dfrac{g_{m2}}{2\pi\,\dfrac{C_1 C_2}{C_1 + C_2}}$

fier to its output. This has an additional advantage in that the *PSRR* has improved as well.

However, care must be taken to avoid parasitic capacitances. An additional node is created at the source of the source follower, which may somewhat degrade the stability.

A resistor R_3 can also be used in place of a source follower (see Fig. 6-54f). It can be realized by means of two MOSTs in their ohmic region, as shown in Fig. 6-54g. In this case, the gain is obtained in the same way as before. It is given by

$$A_v = A_{v0}\frac{1 - (1/g_{m2} - R_3)C_c s}{1 + as + bs^2 + cs^3} \tag{6-181}$$

with
$$a = R_1 C_1 + R_2 C_2 + R_1 C_c \left(1 + \frac{R_2}{R_1} + g_{m2} R_2\right) + R_3 C_c$$

and
$$b = R_1 R_2 C_1 C_2 \left[1 + C_c\left(\frac{1}{C_1} + \frac{1}{C_2}\right) + R_3 C_c\left(\frac{1}{R_1 C_1} + \frac{1}{R_2 C_2}\right)\right]$$

and
$$c = R_1 R_2 R_3 C_1 C_2 C_c$$

The zero drops out provided $R_3 = 1/g_{m2}$. The resultant *GBW* and nondominant pole are listed again in Table 6-12. They are not affected by resistor R_3 because $R_3 C_c$ is negligible in both coefficients a and b. However, a second nondominant or third pole f_3 emerges. It is always at higher frequencies than f_{nd} because $C_1C_2/(C_1 + C_2)$ is always smaller than $(C_1 + C_2)$.

As a result, the positive zero has been converted into a negative pole at higher frequencies and thus its effect is negligible.

This technique has an advantage in that no extra node is introduced. On the other hand, it does not improve the *PSRR*. The main question is how accurately the value of $1/g_{m2}$ can be approached by means of a resistor, or by means of two MOSTs. It proves not to be too difficult to realize this value, within about 20 percent. This is sufficiently accurate to make this technique work. This could be verified by the pole-zero position diagram, with R as a variable.

A cascode transistor T3 can also be used, as shown in Fig. 6-54f. In this case, the gain is given by

$$A_v = A_{v0} \frac{1 + C_c/g_{m3}s}{1 + as + bs^2 + cs^3} \tag{6-182}$$

with
$$a = R_1C_1 + R_2C_2 + R_1C_c \left(\frac{1}{g_{m3}R_1} + \frac{R_2}{R_1} + g_{m2}R_2 \right)$$

and
$$b = R_1R_2C_1C_2 \left[1 + \frac{C_c}{C_2} + \frac{C_c}{g_{m3}} \left(\frac{1}{R_1C_1} + \frac{1}{R_2C_2} \right) \right]$$

and
$$c = R_1R_2C_1C_2C_c/g_{m3}$$

The zero drops out, provided the input impedance of the cascode transistor T3, i.e., $1/g_{m3}$ is small. Zero has vanished and a second-order expression results, providing approximately the same values of *GBW* and phase margin.

This technique has an additional advantage in that the *PSRR* is improved as well (see Fig. 6-48). The main disadvantage is that extra current is required.

6-8-3 Fully-Differential or Balanced OTAs

Amplifiers in which a differential output is available are differential at both input and output terminals. They are called fully-differential amplifiers or balanced amplifiers and their use has been discussed in Sec. 5-5. They are essential for noise insensitive analog circuits. The fully-differential structure provides excellent *PSRR* and *CMRR*, even at high frequencies. Therefore, we can envisage exclusive use of fully-differential structures for all mixed analog-digital circuits in the future.

In this section we focus on some of their design aspects.

Balanced Simple CMOS OTA   It is very easy to convert a single-ended OTA in a balanced OTA. It is sufficient to leave out its output current mirror. From the simple CMOS OTA of Fig. 6-1, the balanced simple CMOS OTA of Fig. 6-55 is readily derived. The differential output is taken between the two drains. Both halves of the circuit thus behave as single-transistor amplifiers with active load. Their gain, GBW, etc. have already been fully analyzed in Sec. 6-1. The biasing, however, is quite different.

Initially we need to fix the average output DC voltage. If this is not done, the average (or common-mode) output voltage $V_{OUT,CM}$ may be too low, pushing the input transistors in the linear region. It may also be too high, pushing the load transistors in the linear region. However, all transistors must be kept in the saturation region in order to ensure high gain. We thus need a common-mode feedback circuit to determine the common-mode output voltage $V_{OUT,CM}$.

The common-mode feedback amplifier of the balanced CMOS OTA consists of transistors T5 through T8 (see Fig. 6-55a). The common-mode equivalent circuit is sketched in Fig. 6-55b. The common-mode output voltage is measured by transistors T5 and T6 and their output signals are added up at node 6, which is called the common-mode summation point. A current mirror with active load (with current I_C) then provides common-mode feedback to the gates of load transistors T3 and T4. As a result, transistors T3 and T4 will carry a current $I_B/2$, whereas transistors T5 and T6 will carry a current $I_C/2$. The average or common-mode DC output voltage $V_{OUT,CM}$ is thus $V_{DD} - V_{GS5}$.

As a result, we obtain two different amplifiers: a differential-mode amplifier (T1 through T4) and a common-mode amplifier (T3 through T8). Note that some transistors are shared. Indeed, transistors T3 and T4 occur in both the differential and

FIGURE 6-55   (a) Balanced simple CMOS OTA. (b) Common-mode equivalent circuit.

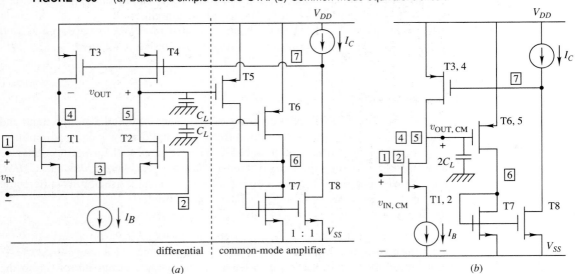

(a)   (b)

the common-mode amplifier. Both amplifiers have their own gain, *GBW*, slew rate, input and output voltage range, noise, etc. A full analysis can thus be given for each amplifier, but we will focus only on the relationship between some characteristics of the differential amplifier with the ones of the common-mode amplifier. These relations can be described by four requirements that must be satisfied by any common-mode amplifier:

1 The GBW_{CM} of the common-mode amplifier must be equal to or larger than the GBW_D of the differential amplifier in order to ensure stable biasing conditions for all frequencies of interest up to GBW_D.

2 The common-mode DC output voltage $V_{\text{OUT},CM}$ must be well stabilized and predictable, i.e., independent of matching between transistors, temperature, etc.

3 The differential amplifier still must provide a maximum output swing, i.e., preferably from the negative supply to the positive supply rail.

4 The differential amplifier still must operate over a maximum common-mode input voltage $V_{\text{IN},CM}$.

Let us verify these requirements on the balanced CMOS OTA of Fig. 6-55a:

1 The GBW_D is $g_{m1}/2\pi C_L$, whereas the $GBW_{CM} = g_{m5}/2\pi C_L$ (see Fig. 6-55b). Thus, for the first requirement it is sufficient to make sure that $g_{m5} > g_{m1}$, which is easily done by use of current source I_C and or V_{GS5} or $(W/L)_5$.

2 The DC output voltage $V_{\text{OUT},CM}$ is determined by transistors T5 and T6. Some mismatch in the current mirror T7,8 may cause a small deviation, which is not all that important. This requirement is thus satisfied.

3 The differential output swing is limited by the input range of the amplifying transistors T5 and T6. This value depends on their values V_{GS5}. From Fig. 4-60a we learn that the maximum swing is about $\sqrt{2}(V_{GS5} - V_T)$, which is usually a lot smaller than the supply voltage. A compromise can be found here.

4 The input common-mode input voltage range $V_{\text{IN},CM}$ is now also limited by the output voltage $V_{\text{OUT},CM}$. It can thus be smaller with common-mode feedback.

In this way, four additional constraints are added in the design plan of a common-mode amplifier. In general, not all requirements can be fulfilled, and this results in a compromise. Let us illustrate this with three circuit examples.

Balanced Symmetrical OTA With Linear MOSTs   A conventional symmetrical OTA is taken from Fig. 6-45, and MOSTs T11 through T13 are added in series with the bottom current mirrors as shown in Fig. 6-56 (Choi et al. 1983). These transistors operate in the linear region. Their V_{DS} is only about 0.2 V. The gate of transistor T13 is connected to ground, whereas the gates of transistors T11 and T12 are connected to the outputs. Since all transistors are matched, the DC common-mode output voltage $V_{\text{OUT},CM}$ will be around 0 V. Indeed, transistors T11 and T12 will change the voltage at node 10 (which is the common-mode summation point),

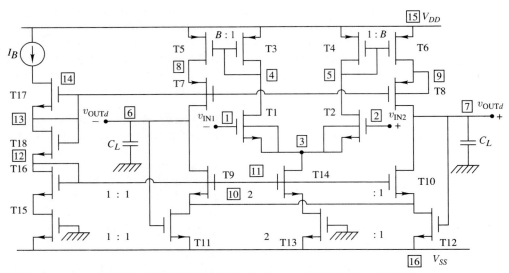

FIGURE 6-56 Balanced symmetrical OTA with MOSTs in the linear region. (Choi et al. 1983)

which changes the $V_{GS9,10}$ and the output currents such that the output voltages are approximately zero volts.

Let us see how this configuration performs:

1 The GBW_D is again $g_{m1}/2\pi C_L$, whereas the $GBW_{CM} = g_{m11}/2\pi C_L$. However, in the linear region the transconductance g_{m11} is quite small: $g_{m11} \approx KP_{11}V_{DS11}$. Hence, $g_{m11} \ll g_{m1}$, which does not fulfill the first requirement. Conmmon-mode large signals (such as overvoltages, etc.) will thus keep this circuit out of operation for time periods of the order of $\tau_{GBW,CM}(= 1/2\pi GBW_{CM})$. This may not harm telephone communications but it certainly harms data transmission systems, in which every bit counts.

2 The DC output voltage $V_{OUT,CM}$ is determined by transistors T11 through T3. Mismatches may cause a considerable deviation in DC output voltage from zero volts and thus this requirement is not fulfilled either.

3 The differential output swing is about the same as with any other cascode symmetrical OTA, provided only a small voltage V_{DS11} is allowed across the linear MOSTs T11 through T13. We form a compromise with the requirement: increasing V_{DS11} increases the GBW_{CM} but decreases the output swing.

4 The input common-mode input voltage range $V_{IN,CM}$ is also about the same as with any other cascode symmetrical OTA. The same comments apply as for the previous requirement.

We conclude that this amplifier performs well for a wide input and output voltage range but not at high frequencies. Also, its DC output voltage is sensitive to mismatches. Let us look at two alternatives.

Balanced Miller symmetrical CMOS OTA with Error Amplifier   In order to increase the GBW_{CM}, a separate amplifier is used in Fig. 6-57 (Haspeslagh and Sansen 1988). The differential amplifier is a Miller symmetrical CMOS OTA derived from Fig. 6-48. Since it has two stages, a compensation capacitance C_c is included.

The output voltages are measured by a separate error amplifier, consisting of transistors M15–20. The common-mode summation point is at the drains of M16 and M17. This signal is then fed to the gate of the input current transistors M5,6.

Since the gates of M16 and M17 are at ground, the output voltages will also be maintained at around zero volts. The error amplifier is differential in order to handle positive and negative output voltage excursions as well.

1 The GBW_{CM} can now be set independently by g_{m15} in the same way as for the balanced CMOS OTA of Fig. 6-55. The first requirement is thus fulfilled.

2 Since the DC output voltage is measured by a differential pair (M15,16 and M17,18), it will be sensitive only to the mismatch of that pair. This configuration is thus fairly insensitive to other mismatches in the main differential amplifier.

3 The output swing will be limited by the input range of the common-mode pair M15,16 and M17,18. This is a weak point indeed. We must design the latter transistors M15–18 for as large a V_{GS15} as possible. However, this will reduce g_{m15} and thus the GBW_{CM} unless large currents are used.

4 The input voltage range is not affected by the common-mode amplifier and so this condition is very easily met.

We conclude that this Miller symmetrical CMOS OTA with a separate error amplifier meets every condition except the third one, i.e., its output voltage swing is too limited.

FIGURE 6-57   Miller symmetry CMOS OTA with error amp balanced (Haspeslagh and Sansen 1988).

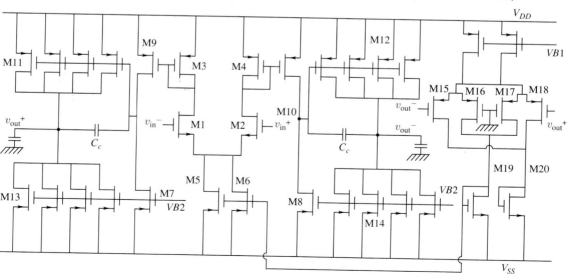

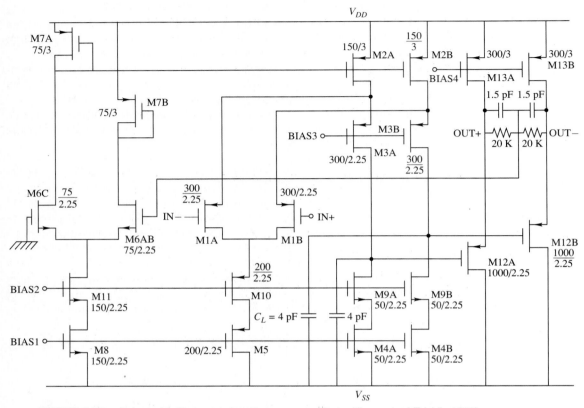

FIGURE 6-58   Balanced folded cascode with error amp. (Banu, Khoury, and Tsividis 1988)

Balanced Folded Cascode Op Amp With Error Amplifier   A separate error amplifier is also used in the circuit of Fig. 6-58 (Banu, Khoury, and Tsividis 1988). The main amplifier is a folded-cascode amplifier, as shown in Fig. 6-50. The load capacitance is $C_L(= 4 \text{ pF})$. The outputs are followed by two source followers with transistors M12, allowing a large output current drive.

The common-mode summation point is at the middle point between the two RC networks at the outputs. This point is fed to a differential pair with transistors M6A and B. The other input of this pair is connected to ground such that this middle point will be around ground itself. The common-mode feedback loop is closed through current mirrors M7 and M2.

The same three requirements are fulfilled as for the previous amplifier. The GBW_{CM} can be set by means of g_{m6}. A differential pair is used as a common-mode amplifier, to avoid excessive problems with mismatches. Also the input voltage range is not affected by the common-mode error amplifier. Let us check the output voltage swing.

The output voltage swing is limited by the current in the source follower, which is available to generate the output swing across the load resistor of 20 kΩ. For this purpose, the source follower transistors M12 are made very large. This requirement is thus fulfilled at the expense of a considerable amount of current (in the source followers).

It can be concluded that the last configuration offers an attractive solution. It fulfills all four conditions but takes more current. Also, a separate amplifier is used for the common-mode feedback. On first sight, this separate amplifier seems to provide only advantages, but we must not forget that such amplifier has more nodes, and thus more nondominant poles, and it is thus difficult to strike the right compromise.

Nevertheless, several compromises must be made. Two interwoven amplifiers must be optimized simultaneously, with respect to speed, noise, etc. This is not a trivial task and we suggest to the reader to first acquire familiarity with single-ended amplifiers before tackling the design of balanced amplifiers. The drawing of a design plan of a balanced amplifier is the *ne plus ultra* of a truly proficient analog circuit designer.

6-9 OP AMP EXAMPLES

In order to illustrate design techniques, we provide a number of configurations of operational amplifiers. Both custom made and standard operational amplifiers are included. For each of them, some important specifications are provided. For the CMOS op amps the transistor dimensions are given as well. In this way they can easily be studied in detail. The reader will find these configurations specifications and dimensions in App 6-2.

None of the amplifiers are actually analyzed in full detail. They are given as examples to be studied by the readers. Some of the design features are withheld, however, for the exercises.

6-9-1 CMOS Op Amp Configurations

Cascode CMOS OTA   The first OTA presented here is a symmetrical OTA, in which cascode transistors have been added (see Fig. AP6-1). The current of the input differential pair is about 10 μA, leading to a *GBW* of 3 MHz with only 12 pF as a compensation capacitance. Also, the *SR* is more than 3 V/μs. These excellent results are partially due to the large current multiplication factor B from M4 to M6, which is 4. The equivalent input thermal noise voltage is high because of the low input current used.

Stages with cascode transistors can be used just about everywhere. An advantage in amplifying stages is that they isolate the input node from the output node, eliminating the Miller effect. They also always increase the output resistance at low frequencies, leading to more low-frequency gain, more low-frequency *CMRR*, etc., but not the *GBW*.

Their main disadvantage is that they limit the output swing. The cascode transistors must be maintained in the saturation region. The drain-source voltage drop must have a minimum value of $V_{DSsat} = V_{GS} - V_T$ above the drain-source voltage of the driver transistor. Since cascode transistors are always small (in W/L), their V_{DSsat} is never small, i.e., one volt or more.

CMOS OTA With High *PSRR*   The second CMOS configuration has been optimized with respect to *PSRR* (see Fig. 6-48 and Fig. AP6-2). It is actually a Miller CMOS OTA, the first stage of which is a symmetrical OTA. The main modification is the addition of cascode transistors M11 and M12 to increase the symmetry of the first stage.

However, the main improvement is caused by transistor M11. This transistor prevents M13 from behaving as a diode at high frequencies, leading to much higher values of $PSRR_{SS}$ (see Sec. 6-6). Moreover, this transistor avoids the presence of the eventual positive zero (Steyaert and Sansen 1990).

Folded Cascode CMOS OTA   The third and last CMOS op amp consists of a folded CMOS OTA (see Fig. 6-50 and Fig. AP6-3). An additional cascode transistor M7 is added in order to increase the output resistance and hence the low frequency gain. Its *GBW* and *SR* are high as is the total current consumption. It is a good example of optimized circuit design.

6-9-2 Bipolar Op Amp Configurations

In order to show that the design techniques are applicable to bipolar operational amplifiers as well, a number of them are discussed. The list starts with very conventional configurations, which are very similar to their MOS counterparts. At the end, some very sophisticated op amps are added, which provide performance hitherto unavailable from CMOS op amps.

Bipolar Op Amp NJM-4558 (JRC)   The first bipolar op amp is a very cheap two-stage Miller amplifier (see Fig. AP6-4). The first stage is a simple OTA running at 20 μA. Its output is connected, over an emitter follower, to a single transistor amplifier with active load. A double emitter follower (with unity gain) forms the output stage. A Miller compensation capacitance connects both high impedance points.

The *GBW* obtained is about the same as for a CMOS op amp with the same input stage current. The *SR* is less here, as expected (see Sec. 6-9-1). The main disadvantage is the large input current. This is a result of the relatively low beta values of the input *pnp* devices.

Note that the biasing circuit is included. It consists of a JFET (or modulated resistance), which allows the Zener diode (reverse *EB* junction) to bias at about 7 V. The resistor in the following transistor determines all the currents.

Bipolar Op Amp LM-4250 (NS)   This op amp has an advantage in that it can run at very low supply voltages, i.e., ± 1.5 V (see Fig. AP6-5). This is a result of the complicated emitter follower (T5–T7) between the first stage and the second one. It provides an output DC voltage that is about the same as its input DC voltage, i.e., about 0.6 V above the V_{EE} supply line.

This op amp can run at very low currents because the current can be set externally by means of T9, but the performance is correspondingly low. For a 10 μA current in the input stage, the GBW is only 0.25 MHz. The SR is low as well, despite the presence of the resistances $R_{3,4}$. The noise performance is bad because of the resistances R_{3-6}. Finally, the input current is high, as for the previous bipolar op amp. Special high beta (100) devices have been used to reduce this input current.

Bipolar Op Amp LM-124 (NS)   This op amp is very similar to the previous one, except for two differences (see Fig. AP6-6). The current of the input stage cannot be set. It is fixed at 6 μA. Also, an emitter follower is used at each input, forming a Darlington pair at each input. As a result, the input current is fairly low, even with lateral *pnp* devices with low beta. An important advantage of this input configuration is the fact that the common-mode input voltage range includes ground. This op amp can thus be used for single-supply battery applications.

Bipolar Op Amp 741   This op amp has been included because it has been the standard general purpose op amp for a long time (see Fig. AP6-7). It has moderate performance for all its specifications.

It has two stages separated by an emitter follower, but in the input stage, the *pnp* devices are replaced by *npn-pnp* combinations that allow for the reduction of the input current. An additional common-mode feedback loop (Q8,9) is then required for stable biasing. Note that all currents are set by transistors Q11,12 and the resistor R_5 of 39 kΩ.

Bipolar Op Amp CA3080 (RCA)   This amplifier is of a special type (see Fig. AP6-8). It is a bipolar OTA. Indeed, the input transistors are followed by three current mirrors. They have unity as current gain with very small error. The output current is thus simply g_{m1} times the input differential voltage. This g_{m1} can be changed by altering the input stage current. The performance is moderate because of the large number of pnp devices used.

Bipolar Op Amp OP-27 (AD-PMI)   This is the first high-performance op amp (see Fig. AP6-9). It offers large GBW and SR, and especially large gain, low offset voltage and low noise. All of this comes, however, at the cost of large current consumption.

It consists of three stages. The first stage uses four cross-coupled input transistors for better matching, and load resistors to allow offset trimming. Also, the input currents are largely compensated (see Sec. 6-5-14). Emitter followers are again used between the two first stages.

The second stage uses *pnp* input transistors with large emitter resistances. Also, their output is partially shorted by R_5. This is necessary to increase the bandwidth of the second stage at the expense of gain. The third stage is a conventional single transistor amplifier with active load. The output stage is particularly attractive because of its symmetry.

The presence of three stages means three high impedance points. For stability they must be connected by three compensation capacitors. This is why several RC networks are present in this circuit. The compensation can only be a result of tedious analyses and several reruns.

The offset can be trimmed to low values such as 10 μV, leading to a 126 dB *CMRR*. This yields a product of 20 V, which is closely related to the Early voltage of the input stage current source transistor.

Finally, the input thermal noise voltage is very low. This is a result of the large current in the input stage (240 μA) and the use of double input transistors with low base resistances.

Bipolar Op Amp NE5534 (Philips-Signetics)   This configuration is similar to the previous one (see Fig. AP6-10). It is again a three stage amplifier and thus at least three compensation capacitors are required. However, the second stage is not a real differential stage. Also, the output stage can deliver more current, as is often required in audio (600 Ω) applications with a large load capacitance. Its high frequency performance is even better than before but its current consumption is higher as well.

Bipolar Op Amp LT1008 (LT)   This is the first op amp with significantly low input current (see Fig. AP6-11). It is a result of the use of super beta transistors at the input with only 2 μA as total input stage current. In addition, input current cancellation circuitry is added. The resultant input current is a mere 30 pA.

The second stage consists of a *pnp* differential pair (Q21,22) and a bootstrapped active load (Q24). This bootstrap (see Exercise 6-34) increases the gain at low frequencies. Its output (at the base of Q28) is connected to an output buffer. As a result, only two gain stages are present, and yet the open loop gain is more than 126 dB.

Resistive loads are used in the first stage. As a result, laser trimming can be used to trim the offset to very low values, leading to very high *CMRR*.

The other specifications are moderate. A biasing block is included. The current through the JFET J1 biases a current reference consisting of Q31-35 in which the current is set by the 3.3 kΩ resistor. The total current consumption is low.

Bipolar Op Amp LM11 (NS)   LM11 is the predecessor of the previous op amp (see Fig. AP6-12). Similar specifications are obtained with similar circuit techniques. Again, super-beta transistors have been embedded.

6-9-3 BIMOS and BIFET Op Amp Configurations

Operational amplifiers benefit as much from the combination of technologies as they do from digital cells. The advantages of both technologies have been indicated many times before and several examples have been presented. A few more examples are now given to illustrate these points.

BIMOS Op Amp CA3140 (RCA)   This is one of the first BIMOS op amps ever made (see Fig. AP6-13). It consists of two stages and an output buffer stage. The input transistors are MOSTs, to reduce the input current and to increase the *SR/GBW* ratio (see Sec. 6-8-1). The second stage consists of a bipolar transistor amplifying device to create sufficient pole splitting.

Note that the current source of the input stage uses a cascode. This increases its output resistance and hence the *CMRR*.

The biasing block is included as well. It consists of a current reference circuit, in which the current is set by the 8 kΩ resistance. The high frequency performance is excellent but the current consumption is relatively large.

BIMOS Op Amp   A recent version of a BIMOS op amp is added to the list (see Fig. AP6-14). It achieves similar performance as before but at much lower current consumption. This is largely due to the smaller linewidths used (3 μm versus 10 μm before). However, the maximum supply voltages are lower.

The input transistors are MOSTs, which reduce the input current and increase the *SR/GBW* ratio. Two emitter followers separate the first stage from the second stage, which consists of an *npn* differential stage with cascode transistors. This increases its output resistance and hence its gain. The output buffer consists of a series of emitter followers. (Rodgers 1989)

BIFET Op Amp LF356 (NS)   By means of ion-implantation, JFETs are easy to add to a bipolar technology. This has resulted in several types of BIFET op amps. A few of the more successful ones are described (see Fig. AP6-15).

The first JFET op amp was the LF356, which consists of two amplifying stages, the first one of which consists of *p*JFETs. This yields low input current and low noise. Also, the *SR/GBW* ratio is high. Its main disadvantage is its current consumption.

Bipolar transistors are used in the second stage to ensure adequate pole splitting. The output stage only contains *npn* transistors and *p*JFETs, yielding high bandwidth.

Since both first stages are differential, common-mode feedback is required for proper biasing (see Sec. 6-8-4). This is realized by only one *npn* transistor with its collector to the sources of the input *p*JFETS.

BIFET Op Amp TL070 (TI)   More recent BIFET op amps are simpler and closer copies of their full bipolar equivalents (see Fig. AP6-16). In this op amp, only the input *pnp* devices have been replaced by *p*JFETs (compared with the NJM-4558 in Fig. AP6-4). The resulting input current is thus low and the *SR/GBW* is high. The input noise voltage is low as well.

BIFET Op Amp LF411 (NS)   This op amp is very similar to the previous one (see Fig. AP6-17). The biasing circuits, however, are significantly different.

BIFET-MOS Op Amp (Das)   In order to conclude this series of op amp configurations, a custom op amp is added that combines all available technologies (see Fig. AP6-18).

It consists of two stages and an output buffer. The input transistors are pJFETs, which results in low input current and low noise. The second stage contains only one MOST with active load. Therefore, a MOST resistance is required in series with the compensation capacitance.

The output stage uses a bipolar transistor to source current to the load. The biasing currents of the input stages can be set at different values from the one of the output stage.

The performance is moderate, except for the noise, which is very low.

This concludes the list of op amps. We repeat that they are not intended as a comprehensive design guide, but merely as a starting point for design issues.

SUMMARY

In this chapter, the analysis and design aspects of operational amplifiers and operational transconductance amplifiers (OTAs) have been covered. We started with the design of a simple CMOS OTA, for which a design plan was spelled out. This OTA was extended with a second stage to form a Miller CMOS OTA. A design plan was given for optimum performance of the GBW, phase margin, etc.

Since this Miller CMOS OTA is often used, it has been analyzed in great detail. The input range and output range examined versus frequency, the settling time, the output impedance, etc. A separate section was devoted to its noise performance, both at low frequencies and at high frequencies.

Another section was then spent on matching, which discussed how matching plays an important role in the offset characteristics and in the $CMRR$ and $PSRR$ at high frequencies. For other characteristics, the performance of the Miller CMOS OTA was calculated and verified with SPICE.

Several other OTA configurations were discussed next. They are the symmetrical CMOS OTA, the cascode OTA, the folded cascode OTA, and finally the OCA (operational current amplifier). They were discussed for both CMOS and BICMOS technologies.

In analog design, there are always plenty of alternatives to consider, some of which were discussed in the second last section. They include the choices: do we design for optimum GBW or SR? Are we required to include positive zero compensation? Do we design single-ended or full-differential circuits?

This chapter concluded with a number of examples of op amps and OTAs. Little detail is given, but each example can serve as a starting point for new designs.

EXERCISES

6-1 Design a simple CMOS OTA (see Fig. 6-1a) for a given GBW, a given load C_L, and a given phase margin (corresponding with $f_{nd} = 3\,GBW$). Give a design plan for all other parameters, showing which parameters are calculated and in what order. Use a simplified model for node capacitance C_{n4}, i.e., use Eq. (6-11b) with $k_3 = 0$. Repeat this:

    a for a given current I_B

    b for a given value of $V_{GS1} - V_T$

c for a given value of $(W/L)_1$

d for a given value of $(W/L)_4$

6-2 Change the biasing current I_B in an existing, simple CMOS OTA (see Fig. 6-1a) with a specific load C_L. Sketch the resulting GBW and phase margin (PM) versus current I_B.

6-3 Design a simple CMOS OTA (see Fig. 6-1a) for a given GBW and a given phase margin (corresponding to $f_{nd} \approx 3\,GBW$). We want to fix the input MOST $V_{GS1} - V_T$ at 0.2 V for large g_m/I_{DS} ratio, and keep $(W/L)_4 = 1$ for minimum size. Give a design plan for the other parameters. Take as node capacitance $C_{n4} \approx k_1 (W/L)_1$, with $k_1 = 10$ fF. Find the required load capacitance C_L, $(W/L)_1$, and I_B. Calculate resulting values for $GBW = 10$ MHz (and $K'_n = 25\ \mu A/V^2$ and $K'_p = 10\ \mu A/V^2$).

6-4 A high-gain stage has the simple CMOS OTA of Fig. EX6-4. Its load is C_L. It is used as an integrator with feedback capacitance C_F. All other capacitances are taken as zero. Give the pole-zero position diagram with C_F as a variable, and mark the interesting break points.

6-5 Take a simple CMOS OTA (see Fig. 6-1a) as a high-gain amplifier for biomedical signals at low frequencies. Therefore, the capacitive load can be omitted. The equivalent input noise is determined mainly by the four transistors. However, the noise contributed by the current source I_B, which is denoted by $i_B = di_B^2$ is not negligible. Calculate the output noise voltage (for grounded inputs) as a result of i_B in the following cases:

a $r_{o1} = r_{o2}$ and $r_{o3} = r_{o4} = \infty$

b $r_{o1} = r_{o2} = \infty$ and $r_{o3} = r_{o4}$

c $r_{o1} = r_{o2}$ and $r_{o3} = r_{o4}$

6-6 Design a Miller CMOS OTA (see Fig. 6-4) for a $GBW = 10$ MHz (with $f_{nd} \approx 3\,GBW$) and $C_L = 5$ pF. Find an expression for the required C_c versus the current I_6 of the second stage. Concerning transistor T6, we know that its $V_{GS6} - V_T = 0.5$ V, because of matching with transistors T3 and T4, and that its $C_{GS6} \approx k_6 (W/L)_6$ is

FIGURE EX6-4   High-gain stage

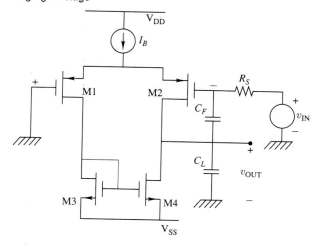

the main contributor to node capacitance C_{n1}. Also, its $k_6 = 6$ fF and parameter $K'_n = 25 \ \mu A/V^2$.

Plot this expression of C_c versus I_6 and find the required current I_6 for $C_c = 1$ pF. How do you interpret this curve?

What are the sizes of the input transistors if $V_{GS1} - V_T = 0.2$ V and $V_{GS3} - V_T = 0.5$ V and $K'_p = 10 \ \mu A/V^2$?

6-7 Design a Miller BICMOS OTA (see Fig. 6-8b) for a $GBW = 10$ MHz (with $f_{nd} \approx 3 \ GBW$) and $C_L = 5$ pF. Develop a design plan, as in the previous exercise, for the npn transistors $\beta = 200$, $\tau = 600$ ps, and $C_{CS} = 0.8$ pF.

6-8 Derive from Eq. (6-25b) an expression for the GBW of the form of Eq. (6-33b) with the input transistors in weak inversion. Also calculate the numerical values for the parameter values used for Fig. 6-11.

6-9 A bipolar Miller op amp has a GBW of 3 MHz and a compensation capacitance of 30 pF. It is used in a gain stage with closed-loop gain of 20 dB. Plot its bandwidth (-3 dB frequency) versus its output signal amplitude (for values up to 10 V) and comment on the breakpoints.

6-10 A bipolar Miller op amp has a GBW of 3 MHz, a SR of 1 V/μs, and a compensation capacitance of 30 pF. It is used in a gain stage with closed-loop gain of $A_{vc} = 20$ dB, where it delivers 2 V output voltage. What is the worst-case settling time (0.1%)? Plot this settling time as a function of the closed-loop gain A_{vc} and comment on the breakpoints.

6-11 A unity-gain buffer uses a Miller CMOS OTA (Fig. 6-4) with a high capacitive load (see Fig. EX6-11). Its GBW is 10 MHz. The large input transistor has $C_{GS} = 3$ pF and $C_{GD} = 0.4$ pF. The package and input pad add a parasitic capacitance of $C_p = 0.3$ pF. Plot the input capacitance versus frequency up to 10 MHz.

6-12 Design a Miller CMOS OTA for Hi-Fi amplification of 40 dB, up to at least 25 kHz with low noise. Its total noise must be less than 20 μV_{RMS} and the $1/f$ noise must be less than 0.1 $\mu V_{RMS}/\sqrt{Hz}$ at 10 Hz (take the same K' and $V_{GS} - V_T$ as in Exercise 6-6). What is the resulting corner frequency?

6-13 A well-designed Miller CMOS op amp (with pMOS input) has a GBW of 3 MHz, a slew rate of 5 V/μs, and 10 nV$_{RMS}/\sqrt{Hz}$ equivalent input noise. The corner frequency is 1 kHz. Its offset voltage is 15 mV. Also, its $CMRR$ is 60 dB and starts rolling off at 300 kHz. Extract as many parameters as you can.

6-14 Redesign the Miller CMOS OTA for better noise performance at high frequencies. Change the current in the second stage (through transistors T1 and T2), such that the maximum noise contribution of the second stage (see Fig. 6-23b) at GBW is only one-tenth (in noise voltage) of the low-frequency noise contribution of the first stage. What is the resulting current?

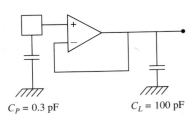

$C_P = 0.3$ pF $C_L = 100$ pF

FIGURE EX6-11   Buffer amplifier.

6-15 A high gain stage has been realized for a DC temperature sensor, as shown in Fig. EX6-15. The sensor provides 10 mV. We have the choice between a cheap MOST op amp with 5 mV offset or a cheap bipolar op amp with 0.5 μA biasing current. Which would you choose? Calculate the gain in both cases and compare.

6-16 Find an expression for the *PSRR* of a single-transistor amplifier with active load and a load capacitance C_L (see Fig. EX6-16).

6-17 Find an expression for the *PSRR* of a CMOS inverter amplifier with a load capacitance C_L (see Fig. EX6-17). Assume that the transconductances g_m have been designed to be the same for both transistors. This is also the case for the output resistances.

6-18 Find an expression for the *PSRR* of a cascode amplifier with resistive load and a load capacitance as seen in Fig. EX6-18). Distinguish four cases:

    a The input voltage v_{IN} and biasing voltage V_{G2} are referred to the negative supply V_{SS}.

    b The input voltage v_{IN} is referred to the negative supply V_{SS}, but the biasing voltage V_{G2} is referred to ground (shown in Fig. EX6-18).

    c The input voltage v_{IN} is referred to the negative supply V_{SS}; the biasing voltage V_{G2} is referred to ground and the cascode transistor M2 does not have a separate well (its bulk is not connected to its source but to the supply V_{SS}).

    d Both the input voltage v_{IN} and biasing voltage V_{G2} are referred to ground. Consider only intermediate and high frequencies.

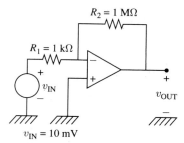

FIGURE EX6-15   High-gain amplifier

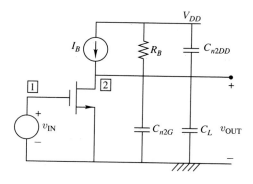

FIGURE EX6-16   Single-transistor amplifier

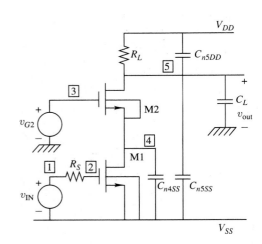

FIGURE EX6-17   CMOS inverter amplifier

FIGURE EX6-18   Cascode stage

6-19 Derive Eq. (6-126).

6-20 Derive Eq. (6-133).

6-21 Give a design plan for a symmetrical CMOS OTA (see Fig. 6-45) with a given *GBW*, a given load C_L, and a given phase margin (e.g., 70°). The gain of the first stage must be $A_{V1} \geq 3$. Give a design plan for all other parameters; i.e., show the parameters calculated in succession. Repeat this:

a for a given current I_B

b for a given value of $(W/L)_1$

c for a given value of $V_{GS1} - V_T$

d for a given value of B

6-22 Design a symmetrical CMOS OTA (see Fig. 6-45) for a $GBW = 10$ MHz (with 70° phase margin) and $C_L = 5$ pF. The first stage gain $A_{v1} = 3$. Also take $B = 3$.

Take as node capacitances $C_{n5} = k(W/L)_1$ and $C_{n6} = k(W/L)_7$ with $k = 10$ fF. Also, $K'_n = 25 \ \mu A/V^2$ and $K'_p = 10 \ \mu A/V^2$.

6-23 Design a symmetrical CMOS OTA (see Fig. 6-45) for a $GBW = 10$ MHz (with $70°$ phase margin) and $C_L = 5$ pF. The first stage gain $A_{v1} = 3$. Use $V_{GS1} - V_T = 0.2$ V for the input transistors, and $V_{GS} - V_T = 0.5$ V for all other transistor pairs, if applicable.

Take as node capacitances $C_{n5} = k(W/L)_1$ and $C_{n6} = k(W/L)_7$ with $k = 10$ fF. Also, $K'_n = 25$ μA/V^2 and $K'_p = 10$ A/V^2.

6-24 Design a symmetrical BICMOS OTA (see Fig. 6-46) as we have done for a CMOS OTA in Exercise 6-23. Its $GBW = 10$ MHz (with $70°$ phase margin) and $C_L = 5$ pF. Use $V_{GS1} - V_T = 0.2$ V for the input transistors. Remember that the node capacitances will be dominated by the collector-substrate capacitances: $C_{CS} = 1.5$ pF for all npn transistors. Also, $K'_p = 10$ μA/V^2.

6-25 Derive an expression for the $PSRR$ of a symmetrical CMOS OTA with a load capacitance of C_L.

6-26 We want to design a cascode symmetrical CMOS OTA (see Fig. 6-47). Its $GBW = 10$ MHz (with $65°$ phase margin) and $C_L = 5$ pF. The first-stage gain A_{v1} must be 3 to reduce the noise. Moreover, the input white noise must not be larger than 10 nV$_{\mathrm{RMS}}/\sqrt{\mathrm{Hz}}$.

Use $V_{GS1} - V_T = 0.2$ V for the input transistors. Take as node capacitances $C_{n5} = k(W/L)_1$ and $C_{n9} = k_6(W/L)_6 = kB(W/L)_6$ with $k = 10$ fF. Also, $K'_n = 25$ μA/V^2 and $K'_p = 10$ μA/V^2.

6-27 A cascode symmetrical CMOS OTA (see Fig. 6-47) is given with $I_B = 25$ μA; $(W/L)_{1,2,9,10} = 20$; $(W/L)_{3,4} = 3$, and all other $(W/L) = 6$. Also, $V_{T0} = 0.8$ V and $V_{DD,SS} = \pm 2.5$ V. Calculate the maximum output voltage swing assuming that all transistors must be kept in the saturation region at all times. Design a biasing network; i.e., what are the sizes of transistors T14 to T18 (using $V_{GS} - V_T = 0.5$ V if necessary); $K'_n = 25$ μA/V^2 and $K'_p = 10$ μA/V^2.

6-28 Design a folded cascode CMOS OTA (see Fig. 6-50) for a $GBW = 10$ MHz (with $70°$ phase margin) and $C_L = 5$ pF. Design it for maximum output voltage swing, assuming that all transistors must be kept in the saturation region at all times (also take $V_{GS} - V_T = 0.2$ V, $V_{t0} = 0.8$ V, and $V_{DD,SS} = \pm 2.5$ V. Calculate the values of $VB1$ and $VB2$. The capacitances $C_{n8} \approx 2k(W/L)_1$ and $C_{n11,12} \approx k(W/L)_9$ with $k = 10$ fF. Use $K'_n = 25$ μA/V^2 and $K'_p = 10$ μA/V^2.

6-29 Design a folded cascode BICMOS OTA (see Fig. 6-51) for a $GBW = 10$ MHz (with $70°$ phase margin) and $C_L = 5$ pF. Design it for maximum output voltage swing, assuming that all transistors must be kept in the saturation region (also take $V_{GS} - V_T = 0.2$ V; $V_{T0} = 0.8$ V, and $V_{DD,SS} = \pm 2.5$ V. Calculate the value of $VB1$. The capacitances $C_{n8} \approx 2k(W/L)_1$ and $C_{n11,12,13} \approx k(W/L)_9$ with $k = 10$ fF. Also, $C_{CS} = C_{jE} = 1.5$ pF for all npn transistors. Use $K'_n = 25$ μA/V^2 and $K'_p = 10$ μA/V^2.

6-30 Design a CMOS OCA (see Fig. 6-52) with a current gain of $B_2 = 10$. With $R_F = 10$ kΩ and $C_L = 10$ pF, the $BW = 1.6$ MHz. We do not want more than $20°$ phase shift at 20 times this frequency. Moreover, the input white noise must not be larger than 4 pA$_{\mathrm{RMS}}/\sqrt{\mathrm{Hz}}$. For this reason $B_1 = 1$.

Use $V_{GS1} - V_T = 0.2$ V for the input transistors. Take as node capacitances $C_{n1} = C_{n5} = k(W/L)_1$ with $k = 20$ fF. Also, $K'_n = 25$ μA/V^2 and $K'_p = 10$ μA/V^2.

6-31 Design a balanced, simple CMOS OTA (see Fig. 6-55) for a $GBW = 10$ MHz (with $70°$ phase margin) and $C_L = 5$ pF. Design it for $GBW_{CM} = 2$ GBW_{DM}. Take $I_B = I_C = 20$ μA and $(V_{GS} - V_T)_{5,6} = 1$ V and $V_{GS} - V_T = 0.2$ V for all other transistors. The capacitance $C_{n6} = k(W/L)_7$ with $k = 20$ fF. Use $K'_n = 25 \ \mu A/V^2$ and $K'_p = 10 \ \mu A/V^2$.

6-32 A folded cascode CMOS OTA with two inputs is shown in Fig. EX6-32. Two parallel inputs are used in order to ensure that the op amp works for all input voltages from one supply voltage to the other (i.e., from "rail to rail"). It is a balanced folded cascode amplifier, but the common-mode amplifier is not shown.

Plot the *GBW* versus the input common-mode range for $V_{DD,SS} = \pm 1.5$ V. Calculate the values of all $V_{B1,2,3,4}$ and the maximum output swing. Calculate all transistor sizes. Current $I_B = 20 \ \mu A$ and $C_L = 5$ pF. All $V_{GS} - V_T = 0.2$ V and $V_{T0} = 0.7$ V. Use $K'_N = 25 \ \mu A/V^2$ and $K'_p = 10 \ \mu A/V^2$.

6-33 The input stage of a fully differential op amp uses positive feedback, as shown in Fig. EX6-33 (Castello, Grassi, and Donati 1990) to increase the input transconductance. Calculate this improvement in gain and gain bandwidth. Take $(W/L)_1 = 20$ and $(W/L)_3 = 15$ (and $I_B = 50 \ \mu A$).

6-34 A simple bipolar OTA (see Fig. EX6-34*a*) is followed by an emitter-follower to provide a low-impedance output. The same emitter-follower is used to bootstrap transistor Q3 in Fig. EX6-34*b*, in order to boost the gain at low frequencies (De Man, Van Parijs, and Cuppens 1977). Calculate the resulting change in gain and in *GBW*, if $C_L = 10$ pF is the only capacitance in play. Take $I_1 = 2I_2 = 100 \ \mu A$; $\beta = 250$, and all $r_o = 1$ MΩ.

FIGURE EX6-32   Folded cascode op amp with double input

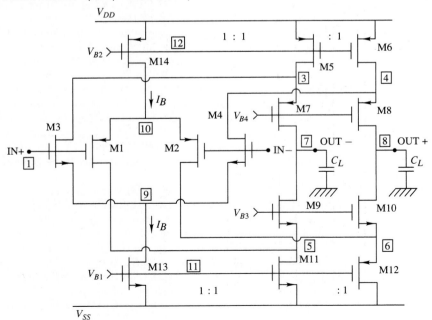

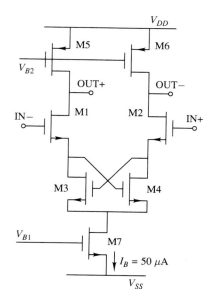

FIGURE EX6-33   High-gain stage with positive feedback

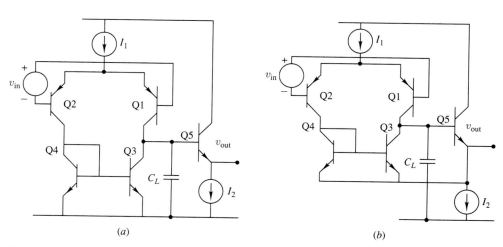

(a)   (b)

FIGURE EX6-34   A differential pair (a) without and (b) with bootstrap

6-35 The balanced folded cascode of Fig. EX6-35 uses a compensation capacitance C_c to increase its gain at high frequencies (Stefanelli et. al., 1993). The common mode amplifier is not shown. Calculate what capacitance C_c is required to compensate the pole generated at the input transistor gate for $R_S = 100$ Ω. Take $I_B = 40$ μA, $C_L = 5$ pF, and all $V_{GS} - V_T = 0.2$ V. Also, $C_{GS1} = 2$ pF and $C_{GD1} = 0.4$ pF. What is the largest value of R_S for which the compensation works?

6-36 The folded cascode CMOS OTA of Fig. EX6-36 is provided with feedforward capacitances C_F to compensate the nondominant pole (Apfel and Gray, 1974; Op't Eynde and Sansen 1990). Calculate the optimum C_F by means of the pole-zero position diagram. Take $I_B = 40$ μA, $C_L = 5$ pF, and all $V_{GS} - V_T = 0.2$ V. Also, $C_{n4,n5} = 0.3$ pF. Use $K'_n = 25$ μA/V^2 and $K'_p = 10$ μA/V^2.

6-37 The folded cascode CMOS OTA of Fig. EX6-37 is provided with regulated or active cascodes (Hosticka 1979; Säckinger and Guggenbühl 1990; Bult and Geelen 1990). This means that local feedback is applied around the cascode transistors to reduce the effect of the node capacitances $C_{n4,n5}$. Calculate the improvement in phase margin in the following cases:

a without node capacitances $C_{n8,n9}$ to ground

b with node capacitances $C_{n8,n9}$ to ground

c with node capacitances $C_{n8,n9}$ to ground and feedforward capacitances C_F (dashed) around the cascode transistors (Sansen and Chang 1990). Find the optimum value of C_F.

Take $I_B = 40$ μA; $C_L = 5$ pF; all $V_{GS} - V_T = 0.2$ V and all r_o's are 2 MΩ. Also, $C_{n4,n5} = C_{n8,n9} = 0.3$ pF, and coupling capacitance C_{n59} between nodes 5 and 9 is $C_{n59} = C_{n48} = 0.2$ pF. Use $K'_n = 25$ μA/V^2 and $K'_p = 10$ μA/V^2.

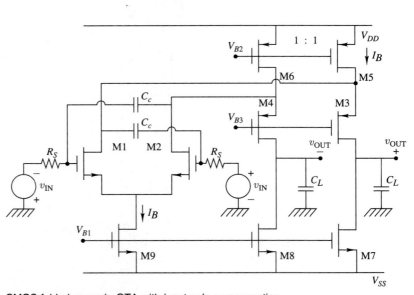

FIGURE EX6-35   CMOS folded cascode OTA with input pole compensation.

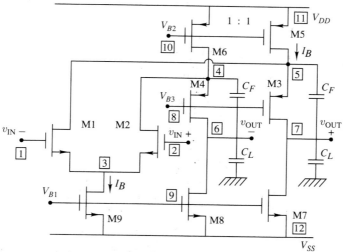

FIGURE EX6-36   Folded cascode OTA with feedforward.

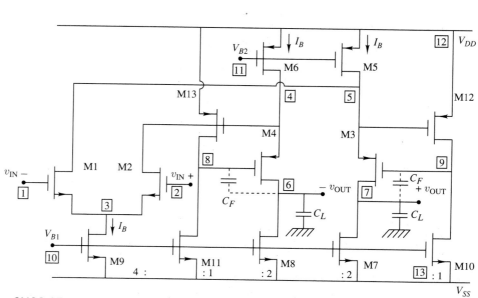

FIGURE EX6-37   CMOS OTA with regulated or active folded cascode and with feedforward.

APPENDIX 6-1: Pole-Zero Doublets and Settling Time

Pole-Zero Doublets in Differential Circuits   Differential circuits have two outputs. A capacitance $C/2$ between both outputs (see Fig. A6-1a) creates a pole at the frequency f_1, given by

$$f_1 = \frac{1}{2\pi RC} \tag{A6-1}$$

because the time constant is $(2R)(C/2)$.

This circuit can be split in two differential half circuits, provided the capacitance is split as well, as shown in Fig. A6-1b. A virtual ground is created between both capacitances C, and therefore both capacitances C can be taken to ground as well (see Fig. A6-1c). Despite the fact that we have two capacitances, we still have only one pole, i.e., the circuit is of first-order.

What happens if the capacitances C (see Fig. A6-2a), or both resistors R, are slightly different? Do we then have two poles that are slightly different or do we have a second-order circuit?

For the analysis, we substitute the transistors by means of current sources with value $g_m v_{IN}/2$. Straight analysis yields the gain

$$A_v = A_{v0} \frac{\left[1 + \left(1 + \frac{\Delta C}{2C}\right) j\frac{f}{f_1}\right]}{\left[1 + j\frac{f}{f_1}\right]\left[1 + \left(1 + \frac{\Delta C}{C}\right) j\frac{f}{f_1}\right]} \tag{A6-2a}$$

The corresponding Bode diagrams are shown in Fig. A6-2b. It is clear that the circuit is still of first-order for both high frequencies although a pole-zero doublet has been created.

Except around the break frequency itself, this Bode diagram can be well approximated by the first-order characteristic (represented as a dashed line in Fig. A6-2b) given by

$$A_v \approx A_{v0} \frac{1}{\left[1 + \left(1 + \frac{\Delta C}{2C}\right) j\frac{f}{f_1}\right]} \tag{A6-2b}$$

the phase of which can be approximated by

$$\varphi = -\arctan\frac{f}{f_1} - \arctan\left(1 + \frac{\Delta C}{C}\right)\frac{f}{f_1} + \arctan\left(1 + \frac{\Delta C}{2C}\right)\frac{f}{f_1}$$

$$\approx -\arctan\left(1 + \frac{\Delta C}{2C}\right)\frac{f}{f_1} \tag{A6-3}$$

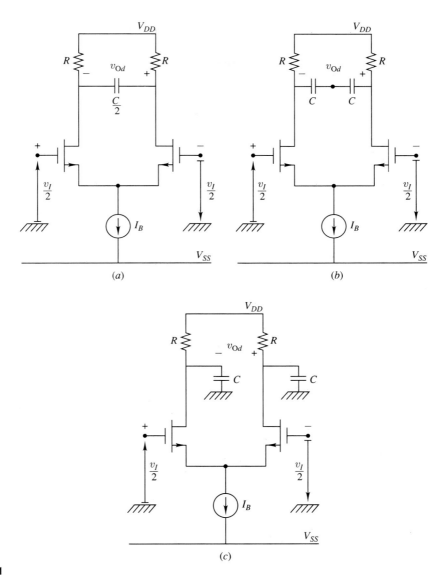

FIGURE A6-1

The error of this last approximation for frequencies lower than $f_1/3$ is barely one degree, and is thus negligible. This approximation can thus be used for calculation of the phase margin, etc.

What happens if the capacitances C are largely different (see Fig. A6-3a)? They have values C_1 and C_2, giving rise to two distinct poles $f_1 = 1/2\pi RC_1$ and $f_2 = 1/2\pi RC_2$. Do we then have a second-order circuit?

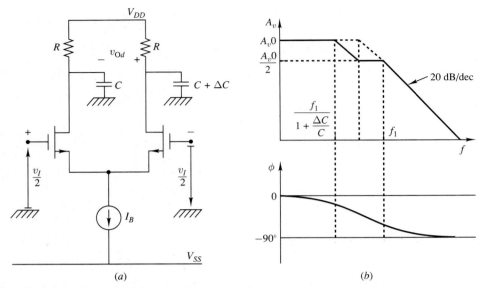

FIGURE A6-2   Differential stage with (a) schematic (b) Bode diagram.

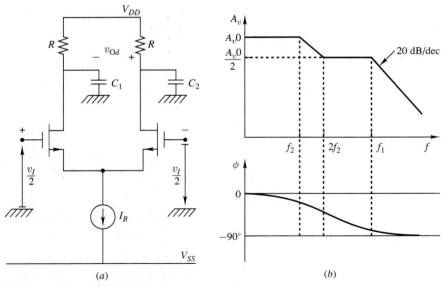

FIGURE A6-3   Differential stage with $C_2 \gg C_1$ (a) schematic (b) Bode diagrams.

Straight analysis yields the gain

$$A_v = A_{v0} \frac{\left(1 + j\dfrac{f}{f_{12}}\right)}{\left(1 + j\dfrac{f}{f_1}\right)\left(1 + j\dfrac{f}{f_2}\right)} \tag{A6-4}$$

in which $1/f_{12} = 1/2f_1 + 1/2f_2$

If we assume $C_1 \gg C_2$ then $f_2 \ll f_1$ and $f_{12} \approx 2f_2$. The corresponding Bode diagrams are shown in Fig. A6-3b. It is again clear that the circuit is still of first-order for both high frequencies. A pole-zero doublet has been created at the lower frequency f_2.

The phase is given by

$$\varphi = -\arctan\frac{f}{f_1} - \arctan\frac{f}{f_2} + \arctan\frac{f}{f_{12}} \tag{A6-5}$$

The phase diagram shows that it is no longer possible to work with approximations.

A further extrapolation of the above problem is illustrated by the circuit shown in Fig. A6-4. It is the simple CMOS OTA, in which only the nondominant pole is withheld. Indeed, the load capacitance, which normally creates the dominant pole, is left out for simplicity. We now must find the pole corresponding to node capacitance C_{n4}.

On first sight, the pole frequency is given by

$$f_{n3} = \frac{g_{m3}}{2\pi C_{n3}} \tag{A6-6}$$

FIGURE A6-4   Simple CMOS OTA with one non-dominant pole (a) circuit (b) Bode diagram.

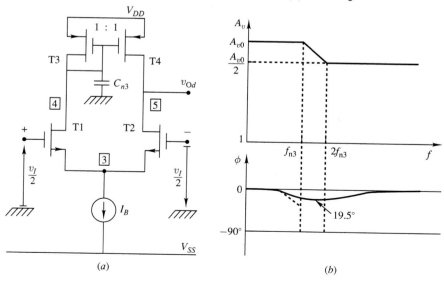

However, straight analysis shows that the gain is actually given by

$$A_v = A_{v0} \frac{1 + j\dfrac{f}{2f_{n3}}}{1 + j\dfrac{f}{f_{n3}}} \tag{A6-7}$$

The corresponding Bode diagram is shown in Fig. A6-4b. We notice that a pole-zero doublet is generated, which leaves the gain at high frequencies at $A_{v0}/2$. The phase shift is maximum at $\sqrt{2}f_{n3}$ and is 19.5°. For frequencies lower than f_{n3}, the phase shift can be approximated by

$$\varphi = -\arctan \frac{f}{f_{n3}} + \arctan \frac{f}{2f_{n3}} \approx -\arctan \frac{f}{2f_{n3}} \tag{A6-8}$$

which is sketched as a dashed line. For frequencies lower than $f_{n3}/3$, the error is less than 0.5°. The latter approximation can thus be used to calculate the phase margin PM of the simple CMOS OTA.

The reason that capacitance C_{n3} generates only a doublet rather than a single pole is that C_{n3} acts only on half the signal. As a result, it merely reduces A_{v0} to $A_{v0}/2$, which is described by a doublet. We conclude that a capacitance on a node creates a pole but that a pole on half the signal also generates a zero at double the pole frequency.

Exactly the same situation occurs with the nondominant pole at node 6 of the symmetrical CMOS OTA (see Fig. 6-45). This node generates additional phase shift as a result of the pole-zero doublet at frequency $g_{m7}/2\pi C_{n6}$.

Settling Time   For a first-order circuit, the settling time is given by Eq. (6-41). The normalized settling time $t_{sN}(\varepsilon)$ is given by

$$t_{sN}(\varepsilon) = \frac{t_s(\varepsilon)}{\tau_{GBW}} \frac{1}{\ln(1/\varepsilon)} \tag{A6-9}$$

in which $\tau_{GBW} = 1/2\pi GBW$. In unity-gain configuration, this normalized settling time $t_{sN}(\varepsilon) = 1$.

In underdamped second-order circuits with PM < 76°, the settling time is given by

$$t_{sN}(\varepsilon) = \frac{1}{k_s}\left[1 + \frac{\ln(1 - k_s/2)}{2\ln(1/\varepsilon)}\right] \tag{A6-10}$$

with

$$k_s = \frac{\sin^2(\text{PM})}{\cos(\text{PM})}$$

This is plotted for $\varepsilon = 10^{-3}$ in Fig. A6-5. It clearly shows that for phase margins between 60 and 70°, we can take unity for $t_{sN}(\varepsilon)$ without large error.

Pole-Zero Doublets and Settling Time   Assume that a pole-zero doublet occurs in the gain-frequency characteristic, as shown in Fig. A6-6a. It occurs at frequency f_{pz} and has a spacing of Δf_{pz}. In unity-gain configuration, the settling time is expected to be described by τ_{GBW} as described in App. 6-1. However, the pole-zero doublet causes a slow settling component with time constant $\tau_{pz} = 1/2\pi f_{pz}$ (Kamath, Meyer, and Gray

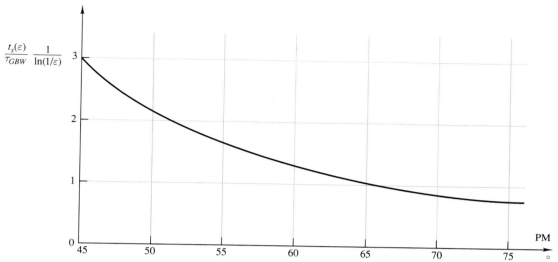

FIGURE A6-5 Normalized settling time for $\varepsilon = 0.1\%$.

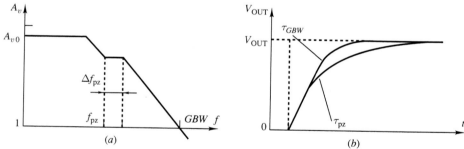

FIGURE A6-6 (a) Bode diagram with (b) doublet causes slow settling.

1974). Its output voltage is given by

$$V_{\text{OUT}} = V_{\text{IN}} \left[1 - \exp\left(-\frac{t}{\tau_{GBW}} \right) + \frac{\Delta f_{pz}}{GBW} \exp\left(-\frac{t}{\tau_{pz}} \right) \right] \tag{A6-11}$$

and is shown in Fig. A6-6b.

Assume that we have a GBW of 10 MHz ($\tau_{GBW} = 16$ ns). Without this slow settling component, we have a settling time of 0.11 μs for $\varepsilon = 10^{-3}$. If coefficient $\Delta f_{pz}/GBW$ is of the order of 1 percent, and $f_{pz} = GBW/10$, then we obtain $\tau_{pz} \ln(10) = 3.7$ μs settling time.

This is a point of concern for feedforward circuits (see Fig. 4-57) and other pole-zero cancellation schemes. If the cancellation is not perfect, a pole-zero doublet is generated, giving rise to excessive settling times.

APPENDIX 6-2: Amplifier Configurations

FIGURE AP6-1   CASCODE CMOS OTA

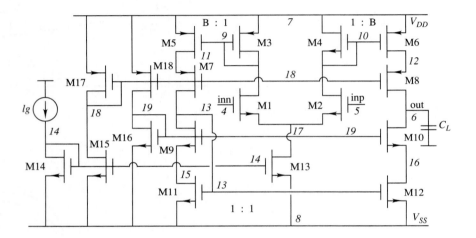

Specifications			Dimensions		
Parameter	Value (at ±2.5 V)	Unit	Transistor	W (μm)	L (μm)
GBW	3	MHz	M1,2	67	10
SR	3.7	V/μs	M3,4	11	5
C_L	12	pF	M5–8	43	5
R_L	5000	kΩ	M9	61	5
A_{v0}	≥ 80	dB	M10	32	5
I_ϵ	< 1	pA	M11,12	15	5
I_{13}	10.7	μA	M13	6	5
I_{12}	21.4	μA	M14	5	30
$I_{17,18}$	5.3	μA	M15	5	8
$dv_{ieq,th}^2$	24	nV$_{RMS}$/$\sqrt{Hz}$	M16	5	22
			M17,18	5	7

FIGURE AP6-2   CMOS OTA WITH HIGH *PSRR* (Steyaert and Sansen 1990)

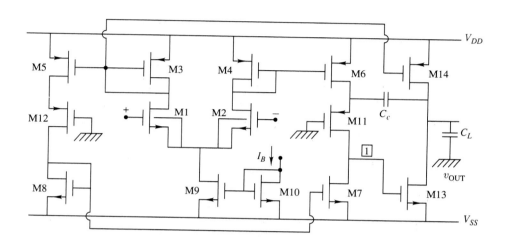

Specifications			Dimensions		
Parameter	Value (at ±2.5 V)	Unit	Transistor	W (μm)	L (μm)
GBW	3.35	MHz	M1,2	40	40
SR	0.4	V/μs	M3–6	20	20
C_L	< 100	pF	M7,8	20	50
C_c	2.5	pF	M9,10	20	20
A_{v0}	≥ 80	dB	M11,12	80	5
$I_\in$	< 1	pA	M13	60	5
I_9	1	μA			
$I_{7,8}$	1	μA			
$I_{13,14}$	10	μA			
$dv^2_{ieq,th}$	47	nV$_{RMS}$/$\sqrt{Hz}$			

FIGURE AP6-3   FOLDED CASCODE CMOS OTA

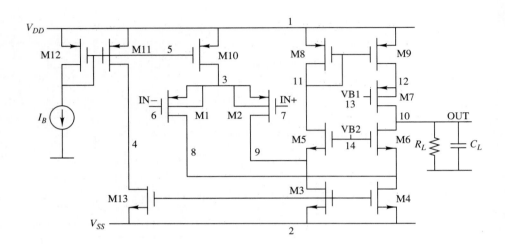

Specifications			Dimensions		
Parameter	Value (at ±2.5 V)	Unit	Transistor	W (μm)	L (μm)
GBW	8	MHz	M1,2	900	5
SR	11	V/μs	M3,4	100	5
C_L	10	pF	M5,6	150	5
C_c		pF	M7	100	5
A_{v0}	≥ 97	dB	M8,9	85	5
I_ϵ	< 1	pA	M10,11,12	300	5
I_{10}	110	μA	M13	100	5
$I_{3,4}$	110	μA			
I_{tot}	440	μA			
$dv^2_{ieq,th}$	4	nV$_{RMS}$/$\sqrt{Hz}$			

FIGURE AP6-4   BIPOLAR OP AMP NJM-4558 (JRC)

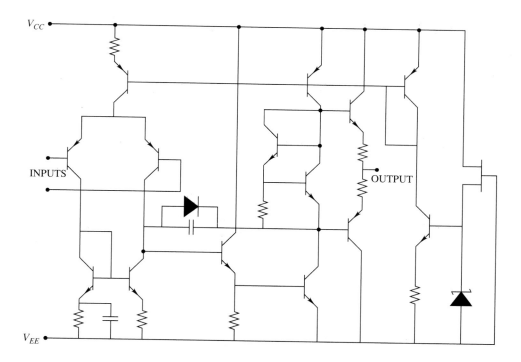

Specifications		
Parameter	Value (at ±15 V)	Unit
GBW	3	MHz
SR	1	V/μs
R_L	> 2	kΩ
C_c	20	pF
A_{v0}	≥ 110	dB
$I_\in$	40	nA
I_{tot}	3.5	μA
I_1	20	μA
$dv^2_{ieq,th}$	47	nV$_{RMS}$/$\sqrt{Hz}$

FIGURE AP6-5   BIPOLAR OP AMP LM-4250 (NATIONAL SEMICONDUCTOR)

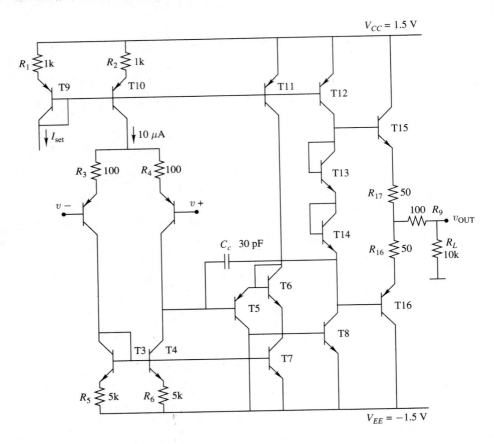

Specifications (at $I_{set} = 10\ \mu A$):		
Parameter	Value (at ±1.5 V)	Unit
GBW	0.25	MHz
SR	0.2	V/μs
R_L	> 10	kΩ
C_c	30	pF
A_{v0}	≥ 110	dB
I_ϵ	50	nA
$I_{9,10}$	10	μA
$I_{11,12}$	14	μA
I_{15}	50	μA
$dv^2_{ieq,th}$	38	nV$_{RMS}$/$\sqrt{Hz}$

FIGURE AP6-6   BIPOLAR OP AMP LM-124 (NATIONAL SEMICONDUCTOR)

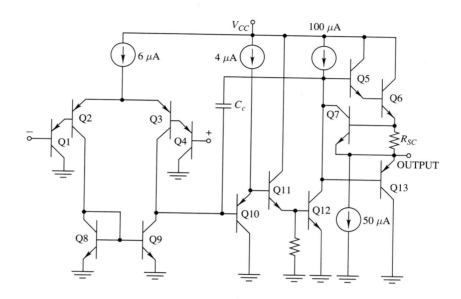

Specifications		
Parameter	Value (at 3 V)	Unit
GBW	0.5	MHz
SR	0.4	V/μs
R_L	> 10	kΩ
C_c	15	pF
A_{v0}	$\geq$ 110	dB
$I_\in$	5	nA
$I_2 + I_3$	6	μA
I_{10}	4	μA
I_{12}	100	μA
I_{tot}	650	μA
$dv^2_{ieq,th}$	68	nV$_{RMS}$/$\sqrt{Hz}$

FIGURE AP6-7 BIPOLAR OP AMP MODEL 741

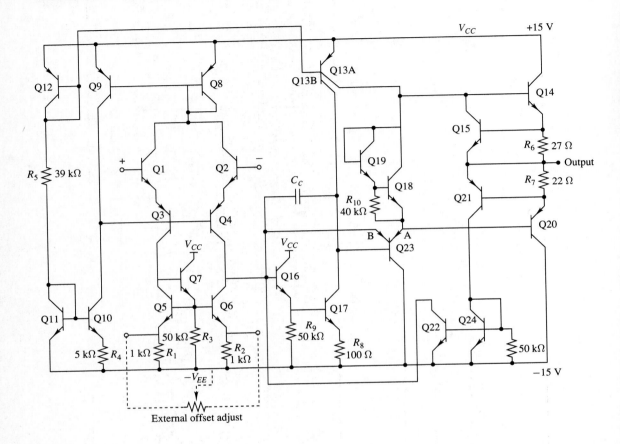

Specifications		
Parameter	Value (at ±15 V)	Unit
GBW	0.8	MHz
SR	0.66	V/μs
R_L	> 10	kΩ
C_c	30	pF
A_{v0}	≥ 90	dB
I_ϵ	50	nA
I_8	20	μA
I_{17}	550	μA
I_{23}	150	μA
$dv^2_{ieq,th}$	14	nV$_{RMS}$/$\sqrt{Hz}$

FIGURE AP6-8   BIPOLAR OP AMP CA3080 (RCA CORP.)

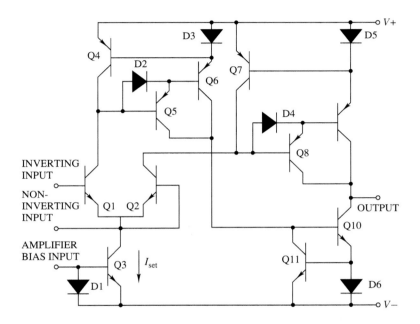

Specifications (at I_{set} = 10 μA):		
Parameter	Value (at 3 V)	Unit
GBW	0.12	MHz
SR	0.25	V/μs
A_{g0}	0.1	mS
$I_\in$	50	nA
I_3	10	μA
I_{10}	10	μA
$dv^2_{ieq,th}$	13	nV$_{RMS}$/$\sqrt{Hz}$

FIGURE AP6-9   BIPOLAR OP AMP OP-27 (PRECISION MONOLITHICS INC)

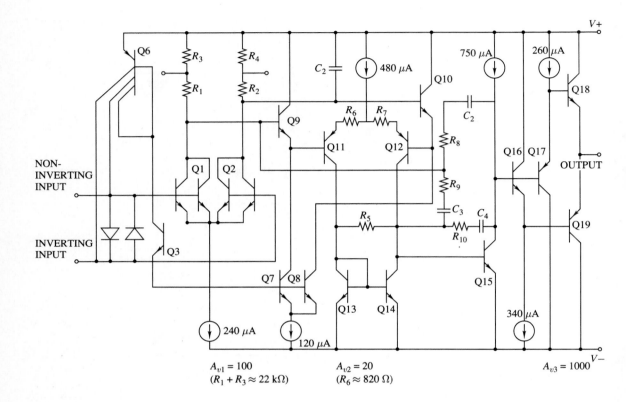

$A_{v1} = 100$
$(R_1 + R_3 \approx 22 \text{ k}\Omega)$

$A_{v2} = 20$
$(R_6 \approx 820 \ \Omega)$

$A_{v3} = 1000$

	Specifications	
Parameter	Value (at ± 15 V)	Unit
GBW	8	MHz
SR	2.8	V/μs
R_L	> 2	kΩ
C_c	?	pF
A_{v0}	≥ 125	dB
$I_\in$	12	nA
$I_1 + I_2$	240	μA
I_{tot}	3000	μA
$dv^2_{ieq,th}$	3	nV$_{RMS}$/$\sqrt{\text{Hz}}$

FIGURE AP6-10   BIPOLAR OP AMP NE5534 (PHILIPS-SIGNETICS)

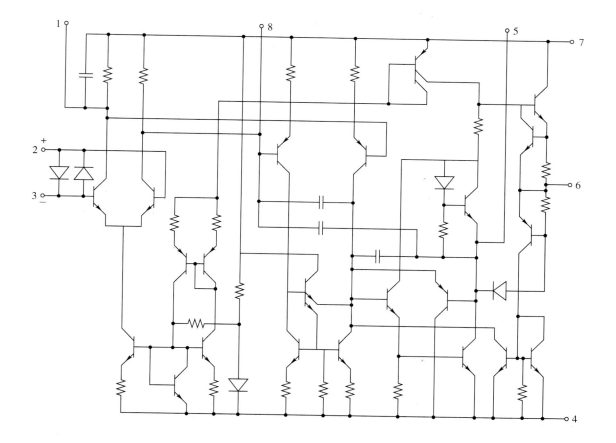

Specifications		
Parameter	Value (at ±15 V)	Unit
GBW	10	MHz
SR	6	V/μs
R_L	> 0.6	kΩ
C_L	100	pF
C_c	22	pF
A_{v0}	≥ 100	dB
$I_\in$	400	nA
$I_1 + I_2$	200	μA
I_{tot}	4000	μA
$dv_{ieq,th}^2$	4	nV$_{RMS}$/$\sqrt{Hz}$

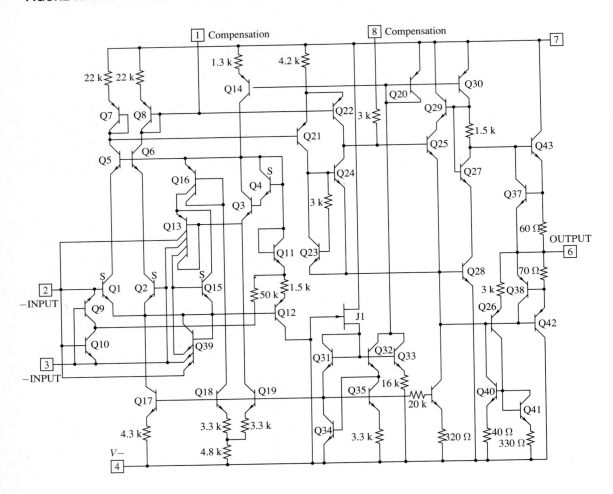

FIGURE AP6-11   BIPOLAR OP AMP LT1008 (LINEAR TECHNOLOGY)

Specifications		
Parameter	Value (at ± 15 V)	Unit
GBW	2	MHz
SR	0.2	V/μs
R_L	> 10	kΩ
C_c	30	pF
A_{v0}	$\geq$ 126	dB
$I_\in$	30	pA
I_{17}	2	μA
I_{tot}	400	μA
$dv^2_{ieq,th}$	14	nV$_{RMS}$/$\sqrt{Hz}$

638

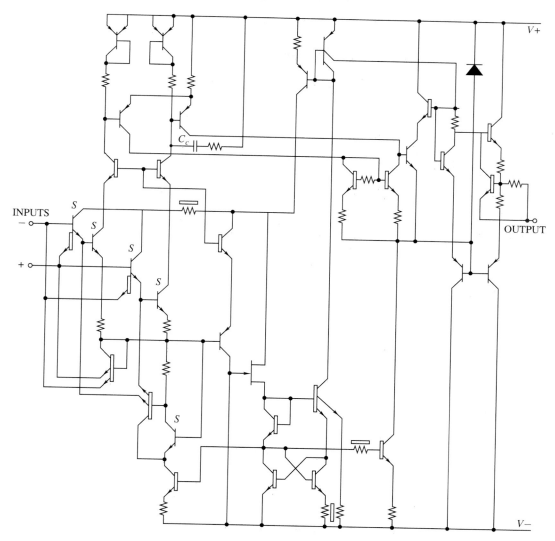

Parameter	Value (at ±15 V)	Unit	Parameter	Value (at ±15 V)	Unit
GBW	0.5	MHz	$I_\in$	20	pA
SR	0.3	V/μs	$I_{1,2}$	0.05	μA
R_L	> 10	kΩ	I_{tot}	300	μA
C_c	30	pF	$dv^2_{ieq,th}$	45	nV$_{RMS}$/$\sqrt{Hz}$
A_{v0}	$\geq$ 120	dB			

Specifications

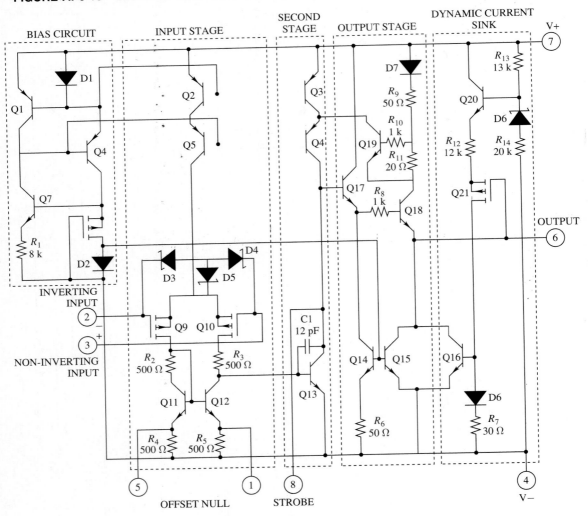

FIGURE AP6-13 BIMOS OP AMP CA3140 (RCA CORP.)

Specifications					
Parameter	Value (at ±15 V)	Unit	Parameter	Value (at ±15 V)	Unit
GBW	4.5	MHz	$I_\in$	10	pA
SR	9	V/μs	2	200	μA
R_L	> 10	kΩ	I_{tot}	4000	μA
C_c	12	pF	$dv_{ieq,th}^2$	35	nV$_{RMS}$/$\sqrt{Hz}$
A_{v0}	≥ 90	dB			

640

FIGURE AP6-14   BIMOS OP AMP (Rodgers and Thurber 1989)

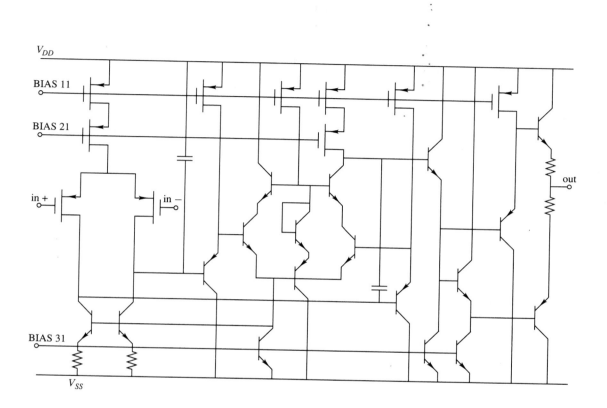

Specifications		
Parameter	Value (at ±15 V)	Unit
GBW	10	MHz
SR	4	V/μs
R_L	> 10	kΩ
C_c	?	pF
A_{v0}	≥ 114	dB
I_ϵ	< 1	pA
$I_1 + I_2$	100	μA
I_{tot}	700	μA
$dv_{ieq,th}^2$	65	nV$_{RMS}$/$\sqrt{Hz}$

FIGURE AP6-15 BIFET OP AMP LF356 (NATIONAL SEMICONDUCTOR)

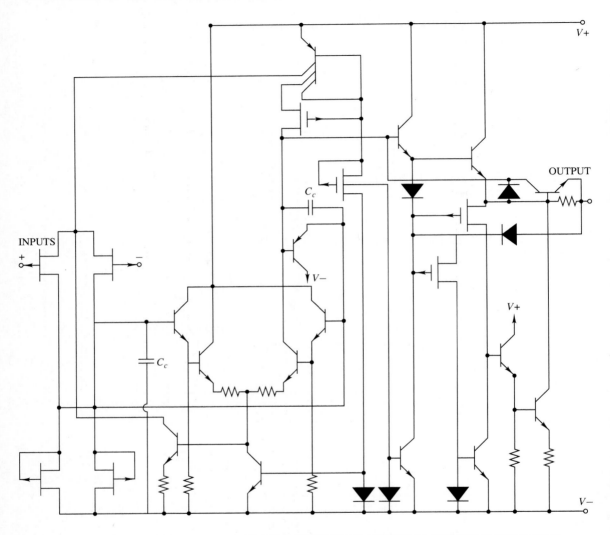

Parameter	Value (at ±15 V)	Unit	Parameter	Value (at ±15 V)	Unit
			Specifications		
GBW	5	MHz	I_ϵ	10	pA
SR	1.5	V/μs	$I_{J1} + I_{J2}$	200	μA
R_L	> 10	kΩ	I_{tot}	4700	μA
C_c	10	pF	$dv_{ieq,th}^2$	12	nV$_{RMS}/\sqrt{Hz}$
A_{v0}	≥ 105	dB			

FIGURE AP6-16   BIFET OP AMP TL070 (TEXAS INSTRUMENTS)

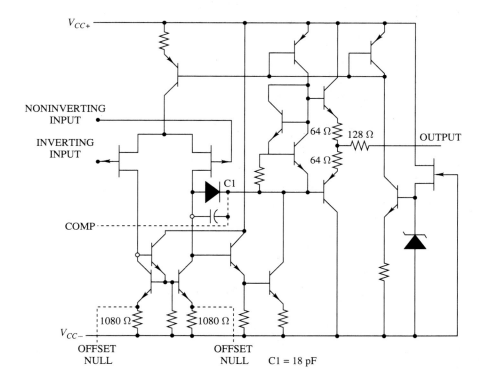

	Specifications	
Parameter	Value (at ±15 V)	Unit
GBW	3	MHz
SR	13	V/μs
R_L	> 10	kΩ
C_c	15	pF
A_{v0}	≥ 106	dB
$I_\in$	30	pA
$I_1 + I_2$	200	μA
I_{tot}	1400	μA
$dv_{ieq,th}^2$	38	nV$_{RMS}$/$\sqrt{Hz}$

FIGURE AP6-17   BIPFET OP AMP LF411 (NATIONAL SEMICONDUCTOR)

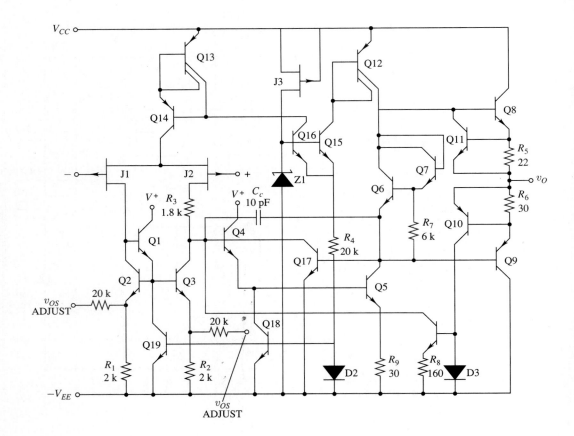

Specifications		
Parameter	Value (at ±15 V)	Unit
GBW	3	MHz
SR	10	V/μs
R_L	> 10	kΩ
C_c	10	pF
A_{v0}	≥ 106	dB
I_ϵ	50	pA
I_{14}	100	μA
I_{tot}	1800	μA
$dv_{ieq,th}^2$	22	nV$_{RMS}$/$\sqrt{Hz}$

FIGURE AP6-18   BIFET-MOS OP AMP (DAS)

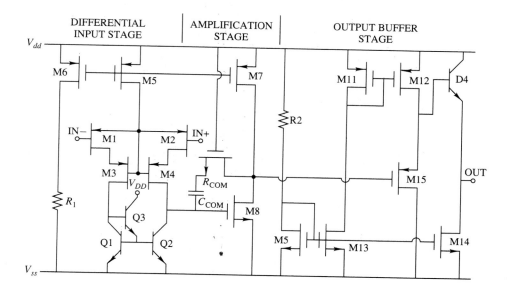

Specifications		
Parameter	Value (at ±15 V)	Unit
GBW	0.3	MHz
SR	0.5	$V/\mu s$
R_L	> 10	$k\Omega$
C_c	10	pF
A_{v0}	≥ 106	dB
I_ϵ	10	pA
I_5	100	μA
$I_{12,14}$	100	μA
I_{tot}	900	μA
$dv_{ieq,th}^2$	6	$nV_{RMS}/\sqrt{Hz}$

REFERENCES

Allen, P., and D. Holberg. 1987. *CMOS Analog Circuit Design.* New York: Holt, Rinehart and Winston.

Apfel, R., and P. Gray. 1974. "A Fast-Settling Operational Amplifier Using Doublet Compression Techniques." *IEEE J. Solid-State Circuits*, vol. SC-9, no. 6, pp. 332–340.

Banu, M., M. Khoury, and Y. Tsividis. 1988. "Fully differential operational amplifier with accurate output balance." *IEEE Journal of Solid-State Circuits*, vol. SC-23, no. 6, pp. 1410–1414.

Bult, K., and G. Geelen. 1990. "A Fast-Settling CMOS Opamp for SC Circuits with 90 dB DC Gain." *IEEE J. Solid-State Circuits*, vol. SC-25, no. 6, pp. 1379–1384.

Castello, R., A. Grassi, and S. Donati. 1990. "A 500 nA Sixth-Order Bandpass SC Filter." *IEEE J. Solid-State Circuits*, vol. SC-25, no. 3, pp. 669–676.

Chang, Z. Y., and W. Sansen. 1991. *Low-Noise Wide-Band Amplifiers in Bipolar and CMOS Technologies.* Norwell, MA: Kluwer Academic.

Choi, T., R. Kaneshiro, R. Brodersen, P. Gray, W. Jett, and M. Wilcox. 1983. *IEEE Journal of Solid-State Circuits*, vol. SC-18, no. 6, pp. 652–664.

Das, C., W. Sansen, and L. Callewaert. 1984. "A monolithic impedance buffer with a compatible JFET-CMOS technology." In *proceedings of 10th ESSCIRC*, pp. 63–66.

Davidse, J. *Analog Electronic Circuit Design*, 1991. Englewood Cliffs, NJ: Prentice Hall.

De Man, H., R. Van Parijs, and R. Cuppens. 1977. "A Low Input Capacitance Voltage Follower in a Compatible Silicon-Gate MOS-Bipolar Technology." *IEEE J. Solid-State Circuits*, vol. SC-12, no. 3l, pp. 217–224.

Gielen, G., and W. Sansen. 1991. *Symbolic Analysis for Automated Design of Analog Integrated Circuits.* Norwell, MA: Kluwer Academic.

Gray, P., and R. Meyer. 1993. *Analysis and Design of Analog Integrated Circuits.* New York: Wiley and Sons.

Grebene, A. 1984. *Bipolar and MOS Analog Integrated Circuit Design.* 2nd ed. New York: Wiley and Sons.

Gregorian, R., and G. Temes. 1986. *Analog MOS Integrated Circuits for Signal Processing.* New York: Wiley and Sons.

Haspeslagh, J., and W. Sansen. 1988. "Design techniques for fully differential amplifiers." In *proceedings of IEEE Custom Integrated Circuits Conference*, pp. 12.2.1–12.2.4.

Hosticka, B. 1979. "Improvement of the Gain of MOS Amplifiers." *IEEE Journal of Solid-State Circuits*, vol. SC-14, no. 6, pp. 1111–1114.

Kamath, B., R. Meyer, and P. Gray. 1974. "Relationship between frequency response and settling time of operational amplifiers." *IEEE Journal of Solid-State Circuits*, vol. SC-9, no. 6, pp. 332–340.

Lakshmikumar, K., R. Hadaway, and M. Copeland. 1989. "Characterization and Modeling of Mismatch in MOS transistors for Precision Analog Design." *IEEE Journal of Solid-State Circuits*, vol. SC-24, no. 5, pp. 1433–1440.

Milcovic, M. 1985. "Current Gain of High-Frequency CMOS Operational Amplifiers." *IEEE Journal of Solid-State Circuits*, vol. SC-20, no. 4, pp. 845–851.

Op't Eynde, F., and W. Sansen. 1993. "A CMOS Wideband Amplifier with 800 MHZ Gain-Bandwidth." Custom Integrated Circuits Conference, pp. 9.1.1.–9.1.4.

Ott, H. W., 1988. *Noise Reduction Techniques in Electronic Systems.* New York: Wiley and Sons.

Pelgrom, M., A. Duimaijer, and A. Welbers. 1989. "Matching properties of MOS transistors." *IEEE Journal of Solid-State Circuits*, vol. SC-24, no. 5, pp. 1433–1440.

Rodgers, B., and C. Thurber. 1989. "A monolithic 5-1/2 digit BIMOS A/D converter." *IEEE Journal of Solid-State Circuits*, vol. SC-24, no. 3, pp. 617–626.

Säckinger, E., and W. Guggenbühl. 1990. "A High-Swing High-Impedance MOS Cascode Circuit." *IEEE J. Solid-State Circuits*, vol. SC-25, no. 1, pp. 289–298.

Sedra, A., and K. Smith. 1987. *Microelectronic Circuits*. CBS College Publishing.

Sansen, W., and Z. Y. Chang. 1990. "Feedforward compensation techniques for high-frequency CMOS amplifiers." *IEEE Journal of Solid-State Circuits*, vol. 25, no. 6, pp. 1590–1595.

Schmoock, J. 1975. "An input stage transconductance reduction technique for high-slew rate operational amplifiers." *IEEE Journal of Solid-State Circuits*, vol. SC-10, no. 6, pp. 407–411.

Stefanelli, B., and A. Kaiser. 1993. "A 2 μm CMOS fifth-order low-pass continuous-time filter for video-frequency applications." *IEEE J. Solid-State Circuits*, vol. SC-28. no. 4, pp. 713–718.

Steyaert, M., and W. Sansen. 1990. "Power Supply Rejection Ratio in Operational Transconductance Amplifiers." *IEEE Trans. Circuits and Systems*, vol. CAS-37, no. 9, pp. 1077–1084.

Swings, K., and W. Sansen. 1993. "ARIADNE: A constraint-based approach to computer-aided synthesis and modeling of analog integrated circuits." *Analog IC's and Signal Processing*, 3, pp. 197–215.

Vittoz, E. A. 1985. "The design of high-performance analog circuits on digital CMOS chip." *IEEE Journal of Solid-State Circuits*, vol. SC-20, no. 3, pp. 657–665.

7

FUNDAMENTALS OF CONTINUOUS-TIME AND SAMPLED-DATA ACTIVE FILTERS

INTRODUCTION

An *electrical filter* or filter circuit can be defined as a network of circuit components (i.e., resistors, capacitors, inductors, and transistors) that operates on or processes electrical signals (Daryanani 1976; Ghausi and Laker 1981; Gregorian and Temes 1986; Schaumann et al. 1990; Schaumann and Laker 1993; Sedra 1989; Unbehauen and Cichocki 1989; Schaumann and Laker 1993). The filter's response $y(t)$ (usually a voltage output signal) will differ from its excitation $x(t)$ (usually a voltage input signal), in accordance with the signal-processing algorithm performed by the filter circuit. Filters can be designed to perform either linear or nonlinear signal processing. Although nonlinear filters are an important class of filters for a variety of applications, the vast majority of filters implemented are designed for linear operation. Hence, our focus in this chapter (and the next chapter, too) is the design of microelectronic *linear filters*. Henceforth, to simplify the terminology, we will use the term filter to imply a linear filter unless noted otherwise.

The term *active filter* refers to a filter that incorporates active device(s) (e.g., transistor) or amplifier circuit(s) in its schematic. Typically, in such a filter, active circuits replace the function of inductors in what would otherwise be a resistor-inductor-capacitor, or RLC circuit. We know that the resonant frequency for a passive RLC circuit is given by

$$f_r = \frac{1}{2\pi\sqrt{LC}} \qquad \text{or} \qquad L = \frac{1}{(2\pi f_r)^2 C} \tag{7-1a}$$

To get a feel for the dimensions of these components let us consider the case where $f_r = 1$ MHz and $C = 100$ pF (i.e., a very large microelectronic capacitor). The corresponding inductor value for this f_r is $L \approx 250$ μH, much too large (by several orders of magnitude) to implement as a planar structure on an IC. Moreover, planar inductors are nonideal due to parasitic capacitance and losses (i.e., low inductor Q). For a fixed f_r, the only way to reduce L in Eq. (7-1a) is to increase C, which in this case is already very large. When f_r is sufficiently high (i.e., ≥ 500 MHz), it can be realized with IC-compatible L (≤ 10 nH) and C (Nguyen and Meyer 1990). In contrast, the f_r realized by an active filter usually is related to an RC product or an equivalent, e.g.

$$f_r = \frac{1}{2\pi RC} \qquad \text{or} \qquad R = \frac{1}{2\pi f_r C} \qquad (7\text{-}1b)$$

Hence, $f_r = 1$ MHz can be achieved with $C = 1$ pF and $R = 1/2\pi f_r C \approx 150$ kΩ. Large R's, say ≤ 10 MΩ, or their equivalent are IC-compatible and can be efficiently implemented in a variety of structures. The specifics of active-filter design and implementation are discussed in Chap. 8.

This chapter is devoted to reviewing the fundamentals of linear-active filtering in the continuous-time and sampled-data domains. For those readers who need to refresh their understanding of sampled-data and discrete-time systems, a brief review of these subjects is provided in App. 7-1. The fundamental schemes for integrated analog filters; namely, circuits based on *active-resistor-capacitor* (or *active-RC*), *active-transconductance-capacitor* (or *active*$-G_m/C$) and *active-switched-capacitor* (or *active-SC*), are introduced in Sec. 7-2. In Secs. 7-1 and 7-3 through 7-6, we examine the various performance requirements for a filter and develop methods for synthesizing efficient numerical transfer functions from frequency response specs. Sensitivity, variability, and their relationship to manufacturing yield, are important criteria for designing and evaluating filter circuits. In Sec. 7-7 we apply models developed in Chap. 3 to evaluate sensitivity, variability, and yield of integrated filters. Typically, circuit design involves a coupling of symbolic analysis and CAD simulation for studying and designing circuits. Symbolic analysis provides insight into circuit behavior and design tradeoffs that would not otherwise be evident. Hence, in Sec. 7-8 we apply a hybrid of discrete-time and analog circuit concepts to facilitate the symbolic analysis of switched-capacitor circuits.

7-1 LINEAR FILTERING CONCEPTS AND DEFINITIONS

Linear filtering, most intuitively described as a spectral selection process, can be represented and specified in several ways. To characterize this process, let us first use our knowledge of elementary signal theory to describe the signals that we will be dealing with. A periodic signal, say $s(t)$ (or $x(t)$, $y(t)$), where $s(t)$ is either a voltage or current defined over the period $T_r = 1/f_r = 2\pi/\omega_r$, can be expressed as the Fourier series

$$s(t) = a_0 + \sum_{k=1}^{\infty} a_k \cos(k\omega_r t) + \sum_{k=1}^{\infty} b_k \sin(k\omega_r t) = \sum_{k=-\infty}^{\infty} S_k e^{jk\omega_r t} \qquad (7\text{-}2a)$$

The real coefficients a_0, a_k, b_k, or complex coefficient S_k, define the spectral components of the signal at particular frequencies $\omega_k = k\omega_r$ rps (a_0 or S_0 is the DC component). More generally, if $s(t)$ is not periodic, it can be expressed by the Fourier integral

$$s(t) = \frac{1}{2\pi} \int_{k=-\infty}^{\infty} S(j\omega)e^{j\omega t} d\omega \qquad (7\text{-}2b)$$

where $\omega = 2\pi f$ is continuous frequency and complex $S(j\omega)$ is the continuous Fourier spectrum of signal $s(t)$.

A linear filter response $y(t)$, with spectrum Y_k or $Y(j\omega)$, is derived by weighting each spectral component of input $x(t)$ by a complex number H_k or $H(j\omega)$, i.e., for periodic signals

$$y(t) = \sum_{k=-\infty}^{\infty} H_k X_k e^{jk\omega_r t} = \sum_{k=-\infty}^{\infty} Y_k e^{jk\omega_r t} \qquad (7\text{-}3a)$$

and for nonperiodic signals

$$y(t) = \frac{1}{2\pi} \int_{k=-\infty}^{\infty} H(j\omega)X(j\omega)e^{j\omega t} d\omega = \frac{1}{2\pi} \int_{k=-\infty}^{\infty} Y(j\omega)e^{j\omega t} d\omega \qquad (7\text{-}3b)$$

In Eq. (7-3b) we see that the filter algorithm is contained in the transfer function $H(j\omega)$, which we conveniently partition into magnitude and phase functions, such that

$$H(j\omega) = \frac{Y(j\omega)}{X(j\omega)} = |H(\omega)|e^{j \arctan\left\{\frac{Im[H]}{Re[H]}\right\}} = M(\omega)e^{j\varphi(\omega)} \qquad (7\text{-}3c)$$

Typically, we express gain in decibels (or dB) and phase in degrees, i.e.,

$$G(\omega) = 20\log_{10} M(\omega)\text{dB} \quad \text{and} \quad \varphi(\omega) = \arctan\left\{\frac{Im[H(j\omega)]}{Re[H(j\omega)]}\right\}\frac{180°}{\pi} \qquad (7\text{-}3d)$$

Combining Eqs. (7-3b) and (7-3c), we see that a linear filter selectively scales the amplitude and adds to the phase of the input via $M(\omega)$ and $\varphi(\omega)$, respectively, i.e.,

$$Y(j\omega) = M_Y(\omega)e^{j\varphi_Y(\omega)} = M(\omega)M_X(\omega)e^{j(\varphi_X(\omega)+\varphi(\omega))} \qquad (7\text{-}4)$$

Filter design then is a two-step process; namely, (1) derive a $G(\omega)$ and/or $\varphi(\omega)$ to achieve a specified performance and (2) synthesize a robust, economical circuit schematic and component values to realize step one.

Equations (7-3) and (7-4), as illustrated in Fig. 7-1, are the essence of linear filtering. Many filters that we will encounter are *gain-shaping filters* where the primary filter function is $G(\omega)$. However, there are a class of *phase-shaping filters* called phase or *delay equalizers*, which are specified by $\varphi(\omega)$ or *group delay*, as defined by

$$\tau(\omega) = -\frac{d\varphi(\omega)}{d\omega} \quad \text{seconds} \tag{7-5}$$

Typically for such filters, we specify $G(\omega)$ to be constant, say 0 dB, for all ω (at least in the range of interest). Delay equalizers and gain-shaping filters are frequently combined in the signal processing of data and video signals that are particularly sensitive to the phasing of spectral components. On the other hand, gain-shaping filters are usually sufficient in the processing of audio and speech signals that are relatively insensitive to phase.

From Eq. (7-3) we see that $y(t)$, for an ideal linear filter, can have only spectral components that are present in $x(t)$. In contrast, a nonlinear filter will produce new spectral components not found in $x(t)$. Nonlinearities appear in linear filters that use active circuits in their implementation, such as op amps and OTAs. When nonlinear behavior occurs in a linear filter, it impairs the filter's performance by producing unwanted harmonic components (e.g., the gray spectral lines at $2f_1$, $f_1 + f_2$, $2f_2$, etc., of output $y(t)$ in Fig. 7-1). This impairment is called *harmonic distortion* (Schaumann et al. 1990; Sedra 1989) and the root-mean-square (rms) sum of all harmonic amplitudes in $y(t)$ is called *total harmonic distortion (THD)*. THD is usually specified as the percentage ratio of the rms sum of harmonic amplitudes to the rms fundamental amplitude. Sources of nonlinear distortion in op amps and OTAs were discussed in Chaps. 5 and 6. Since op amp-based active filters are comprised of one or more op amps embedded in single or multiple negative-feedback loops, nonlinear distortion will be reduced, as discussed in Chap. 5. However, in OTA-based active filters, each open-loop OTA must be individually linearized.

FIGURE 7-1   Filtering illustrated as a spectral weighting process, where the input spectrum is comprised of the three spectral components at frequencies f_k with amplitudes $|X_k|$ for $k = 1$, 2, and 3. The filter, described by the weights $|H_k|$ at f_k, passes the f_1, f_2 components while attenuating the highest frequency components at f_3. In addition, unavoidable nonlinearities in the filter have introduced new spectral components at the sum frequencies $f_1 + f_2$, $f_2 + f_3$, and $f_1 + f_3$, and at the second harmonics of f_k, i.e., $2f_k$. These undesired components, shown in gray, represent harmonic distortion.

7-2   SCHEMES FOR INTEGRATED ANALOG FILTERS

In this chapter and Chap. 8, we will explore three schemes for realizing microelectronic analog filters, namely *active-RC*, *active-G_m/C*, and *active-SC* filters. The first two schemes are continuous-time in nature, and the third is sampled-data; each presents unique advantages and disadvantages that must be weighed by the designer before use in any given application. These approaches, although viewed as being in direct competition with one another, are sometimes used together in complementary system roles. One example is the use of lowpass active-RC filters for anti-aliasing and reconstruction interfaces to a switched-capacitor filter (see Fig. A7-7*b* in App. 7-1). Many features from active-RC circuits and their design lore have been incorporated in synthesis methodologies for active-SC and active-G_m/C filters. Conversely, the current advances in fully integrated active-RC and active-G_m/C filters have been based on the rich technical foundation developed for VLSI active-SC filters.

At this stage let us point out that quality VLSI active-filters, depending upon the implementation approach, can be realized over a wide range of frequencies (50 Hz $\leq f <$ 100 MHz) in CMOS, bipolar, or BICMOS technologies. Equivalent quality VLSI active-SC filters, over a somewhat narrower range (50 Hz $\leq f <$ 1 MHz), are realizable in CMOS and BICMOS technologies. Due to the need for small, high-quality switches, bipolar technology is not viable for active-SC filters. The comparative advantages for active-SC filters are higher precision, greater linearity, and, perhaps, smaller die size and power dissipation. On the other hand, active-RC and active G_m/C filters can achieve higher signal-processing frequencies and, being continuous-time, they are not complicated by the sample-data effects described in App. 7-1. Both switched-capacitor and continuous-time active filters (Gregorian and Temes 1986; Schaumann et al. 1990; Schaumann and Laker 1993; Sedra 1989; Unbehauen and Cichocki 1989) can be implemented with digital logic on the same chip to realize a wide variety of mixed analog/digital VLSI systems, (see Kuraishi et al. 1984; Callias et al 1989).

7-2-1   Active-RC and Active G_m/C Filters

Figures 7-2 and 7-3 represent the variety of schemes available for realizing integrated active-RC filters (Gregorian and Temes 1986; Schaumann et al. 1990; Schaumann and Laker 1993; Sedra 1989; Unbehauen and Cichocki 1989). In Fig. 7-2 we show a typical schematic for a single op amp second-order filter, and in Fig. 7-3 we illustrate the signal-flow graph for a high-order filter comprised of interconnected integrators of the types described in Chap. 5. In both figures, active-RC filters are made up of resistors (R's), capacitors (C's), and amplifier circuits. With the OTA, the functions served by op amps and resistors are combined in the OTA transconductance G_m.

The importance of active-RC filters has been apparent as far back as the 1950's, when it was anticipated that circuits composed of R's, C's, and transistors could take advantage of the solid-state advances occurring at that time better than circuits comprised of L's and C's. It is evident that using active circuits in filters provides

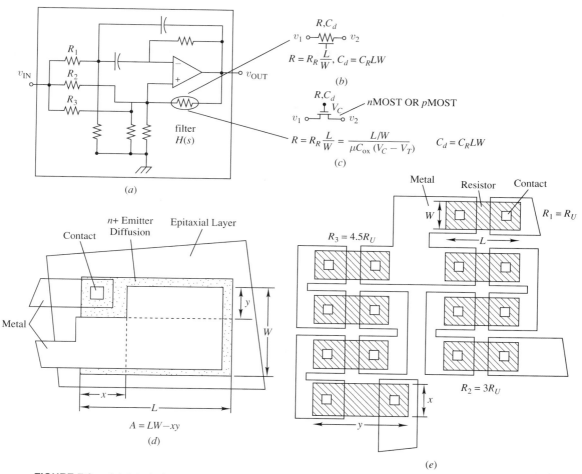

FIGURE 7-2   (a) A typical second-order active-RC filter with input v_{IN} and output v_{OUT}. This filter is realized with R's, C's, and a single op amp. In the IC realization of this schematic, integrated circuit R's are actually distributed RC lines of length L and width W, realized with either (b) a resistive material or (c) a pMOST operating in the triode region. High quality capacitors in bipolar are realized as in (d). The layout strategy for matched resistors is illustrated in (e).

the opportunity to realize gain, i.e., the magnification of voltages, currents, and/or power, at preselected frequencies. Recently, active filters based on the G_m's of OTAs (Fig. 7-3c) have been demonstrated (Geiger and Sanchez-Sinencio 1985; Schaumann and Laker 1993; Schaumann et al. 1990; Sedra 1989; Unbehauen and Cichocki 1989) to provide interesting alternatives to the more traditional resistor op amp-based active filters, particularly at frequencies well above the audio band ($f > 100$ kHz). As seen in Chap. 6, OTAs are realized with simpler circuits, and can achieve significantly higher bandwidths, than op amps. However, as mentioned in Chap. 5, the improved

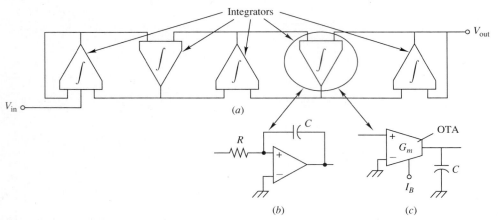

FIGURE 7-3   Many high performance continuous-time active filters are based on the interconnection of integrator blocks, as shown in (*a*). An integrator is realized using either (*b*) the classic negative feedback op amp circuit or (*c*) the operational transconductance amplifier (OTA) based circuit.

high-frequency performance of OTA-based active filters is realized at the expense of reduced linearity.

Active-RC filters, such as those in Figs 7-2 and 7-3, are characterized by transfer functions of the form

$$H(s) = \frac{V_{\text{out}}(s)}{V_{\text{in}}(s)} = \frac{\displaystyle\sum_{i=0}^{M} a_i s^i}{s^N + \displaystyle\sum_{i=0}^{N-1} b_i s^i} = \frac{a_M \displaystyle\prod_{i=1}^{M} (s - \omega_{zi})}{\displaystyle\prod_{i=1}^{N} (s - \omega_{pi})} \tag{7-6}$$

where $M \leq N$, also poles ω_{pi} and zeros ω_{zi} are functions of $1/R_j C_k$ (e.g., Eq. (7-1*b*)) for op amp or G_{mj}/C_k for OTA-based filters, respectively. From elementary filter theory we know that the poles and zeros of passive RC networks are constrained to lie on the negative real axis of the s-plane. The use of op amps (or OTAs) and the application of feedback (inverting and/or noninverting as described in Chap. 5) provide a means to shift the poles and zeros off the real axis and locate them anywhere in the s-plane. In Chap. 8 we will derive design formulas that relate $H(s)$ to the values of the circuit components using techniques studied in Chap. 5. Also, we will examine the important second-order effects due to the practical limits of integrated-circuit op amps, OTAs, and passive components.

The realization of useful integrated active-RC and active-G_m/C filters require high-quality passive components (Unbehauen and Cichocki 1989; Grebene 1984); i.e., linear, low-loss capacitors (Chap. 1 and Fig. 7-2*d*) in the 0.1 pF–100 pF range and linear resistors (Chap. 2-9 and Figs. 7-2*b*, 7-2*c*, and 7-2*e*) in the 100 KΩ to 100 MΩ range. Also required are op amps (Chap. 6) with gain-bandwidths of $GBW \geq$ 1 MHz, and linear, wide bandwidth OTAs (Chap. 6) realizing G_m's in the range

0.1 μS–1000 μS. (Unbehauen and Cichocki 1989; Schaumann and Laker 1993.) The latter is more difficult to achieve over a suitably wide range of input signal levels, as we will discuss in Chap. 8.

It is of paramount importance that all passive and active components be linear, or sufficiently near linear in order to meet THD and dynamic range requirements. Moreover, op amps and OTAs must have sufficient phase margin PM $\geq 60°$ to ensure stability, as described in Chaps. 3 and 6. Since the impedance levels internal to a filter will tend to be high, the output impedances for op amps can be increased ($10 \text{ k}\Omega \leq Z_o \geq 100 \text{ k}\Omega$) to reduce power dissipation and die size. The exception to this trend will be op amps that must also drive off chip loads. Tools and techniques are provided in Chaps. 3, 5, and 6 to synthesize suitable op amps, OTAs and related feedback circuits.

As far as capacitors are concerned, we are fortunate that very high quality IC capacitors (Grebene 1984; Allstot and Black 1983) (e.g., $C_{\text{poly,poly}}$ in Table 2-7) are readily available in most CMOS and bipolar processes, as described in Sec. 2-9. Such capacitors are nearly ideal; i.e., linear, very low loss, and with very small temperature variability. In bipolar processes, capacitors of similar quality can be realized with metal as top plate, SiO_2 dielectric, and heavily doped emitter diffusion as bottom plate, (see Fig. 7-2d). We note that a separate capacitor dielectric layer is more commonly found in CMOS processes than in bipolar processes. In any event, we can assume that ideal (but not precise) capacitors in the 1 pF–100 pF range are generally available. As discussed in Chaps. 1 and 2, IC capacitors (both intended and parasitic) are characterized by a capacitance density (C_o fF/μm^2 or nF/cm^2), and geometry (width W and length L). The value for an IC capacitor of area LW μm^2 and C_o fF/μm^2 is then $C = 10^{-3}C_oLW$ pF. When C is defined in terms of a square unit of $W \times W$ μm^2, then $C = 10^{-3}C_oL/W$ pF and L/W is the number of $W \times W$ units, or squares in LW.

In the case of resistors, several options for bipolar and MOS realizations are presented in Sec. 2-9. These options lead to a wide range of cost-performance tradeoffs, indicated in Table 2-6. The integrated resistors in Table 2-6 are realized using a patterned resistive material of some kind, i.e., thin film, diffusion, and ion-implant (see Fig. 7-2b). In addition, a voltage-controlled resistor (Gregorian and Temes 1986; Sedra 1989; Unbehauen and Cichocki 1989) can be realized in a CMOS process by operating a MOST (either p or n) in the so-called linear (or triode) region, as described in Chap. 1 (see Fig. 7-2c). Henceforth, we will refer to MOST voltage-controlled resistors as MOST-R's or, in particular, an nMOST-R or pMOST-R.

All resistors are characterized by sheet resistance (R_R Ω/□) and geometry (width W and length L). In the case of MOST-R's, we can express an effective sheet resistance $R_R = R_{DSsq}$ in terms of the external control voltage V_C applied to the MOST gate, as given in Eq. (1-9) and repeated in Table 7-1. The value for a resistor of length L μm, width $W\mu$m, and sheet resistance $R_R = R_{DSsq}$ Ω/□ (when □ has dimensions $W\mu$m $\times$ $W\mu$m), is $R = R_{DSsq}(L/W)$. We note that to suitably define linear MOST-R, (see Fig. 7-2c), either the voltage drop v_1 to v_2 must be kept sufficiently small or a linearized MOST-R structure must be used.

TABLE 7-1   TYPICAL ELECTRICAL CHARACTERISTICS FOR IC RESISTORS USED IN FILTERS.

Resistor Type	Sheet resistance R_R $\Omega/\square$	Absolute intrinsic Accuracy $\Delta R/R \pm \%$	Matching accuracy $W = 2$ to $10\,\mu\mathrm{m} \pm \%$	Approximate temperature coefficient $\%/^\circ\mathrm{C}$	Distributed capacitance density C_R $\mathrm{fF}/\mu\mathrm{m}^2$
Bipolar Ion-implanted	100-1000	3	2 to 0.15	0.02	~ 0.1
CMOS p-well	2500	10	2 to 0.2	0.3	~ 0.2
MOST-R $R_{SH} = \dfrac{1}{\beta(V_C - V_T)}$	$< 50\,k$	25	1 to 0.25	0.5	~ 0.7

Matching accuracy between two resistors R_1, R_2 increases as W increases, as $R_1/R_2 \to N$ an integer, and with prudent layout, as illustrated in Fig. 7-2e.

It was noted in Chap. 2 that IC resistors have an associated distributed parasitic capacitance C_R, determined by the particular properties of the dielectric between the resistor structure-and-substrate and the geometry of the resistor (Grebene 1984). The consequences of these capacitances are to shift the pole-zero locations and to increase the order of the filter. This, in effect, limits the bandwidth available from the filter to $f \ll f_{RC}$ in Eq. (2-56). Also, the op amp and OTA are similarly bandlimited as described in Chaps. 5 and 6. In the first-order design of an integrated active-RC filter, we usually make the simplifying assumptions that $f_{RC} = \infty$, op amp $GBW = \infty$, and OTA $BW = \infty$. In subsequent refinements we consider the impacts that finite f_{RC}, GBW, and BW have on the precision of the filter's response at all relevant frequencies. Given that $f/GBW \ll 1$, $f/f_d \ll 1$, and $f/BW \ll 1$, where f is any frequency in the range where precision $G(\omega)$ and $\varphi(\omega)$ are required, a well-designed filter will not be sensitive to these parameters.

To locate precisely the filter poles and zeros in Eq. (7-6), and to hold them fixed with a varying ambient environment (temperature, humidity, etc.), the $1/RC$ or the G_m/C must be defined precisely and held as constant as possible as the ambient environment changes. Based on the electrical characteristics in Table 7-1 it is clear that all the IC resistor realizations are inherently imprecise and vary with temperature. However, if laid out with care, a high degree of matching accuracy can be achieved so that precision ratios of like resistors can be realized, as described in Chap. 3.

A good layout technique is illustrated in Fig. 7-2e, where resistors $R_1 = R_U$, $R_2 = 3R_U$, $R_3 = 4.5R_U$, in the schematic of Fig. 7-2a, are laid out to maximize matching accuracy. In this circuit R_1 is the smallest resistor; hence, we designate its structure (an $L \times W$ resistor and two contacts) as the unit resistance R_U. R_2, the next largest resistor, is an integer (i.e., $N = 3$) multiple of the unit R_U. Hence, its layout is realized with N simple step-and-repeats of the unit R_U. Resistor R_3 is a noninteger (i.e., $N + \delta = 4.5$, where $0 < \delta < 1$) multiple of R_U. Its layout is achieved by repeating R_U $N-1$ times and realizing the $1+\delta$ as a nonunit element with dimensions $x \times y$. One important characteristic of this resistor structure is that the perimeter (P_i/P_j) ratio can always be made equal to the resistor ratio, i.e., $P_i/P_j = R_i/R_j$. Hence, edge undercuts in the definition of the features in Fig. 7-2e will tend to cancel in the resistor ratios (see Exercise 7-7). For NR_U resistors, the segmented layout structure ensures this quality. For $(N+\delta)R_U$ resistors, the final segment's $x \times y$ can be sized such that its perimeter $(P_{1+\delta})$ is $(1+\delta)P_U$, i.e.,

$$\frac{P_{1+\delta}}{P_U} = \frac{x+y}{W+L} = 1+\delta \qquad \text{and} \qquad \frac{R_{1+\delta}}{R_U} = \frac{x}{y}\frac{L}{W} = 1+\delta \qquad (7\text{-}7a)$$

Solving for x and y yields:

$$x = W\frac{(1+\delta)^2(L+W)}{L+(1+\delta)W} \qquad \text{and} \qquad y = L\frac{(1+\delta)(L+W)}{L+(1+\delta)W} \qquad (7\text{-}7b)$$

Note that each R_U has four corners and two contacts. Correspondingly, NR_U resistors have $N \times 4$ corners and $N \times 2$ contacts. Hence, variations in resistance due to these features also will tend to cancel in the ratios. For $(N+\delta)R_U$ resistors, this relationship is achieved only approximately. Consequently, best matching will occur between resistors that are integer multiples of the unit R_U. A similar layout arrangement is recommended for matched capacitors as described in the next subsection.

Since we need precise RC products, matching resistors will not be sufficient to realize precision filters. In Chaps. 1 and 2 we observed that R's and C's (or G_m's and C's) are fabricated using different features or mask levels in all IC processes. Hence, errors or variations in the R's (or G_m's) and C's will be uncorrelated in $1/RC$'s (or G_m/C's). Thus, to achieve precision, either R's or C's must be trimmed or tuned. For example, with thin film R's, precision is usually obtained by laser cutting the resistive pattern to trim the value. In the cases of a MOST-R and OTA G_m, the control voltage V_C and current I_B, respectively, are used to tune these quantities. In fact, adaptive tuning incorporating a phase-frequency locked loop has been used to correct for fabrication errors and time-dependent variations in the ambient environment. It would appear from Tables 2-6 and 7-1 that p-well resistors behaved too poorly to be useful in filters. However, there are applications where these economical (i.e., high resistivity) resistors are adequate. Later in this chapter we will address the problem of filter sensitivity to such component variations and mismatches.

7-2-2   Active-SC Filters

In contrast to the continuous-time active-RC filter, consider the active-SC filter in Fig 7-4a (Ghausi and Laker 1981; Gregorian and Temes 1986; Schaumann et al. 1990; Schaumann and Laker 1993; Sedra 1989; Unbehauen and Cichocki 1989). We see that

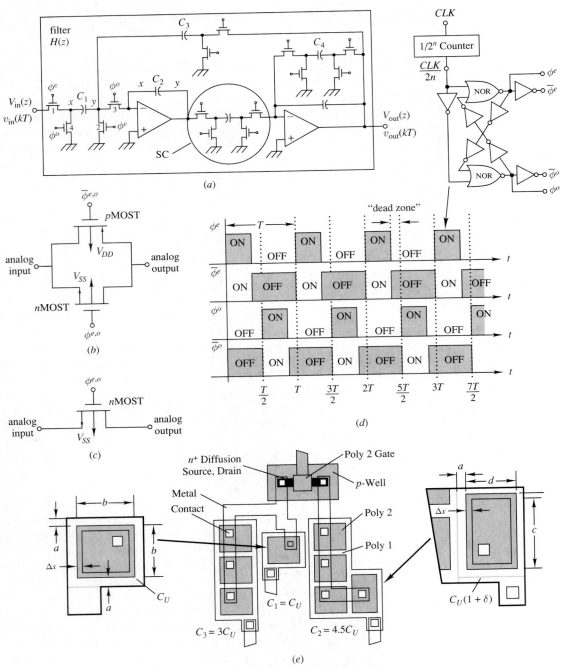

FIGURE 7-4 (*a*) A typical second-order SC filter with input $v_{in}(k)$, $V_{in}(z)$ and output $v_{out}(k)$, $V_{out}(z)$. This filter is comprised of C's, analog switches and two op amps. Realizations of analog switches using complementary and nMOST structures are shown in (*b*) and (*c*), respectively. The timing and digital hardware required to realize ϕ^e, ϕ^o, and compliments are shown in (*d*). The layout practice for matched capacitors is illustrated in (*e*).

active-SC filters are comprised of capacitors (C's), analog switches (or transmission gates), and op amps. The analog switches open and close periodically under the control of orthogonal, square wave-like signals ϕ^e and ϕ^o, each with period T (as shown in Fig. 7-4d). To visualize the operation of a switched capacitor, let us focus our attention in on the switched capacitor composed of capacitor C_1, and switches labeled 1, 2, and 3, 4, controlled by ϕ^e and ϕ^o, respectively, in Fig. 7-4a. With switches 1, 2 ON and 3, 4 OFF, the charge on C_1 follows $v_{in}(t)$, i.e., $q_{C1} = C_1 v_{in}(t)$. The instant switches 1 and 2 turn OFF, say, at $t \simeq T/2$, and the sample $v_{in}(T)$ is captured or recorded on to C_1. If this process repeats with period T, then at each $t \simeq kT/2$, a new sample $v_{in}(kT)$ (with $k = 1, 2, 3, \ldots ,$) will be recorded onto C_1, and the sample rate is $f_s = 1/T$. At $t \simeq kT/2$, and subsequent odd multiples of $T/2$, switches 3 and 4 are ON and 1 and 2 are OFF. At these instants the polarity of C_1 reverses, and C_1 discharges onto C_2 assisted by the virtual ground at the op amp input. As we will see later, virtual grounds and continuous local feedback are essential for robust active-SC filter operation. Consequently, many schemes discussed in Chap. 5 are not useful in practical switched-capacitor circuits, e.g., inverting feedback schemes using only switched-capacitors, all noninverting feedback schemes described in Sec. 5-2, and OTA-based structures in Sec. 5-5. In fact, the ability to achieve sign inversion in a switched-capacitor renders noninverting structures unnecessary.

We note that voltages charging capacitors can be from independent sources such as v_{in}, outputs of op amps, or the voltages held on other capacitors. This sampling process and movement of discrete charge packets (e.g., $q_{C_1}(kT) = C_1 v_{in}(kT)$) via the switching of capacitors is the essence of switched-capacitor filters. Thus, in-depth understanding of the principles of sampled-data systems is essential if the reader is to get maximum benefit from this chapter, and certainly if the reader desires to become a designer of sophisticated active-SC filters. For this purpose we provide in App. 7-1 a brief, but self-contained, review of this material.

Most practical active-SC filters are operated by nonoverlapping biphase control signals, e.g., ϕ^e and ϕ^o in Fig. 7-4d. In our notation we will, from time to time, refer to ϕ^e as either the even-phase or e-phase, and ϕ^o as either the odd-phase or o-phase. We note that additional phases are introduced in some switched-capacitor circuits to reduce DC offsets, $1/f$ op amp noise, and/or low-frequency spurious signals. However, even in such cases the primary signal processing is usually confined to two phases. Although it is convenient to visualize ϕ^e, ϕ^o as ideal 50 percent duty-cycle square waves, nonoverlap of the switch phases is essential for successful switched-capacitor operation. To be specific, the switched-capacitor circuit will fail catastrophically if ϕ^e and ϕ^o switches become turned ON simultaneously. In contrast, ϕ^e and ϕ^o switches that are OFF simultaneously for short periods of time do not interfere with the circuit's proper operation. Hence, to avoid any opportunity for overlap in ϕ^e and ϕ^o, due to unavoidable variations in their finite rise/fall times, duty cycles of 35 to 45 percent are realized, in practice. This timing is illustrated in Fig. 7-4d, where each period T is seen to have a 5 to 10 percent "dead zone," where both ϕ^e and ϕ^o are low.

The analog switches in Fig. 7-4a are realized (Allstot and Black 1983; Grebene 1984; Unbehauen and Cichocki 1989) using the MOST structures in Figs. 7-4b and 7-4c, as discussed in Chap. 1. Note the difference in symbols used to represent an analog switch in Fig. 7-4a, and the nMOST and pMOST in Fig. 7-4b. The analog switch symbol does not have an arrow to designate polarity. At this point, the analog switch symbol represents either realization. Since the CMOS structure in Fig. 7-4b maintains a near constant ON-resistance over the full voltage range $|V_{DD}$ to $V_{SS}|$, typically it is preferred. However, the single nMOST (or NMOS) switch is also used to reduce parasitic capacitance in circuit locations where signals are constrained to very low level, e.g., op amp virtual grounds. To implement the CMOS switch, the nMOST and pMOST must be driven from complement control signals, i.e., $\phi^e, \bar{\phi}^e$ or correspondingly $\phi^o, \bar{\phi}^o$. The timing for the complement controls is illustrated in Fig. 7-4d. It is tempting for the novice to be drawn into the misconception that $\phi^o = \bar{\phi}^e$ or vice versa. Although this relation would be correct if the duty cycles were 50 percent, such an occurrence is impractical. Hence, our use of ϕ^e, ϕ^o rather than $\phi, \bar{\phi}$ avoids confusion on this important detail.

Clock signals ϕ^e and ϕ^o and their complements, if needed, are derived from a precise master source, such as an on-chip crystal oscillator or an external system clock. The master is divided logically to the desired sampling frequency and split into two nonoverlapping phases using cross-coupled NOR gates. If needed, the complements are realized with subsequent inverter stages. Typical digital circuitry needed to perform these operations is shown in Fig. 7-4d. Two gate delays in each of the cross-coupled paths is usually sufficient to realize a suitable dead zone. Although usually not included in published active-SC filter schematics, clock generation is a small, but important, part of the cost of an active-SC filter. Fortunately, this support function is realized with relatively undemanding digital logic and the resulting hardware can be shared over many switched-capacitor subcircuits.

Active-SC filters, like active-RC filters, require and use the same linear, very low loss capacitors (Allstot and Black 1983; Gregorian and Temes 1986; Unbehauen and Cichocki 1989) described in Chap. 1. The basic requirements for op amps used in active-SC filters are similar to those described for active-RC filters. However, due to their sampled-data nature, the open-loop DC gain A_0 and the settling time are more important criteria than the GBW of the dominant pole. The primary electrical requirement for the analog switch is that its ON resistance R_{ON} be sufficiently small, such that $1/R_{ON}C_T \gg 2\pi f_s$ (where $C_T = C + C_p$, C is the intended capacitor, and C_p is the parasitic capacitance connected to the switch) over the full dynamic range of the filter. Typically, $R_{ON} < 10$ KΩ, maintained over the filter dynamic range, is sufficient for this purpose. As noted earlier, the voltage range for maintaining R_{ON} relaxes substantially at the op amp virtual grounds. In any event, the R_{ON} for either structure is adjusted by sizing the W/L of the MOSTs, as described in Chap. 1.

In addition to the R_{ON} specification, there is a conflicting requirement that the gate-source C_{gs} and gate-drain C_{gd} capacitances be as small as possible to reduce the control signal (ϕ^e, ϕ^o) leakage into the filter. It is also desirable to minimize all parasitic capacitances to the substrate or bulk. Fortunately, at the inputs of op amps, which are most sensitive to these effects, the signal amplitude is tightly constrained by the virtual ground; the switches can be made sufficiently small to satisfy both demands. Moreover, the single nMOST (or NMOS) switch in Fig. 7-4c can be effective in these locations, e.g., switch 3 in Fig. 7-4a.

The fundamental innovation[1] in active-SC filters is the functional replacement of the resistor with a switched capacitor. To see how the switched capacitor works, let us turn our attention to Fig. 7-5a, where we show a simple switched-capacitor circuit comprised of switched-capacitor C_1 and capacitor C_2. Once again, the analog switches are controlled by the precision biphase clock signals ϕ^e, ϕ^o (see Fig. 7-4d). Switched-capacitor C_1 synchronously toggles the top and bottom plates of capacitor C_1 between v_1 and v_2, respectively, and ground. Note that in this case the sign of C_1 is not reversed during the switching action. Samples are recorded on C_2 at the precise instant the ϕ^e switches open and disconnect C_2 from the signal path. Furthermore, capacitor C_1 is instantaneously discharged when the ϕ^o switches close, connecting the top and bottom plates of C_1 directly to ground. If q_{C1}, v_1, and v_2 are slowly variable with respect to the clock period T, the circuit equation for the switched-capacitor C_1 (with $C_2 = 0$) can be written as

$$i_{C1}(t) = \frac{dq_{C1}(t)}{dt} = C_1 \frac{dv_{C1}(t)}{dt} \approx C_1 \frac{v_1 - v_2}{T} = \frac{v_1 - v_2}{R_1} \qquad (7\text{-}8a)$$

Hence, we see that the switched-capacitor C_1, with switch period T, serves the function of a resistor R_1, where

$$R_1 \approx \frac{T}{C_1} = \frac{1}{C_1 f_s} \qquad (7\text{-}8b)$$

Since C_1 and f_s typically are on the order of 1 to 100 pF and 100 kHz, respectively, the equivalent R_1 is 10 to 0.1 MΩ. Hence, very large equivalent R's are realized in essentially the space required to realize a few pF's of capacitance and four MOST switches.

---

[1] Switched-capacitor circuits can be found in the literature as far back as the 1950s. Until switched-capacitor techniques were related to MOS technologies by D. L. Fried in 1972, such circuits were largely lab curiosities. Five years later, modern MOS active-SC filters were launched into the limelight with the pioneering work of R. W. Broderson, P. R. Gray, D. A. Hodges, and students at U. C. Berkeley.

FIGURE 7-5   A simple SC circuit and its RC equivalent. In (a) the SC circuit is comprised of C_2 and SC C_1. The timing for the switches is shown in Fig. 7-7d. A functionally equivalent RC circuit is shown in (b).

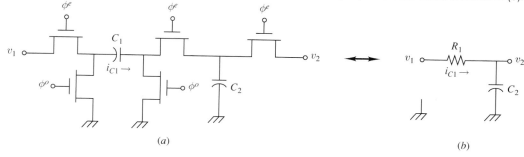

(a)   (b)

If we let $C_2 \neq 0$, the switched-capacitor and RC networks in Fig. 7-5 realize single poles, where

$$\omega_p = \frac{1}{R_1 C_2} \approx f_s \frac{C_1}{C_2} = f_s \gamma_{12} \tag{7-8c}$$

For typical sample rates of 8 kHz $\leq f_s \leq$ 10 MHz, we see from Eq. (7-8c) that ω_p can be adjusted over a wide range via γ_{12}, realized from C_1 and C_2 in the 1 to 100 pF range. In fact, the entire audio range and beyond can be accommodated with values for C_1 and C_2, consistent with VLSI. Moreover, ω_p can be externally scaled to $K\omega_p$ by shifting f_s to Kf_s. This enables us to oversample at $f_s \geq 10 f_N$ (where f_N is the Nyquist frequency defined in App. 7-1) with little penalty. Equation (7-8c) also demonstrates the inherent precision of switched-capacitor circuits in comparison to their RC counterparts.

Active-RC zeros/poles are fixed by values for 1/RC's (or G_m/C's), which we recognize can vary significantly with temperature and processing tolerances. In contrast, the active-SC zeros/poles depend on a crystal controlled f_s and the ratio of capacitors (γ_{12}) of identical structure. With a crystal-based source, sampling frequency f_s is accurately defined (e.g., $|\Delta f_s/f_s| < 0.001$ percent). Hence, the task of realizing precision ω_p reduces to the implementation of precision γ_{12}. This is good news, since realizing critical circuit parameters with ratios of matched components, as described in Sec. 3-4, is the foundation of IC design. In fact, with careful layout (as illustrated in Fig. 7-4e) inherently imprecise MOS capacitors ($|\Delta C_i/C_i| = \pm 20\%$) can be matched, such that $|\Delta \gamma_{ij}/\gamma_{ij}| < 0.1$ percent.

This layout strategy (Gregorian and Temes 1986; Unbehauen and Cichocki 1989; Allstot and Black 1983) is similar in spirit to that suggested for matched resistors in Fig. 7-2e. In this layout, capacitors $C_1 = C_U$, $C_2 = 4.5C_U$, $C_3 = 3R_U$, in the Fig. 7-4a schematic are realized as modular poly1-poly2 structures. The detailed electrical and physical properties of poly1-poly2 capacitors are described in Chap. 2. The top plates, i.e., poly2, of the capacitors are connected to the source, drain of a p-well nMOST, e.g., the switch in Fig. 7-4c. In this circuit, C_1 is the smallest capacitor; hence, we designate its structure [a $b \times b$ poly 2 layer, $(b+a) \times (b+a)$ poly 1 layer and one contact to poly 2] as the unit capacitance C_U. Typically, the value for a is the minimum permitted by the process design rules. C_3, the next largest capacitor, is an $N = 3$ multiple of the unit C_U. Hence, its layout is realized with N simple step-and-repeats of the unit C_U. Capacitor C_2 is a noninteger $N + \delta = 4.5$ multiple of C_U. Its layout is achieved by repeating C_U, $N - 1$ times, and realizing the $1 + \delta$ as a nonunit element with dimensions $c \times d$. Note that the poly 1 bottom plates of the elemental capacitances are accumulated into a single sheet, with added area for a poly 1-metal contact.

An important characteristic of this capacitor structure is that the ratios of perimeter (P_i/P_j) and area (A_i/A_j) can always be made equal to the capacitor ratio, i.e., $P_i/P_j = A_i/A_j = C_i/C_j$. This condition is similar to that recommended for matched resistors. Hence, edge undercuts (Δx) in the definition of the features in Fig. 7-4e will tend to cancel in the capacitor ratios. For NC_U capacitors the segmented layout structure ensures this quality. For $(N + \delta)$ C_U capacitors, the final segment's $c \times d$ can be sized such that its perimeter $P_{1+\delta} = (1 + \delta)P_U$ and area $A_{1+\delta} = (1 + \delta)A_U$, i.e.,

$$\frac{P_{1+\delta}}{P_U} = \frac{c+d}{2b} = 1 + \delta \qquad \text{and} \qquad \frac{A_{1+\delta}}{A_U} = \frac{cd}{b^2} = 1 + \delta \qquad (7\text{-}9a)$$

Solving for c and d yields:

$$c = b\left\{1 + \delta + \sqrt{\delta^2 + \delta}\right\} \qquad \text{and} \qquad d = b\left\{1 + \delta - \sqrt{\delta^2 + \delta}\right\} \qquad (7\text{-}9b)$$

The number of corners and contacts for NC_U capacitors are $N\times$ those of the unit; this relationship is achieved only approximately for $(N + \delta)C_U$ capacitors. As per Eq. 7-8c, realizing matched capacitors in this way will yield precision integrated filters without the laser trimming or sophisticated adaptive tuning schemes required for integrated active-RC schemes.

Returning to Eqs. (7-8), it is important to understand that the approximation Eq. (7-8a) is based on slowly varying $v_{1,2}$, such that $v_{1,2}(t) \approx v_{1,2}(kT)$ in between sampling intervals $(k + 1)T < t \leq kT$. In practice, our sample-data signals will be based on the zero-order-hold or sample-and-hold function described in Fig. 7-6 in App. 7-1. However, we can rigorously define the operation of the switched capacitor C_1 at the discrete sampling instants $t = kT$, by the discrete-time difference equation,

$$\frac{\Delta q_{C1}(kT)}{T} = \frac{q_{C1}(kT) - q_{C1}((k - 1/2)T)}{T} = \frac{C_1 v_1(kT) - C_1 v_2(kT)}{T} \qquad (7\text{-}10a)$$

where $q_{C1}((k - 1/2)T) = 0$, due to the discharging of C_1 to ground during the ϕ^o-phase. Multiplying Eq. (7-10a) by period T, we obtain an expression that relates the charge Δq transferred at $t = kT$ to the terminal voltage samples $v_1(kT)$, $v_2(kT)$ and capacitance C_1, i.e.,

$$\Delta q(kT) = C_1 v_1(kT) - C_1 v_2(kT) \qquad (7\text{-}10b)$$

or in the z-domain (where in App. 7-1 we define $z = e^{sT}$)

$$\Delta Q(z) = C_1 V_1(z) - C_1 V_2(z) \qquad (7\text{-}10c)$$

The fact that C_1 has no memory of past samples $v_1(k-1)T$, $v_2(k-1)T$, is the result of discharging C_1 during the ϕ^o-phase. As we will see later, the forms of Eq. (7-10b) and (7-10c) are typical of discrete nodal-charge equations for switched-capacitor circuits. In any event, at this point Eqs. (7-8) and (7-10) describe an analog circuit operation that lead to significant advances in miniaturization, precision of pole-zero location, functionality, and integration on the same chip as digital VLSI.

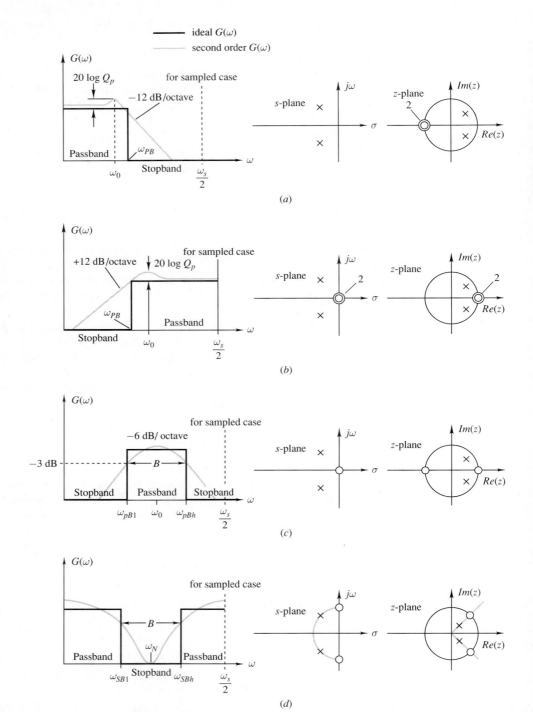

FIGURE 7-6 Filter categories: (*a*) lowpass; (*b*) highpass; (*c*) bandpass; (*d*) band-reject or notch; (*e*) lowpass notch; (*f*) highpass notch; and (*g*) allpass. For each category, the following sketches are provided: (i) the $G(\omega)$ for the ideal filter, (ii) the $G(\omega)$ for a second-order filter, and (iii) the respective s-domain and z-domain pole-zero patterns corresponding to the second order cases in (ii).

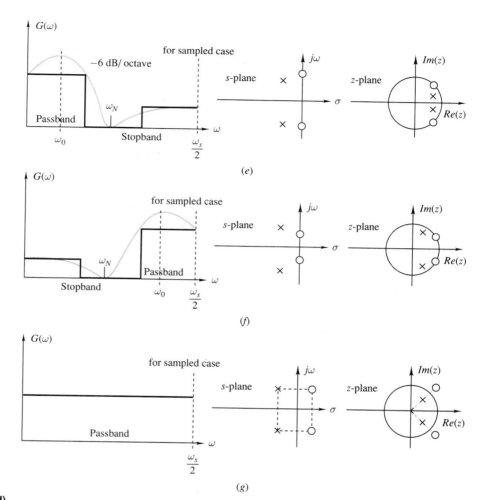

FIGURE 7-6 (cont'd)

In general, based on Eqs. (7-10) and the associated discussion, the input and output voltage samples $(v_{\text{in}}(kT), v_{\text{out}}(kT))$ of active-SC filters are related via a difference equation of the form

$$v_{\text{out}}(kT) + \sum_{n=1}^{N} B_n v_{\text{out}}((k-n)T) = \sum_{n=0}^{M} A_n v_{\text{in}}((k-n)T) \qquad (7\text{-}11a)$$

where A_n, B_n are functions of ratioed capacitors (switched and unswitched); M, N are finite nonnegative integers; and the sampling rate is $f_s = 1/T$. Taking the z-transform of both sides of Eq. (7-11a) and forming the voltage ratio $V_{\text{out}}/V_{\text{in}}$, we write the z-domain filter transfer function as

$$H(z) = \frac{V_{\text{out}}(z)}{V_{\text{in}}(z)} = \frac{\sum_{i=0}^{M} A_i z^i}{z^N + \sum_{i=0}^{N-1} B_i z^i}$$

$$= \frac{A_M \prod_{i=1}^{M} (z - \Omega_{zi})}{\prod_{i=1}^{N} (z - \Omega_{pi})} = \frac{A_M z^{-(N-M)} \prod_{i=1}^{M} (1 - \Omega_{zi} z^{-1})}{\prod_{i=1}^{N} (1 - \Omega_{pi} z^{-1})} \qquad (7\text{-}11b)$$

where $M \leq N$ for IIR filters (see App. 7-1), and the zeros (Ω_{zi}), poles (Ω_{pi}) are functions of capacitor ratios. Later design formulas relating A_i, B_j (or Ω_{zi}, Ω_{pi}) to capacitor ratios will be derived using z-domain techniques (Ghausi and Laker 1981; Gregorian and Temes 1986; Unbehauen and Cichocki 1989), analogous to those in Chap. 5.

We emphasize that the transfer function is the primary link between the filter's performance and its physical realization. That is, once $H(s)$ or $H(z)$ is determined, the designer can immediately estimate many important circuit qualities (e.g., circuit complexity, size or chip die area, sensitivity, and the detailed structure of the magnitude, phase and/or group delay). Moreover, $H(s)$ (or $H(z)$) is the starting point for the synthesis of the filter circuit. Hence, deriving a "good" H from a collection of filter specs is the first step, and in many instances one of the most important steps in filter synthesis.

7-3   FILTER TYPES AND FREQUENCY RESPONSE SPECIFICATIONS

To make a more efficient presentation for the remainder of this chapter, we have elected to integrate the development of continuous-time and sampled-data filters into a single presentation. We believe that this presentation style will enable the reader to more effectively explore the common, as well as unique, opportunities in each domain.

Typically, continuous and sampled filters are classified according to the frequency-domain functions they perform, e.g., lowpass, highpass, bandpass, etc. They are further characterized by the complexity and fine structure of their frequency responses (gain, phase, or group delay). In this section, we define each filter type and discuss how their frequency responses are specified.

The complexity and cost of a filter is directly related to the order of the numerator (M) and denominator (N) polynomials of $H = H(s$ or $z)$ in Eqs. (7-6) and (7-11b). Although practical filters involve wide ranges of M and N, the building blocks of active filters are first- and second-order[2] stages or cells. Using the notation in Eqs. (7-6) and (7-11), these filter-building blocks are represented (for both continuous-time and

---

[2]Second-order active filter-building blocks are also called biquadratic sections, or simply biquads.

sampled-data), respectively, as

$$H(s) = \frac{a_1 s \pm a_0}{s + b_0} \quad \text{and} \quad H(s) = \frac{a_2 s^2 \pm a_1 s + a_0}{s^2 + b_1 s + b_0} \qquad (7\text{-}12a)$$

$$H(z) = \frac{A_1 z \pm A_0}{z + B_0} \quad \text{and} \quad H(z) = \frac{A_2 z^2 \pm A_1 z \pm A_0}{z^2 - B_1 z + B_0} \qquad (7\text{-}12b)$$

We often find $H(z)$ expressed in terms of unit delays or z^{-1}, i.e.

$$H(z) = \frac{A_1 + A_0 z^{-1}}{1 + B_0 z^{-1}} \quad \text{and} \quad H(z) = \frac{A_2 \pm A_1 z^{-1} \pm A_0 z^{-2}}{1 - B_1 z^{-1} + B_0 z^{-2}} \qquad (7\text{-}12c)$$

As we will see in Chapter 8, any filter specification can be realized by a modular active-RC, active-G_m/C, or active-SC filter comprised of first- and/or second-order cells connected in tandem, with and without multiple loops of external feedback.

For biquads with complex zeros and poles, we can express Eqs. (7-12) in the following useful forms: for *continuous-time filters*

$$H(s) = \frac{k \left[s^2 \pm \dfrac{\omega_N}{Q_z} s + \omega_N^2 \right]}{s^2 + \dfrac{\omega_0}{Q_p} s + \omega_0^2} = \frac{k N(s)}{D(s)} \qquad (7\text{-}13a)$$

for *sampled-data filters* (see App. 7-1):

$$H(z) = \frac{k[1 - 2r_z \cos \theta_N z^{-1} + r_z^2 z^{-2}]}{1 - 2r_p \cos \theta_0 z^{-1} + r_p^2 z^{-2}} = \frac{k N(z)}{D(z)} \qquad (7\text{-}13b)$$

The parameters ω_N, ω_0 and Q_z, Q_p are the s-domain null, resonant frequencies, and pole, zero quality factors, respectively. Recall in Chap. 3 that for $Q_p \gg 1$, $\omega_0 \simeq \omega_p$ when ω_p is the pole frequency. Similarly, for $Q_z \gg 1$, $\omega_N \simeq \omega_z$ where ω_z is the zero frequency. In many instances $Q_z = \infty$ and $\omega_N = \omega_z$. Parameters r_z, r_p, and θ_N, θ_0 are the z-domain zero, pole moduli, and arguments, respectively. The constant $k = a_2$ (or A_2) is used to adjust gain $G(\omega)$ at some reference frequency, say $\omega = 0$ or $\omega = \omega_0$ or $\omega = \infty$, to a particular level. We know that, in general, $G(\omega)$ reaches its maximum value near, or at, the resonant frequency ω_0 and its minimum value near, or at, the null frequency ω_N.

As shown in Chap. 3 and App. 7-1, the sharpness of the peak at ω_0 is proportional to the value of Q_p or r_p. Similarly, the sharpness of the minimum at ω_N is determined by Q_z or r_z. Also, as indicated in Eq. (A7-47), r_p, $r_z \to 1$ as Q_p, $Q_z \to \infty$. The exact placement of the maximum and minimum $G(\omega)$'s depends on the values for Q_p and Q_z (or r_p, and r_z) and the relative values of ω_0, ω_N (or θ_0, θ_N). For instance, for $Q_p \gg 1$ (or $r_p \approx 1$) and either $\omega_0 \gg \omega_N$ or $\omega_N \gg \omega_0$, the maximum, or peak of $G(\omega)$ occurs at ω_0 independent of the exact values of ω_N, Q_p, and Q_z. In addition,

$\theta_0 \approx \omega_0 T$ and $\theta_N \approx \omega_N T$, when $Q_p \gg 1$ and $Q_z \gg 1$. In many cases, $1/Q_z = 0$ (or $r_z = 1$); that is the zeros lie on the $j\omega$-axis (or unit circle) and ω_N defines a null where $G(\omega) = -\infty$ dB[3]. Although we constrain the poles to lie in the stable regions of the s, z-planes, the zeros can be placed anywhere. When the zeros lie in the right-half s-plane (or outside the unit circle), the $\pm$ in the numerator of $H(s)$ in Eq. (7-13a) is $-$ (or $r_z > 1$ in Eq. (7-13b)).

In the continuous-time and sampled-data domains, we classify filters into the following generic categories: *lowpass, highpass, bandpass, band-reject* or *notch, lowpass notch, highpass notch,* and *allpass.* The H for these filter categories, each illustrated in Fig. 7-6, are readily identifiable special cases of Eqs. (7-12). Let us now examine each category one by one, starting with the lowpass.

7-3-1   Lowpass

Let us consider first the lowpass (LP) filter in Fig. 7-6a. The LP filter's function is to pass low frequencies ($\omega \leq \omega_{PB}$) and to attenuate high frequencies ($\omega > \omega_{PB}$). Frequency ω_{PB} is the *cutoff frequency*, the frequencies ($0 \leq \omega \leq \omega_{PB}$) are the *passband* and the frequencies ($\omega_{PB} < \omega < \infty$) are the *stopband*. A second-order $G(\omega)$ is illustrated as a gray curve superimposed on the ideal gain response, shown in black. Observe the discrepancy between the second-order response and the ideal response. The ideal filter $G(\omega)$ shows a sharp, steplike transition between passband and stopband. This ideal response, sometimes called a *brick wall* response, cannot be realized with a finite filter circuit. Hence, the ideal response can only be approached asymptotically as the order of H approaches infinity. Fortunately, we can meet a surprisingly large number of practical filter requirements with $N \leq 10$. Analogous arguments can made for all the other filter categories, as well.

Also shown in Fig. 7-6a are the pole-zero patterns for the second-order H's, where

$$H(s) = \frac{k\omega_0^2}{s^2 + \dfrac{\omega_0}{Q_p}s + \omega_0^2} = \frac{kN(s)}{D(s)} \tag{7-14a}$$

and

$$H(z) = \frac{k'(1 + z^{-1})(1 + z^{-1})}{1 - 2r_p \cos\theta_0 z^{-1} + r_p^2 z^{-2}} = \frac{k'N(z)}{D(z)} \tag{7-14b}$$

We set $k' = k/4[1 - 2r_p \cos\theta_0 + r_p^2]$, such that $|H(s = 0)| = |H(z = 1)| = k$. Parameters ω_0, Q_p, and $\omega_s = 2\pi f_s$ participate in defining the structure of $G(\omega)$, as illustrated in Figs. 7-6a and 7-7a. The two zeros at $z = -1$ correspond to the mapping of the two s-plane zeros at $s = \infty$ to the half-sampling frequency in the z-domain.

---

[3]Infinite attenuation is a theoretical value, never achieved in practice. This attenuation, caused by the perfect cancellation of signals within the filter, is limited by second-order effects and noise. In a good design, $G(\omega_z) < -80$ dB.

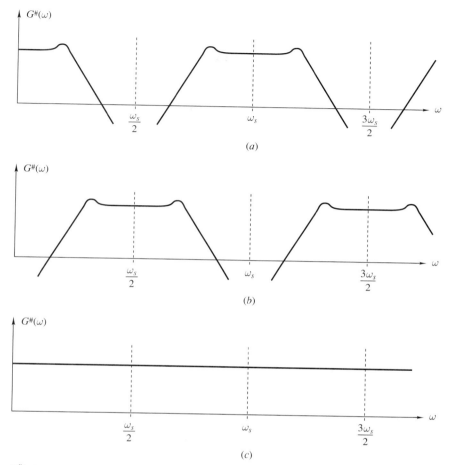

FIGURE 7-7 $G^{\#}(\omega)$ versus ω for selected sample-data filters, illustrating the fold over at odd integer multiples of the $\omega_s/2$. The filter types shown are (a) lowpass; (b) highpass; and (c) allpass.

Note that when the desired DC gain is $G(0) = 20\log(M_0)$ dB, then k and k' in Eqs. (7-14) can be set, respectively, to $k = M_0$ and $k' = M_0/4[1 - 2r_p \cos\theta_0 + r_p^2]$. Due to the repetition in $e^{j\omega T}$, the sampled-data $G^{\#}(\omega)$ in Fig. 7-7a folds over at odd integer multiples of $\omega_s/2$, as described in App. 7-1.

For the sample rates of typical interest in SC filters, the zeros at $z = -1$ have negligible effect on gain response of an LP filter (Ghausi and Laker 1981). Hence, we can exchange one or both $(1 + z^{-1})$ factors in $N(z)$ with either the constant term (specifically 2) or a unit-delay term (specifically $2z^{-1}$). The 2 multiplier is needed to preserve the DC gain, i.e., $(k'N(z)|_{z=1} = 4k')$ in Eq. (7-14b). As we will see in Chap. 8, the use of unit-delay terms in $N(z)$ can be useful in reducing effects due to the finite settling times of op amps, when biquads are connected in tandem chains.

TABLE 7-2 $N(z)$ FOR LOWPASS
z-DOMAIN BIQUADS

LP form[†]	$N(z)$
LP20	$(1 + z^{-1})(1 + z^{-1})$
LP11	$2z^{-1}(1 + z^{-1})$
LP10	$2(1 + z^{-1})$
LP02	$4z^{-2}$
LP01	$4z^{-1}$
LP00	4

[†]The notation LPIJ in Table 5-1 refers to
a lowpass $H(z)$ with I $(1 + z^{-1})$ factors
and J (z^{-1}) factors in $N(z)$.

In any event, the resulting LP $H(z)$'s are simply represented by their $N(z)$'s, as listed in Table 7-2. We note that LP02 and LP01 are the most often used LP functions in active-SC filter design.

7-3-2 Highpass

Consider next the highpass (HP) filter in Fig. 7-6b. The HP filter's function is to pass high frequencies ($\omega \geq \omega_{PB}$) and to attenuate low frequencies ($\omega < \omega_{PB}$). The frequencies ($\omega_{PB} \leq \omega < \infty$)[4] are the passband and the frequencies ($0 < \omega < \omega_{PB}$) are the stopband. As we noted earlier, an ideal brick wall HP can only be approached asymptotically, as N becomes large. The baseband $G(\omega)$ and the pole-zero patterns for $N = 2$ are illustrated in Fig. 7-6b, where

$$H(s) = \frac{ks^2}{s^2 + \dfrac{\omega_0}{Q_p}s + \omega_0^2} = \frac{kN(s)}{D(s)} \tag{7-15a}$$

$$H(z) = \frac{k'(1 - z^{-1})(1 - z^{-1})}{1 - 2r_p \cos\theta_0 z^{-1} + r_p^2 z^{-2}} = \frac{k'N(z)}{D(z)} \tag{7-15b}$$

We set $k' = k/4[1 + 2r_p \cos\theta_0 + r_p^2]$, such that $|H(s = \infty)| = |H(z = -1)| = k$. We see that the s-domain zeros at $s = 0$ are mapped into the z-domain zeros at $z = 1$. Note that if our specification calls for $G(\infty) = 20\log(M_\infty)$ dB[5], then we set $k = M_\infty$

---

[4]In practice, all physical electrical circuits are bandlimited. In the case of integrated active filters, the passband is limited by the finite bandwidth of the op amps and OTAs and the variety of parasitic components that nature provides. Consequently, the HP passband is limited to ($\omega_{PB} \leq \omega < \omega_{BL}$), where in a good design ω_{BL} is well outside the band of interest.

[5]We refer to $G(\infty)$ generically when we design HP filters. However, this gain cannot be measured. Hence, we actually specify $G(\omega_{BL}) = M_\infty$, and we expect that $G(\omega)$ is constant in the vicinity of ω_{BL}, such that $G(\omega_{BL})$ equals the theoretical $G(\infty)$.

for $H(s)$ and $k' = M_\infty/4[1 + 2r_p \cos\theta_0 + r_p^2]$ for $H(z)$. Since the HP $H(z)$ does not have zeros at $z = -1$, it is uniquely described by Eq. (7-15b). In Fig. 7-7b we see that the fold-overs of the HP sampled-data $G^\#(\omega)$ produce a curious train of BP-like bands centered about $\omega = k\omega_s/2$.

7-3-3 Bandpass

Consider next the bandpass (BP) filter in Fig. 7-6c. The BP filter's function is to pass a band of frequencies ($\omega_{PBl} \leq \omega \leq \omega_{PBh}$) and to attenuate both low frequencies ($\omega < \omega_{PBl}$) and high frequencies ($\omega > \omega_{PBh}$), where ω_{PBl} and ω_{PBh} are the low and high cutoff frequencies, respectively. The frequencies ($\omega_{PBl} \leq \omega \leq \omega_{PBh}$) are the passband and the frequencies ($\omega < \omega_{PBl}$ and $\omega > \omega_{PBh}$) are the stopbands. In this case, the resonant or center frequency is $\omega_0 \simeq \sqrt{\omega_{PBl}\omega_{PBh}}$ and the 3 dB bandwidth is $B = \omega_{PBh} - \omega_{PBl}$. Again, the ideal BP can only be realized asymptotically. When $G(\omega)$ is symmetrical about ω_0, then the filter is said to be a *symmetric* BP. The baseband $G(\omega)$ and the pole-zero patterns for the second-order H's are illustrated in Fig. 7-6c, where

$$H(s) = \frac{k\left(\dfrac{\omega_0}{Q_p}\right)s}{s^2 + \dfrac{\omega_0}{Q_p}s + \omega_0^2} = \frac{kN(s)}{D(s)} \qquad (7\text{-}16a)$$

and

$$H(z) = \frac{k'(1 - z^{-1})(1 + z^{-1})}{1 - 2r_p \cos\theta_0 z^{-1} + r_p^2 z^{-2}} = \frac{k'N(z)}{D(z)} \qquad (7\text{-}16b)$$

where $k' = k[D(e^{j\omega_0 T})/N(e^{j\omega_0 T})]$.

In this case, we see that the s-domain zeros at $s = 0$, ∞ are mapped into the z-domain zeros at $z = 1$, -1, respectively. Note that when $Q_p \gg 1$, then the 3 dB bandwidth is $B \approx \omega_0/Q_p$.

As in the LP case, we can exchange the $(1 + z^{-1})$ factor in $N(z)$ with either the constant 2 or a unit delay $2z^{-1}$. The resulting BP $H(z)$'s can be represented by their $N(z)$'s, as listed in Table 7-3. For reasons similar to that of the LP, the predominant BP form used in active-SC filter design is the BP01.

TABLE 7-3   *N(z)* FOR BANDPASS z-DOMAIN BIQUADS

BP form[†]	$N(z)$
BP10	$k(1 + z^{-1})(1 - z^{-1})$
BP01	$2kz^{-1}(1 - z^{-1})$
BP00	$2k(1 - z^{-1})$

[†] The notation BPIJ follows the same reasoning as that for the LPIJ.

7-3-4   Band-Reject

Let us next consider the band-reject (BR) or notch filter in Fig. 7-6d. The BR filter's function is to reject a band of frequencies ($\omega_{SBl} \leq \omega \leq \omega_{SBh}$), while passing both low frequencies ($\omega < \omega_{SBl}$) and high frequencies ($\omega > \omega_{SBh}$). The frequencies ($\omega_{SBl} \leq \omega \leq \omega_{SBh}$) are the stopband and the frequencies ($\omega < \omega_{SBl}$ and $\omega > \omega_{SBh}$) are the passbands. The baseband $G(\omega)$ and the pole-zero patterns for the second-order BR H's are illustrated in Fig.7-6d, where

$$H(s) = \frac{k(s^2 + \omega_N^2)}{s^2 + \dfrac{\omega_0}{Q_p}s + \omega_0^2} = \frac{kN(s)}{D(s)} \tag{7-17a}$$

and

$$H(z) = \frac{k'1 - 2\cos\theta_N z^{-1} + z^{-2}}{1 - 2r_p \cos\theta_0 z^{-1} + r_p^2 z^{-2}} = \frac{k'N(z)}{D(z)} \tag{7-17b}$$

where $k' = k[D(1)/N(1)]$ when $\omega_N \geq \omega_0$ or $= k[D(-1)/N(-1)]$ when $\omega_N \leq \omega_0$.

The "true" BR response occurs when the pole and zero frequencies are coincident, i.e., $\omega_N = \omega_0$. This results in a sharp null at $\omega = \omega_N = \omega_0$, i.e., theoretically $G(\omega_p) = -\infty$ dB, and symmetrical low- and high-frequency passbands about ω_0. Since $r_z = 1$, the zeros of $H(z)$ lie exactly on the unit circle. The symmetry of the notch can be skewed toward a lowpass or a highpass by shifting the zero (or pole) frequency such that $\omega_N \neq \omega_0$ in Eqs. (7-17). That is, we have a lowpass notch (LPN) when $\omega_N > \omega_0$ and a highpass notch (HPN) when $\omega_N < \omega_0$, as shown in Fig. 7-6e and 7-6f, respectively.

7-3-5   Allpass or Delay Equalizer

Thus far we have considered gain-shaping filters specified by either $G(\omega)$, and we have ignored phase. Using the definition for group delay $\tau(\omega)$ in Eq. (7-5) we can derive the following useful expressions: for *continuous-time filters*:

$$\tau(\omega) = -Re\left\{\frac{1}{H(s)}\frac{H(s)}{ds}\right\}\Big|_{s=j\omega} \tag{7-18a}$$

for *sampled-data filters*:

$$\tau(\omega) = -T\left[Re\left\{\frac{z}{H(z)}\frac{H(z)}{dz}\right\}\Big|_{z=e}j\omega T\right] \tag{7-18b}$$

Group delay $\tau(\omega)$ represents the time delay experienced by each and every spectral component of the input signal as it is processed by the filter. In voice and audio applications, ignoring the phase and group delay is usually justifiable because the human ear is insensitive to changes in phase or delay with frequency. However, in ideal data and video transmission systems the phase is linear (i.e., $\varphi(\omega) = -\omega T_0$) with frequency or, equivalently, the group delay is constant ($\tau(\omega) = T_0$) with frequency. When $\tau(\omega) \neq$ constant in such systems, the variation in delay or phase is called *delay distortion* or *phase distortion*. For example, delay distortion produced by modem filters can impair the detection of the logic 1's and 0's contained in data signals resulting in unacceptable transmission errors.

In general, the group delay for a gain-shaping filter will not be constant with frequency. For example, consider the phase and group delay for a continuous-time LP filter with second order $H(s)$ of the form in Eq. (7-14a). These functions can be expressed as follows

$$\varphi_{LP}(\omega) = -\arctan \frac{\omega \omega_p}{Q_p(\omega_0^2 - \omega^2)} \tag{7-19a}$$

and

$$\tau_{LP}(\omega) = \frac{\omega_0}{Q_p} \left(\frac{\omega^2 + \omega_0^2}{(\omega_0^2 - \omega^2)^2 + \left(\dfrac{\omega \omega_0}{Q_p}\right)^2} \right) \tag{7-19b}$$

The phase and group delay in Eqs. (7-19) are plotted in Fig. 7-8 for $Q_p = 0.5$, 0.707, 1, and 10. Note for $Q_p > 0.707$, the group delay peaks near the pole frequency ω_0, and the peak becomes increasingly more pronounced as Q_p increases. Thus, high Q_p gain-shaping filters are seen to produce severe delay distortion.

One means to reduce this distortion is to apply a designer-controlled delay (or phase) equalizer $\tau_C(\omega)$ to add-compensate the original delay $\tau_D(\omega)$ such that the total delay is made more flat, i.e., $\tau_C(\omega) + \tau_D(\omega) \simeq T_0$. This process is illustrated in Fig. 7-9, where $\tau_C(\omega)$ is realized by an allpass (AP) filter.

Typical characteristic AP filters are given in Fig. 7-6g. The ideal AP function is seen to pass all frequencies ($0 \leq \omega \leq \infty$). However, in practice the passband is limited to an upper frequency of ω_{BL}, determined by the second-order effects associated with the implementation. AP biquads are described by the following H's:

$$H(s) = \frac{k\left[s^2 - \left(\dfrac{\omega_0}{Q_p}\right)s + \omega_0^2\right]}{s^2 + \dfrac{\omega_0}{Q_p}s + \omega_0^2} = \frac{kN(s)}{D(s)} \tag{7-20a}$$

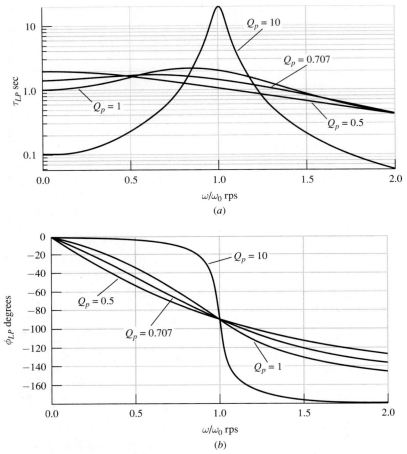

FIGURE 7-8 (a) Group delay τ and (b) phase ϕ versus normalized frequency (ω/ω_0) for second-order lowpass filter with $Q_p = 0.5$, 0.707, 1, and 10.

and

$$H(z) = \frac{k'1 - \dfrac{1}{r_p}2\cos\theta_0 z^{-1} + \dfrac{1}{r_p^2}z^{-2}}{1 - 2r_p\cos\theta_0 z^{-1} + r_p^2 z^{-2}} = \frac{k'N(z)}{D(z)} \qquad (7\text{-}20b)$$

where $k' = k[D(1)/N(1)]$ and $G(1) = G(-1)$.

The phase and group delay for the AP biquad are exactly twice those of the LP biquad (with identical ω_0, Q_p), i.e., $\varphi_{AP}(\omega) = 2\varphi_{LP}(\omega)$ and $\tau_{AP}(\omega) = 2\tau_{LP}(\omega)$. In Fig. 7-7c the sampled-data $G^{\#}(\omega)$ (similarly $\varphi^{\#}(\omega)$ and $\tau^{\#}(\omega)$) is seen to fold over at odd integer multiples of $\omega_s/2$, producing a constant gain from DC up to ω_{BL}.

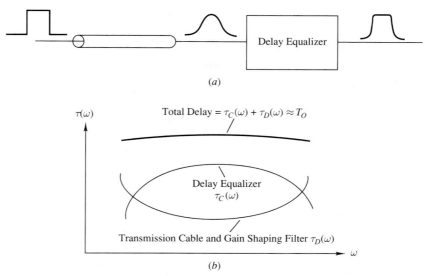

(a)

(b)

FIGURE 7-9   Equalization for delay distortion introduced by transmission cable. (a) schematic showing time domain pulse shapes before and after equalization, and (b) combined group delay characteristics for the transmission cable and gain-shaping filter, delay equalizer, and the total equalized delay.

7-3-6   Basic Filter Specifications

By specifications we mean the set of quantitative objectives that define the range of allowed performance for the filter. The gain, phase and/or group delay, specified for each of several strategic frequencies, are typical first-order performance objectives. For analog filters, these objectives are specified as ranges of values, rather than as specific values, in order to allow for the unavoidable variations in the passive and active components. This manner of specifying filters is illustrated in Fig. 7-10. Here we show that gain-shaping filters are specified typically in terms of five key parameters; namely, maximum passband attenuation (A_{PB}), passband ripple (δ), minimum stopband attenuation (A_{SB}), passband corner frequency(s) (ω_{PB} in rps or f_{PB} in Hz) and stopband corner frequency(s) (ω_{SB} in rps or f_{SB} in Hz). The band of frequencies between a passband and a stopband is referred to as a *transition band*. Shown in Fig. 7-10 are typical gain specifications for LP and BP filters of arbitrary order. In the BP case, we note that, in general, $A_{SB1} \neq A_{SB2}$. However, when $A_{SB1} = A_{SB2}$, the BP is said to be symmetric.

The desired filter gain response $G(\omega)$, and if possible all gain responses $G(\omega) \pm \Delta G(\omega)$ due to components that vary from their design values, must lie within the unshaded region of the filter specification to meet requirements. This unshaded region is often referred to as the *specification window* or the *window of acceptable designs*. When the response for a filter chip falls outside the specification window, at any frequency, the chip is discarded and the yield is reduced. As we described in Chap. 3, the yield Y_{sf}, due to soft failures, can be predicted using sensitivities. The

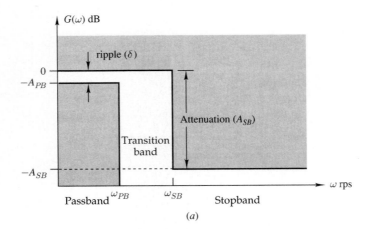

(a)

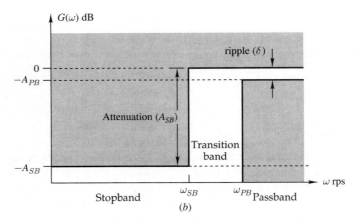

(b)

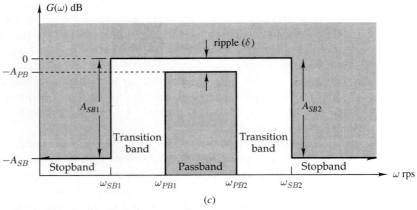

(c)

FIGURE 7-10   Gain $G(\omega)$ specifications for (a) lowpass, (b) bandpass, and (c) bandpass filters.

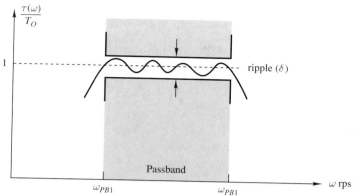

FIGURE 7-11   Group delay specification

specific sensitivity issues associated with filters will be discussed later in this chapter. The specification window not only specifies the range of acceptable gain-response characteristics, but it also provides a large amount of information about the degree of difficulty associated with realizing the filter. The complexity (or order) of the designed filter, for a given A_{SB}, will tend to increase as δ and the width of the transition band(s) ($|\omega_{PB} - \omega_{SB}|$) decrease. Also, for a given δ and $|\omega_{PB} - \omega_{SB}|$, the order will tend to increase as A_{SB} increases.

When a phase or group delay is specified, the gain-shaping filter is designed to meet the gain specifications and a delay equalizer is designed such that the total filter meets the phase or group delay specifications. The constant of the AP filter with frequency $G(\omega)$ allows the designer to partition the synthesis of gain- and group-delay specifications in this way. Usually only delay (or phase) in the passband is of interest, with the out-of-band group delay (or phase) unspecified, as indicated in Fig. 7-11. Since process of delay equalization is additive, not subtractive, the delay at each frequency will be increased. Typically, this added delay is not a problem, if it does not become too large. In communication systems very large delay can cause annoying echoes; hence, in such systems there is a specification that bounds the average inband delay (e.g., T_0 in Fig. 7-11). If the equalized filter is part of a feedback loop, the added delay could cause oscillations or singing to occur. This is a very serious situation, implying that a specification conflict exists that must be resolved at the system level. Conflicting specifications in large systems arise frequently when overall specifications are distributed to subsystems and components. It is important to recognize that specifications are targets, not hard-and-fast rules. Negotiation and reallocation of specifications occur frequently in the early stages of design.

When characterizing active filters, specifications on total harmonic distortion, noise, and/or dynamic range are in the second layer of requirements. We will discuss noise, harmonic distortion, and dynamic range later in this chapter. It should be evident that the discussions related to these criteria in Chaps. 5 and 6, for the op amp and OTA, are directly applicable to our considerations in this chapter.

There are a number of computer programs (Daniels 1974; SIFILSYN; Snelgrove; MATLAB), available on a variety of computer platforms, that can be used to translate the specifications in Figs. 7-10 and 7-11 into a transfer function H, factored into respective poles and zeros. It is not be surprising that, for any specification, there are numerous transfer functions that provide gain and/or phase responses that appear acceptable. Hence, an important part of the design task is to use all the performance and cost objectives to reduce the set of acceptable H's to a single, nominal H. In VLSI filters, the nominal H is that which satisfies gain and/or phase requirements, while balancing filter order and performance margin so that chip area and production yields meet cost objectives. This is no trivial task, but in general we try to keep the order of H as small as possible. One method of obtaining H is to use prototype functions, such as Chebyshev, Butterworth, elliptic, and the like, to configure H's that meet the specifications illustrated in Fig. 7-10 and 7-11. This method is discussed next.

7-4 DETERMINING A NOMINAL H

Transfer functions for IIR filters are either derived from tables (Daryani 1976; Schaumann et al. 1974; Daniels 1974) of prototype polynomials, or by using a computer software package (SIFILSYN; Snelgrove; MATLAB) that computes transfer functions (poles and zeros) from specifications, such as those shown in Fig. 7-10 and 7-11. Similarly, there are computer programs for deriving FIR functions from specifications.

The filter literature (Daniels 1974) contains a large body of IIR filter design-lore based on prototype functions that achieve particular attributes, such as a flat or equiripple passband, equi-ripple stopband, linear phase, and the like. Over the years, before computers were widely used in design, exhaustive tables were compiled for various paramaterized prototype functions, in terms of such filter parameters as ω_{PB}, A_{PB} or δ, A_{SB}, ω_{SB}. Hence, one strategy for deriving a nominal H is to find the lowest order prototype function that fits within the specification window (Figs. 7-10 and 7-11). We emphasize that filter order, which translates directly into chip size and cost for an integrated filter, is a major factor in selecting the best prototype function, but not the only factor. Other parameters, such as values for pole-Q_p's and zero-Q_z's, also influence the chip size and sensitivity to variations in component values.

The most commonly used prototype functions, and their relevant features, are reviewed in Fig. 7-12. For illustrative purposes, the discussion is limited to LP filters. However, the basic conclusions are equally applicable to both HP, BP, and BR filters. It is beyond the scope of this text to consider the detailed development of all the functions depicted in Fig. 7-12, much less the other numerous functions that are available, but not shown. The interested reader is referred to filter texts such as Daryanani (1976), Schaumann et al. (1986), and Daniels (1974), for a more detailed treatment of this subject matter, and additional tables for use in designs. Let us consider some of the more widely used functions.

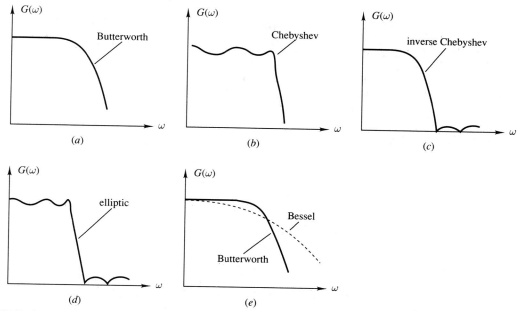

FIGURE 7-12   Gain responses $G(\omega)$ for several lowpass filters based on characteristic functions: (a) Butterworth; (b) Chebyshev; (c) inverse Chebyshev; (d) elliptic; and (e) comparison of Butterworth and Bessel.

7-4-1 Maximally-Flat or Butterworth Filters

Butterworth H's emphasize flatness in the passband. This is achieved at the expense of phase linearity, and to a lesser degree, at the expense of the attenuation slope steepness $(A_{SB}/|\omega_{SB} - \omega_{PB}|)$ in the transition band. Figure 7-12a shows the typical magnitude response of a lowpass Butterworth filter. Its phase response, relative to ideal linear phase, is shown in Fig. 7-13. The LP Butterworth $H(s)$ is an Nth order all-pole function with N zeros at $s = \infty$ (correspondingly, $H(z)$ will have N zeros at $z = -1$). Its magnitude response decreases monotonically with increasing ω, and it achieves infinite attenuation only at $\omega = \infty$. Hence, the asymptotic attenuation (i.e., as $\omega \rightarrow \infty$) is $20N$ dB/decade.

In the s-domain, Butterworth $H(s)$ are based on the maximally flat function

$$|H(j\omega_n)|^2 = H(j\omega_n)H(-j\omega_n) = \frac{k^2}{1 + \varepsilon^2 \omega_n^{2N}} \qquad (7\text{-}21)$$

where N is the order of $H(s)$, $k = |H(j0)|$ is the DC gain, ε is a constant that determines A_{PB}, and $\omega_n = \omega/\omega_{PB}$. Equation (7-21) is derived by requiring that $|H(j\omega)|^2$ be maximally flat at $\omega_n = 0$, i.e., all $2N$-1 derivatives of $|H(j\omega)|^2$ with respect to ω_n (evaluated at $\omega_n = 0$) are set equal to zero. Letting $k = 1$ for the

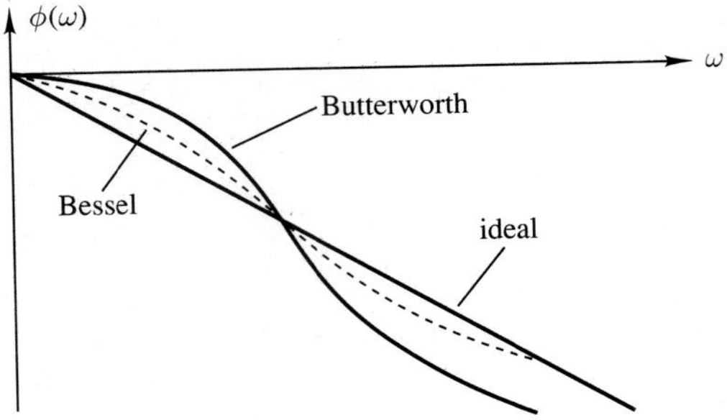

FIGURE 7-13 Comparison of the Butterworth and Bessel phase responses $\phi(\omega)$ to the ideal linear phase.

moment, the gain in dB at the passband edge $\omega_n = 1$ is

$$-A_{PB} = 10 \log \frac{1}{1 + \varepsilon^2} \quad \text{or} \quad \varepsilon = \sqrt{10^{0.1 A_{PB}} - 1} \tag{7-22}$$

Note that when $\varepsilon = 1$, $A_{PB} = 3$ dB and ω_{PB} is the 3 dB cutoff frequency.

The pole locations for Butterworth $H(s)$ are found by taking the left-half plane roots of the denominator of $|H(s_n)|^2$, with $\varepsilon = 1$ and $s_n = s/\omega_{PB}$. The corresponding Butterworth polynomials $D(s_n)$ for $N = 1$ through 5 are tabulated in Table 7-4. Butterworth polynomials for $N > 5$ can be found in any one of the texts cited at the beginning of this section. Lowpass $G(\omega_n)$, for N ranging from 1 to 10, are drawn in Fig. 7-14 to demonstrate the inband and cutoff behavior of Butterworth $H(s)$. We note that a Butterworth $H(z)$ can be obtained from Table 7-4 using Eq. (7-14b), Eq. (A7-46) in App. 7-1 (or the bilinear transform we discuss in the next section), and Table 7-2.

Example 7-1

Consider the design of a lowpass filter with passband $f_{PB} = \omega_{PB}/2\pi = 1$ kHz and DC gain $G(0) = 0$ dB. Determine the Butterworth lowpass $H(s_n)$ required to realize at least 30 dB attenuation (with respect to the gain at DC) at $f = 2$ kHz.

TABLE 7-4 BUTTERWORTH $D(s_n)$ (WHERE $H(s_n) = K/D(s_n)$)

N	$D(s_n)$
1	$s_n + 1$
2	$s_n^2 + \sqrt{2}s_n + 1$
3	$(s_n + 1)(s_n^2 + s_n + 1)$
4	$(s_n^2 + 0.76537s_n + 1)(s_n^2 + 1.84776s_n + 1)$
5	$(s_n^2 + 0.61803s_n + 1)(s_n^2 + 1.61803s_n + 1)(s_n + 1)$

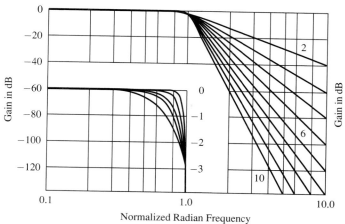

FIGURE 7-14   Butterworth LP $G(\omega)$ for $N = 1$ through 10.

Solution. To determine $H(s_n)$, we must first determine the filter order N. This can be done by using Eq. (7-21), i.e., with $\omega_n = \omega/\omega_{PB} = 2$ we obtain the attenuation at $\omega = 2\pi(2000)$ rps as

$$A_{SB} = -G(\omega)|_{\omega=4000\pi} = 20\log\sqrt{1 + 2^{2N}} = 30 \text{ dB}$$

Solving for N yields $N \geq \ln(10^3 - 1)/2\ln(2) = 4.98$, or rounded to the nearest integer value, $N \geq 5$. Hence, a Butterworth $H(s)$ of at least fifth order is required to meet the 30 dB attenuation specification. This result can be verified in Fig. 7-14. Unless it is desired to meet the attenuation specification with greater margin, we choose $N = 5$ in order to minimize chip area or cost. The resulting $H(s)$ is written by taking the $N = 5$ entry from Table 7-4, i.e.,

$$H(s_n) = \frac{1}{(s_n^2 + 0.61803s_n + 1)(s_n^2 + 1.61803s_n + 1)(s_n + 1)} \qquad (7\text{-}23)$$

Note that $k = 1$ or $G(0) = 0$ dB.

7-4-2   Equi-ripple (Chebyshev) Filters

Chebyshev H, illustrated in Fig. 7-12b, emphasizes the steepness of the attenuation slope in the transition band at the expense of phase linearity and passband flatness. Chebyshev H's are specified by the order (N) and the passband ripple (δ). In return for a finite ripple in the passband, Chebyshev filters offer sharper cutoff (i.e., higher attenuation rate) around the passband edge, as compared to a Butterworth filter with equal N. Correspondingly, Chebyshev step responses exhibit more overshoot due to their higher Q_p's (see Chap. 3). Like the Butterworth case, the Chebyshev LP $H(s)$ is an all-pole function and $G(\omega \to \infty) = -20N$ dB/decade.

In the s-domain, Chebyshev $H(s)$ are based on the equi-ripple function

$$|H(j\omega_n)|^2 = H(j\omega_n)H(-j\omega_n) = \frac{|k|^2}{1 + \varepsilon^2 C_N^2(\omega_n)} \tag{7-24}$$

where $C_N(\omega_n)$ is the Nth order Chebyshev function, ε is a constant that determines δ and A_{PB}, and $\omega_n = \omega/\omega_{PB}$. We see that the gain at DC is $M_0 = |k|/\sqrt{1 + \varepsilon^2 C_N^2(0)}$. The Chebyshev functions are defined by the relations:

$$C_N(\omega_n) = \cos[N\cos^{-1}(\omega_n)] \text{ for } |\omega_n| \le 1 \tag{7-25a}$$

$$= \cosh(N\cosh^{-1}(\omega_n)) \text{ for } |\omega_n| > 1 \tag{7-25b}$$

$$= 2\omega_n C_{N-1}(\omega_n) - C_{N-2}(\omega_n) \tag{7-25c}$$

Equation (7-25c) is a recursive relation that starts with $C_0(\omega_n) = 1$ and $C_1(\omega_n) = \omega_n$, as determined from Eq. (7-25a and 7-25b). We also note that $C_N^2(0) = 1$ (or 0) for N even (or odd) and $C_N(1) = 1$ for all N. Since, in the passband ($\omega_n \le 1$), $|H(j\omega_n)|$ is bounded between a maximum of one and a minimum of $\sqrt{1/(1 + \varepsilon^2)}$, we have

$$\delta = G(1) = 10\log\frac{1}{1 + \varepsilon^2} \quad \text{or} \quad \varepsilon = \sqrt{10^{0.1\delta} - 1} \tag{7-26}$$

The pole locations for the Chebyshev $H(s)$ are found by taking the left-half plane roots of $|D(s_n)|^2$, where $s_n = s/\omega_{PB}$. The Chebyshev polynomials $D(s_n)$ for $N = 1$ through 5 and $\delta = 1$ dB are tabulated in Table 7-5. Higher order $D(s_n)$, for various δ, can be found in several texts, e.g., Daryanani (1976); Schaumann et al. (1990); and Daniels (1974). Lowpass $G(\omega_n)$ for N ranging from 1 to 10 are drawn in Fig. 7-15 to demonstrate the inband and cutoff behavior of 1 dB ripple Chebyshev $H(s)$. The reader is encouraged to make detailed comparisons between these and the corresponding Butterworth responses in Fig. 7-14.

TABLE 7-5   CHEBYSHEV $D(s_n)$ FOR 1 dB RIPPLE
$\delta = 1$ dB ripple ($\varepsilon = 0.5088$)

N	$D(s_n)$
1	$s_n + 1.96523$
2	$s_n^2 + 1.09773s_n + 1.10251$
3	$(s_n + 0.49417)(s_n^2 + 0.49417s_n + 0.99420)$
4	$(s_n^2 + 0.27907s_n + 0.98650)(s_n^2 + 0.67374s_n + 0.27940)$
5	$(s_n^2 + 0.17892s_n + 0.98831)(s_n^2 + 0.46841s_n + 0.42930)(s_n + 0.28949)$

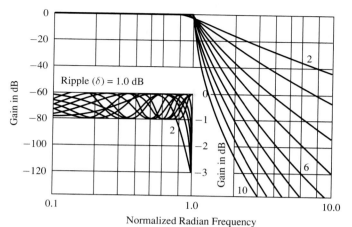

FIGURE 7-15   1 dB ripple Chebyshev LP $G(\omega)$ for $N = 1$ through 10.

Example 7-2

Consider the design of a 1 dB ripple Chebyshev lowpass active-SC filter with passband $f_{PB} = 1$ kHz, DC gain $G(0) = 0$ dB, and sample rate $f_s = 25$ kHz. Determine an $H(z)$ that will realize at least 30 dB attenuation (with respect to the gain at DC) at $f = 2$ kHz.

Solution. Using Eqs. (7-24) and (7-25b), with $\omega_n = 2$, we have the relation for the attenuation at $\omega = 2\pi (2000)$ rps:

$$G(\omega) = -10 \log[1 + \varepsilon^2 C_N^2(\omega_n)]$$
$$= -10 \log \left\{ 1 + \varepsilon^2 \cosh^2[N \cosh^{-1}(\omega_n)] \right\}$$

Hence, for the design in question

$$10 \log[1 + \varepsilon^2 \cosh^2[N \cosh^{-1}(\omega_n)]]|_{\omega_n = 2} \geq A_{SB} = 30 \text{ dB} \qquad (7\text{-}27)$$

Substituting for ε in Eq. (7-26), the relation $\varepsilon^2 = 10^{0.1\delta} - 1$, and solving the resulting expression for N yields

$$N \geq \left[\frac{1}{\cosh^{-1}(\omega_n)} \right] \left[\cosh^{-1} \sqrt{\frac{10^{0.1A_{SB}} - 1}{10^{0.1\delta} - 1}} \right] = 3.66 \qquad (7\text{-}28)$$

Rounding to the nearest integer, we see that the specifications are met with a 1 dB Chebyshev lowpass H of order $N = 4$ or greater. This result can be verified in

Fig. 7-12. We choose $N = 4$ to minimize the silicon area and cost. The $H(s_n)$ is then determined from Table 7-5 and setting $k = 1$.

$$H(s_n) = \frac{0.27563}{(s_n^2 + 0.27907s_n + 0.98650)(s_n^2 + 0.67374s_n + 0.27940)} \quad (7\text{-}29a)$$

To find $H(z)$ from $H(s_n)$ let us normalize f_s and T such that $f_{sn} = f_s/\omega_{PB} = 3.97887$ and $T_n = 1/f_{sn} = 0.25133$ (i.e., $e^{j\omega T} = e^{j\omega_n T_n}$). Hence, $\omega_{01n} = 0.99323$, $Q_{p1} = 3.55906$, $\omega_{02n} = 0.52858$, $Q_{p2} = 0.78455$, and $\theta_{01} = 0.24715$, $r_{p1} = 0.96554$, $\theta_{02} = 0.10237$, $r_{p2} = 0.91882$. Then $H(z)$ can be obtained using Eq. (7-14b) and Eq. (A7-46), i.e.,

$$H(z) = \frac{6.11421E - 5(1 + z^{-1})^4}{(1 - 1.87242z^{-1} + 0.93227z^{-2})(1 - 1.82802z^{-1} + 0.84423z^{-2})} \quad (7\text{-}29b)$$

Comparing the Butterworth example (Example 7-1) with this example, we see that an $N = 5$ Butterworth filter was required to realize $A_{SB} = 30$ dB at $\omega_n = 2$; an $N = 4$, 1 dB ripple Chebyshev filter was found to realize the same A_{SB}. Hence, for a given N, the transition bandwidth can be reduced by increasing δ; in fact, the tradeoff increases for larger N. This conclusion is apparent if we compare Fig. 7-14 and Fig. 7-15.

7-4-3   Cauer (Elliptic) Filters

Cauer (or *elliptic*) type H are equi-rippled in both the passband and the stopband, as shown in Fig. 7-12d. They exhibit a very sharp attenuation slope (i.e., narrow transition band) and infinite attenuation at distinct frequencies within the stopband. Recall in the Chebyshev/Butterworth cases that the stopband loss increases monotonically at the rate of $20N$ dB/decade. Cauer filters are usually found to be the most efficient filter type in terms realizing filter gain specifications (i.e., Fig. 7-10a) with minimum N. Monotonic attenuation beyond ω_{SB} is limited in order to achieve sharper attenuation slope in the transition band. To make this trade the Chebyshev/Butterworth transmission zeros at infinity are replaced with finite transmission zeros that significantly increase the slope of the transition band and limit the stopband attenuation to $\geq A_{SB}$. Cauer H are specified by order N, passband ripple δ, minimum stopband loss A_{SB}, and ratio $\Omega = \omega_{SB}/\omega_{PB}$. We note that in the special case $\delta \to 0$, the passband becomes maximally flat and the resulting H, illustrated in Fig. 7-12c, is called *Inverse Chebyshev*. The mathematical development of the elliptic or Cauer approximation is beyond the scope of this text (see Daniels 1974). Cauer $H(s_n)$, of the form

$$H(s_n) = \frac{N(s_n)}{D(s_n)} = \frac{k \prod_{i=1}^{M} [s_n^2 + \omega_{Ni}^2]}{\prod_{i=1}^{N} [s_n^2 + (\omega_{0i}/Q_{Oi})s_n + \omega_{0i}^2]} \quad (7\text{-}30)$$

have been tabulated for a large number of parameter values (N, δ, Ω, and A_{SB}) in the literature (Schaumann et al. 1990; Daniels 1974). As samples, Cauer $N(s_n)/D(s_n)$ for $2 \leq N \leq 5$, $\delta = 0.5$ dB, and $\Omega = 1.5$, 2.0 are given in Table 7-6. Due to the finite transmission zeros, the asymptotic attenuation (as $\omega \to \infty$) is limited to A_{SB} for N-even and $A_{SB} + 20$ dB/decade for N-odd. The inband and cutoff behavior of $\delta = 0.5$ dB, $\Omega = 1.5$ Cauer filters are shown in Fig. 7-16. In addition, fifth-order filters achieving $\Omega = 1.5$, 2.0 are compared in Fig. 7-17.

Note that the specifications in Examples 7-1 and 7-2 can be realized with the $N = 3$, $\Omega = 2.0$ Cauer H in Table 7-6 with $\delta = 0.5$ dB rather than 1 dB.

7-4-4 Bessel (Linear Phase) Filters

Bessel filters in Fig. 7-12e approximate the linear-phase response of an ideal filter at the expense of reduced attenuation slope in the transition band (Daryanani 1976; Daniels 1974). To illustrate these points, $G(\omega)$ and $\varphi(\omega)$ for Bessel and Butterworth filters, (with identical N) are compared in Figs. 7-12e and 7-13. In practice, it is usually more efficient to realize $G(\omega)$ specifications with a Butterworth, Chebyshev, or a Cauer filter and, when necessary, compensate the resulting phase (or group delay) with an AP delay equalizer to realize $\varphi(\omega)$ specifications.

TABLE 7-6   CAUER $H(s_n)$ FOR 0.5 dB RIPPLE AND $\Omega = 1.5$ AND 2.0

			$\delta = 0.5$ dB ripple and $\Omega = 1.5$	
N	A_{SB}	$N(s_n)$	$D(s_n)$	
2	8.3	$s_n^2 + 3.92705$	$s_n^2 + 1.03153s_n + 1.60319$	
3	21.9	$s_n^2 + 2.80601$	$(s_n^2 + 0.45286s_n + 1.14917)(s_n + 0.76695)$	
4	36.3	$(s_n^2 + 2.53555)(s_n^2 + 12.09931)$	$(s_n^2 + 0.25496s_n + 1.06044)(s_n^2 + 0.92001s_n + 0.47183)$	
5	50.6	$(s_n^2 + 2.42551)(s_n^2 + 5.43764)$	$(s_n^2 + 0.16346s_n + 1.03189)$	
			$(s_n^2 + 0.57023s_n + 0.57601)(s_n + 0.42597)$	
			$\delta = 0.5$ dB ripple and $\Omega = 2.0$	
N	A_{SB}	$N(s_n)$	$D(s_n)$	
2	13.9	$s_n^2 + 7.4641$	$s_n^2 + 1.24504s_n + 1.59179$	
3	31.2	$s_n^2 + 5.15321$	$(s_n^2 + 0.53787s_n + 1.14849)(s_n + 0.69212)$	
4	48.6	$(s_n^2 + 4.59326)(s_n^2 + 24.22720)$	$(s_n^2 + 0.30116s_n + 1.06258)(s_n^2 + 0.88456s_n + 0.41032)$	
5	66.1	$(s_n^2 + 4.36495)(s_n^2 + 10.56773)$	$(s_n^2 + 0.19255s_n + 1.03402)$	
			$(s_n^2 + 0.58054s_n + 0.52500)(s_n + 0.39261)$	

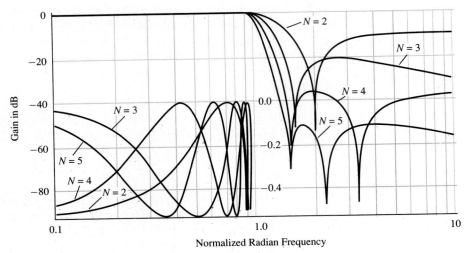

FIGURE 7-16   0.5 dB ripple, $\Omega = 1.5$ Cauer LP $G(\omega)$ for $N = 2$ to 5.

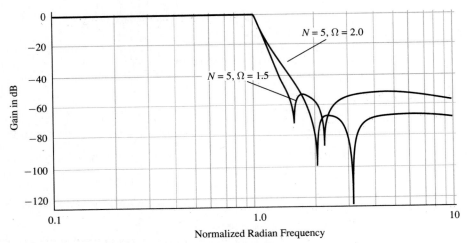

FIGURE 7-17 $N = 5$, 0.5 dB ripple Cauer LP $G(\omega)$ for $\Omega = 1.5$ and 2.0.

7-5 FREQUENCY TRANSFORMS

The *s-to-s transforms* are complex frequency mappings which allow HP, BP, and BR filters to be transformed into LP prototypes, and vice versa. Similarly, the *s-to-z transforms* are complex frequency mappings that allow us to bridge between the *s*- and *z*-domains. Frequency transforms are used primarily to reduce design labor, but often lead to suboptimal circuit realizations. However, in many cases, the practical difference between suboptimal and optimum realizations do not justify the higher design costs to derive a fully optimized design.

7-5-1 *s-to-s* Transforms

Let us first consider the *s*-to-*s* transforms $s_n = f_{XY}(p)$, where $XY = \{HP, BP, BR\}$ in Table 7-7. (Daryanani 1976; Schaumann et al. 1990; Daniels 1974). Here s (or $s_n = s/\omega_{PB}$) is the LP prototype complex frequency and p the transformed complex frequency. In the design of HP, BP, or BR filters, with such features as maximally flat or equi-ripple passbands, it is often expedient to map their requirements into specifications for an LP prototype so that an intermediate $H_{LP}(s_n)$ can be derived from design tables, e.g., Tables 7-4 to 7-6. Reversing the transform enables us to easily obtain the desired $H_{XY}(p)$ from $H_{LP}(s_n)$[6], i.e.,

$$H_{XY}(p) = H_{LP}(s_n)|_{s_n = f_{XY}(p)} \tag{7-31}$$

One inefficiency in this process is that BP filters obtained through this mapping are symmetric, which leads to over-design if the BP requirements are not symmetric. In Table 7-7 we include the HP, BR, and symmetric BP $H_{XY}(p)$ obtained by applying Eq. (7-31) to a simple $N = 1$ Butterworth $H_{LP}(s_n)$. We recall that the parameters $\omega_{PB}, \omega_0, \omega_N, B = \omega_{PBh} - \omega_{PBl}$ were defined in Fig. 7-6. Note that $H_{XY}(p)$ is not normalized. Hence, if a normalized function $H_{XY}(p_n)$ is desired, normalizing the transformed frequency variable p to a convenient frequency, say $p_n = p/\omega_0$ or p/ω_N for BP or BR H_{XY}, is a straightforward procedure.

[6]We note that these frequency transformations and the associated arguments can be applied to any circuit function, including impedance and admittance, i.e., $Z_{XY}(p)$, $Y_{XY}(p)$ can be derived from $Z_{LP}(s_n)$, $Y_{LP}(s_n)$ and vice versa using $s_n = f_{XY}(p)$. A filter schematic can be transformed from that of an LP prototype to a BP, HP, or BR schematic by transforming the Z_{LP}, Y_{LP} for each passive component using f_{XY}.

TABLE 7-7 *s-s* TRANSFORMATIONS

s-s Transformations	$f_{XY}(p)$	$H_{LP}(s_n)$	$H_{XY}(p)$
LP-to-HP: $s_n = f_{HP}(p)$	$\dfrac{\omega_{PB}}{p}$	$\dfrac{1}{s_n + 1}$	$\dfrac{p}{p + \omega_{PB}}$
LP-to-BP: $s_n = f_{BP}(p)$	$\dfrac{p^2 + \omega_0^2}{Bp}$	$\dfrac{1}{s_n + 1}$	$\dfrac{Bp}{p^2 + Bp + \omega_0^2}$
LP-to-BR: $s_n = f_{BR}(p)$	$\dfrac{Bp}{p^2 + \omega_N^2}$	$\dfrac{1}{s_n + 1}$	$\dfrac{p^2 + \omega_N^2}{p^2 + Bp + \omega_N^2}$

7-5-2   *s-to-z* Transforms

In filters s to z transforms are a bridge between the continuous and sampled domains (Ghausi and Laker 1981; Unbehauen and Cichocki 1986; Schaumann et al. 1990; Unbehauen and Cichocki 1989; Tretter 1976). They are used in two ways: (a) to map filter schematics or components, e.g., an integrator, from the s to z; and (b) to map poles and zeros of transfer functions or filter requirements from s to z. With such transforms we seek to map an $F(s)$ into rational $F(z)$ by approximating $z = e^{sT}$ (or $s = 1/T \ln(z)$) with rational first-order functions. Function $F(s)$ can be an impedance, admittance, or transfer function, etc. The s-z transforms listed in Table 7-8 derive their origin from the lore of numerical analysis where differential and integral equations are digitized in order to be solved using a digital computer. When applied to the design of filters, the s-z transforms in Table 7-8; namely, Backward Euler (BE), Forward Euler (FE), Lossless Discrete (LD), and Bilinear (BL), provide contrasting properties. Let us refer to these transforms as $g_{XY}(z)$, with XY = (BE, FE, LD, BL). Since $g_{XY}(z)$ are first-order functions of z, they map Nth order $H(s)$ into Nth order $H(z)$, i.e.,

$$H_{XY}(z) = H(s)|_{s=g_{xy}(z)} = \frac{\sum_{i=0}^{M} a_{XYi} z^{-i}}{1 + \sum_{i=1}^{N} b_{XYi} z^{-i}} \tag{7-32}$$

The detailed form of $H_{XY}(z)$, in particular the coefficients a_{XYi}, b_{XYi}, will vary somewhat with the particular g_{XY}. However, all $g_{XY}(z) \to g(z)$ as $\omega T \to 0$ and the error $|H_{XY}(e^{j\omega T}) - H(j\omega)|$ decreases as $\omega T \ll 1$.

The BE and FE transforms are the simplest mathematically, but also the least accurate. In Table 7-8 this is demonstrated by mapping the integration formula $H(s) = 1/s$ into the z-domain using each of the four transforms. That is, for $s = j\omega$ and $z = e^{j\omega T}$ the integration formula is expressed as

$$\frac{1}{j\omega} \Rightarrow \frac{1}{j\omega}\{1 - \varepsilon(\omega)\}e^{j\varphi(\omega)} \tag{7-33}$$

The magnitude $\varepsilon(\omega)$ and phase $\varphi(\omega)$ of the transformation error are given for each transform in Table 7-8. Clearly, for an exact mapping, the error $\varepsilon(\omega) = \varphi(\omega) = 0$. In fact, only when $\varphi(\omega) = 0$, does the $j\omega$-axis map onto the unit circle and the stability of mapped functions is preserved between the two domains. In contrast we emphasize that the s–s transforms in Table 7-7 are exact.

Note that for LD[7] and BL the phase error is $\varphi(\omega) = 0$. Also, if we use BE and FE integrators in tandem, i.e., $H(z) = H_{BE}H_{FE}$, the total phase error $\varphi(\omega) = \varphi_{BE} + \varphi_{FE} = 0$. As we will see, BE and FE integrators are found in many SC schematics that use $1/g_{XY}(z)$ directly and do not depend on integrators being closely matched to

---

[7]The LD transform was suggested as a means to efficiently realize an accurate digital filter integrator (Bruton 1975). The LD transform cannot be more generally applied because the $z^{-1/2}$ term is not strictly defined in z-transform mathematics.

TABLE 7-8 s TO z TRANSFORMATIONS

s to z Transformations $g_{XY}(z)$	Transformed Integration Formula	$\varepsilon(\omega)$	$\varphi(\omega)$
BE: $s = \frac{1}{T}(1 - z^{-1})$	$\dfrac{T}{2}\dfrac{e^{j\omega T/2}}{j\sin\left(\dfrac{\omega T}{2}\right)}$	$1 - \dfrac{\omega T/2}{\sin\left(\dfrac{\omega T}{2}\right)}$	$\dfrac{\omega T}{2}$
FE: $s = \dfrac{1}{T}\dfrac{1 - z^{-1}}{z^{-1}}$	$\dfrac{T}{2}\dfrac{e^{-j\omega T/2}}{j\sin\left(\dfrac{\omega T}{2}\right)}$	$1 - \dfrac{\omega T/2}{\sin\left(\dfrac{\omega T}{2}\right)}$	$-\dfrac{\omega T}{2}$
LD: $s = \dfrac{1}{T}\dfrac{1 - z^{-1}}{z^{-1/2}}$	$\dfrac{T}{2}\dfrac{1}{j\sin\left(\dfrac{\omega T}{2}\right)}$	$1 - \dfrac{\omega T/2}{\sin\left(\dfrac{\omega T}{2}\right)}$	0
BL: $s = \dfrac{2}{T}\dfrac{1 - z^{-1}}{1 + z^{-1}}$	$\dfrac{T}{2}\dfrac{1}{j\tan\left(\frac{\omega T}{2}\right)}$	$1 - \dfrac{\omega T/2}{\tan\left(\dfrac{\omega T}{2}\right)}$	0

$1/j\omega$. However, BE or FE $g_{XY}(z)$ are rarely used as mappings or replacements for $1/s$ where the errors in Eq. (7-33) are important.

When mapping an $H(s)$ to an $H(z)$, where these errors must be minimized, it is important to use a $g_{XY}(z)$ where $\varphi(\omega) = 0$. The $g_{BL}(z)$ is universally used for this purpose. The $g_{LD}(z)$ was conceived only for the schematic transformation for lossless integrators. With the $g_{BL}(z)$ mapping we can force $\varepsilon(\omega)$ to zero at distinct frequencies by preadjusting the pole and zero locations of the originating $H(s)$. The magnitude error $\varepsilon(\omega) \neq 0$ is due to the nonlinear relationship between frequency points on the $j\omega$-axis and the unit circle. This error, called *warping*, can be reduced to zero at a finite number of frequencies (usually the pole ω_{pi} and zero ω_{zi} frequencies) by *prewharping* their locations to $\hat{\omega}_{pi} \neq \omega_{pi}$, $\hat{\omega}_{zi} \neq \omega_{zi}$ prior to transformation so that

$$\varepsilon(\omega_{pi}) = 1 - \frac{\hat{\omega}_{pi} T/2}{\tan\left(\dfrac{\omega_{pi} T}{2}\right)} = 0 \quad \text{and} \quad \varepsilon(\omega_{zi}) = 1 - \frac{\hat{\omega}_{zi} T/2}{\tan\left(\dfrac{\omega_{zi} T}{2}\right)} = 0$$

after transformation (Ghausi and Laker 1981; Gregorian and Temes 1986; Schaumann et al. 1990; Unbehauen and Cichocki 1989; Tretter 1976). Thus, $g_{BL}(z)$ is applied to the prewharped $H(\hat{s})$. Prewharping is often unnecessary in SC filters because of high sampling rates that set $\omega_{pi} T, \omega_{zi} T \ll 1$, such that $\tan(\omega_{pi} T/2) \approx \omega_{pi} T/2$ and $\tan(\omega_{zi} T/2) \approx \omega_{zi} T/2$.

Let us consider the BL transform of the $N = 2$ LP $H(s)$ in Eq. (7-11a), i.e.,

$$H(s) = \frac{k\omega_0^2}{s^2 + \dfrac{\omega_0}{Q_p}s + \omega_0^2} \tag{7-34a}$$

Applying the BL transform to $H(s)$ yields the following $H(z)$

$$H(z) = \cfrac{\cfrac{k(\omega_0 T)^2}{4 + \cfrac{2\omega_0 T}{Q_p} + (\omega_0 T)^2}(1 + z^{-1})(1 + z^{-1})}{1 - 2\left\{\cfrac{1 - \cfrac{(\omega_0 T)^2}{4}}{1 + \cfrac{\omega_0 T}{2Q_p} + \cfrac{(\omega_0 T)^2}{4}}\right\}z^{-1} + \left\{\cfrac{1 - \cfrac{\omega_0 T}{2Q_p} + \cfrac{(\omega_0 T)^2}{4}}{1 + \cfrac{\omega_0 T}{2Q_p} + \cfrac{(\omega_0 T)^2}{4}}\right\}z^{-2}}$$

$$(7\text{-}34b)$$

Equation (7-34b) is valid for all $\omega_0 T$. We leave it to the reader to verify that when $\omega_0 T \ll 1$, the denominator of Eq. (7-34b) is approximated in Eq. (A7-48). Recall, when $\omega T \ll 1$, that the zeros at $z = -1$ can be eliminated in accordance with Table 7-2.

7-6   NOISE, DC OFFSET, HARMONIC DISTORTION, AND DYNAMIC RANGE

The performance of microelectronic filters is limited by the undesired disturbances (noise, harmonic distortion, DC offset) generated internal and external to the filter (Gregorian and Temes 1986; Schaumann et al. 1990; Unbehauen and Cichocki 1989). When these disturbances fall in the passband of the filter, they alter the character of the desired signal in a manner that cannot be eliminated by linear filtering. Moreover, out-of-band disturbances in sampled filters can alias, as described in App. 7-1, and increase the overall passband disturbance level. Although noise, harmonic distortion, and DC offset are physically very different, we assume that they are small (compared to the desired signal) and that they occur as multiple disturbance sources at various points within the filter. If the active filter is operating linearly, superposition can be used to accumulate the output-referred contributions from all the disturbance sources, i.e.,

$$\hat{Y}(j\omega) = H(j\omega)X(j\omega) + \sum_i H_i(j\omega)D_i(j\omega) = Y(j\omega) + D_o(j\omega) \qquad (7\text{-}35)$$

where $X(j\omega)$ is the desired or undisturbed signal, $D_i(j\omega)$ are the disturbance sources, $Y(j\omega)$ is the desired response with all $D_i = 0$, $D_o(j\omega)$ is the total output-referred disturbance, $H(j\omega)$ is the transfer function between Y and X, and $H_i(j\omega)$ are the transfer functions between the output Y and and disturbances D_i.

At this point, it is useful to distinguish between signal-dependent and signal-independent disturbances. Signal-independent disturbances, such as noise and power-supply hum, are processed by the filter and combined linearly with the desired signal. Consequently, these disturbances set the limit for the lowest level signal that can be processed by the filter, i.e., simply put, if $|X| \ll |D_i|$ then $\hat{Y} \approx D_o$ and Y is essentially lost or buried in the noise. Consequently, we limit the minimum $|X| \geq |X_{\text{MIN}}|$ to guarantee $|X| \gg |D_i|$ and $|Y| \gg |D_o|$.

Signal-dependent disturbances, caused by inherent nonlinearities in the filter, limit the highest signal level that can be processed. In this case $|D_i| = f(|X|)$ are nonlinear functions of input amplitude $|X|$. We noted earlier in the chapter that circuit nonlinearities introduce unwanted harmonic and intermodulation frequency components, e.g., Fig. 7-1, called harmonic distortion. Since the nonlinearities cause $|D_i|$ to increase with increasing $|X|$, we limit $|X| < |X_{MAX}|$, and correspondingly $|Y| < |Y_{MAX}|$, so that the distortion components are small and bounded. We assume that strong nonlinear behavior of any kind is unacceptable; hence, the detailed characterization of such cases is of little practical interest.

DC offset is yet another disturbance contributing to the upper signal-level limit of a filter. Ideally, the DC component of signal Y is zero, and Y swings symmetrically within the limits $|Y_{MAX}|$. Hence, when DC offset occurs, the signal swing becomes asymmetric, causing either the positive or negative swing to cross the $|Y_{MAX}|$ limit prematurely, i.e., $|D_i| = f(|X|, Y_{DC})$ where Y_{DC} is the DC offset. Hence, the occurrence of large Y_{DC} enhances $|D_i|$ and reduces the allowed $|Y_{MAX}|$, and correspondingly reduces the upper signal limit $|X_{MAX}|$.

As we discussed in Chap. 5, noise is a random phenomenon and noise sources are usually assumed to be uniform and uncorrelated. The primary noise sources in active filters are the thermal noise associated with each resistor (the R's in active-RC filters and ON-resistances R_{ON} associated with the MOST switches in active-SC filters), and the combined thermal and $1/f$ noise associated with each op amp or OTA. Unswitched capacitors generate negligible noise. Noise (and harmonic distortion models) for op amps and OTAs are developed in Chaps. 5 and 6. Initially, let us confine our consideration to a continuous-time active filter, where the noise is bandlimited by a filter's frequency response. Using concepts and definitions in Sec. 5-3, we intuitively express the total output noise PSD $S_{no}(\omega)$ as a weighted sum of the PSD's, for the filter's K noise voltage densities $(\overline{v_n^2})$, and M noise current densities $(\overline{i_n^2})$, i.e.,

$$S_{no}(\omega) = \left\{ \sum_{k}^{K} |H_k(\omega)|^2 (\overline{v_{nl}^2}) + \sum_{m}^{M} |R_m(\omega)|^2 (\overline{i_{nm}^2}) \right\} \frac{(V)^2}{Hz} \qquad (7\text{-}36)$$

where $|H_k(\omega)|$ and $|R_m(\omega)|$ are the magnitudes of the voltage transfer and transresistance functions from the K noise voltage sources and M noise current sources, respectively, to the output. Using Eqs. (5-57), we can express the output rms noise voltage as

$$\overline{v_{no}} = \sqrt{\frac{1}{2\pi} \int_{-\infty}^{\infty} S_{no}(\omega) d\omega} \ \ V_{RMS} \qquad (7\text{-}37)$$

Note that the division by 2π inside the radical is due to the change in integration variable from f to ω, i.e., $df = (1/2\pi) d\omega$.

In sampled systems the situation is more complicated due to aliasing and sample-and-hold reconstruction, concepts reviewed in App. 7-1 (Gregorian and Temes 1986; Unbehauen and Cichocki 1989; Fischer 1982). Let us first consider the effect of aliasing. When noise is sampled, wideband noise (e.g., thermal noise and all other out-of-band disturbances) is folded back into the baseband, causing the measured noise to increase. In particular, aliasing occurs if the noise bandwidth $BW_n > f_s/2$. In fact, for ideal impulse sampling, the noise PSDs in baseband and the $k\omega_s$ sidebands are added in accordance with Eq. (A7-13), i.e.,

$$S_n^{\#}(f) = \frac{1}{T^2} \sum_{k=-\infty}^{\infty} S_n(f - kf_s) = \frac{1}{T^2} \sum_{k=-\infty}^{\infty} S_{kn} \qquad (7\text{-}38)$$

where $S_n^{\#}(f)$ is the sampled PSD and $S_n(f) = S_{0n}$ is the fundamental PSD. Equation (7-38) is a power relation, i.e., it is formed by taking $|\cdot|^2$ of the sampled noise via Eq. (A7-13). If S_{0n} are uniform or "white" uncorrelated broadband noise, with amplitude $\eta(V)^2/\text{Hz}$ and bandwidth $BW_n \gg f_s$, then $2\{BW_n/f_s\} - 1$ sidebands alias back into the signal baseband $0 < f < f_s/2$. This process is illustrated in Fig. 7-18 where S_{0n} is a white-noise source with bandwidth $BW_n = 3f_s$. We see from Fig. 7-18 that sidebands ± 1, ± 2, and $+3$ alias back into the band $0 \le f \le f_s/2$. For these practical conditions, Eq. (7-38) can be simplified to the following convenient form

$$S_n^{\#}(f) \approx \frac{2}{T^2} \left(\frac{BW_n}{f_s} \right) \eta \qquad (7\text{-}39)$$

where $S_{kn} = \eta$ for $k = 0, \pm 1, \pm 2, \ldots \pm \infty$ (Fischer 1982). For the case in Fig. 7-18, we see that $2(BW_n/f_s) = 6$ (due to the 6 components $k = 0, \pm 1, \pm 2$, and $+3$) and $S_n^{\#}(f) = (6/T^2)\eta$.

Example 7-3

Consider the noise performance for the simple simpled-data circuit in Fig. 7-19a. The timing for the switch is illustrated in Fig. 7-19d. (a) Derive the output noise power spectral density and output mean-square noise, and (b) calculate the RMS noise for $R_{\text{ON}} = 5$ kΩ, $C = 50$ pF, $f_s = 8$ kHz, $\tau = 0.4$ and Temp $= 300$ K or room temperature.

Solution. (a) We note that the subject switched-capacitor circuit is comprised of a switch, controlled by clock signal ϕ, and a shunt capacitor C. Due to the action of the switch, the circuit has two phases; namely, when $\phi = $ ON and $\phi = $ OFF. When $\phi = $ ON, $v_o(t)$ follows or tracks $v_{\text{in}}(t)$. Let us call this the ON-phase. During this phase $[kT \le t < (k + 1 - \tau)T]$ the ON switch is modeled as a finite resistance R_{ON}. The instant that $\phi = $ OFF, i.e., $t = (k + 1 - \tau)T$, C is left with charge $Q = Cv_{\text{in}}[(k + 1 - \tau)T]$ and the samples $v_o = v_{\text{in}}[(k + 1 - \tau)]T$ are held on C until $\phi = $ ON again. Let us call this the OFF-phase.

To calculate the output noise for this circuit, we set $v_{\text{in}} = 0$ and introduce noise generator $\overline{v_n^2}$ to account for thermal noise associated with R_{ON} of the switch, as shown in Fig. 7-19b. Using the circuit operation described previously and the result

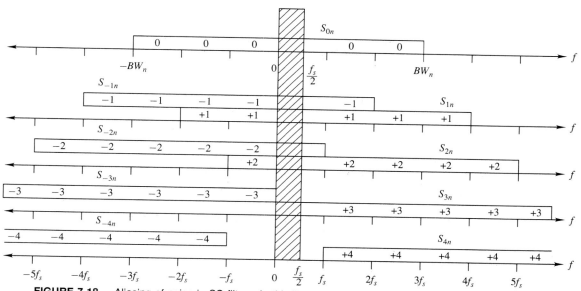

FIGURE 7-18   Aliasing of noise in SC filters. In this illustration the noise source is assumed to be white, uncorrelated with bandwidth $BW_n = 3f_s$.

in Eq. (1-62b) of Chap. 1, we can express the output noise during the ON-phase as

$$\eta = S_{0n}(f)|_{ON} = \frac{1}{2}\left[\frac{4k_B \text{Temp} R_{ON}}{1 + (2\pi f R_{ON}C)^2}\right] = \frac{\overline{v_{no}^2}|_{ON}}{\Delta f} \tag{7-40a}$$

and

$$\overline{v_{no}}|_{ON} = \sqrt{\int_{-\infty}^{\infty} S_{0n}(f)_{ON} df} = \sqrt{\frac{k_B \text{Temp}}{C}} \tag{7-40b}$$

where $\Delta f = 2BW_n$, $BW_n = \dfrac{\pi}{2}\left\{\dfrac{1}{2\pi R_{ON}C}\right\} = \dfrac{1}{4R_{ON}C}$ (recall Eq. (1-63) in Chap. 1) and $k_B = 1.38 \times 10^{-23}$J/K is Boltzmann's constant. The 1/2 factor in Eq. (7-40a) is due to η being defined as a two-sided PSD and Δf spans $-BW_n \leq f \leq +BW_n$. Note that we use k_B and Temp for Boltzmann constant and temperature (rather than k and T) to clearly distinguish these parameters from the sample integer k and clock period T. Using Eqs. (7-40) and (1-63) we can write

$$\eta \approx \frac{1}{\Delta f}\frac{k_B \text{Temp}}{C} = 2k_B \text{Temp} R_{ON} \tag{7-41}$$

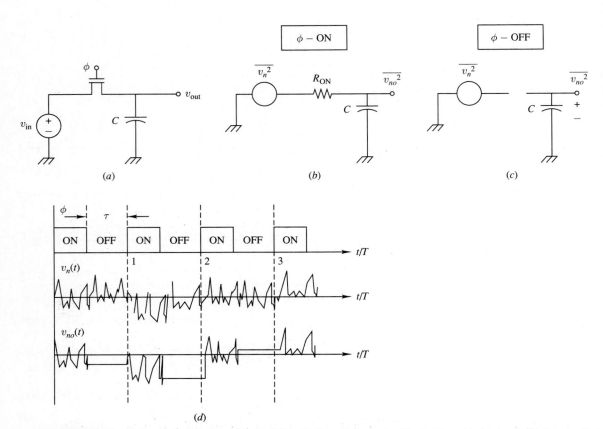

FIGURE 7-19   Noise in sample-data circuits: (*a*) a simple switched-capacitor track-and-hold circuit; (*b*) the circuit and noise source when $\phi = $ ON; (*c*) the circuit and noise source when $\phi = $ OFF; and (*d*) the sketches for the switch timing, input noise, and output noise.

To obtain the noise contributed during the ON-phase to the overall noise, we must scale $\overline{v_{no}^2}$ and η in proportion to the fraction of period T taken by the ON-phase, i.e., $1 - \tau$.

$$\overline{v_{n\text{ON}}} = \sqrt{1 - \tau}\,\overline{v_{no}}|_{\text{ON}} \qquad \text{or} \qquad \eta_{\text{ON}} = (1 - \tau)\eta \qquad (7\text{-}42)$$

In Fig. 7-19*d* the input and output noise waveforms are sketched with the switch timing. The output noise during the ON-phase is seen to follow the input noise (of course with some slight delay associated with $R_{\text{ON}}C$).

During the OFF-phase (i.e., Fig. 7-19*c*), the switch is an open circuit and the noise sampled-and-held on C is

$$v_{no}(t)|_{\text{OFF}} = v_{no}[(k + 1 - \tau)T]|_{\text{ON}} \qquad (7\text{-}43)$$

An illustrative waveform for $v_{no}(t)|_{\text{OFF}}$ is sketched in Fig. 7-19d. Recall from Chap. 1 that thermal noise is white. However, the bandwidth of the output noise from the ON-phase is limited to $BW_n = 1/4R_{\text{ON}}C$. Using the numbers in (b) we calculate that $BW_n = 1$ MHz $> f_s = 8$ kHz; thus, aliasing will occur. Using Eqs. (7-39), (7-41), and sample-and-hold reconstruction (as given in Eqs. (A7-18) in App. 7-1), the PDS for the OFF noise is

$$S_n(f)|_{\text{OFF}} \approx \frac{2}{T^2}\left\{\frac{BW_n}{f_s}\right\}\left\{\tau T \sin c\left(\frac{\pi\tau f}{f_s}\right)\right\}^2 \eta$$

$$= \frac{\eta}{2f_s C R_{\text{ON}}}\tau^2 \sin c\left(\frac{\pi\tau f}{f_s}\right)^2 \tag{7-44}$$

and for $f \ll f_s$, where $\sin c(x) = \sin(x)/x \approx 1$, we can further approximate

$$S_n(f)|_{\text{OFF}} \approx \frac{\tau^2}{2f_s C R_{\text{ON}}}\eta = \frac{\tau^2 k_B \text{Temp}}{f_s C} \tag{7-45a}$$

and

$$\overline{v_{no}}|_{\text{OFF}} \approx \sqrt{S_n(f)|_{\text{OFF}}\Delta f} = \tau\sqrt{\frac{1}{2f_s C R_{\text{ON}}}}\sqrt{\frac{k_B \text{Temp}}{C}} \tag{7-45b}$$

Note that $S_n(f)|_{\text{OFF}}$ is independent of R_{ON}; but $\overline{v_{no}}|_{\text{OFF}}$ scales with $1/R_{\text{ON}}$ since increasing R_{ON} decreases BW_n. When $BW_n \gg f_s$, the total RMS noise is dominated by the OFF component; thus

$$\overline{v_{no}} = \sqrt{\overline{v_{no}^2}|_{\text{ON}} + \overline{v_{no}^2}|_{\text{OFF}}} \approx \overline{v_{no}^2}|_{\text{OFF}}$$

$$= \tau\sqrt{\frac{1}{f_s C R_{\text{ON}}}}\sqrt{\frac{k_B \text{Temp}}{C}} \tag{7-46}$$

The composite noise waveform $v_{no}(t)$ is also illustrated in Fig. 7-19d.

(b) Inserting numerical values for R_{ON}, C, f_s, τ_{OFF}, Temp, and k_B into Eq. (7-46) yields $\sqrt{\frac{k_B \text{Temp}}{C}} \approx 0.09$ nV$_{\text{RMS}}$, $\tau\sqrt{\frac{1}{f_s C R_{\text{ON}}}} \approx 9$; therefore $\overline{v_{no}} \approx 0.8$ nV$_{\text{RMS}}$.

Due to the aliasing expressed in Eqs. (7-39) and (7-44), the alert reader will recognize that the criteria for a low noise op amp designed for use in an active-SC filter is distinctly different than that designed for an active-SC filter. That is, the thermal component of the op amp noise is usually significantly more important than the $1/f$ component for the active-SC case. The opposite priority usually prevails for op amps used in continuous-time circuits where aliasing does not occur. We caution the reader, that, if the output of an active-RC filter is sampled (such as by an A/D converter), then the opportunities for aliasing noise are similar to those in active-SC filters.

The ratio $X_{\text{MAX}}/X_{\text{MIN}}$ represents the *dynamic range* (Gregorian and Temes 1986; Schaumann et al. 1990; Unbehauen and Cichocki 1989), which characterizes the overall robustness and signal-handling capability of the filter. Although the disturbances mentioned are physically very different, they were all assumed small (in comparison with the desired signal) and that they enter the filter at multiple internal nodes. If the active filter is operating nearly linearly, superposition is used to accumulate the output-referred contributions from all the disturbance sources to obtain an estimate of the disturbed output and the dynamic range.

7-7   SENSITIVITY, VARIABILITY, AND YIELD

In this section we will expand upon the concepts introduced in Sec. 3-4 and develop further the sensitivity models that are useful for filter design. We assume, for the developments in this subsection, that the reader is thoroughly familiar with Eqs. (3-84) through (3-89) and their application to yield estimation.

The reader may be tempted into arguing that an optimum design is obtained from an H that uses the extremes of the specification window, i.e., all the white space in Fig. 7-10a. However, the clear-thinking student will quickly conclude that following such an approach in designing integrated analog filters (or any precision analog circuit, for that matter) will lead to poor yields in production, and will no doubt lead to failures in the field, due to drifts with temperature and age. To demonstrate the problem, we show in Fig. 7-20 the effect of component variations on the gain response $G(\omega)$ for 1000 samples of a fifth-order Cauer filter, designed to serve as a receive (or reconstruction) filter for a PCM codec (see Fig. 8-1). Here, component variations are due to fabrication tolerances and ambient temperature in the range $0°C \leq T \leq 60°C$. All 1000 $G(\omega)$'s were found to lie within the widely spaced dashed envelope. Comparing the envelope with the ± 0.125 dB specification window, we observe that the yield is less than 100 percent.

In contrast, we point out that the sensitivity problem for digital filters is different. Precision in digital filters is unambiguously tied to the number of bits used to quantize (or truncate) the coefficients of $H(z)$. Hence, once a design (see Sec. 7-2) is found to fit the specification window, then the design task is to determine the coefficients with the minimum number of bits required to keep the quantized response within the window. Once an acceptable quantized design is found, generally it is robust. Hence, the quantized digital filter can be designed to the limits of the specification window with little effect on yield.

Letting $P = H(\lambda)$, where $\lambda = j\omega$ or $e^{j\omega T}$, we can derive some useful expressions for $S_{x_i}^H$, $Q_{x_i}^G$, and $Q_{x_i}^\varphi$ in terms of the resonant-null frequency and pole-zero Q sensitivities, i.e., using Eqs. (7-13), (A7-51), and (3-86) we derive:

$$S_{x_i}^{H(\lambda)} = \frac{1}{8.686} Q_{x_i}^{G(\lambda)} + j Q_{x_i}^{\varphi(\lambda)} \qquad (7\text{-}47a)$$

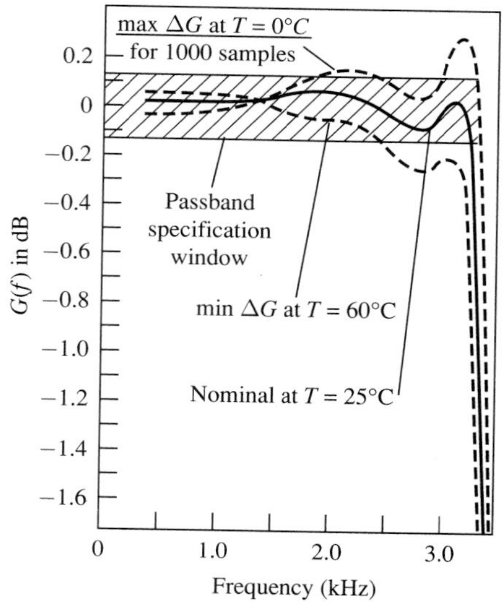

FIGURE 7-20   Computer simulation of worst-case response deviations for 1000 samples of a 5th-order Cauer PCM receive active-RC filter. The component deviations are due to the combined effects of fabrication tolerances and temperature variations over the range $0°C \leq T \leq 60°C$. The dashed curves represent the envelope of worst-case ΔG and the shaded rectangle corresponds to the ± 0.125 dB passband specification window.

where

$$Q_{x_i}^{\varphi(\lambda)} = Im(S_{x_i}^{H(\lambda)}) \qquad \text{and} \qquad Q_{x_i}^{G(\lambda)} = 8.686 Re(S_{x_i}^{H(\lambda)}) \qquad (7\text{-}47b)$$

Let us decompose $S_{x_i}^{H(\lambda)}$ into the following form

$$S_{x_i}^{H(j\lambda)} = S_{x_i}^k + S_{x_i}^{N(\lambda)} - S_{x_i}^{D(\lambda)} \qquad (7\text{-}48)$$

We can conveniently expand Eq. (7-48) in terms of the ω_0, ω_N, Q_p, and Q_z sensitivities, i.e.

$$S_{x_i}^{H(\lambda)} = \left(S_{x_i}^k + S_{\omega_N}^{H(\lambda)}\right)\left(S_{x_i}^{\omega_N} + S_{Q_z}^{H(\lambda)}\right)\left(S_{x_i}^{Q_z} + S_{\omega_0}^{H(\lambda)}\right)\left(S_{x_i}^{\omega_0} + S_{Q_p}^{H(\lambda)}\right)S_{x_i}^{Q_p} \qquad (7\text{-}49)$$

where

$$S_{x_i}^{\omega_0} = \frac{x_i}{\omega_0}\frac{\partial \omega_0}{\partial x_i}, \; S_{x_i}^{Q_p} = \frac{x_i}{Q_p}\frac{\partial Q_p}{\partial x_i}, \qquad \text{also} \qquad S_{x_i}^{\omega_0 T} = S_{\omega_0}^{\omega_0 T} S_{x_i}^{\omega_0} = S_{x_i}^{\omega_0} \qquad (7\text{-}50)$$

and $S_{x_i}^{\omega_N}$, $S_{x_i}^{Q_z}$ and $S_{x_i}^{\omega_N T}$ are defined similarly. In App. 7-1 approximate expressions are derived relating θ_0, r_p, θ_N, r_z to ω_0, Q_p, ω_N, Q_z under the conditions that θ_0, $\theta_N \ll 1$. For highly oversampled active-SC filters, Eqs. (A7-48) and (A7-51) offer insight and are usually sufficient for sensitivity calculations.

Evaluating $S_{\omega_0}^H$, $S_{\omega_N}^H$, $S_{Q_p}^H$, and $S_{Q_z}^H$, using Eqs. (7-13) and (A7-51) for $H(s)$ and $H(z)$, we obtain for the continuous-time active filters

$$S_{\omega_N}^{H(j\omega)} = \frac{N(j\omega)^*}{|N(j\omega)|^2}\left[j\omega\frac{\omega_N}{Q_z} + 2\omega_N^2\right] \tag{7-51a}$$

$$S_{Q_z}^{H(j\omega)} = -\frac{j\omega N(j\omega)^*}{|N(j\omega)|^2}\left(\frac{\omega_N}{Q_z}\right) \tag{7-51b}$$

$$S_{\omega_0}^{H(j\omega)} = -\frac{D(j\omega)^*}{|D(j\omega)|^2}\left[j\omega\frac{\omega_0}{Q_p} + 2\omega_0^2\right] \tag{7-51c}$$

$$S_{Q_p}^{H(j\omega)} = \frac{j\omega D(j\omega)^*}{|D(j\omega)|^2}\left(\frac{\omega_0}{Q_p}\right) \tag{7-51d}$$

Note that superscript * denotes complex conjugate.

For the sampled-data active filters we obtain:

$$S_{\omega_N}^{H(e^{j\omega T})} \approx \frac{N(e^{j\omega T})^*}{|N(e^{j\omega T})|^2}\left[e^{-j\omega T}2\omega_N T\left(\frac{\pm 1}{2Q_z} + \omega_N T\right) - e^{-j2\omega T}\left(\frac{\pm\omega_N T}{Q_z}\right)\right] \tag{7-52a}$$

$$S_{Q_z}^{H(e^{j\omega T})} \approx -\frac{N(e^{j\omega T})^*}{|N(e^{j\omega T})|^2}\left(e^{-j\omega T}\frac{\pm\omega_N T}{Q_z} - e^{-j2\omega T}\frac{\pm\omega_N T}{Q_z}\right) \tag{7-52b}$$

$$S_{\omega_0}^{H(e^{j\omega T})} \approx -\frac{D(e^{j\omega T})^*}{|D(e^{j\omega T})|^2}\left[e^{-j\omega T}2\omega_0 T\left(\frac{1}{2Q_p} + \omega_0 T\right) - e^{-j2\omega T}\left(\frac{\omega_0 T}{Q_p}\right)\right] \tag{7-52c}$$

$$S_{Q_p}^{H(e^{j\omega T})} \approx \frac{D(e^{j\omega T})^*}{|D(e^{j\omega T})|^2}\left(e^{-j\omega T}\frac{\omega_0 T}{Q_p} - e^{-j2\omega T}\frac{\omega_0 T}{Q_p}\right) \tag{7-52d}$$

Equations (7-52) provide insight and are usually sufficient for sensitivity calculations that do not demand high precision. The reader can alternatively find sensitivity relations for $H(z)$ in terms of θ_0, r_p, θ_N, r_z (see Exercise 7-34).

The student can verify that, for specified ω_N, Q_z, ω_0, Q_p, and $\omega_N T \ll 1$, $\omega_0 T \ll 1$, we have the following approximate equalities (in the baseband region where $\omega < \pi/T$):

$$S_{\omega_N}^{H(j\omega)} \approx S_{\omega_N}^{H(e^{j\omega T})}, \quad S_{Q_z}^{H(j\omega)} \approx S_{Q_z}^{H(e^{j\omega T})} \tag{7-53a}$$

$$S_{\omega_0}^{H(j\omega)} \approx S_{\omega_0}^{H(e^{j\omega 0})}, \quad S_{Q_p}^{H(j\omega)} \approx S_{Q_p}^{H(e^{j\omega T})} \tag{7-53b}$$

Moreover, using Eqs. (7-51), (7-52), and (7-47) we can readily determine $Q_{\omega_0}^G$, $Q_{\omega_N}^G$, $Q_{Q_p}^G$, $Q_{Q_z}^G$, and $Q_{\omega_0}^\varphi$, $Q_{\omega_N}^\varphi$, $Q_{Q_p}^\varphi$, $Q_{Q_z}^\varphi$ for both the continuous-time and sampled-data cases. We have plotted in Fig. 7-21 curves for $Q_{\omega_0}^G$, $Q_{Q_p}^G$, $Q_{\omega_0}^\varphi$, $Q_{Q_p}^\varphi$ versus normalized frequency over the range $0 \le \omega/\omega_0 \le 2$. For each sensitivity we show curves for $Q_p = 2, 5$, and 10. In accordance with Eqs. (7-53), these sensitivities are nearly identical for both the sampled-data and continuous-time cases, when the sampling rate is such that $T < 1/(2\omega_0)$ For active-SC filters, this inequality is almost always satisfied in practice.

The curves in Fig. 7-21 are interesting in that they show the relative contributions of $\Delta\omega_0/\omega_0$, $\Delta Q_p/Q_p$ to ΔG, and $\Delta\varphi$ as a function of frequency, i.e.,

$$\Delta G \approx Q^G_{\omega_0} \frac{\Delta\omega_0}{\omega_0} + Q^G_{Q_p} \frac{\Delta Q_p}{Q_p} \qquad \text{and} \qquad \Delta\varphi \approx Q^\varphi_{\omega_0} \frac{\Delta\omega_0}{\omega_0} + Q^\varphi_{Q_p} \frac{\Delta Q_p}{Q_p} \qquad (7\text{-}54a)$$

where

$$\frac{\Delta\omega_0}{\omega_0} \approx \sum_{i=1}^{k_\omega} \left(S^{\omega_0}_{x_i}\right) \frac{\Delta x_i}{x_i} \qquad \text{and} \qquad \frac{\Delta Q_p}{Q_p} \approx \sum_{i=1}^{k_Q} \left(S^{Q_p}_{x_i}\right) \frac{\Delta x_i}{x_i} \qquad (7\text{-}54b)$$

FIGURE 7-21   Plots of (a) $Q^G_{\omega_0}$; (b) $Q^G_{Q_p}$; (c) $Q^\varphi_{\omega_0}$ and (d) $Q^\varphi_{Q_p}$ versus normalized frequency ω/ω_0. Shown are curves for $Q_p = 2$, 5, and 10. These curves also apply to the same sample-data case in the baseband (i.e., $\omega < \pi/T$), when $\omega_0 T < 0.5$.

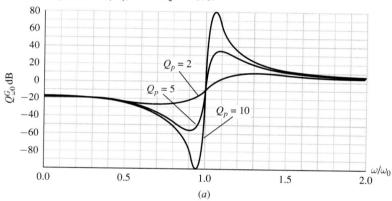

(a)

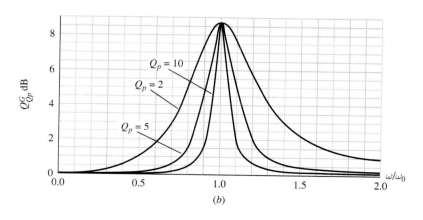

(b)

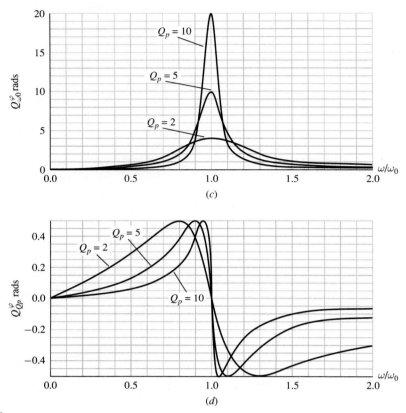

FIGURE 7-21 (cont'd)

and k_ω, k_Q represent the number of elements in the biquad that determine ω_0, Q_p, respectively. Some important and easy to remember points on these sensitivity curves are

(a) At the pole frequency $\omega = \omega_0$ or $\omega/\omega_0 = 1$, where

$$Q_{\omega_0}^G = -8.686 \text{ dB}, \quad Q_{Q_p}^G = 8.686 \text{ dB}, \quad Q_{\omega_0}^\varphi = 2Q_p \text{ rads}, \quad Q_{Q_p}^\varphi = 0 \text{ rads} \qquad (7\text{-}55a)$$

(b) At the 3 dB band edges $\omega = \omega_0 \pm \omega_0/2Q_p$ or $\omega/\omega_0 = 1 \pm 1/2Q_p$, where

$$Q_{\omega_0}^G = \pm 8.686 Q_p \text{ dB}, \quad Q_{Q_p}^G \approx \frac{1}{2} 8.686 \text{ dB}, \quad Q_{\omega_0}^\varphi \approx Q_p \text{ rads}, \quad Q_{Q_p}^\varphi \approx \pm \frac{1}{2} \text{ rads} \quad (7\text{-}55b)$$

In the vicinity of $\omega = \omega_0 \pm \omega_0/2Q_p$, we see that ΔG and $\Delta \varphi$ are predominantly determined by $Q_{\omega_0}^G$ and $Q_{\omega_0}^\varphi$, respectively. Hence, if $|S_{x_i}^{Q_p}| \ll Q_p$, we can approximate

ΔG and $\Delta\varphi$ in the passband as

$$\Delta G \approx Q_{\omega_0}^G \frac{\Delta\omega_0}{\omega_0} \qquad \text{and} \qquad \Delta\varphi \approx Q_{\omega_0}^\varphi \frac{\Delta\omega_0}{\omega_0} \qquad (7\text{-}56)$$

We note that $Q_{\omega_0}^G$ and $Q_{\omega_0}^\varphi$, which depend only on the specifics of the nominal H, increase with the value of Q_p. The $\Delta\omega_0/\omega_0$ and $\Delta Q_p/Q_p$ depend on the biquad circuit sensitivities and the variation of the circuit components. As we will see shortly, maintaining constant yield Y_{sw} for a given biquad with a particular $\Delta\omega_0/\omega_0$ requires that the specification windows for gain and phase be widened in proportion to Q_p.

Using Eqs. (7-54) or (7-56), we can determine ΔG and $\Delta\varphi$, or we can estimate the statistics $\sigma(\Delta G)$ and $\sigma(\Delta\varphi)$ using Eqs. (3-88) and (3-89), respectively. Once again, when we assume that the component variations are gaussian random variables, the ΔG and $\Delta\varphi$ are also gaussian in the linear approximation. The discussion in Sec. 3-4, with regard to component matching and yield, applies directly to the realization of cost-effective integrated active filters.

Let us summarize the main points of this subsection with an example.

Example 7-4

Consider the BP SC biquad in Fig. 7-22a, with sample rate $f_s = 100$ kHz. The timing signals for the analog switches ϕ^e, ϕ^o and the input samples $v_{in}(kT)$ are shown in Fig. 7-22b. Assume the op amps are ideal and that the biquad is designed for $f_0 = (10/\pi)$ kHz and $Q_p = 10$, and the voltage transfer function is given by[8]

$$H(z) = \frac{V_{out}(z)}{V_{in}(z)} = \frac{\dfrac{H}{D}z^{-1}(1 - z^{-1})}{1 - 2\left(1 - \dfrac{AE}{2DB} - \dfrac{AC}{2DB}\right)z^{-1} + \left(1 - \dfrac{AE}{DB}\right)z^{-2}} \qquad (7\text{-}57)$$

With $x_i = A, B, C, D, E$, and H, and the statistics for the capacitor variations $\Delta x_i/x_i$ being $\sigma_i = 0.1$ and $\rho_{ij} = 0.999$: (a) determine the $S_{x_i}^{\omega_0}$ and $S_{x_i}^{Q_p}$, and (b) determine $\sigma(\Delta G)$ and $\sigma(\Delta\varphi)$ at the ± 3 dB band edges. Use approximations where possible.

Solution. Evaluating $\omega_0 T = 2\pi f_0/f_s$ we determine that $\omega_0 T = 0.20 < 0.50$; hence, the conditions for the approximate equalities in Eqs. (7-53) are satisfied and we may use Fig. 7-21 and the sensitivities in Eqs. (7-55) in our analysis. Also, we observe that $Q_p \gg 1$. (a) Comparing Eq. (7-57) with Eq. (7-16b), Eq. (A7-48),

---

[8]At this stage we present this $H(z)$ without derivation. However, we note that $V_{in}(z) = \mathbf{Z}(v_{in}(kT))$ and $V_{out}(z) = \mathbf{Z}(v_{out}(kT))$ as described in App. 7-1. The ϕ-phase switch at the output clearly designates the phase during which $v_{out}^{\#}(t)$ is to be sampled. Timings for switch and signal transitions and sampling instants are important specifications for all switched-capacitor circuits. Simple but rigorous techniques to evaluate $H(z)$'s for active-SC filters will be developed in the next section.

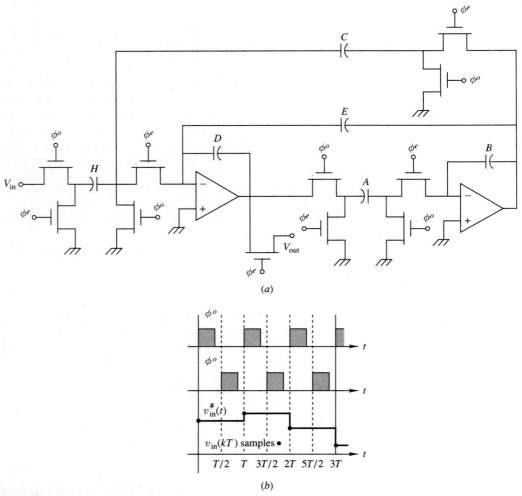

FIGURE 7-22   SC circuit for Example 7-4.

and Table 7-3, we see that Eq. (7-57) is a BP01 and that

$$\omega_0 T \approx \sqrt{\frac{AC}{DB}} \qquad \text{and} \qquad Q_p \approx \frac{1}{E}\sqrt{\frac{DBC}{A}} \qquad (7\text{-}58)$$

Evaluating $S_{x_i}^{\omega_0}$ and $S_{x_i}^{Q_p}$, we obtain (recalling that $S_{x_i}^{\omega_0 T} = S_{x_i}^{\omega_0}$):

$$S_A^{\omega_0} = S_C^{\omega_0} = -S_D^{\omega_0} = -S_B^{\omega_0} = 0.5 \qquad \text{and} \qquad S_E^{\omega_0} = S_H^{\omega_0} = 0 \qquad (7\text{-}59a)$$

$$S_B^{Q_p} = S_C^{Q_p} = S_D^{Q_p} = -S_A^{Q_p} = 0.5, \quad S_E^{Q_p} = -1 \quad \text{and} \quad S_H^{Q_p} = 0 \qquad (7\text{-}59b)$$

(b) Since $Q_p \gg 1$, and according to Eq. (7-52b), all $|S_{x_i}^{Q_p}| \ll Q_p$, we can approximate ΔG and $\Delta\varphi$ with Eq. (7-56). Thus, we may express $\sigma(\Delta G)$ and $\sigma(\Delta\varphi)$ as

$$\sigma(\Delta G) \approx |Q_{\omega_0}^G| \left[\sum_{i=1}^{k_\omega} \left(S_{x_i}^{\omega_0} \right)^2 \sigma_i^2 + \sum_{i=1}^{k_\omega} \left(\sum_{j \neq i}^{k_\omega} S_{x_i}^{\omega_0} \right) S_{x_j}^{\omega_0} \rho_{ij} \sigma_i \sigma_j \right]^{1/2} = |Q_{\omega_0}^G| \kappa_{\omega_0}$$

$$(7\text{-}60a)$$

$$\sigma(\Delta\varphi) \approx |Q_{\omega_0}^\varphi| \left[\sum_{i=1}^{k_\omega} (S_{x_i}^{\omega_0})^2 \sigma_i^2 + \sum_{i=1}^{k_\omega} \left(\sum_{j \neq i}^{k_\omega} S_{x_i}^{\omega_0} \right) S_{x_j}^{\omega_0} \rho_{ij} \sigma_i \sigma_j \right]^{1/2} = |Q_{\omega_0}^\varphi| \kappa_{\omega_0}$$

$$(7\text{-}60b)$$

Using Eq. (7-59a) and the given σ_i and ρ_{ij}, we readily calculate κ_{ω_0}

$$\kappa_{\omega_0} = \left[\sum_{i=1}^{k_\omega} \left(S_{x_i}^{\omega_0} \right)^2 \sigma_i^2 + \sum_{i=1}^{k_\omega} \left(\sum_{j \neq i}^{k_\omega} S_{x_i}^{\omega_0} \right) S_{x_j}^{\omega_0} \rho_{ij} \sigma_i \sigma_j \right]^{1/2} = 0.003 \qquad (7\text{-}61)$$

Hence, using Eqs. (7-60) with Eqs. (7-61) and (7-55b), we obtain the following estimates for $\sigma(\Delta G)$ and $\sigma(\Delta\varphi)$ at the ± 3 dB frequencies:

$$\sigma(\Delta G) \approx |Q_{\omega_0}^G| \kappa_{\omega_0} = 8.686 Q_p (0.003) = 0.26 \text{ dB} \qquad (7\text{-}62a)$$

$$\sigma(\Delta\varphi) \approx |Q_{\omega_0}^\varphi| \kappa_{\omega_0} = Q_p (0.003) = 0.03 \text{ rads (or } 1.7^\circ) \qquad (7\text{-}62b)$$

In practice, these ± 3 dB points will tend to be the most critical gain/phase tests for this, as well as most filters. Hence, the expected yields at these frequencies are usually a good metric for the soft-yield Y_{sw} in Eq. (3-91b). For example, if the specification window at the band edges was $\pm 2\sigma(\Delta G)$ and the chip area[9] required to implement the biquad was $A = 0.02$ cm² in a CMOS process with a defect density of $D = 2/\text{cm}^2$, then a reliable estimate of yield using Eqs. (3-91), (3-92a) and (3-90) is $Y_f \approx Y_{tw} = Y_{sw} Y_{hw} = (2erf(2))(e^{-(.02)(2)}) \approx (0.96)(0.96) = 0.92$, or 92 percent.

7-8 MODELING AND ANALYSIS OF SWITCHED-CAPACITOR FILTERS

Switched-capacitor filters are semicontinuous analog or sampled-data circuits governed by the familiar electronic circuit principles of emittance, loading, and energy conservation (e.g., Kirchhoff's laws). However, the essential information in switched-capacitor voltage signals is found in discrete, periodic samples that are stored on

---

[9]As we will see, the capacitance ratios, hence the chip area (A) required to implement a biquad, increases with Q_p (and also Q_z except when $1/Q_z = 0$) and sometimes with Q_p^2.

the capacitors. These samples are most accurately characterized using discrete-time mathematics, e.g., App. 7-1. If needed, the semicontinuous analog or sampled-data character of switched-capacitor circuits and signals can be incorporated at the end of the analysis, as shown in App. 7-1 (e.g., Fig. A7-6). Finally, switched-capacitor circuits generally exhibit a periodic time-varying behavior that is related to their biphase (ϕ^e, ϕ^o) clocked operation. Periodic time-variance, an unfamiliar concept to most students, can complicate the operation of a switched-capacitor circuit. Moreover, the performance of such a circuit can be significantly altered with only subtle changes to its schematic.

Our primary purpose for this section is to develop systematic pencil-and-paper techniques that result in efficient derivations of symbolic switched-capacitor circuit equations that provide insights to facilitate prudent design. Although CAD simulation, using such tools as SWITCAP (Fang et al. 1983) or SWAP (Silvar-Lisco Co. 1983), is very important for verifying designs, the primary purpose of this section is to develop techniques that support creative, high-quality design prior to intensive computer verification. It is important for the reader to recognize that SPICE is not well-suited to performing transient simulations of switched-capacitor circuits. The variable time-step integration routines do not adapt well to the fast transitions that occur with the periodic opening and closing of switches in each phase. With appropriate MOST models, SPICE can be used to study parasitic charging, clock feedthrough effects, and transient effects that can be suitably examined with a simulation involving only a few clock cycles. However, with the z-domain models to be developed in this section, SPICE can be used to conduct steady-state AC analyses (Meares and Hymowitz 1988).

7-8-1 Periodic Time-Variance in Biphase Switched-Capacitor Filters

The most expedient and intuitive means to explain periodic time-variance is with the aid of examples; hence, consider the biphase switched-capacitor circuits in Figs. 7-23 and 7-24. For this discussion let us assume that the op amps, analog switches, and capacitors are ideal components, and that all capacitors are initially (at $t = 0$) uncharged. It follows that charges residing on capacitors remain undisturbed during the dead zones between phases, when all switches are turned OFF. These are the usual assumptions made in first-order modeling and design of switched-capacitor filters. In Chap. 8 we will examine some high-performance switched-capacitor circuits that inherently reduce typical second-order effects and actually achieve near first-order performance. We note that, in practice, many of the analog switches in these circuits would be realized as CMOS structures (e.g., Fig. 7-4c) and the complements to ϕ^e and ϕ^o would also be required, as shown in Fig. 7-4d.

In Fig. 7-23a we have a circuit comprised of one op amp, switched-capacitors H and C, and an integrator-like feedback capacitor D. Let us call this schematic "circuit 1." Continuous local feedback via D is essential for maintaining stability and linearity independent of switch phase. From Chap. 5 we recall that feedback D forces the op amp inverting input to virtual ground, a condition that, as we will see in Chap. 8, yields marvelous benefits. This circuit is, in fact, a summing integrator, similar in structure to the active-RC summing integrator in Fig. 5-12b. Active-SC integrators,

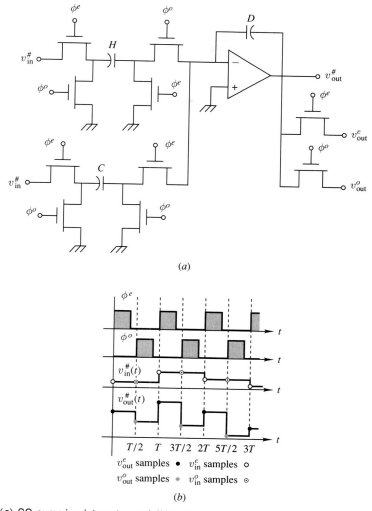

(a)

(b)

FIGURE 7-23   (a) SC summing integrator and (b) timing diagrams for clock signals ϕ^e and ϕ^o, sampled data signals $v_{in}^{\#}(t)$ and $v_{out}^{\#}(t)$, and their respective samples $v_{in}^e(kT)$, $v_{in}^o((k+\frac{1}{2})T)$, $v_{out}^e(kT)$, $v_{out}^o((k+\frac{1}{2})T)$. SCs H and C are phased so that the output samples are time-variant.

which realize the various functions in Table 7-8, represent the core of active-SC filter design. We will discuss active-SC integrators in Sec. 7-8.

The circuit in Fig. 7-24a is identical to "circuit 1" except for switch phase changes in switched-capacitor H. Let us call this schematic "circuit 2". The timing for the switching, the sampled-and-held input $v_{in}^{\#}(t)$, and output $v_{out}^{\#}(t)$ are sketched in parts (b) of these figures. In both cases we assume identical staircase-like sample-data inputs that change value once per clock period T, at the beginning of phase-ϕ^e. In

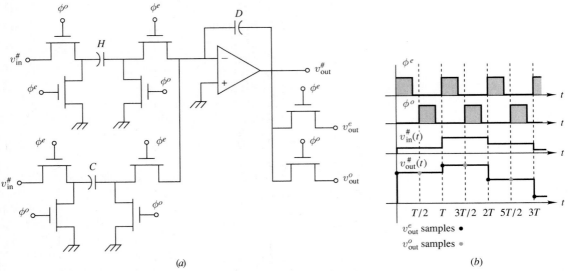

(a)   (b)

FIGURE 7-24   (a) SC summing integrator and (b) timing diagrams. The SC circuit in (a) is similar to the circuit in Fig. 7-23, except the phases for SC H are reversed so that the output samples are time-invariant.

Fig. 7-23b we see that $v_{\text{out}}^{\#}(t)$ for "circuit-1" changes value twice per clock period T. Correspondingly, the output for "circuit-2" changes only once per T, in phase with the input. Both circuits produce identical ϕ^e-phase samples, i.e., $v_{\text{out}}^e(kT)$, a fact the reader will be able to verify later. Due to the continuous feedback of D and the use of near ideal switches and capacitors, $v_{\text{out}}^{\#}(t)$ remains constant through the between phase dead zones. In effect, the dead zone, as long as it is kept reasonable (say 5–20 percent of $T/2$), quietly serves its purpose in the background. It can then be ignored in the first-order analysis, and is rarely a source of any substantive second-order behavior.

Considering the sampled waveforms depicted in Figs. 7-23 and 7-24, it will be convenient to define the voltage samples in the ϕ^e and ϕ^o phases as follows

$$v^e(k) = v^e(kT) = v^{\#}\left(\frac{nT}{2}\right) \qquad \text{for } n = 0, 2, 4, \ldots, \text{ even, } \ldots \qquad (7\text{-}63a)$$

$$\equiv 0 \qquad \text{for } n = 1, 3, 5, \ldots, \text{ odd, } \ldots$$

$$v^o(k) = v^o\left[\left(k + \frac{1}{2}\right)T\right] = v^{\#}\left(\frac{nT}{2}\right) \qquad \text{for } n = 1, 3, 5, \ldots, \text{ odd, } \ldots \qquad (7\text{-}63b)$$

$$\equiv 0 \qquad \text{for } n = 0, 2, 4, \ldots, \text{ even, } \ldots$$

where $k = n/2$ for n even, $k = (n-1)/2$ for n odd. Thus, we observe that $v^e(k)$ and $v^o(k)$ form an interlaced, orthogonal pair of voltage sample sequences. These sequences are separated in time by one-half clock cycle (or $T/2$). The samples in each sequence are periodically spaced by T, i.e., the sample rate is $f_s = 1/T$. Their sum, using superposition, is a composite at double the sample rate $f_s = 2/T$, i.e.,

$$v(n) = v\left(n\frac{T}{2}\right) = v^e\left(\frac{nT}{2}\right)\Big|_{n=\text{even}} + v^o\left(\frac{nT}{2}\right)\Big|_{n=\text{odd}} \qquad \text{for all } n \geq 0 \quad (7\text{-}64)$$

The definitions in Eqs. (7-63) and (7-64) are illustrated in Fig. 7-25. Let us refer to sample sequences where $v^o(k) \neq v^e(k)$ as *phase-dependent* (i.e., switch phase) samples. However, when $v^o(k) = v^e(k)$, the samples are *phase-independent*. The v_o^e, v_o^o in Fig. 7-23b are seen to be phase-dependent and, in contrast, those in Fig. 7-24b are phase-independent.

Staircase-like signals, where the amplitude changes value per $T/2$, such that $v^o(k) \neq v^e(k)$, represents the most general sample data signal we can permit in a two-phase system. The hold period between samples is essential and consistent with the operation of the circuits we are prescribing. In practice, this implies that we can shift the periodic acquisition of samples $v(k)$ any time within the $T/2$ intervals $kT \leq t < (k + \frac{1}{2})T$. For the special case where $v^o(k) = v^e(k)$, this interval extends an additional $T/2$, to $kT \leq t < (k + 1)T$. This interval will become important when we consider the nonideal transient behavior of the op amps. In any case, such sampled-data signals occur and propagate naturally in switched-capacitor circuits, or they can be easily arranged to do so.

Time-variance (or *periodic-time-variance*, to be more precise) is related to the sample-to-sample property of phase-dependence. That is, in general, the behavior seen at the output of a switched-capacitor circuit depends on the particular phase the output is observed. Consequently, we show in Figs. 7-23a and 7-24a three options for sampling $v_{\text{out}}^\# T$; namely,

1 per T, during ϕ^e yielding samples $v_{\text{out}}^e(k)$,
2 per T during ϕ^o yielding samples $v_{\text{out}}^o(k)$, or
3 per $T/2$ (i.e., no switch) yielding $v_{\text{out}} = v_{\text{out}}^e + v_{\text{out}}^o$.

FIGURE 7-25   Decomposition of discrete time samples $v(n)$ into orthogonal components $v^e(k)$ and $v^o(k)$.

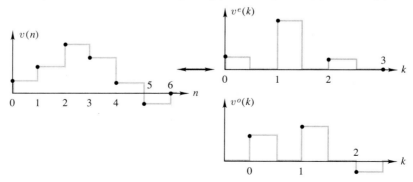

Hence, periodic time-variance and periodic time-invariance can be succinctly defined in terms of the relative phase dependence of input-output samples. Let a switched-capacitor circuit be defined as *periodic-time-variant* if any sequence of phase-independent input samples yields a sequence of phase-dependent output samples, i.e.,

$$v_{in}^o(k) = v_{in}^e(k) \rightarrow v_{out}^o(k) \neq v_{out}^e(k) \tag{7-65a}$$

The circuit is *periodic-time-invariant* when all phase independent-input sequences result in output sample sequences that are also phase-independent, i.e.,

$$v_{in}^o(k) = v_{in}^e(k) \rightarrow v_{out}^o(k) = v_{out}^e(k) \tag{7-65b}$$

Based on these simple definitions, the switched-capacitor "circuit 1" and "circuit 2" are identified as periodic-time-variant and time-invariant, respectively. We see that subtle change in the switch phases of one switched-capacitor (or more) in a circuit may be sufficient to transform a time-invariant circuit into a time-variant circuit, and vice-versa. As we will learn later, active-SC filters are more robust when designed to be time-invariant.

7-8-2 ϕ^e and ϕ^o Decomposition

Topologically, the periodic biphase switching causes the circuit schematic to change with time, alternating between two schematics as the switches open and close. That is, one schematic can be drawn for the ϕ^e-phase (i.e., circuit-ϕ^e) and a second for the ϕ^o-phase (i.e., circuit-ϕ^o). There is a third schematic that arises during the dead zone when all switches are OFF. As stated earlier, we assume that our switched-capacitor circuits are insensitive to the specific length of a reasonable dead zone. In fact, if this assumption is not valid for a particular realization, the circuit is fatally flawed and should not be used. Hence, we ignore this third circuit in first-order analyses. In CAD simulation programs, such as SWITCAP, an additional phase can be defined to model the dead zones. However, the simulation will not reveal any additional information unless sophisticated models are used for the integrated circuit components.

In any event, the two primary schematics are made interdependent via the charges stored on the capacitors during the previous phase. Hence, for any node-p in a switched-capacitor circuit, we can write two interdependent discrete nodal charge equations (e.g., Eqs. (7-10)); i.e., one for each phase:

$$\Delta q_p^e(k) = \sum_{i=1}^{M_{ep}} C_{pi} v_{pi}^e(k) - \sum_{i=1}^{M_{ep}} C_{pi} v_{pi}^o \left(k - \frac{1}{2} \right) \quad \text{during} \quad \phi^e \tag{7-66a}$$

$$\Delta q_p^o(k) = \sum_{i=1}^{M_{op}} C_{pi} v_{pi}^o(k) - \sum_{i=1}^{M_{op}} C_{pi} v_{pi}^e \left(k - \frac{1}{2} \right) \quad \text{during} \quad \phi^o \tag{7-66b}$$

or equivalently in the z-domain,

$$\Delta Q_p^e(z) = \sum_{i=1}^{M_{ep}} C_{pi} V_{pi}^e(z) - z^{-1/2} \sum_{i=1}^{M_{ep}} C_{pi} V_{pi}^o(z) \quad \text{during} \quad \phi^e \qquad (7\text{-}67a)$$

$$\Delta Q_p^o(z) = \sum_{i=1}^{M_{op}} C_{pi} V_{pi}^o(z) - z^{-1/2} \sum_{i=1}^{M_{op}} C_{pi} V_{pi}^e(z) \quad \text{during} \quad \phi^o \qquad (7\text{-}67b)$$

where M_{ep} and M_{op} denote the total number of capacitors C_{pi} connected to node-p during the ϕ^e and ϕ^o phases, respectively. The discrete charge transfers $\Delta q^e(k)$ and $\Delta q^o(k)$ are defined in a manner similar to Eqs. (7-63). Note that the $z^{-1/2}$ ($T/2$ delay) terms are due to the exchange of charges on capacitors that link or bridge the ϕ^e- and ϕ^o-circuits.

This decomposition is best demonstrated by Figs. 7-23 and 7-26. In Fig. 7-26 we partition the active-SC circuit in Fig. 7-23 into the two circuits, i.e., circuit-ϕ^e when ϕ^e = ON, ϕ^o = OFF and circuit-ϕ^o when ϕ^o = ON, ϕ^e = OFF. Note that the dependent voltage sources in both circuits model the transfer of charges between the ϕ^e- and ϕ^o-phases, and take into account the interphase $T/2$ delay. That is, dependent source $v_D^o = v_{\text{out}}^o(k - \frac{1}{2})$ in circuit-ϕ^e is the charge transferred via capacitor-D from the previous ϕ^o-phase (i.e., $T/2$ earlier) to the current ϕ^e-phase. Conversely, $v_D^e = v_{\text{out}}^e(k - \frac{1}{2})$ represents the charge transferred via D from the previous ϕ^e-phase to the current ϕ^o-phase. When a dependent source associated with a particular capacitor is set to zero, e.g., $v_C^o = 0$ in circuit-ϕ^e, it implies that no charge is transferred to the current phase via that capacitor. In this case, we observe that capacitor-C is fully discharged during the previous ϕ^o-phase.

FIGURE 7-26   Decomposition of the SC circuit in Fig. 7-23 into (a) ϕ^e and (b) ϕ^o circuits. The dependent sources model charge linkages between the ϕ^e and ϕ^o phases.

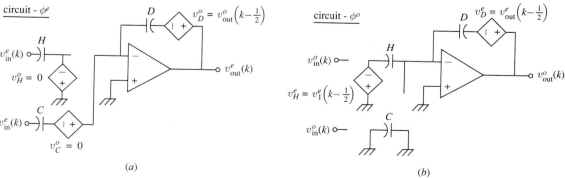

(a) $\qquad\qquad\qquad\qquad\qquad\qquad\qquad$ (b)

The circuit decomposition illustrated in Fig. 7-26 is used in many CAD tools; but it is not well-suited to pencil-and-paper frequency domain analysis. Alternatively, we can combine ϕ^e- and ϕ^o-circuits into a single z-domain model or equivalent circuit as illustrated in Fig. 7-27. In the z-domain equivalent circuit, the coupling between ϕ^e- and ϕ^o-circuits is achieved topologically rather than through dependent voltage sources. In Fig. 7-27 the z-domain circuit has, in general, two inputs and two outputs, one set for each phase; a concept consistent with the decomposition in Fig. 7-26. Hence, two-port switched-capacitor circuits will, in general, be modeled by four-port z-domain models.

The z-domain model for a given switched-capacitor circuit is not unique and must be synthesized from the governing circuit equations (Ghausi and Laker 1981; Unbehauen and Cichocki 1989). Our task is to develop a systematic approach to synthesizing z-domain models, in particular, one that facilitates the acquisition of design intuition with pencil-and-paper analysis. The approach we will use is accomplished in two steps: (1) synthesize z-domain models for each of the basic switched-capacitor elements using Fig. 7-27 as a guideline; and (2) connect the element models in accordance with the originating switched-capacitor circuit schematic to complete the equivalent circuit. The basic switched-capacitor elements are individual unswitched-capacitors, switched-capacitors, op amps, and independent voltage sources. This process is symbolically illustrated in Fig. 7-28, where the individual elements are highlighted within boxes in both the originating schematic (Fig. 7-28a) and the four-port z-domain model (Fig. 7-28b). We see in Fig. 7-28b that all elements are modeled as four-port equivalent circuits. We also split independent (and dependent) sample-data voltage sources into ϕ^e and ϕ^o components. Each component is then modeled as a z-transformed voltage source. Also, each op amp (i.e., a dependent source) is modeled as a pair of op amps, representing the op amp's role in both phases. Each element model and the overall equivalent circuit are drawn consistent with the general layout in Fig. 7-27.

Since it is unwieldly to combine discrete-time and continuous-time mathematics, z-domain analysis limits op amp modeling to frequency independent behavioral models. That is, finite DC gain can be accommodated, but continuous-time properties (e.g., transient response) of op amps cannot be included in our first-order analysis or design. CAD tools, such as SWITCAP, subsequently can be used to examine the

FIGURE 7-27   SC equivalent circuit with port variables $v_{in}^e(z)$ and $\Delta Q_{in}^e(z)$; $\Delta Q_{in}^o(z)$ and $V_{in}^o(z)$; $v_o^e(z), \Delta Q_o^e(z)$; and $v_o^o(z), \Delta Q_o^o(z)$. The 4pz in the lower left corner of the equivalent circuit box is a reminder that the circuit is a four-port and represented in the z-domain.

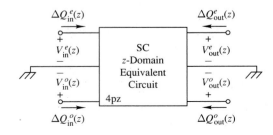

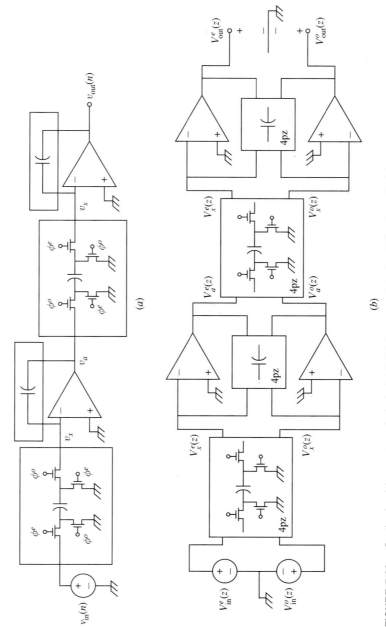

FIGURE 7-28 Synthesis of four-port equivalent circuit (*b*) from an originating SC schematic (*a*). The boxes labeled 4pz represent the four-port z-domain equivalent circuits for the SC elements in the originating schematic.

impact of the op amp's transient response on an active-SC filter's first-order performance. This is done by modeling the continuous-time op amp as a sampled-data subsystem with sample rate, perhaps an order of magnitude higher than that of the active-SC circuit. However, as we will discuss in Chap. 8, time-invariant active-SC filters can be designed to be insensitive to the transient responses of properly designed op amps.

An interesting question is how does the time-variance property of a switched-capacitor circuit impact its z-domain model? The impact is, in fact, quite significant. Time-variant circuits require four-port models. This makes sense since such switched-capacitor circuits, e.g., Figs. 7-23 and 7-26, process and transfer charge during both phases. On the other hand, time-invariant circuits, e.g., Fig. 7-24, process and transfer charge during one phase only. The time-invariant circuit is then idle, or in a hold state, during the alternate phase. The ports representing the idle phase (appearing as open circuits in the model) can be eliminated and the z-domain model reduces to a two-port. Later, the reader can verify that the four-port model in Fig. 7-28b can be reduced to the two-port equivalent circuit in Fig. 7-29; because the circuit in Fig. 7-28a is time-invariant.

To simplify analysis, and more important, to realize a robust design, it is essential to determine if a switched-capacitor circuit is time-invariant, and if not, how it can be made so. Examining Figs. 7-23a and 7-24a can help us develop a rule for making this determination by visual inspection. Returning first to Fig. 7-26a we observe that capacitor D receives charge during both phases; namely from H in ϕ^o and C in ϕ^e. In contrast, the phasing of H in Fig. 7-27a was arranged such that D receives charge only on ϕ^e. The key to time-invariance is maintaining the switching at each op amp virtual ground on a single phase, so that the unswitched feedback capacitors (e.g., D) receive charge on either ϕ^e or ϕ^o, but not both. The inverting configured op amps provide convenient buffering to enable the switched-capacitors at each virtual ground to be independently synchronized to one of the phases. We can now readily verify our earlier claim that the circuit in Fig. 7-28a is time-invariant.

An important byproduct of time-invariant operation is that fewer switches are required in the hardware realization, as can be seen by comparing the circuits in

FIGURE 7-29   When the originating SC schematic is time-invariant, the equivalent circuit reduces to a two-port. The boxes labeled 2pz represent the reduced two-port z-domain equivalent circuits for the SC elements in the originating schematic of Fig. 7-28a.

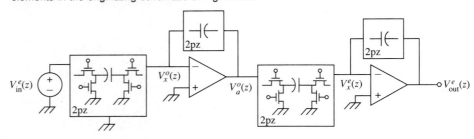

Figs. 7-22 and 7-24. The reader can verify that functioning of H, C, D in the two circuits are identical. However, in Fig. 7-22 the switch pairs of switched-capacitors H and C connected to the op amp input are combined into one common switch pair. In general, this savings can be repeated at every op amp input connected to multiple switched-capacitors. Schematics where switches have been combined in this way are called *switch-shared circuits*. Switch sharing serves to reduce die area and, perhaps more important, the second-order effects associated with switch related parasitic capacitances. Switch sharing also tends to camouflage the identity of the switched-capacitor elements. When it is important to make the composition of the circuit clear, it is helpful to draw the circuit with no shared switches, i.e., as in Fig. 7-24. In practice, it is the switch-shared schematic that is implemented. We note that switch sharing cannot be implemented with the time-variant SC circuit in Fig. 7-23.

7-8-3 Switched-Capacitor *z*-Domain Models

Let us begin by returning to the subject of sample-data voltage sources. As illustrated in Fig. 7-28, each voltage source is split into ϕ^e, ϕ^o components and transformed into the z-domain at sample rate $1/T$. In Fig. 7-30a we show voltage samples changing value per $T/2$ and $V^o \neq V^e$, i.e., a phase-dependent source. Phase-independent sources in Fig. 7-30b and 7-30c change value per T such that $V^o = z^{-1/2}V^e$ and $V^e = z^{-1/2}V^o$, respectively. To facilitate robust, time-invariant switched-capacitor circuit performance, phase-independent voltage sources are preferred, but not always necessary. Verifying the occurence of phase-independent voltages at all internal nodes (e.g., op amp outputs), is another way to check for time-invariance.

The z-domain equivalent circuits for unswitched and switched-capacitors are synthesized from the equilibrium equations characterizing their operation. We must keep in mind that such equivalent circuits are models, not physical circuits. Furthermore, their synthesis is not unique. Let us consider the synthesis of a z-domain model for the inverting switched capacitor in Fig. 7-31a. The discrete-time and z-domain equilibrium equations, of the form of Eqs. (7-66) and (7-67), can be written as follows:

during ϕ^e

$$\Delta q_1^e(k) = Cv_1^e(k) - \left[-Cv_2^o \left(k - \frac{1}{2} \right) \right] \tag{7-68a}$$

$$\Delta q_2^e(k) = 0 \tag{7-68b}$$

during ϕ^o

$$\Delta q_1^o(k) = 0 \tag{7-68c}$$

$$\Delta q_2^o(k) = Cv_2^o(k) - \left[-Cv_1^e \left(k - \frac{1}{2} \right) \right] \tag{7-68d}$$

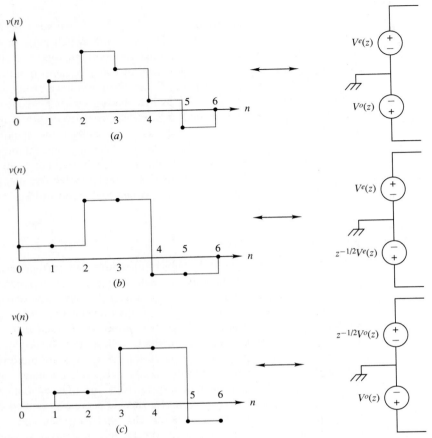

FIGURE 7-30   Z-domain equivalent circuits for independent voltage sources: (a) a phase-dependent source; (b) a phase-independent source starting on ϕ^e phase; and (c) phase-independent source starting on ϕ^o phase.

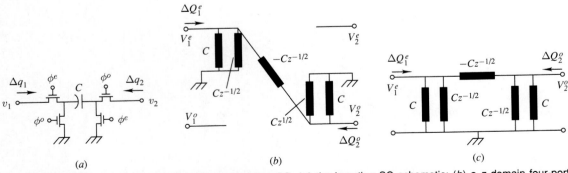

FIGURE 7-31   Equivalent circuits for an inverting SC: (a) the inverting SC schematic; (b) a z-domain four-port equivalent circuit; and (c) a reduced two-port equivalent circuit.

or equivalently, in the **z-domain,**

$$\Delta Q_1^e(z) = CV_1^e(z) + z^{-1/2}CV_2^o(z) \qquad (7\text{-}69a)$$

$$\Delta Q_2^e(z) = 0 \qquad (7\text{-}69b)$$

$$\Delta Q_1^o(z) = 0 \qquad (7\text{-}69c)$$

$$\Delta Q_2^o(z) = CV_2^o(z) + z^{-1/2}CV_1^e(z) \qquad (7\text{-}69d)$$

Note the sign inversion in the left-hand side of Eqs. (7-68a) and (7-68d). This sign inversion models capacitor-C's polarity inversion, as the switches are cycled through the ϕ^e and ϕ^o phases. Also note that Eqs. (7-68b) and (7-68c) take into account that C is disconnected from terminal-1 during ϕ^o and terminal-2 during ϕ^e; hence, no charge is transferred, i.e., $\Delta q_2^e(k) = \Delta q_1^o(k) = 0$.

The z-domain model, synthesized directly from Eqs. (7-69), is shown in Fig. 7-31b. This equivalent circuit represents one of many models that could be synthesized from Eqs. (7-69). The four-port model is comprised of admittance parameters with units $\Delta Q/V$, expressed as functions of the z-transform variable $z = e^{sT}$. These model parameters combine in series and parallel in the same manner as physical circuit admittances, and the equilibrium equations follow the same rules as Kirchhoff's current law (KCL). Note that if we eliminate the open terminals in Fig. 7-31b, and untwist the equivalent circuit so that the ϕ^e, ϕ^o ports are drawn on the same line, we achieve the simpler schematic in Fig. 7-31c. A bonus for using switched capacitors like Fig. 7-31 in time-invariant circuits is that the two open terminals serve no function in the model and the simpler Fig. 7-31c model can be used directly. The most important parameter in the model is the series element $-Cz^{-1/2}$ connecting terminal 1 in ϕ^e to terminal 2 in ϕ^o. This switched capacitor, in fact, simulates a negative resistor of value $-R \approx -1/f_sC$ (recall Eq. (7-8b)) and introduces a sample-data delay of $T/2$. It provides a uniquely simple and elegant means for achieving $180°$ phase shift without needing an inverting amplifier.

For integrator-based active-SC circuits, further simplification can be achieved due to the embedding switched-capacitor elements between ideal voltage sources and op amp virtual grounds. It is no accident that the example active-SC circuits in Figs. 7-23, 7-24, and 7-28 are implemented in this way. In Chap. 8 we show that insensitivity to unavoidable parasitic capacitances is one of the important qualities achievable with active-SC filter structures of this form. The simplifications that occur in the model is demonstrated in Fig. 7-32. Here, just as with physical admittances, equivalent circuit elements shunting either ideal voltage sources (or op amp outputs) or ideal op amp virtual grounds, do not affect the circuit operation. Such elements can be eliminated from the model as shown in Fig. 7-32b.

The steps followed in Eqs. (7-68) and (7-69) and in Figs. 7-31 and 7-32 can be repeated to synthesize the z-domain model for any switched-capacitor element. The results of such exercises are summarized in a library of important models contained

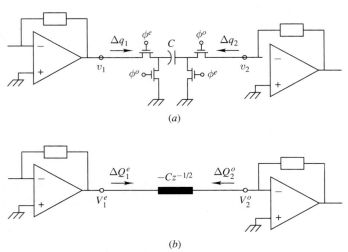

(a)

(b)

FIGURE 7-32 A further reduced equivalent circuit when the SC in Fig. 7-31 is embedded between an ideal voltage source (i.e., an op amp output as shown, or any dependent voltage source, or any independent voltage source) and an ideal virtual ground.

in Fig. 7-33. It should be clear to the reader that a consistent switch of all ϕ^e with ϕ^o, and vice versa, only changes the superscript labels for the terminal variables. Otherwise, the equivalent circuits remain as they are in Fig. 7-33. Please take note of the capacitor with a series switch in Fig. 7-33b. This element is not a switched-capacitor in the sense of the SCs in Figs. 7-33c, d, and e. In function, this is an unswitched capacitor; however, charging or discharging is constrained to one phase, due to the switch (ϕ^e in this case). As we will see, this is an important element that arises in most uses of so-called unswitched capacitors. In the model for this element we introduce another admittance-like model parameter $C(1 - z^{-1})$. The reader can verify that capacitors D and B in Fig. 7-24 operate as Fig. 7-33b and capacitor D in Fig. 7-23 operates as Fig. 7-33a. In fact, all time-invariant active-SC filters use unswitched capacitors functioning as Fig. 7-33b.

Switched capacitors in Figs. 7-33c and 7-33e simulate positive resistors and introduce $T/2$ and 0 sample-data delays, respectively. Figure 7-33d is the inverting switched-capacitor used in Fig. 7-32. Comparing models, we see that Figs. 7-33c and 7-33d are functionally equivalent, but opposite in sign. The $T/2$ delays, represented by $z^{-1/2}$ terms, are a subtle but important characteristics of these elements. Using this library, accurate and intuitive models for any biphase switched-capacitor circuit can be drawn, as shown in Fig. 7-28 or 7-29. The resulting switched-capacitor equivalent circuits are well-suited to the analytical manipulation required in circuit synthesis. Moreover, these models can be coded in SPICE to enable steady-state AC simulations of switched-capacitor filters. Since the model is based in the z-domain, the op amps used in such simulations must be restricted to voltage-controlled voltage sources with frequency independent gains.

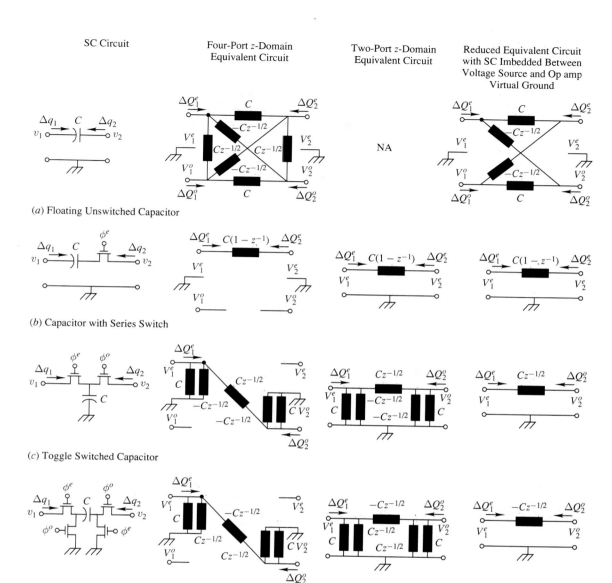

| SC Circuit | Four-Port z-Domain Equivalent Circuit | Two-Port z-Domain Equivalent Circuit | Reduced Equivalent Circuit with SC Imbedded Between Voltage Source and Op amp Virtual Ground |

(a) Floating Unswitched Capacitor

(b) Capacitor with Series Switch

(c) Toggle Switched Capacitor

(d) Inverting Toggle Switch Capacitor

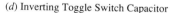

(e) Tracking Switched Capacitor

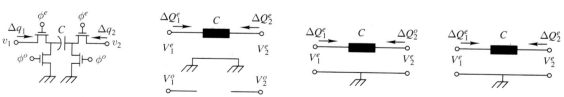

FIGURE 7-33 Library of four-port and two-port z-domain equivalent circuits synthesized for the important SC elements.

Example 7-5

Draw the z-domain model for the switched-capacitor circuit in Fig. 7-34a. Simplify where possible.

Solution. The reader can verify that this circuit is time-invariant; hence, the z-domain model will be of the form in Fig. 7-29. It is then drawn by connecting Figs. 7-33c and 7-33d in accordance with schematic Fig. 7-34b. The desired model is given in Fig. 7-34c. Note that in Fig. 7-34d we take advantage of the cancellation that occurs when elements $2Cz^{-1/2}$ and $-2Cz^{-1/2}$ are combined in parallel. We will discuss this useful circuit in Chap. 8, when we consider parasitic capacitances.

Skillfully applying the equivalent circuit method to the analysis and design of switched-capacitor circuits, we must become thoroughly familiar with the equivalent-circuit library. Hence, we urge the reader to derive and verify each entry in the library.

7-8-4   Active-SC Integrators

The cadre of active-SC circuits that realize z-domain integrating functions in Table 7-8 are the core building blocks of switched-capacitor filter synthesis. Using the elements in Fig. 7-33, several varieties of inverting and noninverting integrators are readily

FIGURE 7-34   SC circuit for Example 7-5: (a) represents the SC circuit and (b) illustrates SCs in the equivalent circuit library. (c) The SC equivalent circuit obtained by cascading the equivalent circuits in Figs. 7-33c and 7-33d, and (d) the simplified equivalent circuit.

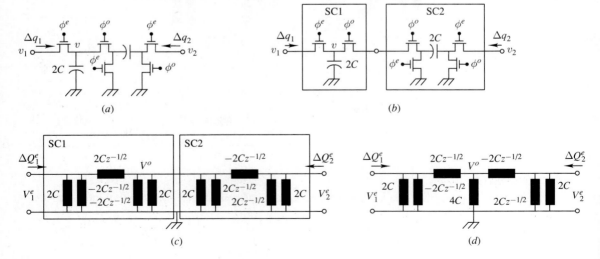

available in single op amp structures similar to Fig. 5-10. Not all the functions in Table 7-8 are available in both polarities using single-ended structures (recall Fig. 5-39). All polarities can be realized when fully balanced structures are used, e.g., Fig. 5-45. Fully balanced structures play an important role in practical active-SC circuit design; hence, their implementation will be addressed separately in Chap. 8.

Since active-SC integrators are used prolifically, it is our purpose here to use Fig. 7-33 to construct a set of integrator z-domain models that can be used to analyze and design many filters. Let us consider three active-SC integrator structures in Fig. 7-35, where the actual hardware schematics are shown to the right of the double arrow and the models to the left. We assume that v_{in} is a phase-independent input voltage, changing in value at the beginning ϕ^e as in Fig. 7-30b. In each case the output samples $v_{out}^e(k)$ and $v_{out}^o(k)$ are made available separately. All three circuits, with ideal op amps, are clearly time-invariant. The phase-independent output samples are made evident by the $z^{-1/2}$ voltage-controlled voltage source at the output of each model. In practice, this ideal output phase-independence will be disturbed by the op amp's nonideal transient response. Fortunately, as we will see in Chap. 8, we can take advantage of the time-invariant nature of these circuits to reduce their sensitivity to this unavoidable behavior.

The equivalent circuits in Fig. 7-35 are obtained by straightforward applications of the methods described in the previous section. We leave it to the reader to verify them. Recalling that the equivalent circuit elements involve $\Delta Q(z)/V(z)$-type admittances, the circuit equations are most conveniently written in terms of KCL, or nodal analysis. To demonstrate the analysis, let us consider the following example.

Example 7-5

For the active-SC integrator in Fig. 7-35a derive the transfer functions for the ϕ^e, ϕ^o output samples to the ϕ^e, ϕ^o input samples, respectively. Let us first define

$$T_{ee}(z) \doteq \frac{V_{out}^e}{V_{in}^e}, \ T_{oe}(z) = \frac{V_{out}^o}{V_{in}^e}, \ T_{eo}(z) = \frac{V_{out}^e}{V_{in}^o}, \quad \text{and} \quad T_{oo}(z) = \frac{V_{out}^o}{V_{in}^o} \qquad (7\text{-}70)$$

Solution. Writing KCL from the model, with an ideal op amp, yields

$$C_1 V_{in}^e + C(1 - z^{-1}) V_{out}^e = 0 \quad \text{and} \quad V_{out}^o = z^{-1/2} V_{out}^e \qquad (7\text{-}71)$$

Hence, we determine that

$$T_{ee}(z) = -\frac{C_1}{C} \frac{1}{1 - z^{-1}} \quad \text{and} \quad T_{oe}(z) = -\frac{C_1}{C} \frac{z^{-1/2}}{1 - z^{-1}} \qquad (7\text{-}72)$$

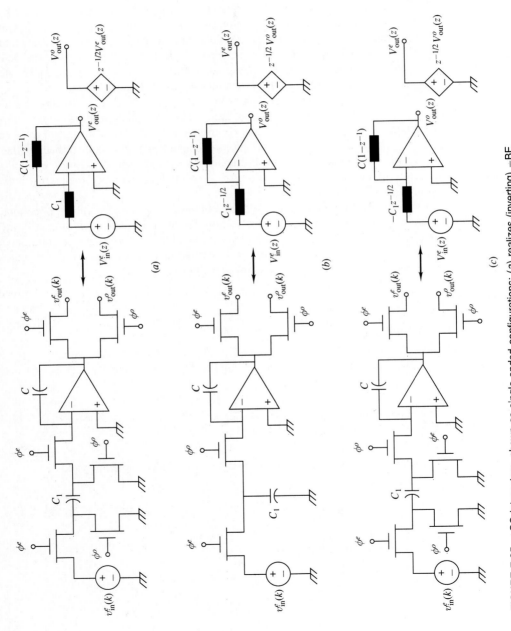

FIGURE 7-35 SC integrators, shown as single-ended configurations: (a) realizes (inverting) −BE or −LD integrators; (b) realizes −FE or −LD integrators; and (c) realizes (noninverting) +FE or +LD integrators during the ϕ^e and ϕ^o, respectively.

With reference to Table 7-8 we recognize T_{ee} and T_{oe} to be BE and LD inverting integrators, respectively. It should be evident to the reader that with the switch phasings shown, V_{in}^o is not transmitted by the circuit and consequently $T_{eo} = T_{oo} = 0$.

Conducting similar analyses of the remaining integrators in Fig. 7-35 we obtain the transfer functions listed in Table 7-9.

In addition, we also list the transfer functions for the inverting bilinear integrator in Fig. 7-36. Unless the input-feed switched capacitors match exactly, i.e., $C_{1A} = C_{1B} = C_1$, there will be a residual (and unavoidable) error in actual realization of $T_{ee}(z)$ in Table 7-9d. In the remarks column of the table we use the notation $\pm$ XY, where $\pm$ refers to the sign of the integrator and XY is the s-to-z mapping used from Table 7-8. From here on we will use this notation to refer to the expressions in Table 7-9 and/or their realizations in Fig. 7-35 and 7-36.

The inquisitive reader may ask what happens to the operation of the circuits in Fig. 7-35 when the switch phasings on C_1 are inverted so that input samples are picked up on ϕ^o rather than ϕ^e. This situation is considered in Fig. 7-37. We see that the impact of the phase changes is to delay the transmission of samples v_{in}^e by $T/2$. This $z^{-1/2}$ can either be kept with the source, as in Fig. 7-37b, or be conveniently joined with the element $-C_1 z^{-1/2}$, as in Fig. 7-37c, to yield $-C_1 z^{-1}$. This is equivalent to the sampling delay available at the output modeled by the $z^{-1/2}$ controlled source.

The summing integrator in Fig. 7-38 calls together many of the concepts developed in this section. This circuit, or one of a vast number of simple variations, is the core building block for integrator based active-SC filters. Hence, we urge the reader to become thoroughly familiar with this circuit. At this point the reader should be prepared to apply z-domain models to the analysis and design of a vast variety of switched-capacitor circuits.

TABLE 7-9   SC INTEGRATORS (NOTE $C_1/C = KT$)

	Integrator Circuit	$T_{ee}(z)$	$T_{oe}(z)$	Remarks
(a)	Fig. 7-35a	$-\dfrac{C_1}{C}\dfrac{1}{1-z^{-1}}$	$-\dfrac{C_1}{C}\dfrac{z^{-1/2}}{1-z^{-1}}$	$-$BE,$-$LD (inverting)
(b)	Fig. 7-35b	$-\dfrac{C_1}{C}\dfrac{z^{-1}}{1-z^{-1}}$	$-\dfrac{C_1}{C}\dfrac{z^{-1/2}}{1-z^{-1}}$	$-$FE,$-$LD (inverting)
(c)	Fig. 7-35c	$\dfrac{C_1}{C}\dfrac{z^{-1}}{1-z^{-1}}$	$\dfrac{C_1}{C}\dfrac{z^{-1/2}}{1-z^{-1}}$	$+$FE,$+$LD (noninverting)
(d)	Fig. 7-36	$-\dfrac{C_1}{C}\dfrac{1+z^{-1}}{1-z^{-1}}$	$-\dfrac{C_1}{C}\dfrac{z^{-1/2}(1+z^{-1})}{1-z^{-1}}$	$-$BL (inverting), iff $C_{1A} = C_{1B} = C_1$

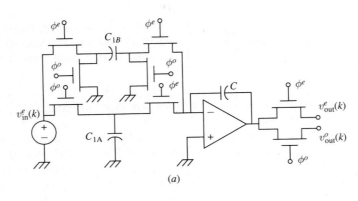

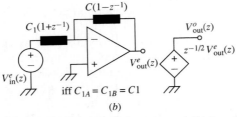

FIGURE 7-36   SC $-BL$ integrator: (*a*) the SC schematic; and (*b*) the z-domain equivalent circuit with $C_{1A} = C_{1B} = C_1$.

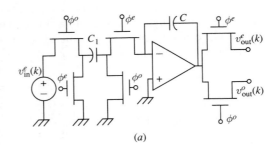

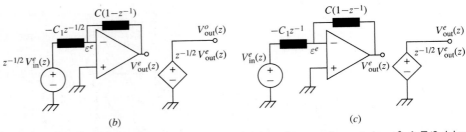

FIGURE 7-37   SC noninverting integrator in Fig. 7-35*c* with SC C_1 phased to sample v_{in} during ϕ^o. A $T/2$ delay after phase-independent v_{in} is assumed to have changed value: (*a*) the SC schematic; (*b*) the equivalent circuit; (*c*) the equivalent circuit with a $z^{-1/2}$ input delay incorporated in the input feed element $-C_1 z^{-1/2}$ to yield $-C_1 z^{-1}$.

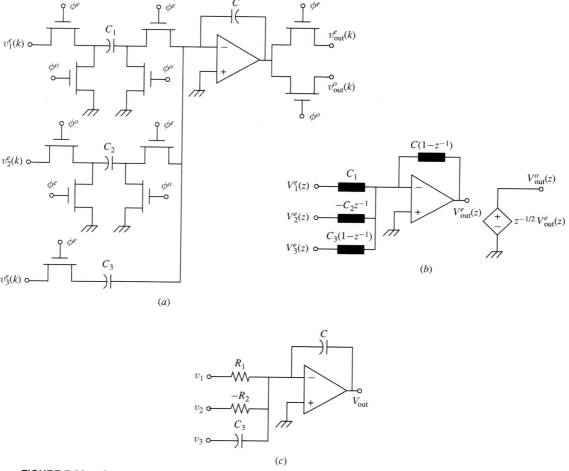

FIGURE 7-38   Summing integrator: (a) SC schematic equivalent; (b) the z-domain equivalent circuit for (a), where v_{in} are assumed to be phase independent and change values at the beginning ϕ^e; and (c) the active-RC equivalent to (a). Note that in (a), a ϕ^e switch is inserted in series with C_3 to block transmission of v_3^o samples.

SUMMARY

By now it should be clear that the design of integrated filters is a challenging endeavor involving the interpretation of complex specifications, the manipulation of systems of analytical expressions, computer modeling, and some down-to-earth circuit design. Design begins with the development of a complete set of filter specifications and ends with a layout, designed and verified to these specifications.

This and the next chapter provide the tools and circuits required to realize integrated continuous-time and sampled-data filters, starting with the user or customer's requirements. In this chapter we examined the process of specifying a filter, developing a suitable numerical $H(s)$ or $H(z)$, and determining estimates of variability and yield. We also developed a toolkit of z-domain models for intuitively analyzing and designing biphase switched-capacitor circuits.

In the next chapter we continue the subject of integrated filters by considering the design and implementation of several proven filter circuits. We remind the reader that an informative appendix to review the fundamentals of sample-data systems follows this summary.

EXERCISES

7-1 The simple RC circuit in Fig. EX7-1 is to be designed in a 3 μm CMOS p-well double-poly technology for a pole frequency of 25 kHz;

    a if $R = 100$ kΩ, calculate the value for capacitor C;

    b estimate the total die area consumed by the RC, if the R is implemented as a p-well resistor with sheet resistance $R_R = 2500$ $\Omega/\square$ (the minimum size p-well square is 6 μm $\times$ 6 μm) and the C is implemented as a single square poly 1-poly 2 capacitor with density $C_o = 5.6$ fF/μm^2 (ignore the spaces between components);

    c discuss the results of **b** in relation to the feasibility of IC integration.

7-2 For the RC in Exercise 7-1:

    a calculate the parasitic capacitance CR associated with the p-well R;

    b calculate the corresponding parasitic pole frequency;

    c compare **b** with the designed pole frequency and discuss your conclusion.

7-3 Find the values for R and C in Exercise 7-1 that minimize the die area required (ignore the spaces between components).

7-4 Repeat Exercise 7-1 with R implemented as a MOST-R, with transistor parameters $K_p = 40$ μA/V^2, $V_T = 0.8$ V, and $V_C = 2$ V.

7-5 For the RC in Exercise 7-4:

    a Calculate the parasitic capacitance CR associated with the MOST-R;

    b calculate the corresponding parasitic pole frequency;

    c compare **b** with the designed pole frequency and discuss your conclusion.

7-6 Repeat Exercise 7-3, after replacing the p-well resistor with a poly-I resistor ($R_r = 25$ $\Omega/\square$ and minimum size square is 3 μm $\times$ 3 μm). Compare the results with those in Exercise 7-3.

7-7 Show that errors due to edge undercuts in the definition of the features in ratioed resistors will tend to cancel when resistor ratios are realized using the layout in Fig. 7-2e.

7-8 Using the resistor layout scheme in Fig. 2-30 with 3 μm line width, draw the minimum area layout for an ion-implanted resistor ($R_R = 1000$ $\Omega/\square$) to realize a value of 106.5 kΩ. The layout rules are the spacing between ion-implant lines is 6 μm and the overlap of the well over the ion-implant is 6 μm.

FIGURE EX7-1

7-9 With $f_s = 100$ kHz, determine the capacitance values for a switched-capacitor to realize equivalent resistances of:

a 10 kΩ;

b 100 kΩ;

c 10 MΩ;

d 100 MΩ;

e 1000 MΩ;

f discuss the results in **a** through **e**.

7-10 The simple switched-capacitor circuit in Fig. EX7-10 is to be designed in a 3 μm CMOS p-well double-poly technology for a pole frequency of 25 kHz:

a if $C_2 = 10$ pF and $f_s = 256$ kHz, calculate the value for capacitor C_1;

b estimate the die area consumed by C_1 and C_2, if they are implemented as a single square poly 1-poly 2 capacitors with density $C_o = 5.6$ fF/μm^2;

c discuss the results of **b** in relation to the feasibility of IC integration.

7-11 The objective of this problem is to design the circuitry in Fig. EX7-11a to provide the requisite switch-control signals for a a switched-capacitor filter. Let CLK be derived from a 2.048 MHz crystal oscillator, let the gate delay for a single inverter be 20 ns, and let the gate delay for a NOR gate be 30 ns. Determine countdown integer n and the number of inverters in the cross-coupled paths required to realize the signals specified in Fig. EX7-11b.

FIGURE EX7-10

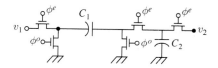

FIGURE EX7-11

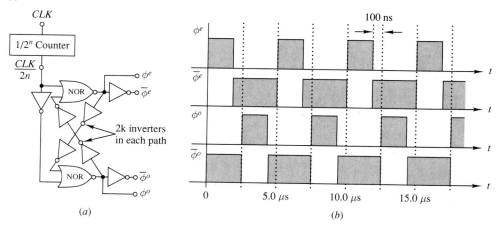

(a)

(b)

7-12 Our objective is to design double-poly CMOS capacitor arrays using the matched layout structure in Fig. 7-4e. Let the unit capacitance, with minimum sized contacts and dimension a, be a square with $b = 20$ μm, realizing $C_U = 1.2$ pF. Draw the layouts that realize capacitors of values
   a 6.25 pF;
   b 12.867 pF.
   All dimensions are to be rounded to a grid of 0.25 μm.

7-13 Let the unit capacitance in Exercise 7-12 have an absolute accuracy of ±2 percent. If a capacitance ratio is to be $N + x$, with $x < 1$, determine the minimum value for x that can be resolved. Assume that all dimensions are rounded to a grid of 0.25 μm and that the oxide layers in both capacitors are identical.

7-14 Consider the NMOS analog switch scheme in Fig. EX7-14. For the nMOST, let $V_t = 0.7$ V, $K = 10$ μA/V^2. The substrate is biased at -3 V. Let control ϕ be $+3$ V or -3 V:
   a for $\phi = 3$ V, calculate the switch resistance and v_{OUT} when $v_S = +3$ V, 0 V, and -3 V;
   b for $\phi = -3$ V, calculate the switch resistance and V_{OUT} when $V_S = +3$ V, 0 V, and -3 V; and
   c discuss the viability of this scheme as an analog switch.

7-15 Consider the CMOS analog switch scheme in Fig. EX7-15. For the nMOST and pMOST, let $|V_t| = 0.7$ V, $K = 10$ μA/V^2, the backgate biases be -3 V and $+3$ V, respectively. Let controls ϕ, $\bar{\phi}$ be $\pm$ 3 V.
   a For $\phi = 3$ V and $\bar{\phi} = -3$ V, calculate the switch resistance and v_{OUT} when $v_S = +3$ V, 0 V, and -3 V;
   b for $\phi = -3$ V and $\bar{\phi} = +3$ V, calculate the switch resistance and v_{OUT} when $v_S = +3$ V, 0 V, and -3 V; and
   c discuss the viability of this scheme as an analog switch.

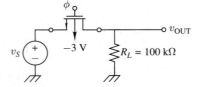

FIGURE EX7-14

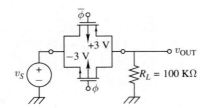

FIGURE EX7-15

7-16 For the nMOST analog switch in Exercise 7-14 and $\phi = +3$ V, determine the range of v_S for which the switch resistance is less than 25 kΩ.

7-17 The CMOS analog switch in Fig. EX7-15 has the same device specifications as that in Exercise 7-15. This switch connects a sinusoidal source $v_S = 0.5 \sin \omega t$ to a capacitive load, represented by $C_L = 100$ pF. Determine the 3 dB bandwidth of this switch.

7-18 Consider the continuous-time signal

$$x(t) = 2\cos(200\pi t) + 3\sin(600\pi t) + 4\cos(1200\pi t) \qquad (EX7\text{-}1)$$

   a Determine the Nyquist rate for this signal;
   b If the sampling frequency is $f_s = 500$ Hz, determine the discrete-time signal obtained after sampling.

7-19 Determine the z-transforms for the following sample-data signals.
   a $x(k) = \{0, 1, -2, 3, -4, 0, 6, 0\}$ for $k = 0, \dots, 7$.
   b $x(k) = \delta(k)$, i.e., $x(k) = 1$ for $k = 0$ and $x(k) = 0$ for $k \neq 0$.
   c $x(k) = \delta(k - n)$, i.e., $x(k) = 1$ for $k = n$ and $x(k) = 0$ for $k \neq n$.
   d $x(k) = u(k)$, i.e., $x(k) = 1$ for $k \geq 0$.
   e $x(k) = u(k - n)$, i.e., $x(k) = 1$ for $k \geq n$ and $x(k) = 0$ for $k < n$.

7-20 Determine the z-transform for the samples obtained when the following continuous-time signals are sampled at $f_s = 1/T$:
   a $x(t) = \alpha^{t/T} u(t)$, where α is real.
   b $x(t) = \{1 - e^{-\beta t}\} u(t)$, where β is real
   c $x(t) = \sin \omega_0 t u(t)$.
   Note that $u(t)$ is the unit step function (i.e. $u(t) = 0$ for $t < 0$ and $u(t) = 1$ for $t \geq 0$).

7-21 Identify the filter types and plot the gain and phase responses for the pole-zero patterns in Fig. EX7-21. Assume that the in-band gains are 0 dB.

FIGURE EX7-21   where:
(a) $p_1, p_1* = -0.3 \pm j1.0$, $p_2 = -2.0$, $z_1 = 2.0$,

(b) for $T = 0.1$ sec, $p_1, p_1* = 0.8\, e^{\pm j0.10}$, $p_2, p_2* = 0.8\, e^{j0.12}$, $z_1, z_1* = e^{\pm j0.13}$,

(c) $p_1, p_1* = -0.2 \pm j0.9$, $p_2, p_2* = -0.2 \pm j1.1$,

(d) for $T = 0.4$ sec, $p_1, p_1* = 0.95\, e^{\pm j0.12}$, $p_2, p_2* = 0.95\, e^{\pm j0.14}$, $z_1, z_1* = e^{\pm j0.125}$, z_2, $z_2* = e^{j\pm j0.135}$.

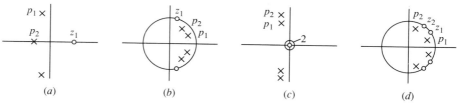

   (a)   (b)   (c)   (d)

7-22 Use the bilinear transform to translate the continuous-time transfer function $H(s)$ in Eq. EX7-2 into the z-domain.

$$H(s) = \frac{(2\pi 10^3)^3}{(s + 2\pi 10^3)(s^2 + (2\pi 100)s + (2\pi 10^3)^2)} \tag{EX7-2}$$

a determine $H(z)$ for $f_s = 3$ kHz, 8 kHz, 128 kHz.

b It will simplify the implementation of $H(z)$ if the zeros at $f_s/2$ are replaced by kz^{-2}. Determine the value for k for each $H(z)$ in **a**.

c Calculate the errors in $|H(z)|$ at 1 kHz and 3 kHz associated with the approximation in **b**.

7-23 Derive Eq. (7-28).

7-24 Consider the filter specifications in Fig. EX7-24: Find the minimum filter orders (N_{MF}, N_{EL}) required to realize maximally flat (*MF*) and elliptic (*EL*) filters, respectively, which satisfy these specifications.

7-25 Find the $H(s)$ for a highpass filter that satisfies the specifications in Fig. EX7-25. In addition, the passband is to be equi-ripple and the stopband rolloff is to be monotonic:

a determine the normalized lowpass prototype specifications;

b determine the normalized lowpass prototype $H_{LP}(\bar{s})$;

c determine the normalized highpass $H_{HP}(s)$, such that $20\log|H_{HP}(j\infty)| = 0$ dB.

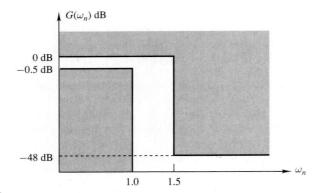

FIGURE EX7-24

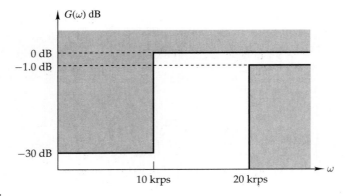

FIGURE EX7-25

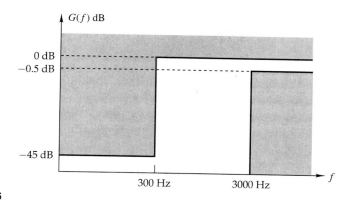

FIGURE EX7-26

7-26 An HP Butterworth filter is to be designed to realize the specifications in Fig. EX7-26. Determine the $H(s)$.

7-27 Determine the Chebyshev $H(s)$ that realizes the filter specifications in Fig. EX7-27.

7-28 Use the bilinear transform to translate the $H(s)$ determined in Exercise 7-25 to an $H(z)$:
a for $f_s = 8$ kHz; and
b $f_s = 128$ kHz.
(Note; this exercise can be accomplished using a symbolic math software tool, such as Mathematica. We encourage students to use such tools when appropriate.)

7-29 Derive the pole locations for the $H(z)$'s obtained from the continuous-time prototype

$$H(s) = \frac{(7\pi \times 10^3)^2}{s^2 + 3.5\pi \times 10^2 s + (7\pi \times 10^3)^2} \qquad \text{(EX7-3)}$$

and $f_s = 16$ kHz, using:
a the forward Euler mapping;
b the backward Euler mapping; and
c the bilinear transform.
Compare and discuss the results of **a** through **c**.

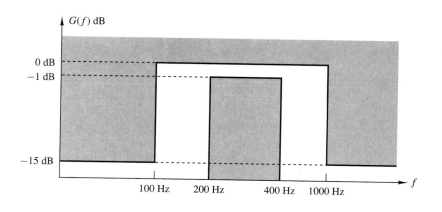

FIGURE EX7-27

7-30 Simpson's integration rule is well-known in numerical analysis as a discrete-time approximation for continuous-time integration. This rule can be expressed as follows

$$s = \frac{3}{T} \left(\frac{1 - z^{-2}}{1 + 4z^{-1} + z^{-2}} \right) \qquad (EX7-4)$$

a Determine the magnitude and phase errors ($\varepsilon(\omega)$ and $\varphi(\omega)$, respectively), as defined in Eq. (7-33).

b Compare the result of **a** with errors associated with the transformations in Table 7-8.

c Describe the advantages and disadvantages of using Eq. (EX7-4) to synthesize sample-data filters.

7-31 Consider the closed-loop amplifier circuit in Fig. EX7-31, where the op amp open-loop gain is $A_0 = 1000$ and the feedback $\beta = 0.01$. If the maximum peak-to-peak output voltage swing is 5 V and the total input referred noise is $\overline{v_{ni}} = 10 \ \mu$V rms, determine the circuit's dynamic range.

7-32 Let output voltage follower in Fig. EX7-32 be sampled at rate f_s and the output noise of the op amp be characterized as follows $\overline{dv_{no}} = 10 \ \mu$V$_{\text{RMS}}/\sqrt{\text{Hz}}$ @ 100 Hz, $0.1 \ \mu$V$_{\text{RMS}}/\sqrt{\text{Hz}}$ @ 10 KHz, and $0.1 \ \mu$V$_{\text{RMS}}/\sqrt{\text{Hz}}$ @ $f > 10$ kHz. Plot the sampled noise for $f_s = 8$ kHz, 16 kHz, and 128 kHz. Assume $\sin x / x = 1$ for all f and that the op amp has a DC gain of $A_0 = 1000$ and a noise bandwidth of 20 MHz.

7-33 Derive Eqs. (7-51a) through (7-51d).

7-34 For a second-order $H(z)$ of the form in Eq. (7-13b), derive the sensitivities of $H(z)$ with respect to $\theta_0, r_p, \theta_N, r_z$ that correspond to the results in Eqs. (7-52).

7-35 Verify that capacitor D in Fig. 7-24 operates as indicated in Fig. 7-33b, and capacitor D in Fig. 7-23 operates as described in Fig. 7-33a.

7-36 Derive the four-port and two-port z-domain equivalent circuits in Fig. 7-33.

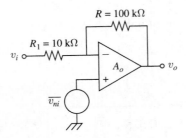

FIGURE EX7-31

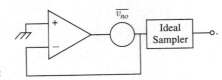

FIGURE EX7-32

7-37 Determine the behavior of the switched-capacitor circuit in Fig. EX7-37:
   a draw the z-domain equivalent circuit;
   b determine the voltage transfer function $H(z) = V_{\text{out}}^e / V_{\text{in}}^e$. Assume that the op amp is ideal.

7-38 Consider the switched-capacitor summing amplifier in Fig. EX7-38, where C_p is a parasitic capacitance associated with the integrated circuit implementation, V_{OFF} is the input referred DC offset of the op amp, and A_0 is the op amp's DC gain:
   a draw the z-domain equivalent circuit;
   b derive the output voltage v_o^e in terms of the inputs v_1^e, v_2^e, v_3^e, v_4^e, and V_{OFF};
   c determine the ideal relationship in **b** when $C_p = 0$, $A_0 = 0$, $V_{\text{OFF}} = 0$.

7-39 Derive the PSD for the output noise of the active-SC integrator in Fig. EX7-39. Assume that the SW2 and the op amp are noiseless, SW1 has an ON resistance of R, the sample rate is $f_s = 1/T$, ϕ^e, ϕ^o are 50 percent duty-cycle clocks, and the op amp $A(s) = \omega_t/s$.

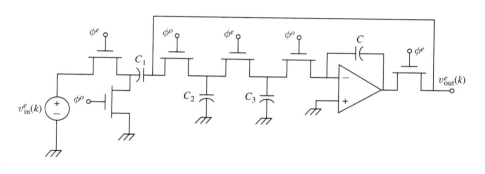

FIGURE EX7-37

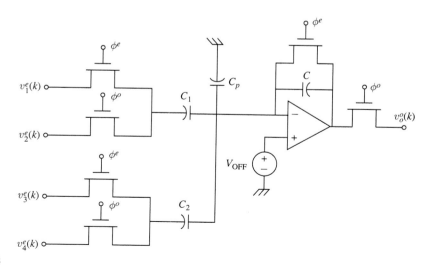

FIGURE EX7-38

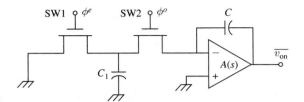

7-40 The equivalent circuits in Fig. 7-32 can be used to model switched-capacitor elements for SPICE simulations.

a Modify the equivalent circuit schematics so that they can be coded as SPICE subcircuits;

b derive the appropriate SPICE code for the subcircuits; and

c simulate the switched-capacitor circuit in Fig. 7-33 using **b**.

(*Hint:* the transmission line model can be used to model $z^{-1} = e^{-j\omega T}$ and $z^{-1/2} = e^{-j\omega T/2}$; and charges can be converted to equivalent scaled-currents).

APPENDIX 7-1: Sampled-Data Signals and Systems

This appendix provides the necessary working background needed to understand and design sampled-data systems, e.g., the switched-capacitor filters in Chaps. 7 and 8. A complete treatment of sampled-data signals and filters would consume an entire book, and as such, is beyond the scope of this text. A comfortable working knowledge of the material in this appendix is the minimum prerequisite to the successful study of the concepts in Chaps. 7 and 8. Although an increasing number of electrical engineering students are studying sampled systems during their undergraduate curriculum, many readers will not have had suffcient exposure to this material when they reach the senior undergraduate or first-year graduate levels. Consequently, we include this material in this text in order to ensure that all readers start with a sufficient baseline knowledge in this important area. Those readers seeking more depth in this area are referred to such excellent texts as Tretter (1976).

A7-1-1 Terminology and Intuition

At this point it is important to clearly distinguish between *continuous-time analog*, *discrete-time* (or *sampled-data digital*) and *sampled-data analog* filters. A system, such as a filter, is said to be a continuous-time analog (or *continuous-time* or, in brief, *continuous*) if the input signal x_{in} and output signal x_{out} are continuous waveforms as shown in Fig. A7-1a. In other words, x_{in} and x_{out} are continuously variable in both amplitude and time. In our mathematical formulae, we make the continuous change in time evident by writing x_{in} and x_{out} as functions of continuous-time variable t, i.e., $x_{in} = x_{in}(t)$ and $x_{out} = x_{out}(t)$. The continuous amplitude is understood in the notation.

In sampled-data filters (analog and digital), the input and output signals are defined by sets of instantaneous values or "snap shots" recorded at discrete, usually periodic, instants. One signal snap shot is referred to as a *sample* and the process of acquiring samples is referred to as *sampling*. The sampled waveforms typically associated with sampled-data digital and analog filters are illustrated in Figs. A7-1b and A7-1c, respectively. Only the signal samples are observable in discrete-time or sampled-data digital filters (or more

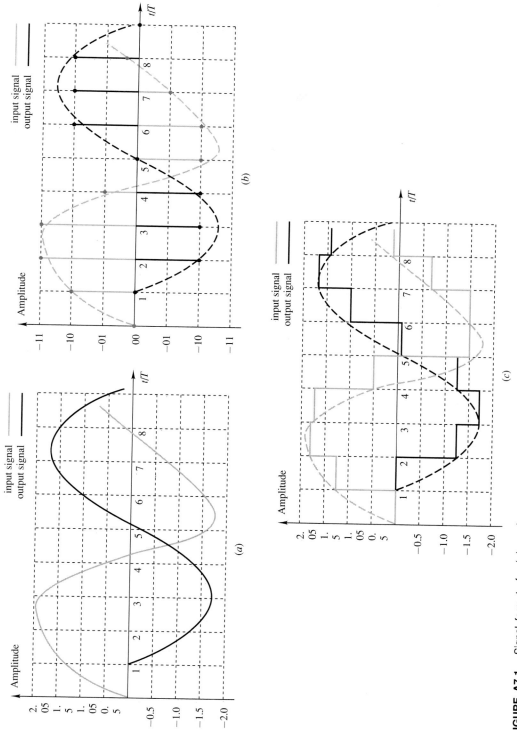

FIGURE A7-1 Signal formats for (a) continuous-time analog, (b) sampled-data digital, and (c) sampled-data analog filters.

simply *digital filters*). Furthermore, the amplitudes of digital signals can assume only a finite number of distinct values. The assignment of specific discrete values of amplitude to ranges of continuous amplitude is referred to as *quantization*. For example, samples quantized to 8 bits must be assigned to one of $2^8 = 256$ distinct levels, or distinct 8 bit digital words. Hence, digital signals are discrete in both time and amplitude. In our mathematical formulae we make the discrete change in time evident by writing x_{in} and x_{out} as functions of sample times ($t = kT$) or the discrete-time integer variable (k), i.e.,

$$x_{in}(k) = x_{in}(kT) \quad \text{and} \quad x_{out}(k) = x_{out}(kT) \qquad (A7\text{-}1)$$

where $k = \text{integer}[t/T]$. The time interval T between successive samples is called the *sampling period* or *sample interval*, and the reciprocal of the sampling period $1/T = f_s$ is called the *sampling rate* (samples per second) or the *sampling frequency* (hertz). Please note that $t = kT$, (for $k = 0, 1, \ldots, \infty$), are the actual sampled time instants in seconds, while integer k represents normalized time that is unitless. When describing digital signals, the discrete amplitude (typically expressed in binary arithmetic), is understood in the notation in Eq. (A7-1).

Digital filters can be implemented using robust digital VLSI. Consequently, they have become very important and are being used in a growing list of applications (Tretter 1976). Since this book's focus is on analog integrated circuits and systems, digital filters will not be discussed further, except when used for comparison, where appropriate.

In sampled-data analog filters, which are truly analog systems, amplitude is continuous and sampling time is discrete. Moreover, unlike digital signals in Fig. A7-1b, sampled-data analog (or more simply *sampled-analog*) signals are well defined at all times in between the discrete sampling instants. In particular, such signals are typically held constant between samples; i.e., $x(t) \equiv x(kT)$ for all $kT < t < (k + 1)T$, as illustrated in Fig. A7-1c. In many cases, sampled analog signals are described in terms of their samples exclusively, using the notation in Eq. (A7-1). Continuous amplitude is understood when we use this notation to describe sampled analog signals.

When we refer to a total sampled-analog signal, defined over continuous-time (i.e., the samples plus all in between values of the waveform), typically we use a modified continuous-time notation of the form

$$x_{in}^{\#}(t) \quad \text{and} \quad x_{out}^{\#}(t) \qquad (A7\text{-}2)$$

The superscript (#) is used in various texts to distinguish sampled analog signals from smooth continuous signals. These signals are sometimes referred to as the *reconstructed signals*. In fact, the *construction* or *reconstruction* of continuous, like signals (of the form shown in Fig. A7-1c) from their respective samples, is inherent to all sampled analog systems. Later in this section we will develop mathematical models for sampling, reconstruction, and other important concepts associated with sampled-data signals and filters.

An important mathematical distinction between continuous-time and sampled-data (analog and digital) systems, is the fact that continuous-time systems are characterized by differential equations and sampled systems are characterized by difference equations. In performing numerical analysis we routinely convert continuous-time differential and integral equations to difference equations for solution, using digital computers. Hence, those who have used the trapezoidal rule, or some other numerical integration algorithm, to compute $y = \int_0^T f(\tau)d\tau$ on a personal computer or programmable calculator have applied sampled-data processing techniques. An interesting exercise is to numerically integrate a function $f(t)$ that can be easily integrated by hand or with the aid of a table as well. We can then compare the hand-calculated (or exact) result with the numerical result as the integration step size ($\Delta\tau \approx d\tau$) is decreased within the interval 0, T. In this exercise we would notice that the difference between the exact and numerical results reduces as the step size decreases, or, in other words, as the number of samples increases. This phenomenon has important ramifications in the performance and design of sampled-data filters, as we will uncover in later sections of this appendix.

To gain further insight into the operation of sampling, let us consider a simple example where we consider the sampling of continuous-time sinusoidal signal

$$x(t) = A\cos(\omega_a t + \phi) = A\cos(2\pi f_a t + \phi) \tag{A7-3}$$

at the sampling rate of f_s samples per second. Let us first determine the expression for the samples $x(k)$. Substituting $t = kT$ into the expression for $x(t)$ yields the following expression for the samples $x(kT), k = 0, 1, 2, \cdots, \infty$

$$x(k) = A\cos(2\pi f_a kT + \phi) = A\cos\left(\frac{2\pi f_a}{f_s}k + \phi\right) \tag{A7-4}$$

Let us now examine two numerical cases of Eq. (A7-4); namely,

$$x_0(t): \quad \text{with } A_0 = 1, \phi_0 = 0°, f_s = 40 \text{ Hz, and } f_a = f_0 = 10 \text{ Hz};$$

and

$$x_1(t): \quad \text{with } A_1 = 1, \phi_1 = 0°, f_s = 40 \text{ Hz, but } f_a = f_1 = 50 \text{ Hz.}$$

The expressions for $x_0(t)$, $x_1(t)$ and the samples $x_0(k)$, $x_1(k)$ are determined by substituting their values for A, ϕ, f_s, and f_a into Eqs. (A7-3) and (A7-4), respectively. That is,

$$x_0(t) = \cos(20\pi t) \quad \text{and} \quad x_0(k) = \cos\left(\frac{20\pi}{40}k\right) = \cos\left(\frac{\pi}{2}k\right) \tag{A7-5}$$

where the samples $x_0(k)$ are spaced $T = 0.025$ seconds apart, or four times per signal period ($T_0 = 1/f_0 = 0.1$ seconds), and

$$x_1(t) = \cos(100\pi t) \quad \text{and} \quad x_1(k) = \cos\left(\frac{100\pi}{40}k\right) = \cos\left(\frac{5\pi}{2}k\right) \tag{A7-6}$$

where the samples $x_1(k)$ occur only 0.8 times per signal period (or four samples per five signal periods).

Using the trigonometric identity $\cos(\alpha k \pm 2\pi k) = \cos(\alpha k)$, and recognizing that $(5\pi/2)k = (\pi/2)k + 2\pi k$, Eq. (A7-6) can be rewritten as

$$x_1(k) = \cos\left(\frac{\pi}{2} + 2\pi\right)k = \cos\left(\frac{\pi}{2}k\right) \tag{A7-7}$$

Comparing the results in (A7-5) and (A7-7), we see the remarkable result that sampling continuous signals $x_0(t)$ and $x_1(t)$ at $f_s = 40$ Hz produces identical samples $x_0(k) = x_1(k)$. But we know $x_0(t) \neq x_1(t)$. This example demonstrates an important phenomenon peculiar to sampled-data systems, refered to as *aliasing*.

Conceptually, aliasing is an ambiguity in the sampling process that occurs when the continuous analog signal sampled has large spectral components at frequencies too high for the sampling process to accurately resolve. This is demonstrated graphically in Fig. A7-2. Here signals $x_1(t)$ and $x_2(t)$ are sampled at frequency $f_s = 1/T$ and quantized to 2 bit digital words, yielding the samples $x_1(k)$ and $x_2(k)$ for $k = 0, 1, \ldots, 7$. We observe that $x_1(k)$ is a much closer approximation to $x_1(t)$ than $x_2(k)$ is to $x_2(t)$. The sampling operation is too slow to accurately follow the high-frequency variation in x_2. Moreover, the sampling process interprets the high-frequency components of x_2 to be at much lower frequencies. To be more precise, these high-frequency components are translated or aliased into the baseband frequency range $|f| < f_c$. For now it suffices to define f_c as the highest frequency component in continuous signal x_i that can be sampled unambiguously at sampling rate f_s. The exact mathematical relationship between f_c and f_s required for unambiguous sampling will be derived later.

In the numerical example we showed that with sampling frequency $f_s = 40$ Hz, the samples for a 50 Hz sinusoidal signal were identical to those of a 10 Hz sinusoidal signal. In other words, the 50 Hz signal was translated or aliased down to 10 Hz, i.e., $f_1 = 50$ Hz is said to be an alias of the frequency $f_0 = 10$ Hz. This result is due to the trigonometric identity $\cos(\alpha k \pm 2\pi k) = \cos(\alpha k)$. The concept can be readily generalized to sampled sinusoidal signals separated by n multiples of 2π, or $\pm 2n\pi$, (i.e., $\pm 2\pi, \pm 4\pi, \pm 6\pi$, etc.). That is,

$$A \cos\left(\frac{2\pi f_0}{f_s} k\right) = A \cos\left(\frac{2\pi f_0}{f_s} k \pm 2n\pi k\right) = A \cos\left(2\pi \left[\frac{f_0 \pm nf_s}{f_s}\right] k\right)$$

In other words, sinusoids (or spectral components of more complex signals) at frequencies $f_n = f_0 + nf_s$, where $n = 0, 1, 2, 3, \ldots$, yield identical samples when sampled at f_s. Hence, all the frequencies f_n are aliases of the frequency f_0. In the case where $f_s = 40$ Hz and $f_0 = 10$ Hz, the frequencies 50 Hz, 90 Hz, 130 Hz, 170 Hz, $\ldots$, and so on, are all seen to be aliases of the baseband frequency 10 Hz.

In any event, it should be clear at this point that aliasing is detrimental. If left unremedied, aliasing results in undesired and uncorrectable behavior. Since aliasing cannot be removed once it occurs, it must be prevented. The act of preventing aliasing is called *anti-aliasing*. Let us interrupt our consideration of these topics in order to develop the mathematical background to pursue them more rigorously.

A7-1-2 Sampling: A Mathematical Model

Mathematically, let us consider an ideal impulse sampling process that extracts from the signal $x(t)$ a sequence of values $\{x(kT)\}$ at the periodic sampling instants $t = kT$. A convenient model is derived by considering the sampled signal $x^{\#}(t)$ to be the product of the continuous signal $x(t)$ and the impulse-sampling function $s(t)$ as shown in Fig. A7-3, i.e.,

$$x^{\#}(t) = x(t)s(t) \tag{A7-8a}$$

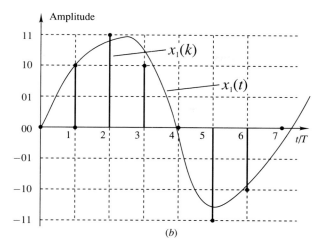

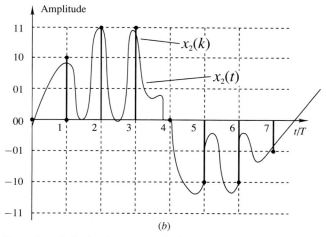

FIGURE A7-2 Examples of aliasing in two sampled systems, where $x_1(t)$ and $x_2(t)$ are continuous-time signals and $x_1(k)$, $x_2(k)$ are digital samples.

where

$$s(t) = \sum_{k=-\infty}^{\infty} \delta(t - kT) \tag{A7-8b}$$

Hence, the sampled signal $x^{\#}(t)$ is written

$$x^{\#}(t) = x(t) \sum_{k=-\infty}^{\infty} \delta(t - kT) = \sum_{k=-\infty}^{\infty} x(t)\delta(t - kT) \tag{A7-9}$$

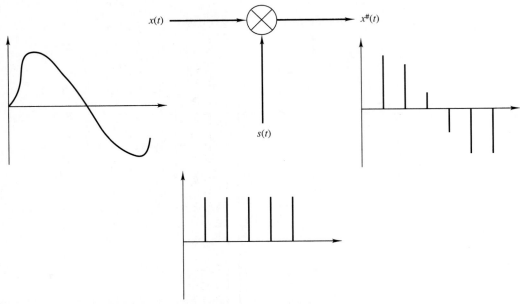

FIGURE A7-3   Modeling the sampling operation as a modulation process.

Using the definition[10] of the delta function, Eq. (A7-9) is rewritten

$$x^{\#}(t) = \sum_{k=-\infty}^{\infty} x(kT)\delta(t - kT) \qquad \text{(A7-10)}$$

From Eq. (A7-10) we see that the sampled signal $x^{\#}$ is an idealized analog signal comprised of a weighted periodic train of impulses with amplitudes equal to the samples of $x(t)$. This is illustrated in Fig. (A7-3). The samples $x(kT)$ in Eq. (A7-10) form an ideal discrete-time sequence. Sampling in switched-capacitor filters is nearly ideal; hence, it is accurately represented by this impulse model. We note that in the case of digital filters, the samples $x(kT)$ would be quantized to N-bit words.

---

[10]Note that the delta function $\delta(t - kT)$ is defined such that

$$\int_{-\infty}^{\infty} \delta(t - kT)dt = 1 \qquad \text{for } t = kT$$

$$= 0 \qquad \text{for } t \neq kT$$

Since the sampling function is periodic, it can be expressed as a Fourier series, i.e.,

$$s(t) = \frac{1}{T} \sum_{k=-\infty}^{\infty} e^{jk\omega_s t} \tag{A7-11}$$

where $C_k = 1/T$ are the Fourier coefficients and $\omega_s = 2\pi f_s = 2\pi/T$ is the sampling frequency in radians-per-second. Substituting Eq. (A7-11) into Eq. (A7-8a) yields

$$x^{\#}(t) = \frac{1}{T} \sum_{k=-\infty}^{\infty} x(t) e^{jk\omega_s t} \tag{A7-12}$$

Taking the Fourier transform of $x^{\#}(t)$, we can derive several important frequency-domain properties of sampled signals. We know that the Fourier transform of a continuous signal $x(t)$ is $\mathbf{F}[x(t)] = X(j\omega)$. In contrast, the Fourier transform of the sampled signal is

$$\begin{aligned} X^{\#}(j\omega) = \mathbf{F}[x^{\#}(t)] &= \mathbf{F}\left[\frac{1}{T} \sum_{k=-\infty}^{\infty} x(t) e^{jk\omega_s t} \right] \\ &= \frac{1}{T} \sum_{k=-\infty}^{\infty} \mathbf{F}[x(t)] e^{jk\omega_s t} \\ &= \frac{1}{T} \sum_{k=-\infty}^{\infty} X(j\omega - jk\omega_s) \end{aligned} \tag{A7-13}$$

From Eq. (A7-13) we see that the sampling operation has introduced new spectral components that arise from the translations of the baseband spectrum $X(j\omega)$ to integer multiples or harmonics of the sampling frequency ω_s. Reflecting on the harmonically rich $x^{\#}(t)$, illustrated in Fig. A7-3, this spectral enhancement is an appropriate result.

To observe the practical significance of Eq. (A7-13), let us contrast the sketch of the spectrum for a continuous bandlimited signal $x(t)$, where $X(j\omega) = 0$ for $|\omega| > \omega_c$, with a sketch of spectrum that results when bandlimited $x(t)$ is sampled at frequency ω_s. Let us first consider the case where the sampling frequency is $\omega_s < 2\omega_c$. These spectra are sketched in Figs. A7-4a and A7-4b, respectively. In Fig. A7-4b we observe that $X^{\#}(j\omega)$ is comprised of repeated translations of the baseband $X(j\omega)$. Moreover, we observe that these repeated baseband spectra overlap. This overlap is a graphic representation of the aliasing phenomenon we conceptualized earlier. Aliasing is seen to introduce an ambiguity into $X^{\#}(j\omega)$ and prevents the eventual recovery of the baseband spectrum $X(j\omega)$. If we increase the sampling frequency to $\omega_s > 2\omega_c$, than the repeated spectra are spread apart such that the overlap disappears, as shown in Fig. A7-4c. In this case the baseband spectrum $X(j\omega)$ can be fully recovered or reconstructed by passing $X^{\#}(j\omega)$ through a continuous lowpass filter of the form shown in Fig. A7-5. The critical sampling frequency $\omega_s = 2\omega_c$ is referred to as the *Nyquist frequency* (ω_{NY}), i.e.

$$\omega_{NY} = 2\omega_c \tag{A7-14}$$

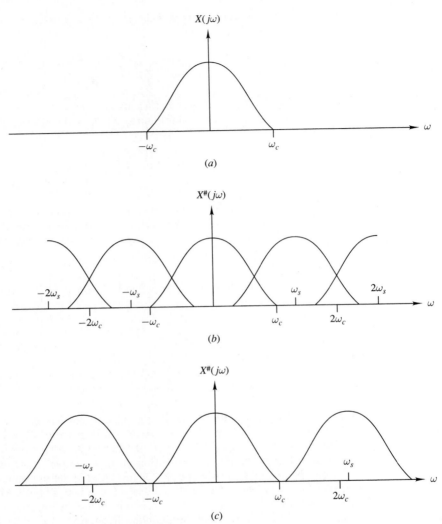

FIGURE A7-4 Spectra for (a) continuous baseband signal $x(t)$, (b) $x(t)$ sampled at $\omega_s < 2\omega_c$, and (c) $x(t)$ sampled at $\omega_s > 2\omega_c$.

Hence, to avoid aliasing, the baseband cutoff must be restricted to $\omega_c \leq \omega_s/2$. If we include both positive and negative frequencies as in Fig. A7-4, the unambiguous limits of the baseband frequency range is

$$-\frac{\omega_s}{2} \leq \omega \leq \frac{\omega_s}{2} \quad \text{or} \quad |\omega| \leq \frac{\omega_s}{2}$$

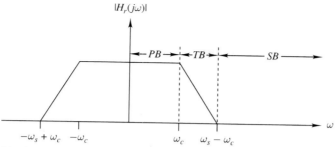

FIGURE A7-5   Sketch of reconstruction filter with transfer function $H_r(j\omega)$, showing positive and negative ω. Note that the abbreviations PB refers to pass band, TB refers to transition band, and SB refers to stop band.

The half-sampling frequency $\omega_s/2$ (or $f_s/2$) is also referred to as the *folding frequency*. Figures A7-4b and A7-4c demonstrate the *Sampling Theorem*[11] established by C. E. Shannon in 1948. The band-limiting of continuous signals to ω_c is achieved by prefiltering (filtering prior to sampling) $x(t)$ with a continuous-time lowpass filter of the type pictured in Fig. A7-5. This prefilter is referred to as an *anti-aliasing filter*. An anti-aliasing filter is one of the essential overhead functions required of all sampled-data systems. Observe that $\omega_s = \omega_{NY}$ is an impractical sampling rate, since this would require the anti-aliasing filter to be an unrealizable brick wall or rectangular filter with discontinuous rolloff at $\omega = \omega_c$. If $\omega_s > \omega_{NY}$, then the anti-aliasing filter can have a finite rolloff and it is realizable. If we further increase ω_s, the anti-aliasing filter can be allowed to rolloff more slowly, and it can be realized with lower order (i.e., fewer components, less silicon area, and less cost).

The tradeoffs associated with sampling frequency vary considerably with the particular implementing technology. For example, in switched-capacitor filters it is not unusual for $\omega_s \gg \omega_{NY}$, perhaps as large as $\omega_s = 20\omega_{NY}$ to $50\omega_{NY}$. Digital filters, implemented in a programmable Digital Signal Processor (DSP) device, such as the Texas Instruments TMS320^{TM}, will usually sample at $\omega_s = 1.5\omega_{NY}$ to $2\omega_{NY}$. Consequently, anti-aliasing for switched-capacitor filters is usually achieved with simple first- and second-order lowpass filters, whereas anti-aliasing for a digital filter could require a fifth-order (or higher) lowpass filter.

To illustrate some of the concepts discussed in this section, let us consider the following signal example

$$x(t) = 2\cos(200\pi t) + 3\sin(600\pi t) + 4\cos(1200\pi t) \qquad \text{(A7-15)}$$

What is the Nyquist rate for this signal? If the sampling frequency is $f_s = 500$ Hz, determine the discrete-time signal obtained after sampling.

---

[11]The Sampling Theorem states that a function $x(t)$, having a Fourier spectrum $X(j\omega)$ such that $X(j\omega) = 0$ for $\omega > \omega_c$, is uniquely described by knowledge of its values at uniformly spaced time instants $T = 2\pi/\omega_s$ with $\omega_s > 2\omega_c$.

The signal $x(t)$ in Eq. (A7-15) is seen to be comprised of components at $f_1 = 100$ Hz, $f_2 = 300$ Hz, and $f_3 = 600$ Hz. Thus, the Nyquist rate is $f_{NY} = 2f_3 = 1200$ Hz. Since $f_s = 500$ Hz $< f_{NY}$, aliasing will occur. Since $f_s/2 = 250$ Hz, the 300 Hz and 500 Hz components will alias into lower frequencies. Using Eq. (A7-5), we can write the sampled signal in the following form

$$x(k) = 2\cos\left(\frac{2\pi}{5}k\right) + 3\sin\left(\frac{6\pi}{5}k\right) + 4\cos\left(\frac{12\pi}{5}k\right)$$

$$= 2\cos\left(\frac{2\pi}{5}k\right) + 3\sin\left(2\pi k - \frac{4\pi}{5}k\right) + 4\cos\left(2\pi k + \frac{2\pi}{5}k\right)$$

To demonstrate the aliasing, let us apply the trigonometric identities $\cos(\alpha k \pm 2\pi k) = \cos(\alpha k)$ and $\sin(\alpha k \pm 2\pi k) = \pm\sin(\alpha k)$, i.e.,

$$x(k) = 2\cos\left(\frac{2\pi}{5}k\right) + 3\sin\left(\frac{-4\pi}{5}k\right) + 4\cos\left(\frac{2\pi}{5}k\right)$$

$$= 6\cos\left(\frac{2\pi}{5}k\right) - 3\sin\left(\frac{4\pi}{5}k\right) \qquad (A7-16)$$

We see that the 600 Hz component has aliased down to 100 Hz and been added to the original 100 Hz component. The 300 Hz component is aliased down to 200 Hz and is reversed in sign. Clearly the original $x(t)$ in Eq. (A7-15) cannot be recovered from $x(k)$ in Eq. (A7-16), or if $f_s < f_{NY}$.

A7-1-3   Reconstruction in Analog Sampled-Data Systems

The construct of a sampled-data $x^\#(t)$ from the $x(k)$, and ultimately the recovery $x(t)$, are operations referred to as *reconstruction*. Conceptually, reconstruction is best described as the interpolation or smoothing of the sampled signal in continuous time. Some form of reconstruction occurs naturally in analog sampled-data systems and it can be enhanced by design with additional lowpass filtering. It is interesting to note that the observation of a sampled signal using a display device such as an oscilloscope, inherently involves recon-struction. We further note that, although ideal, impulse sampling does occur in practice, an ideal impulse reconstructed $x^\#(t)$ requires unlimited bandwidth and is not physically possible. However, it can be approximated with narrow pulse reconstruction where the weighted impulses in Fig. A7-3 are replaced by weighted finite width pulses.

The holding of the signal constant in between samples, as shown in Fig. A7-1c, is a widely used form of reconstruction called a *zero-order-hold* or *sample-and-hold* re-construction. This form of reconstruction occurs inherently in many types of switched-capacitor filters. If additional reconstruction is required, e.g., further smoothing of the sampled-data $x^\#(t)$ in Fig. A7-1c to achieve a smoothly variable or baseband-like $x(t)$ in Fig. A7-1a, than $x^\#(t)$ is to be processed by a continuous-time lowpass filter. This continuous-time lowpass filter is referred to as a *reconstruction filter*, i.e., the filter H_r sketched in Fig. A7-5. The reconstruction filter is designed to attenuate the high-frequency components of $X^\#(j\omega)$, as deemed necessary to achieve the desired amount of smooth-ing or reconstruction. Meanwhile, the baseband components are passed as unaffected as possible.

Let us study the sample-and-hold reconstruction in greater detail, since it occurs often in switched-capacitor filters. This process is demonstrated in Fig. A7-6. To start, consider the impulse response $h_0(t)$ for the sample-and-hold, a pulse of unit amplitude, which starts at time $t = 0$ and falls abruptly to zero at time $t = T$ as shown in Fig A7-6a, i.e.,

$$h_0(t) = 1 \qquad \text{for} \qquad 0 \le t < T$$

$$\text{(A7-17)}$$

$$0 \qquad \text{for} \qquad t > T$$

Referring to Fig. A7-1c, we note that if the sampling period T is made small enough (i.e., the sampling rate becomes large enough), the reconstructed signal is smoothed to closely approximate the continuous signal. Hence, the requirements for a particular reconstruction filter are seen to be tightly coupled to the sampling rate.

The frequency response for the sample-and-hold $H_0(j\omega)$ is determined by taking the Fourier transform of the impulse response $h_0(t)$ in Fig. A7-6a. The resulting

$$H_0(j\omega) = T \frac{1 - e^{j\omega T}}{j\omega T} = T e^{-j\omega T/2} \sin c \left(\frac{\omega T}{2} \right) \qquad \text{(A7-18a)}$$

and

$$|H_0(j\omega)| = T \left| \sin c \left(\frac{\omega T}{2} \right) \right| \qquad \text{(A7-18b)}$$

where $\sin c \ \omega T/2 = \left[(\sin \omega T/2) / (\omega T/2) \right]$. The sin c argument can be expressed in terms of f in Hz by replacing $\omega = 2\pi f$ so that $\omega T/2 = \pi f T = \pi f/f_s$. Note that if the hold time is less than full period T, i.e., τT where $\tau < 1$ is the fraction of the period that the signal is held, the amplitude of H_0 and the argument for the sinc function are scaled by τ. The magnitude response $|H_0(j\omega)|$ is shown in Fig. A7-6b. The spectrum of the reconstructed signal $|X_r(j\omega)|$, sketched in Fig. A7-6c, is then the product of the impulse-sampled spectrum $|X^\#(j\omega)|$ and the sample-and-hold spectrum $|H_0(j\omega)|$, i.e.,

$$|X_r(j\omega)| = |X^\#(j\omega)||H_0(j\omega)| \qquad \text{(A7-19)}$$

Note that $|H_0|$ in Eq. (A7-19) serves as a reconstruction filter. Observe that the high frequency content of $|X^\#|$ is greatly attenuated by $|H_0|$. Also, the baseband spectrum is slightly attenuated near the band edge, due to the shaping of the main lobe of $|H_0|$, and the residues of the repeated spectra from $|X^\#|$ remain, due to the finite sidelobes of $|H_0|$.

The transfer function for a sample-data system, prior to reconstruction, is accurately expressed in the following form

$$H^\#(j\omega) = H_B(j\omega) + HI(j\omega - jk\omega_s) \qquad \text{(A7-20)}$$

where $H_B(j\omega)$ refers to the desired baseband part of $H^\#(j\omega)$, and $HI(j\omega - jk\omega_s) = 1/T \sum_{k=-\infty}^{\infty} H(j\omega - jk\omega_s)$ for $k \ne 0$ are the undesired higher-order components. Corre-

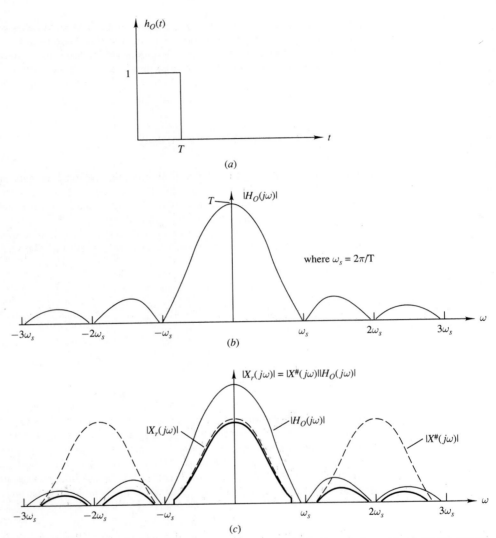

FIGURE A7-6   Reconstruction with sample and hold: (a) impulse response for sample and hold, (b) Magnitude response for sample and hold, and (c) spectrum of reconstructed signal $|X_r(j\omega)|$ superimposed onto the spectra for the impulse sampled signal $|X^\#(j\omega)|$ and the sample and hold $|H_0(j\omega)|$.

spondingly, the sampled-and-held signal spectrum is $|X'_r(j\omega)|$, expressed as

$$|X'_r(j\omega)| = |X^\#(j\omega)||H^\#(j\omega)||H_0(j\omega)| \tag{A7-21}$$

The sample-and-hold $|H_0(j\omega)|$ reduces the undesired higher-order components of $|X^\#(j\omega)|$ $||H^\#(j\omega)|$, as discussed above. Furthermore, the roll-off of $|H_0|$'s main lobe may attenuate $|X^{\#}(j\omega)||H^{\#}(j\omega)|$ beyond that intended by the requirements for $|H_B(j\omega)|$. For $\omega_s < \gamma\omega_{NY}$, with γ in the range between 1.5 to 5 (depending on the specifications for the baseband filter $|H_B(j\omega)||H_0(j\omega)|$, the main lobe roll-off $|H_0|$ may cause intolerable deviations from the specified response. To compensate for this attenuation the sample-data filter $|H_B(j\omega)|$ can be designed or predistorted with an intentional peak to, in effect, cancel the attenuation of H_0, i.e.,

$$|H_B^d(j\omega)||H_0(j\omega)| \approx |H_B(j\omega)| \qquad (A7\text{-}22a)$$

where $|H_B^d(j\omega)|$ is the predistorted baseband response and $|H_B(j\omega)|$ is the desired baseband response.

The baseband attenuation due to $|H_0|$ can be made negligible by increasing the sampling rate such that $\omega_s \gg \omega_{NY} > \gamma\omega_{NY}$, where

$$|H_B(j\omega)||H_0(j\omega)| \approx |H_B(j\omega)| \qquad (A7\text{-}22b)$$

The use of sample rates where $\omega_s \gg \omega_{NY}$ is often referred to as *over-sampling*. As mentioned previously, the sampling rate for a switched-capacitor filter is usually chosen such that the sampling frequency is much higher than the Nyquist rate; in particular, it is common to find $\omega_s = 20\omega_{NY}$ to $50\omega_{NY}$. For such cases, Eq. (A7-22b) is a convenient simplifying equation, in that the frequency response is completely determined by the samples of the unit response and predistortion is usually unnecessary.

Finally, further attenuation of the residual high-frequency components in $|X_r|$ (and $|X_r'|$) can be achieved by following the sample-and-hold (with a continuous lowpass reconstruction filter) of the form illustrated in Fig. A7-5.

A7-1-4   Input/Output Interfaces to the Analog Environment

Since most physical phenomenon are continuous-time in nature, it is important to consider how the various filter schemes discussed interface with the continuous-time environment. The interface needs for each of the filter types are shown in Fig. A7-7. In the case of the continuous-time filter, with transfer function H, the interface is trivial, as illustrated in Fig. A7-7a. In the switched-capacitor filter case, additional functions are required to effect this interface, as depicted in Fig. A7-7b.

From the discussion on aliasing, it should be clear that the input interface must first include an anti-aliasing filter with lowpass transfer function H_a. The anti-aliased continuous-time input is then sampled by a device that presents a sample-and-hold approximation of the continuous-time input to the sampled-data filter. As shown in Sec. 7-8 of Chap. 7, these sampling and sample-and-hold operations are usually performed by switched-capacitor filters with no additional hardware. Nonetheless, dedicated *sample-and-hold circuits* are important components in many sampled-data systems (Gregorian and Temes 1986; Unbehauen and Cichocki 1989; Grebene 1984). The transfer function for a switched-capacitor filter is accurately expressed as the product of the designed filter function and the sample-and-hold, i.e., HH_0. The sampling rate is usually sufficiently high that H need not be predistorted, i.e., $HH_0 \approx H$. The sample-and-hold output of the switched-capacitor filter, although semicontinuous in appearance, is an analog signal. Hence, it can be directly interfaced to the analog environment. If a smooth output is required, the sample-and-hold signal is further processed by a reconstruction filter with lowpass transfer function H_r. Usually, for convenience, $H_r = H_a$.

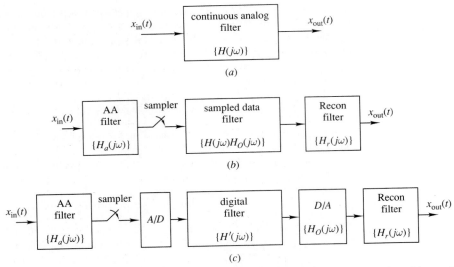

FIGURE A7-7   Interface requirements to the continuous-time environment for (a) continuous analog, (b) sampled analog, and (c) digital filters. Also shown are sketches representing the anti-aliasing filter H_a, the designed filter H, the predistorted (digital filter only) filter H', the sample and hold H_0, and the reconstruction filter H_r.

It is noted that when two or more sampled-data systems are interconnected, e.g., the output of one switched-capacitor filter (SCF) is fed into the input of some other sampled-data network (SDN), sampling in the SCF and SDN must be synchronized so that the SDN samples the output of the SCF in between its steplike changes in value. Otherwise, erroneous results can be obtained. It is interesting that the use of a reconstruction filter to smooth the step transitions in output of the SCF serves to eliminate the need for this synchronization. The realization of anti-aliasing and reconstruction filters for VLSI sampled-data filters are important applications for continuous-time active filters.

Digital filters require all the functions for analog interface associated with switched-capacitor filters, as illustrated in Fig. A7-7c. In addition, the input samples must be quantized, as previously discussed, and translated into digital words. This requires a device referred to as an *analog-to-digital converter* or *A/D converter*. N bit A/D conversion is simply the process of converting continuous-time and amplitude into discrete-time and digital (or quantized) amplitude; encompassing the operations of sampling, quantization and representation of the samples in some digital format (e.g., N-bit binary). We note that a properly designed A/D converter has a unity-transfer function and linear phase across the band of interest. At the output, this process must be reversed and the digital sampies translated into a reconstructed analog signal (usually a sample-and-hold waveform similar to that in Fig. A7-1c). This process is referred to as *digital-to-analog conversion* or D/A *conversion*. This function is performed by a device called a D/A *converter*. A properly designed D/A converter has the transfer function of a sample-and-hold, namely H_0. A/D and D/A converters are important sampled-data systems in their own right. Since we pay a significant price for over-sampling in digital filters, the designed filter is usually predistorted to compensate for the H_0 of the D/A converter.

Obviously, switched-capacitor filters do not require A/D and D/A conversion to interface with the continuous analog domain. The use of over-sampling significantly reduces the complexity of both the anti-aliasing and reconstruction filters, and eliminates the need for predistortion. As shown in Chap. 8, the cost of over-sampling is not significant. In addition, over-sampling reduces noise associated with spurious signals entering the filter through parasitic connections to power supplies, and to the clock lines that operate the switches.

A7-1-5   Use of the *z*-Transform in the Analysis of Sampled-Data Systems

The use of the z-transform simplifies the analysis of sampled-data systems by mapping linear difference equations into algebraic equations that are much easier to solve. Furthermore, by studying the z-domain poles and zeros, the designer obtains valuable insight into the behavior of the system. For example, gain and phase responses are readily determined from z-domain transfer relations. Thus, sampled-data systems can be specified in terms of well-known frequency domain quantities.

The definition of the z-transform arises naturally from the description of sampled systems. To demonstrate this fact, let us first consider the impulse-sampled signal $x^{\#}(t)$ given in Eq. (A7-12), i.e.,

$$x^{\#}(t) = \sum_{k=-\infty}^{\infty} x(kT)\delta(t - kT) \qquad \text{(A7-23)}$$

Taking the Laplace transform of $x^{\#}(t)$ in Eq. (A7-23) yields

$$X^{\#}(s) = \mathbf{L}[x^{\#}(t)] = \sum_{k=-\infty}^{\infty} x(kT)e^{-ksT} \qquad \text{(A7-24)}$$

Let us make the change of variables,

$$z = e^{sT} \qquad \text{(A7-25)}$$

which when substituted into Eq. (A7-24) yields

$$X(z) = \mathbf{Z}[x^{\#}(t)] = \sum_{k=-\infty}^{\infty} x(kT)z^{-k} \qquad \text{(A7-26)}$$

Function $X(z)$ is referred to as the z-transform of $x^{\#}(t)$, where z is the z-transform complex frequency variable. The z- and Laplace transforms are related, according to Eq. (A7-25), as well as for the sinusoidal steady state $s = j\omega$ and $z = e^{j\omega T}$. As with the Laplace transform, we can define both one-sided and two-sided z-transforms. These definitions are, respectively,

$$\mathbf{Z}_I[x(k)] = X_I(z) = \sum_{k=0}^{\infty} x(kT)z^{-k} \qquad (A7\text{-}27a)$$

$$\mathbf{Z}_{II}[x(k)] = X_{II}(z) = \sum_{k=-\infty}^{\infty} x(kT)z^{-k} \qquad (A7\text{-}27b)$$

The z-transforms in Eq. (A7-27) are seen to be an infinite power series; hence, they exist only for those values of z for which these series converge. The *region of convergence* (ROC) is then defined as the set of z's for which $X_I(z)$ (or $X_{II}(z)$) attain finite values. Thus, any time we site a z-transform we should specify its ROC, otherwise the situation is incomplete and ambiguous. In this text we exclusively deal with signals and systems with startup at $t = 0$; hence, we will use only the one-sided z-transform. We can then simplify our notation by eliminating the subscript (I) in our use of Eq. (A7-27a). Henceforth, the one-sided z-transform will be referred to as $\mathbf{Z}[x(kT)]$, or the z-transform.

Let us now illustrate these concepts by deriving the z-transform for the following function:

$$x(k) = \{1, 2, 3, 4, 5, 0, 7\} \quad \text{for} \quad k = 0, \ldots, 6 \qquad (A7\text{-}28)$$

Using the definition for the z-transform in Eq. (A7-27a) yields:

$$\begin{aligned} X(z) &= 1z^{-0} + 2z^{-1} + 3z^{-2} + 4z^{-3} + 5z^{-4} + 0z^{-5} + 7z^{-6} \\ &= 1 + 2z^{-1} + 3z^{-2} + 4z^{-3} + 5z^{-4} + 7z^{-6} \end{aligned} \qquad (A7\text{-}29)$$

The ROC is the entire z-plane. From this example we can see that the ROC for finite duration signals is the entire z-plane, except for, possibly, $z = 0$. The coefficient of z^{-k} is always the value of the signal sample at time $t = kT$. Finite duration signals occur in such systems as finite impulse response (FIR), digital filters, transversal surface acoustic wave (SAW) filters, and phased-array antennas. Such systems do not use any feedback (i.e., as described in Chap. 2) in their realizations.

Most continuous-time and sample-data filter systems utilize feedback, realizing impulse responses $h(t)$ and unit responses $h(k)$ that are infinite in duration. Such filter systems include active-RC and active-SC filter schemes discussed in Chaps. 7 and 8, as well as infinite impulse response (IIR) digital filters. We note that the unit excitation $\delta(k)$ (see Exercise 7-19) is analogous to the continuous-time impulse excitation $\delta(t)$. From Eq. (A7-27a), we see that an infinite duration signal leads to an infinite series z-transform. Within its ROC, an infinite series can always be found to converge to a compact closed form. Usually it will be more convenient to use the closed-form expression, rather than the infinite series.

For example, let us consider the z-transform for the unit response

$$h(k) = e^{-akT} \quad \text{for} \quad 0 \le k \le \infty, \qquad (A7\text{-}30)$$

with sampling rate $f_s = 1/T$. Simply substituting the values for $h(k)$ (above) into Eq. (A7-27a) yields the desired z-transform

$$H(z) = \sum_{k=0}^{\infty} e^{-akT} z^{-k} \tag{A7-31a}$$

Eq. (A7-31a) is recognized as a geometric series that converges to the closed form

$$H(z) = \frac{1}{1 - e^{-aT} z^{-1}} \quad \text{for the ROC} \quad |z| > e^{-aT} \tag{A7-31b}$$

Recall that in the continuous-time domain, the Laplace transform of the impulse response $h(t) = e^{-at} u(t)$ is

$$H(s) = \frac{1}{s+a} \tag{A7-32}$$

A z-domain equivalent to $H(s)$ can be derived by taking the z-transform of the sample sequence obtained by sampling $h(t)$ at $f_s = 1/T$, i.e., Eq. (A7-30). The equivalent $H(z)$ is then Eq. (A7-31b). A special case occurs when $e^{-at} = 1$ or $a = 0$, i.e.,

$$X(z) = \frac{1}{1 - z^{-1}} \tag{A7-33}$$

Since a large body of filter-design knowledge exists in the s-domain, it is often convenient to translate filter specifications or $H(s)$'s from the s-domain to the z-domain. The equivalence between $H(s)$ and $H(z)$ demonstrated in Eqs. (A7-31b) and (A7-32) is called the *matched z-transform* (Tretter 1976). Later we will consider other conversion methods. Also, in Sec. 7-5 we show that $1/(1 - z^{-1})$ is one of the z-domain approximations for the integration operator $(1/s)$.

The $H(z)$ in Eq. (A7-31b) (and its equivalent $H(s)$) represents a single-pole system with pole at $z = e^{-aT}$. An important class of sample-data filters are those that realize a damped sinusoidal unit response of the form $h(k) = [e^{-akT} \cos \omega_0 k T]u(k)$. To determine the $H(z)$, let us first express $h(k)$ as a sum of complex exponentials, i.e.,

$$h(k) = \frac{1}{2} e^{-akT + j\omega_0 kT} u(k) + \frac{1}{2} e^{-akT - j\omega_0 T} u(k)$$

with

$$H(z) = \frac{1}{2} \mathbf{Z}\{e^{-akT} e^{j\omega_0 kT} u(k)\} + \frac{1}{2} \mathbf{Z}\{e^{-akT} e^{-j\omega_0 kT} u(k)\} \tag{A7-34}$$

Applying Eq. (A7-31b) to each term of Eq. (A7-34), we obtain

$$\mathbf{Z}\{e^{-akT} e^{j\omega_0 kT} u(k)\} = \frac{1}{1 - e^{-aT} e^{j\omega_0 T} z^{-1}} \quad \text{with ROC} \quad |z| > e^{-aT}$$

and

$$\mathbf{Z}\{e^{-akT}e^{-j\omega_0 kT}u(k)\} = \frac{1}{1 - e^{-aT}e^{-j\omega_0 T}z^{-1}} \qquad \text{with ROC} \quad |z| > e^{-aT}$$

Hence, combining terms, we obtain

$$H(z) = \frac{1 - e^{-aT}\cos\omega_0 T z^{-1}}{1 - e^{-aT}2\cos\omega_0 T z^{-1} + e^{-2aT}z^{-2}} \qquad \text{with ROC} \quad |z| > e^{-aT} \qquad \text{(A7-35)}$$

Note that the $H(z)$'s in Eqs. (A7-31b) and (A7-35) are both formed as the ratio of two polynomials in successive powers of z^{-1}. This important family of z-transformed unit responses is more generally expressed as

$$H(z) = \frac{N(z)}{D(z)} = \frac{a_0 + a_1 z^{-1} + \ldots + a_M z^{-M}}{1 + b_1 z^{-1} + \ldots + b_N z^{-N}} = \left(\frac{\sum_{n=0}^{M} a_n z^{-n}}{1 + \sum_{n=1}^{N} b_n z^{-n}} \right) \qquad \text{(A7-36a)}$$

We note that Eq. (A7-36a) can also be expressed in successive powers of z^{+1} by multiplying and dividing $X(z)$ by either z^N / z^N if $N \geq M$ or z^M / z^M if $M > N$, i.e.,

$$H(z) = z^{N-M} \frac{a_0 z^M + a_1 z^{M-1} + \ldots + a_M}{z^N + b_1 z^{N-1} + \ldots + b_N} = z^{N-M} \left(\frac{\sum_{n=0}^{N} a_n z^{M-n}}{1 + \sum_{n=1}^{N} b_n z^{N-n}} \right) \qquad \text{(A7-36b)}$$

We note that Eqs. (A7-36) are used interchangeably. It is often useful to express $H(z)$ in factored form, i.e.

$$H(z) = \frac{a_0(1 - \alpha_1 z^{-1})(1 - \alpha_2 z^{-1})\ldots(1 - \alpha_M z^{-1})}{(1 - \beta_1 z^{-1})(1 - \beta_2 z^{-1})\ldots(1 - \beta_N z^{-1})} \qquad \text{(A7-37a)}$$

$$= a_0 z^{N-M} \frac{(z - \alpha_1)(z - \alpha_2)\ldots(z - \alpha_M)}{(z - \beta_1)(z - \beta_2)\ldots(z - \beta_N)} \qquad \text{(A7-37b)}$$

where $z = \alpha_i$ and $z = \beta_i$ define, respectively, the zeros and poles for $H(z)$. We note that since a_n and b_n are real numbers, the α_i and β_i are either real, or occur in complex conjugate pairs.

To gain insight from the inspection of $H(z)$, let us examine the mapping $z = e^{sT}$ in greater detail. Let us start by expressing s as a complex variable $s = \sigma + j\omega = Re(s) + jIm(s)$. Correspondingly,

$$z = Re(z) + jIm(z) = e^{\sigma T}e^{j\omega T} = |z|e^{j\phi(z)} \qquad \text{(A7-38)}$$

Referring to Fig. A7-8 and Eq. (A7-38), we observe that the origin $s = 0 + j0$ maps into the point $z = 1$. Also, the s-plane real-axis $-\infty \leq \sigma \leq \infty$, maps into z-plane positive-real

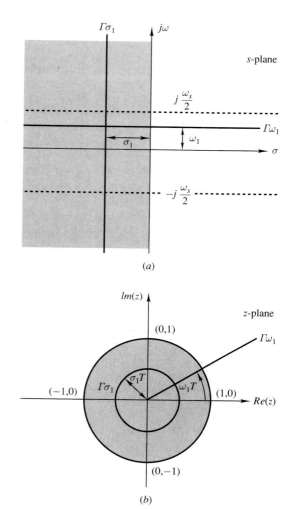

FIGURE A7-8 Mapping between the s- and z-domains via $z = e^{sT}$.

axis $0 \leq Re(z) \leq \infty$ and points on the s-plane $j\omega$-axis map into points onto the z-plane unit circle (i.e., $|z| \equiv 1$). Points in the left-half s-plane map inside the z-plane unit circle (i.e., $|z| < 1$), and points in the right-half s-plane map outside the z-plane unit circle (i.e., $|z| > 1$). In particular, a line parallel to the s-plane $j\omega$-axis, passing through $\sigma = \sigma_1$, maps onto a z-plane circle (Γ_{σ_1}) of radius $|z| = e^{\sigma_1 T}$. A line parallel to the s-plane σ-axis, passing through $j\omega = j\omega_1$, maps onto a z-plane ray (Γ_{ω_1}), extending outward from the origin (0, 0) at an angle $\phi = \omega_1 T$. Finally, we note that for the frequency range $-\omega_s/2 \leq \omega \leq \omega_s/2$, the angle $\phi(z)$ uniquely lies within the 2π interval $-\pi \leq \phi(z) \leq \pi$. Hence, for successive intervals of ω, e.g., $\omega_s/2 \leq \omega \leq 3\omega_s/2$, such that $|\omega| \geq \omega_s/2$, the phasor simply continues rotating in a redundant fashion, through the angles $-\pi \leq \phi(z) \leq \pi$. As we saw in the previous section, this gives rise to the repeated replicas of the baseband spectrum.

Identifying the z-plane poles and zeros of $H(z)$ provides important insights into the behavior of the sampled signal. Consider, for example, the single-pole z-domain function

$$H(z) = \frac{1}{1 - \alpha z^{-1}} \tag{A7-39}$$

Note that with $\alpha = e^{-aT}$, $H(z)$ in Eq. (A7-31b) is of the same form as Eq. (A7-39). Depending on the location of the pole at $z = \alpha$, there are six different categories of unit responses $h(k)$ that can arise from this $H(z)$, as illustrated in Fig. A7-9. These categories are

1 If $\alpha > 1$, the pole is on the right half of the $Re(z)$ axis and outside the unit circle. Consequently, $h(k)$ diverges and the system is said to be unstable. This category of response is analogous to the continuous situation, where the real-axis pole lies to the right of the s-plane's origin. Any switched-capacitor filter providing a unit response of this form is said to be unstable.

2 If $\alpha = 1$, the pole is at the intersecection of the $Re(z)$ axis and the unit circle at $z = 1 + j0$. Consequently, $h(k) = u(k) = 1$ for all k. This category is analogous to the continuous-time situation, where the real-axis pole lies at s-plane's origin.

3 If $0 < \alpha < 1$, the pole is on the right half of the $Re(z)$ axis and inside the unit circle. Consequently, $h(k)$ decays and the switched-capacitor filter is said to be stable. This category of response is analogous to the continuous situation, where the real-axis pole lies in the left half of the s-plane.

4 If $-1 < \alpha < 0$, the pole is on the left half of the $Re(z)$ axis and inside the unit circle. In this case, $h(k)$ is seen to be a decaying sequence of samples alternating between positive and negative values. The period, i.e., the time interval between successive samples of the same sign, is exactly $2T$. Hence, $h(k)$ is a damped oscillating sequence with a frequency $f_s/2 = 1/2T$. This case, and the two that follow, have no analogy in the continuous-domain lore of single-pole systems. In any event, sample-data filters that exhibit this $h(k)$ are stable.

FIGURE A7-9   Pole locations for $H(z) = 1/1 - \alpha z^{-1}$ and corresponding $h(k)$ for (1) $\alpha > 1$, (2) $\alpha = 1$, (3) $0 < \alpha < 1$, (4) $-1 < \alpha < 0$, (5) $\alpha = -1$, and (6) $\alpha < -1$.

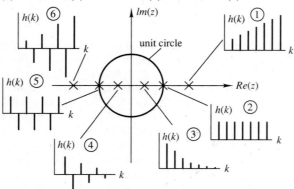

5 If $\alpha = -1$, the pole is at the intersection of the $Re(z)$ axis and the unit circle at $z = -1 + j0$. Based on the previous result, we see that $h(k)$ is a sequence of alternating $+1$'s and -1's with a period of $2T$. Hence, this alleged first-order system oscillates at $f_s/2$.

6 If $\alpha < -1$, the pole is on the left half of the $Re(z)$ axis and outside the unit circle. Consequently, the unit response alternates in sign at frequency $f_s/2$ and diverges in an exponential fashion. Any sample-data filter providing a unit response of this form is unstable.

To see the problem in categories 4–6 more clearly, let us refer to the analogy between the $H(z)$'s in Eqs. (A7-39) and (A7-31b), i.e., $\alpha = e^{-aT}$. But here α is a negative-valued real number that can be expressed in polar form as $\alpha = |\alpha|e^{j\pi}$. Thus, solving for a in the relation $|\alpha|e^{j\pi} = e^{-aT}$ reveals that a must be complex, i.e.,

$$a = -\frac{\ln|\alpha|}{T} + j\frac{\pi}{T} = -\frac{\ln|\alpha|}{T} + j\frac{\omega_s}{2} \qquad \text{(A7-40)}$$

This result implies that the equivalent s-domain pole is not real-valued, and, in fact, the equivalent s-domain system is not first-order. Hence, oscillation or resonance at the half-sampling rate can be efficiently realized in sample-data systems.

A7-1-6 Conversions Between $H(s)$ and $H(z)$

Due to the wealth of literature on continuous-time filter design, it is often convenient to convert $H(s)$ to $H(z)$. When s and z are related by $s = (1/T)\ln z$, the lossless mapping of even a first-order $H(s)$ leads to an infinite-order $H(z)$. Thus, the conversion problem is to adequately approximate $H(s)$ with finite-order $H(z)$. More specifically, the objective is to convert the Nth-order $H(s)$ to a closely equivalent Nth-order $H(z)$, using a first-order transformation. By preserving order, the realizations for both functions will have similar complexity. Several interesting approximate mappings have been used in the literature. Some of the more interesting mappings are compared in Sec. 7-5-2.

One such mapping is the matched z-transform. To facilitate our discussion, let us consider the two-pole $H(s)$ illustrated in Fig. A7-10a; i.e.,

$$H(s) = \frac{k\lambda_1\lambda_2}{(s - \lambda_1)(s - \lambda_2)} = \frac{k\omega_0^2}{s^2 + \left(\dfrac{\omega_0}{Q_p}\right)s + \omega_0^2} \qquad \text{(A7-41)}$$

where ω_p is the pole frequency, Q_p is the pole-quality factor, and $k = |H(j0)|$ is the gain at DC. The poles of $H(s)$ are located at

$$\lambda_{1,2} = -\frac{\omega_0}{2Q_p} \pm j\omega_0\sqrt{1 - \frac{1}{4Q_p^2}} = -\sigma_p \pm j\omega_p \qquad \text{(A7-42)}$$

In Chap. 3 we explored the relationships between Q_p to the amount of peaking in the magnitude response $|H(j\omega)|$ and the degree of overshoot in the step response. Note that for high Q_p or $Q_p \gg 1$, which occurs frequently in the design of sharp cutoff filters, $\omega_0 \approx \omega_p$.

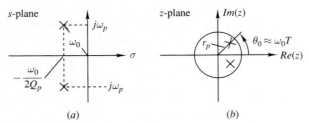

FIGURE A7-10   (a) Pole positions for complex two-pole $H(s)$, and (b) corresponding pole positions for $H(z)$.

Correspondingly, a two-pole $H(z)$ can be derived by transforming the pole locations $\lambda_{1,2}$ by the matched z-transform (e.g., Eq. (A7-31b)), such that

$$\beta_{1,2} = e^{\lambda_{1,2}T} = r_p e^{\pm j\theta_0} \tag{A7-43}$$

The resulting function, illustrated in Fig. A7-10b, is

$$H(z) = \frac{k(1 - \beta_1)(1 - \beta_2)}{(1 - \beta_1 z^{-1})(1 - \beta_2 z^{-1})} = \frac{k(1 - 2r_p \cos\theta_0 + r_p^2)}{1 - 2r_p \cos\theta_0 z^{-1} + r_p^2 z^{-2}} \tag{A7-44}$$

Note that the numerator for $H(z)$ has been chosen so that $|H(e^{j0T})| = |H(1)| = k$. Note that comparing Eqs. (A7-35) and (A7-44) that $e^{-aT} = r_p$ and $\omega_0 T = \theta_0$. The equivalence between z-domain pole parameters r_p, $\cos\theta_p$, and the s-domain parameters Q_p, ω_0 can be found by manipulating Eq. (A7-43), i.e.,

$$\beta_1 = r_p e^{j\theta_0} = e^{\lambda_1 T} = e^{(-\sigma_p + j\omega_p)T} = e^{-\sigma_p T} e^{j\omega_p T} \tag{A7-45}$$

where σ_p and ω_p are defined in Eq. (A7-42). Solving for r_p and θ_0 yields

$$r_p = e^{-\sigma_p T} = e^{-(\omega_0 T / 2Q_p)} \quad \text{and} \quad \theta_0 = \omega_p T \simeq \omega_0 T \tag{A7-46}$$

When we highly over-sample, such that $\omega_p T \ll 1$, further approximation can be achieved by expressing $r_p = e^{\sigma_p T}$ and $\cos\theta_0$ in truncated Taylor series, i.e.,

$$e^{-x} = 1 - x + \frac{x^2}{2!} - \frac{x^3}{3!} + \ldots \approx 1 - x \quad \text{for} \quad x \ll 1$$

$$\cos(y) = 1 - \frac{y^2}{2!} + \frac{y^3}{3!} - \ldots \approx 1 - \frac{y^2}{2} \quad \text{for} \quad y \ll 1$$

where the ROCs for e^{-x} and $\cos y$ are all real values of x and y, respectively. Thus, for $\omega_p T \ll 1$ and $\omega_0 T \ll 1$, we can write the following approximate relations for $\cos \theta_0$ and r_p:

$$\cos \theta_0 \approx 1 - \frac{(\omega_0) T^2}{2} \qquad \text{and} \qquad r_p \approx 1 - \frac{\omega_0 T}{2 Q_p} \tag{A7-47}$$

Substituting Eqs. (A7-47) into Eq. (A7-44), $H(z)$ can be expressed in the following approximate form

$$H(z) \approx \frac{k \dfrac{(\omega_0 T)^2}{2}}{1 - 2\left\{1 - \dfrac{\omega_0 T}{2 Q_p} - \dfrac{(\omega_0 T)^2}{2}\right\} z^{-1} + \left\{1 - \dfrac{\omega_0 T}{Q_p}\right\} z^{-2}} \tag{A7-48}$$

Equations (A7-43), (A7-44) and (A7-48) can be generalized for the case where the transmission zeros are at finite frequencies (i.e., ω_N, Q_z, and θ_z, r_z), such that

$$H(s) = \frac{k\left[s^2 \pm \dfrac{\omega_N}{Q_z} s + \omega_N^2\right]}{s^2 + \dfrac{\omega_N}{Q_p} s + \omega_N^2} \tag{A7-49}$$

$$H(z) = \frac{k(1 - 2r_z \cos \theta_N z^{-1} + r_z^2 z^{-2})}{1 - 2r_p \cos \theta_0 z^{-1} + r_p^2 z^{-2}} \tag{A7-50}$$

$$\approx \frac{k\left[1 - 2\left\{1 \mp \dfrac{\omega_N T}{2 Q_z} - \dfrac{(\omega_N T)^2}{2}\right\} z^{-1} + \left\{1 \mp \dfrac{\omega_N T}{Q_z}\right\} z^{-2}\right]}{1 - 2\left\{1 - \dfrac{\omega_0 T}{2 Q_p} - \dfrac{(\omega_0 T)^2}{2}\right\} z^{-1} + \left\{1 - \dfrac{\omega_0 T}{Q_p}\right\} z^{-2}} \tag{A7-51}$$

When $\pm$ in the numerator of Eq. (A7-49a) is $-$, or the $\mp$ in Eq. (A7-51) is $+$, the zeros lie in the right-half s-plane or outside the unit circle, such that $r_z > 1$.

We caution the reader that the approximations in Eqs. (A7-48) and (A7-51) are usually too imprecise to be used as a transformation between $H(s)$ and $H(z)$, or vice versa. The errors in approximating r_p^2 and $r_p \cos \theta_0$ in these relations are about

$$|\Delta r_p^2| \approx \frac{1}{2}\left(\frac{\omega_0 T}{Q_p}\right)^2 \qquad \text{and} \qquad |\Delta r_p \cos \theta_0| \approx \frac{1}{4}\left(\frac{\omega_0 T}{Q_p}\right)^2$$

To see the problem quantitatively, let us look at a simple example where $f_p = 3$ kHz, $Q_p = 1$, and $f_s = 128$ kHz; thus $|\Delta r_p^2| \approx 0.01$ and $|\Delta r_p \cos \theta_0| \approx 0.005$. In this magnitude, Δ's would introduce deviations in $G(\omega)$ on the order of 0.1 dB. Hence, they are best used where they lend insight, or to simplify calculations such as sensitivity (see Sec. 3-4 and 7-7), where high precision is not essential. In Sec. 7-5-2 we introduced several transforms, including the well-known bilinear transform, to translate $H(s)$ to $H(z)$.

We have now covered the topic of sampled systems in sufficient depth for the reader to pursue the design of switched-capacitor filters. Since we can never learn too much about these fundamental concepts, we encourage interested readers to pursue further study of sampled systems by taking courses and/or pursuing self study, using any one of several excellent texts listed at the end of this chapter.

REFERENCES

Allstot, D. A., and W. C. Black. 1983. "Technological Design Considerations for Monolithic MOS Switched-Capacitor Filtering System." *Proc. IEEE*, vol. 71, no. 8, pp. 967–986.

Bruton, L. T. 1975. "Low Sensitivity Ladder Filters." *IEEE Transactions on Circuits and Systems*, vol. CAS-22, March, pp. 168–176.

Callias, F., F. H. Salchli, and D. Girard. 1989. "A Set of Four ICs in CMOS Technology for a Programmable Hearing Aid." *IEEE J. Solid-State Circuits*, vol. SC-24, no. 12, pp. 301–312.

Daniels, R. W. 1974. *Approximation Methods for Electronic Filter Design.* New York: McGraw-Hill.

Daryanani, G. 1976. *Principles of Active Network Synthesis and Design.* New York: Wiley and Sons.

Fang, S. C., Y. Tsividis, and O. Wing. 1983. "SWITCAP: A Switched-Capacitor Network Analysis Program." Parts I and II. *IEEE Circuits and Systems Magazine.* Sept. and Dec.

Fischer, J. H. 1982. "Noise Sources and Calculation Techniques for Switched Capacitor Filters," *IEEE J. Solid-State Circuits,* vol. SC-17, no. 8, pp. 742–752.

Geiger, R. L., and E. Sanchez-Sinencio. 1985. "Active Filters Using Operational Transconductance Amplifiers: A Tutorial." *IEEE Circuits and Devices Magazine*, vol. 1, no. 3, pp. 20–32.

Ghausi, M. S., and K. R. Laker. 1981. *Modern Filter Design: Active-RC and Switched Capacitor*, Englewood Cliffs, NJ: Prentice-Hall.

Grebene, A. B. 1984. *Bipolar and MOS Analog Integrated Circuit Design.* New York: Wiley and Sons. 1984.

Gregorian, R., and G. C. Temes. 1986. *Analog MOS Integrated Circuits for Signal Processing.* New York: Wiley-Interscience.

Kuraishi, Y., K. Nakayama, K. Miyadera, and T. Okamura. 1984. "A Single-Chip 20-Channel Speech Spectrum Analyzer Using a Multiplexed Switched-Capacitor Filter Bank." *IEEE J. Solid-State Circuits.* vol. SC-19, no. 12, pp. 964–970.

MATLAB: *Control Systems Toolbox User's Guide, Signal Processing Tool Box User's Guide.* South Natic, MA: The MathWorks, Inc.

Meares, L. G., and C. E. Hymowitz. 1988. *Simulating With SPICE.* San Pedro, CA: Intusoft.

Nguyen, N. M., and R. G. Meyer. 1990. "Si IC-Compatible Inductors and LC Passive Filters." *IEEE J. of Solid State Circuits*, vol. 25, no. 4, pp. 1028-1031.

Oliver, B. M., J. R. Pierce, and C. E. Shannon. 1948. "The Philosophy of PCM." *Proceedings IRE*, vol. 36, Nov., pp. 1324–1331.

Schaumann, R., M. S. Ghausi, and K. R. Laker. 1990. *Design of Analog Filters*. Englewood Cliffs, NJ: Prentice-Hall.

Schaumann, R., and K. R. Laker. 1993. In "Active Filter Design." *Reference Data for Engineers: Radio, Electronics, Computer, and Communications*, 8th Ed., edited by E. C. Jordan. Indianapolis, IN: Howard W. Sams and Co.

Sedra, A. S. 1989. "Miniaturized Active RC Filters." *Miniaturized and Integrated Filters*, edited by S. K. Mitra and C. F. Kurth. New York: Wiley-Interscience.

SIFILSYN Software for Filter Analysis and Design. Santa Clara, CA: DGS Associates.

Snelgrove, W.M. *FILTOR2-A Computer-Aided Filter Design Package*. Toronto: University of Toronto Press

SWAP: A Switched Capacitor Network Analysis Program. 1983. Heverlee, Belgium: Silvar-Lisco Company.

Tretter, S. A. 1976. *Introduction to Discrete-Time Signal Processing*. New York: Wiley and Sons.

Unbehauen, R., and A. Cichocki. 1989. *MOS Switches-Capacitor and Continuous-Time Integrated Circuits and Systems*. Berlin: Springer-Verlag.

8

DESIGN AND IMPLEMENTATION OF INTEGRATED ACTIVE FILTER SUBSYSTEMS

INTRODUCTION

Historically, active filters have been implemented with various degrees of integration (Ghausi and Laker 1981; Gray et al. 1980; Grebene 1984; Gregorian 1986; Moschytz 1986; Schaumann, Ghausi, and Laker 1990; Sedra 1985; Sedra 1989; Toumazou 1990). In recent years, the microelectronic technologies (e.g., CMOS and bipolar), filter architectures, and design techniques have emerged that allow the realization of very high quality fully-integrated active filters. Moreover, sophisticated analog and digital functions can and do coexist on the same very large scale integrated (VLSI) chip. This development, coupled with the exponential growth in the number of devices fabricated on a single chip (this number has doubled each year since the early 1960s), has resulted in the implementation of single-chip mixed analog/digital systems. Only a few years ago, these systems required several chips and in some cases multiple circuit boards. In these new, mixed signal chips, the integrated active filter is one of several important analog and digital subsystems. As illustrated by the PCM codec chip in Fig. 8-1, it is common to find more than one integrated filter in a VLSI system. The highest demand for VLSI analog/digital systems has been in the areas of information acquisition and voice/data telecommunications, e.g., PCM codecs (an example of which is shown in Fig. 8-1), line interface subsystems, modems for a variety of data rates, and the like (Geiger, Allen, and Strader 1990; Gray, Hodges, and Broderson 1980; Grebene 1984).

VLSI information acquisition systems, such as that depicted in Fig. 8-2, provide the means for accurately detecting, acquiring, and conditioning various physical data for processing, storage, and/or action by a digital computer. Applications for these systems are in the areas of robotics, high energy physics, x-ray spectroscopy, medical instruments, chemical process control, monitoring the performance and fatigue of

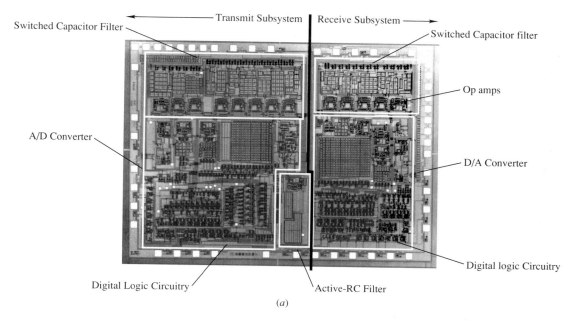

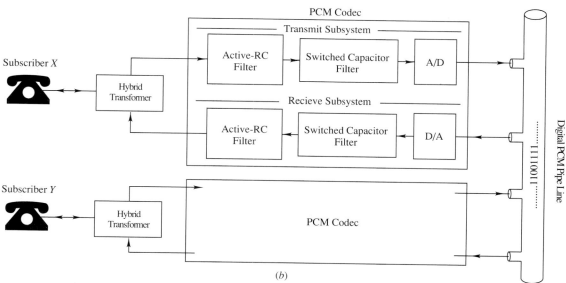

FIGURE 8-1 A typical VLSI analog/digital system floor plan. The example shown is a PCM codec realized in 5 μm CMOS. The left side of the chip contains the transmit subsystem (active-RC filter, switched-capacitor filter and A/D converter) and the right side contains the receive subsystem (D/A converter and switched-capacitor filter). Digital logic circuitry is embedded in the realizations of the A/D and D/A converters. Op amps are embedded in the active-RC and switched-capacitor filters. (a) The floor plan of the PCM codec superimposed on a photo of the actual chip. (b) The block diagram of the PCM codec system as it is used in telephony. All blocks are included on the chip (except the telephones at the input of the transmit and the output of the receive subsystems, and the digital channel linking subscribers X and Y).

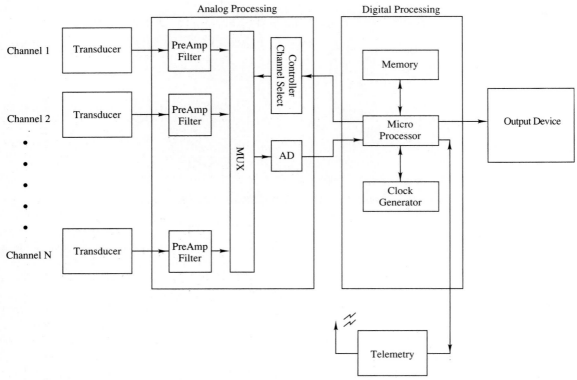

FIGURE 8-2   A VLSI multi-channel information acquisition system, showing an $N \times 1$ transducer array with associated analog processing, digital processing, and telemetry functions. The telemetry function is used in remote sensing applications. (Steyaert and Sansen 1990)

mechanical systems, and automated manufacturing, to name a few. Such systems integrate one or more sensors (or detectors) on a single chip, with linear analog signal conditioning, A/D conversion, and perhaps a custom microprocessor or digital signal processor. Linear signal conditioning will typically include a low-noise, high-gain linear amplifier to magnify what are usually very small signals, and an integrated filter to eliminate spurious (or undesired) signals and DC biases, as shown in Fig. 8-3.

Most integrated filters are implemented in CMOS due to the advantages of low power dissipation, the ability to mix analog and digital subsystems compactly on the same die, and the near ideal quality of such components as capacitors and analog switches. Some filters, particularly high frequency continuous-time filters (e.g., for video applications), have been realized in bipolar (Moulding et al. 1980) and in CMOS (Silva et al. 1993). It is expected that BICMOS, combining CMOS and bipolar transistors, will be used for some high-end analog systems. However, given the relative simplicity of the CMOS process, we expect CMOS to continue to be the dominant fabrication technology. We note that interesting GaAs active filters (Toumazou et al.

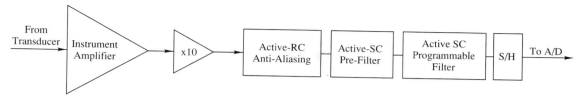

FIGURE 8-3 The block schematic of a typical signal conditioning path for an information acquisition system. The path includes a low-noise instrumentation amplifier that ensures high input impedance and a high common-mode rejection ratio, a ×10 amplifier to further amplify the sensed signal, an active-RC filter for bandlimiting the amplified input signal in preparation for sampling, a switched-capacitor pre-filter to reduce offsets and out-of-band noise, a switched-capacitor programmable filter to customize the processing to specific applications, and a switched-capacitor sample-and-hold (S/H) circuit that feeds an A/D converter. (Steyaert and Sansen 1990)

1990) have been demonstrated in research labs, but we do not expect GaAs to play a major role in applications where precision signal conditioning is required.

This chapter builds on the materials in Chaps. 5–7 to design and implement practical continuous-time and sampled data integrated active filters. Once a filter has been properly specified and a suitable numerical transfer function synthesized, the designer selects a filter schematic (or set of candidate schematics), executes the design of the filter (or candidate filters) to determine component values, evaluates the design (or candidate designs) using CAD tools, and implements the final design in a suitable IC technology. In this chapter we review concepts, circuit designs, filter schematics, and filter design lore that have been found to result in robust integrated filters. That is, filters that are well suited to a broad range of specifications, e.g., those illustrated in Figs. 8-1 through 8-3.

Continuous-time and sampled data realizations are considered with equal emphasis. In particular, we focus on design and implementation using modular structures. In this regard, op amps, OTAs, and the passive structures described in previous chapters are the building blocks used here to realize a variety of integrated filters.

8-1 PARASITIC CAPACITANCES IN INTEGRATED FILTERS

The achievement of many practical filter specifications requires circuits capable of realizing transfer function coefficients with 10–12 bits of precision and processing signals encompassing a dynamic range of 80 dB or more. Perhaps the most humbling experience for a novice integrated filter designer is the recognition that this degree of robustness must be achieved with IC components connected to undesired parasitic components that are often of comparable value.

In discrete electronics, parasitic is a term often used to describe a weak second-order effect that can be ignored in a first-order model under certain conditions, say at low frequencies. An example of such a second-order effect is the inductance of a wire lead. Parasitics in an integrated circuit also include real, but unintended, components that arise from unavoidable overlaps in features on different mask levels and the substrate (Geiger, Allen, and Strader 1990; Ghausi and Laker 1981; Gray and Meyer 1984; Moschytz, 1986). Parasitics of this kind are not necessarily weak second-order effects, but are often comparable to, and interfere with, the operation of intended components (as illustrated in Example 1-9). To further complicate matters, some components that are taken for granted in discrete circuit design, most notably resistors, are inherently nonlinear and distributed (Ghausi and Kelly 1968).

If left unattended, parasitic components can impair the performance of the filter by modifying its frequency response, providing feed-in paths for spurious signals and, in some cases, introducing nonlinearity. Some of the parasitics establish RC time constants that limit high frequency performance, as in discrete circuits. In effect, the integrated filter is embedded in a multi-input parasitic network that both alters its electrical characteristics and connects its nodes to spurious inputs from power supplies and clock feeds. The integrated filter designer is challenged to achieve a circuit realization that neutralizes both the component nonlinearities and parasitics to the extent that they become nondominant contributors to the filter's soft-yield. Hence, the magnitudes of the parasitic components, and the filter circuit's sensitivities to their presence, are of equal concern. In Secs. 8-2, 8-3, and 8-5 we explore the impact of parasitics, and offer methods for coping with their existence.

The most prolific parasitic components tend to be capacitances. Their values range from being insignificant (i.e., < 10 fF) to a few tenths of pF, and some are voltage dependent. As evident in Chaps. 1 and 2, parasitic capacitances occur in all IC technologies (Geiger, Allen, and Strader 1990; Ghausi and Laker 1981; Gray and Meyer 1984). Their values depend on the geometries and dielectric qualities of materials peculiar to a given process. Figure 8-4 (see color plate 1) shows the cross-section of a typical p-well CMOS process, illustrating the structures for a p-well nMOST, a pMOST, and a poly 1-poly 2 capacitor. Superimposed are circuit symbols, drawn in black, that define the poly 1-poly 2 capacitor C_A and the pMOST-R of value R_A. The important parasitics, modeled as lumped capacitances, are indicated with capacitor symbols drawn in gray. These parasitics impact, at times significantly, the performance of active-RC and SC integrated filters.

With a little imagination, the reader can visualize the pMOST, with source-drain terminals (1) and (2) and gate control x, either serving as a MOST-R with $x = V_C$ such that $R = R_A$ (as per Fig. 7-2c) or one-half of a CMOS switch with $x = \bar{\phi}^{e,o}$ (as per Fig. 7-4b). Capacitor C_A, with top and bottom plates connected to terminals (3) and (4), respectively, is the only intentionally fabricated capacitance. Since it will be important to distinguish between (intentional) capacitor top and bottom plates in our schematics, we assign the "straight line" in the capacitor symbol to the top plate and the "curved line" to the bottom plate. From Chap. 2 we know that the value of C_A depends on the geometric dimensions of the Poly 2-oxide-Poly 1 overlap, and on the thickness and dielectric properties of the capacitor oxide. Moreover, significant care has been taken to lay out C_A, and all other intentional capacitors, to achieve a high degree of matching, e.g., Fig. 7-4d. As we will see, parasitics are indeed "flies in the ointment."

Many of the parasitic C's, namely, C_{GS}, C_{GD}, C_{jD}, and C_{jS}, are associated with the MOST model described in Chap. 1. The expressions for each, in the three MOST operating regions, are summarized in Table 8-1. Source and drain-to-bulk capacitances C_{jS} and C_{jD} are voltage dependent and consequently enhance nonlinear distortion. The relations for voltage dependent C_{jSB} and C_{jDB} can be found in Table 1-5. All the MOST parasitics scale in direct proportion with the geometric dimensions of the MOST (i.e., W, L_{eff}, L_D, A_S, A_D defined in Chap. 1). Hence, their values are only within the control of the designer insofar as the need to keep the MOSTs as small as a prudent electrical design permits. Recall that the amount of C_{oxt}, the gate-to-channel capacitance, in C_{GS} and C_{GD}, varies with the operating region and $C_{oxt} = C_{ox} W L_{\text{eff}} \gg C_{GS0}, C_{GD0}$.

Parasitic C_R represents the accumulated capacitance formed by the metal interconnect level, i.e., metal-to-substrate over field oxide. It is determined by C_{oxm}, defined in Table 1-7, and the dimensions of the route $L_R \times W_R$. C_R's are very much within the control of the designer, and they can be minimized (at least the critical ones) in a well planned layout. Parasitic C_B is formed by the Poly 1 bottom plate associated with C_A, and the field oxide and substrate. C_B scales directly with the dimensions of the poly 1 bottom plate $L_B \times W_B$, that underlies the entire C_A structure (recall Fig. 7-4d). It also depends on C_{oxp}, the capacitance associated with poly 1-to-substrate over field oxide. Hence, the value of C_B is not usually within designer control and will always be a fixed percentage of C_A. The relations for parasitics C_R and C_B are also listed in Table 8-1.

Example 8-1

With $C_{oxp} = 6.5$ nF/cm^2, calculate the bottom-plate parasitic capacitances C_{B1} and C_{B2} for the double-poly capacitors C_1 and C_2 in Fig. 8-5 (see color plate 1).

Solution. From the dimensions, the areas for the bottom plates of C_1 and C_2 are, respectively, $A_1 = 778$ μm$^2 = 778 \times 10^{-8}$ cm^2 and $A_2 = 7264$ μm$^2 = 7264 \times 10^{-8}$ cm^2. Thus, $C_{B1} = C_{oxp} A_1 = 0.05$ pF and $C_{B2} = C_{oxp} A_2 = 0.47$ pF.

TABLE 8-1   PARASITIC CAPACITANCES (WHERE $C_{oxT} = C_{ox} W L_{\text{eff}}$ AS PER TABLE 1-5)

	Region		
	Cutoff	Triode	Saturation
C_{GS}	$C_{GS0} = C_{ox} W L_D$	$C_{GS0} + \frac{1}{2} C_{oxt}$	$C_{ox} W L_D + \frac{2}{3} C_{oxt}$
C_{GD}	$C_{GD0} = C_{ox} W L_D$	$C_{GD0} + \frac{1}{2} C_{oxt}$	C_{GD0}
C_{jS}	$\approx C_{jSB} A_S$	$\approx C_{jSB} A_S + \frac{1}{2} C_{BC}$	$\approx C_{jSB} A_S + \frac{2}{3} C_{BC}$
C_{jD}	$\approx C_{jDB} A_D$	$\approx C_{jDB} A_D + \frac{1}{2} C_{BC}$	$\approx C_{jDB} A_D$
C_R		$C_{oxm} W_R L_R$	
C_B		$C_{oxp} W_B L_B$	

Note that all parasitics connect the signal path of the intended integrated circuit to the bias and control voltages. Let us refer to the intended AC signal input as X_{in}, the AC output as X_{out}, and the bias/control voltages as B_i. To the extent that B_i are well-behaved, the parasitics are connected between the signal path and AC ground, and their primary effect is to degrade the integrated filter's precision. The voltage dependent parasitic C's also introduce additional nonlinear distortion. When the bias and control voltages are not well-behaved, and contain AC components, they contribute to the system noise and degrade dynamic range.

These two phenomenon are best considered using superposition. That is, we evaluate the impact on precision and dynamic range, respectively, using the following transfer relations:

$$X_{\text{out}}|_{B_{\text{in}}=0} = H(j\omega)X_{\text{in}} \tag{8-1a}$$

and

$$X_{\text{out}}|_{X_{\text{in0}}} = \sum_i H_i(j\omega)B_i \tag{8-1b}$$

The $B_i = 0$ represent the connections to AC ground mentioned above. In Sec. 8-3, we address Eq. (8-1a) and explore methods for reducing the involvement of parasitics in the signal path performance. In Sec. 8-5, we examine the full impact of Eq. (8-1b).

8-2 DESIGN OF PRACTICAL INTEGRATED FILTER COMPONENTS

By applying good layout practice, the magnitudes of many parasitic components can be reduced and perhaps made negligible. Good layout practice includes: (1) making all signal routes, especially the critical ones, as short as possible, (2) using the smallest geometries possible, (3) realizing low resistance routings for power, ground, and critical signals (e.g., make these routes entirely in metal), and (4) maximizing physical and electrical isolation between analog and digital circuitry. In addition, clever circuit techniques can lead to reduced sensitivities to the parasitic components, especially to the most critical ones. To successfully combat parasitics it is prudent to attack with the combination of a good layout and a clever design. It is also prudent to include as many critical parasitic components as possible in computer simulations used to verify a design.

In Chaps. 1 and 2 we review the variety of passive and active components available in MOS and bipolar technologies. Chapter 6 was devoted to the transistor level design of op amps and OTAs suitable for a broad range of applications. In this section we examine the nonideal behavior of several integrated filter components and their interaction with the parasitic capacitances listed in Table 8-1. Where needed and available, design strategies will be offered that reduce the nonideal behavior and the size of the parasitic capacitances. Let us start with the capacitor in Fig. 8-6.

8-2-1 Poly 1-Poly 2 Capacitor

The capacitor C_A in Fig. 8-6 is connected to the substrate bias V_{DD} from the top plate (terminal 3) via C_R and the bottom plate (terminal 4) via C_B. To the extent that V_{DD} is an ideal DC source, its terminal is at AC ground. We note that both parasitics are

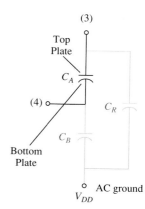

FIGURE 8-6   Lumped model for poly 1-poly 2 capacitor of value C_A in black, with parasitic capacitances C_R and C_B in gray.

linear, as indicated in Table 8-1. In the literature, C_R is often referred to as the top plate parasitic and C_B as the bottom plate parasitic. This model applies to both CMOS (Fig. 7-4e) and bipolar capacitors (Fig. 7-2d). As noted earlier, aside from parasitics, the C_A realizations discussed in Sec. 7-2 are very near ideal in behavior.

In discrete circuits, capacitors are considered symmetrical with regard to the top and bottom plates. When parasitics are taken into account, we see that this symmetry (in Fig. 8-6) is an oversimplification for integrated capacitors. In fact, the impact of C_B can be minimized when the bottom plate (4) is connected to either ground or to the output of an ideal (dependent or independent) voltage source. We prefer, if possible, to connect the top plate (3) to an op amp virtual ground.

8-2-2 MOST Analog Switch

The circuit model for a pMOST or nMOST operating as a switch is shown in Fig. 8-7 (Allstot and Black 1983; Gray and Meyer 1984). The MOST is controlled by clock $\phi^{e,o}$ (i.e., ϕ^e or ϕ^o) and backgate bias V_B. Recall that for a pMOST, $V_B = V_{DD}$ and for an nMOST, $V_B = V_{SS}$ or ground. Under the control of $\phi^{e,o}$ the MOST alternates between the cutoff and triode regions, which constitute the switch's OFF and ON states, respectively. Many of the parasitics (C_{jD}, C_{jS}, C_{GD}, and C_{GS}) in Fig. 8-7 are associated with the MOST switch. C_{R1} and C_{R2} are due to the routing to terminals (1) and (2), respectively. Since C_{jD} and C_{jS} are voltage dependent, they are potential sources of nonlinear distortion. The other parasitics are linear. The relations for all the parasitics C's are listed in Table 8-1. In addition, we see that C_{R1}, C_{R2} and C_{jD}, C_{jS} AC-couple the switch signal path to V_{DD} and V_B (which can also be V_{DD}), respectively. Parasitics C_{GD} and C_{GS} couple the signal path to the clock $\phi^{e,o}$.

In its operation as a switch, the MOST is a variable resistor with, ideally, a very large resistance (i.e., $R_{OFF} \to \infty$) when the switch is OFF, and a very small resistor (i.e., $R_{ON} \to 0$) when the switch is ON. When cut off, the MOST is very nearly an open circuit, with $R_{OFF} > 10^{10}\ \Omega$. The parasitics for the OFF state are shown

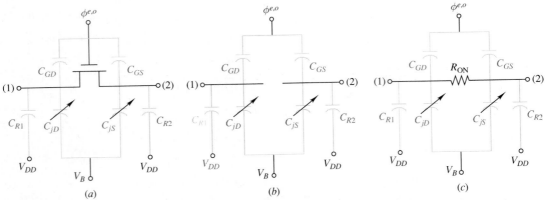

FIGURE 8-7 p or nMOST switch: (a) the circuit with back gate bias V_B and control clock $\phi^{e,o}$; (b) model for the OFF state; and (c) the model for the ON state. Parasitic capacitances are shown in gray.

in Fig. 8-7b; and the cutoff MOST is well approximated by an open circuit. In the ON state, the MOST and its parasitics are shown in Fig. 8-7c. The switch R_{ON} (i.e., R_{DS} in Eq. (1-34)) is determined by the instantaneous value of V_{GS} and the geometric dimensions $W \times L$ of the MOST. Also, as $R_{ON} \to 0$, then $v_{DS} = v_{12} \to 0$, which naturally suppresses the MOST nonlinearities. Expressions for the parasitic capacitances in the cutoff and triode regions are listed in Table 8-1. For switched-capacitor filters it is important that R_{ON} be sufficiently small, so as not to interfere with charge transfer during $\phi^{e,o}$. Hence, for a given switch S_i, the designer must set $W_i \times L_i$ such that $R_{ONi}C_{Ti} \ll \eta T$. Where C_{Ti} is the total capacitance (intentional + parasitic) connected to the MOST S_i's source or drain terminal, $\eta < 0.5$ (or 50 percent) is the duty cycle for $\phi^{e,o}$, and ηT is the time allowed for C_{Ti} to charge. It is highly desirable to standardize on one switch size; hence, $W_i = W$ and $L_i = L$ is conservatively set such that $R_{ON}C_{Tmax} \ll T/2$, where C_{Tmax} is the maximum C_{Ti} in the switched-capacitor circuit.

The objective of $R_{ON} \to$ small requires $W/L \to$ large. At the same time, we seek to make the parasitic capacitances in Fig. 8-7 small, which requires area $WL \to$ small. To examine these conflicting objectives, let us consider some numbers.

Example 8-2

Let the analog switches in an active-SC filter be realized as single nMOSTs. Assume that the capacitance connected to any given switch is bounded by $C_{Ti} \leq 10$ pF, the MOST switch is designed for an $R_{ON} \approx 5$ kΩ, and that the $\phi^{e,o}$ duty cycle is $\eta = 40$ percent. Determine the highest sample rate f_s that can be supported if the switch time constant is to constitute less than 10 percent of the time available to charge C_{Ti}. Since the value of R_{ON} increases continuously along the charging cycle, as shown in Fig. 1-17c, assume that $R_{ON} \approx 5$ kΩ occurs at the point where the voltage across C_{Ti} reaches half its final value.

Solution. From the data above, $R_{ON}C_{Tmax} \leq 5 \times 10^{-8}$ sec. Hence, if we choose to limit $R_{ON}C_{Tmax}$ to less than 10 percent of ηT, then $\eta T > 0.5$ μsec or $T > 1.25$ μsec. Hence, the sample rate is limited to $f_s = 1/T < 800$ kHz. Note that if $\eta \approx 0.5$, then $f_s < 1$ MHz. We see that the requirement for $\eta < 0.5$, to avoid overlap, further reduces the high frequency capability of the technology. Clearly, η cannot be made arbitrarily small.

From Chap. 1, $R_{ON} < 10$ kΩ is achievable with a MOST switch of minimum geometry, i.e., $W/L = 1$. Schematics and layouts for two NMOS switches are shown in Fig. 8-8a and 8-8b (*see color plate 2*). These configurations are for the single-pole-double-throw and double-pole-double-throw switches, respectively. Recalling the SC integrator structures in Fig. 7-35 one can see that the double-pole type switch occurs frequently in SC circuits. Thus, it behooves us to have an efficient layout for this structure, such as Fig. 8-8b. Furthermore, a CMOS double-pole double-throw switch can be constructed by adding complementary *p*MOSTs in parallel to the *n*MOSTs, as shown in Fig. 8-8c. The CMOS structure reduces R_{ON} and increases R_{OFF} by an order of magnitude, respectively (see Exercises 7-14 and 7-15). Note that at op amp virtual grounds, where $v_{GS} \gg V_T$, R_{ON} can be kept sufficiently small with a simple NMOS switch, shown in Fig. 8-8b. Thus, to realize high performance switches while minimizing parasitics, we generally use NMOS switches at op amp virtual grounds and CMOS switches everywhere else. The MOSTs in both structures will be of minimum $W \times L$, unless otherwise noted. The prudent designer will reexamine the sufficiency of minimum switch dimensions, at the nodes of largest C_{Ti}, once the values for the capacitors are set in the design.

Example 8-2 demonstrates one of the costs of switched-capacitor realization, namely, the inefficient use of technology bandwidth. The bandwidth requirement for the technology is dictated by the sample rate f_s, rather than the frequency requirements for the filter. Since switched-capacitor filters are usually highly oversampled ($f_s > 20f_C$ where f_C is the filter cutoff frequency—see App. 7-1), this inefficiency can be a heavy burden. This is particularly evident when filter critical frequencies are well above the audio range. In this area, continuous-time filters, which do not carry this burden, have an implementation advantage. In effect, with switched-capacitor filters, we sacrifice bandwidth in order to realize filter-time constants with substantially increased precision.

8-2-3   Linearized MOST Resistor

When operated in the triode region, the *p*MOST-R or *n*MOST-R (Geiger, Allen, and Strader 1990; Gregorian and Temes 1986; Unbehauen and Cichocki 1989) in Fig. 8-9a, is a voltage-controlled, nonlinear distributed RC line. Recall that triode operation occurs when $v_{DS} < v_{GS} - V_T$ for an *n*MOST (or $v_{DS} > v_{GS} - V_T$ for a *p*MOST) and V_T is defined in Eqs. (1-7). The MOST-R, in its simplest form, is essentially an ON analog switch with $R_{ON} = R_A$. However, in the case of a MOST-R we want R_A to be large. Also, v_{DS}, the voltage drop across R_A, is no longer constrained by device operation to be small. Our objective is to realize a linear voltage-controlled R_A over a broad range of v_{DS}. Suitably linearized, the MOST-R can be represented by the small signal model in Fig. 8-9b. The capacitance of the RC line is gate-to-channel parasitic C_{oxt}. We note that Fig. 8-9b can be used in form to model any CMOS or bipolar integrated resistor listed in Table 7-1. For ohmic material type resistors, i.e., p-well, ion-implanted or thin-film R's, V_C and parasitics C_{GD} and C_{GS} disappear from the model. However, p-well resistors have distributed capacitances similar to C_{oxt} and a voltage dependent capacitance to the bulk similar to $C_{JD,S}$.

To examine the performance of this MOST-R (Gregorian and Temes 1986; Czarnul 1986; Khorramabadi and Gray 1984; Nedungadi and Viswanathan 1985; Tsividis, Banu, and Khoury 1986; Unbehauen and Cichocki 1989), let us return for a moment to the MOST model in Sec. 1-4 for the condition $v_{GS} = $ large, $v_{DS} = $ large, $v_{BS} \neq 0$. In Eq. (1-16), current i_{DS} is written in a general form to include all nonlinearities and the body effect. Substituting $v_{GS} = V_C - v_S$, $v_{BS} = V_B - v_S$ and $v_{DS} = v_D - v_S$ from Fig. 8-9a into Eq. (1-16), we can write i_{DS} for an nMOST in the triode region as follows

$$i_{DS} = \beta\{(V_C - V_T)(v_D - v_S) - \frac{1}{2}[(v_D)^2 - (v_S)^2] \tag{8-2}$$

$$+ \gamma \frac{2}{3}[(v_D - v_{BS} + 2|\phi_F|)^{3/2} - (v_S - v_{BS} + 2|\phi_F|)^{3/2}]\}$$

where $\beta = \mu C_{ox}(W/L)$ and $V_T = V_{T0} + \gamma(\sqrt{2|\phi_F| - v_{BS}} - \sqrt{2|\phi_F|})$. We note that for a pMOST, Eq. (8-2) is modified by interchanging V_C and V_T, and replacing $+\gamma$ with $-\gamma$. Also, recall from Eqs. (1-6) that V_{T0} is free of back-gate effects.

FIGURE 8-9 p or nMOST-R: (a) a single MOST circuit with control voltage V_C; and (b) small signal, lumped equivalent model. Parasitic capacitances are shown in gray.

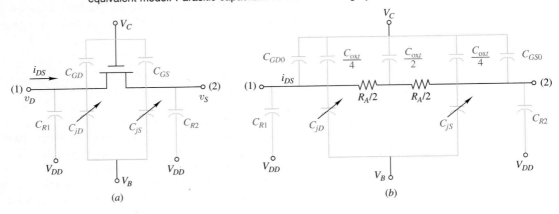

Expanding 3/2 power terms in Eq. (8-2) into a Taylor series with respect to v_D and v_S (i.e., assuming $v_D \approx v_S \approx 0$), we can express i_{DS} in the following form:

$$i_{DS} = a_1(v_D - v_S) - \{a_2[(v_D)^2 - (v_S)^2] - a_3[(v_D)^3 - (v_S)^3] + ...\} \qquad (8\text{-}3a)$$

$$= \beta(V_C - V_T)(v_D - v_S) - i_{NL}(v_D, v_S) \qquad (8\text{-}3b)$$

where all the nonlinear terms are lumped into current i_{NL}. The two most significant terms in this expansion (Tsividis, Banu, and Khoury 1986) are $a_1(v_D - v_S)$ and $a_2[(v_D)^2 - (v_S)^2]$, where

$$a_1 = \beta(V_C - V_T) \qquad \text{and} \qquad a_2 = \frac{\beta}{2}\left[1 + \frac{\gamma}{2\sqrt{2|\phi_F| - v_{BS}}}\right] \qquad (8\text{-}3c)$$

Hence, the small signal (i.e., v_{DS} = sufficiently small $\ll V_C$) R_A is formed by the ratio i_{DS}/v_{DS} with $i_{NL} = 0$, i.e.,

$$R_A = \frac{v_{DS}}{i_{DS}} = \frac{1}{\beta(V_C - V_T)} = \frac{L/W}{\mu C_{ox}(V_C - V_T)} \qquad (8\text{-}4)$$

When suitably linear, R_A is seen to be independent of v_{DS}.

Example 8-3

To get a feel for the magnitudes of the numbers involved: calculate (a) the linear and second-order terms for the conductance i_{DS}/v_{DS} and (b) the effective linear resistance R_A for an nMOST of $L/W = 10$ using the device parameters in Table 1-1.

Solution. Using Eqs. (8-3), let us form the ratio i_{DS}/v_{DS} and truncate the expression after two terms, i.e.,

$$\frac{i_{DS}}{v_{DS}} = a_1 + a_2(v_D + v_S)$$

Let $V_C = 3.0$ V, $V_B = -3$ V, $v_D = 1$ V, $v_S = 0$ V, and from Table 1-1 we get $\gamma = 0.92$ V$^{1/2}$, $V_{T0} = 0.6$ V, $2\phi_F = 0.6$ V, $\mu C_{ox} = KP = 40$ μA/V^2. (a) Substituting this data into Eq. (8-3c) we obtain $V_T = 1.9$ V, and

$$a_1 = 44 \ \mu\text{A/V or } 44 \ \mu\text{S} \quad \text{and} \quad a_2(v_D + v_S) = 24.9 \ \mu\text{A/V or } 24.9 \ \mu\text{S}.$$

We see that a_2 is not negligible, and can only be reduced relative to a_1 by reducing v_D (and v_S) to a very small level. (b) the resistance $R_A = 1/a_1 = 22.73$ kΩ.

We see in Eq. (8-4) that R_A is controlled by the MOST dimensions $W \times L$ and control voltage V_C. Typically, the nominal value for R_A is set by $W \times L$, and V_C is used to tune or adaptively adjust the value over a range of about ± 10 percent. When matched R's are required, a layout strategy similar to that in Fig. 7-2e is used. The MOST parasitics increase with area WL, and are largely determined by the resistor value. The relations for the MOST parasitics $C_{GS}, C_{GD}, C_{jS}, C_{jD}$ in the triode region are listed in Table 8-1. Since C_{jD}, C_{jS} are voltage dependent, they are sources of nonlinearity, independent of the status of R_A. Note that C_{GS}, C_{GD} (or C_{GS0}, C_{GD0}, and C_{oxt}) AC-couple the terminals of the resistor directly to the control voltage V_C. V_C is either a DC source or a very slow varying-control signal from an adaptive tuning loop.

As it stands, the nonlinearity in Eqs. (8-2) and (8-3) severely limits the functionality of the MOST-R. However, using resistor structures (Gregorian and Temes 1986; Czarnul 1986; Tsividis, Banu, and Khoury 1986; Unbehauen and Cichocki 1989) in Fig. 8-10, the nonlinearity in Eq. (8-3b) can largely be canceled in an elegant fashion. Such structures significantly extend the range of linear operation for the MOST-R. One recommended structure (Gregorian and Temes 1986; Tsividis Banu, and Khoury 1986) is illustrated in Fig. 8-10a, where we show a differential pair of matched MOSTs T1 and T2 used to simulate the differential resistor pair in Fig. 8-10b. In this structure the drains of the MOSTs are driven with a differential voltage $\pm v_D$ and both sources are constrained to v_S, although they are not physically connected.

To evaluate the operation of this structure, let us first form the currents i_{DS}^+ and i_{DS}^- through the differential paths using Eq. (8-3b), i.e., for nMOSTs

$$i_{DS}^+ = \beta(V_C - V_T)(v_D - v_S) - i_{NL}(v_D, v_S) \qquad (8\text{-}5a)$$

$$i_{DS}^- = \beta(V_C - V_T)(-v_D - v_S) - i_{NL}(-v_D, v_S) \qquad (8\text{-}5b)$$

FIGURE 8-10   Linearized MOST-R structures: (a) two matched MOSTs (p or n) with differential input; (b) lumped equivalent model (parasitics not shown); and (c) four matched MOSTs (for linear operation $V_{C4} = V_{C1}$ and $V_{C3} = V_{C2}$).

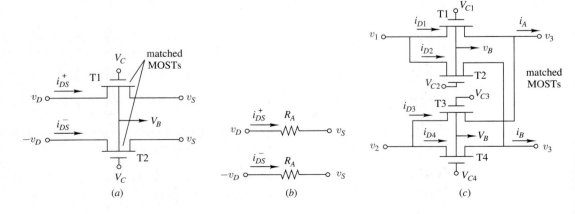

In writing these expressions, we assume that MOSTs T1 and T2 are matched such that $\beta_1 = \beta_2 = \beta$ and $V_{T01} = V_{T02} = V_{T0}$. Nonlinear $i_{NL}(v_D, v_S)$ can be conveniently expressed in terms of even and odd nonlinear terms, i.e.,

$$i_{NL}(v_D, v_S) = g_e(v_D) + g_o(v_D) - (g_e(v_S) + g_o(v_S)) \tag{8-6}$$

where $g_e(v)$ and $g_o(v)$ are even and odd nonlinear functions of v, respectively, such that $g_e(-v) = g_e(v)$ and $g_o(-v) = -g_o(v)$. Substituting Eq. (8-6) into Eqs. (8-5) yields

$$i_{DS}^+ = \beta(V_C - V_T)(v_D - v_S) - \{g_e(v_D) + g_o(v_D)$$
$$- [g_e(v_S) + g_o(v_S)]\} \tag{8-7a}$$

$$i_{DS}^- = \beta(V_C - V_T)(-v_D - v_S) - \{g_e(v_D) - g_o(v_D)$$
$$- [g_e(v_S) + g_o(v_S)]\} \tag{8-7b}$$

All the nonlinearities except $g_o(v_D)$ are removed when we take the difference of these two currents, i.e.,

$$i = i_{DS}^+ - i_{DS}^- = \beta(V_C - V_T)(2v_D) - 2g_o(v_D) \approx \beta(V_C - V_T)(2v_D) \tag{8-8}$$

Typically, $g_o(v_D)$ is very small (e.g., ≤ 0.1 percent of the linear component); hence, Eq. (8-8) can be accurately truncated to the desired result, i.e.,

$$i = i_{DS}^+ - i_{DS}^- \approx \beta(V_C - V_T)(2v_D) \tag{8-9a}$$

and

$$R_A = \frac{2v_D}{i_{DS}^+ - i_{DS}^-} = \frac{1}{\beta(V_C - V_T)} \tag{8-9b}$$

Thus, in the triode region, where $v_D < V_C - V_T$, R_A in Eq. (8-9b) is independent of v_S and v_D over a broad range of v_{DS}. Mismatches in β's and V_{T0}'s of T1 and T2 will proportionately degrade the cancellations forced in Eq. (8-8). The equivalence between Figs. 8-10a and 8-10b is then established. We leave it to the reader to verify that spurious signals fed through the parasitics from V_{DD} (or V_C), as per Fig. 8-9b, will also be canceled when i is formed in Eq. (8-8). For pMOSTs, we interchange V_C and V_T in Eqs. (8-5) through (8-9).

In Fig. 8-10c, we show another interesting structure, comprised of four matched MOSTs (T1, T2, T3, and T4) controlled by V_{C1}, V_{C2}, V_{C3}, and V_{C4} (Czarnul 1986). We leave it for the reader to verify that if we form the difference $i = i_A - i_B$ with $V_{C4} = V_{C1}$ and $V_{C3} = V_{C2}$ all nonlinearities cancel, even $g_o(v_D)$ in Eq. (8-8). Hence, after clearing all the canceled terms, we have for nMOSTs

$$i = i_A - i_B = \{\beta(V_{C1} - V_T) - \beta(V_{C2} - V_T)\}(v_1 - v_2) \tag{8-10a}$$

$$= \beta(V_{C1} - V_{C2})(v_1 - v_2) \tag{8-10b}$$

Thus, in this structure, the R_A is also independent of V_T and the associated body effect, where

$$R_A = \frac{1}{\beta(V_{C1} - V_{C2})} \qquad (8\text{-}11)$$

Furthermore, R_A depends on the difference of control voltages V_{C1} and V_{C2}. This relationship serves to cancel any spurious AC signals common to the V_{Ci}. For pMOSTs, due to the interchange of V_{Ci} and V_T, V_{C1} and V_{C2} interchange in Eq. (8-11).

We note that the structure of Fig. 8-10c can be used in a balanced, differential manner with $v_1 = v_D$ and $v_2 = -v_D$. Then, $v_1 - v_2 = 2v_D$, and Fig. 8-10c realizes the differential resistor pair in Fig. 8-10b. However, in contrast to Eqs. (8-8) and (8-9), R_A in Eq. (8-11) is independent of all nonlinearities and the body effect via V_T. The reader can verify that any spurious signals common to i_A and i_B will also cancel when i is formed in Eq. (8-10). The fact that we assume that all transistors are matched (i.e., $\beta_i = \beta$ and $V_{T0i} = V_{T0}$) and operating in the triode region, i.e., $v_1, v_2 < \min[V_{C1} - V_T, V_{C2} - V_T]$ is worth repeating. Once again, the cancellations achieved in Eq. (8-10) will degrade in proportion to the degree of mismatch that occurs among the four MOSTs.

In Figs. 8-10a and 8-10c, the designer has a choice of two linearized MOST-R structures. Figure 8-10a is simpler, but Fig. 8-10c is more robust to the degree that all MOSTs are matched. Also, Fig. 8-10a must be used in a balanced differential structure to achieve linearity. Hence, it can only be used to realize integrated matched resistor pairs in fully-balanced, differential active-RC circuits such as Fig. 5-43. On the other hand, Fig. 8-10c can be used to realize a matched pair of resistors in either balanced or unbalanced (i.e., where $v_2 \neq -v_1$) circuits.

8-2-4 Linearized OTA Transconductance

Our purpose in this section is to explore the use of the OTA (Bazanezhad and Temes 1984; Gregorian and Temes 1986; Khorramabadi and Gray 1984; Nedungadi and Viswanathan 1984; Park and Schaumann 1986; Torrance, Viswanathan, and Hanson 1985; Tsividis, Czarnul, and Fang 1986; Unbehauen and Cichocki 1989; Silva et al. 1993) as a linear voltage-controlled current source (*VCCS*) or transconductance G_m, as described in Sec. 5-5, to realize active-G_m/C filters. Since OTAs can be realized in CMOS and bipolar, active-G_m/C filters can be realized in either technology. For this application, OTAs are operated in a local open loop. This enables the designer to use the intrinsic bandwidth of the technology more efficiently, but the benefits of feedback that assist the operation of OTAs and op amps in many other applications are sacrificed.

Design relations were developed in Chaps. 4 and 6 for the basic CMOS OTA, redrawn in Fig. 8-11. This circuit is comprised of an nMOST differential pair, a 1:1 pMOST current mirror, and a bias current $2I_A$ set such that T1 and T2 are in saturation. From the analysis in Sec. 4-7, we know that the pertinent relationships describing the large signal behavior for this circuit, with matched T1, T2, (i.e., $\beta_1 = \beta_2 = \beta$ and $V_{T1} = V_{T2} = V_T$) are given by

$$i_{D1} = \frac{\beta}{2}(v_{GS1} - V_T)^2, \; i_{D2} = \frac{\beta}{2}(v_{GS2} - V_T)^2, \text{ and } 2I_A = i_{D1} + i_{D2} \qquad (8\text{-}12)$$

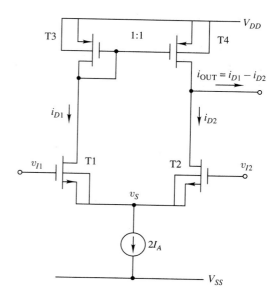

FIGURE 8-11 Basic CMOS OTA, with nMOST differential pair, pMOST current mirror and bias current $2I_A$.

where $v_{GS1} = v_{IN1} - v_S$ and $v_{GS2} = v_{IN2} - v_S$. Eliminating V_T, currents i_{D1} and i_{D2} can be expressed as follows

$$i_{D1} = I_D + i_d = I_A + \sqrt{\frac{\beta I_A}{2}} \Delta v_{IN} \sqrt{1 - \frac{\beta}{8I_A}(\Delta v_{IN})^2} \qquad (8\text{-}13a)$$

$$i_{D2} = I_D - i_d = I_A - \sqrt{\frac{\beta I_A}{2}} \Delta v_{IN} \sqrt{1 - \frac{\beta}{8I_A}(\Delta v_{IN})^2} \qquad (8\text{-}13b)$$

and the output current

$$i_{OUT} = i_{D1} - i_{D2} = 2i_d = \sqrt{2\beta I_A} \Delta v_{IN} \sqrt{1 - \frac{\beta}{8I_A}(\Delta v_{IN})^2} \qquad (8\text{-}13c)$$

Expanding Eq. (8-13c) into a Taylor series shows that i_{OUT} has only odd harmonics, i.e.,

$$i_{OUT} \approx \sqrt{2\beta I_A} \Delta v_{IN} - \frac{1}{8}\sqrt{\frac{\beta^3}{2I_A}}(\Delta v_{IN})^3 = a_1 \Delta v_{IN} + a_3 (\Delta v_{IN})^3 \qquad (8\text{-}13d)$$

where $\Delta v_{IN} = v_{IN1} - v_{IN2}$, i_d is the incremental drain current due to Δv_{IN}, and $\Delta v_{IN} \leq 2\sqrt{I_A/\beta}$ for T1, T2 to remain in saturation.

We see in Eqs. (8-13c) and (8-13d) that i_{OUT}, and hence $G_m = i_{OUT}/\Delta v_{IN}$, is nonlinear in Δv_{IN}. Only for $\Delta v_{IN} \ll 4\sqrt{I_A/\beta}$ is i_{OUT} linear, and

$$G_m = \frac{i_{OUT}}{\Delta v_{IN}} = \sqrt{2\beta I_A} \qquad (8\text{-}14)$$

A similar analysis can be done for a bipolar differential pair, revealing that the nonlinear dependence of the collector current on Δv_{IN} is of an exponential rather than a square form in Eq. (8-12). Note that G_m can be tuned by adjusting I_A, which is similar to the role of V_C in tuning the MOST-R. Also, the range of Δv_{IN} for which Eq. (8-14) is valid is proportional to $\sqrt{I_A}$.

Example 8-4

To get a feel for the magnitudes of the numbers involved: calculate (a) a_1 and a_3 expansion terms for the current i_{OUT} and (b) the effective linear transconductance G_m for the CMOS OTA in Fig. 8-9. For these calculations let $KP = \mu C_{ox} = 40\ \mu A/V^2$, $W/L = 1$, and $2I_A = 20\ \mu A$.

Solution. These numbers lead to (a) $a_1 = 40\ \mu A/V, a_3 = 3.5\ \mu A/V^3$ and (b) $G_m \approx a_1 = 40\ \mu S$ if $\Delta v_{IN} \ll 2$ V. Note that the limit $4\sqrt{I_A/\beta}$ can be increased by either increasing I_A or decreasing β (i.e., increasing L/W). Making either very large is disadvantageous; i.e., increasing I_A increases power dissipation and increasing L/W increases die area. Furthermore, since filter time constants are determined by $C/G_m = \tau$, the scaling of G_m due to increases in I_A and/or L/W for linearity will necessitate a proportional scaling of C.

We conclude that the linearity of the simple OTA in Fig. 8-11 can be enhanced only by increasing die area and/or increasing power dissipation. Thus, it would be useful to find a scheme that increases the intrinsic linear range for Δv_{IN}.

To increase this range, let us consider an interesting scheme (Nedungadi and Viswanathan 1984) where the bias $2I_A$ current in Fig. 8-11 is designed to depend on Δv_{IN} with the relationship

$$2I_A \rightarrow 2i_A = 2I_B + \frac{\beta'}{2}(\Delta v_{IN})^2 \qquad (8\text{-}15)$$

Multiplying and dividing Eq. (8-13c) by $\sqrt{2I_A}$ and replacing I_A with i_A yields

$$
\begin{aligned}
i_{out} &= \sqrt{\beta}\,\Delta v_{IN}\sqrt{2I_A - \frac{\beta}{4}(\Delta v_{IN})^2} \\
&= \sqrt{\beta}\,\Delta v_{IN}\sqrt{2I_B + \frac{\beta'}{2}(\Delta v_{IN})^2 - \frac{\beta}{4}(\Delta v_{IN})^2} \qquad (8\text{-}16)
\end{aligned}
$$

where we substituted Eq. (8-15) for $2i_A$.

The nonlinearity in Eq. (8-16) cancels when we set $\beta' = \beta/2$ and the resulting linearized G_m is the same as Eq. (8-14), but with I_A replaced with I_B. Note that nonlinearity due to the short channel effect $1 + \lambda v_{DS}$ in Eq. (1-20) is not canceled with this method and can be reduced only by increasing the channel length L for the nMOSTs.

An implementation of this concept is shown in Fig. 8-12, where we have differential pair T7, T8 and current mirror T3, T4, as in Fig. 8-11. The requisite bias current in Eq. (8-15) is realized by nMOSTs T1, T2, T5, and T6 with bias currents $(\gamma + 1)I_B$. With this scheme, $2i_A$ is realized by the sum of the T1 and T2 drain currents, i.e., $2i_A = i_{D1} + i_{D2}$. The fact that this sum realizes a current with the relationship in Eq. (8-15) should be evident from Eqs. (8-13). The circuitry involved in defining this current is highlighted in gray. The final nMOST T9 serves to shift current $2i_A$ from node A to node B. Bias current αI_B is chosen to maintain T9 in saturation over the full input range. The β's for T1, T2, T7, T8 are matched such that $\beta_1 = \beta_2 = \beta_7 = \beta_8 = \beta$ and the β's for T5, T6 are matched such that $\beta_5 = \beta_6 = \gamma\beta$.

For this circuit, it can be shown that

$$2i_A = i_{D1} + i_{D2} = 2I_B + (i_1 - i_2)$$

$$= 2I_B + \frac{\gamma(\gamma - 1)}{(\gamma + 1)^2}\beta(\Delta v_{IN})^2 \qquad \text{(8-17)}$$

FIGURE 8-12   Nedungadi-Viswanathan OTA compensated to realize linearized transconductance G_m (Nedungadi and Viswanathan 1984).

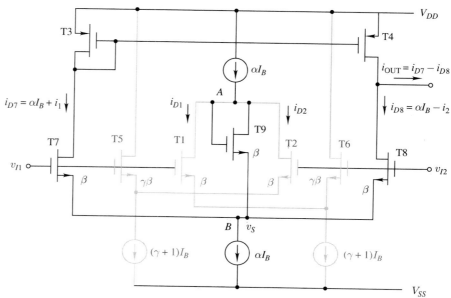

where T1, T2, T5, T6, T7, and T8 are in saturation when $\Delta v_{IN} \leq \sqrt{2(\gamma + 1)I_B/\gamma\beta}$, and T9 is in saturation when $\alpha \geq 4\gamma/(\gamma + 1)$. Comparing Eqs. (8-17) and (8-15), we see that for linear operation

$$\beta' = \frac{2\gamma(\gamma - 1)}{(\gamma + 1)^2}\beta = \frac{\beta}{2} \quad \text{or} \quad \frac{(\gamma + 1)^2}{\gamma(\gamma - 1)} = 4 \tag{8-18}$$

Solving Eq. (8-17) for γ yields $\gamma = 2.155$ and, correspondingly, $\alpha \geq 2.732$. The linearized G_m is given by

$$G_m = \frac{i_{OUT}}{\Delta v_{IN}} = \sqrt{2\beta I_B} \tag{8-19}$$

for the full range $\Delta v_{IN} \leq 1.711\sqrt{I_B/\beta}$, where $i_{OUT} = i_{D7} - i_{D8}$. This is a considerable improvement over the linearity range for the simple differential pair in Fig. 8-11.

We point out that other linear and tunable G_m schemes have been offered. One scheme, interesting in its inherent simplicity, is shown in Fig. 8-13a (Park and Schaumann 1986). The circuit, based on the CMOS inverter, realizes a linearized $i_{OUT} = -G_m v_{IN}$ where G_m is proportional to the difference in control voltages $V_{C1} - (-V_{C2})$; i.e.,

$$G_m = \frac{i_{OUT}}{v_{IN}} = 4\beta_{\text{eff}}(V_{C1} + V_{C2} - \Sigma V_T) \tag{8-20a}$$

FIGURE 8-13   Alternative CMOS linearized transconductance elements: (a) based on the CMOS inverter (Park and Schaumann 1986); and (b) based on the MOST-R (Tsividis, Czarnul, and Fang 1986).

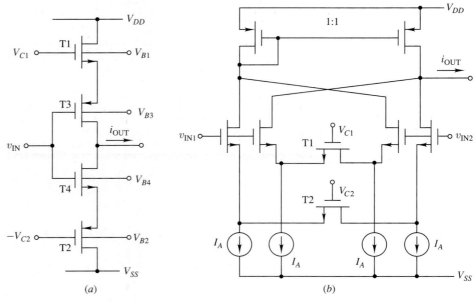

where $\beta_{\text{eff}} = \beta_n\beta_p/(\sqrt{\beta_n} + \sqrt{\beta_p})^2$ and $\Sigma V_T = 1/2\{V_{Tn1} + V_{Tn4} + |V_{Tp2}| + |V_{Tp3}|\}$. All n and pMOSTs are respectively matched (i.e., $\beta_{Tn1} = \beta_{Tn4} = \beta_n$ and $\beta_{Tp2} = \beta_{Tp3} = \beta_p$) and biased in the saturation region. We leave it to the reader to verify this circuit [see Exercise 8-6]. The parasitics and the resulting frequency response for OTA structures has been covered in significant detail in Chaps. 4 and 6. When we design active-G_m/C filters, we rely on models developed in these chapters.

The linearized transconductor in Fig. 8-13b presents another compelling alternative to the more conventional OTA and inverter-based structures (Tsividis, Czarnul, and Fang 1986). In this circuit, the G_m is derived from a cross coupled pair of matched MOST-R's (T1, T2) operating in the triode region. Nonlinearities (including body effect terms) are canceled in the manner described for the MOST-R structure in Fig. 8-10c. In this configuration, and similarly the one in Fig. 8-13a, the G_m is controlled with gate voltages V_{C1} and V_{C2} rather than the bias current I_A, i.e.,

$$G_m = \frac{i_{\text{OUT}}}{(v_{\text{IN1}} - v_{\text{IN2}})} = \beta(V_{C1} - V_{C2}) \qquad (8\text{-}20b)$$

where β is the transconductance gain for MOSTs T1, T2. The back gates of T1, T2 are connected to V_{SS}. Hence, the biasing of the source followers and active loads are unaffected by any tuning of G_m. Also, the fact that G_m is determined by the difference of two control signals enable one to cancel any common spurious AC coupled to these controls. Once again, we leave it to the reader to verify the operation of this circuit. As one would expect, the dominant parasitics for this transconductor are those of the MOST-R in Fig. 8-9b.

8-3 PARASITICS AND FILTER PRECISION

Parasitics can combine with the intentional components to either modify the filter coefficients (e.g., Fig. 8-14a) or, perhaps worse, create unwanted poles and zeros (e.g., Fig. 8-14b). (Allstot and Black 1983; Ghausi and Laker 1981; Grebene 1984;

FIGURE 8-14   Parasitic capacitances introducing (a) error in filter coefficients when a dominant parasitic adds to an intentional component of a like kind; and (b) introducing an undesired pole (or zero) when a dominant parasitic combines with an intentional component of a different kind.

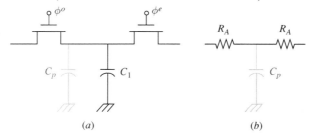

(a)   (b)

Gregorian and Temes 1986; Moschytz 1986; Schaumann, Ghausi, and Laker 1990; Sedra 1985, Sedra 1989; Toumazou et al. 1990; Unbehauen and Cichocki 1989). In texts on discrete circuits, the reader is usually instructed to compensate for measured or estimated parasitics by modifying intentional components. This process is called *predistortion*. For example, in Fig. 8-14a, let the measured parasitic and the desired capacitance be $C_p = \delta$ pF and $C_1 = N$ pF, respectively. In principle, we can compensate for the presence of C_p by predistorting C_1 to $C_{1d} = N - \delta$ pF, such that the total is the desired value $C_p + C_{1d} = N$ pF. Because C_1 and C_p involve different mask levels, they have no opportunity to track or match (statistically or otherwise). Hence, the universal application of a one-time mask correction to C_1 in order to compensate C_p, as above, could be marginally better (or worse) than making no correction. This is consistent with our discussion on sensitivity and variability in Sec. 7-7.

Consequently, due to the independent statistics and differing dependencies on temperature, etc., predistortion can only be effective if C_1 is customized for every chip and continuously adjusted for changes in the ambient environment. To do so would require one to measure or infer the values of C_p under some test condition. Furthermore, changes to C_p due to temperature, etc., would need to be monitored and compensated for in real time—a pretty tall order—although continuous tuning in this way is feasible for some cases using the on-chip control systems described later in Sec. 8-4. However, tuning is not a universal solution. First, tuning increases, perhaps significantly, the cost of the integrated filter. Second, since C's are not easily tunable, switched-capacitor filters are not candidates for this approach. Hence, before pursuing tuning as a means to gain precision, let us explore what can be achieved with prudent layout and shrewd structural design.

In the absence of tuning, the designer can either reduce the relative magnitudes of the parasitics or reduce the filter's sensitivities to the parasitics, or both. Note that one could make the semantic argument that tuning is an exercise of the latter option. In the previous section we described prudent layout rules for minimizing the relative magnitude of parasitics (i.e., relative to the magnitudes of the intentional components). For example, it is of no value to reduce C_B in Fig. 8-6a by scaling down the physical size and magnitude of C_A. However, C_R can be reduced independently of C_A, and every step should be taken to do so.

Let us consider circuit techniques that isolate and neutralize parasitics, or at least reduce circuit sensitivities to them. For the purposes of this discussion, generality will not be lost if we assume that all bias terminals in Figs. 8-6, 8-7, and 8-9 (e.g., V_{DD}, V_B, V_C) are at AC ground. Later, in Sec. 8-5, we remove this assumption and consider the consequences of spurious AC signals coupled to these bias terminals, e.g., $v_{DD} = V_{DD} + v_{dd}$.

8-3-1   Reducing the Effect of Parasitics on Filter Precision

With bias terminals at AC ground, most of the parasitic C's in Figs. 8-6 and 8-9 have one plate connected to ground. There are two simple strategies that serve as the first line of defense for dealing with such parasitics: (a) the use of op amps to buffer the terminals of integrated elements to neutralize their associated parasitics;

and for those parasitics that cannot be otherwise neutralized, (b) the manipulation of the circuit structure to minimize parasitic occurrences as nonadditive elements (e.g., Fig. 8-14b). The buffering referred to in (a) is achieved by isolating grounded parasitics between voltage sources and virtual grounds. Active-G_m/C circuits that use OTAs, or alternative transconductance realizations, are disadvantaged from this point of view, since such circuits do not naturally provide this buffering. Hence, prudent design practice for active-G_m/C filters stresses the application of strategy (b) (Schaumann, Ghausi, and Laker 1990).

All is not lost, even when parasitics cannot be eliminated or neutralized by structure, and reductions through careful layout have not sufficiently reduced their impact. Filter structures that have low sensitivities to variations in the intentional components will also have reduced sensitivities to parasitics (particularly the additive ones). In Sec. 8-10, we consider the realization of active filters (SC, RC, and G_m/C) that simulate the very low sensitivity properties of passive LC ladder filters. Also, in Sec. 8-4, we develop closed-loop subsystems for on-chip tuning. In the case of active-SC filters, tuning is usually unnecessary.

Buffering switched-capacitors, C's, and R's between an ideal voltage source (or an op amp output) and an op amp virtual ground, neutralizes many of the parasitic capacitances encountered in Fig. 8-4. This is illustrated in Fig. 8-15a, where poly 1-poly 2 capacitor C_A is connected as suggested. To the extent that v_{in} is an ideal voltage-controlled voltage source (VCVS) and v_ε is an ideal virtual ground, parasitics C_B and C_ε are neutralized and play no role in the signal transmission. Included in C_ε is the input capacitance of the op amp C_{IN}. Note that, as suggested earlier, the bottom plate of C_A is connected to the voltage source and the top plate to virtual ground. For comparison, in Fig. 8-15b, capacitor C_A is replaced by two capacitors in series. The parasitics shunting the op amp output and virtual ground are neutralized as before, and left out of the circuit. However, the combined parasitic $C_R + C_B$ at the common node alters the gain between v_{in} and v_{out}.

In examining the use of the integrated resistor, let us consider the circuit in Fig. 8-16. The output stage is seen to be an inverting integrator with time constant

FIGURE 8-15   Effect of parasitic C's when integrated circuit elements are used in filter circuits (a) a poly 1-poly 2 C_A buffered between two ideal op amps to neutralize parasitic C's; (b) parasitic C's are only partially neutralized when C_A in (a) is replaced by two C_A's in series.

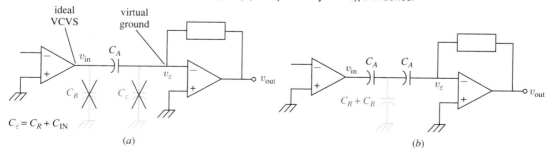

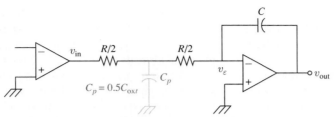

FIGURE 8-16   An inverting integrator implemented with a MOST-R and a poly 1-poly 2 capacitor C. All parasitics except $C_p = 0.5C_{oxt}$ have been neutralized by the ideal op amps.

$\omega_t = 1/RC$. Buffering the resistor as before, we can neutralize all the parasitics except $C_p = C_{oxt}/2$, which is part of the distributed capacitance. Hence, the integrator has an extra parasitic pole at $\omega_p = 4/RC_p$. Since we cannot neutralize C_p, we want $\omega_t/\omega_p \ll 1$ so that its effect is made negligible. Since $R \propto L/W$ and $C_p \propto LW$, then

$$\omega_t \propto \frac{W/L}{C} \quad \text{and} \quad \omega_p \propto \frac{1}{L^2}; \quad \text{hence,} \quad \omega_t/\omega_p \propto \frac{LW}{C}$$

which suggests that W be set to the minimum value and that L is adjusted to attain the desired value of R. The designer can further control ω_t/ω_p by scaling the resistors by R/k (i.e., L/k) and the capacitors by kC which reduces ω_t/ω_p by $1/k^2$. In effect, die area is traded for reduced parasitic effect.

In the case of a switched capacitor, such as Fig. 8-17a, where the bottom plate of C_1 is connected to system ground, C_B is neutralized, as are C_{p1} and C_{ε}. However, C_{p2} and C_{p3} add directly to C_1, as illustrated in Fig. 8-17b. We define the C_{pi}'s to include parasitics due to routing C_{Ri} and switch junctions C_{ji} (where for simplicity we assume $C_{j1} = C_{j2} = C_j$). Consequently, $C_p = C_{p2} + C_{p3}$ introduces a gain error and contributes to the circuit's overall nonlinear distortion. The small-signal effects of C_p can be analyzed using the z-domain equivalent circuit method, illustrated in Fig. 8-17c. The equivalent circuit is similar to that in Fig. 7-35b, with the addition of the $C_p z^{-1/2}$ element shown in gray to account for the parasitic. The resulting transfer functions are

$$T_{oe}(z) = -\frac{C_1 + C_p}{C}\frac{z^{-1/2}}{1 - z^{-1}} \quad \text{and} \quad T_{ee}(z) = -\frac{C_1 + C_p}{C}\frac{z^{-1}}{1 - z^{-1}} \quad (8\text{-}21)$$

To use this circuit, the designer must first make C_p as small as possible, then scale C_1 so that the sensitivity of T_{oe} (or T_{ee}) to parasitic C_p is less than some design objective $\alpha \ll 1$, i.e.,

$$S_{C_p}^{T_{oe}} = \frac{1}{1 + \dfrac{C_1}{C_p}} < \alpha \quad \text{or} \quad \frac{C_1}{C_p} > \frac{1}{\alpha} \quad (8\text{-}22)$$

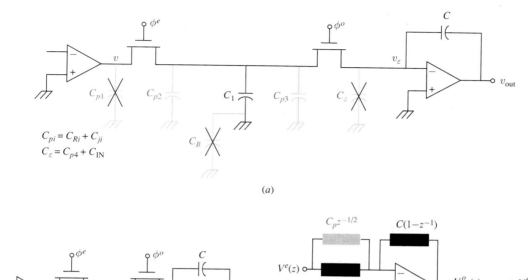

$$C_{pi} = C_{Ri} + C_{ji}$$
$$C_{\varepsilon} = C_{p4} + C_{IN}$$

(a)

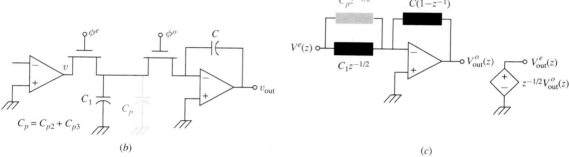

$$C_p = C_{p2} + C_{p3}$$

(b)

(c)

FIGURE 8-17   Inverting −LD,−FE integrator of Fig. 7-35b, comprised of toggle SC C_1 and integrating capacitor C: (a) with all parasitics shown (for simplicity we assume $C_{jS} = C_{jD} = C_j$); (b) parasitics neutralized by the op amps and the grounded bottom plate of C_1 are removed, leaving C_p; (c) the z-domain equivalent circuit for (b).

Ultimately, C must also be scaled upward by the same factor so that the gain C_1/C remains fixed. Hence, the only recourse is to increase die area, perhaps substantially since $\alpha = 10^{-4}$ or 0.01 percent may be required to reduce $S_{C_p}^{T_{oe}}$ to an acceptable level.

Another active-SC circuit with an interesting parasitic condition is illustrated in Fig. 8-18. We leave it to the reader to show that in this circuit, C_p contributes to a parasitic zero. It can also be verified that this circuit is functionally equivalent to the one in Fig. 7-35a. Fortunately, the effect of such parasitics can be further minimized by the structural design of the switched-capacitor. Such structures are said to be *parasitic insensitive*, a condition that is the subject of the next section.

In any event, the value of inverting feedback-configured op amps (i.e., virtual ground input and voltage source output) to neutralize many of the parasitics encountered is clearly significant. Since OTAs are open loop voltage-controlled current sources (*VCCS*) or transconductance amplifiers (Chaps. 5 and 6), we cannot expect them to provide any parasitic buffering. Hence, for active-G_m/C filters we rely on structures that place parasitics in additive locations and have very low component sensitivities.

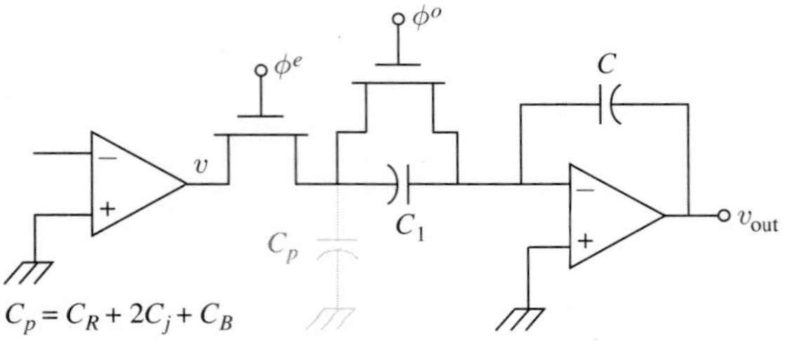

FIGURE 8-18 A classic inverting $-$BE,$-$LD integrator. Everything but C_p can be neutralized by the ideal op amps.

$$C_p = C_R + 2C_j + C_B$$

8-3-2   Parasitic Insensitive Switched-Capacitor Structures

A switched-capacitor structure is parasitic insensitive when *all* parasitics are neutralized. An important contributor to neutralizing parasitics is the embedding of switched-capacitors between ideal voltage sources and op amp virtual grounds (Ghausi and Laker 1981; Gregorian and Temes 1986; Moschytz 1986; Schaumann, Ghausi, and Laker 1990; Unbehauen and Cichocki 1989).

Consider the active-SC inverting integrator in Fig. 8-19a, with all the parasitic capacitances C_{pi} shown in gray. Note that C_{p2} and C_{p3} involve two switches, and thus the $2C_{ji}$ contribution. Recall that this is the inverting $-$BE, $-$LD integrator in Fig. 7-35a. After removing the parasitics (C_{p1} and C_ε) clearly neutralized by the op amps, we are left with the circuit in Fig. 8-19b. To investigate the impact of C_{p2} and C_{p3}, let us examine their function in both the switch phases shown in Figs. 8-19c and 8-19d. First, in the ϕ^e phase in Fig. 8-19c, we see that both parasitics are neutralized by the op amps. During the ϕ° phase in Fig. 8-19d, both parasitics are discharged to system ground and are unquestionably neutralized. The same arguments can be repeated to show that the noninverting +LD, +FE integrator in Fig. 7-35c is also parasitic insensitive. This should not be surprising, as the switched capacitors are similarly structured.

Parasitic insensitivity has been achieved to the extent that the op amps are ideal. As the DC gains for compact, low power, CMOS op amps are usually $A_0 > 10^4$ in the frequency range of interest, the relative contribution of the parasitics are significantly reduced (i.e., by $\approx 1/A_0$). We leave it to the reader to show that $1/A_0 = 10^{-4}$ in parasitic insensitive structures is equivalent to $\alpha = 10^{-4}$ in Eq. (8-22).

Example 8-5

Let us consider the parasitic insensitive integrator in Fig. 8-20. Let $C_1 = 1$ pF, $C = 10$ pF, $C_{pi} = 0.03$ pF, $C_\varepsilon = 1$ pF and $A_0 = 1000$. Determine the resulting error in $H(z)$ from the ideal $-$BE integrator.

Solution. The z-domain equivalent circuit, which includes the nonideal components, is shown in Fig. 8-20. Analyzing them, we find that

$$\left[C - \frac{C_1 + C_{p3} + C_\varepsilon}{A_0} - \left(C - \frac{C_\varepsilon}{A_0} \right) z^{-1} \right] V_{\text{out}}^e + C_1 V_{\text{in}}^e = 0$$

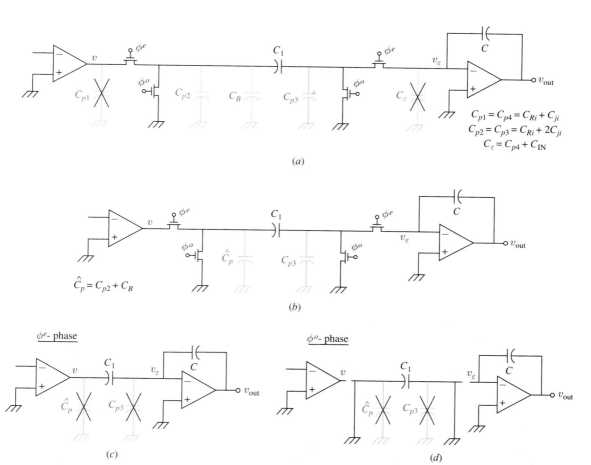

FIGURE 8-19   The $-$BE,$-$LD integrator in Fig. 5-34a: (a) redrawn showing all relevant parasitics, and (b) with parasitics clearly neutralized by op amps removed. The circuit in (b) is redrawn for the ϕ^e phase in (c) and the ϕ^o phase in (d).

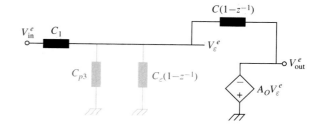

FIGURE 8-20   Z-domain equivalent circuit for the $-$BE integrator in Example 8-5. The op amp DC gain is A_0.

Solving for $H(z) = V_{\text{out}}^e / V_{\text{in}}^e$ and approximating $1/(1-\delta) \approx 1+\delta$, we obtain

$$H(z) \approx \frac{-\dfrac{C_1}{C}\left[1 + \dfrac{C_1 + C_{p3} + C_\varepsilon}{CA_0}\right]}{1 - \left[1 + \dfrac{C_1 + C_{p3}}{CA_0}\right]z^{-1}} = \frac{-\alpha(1 + \Delta\alpha)}{1 - (1 + \Delta p)z^{-1}}$$

where the effects of the parasitic capacitances are not zero, but significantly scaled by $(1/A_0 = 10^{-4})$ such that

$$\Delta\alpha = \frac{C_1 + C_{p3} + C_\varepsilon}{CA_0} = 0.0002 \quad \text{and} \quad \Delta p = \frac{C_1 + C_{p3}}{CA_0} = 0.0001$$

Later, we show that the structures in Fig. 7-35a ($-$BE, $-$LD) and 7-35c ($+$LD, $+$FE) represent a sufficient set of building blocks to construct parasitic insensitive switched-capacitor circuits that realize the full range $H(z)$'s described in Secs. 7-3 and 7-4. However, there are designs where the lack of a parasitic insensitive equivalent to the switched-capacitor toggle in Fig. 7-33c, or the $-$LD, $-$FE integrator in Fig. 7-35b, leads to large capacitance ratios. Also, several important functions, such as the $-$BL integrator in Fig. 7-36, cannot be realized with parasitic insensitivity. More importantly, the sample-and-hold quality of the toggle switched-capacitors, i.e., Figs. 7-33c and 7-33d, will later prove to be of value in desensitizing active-SC filters to the unavoidable transient responses of practical op amps. Such transients cause op amp outputs to deviate from the strict signal assumptions (i.e., sample-and-hold) in Fig. 7-25, on which we base the integrity of the z-domain design. Since only the inverting toggle switched-capacitor in Figs. 7-33d and 7-35c can be incorporated in a parasitic insensitive structure, our design capability at this point is somewhat limited.

This situation can be addressed with the interesting structure in Fig. 8-21a (*see color plate 3*), where switched capacitors C_A and C_B are connected in tandem at the input without op amp buffering (Fleischer, Ganesan, and Laker 1981). This circuit, as we will verify, can be made functionally equivalent to the parasitic sensitive $-$LD, $-$FE integrator in Fig. 7-35b. However, in this case, if the switched capacitors are "matched," their electrical interaction will greatly reduce the sensitivities to the parasitic C_{pi}'s in contrast to the situation in Fig. 8-17. We will define "matched switched capacitors" shortly.

Eliminating the parasitics that were obviously neutralized by the op amps, we are left with C_{p1} and C_{p2}, illustrated in Figs. 8-21a and 8-21b. Observe that C_{p1} and C_{p2} are each formed by two half-switches (one driven by ϕ^e and the other by ϕ^o) and routing as shown in green and red, respectively. The two parasitics are indeed physically identical, and can be matched such that $C_{p1} = C_{p2}$ with careful layout. This matching is illustrated in Fig. 8-21c. From the equivalent circuit,

$$T_{eo}(z) = -\frac{\dfrac{C_B}{2C}z^{-1/2}}{1 - z^{-1}}\left[\frac{2(C_A + C_{p1})}{C_A + C_B + C_{p1} + C_{p2}}\right] \tag{8-23}$$

If the tandem SC's are "matched" such that $C_A = C_B = 2C_1$ and $C_{p1} = C_{p2} = C_p$, then Eq. (8-23) can be rewritten as

$$T_{eo}(z) = -\frac{\frac{C_1}{C}z^{-1/2}}{1-z^{-1}}\left(\frac{4C_1 + 2C_p}{4C_1 + 2C_p}\right) = -\frac{\frac{C_1}{C}z^{-1/2}}{1-z^{-1}} \tag{8-24}$$

Once again, the parasitics cancel and the equivalent circuit in Fig. 8-21b reduces to Fig. 8-21d, but without the residue parasitic in Fig. 8-17c. Recalling Fig. 7-33, we can develop a noninverting dual circuit to Fig. 8-21. This active-SC integrator and its equivalent circuit, realizing a +FE and a $+z^{-1/2}$FE, is shown in Fig. 8-22d. The extra $z^{-1/2}$ delay, available if the output sample is taken during ϕ^e, will prove useful later

FIGURE 8-22 Parasitic insensitive integrator structures: (a) −BE, −LD; (b) +LD, +FE; (c) −LD, −FE; (d) +FE, $+z^{-1/2}$FE.

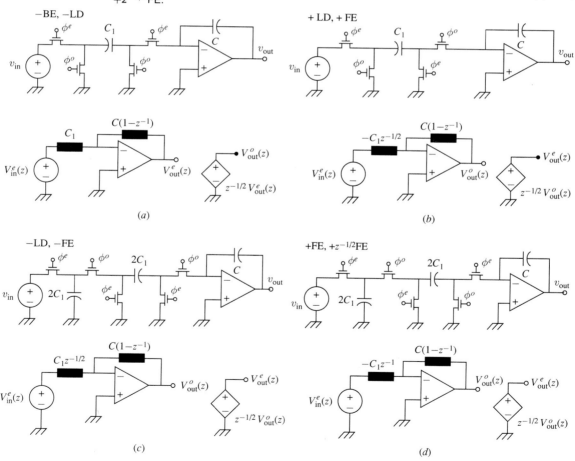

when we deal with op amp transients. In fact, Fig. 8-22 displays the full and powerful bag of parasitic insensitive tricks. With these four building blocks, the designer can implement any specified $H(z)$ with parasitic insensitivity while optimizing other important factors, such as capacitance area and sensitivity to op amp transients.

8-4   AUTOMATIC ON-CHIP TUNING

We have shown that one can realize very precise capacitor ratios with the matched layout method in Fig. 7-4e and achieve parasitic insensitivity with the structures in Fig. 8-22. Consequently, precision active-SC filters are realized without tuning or element adjustment of any kind. However, pointed out several times, the situation is quite different for the RC's and C/G_m's in continuous-time active filters. In these cases, tuning is an essential strategy for achieving precision control of these inherently imprecise quantities (Banu and Tsividis 1985; Gregorian and Temes 1986; Kozma, Johns, and Sedra 1991; Krummenacher and Joehl 1988; Lopresti 1977; Schaumann, Ghausi, and Laker 1990; Van Peteghem and Song 1989; Silva et al. 1993).

At this point the reader may visualize the process of tuning a filter as analogous to the task of adjusting the graphic equalizer for a high quality audio system. The process, no doubt, is similar, but the tuning of a graphic equalizer involves the adjustment of only five or six parameters, and the quality of the result is subjective. Moreover, it may take several tens of seconds or more to accomplish this relatively simple task. This is not a problem, since the audio can still be enjoyed before and during the adjustment. In the case of a continuous-time active filter, tuning is usually essential and many parameters must be adjusted before transmission requirements are satisfied. To further complicate matters, the tuning must be fast (accomplished in less than 10^{-3} seconds) so as not to interfere with the normal use of the filter.

To appreciate what is involved in the tuning of a filter, let us assume that we are required to realize a transfer function $H(s, \mathbf{x}, \mathbf{c})$, where $\mathbf{c}$ is the vector of tunable circuit parameters (i.e., the R's or G_m's) and $\mathbf{x}$ is the vector of the remaining circuit parameters, which are left fixed (e.g., C's, op amp GBW's, and parasitics). Since both $\mathbf{x}$ and $\mathbf{c}$ are subject to statistical fabrication errors and variations due to changes in the ambient environment, we can write

$$\mathbf{x} = \mathbf{x}_0 + \Delta\mathbf{x} \text{ and } \mathbf{c} = \mathbf{c}_0 + \Delta\mathbf{c} + \Delta\mathbf{c}_t \qquad (8\text{-}25a)$$

where $\mathbf{x}_0$ and $\mathbf{c}_0$ are the nominal values, $\Delta\mathbf{x}$ and $\Delta\mathbf{c}$ are the statistical changes, and $\Delta\mathbf{c}_t$ are the tuning adjustments. Our objective is to develop a tuning system that automatically adjusts $\Delta\mathbf{c}_t$ such that

$$H(s, \mathbf{x}, \mathbf{c}) = \frac{N(s, \mathbf{x}_0 + \Delta\mathbf{x}, \mathbf{c}_0 + \Delta\mathbf{c} + \Delta\mathbf{c}_t)}{D(s, \mathbf{x}_0 + \Delta\mathbf{x}, \mathbf{c}_0 + \Delta\mathbf{c} + \Delta\mathbf{c}_t)} = H(s, \mathbf{x}_0, \mathbf{c}_0) \qquad (8\text{-}25b)$$

where N and D are Mth- and Nth- (where $M \leq N$) order polynomials, respectively. Referring back to Eq. (7-6), $H(s, \mathbf{x}, \mathbf{c})$ is determined by the values of $M + N + 1$ coefficients, or, equivalently in Eq. (7-13a), $(M + N/2)$ resonant-notch frequencies,

$(M + N/2)$ pole-zero Q's, and the value of a gain constant. The net result is that if Eq. (8-25b) can be made to hold at $N + M + 1$ frequency points, it will also hold through the entire frequency domain. In general, all of these quantities are interrelated functions of $\mathbf{x}$ and $\mathbf{c}$. Clearly, we are describing a task that is of far greater complexity and precision than the subjective tuning of an audio system.

In the previous section, we saw that the values of MOST-R's and OTA-G_m's are proportional to DC control signals V_C and I_A, respectively. Moreover, from the previous paragraph, it should be obvious that the realization of Eqs. (8-25) requires that $\mathbf{c}$ be of dimension $(N + M + 1) \times 1$. This is generally not a problem, as active-RC filters are frequently comprised of more than $N + M + 1$ R's or G_m's. Hence, a method for realizing Eq. (8-25b) is to measure gain/phase at $N + M + 1$ frequencies and then solve $N + M + 1$ simultaneous equations to determine $\Delta\mathbf{c}_t$. Elegant implementations of this algorithm have been used quite successfully to control the laser trimming of active-RC filters (Lopresti 1977). While such algorithms have worked well for the off-chip, one-time tuning of discrete and hybrid filters (Ghausi and Laker 1981; Gregorian and Temes 1986), the hardware requirements alone render them impractical for on-chip tuning. How then do we use a small number of controls (usually $\ll N + M + 1$) to affect fine coordinated adjustments to R's (or G_m's), such that the equality in Eq. (8-25b) is realized robustly and economically?

8-4-1   On-Chip Tuning Strategies

The generally adopted solution is to incorporate the continuous-time filter into a feedback or closed-loop control subsystem, which locks the filter (i.e., its tunable parameters) to a set of stable references (Banu and Tsividis 1985; Gregorian and Temes 1986; Kozma, Johns, and Sedra 1991; Krummenacher and Joehl 1988; Schaumann, Ghausi, and Laker 1990; Van Peteghem and Song 1989). Such closed-loop strategies usually involve the following steps, performed in sequence:

1 Measure the actual filter performance (e.g., $H(s, \mathbf{x}, \mathbf{c})$ or $G(s, \mathbf{x}, \mathbf{c})$ and/or $\varphi(s, \mathbf{x}, \mathbf{c})$).

2 Compare actual performance in (1) with a standard or reference (e.g., related to $H(s, \mathbf{x}_0, \mathbf{c}_0)$ or $G(s, \mathbf{x}_0, \mathbf{c}_0)$ and/or $\varphi(s, \mathbf{x}_0, \mathbf{c}_0)$).

3 Determine the error, i.e., the difference between (1) and (2).

4 Calculate and apply a correction ($\Delta\mathbf{c}_t$) to the filter to reduce the error determined in (3).

If the tuning is iterative, then steps 1–4 are repeated until the error is reduced to either zero or to an acceptably low level.

A block diagram for a *closed loop tuning subsystem* that realizes the above objectives is illustrated in Fig. 8-23. Most automatic tuning schemes start with a reference signal X_{ref} at a very accurate and stable reference frequency ω_{ref}, derived from the system clock. If possible, ω_{ref} should be selected in the stop band of the filter to reduce the opportunity for X_{ref} to crosstalk into the information-carrying signal path

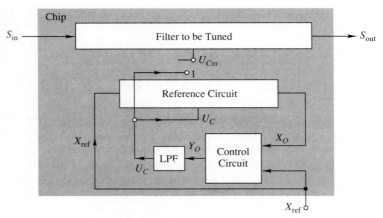

FIGURE 8-23   Block diagram for an indirect on-chip closed loop tuning subsystem.

(S_{in} to S_{out}). In this scheme, the tuning is conducted with the aid of a reference circuit, e.g., an oscillator or second-order filter stage, made from the same components as the filter to be tuned. The particular algorithm used to conduct the tuning is realized in the control circuit. Such schemes perform *indirect tuning*, since the actual tuning is done on the reference circuit and only the converged tuning signal is passed on to the filter. An obvious advantage of this indirect method is that the filter is free to process S_{in} while tuning converges off-line with the reference circuit. The price paid is that the components in the filter and reference circuit must be very closely matched (at least as well matched as the like components within the filter), or unacceptable tuning errors may occur. To see how this scheme works, let us closely examine Fig. 8-23.

In this scheme, X_{ref} is applied to the reference and control circuits, producing response X_o at the output to the reference circuit. Signal X_o is then fed to the control circuit to produce the tuning signal Y_o. Tuning output Y_o is filtered by the lowpass filter (LPF) to produce DC voltages/currents (e.g., U_C) required to adjust the R's or G_m's. If the control circuit reaches a steady state $U_C = U_{Css}$ in an iterative fashion, U_C is continuously applied to the reference circuit until convergence is achieved. Switch 1, in Fig. 8-23, connects the filter to the U_C when steady state is achieved, i.e., when U_C is constant or very nearly so. Only U_{Css} is applied to the filter. Note that it may be more practical to realize U_C as a correction term rather than the total control signal, i.e., let $U_{CT} = U_B \pm U_C$, where U_B is a DC bias fixed at some nominal value and $\pm U_C$ is a correction term applied in series. This way, if no correction is applied, the filter and reference are functional with all R's or G_m's biased within approximately ± 20 percent of their desired values with U_B. Whether tuning is enabled or not, the filter processes S_{in} without interruption.

An alternative scheme, shown in Fig. 8-24, avoids the requirement for a match between a reference circuit and the filter by tuning the filter directly. Such schemes are said to perform *direct tuning*. This not only eliminates the mismatch issue, it also

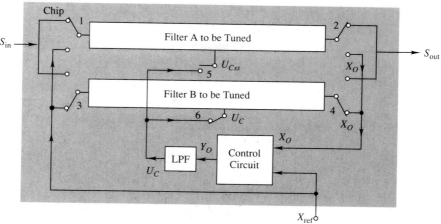

FIGURE 8-24   Block diagram for a direct on-chip closed loop tuning subsystem.

opens the tuning to more general algorithms, such as least mean square (LMS) adaptive methods (Kozma, Johns, and Sedra 1991). The obvious disadvantage of direct tuning schemes is that the filter must be duplicated (e.g., tunable filter A and tunable filter B) so that tuning can be done off-line without interrupting the filter operation. The functioning of this scheme is similar to the indirect scheme, except that in this case, filters A and B are alternately taken out of service via switches 1-6 to conduct the required tuning. Once $U_C = U_{Css}$, the tuned filter (in this case filter A) is put back in service and filter B is taken out of service to be tuned. Filter B is kept tuned and ready for service to replace filter A when filter A requires retuning. This process continues through the full service life of the filter. In practice, we must be careful when bringing filters A or B into service, so as to allow each to reach a sinusoidal steady state. Hence, it is recommended that switches 1-4 be sequenced so that, initially, S_{in} is connected while the filter output is left open. Once the transients decay, and a sinusoidal steady state is reached, the filter output can be safely connected to the signal path.

To illustrate the tuning of an imprecise RC product, let us consider the passive RC filter in Fig. 8-25a, which realizes a single real-axis pole at $s = -1/RC$. Let R be a suitably linear MOST with $R(\beta, V_C)$ given in Eq. 8-9b. The voltage transfer function for this filter is given by

$$H(\omega, C, R(V_C)) = \frac{V_{out}}{V_{in}} = \frac{1}{j\omega RC + 1} = \frac{1}{j\omega \dfrac{C}{\beta(V_C - V_T)} + 1} \tag{8-26}$$

Clearly, if the RC product changes from the nominal $R_o C_o$, due to variations ΔR and ΔC, then the error can be reduced to zero by tuning R via V_C. This adjustment is most readily determined by comparing the output of $H(\omega, C, R(V_C))$ with that of a known

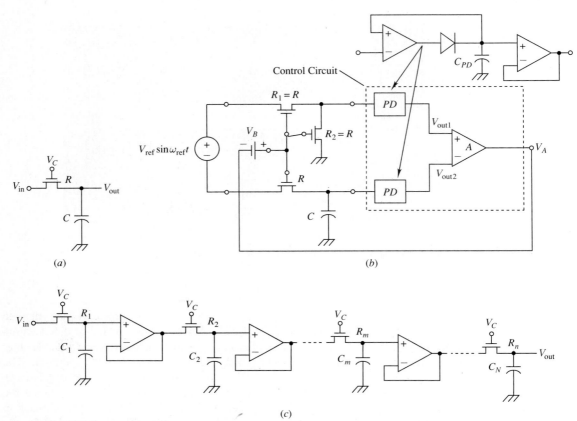

FIGURE 8-25 Tuning illustration: (a) simple integrated RC lowpass filter comprised of a linear MOST-R and a poly 1-poly 2 capacitor C; (b) a closed loop tuning scheme to tune the RC product by detecting and comparing the peak outputs of a voltage divider reference and the RC filter at a very accurate reference frequency ω_{ref}; and (c) a filter with N buffered RC stages realizing real poles at $s = -1/R_iC_i$.

reference circuit at an accurate reference frequency ω_{ref} and an arbitrary voltage V_{ref}. V_{ref} should be at a convenient level—well within the linear ranges of the reference circuit and filter.

A suitable implementation of this tuning strategy is shown in Fig. 8-25b (Gregorian and Temes 1986; Schaumann, Ghausi, and Laker 1990). The reference circuit is seen to be a MOST-R voltage divider with $R_1 = R_2 = R$, nominally, for maximum matching. Also, V_C in Eq. (8-26) is realized in this scheme as the combination of a fixed bias V_B in series with a variable control V_A, such that $V_C = V_B \pm V_A$. The tuning is accomplished by comparing the peak amplitudes of the outputs from reference V_{out1} and filter V_{out2}, using a differential amplifier of gain A. Comparator output V_A is fed back to the reference to complete the loop; and it is also fed to the filter.

In the frequency domain, the outputs of the peak detectors (PD), are given by

$$V_{out1} = \frac{R_2}{R_2 + R_1} V_{ref} \quad \text{and} \quad V_{out2} = \frac{V_{ref}}{\sqrt{(\omega_{ref}CR)^2 + 1}} \qquad (8\text{-}27)$$

A circuit realization for the PDs is shown as an insert in Fig. 8-25b (Schaumann, Ghausi, and Laker 1990). The control voltage V_A is then written as

$$V_A = A(V_{out1}(j\omega_{ref}) - V_{out2}(j\omega_{ref})) = A\left\{ \frac{1}{k} - \frac{1}{\sqrt{(\omega_{ref}RC)^2 + 1}} \right\} V_{ref} \qquad (8\text{-}28a)$$

where $k = 1 + R_1/R_2$. Recognizing that gain A is usually very large, ideally such that $A \to \infty$, we can rewrite Eq. (8-28a) as

$$\frac{1}{k} - \frac{1}{\sqrt{(\omega_{ref}RC)^2 + 1}} = \frac{1}{A}\frac{V_A}{V_{ref}}\big|_{A\to\infty} \to 0 \qquad (8\text{-}28b)$$

i.e., $V_{out1} \approx V_{out2}$ and we force $\sqrt{(\omega_{ref}RC)^2 + 1}) \approx k$ and $V_A \approx 0$. The two magnitudes are said to be locked and this control structure is a *magnitude locked loop* or MLL. Solving Eq. (8-28b) for RC, it follows that

$$RC \to \frac{1}{\omega_{ref}}\sqrt{\left(1 + \frac{R_1}{R_2}\right)^2 - 1} \qquad (8\text{-}29)$$

with, nominally, $R_1 = R_2$.

Equation (8-29) relates the precision of the *tuned* RC product to a very stable ω_{ref} and the ratio of two matched components. This relation is very similar in spirit to the situation that inherently occurs in an active-SC filter (i.e., Eq. (7-8c)).

To close the loop, let us assume that ω_{ref} is chosen such that $((\omega_{ref}RC)^2 \gg 1$. This choice conveniently simplifies Eq. (8-28a) and places ω_{ref} harmlessly in the filter stopband. Rewriting V_A in Eq. (8-28a), we obtain

$$V_A = A\left(\frac{1}{k} - \frac{p_{RC}}{\omega_{ref}}\right) V_{ref} \qquad (8\text{-}30)$$

where $p_{RC} = 1/RC$. Let us also assume that p_{RC} changes from its nominal value $(p_{RC})_0$ due to an error in both R and C such that

$$p_{RC} = (p_{RC})_0 + \varepsilon_{RC} \qquad (8\text{-}31a)$$

where ε_{RC} is the resulting error. Note that with Eq. (8-28b), $(p_{RC})_0 \to \omega_{\mathrm{ref}}/k$. Referring to Fig. 8-25b and Eq. (8-25), we know that p_{RC} is also related to control voltage V_A, i.e.,

$$p_{RC} = \frac{\beta}{C}(V_B + V_C - V_T) = (p_{RC})_0 + \Delta p_{RC} - (\varepsilon_{RC})_T \tag{8-31b}$$

where $(p_{RC})_0 = (\beta/C)V_B$, $(\varepsilon_{RC})_T = (\beta/C)V_T$, and $\Delta p_{RC} = (\beta/C)V_A$ is the change due to tuning. The error term $(\varepsilon_{RC})_T$, which is due to uncertainties in the threshold voltage, can be incorporated into ε_{RC} such that

$$p_{RC} = (p_{RC})_0 + \varepsilon_{RC} + \frac{\beta}{C}V_A \tag{8-31c}$$

Substituting Eq. (8-31c) into Eq. (8-30), we find that

$$V_A = A\left\{ \frac{1}{k} - \frac{1}{\omega_{\mathrm{ref}}} \left[(p_{RC})_0 + \varepsilon_{RC} + \frac{\beta}{C}V_A \right] \right\} V_{\mathrm{ref}} \tag{8-32}$$

Solving Eq. (8-32) for V_A yields

$$V_A = \frac{-A\dfrac{\varepsilon_{RC}}{\omega_{\mathrm{ref}}}V_{\mathrm{ref}}}{1 + A\dfrac{\beta}{C\omega_{\mathrm{ref}}}V_{\mathrm{ref}}}\bigg|_{A\to\infty} \approx -\frac{C\varepsilon_{RC}}{\beta} \tag{8-33}$$

Hence, as we concluded earlier, V_A converges to zero as the tuning loop forces error ε_{RC} to zero.

To generalize this example, let us visualize the tuned RC filter as being comprised of N real poles defined by $p_i = 1/R_i C_i$ for $i = 1, \ldots, N$. The corresponding circuit is shown in Fig. 8-25c. To tune this filter, we could replicate Fig. 8-25b N times for N reference frequencies $(\omega_{\mathrm{ref}})_i$, e.g., analogous to the scheme described previously in Eqs. (8-25). Alternatively, we can designate one of the N poles as the reference pole, say $p_m = 1/RC$, and the remaining $i \neq m$ poles are anchored to p_m by the relation

$$p_i = k_i p_m \tag{8-34}$$

where k_i are ratios of matched components. The reference pole p_m is then tuned, as described in Fig. 8-25b, and the stable control V_A is distributed to all the R's. One realization of this strategy is to set all the resistors nominally to $R_{0i} = R_0$, and adjust the nominal pole locations by calculating C_{0i} such that $C_{0i}R = C_i R_i$ and $k_{0i} = C_0/C_{0i}$. The key to this strategy is to have one V_A serve all the R_i's. Hence, different values for R_i can be accommodated by fixing V_A and scaling R_{0i} via β_{0i} (i.e., W_{0i}/L_{0i}). In either case, since the actual $k_i = CR/C_i R_i$ and with p_m anchored to ω_{ref} by Eq. (8-29), the precision of the p_i's is set by ratios of matched R_i's and C_i's.

In general, however, we know that most practical filters are comprised of complex conjugate pairs of poles and zeros. The tuning system in Fig. 8-25b addresses only the tuning of the real parts of these poles and zeros. Contemporary schemes are of the indirect type, based on the functional tuning of resonant-notch frequencies $\omega_{0,N}$ and quality factors $Q_{p,z}$. Recall that the relationship between these parameters and pole/zero locations is shown in Fig. 3-18. Filter structures that tend to isolate $(\omega_{0,N})$'s and $(Q_{p,z})$'s to independent R's or G_m's are best suited to this form of tuning. Hence, the ease of tuning, or *tunability* (for a particular tuning scheme), is an important criterion (along with sensitivity, dynamic range, die area, power dissipation, etc.) in selecting an active filter structure. Figure 8-26 shows a block diagram for an indirect tuning subsystem to tune the R's (or G_m's), which compensates for the deviations in $\omega_{0,N}$ and $Q_{p,z}$ caused by fabrication errors and changes in the ambient environment. In general, it is most convenient to conduct the tuning of the reference via poles, i.e., ω_{0i} and Q_{pj}, where i and j need not be equal. The remaining pole/zero $\omega_{0,N}$'s and $Q_{p,z}$'s can be anchored to the reference, as per Eq. (8-34).

In general, these two tuning tasks require separate reference signals (X_{rf} and X_{rQ}) and separate reference circuits (circuits 1 and 2, both realized from the components matched with the tunable filter). For $\omega_{0,N}$ tuning, the control circuit in Fig. 8-26 is a phase comparator, which detects the difference in the phases of X_{rf} and X_{of}. Usually, reference circuit 1 is a *voltage-controlled oscillator* (VCO) and the tuning loop is a *phase locked loop* (PLL). For $Q_{p,z}$ tuning, the control circuit is an amplitude comparator, which detects the difference in the peak values of X_{rQ} and X_{oQ}. This is in fact an MLL-based control system, similar to that described in Fig. 8-25.

FIGURE 8-26   Block diagram for an indirect on-chip closed loop tuning subsystem based on separate frequency and Q control.

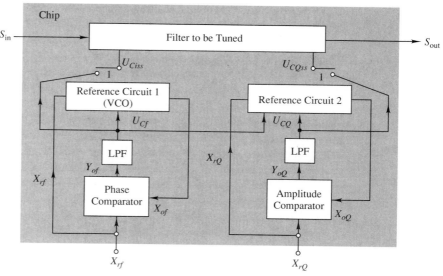

Frequency and Q_p tuning produce independent control signals U_{Cf} and U_{CQ}, respectively. However, U_{Cf} must be fed to reference circuit 2 so that frequency errors do not interfere with the tuning of Q_p. Since $Q_p = \infty$ for the VCO, U_{CQ} is not fed back to reference circuit 1. The steady states U_{Cfss} and U_{CQss} are applied directly to the R's or G_m's selected by the designer to control $\omega_{0,N}$'s and $Q_{p,z}$'s. Let us now look at each of these tuning tasks in more detail.

8-4-2   Frequency Tuning with PLL

As observed in Eq. (7-56), the ΔG and $\Delta\phi$ for many practical filters are dominated by $\Delta\omega_0$ and $\Delta\omega_N$. Hence, the purpose of frequency tuning is to make $\Delta\omega_{0,N}$ as small as possible by phase locking the $\omega_{0,N}$'s to an accurate reference frequency.

A PLL-type tuning block, with the phase detector implemented as an exclusive OR (EXOR) gate, is shown in Fig. 8-27a. The op amp comparators serve to square up the otherwise sinusoidal inputs, as shown in Fig. 8-27b. The function of the phase detector is to provide an output voltage proportional to the phase difference of two periodic signals at the same frequency. We point out that there are several alternative realizations for the phase detector, such as an analog multiplier (Grebene 1984). The operation proceeds as follows: (a) the phase detector compares the reference signal x_{rf} with the output of the VCO x_{of} to produce an error signal y_o; (b) the loop LPF (usually a single pole) extracts the average value of y_o, while eliminating all undesirable high-frequency components; (c) an error signal U_{Cf} is applied to the VCO, which corrects the detected phase error ϕ_ε. When steady state is reached and the PLL is locked, the output of the loop LPF is a DC signal $u_{Cf}(t) = U_{Cf}$. In Fig. 8-27c, the output U_{Cf} is plotted versus τ. Time shift τ, illustrated in Fig. 8-27b, is converted to ϕ_ε and vice versa by the relation $\phi_\varepsilon = 2\pi\tau/T$. Thus, the maximum phase range of the detector is seen in Fig. 8-27c to be $-\pi/2 \le \phi_\varepsilon \le \pi/2$.

The operation of the basic PLL can best be described by starting with the output of the phase detector; i.e.,

$$y_o = x_{rf} \oplus x_{of} \tag{8-35}$$

The result of this operation is shown graphically in Fig. 8-27b. Thus, assuming that the LPF has DC gain H_0 and a passband $\omega < 2\omega_{rf}$, the output of the LPF is

$$U_{Cf} = 4H_0 Y_M \frac{\tau}{T} = \frac{2}{\pi} H_0 Y_M \phi_\varepsilon = K_u \phi_\varepsilon \tag{8-36}$$

where U_{Cf} is the average value as described in Fig. 8-27c and Y_M is the amplitude of the square wave y_o in Fig. 8-27b.

We can assume that the VCO's free-running output frequency ω_F (i.e., the VCO frequency when $U_{Cf} = 0$), is different from the reference frequency ω_{rf}, and that there is a phase difference of $\theta(t)$. Thus, the total instantaneous phase error can be expressed as follows

$$\phi_\varepsilon(t) = (\omega_F - \omega_{rf})t - \theta(t) = \Delta\omega_F t - \theta(t) \tag{8-37}$$

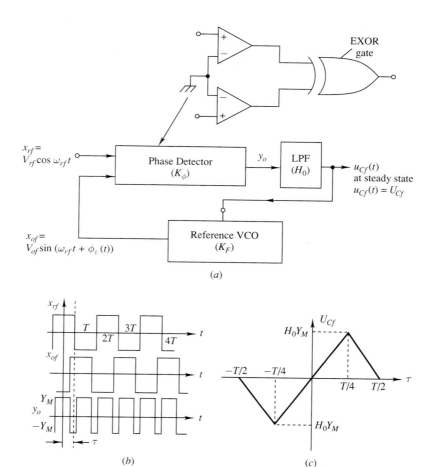

FIGURE 8-27   PLL-based frequency tuning scheme: (a) the tuning loop with the phase detector realized as an EXOR gate; (b) the timing of the EXOR inputs and output showing the phase error as a time shift τ; and (c) the phase detector's U_{Cf} versus τ transfer characteristic.

In usual VCO operation, the instantaneous change of phase, and consequently the frequency, is made proportional to the applied signal $u_{Cf}(t)$; thus

$$\frac{d\theta(t)}{dt} = K_F u_{Cf}(t) \tag{8-38}$$

An equation for the instantaneous value of $\phi_\varepsilon(t)$ is then obtained by differentiating Eq. (8-37) with respect to t and substituting Eqs. (8-38) and (8-36) into the result, i.e.,

$$\frac{d\phi_\varepsilon(t)}{dt} + K_F K_u \phi_\varepsilon(t) = \Delta\omega_F \tag{8-39}$$

Recall that $\Delta\omega_F$ is the initial open-loop frequency error of the VCO.

Without attempting to solve Eq. (8-39), we recognize that at steady-state $d\phi_\varepsilon(t)/dt = 0$. Hence, the residual steady-state error is

$$(\phi_\varepsilon)_{ss} = \frac{\Delta\omega_F}{K_F K_u} = \frac{\Delta\omega_F}{K} \tag{8-40}$$

where $K = K_F K_u > |\Delta\omega_F|$ is the system loop gain. With Eq. (8-40) and (8-36), the steady-state error signal is

$$U_{CF} = K_u \frac{\Delta\omega_F}{K} = \frac{\Delta\omega_F}{K_F} \tag{8-41}$$

and the VCO output equals

$$x_{of}(t) = V_M \sin\left(\omega_{rf}t + \frac{\Delta\omega_F}{K}\right) \tag{8-42}$$

The steady-state error signal adjusts itself such that the VCO frequency is locked to the reference frequency ω_{rf} with a small residual phase error. Note that the final rate of convergence, with a single pole LPF, is exponential with the rate set by loop gain K. It is clearly desirable to have K as large as possible.

8-4-3   *Q* Tuning with MLL

For applications that require medium to high values of $Q_{p,z}$, the automatic tuning of $Q_{p,z}$ is necessary to control the fine shape of the filter response (e.g., passband ripple, roll off in the transition band). Based on the sensitivity arguments in Sec. 7-7, we interpret $Q_{p,z}$ tuning as a second-order correction that is applied to the filter where the $\omega_{0,N}$ have been successfully tuned. In fact, $Q_{p,z}$ tuning always requires properly tuned $\omega_{0,N}$ frequencies, i.e., U_{Cf} in Fig. 8-26.

A simple Q tuning system (Unbehauen and Cichocki 1989) can be achieved by making use of the fact that, in a transfer function, Q-errors and magnitude errors are closely related, particularly at the resonant frequencies ω_0 (see Sec. 7-7). Such a scheme is shown in Fig. 8-28, which operates similarly to the scheme in Fig. 8-25b. To illustrate the method, consider the simple second-order LP function of Eq. (7-14a), i.e.,

$$H(s) = \frac{k\omega_0^2}{s^2 + \dfrac{\omega_0}{Q_p}s + \omega_0^2} \tag{8-43}$$

Assuming ω_0 has been tuned correctly, we find that $M_p = |H(j\omega_0)| = kQ_p$, where Q_p is untuned and $Q_p = Q_{p0} + \Delta Q_p$. Since k is usually set by a ratio of matched components, it can be assumed to be accurate. Therefore, any Q-error ΔQ_p appears

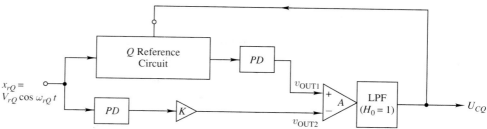

FIGURE 8-28 MLL-based Q tuning scheme.

as a magnitude error ΔM_p from nominal ($M_{p0} = kQ_{p0}$), i.e., if $\omega_{rQ} = \omega_0$

$$M_p = M_{p0} + \Delta M_p = k(Q_{p0} + \Delta Q_p) \tag{8-44a}$$

or

$$\Delta M_p = k\Delta Q_p \tag{8-44b}$$

Equation (8-44b) is the key to the Q-tuning scheme in Fig. 8-28, which operates as follows: (a) determine M_p using a peak detector; (b) determine ΔM_p by comparison of M_p with a known reference; and (c) with k known, deduce ΔQ_p via Eq. (8-44b).

The Q-reference circuit is designed to mimic all relevant Q-errors of the filter circuit. We note that the two PD's are identical. Also, parameters K and A represent the gains for a DC amplifier and a comparator, respectively. It is assumed that all frequency parameters of the filter and reference are tuned correctly by means of a suitable frequency control loop, described in the previous section. Control signal U_{CQ} is returned to both the reference and the filter to adjust the R's (or G_m's) designated by the designer to tune the quality factors.

Referring to Fig. 8-28, the outputs of the two peak detectors are readily expressed as

$$v_{OUT1} = M(\omega_{rQ})V_{rQ} \quad \text{and} \quad v_{OUT2} = KV_{rQ} \tag{8-45}$$

so that the DC Q-control voltage U_{CQ} is

$$U_{CQ} = A(v_{OUT1} - v_{OUT2}) = A[M(\omega_{rQ}) - K]V_{rQ} \tag{8-46}$$

where $\omega_{rQ} = \omega_0$ is an accurate reference frequency and V_{rQ} is a convenient reference voltage. From Eq. (8-46) we have

$$M(\omega_{rQ}) - K = \frac{1}{A}\left[\frac{U_{CQ}}{V_{rQ}}\right]\Big|_{A\to\infty} \approx 0 \tag{8-47}$$

Equation (8-47) forces $K \approx M(\omega_{rQ})$ or $K V_{rQ} \approx M(\omega_{rQ}) V_{rQ}$, and the amplitudes of v_{OUT1} and v_{OUT2} are locked together.

Let us assume that the Q-reference circuit is a second-order LP filter (i.e., with $H(s)$ in Eq. (8-43)), that is representative of the circuitry of the filter such that error ΔQ_p is observed, as in Eq. (8-44a). If we design the K of the DC amplifier to equal the nominal amplitude $M_{p0} = k Q_{p0}$, but allow for a (small) fabrication error ΔK in the definition of K, Eq. (8-44a) yields

$$k(Q_{p0} + \Delta Q_p) = K + \Delta K \qquad (8\text{-}48a)$$

or

$$\Delta Q_p = \frac{\Delta K}{k} \qquad (8\text{-}48b)$$

We see that the precision of Q_p is limited by the precision of the matched components that comprise k of the reference filter and K of the DC amplifier. If we further assume that the application of control U_{CQ} to the reference circuit causes Q_p to change linearly, i.e., $\Delta Q_p = -K_Q U_{CQ}$, then the closed-loop arguments in Eqs. (8-30) through (8-33) directly apply to this case. Hence, we have

$$U_{CQ} = A(k Q_{p0} - K - \Delta K - k K_Q U_{CQ}) V_{rQ} \qquad (8\text{-}49)$$

which, if solved for U_{CQ}, yields

$$U_{CQ} = \frac{-A \Delta K V_{rQ}}{1 + A K_Q k V_{rQ}} \Big|_{A \to \infty} \approx -\frac{\Delta K}{K_Q k} \qquad (8\text{-}50)$$

Equation (8-50) is clearly analogous to Eq. (8-33), which is associated with Fig. 8-25b.

At the time of this writing, the development of on-chip tuning schemes for continuous-time integrated filters is a subject of active research. Although several interesting and practical schemes have been offered thus far, other excellent and perhaps superior schemes are expected to emerge. We see adaptive signal processing techniques, e.g., in Kozma, Johns, and Sedra (1991) and Silva et al. (1993), as providing the seeds for the next generation of tuning schemes.

8-5 *PSRR*, CLOCK FEEDTHROUGH, AND DC OFFSET

Here we address the noninformation signal inputs that are capacitance coupled via the parasitics to the signal path of the integrated filter, as shown in Figs. 8-4 through 8-10. In active-SC filters, this situation is exacerbated by the sampling in the signal path. (Allstot and Black 1983; Gregorian and Temes 1986; Marsh et al. 1981; Martin 1982; Moschytz 1986; Shieh, Patil, and Sheu 1987; Unbehauen and Cichocki 1989; Van Peteghem 1988).

The signals of concern here are the power supplies V_{SS} and V_{DD}, switch clocks $\phi^{e,o}$, the control biases for MOST-R's and G_m's, and the op amp DC offset V_{OS}. Clearly, the feedthrough of clocks $\phi^{e,o}$ is a behavior that is unique to active-SC filters. Power supply rejection and DC offset have been discussed extensively in Chap. 6. The reader studying chapters out of sequence is encouraged to peruse Secs. 6-6 and 6-7 before proceeding on.

Our purpose here is to examine layout and/or circuit structures that increase the filter's robustness, insofar as DC offset, clock feedthrough, and the *PSRRs* are concerned.

8-5-1 Clock Feedthrough and DC Offset Cancellation

In many filters, it is important to minimize residual DC voltages that appear at the signal output terminal. The primary concern is that the resulting loss of signal symmetry about 0 V (or $V_{DD}/2$ for single supply systems) degrades dynamic range. Hence, designers of filters with requirements that call for high gain ($\geq$ 20 dB) or high dynamic range must be especially concerned about DC offsets. As shown in Fig. 8-29, op amp DC offsets and clock feedthrough are the principal contributors. In this schematic we clearly distinguish between the use of complementary and single channel (n or p) switches. As pointed out in Sec. 7-2, the virtual ground affords us the opportunity to use a single channel switch (shown as an n-channel) at the inverting input to the op amp.

Two different mechanisms are responsible for the clock feedthrough: (a) the capacitance coupling via C_{GS} and C_{GD} of the switches at the op amp input; and (b) the *channel pumping* or *charge injection* effects (Allstot and Black 1983; Gregorian and Temes 1986; Shieh, Patil, and Sheu 1987; Unbehauen and Cichocki 1989; Van Peteghem 1988). Charge injection is a phenomenon in which some fraction of the charges stored in the channels of MOST switches, when turned ON, are discharged onto associated capacitors (say C_1 and C in Fig. 8-29) as they turn OFF. Since the MOST switches are turning ON and OFF periodically with clock f_s, this charge injection occurs with the same periodicity. This rather complex and difficult to model phenomenon is related to the changes in C_{GS} (and C_{js}), noted in Table 8-1 as the

FIGURE 8-29   Circuit model for DC offset and clock feedthrough due to capacitive coupling to ϕ^e and ϕ^o.

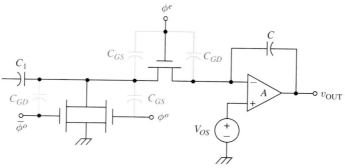

MOSTs make the transition from triode to cutoff operation. In Fig. 8-29, the clock feedthrough transferred to the signal path is proportional to $C_{GD,S}/C$. Once coupled to the signal path, the clock feedthrough, with frequency f_s, is sampled by a later stage and aliased down to DC. Clock feedthrough, passed continuously via unswitched capacitors to the output, appears as a high-frequency spurious signal superimposed on the information signal. This component of the clock feedthrough is conveniently removed with the continuous reconstruction filter.

For a single ended open-loop op amp, with open-loop gain A and the DC offset modeled as in Fig. 5-28b, the voltages at the input and output of the op amp are

$$v_X = v_{\text{in}} \text{ and } v_{\text{OUT}} = -A(v_{\text{in}} - V_{OS}) \tag{8-51}$$

Based on considerations in Sec. 6-6, V_{OS} can be reduced to the millivolt range. If this is not sufficient, local *autozeroing* (Gray, Hodges, and Broderson 1980; Gregorian and Temes 1986) using switched-capacitor techniques as in Fig. 8-30a, can reduce the offset by an order of magnitude or more. In this circuit, using a *chopper stabilizing* technique, V_{OS} is first stored on C_{AZ} during a measurement phase ϕ_1 and combines with the signal during the operation phase ϕ_2 (Gregorian and Temes 1986; Unbehauen and Cichocki 1989). The timing for ϕ_1 and ϕ_2, illustrated in Fig. 8-30b, is somewhat arbitrary. Note that the operation phase is significantly longer than the measurement phase, i.e., $T_2 \gg T_1$ and the period for the measurement samples is T. Many-clocked systems, particularly A/D converters, allocate a time slot to perform autozeroing on an infrequent but periodic basis. In an active-SC filter, ϕ_1 would be third phase, perhaps inserted into the dead zone between ϕ^e and ϕ^o. Note that the ϕ_1 switches carry only small DC offsets and hence are implemented as single-channel MOSTs.

The operation of the autozero is relatively simple. During the measurement phase, with ϕ_1 ON, the v_{OUT} is shorted back to v_X and the bottom plate of C_{AZ} is shorted

FIGURE 8-30   Autozeroing of op amp DC offset: (a) a chopper-stabilized structure to cancel op amp DC offsets, and (b) representative timing for the switches.

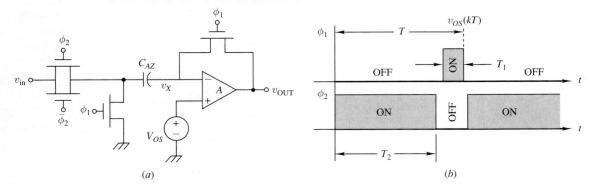

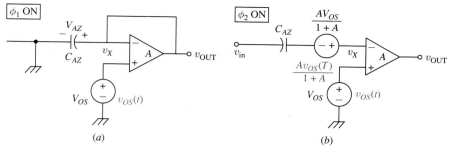

FIGURE 8-31 Operation of the autozero circuit in Fig. 8-27: (a) circuit during ϕ_1 phase, and (b) circuit in ϕ_2 phase. Changes to the model when v_{OS} is slowly time varying are indicated in gray.

to ground, as shown in Fig. 8-31a. According to Eq. (8-51) we now have

$$v_X = -A(v_X - V_{OS}) \text{ and } v_X = \frac{A}{1+A}V_{OS} \approx V_{OS} \qquad (8\text{-}52)$$

where $v_X = V_{AZ}$. During the operation phase, when ϕ_2 ON, feedback around the op amp is opened and C_{AZ} is put into the signal path, as illustrated in Fig. 8-31b. Using Eqs. (8-51) and (8-52), we have

$$v_X = v_{in} + V_{AZ} = v_{in} + \frac{A}{1+A}V_{OS} \qquad (8\text{-}53a)$$

and

$$v_{OUT} = -A\left(v_{in} + \frac{A}{1+A}V_{OS} - V_{OS}\right) = -A\left(v_{in} + \frac{1}{1+A}V_{OS}\right) \qquad (8\text{-}53b)$$

Hence, during the operation phase, V_{OS} is attenuated by $1/(1+A)$ and goes to zero as A becomes large. For example, if $V_{OS} = 10$ mV and $A \geq 1000$, then the DC offset at the output will be reduced to $V_O \leq 10$ μV.

This technique is also used to cancel op amp $1/f$ noise, which varies slowly in contrast to the period of ϕ_1 (Gregorian and Temes 1986; Unbehauen and Cichocki 1989). Note that there is a delay of T_d between measurement and operation. That is, during each ϕ_2 phase, a slow varying $v_{OS}(t)$ is subtracted from the $\{A/(1+A)\}v_{OS}(kT)$ stored on C_{AZ}. This reduces the cancellation in Eq. (8-53b) as $1 - e^{-j\omega T}$. This effect is fundamental to all chopper-stabilized systems. It should not be surprising to the reader that the thermal noise of the op amp will not be canceled, and in fact will be enhanced by the sampling. Also, the switched C_{AZ} introduces kT/C noise, which adds to the overall system rms noise.

Clock feedthrough can be reduced through means involving layout and circuit techniques (Gregorian and Temes 1986; Martin 1982; Unbehauen and Cichocki 1989) similar to the chopper-stabilized structure in Fig. 8-30. In this layout it should be clear that $C_{GD,S}/C$ is minimized by sizing the switches at the op amp input as small as possible (minimizing $C_{GD,S}$) and scaling C as large as possible. If we scale C and C_1 by k, the signal transfer is certainly unaffected, but the clock feedthrough is reduced by $1/k$. Fortunately, in most active-SC filters, which oversample such that $f_S \gg f_N$ (see App. 7-1), the integrating capacitor C in Fig. 8-29 will tend to be among the largest capacitors in the filter. The use of minimum sized, single-channel switches at the op amp input is consistent with this objective.

In addition to these layout steps, cancellation circuits such as Fig. 8-32 can be used (Martin 1982). In this circuit, the layout (components and parasitics) connected to the negative op amp input is replicated and inserted in series with the positive input. To the degree that the two layouts match, the clock feedthrough is reduced by the common-mode rejection of the op amp. Unlike the autozeroing circuit, the sampling in this scheme does not interfere with the degree of cancellation realized. Since the kT/C noise introduced by the two SC's C_1 are not correlated, noise is not canceled with the clock feedthrough. Hence, it is likely that system noise of the canceled circuit will be a bit larger than the integrator without cancellation. Moreover, the die area for the integrator is increased by 50 percent or more.

Akin to clock feedthrough is the feed of spurious AC on the MOST-R control V_C (or the G_m control I_A) into the filter. Since AC on these controls modulates the values of R and G_m, the impact on performance can be severe. In practice, in order to realize the required precision, V_C (or I_A) is tuned using the closed loop schemes described in the previous section. The lowpass filters (LPFs) in Figs. 8-23 through 8-28 conveniently cleanse these controls of any spurious AC introduced at or before the control loop.

FIGURE 8-32   Active-SC integrator with clock feedthrough cancellation.

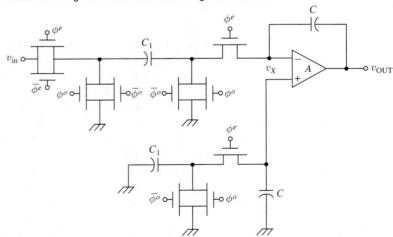

8-5-2   Layout Measures to Improve *PSRR*

In Chap. 6 we introduced the unavoidable fact that practical DC power supplies cause V_{SS} and V_{DD} to be corrupted by spurious AC components generated within the power supplies and introduced by on-chip interactions with digital circuitry, i.e.,

$$v_{SS}(t) = V_{SS} + v_{ss}(t) \text{ and } v_{DD}(t) = V_{DD} + v_{dd}(t) \tag{8-54}$$

This spurious AC (v_{ss} and v_{dd}) is sometimes referred to in filter specifications as power supply noise or ripple. Fortunately, much of the so-called power supply noise is actually deterministic, not random. Hence, couplings that are electrically equivalent are highly correlated.

The ability for an op amp, a filter, or a system to suppress $v_{SS}(t)$ and $v_{DD}(t)$ is measured by the so-called power supply rejection ratios ($PSRR_{DD}$ and $PSRR_{SS}$). We generalize the definitions in Eqs. (6-103) to accommodate the frequency dependent *PSRR*s for a filter, i.e.,

$$PSRR_{DD}(\omega) = 20 \log \frac{M(\omega)}{M_{DD}(\omega)} = G(\omega) - G_{DD}(\omega) \text{ in dB} \tag{8-55a}$$

and

$$PSRR_{SS}(\omega) = 20 \log \frac{M(\omega)}{M_{SS}(\omega)} = G(\omega) - G_{SS}(\omega) \text{ in dB} \tag{8-55b}$$

where M, G and M_{XX}, G_{XX} are the filter's information signal gain ($V_{\text{out}}/V_{\text{in}}$) and power supply gain functions (V_{out}/V_{xx}), respectively.

Note that the DC components V_{SS} and V_{DD} can drift with temperature, with age, and from supply-to-supply by about ± 10 percent. These static variations, not to be confused with the AC variations in Eq. (8-54), serve to alter the DC characteristics of the MOSTs and BJTs described in Chaps. 1 and 2. Intuitively, we expect that a circuit highly sensitive to static power supply variations is also likely to have poor *PSRR*s. Be that as it may, absolute static power supply variations can contribute to the random variations in the filter characteristics, and any resulting asymmetry (i.e., $|V_{SS}| \neq |V_{DD}|$) can degrade device matches designed to reduce DC offset and nonlinear distortion. Following the design practice prescribed in Chap. 6 and Sec. 8-2, static power supply variations should have little impact on the performance of active filters.

As established in Chap. 6, high values of $PSRR_{DD}$ and $PSRR_{SS}$ can be realized in op amps and OTAs at low frequencies, but they degrade at high frequencies as the active circuit's second-order effects increase in importance. The need for good *PSRR*s is particularly true for active-SC filters, where the high-frequency components on power supply lines are sampled and aliased into the filter's passband, as illustrated in Fig. 7-18. Hence, by hook or by crook, good *PSRR*s at high frequencies must be realized. Except for sampling, a major exception indeed, the *PSRR* problems for continuous-time and switched-capacitor filters are similar. We thus focus our discussion on active-SC filters realized in CMOS.

Like clock feedthrough, $PSRR_{DD}$ and $PSRR_{SS}$ are heavily determined by the parasitic capacitance couplings in Fig. 8-4 (*see color plate 1*) between the signal path and v_{DD} and v_{SS}, respectively. In addition to setting the DC operating conditions for the active devices, recall that V_{DD} is also the bias for the CMOS substrate. The variety of coupling paths are indicated in Fig. 8-33 for a typical active-SC integrator. The most important couplings are those closest to the op amp input where spurious charges are transferred directly to the integrating capacitor C. First, in Fig. 8-33a, we show two capacitance couplings to v_{DD} that are external to the op amp, namely, C_R and C_J, at the routing and switch junctions, respectively. As described in Sec. 6-7, v_{DD} enters the op amp signal path via the normal operation of the MOSTs, represented by the *VCVS* A_{DD}, and via parasitic capacitors, represented by C_I. Recall that the ratio A_v/A_{DD} is the op amp's $PSRR_{DD}$. In addition, when the ON level for ϕ^e and ϕ° is derived from v_{DD}, the C_{GS}'s and C_{GD}'s for the MOST switches provide an indirect coupling. Consequently, some power supply noise couples along with the clock feedthrough. The representation for v_{SS} in Fig. 8-33b is similar to that for v_{DD}, with the significant difference being no capacitance couplings to v_{SS}, except the possibly indirect couplings via the OFF level of ϕ^e and ϕ°. Hence, in CMOS active-SC filters (and for that matter active-RC and active-G_m/C) filters, $PSRR_{SS} \gg PSRR_{DD}$.

Attempting to increase the *PSRR* is akin to pealing an onion with many layers of skin. The direct path *PSRR*s can be slightly increased with a well-engineered layout designed to reduce the size of dominant parasitic feeds. In the first layer of the "onion," we reduce the $W \times L$ of the important parasitic couplings with a tight layout and, where electrically feasible, by using small transistors. This serves to minimize the all important transfer gains C_R/C, C_J/C and C_I/C. Adopting the design methods offered in Sec. 6-7, the op amp's A_{DD} and A_{SS} are made as small as possible.

The creative use of mask levels, e.g., p-well (or n-well), can be used to partially decouple some parasitics from the supply lines. This is illustrated in Fig. 8-34 (*see color plate 2*). The purpose here is to surround the capacitors, the switch, and as much routing (to the op amp input) as possible, in a grounded p-well, as shown in Fig. 8-34a. Two connections for the p-well are indicated, namely, to ground for the shields under capacitors and routing, and to V_{PW} for the shields under nMOST switches. Bias V_{PW} (about -3.5 V for a ± 5 V system) is generated on-chip using a voltage reference (Marsh et al. 1981). Such a scheme, illustrated in Fig. 8-36a (on page 807), uses a simple current mirror to generate $V_{REF} = R I_{REF}$. The desired V_{PW} is derived by amplifying V_{REF} by $-K$. The voltage reference serves to provide a buffer between the p-well bias V_{PW} and v_{DD}, v_{SS}, sacrificing 1 or 2 dB in signal swing.

If the p-well under the capacitors and routing could be made into a perfect ground plane, the "shielded" capacitance couplings to the signal path could be safely tied to ground rather than to v_{DD}. Unfortunately, due to the 2.5 k$\Omega/\square$ sheet resistance (see Table 7-1) for the p-well and the limited physical contacts that can be made to ground, the connection to ground is via a parasitic resistance R_{pW}. This is indicated in the schematic of Fig. 8-34b. Consequently, the effectiveness of the shield diminishes with

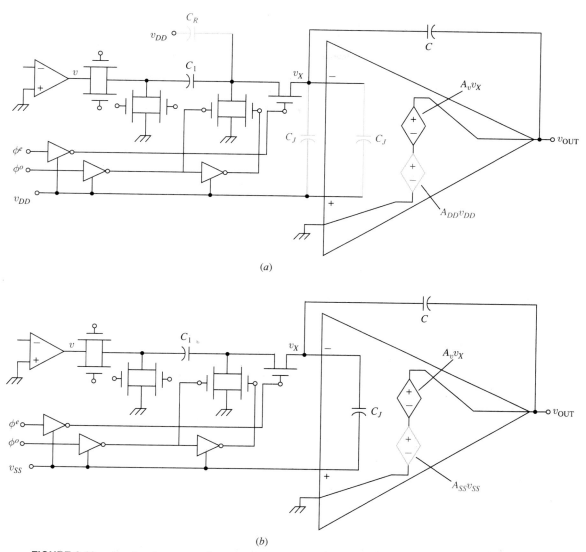

FIGURE 8-33 Dominant sources of power supply coupling in CMOS SC filters: (a) from V_{DD} and (b) from V_{SS}.

frequency and as R_{pW} increases with physical distance from the ground contact. With careful attention to ground contacts, experience has proven these steps to yield a 5 to 10 dB improvement in $PSRR_{DD}$ and $PSRR_{SS}$ at low frequencies (Marsh et al. 1981). Note that C_{B1}, C_{R1} are poly-to-substrate parasitic capacitances in field-oxide, and C_{B2}, C_{R2} are p-well-to-substrate parasitic capacitances. The p-well-to-substrate capacitance density is large, on the order of 5 to 10 times the poly-to-substrate capacitance density ($C_{oxp} = 6.5 \text{ nF/cm}^2$). Thus, we find that $C_{B2} \gg C_{B1}$ and $C_{R2} \gg C_{R1}$.

Example 8-6

Consider the simple circuit in Fig. 8-35a with capacitor $C = 10$ pF and an un-shielded parasitic capacitance $C_{p1} = 0.05$ pF. Alternatively, we can shield the circuitry contributing to C_{p1} in a grounded p-well, as described in Fig. 8-34. For the shielded circuit in Fig. 8-35b, let us assume that $R_{pW} = 10$ kΩ and $C_{p2} = 1$ pF. Compute the voltage ratio v_{out}/v_{DD} for the unshielded and shielded cases.

Solution. The v_{out}/v_{dd} voltage ratios for Fig. 8-35a and 8-35b are found to be, respectively,

$$|\frac{V_{out}}{V_{dd}}|_a = \frac{C_{p1}}{C} \quad \text{and} \quad |\frac{V_{out}}{V_{dd}}|_b = \frac{C_{p1}}{C}\frac{\omega C_{p2} R_{pW}}{\sqrt{1 + \omega^2 R_{pW}^2 (C_{p1} + C_{p2})^2}}$$

or

$$|\frac{V_{out}}{V_{dd}}|_b = |\frac{V_{out}}{V_{dd}}|_a A(\omega)$$

where $A(\omega) = \omega C_{p2} R_{pW}/\sqrt{1 + \omega^2 R_{pW}^2 (C_{p1} + C_{p2})^2}$ is the attenuation due to the p-well shield. Inserting the numbers for C, R_{pW}, C_{p1}, and C_{p2}, we obtain

$$|\frac{V_{out}}{V_{dd}}|_a = 0.005(-46\text{dB}) \quad \text{and} \quad A(\omega) \approx \frac{\omega \times 10^{-8}}{\sqrt{1 + \omega^2 \times 10^{-16}}}$$

Note that for:

$\omega \ll 10^8$ rps or $f \ll 15.9$ MHz $A(\omega) \approx 2\pi f \times 10^{-8}$,
$\omega = 10^8$ rps or $f = 15.9$ MHz, $A(\omega) = 0.707$ (−3 dB)
$\omega \gg 10^8$ rps or $f \gg 15.9$ MHz $A(\omega) \approx 1$ (0 dB)

FIGURE 8-35   Circuits for Example 8-6: (a) Integrator summing node with unshielded parasitic C_{p1} and (b) with the circuitry comprising C_{p1} shielded in a p-well with resistance R_{pW} and capacitance C_{p2}.

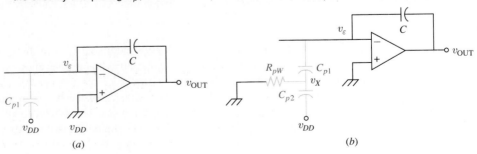

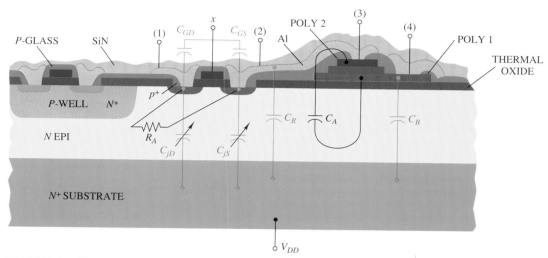

FIGURE 8-4 The parasitic capacitances, in a typical dual poly, p-well CMOS process, which are deemed most important in the realization of integrated filters. Symbols for the parasitic capacitances and the one intentional capacitor are shown in gray and black, respectively.

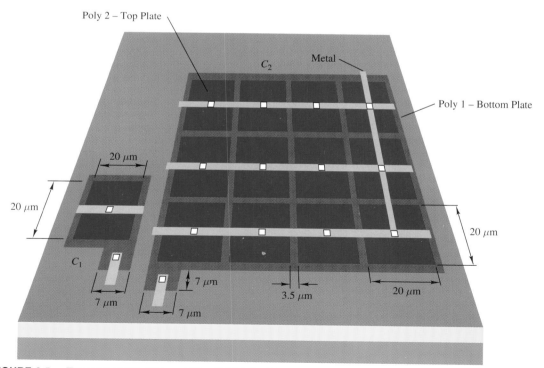

FIGURE 8-5 Top view of unit (C_1) and 12 unit (C_2) double-poly capacitors.

Color plate 1

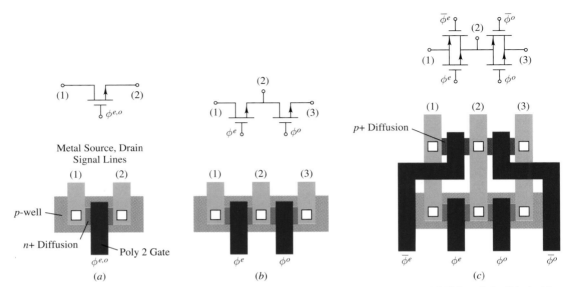

FIGURE 8-8 Analog switch schematics and layouts: (a) single-pole-double-throw NMOS switch, (b) double-pole-double-throw NMOS switch, and (c) double-pole-double-throw CMOS switch.

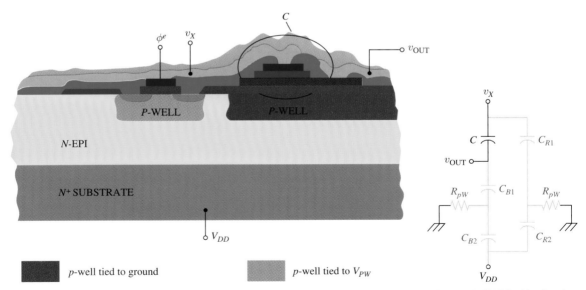

FIGURE 8-34 p-well shields to increase $PSRR_{DD}$ and $PSRR_{SS}$: (a) cross-section of a p-well CMOS chip showing circuitry and p-well shields at the op amp input; (b) circuit schematic showing impact of grounded p-well on parasitics associated with capacitor C.

Color plate 2

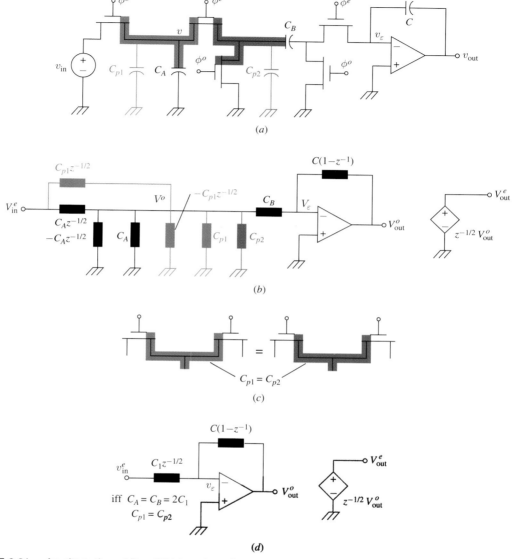

FIGURE 8-21   An alternative $-$LD, $-$FE integrator using two tandem SC's at the input: (a) the circuit showing parasitics C_{p1} and C_{p2} in green and red, respectively. The z-domain equivalent circuit for (a) is shown in (b), with all components due to parasitics in their respective colors. In (c) we show that the top plate parasitics C_{p1} and C_{p2} can be made equal by careful matching of the layout. When the SC's are matched, i.e., $C_A = C_B = 2C_1$ and $C_{p1} = C_{p2} = C_p$, all the parasitics in (c) cancel and (c) reduces to (d).

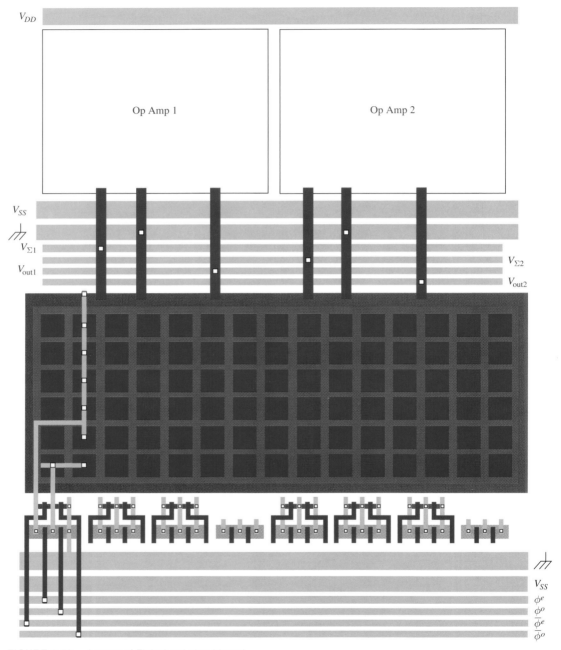

FIGURE 8-53 Layout of Fleischer-Laker biquad.

Color plate 4

The indirect sources via the switch clocks ϕ^e, ϕ^e can be virtually eliminated if the ON, OFF levels $\pm V_{SW}$ are developed with a voltage reference (say ± 3 V for ± 5 V supplies) as above. In fact, one bias generator can realize V_{PW} and $\pm V_{SW}$, as illustrated in Fig. 8-36a. The levels are readily changed by biasing the clock drivers, which deliver ϕ^e and ϕ° to the switch gates from $\pm V_{SW}$ rather then V_{SS} and V_{DD} as shown in Fig. 8-36b. Since $(C_{GS})_{ON} > (C_{GS})_{OFF}$, decoupling the ON level from v_{DD} has a larger impact.

To the degree that the layouts at positive and negative op amp inputs in Fig. 8-32 match, $PSRR_{DD}$ and $PSRR_{SS}$ are enhanced by the common-mode rejection of the op amp along with the clock feedthrough. Experience with cancellation schemes, based on $|X| - |Y| \rightarrow 0$, dictates the reduction of $|X|$ and $|Y|$ as much as possible before cancellation. Hence, some or all of the schemes described should be used concurrently with a cancellation structure. In the next section we explore the use of balanced differential structures (e.g., Figs. 5-39 through 5-46) to increase $PSRR$.

Additional increases in $PSRR$ can be obtained with the aid of external passive components, strategically placed to filter, bypass, or lowpass filter the power supply feeds to the pins of the chip. The impact of bypassing depends on the degree to which ohmic losses in the power supply, and ground bussing within the chip, have been minimized. Obviously, ground loops are not allowed. In mixed analog/digital systems it is standard practice to provide separate grounds for analog and digital circuitry, tied to a single point (if possible) of the chip. To reduce system costs, it is usually an objective, if not a requirement, for the chip to meet all specifications with zero or minimum bypassing.

FIGURE 8-36   On-chip bias generation for V_{PW} and $\pm V_{SW}$: (a) an illustrative scheme based on simple current mirror reference; and (b) distribution of $\pm V_{SW}$ to clock drivers.

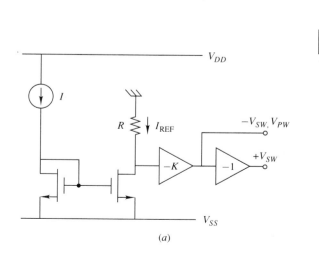

(a)

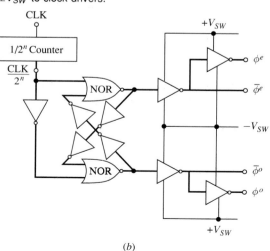

(b)

8-5-3   Balanced Active-RC and Active-SC Design

In Eq. (5-62), we found that a balanced differential design, as per Figs. 5-40 through 5-46 and 5-50, produces two benefits. First, correlated disturbances v_D at the two op amp inputs are attenuated by the op amp *CMRR*, and second, the signal swing is doubled. The critical tasks are then the design and implementation of a balanced differential op amp or OTA (see Sec. 6-9-3). (Gregorian and Temes 1986; Schaumann, Ghausi, and Laker 1990; Unbehauen and Cichocki 1989). If we let disturbance v_D in Fig. 5-43 denote V_{SS}, V_{DD} or clock feedthrough, the analysis in Sec. 5-4 is directly applicable to our objectives. Similarly, parasitic insensitivity is realized throughout the signal path. For MOST-R-based active-RC filters, a balanced differential operation is crucial to the success of linearization schemes, based on the differential MOST-R in Fig. 8-10b. However, the four MOST structures in Fig. 8-10c achieve linearization in the absence of a balanced output. Note that the linearized G_m's in Figs. 8-11 and 8-12 do not have a balanced differential output. Using Fig. 5-50, a balanced linearized G_m structure can be realized using two linear single-ended OTAs.

We determined in Sec. 5-4 that the dynamic range improves by $2/\sqrt{2}$, even if the *PSRR*s were left unchanged. In contrast, the dynamic range for the single-ended cancellation structure in Fig. 8-32 is degraded by $1/\sqrt{2}$. Also, we outlined in this section a systematic process for translating single-ended active-RC designs to balanced differential designs. We observed that the differential output led to some structural advantages, e.g., the single amplifier noninverting integrator in Fig. 5-45. For active-SC filters, this structural versatility is a valuable byproduct. For example, all the z-domain integration formulas in Table 7-8 can be realized in either inverting or noninverting parasitic insensitive structures. We leave it to the reader to verify this claim. Later, we show examples where the differential outputs are used to reduce the total capacitance required for the realization and to lower sensitivities to the capacitor ratios.

The price paid for the various advantages of balanced differential operation is at least a doubling of the circuitry and power dissipation. Consequently, it is not a universal solution. In fact, designs that are very sensitive to power and or cost (e.g., for battery-powered consumer products) are usually realized with single-ended structures. In any event, because singled-ended structures are simpler, take up less page space, and are perhaps less confusing to the novice reader, we usually present filter structures this way. Later, however, we will discuss the structural flexibility of the balanced differential structure. Otherwise, it will be assumed that an equivalent balanced differential structure can always be obtained by the straightforward translation of a single-ended structure (i.e., as described in Sec. 5-4). Of course, to realize the actual circuit we must have an accurate balanced differential op amp (see Sec. 6-9-3), available to replace the single-ended op amp.

8-6   FIRST-ORDER AND BIQUADRATIC FILTER STAGE REALIZATIONS

Active filter design is largely modular in nature, a fact that lends itself to poly cell design approaches and programmable filters. Here we build upon the techniques in this and previous chapters to increase the level of design to arbitrary first- and second-order filter stages. As described in Sec. 8-9, such stages are interconnected in either tandem or multiple-loop feedback structures to realize higher order filters with a variety of unique properties.

The realization of integrated filters in VLSI technologies has changed much of the conventional wisdom found in traditional active filter texts and literature. One such recently discarded "rule of thumb" was to choose an active filter circuit that required the minimum number of capacitors, i.e., one C per pole or pole/zero pair. Such active-RC filter circuits were said to be canonical structures. The minimum C objective followed from the economics of discrete and thin film technologies, in which precision resistors were less costly and available over a broader range of values than precision capacitors. Of course, resistors are trimmable and capacitors are not. In integrated filters, particularly when implemented in CMOS, capacitors are the more robust components. In continuous-time filters, resistors and transconductances are trimmable, but are otherwise not ideally behaved, e.g., nonlinear. In active-SC filters, the switched capacitors or resistor analogs introduce clock feedthrough and kT/C noise. Hence, in integrated filters, the more robust structures will tend to minimize the number of R's, G_m's, or their equivalents. For continuous-time filters, there must be sufficient R's or G_ms to perform the automatic tuning described in Sec. 8-4.

Another convention that has fallen into disfavor is the attempt to minimize the number of op amps. This stems again from hybrid design and low scale analog integration, when a chip of one or two op amps was considered a complex IC. The economies of scale were such that significant savings could be achieved by minimizing the number of op amps used. Although op amps in integrated filters are not problem-free—they add noise, introduce nonlinear distortion and consume power—they are viewed as components similar to resistors and capacitors. In fact, as seen in Fig. 8-1, capacitors rather than op amps consume the most die area in active-SC filters. As observed in Sec. 8-3, op amps serve to isolate and neutralize parasitics. Consequently, most minimum op amp structures, which were promoted for hybrid realization, have proven to be impractical for realizing precision integrated filters. In addition, op amps can isolate parameters to facilitate on-chip tuning, as described in Sec. 8-4.

8-6-1 Realizing Real Poles and Zeros

First-order $H(s)$ and $H(z)$ in Eqs. (7-12) are readily realized by starting with the basic integrator. Equations (7-12) are rewritten below for convenience

$$H(s) = \frac{a_1 s \pm a_0}{s + b_0} \quad \text{and} \quad H(z) = \frac{A_1 \pm A_0 z^{-1}}{1 - B_0 z^{-1}} \qquad (8\text{-}56)$$

In Fig. 8-37 we show realizations for the important generic first order $H(s)$ and $H(z)$; namely, LP (Figs. 8-37a–c), HP (Figs. 8-37d–f), and AP (Figs. 8-37g–i). The implementations shown are for a balanced differential MOST-RC, a single-ended OTA-based G_m/C, and a single-ended switched capacitor. For the MOST-RC real-

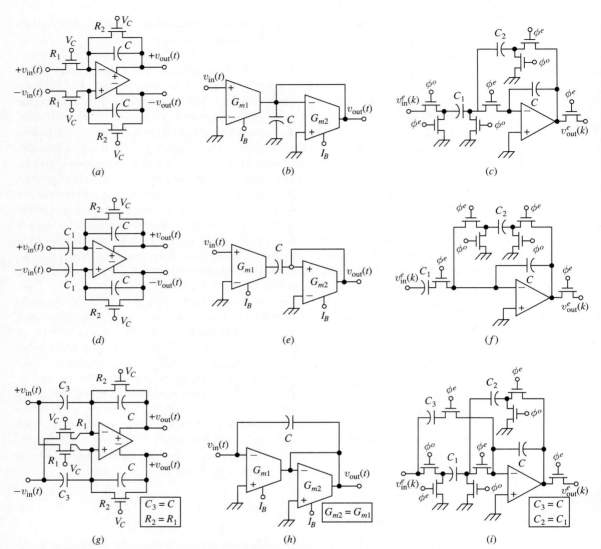

FIGURE 8-37   Generic integrated first-order active-RC, active-G_m/C, active-SC realizations. Circuits $(a–c)$ are LP, $(d–f)$ are HP, and $(g–i)$ are AP.

izations, balanced differential design is used to linearize the MOST-R's, as described in Sec. 8-2-3. Schemes to realize OTAs with linear G_m's over a wider range of signal conditions were developed in Sec. 8-2-4. We leave it to the reader to translate the single-ended active-G_m/C and active-SC implementations into balanced differential equivalents, as described in Sec. 5-4 and 5-5. Note that the active-G_m/C circuits are comprised of the OTA building blocks shown in Fig. 5-48. The symbolic transfer functions for each of the circuits, determined for ideal op amps and OTAs, are listed in Table 8-2.

The design formulas for a given integrator capacitor C are also listed in Table 8-2. These formulas are derived by simply equating the coefficients of the numerical $H(s)$ or $H(z)$ in Eqs. (8-56) with those of the corresponding coefficients of the symbolic $T(s)$ or $T(z)$ in Table 8-2. The actual component values are then scaled in accordance with the designer's choice for the value of C. This choice involves a case-by-case tradeoff of die area versus the magnitude of second-order effects due to parasitics. In general, the die area increases with increasing C, but in the case of MOST-RC (or G_m/C) circuits there is an optimum balance between C's and R's (or G_m's) that minimizes the die area they consume. For example, consider the implementation of the R and C for a simple RC product where $RC = \beta$ and β is a fixed constant. Let us assume that die areas for the R and C are A_R and A_C, respectively, and the total RC die area is $A_T = A_R + A_C$. It can be shown (see Exercise 8-8) that the values for R and C that yield the minimum A_T occur when $A_R = A_C$.

Although the switch-reduced schematics are shown for active-SC realizations, the reader should not have difficulty drawing the z-domain equivalent circuits and verifying the $T(z)$'s in Table 8-2. Usually, the sign of $T(s)$ or $T(z)$ is unimportant, and

TABLE 8-2 $T(s), T(z)$ AND DESIGN FORMULAS FOR FIRST-ORDER CIRCUITS IN FIG. 8-37

	MOST-RC	OTA G_m/C	switched-capacitor
LP	(a) $T(s) = \dfrac{-1/CR_1}{s + \dfrac{1}{CR_2}}$	(b) $T(s) = \dfrac{G_{m1}/C}{s + \dfrac{G_{m2}}{C}}$	(c) $T(z) = \dfrac{\dfrac{C_1}{C + C_2} z^{-1}}{1 - \dfrac{C}{C + C_2} z^{-1}}$
	Hence, $R_1 = \dfrac{1}{a_0 C},\ R_2 = \dfrac{1}{b_0 C}$	Hence, $G_{m1} = a_0 C,\ G_{m2} = b_0 C$	Hence, $C_1 = \dfrac{A_0}{B_0} C,\ C_2 = \dfrac{1 - B_0}{B_0} C$
HP	(d) $T(s) = \dfrac{-sC_1/C}{s + \dfrac{1}{CR_2}}$	(e) $T(s) = \dfrac{sG_{m1}/C}{s + \dfrac{G_{m2}}{C}}$	(f) $T(z) = \dfrac{-\dfrac{C_1}{C + C_2}(1 - z^{-1})}{1 - \dfrac{C}{C + C_2} z^{-1}}$
	Hence, $C_1 = a_1 C,\ R_2 = \dfrac{1}{b_0 C}$	Hence, $G_{m1} = a_1 C,\ G_{m2} = b_0 C$	Hence, with $A_0/A_1 \equiv 1$, $C_1 = \dfrac{A_1}{B_0} C,\ C_2 = \dfrac{1 - B_0}{B_0} C$
AP	(g) $T(s) = \dfrac{s - \dfrac{1}{CR_1}}{s + \dfrac{1}{CR_2}}$	(h) $T(s) = -\dfrac{s - \dfrac{G_{m1}}{C}}{s + \dfrac{G_{m2}}{C}}$	(i) $T(z) = \dfrac{-\dfrac{C_3}{C + C_2}\left(1 - \dfrac{C_3 + C_1}{C_3} z^{-1}\right)}{1 - \dfrac{C}{C + C_2} z^{-1}}$
	Hence, with $a_1 \equiv 1,\ a_0 \equiv b_0$ $R_1 = R_2 = \dfrac{1}{b_0 C},\ C_3 = C$	Hence, with $a_1 \equiv 1,\ a_0 \equiv b_0$ $G_{m1} = G_{m2} = b_0 C$	Hence, with $A_0/A_1 \equiv 1/B_0$ $C_1 = C_2 = \dfrac{1 - B_0}{B_0} C,\ C_3 = C$

hence we show some stages in Fig. 8-37 as inverting and others as noninverting. For MOST-RC filters, the sign can be changed by simply switching the differential inputs. Using the inverting input to G_{m1} as the signal input in Figs. 8-37b and 8-37e will similarly invert their respective $T(s)$'s. Various inverting and noninverting first order LP $H(z)$'s can be realized by straightforward applications of the active-SC integrator structures discussed in Sec. 8-3.

Let us briefly consider the consequences of nonideal op amps. If the op amp used in an active-RC realization has finite DC and AC characteristics, the gain and phase of the filter will deviate from its ideal frequency response (Ghausi and Laker 1981; Gregorian and Temes 1986; Schaumann, Ghausi, and Laker 1990; Unbehauen and Cichocki 1989). The specific nature of the deviation will be a function of the op amp's open-loop characteristic and the filter's desired closed-loop response. This was described in some detail in Secs. 5-2 and 5-3. For single-pole compensated op amps, where we can approximate the actual op amp open-loop gain as $A(s) \approx \omega_t/s$, the troublesome phase error can be reduced using the active compensation schemes in Fig. 5-23. In active-G_m/C realizations, the finite bandwidth of the OTAs will cause a similar gain and phase error. However, due to the simplicity of the OTA (as compared to a full op amp), active-G_m/C filters can be pushed to higher frequencies before the OTA GBW impacts the filter's closed-loop response $T(s)$.

For active-SC realizations, the samples $v_{in}(kT)$ are assumed to be phase independent; changing once per clock period T at the beginning of ϕ^e. Thus, given ideal op amps, the circuits are parasitic insensitive and output samples $v_{out}(kT)$ are also phase independent. When we take into account the nonideal op amp, its finite DC gain produces an error in $T(z)$, equivalent to analogous active-RC cases studied in Chap. 5. This error can be readily evaluated and studied using the equivalent circuits. However, the op amp's AC characteristics impact $T(z)$ in a much different manner due to the sampling (Gregorian and Temes 1986; Laker, Ganesan, and Fleischer 1985; Martin and Sedra 1981; Unbehauen and Cichocki 1989). For the continuous-time cases in Chap. 5, we saw that it was the steady-state AC op amp characteristics that determined the error $\varepsilon_{rr}(j\omega)$. In active-SC filters, the transient or settling characteristics of the op amp cause the op amp outputs to deviate from the ideal staircase waveforms in Figs. 7-22 and 7-23. Hence, the instantaneous samples taken by the switched capacitors are in error. Although the process is intuitively simple, the mathematical analysis is quite complex (Gregorian and Temes 1986; Unbehauen and Cichocki 1989). We discuss this effect further and recommend remedies in Sec. 8-9-2. As we will see, assuming properly designed op amps, we can reduce the AC related error to a negligible value with subtle alterations of the active-SC architecture. Hence, the DC gain related error will remain the predominant contributor to ε_{rr}.

Following the arguments in Chap. 5, the DC gain-related error can be determined using the z-domain equivalent circuits. For this purpose, let us define the resulting error analogous to Eq. (5-8a), i.e.,

$$T_A(z) = T(z) \left\{ \frac{1}{1 + \varepsilon_{rr}(z)} \right\} \text{ and } \varepsilon_{rr}(j\omega) = \varepsilon_{rr}(z)|_{z=e^{j\omega T}} \qquad (8\text{-}57)$$

where $T_A(z)$ is the actual transfer function, $T(z)$ is the ideal transfer function in Table 8-2, and ε_{rr} is the error. Consider the LP active-SC circuit in Fig. 8-37c with $T(z)$ given in Table 8-2. The equivalent circuit, with the op amp modeled as a VCVS having DC gain A_0, is shown in Fig. 8-38. The resulting $\varepsilon_{rr}(z)$ can be found by analyzing this equivalent circuit and manipulating $T_A(z)$ into the form of Eq. (8-57), i.e.,

$$\varepsilon_{rr}(z) = \frac{1}{A_0}\left\{1 - \frac{\dfrac{C_1}{C+C_2}z^{-1}}{1 - \dfrac{C}{C+C_2}z^{-1}}\right\} \qquad (8\text{-}58a)$$

When $C_2 \ll C$, which is typical due to oversampling, we find the steady-state error $\varepsilon_{rr}(j\omega)$ to be

$$\varepsilon_{rr}(j\omega) \approx m_{rr}(\omega) + j\varphi_{rr}(\omega) \approx \frac{1}{A_0}\left(1 + \frac{C_1}{2C}\right) - j\left(\frac{1}{2A_0}\right)\frac{C_1/C}{\tan\left(\dfrac{\omega T}{2}\right)} \qquad (8\text{-}58b)$$

Note that the error is reduced as C increases, such that $C \gg C_1$, and then $m_{rr}(\omega) \approx 1/A_0$ and $\varphi_{rr}(\omega) \approx 0$. Once again, due to oversampling, $C \gg C_1, C_2$, which reduces $\varepsilon_{rr}(j\omega)$ along with all the parasitic effects that scale with C. We leave it to the reader to examine the DC op amp gain-related errors for the other first-order switched-capacitor circuits in Fig. 8-37.

It should be evident to the reader that the LP realization in Fig. 8-37c is not bilinear. In the majority of applications, where f_s is much larger than the Nyquist rate, this realization is both efficient and robust. However, for those cases where a bilinear first order LP stage is required, two alternatives are presented in Fig. 8-39. The first is a single-ended structure that takes advantage of the switched-capacitor tandem in Fig. 8-21 to assist in the realization of the zero at $z = -1$. However, this requires that the C_1's be matched. The second is a fully-balanced differential configuration that takes advantage of the balanced inputs $\pm v_{in}$. In this structure, the requisite zero is realized by performing the subtraction $[V_{in} - (-z^{-1}V_{in})]$ directly within switched-capacitor C_1, avoiding the opportunity for mismatch.

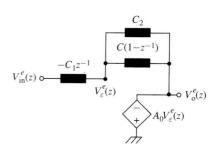

FIGURE 8-38 *Z*-domain equivalent circuit for the SC LP in Fig. 8-37c with nonideal op amp with finite DC gain A_0.

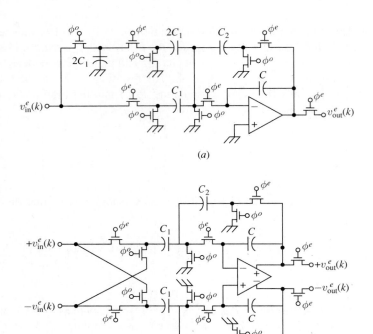

(a)

(b)

FIGURE 8-39   Bilinear first-order LP SC realizations: (a) a single-ended implementation, and (b) a fully-balanced differential implementation taking advantage of the balanced inputs.

Example 8-7

Design (a) an active-RC (using MOST-R's), (b) an active-G_m/C, and (c) an active-SC first-order AP filters to realize a 90° phase shift and a gain of 0 dB at 10 kHz. Let $C = 10$ pF and the sample rate for the active-SC circuit be $f_s = 256$ kHz.

Solution. From the 90° phase and 0 dB gain specification, we determine the numerical $H(s)$ to be

$$H(s) = \frac{s - \omega_p}{s + \omega_p} = \frac{s - 2\pi(10^4)}{s + 2\pi(10^4)} \tag{8-59a}$$

Applying the bilinear transform in Table 7-8, with $T = 1/f_s$, we obtain an equivalent numerical $H(z)$, i.e.,

$$H(z) = \frac{2 - \omega_p T}{2 + \omega_p T} \frac{1 - \left(\dfrac{2 + \omega_p T}{2 - \omega_p T}\right) z^{-1}}{1 - \left(\dfrac{2 - \omega_p T}{2 + \omega_p T}\right) z^{-1}} = 0.7814 \frac{1 - 1.2798 z^{-1}}{1 - 0.7814 z^{-1}} \tag{8-59b}$$

Using the design formulas in Table 8-2, with $C = 10$ pF, and the numerical $H(s)$ and $H(z)$, we determine that

    a for the active-RC design: $R_1 = R_2 = 1/(2\pi \times 10^4 \times 10^{-11}) = 1.5915$ MΩ and $C_3 = 10$ pF.

    b for the G_m/C design: $G_{m1} = G_{m2} = 2\pi \times 10^4 \times 10^{-11} = 0.6283$ μS.

    c for the active-SC design: $C_1 = C_2 = \{(1 - 0.7814)/0.7814\} \times 10^{-11} = 2.7975$ pF and $C_3 = 10$ pF.

8-6-2 Types of Biquads

The biquad or second-order filter that realizes Eq. (7-13) is perhaps the most extensively covered filter circuit in the literature (Ghausi and Laker 1981; Grebene 1984; Gregorian and Temes 1986; Moschytz 1986; Schaumann, Ghausi, and Laker 1990; Sedra 1985; Sedra 1989; Unbehauen and Cichocki 1989). This attention stems from the biquad's simplicity and its importance in the realization of modular filters. The numerous qualities expected in an integrated biquad circuit, namely, small die size, low power dissipation, insensitivity to variations in the passive components, insensitivity to the nonidealities of the active devices, immunity to parasitics, low noise, high dynamic range, and high *PSRR*s, are essentially independent of whether the circuit implemented in active-RC with MOST-R's, active-G_m/C with OTA G_m's, or active-SC. Continuous-time filters must also be tunable on-chip, as described in Sec. 8-4. Hence, it should not be surprising that only a small number of the circuit structures covered in the general literature have emerged as structures of choice for a majority of applications.

There are three classes of biquads in the literature, each with numerous variations and special cases. These classes are (1) single op amp biquads, (2) double op amp biquads based on the generalized impedance converter, and (3) triple (or more) op amp biquads.

Single Amplifier Biquads   The motivation for single op amp biquads (Ghausi and Laker 1981; Schaumann, Ghausi, and Laker 1990) stems from the objective (which has fallen into a state of disuse) to minimize op amps. The two circuits in Fig. 8-40 have been widely discussed in the literature and used in practice. The first circuit in Fig. 8-40*a* is a general biquad introduced by Friend (1975). It comprises one op amp, two capacitors, and eight resistors; i.e., the minimum number of capacitors and op amps. The circuit implementation is optimized for hybrid IC realization and all the resistors are laser trimmable. The price paid for the use of a single amplifier is complex tuning, which involves the interdependent tuning of all eight resistors. Moreover, the circuit is rather sensitive to parasitic C's at the circled nodes. These parasitics produce unwanted poles and zeros. These penalties, although minor or nonexistent in hybrid implementation, render such circuits impractical as precision integrated filters.

The second circuit in Fig. 8-40*b* is an LP single amplifier biquad due to Sallen-and-Key, as discussed in Ghausi and Laker (1981). Although this simple circuit was proposed in 1955, it is still widely used today to realize the on-chip continuous-time LP anti-aliasing and reconstruction filters (see App 7-1) for active-SC filters. In

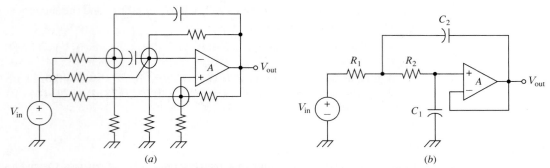

FIGURE 8-40   Single amplifier active-RC biquads: (a) Friend general biquad, and (b) Sallen and Key LP biquad.

CMOS, the R's are realized as simple untrimmed p-well resistors and the C's are poly 1-poly 2 capacitors. They key to the success of this circuit, for these applications, is that the only precision requirement on the LP filter is the DC gain. Due to the high degree of oversampling, ω_0 can usually be located well outside the baseband of the active-SC filter and sufficiently below f_s such that $|\Delta\omega_0/\omega_0| < 50$ percent, as long as the lack of precision in the RC's do not interfere with operation of the filter.

An analysis of Fig. 8-40b, with the open-loop op amp gain designated as $A(s)$, yields the following symbolic transfer function:

$$T(s) = \frac{\left(1 - \dfrac{1}{A(s)}\right) \dfrac{1}{R_1 R_2 C_1 C_2}}{s^2 + s\left[\dfrac{1}{R_1 C_1} + \dfrac{1}{R_2 C_1} + \dfrac{1}{R_2 C_2}\dfrac{1}{A(s)}\right] + \dfrac{1}{R_1 R_2 C_1 C_2}} = \frac{k\omega_0^2}{s^2 + \dfrac{\omega_0}{Q_p}s + \omega_0^2}$$

$$(8\text{-}60)$$

where we have assumed that $1/A(s) \ll 1$. The filter's DC gain is $T(j0) = 1 - 1/A(s)$, independent of the values for the R's and C's. If the op amp's $A(s)$ is compensated for a one pole roll off such that

$$A(s) = \frac{A_0 p}{s + p} = \frac{\omega_t}{s + p} \tag{8-61}$$

Thus, we have $T(j0) = 1 - 1/A_0$. For an anti-aliasing or reconstruction filter, it is important that $T(s)$ does not add error to the active-SC filter's $H(z)$. Hence, with $f_s \gg f_{NY} = 2\omega_C$ (f_{NY} is the Nyquist frequency) as described in App. 7-1, ω_0 can be chosen such that $\omega_s \gg \omega_0 \gg \omega_C$. Also, with Q_p chosen for a maximally flat or Butterworth response, the reader can verify that the most important source of error is due to variations in the anti-aliasing filter's low frequency gain, i.e., $\Delta T(j0)$. The fact that $T(j0)$ is independent of the R's and C's leaves $1 - 1/A_0$ as the only source of deviation from the ideal $T(j0) = 1$. Conservatively, an op DC gain of $20\log A_0 = 60$ dB permits $G(0) = 20\log T(j0)$ to be realized to within ± 0.0086 dB.

The other important specification in the design of an anti-aliasing filter is the attenuation $1/G(\omega_A)$, provided at the first alias frequency $\omega_A = 2\pi f_s - \omega_C$, where $\omega_0 \ll \omega_A$ due to oversampling. The specification for $G(\omega_A)$ and a conservative or worst case estimate of the anticipated variation in ω_0 (due to $\Delta R's$, $\Delta C's$, ω_t and parasitics) usually sets the lower limit on f_s. The reader has the opportunity to perform a detailed anti-aliasing filter design in Exercise 8-22. For convenience, the reconstruction filter is usually realized as a copy of the anti-aliasing filter. This can lead to overdesign, due to the $\sin x/x$ roll off attributed to the sample-and-hold described in App. 7-1. In any event, the Sallen-and-Key biquad is very well matched to the anti-aliasing and reconstruction requirements of active-SC filters. With unity gain, it provides the requisite precision at low frequencies, i.e., $T(j\omega) = T(j0)$ for $0 \leq \omega \leq \omega_C \ll \omega_0$. Except for this special case, this biquad is not particularly well suited for realizing precision integrated filters.

Two Amplifier Biquads Based on the GIC   The GIC, or generalized impedance converter, has been widely used in hybrid active-RC filter realizations and represents an important body of active-RC literature (Ghausi and Laker 1981; Schaumann, Ghausi, and Laker 1990). Its primary attribute is that it can be designed to be relatively insensitive to the op amp ω_t's. In Fig. 8-41, we show a typical GIC BP biquad (Schaumann, Ghausi, and Laker 1990). Similar to the situation for single amplifier biquads, GIC-based structures are not well-suited to the realization of integrated filters, due to the unavoidable parasitics at the circled nodes.

Multiple Amplifier State Variable Based Biquads   The two-integrator or state variable loop has emerged as one of the most basic structures in integrated filter realization. This loop, shown in Fig. 8-42a, is a simple circuit comprised of inverting and noninverting integrators connected in a closed loop. This loop determines the natural frequencies, i.e., resonant frequencies, in accordance with

$$s^2 + K_{CD}K_{AB} = s^2 + \omega_0^2 = 0 \qquad (8\text{-}62a)$$

FIGURE 8-41   GIC-based two op amp LP biquad.

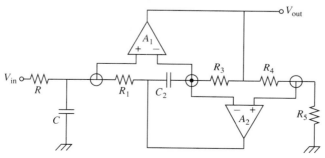

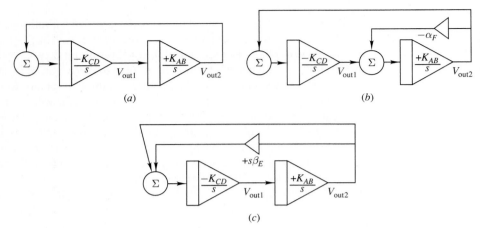

FIGURE 8-42 The state variable two-integrator resonant loops: (a) lossless loop, (b) a stable loop achieved by damping the noninverting integrator via local feedback $-\alpha_F$, and (c) a stable loop achieved by damping the resonator via feedback $s\beta_E$.

where K_{CD} and K_{AB} are the gains of the inverting and noninverting integrators, respectively. The equivalent sample data resonant loop can be derived by replacing each integrator with either their $\pm$LDI counterparts or with a $-$BE, $+$FE tandem, as indicated in Sec. 7-8-4. That is, using the s-to-z transforms in Table 7-8 with a sample rate of $f_s = 1/T$, we have

$$\left(-\frac{K_{CD}}{s}\right)\left(+\frac{K_{AB}}{s}\right) \rightarrow \left(-\frac{K_{CD}T}{1-z^{-1}}\right)\left(+\frac{K_{AB}Tz^{-1}}{1-z^{-1}}\right)$$

$$= \left(-\frac{K_{CD}Tz^{-1/2}}{1-z^{-1}}\right)\left(+\frac{K_{AB}Tz^{-1/2}}{1-z^{-1}}\right)$$

which yields the following z-domain characteristic equation

$$1 - \{2 - K_{CD}K_{AB}T^2\}z^{-1} + z^{-2} = 1 - \{2 - (\omega_0 T)^2\}z^{-1} + z^{-2} = 0 \qquad (8\text{-}62b)$$

The poles described in Eqs. (8-62) are made stable by damping one of the integrators or by damping the resonator.

Damping the noninverting integrator with local feedback $-\alpha_F$, as indicated in Fig. 8-42b, yields a complex pole pair, described by the following characteristic equation

$$s^2 + \alpha_F K_{AB}s + K_{CD}K_{AB} = s^2 + \frac{\omega_0}{Q_p}s + \omega_0^2 = 0 \qquad (8\text{-}63)$$

In Fig. 8-43, we show various active filter realizations of this loop, starting with the classic active-RC loop Fig. 8-43a (Ghausi and Laker 1981; Unbehauen and Cichocki

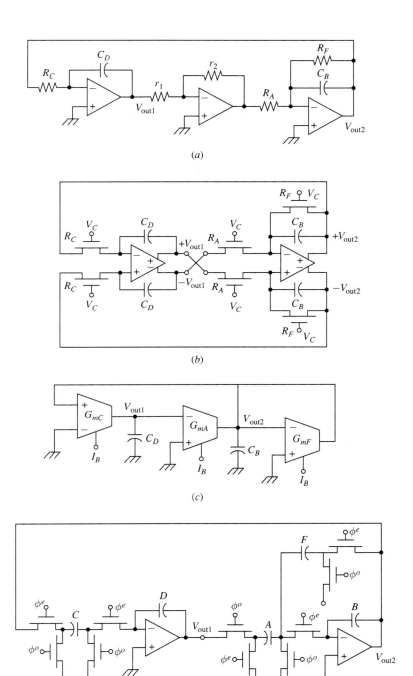

FIGURE 8-43 Circuit realizations of the α_F-based loop in Fig. 8-42b: (a) active-RC, (b) active-RC with MOST-R's, (c) active-G_mC with OTA G_m's, and (d) active-SC.

1989). Note that the noninverting damped integrator is realized in a brute-force fashion, i.e., an inverting amplifier (where $r_1 = r_2$) in tandem with an inverting damped integrator. Alternatively, the active-compensated noninverting integrator structures given in Fig. 5-23e can be used. In Figs. 8-43a–d we illustrate active-RC (basic), active-RC with MOST-R's, active-G_m/C with OTA G_m's and active-SC realizations of the stable resonant loop.

Assuming ideal op amps and passive components, the characteristic equations for these resonators are, respectively,

$$s^2 + \frac{1}{R_F C_B}s + \frac{r_2}{r_1}\frac{1}{R_C C_D R_A C_B} = 0 \qquad (8\text{-}64a)$$

$$s^2 + \frac{1}{R_F C_B}s + \frac{1}{R_C C_D R_A C_B} = 0 \qquad (8\text{-}64b)$$

$$s^2 + \frac{G_{mF}}{C_B}s + \frac{G_{mC} G_{mA}}{C_D C_B} = 0 \qquad (8\text{-}64c)$$

$$1 - \left[\frac{2DB + DF - AC}{D(B + F)}\right] z^{-1} + \frac{DB}{D(B + F)} z^{-2} = 0 \qquad (8\text{-}64d)$$

Note that the integrator loops in Figs. 8-43b–c do not require a third op amp for sign inversion. Also, all the loops except the MOST-R circuit in Fig. 8-43b use two capacitors (unswitched)—the minimum number for a second order loop. In this case, a fully-balanced differential structure is used to realize linearized MOST-R's, and hence two capacitors are used in each path. As noted earlier, fully-balanced differential structures can also be used for active-G_m/C, active-RC, and active-SC filters to increase PSRRs. It is important that most, if not all, parasitics are either neutralized or significantly reduced. The active-G_m/C resonator utilizes grounded capacitors, thus minimizing the opportunity for creating unwanted parasitic poles and zeros. Moreover, ω_0 and Q_p can be independently tuned by adjusting two resistors in sequence. For example, in Fig. 8-43b, we first adjust R_C to tune ω_0 and then adjust R_F to set Q_p. As noted earlier, tuning is unavoidable in precision continuous-time filters. We leave it to the reader to examine the virtues of the other cases.

In Fig. 8-42c, we show that we also dampen the resonator by applying feedback $s\beta_E$, yielding

$$s^2 + \beta_E K_{CD} K_{AB} s + K_{CD} K_{AB} = 0 \qquad (8\text{-}65a)$$

In Figs. 8-44a and 8-44b, we show active-RC realizations with MOST-R's and active-SC realizations of this scheme. Here we see that the integrators are lossless and that the derivative feedback $s\beta_E$ in Fig. 8-42c is realized via a capacitor (i.e., C_E and E, respectively). Note that this resonator structure does not easily map into a practical active-G_m/C circuit. This is due to the high input/output impedances of the G_m VCCS's that would interact with the capacitance feedback. In any event,

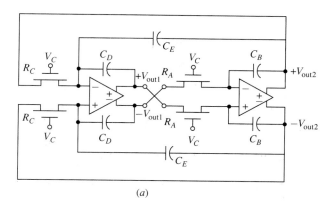

(a)

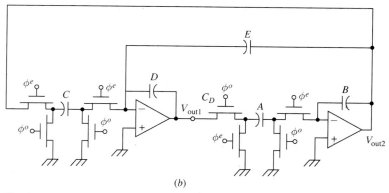

(b)

FIGURE 8-44 Circuit realizations of the $s\beta_E$-based loop in Fig. 8-42c: (a) active-RC with MOST-R's, and (b) active-SC.

Figs. 8-44a and 8-44b, respectively, realize the following characteristic equations

$$s^2 + \frac{C_E}{C_D}\frac{1}{R_A C_B}s + \frac{1}{R_C C_D R_A C_B} = 0 \tag{8-65b}$$

$$1 - \left[\frac{2DB - AE - AC}{DB}\right]z^{-1} + \frac{DB - AE}{DB}z^{-2} = 0 \tag{8-65c}$$

Once again, Eqs. (8-65) are derived with ideal components. Note that these $s\beta_E$ loops use three capacitors, one more than the minimum number of capacitors required for the α_F loops. However, as we will see in the next section, active-SC biquads realized with this loop structure can lead to significant reductions in total capacitance and a corresponding savings in die area. Otherwise, the sensitivities, parasitic properties, and overall performance are similar to α_F loops. An interesting design-tuning strategy for the active-RC case in Fig. 8-44*a* is to constrain $R_C = R_B = R$, and design ω_0 and Q_p by setting the values for capacitors C_D and C_E, respectively. The MOST-R's R_B and R_C can be closely matched and the value R tuned as described in Sec. 8-4.

For the sampled data loop, with a large Q_p, the z^{-1} coefficient must be specified precisely. Since this coefficient is essentially the resonant frequency term, as indicated in Eq. (8-62*b*), this intuitive claim is consistent with the sensitivity evaluations discussed in Sec. 7-7. In digital filter literature, many *z*-domain resonant structures have been studied and used. The reader may find it interesting to know that one structure was devised to accurately realize this coefficient with a finite precision digital word for cases when $\omega_0 T \ll 1$ (Agarwal and Burrus 1975). The characteristic equation for this digital structure is given by

$$1 + (2 - \beta_1)z^{-1} + (1 - \beta_2)z^{-2} = 0 \tag{8-66}$$

where β_1 and β_2 are finite precision digital words. The strong analogy between Eq. (8-66) and Eqs. (8-64*d*) and (8-65*c*) are quite evident.

8-7 FLEISCHER-LAKER ACTIVE-SC BIQUADS

In this section we consider the parasitic insensitive active-SC biquad structure shown in Fig. 8-45 (Ghausi and Laker 1981; Gregorian and Temes 1986; Moschytz 1986; Schaumann, Ghausi, and Laker 1990; Unbehauen and Cichocki 1989). This structure is seen to incorporate both the α_F and $s\beta_E$ resonant loops in Figs. 8-43*d* and 8-44*b*. Here we show the switched reduced schematic; which lessens the die area for the biquad layout while reducing clock feedthrough and enhancing the *PSRRs*. We recommend that the switches at the op amp inputs be realized using the CMOS scheme in Fig. 8-29. The reader can readily verify that the biquad is time-invariant, and with the phase independent input shown in Fig. 8-45, the op amp outputs are similarly phase-independent.

The structure is general, in that it is capable of realizing all stable *z*-domain biquadratic transfer functions of the form given in Eqs. (7-12*c*) or (7-13*b*). For convenient reference, these expressions are rewritten below, i.e.,

$$H(z) = \pm \frac{A_2 \pm A_1 z^{-1} \pm A_0 z^{-2}}{1 - B_1 z^{-1} + B_0 z^{-2}} = \pm \frac{kN(z)}{D(z)} \tag{8-67a}$$

or, for complex poles and zeros near the unit circle,

$$H(z) = \frac{\pm k[1 - 2r_z \cos\theta_N z^{-1} + r_z^2 z^{-2}]}{1 - 2r_p \cos\theta_0 z^{-1} + r_p^2 z^{-2}} = \frac{kN(z)}{D(z)} \tag{8-67b}$$

$$\approx \frac{\pm k\left\{1 - 2\left[1 \pm \dfrac{\omega_N T}{2Q_z} - \dfrac{(\omega_N T)^2}{2}\right]z^{-1} + \left[1 - \left(\pm\dfrac{\omega_N T}{Q_z}\right)\right]z^{-2}\right\}}{1 - 2\left[1 - \dfrac{\omega_0 T}{2Q_p} - \dfrac{(\omega_0 T)^2}{2}\right]z^{-1} + \left[1 - \dfrac{\omega_0 T}{Q_p}\right]z^{-2}} \tag{8-67c}$$

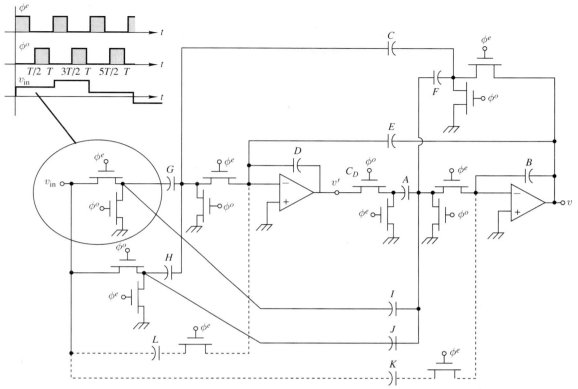

FIGURE 8-45   General parasitic insensitive active-SC biquad with schematic drawn in switch reduced form. The switch timing and form of sampled data input are also shown.

Equations (8-67a) and (8-67b) represent the numerical transfer function to be realized as determined using the techniques given in Sec. 7-3 and 7-4. The approximation in Eq. (8-67c) provides an insightful analog between familiar continuous-time filter parameters (ω_0, Q_p, ω_N, Q_z) and sample-data parameters (θ_0, r_p, θ_N, r_z). As discussed in App. 7-1, while this approximation improves as $\omega_0 T$, $\omega_N T \ll 1$, it is not sufficiently precise to serve as a substitute for the bilinear transform. It is best used for insight and to evaluate trends, where precision is not important.

The kernel (Ghausi and Laker 1981; Schaumann, Ghausi, and Laker 1990) of this biquad is the two-integrator loop formed by capacitors B, D, A, and C, which we conveniently refer to as the $ABCD$ loop. Alone, the $ABCD$ loop realizes Eq. (8-62b), or $D(z)$ in Eq. (8-67b) with $r_p = 1$, and resonates at ω_0 or $\theta_0 = \omega_0 T$. As described in the previous section, loop stability is realized with either E or F (Ghausi and Laker 1981). In either case, the poles are shifted inside the unit circle such that $r_p < 1$. Various combinations of feed-in SC's G, H, I, J and/or capacitors K, L are used to realize $kN(z)$ (Ghausi and Laker 1981). Capacitors K and L, connected with dashed lines, will be shown to be convenient discretionary parameters that can be used to reduce total capacitance and/or sensitivity. The switches on the top plates of K, L break the continuous paths through the otherwise unswitched capacitors during the unwanted phase (in this case ϕ^o). This also simplifies the z-domain models for K, L as per Fig. 7-33b. If we could guarantee that the biquad input v_{in} is always an ideal "staircase" signal, as shown in Fig. 8-45, these switches would be unnecessary. Since this is not the case, we recommend that the prudent designer include these switches in the realization. We leave it to the reader to show that their location at the top plates of K, L are best for $PSRR_{DD}$.

To evaluate the biquad, we start with the z-domain equivalent circuit shown in Fig. 8-46. Note that the switching for A and the switching for H and J have been chosen to acquire the ϕ^e samples of v' and v_{in}, respectively, on the ϕ^o phase that immediately follows. This explains the additional $T/2$ delay in their respective z-domain equivalents. At this point, the reader should have little difficulty verifying or analyzing this equivalent circuit. The biquad provides two op amp outputs, $V(z)$ and $V'(z)$; each forming different but related transfer functions with $V_{in}(z)$, i.e.,

$$T(z) = \frac{V^e(z)}{V_{in}^e(z)}$$

$$= -\frac{D\hat{I} - \{D(\hat{I} + \hat{J}) - A\hat{G}\}z^{-1} + \{D\hat{J} - A\hat{H}\}z^{-2}}{D(F + B) - \{2DB - A(C + E) + DF\}z^{-1} + \{DB - AE\}z^{-2}}$$

$$(8\text{-}68a)$$

FIGURE 8-46 Z-domain equivalent circuit for the general active-SC biquad in Fig. 8-45.

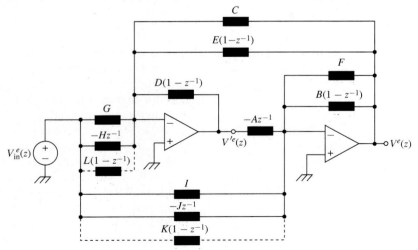

and

$$T'(z) = \frac{V'^e(z)}{V_{in}^e(z)} \tag{8-68b}$$

$$= -\frac{\{\hat{I}(C+E)-\hat{G}(F+B)\}+\{(\hat{G}+\hat{H})B+F\hat{H}-(\hat{I}+\hat{J})E-C\hat{J}\}z^{-1}+\{E\hat{J}-B\hat{H}\}z^{-2}}{D(F+B)-\{2DB-A(C+E)+DF\}z^{-1}+\{DB-AE\}z^{-2}}$$

Where

$$\hat{G}=G+L, \quad \hat{H}=H+L, \quad \hat{I}=I+K, \quad \text{and} \quad \hat{J}=J+K; \tag{8-68c}$$

also, $V^\circ(z) = z^{-1/2}V^e(z)$ and $V'^\circ(z) = z^{-1/2}V'^e(z)$. Later we show a family of intuitive structural transformations that can be used to select the best combination of G, H, I, J, K, and L.

It should be evident that the biquad in Fig. 8-45 is rarely required in its full form, i.e., with all twelve capacitors. The BP biquad in Fig. 7-22, examined in Example 7-4, is one of numerous special cases of this general structure. The value of the general structure is that it provides a systematic framework for designing numerous special-case biquads for a vast variety of z-domain functions (e.g., Sec. 7-3) with common properties (e.g., parasitic insensitivity and low ω_0, Q_p sensitivities). The structure's design is then reduced to the prudent and creative selection of either E or F for damping and the best combination of G, H, I, J, K, and L to realize $kN(z)$. Typically, this selection focuses on minimizing the total capacitance required for the realization and, where relevant, minimizing the ω_N, Q_z sensitivities. The design is completed by dynamic-range scaling the op amp outputs and determining values for the capacitors; important tasks that we describe shortly. With numerous special cases of Fig. 8-45 used throughout the industry, it is fair to say that the value of this structure has been field proven. Also, several interesting variances to Fig. 8-45 have been offered to improve certain aspects of performance, such as capacitor area efficiency (Huang and Sansen 1987) and sensitivity to op amp settling effects (Gregorian and Temes 1986; Laker, Ganesan, and Fleischer 1985; Martin and Sedra 1981; Unbehauen and Cichocki 1989).

Equations (8-68) provide the designer with yet another discretionary choice. In most designs, one output will be primary and the other secondary. By primary we mean that the $H(z)$ for a given filter is realized on the basis of the transfer function between the primary output and the input. In an ideal world, the secondary output would then be superfluous. However, in practice, the secondary output must be monitored and properly scaled to realize a high dynamic range (Ghausi and Laker 1981; Schaumann, Ghausi, and Laker 1990). The poles for $T(z)$ and $T'(z)$ are identical, but the zeros in $T'(z)$ are formed in a much more complicated fashion than in $T(z)$ (Ghausi and Laker 1981). Experience has proven that designs based on $T(z)$ as the primary function typically produce superior realizations. Hence, we pursue only designs via $T(z)$ and leave the development of $T'(z)$ design relations as exercises for the reader. We will return to $T'(z)$ when dynamic range is considered.

8-7-1   Evaluation of the General Active-SC Biquad

It is convenient here to differentiate between the use of E and F for pole damping. Let us refer to the biquad where $E \neq 0, F = 0$ as the E-circuit and the biquad with $F \neq 0, E = 0$ as the F-circuit. The differences between the E- and F-circuits may seem subtle, but the difference in total capacitance (i.e., die area) for equivalent designs can be significant.

We rewrite E- and F-circuit transfer functions, with $V(z)$ as the primary output, in the form of Eq. (8-67b); i.e.,

$$T_E(z) = \frac{V^e(z)}{V^e_{in}(z)} = -\frac{\left(\dfrac{\hat{I}}{B}\right)\left[1 - 2\left[\dfrac{\hat{I} + \hat{J}}{2\hat{I}} - \dfrac{A\hat{G}}{2D\hat{I}}\right]z^{-1} + \left[\dfrac{\hat{J}}{\hat{I}} - \dfrac{A\hat{H}}{D\hat{I}}\right]z^{-2}\right]}{1 - 2\left[1 - \dfrac{A(C + E)}{2DB}\right]z^{-1} + \left[1 - \dfrac{AE}{DB}\right]z^{-2}}$$

(8-69a)

and

$$T_F(z) = \frac{V^e(z)}{V^e_{in}(z)} = -\frac{\left(\dfrac{\hat{I}}{B + F}\right)\left\{1 - 2\left[\dfrac{\hat{I} + \hat{J}}{2\hat{I}} - \dfrac{A\hat{G}}{2D\hat{I}}\right]z^{-1} + \left[\dfrac{\hat{J}}{\hat{I}} - \dfrac{A\hat{H}}{D\hat{I}}\right]z^{-2}\right\}}{1 - 2\left[\dfrac{2B + F}{2(B + F)} - \dfrac{AC}{2D(B + F)}\right]z^{-1} + [\dfrac{B}{B + F}]z^{-2}}$$

(8-69b)

The initial step in the design of a biquad is to equate the numerical $H(z)$ of Eq. (8-67b) with the symbolic circuit $T_E(z)$ and $T_F(z)$ in Eqs. (8-69). Comparing the coefficients of these equations, we derive expressions that relate the sample-data parameters $\{\cos\theta_0, r_p, \cos\theta_N, r_z,$ and $k\}$ to the biquad's capacitors $\{A, B, C, D, E, F, \hat{G}, \hat{H}, \hat{I},$ and $\hat{J}\}$. These expressions are listed in Table 8-3.

For design purposes, capacitors or capacitor ratios can be expressed in terms of the sample-data parameters listed in Table 8-4. Note that there are ten capacitors (or twelve if K and L are included) available to set the five parameters that define the transfer function. Hence, there are a number of discretionary choices that can be used to optimize other performance and design criteria, e.g., sensitivity, dynamic range, and die area. Later, we dissect and examine these options in greater detail.

Comparing the coefficients Eqs. (8-67c) and (8-69), we can derive an insightful set of approximate expressions that relate the frequency-domain parameters $\omega_0, Q_p, \omega_N,$ and Q_z to the biquad capacitors. These expressions are listed in Table 8-5.

Note that this particular arrangement reveals that $\hat{G} > \hat{H}$ for ω_z to be defined. Not surprisingly, pole-zero frequencies ω_0, ω_N are proportional to the sampling frequency $f_s = 1/T$. In addition, capacitor ratios (and thus the die area), tend to increase in proportion to $f_s/\omega_0, f_s/\omega_N, Q_p,$ and Q_z. In the cases of ω_N and Q_z, the resulting growth in capacitance ratios can be retarded by use of the $\hat{G} - \hat{H}$.

TABLE 8-3   BIQUAD PARAMETERS

	E-Circuit	F-Circuit
r_p	$0 < \sqrt{1 - \dfrac{AE}{DB}} < 1$	$0 < \sqrt{\dfrac{B}{B+F}} < 1$
$\cos\theta_0$	$\dfrac{1}{r_p}\left\{1 - \dfrac{A(C+E)}{2DB}\right\} > 0$	$\dfrac{1}{r_p}\left\{\dfrac{2B+F}{2(B+F)} - \dfrac{AC}{2D(B+F)}\right\} > 0$
k	$\dfrac{\hat{I}}{B} > 0$	$\dfrac{\hat{I}}{B+F} > 0$
r_z	$\sqrt{\dfrac{\hat{J}}{\hat{I}} - \dfrac{A\hat{H}}{D\hat{I}}} > 0$	$\sqrt{\dfrac{\hat{J}}{\hat{I}} - \dfrac{A\hat{H}}{D\hat{I}}} > 0$
$\cos\theta_N$	$\dfrac{1}{r_z}\left\{\dfrac{\hat{I}+\hat{J}}{2\hat{I}} - \dfrac{A\hat{G}}{2D\hat{I}}\right\} > 0$	$\dfrac{1}{r_z}\left\{\dfrac{\hat{I}+\hat{J}}{2\hat{I}} - \dfrac{A\hat{G}}{2D\hat{I}}\right\} > 0$

TABLE 8-4   BIQUAD CAPACITOR RATIOS $(\gamma = A\hat{H}/D\hat{I})$

	E-Circuit	F-Circuit
$\dfrac{AE}{DB}$	$1 - r_p^2 > 0$	—
$\dfrac{F}{B}$	—	$\dfrac{1 - r_p^2}{r_p^2} > 0$
$\dfrac{AC}{DB}$	$1 + r_p^2 - 2r_p\cos\theta_0 > 0$	$\dfrac{1 + r_p^2 - 2r_p\cos\theta_0}{r_p^2}$
$\dfrac{\hat{I}}{B}$	$k > 0$	$r_p^2 k > 0$
$\dfrac{\hat{J}}{\hat{I}}$	$\gamma + r_z^2 > 0$	$\gamma + r_z^2 > 0$
$\dfrac{A\hat{G}}{D\hat{I}}$	$\gamma + r_z^2 - 2r_z\cos\theta_N > 0$	$\gamma + r_z^2 - 2r_z\cos\theta_N > 0$

The ω_0 and Q_p sensitivities can be readily determined from Table 8-5. Observe that ω_0 and Q_p are controlled by the ratios of only four or five capacitors; the minimum number for an active-SC biquad.

After scanning Tables 8-6 and 8-7, we conclude that the E- and F-circuits are equivalent in terms of sensitivity. The ω_0 and Q_p sensitivities are minimal and set by the biquad's circuit structure.

In contrast, the ω_N and Q_z sensitivities are very much at the disposal of the designer, dictated by the choices made in selecting the combination of $G, H, I, J, K,$ and L for the realization. These sensitivities are listed in Table 8-8. This table is a valuable tool for comparing and selecting structures to realize $H(z)$'s having com-

TABLE 8-5 FREQUENCY-DOMAIN PARAMETERS ($\hat{G} > \hat{H}$)

	E-Circuit	F-Circuit
ω_0	$\approx f_s \sqrt{\dfrac{AC}{DB}}$	$\approx f_s \sqrt{\dfrac{AC}{D(B+F)}}$
$\dfrac{\omega_0 T}{Q_p}$	$\approx \dfrac{AE}{DB}$	$\approx \dfrac{F}{B+F}$
Q_p	$\approx \dfrac{1}{E}\sqrt{\dfrac{BCD}{A}}$	$\approx \sqrt{\dfrac{AC}{DF}\left(1+\dfrac{B}{F}\right)}$
ω_N	$\approx f_s \sqrt{\dfrac{A(\hat{G}-\hat{H})}{D\hat{I}}}$	$\approx f_s \sqrt{\dfrac{A(\hat{G}-\hat{H})}{D\hat{I}}}$
$\mp\dfrac{\omega_N T}{Q_z}$	$\approx 1 - \dfrac{\hat{J}}{\hat{I}} + \dfrac{A\hat{H}}{D\hat{I}}$	$\approx 1 - \dfrac{\hat{J}}{\hat{I}} + \dfrac{A\hat{H}}{D\hat{I}}$
Q_z	$\approx \dfrac{\sqrt{AD\hat{I}(\hat{G}-\hat{H})}}{D(\hat{J}-\hat{I}) - A\hat{H}}$	$\approx \dfrac{\sqrt{AD\hat{I}(\hat{G}-\hat{H})}}{D(\hat{J}-\hat{I}) - A\hat{H}}$

TABLE 8-6 ω_0 SENSITIVITIES

	$S_A^{\omega_0}$	$S_B^{\omega_0}$	$S_C^{\omega_0}$	$S_D^{\omega_0}$	$S_E^{\omega_0}$	$S_F^{\omega_0}$
E-Circuit	$\dfrac{1}{2}$	$-\dfrac{1}{2}$	$\dfrac{1}{2}$	$-\dfrac{1}{2}$	0	—
F-Circuit	$\dfrac{1}{2}$	$-\dfrac{1}{2}\dfrac{B}{B+F}$	$\dfrac{1}{2}$	$-\dfrac{1}{2}$	—	$-\dfrac{1}{2}\dfrac{F}{B+F}$

TABLE 8-7 Q_p SENSITIVITIES

	$S_A^{Q_p}$	$S_B^{Q_p}$	$S_C^{Q_p}$	$S_D^{Q_p}$	$S_E^{Q_p}$	$S_F^{Q_p}$
E-Circuit	$-\dfrac{1}{2}$	$\dfrac{1}{2}$	$\dfrac{1}{2}$	$\dfrac{1}{2}$	-1	—
F-Circuit	$\dfrac{1}{2}$	$\dfrac{1}{2}\dfrac{B}{B+F}$	$\dfrac{1}{2}$	$-\dfrac{1}{2}$	—	$-\dfrac{1}{2}\left(1+\dfrac{F}{B+F}\right)$

plex transmission zeros, e.g., LPN, HPN, BR, and AP functions. Yields can be estimated using Eqs. (7-54) and entries from Table 8-6 through 8-8. Earlier, in Example 7-4, yield was estimated for a biquad realizing a BP11 $H(z)$. Note that for matched capacitors, e.g., Fig. 7-4e, the correlation among capacitors within a biquad can be $\rho > 0.9$.

TABLE 8-8 ω_N AND Q_z SENSITIVITIES $\left(U = 1/\gamma\left\{\hat{J}/\hat{I} - 1\right\}$ AND $\gamma = A\hat{H}/D\hat{I}\right)$

	$S_A^{\omega_N}$	$S_D^{\omega_N}$	$S_{\hat{G}}^{\omega_N}$	$S_{\hat{H}}^{\omega_N}$	$S_{\hat{i}}^{\omega_N}$	$S_{\hat{j}}^{\omega_N}$
E- and F-Circuits	$\dfrac{1}{2}$	$-\dfrac{1}{2}$	$\dfrac{1}{2}\dfrac{\hat{G}}{\hat{G}-\hat{H}}$	$-\dfrac{1}{2}\left[\dfrac{\hat{H}}{\hat{G}-\hat{H}}\right]$	$-\dfrac{1}{2}$	0
	$S_A^{Q_z}$	$S_D^{Q_z}$	$S_{\hat{G}}^{Q_z}$	$S_{\hat{H}}^{Q_z}$	$S_{\hat{i}}^{Q_z}$	$S_{\hat{j}}^{Q_z}$
E- and F-Circuits	$\dfrac{1}{2}+\dfrac{1}{U-1}$	$\dfrac{1}{2}-\dfrac{U}{U-1}$	$\dfrac{1}{2}\dfrac{\hat{G}}{\hat{G}-\hat{H}}$	$-\dfrac{1}{2}\left[\dfrac{\hat{H}}{\hat{G}-\hat{H}}\right]+\dfrac{1}{U-1}$	$\dfrac{1}{2}+\dfrac{(1/\gamma)}{U-1}$	$-\dfrac{\hat{J}}{\hat{I}}\dfrac{(1/\gamma)}{U-1}$

Insofar as sensitivity is concerned, we must examine the impact of op amp finite gain on the performance of the biquad expressed in Eqs. (8-69) and Table 8-3. This impact is most visibly and conveniently evaluated with regard to the basic undamped resonant $ABCD$ loop. Here we consider only the effect of the op amps' DC gains A_0, ignoring their transient responses. In Sec. 8-9, we develop methods for significantly reducing the impact of op amp transient responses, leaving the op amp DC gain effects as the baseline. Hence, the DC gains of the two op amps will limit the precision of the biquad, even if the capacitor ratios could be realized with infinite precision.

Evaluating the $ABCD$ loop, as we did for the first order circuit in Fig. 8-38, we assume that the op amps are matched such that the DC gains are equal, i.e., $A_{01} = A_{02} = A_0$. We leave it to the reader to draw the equivalent circuit and to conduct the analysis as a home exercise. Recognizing that $1/A_0 \ll 1$ such that terms involving $1/A_0^2$ are negligible, the characteristic equation for the nonideal $ABCD$ loop is approximately

$$1 - \left[2 - \frac{AC}{DB}\left(1 + \frac{2}{A_0}\right) - \frac{1}{A_0}\left(\frac{A}{B} - \frac{C}{D}\right)\right]z^{-1}$$

$$+ \left[1 - \frac{1}{A_0}\left(\frac{A}{B} - \frac{C}{D}\right)\right]z^{-2} = 0 \tag{8-70a}$$

Hence, comparing Eq. (5-70a) with Eq. (8-67c), we obtain

$$\omega_0 T \approx \sqrt{\frac{AC}{DB}\left(1 + \frac{2}{A_0}\right)} \quad \text{and} \quad \frac{\omega_0 T}{Q_p} \approx \frac{1}{A_0}\left(\frac{A}{B} - \frac{C}{D}\right) \tag{8-70b}$$

We see that the impact of A_0 is to shift ω_0 slightly upward and to either enhance Q_p when $C/D > A/B$ or reduce Q_p when $A/B > C/D$. In the case of the undamped resonator, Q_p enhancement implies that the poles are shifted outside the unit circle.

8-7-2   Synthesis of Practical Active-SC Biquads

Synthesis (and our intuition) is enhanced if we simplify the circuit by initially eliminating some of the discretionary choices. At the outset, we set the following capacitors:

$$A = B = D = 1 \tag{8-71}$$

Later, we restore the design flexibility sacrificed in Eq. (8-71). In this regard, A and D, will be used to independently adjust the gain constants associated with T and T' to maximize dynamic range, as mentioned previously.

Capacitors B and D control the admittance levels at their respective op amp summing junctions. Thus, two groups of capacitors, $\Sigma_1 = (C, D, E, G, H, L)$ and $\Sigma_2 = (A, B, F, I, J, K)$, can be arbitrarily and independently scaled without change to T and T'. Setting $B = D = 1$ is equivalent to normalizing the values for each of these capacitor groupings by D and B, respectively. Until this point, the comparative advantage of E versus F is transparent to the designer. Experience suggests using some rules-of-thumb, but for many cases it is prudent to carry E- and F-circuit designs to completion so that their die areas can be compared. Since the two circuits are very similar in structure, this requires minimal extra work.

Combining Eqs. (8-71) and Eqs. (8-69) yields the following simplified E- and F-circuit transfer functions, respectively,

$$T_E(z) = -\frac{\hat{I}\left\{1 - \left[\dfrac{\hat{I} + \hat{J} - \hat{G}}{\hat{I}}\right] z^{-1} + \left[\dfrac{\hat{J} - \hat{H}}{\hat{I}}\right] z^{-2}\right\}}{1 - 2\left[1 - \dfrac{C + E}{2}\right] z^{-1} + (1 - E)z^{-2}} \tag{8-72a}$$

$$T_F(z) = -\frac{\dfrac{\hat{I}}{1 + F}\left\{1 - \left[\dfrac{\hat{I} + \hat{J} - \hat{G}}{\hat{I}}\right] z^{-1} + \left[\dfrac{\hat{J} - \hat{H}}{\hat{I}}\right] z^{-2}\right\}}{1 - 2\left[\dfrac{2 + F - C}{2(1 + F)}\right] z^{-1} + \left[\dfrac{1}{1 + F}\right] z^{-2}} \tag{8-72b}$$

The pole locations for T_E, T_E' and T_F, T_F' are determined by C, E and C, F, respectively. Their zero locations are realized by $\hat{G}, \hat{H}, \hat{I}$, and $\hat{J}$. Note that with $A = B = D = 1$, the $D(z)$ and $N(z)$ for T_E and T_F are controlled by different sets of capacitors, i.e., the pole-zero locations can be set independent of one another. In Fig. 8-47 we show the realizable E- and F-circuit pole locations by plotting coefficients $B_0 = r_p^2$ versus $-B_1 = r_p \cos \theta_0$. The stable pole locations occur only when B_0 and $-B_1$ are within the filled triangle. In Fig. 8-47a, the E-circuit realizes all the possible stable pole locations and the F-circuit, in Fig. 8-47b, realizes all the stable locations except for the real poles on alternate sides of $z = 0$. Note that no combination of capacitor values or variations can force high-Q_p poles to instability in either circuit. However, finite op amp DC gains can enhance Q_p, as observed in Eq. (8-70b), and possibly lead to instability even though the ideal circuit is perfectly

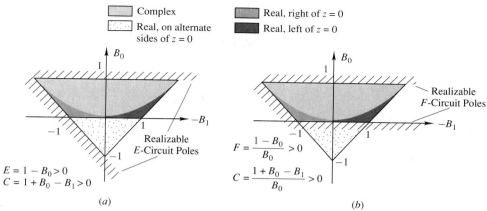

FIGURE 8-47   Realizable pole locations for (a) *E*-circuit and (b) *F*-circuit.

stable. We leave it to the reader to verify that arbitrary zero locations are realizable with either circuit.

Thoughtful study of the equivalent circuit in Fig. 8-46 and Eq. (8-68c) reveals an interesting set of transformations between the switched-capacitor pairs (I, J) and (G, H) and capacitors K and L, respectively. These relationships are illustrated for I, J, and K in Fig. 8-48. A crucial assumption in deriving the equivalencies in

FIGURE 8-48   Switched-capacitor element transformations.

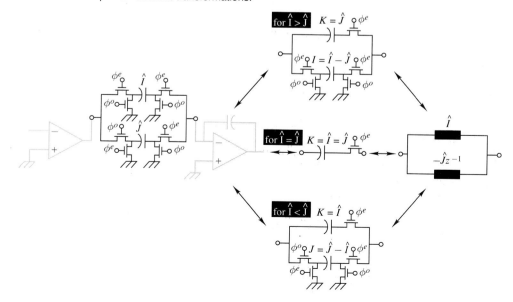

Fig. 8-48 is that the switched-capacitor elements are buffered between an ideal voltage source and virtual ground. Interchanging I, J, and K with G, H, and L, and these transformations can be used to manipulate the structure at either or both op amp inputs. Combining Eq. (8-68c) with the structural transformations in Fig. 8-48, we have (a): $I = J = 0$ and $K = \hat{I}$ when $\hat{I} = \hat{J}$; (b): $J = 0, I = \hat{I} - \hat{J}$ and $K = \hat{J}$ when $\hat{I} > \hat{J}$, and (c): $I = 0, J = \hat{J} - \hat{I}$ and $K = \hat{I}$ when $\hat{I} < \hat{J}$.

The net result is that Fig. 8-45 represents a powerful family of active-SC biquad circuits. Given the famous SC-to-R equivalence, it is intriguing that when $\hat{I} = \hat{J}$, the parallel combination of these two switched-capacitors $(\hat{I}, \hat{J})$ is equivalent to a single unswitched-capacitor $K = \hat{I} = \hat{J}$. Intuitively, using K rather than $\hat{I}, \hat{J}$, we expect to reduce both total capacitance and sensitivity. In fact, the $1/Q_z$ sensitivities are significantly reduced, as can be verified by using Table 8-8 (i.e., $U = 0$). The relationships for $\hat{I} > \hat{J}$ and $\hat{I} < \hat{J}$ yield similar advantages. For example, if a design requires $\hat{I} = 13$ pF and $\hat{J} = 12$ pF, the $\hat{I} > \hat{J}$ transformation yields an alternative set of elements $I = \hat{I} - \hat{J} = 1$ pF and $K = \hat{J} = 12$ pF. Note, however, that like all good things, the transformations in Fig. 8-48 reach their limit when $\hat{I} \approx \hat{J}$ such that $|\hat{I} - \hat{J}| \ll 1$. At this extreme, the use of $\hat{I}$ and $\hat{J}$ can be shown with the aid of Table 8-8 to yield very large sensitivities, due to the small difference of two large quantities. On the other hand, using the $\hat{I} > \hat{J}$ or $\hat{I} < \hat{J}$ transformations yields very large capacitance spreads. In this extreme case, neither alternative is ideal; but the designer can choose to trade sensitivity for die area or vice versa.

Proceeding with the synthesis of $T_{E,F}(z)$, the natural sequence first realizes $D(z)$ followed by $kN(z)$. The design can start with either an $H(s)$ prototype or an $H(z)$. $H(s)$ can be mapped into $H(z)$ using the bilinear transform described in Sec. 7-5-2. If we start with $H(s) = N(s)/D(s)$, we let the $D(\hat{s})$ for the prewharped s-domain transfer function be

$$D(\hat{s}) = \hat{s}^2 + \hat{b}_1\hat{s} + \hat{b}_0 \tag{8-73}$$

where $\hat{s}$ is the prewharped frequency variable. Substituting the bilinear transform in Table 7-8 for $\hat{s}$, and equating the coefficients of the resulting z-domain polynomial with those of the $D(z)$'s for the symbolic $T_{E,F}$ in Eqs. (8-72), yields

$$E = \frac{\hat{b}_1 T}{1 + \hat{b}_1(T/2) + \hat{b}_0(T^2/4)} \quad \text{and} \quad C = \frac{\hat{b}_0 T}{1 + \hat{b}_1(T/2) + \hat{b}_0(T^2/4)} \tag{8-74a}$$

and

$$F = \frac{\hat{b}_1 T}{1 - \hat{b}_1(T/2) + \hat{b}_0(T^2/4)}, \quad C = \frac{\hat{b}_0 T}{1 - \hat{b}_1(T/2) + \hat{b}_0(T^2/4)} \tag{8-74b}$$

where T is the sampling period. If the design starts with an $H(z)$, relations for C, E and C, F are determined by equating the coefficients of $D(z)$ in Eq. (8-67a) with the denominators of symbolic $T_{E,F}$. The resulting relations are

$$E = 1 - B_0, \quad C = 1 + B_0 - B_1 \tag{8-75a}$$

and

$$F = \frac{1 - B_0}{B_0} C = \frac{1 + B_0 - B_1}{B_0} \tag{8-75b}$$

Once values for C, E or C, F have been fixed, values for G, H, I, J, K, and L are determined from a suitable numerator function, thus defining the desired zero locations.

Design equations for determining G, H, I, J, K, and L for $T_{E,F}$ and $T'_{E,F}$ realizations can be found in Ghausi and Laker (1981). In Table 8-9, for the E-circuit, we summarize the $\hat{G}, \hat{H}, \hat{I}$, and $\hat{J}$ design formulas and a typical realization for each of the generic $H(z)$ in Sec. 7-3. The corresponding F-circuit values are easily obtained by multiplying E-circuit values by $1 + F$. Using these design formulas and Fig. 8-48, numerous alternative designs can be developed.

Figures 8-49a and 8-49b show E- and F-circuits that implement LPN (or HPN or BR) $H(z)$ according to Table 8-9. We see that the LPN (etc.), with $1/Q_z = 0$, can be realized with $H = 0$ and $K = \hat{I} = \hat{J}$ such that $\hat{I} - \hat{J} \equiv 0$ and $\hat{H} \equiv 0$. For this choice, $S_x^{Q_z} \equiv 0$ and the $S_x^{\omega_N}$ are minimal. Moreover, the use of K rather than I, J reduces capacitance and eliminates several switches. An F-circuit realization for an HP $H(z)$ is shown in Fig. 8-49c. The HP can be viewed as a special case of the HPN with $G = 0$, i.e., as $G \to 0$, the zeros shift around the unit circle to $z = -1$. In Fig. 8-49d, we have an LP01 at the primary output V. We leave it for the reader to verify that the secondary output V' is BP00.

With the poles and zeros realized, capacitors A, D, and B are adjusted to scale the dynamic range, Σ_1, and Σ_2, respectively. Here we assume that the gain at the primary output, namely T, is specified at all frequencies by $H(z)$ and the gain at the secondary output, namely T', is unspecified. Hence, the gain levels of T' are left to the discretion of the designer to achieve other design criteria. Let us also assume that the filter is required to process both large and small signals. Clearly, an overload of any one of the two op amps will produce dynamic range-limiting harmonic distortion. It is easy to convince ourselves, given an active filter with N op amps, that the best we can do is design the filter such that all N op amps overload at the same level. In dynamic range scaling, we simply adjust the gain level at the secondary output to ensure that the secondary op amp never overdrives ahead of the primary op amp.

This task is accomplished by scaling A so that the maximum levels at the op amp outputs are equalized, as shown in Fig. 8-50, i.e.,

$$\max_{0 \le \omega < \infty} V'(\omega) = \max_{0 \le \omega < \infty} V(\omega) \text{ or } \max_{0 \le \omega < \infty} |T'_{E,F}(\omega)| = \max_{0 \le \omega < \infty} |T_{E,F}(\omega)|$$

$$\text{or } \max_{0 \le \omega < \infty} G'_{E,F}(\omega) = \max_{0 \le \omega < \infty} G_{E,F}(\omega) \tag{8-76}$$

TABLE 8-9 *E*-CIRCUIT ZERO-PLACEMENT DESIGN FORMULAS AND A TYPICAL DESIGN

Filter Type	$\hat{G}, \hat{H}, \hat{I}, \hat{J}$ Design Formulas	Typical Design
LP20	$\hat{I} = \lvert k \rvert,\ \hat{J} - \hat{H} = \lvert k \rvert$ $\hat{I} + \hat{J} - \hat{G} = -2\lvert k \rvert$	$K = \lvert k \rvert,\ G = 4\lvert k \rvert$ $H = I = J = L = 0$
LP11	$\hat{I} = 0,\ \hat{J} - \hat{H} = \pm\lvert k \rvert$ $\hat{I} + \hat{J} - \hat{G} = \mp\lvert k \rvert$	$J = \lvert k \rvert,\ G = 2\lvert k \rvert$ $H = I = K = L = 0$
LP10	$\hat{I} = \lvert k \rvert,\ \hat{J} - \hat{H} = 0$ $\hat{I} + \hat{J} - \hat{G} = -\lvert k \rvert$	$I = \lvert k \rvert,\ G = 2\lvert k \rvert$ $H = J = K = L = 0$
LP02	$\hat{I} = 0,\ \hat{J} - \hat{H} = \pm\lvert k \rvert$ $\hat{I} + \hat{J} - \hat{G} = 0$	$H = \lvert k \rvert$ $G = I = J = K = L = 0$
LP01	$\hat{I} = 0,\ \hat{J} - \hat{H} = 0$ $\hat{I} + \hat{J} - \hat{G} = \mp\lvert k \rvert$	$G = \lvert k \rvert$ $H = I = J = K = L = 0$
LP00	$\hat{I} = \lvert k \rvert,\ \hat{J} - \hat{H} = 0$ $\hat{I} + \hat{J} - \hat{G} = 0$	$I = \lvert k \rvert$ $G = H = J = K = L = 0$
BP10	$\hat{I} = \lvert k \rvert,\ \hat{J} - \hat{H} = -\lvert k \rvert$ $\hat{I} + \hat{J} - \hat{G} = 0$	$L = \lvert k \rvert,\ I = \lvert k \rvert$ $G = H = J = K = 0$
BP01	$\hat{I} = 0,\ \hat{J} - \hat{H} = \mp\lvert k \rvert$ $\hat{I} + \hat{J} - \hat{G} = \mp\lvert k \rvert$	$J = \lvert k \rvert$ $G = H = I = K = L = 0$
BP00	$\hat{I} = \lvert k \rvert,\ \hat{J} - \hat{H} = 0$ $\hat{I} + \hat{J} - \hat{G} = \lvert k \rvert$	$I = \lvert k \rvert$ $G = H = J = K = L = 0$
HP	$\hat{I} = \lvert k \rvert,\ \hat{J} - \hat{H} = \lvert k \rvert$ $\hat{I} + \hat{J} - \hat{G} = 2\lvert k \rvert$	$K = \lvert k \rvert$ $G = H = I = J = L = 0$
LPN HPN BR	$\hat{I} = \lvert k \rvert,\ \hat{J} - \hat{H} = \lvert k \rvert$ $\hat{I} + \hat{J} - \hat{G} = 2\lvert k \rvert \cos\theta_N$	$K = \lvert k \rvert,\ G = 2\lvert k \rvert (1 - \cos\theta_N)$ $H = I = J = L = 0$
AP	$\hat{I} = \lvert k \rvert,\ \hat{J} - \hat{H} = \lvert k \rvert \dfrac{1}{r_p^2}$ $\hat{I} + \hat{J} - \hat{G} = 2\lvert k \rvert \dfrac{1}{r_p} \cos\theta_0$	$k = \lvert k \rvert,$ $G = \lvert k \rvert \left(1 + \dfrac{1}{r_p^2} - \dfrac{1}{r_p} \cos\theta_0 \right)$ $J = \lvert k \rvert \left(\dfrac{1}{r_p^2} - 1 \right)$ $H = I = L = 0$

The primary gain level is kept fixed by counterbalancing it with a proportionate scaling of D. For example, let Eq. (8-76) be satisfied by scaling $T'_{E,F}$ by a constant μ, i.e.,

$$T'_{E,F} \to \mu T'_{E,F} \tag{8-77a}$$

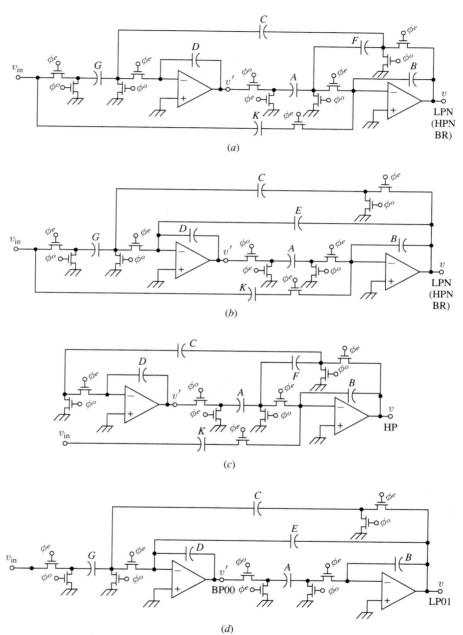

FIGURE 8-49   Examples of biquad realizations: (a) F-circuit LPN (HPN or BR), (b) E-circuit LPN (HPN or BR), (c) F-circuit HP, and (d) E-circuit LP01 or BP00.

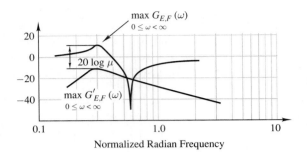

FIGURE 8-50   Dynamic range scaling using $G_{E,F}(\omega)$ and $G'_{E,F}(\omega)$.

Then, $T_{E,F}$ is held fixed if A and D are simultaneously adjusted such that

$$(A, D) \rightarrow \left(\frac{1}{\mu} A, \frac{1}{\mu} D \right) \tag{8-77b}$$

Determining μ to satisfy Eq. (8-76) can be done in a straightforward manner by plotting $|T'_{E,F}|$ and $|T_{E,F}|$ (or $G'_{E,F}$ and $G_{E,F}$ in dB) as functions of frequency, with sufficient detail to estimate the maxima by eye. Alternatively, V and V' can be calculated with the aid of an AC circuit analysis program.

Once satisfactory gain levels have been obtained at both outputs, the final step in the design is to use D and B to scale Σ_1 and Σ_2, respectively, to convenient implementable values. A convenient scaling is to adjust Σ_1 and Σ_2 by constants ν and κ, respectively, so that the minimum capacitances are normalized to one unit, or $1 \times U$, i.e.,

$$(C, D, E, G, H, L) \rightarrow (\nu C, \nu D, \nu E, \nu G, \nu H, \nu L), \, s.t. \min_{X \varepsilon \Sigma_1}(\nu X) = 1 \tag{8-78a}$$

$$(A, B, F, I, J, K) \rightarrow (\kappa A, \kappa B, \kappa F, \kappa I, \kappa J, \kappa K), \, s.t. \min_{X \varepsilon \Sigma_2}(\kappa X) = 1 \tag{8-78b}$$

where X is any one of the biquad capacitors A through L. The capacitor values implemented on chip are calculated by multiplying the normalized values in Eqs. (8-78) by the actual unit value in pF; e.g., if $U = 1.5$ pF and $D = 32.56$, then the implemented $D \rightarrow D \times U = 48.84$ pF. Clearly, the Σ_1 and Σ_2 need not be scaled to the same minimum unit. In die area sensitive designs, this flexibility may be exploited.

In the following section, some illustrative examples are given. The first example is an LPN circuit for which the design is followed through step-by-step to illustrate the design procedure. The second example is an AP circuit where $\hat{G}, \hat{H}, \hat{I},$ and $\hat{J}$ are manipulated to achieve and optimum design.

8-7-3 Examples

The first example is the step-by-step design of an LPN biquad, from an $H(z)$ to final integrable capacitor values. In the second example we consider the design and realization of an AP biquad.

Example 8-8

Realize the following LPN $H(z)$:

$$H(z) = 0.89093 \frac{1 - 1.99220z^{-1} + z^{-2}}{1 - 1.99029z^{-1} + 0.99723z^{-2}} \tag{8-79}$$

where $f_s = 128$ kHz (or $T = 7.8125$ μsec). This $H(z)$ provides a notch frequency at $f_N = 1800$ Hz, a peak corresponding to a quality factor of $Q_p = 30$ at $f_0 = 1700$ Hz, and a DC gain of 0 dB. Design both E- and F-circuits for maximum dynamic range and for a minimum capacitance of $U = 1$ pF. Compare the total capacitance required to realize both designs.

Solution. The reader may be alarmed by the high degree of numerical precision in the coefficients of $H(z)$ in Eq. (8-79). Since capacitor ratios are used to realize only the departures from -2 and $+1$ for the z^{-1} and z^{-2} coefficients, respectively, the precision required is not a problem and is consistent with the sensitivities in Tables 8-6 to 8-8. This property occurs with all Agarwal-Burrus like structures, i.e., Eq. (8-66).

First, let us calculate the raw, normalized capacitance values (with $A = B = D = 1$) using Eqs. (8-75) and the LPN entry in Table 8-9. The resulting unscaled capacitor values for the E- and F-circuit designs are listed in Table 8-10. To adjust

TABLE 8-10   LPN REALIZATION FOR EXAMPLE 8-8

	E-Circuit				F-Circuit		
Cap	Unscaled Values	Dynamic Range Adjusted Values	Final Values (pF)	Cap	Unscaled Values	Dynamic Range Adjusted Values	Final Values (pF)
A	1.0000	0.08333	1.0000	A	1.0000	0.08333	29.9748
B	1.0000	1.0000	12.0004	B	1.0000	1.0000	359.7122
C	0.00694	0.00694	2.5054	C	0.00696	0.00696	1.0000
D	1.0000	0.08333	30.0830	D	1.0000	0.08333	12.0072
E	0.00277	0.00277	1.0000	E	—	—	—
F	—	—	—	F	0.00278	0.00278	1.0000
G	0.00694	0.00694	2.5054	G	0.00696	0.00696	1.0000
K	0.89093	0.89093	10.6916	K	0.89340	0.89340	321.3669
ΣC(pF)	—	—	59.8	ΣC(pF)	—	—	726.1

the dynamic range, we need to first determine the peak or maximum voltage gain levels at V and V'. The maximum voltage gain levels at the primary outputs of both the E- and F-circuits are identical and occur at ω_0; hence,

$$\max_{0 \leq \omega < \infty} G_{E,F}(\omega) \approx 10.6 \text{ dB} \tag{8-80a}$$

The peak gain in Eq. (8-80a) is quite large due to $Q_p = 30$. However, the maximum gain level at the secondary output is significantly lower, i.e.,

$$\max_{0 \leq \omega < \infty} G'_{E,F}(\omega) \approx -11.0 \tag{8-80b}$$

Note that the gain peaks in Eqs. (8-80) need not be determined precisely. To equalize the gain peaks, in accordance with Eq. (8-76), the maximum $G'_{E,F}(\omega)$ in Eq. (8-80b) must be increased by $+21.6$ dB to 10.6 dB. Thus, the required linear scale factor is

$$\mu = \log^{-1} \frac{21.6}{20} \approx 12.0.$$

Scaling A and D by μ, as directed in Eq. (8-77b), yields the dynamic range-adjusted values in Table 8-10.

Scanning the unscaled and dynamic range adjusted capacitor values, there appears to be no difference in the E- and F-circuit designs as far as capacitance values are concerned. Earlier, we established that their sensitivities are equivalent. Let us then carry the designs to completion and scale the admittance levels at the two summing junctions so that the minimum capacitance value is 1 pF.

Comparing the dynamic range adjusted values for both the E- and F-circuits in Table 8-10, we find that the minimum capacitors within Σ_1 and Σ_2 in Eqs. (8-78) are

$$E\text{-Circuit: min. } \Sigma_1 = E = 0.00277 \text{ and min. } \Sigma_2 = A = 0.08333 \tag{8-81a}$$

$$F\text{-Circuit: min. } \Sigma_1 = C = 0.00694 \text{ and min. } \Sigma_2 = F = 0.00278 \tag{8-81b}$$

Hence, for the E-circuit, $\nu = 1/0.00277$ and $\kappa = 1/0.08333$. For the F-circuit, $\nu = 1/0.00694$ and $\kappa = 1/0.00278$. Scaling the capacitors as indicated in Eqs. (8-78) yields the "final" values listed in Table 8-10.

Comparing these "final" realizations, we discover that the F-circuit requires nearly twelve times the total capacitance of the E-circuit! This difference occurs even though the unscaled and dynamic range adjusted values seem almost identical. Experience has established that the E-circuit will usually require significantly lower ΣC when $Q_p \gg 1$ (and/or $Q_z \gg 1$) and $\omega_0 T \ll 1$ (and $\omega_N T \ll 1$). Otherwise, the F-circuit yields the lower ΣC realization. One famous example in which the F-circuit realizes a sizable ΣC advantage is the 50/60 Hz HPN for PCM codecs, realized with $f_s = 8$ kHz (Marsh et al 1981). The $H(z)$ for this application is given by

$$H(z) = 0.93906 \frac{1 - 1.99778z^{-1} + z^{-2}}{1 - 1.87195z^{-1} + 0.88219z^{-2}} \qquad (8\text{-}82)$$

The upper cutoff frequency for this filter is 300 Hz and the high-frequency gain is 0 dB. After all scaling is complete, the designs result in $\Sigma C = 143$ pF for the E-design and $\Sigma C = 68$ pF for the F-design, each with a minimum capacitance of 1 pF. However, no rigorous proof exists for these trends, nor has any definite rule of thumb been established. Hence, we recommend that the prudent designer carry both E- and F-circuit designs to completion so that they can be meaningfully compared. Fortunately, the design of these biquads is simple and highly repetitive. The experimental response for the LPN E-circuit realization is shown in Fig. 8-51.

Example 8-9

Realize the following AP $H(z)$:

$$H(z) = 0.98299 \frac{1 - 1.99832z^{-1} + 1.01730z^{-2}}{1 - 1.96433z^{-1} + 0.98299z^{-2}} \qquad (8\text{-}83)$$

where $f_s = 128$ kHz (or $T = 7.8125$ μsec). This $H(z)$ provides $f_0 = f_N = 2801.5$ Hz and $Q_p = -Q_z = 7.98$; a flat gain of 0 dB. Compare the total capacitance required to realize the three AP circuits in Fig. 8-52. Note that Fig. 8-52a represents two circuits; the first with $L = 0$, which we call the G, J, K circuit and the second with $L \neq 0$, which we call the G, J, K, L circuit. The third circuit is a balanced differential realization that we call the $G, K, -L$ circuit.

Solution. Since, $Q_p = -Q_z \gg 1$ and $\omega_0 T = \omega_N T \ll 1$, let us pursue the E-circuit design. The reader can repeat the process for F-circuit realizations.

Figure 8-52a, with L in gray, shows two E-circuit AP realizations, i.e., with $L = 0$ and with $L \neq 0$. Given the previous LPN example, the G, J, K circuit with

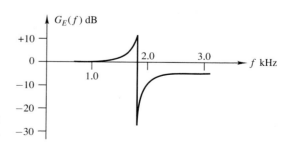

FIGURE 8-51   Experimental response of the $Q_p = 30$ LPN E-circuit realization in Table 8-10.

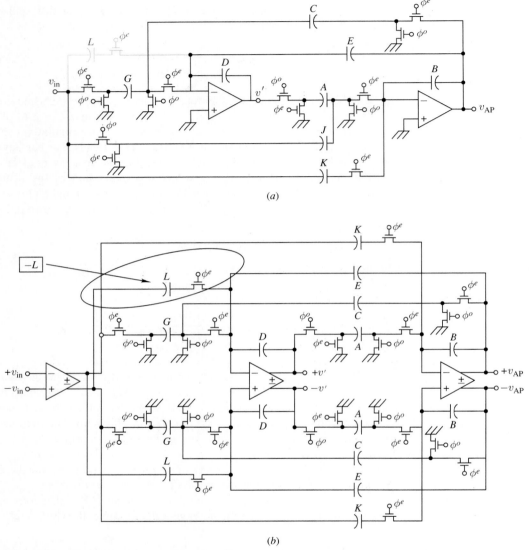

(a)

(b)

FIGURE 8-52   Low sensitivity AP biquads: (a) optimized single-ended *E*-circuit, and (b) superior balanced *E*-circuit.

$L = 0$ is a natural choice for an AP. That is, with $I = J = 0$, the zeros lie exactly on the unit circle. With $I \neq 0$, the zeros can be shifted inside the unit circle. With $J \neq 0$, they can be shifted outside the unit circle to the AP locations designated in Fig. 7-6g. The design formulas for the capacitor ratios in terms of the sample-data parameters r_p, $r_p \cos \theta_0$, r_z, and $r_z \cos \theta_N$ for this circuit are given in Table 8-11.

Also, for comparison and to evaluate sensitivities, expressions for ω_0, Q_p, ω_N, and Q_z are given in Table 8-12. It should be evident that the sensitivities of ω_N, Q_z are minimum. However, the $K/J = Q_z/(\omega_N T)$ ratio becomes very large as $Q_z \gg 1$ and $\omega_N T \ll 1$. In contrast, the equally large $Q_p/(\omega_0 T) = DB/AE$ is helped by being formed by the product of two ratios. By letting $L \neq 0$, a subtraction is introduced into the denominator of Q_z in Table 8-12 via $\gamma = AL/DK$. Controlled by the value of L, the designer can adjust the effect of the subtraction to optimally

TABLE 8-11   AP BIQUAD CAPACITOR RATIOS (γ = DISCRETIONARY PARAMETER)

	G, J, K	G, J, K, L	G, K, −L
$\dfrac{AE}{DB}$	$1 - r_p^2$	$1 - r_p^2$	$1 - r_p^2$
$\dfrac{AC}{DB}$	$1 + r_p^2 - 2r_p \cos\theta_0$	$1 + r_p^2 - 2r_p \cos\theta_0$	$1 + r_p^2 - 2r_p \cos\theta_0$
$\dfrac{K}{B}$	k	k	k
$\dfrac{J}{K}$	$r_z^2 - 1$	$r_z^2 - 1 + \gamma$	—
$\dfrac{AG}{DK}$	$1 + r_z^2 - 2r_z \cos\theta_N$	$1 + r_z^2 - 2r_z \cos\theta_N$	$1 + r_z^2 - 2r_z \cos\theta_N$
$\dfrac{AL}{DK}$	—	γ	$r_z^2 - 1$

TABLE 8-12   AP FREQUENCY-DOMAIN PARAMETERS FOR THREE *E*-CIRCUIT REALIZATIONS IN FIG. 8-52 (γ = DISCRETIONARY PARAMETER).

	G, J, K	G, J, K, L	G, K, −L
ω_0	$\approx f_s \sqrt{\dfrac{AC}{DB}}$	$\approx f_s \sqrt{\dfrac{AC}{DB}}$	$\approx f_s \sqrt{\dfrac{AC}{DB}}$
$\dfrac{\omega_0 T}{Q_p}$	$\approx \dfrac{AE}{DB}$	$\approx \dfrac{AE}{DB}$	$\approx \dfrac{AE}{DB}$
Q_p	$\approx \dfrac{1}{E}\sqrt{\dfrac{BCD}{A}}$	$\approx \dfrac{1}{E}\sqrt{\dfrac{BCD}{A}}$	$\approx \dfrac{1}{E}\sqrt{\dfrac{BCD}{A}}$
ω_N	$\approx f_s \sqrt{\dfrac{AG}{DK}}$	$\approx f_s \sqrt{\dfrac{AG}{DK}}$	$\approx f_s \sqrt{\dfrac{AG}{DK}}$
$\pm \dfrac{\omega_N T}{Q_z}$	$\approx \dfrac{J}{K}$	$\approx \dfrac{J}{K} - \gamma$	$\approx \dfrac{AL}{DK}$
Q_z	$\approx \dfrac{1}{J}\sqrt{\dfrac{AKG}{D}}$	$\approx \dfrac{1}{J - \gamma K}\sqrt{\dfrac{AKG}{D}}$	$\approx \dfrac{1}{L}\sqrt{\dfrac{KGD}{A}}$

trade Q_z-sensitivity for reduced ΣC (Laker, Ganesan, and Fleischer 1985). It was found that $L = 2.000$ yields a good balance.

Finally, in Fig. 8-52b, we show a balanced differential Fleischer-Laker biquad optimized for an AP. In this circuit we take advantage of the differential input to realize a $-L$ by cross coupling the inputs to L. For this case, we see in Table 8-12 that formulas for ω_N, Q_z exactly parallel ω_0, Q_p. The design formulas for this circuit are given in Table 8-11. This same idea can be applied to the other feed-in capacitors $\hat{G}$, $\hat{H}$, $\hat{I}$, and $\hat{J}$, so that

$$\hat{G} = \pm G \pm L \quad \hat{H} = \pm H \pm L \quad \hat{I} = \pm I \pm K \quad \text{and} \quad \hat{J} = \pm J \pm K \tag{8-84}$$

yielding an abundance of fresh alternatives not available in the single-ended realization.

The final capacitance values for all three realizations of Eq. (8-83) are listed in Table 8-13. Note that $K/J = 57.8$ and $\Sigma C = 153$ pF for the G, J, K realization. By inserting $L = 2.000$, K/J is reduced to 19.27 and ΣC to 67 pF. In the balanced case, even with the doubling of all capacitors, $\Sigma C = 57$ pF. Also listed in Table 8-13 are the peak standard deviations for gain $\sigma(\Delta G)$ and group delay $\sigma(\Delta\tau)$, estimated for independent gaussian capacitors with $\sigma_C = 0.001$ for all A through L. Peak values are the largest values as functions of ω. We see that the σ's for all three realizations are quite comparable, as the relations in Tables 8-11 and 8-12 suggest.

TABLE 8-13   AP CAPACITOR VALUES AND σ's

Cap	Final Values (pF) G, J, K	Final Values (pF) G, J, K, L	Final Values (pF) G, K, −L
A	16.090	5.491	1.000
B	58.800	19.600	3.654
C	1.097	1.097	1.097
D	16.090	16.470	16.090
E	1.000	1.000	1.000
G	1.097	1.097	1.097
J	1.000	1.000	—
K	57.800	19.270	3.591
L	—	2.000	1.000
ΣC (pF)	153.0	67.0	$2 \times 28.5 =$ 57.0
$\sigma(\Delta G)$ (dB)	0.068	0.073	0.049
$\sigma(\Delta\tau)$ (μ sec)	17.6	16.8	12.3

When implementing active-SC filters on the chip, it is usually efficient to arrange the layout so that op amps, switches, capacitors, clock lines, and analog signal lines are in separate areas. This also allows the designer to keep analog signal lines isolated from clock and other digital signal-carrying lines. One such layout is shown in Fig. 8-53 (*see color plate 4*), where the op amps are arranged in the top row, ground and AC signal lines in the next row, followed by rows of capacitors, switches, and clock lines. Shown in Fig. 8-53 is the circuitry required to realize a Fleischer-Laker biquad, with *p*-well shielding (i.e., for capacitors and summing node *n*MOST double-pole-double-throw switches) to increase the *PSRR*.

8-8 INTEGRATED CONTINUOUS-TIME FLEISCHER-LAKER TYPE BIQUADS

The design process and the circuit realizations for state variable active-RC and active-G_m/C biquads, with resonant loops described in Figs. 8-42 and 8-43, strongly parallel the developments for the active-SC biquads in the previous section. The structures that follow have been constructed to retain as many properties of the Fleischer-Laker active-SC biquad as possible.

8-8-1 Active-RC Biquads using MOST-R's

Let us first consider the general biquad in Fig. 8-54, where the resistors are realized with MOST-R's. To emphasize and take advantage of the strong analogy with the active-SC biquad, we have labeled the R's and C's to show correspondence on a component-by-component basis. Although not a practical circuit, the components are more clearly shown in the single-ended "RC" equivalent in Fig. 8-54*d*. Assuming ideal op amps and MOST-R's, the voltage transfer function to the primary output V_{out2} can be written as

$$T_E(s) = $$

$$\left(\frac{-C_K}{C_B}\right) \frac{s^2 + \left(\frac{1}{R_I C_K} - \frac{1}{R_J C_K} + \frac{C_L}{C_D}\frac{1}{R_A C_K}\right)s + \frac{1}{R_A C_K C_D}\left(\frac{1}{R_G} - \frac{1}{R_H}\right)}{s^2 + \frac{C_E}{C_D}\frac{1}{R_A C_B}s + \frac{1}{R_C C_D R_A C_B}} \tag{8-85a}$$

$$T_F(s) = $$

$$\left(\frac{-C_K}{C_B}\right) \frac{s^2 + \left(\frac{1}{R_I C_K} - \frac{1}{R_J C_K} + \frac{C_L}{C_D}\frac{1}{R_A C_K}\right)s + \frac{1}{R_A C_K C_D}\left(\frac{1}{R_G} - \frac{1}{R_H}\right)}{s^2 + \frac{1}{R_F C_B}s + \frac{1}{R_C C_D R_A C_B}} \tag{8-85b}$$

Once again, we differentiate between "E" and "F" type damping. The ideal relations between ω_0, Q_p, ω_N, Q_z, and the components are listed in Table 8-14. We leave it to the reader to verify these relations. Note that the use of $C_K > 0$ and $R_G > 0$ (with

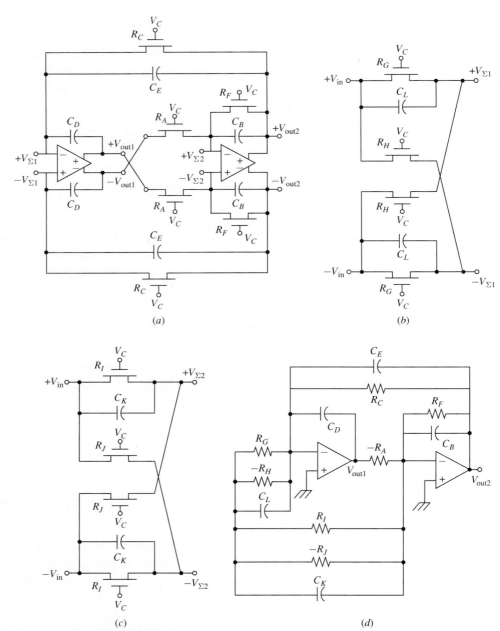

FIGURE 8-54 General integrated active-RC biquad: (*a*) resonator permitting the realization of either the $-\alpha_F$ or $s\beta_E$ loops, (*b*) zero forming feeds into $\pm V_{\Sigma 1}$, (*c*) zero forming feeds into $\pm V_{\Sigma 2}$, and (*d*) the single-ended equivalent to (*a*).

TABLE 8-14   ACTIVE-RC BIQUAD PARAMETERS $1/R_G > 1/R_H$

	E-Circuit	F-Circuit
ω_0	$\sqrt{\dfrac{1}{R_C C_D R_A C_B}}$	$\sqrt{\dfrac{1}{R_C C_D R_A C_B}}$
$\dfrac{\omega_0}{Q_p}$	$\dfrac{C_E}{C_D}\dfrac{1}{R_A C_B}$	$\dfrac{1}{R_F C_B}$
Q_p	$\dfrac{C_D}{C_E}\sqrt{\dfrac{R_A C_B}{R_C C_D}}$	$R_F\sqrt{\dfrac{C_D}{R_C R_A C_B}}$
ω_N	$\sqrt{\dfrac{1}{R_A C_K C_D}\left(\dfrac{1}{R_G}-\dfrac{1}{R_H}\right)}$	$\sqrt{\dfrac{1}{R_A C_K C_D}\left(\dfrac{1}{R_G}-\dfrac{1}{R_H}\right)}$
$\pm\dfrac{\omega_N}{Q_z}$	$\dfrac{1}{R_I C_K}-\dfrac{1}{R_J C_K}+\dfrac{C_L}{C_D}\dfrac{1}{R_A C_K}$	$\dfrac{1}{R_I C_K}-\dfrac{1}{R_J C_K}+\dfrac{C_L}{C_D}\dfrac{1}{R_A C_K}$
Q_z	$\dfrac{\sqrt{\dfrac{C_K}{R_A C_D}\left(\dfrac{1}{R_G}-\dfrac{1}{R_H}\right)}}{\dfrac{1}{R_I}-\dfrac{1}{R_J}+\dfrac{C_L}{C_D}\dfrac{1}{R_A}}$	$\dfrac{\sqrt{\dfrac{C_K}{R_A C_D}\left(\dfrac{1}{R_G}-\dfrac{1}{R_H}\right)}}{\dfrac{1}{R_I}-\dfrac{1}{R_J}+\dfrac{C_L}{C_D}\dfrac{1}{R_A}}$
k	$\dfrac{C_K}{C_B}$	$\dfrac{C_K}{C_B}$

$C_L = 0$ and $R_H = R_I = R_J = 0$) results in a BR (or LPN or HPN) biquad, where for ideal op amps $1/Q_z \equiv 0$. This and several other useful features of the active-SC biquad translate over to the active-RC analog.

The design process associated with selecting the raw component values, optimizing dynamic range, and scaling the impedance levels at both op amp inputs, is nearly identical to that described for the active-SC biquad. The one difference lies in the criteria used for the impedance scaling. In this case, we may choose to constrain integrating capacitors C_B and C_D such that $C_D = C_B = C_M$ and then scale C_M to achieve the desired trade between die area and performance, e.g., to minimize total die area as illustrated in Exercise 8-34. Alternatively, we may scale all the raw component values so that the smallest component, either R or C, equals the designated unit resistance R_U or capacitance C_U.

To evaluate the impact of the finite op amp gains and the distributed parasitic capacitances associated with the MOST-R's, let us examine the undamped state variable loop (i.e., Fig. 8-42a with $1/R_F = 0$). Let us also simplify matters, with little loss of generality, by considering the single-ended equivalent of the loop. Hence, modeling the op amp gains as $A_1(s) = A_2(s) = \omega_t/s$, and the MOST-R's as shown in Fig. 8-16, our circuit is drawn in Fig. 8-55. The characteristic equation for this nonideal loop,

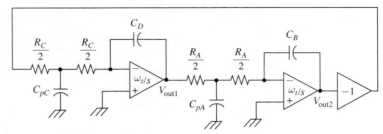

FIGURE 8-55   Undamped active-RC state variable loop with finite gain op amps and nonideal MOST-R's.

after much algebraic manipulation, is approximately expressed as

$$s^2 - 2\omega_0 \left(\frac{\omega_0}{\omega_t} + \frac{\omega_0}{4\omega_d} \right) s + \omega_0^2 \left(1 - \frac{2\omega_0}{\omega_t} \right) = 0 \qquad (8\text{-}86)$$

where we have assigned $\omega_0 = 1/R_C C_D = 1/R_A C_B$ and $\omega_d = 1/R_C C_{pC} = 1/R_A C_{pA}$. Note that the Q_p is enhanced by the phase shifts due to ω_t and ω_d. We also see that the pole frequency is reduced. In principle, we can predistort the R's and C's to compensate for these shifts, but in practice this is not very effective. First, ω_t and ω_d are highly variable. Moreover, they are defined by parameters that do not track any of the other circuit components. Alternatively, the active compensation techniques described in Sec. 5-3 can be used to reduce the effect of ω_t. In any case, it is good practice to reduce the C_p's as much as possible in the layout of the R's. The closed-loop tuning described in Sec. 8-4 tends to counter the errors in Eq. (8-86).

To explore the precision and tuning of these biquads, let us focus our attention on the pole locations defined by ω_0 and Q_p. Let us then refer to the ω_0, Q_p realized by the E-circuit as ω_{0E}, Q_{pE} and realized by the F-circuit as ω_{0F}, Q_{pF}. We observe in Table 8-14 that ω_0 is formed the same way in both structures. Hence, the precision of the realized ω_0 and its tuning are the same in both cases, i.e., $\omega_{0E} = \omega_{0F}$. In Table 8-14, we find for the E-circuit that Q_{pE} is formed as the product of one R-ratio and two C-ratios, and its resistors R_A, R_C must be set when tuning ω_{0E}. This can be accomplished by routing one control signal V_C to both R_A and R_C, such that $R_A = R(V_C)$ and $R_C = \alpha R(V_C)$. Thus, once ω_{0E} is tuned, Q_{pE} is also tuned, and its precision depends on the matching accuracy of C_E/C_D, C_B/C_D and $R_A(V_C)/R_C(V_C)$. In contrast, the F-circuit Q_{pF} can be independently tuned by adjusting $R_F = R_F(V_{CF})$. As mentioned in Sec. 8-4, the tuning of Q_{pF} depends upon a tuned ω_{0F} (and a fixed R_A and R_C). The precision of the tuned Q_{pF} is then determined by the matching accuracy of C_B/C_D, $R_F(V_{CF})/R_A(V_C)$ and $R_F(V_{CF})/R_C(V_C)$. Alternatively, we could route V_C to R_F so that $R_F = \beta R(V_C)$; thus choosing not to independently tune R_F. This simplifies the tuning and the associated on-chip hardware but it sacrifices the opportunity to compensate for effects that are not observed when ω_{0F} is tuned. Note that since Q_{pE} is more dependent on the capacitor ratios than Q_{pF}, we can intuitively argue that Q_{pE} can be realized with better precision.

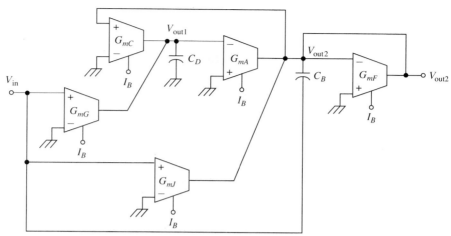

FIGURE 8-56   General integrated active-G_m/C biquad. Note that $G_{mJ} > 0$ locates the complex zeros in the right-half of the s-plane. If the input terminals to G_{mJ} are inverted, than a G_{ml} is realized and the zeros lie in the left-half of the s-plane.

8-8-2   Active-G_m/C Biquads using MOST-G_m's

A general "F" type active-G_m/C biquad is shown in Fig. 8-56, with the transfer function to the primary output V_{out2} given by

$$T_F(s) = \frac{s^2 - \dfrac{G_{mJ}}{C_D}s + \dfrac{G_{mA}G_{mG}}{C_D C_B}}{s^2 + \dfrac{G_{mF}}{C_B}s + \dfrac{G_{mC}G_{mA}}{C_D C_B}} \tag{8-87}$$

Note that when $G_{mJ} = 0$, $1/Q_z \equiv 0$. Also note that feeding the bottom plate of C_B to the input provides the feed-forward path realized with C_K in the active-RC biquad. Also, inverting the polarity at the inputs to G_{mJ} will serve to locate the zeros in the left-half plane. The balanced differential realization of this general active-G_m/C biquad is shown in Fig. 8-57. The design formulas are given in Table 8-15. A suitable realization of the "E" type biquad has not been found in active-G_m/C. It is assumed that the precautions described in Sec. 8-2 have been followed to ensure sufficient linearity.

For this active-G_m/C filter, the nonidealities are primarily due to the parasitic conductances and capacitances at the input/output terminals of the OTA (as indicated in Fig. 5-49). Let us evaluate the impact of these parasitics on the performance of an active-G_m/C undamped state variable loop (i.e., Fig. 8-43b with $G_{mF} = 0$). This circuit, drawn in Fig. 8-58, yields the following characteristic equation

$$s^2 + \left(\frac{g_{oC}}{C_D + C_{iA}} + \frac{g_{oA}}{C_B + C_{iC}}\right)s + \frac{G_{mC}G_{mA} + g_{oA}g_{oC}}{(C_D + C_{iA})(C_B + C_{iC})} = 0 \tag{8-88a}$$

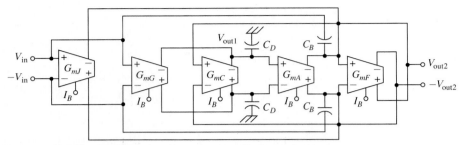

FIGURE 8-57 Balanced differential realization of the general active-G_m/C biquad in Fig. 8-51.

TABLE 8-15 ACTIVE-G_m/C BIQUAD PARAMETERS

	E-Circuit	F-Circuit
ω_0	—	$\sqrt{\dfrac{G_{mC}\,G_{mA}}{C_D C_B}}$
$\dfrac{\omega_0}{Q_p}$	—	$\dfrac{G_{mF}}{C_B}$
Q_p	—	$\dfrac{1}{G_{mF}}\sqrt{\dfrac{G_{mC}\,G_{mA}\,C_B}{C_D}}$
ω_N	—	$\sqrt{\dfrac{G_{mG}\,G_{mA}}{C_D C_B}}$
$-\dfrac{\omega_N}{Q_z}$	—	$\dfrac{G_{mJ}}{C_D}$
Q_z	—	$\dfrac{1}{G_{mJ}}\sqrt{\dfrac{G_{mG}\,G_{mA}\,C_D}{C_B}}$
k	—	1

or, approximately,

$$s^2 + \left(\frac{g_{oC}}{C_D + C_{iA}} + \frac{g_{oA}}{C_B + C_{iC}}\right)s + \frac{G_{mC}G_{mA}}{C_D C_B}\left(1 + \frac{g_{oA}g_{oC}}{G_{mC}G_m} - \frac{C_{iA}}{C_D} - \frac{C_{iC}}{C_B}\right) = 0$$

$$(8\text{-}88b)$$

In this case we see that Q_p is reduced and ω_0 will increase or decrease by a small amount, depending on the relative values of the components and parasitics. These effects are small insofar as $g_{oC}, g_{oA} \ll G_{mC}, G_{mA}$ and $C_{iC}, C_{iA} \ll C_D, C_B$. Closed-loop tuning will tend to counter these errors, along with imprecision in the G_m/C's. Note that the tuning and precision of this biquad are similar to that described for the "F" type active-RC biquad.

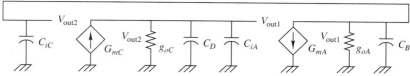

FIGURE 8-58   Undamped active-G_m/C state variable loop with finite parasitics.

8-9   HIGH ORDER FILTER IMPLEMENTATION USING CASCADED STAGES

Rarely is one requested to design and realize only a first- or second-order filter, as most practical filters are more complex. However, our modular approach allows us to implement a wide range of filter requirements using simple interconnections of first- and/or second-order filter stages. In this section, we consider the realization of a high-order integrated filter as a cascade or tandem connection of first- and second-order active filter stages. Cascade design is highly modular, capable of realizing any $H(s)$ or $H(z)$, and relatively easy to design, implement, and tune (if necessary). The price paid for these advantages is sensitivity. In Sec. 8-10, we present an alternative approach, based on passive ladder filters. Active ladders, as they are called, offer significantly improved sensitivities. They are best suited to LP and BP filters, where cascade design is completely general.

8-9-1   Cascading First- and Second-Order Filter Stages

Cascade design (Ghausi and Laker 1981; Gregorian and Temes 1986; Moschytz 1986; Schaumann, Ghausi, and Laker 1990; Unbehauen and Cichocki 1989) is based on the simple tandem interconnection of N first-order and biquad stages, as shown in Fig. 8-59. If the stages are noninteracting, the overall transfer function is the product of the individual stage transfer functions, i.e., in the s-domain,

$$T(s) = \prod_{i=1}^{N} T_i(s) = \frac{kN(s)}{D(s)} = \left[\prod_{i=1}^{N} k_i\right]\left[\prod_{i=1}^{N} \frac{N_i(s)}{D_i(s)}\right] \qquad (8\text{-}89)$$

By noninteracting, we mean that at any stage, say the ith stage, the output impedance $Z_{\text{out}i}$ is not loaded by the input impedance $Z_{\text{in}i+1}$ of the succeeding stage, i.e., $|Z_{\text{out}i}| \ll |Z_{\text{in}i+1}|$. In op amp-based active filters, this condition is inherently realized for $\omega \ll \omega_t$.

FIGURE 8-59   Cascade structure.

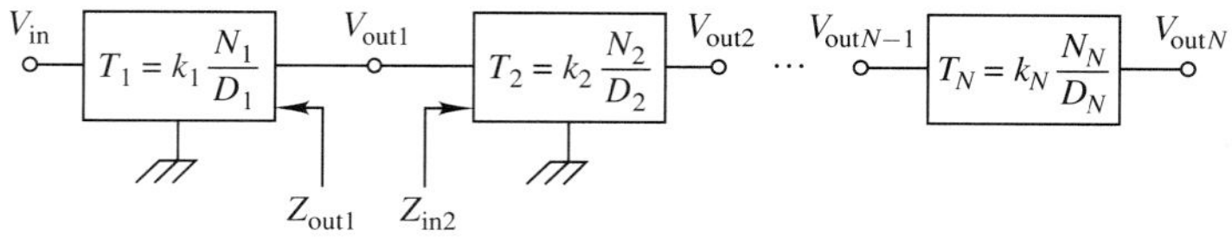

However, due to the high input and output impedances of the OTA *VCCS*, active-G_m/C filters require interstage buffering. The required buffers are usually realized as simple unity-gain source follower (or emitter follower) stages, described in Sec. 4-3. Furthermore, output buffering is generally required to drive external loads. Typically, when $N = $ even, $T(s)$ is realized as a cascade of N biquads. When $N = $ odd, $T(s)$ is realized as a cascade of $N - 1$ biquads and one first-order stage.

Let us examine the relationship between variations in the stage $T_i(s)$'s, i.e., $\Delta T_i/T_i$ and the overall function $\Delta T/T$, which are only valid where $T_i(s) \neq 0$ and $T(s) \neq 0$ Techniques for estimating $\Delta T_i/T_i$, due to statistical and deterministic variations in the components, were given in Sec. 7-7. Hence, if $T(s)$ varies due to changes in the components of the $T_i(s)$'s, we can write for a particular frequency ω_a:

$$T(j\omega_a)\left[1 + \frac{\Delta T(j\omega_a)}{T(j\omega_a)}\right] = \prod_{i=1}^{N} T_i(j\omega_a) \prod_{i=1}^{N}\left[1 + \frac{\Delta T_i(j\omega_a)}{T_i(j\omega_a)}\right] \qquad (8\text{-}90a)$$

or

$$\frac{\Delta T(j\omega_a)}{T(j\omega_a)} = 1 - \prod_{i=1}^{N}\left[1 + \frac{\Delta T_i(j\omega_a)}{T_i(j\omega_a)}\right] \qquad (8\text{-}90b)$$

If $\Delta T_i(j\omega_a)/T_i(j\omega_a) \ll 1$, we can simplify Eq. (8-90b) to a more intuitive form, i.e.,

$$\frac{\Delta T(j\omega_a)}{T(j\omega_a)} = \sum_{i=1}^{N} \frac{\Delta T_i(j\omega_a)}{T_i(j\omega_a)} \qquad (8\text{-}91)$$

Equation (8-91) states that the variation in the cascade transfer function, for sufficiently small changes, is the sum of the individual stage transfer function variations. Similar results can be derived for variations in gain ($G(\omega_a)$ in dB), phase or group delay. From a design point of view, Eq. (8-91) implies that $\Delta T/T$ can only be reduced by decreasing the variabilities of the individual stages. Hence, the prudent designer will use low sensitivity and parasitic insensitive stage designs wherever possible. Clearly, results that parallel Eqs. (8-89) to (8-91) can be readily written in the z-domain for sampled data filters.

Equations (8-89) through (8-91) and Fig. 8-59 largely define the design tasks for cascade synthesis and realization. However, there are some subtle design choices that may not be obvious from the presentation thus far. The design process is as follows:

1 *The required numeric H(s or z) is determined using techniques described in Sec. 7-4.*

2 *We factor the numerator N(s or z) and denominator D(s or z) of H(s or z) into their respective root functions. Imaginary and complex conjugate roots are combined into quadratic polynomials.*

It may seem that one can arbitrarily combine the roots of $N(s$ or $z)$ and $D(s$ or $z)$ to form the $T_i(s$ or $z)$ in Eq. (8-89). After all, $H(s)$ is realized no matter how we pair the poles and zeros and order the stages in the tandem. However, the variability and, in particular, the dynamic range of the cascade, are in fact impacted by how this pairing and ordering is done (Ghausi and Laker 1981; Schaumann, Ghausi, and Laker 1990).

In the previous section, we saw that the maximum undistorted signal voltage that a filter can process is limited, depending on the operating frequency, by the power supply or by the linearity or overload of the op amps. Let us label this maximum signal level $V_{out\,(max)}$ and assume that it is measured at the primary output of the biquadratic section. We must make sure that the signal level at any section output, $|V_{outi}(j\omega)|$, satisfies

$$\max|V_{outi}(j\omega)| < V_{out(max)} \text{ for } 0 \le \omega < \infty \text{ and } i = 1, \ldots, N \qquad (8\text{-}92)$$

Note that this condition must indeed be satisfied for all frequencies, and not only in the passband; large signals outside the passband must not be allowed to overload and saturate the op amps. The lower limit of the useful signal range is set by the noise floor. If, in the passband of a cascade filter, the signal at an internal stage becomes very small, it must be amplified back up to the prescribed output level. Since from any point in the cascade of filter stages, say at the output of stage i, signal and noise are amplified by the same amount, namely,

$$V_{outN}(j\omega) = \prod_{j=i+1}^{N} T_j(j\omega) V_{outi}(j\omega) \qquad (8\text{-}93a)$$

we may conclude that the signal-to-noise ratio will suffer if any $V_{outi}(j\omega)$ suffers significant inband attenuation, i.e., if it is permitted to become too small. Equation (8-93a) also represents the noise gain from the output of section i to the filter output. Thus, the second condition to be satisfied by the output voltage of any biquad is

$$\min|V_{outi}(j\omega)| \rightarrow \text{ maximized for } \omega_L \le \omega \le \omega_U \text{ and } i = 1, \ldots, N \qquad (8\text{-}93b)$$

Of course, we are concerned here only with signal frequencies between the lower and upper passband corners, ω_L and ω_U, respectively, because in the stopband, signal-to-noise ratio is of no interest.

Pole-zero pairing, section ordering and gain scaling are to be chosen (Ghausi and Laker 1981; Schaumann, Ghausi, and Laker 1990) such that the conditions of Equations (8-93) are satisfied. Once this is complete, the dynamic range scaling of the individual sections can be completed as described in the previous section. Space does not permit us to develop these concepts and procedures in any greater detail. Hence, we only state some general rules of thumb. To optimize pairing and ordering for a particular set of filter requirements necessitates the use of CAD tools such as FILSYN (Szentirmai). The curious or otherwise interested reader is referred to any of several active filter texts listed in the references for more details on this process. Continuing with the design steps we have:

3 *Equations (8-93) are best satisfied by pairing the highest Q_{pi} poles with the closest zeros, such that the distance $|p_i - z_i|$ is minimized. The remaining roots of $N(s\ or\ z)$ and $D(s\ or\ z)$ can usually be arbitrarily paired to form the rest of the $T_i(s\ or\ z)$ with little impact.*

4 *The order of stages that best satisfies Eqs. (8-93) is somewhat more subtle, requiring computer assistance and intuition gained by experience. However, it is often desirable to start the cascade with either an LP or a BP to eliminate unnecessary high frequency components, which could cause nonlinear behavior in subsequent stages due to op amp slew limits. In other applications, where the presence of a particularly strong unwanted tone, such as 50/60 Hz power hum, could overdrive certain subsequent stages, the cascade is started with an HP stage. It is also common to end a cascade with an HP or BP stage to eliminate DC offset and other spurious signals produced within the filter.*

5 *The gain constants k_i are scaled to equalize the gain maxima as described in previous sections and such that the end-to-end gain constant k in Eq. (8-89) is realized.*

6 *The best biquad structures for each of the T_i are chosen from the point of view of sensitivity, parasitics, die area, etc. For example, in an active-SC cascade realization, we typically find a combination of E- and F-circuits used to optimize the design of each section.*

7 *Finally, we design and implement the requisite first- and second-order stages, as described in the previous section.*

These design steps are technology and filter-type independent. We next focus on several interesting issues associated with the realization of cascade active-SC filters. In the next subsection, we examine remedies to the problem of op settling and in Sec. 8-9-3 we apply these remedies to the realization of a delay equalizer, comprised of a cascade AP stage. Cascaded AP stages are particularly treacherous and can be very sensitive to any phase dependence caused by op amp transients.

8-9-2 Time-Staggered Active-SC Stages

The adverse effects on active-SC filter performance, due to the nonideal op amp transient behavior, have been well documented (Gregorian and Temes 1986; Sansen, Qiuting, and Halonen 1987; Unbehauen and Cichocki 1989). Perhaps the most prominent of these effects are the gain and phase errors that occur due to the op amp's unavoidable finite DC gain and settling behavior (Gregorian and Temes 1986; Unbehauen and Cichocki 1989). Also, the op amp's slewing, in response to the sudden step-like changes in input (albeit small), introduces some additional charge transfer error and nonlinear distortion. These slew-induced effects can be controlled in the design of the op amp's input differential stage by making the stage's transconductance G_m as large as possible (Sansen, Qiuting, and Halonen 1987).

The gain and phase errors can become quite severe when samples must propagate through chains of several unsettled op amps during a single-clock phase. For example, consider the cascade of two LPN biquads shown in Fig. 8-60. During ϕ^e, a chain traversing three op amps (via K_1, K_2, and C_2) is seen to exist. The error at the output

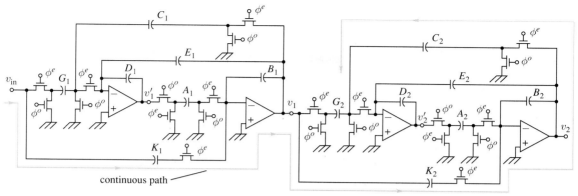

FIGURE 8-60   Cascaded active-SC LPN (HPN or BR) stages showing the continuous paths through multiple op amps.

of the third op amp will invariably be much larger than that at the first op amp output. Chains of two or more op amps, connected within a single clock phase, occur both within single biquad stages and through tandem connected biquad stages.

The settling problem is depicted in Fig. 8-61 for the cases of overdamped (no overshoot) and underdamped (overshoot followed by ringing) op amp dynamics. Under-

FIGURE 8-61   The op amp settling problem. Shown are the transient responses for overdamped and underdamped op amps superimposed on the active-SC filter bi-phase clocks. Also illustrated is the impact that the sampling point has on the settling error actually propagated with each sample.

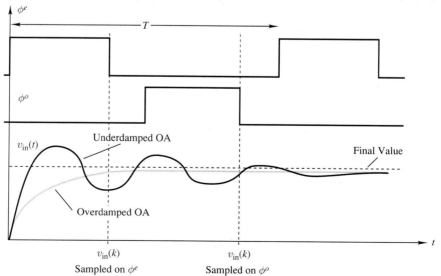

damped transients occur in second- and higher-order systems when the phase margin PM is not sufficiently large (i.e., PM $<76°$ for second-order systems). The characteristics of op amp settling are discussed in Chap. 6. Settling time is closely related to op amp GBW via Eq. (6-41). For a one-pole model, the op amp outputs change in value in accordance with

$$\{\Delta v_{\text{in}}(t)\}_a \approx \alpha \Delta v_{\text{in}}(kT)(1 - e^{-t/\tau_p}) \tag{8-94}$$

where $\{\Delta v_{\text{in}}(t)\}_a$ is the actual sample update, $\Delta v_{\text{in}}(kT)$ is the ideal sample update, and τ_p is the op amp time constant. Constant α, ideally unity, is a function of the op amp DC gain A_0. The net result is that the voltage sample taken at the op amp output is in error. The error has two components: first, a fixed (steady-state) error due to $1/A_0$, as described in Chap. 5; and a settling error due to e^{-t/τ_p}. For example, sampling v_{in} after only $4.6\tau_p$ introduces an additional one percent error; while sampling after $6.9\tau_p$ adds only a 0.1 percent error. When the op amp transients are underdamped, the settling error can either add or subtract from the steady-state error due to $1/A_0$. Moreover, settling errors can accumulate rapidly as a sample propagates, within a given clock phase, through a large chain of op amps. Analytical evaluation of the settling error is tedious, even for a first order active-SC stage (Gregorian and Temes 1986; Unbehauen and Cichocki 1989). Hence, switched-capacitor CAD analysis tools, such as SWITCAP (Fang, Tsividis, and Wing 1983) are recommended for such evaluations.

In Fig. 8-61, we show the op amp output changing in value at the beginning of ϕ^e. In our z-domain analysis, we assume that v_{in} changes instantaneously to its ideal final value and remains constant for T seconds. Significant variations from the desired gain $G(\omega)$ and group delay $\tau(\omega)$ can occur when the phase independence of the op amp outputs deteriorates, i.e., $v_{\text{in}}(kT) \neq v_{\text{in}}((k+1/2)T)$. To combat the problem, the designer usually has the luxury to choose whether to take the sample on ϕ^e or ϕ°, i.e., to wait another $T/2$ for the op amp to settle as shown in Fig. 8-61. The only penalty for this wait is a latency delay of $T/2$ per biquad stage. This latency is important only if the active-SC filter is in a feedback loop or some time-critical path. Introducing such $T/2$ delays serves to break the op amp chains, and isolate the settling error.

To find a remedy, let us first consider op amp chains that run between tandem biquadratic filter stages. In order to break these chains, we introduce the $T/2$ delays between the stages suggested in Fig. 8-61 by simply alternating switch phasings from biquad to biquad. This technique, known as *staggering*, is shown in Fig. 8-62 (Allstot and Black 1983; Laker, Ganesan, and Fleischer 1985; Martin and Sedra 1981; Unbehauen and Cichocki 1989). Note that in order to transmit the correct (i.e., properly delayed) signal, the K capacitors need to be opened during the unwanted clock phase. We have already taken care of this with the series switch at the top plate of K. Although staggering is illustrated for cascaded E-circuits, all the techniques and results to be presented extend to F-circuits with only minor modifications.

The method of staggering demonstrated in Fig. 8-62 for two LPN (HPN or BR) biquad stages is clearly extendable to an arbitrary number of similar stages. It may be used to realize a cascade connection of all useful types of biquadratic transfer functions, the sole exception being the single-ended AP biquad. The problem stems

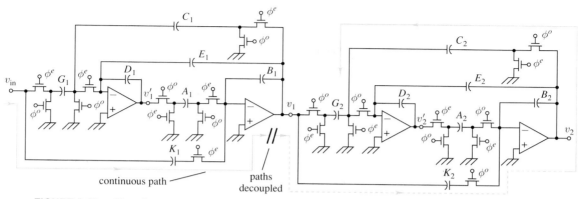

FIGURE 8-62   Use of staggering between stages to implement the delayed sampling illustrated in Fig. 8-56.

from the fact that, regardless of which all-pass implementation in Fig. 8-52a is used, there is always a residual J capacitor. If such biquads were staggered, the J capacitor would not acquire the proper input sample, i.e., the sample "previously" transmitted via I or K. Moreover, it would transfer the sample to B during the incorrect phase. Hence, the proper transfer function would not be realized. Note that the same problem occurs when $H \neq 0$.

To obtain the proper transfer function, extra delay must be introduced into the J capacitor path. This delay can be realized by replacing each of the J capacitors in Fig. 8-52a with the tandem pair of switched capacitors in Fig. 8-22d. It has been shown that this tandem switched-capacitor circuit realizes the desired $-Jz^{-3/2}$ and can be implemented with insensitivity to all parasitics. The resulting staggered cascade of AP biquads is illustrated in Fig. 8-63. Now all feed-ins to each biquad are synchronized to a single phase, eliminating the sensitivity to $v_{\text{in}}(kT) \neq v_{\text{in}}((k + 1/2)T)$. Note that since only G, K, and $-L$ (not J) are used in the balanced differential AP biquad in Fig. 8-52b, it is staggered using circuitry similar to Fig. 8-63. We see that staggering always results in the complete decoupling of successive stages. This ensures that any existing settling errors are localized to each biquad stage separately, thereby eliminating some complex and potentially very harmful interactions. Note that when a first order AP is required, switched-capacitor C_1 in Fig. 8-37i can be implemented using the tandem J to achieve the same benefit.

Next, we consider the op amp chains within single biquadratic stages. Chains connecting two op amps via capacitors C and E are seen to be present in all the biquads shown, including the general biquad in Fig. 8-45. The KBC chain can be broken by reversing all the switch phases associated with C, i.e., B and D update on opposite phases (Martin and Sedra 1981). While this may result in improved performance, there are many situations where the performance is perfectly adequate without reversing the phases of the C-switches. Extensive simulations have confirmed this conclusion, especially in cases where $D \gg G, C$, and E. This tends to be the

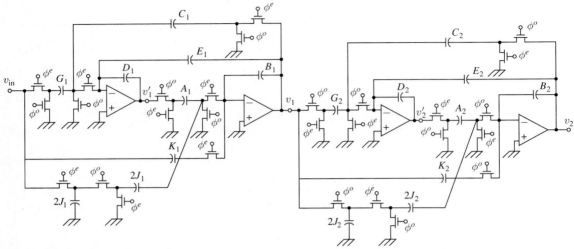

FIGURE 8-63 Staggered AP biquad stages where the feed-ins have been synchronized to sample their respective inputs all on ϕ^o and T seconds after the op amp transient begins.

case whenever $\omega_0 T, \omega_N T \ll 1$. Having a relatively large D has two benefits. First, it leads to a feedback factor close to unity, so that the integrator's loop gain-bandwidth product is not substantially less than the op amp gain-bandwidth product. Thus, the op amps inherent settling time is not compromised. Second, since A does not sample v' until the phase-succeeding input transfers to D, the settling of v' can continue for $T/2$ after C is disconnected. Note that the switch phasings shown in Fig. 8-45 have several advantages in that they were chosen to maintain phase independence and to maximize switch sharing.

8-9-3 Settling Error Analysis of Delay Equalizers Realized as a Cascade of Active-SC AP Stages

As an example, let us consider the design of a unity-gain eighth-order active-SC delay equalizer, realized as a cascade of four AP biquads. The AP biquads are characterized as follows (Laker, Ganesan, and Fleischer 1985):

AP1: $f_{01} = f_{N1} = 982$ Hz and $Q_{p1} = -Q_{z1} = 1.50$

AP2: $f_{02} = f_{N2} = 1529$ Hz and $Q_{p2} = -Q_{z2} = 2.28$

AP3: $f_{03} = f_{N3} = 2071$ Hz and $Q_{p3} = -Q_{z3} = 3.07$

AP4: $f_{04} = f_{N4} = 2631$ Hz and $Q_{p4} = -Q_{z4} = 3.84$

The sampling rate is $f_s = 200$ kHz and a clock duty cycle is assumed to be near 50 percent. This results in a switch closure time of about 2.5 μsec in each phase. The op amps are assumed to be single pole systems with conservative low-frequency gain ($A_0 = 7500$) and gain-bandwidth product ($GBW = 800$ kHz or

$\tau_p = 1/(2\pi GBW) \approx 200$ nsec at unity gain). All simulation results were obtained using the SWITCAP (Fang, Tsividis, and Wing 1983). Since this switched-capacitor circuit simulator supports multiple-switching frequencies, transient effects are computed by simulating resistors in the one-pole op amp models as switched capacitors that are very rapidly switched. The results shown were obtained using a 100 MHz sampling rate within the simulated op amp model.

A first-order op amp model is chosen to provide a simple comparison between the various cases to be studied and to reveal the true trends. Extensive simulations have shown that using realistic, i.e., second- or third-order, op amp models often yields inconclusive results. In effect, due to overshoots and undershoots in the transient responses of real op amps, simulation results can sometimes show misleading temporary improvements in settling errors, due to the coincidental matching of the sampling instants and a zero crossing of the op amp transient response. While such results might be valid for the particular case under evaluation, they are critically dependent on the precise op amp (transistor level) characteristics, which vary statistically from unit to unit. Since SWITCAP is not a transistor level simulator, its results, insofar as op amp settling is concerned, are best used to reveal trends that are independent of transistor level effects not modeled. In fact, linear gain and phase errors due to unsettled op amps can be simulated by introducing equivalent errors in the values of capacitors that are fed by the op amps' outputs. Consequently, low sensitivity circuits are likely to have increased tolerance to the nonideal transient responses of op amps.

Figure 8-64a shows the deviations from the ideal flat amplitude response when all eight op amps have the previously specified A_0 and GBW (Laker, Ganesan, and Fleischer 1985). Both staggered and unstaggered designs are evaluated and compared. Note that the internal settling properties of all the AP biquad structures in Fig. 8-52 are quite similar. The use of staggering provides an order of magnitude improvement in the gain error ΔG. The very small residual error for the staggered case is due to the finite DC gain ($A_0 = 7500$) of the op amps. This fact is demonstrated in Fig. 8-64a, where the response is for the same staggered design, but with op amps where $A_0 = 7500$ and $GBW = \infty$. The magnitude of this DC gain related error is not affected by the staggering, and depends on the low sensitivities of the biquads. From this point of view, all the low sensitivity AP structures in Fig. 8-52 yield equivalent results. Similar improvements in performance are evident in Fig. 8-64b, where the delay deviations are displayed. Results for the unstaggered case indicate that the maximum error is about 30 μsec which, while reasonable, is certainly unsuitable for precision applications. Except for the expected 10 μsec latency due to the four $T/2$ delays introduced by staggering, the worst-case errors for the staggered case are well under 1 μsec.

An alternative comparison of the behavior of these circuits is shown in Fig. 8-64c. These curves display the maximum magnitude error for each of the two cases as a function of the op amps' GBW, with A_0 kept fixed at 7500. In this comparison, staggering is seen, for a given bound on $|\Delta G|$, to permit the use of op amps with roughly half the GBW as the unstaggered case. In high-frequency applications, this could be significant. Figure 8-64 represents very good news indeed, suggesting that staggering substantially reduces the op amp linear transient-related errors. Moreover, these errors

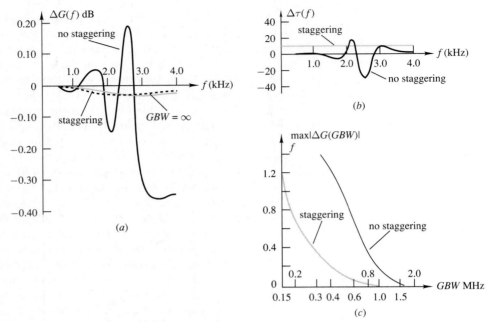

FIGURE 8-64 Effect of finite op amp bandwidth on the performance of fourth-order delay equalizer comprised of a cascade of two AB biquads: (a) error in gain response versus frequency, (b) error in group delay versus frequency, (c) maximum gain error versus the op amps' *GBW*. Compared are unstaggered and staggered realizations. These results represent a compendium of simulations obtained using SWITCAP.

can be made negligible if the application can afford op amps designed to settle to 0.1 percent of the final value within $T/2$. In any event, active-SC delay equalizers that satisfy the stringent requirements of most data communications applications can only be realized with staggering. We note in passing that an incidental benefit of the use of the tandem J in Fig. 8-22d and Fig. 8-63 is a reduction in total capacitance. The opportunity for gaining a factor of 2 reduction in the scaling of Σ_2 occurs whenever $J = 1$ (after dynamic range scaling).

8-10 HIGH ORDER FILTER IMPLEMENTATION USING ACTIVE LADDERS

In the previous chapter, we observed the advantages of cascade architecture, namely, its high degree of modularity, its generality, and the simple noninteracting relationship between the overall transfer function (as well as the gain, phase, and group delay) and those of its stages, as given in Eq. (8-89). Once the designer has completed the pole-zero pairing and gain distribution, the design labor is reduced to the synthesis of first- and second-order stages. The price paid for these advantages is sensitivity, or variability, as described in Eq. (8-91). In general, we recommend the use of cascade design for quick turnaround and for less demanding specifications that can tolerate the larger variability.

Many years ago, as related in Ghausi and Laker (1981) and Schaumann, Ghausi, and Laker (1990), Orchard proved that resistive terminated passive LC ladder filters are inherently insensitive to component variations, particularly in their passband. He also conjectured that active ladders, which simulate the operation of such passive ladders, would retain similarly low sensitivities. The class of active ladder filters that we are concerned with is derived by simulating the node and mesh equations of passive resistor-terminated LC ladder filters (Schaumann, Ghausi, and Laker 1990). Active ladder filters of this kind, illustrated in Fig. 8-65, are said to mimic the signal flow graph of their passive counterparts. We see in Fig. 8-65 that the terminations at both input and output are resistors and that otherwise the filter is "lossless" LC. That is, Z_{LCin} and Y_{LCin} correspond to LC one-port impedances and admittances, respectively. Usually, the design of an active ladder filter is based on the pre-synthesis of a suitable passive ladder prototype. CAD tools such as FILSYN can assist in obtaining this prototype (Szentirmai). It is beyond the scope of this text to develop the theory of passive ladder synthesis. The interested reader can find this material in several texts, such as Schaumann, Ghausi, and Laker (1990). Hence, we assume that the desired passive prototype is in hand.

As we will see, the active simulation results in the interconnection of first- or second-order sections in a multiple-loop negative-feedback network, emulating the elemental interactions that occur in the passive prototype. Once again, the principle advantage of active ladder filters is the very low sensitivity or variability inherited from their passive prototypes. Intuitively, the low sensitivity is attributed to the multiple loops of negative feedback. Recall that the derivation of Eq. (3-15) showed that the closed-loop gain sensitivity is inversely proportional to the amount of feedback $1 + \mathcal{A}\mathcal{H}$. The price paid for sensitivity reduction is that the design is complicated, and adequately developed only for certain classes of filters, such as LP, LPN, and BP. Important filter types such as the AP are not realized as active ladders. Nonetheless, when the filter requirements are demanding, an active ladder design may be the only means to meet specifications. Certainly, in integrated filters, where components are highly variable and tuning is expensive, active ladders are used when required and feasible (Ghausi and Laker 1981; Grebene 1984; Gregorian and Temes, 1986; Moschytz 1986; Schaumann, Ghausi, and Laker 1990; Sedra 1985; Sedra 1989; Toumazou; Unbehauen and Cichocki 1989).

FIGURE 8-65   A typical double-resistive terminated LC ladder.

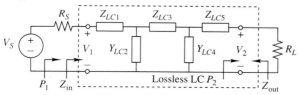

8-10-1   Sensitivity

To intuitively and analytically explore sensitivity, we introduce the concept of *reflection zeros*, used in the literature on passive LC ladder filters. We must first define a real rational function $K(s)$ such that for the numeric transfer function, we have

$$|H(j\omega)|^2 = \frac{1}{1 + |K(j\omega)|^2} \tag{8-95}$$

where $K(s) = 0$ at $s = \pm j\omega_{ri}$, namely, the reflection zeros. Readers familiar with passive filter or transmission line theory will recognize that $|K(j\omega)|$ is similar to the classic definition of the reflection coefficient. Since $|H(j\omega_{ri})| \equiv 1$ (or $G(\omega_{ri}) \equiv 0$ dB), ω_{ri} also corresponds to the gain peaks (or loss minima) in the filter response. To illustrate, Fig. 8-66a shows the reflection zeros for a fourth-order elliptic LP response.

We know from our study of elementary circuit theory that the gain response for a passive circuit is constrained to $G(\omega) \leq 0$ dB. Moreover, if R_S and R_L are chosen such that maximum power is transferred at $\omega = \omega_{ri}$, i.e. $P_1(j\omega_{ri}) = P_2(j\omega_{ri})$ or $R_S = Z_{\text{in}}(j\omega_{ri})$ and $R_L = Z_{\text{out}}(j\omega_{ri})$ in Fig. 8-65, then the passive ladder filter will indeed realize $|K(j\omega_{ri})| = 0$ and $G(\omega_{ri}) = 0$ dB.

To evaluate sensitivity, let us assume that component x_i of a passive ladder is varying about its nominal x_{i0}, such that $x_i = x_{i0}(1 + \Delta x_i/x_{i0})$. From Sec. 7-7, we write the sensitivity of the active ladder transfer function $T(j\omega)$ to component x_i as

$$S_{x_i}^{T(j\omega)} = \frac{1}{8.686} Q_{x_i}^{G(j\omega)} + j Q_{x_i}^{\varphi(j\omega)} \tag{8-96}$$

FIGURE 8-66   Passive ladder sensitivity: (*a*) the reflection zeros ω_{ri} for a fourth-order elliptic LP $H(s)$, and (*b*) illustration of Orchard's argument for zero sensitivity for L's and C's at ω_{ri}.

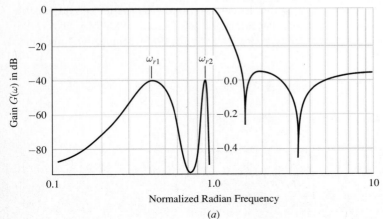

(*a*)

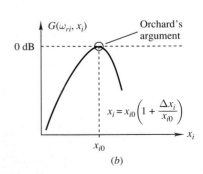

(*b*)

We also sketch, in Fig. 8-66b, the gain $G(\omega)$ at one of the reflection zeros ω_{ri}, as component x_i varies from x_{i0}. From the preceding discussion, we state that $G(\omega_{ri}, x_{i0}) \equiv 0$ dB if R_S and R_L are selected for maximum power transfer. Consequently, $G(\omega_{ri}, x_i)$ must have the parabolic shape indicated, with the peak at precisely ω_{ri} when $x_i = x_{i0}$. Consequently,

$$Q_{x_i}^{G(j\omega)} = 0 \text{ at } \omega = \omega_{ri} \text{ and } x_i = x_{i0} \tag{8-97}$$

This classic result, established by Orchard, has inspired passive ladder simulation in active-RC, -SC, and digital filters. It is important to note that Eq. (8-97) only applies when terminations R_S and R_L are fixed at maximum power transfer. Since, in practice, the R's vary from their nominal values, the sensitivities are not quite zero. However, the degradation of Eq. (8-97) is slow and well-behaved; hence, the sensitivities are still very low. Although Orchard's elegant arguments were based on the magnitude response, it can be shown that the phase sensitivities are also quite low in the passband (Ghausi and Laker 1981; Schaumann, Ghausi, and Laker 1990).

The astute reader may question what happens in an active filter where $G(\omega)$ is not limited to 0 dB by passivity. The answer is that the basic parabolic shape in Fig. 8-66b is retained through the translation. For example, Fig. 8-67 displays the Monte Carlo simulations for cascade, active ladder, and passive ladder realizations

FIGURE 8-67   Monte Carlo simulation of $\sigma(\Delta G)$ for cascade, active ladder, and passive ladder realizations for a fourth-order Butterworth BP response.

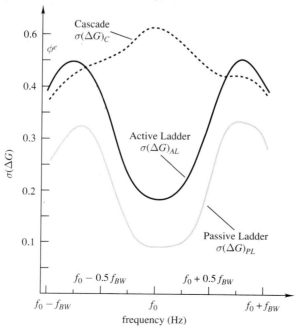

of a fourth-order Butterworth BP response. Here, $\sigma(\Delta G)$ is plotted as a function of frequency, where f_o and f_{BW} are the fourth-order filters' center frequency and 3 dB bandwidth, respectively. The statistics for passive components are zero mean gaussian, with $\sigma_i = 0.001$ (or 0.1 percent) and $\rho_{ij} = 0$. Also, all active elements in the cascade and active ladder are assumed to be ideal. The details of the individual designs are unimportant at this point; Fig. 8-67 simply conveys the trends.

The advantage $\sigma(\Delta G)_{PL}, \sigma(\Delta G)_{AL} \ll \sigma(\Delta G)_C$ for the ladder designs, in the passband, is quite apparent. The appearance of an upward "DC" bias in $\sigma(\Delta G)_{AL}$ as compared to $\sigma(\Delta G)_{PL}$, such that $\sigma(\Delta G)_{AL} > \sigma(\Delta G)_{PL}$, is primarily due to the simple fact that the active ladder uses at least twice as many components than the passive ladder. Note also that at frequencies $f_0 + 0.5f_{BW} < f < f_0 - 0.5f_{BW}$, $\sigma(\Delta G)_C < \sigma(\Delta G)_{AL}$. This advantage for the cascade design, at the band edges and in the transition band, is a common occurrence and needs to be taken into account if precision in the gain or phase at these frequencies is required. We also point out that for these frequencies, and for responses on which the passband is not "flat" or equi-ripple, inserting losses into the ladder can improve $\sigma(\Delta G)$ (and also $\sigma(\Delta \phi)$). The interested reader is referred to Ghausi and Laker (1981) for a further description of this and other low sensitivity multiple-loop feedback structures.

8-10-2 Realization Using Signal Flow Graphs

One intuitive tool for translating a passive ladder prototype into a suitable active ladder realization is the signal flow graph. In the signal flow graph, we map the passive ladder circuit and its elements to an equivalent interconnected collection of mathematical operations. An active ladder is then derived to simulate the signal flow graph. The resulting active ladder can be active-RC, active-G_m/C, or active-SC. For the active-SC filter, the signal flow graph is either developed in the z-domain or translated into the z-domain using Table 7-8.

To illustrate this process, let us first consider the simulation of the floating inductor of value L and shunt capacitor of value C in Figs. 8-68a and 8-68b, respectively. We know that the circuit equations for these two elements are

$$I = \frac{V_1 - V_2}{sL} \quad \text{and} \quad V = \frac{I_1 - I_2}{sC} \tag{8-98}$$

The idea is to simulate Eqs. (8-98) with an active circuit. Initially, we translate the currents into voltages by scaling current and admittance by a resistance R and an impedance by $1/R$, i.e.,

$$\hat{V} = IR = \frac{V_1 - V_2}{sL/R} \quad \text{and} \quad V = \frac{I_1 R - I_2 R}{sCR} = \frac{\hat{V}_1 - \hat{V}_2}{sCR} \tag{8-99}$$

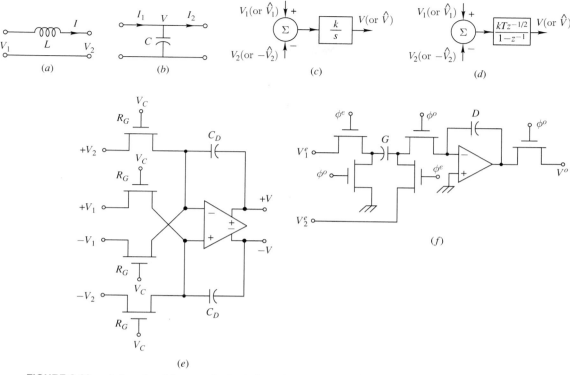

FIGURE 8-68 Active signal flow graph simulations: (a) floating inductor, (b) shunt capacitor, (c) s-domain signal flow graph, (d) z-domain signal flow graph, (e) MOST-RC simulation, and (f) SC simulation.

At this point R is arbitrary, but later in the process, R is used to scale the components to convenient values. We represent Eqs. (8-99) with the common flow in Fig. 8-68c, where $k = R/L$ or $1/RC$. The active-RC circuit in Fig. 8-68e is a straightforward implementation of this flow graph, where $R_G = R$ and $C_D = C$ or $C_D = L/R^2$. We leave it to the reader to draw the active-G_m/C realization of Fig. 8-68c. An active-SC realization follows directly from the translation of Fig. 8-68c into the z-domain, using either the BL or LD transforms in Table 7-8. Using the LD transform we obtain the flow graph in Fig. 8-68d and the active-SC circuit in Fig. 8-68f, where for $D = C$, $G = T/R = 1/f_s R$ for the shunt capacitor simulation and $D = L/R$, $G = T/R$ for the floating inductor simulation. In this circuit, the sample $V_1^e - V_2^e$ is stored on G during ϕ^e, and then inverted and accumulated on D during ϕ^o. Note that the LD transform maps the switched capacitor G into an equivalent resistor and vice versa. It is important to keep close track of the phasings for the input and output samples so that the $z^{-1/2}$ delay is maintained.

To generalize, let us consider the arbitrary LC ladder network in Fig. 8-69, comprised of series LC admittances Y_i and LC shunt impedances Z_i, with branch currents

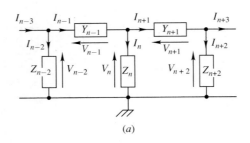

(a)

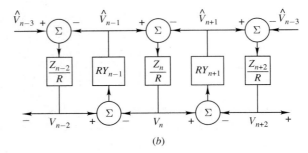

(b)

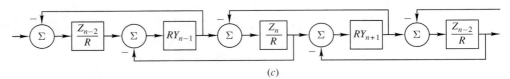

(c)

FIGURE 8-69   Signal flow graph for an arbitrary LC ladder: (a) the LC ladder section, (b) a signal flow graph simulation for (a) and Eqs. (8-100), and (c) a rearrangement of (b) into a leap frog structure.

I_i and node voltages V_i. The resistor terminations are not shown. Writing the circuit equations we obtain

$$V_{n-2} = Z_{n-2}(I_{n-3} - I_{n-1}) \qquad (8\text{-}100a)$$

$$I_{n-1} = Y_{n-1}(V_{n-2} - V_n) \qquad (8\text{-}100b)$$

$$V_n = Z_n(I_{n-1} - I_{n+1}) \qquad (8\text{-}100c)$$

$$I_{n+1} = Y_{n+1}(V_n - V_{n+2}) \qquad (8\text{-}100d)$$

$$V_{n+2} = Z_{n+2}(I_{n+1} - I_{n+3}) \qquad (8\text{-}100e)$$

Again scaling all impedances by $1/R$, and all currents and admittances by R, we obtain

$$V_{n-2} = \frac{Z_{n-2}}{R}(\hat{V}_{n-3} - \hat{V}_{n-1}) \qquad (8\text{-}101a)$$

$$\hat{V}_{n-1} = Y_{n-1}R(V_{n-2} - V_n) \qquad (8\text{-}101b)$$

$$V_n = \frac{Z_n}{R}(\hat{V}_{n-1} - \hat{V}_{n+1}) \qquad (8\text{-}101c)$$

$$\hat{V}_{n+1} = Y_{n+1}R(V_n - V_{n+2}) \qquad (8\text{-}101d)$$

$$V_{n+2} = \frac{Z_{n+2}}{R}(\hat{V}_{n+1} - \hat{V}_{n+3}) \qquad (8\text{-}101e)$$

The signal flow graph simulation of Eqs. (8-101) is shown in Fig. 8-69*b*. Rearranging the stages horizontally, we obtain an alternative *leap frog* arrangement in Fig. 8-69*c* (Ghausi and Laker 1981; Schaumann, Ghausi, and Laker 1990). We leave it to the reader to verify these flow graphs. Examining Eqs. (8-101), we note that if the LC ladder shunt Z_i's are simple capacitors and the series Y_i's are simple inductors, then all the Z_i/R's and Y_i/R's are of the form k_i/s. In such a case, namely, an all-pole LP LC ladder, the active simulation is a straightforward integrator-based circuit. When the LC ladder to be simulated is not an all-pole LP, the Z_i's and Y_i's are LC subnetworks and the active realization is no longer straightforward.

8-10-3 Realizing All Pole LP Filters

Let us consider the fifth-order all-pole LP passive ladder in Fig. 8-70. Following the steps in the previous section, the circuit equations (after scaling by R) are written as follows:

$$\hat{V}_{\text{in}} = \frac{R}{R_a}(V_{\text{in}} - V_1) \qquad (8\text{-}102a)$$

$$V_1 = \frac{1}{sC_1R}(\hat{V}_{\text{in}} - \hat{V}_2) \qquad (8\text{-}102b)$$

$$\hat{V}_2 = \frac{R}{sL_2}(V_1 - V_3) \qquad (8\text{-}102c)$$

$$V_3 = \frac{1}{sC_3R}(\hat{V}_2 - \hat{V}_4) \qquad (8\text{-}102d)$$

$$\hat{V}_4 = \frac{R}{sL_4}(V_3 - V_5) \qquad (8\text{-}102e)$$

$$V_{\text{out}} = \frac{1}{sC_5R}(\hat{V}_4 - \hat{V}_6) \qquad (8\text{-}102f)$$

$$\hat{V}_6 = \frac{R}{R_b}V_{\text{out}} \qquad (8\text{-}102g)$$

The signal flow graph for Eqs. (8-102) is shown in Fig. 8-71. Here we see that the signal flow graph is comprised of five integrators interconnected in leap frog

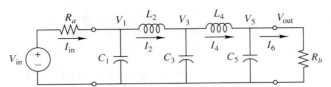

FIGURE 8-70   Fifth-order all-pole passive ladder filter.

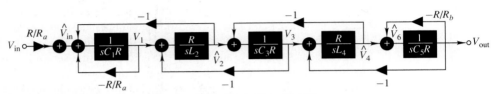

FIGURE 8-71   A signal flow graph simulation for Fig. 8-70 and Eqs. (8-101).

fashion. Note that the terminations R_a and R_b map into local feedback loops around the first and last integrators. Examining the active simulations for the terminations in Fig. 8-72 more closely, we observe that they are actually damped integrators. By combining Figs. 8-72 and 8-71, we obtain the alternative flow graphs in Fig. 8-73. Since the feedback is around pairs of integrators, we can, if convenient, invert the signs of all the integrators as in Fig. 8-73a or invert alternate integrators as in Fig. 8-73b, which eliminates the sign inversions in the feedback loops.

Figure 8-74a shows a MOST-RC realization of the input termination in Fig. 8-72b, where $C_D = C_1$, $R_F = R_a$, $R_G = R_a$, and $R_C = R$. Similarly, we show a G_m/C realization in Fig. 8-74c, where $C_D = C_1, G_{mF} = 1/R_a$, $G_{mG} = 1/R_a$, and

FIGURE 8-72   Manipulation of the signal flow graphs for terminations R_a and R_b in Fig. 8-71.

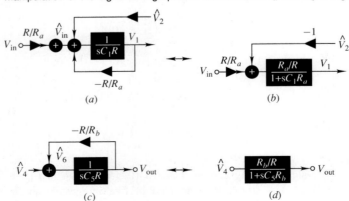

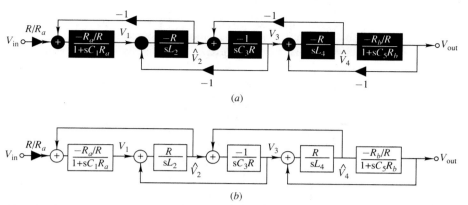

FIGURE 8-73   Alterative flow graphs for Fig. 8-70 and Eqs. (8-102) using the equivalents in Fig. 8-72. In (a) all the integrators are inverting and (b) alternate integrators are inverting.

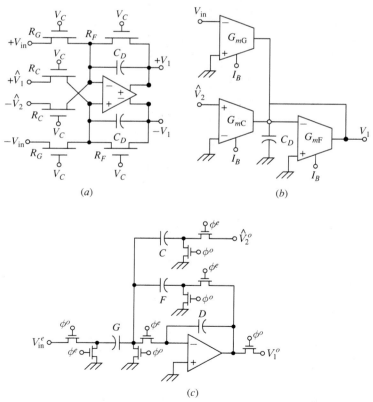

FIGURE 8-74   (a) Active-RC, (b) active-G_m/C and (c) active-SC realizations of the input termination in Fig. 8-73.

$G_{mC} = 1/R$. Recall that in Fig. 8-68f, we realized the undamped active-SC integrator by LD-transforming the s-domain signal-flow graph in Fig. 8-68c. Unfortunately, applying the LD transform to the signal flow graph for the termination does not result in a realizable flow graph. We leave it to the reader to verify and explain this claim. One alternative is to realize the termination in a BE form, such as switched-capacitor C_2 in Fig. 8-37c or switched-capacitor F in Fig. 8-43d. This alternative, shown in Fig. 8-74c, yields a termination phase error of $\omega T/2$, as given in Table 7-8. For highly oversampled active-SC realizations where $\omega T/2 \ll 1$, a simple solution is to slightly predistort F to compensate for the error. If the error is small, there is little penalty for this quick fix. However, if the error is large, the low sensitivity of the ladder realization may be somewhat compromised by the adjustment. That is, the maximum power transfer will no longer occur. Hence, a more elegant solution is to realize the termination without error via the BL transform (Gregorian and Temes 1986; Schaumann, Ghausi, and Laker, 1990; Unbehauen and Cichocki 1989).

As with biquads and cascade design, the outputs of all the op amps need to be scaled to optimize for dynamic range. Also, once dynamic-range scaling is completed, the capacitors at each op amp input can be impedance scaled to realizable values, e.g., $C_{min} = 1$ pF. The active ladder in Fig. 8-73b has been modified in Fig. 8-75 to include adjustable gains k_i to implement dynamic-range scaling. Consequently, the feedback gains are adjusted by $1/k_i k_j$ and the input gain by $1/k_1 k_2 k_3 k_4 k_5$. This scaling is usually accomplished with the aid of a computer simulation that shows the op amp outputs as functions of frequency. The reader should recognize that the scaling in Fig. 8-75 requires no additional hardware.

Single-ended active-RC implementations of the signal flow graphs in Figs. 8-73a and 8-75 are shown in Figs. 8-76a and 8-76b, respectively. Note that the signal flow graph in Fig. 8-73a, comprised of all inverting integrators, requires five op amps for the integrators and four additional op amps to realize the -1 feedback gains. In contrast, the realization in Fig. 8-76b requires two added op amps to realize the noninverting integrators. With balanced differential realizations, these extra inverting amplifiers would not be required. The important difference in these two realizations can be observed by a close examination of the two-integrator loops in both circuits when the op amps are nonideal. Let us assume that all op amps are matched and compensated for a one pole response such that $A(s) \approx \omega_t/s$. Typical loops in each circuit are circled in Fig. 8-76 for this purpose. Our objective is to estimate the error

FIGURE 8-75   The active ladder flow graph in Fig. 8-73b is modified to allow dynamic range scaling.

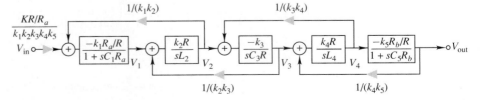

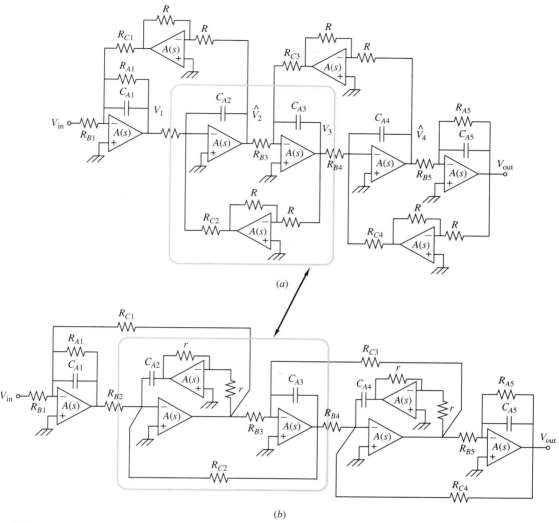

(a)

(b)

FIGURE 8-76   Single-ended active-RC realizations of the flow charts in (a) Fig. 8-73a and (b) Fig. 8-75.

$\varepsilon_{rr}(j\omega)$ due the nonideal op amps in each loop. This is best accomplished using the results in Fig. 5-23. The $\varepsilon_{rr}(j\omega)$ for the loop in Fig. 8-76a, comprised of two inverting integrators and one inverting amplifier, is estimated to be

$$\varepsilon_{rr}(j\omega) \approx \frac{1}{\omega_t}\left(\frac{1}{R_{C2}C_{A2}} + \frac{1}{R_{B3}C_{A3}}\right) - j\frac{4\omega}{\omega_t} \qquad (8\text{-}103a)$$

Similarly, for the loop in Fig. 8-76b comprised of inverting and noninverting integrators, we have

$$\varepsilon_{rr}(j\omega) \approx \frac{1}{\omega_t}\left(\frac{1}{R_{C2}C_{A2}} + \frac{1}{R_{B3}C_{A3}}\right) + j0 \qquad (8\text{-}103b)$$

Hence, the important phase error is made negligible by the active compensation and the matching among the op amps. As pointed out in Fig. 5-46, this compensation can also be achieved in a balanced differential realization.

The active-SC realization of the two-integrator loop used in Fig. 8-75 can be realized with no transform-related phase error by using either a +LD, −LD or a +FE, −BE loops. The latter is shown in Fig. 8-77. Note that repeating this timing through all the two-integrator loops, including the terminations, results in a natural pairwise staggering, i.e., there is a T delay for every other op amp. Consequently, active-SC ladder designs are usually robust with regard to op amp settling.

8-10-4 Realizing Symmetric All-Pole BP Filters

All-pole, symmetric BP active ladders are conveniently developed by simply LP-to-BP transforming a suitable LP ladder (Ghausi and Laker 1981; Schaumann, Ghausi, and Laker 1990). The LP-to-BP transform is given in Table 7-7. Using the notation in Table 7-7, let s be the LP complex frequency and p the BP complex frequency. With the following definitions, the flow chart in Fig. 8-75 can be redrawn in the form of Fig. 8-78a, i.e.,

$$T_1(s) = \frac{-k_1/RC_1}{s + \dfrac{1}{R_aC_1}} \qquad T_2(s) = \frac{k_2R/L_2}{s} \qquad T_3(s) = \frac{-k_3/RC_3}{s}$$

$$T_4(s) = \frac{k_4R/L_4}{s} \quad \text{and} \quad T_5(s) = \frac{-k_5/RC_5}{s + \dfrac{1}{R_bC_5}} \qquad (8\text{-}104)$$

FIGURE 8-77   The active-SC two-integrator loop: (a) the z-domain flow chart and (b) the active-SC circuit realization.

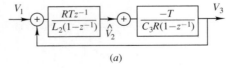

(a)

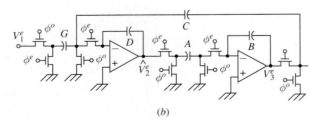

(b)

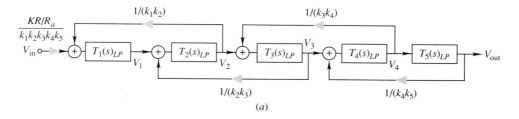

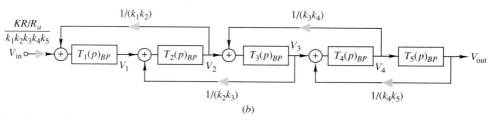

FIGURE 8-78   Symmetric all-pole BP ladder design: (*a*) a prototype fifth-order LP flow chart and (*b*) the transformed BP coupled biquad flow chart.

Applying the LP-to-BP transformation to Eqs. (8-104) yields

$$T_1(p) = \frac{-k_1 Bp/RC_1}{p^2 + p\dfrac{B}{R_a C_1} + \omega_0^2} \qquad T_2(p) = \frac{k_2 RBp/L_2}{p^2 + \omega_0^2} \qquad T_3(p) = \frac{-k_3 Bp/RC_3}{p^2 + \omega_0^2}$$

$$T_4(p) = \frac{k_4 RBp/L_4}{p^2 + \omega_0^2} \qquad \text{and} \qquad T_5(p) = \frac{-k_5 Bp/RC_5}{p^2 + p\dfrac{B}{R_b C_5} + \omega_0^2} \qquad (8\text{-}105)$$

where B is the 3 dB bandwidth of the fifth-order LP and ω_0 is the center frequency for the transformed tenth-order BP. Note that the $T_i(p)$ are BP biquads tuned to the same pole frequency $\omega_{0i} = \omega_0$ and

$$\frac{\omega_0}{Q_1} = \frac{B}{R_a C_1} \qquad \frac{\omega_0}{Q_5} = \frac{B}{R_b C_5} \qquad \text{and} \qquad \frac{\omega_0}{Q_2} = \frac{\omega_0}{Q_3} = \frac{\omega_0}{Q_4} = 0 \qquad (8\text{-}106)$$

The resulting BP signal flow graph, shown in Fig. 8-78*b*, is referred to as a *coupled biquad* structure. The BP biquad $T_i(p)$ can be realized using the low sensitivity continuous-time biquads described in Sec. 8-8.

Also, second-order BL BP functions can be realized using Fleischer-Laker biquads. Thus, active-SC realizations of Fig. 8-78*b* can be obtained by BL-transforming the $T_i(p)$ into the *z*-domain (Ghausi and Laker 1981). The details of this exercise are left to the reader.

8-10-5   Realizing Finite Transmission Zeros

Realizing active ladders with finite transmission zeros, rather than as straightforward all-pole ladders, requires some pre-manipulation of the originating passive ladder's flow graph. Consequently, different manipulations result in similar but different simulations. An intuitive approach for dealing with transmission zeros is shown Fig. 8-79 (Allstot et al. 1978; Jacobs et al. 1978). Alternative approaches can be found in Gregorian and Temes (1986), Schaumann, Ghausi, and Laker (1990), and Unbehauen and Cichocki (1989).

As indicated in Fig. 8-79a, the transmission zeros are realized in passive ladders as series LC tank circuits, e.g., the parallel combination of L_2, C_2. The equations at the two nodes of this circuit are

$$s(C_1 + C_2)V_1 + \frac{1}{sL_2}V_1 - \frac{1}{sL_2}V_3 - sC_2V_3 = 0 \qquad (8\text{-}107a)$$

$$s(C_3 + C_2)V_3 + \frac{1}{sL_2}V_3 - \frac{1}{sL_2}V_1 - sC_2V_1 = 0 \qquad (8\text{-}107b)$$

The direct signal flow graph simulation of these equations leads to the use of integrators and differentiators. In Chap. 5, we recommended that differentiators be avoided to avoid instability. It can be shown that embedded capacitance π-networks (e.g., C_1, C_2, C_3 in Fig. 8-79a) or inductive T-networks, will introduce the undesirable differentiators. A simple modification to eliminate the π-network is shown in Fig. 8-79b. The approach is to simulate the function of series C_2 by adding C_2 to shunt C_1 and C_3, and introducing two cross-coupled voltage-controlled current sources (VCCS's) sC_2V_3 and sC_2V_1 so that Eqs. (8-107) remain realized. The structure in Fig. 8-79b is an all-pole LP structure, which we know how to handle, and the two VCCS's are realized as capacitance feeds into the appropriate integrators.

To demonstrate, let us consider the fifth-order elliptic LP passive ladder in Fig. 8-80a. Applying the modification in Fig. 8-80b to series capacitors C_2 and C_4

FIGURE 8-79   Realization of active ladders with finite transmission zeros: (a) a section of an LC ladder realizing a transmission zero when $sL_2||1/sC_2 = \infty$, and (b) a simulation of (a) that does not require differentiators in the flow graph.

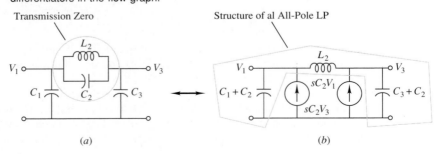

(a)   (b)

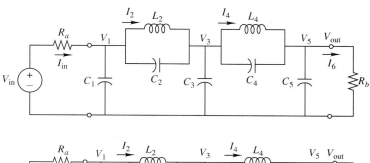

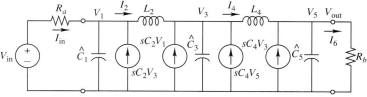

FIGURE 8-80   A fifth-order passive ladder used to realize a fifth-order elliptic LP $H(s)$: (a) the unmodified ladder and (b) the ladder modified as indicated in Fig. 8-79b.

yields the desired prototype in Fig. 8-80b, where $\hat{C}_1 = C_1 + C_2$, $\hat{C}_3 = C_2 + C_3 + C_4$, and $\hat{C}_5 = C_4 + C_5$. Scaling by R as prescribed for the all-pole case, the resulting circuit equations for Fig. 8-80b are

$$\hat{V}_{in} = \frac{R}{R_a}(V_{in} - V_1) \tag{8-108a}$$

$$V_1 = \frac{1}{s\hat{C}_1 R}(\hat{V}_{in} - \hat{V}_2) + \frac{C_2}{\hat{C}_1}V_3 \tag{8-108b}$$

$$\hat{V}_2 = \frac{R}{sL_2}(V_1 - V_3) \tag{8-108c}$$

$$V_3 = \frac{1}{sC_3 R}(\hat{V}_2 - \hat{V}_4) + \frac{C_2}{\hat{C}_3}V_1 + \frac{C_4}{\hat{C}_3}V_5 \tag{8-108d}$$

$$\hat{V}_4 = \frac{R}{sL_4}(V_3 - V_5) \tag{8-108e}$$

$$V_{out} = \frac{1}{sC_5 R}(\hat{V}_4 - \hat{V}_6) + \frac{C_4}{\hat{C}_5}V_3 \tag{8-108f}$$

$$\hat{V}_6 = \frac{R}{R_b}V_{out} \tag{8-108g}$$

The resulting signal flow graph is shown in Fig. 8-81. This signal flow graph is recognized to be the fifth all-pole LP graph in Fig. 8-71, embedded in a network of capacitance feeds shown in gray. The signs of the integrators can be manipulated as

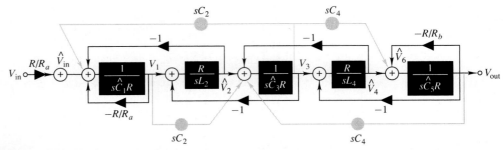

FIGURE 8-81   The signal flow graph for the passive ladder in Fig. 8-80*b*, requiring only integrators and capacitive feeds.

described in Figs. 8-81 and 8-75, with appropriate care taken to keep the signs and gains through the capacitance feeds consistent with the rest of the flow graph. The generalized integration and summing can be realized using the active-RC circuit in Fig. 5-12*c* or the active-SC circuit in Fig. 7-38*b*.

SUMMARY

In this chapter, we developed many different circuits for realizing robust sample-data and continuous-time integrated filters of arbitrary order and function. These circuits were realized in three integrated filter technologies, namely, active-RC, active G_m/C, and active-SC. In Table 8-16 we highlight some of the merits and demerits of these filter technologies. Active-RC and active-SC filters are relatively mature technologies and hence it is unlikely that they will experience any dramatic changes in the near future. Active-G_m/C filters, which use open-loop OTAs as *VCCS*'s, are fundamentally different from classical active filters, which use closed-loop op amps to realize feedback controlled *VCVS*'s. Integrated active-RC and active-SC filters have largely evolved out of the classical active filter model. Because the active-G_m/C filter deviates from the classical model and offers potential for applications up to VHF, it is a very prevalent topic within the circuits-and-systems research community. Integrated active-RC filters will likely benefit from related research in adaptive tuning and self-calibration.

Let us then conclude with a detailed, step-by-step flowchart for using the concepts and circuits described in this chapter and Chap. 7. The objective is to design and realize manufacturable and cost-effective integrated filters that satisfy customer requirements. It should be clear that integrated filter design is a far more challenging engineering exercise than the calculation of passive component values. The design begins with the development of a complete set of filter specifications as described in Chap. 7. Based on these data, decisions are made that lead to the engineering of a complete filter system (e.g., filter, clocks, on-chip tuning, etc.). Next, the filter structures (cascade, active-ladder, *E* or *F* type biquads) and the associated circuits (e.g., op amps, OTAs, MOST-R's, etc.) are designed. This segment of the design includes the selection of

TABLE 8-16   COMPARISON OF INTEGRATED ACTIVE FILTER TECHNOLOGIES

Active-SC	Active-RC (with MOST-R's)	Active-G_m/C
MERITS:	**MERITS:**	**MERITS:**
- Very high precision with no tuning.	- High-to-moderate precision with tuning.	- Moderate precision with tuning.
- Realize some functions with no continuous-time equivalent.	- Uses classical active-RC structures.	- Structures based on simple open-loop OTAs.
- Small die area and low power dissipation at $f < 20$ kHz.	- Small die area and low power dissipation at $f < 100$ kHz.	- Small die area and low power dissipation at $f < 10$ MHz.
- Parasitic insensitive.	- Feedback reduces sensitivity to parasitics.	- Integrates with digital CMOS and bipolar.
- Realizes "E" and "F" biquads.	- Realizes "E" and "F" biquads.	- Realizes "F" biquads.
- Integrates with digital CMOS.	- Integrates with digital CMOS	- No sample-data effects.
	- No sample-data effects.	- Efficient use of bandwidth.
DEMERITS:	**DEMERITS:**	**DEMERITS:**
- Sample-data effects (increased noise, reduced *PSRR*, aliasing).	- Requires on-chip tuning.	- Requires on-chip tuning.
- Require support circuits for digital clocks & anti-aliasing/reconstruction filters.	- Requires support circuits for closed-loop tuning.	- Requires support circuits for closed-loop tuning.
- Fully-balanced-differential structures for best *PSRR* and high dynamic range.	- Requires fully-balanced-differential structures for linearity.	- Fully-balanced-differential structures for high dynamic range.
- Inefficient use of bandwidth (i.e., oversampling).	- Use of op amps and large feedback limit use of bandwidth.	- Difficult to desensitize to parasitics.
- Not well suited to high frequency applications.	- Not well suited to high frequency applications.	- OTAs are voltage-controlled current sources.
- Not realizable in bipolar.	- Not realizable in bipolar.	- Minimum use of feedback.
		- Not suited to realizing "E" type biquad.

passive component values. The process concludes with a layout of the integrated filter that has been simulated and verified to meet the customer's specifications.

Many steps must occur along the way, as described below:

   I. Develop filter specifications from customer requirements.

  II. Determine if realization is to be continuous-time or sampled-data.

      A. If active-SC:

         1. Determine I/O sample rates and requirements.

         2. Determine needs and specifications for support functions (i.e., crystal oscillator, anti-aliasing, reconstruct filters, clock control logic, drivers, etc.).

         3. Select sample rates for the active-SC filter.

         4. Which technology, CMOS or BICMOS?

         5. Determine op amp requirements.

         6. Design and SPICE simulate op amps if necessary.

         7. Design support functions if necessary.

    B. If continuous-time:
        1. Determine if active-RC or active-G_m/C.
        2. Which technology? i.e., CMOS, BICMOS, or bipolar (G_m/C only).
        3. Determine op amp or OTA requirements.
        4. Design and SPICE simulate op amps or suitably linear OTAs if necessary.
        5. Develop autotuning strategy.
III. Determine the required numeric $H(s)$ or $H(z)$.
IV. Develop test strategy.
V. Determine if cascade or active ladder implementation.
    A. If cascade:
        1. Decompose into first- and second-order stages; i.e., pairing and ordering.
        2. Scale stage gains to maximize dynamic range.
        3. If active-SC; set up the cascade in staggered form.
        4. Calculate the raw or normalized component values for all the stages.
        5. Adjust gain levels at each op amp or OTA to maximize dynamic range.
        6. Scale components to achieve area, precision, dynamic range requirement, or make appropriate tradeoffs.
    B. If active ladder:
        1. Design passive LC ladder prototype.
        2. Develop signal flow graph without differentiators.
        3. If active-SC; transform flow chart into z-domain.
        4. Design for raw or normalized element values.
        5. If continuous-time, use active matching to minimize accumulated phase errors due to op amp ω_t's.
        6. Scale levels at each op amp or OTA output to maximize dynamic range.
        7. Scale components to achieve area, precision, dynamic range requirement, or make appropriate tradeoffs.
VI. Design support functions.
    A. If active-SC; design clock generation subsystem, anti-aliasing, and recon-struction filters.
    B. For continuous-time filters, design autotuning subsystem.

It should be recognized that the sequence outline above is not necessarily a serial, single-pass process. During design, particularly when faced with stringent require-ments, simulations performed in a given step may suggest that a decision made earlier in the sequence needs to be changed. Although we would like to avoid the added costs and schedule slippage associated with backtracking, it is obviously best to determine the need for such changes as early in the process as possible.

EXERCISES

8-1 Let the capacitor oxide for two unit double-poly capacitors, namely C_1 and C_2, vary linearly as indicated in Fig. EX8-1. We are concerned with the precision of capacitor ratio $\alpha = C_2/C_1$.
    a Determine the approximate error $\Delta\alpha/\alpha$ due to this oxide gradient.

b Let C_2 be comprised of $8C_1$ and let the capacitor oxide vary as in Fig. EX8-1, radially in any direction from the center of C_1. Draw the top view of the layout of C_1 and C_2 that minimizes $\Delta\alpha/\alpha$. Explain your configuration.

8-2 Let the analog switches in an active-SC filter be realized as CMOS pairs (e.g., Fig. 8-8c). Assume that the capacitance connected to any given switch is bounded by $C_{Ti} \leq 50$ pF, the CMOS switch is designed for an $R_{ON} \approx 5$ kΩ, and that the $\phi^{e,o}$ duty cycle is 40 percent.

a Determine the highest sample rate f_s that can be supported if the switch time constant is to constitute less than 5 percent of the time available to charge C_{Ti}.

b Estimate the parasitic capacitances.

8-3 An NMOS single-pole-double-throw switch has a $v_{GS} > V_T$ and its drain is open-circuit. What is v_{DS}? Explain your answer.

8-4 Consider the differential MOST-R circuit in Fig. EX8-4. Using the MOST-R model in Fig. 8-9b, show that spurious signals fed through the parasitic capacitors from V_{DD} are ideally canceled when v_{out} is formed.

8-5 Consider the circuit in Fig. EX8-5, comprised of four matched MOSTs (T1, T2, T3, and T4) controlled by V_{C1}, V_{C2}, V_{C3}, and V_{C4}. Show that by forming the difference $i = i_A - i_B$, with $V_{C4} = V_{C1}$ and $V_{C3} = V_{C2}$, *all* nonlinearities cancel.

8-6 Verify that the CMOS inverter in Fig. 8-13a realizes a linear G_m given by Eq. (8-20a). What are the operating conditions for this operation?

8-7 Verify that the MOST-R based structure in Fig. 8-13b realizes a linear G_m given by Eq. (8-20b). What are the operating conditions for this operation?

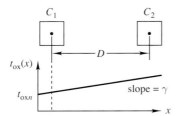

FIGURE EX8-1

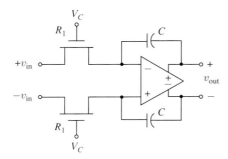

FIGURE EX8-4

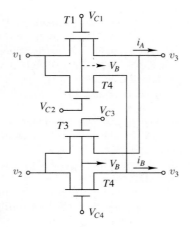

FIGURE EX8-5

8-8 A simple CMOS inverting active-RC integrator is to be designed using a p-well resistor and a poly 1-poly 2 capacitor. The design objective is $1/RC = \beta = 2\pi$ (20 kHz) with minimum total RC area.
   a Determine the relationship between R, C, and β for a minimum RC die area design.
   b Using the data in Table 7-1 and a minimum size p-well square of 6 $\mu m \times 6$ μm, find the values for R, C, and die area.
8-9 Consider the active-SC circuit in Fig. EX8-9 (also shown in Fig. 8-18). What is the error in the voltage ratio $V_{out}(z)/V(z)$ due to parasitic capacitance C_p?
8-10 **a** Derive the voltage transfer functions for the active-SC circuit in Fig. EX8-10, assuming all components are ideal.
   b Derive the effect that parasitic capacitances have on the AC operation of this circuit.
8-11 Repeat Exercise 8-10 for the active-SC circuit in Fig. EX8-11.
8-12 Verify Eq. (8-23).
8-13 Develop a bilinear integrator that is minimally sensitive to parasitic capacitances (i.e., insensitive or compensated).
8-14 Verify the MLL result in Eq. (8-29).

FIGURE EX8-9

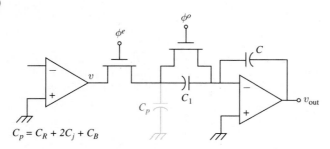

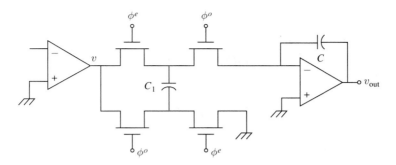

FIGURE EX8-10

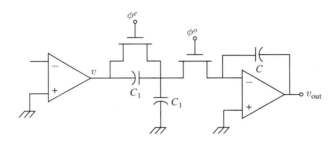

FIGURE EX8-11

8-15 **a** If the resistor ratio R_1/R_2 has an error of δ percent, determine the corresponding error in the tuned RC product.
   b Determine the error in RC when the comparator has an infinite gain, say of $A = A_0$.
   c Determine the error in RC that occurs when the two peak-detectors are mismatched by ε percent.

8-16 Develop a block diagram for a tuning system to correct for the error depicted in Fig. EX8-16. Explain the operation of your block diagram.

8-17 For the other first-order switched-capacitor circuits in Fig. 8-37, derive the frequency response errors that arise when the op amp DC gains are finite (say A_0).

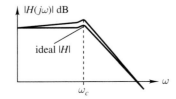

FIGURE EX8-16

8-18 For the active-SC circuit in Fig. EX8-18 find:

  a the transfer function $H(z) = V_{out}(z)/V_{in}(z)$;

  b the values of C_1/C for which the circuit stable; and

  c the function this circuit performs when $C_1 = C$. Assume that v_{in} changes on ϕ^e and is held for the full-clock period.

8-19 Consider the active-SC circuit in Fig. EX8-19, where V_{off} represents the input-referred DC offset voltage of the op amp. Derive the transfer functions:

  a V_{out}/V_{in}

  b V_{out}/V_{off}

FIGURE EX8-18

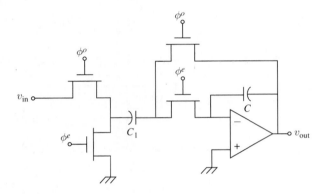

FIGURE EX8-19

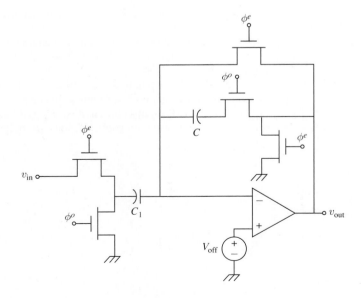

8-20 Use the circuit in Fig. EX8-19 to implement a full-clock period delay stage that is compensated for DC offset.

8-21 Consider the active-RC circuit in Fig. EX8-21a.

    a If the two R_1's are mismatched by Δ_R, what is the resulting effect on $+v_{\text{out}}$ and $-v_{\text{out}}$?

    Assume the balanced-differential op amp is ideal.

    b Let $\Delta_R = 0$, determine the effect on $+v_{\text{out}}$ and $-v_{\text{out}}$ if the balanced-differential op amp is realized as in Fig. EX8-21b with $A_i = A_0\omega_t/s$.

8-22 Design a Sallen-and-Key active-RC biquad (Fig. 8-40b) to realize an anti-aliasing (AA) filter for a sample-data system with a baseband limited $f \leq 3.5$ kHz and a sample rate of $f_s = 256$ kHz. The AA filter is to achieve attenuation of ≥ 30 dB at $f_s - f_c$ and ≤ 0.05 dB attenuation for $f \leq f_c$.

    a Determine the poles f_0 and Q_p that realize these specifications.

    b If the R's are realized as p-well diffusions (5kΩ/$\square$), and the C's as double-poly capacitors (0.11 nF/cm^2), determine the values for the R's and C's that minimize the total area required for the passive components.

    c Determine the dimensions for the R's and C's. The minimum size p-well square is assumed to be 6 $\mu m \times 6$ μm.

8-23 Consider the Fleischer-Laker biquad in Fig. 8-45:

    a Verify the z-domain equivalent circuit in Fig. 8-46.

    b Derive the $\frac{AC}{DB}$ and $\frac{A\hat{G}}{D\hat{I}}$ entries in Table 8-4 and the ω_0, θ_p, ω_N, θ_z entries in Table 8-5.

8-24 Verify the ω_0 and Q_p sensitivities for capacitors A, B, C, and E for the E-circuit in Tables 8-6 and 8-7.

8-25 Verify the ω_N, Q_z sensitivities in Table 8-8.

8-26 Verify the switched-capacitor transformations in Fig. 8-48.

FIGURE EX8-21

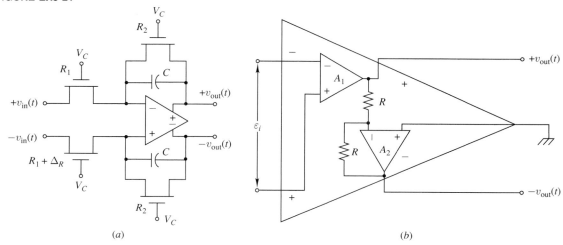

(a)   (b)

8-27 The task is to design a second-order bandpass (BP) switched-capacitor circuit with $f_0 = 1633$ Hz, $Q_p = 16$, and $G(j2\pi f_0) = 0$ dB. With $f_s = 8$ kHz and $C_{min} = 1$ pF. Design the following Fleischer-Laker biquad to these specifications:
  a BP10.
  b BP00.
  Compare **a** and **b**. Both designs should be properly scaled for maximum dynamic range and a 1 pF minimum capacitance.

8-28 A switched-capacitor filter is required to reject 60 Hz power hum. The requisite response is a second-order highpass notch (HPN) with $f_0 = 300$ Hz, $Q_p = 0.707$, $f_z = 60$ Hz, and $G(j\infty) = 0$ dB. Design Fleischer-Laker biquads:
  a Using E-damping
  b F-damping.
  c Compare the two designs.
  The designs are to be scaled for maximum dynamic range and a 1 pF minimum capacitance.

8-29 Draw a layout for the switched-capacitor circuit designed in Exercise 8-28. Assume a 3.5 mm double-poly, p-well CMOS technology with a poly I-poly II capacitance density of 0.12 nF/cm^2. In the layout, take prudent steps to maximize the precision and *PSRR*.

8-30 For the circuit in Fig. EX8-30:
  a show that it realizes a noninverting bilinear bandpass (+BP10) $H(z)$ from the input (V_{in}) to output (V_{out1}) and an inverting bilinear bandpass (−BP01) $H(z)$ from input (V_{in}) to output (V_{out2}).
  b design the circuit to realize an $f_0 = 4$ kHz, $Q_p = 5$, $G(f_0) = 0$ dB, and $f_s = 128$ kHz. Calculate the unscaled capacitor values only.

8-31 Consider the circuit in Fig. EX8-31:
  a derive the transfer functions V_{out1}/V_{in} and V_{out2}/V_{in}; and
  b compare the performance of this circuit with that in Fig. EX8-30.

8-32 Consider the following two LPN switched-capacitor biquads in Fig. EX8-32.
  a Derive the design equations for both circuits, i.e., the relations for each of the capacitors in terms of z-domain coefficients A_0, A_1, A_2, B_0, and B_1 in Eq. (8-67a).

FIGURE EX8-30

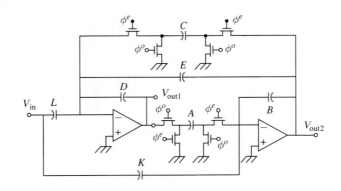

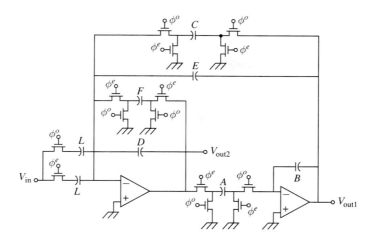

FIGURE EX8-31

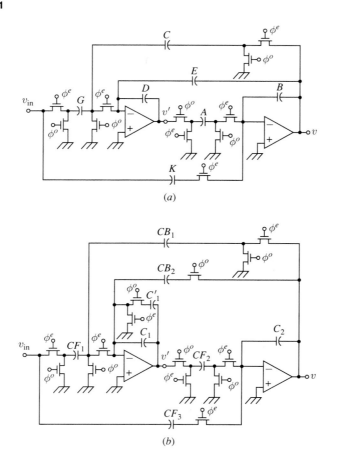

(a)

(b)

FIGURE EX8-32

b Design both circuits for $f_0 = 1$ kHz, $f_N = 2.5$ kHz, $Q_p = 30$, $G(f_0) = 0$ dB, and $f_s = 128$ kHz (scale both circuits for maximum dynamic range and for minimum capacitance of 1 pF).

c Compare the two designs.

8-33 Evaluate the impact of finite DC op gains (A_0) on the performance of the LPN biquads in Fig. EX8-32.

8-34 Consider the integrated active-RC circuits in Fig. 8-54:

a design (determine the R and C values) for a balanced realization of the filter requirements in Exercise 8-32. Scale the circuit for maximum dynamic range and the minimum total area for the MOST-R's and C's. Use the process parameters for the 3 μm p-well CMOS process given in Tables 1-1 and 1-7.

b Determine the dimensions for the MOST-R's and C's.

8-35 Repeat Exercise 8-34 for the active-$G_m C$ biquad in Fig. 8-56.

8-36 Assume, for the Fleischer-Laker biquad, that the primary transfer function is the output of the first op amp, i.e., $T'(z)$. Develop the design relations for $T'(z)$ that parallel those in Eqs. (8-75) and Table 8-9.

8-37 Using the minimum number of capacitors:

a determine a Fleischer-Laker biquad for realizing a bilinear low-pass (LP11) response; and

b design the circuit developed in **a** for a maximally-flat response with $f_0 = 4$ kHz, $G(0) = 0$ dB, and $f_s = 128$ kHz. Calculate the unscaled capacitor values only.

8-38 Design the following fifth-order elliptic LP transfer function as a cascade of switched-capacitor first- and second-order active-SC stages:

$$H(s_n) = 2.15 \times \frac{1}{s_n + 16.8} \times \frac{s_n^2 + (43.2)^2}{s_n^2 + 19.4 s_n + 400.34} \times \frac{s_n^2 + (29.2)^2}{s_n^2 + 4.72 s_n + 507.33}$$

Let $f_s = 128$ kHz. Scale the design for maximum dynamic range and for minimum capacitance of 1 pF.

8-39 Design a switched-capacitor ladder filter to implement a fifth-order elliptic response with $\delta = 1$ dB, $f_{PB} = 3$ kHz, $f_{SB} = 5.685$ kHz, and $A_{SB} > 60$ dB, and $f_s = 128$ kHz. Use the schematic in Fig. 8-80a as the passive LC prototype with the following element values: $R_a = R_b = 50 \ \Omega$, $C_1 = 2.00737 \ \mu$F, $C_2 = 0.29643 \ \mu$F, $C_3 = 2.86680 \ \mu$F, $C_4 = 0.11053 \ \mu$F, $C_5 = 2.17013 \ \mu$F, $L_2 = 2.42969$ mH, and $L_4 = 2.72208$ mH. Calculate the unscaled capacitor values for the switched-capacitor ladder realization.

(Optional Project: Scale the component values of the switched-capacitor circuit for maximum dynamic range and to minimize the total capacitance; with the constraint that the minimum capacitance is 1 pF. Compare the resulting design with that in Exercise 8-38 with regard to silicon area, estimated yield, and noise.)

REFERENCES

Agarwal, R. C., and C. A. Burrus. 1975. "New Recursive Digital Filter Structures Having Very Low Sensitivity and Roundoff Noise." *IEEE Trans. Circuits and Syst.*, vol. CAS-22, no. 122, pp. 921–927.

Allstot, D. J., R. W. Broderson, and P. R. Gray. 1978. "MOS Switched-Capacitor Ladder Filters." *IEEE J. Solid-State Circuits*, vol. SC-13, no. 6, pp. 806–814.

Allstot, D. A., and W. C. Black. 1983. "Technological Design Considerations for Monolithic MOS Switched-Capacitor Filtering System." *Proc. IEEE,* vol. 71, pp. 967–986.

Banu, M., and Y. Tsividis. 1985. "An Elliptic Continuous-Time CMOS Filter with On-Chip Automatic Tuning." *IEEE J. Solid-State Circuits,* vol. SC-20, pp. 1114–1121.

Bazanezhad, J. N., and G. C. Temes. 1984. "A Linear NMOS Depletion Resistor and its Application in an Integrated Amplifier." *IEEE J. Solid-State Circuits*, vol. SC-19, pp. 932–938.

Czarnul, Z. 1986. "Modifications of the Banu-Tsividis Continuous-Time Integrator Structure." *IEEE Trans. Circuits Syst.,* vol. CAS-33, no. 7, pp. 714–716.

Fang, S. C., Y. Tsividis, and O. Wing. 1983. "SWITCAP: A Switched-Capacitor Network Analysis Program." Parts I and II, *IEEE Circuits and Systems Magazine*, Sept-Dec.

Fleischer, P. E., A. Ganesan, and K. R. Laker. 1981. "Parasitic Compensated Switched Capacitor Circuits." *Electron. Lett.*, vol. 17, no. 24, pp. 929–931.

Geiger, R. L., P. E. Allen, and N. R. Strader. 1990. *VLSI Design Techniques for Analog and Digital Circuits*, New York: McGraw-Hill.

Ghausi, M. S., and J. Kelly. 1968. *Introduction to Distributed Parameter Networks.* New York: Holt, Rinehart & Winston.

Ghausi, M. S., and K. R. Laker. 1981. *Modern Filter Design: Active-RC and Switched Capacitor.* Englewood Cliffs, NJ: Prentice-Hall.

Grebene, A. B. 1984. *Bipolar and MOS Analog Integrated Circuit Design.* New York: Wiley and Sons.

Gregorian, R., and G. C. Temes. 1986. *Analog MOS Integrated Circuits for Signal Processing.* New York: Wiley-Interscience.

Gray, P. R., D. A. Hodges, and R. W. Broderson, eds. 1980. *Analog MOS Integrated Circuits.* New York: IEEE Press Selected Reprint Series/Wiley.

Gray, P. R., and R. G. Meyer. 1984. *Analysis and Design of Analog Integrated Circuits.* New York: Wiley and Sons.

Huang, Q., and W. Sansen. 1987. "Design Techniques for Improved Capacitor Area Efficiency in Switched-Capacitor Biquads." *IEEE Trans. Circuits and Syst.,* vol. 33, no. 121, pp. 1590–1598.

Jacobs, G. M., D. J. Allstot, R. W. Broderson, and P. R. Gray. 1978. "Design Techniques for MOS Switched Capacitor Ladder Filters." *IEEE Trans. Circuits and Syst.,* vol. CAS-25, pp. 1014–1021.

Khorramabadi, H., and P. R. Gray. 1984. "High-Frequency CMOS Continuous-Time Filters." *IEEE J. Solid-State Circuits*, vol. SC-19, pp. 963–967.

Kozma, K. A., D. A. Johns, and A. S. Sedra. 1991. "Automatic Tuning of Continuous-Time Filters Using an Adaptive Filter Technique." *IEEE Trans. Circuits Syst.*, vol. 38, no. 11, pp. 1241–1248.

Krummenacher, F., and N. Joehl. 1988. "A 4-MHz CMOS Continuous-Time Filter with On-Chip Automatic Tuning." *IEEE J. Solid-State Circuits*, vol. SC-23, pp. 750–758.

Laker, K. R., A. Ganesan, and P. E. Fleischer. 1985. "Design and Implementation of Cascaded Switched Capacitor Delay Equalizers." *IEEE Trans. Circuits Syst.,* vol. CAS-32, pp. 700–711.

Lopresti, P. V. 1977. "Optimum Design of Linear Tuning Algorithms." *IEEE Trans. Circuits. Syst.*, vol. CAS-24, no. 3, pp. 144–151.

Marsh, D. G. 1981. "A Single-Chip CMOS CODEC with Filters." *IEEE J. Solid-State Circuits*, vol. SC-16, 308-315.

Martin, K. 1982. "New Clock Feedthrough Cancellation Technique for Analog MOS Switched-Capacitor Circuits." *Electron. Lett.*, vol. 18, no. 2, pp. 39–40.

Martin, K., and A. S. Sedra. 1981. "Effects of the Op Amp Finite Gain and Bandwidth on the Performance of Switched-Capacitor Filters." *IEEE Trans. Circuits Syst.*, vol. CAS28, pp. 822–829.

Meares, L. G., and C. E. Hymowitz. 1988. *Simulating With SPICE*, San Pedro, CA: Intusoft.

Moschytz, G. S., ed. 1986. *MOS Switched Capacitor Filters*, New York: IEEE Press Selected Reprint Series/Wiley.

Moulding, K. W., J. R. Quartly, P. J. Rankin, R. S. Thompson, and G. A. Wilson. 1980. "Gyrator Video Filter IC with Automatic Tuning." *IEEE J. Solid-State Circuits*, vol. SC-15, pp. 963–968.

Nedungadi, A., and T. R. Viswanathan. 1984. "Design of Linear CMOS Transconductance Elements." *IEEE Trans. Circuits Syst.*, vol. CAS-31, pp. 891–894.

Park, C. S., and R. Schaumann. 1986. "A High-Frequency CMOS Linear Transconductance Element." *IEEE Trans. Circuits. Syst.*, vol. CAS-33, pp. 1132–1138.

Sansen, W. M. C., H. Qiuting, and K. A. I. Halonen. 1987. "Transient Analysis of Charge Transfer in SC Filters-Gain Error and Distortion." *IEEE J. Solid-State Circuits*, vol. SC-22, no. 2, pp. 268–276.

Schaumann, R., M. S. Ghausi, and K. R. Laker. 1990. *Design of Analog Filters*. Englewood Cliffs, NJ: Prentice-Hall.

Sedra, A. S. 1989. "Miniaturized Active RC Filters." In *Miniaturized and Integrated Filters*, edited by S. K. Mitra and C. F. Kurth. New York: Wiley-Interscience.

Sedra, A. S. 1985. "Switched-Capacitor Filter Synthesis." In *Design of MOS VLSI Circuits for Telecommunications*. edited by Y. Tsividis and P. Antognetti. Englewood Cliffs, NJ: Prentice-Hall.

Sedra, A. S., and K. C. Smith. 1987. *Microelectronic Circuits*. New York: Holt, Rinehart & Winston.

Shieh, J-H, M. Patil, and B. J. Sheu. 1987. "Measurement and Analysis of Charge Injection in MOS Switches." *IEEE J. Solid-State Circuits*, vol. SC-22, no. 2, pp. 277–281.

Silva-Martinez, J., M. Steyaert, and W. Sansen. 1993. *High-Performance CMOS Continuous-Time Filters*. Norwell, MA: Kluwer Academic.

Snelgrove, W. M. and A. Shoval. 1992. "A Balanced 0.9-mm CMOS Transconductance-C Filter Tunable Over the VHF Range." *IEEE J. Solid-State Circuits*, vol. 27, no. 3, pp. 314–323.

Steyaert, M., and W. Sansen. 1990. "Low-Power Monolithic Signal-Conditioning System." *IEEE J. Solid-State Circuits*, vol. 25, no. 2, pp. 609–612.

Szentirmai, G. *S/FILSYN Software for Filter Analysis and Design*. Santa Clara, CA: DGS Associates.

Torrance, R. R., T. R. Viswanathan, and J. V. Hanson. 1985. "CMOS Voltage to Current Transducers." *IEEE Trans. Circuits Syst.*, vol. CAS-32, no. 11, pp. 1097–1104.

Toumazou, C., F. J. Lidgey, and D. G. Haigh, eds., *Analogue IC Design: The Current-Mode Approach*, London: Peter Peregrinus Ltd.

Toumazou, C., D. G. Haigh, K. Steptoe, S. J. Harrold, J. I. Sewell, and R. Bayruns. 1990. "Design and Testing of a GaAs Switched Capacitor Filter." *Proceedings 1990 IEEE Int. Symp. on Circuits and Systems*, 90CH2868-8, pp. 2825–2828.

Tsividis, Y., M. Banu, and J. Khoury. 1986. "Continuous-Time MOSFET-C Filters in VLSI." *IEEE Trans. Circuits Syst.*, vol. CAS-33, *Special Issue on VLSI Analog and*

Digital Signal Processing, pp. 125–140. Also in *IEEE J. Solid-State Circuits,* vol. SC-21, pp. 15–30.

Tsividis, Y., Z. Czarnul, and S. C. Fang. 1986. "MOS Transconductors and Integrators with High Linearity." *Electron. Lett.*, vol. 22, pp. 245–246, 619.

Unbehauen, R., and A. Cichocki. 1989. *MOS Switched-Capacitor and Continuous-Time Integrated Circuits and Systems*, Berlin: Springer-Verlag.

Van Peteghem, P. M. 1988. "On the Relationship Between *PSRR* and Clock Feedthrough in SC Filters." *IEEE J. Solid-State Circuits*, vol. 23, no. 4, pp. 997–1004.

Van Peteghem, P. M., and R. Song. 1989. "Tuning Strategies in High-Frequency Integrated Continuous-Time Filters." *IEEE Trans. Circuits Syst.,* vol. 36, no. 1, pp. 136–139.

INDEX

Heterick Memorial Library
Ohio Northern University

DUE	RETURNED	DUE	RETURNED
1. OCT 14 '96	OCT 14 96	13.	
2. 12-27-9	DEC 10 1996	14.	
3. 9-5-9	AUG 27 1997	15.	
4. 11/26/97	NOV 25 1997	16.	
5. 5-18-98	JUN 1 8 1998	17.	
6. 12-16-98	DEC 1 8 1998	18.	
7.		19.	
8.		20.	
9.		21.	
10.		22.	
11.		23.	
12.		24.